# NIV
## *Compact Bible Commentary*

# NIV
## *Compact Bible Commentary*

John Sailhamer

**ZONDERVAN**™

GRAND RAPIDS, MICHIGAN 49530

# ZONDERVAN™

*The NIV Compact Bible Commentary*
Copyright © 1994 by John H Sailhamer

Requests for information should be addressed to:
Zondervan, *Grand Rapids, Michigan 49530*

## Library of Congress Cataloging-in-Publication Data

Sailhamer, John.
    NIV bible commentary  /  by John H. Sailhamer.
        p.    cm.
    ISBN 0-310-22868-9 (softcover)
    1. Bible — Commentaries.    I. Bible. English. New International 1994.
II. Title.
BS491.2.S255                                                                    93–41129

Printed in the United States of America

02  03  04  /DC/  20  19  18  17  16  15  14  13

# Contents

| | | | |
|---|---|---|---|
| Preface | 7 | Obadiah | 420 |
| Introduction | 8 | Jonah | 421 |
| Abbreviations | 10 | Micah | 423 |
| | | Nahum | 425 |
| Genesis | 11 | Habakkuk | 427 |
| Exodus | 63 | Zephaniah | 429 |
| Leviticus | 106 | Haggai | 431 |
| Numbers | 120 | Zechariah | 433 |
| Deuteronomy | 146 | Malachi | 436 |
| The Deuteronomic History | 175 | Matthew | 437 |
| Joshua | 179 | Mark | 451 |
| Judges | 202 | Luke | 470 |
| Ruth | 213 | John | 485 |
| 1 Samuel | 216 | Acts | 497 |
| 2 Samuel | 238 | Romans | 515 |
| 1 Kings | 250 | 1 Corinthians | 533 |
| 2 Kings | 264 | 2 Corinthians | 540 |
| 1 Chronicles | 273 | Galatians | 544 |
| 2 Chronicles | 287 | Ephesians | 547 |
| Ezra | 302 | Philippians | 550 |
| Nehemiah | 305 | Colossians | 552 |
| Esther | 309 | 1 Thessalonians | 555 |
| Job | 312 | 2 Thessalonians | 557 |
| Psalms | 315 | 1 Timothy | 559 |
| Proverbs | 350 | 2 Timothy | 563 |
| Ecclesiastes | 356 | Titus | 565 |
| Song of Songs | 359 | Philemon | 566 |
| The Prophetic Literature | 362 | Hebrews | 567 |
| Isaiah | 363 | James | 574 |
| Jeremiah | 375 | 1 Peter | 577 |
| Lamentations | 385 | 2 Peter | 580 |
| Ezekiel | 387 | 1 John | 583 |
| Daniel | 396 | 2 John | 586 |
| Hosea | 414 | 3 John | 587 |
| Joel | 416 | Jude | 588 |
| Amos | 418 | Revelation | 590 |

# Preface: A Note to the Reader

Having spent a good many hours pouring over the manuscript of this book, it occurs to me that a few initial comments to you, the reader, on its purpose and usefulness might be in order. There are many different kinds of commentaries on the Bible—just as there are many reasons why one would want to use a commentary. Technical commentaries are essential for a detailed, close study of a biblical passage. Devotional commentaries help the reader see the application of a biblical passage to his or her life. Bible survey commentaries give the reader an overview of the contents of each book of the Bible. *The NIV Compact Bible Commentary* does not fit exactly into any of those categories. It is not a technical commentary, even though it is based on a thorough technical reading of the Bible in both Hebrew and Greek. It is not, strictly speaking, a devotional commentary, in that its focus is on the meaning of the text rather than on a particular life application. That does not mean, of course, that its ultimate purpose is not to enable you to apply the Bible to your life situations. It is our view that we can only apply the Bible to our lives when we actually understand its meaning. Nor is this commentary a Bible survey, though in reading it one will certainly get a survey of the entire Bible.

What then is the purpose of the commentary that lies before you? The best way to describe it is to say that it was written to aid you in reading the Bible on your own. There is no substitute for reading the Bible. It is God's Word. Nothing, not even the most brilliant commentary in the world, can take its place—nor should it aim to take its place. The purpose of this commentary is to provide you with a ready and instant help in understanding the Bible while you are reading it. We believe that what is usually lacking in reading the Bible is a sense of what the whole of the Bible is about. We easily get lost in the details. Those details would make more sense if we knew what they were about from the point of view of an entire book or the whole Bible. They obviously made sense to the biblical writers, but then, they knew what and why they were writing. We hope, then, that this commentary will give you a sense of the whole Bible and how that impacts on the meaning of a particular passage. If you were to spend many hours and read the Bible through several times, you would find the details beginning to make more and more sense. The purpose of the commentary is to provide you with just such a perspective. It attempts to show how the Bible fits together and how the parts fit into the whole. There are great themes in the Bible. This commentary develops those themes throughout the Bible and shows how those themes and the images that depict them come to place in each passage.

It remains for me to express appreciation to Ed van der Maas, Acquisitions Editor at Zondervan Publishing House, who first suggested the idea for this book to me, and to Verlyn D. Verbrugge, Senior Development Editor, for seeing it through to completion.

# Introduction

The Bible is a book made up of many books. These books were written over many centuries of time by authors with vastly different backgrounds and cultures. Many are well known: Moses, David, Solomon, Ezra, Paul. These men, and others like them, are not only the leading characters in the Bible, they are also the leading producers of the Bible. A surprisingly large number of the biblical authors, however, are nameless. Who wrote the books of Kings, for example, or Chronicles? Who wrote the book of Hebrews?

Fortunately, the answers to such questions are not of major consequence in understanding the Bible. We know the Bible and the books of the Bible by reading them. It is true that some kinds of books (e.g., a diary) require a certain amount of information about its author before it can be properly understood. Other books, like works of literature and history, are written so that we do not have to know the author to understand and appreciate his or her work. What we need to know is given to us as we read the text. The Bible is that way. It is written simply to be read.

The Bible is a unique book. It is one of a kind. It is the Word of God. What does that mean to us as we study and teach the Bible? Basically it means two things: (1) The Bible is divine revelation; (2) the Bible is divinely inspired.

The Bible teaches that God has left signs of his existence and power in his work of creation. From the world around us and from within ourselves, we can see evidences of God's glory. From the world we can see that he is a powerful and wonderful God. From within our own conscience we can know that he is a personal and holy God. But there is a limit to what can be known about God in that way. For example, apart from the Bible we cannot know God's will or God's love for us. We may know that we need God's grace and mercy, but without God himself speaking to us we cannot know how to receive it. In the Bible, therefore, God has revealed his will for us. He speaks to us in the Bible.

But how does it do that? It does so by being a book—it uses letters, words, sentences, and paragraphs. The Bible is a written text. If we can read, we can understand it. This all sounds elementary, but it is important to say this. Sometimes the idea is cast about that the Bible is nothing more than human thoughts and aspirations about God. The Christian idea of revelation is much more than that. The Bible may be human words, but those words express the very words that God wants us to know.

But how can human words express God's will? The answer to that question leads to the notion of inspiration. The Bible teaches that the books of the Bible were written by human beings who were "carried along" in their writing by the Holy Spirit (2Pe 1:21). The Bible is not any more specific than that, however. It does not tell us how the Holy Spirit moved these writers so that their writings expressed God's will. There are thus some unanswered questions. Given that fact, we should not attempt to explain it in any more detail. As far as we know, God did not dictate the words of the Bible to the writers, but neither did he merely give them suggestions on what to write, leaving the choice of words to them. There is really no description of the process by which God inspired certain persons to write Scripture. What we do have, however, is clear statement that the written words, as we now have them in the Bible, are "God-breathed" (2Ti 3:16). What the human writers wrote, God intended to say to us. We can thus know God's will if we study and reflect on Scripture.

It is one thing to talk about the Bible in general terms, but just exactly what Bible are we talking about? Isn't there some disagreement on what books are in the Bible? The answer, of course, is yes, but there is not as much disagreement as one might think. The standard for what books are in the Bible and what books are not is called "the canon." The word *canon* itself means "yardstick" in Greek.

For the first part of the Bible, the Old Testament, the standard was determined very early, long before the birth of Jesus. We have little direct knowledge of the process, but we can say with certainly that the Old Testament that we have today is the same as that of Jesus. It was the accepted standard of the Jews in the first century.

In some parts of the Christian church, before the time of printing, additional books were put alongside the canon of the Old Testament in some manuscripts. These were popular works that were used in worship and devotion. Later on some of these works were taken to be part of the canon of the Bible by the Roman Catholic Church and the Eastern Orthodox churches, though not having exactly the same authority as the Bible. These books, called the Apocrypha, are thus included in their Bibles.

There is no dispute about the canon of the New Testament. At an early stage in the history of the church, the New Testament canon was closed. No additional books have been added.

What was the basis for including a book in the canon of the Old and New Testaments? What makes a book a part of the Bible? For both Testaments, the criterion was twofold: (1) universal acceptance among God's people—Israel for the Old Testament and the church for the New Testament; (2) internal witness of the Holy Spirit. The Spirit of God bore witness to the early readers of Scripture that these books and no others were the inspired Word of God.

How do we know the early church accepted the right books and genuinely witnessed the Spirit's confirmation? This is really the most important question. For the Old Testament we have the additional confirmation of Jesus. Throughout his ministry, in his words and actions, Jesus quoted and used the Scriptures as God's Word. To accept the authority of Jesus is to accept the authority of the Old Testament. For the New Testament we have the confirmation of the apostles. Thus the additional basis for the acceptance of the New Testament books is apostolic authority. The apostles were those who had received direct instruction from Jesus during his earthly ministry. It is their acceptance and confirmation of the canon of the New Testament that assures us of its authority in our lives today.

# Abbreviations

## Books of the Bible

| | | | |
|---|---|---|---|
| Ge | Genesis | Lk | Luke |
| Ex | Exodus | Jn | John |
| Lev | Leviticus | Ac | Acts |
| Nu | Numbers | Ro | Romans |
| Dt | Deuteronomy | 1Co | 1 Corinthians |
| Jos | Joshua | 2Co | 2 Corinthians |
| Jdg | Judges | Gal | Galatians |
| Ru | Ruth | Eph | Ephesians |
| 1Sa | 1 Samuel | Php | Philippians |
| 2Sa | 2 Samuel | Col | Colossians |
| 1Ki | 1 Kings | 1Th | 1 Thessalonians |
| 2Ki | 2 Kings | 2Th | 2 Thessalonians |
| 1Ch | 1 Chronicles | 1Ti | 1 Timothy |
| 2Ch | 2 Chronicles | 2Ti | 2 Timothy |
| Ezr | Ezra | Tit | Titus |
| Ne | Nehemiah | Phm | Philemon |
| Est | Esther | Heb | Hebrews |
| Job | Job | Jas | James |
| Ps | Psalms | 1Pe | 1 Peter |
| Pr | Proverbs | 2Pe | 2 Peter |
| Ecc | Ecclesiastes | 1Jn | 1 John |
| SS | Song of Songs | 2Jn | 2 John |
| Isa | Isaiah | 3Jn | 3 John |
| Jer | Jeremiah | Jude | Jude |
| La | Lamentations | Rev | Revelation |
| Eze | Ezekiel | | |
| Da | Daniel | | |
| Hos | Hosea | | |
| Joel | Joel | | |
| Am | Amos | | |
| Ob | Obadiah | | |

## Other Abbreviations

| | |
|---|---|
| c. | about |
| cf. | compare |
| ch(s). | chapter(s) |
| e.g. | for example |
| etc. | and so on |
| i.e. | that is |
| NT | New Testament |
| OT | Old Testament |
| v(v). | verse(s) |
| ff. | following verses |

| | |
|---|---|
| Jnh | Jonah |
| Mic | Micah |
| Na | Nahum |
| Hab | Habakkuk |
| Zep | Zephaniah |
| Hag | Haggai |
| Zec | Zechariah |
| Mal | Malachi |
| Mt | Matthew |
| Mk | Mark |

# Genesis

## Introduction

Genesis is a part of the Pentateuch (the first five books of the Bible), which Jewish tradition and the NT have ascribed to Moses (cf. Jn 1:17; 5:46; 7:19, 23). Nowhere in the work itself does the author identify himself, but throughout the pentateuchal narratives it is Moses who is most closely associated with the writing of the material contained in them (Ex 17:14; 20:1; cf. also Jos 8:31–32).

Genesis records two types of events: those that happened on a global or even cosmic scale (e.g., Creation, the Flood) and those that happened in a relatively isolated, localized way (e.g., Noah's drunkenness, Abraham's visions). By far most events in Genesis happened in a limited sphere of time and location and can best be described as "family matters."

The purpose of Genesis is intricately bound up with the purpose of the Pentateuch as a whole. Several purposes can be identified. (1) The author shows how events of the past are pointers of those in the future. For example, the sojourn of Abraham in Egypt and later in Gerar, both because of a famine (Ge 12:10–20; 20:1–18), and Isaac's sojourn in Gerar, also because of a famine (26:1–11), foreshadow Ge. 41–Ex 12, Israel's sojourn in Egypt that came about as a result of the famine recorded in the Joseph story.

(2) A close study of Ge 1:1–2:4a shows that the author was mainly concerned about three specific subjects: God, man and woman, and the land. He tells us that God is the owner of the land; he created and prepared it, and he can give it to whomever he chooses (Jer 27:5).

(3) God is the Creator of the universe. Because Israel came to know God in a close and personal way, they tended to nationalize God as the God of Israel alone (Mic 3:11). Over against this lesser view of God stands the message of Genesis with its clear introduction to the God who created the universe and who has blessed all humanity.

(4) The most prominent event in the whole Pentateuch is the covenant between God and Israel established at Mount Sinai. That covenant relates directly back to God's initial desire to bless the human race (Ge 12:1–3). About that theme we can say three things: (a) The covenant at Sinai was God's plan to restore his blessing to the human race *through the descendants of Abraham.* (b) However, the covenant at Sinai failed to restore that blessing because Israel failed to trust God and to obey his will. (c) But the author goes on to demonstrate that God's promise to restore the blessing will ultimately succeed because God himself promised to give Israel, at some future date, a heart that would trust and obey him (Dt 30:1–10). In other words, the entire outlook of the Pentateuch looks to the future as the time when God's faithful promise would be fulfilled.

# I. Introduction to the Patriarchs and the Sinai Covenant (1:1–11:26)

Chapters 1–11 introduce both the book of Genesis and the entire Pentateuch (the first five books of the Bible). They set the stage for the narratives of the patriarchs (Ge 12–50) as well as provide the appropriate background for understanding the central topic of the Pentateuch: the covenant God made with Israel at Mount Sinai (Ex 1–Dt 34).

## A. The Land and the Blessing (1:1–2:25)

### 1. The God of creation (1:1)

The Creator is identified as "God," the God of the fathers and of the covenant at Sinai. By identifying God as the Creator, a crucial distinction is introduced between the God of Israel and the idol gods of the nations. This verse also explains the origin of all that exists in the universe, affirming that God alone is eternal and that all else owes its origin and existence to him.

## 2. Preparation of the land (1:2–2:3)

Verse 2 describes the condition of the land just before God prepared it for the human race (cf. Isa 45:18): it was "formless and empty" with "darkness" over it, and it was covered with water. The remainder of the account portrays God's preparing the land for man and woman. The land was awaiting God's call to light and life. The Spirit of God, in the initial stages of Creation, was hovering over the unformed world like an eagle "hovering" over its young with great concern (cf. Dt 32:11).

The sun, moon, and stars must be included in the usual meaning of the phrase "heavens and the earth"; they were created in v.1. Verse 3 thus describes the appearance of the sun through the darkness. The division between "the day" and "the night" leaves little room for an interpretation of the "light" in v.3 as other than that of the sun.

The frequent repetition "And God saw" (vv.4, 10, 12, et al.) describes the "seeing" activity of God, which the author wishes to emphasize about God (cf. the "God who sees" in 16:13; see also 6:5; 11:5; 18:21). Here God sees that which is *beneficial* for the human race. He is the one who both knows what is "good" for humankind and is intent on providing it. Thus the author prepares us for the tragedy of ch. 3, where the rebellious attempt by man and woman to gain the knowledge of "good and evil" for themselves is seen not only as sin but also as folly.

On the second day God made the "expanse," that is, the sky—a term that refers not only to the place of the sun, moon, and stars (v.14) but also to where the birds fly (v.20). The "waters above" the sky is likely a reference to the clouds (cf. 7:11–12; 2Ki 7:2; Ps 104:3).

There are two distinct acts of God on the third day: the preparation of the dry land and the seas, and the furnishing of the dry land with vegetation. Both these acts are called "good," doubtless because they are for the benefit of humankind. Water is an obstacle standing in the way of inhabiting the dry land; it must be removed before humans can enjoy God's gift of the land. God then furnished the land with seed-bearing plants and fruit trees. Since in ch. 2 Moses stresses how God furnished the "garden" with trees "good for food," the focus here is on that part of God's creation that ultimately becomes the Garden of Eden.

We have already mentioned that the sun, moon, and stars were created on the first day. What then took place on the fourth day? The lights that God had created were given a *purpose*, namely, "to separate the day from the night" and "to mark seasons and days and years." Behind this narrative is also the writer's concern to emphasize that God alone created the lights of the heavens, and thus no one else (and certainly no other god) is to be given the glory and honor due only to him.

The creation of living creatures is divided into two days. On the fifth day God created the sea and the sky creatures, and on the sixth day he created the land creatures—including man and woman. The word for "created" is used only six times in the Creation account (1:1, 21, 27; 2:3); elsewhere the word "to make" is used to describe God's actions. Why is "create" used with reference to the "great creatures of the sea" (v.21)? Here we have the beginning of a new stage in Creation, namely, that of "living beings."

For the first time the notion of "blessing" appears. The blessing of the creatures of the sea and sky is identical with the blessing of humankind, with the exception of the "dominion," given only to man and woman. As soon as "living beings" are created, the notion of "blessing" is appropriate because the blessing relates to the giving of life.

The account of the creation of the land creatures on the sixth day distinguishes two types: "living creatures" that dwell on the land and people. The former are divided into three groups: "livestock," "creatures that move along the ground," and "wild animals." (v.24). Here again the author begins with the divine command—"And God said"—and then follows it with a comment—"God made." Verse 25 adds the important clarification that although vegetation was produced from the land, the living creatures were made by God himself (cf. ch. 2).

The beginning of the creation of the human race is marked by the usual "And God said." However, this time God says, "Let us make." Furthermore, in this account it is specified that the man and the woman were made "in our [God's] image," not merely "according to his own kind." Their image is not simply that of the human being; they share a likeness to the Creator. The creation of humankind is specifically noted as a creation of "male and female," stressing the fact that God created "man" as "male and female." Finally, only human beings have been given dominion in God's creation, a dominion expressly stated to be over all other living creatures.

Many attempts have been made to explain the plural forms: "Let *us* make man in *our* image, in *our* likeness": e.g, (1) the plural is a reference to a plurality in God, hence a hint of the Trinity; (2) the plural is a reference to God and his heavenly court of angels; (3) the plural is an attempt to avoid the idea of an immediate resemblance of humans to God; (4) the plural is an expression of deliberation on God's part as he sets out to create the human race. Of these op-

tions, the first one is by far the best. God created humankind through an expression of his own plurality. That divine plurality anticipates the human plurality of the man and woman, thus casting the human relationship between man and woman as a reflection of God's own personal relationship within himself.

The importance of the "blessing" cannot be overlooked since it remains a central theme throughout Genesis and the Pentateuch. Living creatures were already blessed on the fifth day (v.22); now the blessing extends to all God's living creatures, including human beings. The blessing itself is primarily "posterity." Already, therefore, the fulfillment of the divine blessing is tied to humankind's "seed" and the notion of "life"—two themes that will later dominate the narratives of Genesis (cf. 2:16–17; 12:1–3).

The seventh day is set apart from the first six. On this day God does not "speak," nor does he "work" as he had on the previous days. Rather, he "blessed" the day and "made it holy." The reader is left with a somber reminder, stated three times, of only one fact: God did not work on the seventh day. If the purpose of pointing to the "likeness" between humans and their Creator was to call on the readers to be more like God (e.g., Lev 11:45), then the seventh day stresses that very thing: they must "rest" on the seventh day (cf. Ex 20:8–11; Ps 95:11; Heb 3:11).

### 3. The gift of the land (2:4–24)

This account begins by describing the condition of the land before the creation of the first man (cf. 1:2). The focus is on those parts of the land that will be directly affected by the Fall (3:8–24). The narrative stresses that before Adam was created (v.7), the effects of his rebellion and the Fall had "not yet" been felt on the land. In the subsequent narratives, each part of the description of the land in vv.4–6 is specifically identified in the results of the fall of humankind. The "shrub of the field" and "plant of the field" anticipate the "thorns and thistles" and "plants of the field" that come (in 3:18) as a result of the curse. Similarly, the fact that the Lord God had not yet "sent rain on the earth" prepares us for the Flood narratives (7:4). The reference to "no man to work the ground" points to the time when the man and woman are cast from the garden "to work the ground" (3.23). We are also told that a land was prepared for humankind. In the description of that land, however, we catch a glimmer of the time when humans would become aliens and strangers in a foreign land.

The description of the creation of the first man in v.7 differs significantly from that of ch. 1. Though made in God's image, the first man did not begin as a "heavenly creature"; he was made of the "dust of the ground." This anticipates his destiny in the Fall, when he would again return to the "dust" (3:19).

Much attention is given to the description of the "garden." We are told that the Lord God planted the garden and "put" the man there. This garden was planted "in the east, in Eden." The word "Eden" appears to be a specific place; it means "delight" and evokes a picture of idyllic delight and rest. "In the east" is striking because elsewhere in Genesis, "eastward" is associated with judgment and separation from God (e.g., 3:24; 11:2; 13:11). The garden is not actually called the "garden *of* Eden" but the "garden *in* Eden," a designation found only here. Thus the garden was planted in Eden, which apparently was a location larger than the garden itself; and, if "in the east" is taken with reference to Eden itself, the garden was on its eastern side.

In the garden were beautiful, lush trees, including the elusive "tree of life" and "the tree of the knowledge of good and evil"; there was also a river with four "headwaters." Care is given to locate the rivers and to describe the lands through which they flowed. The lands were rich in gold and precious jewels, and their location was closely aligned with the land later promised to Abraham and his descendants. Later on associations were made between the Garden of Eden and the land promised to the fathers (cf. Isa 51:3; Eze 36:35; Joel 2:3; Zec 14:8; Rev 22:1–2).

The exact location of the Garden of/ in Eden has long been a topic of debate. Two rivers mentioned can be identified with certainty, the Euphrates and the Tigris; it is difficult to identify the other two. The mention of those two links the Garden of Eden and the Promised Land. It can hardly be a coincidence that these rivers, along with the "River of Egypt," later play a role in marking boundaries of the land promised to Abraham (15:18).

Beginning in v.15, the author gives two purposes that God had in putting the man in the garden. (1) By using a different verb for "put" here, the author suggests that the man was placed into the garden where he could "rest," be "safe," and have fellowship with God (3:8). (2) The man was put in the garden to worship God and to obey him. His life in the garden was to be characterized by worship and obedience. "To worship and to obey" is a better translation than "to work it and take care of it" (v.15), for that is later said to be a result of the Fall (3:23). This interpretation suits the larger ideas of the narrative. Throughout ch. 2 the author has consistently and consciously developed the idea of the human being's "likeness" to God along the same lines as the major themes of the Pentateuch as a whole, namely, the theme of worship and Sabbath rest.

With this in mind, it is understandable that we read for the first time in v.16 that "God commanded" the man whom he had created. Enjoyment of God's good land is contingent on "keeping" God's commandments (cf. Dt 30:16). The inference is that God alone knows what is good for the man and what is not good for him. To enjoy the "good" he must trust God and obey him. If he disobeys, he will have to decide for himself what is good and what is not good. To people today such a prospect may seem desirable, but it is the worst fate that could have befallen the human race; for only God knows what is good for them.

Having put this in general terms in vv.16–17, the author turns in the remainder of ch. 2 to set forth a specific example of God's knowledge of the "good"—the creation of the woman. When he sees the man alone, God says, "It is not good for the man to be alone." At the close of ch. 2, the author puts the final touch on his account of what it means for human beings to be "in God's image and likeness." This entails a "partnership" (NIV, "a suitable helper") of the man with his wife. The point is that there is no helper to correspond to the man. A special act of creation of the woman is therefore necessary. Man needs a helper to care for the garden and to provide support in a general sense. And in light of the importance of the blessing in 1:28, the "help" envisioned also involves the bearing of children.

Just as at other crucial points when a new relationship is initiated (e.g., 15:12; 28:11), the recipient of God's provision sleeps while God acts. The purpose of the sleep portrays a sense of passivity and acceptance of the divine provision (cf. Ps 127:2). Woman, made of the same substance as the man, now stands at the side of her husband (from where her rib came) to be his helper. The man's jubilant response in v.23 reflects back on, but also goes beyond, the narrative account in vv.21–22. Whereas in the earlier account only "rib" is mentioned, now "bone of my bones" is

mentioned, and the closing of the man's "flesh" anticipates "flesh of my flesh."

Clearly the naming of the animals is part of the story of the creation of the woman, for in the conclusion of v.20 the author remarks, "But for Adam, no suitable helper was found." The author saw in the man's naming the animals his search for a suitable partner. That no suitable partner was found shows that the man was *not like* the other creatures. In contrast, his words "bone of my bones and flesh of my flesh" show that he recognized his own likeness in the woman.

## B. The Land and the Exile (2:25–3:24)

### 1. Disobedience (2:25–3:7)

A more studied attempt to treat the problem of evil and temptation to sin cannot be found in all Scripture. Genesis 2:25 clearly links the account of the land and the blessing (1:1–2:24) with that of the Fall (3:1–24). The reference to "both" the man and his wife looks back to the previous narrative, while their description as "naked, and . . . no shame" anticipates the central problem that follows. The nakedness had a deeper meaning than merely being without clothes. The Hebrew word used is *arom,* which sounds almost the same as the word *arum* (meaning "crafty") in 3:1. This provides an immediate connecting link with the previous narrative and a presage to the events and outcome of the subsequent story. It also gives an immediate clue to the potential relationship between the serpent's "cunning" and the innocence implied in the "nakedness" of the couple.

The description of the snake as more "crafty" than any of the creatures suggests a relationship between the Fall and humankind's quest for wisdom. The disobedience of our first parents is not so much an act of great wickedness or a great transgression as it is an act of great folly. They had all the "good" they needed, but they wanted more—they wanted to be like God. Moreover, the wisdom that the serpent promised ultimately led to the curse (v.14).

The snake speaks only twice, but that is enough to offset the balance of trust and obedience between the man and the woman and their Creator. The centerpiece of the story is the question of the knowledge of the "good and evil." The snake implied that God was keeping this knowledge *from* the man and the woman, while the sense of the narratives in the first two chapters has been that God was working his knowledge *for* the man and the woman (e.g., 1:4, 10, 12). In other words, the snake's statements directly challenge the central theme that God will provide the "good" for the human race if they will only trust and obey him.

The woman's thoughts in the last moments before the Fall were that she "saw that the ... tree was good." Up until now the expression has only been used of God. Thus the temptation is not presented as a general rebellion from God's authority but rather a quest for wisdom and "the good" apart from God's provision. Ironically, that which the snake promised did, in fact, come about: the man and the woman became "like God" in recognizing the difference between good and evil as soon as they ate of the fruit. The sad part, however, lies in the fact that they were already "like God" because they had been created in his image (1:26).

When they ate of the fruit and their eyes were opened, it was not the "good" that they saw and enjoyed. Rather, their new knowledge was that of their own nakedness; no longer were they like God, and they were no longer even like each other: they were ashamed of their nakedness, and they sewed leaves together to hide their differences from each other. They sought wisdom but found only vanity and toil.

## 2. Judgment (3:8–20)

The judgment scene opens with the "sound" of the Lord's coming, a common form of expression for the Lord's call to obedience (cf. Dt 5:25; 8:20; 13:18; et al.). Appropriately the scene of the curse opens with a subtle but painful reminder of the single requirement for obtaining God's blessing— obedience to God's command. This passage foreshadows the coming of the Lord at the mountain of Sinai, where the people also "heard the sound of the LORD our God." In both instances fear prevailed. In the present instance, Adam and his wife fled to the trees at the first sound of the Lord in the garden. Note how trees play a central role in depicting humanity's changing relationship with God. In chs. 1–2 fruit trees symbolize God's bountiful provision. In ch. 3 they become the ground for inciting the man and the woman to rebel and the place where they seek to hide from God. Finally, when the man and the woman are cast out of the garden, their way is barred from "the tree of life" (v.24).

Before meting out the judgment, God's only words to the rebellious pair come as questions (cf. 4:9–10; 18:21). Skillfully, by repeating "naked," the author allows the man to be convicted with his own words. Then, to show that alienation between the man and the woman went far beyond the shame that each felt in the presence of the other, the man cast blame on the woman and, obliquely, on God. His words are an ironic reminder of God's original intention in 2:18. As a measure of the extent of the Fall, he now sees God's good gift as the source of his trouble.

The record of the curse of the snake, the woman, and the man (vv.14–20) tells the story of the beginning of a great struggle, a struggle that will find its conclusion only by an act of some distant "seed." Regarding the snake, whereas once he was "crafty," now he is "cursed . . . above all the livestock and all the wild animals"—he must "crawl on [his] belly and . . . eat dust all the days of [his] life." This curse does not necessarily suggest that previously the snake had walked as the other land animals. The point is rather that for the rest of his life, when the snake crawls on his belly, he will "eat dust," an expression of shame and total defeat (cf. Isa 65:25; Mic 7:17).

The fates of the snake and the woman embody the fates of their seed. The "enmity" is said to be between the snake and the woman and between their respective "seeds." In the second half of v.15, God says that the "seed" of the woman ("he") will crush the head of the snake ("your head"). The woman's "seed" is certainly intended to be understood as a group (or individual) that lies the same temporal distance from the woman as the "seed" of the snake does from the snake itself. Yet what this seed crushes is the head of the snake himself. That is, though the "enmity" may lie between the two "seeds," the goal of the final crushing blow is not the "seed" of the snake but the snake itself. The author seems intent on treating the snake and his "seed" together, as one. When that "seed" is crushed, the head of the snake is crushed.

More is at stake in this brief passage than the reader is at first aware of. No attempt is made here to answer the question of the snake's role in the temptation over against that of a higher being—Satan. Later biblical writers, however, certainly saw Satan behind the deed of the snake (cf. Ro 16:20; Rev 12:9).

Verse 15 contains a puzzling yet important ambiguity: Who is the "seed" of the woman? The purpose of this verse has not been to answer that question but rather to raise it. The remainder of the book is the author's answer.

The judgment against the woman relates first to her sons and then to her husband. She will bear children in increased pain or toil, and her husband will "rule over" her. The woman and her husband were to have enjoyed the blessing of children (1:28) and the harmonious partnership of marriage (2:18, 21–25). The judgment states that what the woman once was to do as a blessing had become tainted by the curse. Life's greatest blessing for her would experience the painful consequences of her rebellion against God.

We must not overlook, however, the relationship between the promise of v.15 and the words God spoke to the woman in v.16. God had promised that the final victory would be through the "seed" of the woman. When the man and the woman were first created, childbirth was at the center of the blessing that their Creator had bestowed on them (1:28). Now, after the Fall, childbirth (even though its pain is linked to the Fall) is again to be the means through which the snake would be defeated and the blessing restored. In the pain of the birth of every child, there was to be a reminder of the hope that lay in God's promise. Birthpangs are not merely a reminder of the futility of the Fall; they are as well a sign of an impending joy (Ro 8:22–24; cf. Mt 24:8).

Because of the curse, the man could no longer "freely eat" of the "good land" that was provided by the Creator. Throughout chs. 2–3, the ongoing relationship between human beings and the Creator is linked with the theme of "eating." God's blessing and provision for the man's food are first noted in 2:16. Then it was exactly over the issue of "eating" that the tempter raised doubts about God's ultimate goodness and care for the man and his wife (3:1–3). Finally, the pair's act of disobedience is that "she ate it . . . and he ate it" (3:6). Understandably, then, "eating" is related to the judgment on the man. ("Eating" and humanity's relationship to God surface again in Lev 11 and Dt 14 on clean and unclean food and in Lev 23 on eating as participation in the feasts of God.)

As the result of human rebellion, the description of the "land" reverses its description in ch. 2 (see comment on 2:4–24). This opens the way for the motif of "a new heaven and a new earth" (Rev 21:1; cf. Isa 65:17; Ro 8:22–24). Similarly, v.19 shows the reversal of the man's condition. Before the Fall he was taken from the ground and given the "breath of life" (2:7). Now he must return to the dust from which he was taken. Thus the promised verdict of death had come about (2:17). A further reminder of the effect of the Fall is the connection between the man's name, "Adam" (v.20), and the "ground" (*adamah*) from which he was taken. Adam again named his wife, this time calling her "Eve" and pointing to her destiny as "the mother of all the living"—her previous name (2:23) pointed to her origin ("out of man").

### 3. Protection (3:21)

The mention of the type of clothing that God made—"garments of skin," i.e., tunics—is perhaps intended to recall the state of the man and the woman before the Fall: "naked" and "no shame" (2:25). The author may also be anticipating the notion of sacrifice in the animals slain for the making of the skin garments (cf. Ex 28:42).

### 4. Exile (3:22–24)

The verdict of death consisted of being cast out of the garden and barred from the Tree of Life, cut off from the protective presence of community with God in the garden (cf. 4:14). Ironically, when the human race, who had been created *like* God (cf. 1:26), sought to "be like God" (3:5–7), they found themselves after the Fall no longer *with* God. Their happiness does not consist of their being *like* God so much as it does their being *with* God (cf. Ps 16:11).

The depiction of the garden and the Tree of Life guarded by cherubim after the Fall anticipate God's plan to restore blessing and life to the human race in the covenant at Sinai and in the law (Ex 25:10–22). Only through the covenant can human fellowship with God be restored (Ex 25:22), whereby humans return to the state enjoyed in Ge 2:15, as people who serve God, obey his will, and enjoy his blessing. At this point in the narrative, "east" only signifies "outside the garden" (but cf. 11:2; 13:11).

### C. Life in Exile (4:1–26)

#### 1. Worship (4:1–8)

Eve's first words after the Fall are likely a form of a boast, that just as the Lord had created a man, so now she had created a man, expressing her confidence in her own ability to fulfill the promise of 3:15. This interpretation fits in with a recurring theme in the narratives of this book that human effort cannot obtain a blessing that only God can give (cf. ch. 11; 16:1–4). Note also the contrast between Eve's words here at the beginning, "*I* have brought forth a *man*," with her closing acknowledgment, "*God* has granted me another *seed*" (v.25).

The narrative of Cain and Abel teaches a lesson on the kind of worship that is pleasing to God—that which springs from a pure heart. How so? We must first note that according to vv.3–4, both offerings, in themselves, were acceptable to God—they are both described as "offerings," and they are both "firstfruits" offerings. Whatever the specific cause of God's (unstated) rejection of Cain's offering, the narrative ultimately focuses our attention on Cain's twofold attitude of anger: (1) anger against God (v.4b) and (2) anger against Abel (v.8). By stating the problem in this way, the author surrounds his lesson on "pleasing offerings" with a subtle narrative warning: "By their fruit you will recognize them" (Mt

7:20). God pleaded with Cain to "do what is right" or face the consequences of shedding innocent blood and exile from the land (cf. v.12; cf. Jer 7:5–7).

Possibly the present narrative should be read in light of the rules about the "cities of refuge." The purpose of the cities was to ensure that "innocent blood will not be shed in your land" (Dt 19:10), which, of course, is the central point of the Cain and Abel narrative (v.10). The law (Dt 19:11) specifies that a guilty murderer is one who "rises up" (NIV, "assaults") against his neighbor and slays him. Here in Ge 4:8 it states that "while they were in the field, Cain attacked [lit., rose up (against)] Abel and killed him." According to Deuteronomy, Cain's offense was punishable by death. That God showed mercy on him and that later in the story God's mercy was connected with Cain's building a city suggests more than coincidental relationship between the story of Cain and the cities of refuge.

### 2. Repentance (4:9–15a)

As in ch. 3, when the Lord came in judgment, he first asked questions (v.9) and then meted out the punishment (vv.11–12). The picture of Cain's judgment is remarkably similar to the exile that Israel was warned of in Dt 28:16–18 (cf. Isa 26:21; 27).

Both the sense of "bear" in v.13 and the Lord's response to Cain in v.15 suggest that his words must not be understood as a complaint about his punishment but rather as an expression of remorse and repentance over the extent of his "iniquity." In v.14 Cain acknowledged that God's punishment (v.12) could result in his own death since he would not have the protection of an established community. Like his parents who were driven out of their home in God's judgment, the penalty of death to be carried out against Cain was banishment from a protective community.

### 3. Protection (4:15b–24)

The background of the cities of refuge (Nu 35:9–34) may provide a clue to the sense of the "sign" or "mark" given "to" or "for" (not "on") Cain. Its purpose was to provide Cain with protection from vengeance. Though the sign is not explicitly identified, the narrative continues with an account of Cain's departure to the land of Nod, "east of Eden," where he built a city. In light of the purpose of the later cities of refuge, it may be significant that the "sign narrative" is followed by the "city narrative." Cain's city may have been intended as the "sign" that gave divine protection to him from anyone who might attempt to avenge Abel's death (cf. Nu 35:12). Even in Lamech's day Cain's city was a place of refuge for the "manslayer" (see comments below).

The remainder of the chapter is devoted to the "culture" that developed in the context of the "city" that Cain built. The primary components of city life were animal husbandry (Jabal, v.20), arts (Jubal, v.21), craftsmanship (Tubal-Cain, v.22), and, apparently, law (Lamech, vv.23–24). Lamech's words to his two wives are frequently read as an example of a boasting arrogance and rebellion. But in the context of the Mosaic Law and the teaching regarding the cities of refuge, his words appear to be an appeal to a system of legal justice. The Mosaic Law provided for the safe refuge of any "manslayer" until a just trial could be held (Nu 35:12). Lamech, by referring to the "avenging of Cain" (cf. v.24), made it known that in his city he too had been "avenged."

To show that he had not shed innocent blood, Lamech appealed to the fact that he killed a man "for wounding" and "for injuring" him. He did not "hate his neighbor, lie in wait for him, rise up against him, and kill him" (cf. Dt 19:11), as Cain had done, but rather based his appeal on a plea of self-defense. Lamech's appeal bears striking resemblances to the principle of lex talionis (Ex 21:25). The force of the principle was to insure that a given crime was punished only by a just penalty. If Cain, who killed his brother with malice, could be avenged, then Lamech would surely be avenged for killing in self-defense, that is, for "wounding" him.

### 4. Blessing (4:25–26)

Though Cain's sons prospered and became the founders of the new world after the Fall, the focus turns from the line of Cain to the new son born "in place of Abel." Once again, the author betrays his interest in the "seed" of the woman. A pattern is established that will remain the thematic center of the book. The promised seed comes not through the heir apparent but through the one whom God chooses. Cain takes his place as one of those who were not to become a part of the line of the "seed" (cf. Japheth, 10:2–5; Ham, 10:6–20; Nahor, 11:29; 22:20–24; Ishmael, 17:20; Lot, 19:19–38; Esau, ch. 36). The importance of the line of Seth is underscored by the fact that in his day people already practiced true worship of God.

### D. The Story of Noah (5:1–10:32)

A major break is signaled at the beginning of ch. 5 by the new heading: "This is the written account of Adam's line." This section, which concludes at 9:29, is built around a list of ten of the descendants of Adam, concluding with Noah. After Noah's death is recorded (9:29), a new list of his sons begins, ending with the birth of Abraham (11:26). The interweaving of narrative and genealogical lists occurs throughout Genesis.

### 1. Prologue (5:1–3)

The prologue to the Noah story does three things. (1) It redirects the reader's attention back to the course of events in ch. 1 with the "likeness" of God motif. (2) It also ties ch. 5 together

with 4:25–26 by continuing the pattern of "birth" and "naming." Just as God made a man in his likeness and named him Adam, so Adam fathered a son "in his own likeness" and named him Seth. Clearly, although Adam is the father of Seth and Seth the father of Enosh, etc., God is the Father of them all. (3) The reference to God's "blessing" humankind relates back to the Fall. God's original plan of blessing, though thwarted by human folly, will be restored through the seed of the woman (3:15), the seed of Abraham (12:3), and the "Lion of the tribe of Judah" (49:8–12; cf. Rev 5:5–13).

### 2. The sons of Adam (5:4–32)

The genealogical list in ch. 5 is nearly identical in form to that of 11:10–26, the genealogy of Shem. The only difference is the inclusion of the clause "and then he died" (ch. 5). The death of each patriarch is underscored to highlight the exceptional case of Enoch, who "walked with God" and who did not die. The pronouncement of death, in other words, is not the last word; a door is left open for a return to the Tree of Life. Enoch found that door by "walking with God" and has become a paradigm for all who seek life.

Regarding Noah, the last one mentioned in this list, two points in particular call for attention. (1) He will bring comfort from the labor and painful toil of the curse (v.29). Likely that comfort was the salvation of humankind in the ark and the reinstitution of the sacrifice after the Flood (cf. 8:21). (2) Noah's rescue from death in the Flood receives the same explanation for Enoch's rescue from death ("he walked with God"). When Noah did finally die (9:29), it came only after the story of his sin of drunkenness (9:18–27).

### 3. Epilogue (6:1–4)

At the conclusion of the list of patriarchs and before the account of the Flood, the author summarizes the state of affairs of Adam's descendants (cf.

10:31–32; 11:27–32; Ex 1:7.) His main emphasis here is that Adam's children, the sons of God (cf. 5:1), greatly increased in number, married, and continued to have children; i.e., it presents a picture of everyday affairs (cf. Mt 24:38–39).

The sense of v.3 is clear if read within the context of what precedes and follows. After creating humans as male and female, God "called them man [Adam]" (5:2), which obviously had a wider scope than the personal individual of ch. 4. After focusing on the lives of ten individuals in ch. 5, God speaks a second time about "man" (6:3). The ages of the men in those intervening verses stand in stark contrast to the "one hundred and twenty years" mentioned in this verse. The inference is that it was God's Spirit dwelling with these men that gave them their long lives. The sad reality is that such long lives belonged to another age and that they were exceptions rather than the rule. Thus the author continues to show the ages of the men of the book and notes that generally their ages grow increasingly shorter (cf. 11:10–26). At the close of the Pentateuch we finally reach an individual, Moses, who is specifically mentioned as dying at the age of 120 years (Dt 34:7).

"Nephilim" elsewhere in the Pentateuch refers to the great men who were in the land of Canaan at the time of the Exodus (Nu 13:32–33). Here "Nephilim" appears to refer to the great men of antiquity. Since the author has just referred to ten such great men (ch. 5), perhaps these were the "men of renown."

### 4. The Flood (6:5–9:17)

Genesis 6:5–12 forms the introduction proper to the Flood story. Its cause is tied directly to the earlier account of the fall of humankind (ch. 3). Although people had obtained the "knowledge of good and evil," it had not been beneficial. They were far better off when they

had to trust God for "the good." The grief and pain of human sin were not something that only humans felt. God himself grieved over it. Noah, however, found favor with God.

The Flood account begins in 6:9 with the description of Noah's righteousness. The main purpose of the story is not to show why God sent a flood but rather why God saved Noah. His "righteousness" stands in contrast with the "violence" of "all the people." In other words, God saved Noah because he "walked with God" and did not "corrupt" God's way (cf. 5:22–24). His life becomes a model of the kind of life that finds grace in the sight of God. It is simple obedience to God's commands and trust in his provision (cf. Heb 11:7).

The list of specifications for the ark in 6:13–15 is not so much for us to see what the ark looked like but rather to appreciate the meticulous care Noah exercised as he obeyed God's will. The exact nature of the material that the ark was made from is unknown. The meaning of NIV's "cypress wood" remains a mystery. This wood was sealed with "pitch," another rare word found only here. For a wooden vessel, the ark was enormous. It was constructed with three stories, each with separate compartments; it had an opening for light and a door in its side. Obviously the structure consisted of more features than those enumerated in this brief description.

In 7:1–5 God commands Noah to enter the ark prior to the coming rains. The emphasis of the section lies in the special provisions for the "clean animals," suggesting that in the ark Noah and his family ate only "clean meat" (cf. Lev 7:19–21). As entrance into the tabernacle was possible only with an offering of unblemished animals, so too Noah's entry into the ark is tied to his taking with him "seven pairs" of every clean animal. The sacrificial importance of these "clean animals" is seen in 8:20–21.

What is most apparent in the description of the onset of the Flood (7:6–24) is the focus on the occupants of the ark. With great detail the procession of those entering the ark passes by the reader. Only at the conclusion of ch. 7, when the ark is resting safely over the highest mountains in the surging flood, does the author cast his glance on those who were not spared by the ark (vv.21–23). Even then the author's attention on these people is motivated less by the reason why they perished than by the reason why Noah and those with him in the ark survived: they had done "as God had commanded" (7:9, 16; cf. v.5; 6:22). Obedience to the Lord is the way to salvation.

Chapter 8 begins by emphasizing that those in the ark had to wait before God sent his deliverance. God began to stop the flow of the waters and to remove the sources of the floods. But it still took much time before Noah could disembark on dry land. He had to wait patiently. At the end of forty days, after the ark came to rest, Noah began to look for signs of his impending deliverance. He sent out a raven and a dove, but no signs of dry land appeared. Noah continued to wait. By the time Noah knew that the dry lands had appeared, he had waited exactly one year (cf. 7:6, 11; 8:13–14). But even then Noah could only open the window to look out of the ark. He still had to wait for God's command before leaving the ark (8:15–17).

The image that emerges from this portrait of Noah is that of a righteous and faithful *remnant* (see 7:23), patiently waiting for God's deliverance (cf. Isa 8:17–18; 40:31; Jas 5:7–11). Henceforth "the Flood" is synonymous with eschatological judgment (Isa 8:7–8), and Noah's deliverance is an image of the salvation of the faithful (Mt 24:37–39).

Noah left the ark only at God's command (8:15–19). The description, though condensed, closely follows the Creation pattern in ch. 1, suggesting a return to the work of Creation. Significantly, at this point the author takes up a lengthy account of the *covenant* (8:20–9:17). The restoration of God's creation was founded on the establishment of a covenant. By Noah's altar and offering, the whole of the state of humankind before the Flood is reestablished. The human race is still fallen (9:21), but through an offering on the altar they may yet find God's blessing. It is also significant that as in ch. 1, the focus of the author's interest in "man" after the Flood is his creation in God's image (9:6).

There is a striking thematic parallel between the picture of God's calling Noah out of the ark (8:15–20) and his later call of Abraham (12:1–7). Both Noah and Abraham represent new beginnings. Both are marked by God's promise of blessing and his gift of the covenant. The covenant with Noah plays an important role in the restoration of blessing, for it lies midway between God's original blessing of all humankind (1:28) and God's promise to bless "all peoples on the earth" through Abraham (12:1–3).

Also significant are the close associations between Noah and Moses, specifically between Noah's altar and Moses' altar at Mount Sinai following the Exodus (Ex 24:4–18) and between God's covenant with Noah and his covenant at Sinai. The latter covenant is not really a new act but a return to God's original promises.

### 5. Noah's drunkenness (9:18–29)

These verses conclude the Flood story and introduce the short episode of Noah's drunkenness. What should not be overlooked in this particular transitional unit is the identification of Canaan as one of the sons of Ham. This is crucial to what follows (cf. vv.22, 25).

Just as in the Creation God planted a garden for people to enjoy, so now Noah plants an orchard. The outcomes are remarkably similar. Noah ate of the fruit of his orchard and became naked (cf. 2:25; 3:7). That is, even after the salvation from the Flood, enjoyment of God's good gifts by the human race could not be sustained. Noah, like Adam, sinned, and the effects were felt in the sons and daughters that followed.

Ham looked on his father's nakedness. Shem and Japheth instead covered it without looking on him. The author's main intent is to show simply the contrast between the deeds of Ham and those of Shem and Japheth, a contrast that becomes the basis for the curse and the blessing that follow. We can understand the impact of this contrast by looking at the Fall in ch. 3. In covering their father's nakedness, Shem and Japheth were like Adam and Eve (3:7) and God (3:21), who did not look on human nakedness but covered it (cf. 2:25). Ham did not follow that lead. His actions were more like those of whom God warned later in the Torah, those who "expose their own nakedness" before God and others (cf. Ex 20:26). The sons of Noah, therefore, belong to two groups of people, those who like Adam and Eve hide the shame of their nakedness, and those who like Ham (or rather the Canaanites) have no sense of their shame before God. To the one group, the line of Shem, there will be blessing (v.26); but to the other, the Canaanites (not the Hamites), there can only be a curse.

### 6. The line of Noah (10:1–32)

The author's purpose in giving a list of names at this point can be seen in his statement at 10:32. These names give a panoramic view of the nations as a backdrop for the rest of the book and beyond. There are exactly seventy nations represented in the list, which symbolizes the totality of nations. In other words, "all nations" find their ultimate origins in the three sons of Noah.

Though the author is about to narrow his focus to the "seed of Abraham" and the "sons of Israel," he first lays a solid foundation for his ultimate purpose in God's choice of Abraham: through his "seed" God's blessing will be restored to "all peoples on earth" (12:3). It is not without purpose that the author reminds his readers that the total number of Abraham's "seed" at the close of Genesis is also "seventy" (46:27; cf. Ex 1:5).

The list begins with "the sons of Japheth" (10:2–5), "the maritime peoples" (v.5), i.e., those who make up the geographical horizon of the author, a kind of "third world" over against the nations of Ham (Canaan) and Shem. Later, when the focus is on the establishment of God's universal kingdom, these nations again come into view to show that God's plan includes all peoples (Ps 72:8, 10).

A pattern in the author's selection is clearly discernible in the list of the sons of Japheth. Fourteen names are listed in all: seven sons of Japheth, then seven grandsons. The author has omitted the sons of five of the seven sons of Japheth (Magog, Madai, Tubal, Meshech, and Tiras), listing only the sons of Gomer and Javan. Thus his intention is not to give an exhaustive list but rather a "complete" list, one that for him revolves around the number seven.

The list of the sons of Ham (vv.6–12) begins as the list of the sons of Japheth does, with the simple naming of Ham's four sons. Then the grandsons of the first listed (Cush) are given. But before going on to the next son (Mizraim), the great-grandsons (sons of Raamah) are listed. The end result is a list of "seven sons"—a complete list. Immediately following this are the exploits of Nimrod and his cities, introducing the city of Babylon, the subject of 11:1–9. The genealogy continues with a list of the sons of Mizraim, again seven names. This is the last list of the numerical pattern "seven." The remainder of the lists of names appears to be influenced by no particular numerical pattern except the total number of "seventy nations" that dominates the list of names. The exact boundaries of the area of Canaan (v.19) are singled out since that area lay at the heart of the purpose of the book. This was the land promised to Abraham, though "at that time the Canaanites were in the land" (12:6).

Regarding the sons of Shem (vv.21–31), the reference in v.21 to Shem and Japheth without Ham recalls Noah's blessing of Shem and Japheth in 9:26–27, where Canaan is also excluded. The list of descendants of Shem is also highly selective, focusing on Eber's son Joktan. Significantly, a second genealogy of Shem is given after the account of the building of Babylon (11:1–9), and there the line is continued to Abraham through Eber's first, Peleg (11:10–26). Thus a dividing line is drawn through the descendants of Shem on either side of the city of Babylon, falling between the two sons of Eber. One line of Joktan leads to the building of Babylon and the line of Peleg to the family of Abraham.

The final verse of ch. 10 again takes up the theme of the division of the nations, providing a context for the narrative of the city of Babylon that follows. What has been described "geographically and linguistically" in ch. 10 is described "theologically" in ch. 11—namely, God's judgment of Babylon and his dispersion of the nations.

## E. The City of Babylon (11:1–9)

As just mentioned, the oneness of the people up to this point divides in the two sons of Eber (10:25). The first scene (of Babylon) opens with a movement "eastward" to the "plain in Shinar." Recall that both the man and woman and Cain moved eastward after

being cast out from the presence of God (3:24; 4:16). When Lot divided from Abraham, he moved "toward the east" (13:10–12). When a person in the Bible goes "east," he leaves the land of blessing and goes to a land where his hopes turn to ruin (e.g., Babylon and Sodom).

The word "name" plays a central role here. First, the builders of the city wanted "to make a name" for themselves. The conclusion of the story returns to the "name" of the city, ironically associating it (Babylon/Babel) with the confusion of their language. "Scattered" is another key word. The purpose of the city was so that its inhabitants would not "be scattered over the face of the whole earth." Ironically, at the conclusion of the story it is the Lord who "scattered" the builders from the city "over the face of the whole earth." The expression "the whole land" ("world" or "earth") is a third key term in the story. The people had left "the whole world" (11:1) to build a city in the east. The purpose of that city was to keep them from being scattered throughout "the whole earth." But in response the Lord reversed their plan and scattered them over "the face of the whole earth."

The focus of the author since the beginning chapters of this book has been both on God's plan to bless humankind by providing them with that which is "good" and on human failure to trust God and enjoy the "good" God had provided. The characteristic mark of this failure has been the attempt by humans to grasp the "good" on their own, as the builders of the tower were attempting to do. The author has centered his description of God's blessing on the gift of the land (1:28). The good land is the place of blessing. To leave this land and to seek another is to forfeit the blessing of God's good provisions. It is to live "east of Eden."

### F. The Line of Shem (11:10–26)

This list of ten descendants of Shem, like that of Adam in ch. 5, draws the line of the "faithful" (Noah to Abraham) and bypasses the "unfaithful" (10:26–30). These verses show that God's promise concerning the seed of the woman cannot be thwarted by the confusion and scattering of the nations at Babylon. Though the offspring of Noah were scattered at Babylon, God preserved a line of ten great men from Noah to Abraham.

## II. Abraham (11:27–25:11)

### A. The Line of Abraham (11:27–32)

The genealogy that precedes the narrative of Abraham provides the necessary background for understanding the events in his life. Thus far the author has usually listed ten names between important individuals, but this short list has only eight names. Who is the ninth and, more importantly, the tenth? As the narrative unfolds, they are the two sons of Abraham, "Ishmael" (16:15) and "Isaac" (21:3). This introduction, then, anticipates the birth of Isaac, the tenth name.

Interspersed in the list of names is the brief notice that Terah and his family, including Abram and Lot, had left Ur of the Chaldeans and traveled as far as Haran, en route to the land of Canaan. There is no mention of the call of God until 12:1, presumably after the death of Terah (v.32b). It appears, then, that Abram was called to leave his homeland while in Haran—after his father's death and not while in Ur. Furthermore, 12:4–5, which recounts Abram's obedient response to God's call, explicitly states that he "set out from Haran."

A second look, however, suggests that the author intended us to understand the narrative differently. How so? Verses 27–32 show that Abram's birth took place in Ur of the Chaldeans, not Haran. Thus the command given to Abram to leave the place of his birth (12:1; NIV, "your country") could only have been given at Ur. Putting the call of Abram within the setting of Ur aligns this narrative with themes in the later prophetic literature and connects his call (12:1–3) with the dispersion of the city of Babylon (11:1–9), thus making Abraham prefigure all those future exiles who, in faith, wait for the return to the Promised Land (cf. Mic 7:18–20).

### B. The Call of Abram (12:1–9)

Abram, like Noah, marks a new beginning as well as a return to God's original plan of blessing "all peoples on earth" (cf. 1:28). Notable is the frequent mention of God's "blessing" throughout the narratives of Abram and his descendants (12:1–3; 13:15–16; 15:5, 18; et al.). He is represented as a new Adam and his seed as a second Adam, a new humanity. Those who "bless" him, God will bless; those who "curse" him, God will curse. The way of *life and blessing,* which was once marked by the "tree of the knowledge of good and evil" (2:17) and then by the ark (7:23b), is now marked by identification with Abram and his seed.

The identity of the seed of Abraham is one of the chief themes of the following narratives. At the close of Genesis (49:8–12), a glimpse of his future seed is briefly allowed. This one seed who is to come, to whom the right of kingship belongs, will be the "lion of the tribe of Judah" (cf. 49:9); and "the obedience of the nations is his" (49:10).

The account of Abram's entry into the land of Canaan is selective. Only three sites are mentioned: Shechem, a place between Bethel and Ai, and the Negev. Significantly, these are the same three locations visited by Jacob when he returned to Canaan from Haran (chs. 34–35), as well as the same sites occupied in the account of the conquest of the land under Joshua.

## C. Abram in Egypt (12:10–13:4)

Verse 10 opens with a notice that a famine forced Abram to seek refuge in Egypt. This is the first occurrence of the recurring theme of the threat to God's promise recorded in 12:1–3. In nearly every episode that follows, God's promise of "numerous seed," "blessing to all peoples on earth," or the "gift of the land" is placed in jeopardy by the actions of the characters of the narrative. The promise looks as if it will fail. In the face of such a threat, however, God remains faithful to his word and safeguards the promise.

The account of Abram's sojourn in Egypt (as well as in Gerar, ch. 20; and Isaac's sojourn in Gerar, ch. 26) parallels in many respects the account of God's deliverance of Israel from Egypt (Ge 41–Ex 12). Both passages have a similar message. Abram's stay in Egypt prefigures Israel's later stay in Egypt (both initiated by a famine). Behind the situations stands a faithful, loving God. What he has done with Abram, he will do for his people today and tomorrow.

## D. The Lot Narratives (13:5–19:38)

### 1. Abram and Lot (13:5–18)

The narrative here is governed by the theme of "struggle" and shaped around the "separation" (vv.9, 11, 14) that ensues. At its conclusion stands the second statement of God's promise to Abram. Just as the first statement of the promise was preceded by his separation (10:32; 12:1), so the second statement of the promise is put in the context of Abram's separation from his closest kin, Lot. Significantly, the final statement of the promise to Abraham comes immediately after he has demonstrated his willingness to be separated from his only son and heir, Isaac (22:15–18).

Abram's separation from Lot also carries the theme of the promise into jeopardy. Ironically, Abram is on the verge of giving the Promised Land to Lot, who later (19:37–38) became the father of the Ammonites and the Moabites. These people throughout Israel's subsequent history (Dt 23:3–6; Ezr 9:1) were the primary obstacle to the fulfillment of the promise. But Lot "chose" to go "east," which foreboded disaster; so Abram remained in the land. Thus God's promise was secure, in spite of Abram's passivity.

The land Lot chose was "like the garden of the LORD" and "like the land of Egypt," a positive description within the context of Genesis. But there is a subtle foreshadowing of the fatal results of Lot's choice in the geographic marker "toward Zoar," where Lot fled for safety from the destruction of Sodom and Gomorrah (19:22).

Definite ties connect Lot's separation from Abram to the separation of the nations at Babylon (11:1–9). The account of the dispersion of the nations closes in 10:32b with a reference to the nations being "spread out [i.e., separated] over the earth after the flood." Then the narrative of the dispersion of Babylon opens with the people of the land traveling "eastward" (11:2). Similarly, Lot traveled "towards the east" when he "parted" (separated) from Abram (13:11). Following the separation of the nations at Babylon, the narrative resumes with Abram traveling throughout the land of Canaan, receiving it as a promise, and then building an altar in response to God's promise (12:1–9). So also, after Lot separated to Sodom, Abram traveled throughout the land of Canaan, received it a second time as a promise, and built an altar in response (v.18).

### 2. Abram and the nations (14:1–24)

At first glance the ties between chs. 13 and 14 seem meager. The narrative begins abruptly by a reference to the time of Amraphel, and the location moves from Hebron (13:18) to an international arena and the wars of four kings. Lot is the link between the two accounts. Immediately following the report of his capture, the narrative returns to Hebron (14:13b), where Abram is brought into the center of the account of the battle with the four kings (vv.14–17). The mention of "Mamre" at vv.13, 24 returns us to the scene at the close of ch. 13.

"The LORD," the God whom Abram worshiped at Hebron (13:18), is the "creator of heaven and earth" (14:22), and he delivers the four kings of the east into Abram's hands. Abram asks nothing from the kings of this world (vv.22–23), and he is the only one who proves able to live peacefully in the land. As 12:3 has forecast, those who join with him (v.13b) will enjoy his blessing (v.24b); those who separate from him, as Lot had done (13:12), will suffer the same fate as Sodom and Gomorrah (14:11–12).

Shinar (v.1) has already been identified with Babylon (10:10; 11:2, 9); its king is mentioned in the narrative, thus aligning the account with the theme of "Babylon." Elsewhere throughout the chapter Kedorlaomer is always first among the four kings (vv.4, 5, 9, 17). Although little information is given about the actual battles other than that the kings of Sodom and Gomorrah were soundly defeated and routed, the account is overladen with geographical and political details. What is important in this narrative is that the events recorded were global in scope and ended in the disgraceful defeat of the kings of Sodom and Gomorrah.

In v.12 the perspective changes markedly from the war with the four eastern kings to the fate of Lot. The ultimate cause of his unfortunate fate was that "he was living in Sodom," a hint of the blessing in the land for those who align themselves with Abram (12:1–3; 13:14–17) and the fate of all those who separate themselves from him. Lot's fate is the first stage in a lesson that will bring him still further in need of the intercession of Abram (18:23–32). Twice

Abram intervenes for Lot: here he rescues Lot in the war with Babylon and later his intercession (18:23–32; 19:29) effects Lot's deliverance. The picture of Abram that emerges here is the same as that in 20:7: "He is a prophet, and he will pray for you and you will live."

The scene returns in v.13 to Abram and his three friends at Hebron, strangely unaffected by the events of the previous narrative. In this brief scene Abram musters a select army, defeats the four kings, and returns Lot with the rest of the captives. After his return, Abram was met by two kings in the "King's Valley" (v.17). Melchizedek appears suddenly as if out of nowhere and just as quickly is gone. The insertion of this encounter into the section dealing with the king of Sodom suggests that it must be read as the background to Abram's encounter with the king of Sodom. Thus a contrast is established between Abram's responses to the king of Salem and the king of Sodom: one is positive, the other negative.

Lying behind these responses is the contrast between the offers of the two kings. The king of Salem brings "bread and wine" as a priestly act and acknowledges that it was the "God Most High, Creator of heaven and earth," who delivered the adversaries into Abram's hand. Abram's response to Melchizedek appropriately recognizes the validity of his offer as well as of his priesthood: Abram paid a tithe (see Nu 18:21). The king of Sodom, on the other hand, offered Abram all the "goods" recovered in the battle. Abram would have nothing to do with an offer of reward from him, for his reward would come from the Lord (cf. 15:1, 14b); Abram was a man of faith. At the same time, Abram laid claim to rightfully own what his young men had eaten (cf. Dt 20:14b), and he also recognized that his three friends had their own rightful share in the spoil.

### 3. Abram and the covenant (15:1–21)

God's address to Abram is in the elevated style typical of later prophetic literature (vv.1, 4; cf. Jer 34:12). Like the seer Balaam (Nu 24:4, 16), Abram saw the word of the Lord "in a vision." For the first time it is recorded that he spoke to God. Previously when God spoke to him, Abram obeyed but did not speak in return. Here he raised a question of how the promise would be fulfilled. In fact, he raised so many questions that we are reminded of his unwavering faith (v.6).

Abram's questions provide the backdrop for the central issue of the chapter: God's apparent delay in fulfilling his promises. The issue at stake is the same one faced by Jeremiah. God's people, instead of enjoying the promised blessing, find themselves about to enter captivity in Babylon. The promise appears to have come to naught (cf. Jer 25:11), but God reveals that the time of exile has a limit (v.12). Similarly, Abram must wait in faith for the fulfillment of the promise, being counted righteous in his faith (v.6), but realizing that the promise was afar off to another generation (vv.15–16; cf. Heb 11:13).

What was Abram afraid of here (v.1)? God's first words relate back to Abram's fear for the final outcome of God's promise to make his "offspring like the dust of the earth" (13:16; cf. v.2). Abram's questions betray also that fear. He has little reason to hope that God will remain faithful to his word. Significantly, Abram's next words to the Lord (17:18) also reveal doubt. On the other hand, when he is silent, his actions always exhibit faith.

The appeal to the number of the stars of "the heavens" recalls Abram's own words in 14:22, where his hope for reward was based solely on the "Creator of heaven and earth." If the Lord was the Creator of the great multitude of stars, he was able to give him an equal number of descendants (cf.

22:17; 26:4; Ex 32:13; Dt 1:10; 28:62). God's faithfulness in the past was the basis for Abram's trust in the future.

God was about to enter a "covenant" (v.18) with Abram that would be the basis of all God's future dealings with him and his offspring (vv.7–21). Verse 6 sets the record straight: Abram had believed in the Lord and had been accounted righteous. The "covenant" did not make him "righteous"; rather, it was through his "faith" that he was reckoned righteous.

Verses 7–16 recount the establishment of a covenant between the Lord and Abram. The opening statement is virtually identical to that of the Sinai covenant (Ex 20:2); God's covenant is grounded in a past act of divine salvation (cf. Ge 11:28, 31). The coming of God's presence in the awesome fire and darkness of Mount Sinai (Ex 19:18; 20:18; Dt 4:11) is clearly foreshadowed in Abram's pyrotechnic vision (vv.12, 17). In the Lord's words, the connection between Abram's covenant and the Sinai covenant is explicitly made by means of the reference to the four hundred years of bondage of his descendants and their subsequent exodus.

In v.17, the act of dividing the animals and walking through the parts was apparently an ancient form of contractual agreement (cf. Jer 34:18). While the meaning of the details may remain a mystery, fortunately the writer of Genesis has explained the custom: "On that day the LORD made a covenant with Abram." The sudden and solitary image of the birds of prey that Abram must drive away (v.11) give a fleeting glimpse of the impending doom that awaits Abraham's seed, but it also points to the protective care of God's promises (cf. Mt 24:28).

In vv.18–21 the author again draws the promise of the land back into the narrative by concluding with a description of the geographical boundaries of the covenant land. The borders of the

Promised Land appear to coincide with the border of the Garden of Eden (cf. 2:10–14).

### 4. Hagar (16:1–16)

The mention of Hagar's geographical origin in Egypt links this account to 15:18b–21. Twice we read that Hagar, *the Egyptian,* "despised" Sarai (cf. 12:3). As a consequence, Hagar was forced into the "desert" (v.7), where she was to stay until she submitted herself again to Sarai. Only then did the Lord offer Hagar a blessing (v.10; cf. 17:2, 20).

To deal with her barrenness, Sarai's plan of offering her maid to her husband so that she could bear him an heir was apparently acceptable within the social custom of the day. That plan, however, was one more example of the futility of human effort to achieve God's blessing. Although successful, the plan does not meet with divine approval (17:15–19; cf. 11:1–9; 12:10–20; 13:1–12; 14:21–24).

The location shifts to the desert, to the "spring that is beside the road to Shur." In other words, Hagar was returning to Egypt (see 25:18). The angel of the Lord greets her with a question and then offers a blessing to the distraught handmaid. The child to be born to her will be named "Ishmael" because the Lord "has heard" (a play on words, since both terms are built on the same Heb. root) her "misery." The key term throughout the chapter is "misery," which occurs as a noun in v.11b and as a verb in v.6 ("mistreated") and v.9 ("submit"). Hagar was afflicted by Sarai (v.6); she was told to put herself back under that affliction (v.9); and the Lord heard her affliction (v.11).

The second half of Hagar's "blessing" did not portend well for her son: he would be a "wild donkey of a man" (a Hebrew word with similar sound to the word "Paran"). In 21:21 Ishmael is said to be "living in the Desert of Paran." Ishmael was to dwell on the outskirts of civilization and in hostility to his brothers, especially his future brother Isaac.

The final section of ch. 16 consists of Hagar's naming of God and the birth of Ishmael. The two events go together in that the birth of the child was the confirmation of the name given to God in this section: "the God of seeing."

### 5. Abram, Sarah, and Ishmael (17:1–27)

Abram was eighty-six years old when Ishmael was born (16:16). At the beginning and close of ch. 17, his age is given as ninety-nine (vv.1a, 24). Thus his age functions as a framework. The Lord's first speech to Abram establishes the interpretive boundaries for the rest of the chapter and establishes the fact that the events of this chapter represent the making of a covenant between the Lord and Abram. The substance of the covenant is the promise of abundant descendants.

God is immediately identified as the "LORD," the God of the covenant at Sinai (Ex 3:15). Within the narrative, however, he identified himself to Abram as "God Almighty." After doing so, he gives a brief synopsis of the covenant, stressing Abram's obligation: "Walk before me and you will be blameless" (lit. tr.) and the divine promise: "[I] will greatly increase your numbers." But had not God already "made" a covenant with Abram in 15:18? Why did he do so a second time? The two covenants are, in fact, two distinct aspects of God's single covenant with Abram—one stresses the promise of the land (15:18–21) and the other the abundance of descendants (17:2).

The report of Abram's response is also brief: Abram "fell facedown" (v.3), a sign of deep respect. In his response to the Lord's second speech (v.17), he not only "fell facedown" but he also "laughed." When Abram heard that God would greatly increase his descendants, he responded with respect and submission. But when he heard *how*

God would carry out his plan, his respect contained a tinge of laughter.

God's second speech is divided into three sections by the clause "and God said." Each section deals respectively with one of the parties of the covenant (the "LORD," "Abram," and "Sarai"). The substance of each section is memorialized by a specific sign: the change of Abram's name to "Abraham" ("father of many nations"), the circumcision of all males, and the change of Sarai's name to "Sarah" ("princess"). God's part of the covenant consists of two promises: abundant descendants and eternal faithfulness. Abraham's descendants who belong to this covenant will owe their existence to God alone.

The choice of the word "fruitful" in v.6 and "increase your numbers" in v.2 recalls the blessing of all humankind in 1:28 and its reiteration in 9:1, showing that the covenant with Abraham is the means God uses to channel his blessings to all people.

A new element is added in v.6b: "kings will come forth from you." This anticipates not only Abraham's descendants recorded in Samuel and Kings but, more importantly, provides a link between the general promise of blessing through the seed of Abraham and the subsequent focus of that blessing in the royal house of Judah (49:8–12; Nu 24:7–9). The notion that the blessing would come from a king is not new (cf. 14:18–19), but the idea that this king would come from the seed of Abraham is new.

The focus of vv.7–8 lies in the repetition of the term "everlasting," applied to both the covenant and the land. The promises in these verses were given before (cf. 13:14–15; 15:18–21); however, here the everlasting nature of these promises is in view. Eternality was certainly implied in the "forever" of the "land" promise (13:15); but when the "covenant" was granted in ch. 15, there was not yet a mention of its being "eternal." Central here then is God's everlasting faithfulness.

Abraham's part in the covenant consisted of obedience, particularly that "every male among you . . . must be circumcised." To keep the covenant was to practice circumcision faithfully; to "break" the covenant was to be "uncircumcised." But the whole of the covenant was not simply the rite of circumcision, for that was to "be the sign of the covenant."

Sarah's part in the covenant was to be the mother of nations, and "kings of peoples will come from her." As with Abraham, her new name—Sarah—was a sign of her part in the covenant.

Abraham's response in v.17—"fell facedown" and "laughed"—is unexpected. His own words uncover the motivation behind his laughter. In 18:12, when Sarah also responded to God's promise with laughter, her laughter was met with divine disapproval. The absence of such a rebuke here suggests that Abraham's laughter does not so much reflect a lack of faith as it does a limitation of his faith. Abraham's faith must grow if he is to continue to put his trust in God's promise. One clear purpose in Abraham's laughter is that the Hebrew expression "he laughed" foreshadows the name "Isaac." Throughout the remainder of the narratives surrounding the birth of Isaac, a key word within each major section is "laughter": Sarah "laughed" (18:12); Lot's sons-in-law laughed (19:14); all who heard of Sarah's birth to Isaac would "laugh" (21:6); the son of Hagar laughed (21:9b; NIV, "was mocking") at Isaac; finally, Isaac's own failure to trust in God (26:7) was uncovered when the Philistine king saw him "laughing" (26:8b; NIV, "caressing"). Thus the power of God and the limitations of human faith are embodied in that most ambiguous of human acts, laughter.

The third divine speech extends the covenant to include Isaac, who is to be born of Sarah, and consequently excludes Ishmael, the son of Hagar. Thus Isaac is here brought to the level of a participant in the original covenant, and the identification of the covenant "offspring" of Abraham is made more specific.

Although Ishmael has been excluded from the covenant with Abraham, he and his descendants are still to live under the blessing of God. In fact, in his blessing of Ishmael, God reiterated both his original blessing of all humanity in 1:28 and his blessing of Abraham in 12:2. Just as the "offspring" of Isaac would form a great nation of twelve tribes (49:1–27), so the "offspring" of Ishmael, under God's blessing, would form a great nation of twelve rulers (cf. 25:13–15).

Abraham's final response (v.23) shows that he obeyed the covenant; he circumcised all the male members of his household "as God told him." Such obedience reflects the injunction given in v.1: "Walk before me and be blameless" (cf. 5:22, 24; 6:9). Abraham and Noah are examples of those who obeyed the covenant and were therefore "blameless."

### 6. Three visitors (18:1–33)

The narrative in ch. 18 begins in the same way as ch. 17, with the Lord appearing to Abraham. This helps clarify at the outset who the three men were who visited Abraham and what their mission was. The mention of the "great trees of Mamre" reestablishes the location of Abraham during these events (cf. 13:18).

The narrative of the arrival of three men at Abraham's tent is complicated by several uncertainties. (1) The relationship between the three men and the appearance of the Lord (v.1a) is not explicit. (2) There seems to be a conscious shift in number: in v.3, Abraham's address uses the singular "you," while vv.4–9 use the plural "you." (3) What is the nature of the relationship between

these uncertainties and their counterparts in ch. 19 (i.e., the relationship between the "two angels" [19:1a] and the Lord, who "rained down burning sulfur on Sodom and Gomorrah" [19:24]). Such irregularities result from a conscious attempt to stress at one and the same time two equally important views of God: his immanent *presence* and his transcendent, sovereign *power.* Take, for example, the interchange between the singular and plural in v.3 and vv.4ff. Those passages that speak of God's making himself known through words, visions, and angels pose no difficulty in light of the strict prohibition against the presentation of God in any physical form (Dt 4:15). But what about when it is expressly stated that God "appeared" to someone (12:7; 17:1; 18:1)? How can God "appear" and yet say "my face must not be seen" (Ex 33:23)? By carefully identifying and distinguishing the three characters in the narrative by means of the singular and plural "you," the author is able to show that the Lord's appearing to Abraham and the visit of the three men are one and the same event. God appeared to Abraham, but not "face to face" in his own physical form.

There are close similarities between the account of Abraham's visit by "three men" and Lot's visit by the "two angels/men" (19:1–2). In ch. 18 Abraham is sitting "at the entrance to his tent," whereas in ch. 19 Lot is "sitting in the gateway of [Sodom]" (v.1). Second, when Abraham "saw" the men, he ran "to meet them" and "bowed low to the ground" and said, "O Lord, if now" (NIV, "If . . . my lord"); so also Lot in ch. 19, when he "saw" the angels/men, he got up "to meet them" and "bowed down with his face to the ground" and said, "Behold now, O lords" (NIV, "My lords"). One primary difference between the two accounts is the way the visitors are greeted. Abraham addressed them as "Lord" and appropriately used the singular to address all three men in v.3 (see above). Having just entered a covenant with the Lord (ch. 17), Abraham recognized the Lord when he appeared to him, whereas Lot, who then lived in Sodom, did not recognize the Lord.

The three men inquired about Sarah but spoke only to Abraham. Abraham and particularly Sarah were too old to have children. Throughout this story, the main obstacle to the fulfillment of the promise was Sarah's age (cf. 25:1–4). It is repeatedly stressed that for her to have a child was not simply unlikely; it was impossible (v.14; NIV, "too hard")!

Sarah therefore laughed at the idea that she might yet bear a child. In the Lord's question to Abraham about Sarah's laughter, he subtly changes the wording of Sarah's thoughts, revealing that he was not simply restating her thoughts but was interpreting them as well. First, the Lord restated Sarah's somewhat ambiguous statement—"After I am worn out, . . . will I now have this pleasure?"—as simply "Will I really have a child?" Then he took Sarah's statement about her husband—"my master is old"—and reshaped it into a statement about herself: "now that I am old." Finally, he went beyond her actual words to their intent: "Is anything too hard for the LORD?" The underlying issue, then, is the physical impossibility of the fulfillment of the promise through Sarah. Once the physical impossibility of Sarah's giving birth was firmly established, the Lord repeated his promise to Abraham.

As the three men arose (v.16) and looked out toward Sodom, Abraham accompanied them to send them off. With a seemingly insignificant gesture, the three men "looked down toward Sodom," the doomed city of the next chapter. The Lord then mused to himself about whether he should reveal his plans for Sodom to Abraham. Verse 18 looks back to the original promise of 12:2–3 that Abraham would become a "great . . . nation" and that "all the nations on earth will be blessed through him."

Verse 19 expands on the ideas of 17:1. The Lord puts into words what has been a central part of the narrative, namely, Abraham's election: "I have chosen him." Second, the Lord expresses his purpose in choosing Abraham—"to keep the way of the LORD," so that Abraham and his descendants may do "what is right and just." Only then will the Lord fulfill what he had promised to Abraham. The notion of an internalized obedience is remarkably close to the terms of the "new covenant" (Jer 31:33) and is rooted in the theology of Dt 30:6.

Beginning in v.20, the Lord addresses Abraham. His words answer the question in v.17, revealing at this point that he will go down to investigate the wickedness of Sodom and Gomorrah.

In v.22, the men (presumably all three) leave to go to Sodom. Note that the narrative first states that the Lord said, "I will go down and see" (v.21), and then "the men turned away and went toward Sodom." But if three men left Abraham, why did only "two messengers" (19:1) arrive in Sodom? What happened to the other "man"? The most common explanation is that the remaining "man" is a "christophany," i.e., an appearance of the Second Person of the Trinity in human form, before the Incarnation. When the text says that "the men turned away and went toward Sodom" and that "Abraham remained standing before the LORD," one of the men must have stayed behind with Abraham. Thus this man may have been the preincarnate Christ, accompanied by two "angels."

The central issue in vv.23–33 is expressed in Abraham's question at the end of v.25. The Lord's answer is a resounding yes; the Lord would do right.

Abraham then started with a question about fifty righteous people in a city and concluded with the question of ten righteous ones. Why stop at ten? Did he not care about Lot and his family who only numbered four? Since the sequence of fifty down to ten, in units of ten, would naturally end with ten, Abraham would not have gone to zero righteous people, for he was concerned only with the salvation of the righteous amid the unrighteous, not with the destruction of the wicked.

In Abraham's concern for Lot, the narrative addresses the larger issue of God's treatment of any righteous person in his judgment of the wicked. When the city of Sodom was destroyed, Lot was taken out of it. Thus we have the answer to what God would do if less than ten righteous were found in the city. It should also be pointed out, however, that though Sodom was not spared for Lot's sake, the little city of Zoar was spared on Lot's behalf.

### 7. Lot and Sodom (19:1–38)

According to v.18, the men visiting Lot are represented as a visitation of the Lord (v.18; cf. NIV mg.). They came to carry out the Lord's retribution against the wickedness of the city (v.13b); but in response to Abraham's prayer for the righteous (18:23–32), they also had come to rescue Lot (19:29).

The depiction of the events at Lot's house on the eve of the destruction of Sodom and Gomorrah justifies the divine judgment on the two cities. Even Lot, the righteous one who was ultimately rescued, was tainted by his association with Sodom. Unlike Abraham, he appears insensitive to God's presence with the messengers, addressing them only as "sirs" (v.2; NIV, "lords"). His suggestion that the men of the city take his own daughters and do with them what they please can hardly be taken as a sign of his good character. In fact, in an ironic turn of events, Lot

himself later inadvertently carried out his own horrible proposal (vv.30–38).

The messengers clearly stated their twofold purpose (vv.12–14): they had been sent to destroy the city and to rescue Lot and his family. The response of the two "sons-in-law" shows that they are at one with the rest of the men of the city. This provides a further vindication of the divine punishment that was to follow.

In contrast to the men of Sodom who blindly groped for the door of Lot's house, Lot and his family were taken by the hand and led out of the city to safety at the break of day (vv.15ff.). The rescue of Lot was in response to the prayer of Abraham, for the angels' words explicitly recall the words Abraham used (cf. 18:23; 19:15, 17; see esp. 19:29).

This section suggests that Lot was a righteous man living amid the unrighteous, who was rescued from the fate of the wicked through the intercession of God's chosen one. Surprisingly, however, the basis of God's saving Lot was not his righteousness but because "the LORD was merciful" (v.16). Lot's "righteousness" (cf. 2Pe 2:7) comes only from the connection established between Abraham's prayer "for the righteous" in ch. 18 and the events of Lot's rescue in ch. 19. In the account of the rescue itself, the emphasis is on God's compassion. Lot acknowledges in v.19 that he had found "favor" and "kindness" before God.

At the conclusion of Lot's rescue, he requested shelter in the nearby city of Zoar. In granting the request, the Lord saved that city from destruction. Thus Lot's rescue is a result of two prayers—Abraham's and his own. God had promised not to destroy the city "on behalf of" the righteous in it. So now, though Sodom was destroyed, Zoar was saved from the destruction on account of Lot, the righteous one living in it.

Before the onset of the description of God's judgment, we are reminded of two things. First, "the sun had arisen over the land," and second, "Lot reached Zoar [safely]." The Bible often pictures the "sunrise" as an image of divine salvation for the righteous and divine judgment on the wicked (Isa 9:2; Mal 4:1–2). Then follows the classic image of the fate of every wicked one: "The LORD rained down burning sulfur on Sodom and Gomorrah."

Lot's wife (v.26) and Abraham (v.28) both "looked" at the destruction of the cities, but with very differing consequences. Lot's wife became a "pillar of salt" because she "looked back," thus disobeying the words of the rescuers (v.17). Abraham, on the other hand, looked from a vantage point consistent with the men's words in v.17. They said, "Don't stop anywhere in the plain," and so Abraham "returned to the place where he had stood before the LORD. He looked down toward Sodom and Gomorrah, toward all the land of the plain" (vv.27–28). Unaware of the warning to Lot and his family, Abraham obeyed and escaped the destruction.

Verse 29 is a clear reminder of Abraham's role in Lot's rescue. This carries through the theme of God's promise—in Abraham and his offspring "all peoples on earth will be blessed" (12:3). Ironically, in his own drunkenness Lot carried out the shameful act that he himself had suggested to the men of Sodom (19:8): he lay with his own daughters. The account is remarkably similar to the story of the last days of Noah after his rescue from the Flood (9:20–27). There, as here, the father becomes drunk and uncovers himself in the presence of his children with negative consequences. Thus, at the close of the two great narratives of divine judgment, those who were saved from God's wrath subsequently fell into a form of sin reminiscent of those who died in the judgment.

Lot is mentioned as the father of the Moabites and the Ammonites in Dt 2:9, 19, a passage that stresses their relationship to Israel. Both the Moabites and the Ammonites continued to play an important role in later biblical history.

### E. Abraham and Abimelech (20:1–18)

The focus of chs. 20 and 21 is the relationship between Abraham and the nations. Abraham's role is as a prophetic intercessor, as in the promise "all peoples on earth will be blessed through you" (12:3). He prayed for the Philistines (20:7), and God healed them (v.17). In the narrative Abimelech plays the role of a "righteous Gentile" with whom Abraham could live in peace and blessing. There is an implied contrast in the narratives between chs. 19 (Lot, the one who pictures the mixed multitude) and 20 (Abimelech, the righteous sojourner).

Abraham left the "great trees of Mamre" (18:1, 33) and traveled into "the Negev" to sojourn in Gerar, the "land of the Philistines" (21:34). There Sarah was taken into Abimelech's house. The narrative here is much briefer than the similar event in ch. 12. Clearly the focus is not so much the fate of Sarah as it is that of the Philistines. Many of the details are withheld until Abraham is given an opportunity to speak on his own behalf (vv.11–13). At that point his actions cast more light on the Philistines' inner motives than on his own. Abraham's words show that he had mistakenly judged the Philistines to be a wicked people, but their actions proved otherwise.

The narrative goes to great lengths to demonstrate the innocence of Abimelech. Thus his appeal to his innocence contrasts sharply to Abraham's deception. Indeed, in v.6 God himself concurred with Abimelech. Abimelech, however, was in immediate need of a warning lest he lose his innocence by mistreating Abraham's household.

Abraham's wife was to be returned, and Abraham the prophet must pray in behalf of the life of Abimelech. The surprising outcome of God's visit of Abimelech is that he responded immediately by rising early in the morning and declaring his dream to his servants and then to Abraham. The Philistines responded quickly and decisively to God's warning (cf. Jnh 3:6–9).

Abraham's reply seems intended not only to justify his action with Sarah in the present narrative but also to provide a larger picture for understanding his similar actions while in Egypt in ch. 12. Though we have followed the life of Abraham closely since he left his father's house in ch. 11, this is the first we have heard of Abraham's familial relationship with Sarah. In the last analysis we are left only with the opinion of Abimelech himself, who undoubtedly accepted Abraham's explanation and faulted only himself in this unfortunate situation. Just how sincerely Abimelech accepted Abraham's story can be seen in the fact that in speaking to Sarah he called Abraham "your brother" and attempted to restore the broken relationship with expensive gifts.

Abraham accepted the gifts from the Philistines and offered a prayer on their behalf in return (v.17). Only at this point do we discover the nature of God's words to Abimelech in v.7. The Lord had "closed up every womb in Abimelech's household."

## F. Abraham and Isaac (21:1–25:11)

### 1. The birth of Isaac (21:1–7)

Verse 1 picks up the narrative from 18:10. Strangely, the news of the birth of Isaac has been delayed and treated anticlimactically. The author has paid more attention to the *announcement* of the birth of the son in ch. 18 than to *accomplished fact.* Isaac's birth came about "as [the LORD] had said," stressed three times in vv.1–2. Thus the narrative calls attention to God's faithfulness to his word.

The importance of the announcement of Isaac's birth is seen in the statement that "the LORD was gracious" (v.1), which focuses on God's attentive care and concern. Also important is the reminder that Isaac was the "son . . . in [Abraham's] old age" and that he was born "at the very time God had promised him." The narrative goes on to emphasize Abraham's obedience (v.4; cf. 17:12) and specific age (v.5; cf. 17:1, 24).

### 2. Hagar and Ishmael (21:8–21)

The celebration of Isaac's coming of age led to the expulsion of Ishmael. The similarities between this chapter and ch. 16 are notable. As we have had occasion to note before, the author has often foreshadowed later events in earlier ones, in order to draw connections between important narratives. In this case the Lord's promise to Hagar (16:11–12) was recounted in a strikingly similar fashion to that of the fulfillment of the promise (vv.18–21).

### 3. Abraham and Abimelech (21:22–34)

The reappearance of Abimelech shows that Abraham was still living with the Philistines (cf. v.34). This is a reminder that Abraham did not live out all his days in the Land of Promise but spent many days in exile. Even Isaac, the son of the promise, was not born in the Land of Promise but in exile and had to sojourn there with his father, who "wandered from nation to nation, from one kingdom to another" (Ps 105:13; cf. Heb 11:8–13). Abraham in exile typifies God's care of the righteous who must suffer while waiting to enter the land. The servants of Abimelech had stolen Abraham's wells. But because God was with Abraham in all that he did, he made a covenant with their king, and all was restored to him.

### 4. The binding of Isaac (22:1–14)

The clear statement that "God tested Abraham" reveals the Lord's real purpose in this incident. There is no thought of an actual sacrifice of Isaac in the narrative, though in the mind of Abraham within the narrative that was the only thought that was entertained. The abruptness of God's request surprises us as much as it would have Abraham, and we are as much in the dark about the intention of God's ways as Abraham was.

Noteworthy is the way the narrative excessively and deliberately details Abraham's preparation for the journey and the journey itself. No one says anything until Isaac finally breaks the silence; the question he raises serves only to heighten the anguish of the Lord's request. When Abraham finally speaks, his reply to Isaac's question anticipates precisely the final outcome of the story: "The LORD will provide." These words not only attempt to calm the curious Isaac but are a settled expression of Abraham's trust in God.

Few narratives can equal the dramatic tension of the last moments before God interrupts Abraham's action and calls the test to a halt. His actions are described in exaggerated detail. At the last dramatic moment the Lord intervened and, as Abraham had already anticipated, provided a substitute. Abraham therefore named the altar he had built "The LORD will provide."

### 5. The angel of the Lord (22:15–19)

At the end of the narrative is a "second" encounter between Abraham and the angel of the Lord, one that happened shortly after the first (i.e., after Abraham had finished the burnt offering). The reason why it is called a "second" encounter is to show that the renewal of God's original promises to Abraham was not based on Abraham's specific actions in carrying out the test but rather on his faith and the obedience he showed through this test.

The promise reiterated here is similar to that of the earlier chapters. The promise of "blessing" recalls 12:2. The increase of Abraham's "descendants" is similar to 13:16; 15:5; and 17:2. The view of the "nations'" enjoyment of and participation in Abraham's blessing resembles 12:3 and 18:18. The reference to Abraham's act of obedience as the basis of the promise recalls 18:19. Perhaps, also, the reference to Abraham's descendants possessing the "cities of their enemies" (v.17) refers to the gift of the "land" (12:7; 13:15; 15:18; 17:8).

### 6. The relatives of Abraham (22:20–24)

Immediately after the reiteration of the promise of a great multitude of descendants comes a notice regarding the increase of the family that Abraham and Sarah had left behind in their homeland. The twelve names in the list suggest an intentional comparison with the twelve sons of Jacob or the twelve sons of Ishmael in 25:12–15. The central purpose of the list is to introduce the future bride of Isaac, Rebekah, and to show that she was of the lineage of Milcah and not of Reumah.

### 7. Machpelah and Sarah's death (23:1–20)

Sarah died in Hebron, and Abraham apparently came there from Beersheba (cf. 22:19) to mourn her death. The point of ch. 23 is to show how Abraham, in a fair manner, first came into legal possession of a parcel of land in Canaan. Through what appears to be a hard bargain, Abraham bought not only a cave for the burial of his wife but also a large field with many trees. This became an important burial site for the patriarchs and their wives (cf. 49:30–32; 50:13). Just as Abraham would not accept a gift from the king of Sodom (14:23), so here he refused to accept the parcel of land as a gift. Apparently against the wishes of the Hittites, he paid the full price. God, not another human being, was the source of Abraham's hope of blessing. His purchase of land embodied his hope in God's promise that one day all the land would belong to him and his descendants (cf. Jer 32:6–15).

### 8. A bride for Isaac (24:1–67)

Abraham's concern that God's promise would come to the descendants of Isaac is evidenced in the oath Abraham made with his servant, which makes two important points regarding the future of his descendants. (1) They were not to be mixed with the inhabitants of Canaan—a further expression of the notion of the line of blessing and the line of curse (cf. 9:25–27). The seed of Abraham must be kept separate from the seed of Canaan. (2) Abraham's descendants are not to return to the land of their fathers. Canaan is their home, and Abraham is careful to ensure that Isaac not be taken back to the ancestral home.

Once again the faith of Abraham stands out. The questions raised by the servant provide the occasion. As so many times before, Abraham's reply proves to be both prophetic—it anticipates the final outcome of the story—and thematic—it provides the central motive of the narrative, that God would go before the servant to prepare his way.

Once in Nahor, the servant spelled out specifically the nature of the sign he sought from the Lord (vv.12–14). God did prepare the way, bringing the young girl in question on the scene even before the servant finished speaking. All the details of her background are given as soon as she enters the picture. While the servant is unaware of the actual identity of the girl, we know that she is Rebekah, the daughter of Bethuel, the son of Milcah. Clearly, the Lord has answered the servant's prayer. God had indeed sent "his angel" (v.7) out ahead of him to prepare the way. Such divine preparation for the descendants of Abraham and the line of the blessing

must be accompanied by the kind of appreciation that is seen in the servant in vv.26–27.

After meeting Laban and his household, the servant retells the episode. Rather than a mere repetition, however, this retelling asserts the central points of the first narrative. Originally Abraham said only generally that God would send an angel and that the servant would find a wife for Isaac (v.7). When the servant retold the story, however, he added the idea that the angel would make his "journey a success" (v.40) by gaining a wife for Isaac from his own family. The further detail makes the miracle of God's provision even grander.

At the conclusion of the servant's account, Laban and Bethuel acknowledge that it was the Lord who prepared the way for the servant to meet Rebekah. Thus several witnesses testify that these events were the work of God: the narrator (vv.15–16), the servant (vv.26–27), and Laban and Bethuel (v.50). The final witness is Rebekah herself, who agreed to return with the servant to Isaac. The simplicity of her response (v.58) reveals the nature of her trust in the God of Abraham (cf. Ru 1:16).

The importance of the blessing of Rebekah by her family (vv.59–60) lies in the similarity of this blessing to that given to Abraham by the Lord in 22:17. The Lord has carefully chosen this wife for Isaac, and in his plan the same blessing is given to both Isaac and his bride.

In v.62 Isaac enters the narrative for the first time, just as the servant is bringing the young woman to him. They both lift up their eyes and see the other in the distance. The final remarks (vv.66–67) again show that God guides those who put their trust in him. When Isaac took Rebekah as his wife, he loved her and was comforted with her after the death of his mother. So Rebekah follows Sarah in the line of the descendants of Abraham.

### 9. Abraham's death (25:1–11)

After the death of Sarah, Abraham took another wife, Keturah. The narrator pictures Abraham's life after Sarah's death as that of a completely rejuvenated old man. He continued to be rewarded with the blessing of many offspring. But only Isaac had any share in the promised blessing.

Surprisingly little attention is given to the details of Abraham's death. The length of his life is given, which connects him to the patriarchs (cf. 11:32). That Abraham died "at a good old age" recalls the word of the Lord in 15:15. The mention of Abraham's "good old age" contrasts to Jacob's "few and difficult" (lit., "evil") years (47:9). This narrative thus picks up the "good" and "evil" theme begun in the first chapters of the book and carries it through to the end (cf. 50:20). The final resting place of Abraham was in a portion of the Promised Land that he rightfully owned—the field purchased from Ephron the Hittite.

There are relatively few narratives devoted to the theme of "blessing" in the life of Isaac; most are in ch. 26. All the more important, then, is this brief statement that God blessed Isaac, a reminder that his was the line of the divine blessing (cf. 17:21).

## III. The Account of Ishmael (25:12–18)

The Isaac stories open (cf. v.11) with a final statement regarding the line of Ishmael, consisting of a genealogy of the twelve leaders of Ishmael's clan, a report of the length of his life, and a report of his death. The number twelve appears again to be a deliberate attempt to set these individuals off as founders of a new and separate people (see comment on 22:20–24; cf. 17:20). No mention is made of Ishmael's blessing in 17:20, and we hear nothing more about him in Genesis. The descendants of Ishmael, however, continue to play a part in the Genesis narratives (28:9; 36:3; 37:27–28; 39:1).

## IV. The Account of Isaac (25:19–35:29)

### A. The Birth of Jacob and Esau (25:19–28)

There are marked similarities between the introductions to the Abraham (11:27–32) and the Isaac narratives (25:19–26). Abraham's brother, Haran, died before his father; Isaac's brother Ishmael died before his brothers (25:18b). Abraham took a wife, and she was barren (11:30); Isaac took a wife, and she was barren (25:20–21). Both narratives contain an element of struggle between brothers. Abraham was accompanied by Lot from birth, and Jacob was accompanied by Esau from birth (25:22–24). In the struggles that ensued, Abraham was "separated" from Lot (13:9, 11, 14) and Jacob was "separated" from Esau (25:23).

The "account of Abraham's son Isaac" (v.19) almost immediately turns out to be about the sons of Isaac rather than Isaac himself. Although an important link in the line of Abraham, as an individual character Isaac is given little attention, except for ch. 26.

Isaac, like Esau later (26:34), was forty years old when he took a wife, Rebekah. Because Rebekah was barren, Isaac prayed for his wife (cf. 20:17); the Lord answered, and she bore two sons. The barrenness of both Sarah and Rebekah, as well as Rachel (29:31) and Leah (29:35), reiterates the point that the promised blessing through the chosen seed of Abraham is not to be accomplished solely by human effort. The fulfillment of the promise at each crucial juncture requires a specific act of God.

A central theme throughout Genesis—the struggle between brothers—begins in the womb of Rebekah (cf. 9:20–27; 13:7–12; 21:9; 29–31; 37–50). The point is not that the struggles were necessary for the accomplishment of the will of God but that God's will was accomplished in spite of the conflict. Another important motif is that "the older will serve the younger." From ch. 4 the narrative has portrayed God choosing and approving the younger and the weaker through whom he would accomplish his purpose and bring about his blessing (cf. 4:1–5, 26–5:8; 17:18–19; 29:18; 37:3; 49:8). God's promised blessing was not a natural right but was extended solely by his grace (cf. Mal 1:1–5; Ro 9:10–13).

## B. Selling the Birthright (25:29–34)

The story of Esau's rejection of his birthright is a narrative example that God's choice of Jacob over Esau did not run contrary to the wishes of either. Esau, though he had the right of the firstborn, "despised" his birthright, while Jacob went to great lengths to gain it. Thus, when in God's plan Esau lost his birthright and consequently his blessing, there was no injustice dealt him.

## C. Isaac and Abimelech (26:1–35)

Each brief narrative of Isaac parallels a similar situation in the life of Abraham. The short span of one chapter shows how Isaac's whole life is a retelling of what happened to his father. The lesson conveyed is of God's continuing faithfulness.

As in the days of Abraham (12:10–20; 20:1–18), famine struck during the life of Isaac. At first we are told only that Isaac went down to Gerar to Abimelech; but in the warning Isaac received in the vision of v.2, we are informed that he was on his way to Egypt. No explanation is given why he should not go to Egypt, except that he is to "live in the land." The Lord's warning became the occasion for a formal restatement of the blessing. In the face of the impending famine, the Lord promised to be with Isaac, to bless him, to make his seed great, to give him the land, and to bless all the nations of the land in him (cf. 12:2–3, 7).

The Lord then added a remarkable note: Abraham "kept my requirements, my commands, my decrees and my laws" (cf. Dt 11:1). Did Abraham know the law? If so how? If not, what was the meaning of the Lord's words? At several points Abraham acted in accordance with the law—particularly the law as recorded in Deuteronomy; yet he never actually had a knowledge of that law. For example, in ch. 14 Abraham's actions followed quite closely the stipulations of Dt 20; he obeyed the law from the heart (cf. Dt 30:6; Jer. 31:33). He is the ultimate example of true obedience. Thus, Abraham, a man who lived in faith (Ge 15:6), could be described as one who kept the law.

There are several similarities between Isaac and Abraham in vv.6–11. Both "stayed in Gerar" (cf. 20:1). Each devised a scheme with his wife, calling her his "sister" (cf. 20:2). Each was rebuked by the Philistine king, Abimelech, for the great shame he might have brought on his people (cf. 20:9). Such similarities can hardly be coincidental. Unlike the same incident in the life of Abraham, however, it was not God who warned Abimelech not to touch the patriarch's wife (20:6), but Abimelech himself. It was Abimelech himself who said that anyone who touched the woman would "surely be put to death" (cf. 20:7).

Though earlier Abimelech was said to have been "pure of heart" (20:6; NIV, "clear conscience"), his actions in ch. 26 alone show that his heart was right. As soon as he discovered that Rebekah was not Isaac's sister, he feared that a great shame (NIV, "guilt") would come upon his people. Clearly the picture that emerges is of a righteous, even pious Gentile who did what was right. A wider picture of the nations emerges here—both as wicked and deserving judgment and as righteous.

In vv.12–13, just as Abraham prospered while sojourning among the Gentiles (12:16; 20:14), so Isaac prospered while sojourning with Abimelech. The source of Isaac's prosperity was that "the LORD blessed him." This is the second reference to Isaac's blessing, underscoring the connection between Isaac's prosperity and God's promise to Abraham in 12:2.

Just as Abraham's prosperity became the occasion for the conflict between his shepherds and Lot's (13:5–7), so Isaac's wealth angered the Philistines (vv.14–22) and conflict developed. As the name given to the well—"Rehoboth"—shows, there was a progressive resolution of the conflict as Isaac continued to move away from the Philistines and dig new wells. After finding no conflict at Rehoboth, they said, "We will flourish in the land" (cf. 1:28).

As the Lord had spoken to Abraham after he had separated from Lot and renewed his promise of land and great prosperity (13:14–17), so now after Isaac returned to Beersheba, the Lord appeared and renewed the promise (vv.23–25). For a third time it is said that the Lord would bless Isaac (cf. vv.2, 12). Like his father (12:7; 13:3–4), Isaac responded by building an altar and worshiping God.

Earlier Abimelech, acknowledging God's presence with Abraham (21:22), sought to enter into a covenant with him (21:27). Likewise, Abimelech acknowledged the Lord's presence with Isaac and sought to enter into a covenant with him (vv.26–31). Isaac, like Abraham, was the source of blessing to those who sought him out. Both trusted God and lived "in peace" with their neighbors.

The final picture of Isaac in this chapter is the discovery of a new well on the same day that Isaac had made peace with his neighbors. Consequently the writer associates the name of the city, "Beersheba" (lit., "well of the seven/oath"; cf. 21:31), with the "oath."

Initially the short notice of the marriage of Esau (vv.34–35), who had despised his birthright (25:29–34), to two Hittite women seems insignificant. But this forms the background to the central event in ch. 27, the blessing of Jacob. These preliminary notices put into perspective the cunning deed of Jacob and Rebekah and demonstrate that Esau was not fit to inherit the blessing.

## D. The Stolen Blessing (27:1–40)

There are several elements in this story that heighten the suspense and highlight the deception of Jacob; thus Jacob's name, which means "the deceiver" (cf. v.36), has been appropriately chosen. Isaac is depicted as too old and too blind to distinguish between his two sons. This makes the story more believable and more suspenseful; perhaps it is also an attempt to ease Isaac's culpability. Isaac's insistence on a "good meal" before the blessing recalls Esau's own trading of the birthright for a pot of stew and thus casts Isaac and Esau in similar roles. The suspense of the story is carried right to the end, where Jacob is shown leaving at the same moment as Esau returns from the hunt (cf. v.30).

The goal of Jacob's strategy was to wrest the blessing from Isaac. Although Isaac did not appear completely convinced that he was speaking to Esau, in the end he blessed Jacob. This theme of "blessing" points out the relationship of this narrative both to the narratives that precede and those that follow. The promise to Abraham (12:2–3) is alluded to in the final words of Isaac's blessing (v.29). Similarly, his blessing foreshadows Jacob's later prophecy concerning the kingship of the house of Judah (cf. 49:8). Thus the words of Isaac are a crucial link in the development of the theme of the blessing of the seed of Abraham.

The reverse side of the blessing of Jacob is the disappointment and anger of Esau. He is presented as a tragic figure, a victim of his more resourceful and daring brother. His anguish on hearing about his misfortune of losing the blessing recalls 25:21–34, when he lost his birthright. Within the narrative, Isaac recounted the main points of the blessing given to Jacob a second time, underscoring the fact that he had blessed Jacob rather than Esau. Finally, with Esau in tears, Isaac answered his pleas for a blessing with a third reiteration of the central point of Jacob's blessing: "You will serve your brother." The blessing was irretrievably lost to Esau and would certainly be fulfilled in Jacob.

### E. Jacob's Flight From Beersheba (27:41–28:5)

Jacob's scheme not only resulted in his obtaining the blessing from Isaac, but it also became the occasion for Jacob's journey to the house of Laban. The picture of Esau at the conclusion of this story is that of a bitter, spiteful brother. He made plans to kill Jacob and regain by force his birthright and blessing. Again Rebekah thwarted the plans, having Isaac send Jacob back to her homeland to find a wife. As in many of the narratives of Genesis, Isaac's words of blessing to the departing Jacob precisely anticipate the eventual outcome of the ensuing story: Jacob would visit Laban "for a while," Esau's anger would subside (see ch. 33), and Jacob would find a wife and return as a great assembly of people. Within Isaac's farewell blessing is a final reiteration of the central theme of the preceding narrative: The promised blessings of Abraham and of Isaac were now the promised blessings of Jacob.

### F. Esau's Bitterness (28:6–9)

The final picture of Esau in this narrative is that of a bitter son now seeking to spite his parents through deliberate disobedience. The marriage of Esau to the daughter of Ishmael reminds us that the promised offspring of Abraham was determined, not by the will of human beings, but by the will of God. The families of the two "older" sons (Ishmael and Esau) were united in the marriage, but neither received the blessing promised to Abraham.

### G. Jacob at Bethel (28:10–22)

Jacob, like Abraham (ch. 15), received a confirmation of the promised blessing in "a dream" while sleeping. In both instances a divine confirmation was given about the establishment of the same covenant of promise. In a remarkably similar fashion, both chapters turn to a future exile and return—Abraham's descendants in Egypt and the Lord's deliverance in the Exodus; Jacob's sojourn to Haran and his return to the land promised to Abraham. In both cases the promise was that God would not forsake them and would return them to their land.

The Lord's words in v.15 become the guiding principle that governed the course of Jacob's life. When he returned from Laban's house after many years, he went back to the same place, Bethel; there God again blessed him, promised to give him the land he had already promised to Abraham (35:12), and reaffirmed his decision to make Jacob's descendants into a great nation (35:11). On both occasions Jacob erected a "pillar" and named the place "Bethel" (35:14–15). In other words, at both ends of the Jacob narratives is the reminder that God was with him in all that he did and that God was faithful to his promises.

### H. Jacob and Rachel (29:1–14a)

Jacob was sojourning as an exile from the Promised Land in "the land of the eastern peoples." His journey to find a wife is similar to that of Abraham's servant who sought a wife for Isaac. In ch. 24 the words of the servant guide the narrative and show that it was God alone who directed him to the right young woman for Isaac. In this chapter, however, Jacob is relatively silent. He does not reflect on God's guidance nor on the Lord's promise to be with him wherever he goes (28:15). It is his actions, not his words, that tell the story of God's help and guidance.

First, as with the servant in ch. 24, God directs Jacob to the well where Rachel is watering her flocks. Whereas earlier Rebecca had given water to Abraham's servant and camels, here Jacob single-handedly removed the rock from the well and gave water to Rachel's sheep. Then, in a great show of emotion, Jacob kissed her and cried with a loud voice. Clearly Jacob saw in these circumstances the guiding hand of God (cf. 24:27).

## I. Jacob's Marriages (29:14b–30)

For the first time Jacob became the object of deception; Laban turned the tables on him. In the case of the blessing (ch. 27), Jacob had exchanged the younger for the older; here, however, Laban exchanged the older for the younger. The seven extra years that Jacob had to serve Laban appear as a repayment for his treatment of Esau.

Jacob was indignant. But he was left speechless by Laban's reply in v.26. After that the narrative indicates only that Jacob conceded. Without realizing it, Laban's words recall the very circumstances that had led Jacob on his present journey. His past had caught up with him, and he had to accept the results and serve Laban seven more years. At first it had looked as if Jacob's journey was in fact following the course that Rebekah had anticipated (27:44). Thus we are not surprised to read that Jacob's first seven years of working for Laban seemed as if they were "only a few days." But with the discovery of Laban's trick, seven more years were added to Rebekah's "little while"; and

Jacob's—and Rebekah's—plans began to unravel.

## J. The Birth of Jacob's Sons (29:31–30:24)

In a way that recalls the beginning of the Abrahamic narratives (11:30), a central problem is introduced: The Lord opened Leah's womb, "but Rachel was barren." It is at first surprising that the Lord was behind Rachel's barrenness. In the preceding chapter God had promised that Jacob's descendants would be more numerous than the "dust of the earth." But now he had made Rachel, Jacob's intended wife, barren. God apparently intended Jacob to have Leah as wife. Jacob sought to build a family through Rachel, but God opened Leah's womb. Jacob's schemes, therefore, which had brought him fortune thus far, were crumbling further. Human schemes can never carry out the plans of God. Jacob too would have to depend on God to bring about the divine blessing.

In the conflict that ensued between Jacob and his two wives over the births of their sons, the pattern is set for the remainder of the narratives in Genesis. One of Leah's sons was Judah, while Rachel was the mother of Joseph. Though all twelve sons are important, Joseph and Judah stand out markedly in the following narratives. Both are used by God in important ways, but each has a different role to play in bringing about God's blessing.

In the end the Lord did hearken to Rachel, and her son Joseph was born (30:22). Nevertheless, as Jacob's words to Rachel underscore (30:2), it was God who had withheld sons from Rachel, resulting in his descendants being built from Leah. Even after Leah had ceased bearing children, she managed to have two more sons and a daughter by Jacob. Just as Jacob had purchased the birthright for a pot of stew (25:29–34), so also Leah purchased the right to more children by Jacob with the mandrakes of her son Reuben. All the ensuing conflict and tension between Joseph and his brothers—and particularly Joseph and Judah—are anticipated and foreshadowed here.

## K. Jacob and Laban's Sheep (30:25–43)

After the account of the birth of Jacob's sons, we have the first mention of his planned departure from Haran. Laban, seeking the Lord's blessing on behalf of Jacob, wanted to settle his account for the work Jacob had done for him over the years. So he asked Jacob to name his wages. Laban's offer apparently contained a request that Jacob stay on with him and continue to watch over his herds. Jacob struck a bargain with Laban that resulted in great blessing and wealth for Jacob.

The blessing did not come, however, from Laban; rather it was a gift from God (cf. Abraham's wealth in 14:21). What Jacob took was the right to stay on, to shepherd Laban's flocks, and to keep a part of the herd. In their deal, Jacob was to keep all the speckled or spotted goats and all the black sheep. From this he would build his own herds.

The passage is surely to be read as an example of the Lord's promise in ch. 28 to be with Jacob during his sojourn in the east. Jacob's clever use of the peeled poplar branches was not so much intended to demonstrate his resourcefulness as it was to further the theme of God's continued faithfulness to his word. The clue to the meaning of the passage is v.43, which clearly recalls God's blessing of both Abraham (12:16) and Isaac (26:14). Thus the events of this chapter are put within the larger context of the themes developed throughout the book, namely, God's promise of blessing and his faithfulness to that promise. In the next chapter, Jacob openly acknowledges to his wives that it was God who had taken Laban's herds and given them to him (31:9).

## L. Jacob's Flight From Laban (31:1–21)

Just as Isaac's wealth had made the Philistines jealous (26:14), so Jacob learned that Laban was now angry and jealous of his wealth. At this time the Lord directed Jacob to return to the land of his fathers (v.3), a passage that recalls God's promise to be "with" Jacob (28:15); thus Jacob's life again points toward Bethel, the place of the original promise.

This is the middle point of the narrative and life of Jacob. He was on his way back to Bethel. Later on Jacob looked back at this point (32:10) and repeated the Lord's words of comfort and promise. However, instead of the promise "I will be with you," he recalled God's words as "I will make you prosper." Thus Jacob expands and comments on the sense of God's promise to be "with" him.

Jacob's words of explanation in vv.5–13 repeat the primary events of the preceding chapter. He insists that the Lord was repaying him for Laban's mistreatment. The events were all part of the outworking of God's plan, the plan that began at Bethel and included the Lord's promise to be with him. Even Laban's change of attitude toward Jacob and the jealousy of his sons are seen as part of the plan of God.

Jacob's wives were willing to leave their own family and go with him to the land of Canaan (cf. 24:58; Ru 1:16). More important, they were ready to put their trust in God and seek his blessing. Despite this positive response, an ominous note is sounded about Rachel's stealing of Laban's "household gods" (v.19), gods that would presumably procure the headship of her father's goods. This event bears both a similarity and a contrast to Jacob's stealing his father's blessing when fleeing from home to find a wife (ch. 27). In both cases the younger stole what rightfully belonged to the elder. But (cf. v.32)

Jacob did not know that Rachel had taken the gods. In addition, Rachel's covert action is matched by Jacob's deception in departing from Laban secretly.

## M. Jacob Overtaken by Laban (31:22–55)

The dispute over the stolen household gods gives an occasion for the writer to restate his central theme (v.42): Jacob's wealth had not come through his association with Laban but through God's gracious care during Jacob's difficult sojourn. The narrative concludes with an account of a covenant between Jacob and Laban. Just as Isaac parted ways with Abimelech by entering into a covenant (26:28–31), so also Jacob and Laban parted ways with a covenant.

## N. Jacob's Meeting With Angels (32:1–2)

The events of this chapter are couched between two encounters of Jacob with angels (vv.1, 25; the "man" at Peniel was probably an angel). Thus it recalls a similar picture of the Promised Land in the early chapters of Genesis, when the land was guarded on its eastern borders by angels (3:24). It can hardly be accidental that as Jacob returned from the east, he was met by angels at the border of the Promised Land.

## O. Messengers Sent to Esau (32:3–22)

Chapters 32–33 emphasize the wealth of Jacob and the reconciliation between Jacob and Esau. They are filled with suspense. Like Jacob, we are not sure what Esau intended in gathering four hundred men to meet Jacob on his return. The last we heard from Esau was his intention to kill Jacob in revenge for stealing the blessing (27:41). Jacob's fear that Esau had now come to do just that seems well founded. In light of this, his prayer for safety and his appeal to the covenant promises of God play a crucial role in reversing the state of affairs.

True to form, Jacob made elaborate plans to save himself and his family in the face of Esau's potential threat. He provided his servants with abundant gifts for Esau and instructed them carefully on how to approach Esau when they met. Here again Jacob appears as the planner and the schemer. However, it was not Jacob's plan that succeeded but his prayer. When he met with Esau, he found that Esau had already had a change of heart. Running to meet Jacob, Esau embraced and kissed him and wept (33:4). Jacob's plans and schemes had come to naught, for God had prepared the way.

## P. Jacob's Wrestling Match (32:23–32)

Jacob's wrestling with "a man" (likely an angel) epitomizes his whole life. He had struggled with his brother (chs. 25, 27), his father (ch. 27), and his father-in-law (chs. 29–31); and now he struggles with God (ch. 32). His own words express the substance of these narratives about him: "I will not let you go unless you bless me." Here is a graphic picture of Jacob's continual struggle for the blessing (v.28).

Significantly, Jacob emerges victorious in his struggle, for the angel "blessed him." The name "Peniel" is an important name because it identifies the one with whom Jacob was wrestling as God. His remark that he had seen God face to face did not necessarily mean that the individual he wrestled with was actually God. Rather, when one saw the "angel of the LORD," it was appropriate to say that he had seen the face of God (e.g., Jdg 13:22).

## Q. Jacob's Meeting With Esau (33:1–17)

When Jacob saw Esau and the four hundred men approaching, he divided his entourage again (cf. 32:7–8). He showed his preference for Rachel and

Joseph by putting them last. Esau's greeting was totally unexpected. Jacob had expected revenge from Esau, or, if not revenge, then heavy bargaining and appeasement. But, seemingly in response to Jacob's prayer (cf. 32:11), Esau had had a change of heart. This change is depicted graphically in the contrast between Jacob's fearful approach and Esau's eager excitement to see his brother. All of Jacob's plans pale in the light of Esau's joy. Ironically, the four hundred men accompanying Esau turned out to be not for battle and for taking spoils, but for safeguarding the final stage of Jacob's journey. Once again we see Jacob as one who has gone to great lengths to secure his own well-being but whose efforts have proved pointless. Jacob continued to scheme and plan; yet God's own plans ultimately made Jacob's plans worthless.

This reconciliation of the brothers and Esau's partaking of the blessing that Jacob had received (v.11) picture the ultimate fulfillment of God's promise to Abraham: "All peoples on earth will be blessed through you" (12:3).

### R. Jacob at Shechem (33:18–34:31)

This section forms a transition in the narrative between Jacob's sojourn in the east and the events of the later years of his life in the land of Canaan. As he left Canaan (ch. 28), Jacob vowed that if God would be with him and watch over him by returning him to the land "safely," he would give to God a tenth of all he had (28:20–22). The narrative has been careful to follow the events in Jacob's life that have shown the Lord's faithfulness to his promise.

Jacob returned to Bethel in ch. 35 and built an altar there, but no mention is made of his giving a "tenth" to the Lord. Perhaps the altar in 33:20 and in 35:7 and the offerings, or perhaps the "hundred pieces of silver" (33:19), represented that "tenth." The portion of land purchased by Jacob plays an important role in the later biblical narra-

tives, for on this land the Israelites buried the bones of Joseph (Jos 24:32); thus they represented their hope in God's ultimate fulfillment of his promise of the land.

The birth of Dinah was recorded without much comment in 30:21. But once Jacob and his descendants had departed from Paddan Aram and settled in the vicinity of Shechem (33:18–20), Dinah became the center of the conflict between Jacob and the inhabitants of Canaan. The point of the narrative is to reiterate one of the portraits of Jacob as a man who planned and schemed for what appears to be his own ends, but who in the end actually accomplished God's purposes. Here God's purpose in setting apart the descendants of Abraham comes into jeopardy with the proposed union between Dinah and Shechem. Twice we are informed that the purpose of the marriage was that the family of Jacob should become "one people" (vv.16, 22) with the inhabitants of Canaan. This runs counter to Abraham's admonition (24:3), Rebekah's fear (27:46), and Isaac's command (28:1).

Though Shechem genuinely loved Dinah, the point is that he laid with her, apparently against her will, and thus humiliated her. Simeon and Levi's final words express clearly how they viewed the situation: "Should he have treated our sister like a prostitute?" (v.31).

Jacob was curiously silent about the incident. When he heard what had happened to Dinah, he waited for the return of his sons. It is significant that now the sons of Jacob, not Jacob himself, carried out deception; and at the end of the story Jacob admonished his sons for their actions. His type of plans and schemes were the plans and schemes of his sons. Their bitterness and anger show that they would not let such an act go unpunished. Jacob's last words to Simeon and Levi concerning the events of this chapter were harsh indeed (see 49:6–7).

In ch. 17 the rite of circumcision was given as a sign (v.11) of the unity of the covenant people and their separation from the rest of the nations. It was a sign of the covenant promise that Abraham would become the father of "many nations" (17:5). But in the way the sons of Jacob carried out the request that these Canaanites be circumcised, it offers a curious reversal of God's intention. They offered circumcision as a means for the two families to become "one people." The Canaanites were not joining the offspring of Abraham; rather, the descendants of Abraham were joining with the Canaanites. This point is stressed in Hamor and Shechem's report to their countrymen (v.23).

When the sons of Jacob carried out their deception to the end, their actions did not go unrebuked by their father (v.30). That the sons' reply stands as the last words of the narrative shows that their motive had not been mere plunder but the honor of their sister.

## S. Jacob's Return to Bethel (35:1–15)

This chapter opens with a reference back to the appearance of the Lord to Jacob at Bethel (28:10–15). As Jacob had once fled to Bethel to escape the anger of his brother Esau, so now the Lord tells Jacob to return to Bethel and live there because of the trouble that Simeon and Levi had stirred up. When Jacob obeyed, the Lord delivered him from the anger of the Canaanites who dwelt nearby. Significantly, Jacob called God the one "who answered me in the day of my distress and who has been with me wherever I have gone" (v.3). That summarizes the God who has been active throughout the Jacob narratives. God remained faithful to his promises and delivered Jacob from every distress.

The only previous mention of the "gods" that Jacob's household might have had is the "household gods" (31:19) that Rachel stole from her father. These may be included in the term "foreign gods," but in light of the "rings in their ears," it is likely that Jacob's household had picked up other religious objects while living in Shechem. Jacob and his family now left such things behind and purified themselves in preparation for their journey to Bethel.

The arrival at Bethel marked the end of Jacob's journey and the final demonstration of the faithfulness of God. He had been with Jacob throughout his journeys, and now Jacob had returned to Bethel in safety. As Abraham and Isaac had done on numerous occasions, Jacob built an altar and named it in commemoration of the Lord's appearance to him there when he left for Haran (cf. 28:10–22). In response the Lord appeared again to Jacob and "blessed him." For a second time Jacob's name was changed to "Israel" (cf. 32:28). The point of this second renaming was to give the name "Israel" a more neutral or even positive connotation, thus removing the notion of "struggle" associated with the wordplay in 32:28. Jacob's successive names reveal his standing before God.

The importance of God's words to Jacob in vv.11–12 cannot be overemphasized. (1) God's words recall clearly the primeval blessing of Creation (1:28) and hence show God to be still "at work" in bringing about the blessing to all humanity through Jacob. (2) For the first time since 17:16, mention is made of royalty in the promised line. (3) The promise of the land, first given to Abraham and then to Isaac, was renewed here with Jacob. Thus within these two verses several of the major themes in Genesis come together.

## T. Benjamin's Birth and Rachel's Death (35:16–20)

Rachel, Joseph's mother and Jacob's favorite wife, died giving birth to her second son, Benjamin. That account follows closely on 29:32–30:24. There the last son to have been born was Rachel's first son, Joseph, at which time Rachel had said, "May the LORD add to me another son" (30:24). Apparently looking back to that request, Rachel's midwife said, "Don't be afraid, for you have another son." Rachel named the son "Ben-Oni" as she lay dying, meaning "son of my trouble." Jacob, however, making a wordplay on "Oni," which can mean either "trouble" or "wealth," named him "Benjamin" (lit., "son of my right hand"), reinterpreting the name given by Rachel to mean "son of my wealth or good fortune."

The site of Rachel's burial, Ephrath, was clearly identified with the city of Bethlehem, an important place in biblical history (cf. 1Sa 17:12; Mic 5:2). This passage continued to play an important role in later biblical texts (cf. 48:7; Jer 31:15; Mic 5:2; Mt 2:18).

## U. The Sons of Jacob (35:21–26)

Because of their horrendous conduct, the three oldest sons of Jacob fell from favor (see ch. 34 for the violence of Simeon and Levi). Now Reuben engages in misconduct and forfeits his claim to be the favored son. The next brother in line was Judah, a son of Leah.

A major turning point is about to occur in Jacob's story. Two lines that have thus far run parallel are about to converge. Jacob has two wives, each representing a possible line through which the promise will be carried on. Just as Abraham had two sons and only one was the son of promise, and just as Isaac had two sons and only one was the son of the blessing, so now Jacob, though he has twelve sons, has two wives (Leah and Rachel), and each has a son (Judah and Joseph) that can rightfully contend for the blessing. As the Jacob narratives have already anticipated, in the end it was Judah, the son of Leah, and not Joseph, the son of

Rachel, who gained the blessing (49:8–12), even though the rest of Genesis focuses primarily on Joseph. But that is no indication of the final outcome.

## V. The Death of Isaac (35:27–29)

The Jacob narratives end with the death of his father, Isaac. This notice shows the complete fulfillment of God's promise to Jacob (28:21). According to Jacob's vow, he had asked that God watch over him during his sojourn and return him safely to "my father's house." Thus the conclusion of the Jacob narrative marks the fulfillment of these words.

## V. The Account of Esau (36:1–43)

The separation of Jacob and Esau is cast in the same form as the separation of Abraham and Lot (ch. 13). The possessions of the two brothers were too great, and the land was not able to sustain both of them (v.7; cf. 13:6); so just as Lot parted from Abraham and went eastward, so Esau parted from Jacob and went to Seir. The heirs of the promise remained in the land, and the other son and his family moved eastward.

In vv.9–43, the writer shows the progress and well-being of the line of Esau. He carefully notes that Esau is, in fact, "Edom." The repeated identification of Esau as Edom throughout the chapter prepares us for the future importance of Edom during Israel's later history.

The unusually long genealogy of Esau is made up of several smaller units. The first list (vv.9–14), the sons of Esau, is largely dependent on the brief narratives regarding Esau's wives (26:34; 28:9; 36:3). Verse 10 divides the sons of Esau into two groups: the sons of Adah and the sons of Basemath. Adah's sons (and grandsons) are listed in vv.11–12, then Basemath's in v.13, and finally Oholibamah's in v.14. Verses 15–19 list the tribal "chiefs" of the sons of Esau, beginning with the eldest, Eliphaz, and again grouped according to their mothers.

The next list (vv.20–29) is a list of "the sons of Seir the Horite, who were living in the region," followed by their tribal "chiefs." Seir is ordinarily the name of the geographical territory occupied by the Edomites, but here it refers to an individual whose descendants occupied the territory of Edom (cf. 2Ch 25:11, 14).

The list of Edomite kings (vv.31–39) is introduced by the heading, "These were the kings who reigned in Edom before any Israelite king reigned." This presupposes a knowledge of the kingship in Israel, or at least an anticipation of the kingship. Thus it is a part of those texts (e.g., 17:6, 16; 35:11) that look forward to the promises of Ge 49:10; Nu 24:7, 17–18; and Dt 17:14–20 (cf. 1Sa 2:10).

The chapter closes with a final list of the tribal "chiefs" of Esau's clan. Several names in this list overlap with those in vv.10–14.

## VI. The Account of Jacob (37:1–49:33)

### A. Jacob in the Land (37:1)

Jacob is back in the Land of Promise but is still living there as a sojourner, like his father and grandfather before him (cf. Heb 11:13). He too is awaiting the fulfillment of God's promises. Verse 1 is a fitting transition to the narratives that trace the course of events by which the sons of Jacob left the Land of Promise and entered the land of Egypt.

### B. Joseph's Dreams (37:2–11)

The formal title "This is the account of Jacob" belies the remaining narrative, which is not about Jacob but about Joseph and, later, Judah. Joseph, along with his brothers, is a shepherd of his father's sheep. We are told that Joseph brought a "bad report" about his brothers to his father and that Jacob loved him more than the other brothers because he was the son born to him in his old age. Jacob's special love for Rachel (29:30) had carried over to that of her son, Joseph. The story of Joseph is filled with wordplays and reversals; thus, it seems likely that the reference to the "bad report" foreshadows the brothers' intended "evil" (NIV, "harm") spoken of in 50:20.

The "richly ornamented robe" Jacob made for Joseph illustrates the father's preferential love for Joseph. His preferred status was the central problem that angered his brothers and turned them against him. Eventually their anger resulted in a plan to do away with him altogether. But first, adding to their hatred, Joseph recounted two dreams, both of which end with the image of his brothers "bowing down" to him. This foreshadows the conclusion of the story where, as ruler of the land of Egypt, his brothers "bowed down" (42:6) to him, and Joseph "remembered his dreams about them" (42:9).

Why two dreams? For an answer we must go to Joseph's own words in 41:32, where he explained to the Pharaoh that the twofold occurrence indicates that a matter has been firmly decided by God. The significance of the dreams is seen in the words of Joseph's brothers: "Will you actually rule us?" The meaning behind the "bowing down" in the dreams is that of royalty and kingship. The irony of the narrative is that in the end such royal honor did not reside in the house of Joseph but in the house of Judah (49:10).

### C. Joseph's Journey to Egypt (37:12–36)

On a mission from his father, Joseph found his brothers in Dothan. The purpose of this small account can be seen by comparing it with the brief and similar prelude to the second part of the story, where Joseph and his brothers meet again in Egypt (chs. 42–44). Here, when Joseph's brothers "saw him" approaching, they "plotted to kill him." In the same way, when Joseph first "saw his brothers" in Egypt (42:7), he disguised himself and then planned a scheme that, at least on the surface, looked as if he intended to kill them. The symmetry reinforces the sense that every event is providentially ordered.

Both details of the brothers' plans and their motivation are given. Behind those plans lie Joseph's two dreams, which foreshadowed the divine plan. Little did they suspect that the very plan that they were scheming was to lead to the fulfillment of those dreams. The reference to Joseph's coat in v.23 highlights the central conflict in the story.

The reference to Reuben, who planned to save Joseph from his brothers' hands, is countered later by a similar reference to Judah, who also played an important role in keeping Joseph alive (vv.26–27). Again we can see the central importance of Jacob's last words regarding Judah in 49:8–12. In the end Judah is the one who is placed at the center of the narrative's focus on the fulfillment of the divine blessing. His descendants will ultimately figure in the coming of the Promised Seed.

An important turn of events occurs with the arrival of the "Ishmaelites." They become the occasion for Judah to enter the story with the suggestion that the brothers could "sell [Joseph] to the Ishmaelites." The brothers did so, and the Ishmaelites (also called "Midianites" in this narrative) take Joseph to Egypt with them.

When the focus of the narrative returns to Reuben and to the outcome of his plan to deal with Joseph, ironically it serves only to underscore the role of Judah in the actual rescue of Joseph. Reuben had no part in the plan to sell Joseph to the Ishmaelites. Ultimately, it was Judah who saved the life of Joseph.

The brothers now must fall back on their original plan of telling their father that a "ferocious" (lit., "evil") animal had killed Joseph. Once again the coat

provides the narrative link in the story. The symbol of the brothers' original hatred for Joseph becomes the means of the father's recognition of his loss. In the end the blood-stained coat is all that remains of Joseph; on seeing it Jacob tore off his own coat and exchanged it for sackcloth. Jacob's own fate and that of his sons is thus briefly sketched out in this opening narrative. What happened to Joseph foreshadows all that will happen to the sons of Jacob. They will be carried down into Egypt and will be put into slavery. In this sense, then, Jacob's final words, "in mourning will I go down to the grave [Sheol] to my son," foreshadow the end of the Joseph stories. Jacob goes down (46:3–4) to Egypt to see his son and then dies (50:24–26).

## D. Judah and Tamar (38:1–30)

This narrative has only a loose connection with the Joseph story. Its inclusion creates time for that story to develop in Egypt. The first verse notes only that these events occurred "at that time." In the overall strategy of the book, however, this chapter plays a crucial role.

The narrative begins with the mention of Jacob's three sons (cf. the three sons of Adam, Noah, and Terah). Two sons died because of the evil they did. The point of this introductory information is to show that the continuation of the house of Judah lay in Judah's hands. The narrative that follows shows that he does nothing to further his own household. It takes the "righteousness" of the woman Tamar (v.26) to preserve the seed of Judah. The story thus falls in line with the other patriarchal narratives outside the story of Joseph, which show the promised offspring in jeopardy and the patriarch showing little concern for its preservation. Just as in ch. 20, for example, where the seed of Abraham was protected by the "righteous" (NIV, "innocent") Abimelech, here it is the "righteous" woman Tamar who is ultimately responsible for the survival of the descendants of the house of Judah.

The text makes it clear that Judah's wife was a Canaanite, the daughter of Shua (v.3). Thus, the promise made to Abraham was in jeopardy, confirming the worst fears of Abraham (24:3) and Isaac (28:1). Through Tamar's clever plan, however, the seed of Abraham was preserved by not being allowed to continue through the sons of the Canaanite. Instead, it was continued through Judah and Tamar (who was probably not a Canaanite). The genealogy at the close of the narrative underscores this point.

Tamar's plan resembles that of Jacob and Rebekah (ch. 27). Just as Rebekah schemed to get her husband's blessing for the younger son, to whom God had promised it, so here Tamar schemed to get the blessing of the firstborn when her father-in-law refused to give her his son Selah.

The whole of the Jacob narratives reaches a fitting summary in the brief account of the birth of Perez and Zerah (vv.27–30). As the Jacob narrative began with an account of the struggle of twins (25:22), so now the final story is marked by a similar struggle. In both cases the struggle resulted in a reversal of the right of the firstborn and the right of the blessing; the younger (Perez) gained the upper hand over the elder (Zerah); in Nu 26:20, Perez is regarded as the firstborn.

## E. Joseph in the House of Potiphar (39:1–23)

Fully conscious of the intervening Judah narrative, the text resumes the account of Joseph, taking up where ch. 37 left off. Verse 2 establishes the overall theme of the narrative: "The LORD was with Joseph and he prospered." Verses 3–6 relate the theme to the specific series of events to follow: Joseph's blessing from the Lord is recognized by his Egyptian master, and Joseph is put in charge of his household. Joseph's sojourn in Egypt, like that of his father, Jacob (30:27), has resulted in an initial fulfillment of the Abrahamic promise that "all peoples on earth will be blessed through you" (12:3). Thus "the LORD blessed the house of the Egyptian because of Joseph." Such a thematic introduction alerts the reader to the underlying lessons intended throughout the narrative. This is not a story of the success of Joseph; rather it is a story of God's faithfulness to his promises.

This story about Joseph reverses a well-known plot in the patriarchal narratives. Whereas before it was the beautiful wife of a patriarch who was sought by a foreign ruler (12:11; 26:7), now it was Joseph, the handsome patriarch himself, who was sought by the wife of the foreign ruler. Whereas in the earlier narratives it was either the Lord (12:17; 20:3) or the moral purity of the foreign ruler (26:10) that rescued the wife, here it was Joseph's own moral courage that saved the day. Whereas earlier the focus had been on God's faithfulness in fulfilling his covenant promises, in the story of Joseph attention is turned to the human response. That is, Abraham, Isaac, and Jacob repeatedly fell short of God's expectations, in spite of their faith. Joseph, however, is a striking example of one who always responded in total trust and obedience to God's will. His narratives give expression to that part of the promise found in 18:19: "that they may do righteousness and justice so that the LORD may fulfill what he has promised to Abraham" (pers. tr.). Humans do play a role in the fulfillment of God's plan. When God's people respond as Joseph responded, then their way and God's blessing will prosper. Significantly, in all the book of Genesis only Joseph is described as one who was filled with the Spirit of God (41:38).

The epilogue (vv.21–23) emphasizes that God turned an intended evil against Joseph into a good. God was with Joseph and prospered his way. Lying behind the course of events is the lesson that the whole of the Joseph narratives teach: "You intended to harm me, but God intended it for good" (50:20).

## F. Joseph in Jail (40:1–23)

Chapter 40 represents an intermediary stage in the development of the plot of the Joseph story. Joseph had been cast into jail and had risen to a position of prominence there. Two incarcerated royal officials each had a dream that Joseph correctly interpreted. Though the surviving official soon forgot the matter, when Pharaoh later had a dream himself, the butler remembered the events of this chapter and told the king about Joseph. The picture of Joseph that comes through these events is that of one who, like Daniel, can interpret dreams and mysteries. He discerns the course of future events that to others lies in total darkness.

The sense of the cupbearer's dream may seem self-evident, but as the sense of the baker's dream shows, such apparently self-evident meanings are by no means certain. Who could, on the face of it, discern between the two dreams? One is favorable and the other not so. The one who can tell the difference is Joseph, "one in whom is the spirit of God" (41:38; cf. 40:8). He is set apart from all those who have preceded him in the book. He is "discerning and wise" (41:39), and "things turned out exactly as he interpreted them" (41:13). Whereas Abraham was a "prophet" (20:7), Joseph is a wise man (cf. 41:39). Whereas Abraham sees the course of future events "in a vision" (15:1), Joseph discerns (41:39) the course of the future in the mysterious dreams of others.

## G. Joseph's Interpretation of Pharaoh's Dreams (41:1–36)

The central theme of ch. 41 is expressed by Joseph in v.32: "The matter has been firmly decided by God, and God will do it soon." The two dreams with the same meaning show that God would certainly bring about what was foreseen in the dreams. In the previous chapter the "two" officials of the king each had a dream—one good, the other bad. After "two years" the king himself had "two" dreams; one part of each dream was good (v.29) and the other bad (vv.27, 30).

Pharaoh's two dreams are more transparent than those of the two officials, for the sense of the two dreams was seen in the elements of the dream. Seven good cows and seven good heads of grain are seven good years; seven ugly cows and seven blighted heads of grain are seven bad years to follow. Nevertheless, all the king's magicians and wisemen were unable to give their meaning (cf. Da 2:4–12). Joseph not only was able to interpret the dreams, but, more importantly, he advised Pharaoh how to prepare for what was to come. It is his wisdom, which consisted more in planning and administration than in a knowledge of secret mysteries, that is prominent in this story.

Though the cupbearer had forgotten about Joseph, he now recalled that Joseph's interpretation had stood the test of time. As it turns out, even the cupbearer's forgetfulness worked in Joseph's favor since just at the opportune moment he remembered Joseph and recounted his wisdom before the king. Thus, this episode emphasizes both the wisdom of Joseph and the sovereign workings of God.

The emphasis on the "good" and "evil" in Pharaoh's dreams represents Joseph's ability to distinguish between the "good" and the "evil." It is clear that ultimately such knowledge comes only from God (v.39). Thus the lesson of the early chapters of Genesis is artfully repeated in these last chapters. In light of such considerations, it can hardly be accidental that Joseph's plan seemed "good" to the pharaoh and all his servants.

## H. Joseph's Exaltation Over Egypt (41:37–57)

The account of the king's appointment of Joseph over all his kingdom recalls Adam in chs. 1–2. Just as Adam was dependent on God for his knowledge of "good and evil," so Joseph knows what is good for Egypt and what is bad. Just as Adam is made God's "vicegerent" to rule over all the land, so Joseph is portrayed here as the pharaoh's "vicegerent" over all his land. As Adam was made in God's image to rule over all the land, so the king here gave Joseph his "signet ring" and dressed him in royal garments. Just as God provided a wife for Adam in the garden and gave the man all the land for his enjoyment, so the king gave a wife to Joseph and put him over all the land.

At many points in the story, Joseph appears as the "ideal" of a truly wise and faithful man. By his obedience, he accomplished all that Adam failed to do. This story reflects what might have been had Adam remained obedient to God and trusted him for the "good." At the same time it anticipates what might yet be, if only God's people would, like Joseph, live in complete obedience and trust in God. Therefore the story of Joseph looks forward to one who was yet to come, the one from the house of Judah to whom the kingdom belongs (cf. 49:10). Thus the tension between the houses of Joseph and Judah is resolved by making the life of Joseph into a picture of the one who is to reign from the house of Judah.

## I. Joseph's Brothers in Egypt (42:1–28)

The preceding chapter recorded Joseph's rise to power; the present one turns to the divine purpose behind his miraculous rise. The narrative continues with Jacob, who has been out of the picture since 37:34. As frequently happens, the words spoken at the beginning of the story foreshadow the outcome. Jacob, sending his sons to Egypt, said, "Go down there . . . so that we may live and not die" (cf. 45:5).

The twelve sons of Jacob are divided into two groups throughout the story. There are the "ten of Joseph's brothers" (v.3) and the two sons of Jacob by Rachel—Joseph and Benjamin. These two sons are contrasted specifically with two sons of Leah—Reuben and Judah. These latter two play an important and similar role in the narrative. They speak on behalf of the other brothers and are the catalysts in the resolution of the plots instigated by Joseph. It was Judah, however, who saved the day by offering himself as a pledge for the young lad Benjamin, and later by offering himself as a substitute for Benjamin; and it was Judah who repeated Jacob's own thematic words "that we and you and our children may live and not die" (43:8; cf. 42:2).

Joseph created conflict and tension throughout the narrative, a tension that Judah ultimately resolved. When his brothers approached Joseph to buy grain, he "pretended to be a stranger" (v.7) and spoke harshly, accusing them of being spies. Verse 9 reveals that Joseph's schemes and plans against his brothers were motivated by the dreams of the earlier narratives and not by revenge for what his brothers had done to him.

In response to Joseph's accusation that they were spies, the brothers defended their integrity by saying, "Your servants are twelve brothers"; but lest their integrity be found wanting, they added: "and one is no more." Joseph's schemes have provoked the first hint that the evil deed accomplished long past may yet rise up against them. But when the brothers recounted this event to their father (v.32), they used a different order from that of v.13. Here they mentioned first the "one who is no more"; but when they tell their father about Joseph's accusations and their response, they mention last the "one [who] is no more" and then tell of Benjamin who is home with their father. Though subtle, such a reversal suggests that their memory of what they did to Joseph was beginning to rub on their consciences.

Joseph devised two plans to test his brothers. (1) "One" of the brothers should return for the youngest and the rest remain in prison. (2) After three days the second plan was announced: "one" of the brothers was to remain behind and the others were to return to get the youngest. The focus is on the "one" brother who rescues the others. Within the narrative this "one" brother appears to be an echo of the "one [who] is no more." No wonder, then, that the brothers conclude that their present distress has been caused by what they did to Joseph. Reuben's words focus on the central point: "Now we must give an accounting for his blood." Their "guilt" was coming back on them and calling for justice. Remarkably, however, Joseph had already forgiven his brothers of the evil they had done to him, for he had to turn away from them to hide his sorrow for the distress he was causing. What awaited the brothers was not the "evil" they intended for Joseph but the "good" God intended for them through Joseph (50:20).

Joseph's next plan was to fill the brothers' sacks with the money that they had used to buy grain. This terrified them, for on seeing the money, they asked, "What is this that God has done to us?" (v.28). However they might have meant it, their words have a ring of truth about them. Though we know it was Joseph who ordered the money put back into their sacks, their words point us to the work of God, confirming the direction the narrative appears to be taking. God was behind everything that was happening; he was working out his purposes.

## J. Joseph's Brothers Return for Benjamin (42:29–38)

The events of ch. 42 are now retold in an abbreviated form by the brothers, focusing on the plan of Joseph for bringing the youngest son to Egypt. As if he knew all that had happened between his sons and Joseph, Jacob's words in v.36 ring truer than he would ever have suspected. The brothers had deprived him of Joseph, and it was because of them that Simeon was not now with them and that Benjamin was to be taken away. Thus the brothers receive another reminder of the guilt that lingered over their treatment of Joseph.

In the face of Jacob's words, Reuben's response (v.37) was unusual. While he certainly meant his words to insure confidence regarding Benjamin, within the context of the narrative, it only added insult to injury. Jacob's reply to Reuben not only summarily dismissed Reuben's pledge, but it raised one more time the matter of the loss of Joseph.

## K. Joseph's Identity (43:1–45:28)

### 1. The second trip to Egypt (43:1–34)

In keeping with the general motif of "pairs" of events throughout the Joseph narratives, this story now begins the "second" journey of the sons into Egypt. The famine was still in the land, and the grain purchased earlier was gone; so the father sent his sons back for more. This time Judah insisted on taking Benjamin back with them. In persuading his father, Judah offered to take full responsibility for Benjamin. That both Reuben and Judah had suggested ways Benjamin could be safely taken to Egypt recalls the events of ch. 37 and the brothers' maltreatment of Joseph (37:21, 26). Here they attempt to save Benjamin from the plan Joseph had initiated against the brothers.

Jacob gave in. Just as it was Judah's plan that ultimately saved the life of Joseph (37:26), so now his plan saved the life of Simeon and, in the end, of Benjamin. Jacob's farewell words in v.14 (note especially the word "mercy") provide the narrative key to what follows. When Joseph saw Benjamin (v.29), we are told that "his mercy" (v.30; untr. in NIV) was kindled toward his brother. Note in these words of Jacob that the compassion that Joseph was to find toward his brothers was given by "God Almighty." Behind everything God was still unfolding his plan.

Curiously, the whole problem of the brothers' being "spies" (42:9) is not raised again. But when the brothers were ushered into the royal house of Joseph, they were positive that nothing good was going to come of this (though we as the readers know that their fears were misguided). When the brothers repeated to the steward how they found the money in their grain sacks, we see why they were so anxious. Apparently the steward had been in on Joseph's secret plan all along. Unwittingly he expresses one of the central themes of the book: "Your God, the God of your father, has given you treasure."

Joseph, still unrecognized, was conspicuously careful to ask about the well-being of the brothers' father and the lad, Benjamin, whom they had brought back with them. The brothers had come expecting to be made into servants, but now it was they who were being served. The text simply states that the brothers were "dismayed" (NIV, "in astonishment"). They asked no questions and seemed to accept the words of Joseph's steward (v.23) and Joseph's words to Benjamin (v.29) as the most plausible solution.

### 2. The silver cup (44:1–34)

Once more Joseph tricked his brothers by having his cup and Benjamin's money returned in Benjamin's sack of grain. The question the steward asked

them carries on the central issue of the Joseph narratives: the contrast between the "evil" done by the brothers and the "good" intended and accomplished by God (cf. 50:20). It implicitly includes, therefore, the brothers' mistreatment of Joseph in ch. 37, even though the steward may not have known about that situation. A residue of guilt still hung over their heads; and almost everywhere they turned, they heard an echo of it.

Joseph's plan worked as expected. Not knowing that the cup and money were in Benjamin's sack, the brothers made a rash vow, putting the life of Benjamin and their own freedom in jeopardy. When the cup was discovered, their response was one of complete hopelessness. "They tore their clothing in a rage" (lit. tr.) and returned to the city. Curiously, that response mirrored their father's response when he heard their earlier report about Joseph (37:34).

While it had looked as if Joseph was working a slow revenge on his brothers, his purpose was not vengeance but repentance. Through his schemes his brothers were becoming aware of their guilt and were ready to acknowledge it. The rhetorical answer to their questions (v.16) is that they have nothing to say and cannot show their innocence. Thus they draw the conclusion that "God has uncovered your servants' guilt."

Though the brothers have only the immediate issue of the lost "cup" in mind, within the compass of the entire Joseph narrative, their words take on the scope of a confession of their former guilt as well. We know that the brothers did not take the cup, and we also know that the brothers know they did not take the cup. So when they speak of God "uncovering [their] guilt," we are forced to generalize that sense of guilt. In his response Joseph steered the matter in a direction that even more closely resembles his brothers' treatment of him. The young lad was to be sold into slavery in Egypt, and the brothers were to return to their father.

In Judah's final speech (vv.18–34), he retold the whole of the Joseph story. His own retelling reveals the brothers' perception of the events as well as the hopelessness of their situation. The overall sense of Judah's version is that the brothers have been mistreated, suggesting that if anyone was to blame, it was Joseph, for he had initiated the series of mishaps that led to their present predicament. Judah's words, however, reveal something more to the reader than even he intended; they show that the fault did not lie with Joseph but with the "evil" intention of the brothers toward Joseph, for the issue of the brothers' mistreatment of Joseph again surfaces. Curiously, at this point Judah said of Joseph, "[He] is dead," rather than "[he] is no more" (42:13)—an expression that does not imply death (cf. 5:24; 42:36). Thus, Judah has added a dimension to the story as told to Joseph: an admission that they had intended to kill Joseph. This "slip of the tongue" suggests their guilt.

Judah's account raises even further the issue of the brothers' guilt regarding Joseph in his account of Jacob's response to the demand that Benjamin be taken to Egypt. On that occasion Jacob had said, "You know that my wife bore me two sons. One of them went away from me, and I said, 'He has surely been torn to pieces.'" How could Judah recount the story this way? He surely knew that Jacob's words were mistaken, that they had sold Joseph into slavery. But that form of the story would require admitting to a guilt even greater than that of which they were presently accused. Through Judah's speech, therefore, the reader is again reminded of the brothers' guilt. Nevertheless, it was Judah who intervened on behalf of Benjamin and ultimately his words that saved the day.

### 3. Joseph's revelation (45:1–28)

Joseph had taken no personal enjoyment in deceiving his brothers. When he could hold back no longer, he revealed his true identity. In his words of explanation and comfort to his brothers, Joseph returned once again to the central theme of the narrative: though the brothers had intended evil, God was ultimately behind it all and had worked it out for the good. Here and in 50:20, this theme is no longer merely hinted at; it is given full expression by Joseph. He affirms that it was not the brothers who sent him to Egypt; it was God. And God had a purpose for it all: to accomplish a "great deliverance" (v.7). And in describing how God had taken care of him, Joseph alluded to the brothers' initial comment regarding his dreams as a young lad (37:8), for he was now "ruler of all Egypt."

In the second part of his speech (vv.9–20), Joseph made plans to bring his father to Egypt. In the midst of the famine, the sons of Israel were to be well provided for in Goshen, the "good" (vv.18, 20; NIV, "best") of the land of Egypt (cf. 1:31).

At first, when Jacob heard the news that Joseph was alive, he "was stunned" (v.26) and "did not believe." But when he heard everything that Joseph had said and saw all that he had sent to take him back to Egypt, "the spirit . . . of Jacob revived," and he set out to go to him. A new dimension occurs in Jacob's faith.

### L. Jacob's Journey to Egypt (46:1–7)

Before Jacob went to Egypt, he traveled to Beersheba, built an altar there, and offered sacrifices to the God of his father, Isaac. Earlier, the Lord had said to Isaac, "Do not go down to Egypt" (26:2); but now he said to Jacob in a night vision, "Do not be afraid to go down to Egypt." Such a change in attitude indicates that the Lord was following a specific plan with regard to his people. The words God spoke to Jacob reiterate the promise to Abraham (12:2), but they also add that God would perform this in Egypt. After they had become "a great nation" in Egypt, he would then bring them back to the Promised Land. This was the second "vision" in which God revealed his future plans with the offspring of Abraham (cf. 15:1, 13–14).

Special attention is given to the journey of Jacob and his household into Egypt. Just as Abraham had left Ur and journeyed to Canaan (12:4–5), so now Jacob left Canaan and journeyed to Egypt. Both men were leaving the land of their birth in obedience to the will of God, and the obedience of both plays a pivotal role in God's election of the offspring of Abraham. Thus vv.6–7 emphasize by repetition that "all his offspring" went with Jacob into the land of Egypt.

## M. Jacob's Sons in Egypt (46:8–27)

The list of names in these verses appears to have been selected so that the total numbers "seventy" (v.27). It can hardly be coincidental that the number of nations in Ge 10 is also "seventy." Just as the "seventy nations" represent all the descendants of Adam, so now the "seventy sons" represent all the descendants of Abraham, Isaac, and Jacob. What we see is a demonstration of the theme in Dt 32:8, that God apportioned the boundaries of the nations (Ge 10) according to the number of the sons of Israel. Thus the new nation of Israel is as a new humanity and Abraham as a second Adam. The blessing that is to come through Abraham and his offspring is a restoration of the original blessing of Adam, a blessing that was lost in the Fall.

## N. Settling in Goshen (46:28–47:12)

Curiously, it was Judah, not Joseph, who "pointed out the way" (NIV, "to get directions") for the sons of Israel into the land of Goshen. Once again Judah is singled out for special atten-

tion over against Joseph. Such a special focus on Judah highlights his crucial role in God's plan to bring about Israel's deliverance (cf. 49:8–12).

Chapter 46 ends with Joseph's plan to secure the land of Goshen as a dwelling place for the sons of Israel. The plan was simply to tell the pharaoh that they were shepherds. Since the Egyptians hated shepherds, this would allow the Israelites to live by themselves in Goshen. That plan succeeded. In fact, Pharaoh's response in ch. 47 was even more generous than the previous narrative would have suggested. In addition to allowing Joseph's brothers to settle in Goshen, he put them in charge of his own livestock. In these two brief narratives, Joseph and Judah are placed in marked contrast. Judah led the brothers to the land of Goshen, but it was Joseph's wise plan that resulted in their being able to live there.

The central concern of 47:7–10 is to show that Jacob "blessed Pharaoh" (mentioned twice) when he was brought before him. Lying behind this narrative is God's promise to Abraham that he would bless those who blessed the offspring of Abraham. The passage shows that in Joseph and Jacob, the promise to Abraham was being fulfilled with the nations.

Jacob's words to the pharaoh in 47:9 reflect the later promise that those who honor father and mother would "live long and that it may go well with you in the land" (Dt 5:16). Jacob, who deceived his father to gain the blessing, indicates that his years were few and difficult. While Abraham had obeyed God and lived long in the land (Ge 26:5), Jacob's years were short and difficult, and his final years were not in the land that God had promised to give them.

## O. Joseph's Rule in Egypt (47:13–27)

The narrative returns to the story line of 41:57 with an account of the affairs of Joseph in Egypt and his work on behalf of the pharaoh; his dealings with the Egyptian people mirror the story about Jacob and his family. It opens with the Egyptians seeking to buy grain from Joseph: "Why should we die before your eyes?" (cf. 42:2). Then it continues with the account of their return to Joseph "the second year" (NIV, "the following year"; cf. 45:6), in which they express the desire "that we may live and not die" (cf. 43:8; 45:5). Throughout these narratives the theme was repeatedly expressed that Joseph's wisdom and administrative skills "saved lives" (47:25; cf. 45:5). Furthermore, through God's wisdom given to this descendant of Abraham, the nations were receiving a blessing (cf. 12:2–3).

Note also the ironic twist given here to the earlier Joseph narrative. The whole of the story of Joseph and his brothers began with Joseph being sold (37:28) into slavery (39:17) for twenty pieces of silver (37:28). Now, Joseph was selling the whole of the land of Egypt into slavery and taking their "money" (v.18), while the offspring of Abraham became "fruitful," "increased greatly in number" (v.27), and were living safely and prosperously in Goshen (cf. 1:28).

### P. Jacob's Deathbed (47:28–49:33)

#### 1. Jacob's burial instructions (47:28–31)

Seventeen years later, the time had come for Jacob to die (47:28), but two crucial chapters remain. Jacob's only request (cf. 24:2) was that he not be buried in the land of Egypt. The same theme is taken up in ch. 50, when Joseph makes his sons swear that they will carry his bones back to the Promised Land (see Jos 24:32). A central element of the covenant with Abraham was the promise of the land. The request of the patriarchs to be buried in the land "with their fathers" emphasizes their trust in the faithfulness of God to his word.

As early as the rivalry between Leah, Judah's mother, and Rachel, Joseph's mother (ch. 30), the question of the preeminence of one of the brothers over the other has occupied a central role. In chs. 48 (the blessing of Joseph) and 49 (the blessing of Judah) the issue comes to a final resolution in the choice of one from the tribe of Judah who would reign over the rest of the brothers (49:8–10).

### 2. Ephraim and Manasseh blessed (48:1–22)

Chapter 48 has fittingly concluded the Joseph narratives. As in the earlier patriarchal narratives, the blessing of the father is passed along to the next generation. Two features stand out here. (1) As earlier, it was the younger son, Ephraim, who received the blessing of the firstborn rather than the older, Manasseh (v.19), thus continuing the well-worn theme that the blessing did not follow the lines of natural descent or natural right. The blessing was a gift bestowed on those who could not claim it as a right. (2) The blessing recorded here is largely subordinated to and superseded by the blessing for Judah in ch. 49, who plays the dominant role in the continuing story of the promise and the blessing. From him comes the house of David, and from David comes the Messiah. The role of Ephraim and Manasseh, whose descendants were ultimately exiled and lost in the Dispersion, pales quickly in the light of the rising star of David.

As soon as the frail Jacob saw Joseph and his two sons, he revived (v.2) and prepared to bestow God's blessing on the house of Joseph. Jacob recalled God's promise to him at Bethel (35:9–13) by repeating the Lord's words almost verbatim. But two alterations are significant. (1) In 35:11 the Lord had said, "Be fruitful and increase in number. A nation and a community of nations will come from you." But as Jacob retold the story to Joseph here, he stressed that *God* (cf. "I" in v.4) was the one who would bring about all that had been promised. That is, Jacob emphasized that aspect of the blessing that had been the theme of the Joseph narratives: God ultimately will bring about all that he has promised. (2) As Jacob recounted God's promise in 35:11 of the land, he added "as an everlasting possession" in 48:4—a reference all the way back to 17:8 (cf. 13:15).

Ephraim and Manasseh were taken into the family of Jacob and were to be treated as his own sons. They, along with the other sons of Jacob, would inherit the promise of Abraham. Henceforth the families of Ephraim and Manasseh were counted among the sons of Jacob and later became two of the most important tribes of Israel. Just as Rachel had borne Jacob "two sons" (44:27, Joseph and Benjamin) at a time when he was about to enter the land of Canaan (48:7), so also Joseph had given Jacob "two sons" at the time when he was about to enter Egypt. Such symmetry suggests that Ephraim and Manasseh are seen as replacements of Joseph and Benjamin, which furthers the sense of divine providence behind Jacob's life.

The blessing of Ephraim and Manasseh is recounted in great detail (vv.8–14). Since the account of Jacob's blessing his sons in ch. 49 does not mention these two sons, the present account augments ch. 49. Great care is taken to emphasize that in the blessing of these two sons, Ephraim, the younger, was given the blessing of the firstborn (v.20b).

The first blessing (vv.15–16) appears to be of Joseph rather than the two sons, but in the blessing itself, reference is made to "these boys" (v.16), and that blessing ultimately focuses on them. This blessing is a storehouse of key thematic terms. God is identified as the "God before whom my fathers Abraham and Isaac walked," thus connecting Jacob's faith in God both to his immediate forefathers and to those who preceded Abraham and Isaac (see 5:22, 24; 6:9). The faith of the early fathers was one with that of the patriarchs— they walked with God.

God is also described as "my shepherd" and as "the Angel who has delivered me from all harm." It is unusual that God himself should be described as "the Angel," since earlier in the book it is said that God sent "his angel" (24:7) or simply that one of the patriarchs was visited by "the angel of the LORD" (22:11).

The blessing of the two sons picks up the theme of the promise to Abraham. They were to be called by Jacob's "name" and the "name" of Abraham and Isaac. They were to "increase greatly," just as God had promised Abraham in 12:2.

The central concern of vv.17–20 again underscores that Ephraim, the younger son, was given preeminence over Manasseh. Though nearly blind himself (v.10), Jacob appeared to be making the same mistake that his father, Isaac, had when Jacob deceived him (ch. 27). When Joseph attempted to correct him, he stated his intentions clearly: "His younger brother will be greater than he." Thus receiving the blessing offered by God does not rest with one's natural status in the world. On the contrary, it is based solely on God's grace.

### 3. Jacob's sons blessed (49:1–28)

Jacob's last words to his sons are the occasion for a final statement of the book's major theme since 1:28 and 12:2–3: God's plan to restore the lost blessing through the offspring of Abraham. The key to understanding his last words lies in the narrative framework that surrounds them: Jacob was speaking about those things that would happen "in days to come" (see also Nu 24:14–24; Dt 31:29). On all three occasions the subject matter introduced by this phrase is that of God's future deliverance of his chosen people. At the center of that deliverance stands a king (Ge 49:10; Nu 24:7; Dt 33:5). Here in Ge 49 that king is connected with the house of Judah.

At the close of Jacob's discourse (v.28), the writer draws a line connecting Jacob's words in this chapter to this theme of "the blessing" (actually repeated three times). As Jacob's last words look to the future, he draws on the past—God's blessing of all humanity. The order of the sons follows roughly the order of the record of their birth (chs. 29–30). The sons of Leah lead the list, followed by the sons of the handmaidens, Bilhah, Zilpah, again Bilhah, and then the sons of Rachel.

Reuben (vv.3–4): The key to this saying is the statement, "You will no longer excel." Though Reuben has excelled, he loses the right of the firstborn because he violated the honor of his father (cf. 35:22).

Simeon and Levi (vv.5–7): These two sons are grouped together because they instigated the bloodshed against the city of Shechem (34:25). Here Jacob gives his final verdict on their action: their two tribes would not have their own portion in the inheritance of the land. As fulfillment, the tribe of Simeon virtually disappears from the biblical narratives after the time of the Conquest, and the tribe of Levi becomes the priestly tribe and receives no inheritance in the apportioning of the land.

Judah (vv.8–12): Jacob's prediction for the tribe of Judah pictured him as the preeminent son. Though not having the right of the firstborn (which went to Joseph; cf. 48:5), Judah had been chosen over all the others as the royal tribe. We now see why it has been so important to the writer to stress throughout this book that God's blessing does not necessarily come through the natural right of the firstborn. Unlike the imagery used of the other sons, the words of Jacob regarding Judah are transparent. He is described as a victorious warrior who returns home from battle and is greeted by the shouts of praise from his brothers. The parallelism of v.8 is extended by the statement, "Your father's sons will bow down to you." It is difficult not to see in this an intentional allusion to the dream of Joseph (37:10). What happened to the house of Joseph has been picked up by way of this image and transferred to the future house of Judah.

The image of the victorious warrior is extended with the picture of Judah as a "lion's cub," pictured as sleeping in its den after having just devoured its prey. The question at the end of v.9 speaks for itself. In v.10 the picture is filled out with a description of the young warrior as a king. He is the one who holds the "scepter" and the "ruler's staff." Judah will hold that status among the tribes of Israel until one comes "to whom it belongs."

The most startling aspect of this description comes next: "and the obedience of the nations is his." The use of the plural word "nations" rather than the singular "nation" suggests that Jacob had in view a kingship that extends beyond the boundaries of the sons of Israel to include other nations as well. There may be an anticipation of this view in the promise of God to Jacob in 48:4 (cf. 28:3): "I will make you a community of peoples." In any case, later biblical writers were apparently guided by texts such as this in formulating their view of the universal reign of the future Davidic king (e.g., Ps 2:8; Da 7:13–14; Rev 5:5, 9).

Then Jacob draws an extended picture of the reign of this one from the tribe of Judah (vv.11–12). In his day there will be plenty for everyone. Poetically this idea of plentitude is expressed with the images of the donkey tethered to the choicest of vines and clothing washed in vintage wine. Wine, the symbol of prosperity and blessing, will be so plentiful that even the choicest vines will be put to such everyday use as tethering the animals of burden, and vintage wine will be as commonplace as wash water. The eyes of this king are darker than wine and his teeth whiter than milk. He is a picture of strength and power. Later writers drew heavily from the imagery of this short text in their portrayal of the reign of the coming Messiah (cf. Isa 63:1–6; Rev 19:11, 13, 15).

Jacob's words regarding the remaining sons, with the exception of Joseph, are noticeable not only for their brevity, but also for their cryptic allusions to epic events that at the time lay yet in the future. Their destinies are, in most cases, based on a wordplay of the son's name. The central theme uniting each image is that of prosperity and blessing.

Zebulun (v.13): The Hebrew name Zebulun, meaning "lofty abode," "will live" (lit., "abide") by the seashore and extend his borders as far as Sidon (but cf. Jos 19:10–16).

Issachar (vv.14–15): His name is a play on the word "wages" (cf. 30:18). He is pictured as a strong donkey who sees that his land of rest is good and applies his back to the burden. The expression "he sees how good is his resting place" alludes to the expression in ch. 1—"and God saw that it was good"—and the "resting place" aligns the words of Jacob with the theme of the future rest that God will give his people in the Promised Land (cf. Ps. 95:11).

Dan (vv.16–17): His name is a play on the expression "he will judge" (30:6); he is the one who will judge his people. Though the sense of the snake image used here is unclear, Jacob's final words regarding Dan show that the image was meant in a positive way: "I look for your deliverance, O LORD"—an expression of hope in the Lord's deliverance. That hope is of a future prosperity for all the tribes and a future victory over all their enemies.

Gad (v.19): This brief statement contains a wordplay on nearly every word. It falls in line with the others by following in the path of the prophecy regarding Judah, giving expression to the hope of the final defeat of the enemy.

Asher (v.20): This statement has no clear wordplays, and its meaning is self-evident. In the future Asher's sons will enjoy great abundance and rich delicacies.

Naphtali (v.21): These words are also brief. Like the others, they present a picture of great future prosperity and abundance.

Joseph (vv.22–26): In substance Jacob's statements here repeat much of what was said about the other brothers after Judah. The difference, however, is the repetition of the word "blessing." While the other brothers receive pictures of future well-being and thus figuratively receive a future blessing, Jacob's words to Joseph make the "blessing" explicit. These words fall in line with all those earlier passages that promise "blessings"; thus they prepare the way for Jacob's final remarks in v.28. The reference to the "Shepherd" in v.24 alludes to 48:15.

Benjamin (v.27): The picture here resembles Judah's. Both depict the patriarch's future in terms of a victorious conquest over the enemy. In both the conqueror is a vicious predator, the lion and the wolf. But the stark simplicity of the words to Benjamin brings out the sense of sudden victory and conquest in stronger terms than the imagery of Judah.

In v.28, the writer sums up Jacob's words to his sons in terms of the theme of the blessing (see comment at the beginning of this section). This theme has been evident in all the sons after Judah, both in defeating enemies and in experiencing great prosperity and abundance. Behind this great prosperity lies the Garden of Eden. When the one comes to whom the kingship truly belongs (v.10), there will once again be the peace and prosperity that God intended all to have in the Garden of Eden.

### 4. Jacob's burial instructions repeated (49:29–33)

As he lay dying, Jacob once more (cf. 47:29–30) requested his sons to bury him in the Land of Promise with his fathers, specifically at "Machpelah," the cave purchased by Abraham in ch. 23 where he, Sarah, Isaac, Rebekah, and Leah were buried. This request renews our awareness of the promise of the land—that Jacob's seed would live in peace in the land promised to Abraham and Isaac. Jacob's faith in God's promises remained firm to the end. With such an expression on his lips, "he . . . breathed his last and was gathered to his people."

### Q. Jacob's Death and Burial (50:1–14)

Over half of the final chapter describes the mourning and burial of Jacob. Joseph himself mourned, as did the Egyptians. The pharaoh granted a special request to bury Jacob in his homeland, and a large entourage was provided as a burial procession to carry his body back to Canaan.

Why such detail over the burial of Jacob, in contrast to the mere notice of death and burial for the other patriarchs? A motive may be in the writer's focus in these latter chapters on God's faithfulness to his promise of the land and on the hope of God's people in their eventual return to the land. In later prophetic literature, a recurring image of the fulfillment of the promise to return to the land pictures returning Israel accompanied by many from among the nations (e.g., Isa 2:2–3; Zec 8:23). It is difficult not to see the same imagery at work in the present narrative: Jacob, in his final return to the Land of Promise, was accompanied by a great company of the officials and elders of the land of Egypt, along with the mighty army of the Egyptians. Thus his burial foreshadows the time when God "will bring Jacob back from captivity and will have compassion on all the people of Israel" (Eze 39:25).

## VII. The Final Joseph Narrative (50:15–26)

### A. Joseph's Forgiveness (50:15–21)

The narrative turns one final time to Joseph and his brothers and to the central theme of the Joseph narratives: "You intended to harm [lit., evil] me, but God intended it for good . . . [to] the saving of many lives" (45:5–7). Behind the entire Joseph story lies the unchanging plan of God—the same plan introduced at the beginning of the book, when God saw that what he had created was "good" (1:4–31). Through his dealings with the patriarchs and Joseph, God in his faithfulness had continued to bring about his good plan.

The last description of Joseph's dealings with his brothers is that "he comforted [NIV, reassured] them and spoke kindly to them." It is again difficult not to see in this picture a foreshadowing of the future community of the children of Israel in exile awaiting their return to the Promised Land (cf. Isa 40:1–2).

### B. Summary of Joseph's Life and Death (50:22–26)

Though his words are few, the final statement of Joseph to his sons gives the clearest expression of the kind of hope taught in these narratives. As had his father Jacob, Joseph wanted his bones returned to the Promised Land and made his sons swear to return them when they returned. He expressed clearly his hope and trust that God would bring them back (v.25).

The book of Genesis ends with the Israelites "in Egypt." But the narrative does not end here. As in earlier segments of the book, the death of the patriarch is followed immediately in the next book by a list of names that begins a narrative of the events in the lives of the next generations (compare Ge 50:26–Ex 1:5 with Ge 35:29–36:43).

# Exodus

## I. The Oppression of the Israelites (1:1–22)

The story of Exodus continues without interruption from the book of Genesis by recounting the genealogical list of Jacob's sons who came down to Egypt (1:1–5; cf. Ge 46:3). The total number of persons given here is seventy, the same as the number of nations listed in Ge 10, that is, the descendants of Adam and Noah (see comments on Ge 46:8–27).

Verse 6 marks an important starting point for the next series of events. It recounts the passing of the old generation. Verse 7 is a transitional verse, passing over the majority of the 400 years that Israel was in Egypt (cf. 12:40). The structure of the narrative thus follows the prophetic word about Israel's future given to Abraham in Ge 15:13, "Then the LORD said to him, 'Know for certain that your descendants will be strangers in a country not their own, and they will be enslaved and mistreated four hundred years.'" During this time, Israel had grown into a nation: "the land was filled with them" (referring to the "land of Goshen," not to the whole of the land of Egypt; cf. Ge 47:6).

Verse 8 brings us into the time frame of the major events of this book. Many generations have passed, the children of Israel have greatly increased in number (cf. Ge 12:2), and "a new king" (probably meaning "a new dynasty") had arisen over Egypt. Many identify this new dynasty with that of the Hyksos, an Asiatic people who reigned over Egypt during the Second Intermediate Period (1786–1558 B.C.). The identity of the king, however, was not a concern of the writer of the Pentateuch.

The new king quickly moved to prevent the Israelites from using their great strength to gain their freedom. The first measures taken proved fruitless. In fact, as the narratives progress we can see that the king's efforts begin to work against themselves, only helping to increase and multiply the number of the people further (v.12).

There is an apparent irony behind the narratives of Ex 1 and 2. The more the king tries to thwart God's blessing, the more that blessing increases. Down to the last measure taken by the Egyptian king the theme of a "providential irony" is evident in these events. The author's point is clear enough: God is at work in these events to bring about his plan, and no one, not even the great power of the Gentile nations, can stand in his way (cf. Isa 45).

We can see the irony at work in the king's command that all Hebrew male children be cast into the Nile. Although the mother of Moses obeys the king's command, she does so in a way that recalls the story of God's salvation of Noah in days of the flood—the child is put into an "ark" and then cast into the water. Such shaping of the narrative is clearly intended to show that a sovereign God is at work in Israel's history.

It is interesting to note that the author of the Pentateuch has placed two similar narratives on either side of his lengthy treatment of the Exodus and wilderness wanderings. The two narratives are Ex 1–2 (the Egyptian king's attempt to suppress Israel) and Nu 22–24 (the Moabite king's attempt to suppress Israel). Both narratives focus on the futility of the attempts of the nations to thwart God's plan to bless the seed of Abraham.

## II. The Preparation of a Deliverer—Moses (2:1–25)

In ch. 2 we are given a narrative glimpse of what one family did to protect their newborn son from the decree of the pharaoh. The son was, in fact, the deliverer, Moses. His mother hid him for three months. Then, when she could no longer hide the baby, she constructed a reed basket (an "ark"), sealed it, and placed the baby "in the Nile River" (v.3)—ironically, just as the king of Egypt had decreed (1:22). Furthermore, not only was the child saved by carrying out the decree of the king, but he was saved, in fact, by the pharaoh's own daughter. The writer has not wasted our time with stories about the hardships of the people in general. He has, rather, focused on the life of a single child. Not only was this one of the Hebrew children that the king was attempting to kill; this was, in fact, the very child whom the Lord had intended to bring his people up out of the land—the very eventuality that the king of Egypt feared most (1:10). The king's grand scheme was thwarted by what is cast as a kind of "mere coincidence." We, the readers, have a privileged view of the whole of the process. Such use of "irony" is common in the OT narratives. It shows that God is indeed at work in the affairs of the world and that, despite human efforts to the contrary, he will bring about his purposes.

The fact that the Egyptians used the Nile River to kill the young Israelite boys becomes a part of a larger strategy within the narrative to show God's ultimate vindication of evil. When the people were delivered by the hand of Moses, the first plague against the Egyptians was directed toward the Nile River (it becomes blood), and the last plague was directed against the sons of the Egyptians (the firstborn was killed).

Verse 23 marks another important transitional stage in the events of the book. As in 1:8, this new stage is marked by the rise of a new king. Moses has been in the wilderness, where he had escaped for his life, and now he is free to return to Egypt.

In v.24 the writer gives us the all-important clues to the meaning of the events that are about to be recounted. When the Israelites cried out to the Lord for help, God not only heard their cry, he also "remembered his covenant" with Abraham, Isaac, and Jacob (cf. Lev 26:42). Just as God had "remembered" Noah in the ark and rescued him (Ge 8:1), so now God turns to bring his people up out of bondage and into the land he had promised to their forefathers. The point of the narrative is to show that the basis of God's dealings with Israel was and is his covenant promises to Abraham.

The emphasis on God's covenant promises to the patriarchs, found here so clearly stated within these narratives, is also found in the message of the later prophets. The prophet Micah, for example, sees God's promises to Abraham and Jacob as the basis on which Israel's hope in God's future salvation can rest, "You will again have compassion on us; you will tread our sins underfoot and hurl all our iniquities into the depths of the sea. You will be true to Jacob and show mercy to Abraham, as you pledged on oath to our fathers in days long ago" (Mic 7:19–20). Moreover, God's work of redemption in sending his Son, Jesus, is viewed in the NT as a fulfillment of these same promises to Abraham and the patriarchs (Lk 1:54–55). The "exodus from Egypt" thus becomes an important biblical image of God's faithfulness in remembering his promises and sending his Redeemer. In this account of the Exodus itself we can see the same concerns already at work. The call of Moses already anticipates and foreshadows the future Redeemer. It is not by chance that henceforth in the Pentateuch, the mediator, Moses, becomes one of the central narrative vehicles for depicting the messianic hope (cf. Dt 34:10).

## III. The Call of Moses (3:1–4:31)

### A. God Calls Moses (3:1–10)

The first result of God's "remembering his covenant" with Abraham is his call of Moses, a deliverer. God began his discourse with Moses with a warning not to come near to him because he is holy. As we will later see, the idea of God's holiness will prove to be a central theme in the remainder of the book. In fact, the whole of the structure of Israel's worship of God at the tabernacle is based on a view of God as the absolutely Holy One who has come to dwell in their midst. We should not lose sight of the fact, however, that at the same time that God warned Moses to stand at a distance, he also spoke to him "face to face." The fact that God is a holy God should not be understood to mean he is an impersonal force—God is holy yet intensely personal. This is a central theme in the narratives of the Sinai covenant that follow.

God identified himself to Moses as the "God of your father, the God of Abraham, the God of Isaac and the God of Jacob" (v.6), and proceeded to tell Moses of his plan: Moses was to be the one who would deliver the Israelites from bondage in Egypt and to bring them into the land promised to their forefathers (vv.7–10). He was to form them into a nation with the worship of God as its central concern.

## B. Moses' Response to God's Call (3:11–4:31)

Moses immediately realized the responsibility of his task and replied to God, "Who am I?" We should probably not understand his question as an expression of doubt or fear. It appears rather to derive from a genuine humility. Moses was now a shepherd, and we know from the preceding narratives that the Egyptians did not have dealings with such men (cf. Ge 46:34). Moses knew well that he would have no official recognition among the Egyptians.

God responded to Moses' question, not by building up Moses' confidence in himself, but by the reassurance that he would be with him in carrying out his task. Thus God's words here restate and reinforce the lesson of the earlier

Joseph narratives. As with Joseph, God would provide the kind of recognition Moses would need before the pharaoh by "signs" and "great wonders" that he would perform through Moses. The signs Moses was to give to the people and to the king were miraculous signs that would demonstrate God's power.

It should be noted, however, that the sign given to Moses in 3:12 itself called for faith: "When you have brought the people out of Egypt, you shall worship God at this mountain." Within the narratives of the Pentateuch, the reader is well aware that this specific sign would be fulfilled in Ex 19. Thus when viewed as an element of the text, God's word of assurance to Moses has more certainty to it than might, at first, have appeared. It is a sign to the reader as much as to Moses.

Moses' next response has prompted much discussion among biblical scholars and theologians: he said, "Suppose I go to the Israelites and say to them, 'The God of your fathers has sent me to you,' and they ask me, 'What is his name?' Then what shall I tell them?" In other words, Moses realized that what he was being called to do would meet with opposition in Egypt. Moreover, the nature of the opposition would be theological. The people would want to know about the God whom they were to follow into the wilderness.

When Moses asked about the "name" of God, he was asking more than just the identity of God. He was asking a question about the very nature of God. Within the world of the biblical text, the name was the expression of the very nature of its bearer (cf. 1Sa 25:25). Just as Adam's naming the animals meant that he was looking at their essential nature—looking, in fact, for a "suitable partner"—so the "name" was an expression of the very essence of the one who bears the name.

Thus when Moses asked God's name, the answer he received may not seem like the answer we would have expected. In some translations, the Lord's answer looks even more like an evasion of the question itself. God simply replied, "I AM WHO I AM." If Moses was, in fact, seeking to know God's essential nature in asking for his name, then the answer he received from the Lord was precisely that which he sought. The Lord's reply, "I AM WHO I AM" may be paraphrased to say, "It is I who am with you." Thus in his reply to Moses, the Lord lets it be known to the Israelites, "the One who promises to be with you" has sent Moses to you.

In the following verse, the actual name of God, *Yahweh* (ASV, "Jehovah"), is used. Its association with the expression "I AM WHO I AM" suggests that the Hebrew name *Yahweh* is meant to convey the sense of "He who is present" or "He who has promised to be present with his people." In giving this name to Moses, then, God not only promises to be present with him and his people, but he also gives them a name that recalls the promise itself, "He who is with us."

In the English Bible, the Hebrew *Yahweh* is translated as "LORD" (all capital letters), not as "Yahweh." Why? It is because the English Bible follows an ancient Jewish custom of not pronouncing the divine name. Rather than reading *Yahweh* in the synagogue or in private reading, the Jews replaced the name of God by the word *Adonai*. The English translation "LORD" is an attempt to follow this custom and to distinguish the occurrence of the divine name *Yahweh* from the occurrences of the divine name *Adonai* ("Lord") in the text. "LORD" occurs when the Hebrew text has *Yahweh* and "Lord" when the Hebrew text has *Adonai*.

God's words to Moses in 3:16–22 are an important link in the structure of the pentateuchal narratives. His words first reflect back to the promise of God to the patriarchs in the mention of the "God of your fathers—the God of Abraham, Isaac and Jacob" (v.16). God then turns his attention to the events that are now about to be recorded—Moses' confrontation with the pharaoh. As is the case in many biblical narratives, the description that God gives of these events before they actually happened proves to be a near replica of those events as they were then recorded in the narrative (e.g., Ge 12:10–20). It is important to take note of this feature of the narrative because it is one of the ways the Scriptures attempt to show God's sovereign control over all the various events narrated in the Pentateuch. We, the readers, are allowed to view the events from a divine perspective. God describes what is about to happen, and the narrative follows the same pattern in depicting the events. We should note, however, that even though the events of the Pentateuch turn out as expected from such a vantage point, we often find in the narration of the events that there are significant modifications.

When such modifications do occur within these narratives, they are usually a result of human actions not anticipated in the initial preview. Moses, Israel, or the Egyptians do something unexpected. Hence the narratives, as they unfold the events, remain open to human action; they are not merely determined by God. God knows what will happen, but there is room in the narrative for human actions. For example, in the present narrative, when God first describes to Moses what will happen when he goes before the pharaoh, the role of Aaron as the speaker for Moses is not specifically mentioned. Aaron only comes into the picture because of Moses' reluctance to obey God's call. Moreover, when God recounts the events about to transpire, he anticipates the obedience of the people (3:18). This obedience is, in fact, explicitly and verbally realized in ch. 4 after Moses shows them the signs (4:31). However, as the narrative now stands, the obedience of the people was short-lived. In ch. 6 it is recounted that the people proved to be disobedient "because of a lack of spirit" (6:9). Thus, though God's words prove determinative for the events of the narrative, they do not preclude the new directions taken by human actions. Such narrative features are subtle, yet they are important guideposts for appreciating the sense and meaning of the biblical narratives.

The importance of this section, then, is not only that it gives the readers an overview of the series of events that are about to be recounted and a preview of their outcome, but also, even more importantly, these words, spoken before the events themselves, show that God was in control of the outcome. The pharaoh's choice not to let the people go was known already by God as he sent Moses before him. God's words show further that ultimately the pharaoh would let God's people go, but not without an occasion for demonstrating God's "wonders" in their midst. Thus the Exodus is already in view at the start.

This section ends with a reference to God's promise to Abraham in Ge 14:14 that his people would go out of Egypt with great wealth (Ex 3:22). This was fulfilled in 12:35 when "the Israelites did as Moses instructed and asked the Egyptians for articles of silver and gold and for clothing."

Again, in 4:1, Moses asked a question that revealed his understanding of the true gravity of the task God had given him: "What if they do not believe me and say, 'The LORD did not appear to you'?" In answer to this question, God gave Moses three "signs": (1) his staff became a snake (vv.2–5); (2) his hand became leprous (vv.6–7); (3) the water from the Nile River became blood when poured out (v.9).

In each of these signs there is the unmistakable mark of God's creative power. These signs were not intended for the Egyptians, but rather for the Israelites. They were signs that the Lord was present with Moses and were intended to produce assurance and faith in the Israelites that Moses had been sent by God. To this end the signs achieved their purpose (see 4:31, "and they believed").

Moses raised one final objection—he was not an eloquent speaker. Again, the Lord's response is an appeal to his creative power: "Who gave man his mouth? Who makes him deaf or mute? Who gives him sight or makes him blind? Is it not I, the LORD?" Then the Lord repeated his promise: "I . . . will teach you what to say" (4:12). At this point Moses appeared to overstep his mark and resisted too much. The Lord was angered by Moses' refusals, but he again provided an answer to Moses' objection: Aaron would go with him and speak for him.

Through the entire narrative, Moses is seen as a reluctant but ultimately willing leader. The writer has shown that the kind of leadership that Moses provided was not motivated by a hunger for power. It was a divine call, and God alone would be able to fulfill the task. With such leadership God would do his work, and the people would follow in faith (4:31).

As Moses prepared to return to Egypt to deliver God's people, the Lord warned him of his larger purposes, "I will harden [Pharaoh's] heart so that he will not let the people go" (4:21). Further on in the narrative (7:3–5) the divine purpose for hardening the pharaoh's heart is given—so that "the Egyptians will know that I am the LORD." God's desire was to make himself known to the Egyptians.

A nearly inexplicable event occurs in the brief narrative of Moses' return to Egypt (4:24–26). As Moses was resting for the night, the Lord sought to kill him. His life was spared only because his wife, Zipporah, immediately circumcised her son and laid the foreskin at Moses' feet. After that she said, "You are a bridegroom of blood to me" (4:26), and the Lord withdrew from him and his life was spared.

We are apparently to see this as a form of judgment or warning regarding the necessity of keeping the commandment of circumcision. It is impossible to reconstruct the details of the incident recorded here, and fortunately it is not necessary to do so. The point is clear enough, however. God takes his word seriously, and thus he must be obeyed. Here, at the outset of Israel's covenant with God, the reader is reminded of the importance of obedience and the dire consequences of disobedience. At several other points in the narrative (e.g., see Ge 32:22–32; Ex 33:2–3; Nu 11:1–3), the writer uses such opaque and ominous narratives to remind the readers of God's serious intention that Israel obey his commandments and walk in his ways (see comments on Nu 11:1–3).

A confirmation of this reading of the story comes in the immediately following narrative. When Moses and Aaron ask the pharaoh to let their people go into the wilderness to worship and sacrifice to God, the reason they give is "or he may strike us with plagues or with the sword" (5:3). The present narrative (4:24–26) shows that their reasons were not without merit. The Lord had already confronted Moses to strike him down; there was thus good reason to fear lest he meet them also with plagues or the sword.

It is probably also true that if it was the son of Moses whose life was threatened (which is a possible meaning of the Hebrew text), then this narrative is intended as an anticipation of the last plague, the death of the firstborn of the Egyptians, and of the blood displayed on the doorposts of the Israelite homes, which protected their own firstborn. It is thus not unintentional that a reference is made to the death of the firstborn of Egypt and the salvation of the Israelites in the immediately preceding verses (4:22–23).

# IV. The Deliverance From Egypt (5:1–15:21)

## A. Oppression Worsens; Promises Renewed (5:1–6:30)

### 1. The pharaoh's refusal to free God's people (5:1–3)

After the events of 4:27–31, where the people believed the signs that Moses performed and were ready to accept his leadership, Moses and Aaron went in to the pharaoh to request permission to leave Egypt for three days. The pharaoh's negative response to their request provides the theological setting for the following narratives. He asked, "Who is the LORD that I should obey him? . . . I do not know the LORD" (5:2). These words form the "motivation" for the events that follow—events designed to demonstrate who the Lord is (cf. 7:5). Within the narratives the pharaoh and the Egyptians do learn the lesson (8:19; 9:20, 27; 10:7). But a larger purpose also emerges: The plagues were to be recounted "to your children and grandchildren . . . that you may know that I am the LORD" (10:2). Finally, the reader also needs to learn this same lesson.

### 2. Israel's oppression increased (5:4-18)

The second part of the pharaoh's response also sets the stage for the events that follow. He increased their labor by cutting the supply of straw for making bricks. Thus, as at the beginning of the book, the pharaoh made Israel's labor more difficult and the people now cried out in their distress (cf. 2:23; 5:15). In 2:33 the cry of the people went up before God. By contrast here, in 5:15, the cry of the people is before the pharaoh. It is as if the author wants to show that the pharaoh was standing in God's way; thus he provides another motivation for the plagues that follow.

### 3. The Lord's plan announced (5:19–6:1):

The Israelite leaders are powerless before the pharaoh. By drawing this out, the narrative has begun to stress the importance of the kind of leadership exemplified in Moses. The key to the effective work of Moses is shown clearly here at the beginning, "Then the LORD said to Moses, 'Now you will see what I will do to Pharaoh'" (6:1). The work of Moses was the work of God. Thus Moses is not portrayed here as a miracle worker. Rather, he is the Lord's servant. God does the work while Moses merely watches. As if to stress this aspect of the narrative, the Lord repeats to Moses twice that the work that is about to be carried out through him was by the "mighty hand" of the Lord (6:1).

Moses' own words to God in 5:22–23 stress further God's role in the work that is about to be done. By allowing us to listen to Moses' prayer to God, the author uncovers Moses' own view of his calling. It was God's work, and Moses was sent by God to do it.

### 4. God, Moses, and the Patriarchs (6:2–8)

Because the previous narratives have laid such great stress on the fact that it was God alone who would carry out his work through Moses, the author delays the action of the narrative momentarily in order to further identify the nature of God's relationship to Moses and make his plan more specific. God had already made his name known to Moses in ch. 3. Here in ch. 6 this relationship between God and Moses is contrasted with his previous relationship to the patriarchs. The patriarchs did not know God "by [his] name the LORD" as did Moses and the Israelites. Abraham, Isaac, and Jacob knew God as El Shaddai. The author does not say the patriarchs did not know the name of

"LORD." He says, rather, "I did not make myself known to them [by the name LORD]"; instead, he was known as "God Almighty" (i.e., El Shaddai; v.3). In the book of Genesis, of course, the patriarchs do use the name "LORD" (Ge 15:2,7); but when God "appeared" to the patriarchs (e.g., Ge 17:3), it was as El Shaddai. Thus when Ex 6:3 says "I appeared to Abraham . . . as God Almighty" and not as "LORD," it accurately reflects the wording of the Genesis narratives. God "appeared" to him "in a vision." The present text suggests that unlike the patriarchs, Moses "knew the LORD," not by means of a vision, but "face to face" (Dt 34:10).

This small section of narrative also sketches out the argument of the whole of the Pentateuch. God made a covenant with the patriarchs to give them the land of Canaan (6:4). He remembered his covenant when he heard the cry of the Israelites in Egyptian bondage (v.5). He is now going to deliver Israel from their bondage and take them to himself as a people and be their God (v.6). He will also bring them into the land that he swore to give to their fathers (v.8). The die is cast for the remainder of the events narrated in the Pentateuch. Moses refuses again and is commanded by God to go (vv.9–13).

In light of the Israelites' obedience to God and hearkening to Moses in 4:31, it is surprising to find that they so quickly have disobeyed (6:9). The author, however, is quick to remind us that their own "discontentment" and the hard work were the cause. Even Moses questions God when he is told to go before the pharaoh and speak. If the people of Israel will not hearken to him, why would the pharaoh (v.12)? Moses appears to falter along with the people, losing sight of what has been a central theme in the narratives thus far—it was God, not Moses, who was to bring the people out of Egypt. Unlike ch. 4, in this narrative Moses' objections are cut short by God's command: God "spoke to Moses and Aaron . . . and he commanded them to bring the Israelites out of Egypt" (6:13,26).

In the last analysis, then, the Exodus was a work of God; even Moses and Aaron had to be commanded to bring the people out. There is a pattern here repeated many times throughout the remainder of the pentateuchal narratives. God's initial call for faith and trust is met with doubt and fear. God then responds with a simple call for obedience. This call for obedience, however, does not rule out or replace the necessity of faith and trust, nor does it render the use of "signs" unnecessary (cf. 6:28ff.; 10:1ff.).

### 5. The family of Moses and Aaron (6:14–27)

As the summary statements at the conclusion of this section suggest, the purpose of this list of names is to identify the leading characters of the following narratives, Moses and Aaron. That the purpose of the list is specifically to introduce Moses and Aaron can be seen in the fact that the list of names is only a fragment of a list of the twelve sons of Jacob (cf. Ge 49:1–27). The beginning of the list of tribal names is abbreviated, and it ends abruptly after the families of Levi, i.e., the family of Moses and Aaron (cf. Nu 26:59). This concern to give the "lineage" of the central characters of the narratives has been manifest in the Pentateuch from the beginning (cf. Ge 5; 10; 46).

### 6. Summary (6:28–30)

After the insertion of the list of names in 6:14–27, the writer summarizes the material of the earlier narrative. We are taken back to Moses' objection, "Since I speak with faltering lips, why would Pharaoh listen to me?" (v.30). What was earlier given as a simple command by God to go before the pharaoh (6:13) is now expanded into the instructions for carrying out the

"signs," or plagues, against the Egyptians.

## B. The Plagues (Signs) (7:1–12:36)

### 1. The purpose of the plagues (7:1–7)

The purpose of the "plagues" (signs) is suggested in vv.3–5, where God told Moses that he would harden the pharaoh's heart that he might send signs and wonders upon Egypt. These signs were designed to demonstrate God's power to the Egyptians (v.5) as well as to the Israelites (9:16). God was not out to destroy the Egyptians. As is repeatedly stressed in Scripture, his plans and ways are aimed at the salvation and blessing of all the nations (Ge 12:3). Behind such narratives lies the same theological hope as outlined by the prophet Isaiah, who speaks of God's plans and purposes in dealing with Israel and the nations: "So the LORD will make himself known to the Egyptians, and in that day they will acknowledge the LORD. . . . The LORD will strike Egypt with a plague; he will strike them and heal them. They will turn to the LORD, and he will respond to their pleas and heal them. . . . In that day Israel will be the third, along with Egypt and Assyria, a blessing on the earth. The LORD Almighty will bless them, saying, 'Blessed be Egypt my people, Assyria my handiwork, and Israel my inheritance'" (Isa 19:21–25).

It is possible to argue that the "signs" themselves are directed against the Egyptians' concept of the universe. Within Egyptian religion, the universe existed in a harmonious whole, with each part contributing to the well-balanced system. The Egyptian word for this was ma'at. It was the responsibility of the king, for example, as the incarnate god on earth, to maintain this balance, this ma'at. The purpose of the "plagues" was thus to challenge this basic concept by showing that the king was, in fact, powerless before Israel's God (12:12).

What we see in the "plagues," then, is an unmasking of the pharaoh's claims to deity and to his claim to rule the universe. The pharaoh was, in effect, taking credit for something in which he had no part, and the signs that Moses performed demonstrated that to both the Egyptians and the Israelites. In recording these events, the writer of the Pentateuch shows that only the Lord is truly God (see 10:1–2). Ultimately each of the plagues led up to the final plague—the death of the firstborn. As the firstborn of the pharaoh, the king's own son was thought to be a second incarnate god.

No doubt there is some truth to this assessment of the intention of the plagues. One must be careful, however, to note that there is no clear indication that the author of the Pentateuch intends his readers to see the plagues in this way. There is no mention of the Egyptian concept of *ma'at* in the text itself, nor is there any indication that the author assumes his readers are familiar with the theology of the religion of Egypt. It seems more likely that the author is portraying the events of the plagues to a primarily Israelite audience, or at least one who understands the world in terms of the theology of the Pentateuch. As such there need be nothing more intended in this series of plagues than this general but all important point: the God of the covenant, the Creator of the universe, is superior to the powers of the nations—whether those powers be merely political and military powers, or, in fact, powers that rely on magic and "secret arts."

## 2. Signs (7:8–12)

As Moses and Aaron approached the pharaoh, they were given a sign to perform before the king in order to demonstrate the validity of their mission. Aaron threw down his staff before the pharaoh, and it became a snake (or perhaps more accurately, a crocodile, v.10). The narrative presents this act as wholly a divine sign, not the result of any magic on Aaron's part. In contrast, we are told that the pharaoh's own magicians were able to repeat the sign using their "secret arts" (v.11). The narrative shows clearly, however, that there was a real difference in what Moses did. God was working through Moses to accomplish his own plan.

Even though the Egyptian magicians were able to reproduce the sign, the Lord demonstrated his power all the more in the fact that their own snakes were swallowed by those of Moses and Aaron (v.12). The Egyptian magicians' secret arts consisted of a form of hypnosis of the snakes into an immobile state of catalepsy, making them appear as rods until the spell was broken.

The writer is careful to point out that the events being recorded were already known by God before they came to pass (see vv.3, 13a, the beginning and end of this narrative).The writer then adds, "just as the LORD had said." (v.13b). Such an emphasis on the work of God in hardening the heart of the pharaoh is intended to explain the condition of the pharaoh at the beginning of the first of the ten plagues. In v.14, as God sends the first plagues, we are told only that "Pharaoh's heart was [already] unyielding."

This introductory narrative thus ensures that the work of God in hardening the pharaoh's heart is not missed throughout the narrative of the ten plagues. The consistent refusal to let the Israelites go is traced back to the Lord's hardening of the pharaoh's heart. Note the recurring statement, "just as the LORD had said" (7:13a, 22b; 8:15; 9:12).

## 3. The first plague: The Nile becomes blood (7:14–25)

The narrative suggests that the waters of the Nile, in fact, became blood. It may be that the color of the Nile was simply red like that of blood (cf. the moon turning to blood in Joel 3:4).

There may have been a "red tide" in the Nile—a pollution of the Nile caused by heavy flooding of the Nile valley, bringing large deposits of red dirt from its source in the South and possibly causing an excessive amount of microorganisms that give off a reddish color in the water. This is not to say that what happened was merely a natural phenomenon, even though such "red tides" are known to occur in the Nile River. The point of the narrative is that the Lord, the God of the covenant, and not the pharaoh, the king of Egypt, is able to control the balance of nature.

The further intensification of this plague in v.19, however, suggests that more was involved than a mere "red tide" in the Nile. Not just the Nile was affected; rather, it was the whole of the water sources in Egypt, including all the pools of water and water containers. This suggests that the narrative intends to teach that the water of the Egyptians did, in fact, become blood.

Curiously enough, however, the Egyptian magicians were able to duplicate the sign (v.22), suggesting that not "all of the water" of Egypt had been affected. As is often the case in the everyday language of the biblical narratives, the sense of "all" can be limited by the immediate context. In any event, after the Egyptian magicians carried through with their duplication of the signs, there was no "fresh water" available to drink (v.24). Since the Egyptians had to resort to digging for their water along the banks of the Nile (v.24), it is possible that the Egyptian magicians found fresh water for their duplication of the sign by the same means.

### 4. The second plague: The frogs (8:1–15)

The frog, along with most creatures in the natural world, was worshiped by the ancient Egyptians. It was considered the giver of the breath of life, and thus it became a symbol of life. At the word of Moses' God, the frogs overwhelmed the Egyptians, and the king had to plead with Moses to have them removed. In answer to the prayer of Moses, on the following day, all the frogs in the land died. Already the pharaoh shows signs of giving in to Moses' request, particularly in the midst of a plague (8:8). When the plague subsided, however, the pharaoh had a change of heart. We are again reminded that the hardness of his heart "was just as the LORD had said" (v.15).

### 5. The third plague: Gnats (8:16–19)

The importance of this plague lies in the fact that the Egyptians were unable to reproduce it. When they could not succeed, the magicians concluded that "this is the finger of God"—God was truly producing this sign; it was not a trick like their own (8:19). This is the point in the narrative where we, the readers, see that the Egyptian magicians were using tricks in their earlier signs. Their confession plays an important role in uncovering the writer's real purpose in recounting these events.

### 6. The fourth plague: Swarms of flies (8:20–32)

Another new element is introduced with this plague—the Israelites were set apart from the swarms of flies, and only the Egyptians were affected (v.22). In the Hebrew text this is called a "deliverance" for the people of Israel (see NIV note), as in Isa 50:2, "Was my arm too short to ransom you?"

Again the pharaoh appeared ready to give in to the request to let the people go to worship God. He set a limit, however, by not letting them leave the land (v.25). When Moses appealed to him, he gave in further but was vague on what limits he intended for them, "You must not go very far" (v.28). Though Moses already anticipated the pharaoh's change of heart (v.29), he nevertheless prayed for the removal of the swarms (vv.30–31). As is expected, the pharaoh hardened his heart.

### 7. The fifth plague: Pestilence on the livestock (9:1–7)

The words of Moses to the pharaoh proved true. All the livestock of the Egyptians died of disease and yet not one of the livestock of the Israelites was affected. Moses was not called in this time. The pharaoh's heart hardened and he did not let the people go.

### 8. The sixth plague: Boils on the Egyptians (9:8–12)

The report of this plague resumes the general pattern of the earlier plagues in referring at the end to God's promise to harden the heart of the pharaoh (7:3). Moreover, the author explicitly states that "the LORD hardened Pharaoh's heart" (v.12). On the other hand, the nature of Moses' actions in this plague was unique. He had to throw soot into the air so that the dust would become boils over all the Egyptians.

In this account we learn that the magicians were still hard at work opposing the signs of Moses. A new twist, however, is introduced here. Their problem now was not that they could not duplicate the sign—something they would not likely have wanted to do; rather, they could not "stand before Moses because of the boils." This shows that, like some earlier plagues, the Israelites were not affected by the boils. It also provides a graphic picture of the ultimate failure of the magicians to oppose the work of Moses and Aaron; they lay helpless in their sickbeds.

### 9. The seventh plague: Hailstorms (9:13–35)

The result of the hailstorms was the destruction of the Egyptians' crops and livestock, i.e., "all that was left in the fields." Again, the Israelites were safe in Goshen. The Lord's words to the pharaoh in this plague greatly expand on the purpose of the plagues developed so far in the narrative. Up to this point, that purpose has been described generally as so that "the Egyptians will know that I am the LORD" (7:5). That purpose is now expanded to include "that you [Pharaoh and the Egyptians] may know that there is no one like me in all the earth" (9:14)—an idea that comes close in meaning to the first commandment (20:2–6)—and "that my name might be proclaimed in all the earth" (9:16)—resembling the second commandment (20:7). This narrative thus grounds the commandments in the historical acts of God in the Exodus.

### 10. The eighth plague: Locusts (10:1–20)

With the eighth plague, a new element is introduced into the purpose of the plagues. As before, God hardened the pharaoh's heart so that he might perform the signs; but this time the sign was not to Egypt and the pharaoh. It was rather for Israel and their children, "that you may tell your children and grandchildren how I dealt harshly with the Egyptians . . . that you may know that I am the LORD" (v.2).

As the narrative now stands, it presents a fickle pharaoh. He first appeared to consent to the Israelites' request to leave the land with all their families and possessions (vv.8–10). But then, just as quickly, it becomes clear that he intended to hold back their families and send only the men (v.11). With this Moses and Aaron were driven out of the kings' presence, and the plague was called down on the Egyptians.

The NIV, along with other translations, renders the pharaoh's words as if he is speaking sarcastically, "The LORD be with you—if I let you go, along with your women and children [as you are requesting]." This may, in fact, be the case. As it stands, however, there is not much evidence for such a reading within the text, and the picture of a halting confused pharaoh plays well here at the conclusion of the plague narratives. It shows that Moses and Aaron are beginning to get on his nerves.

## 11. The ninth plague: Darkness (10:21–29)

There is a marked finality to the ninth plague. (1) The pharaoh was down to his last ruse. The women and children could go but not the livestock. This was unacceptable to Moses because the livestock were needed for offerings. (2) The darkness of the plagues signaled the end to the plagues. Just as the world had begun in total darkness (Ge 1:2), so now the land of Egypt returned to that state. There is thus a narrative finality to the ninth plague. (3) Moses and Aaron were warned by the pharaoh never to return to him again. All future opportunities for signs were thus removed.

There was still, however, "one more plague" to be unleashed against Egypt. There is a hint of that plague in the pharaoh's own last concession to Moses: "your women and children may go with you" (v.24). Little did he know of the bitter irony contained in his words. The reader, however, is well aware of the sense his words have. The children of the Israelites would go free, but "every firstborn son in Egypt will die" (11:5). In spite of the fact that they had been warned not to return to the pharaoh, Moses and Aaron had to return to warn the Egyptians of the last plague (cf. 11:4–8). When Moses said, "I will never appear before you again" (v.29), it may be that his words to the pharaoh here also included the announcement of the last plague.

With the eighth and ninth plagues the narrative shows that the pharaoh was resisting the request of Moses beyond all reasonable limits. Even his own servants appear to scold him with the remark, "Do you not yet realize that Egypt is ruined?" (10:7). But the pharaoh continued to hold out because, as the narrative stresses, the Lord had hardened his heart. The more the king resisted, the stronger the message of the narrative came through. The plagues were "signs" to show the power of God.

## 12. The last plague (11:1–12:36)

Looking at the last plague in terms of what it must have meant for the Egyptians and quite apart from the sense given to the plagues in the biblical account, we can easily see that it was the most severe, both personally and theologically. Not only was it a severe blow to each Egyptian household who lost an elder son, but it was a powerful blow to the Egyptians' idea of royal succession. In ancient Egypt the eldest son of the king was considered a god. It is interesting that the king who followed the pharaoh of the Exodus (Thutmose IV) was not the eldest son. In one of his own inscriptions, he attributes his kingship to the premature death of an elder brother.

Within the context of the biblical narrative, however, we can see that the last plague is central to God's further dealings with Israel. It was memorialized for the Israelites in the celebration of the Passover (ch. 12) and the Feast of Unleavened Bread (ch. 13). Moreover, it was on the basis of the last plague that God was able to claim the "firstborn" for himself and ultimately to substitute the Levitical priesthood for Israel's firstborn (13:1–2; Nu 3:13, 41). Thus by means of the account of the last plague the author of the Pentateuch introduces into the Exodus narrative in a clear and precise way the notion of redemption from sin and death.

The idea of salvation from slavery and deliverance from Egypt is manifest throughout the early chapters of Exodus. The idea of redemption and salvation from death, however, is the particular contribution of the last plague, especially as it is worked into the narrative by the author. Hence the commemoration of the Passover was to be more than a remembrance of God's deliverance of Israel from slavery and oppression. It was also a commemoration of salvation from the "angel of death" sent against anyone who did not enter into the Passover. By means of this plague, then, the writer is able to bring the Exodus narratives into the larger framework of the whole of the Pentateuch and particularly that of the early chapters of Genesis. In the midst of the judgment of death, God provides a way of salvation for the promised seed (Ge 3:15). Like Enoch (5:22–24), Noah (6:9), and Lot (19:16–19), those who walk in God's way will be saved from death and destruction.

The biblical texts describing the Passover are a mixture of narrative and instruction. As the writer recounts the events of the Exodus, he also inserts instructions regarding how the event of the Passover is to be commemorated by later generations. The Israelites celebrated the first Passover feast before they left Egypt and hence needed to know these instructions. There are additional features of the Passover celebration, however, that are here addressed specifically to later generations.

On the tenth day of the month of Abib, each household selected a lamb for a sacrifice. It was to be kept for four days; the text does not give a reason why. There are several traditional answers to this question, but none of them is inherently convincing. Suggestions are: (1) The lamb was chosen several days early to avoid the last minute rush and final preparations for leaving Egypt. (2) It was to allow sufficient time for observing the animal to ensure that it was "without blemish." (3) It was kept during this period of time to allow for reflection on God's salvation and grace shown in the Exodus. (4) There may also be a reason that is tied to the ninth plague of darkness (10:22). By choosing the animal on the tenth day, the three days of darkness would have been avoided. The fourteenth, then, would have been the next day in which there was light.

On the fourteenth day of Abib the animal was slain "at twilight" and eaten. Since twilight marked the end of the day, it would have been the fifteenth of Abib (Nu 33:3) when, at midnight (12:29), the Lord struck the firstborn of Egypt and the Israelites were swiftly sent out of the land by the Egyptians. They departed from Rameses and rather than take the nearest route into the land of Canaan (13:17–18), they turned eastward to Succoth (12:37) and from there to Etham (13:20) on their way to Sinai (14:2).

In the future commemoration of this event, the Feast of Unleavened Bread was to begin on the same day as the Exodus, the fifteenth of Abib (12:17; Lev 23:6; Nu 28:17; 33:3). This was also reckoned as the "evening" of the fourteenth of Abib (Ex 12:18) since it was to follow the Passover. The Feast of Unleavened Bread, then, lasted from the fifteenth to the twenty-first of Abib (12:18).

The Feast of Passover was inaugurated to commemorate the birth of the nation of Israel. The fact that this feast marked a new beginning can be seen in the inauguration of a new calendar shaped around this event as the first event of the year. The feast was also intended to remind Israel of the Lord's salvation when he "passed over" their houses and delivered their firstborn (12:13, 27). The bitter herbs eaten with the meal were to remind Israel of the bitter days of bondage in Egypt, and the unleavened bread was to remind them of God's quick deliverance (12:33–34, 39).

Later biblical writers are careful to remind us that key biblical events happened during the time of the celebration of the Passover. We are told, for example, that Joshua led Israel through the Jordan and into the Promised Land during the time of the Passover Feast (Jos 4:19). Also, Jesus rode into Jerusalem at the time of the preparation for the

Passover Feast. Jewish tradition said that on the Passover day the Messiah would come to save God's people; in the Gospels, Jesus is shown as the one who fulfilled that expectation. He is the Lamb of God, slain during the days of the Passover Feast (Jn 18:28). According to Paul, "Christ, our Passover lamb, has been sacrificed" (1Co 5:7; cf. also v.8). For Peter, Christ was "a lamb without blemish or defect, chosen before the creation of the world" (1Pe 1:19–20). In the last book of the Bible, Christ, the Passover Lamb, stands at the center of John's vision of the future redemption of the heavens and earth when all creatures in heaven and on earth sing, "Worthy is the Lamb, who was slain" (Rev 5:12).

The instructions to Moses and Israel on the eve of the Exodus are recorded here in such a way that they provide the directions for celebrating the Passover throughout all future generations. Though much has been added in later traditions to the celebration of the Passover, the instructions given here are quite simple. A male yearling lamb without blemish was slain and its blood put on the doorposts. After it was properly cooked, it was eaten with unleavened bread and bitter herbs. Anything not eaten was to be destroyed with fire by morning. Those eating the meal were to be dressed for travel and ready at any point to leave. Instructions relating to the later celebrations of the Passover are given in 12:43–49.

According to Jewish tradition, some instructions given in these chapters were intended only for the first Passover in Egypt and were not practiced later. These are (1) taking the lamb on the tenth day, (2) applying the blood to the doorposts, and (3) eating the meal in haste. In the later description of the celebration of the Passover in the Pentateuch, these elements are omitted (Lev 23:5ff. Nu 9:2ff.; 28:16–17; Dt 16:1ff.).

The night of the Passover was to be remembered throughout all generations by means of the Feast of Unleavened Bread. The instructions regarding this feast were not given to Israel to be carried out the night of the first Passover, but are included here because this feast was later to play an important part in the celebration of the Passover.

The description of the Feast of Unleavened Bread is, like that of the Passover, very simple. Beginning on the evening of the fourteenth of Abib, the Israelites were to go without yeast in their food for seven days. The first day and the seventh day were to be special days in which they were to cease from all unnecessary work and gather together in a holy assembly. A similar set of instructions is given in 13:3ff. (cf. 23:15). In those instructions, some of the features of the Passover meal are combined with that of the Feast of Unleavened Bread.

The people were instructed to put the blood of the lamb on their doorposts (12:21–23). That was the only way they could avert the "destroyer." Though the text does not explicitly state it, the overall argument of the Pentateuch suggests that their obedience to the word of the Lord in this instance was an evidence of their faith and trust in him (see Heb 11:28).

The purpose of the Passover was to remind God's people of his gracious act of deliverance. When the children saw the feast, they were to ask, "What does this ceremony mean?" The parents could then tell them of God's grace and love. Unfortunately, after Israel settled in Canaan, the Passover was not always celebrated as it should have been (cf. 2Ki 23:22–23; 2Ch 30:2–3, 17–20; 35:18). Thus there was little occasion for teaching God's great acts. Already after the death of Joshua, for example, "another generation grew up, who knew neither the LORD nor what he had done for Israel" (Jdg 2:10).

On the night of the Passover, the Lord went through the land to strike down the firstborn of the Egyptians. He sent his "destroyer" (12:23) to those houses not marked by the blood of the lamb. As elsewhere in Scripture, the Lord's work was carried out by angels (cf. 2Sa 24:14–15; Ps 78:49).

It has long been recognized that a certain symmetry exists between Egypt's treatment of Israel in the early chapters of Exodus and God's treatment of Egypt in the present text. As Egypt had killed all the Israelite sons (1:22) and had oppressed God's firstborn, Israel (4:22–23), so now their firstborn were taken, and they were avenged for the mistreatment they had done.

### 13. The Exodus (12:31–36)

The author is careful to draw a connection between the wealth of the Egyptians given to the Israelites and God's promise of wealth and blessing to the patriarchs. Thus the promise to Abraham was fulfilled—"They shall come out with great wealth" (Ge 15:14).

### C. The Exodus (12:37–13:16)

### 1. Travel from Egypt (12:37)

The Israelites were living in Rameses (1:11), an ancient city in the delta region of Egypt. This was the area of Goshen allotted to them by the Egyptians in the days of Joseph (Ge 47:11). From there they traveled to Succoth in route to Mount Sinai. This would have taken them southeastward about a day's journey from Rameses. The present location of many of their camps in the wilderness remains uncertain, even that of Mount Sinai itself. It is important to note, however, that the general history and geography of the whole of the area is quite well known; hence, we have an accurate picture of the conditions of their travel even though we cannot identify most of the sites named here. For the most part they likely used the established trade routes that ran through the area connecting Egypt with the regions to the East. Because of the small amount of annual rainfall, their travel would have taken them either over dry and dusty flatlands or through precipitous mountain ranges. This region was not capable of supporting even small numbers of settlers, let alone the number of Israelites in the Exodus (perhaps over two million). As the biblical narrative makes abundantly clear, they could not have survived without the miraculous provisions of water, food, and clothing (Dt 8:2–5).

### 2. Mixed multitude (12:38)

The author notes that a great many non-Israelites went out with the Israelites. The identity of this group and their relationship to Israel is the subject of considerable discussion. A common interpretation is that they were "proselytes" who had abandoned their pagan gods to follow the God of Israel. However, it may well be that the author intends us to understand them not as true proselytes, but as those who had followed the Israelites out of Egypt only because they had seen the miracles Moses performed. Later in Nu 11:4 this group is called "the rabble" and is seen as the cause of Israel's incessant complaining against God's good provisions. Just as Abraham had brought Lot with him out of Ur (Ge 12:5), so Israel is accompanied by the "mixed multitude" (cf. also the "mixed multitude" in Ne 13).

Just as the Lord had brought Abraham out of Egypt with great wealth and reward (Ge 13:1–2), so we are again reminded that Israel left Egypt with many possessions.

### 3. Unleavened bread in haste (12:39)

Having left Egypt in haste the night before, the Israelites now must prepare their food with unleavened bread. The writer reminds us of this here as a way of explaining the Feast of Unleavened Bread. Earlier he has given the instructions for celebrating the feast, but only here does he provide its explanation.

### 4. Chronological note (12:40–41)

The time of Israel's sojourn in Egypt is calculated "to the very day," that is, 430 years. In Ge 15:13 the time is given in the round number of 400 years. The 430 years, however, appears to be important in the remaining chronologies of the Bible. If the number of years from the Judges to the moving of the ark to Jerusalem (1Sa 7:2) are added, without attention to overlapping periods, the total is 430. The period of Davidic kingship is also 430 years. These three sets of 430 add up to 1,290—the same number (of days) given in Daniel for the time period before the building of the new temple (Da 12:11).

### 5. Instructions for future observance (12:42–51)

These additional instructions for the Passover Feast look to the time when Israel would dwell in their own land, living in their own cities and towns and in close contact with the world about them. Thus the basic question is whether "foreigners" could also eat the Passover meal. The answer is no; only permanent members of the community of God's people could partake.

One of the details of the Passover ritual was later to become an important element in the identification of Jesus as the Passover lamb: "Do not break any of the bones" (v.46). On the basis of this element of the Passover, the gospel of John draws a connection between Jesus and the Passover lamb (Jn 19:31–36); the NT authors often read these OT texts with an eye to their meaning for the events in the life of Jesus.

### 6. Firstborn of Israel set apart (13:1–2)

From the context alone we can conclude that the firstborn were set apart for the Lord because he had "passed over" them in the destruction of the

firstborn of Egypt. They thus belonged to him and, as later was seen with the Levites, they were to serve him in worship (cf. 13:11–16; also Nu 3:13, 41). The "consecration to the LORD" was carried out in two ways. (1) The firstborn was to be set apart from ordinary affairs of life and given over to God's service; they evidently were the priests mentioned in Ex 19:22; 24:5. This was carried over to the sons of Levi when they became priests (Nu 3:41). (2) The firstborn could also be "redeemed" by a payment of money (Nu 18:15–17).

### 7. Instructions for commemoration of the Feast of Unleavened Bread (13:3–10)

A similar set of instructions has already been given in 12:14–20. There are several differences in emphasis between the two passages, however. This one gives a more prominent place to the Feast of Unleavened Bread in the commemoration of the night of the Passover and the exodus from Egypt. In times when there was no possibility of celebrating the Passover Feast (i.e., after the destruction of the temple in Jerusalem), the Feast of Unleavened Bread could still function as the time of remembrance of what God had done for Israel.

Other differences focus attention on varying aspects of the Feast. For example, in ch. 12, the emphasis falls on the importance of correct celebration of the Feast by stressing the stringent penalties for eating leavened bread (12:19). Here, however, the emphasis falls on the continual celebration of the Feast, stressing the fact that it is to be observed "at the appointed time year after year." Whereas during the Passover meal the great deeds of God were to be retold in response to the question of the children (12:26), the Feast of Unleavened Bread itself was to be the occasion for the retelling of God's acts. There was thus no need to wait for the children to ask.

## 8. Redemption of the firstborn (13:11–16)

Because God had redeemed the firstborn of Israel on the night of the Exodus, it was the duty of the people to devote every firstborn male to the service of worship. The firstborn of the clean animals was to be devoted to the Lord by its being offered as a sacrifice. The firstborn of the unclean animals (e.g., donkeys) and of human beings were to be redeemed by substitution (cf. Nu 18:15)—a sheep in the case of unclean animals and money in the case of the firstborn male child (Nu 18:16). Later the tribe of Levi assumed the role of the firstborn and were set apart for service in the tabernacle (Nu 3:12–13, 45). Even then, however, a redemption price was still to be paid to the Levites (Nu 18:14).

## D. The Crossing of the Red Sea (13:17–15:21)

### 1. Travel from Egypt (13:17–20)

The shortest route to the land of Canaan was the well-guarded route that led directly up the coastline and was the main artery of Egypt's defenses against their northern neighbors. The writer gives here an interesting glimpse into God's plans and purposes in dealing with his people. He knew they were not ready for battle and that at the sight of war they would flee back to bondage in Egypt. He thus led them another way—a way that turned out to be no more successful for this generation of his people and one that would not be without its own hardships and temptations to return to Egypt (e.g., 14:12; Nu 14:1–4).

We should also note that the way in which God led them did not exclude war (cf. ch. 17). The NIV gives the impression in v.18 that the people were heavily equipped for war. The Hebrew text, however, only suggests that as they marched out of the land, they formed orderly columns of fifty men abreast, according to the military cus-tom of the day, "in battle array." But since they engaged in war with the Amalekites shortly after this, they obviously were armed.

In Ge 50:24–25 Joseph's faith in God's promise to give the Israelites the land of Canaan had led him to pass on a charge to his brothers and the future generations in Egypt that his bones were to be returned to the Promised Land. The writer reminds us of the fulfillment of that promise. Even in the later prophetic literature (Eze 37:11ff.), the bones of the faithful serve as a sign that the promise of the land still awaits its fulfillment.

On the second day of their journey (the sixteenth of Abib) they came to Etham, at the "edge of the desert"; this would put it along where the Suez Canal is located today.

### 2. Pillar of cloud and fire (13:21–22)

The purpose of the pillar of cloud was to guide the Israelites through the desert. It thus went before the people, and they followed it. A second pillar, the pillar of fire, was to give them light at night. The Lord went with the people in the cloud and the fire. Later, after building the tabernacle, the cloud and the fire rested on the tabernacle. If the cloud moved, the people followed. If it did not, the people remained at their present camp (40:34ff; Nu 9:15–23).

The cloud and the fire have other uses in the subsequent narratives. At one point, for example, they joined forces against the Egyptians (14:19–20). The pillar of cloud separated the camp of the Egyptians from the Israelites and shielded the light of the pillar of fire from the camp of the Egyptians.

In the NT the apostle Paul identifies the cloud, along with the Red Sea in the wilderness, as the place of the Israelites' "baptism into Moses" (1Co 10:2).

### 3. Crossing the Red Sea (14:1–31)

In interpreting the account of the crossing of the Red Sea we must acknowledge that the exact geographical setting of many of the events is uncertain. The most important location is the "Red Sea" (or as it is called in the Hebrew Bible, the "Reed Sea"). We should not let the name "Reed Sea" lead us to think that the sea was merely a marshland and that the biblical account of the dividing of the waters has been exaggerated. In 1Ki 9:26 it is the same "Sea of Reeds" that served as the port of Solomon's fleet of ships. This would have been a large and deep body of water. In any event we know from the account in Exodus that the Israelites passed through this large body of water on dry land and that the Egyptians following them were drowned when the waters poured back over them.

The Lord had a specific purpose in mind in having Israel cross the sea; it was to be another occasion to reveal his superiority over the power of the Egyptians and to show that he alone was to be honored as Lord (v.4). To accomplish this purpose, the Lord first instructed Israel to fall back into Egyptian territory (v.2) and thus led them to believe that the Israelites were wandering aimlessly in the land, afraid to go out into the desert. Second, the pharaoh's heart was hardened (vv.4, 8, 17), and he set out to regain control of the Israelites (vv.6–7).

The immediate response of the Israelites when they saw the Egyptians was fear and mistrust. Moses, however, stood out as a faithful leader, admonishing the people to be courageous and to "stand by and see the salvation of the LORD which he will accomplish for you today" (v.13). Moses here demonstrates the necessity of godly leadership and trust. Throughout the rest of the Bible there are similar examples of godly leadership in men like Joshua, Gideon, David, Josiah, Ezra, and Nehemiah, and women such as Deborah, Ruth, and Esther.

The end result of Moses' example and leadership is the establishment of the faith of the people themselves. When they saw the Lord fight for them and the defeated Egyptians lying along the shore of the sea, they "feared the LORD and put their trust in him and in Moses his servant" (v.31). The concepts of faith and trust in God play an important role for the writer of the Pentateuch. Just as Abraham believed God and was counted righteous (Ge 15:6), so the Israelites, under the leadership of Moses, also believed God. The writer presumably wants us to conclude that here in the desert God's people were living a righteous life of faith, like Abraham. As they headed toward Sinai, their trust was in the God of Abraham who had done great deeds for them. It was only natural that they broke out into a song of praise in the next chapter. On the negative side, however, we should not lose sight of the fact that only too quickly these same people would forget the great work of God and make a golden calf (Ps 106:11–13).

The depiction of the crossing of the sea is in many respects even grander than the most elaborate Hollywood movies, such as Cecil B. deMille's classic film, *The Ten Commandments*. If the number of adult males was at least 600,000 (12:37), there would certainly have been over two million people, plus their livestock, in the whole of the assembly. For so many people to pass through the sea in one night, the width of the parting of the sea would have been at least several miles.

A caution should be sounded here regarding the description of the crossing of the sea in the narrative portions of ch. 14 and the poetic portions of ch. 15. The way events are described in poetry is different from historical narrative. Poetry contains a great deal of stock imagery—word pictures used to depict themes and ideas rather than actual events. Thus if the depiction of the crossing of the sea in chs. 14 and 15 is compared, one will notice some dissimilarities in the two accounts. In the narrative, for example, the Egyptian armies are drowned when the parted sea folds back over them. In the poem of ch. 15, however, their defeat is expressed by means of the poetical image of the Lord hurling them into the sea (15:4b), where "they sank to the depths like a stone" (15:5b). A possible motive behind this image is 1:22, where the same expression occurs for the pharaoh's command to throw the Israelite children into the river. Thus God did to the Egyptians that which they had done to Israel.

It is common in the biblical text to describe the work of God in terms of his angels, or his angel (i.e., the "angel of the LORD"). Just as often, however, the biblical writers speak in terms that show God acting directly with his people. Such is the case in chs. 13–14. In 13:21, for example, the Lord went with the Israelites in the cloud and fire, whereas in 14:19, the "angel of God" accompanied them in the cloud.

### 4. The song of Moses (15:1– 21)

God's defeat of the Egyptians and deliverance of Israel in the crossing of the sea provide the occasion for a hymn of praise sung by Moses and the Israelites. Both its introduction (v.1) and conclusion (v.19) make this context clear. The scope of the song itself, however, goes far beyond the event of the crossing of the sea to include the conquest of the land of Canaan (vv.13–16) and the establishment of the city of Jerusalem as the location of the Temple (vv.17–18). There seems to be no doubt that we are to understand Moses's words as prophetic. Just as with Abraham (Ge 15:13ff.) and Jacob (Ge 49:1ff.) before him, and Balaam (Nu 23–24) after him, Moses is here cast in the role of a prophet (cf. Dt 18:15), telling of God's continued work for his people in the future. Even Miriam, who led the women in singing this song, is called here a "prophetess" (v.20). This is yet another example of the fact that the Pentateuch as a whole is not merely concerned with God's work in the past, but is also interested in his work that lies in the future.

The poetic imagery that dominates the song is that of the Lord as a mighty warrior, e.g., "The LORD is a warrior; the LORD is his name" (v.3). The weapon of this warrior is not only his great strength, but also the mighty waters of the sea, with which he shattered the enemy. There are images here reminiscent of the struggle portrayed in Ge 3:15. As is the case throughout the poetry of the Bible, God's power is depicted most graphically with reference to his control over his creation. Thus the view of God in Ge 1 can be seen clearly in this poem.

In the poem, God is depicted as one of the judges of Israel, like Samson (Jdg 13ff.) delivering the nation from the oppression of the Philistines (15:14), or like Ehud (Jdg 3:12ff.) sending trembling through the leaders of Moab (15:15). Throughout the poem, however, the picture of God's great deeds foreshadows most closely that of David, who defeated the chiefs of Edom, Philistia, and Canaan and made Mount Zion the eternal home for the Lord's sanctuary (15:17). Curiously enough, many of the poems in the Pentateuch seem to foreshadow events in the life of David as well as to go far beyond him to even greater days in the future (cf. Ge 49:8–12; Nu 24:17–19). In many respects, this song of Moses resembles Ps 78, which rehearses God's great deeds of the past and then moves on to describe God's work through David.

## V. The Wilderness Wanderings (15:22–18:27)

### A. God's Provision for Israel in the Desert (15:22–27)

After the destruction of the pharaoh's army in the sea, the Israelites continued their journey eastward into the Desert of Shur. Shur was a large semidesert region east of the Egyptian border frontier. After three days without finding water, they arrived at Marah. There the Lord began to provide for the people, and the people learned to depend on his provision.

There is an important narrative lesson in the incident of the bitter waters. When the people were helpless and thirsty, Moses called out to the Lord for help. The Lord answered Moses by giving him an "instruction" on how to make the water sweet. When they followed the "instruction," the water became sweet and their thirst was satisfied (v.25). In the Hebrew text, the word "instruction" means divine instruction. There is then a lesson about God's instructions to Israel in this incident: God's people must "listen carefully to the voice of the LORD [their] God" (v.26). His instruction would be sweet to them and satisfy their thirst.

The mention of "a decree and a law" (v.25b) for Israel and of Israel's being called upon to listen to the Lord's "commands" and "decrees" before the time of the giving of the Law at Sinai raises many questions. Already at this stage in their journey God had made known his will to the Israelites in concrete laws, such as the commands for keeping the Sabbath and those necessary for the administration of justice. We may posit a distinction between God's initial giving of the law to Israel, which was not too burdensome to bear, and God's giving of the detailed laws at Sinai after the incident of the Golden Calf (ch. 32). The Law was originally intended to teach God's people what was "right in his eyes" (15:26). After the failure of the people in the incident of the golden calf, however, more stringent measures were taken to keep the people from falling away into idolatry. Paul appears to have this view of the secondary nature of the Mosaic law in Gal 3:19, where he says that the Mosaic

law "was added because of the transgressions."

Having learned the lesson of dependence on God and listening to his voice, the people moved on to Elim where they found abundant water and nourishment (15:27).

## B. The Manna and the Quail (16:1–36; Nu 11:4–35)

The chapter opens on the fifteenth day of the second month (Iyar). The Israelites had been in the desert one month. The gathering of the manna and quail began on the sixteenth of Iyar.

After leaving Elim en route to Mount Sinai, the Israelites found themselves in the "Desert of Sin" ("Sin" is related to the name "Sinai"). Here, again, they were tested by the Lord to see if they would "follow [his] instructions" (lit., "[his] law"; v.4). This test is brought on by the grumblings of the people over the shortage of food in the desert. They saw themselves as no better off than the Egyptians who died "by the LORD's hand" when he brought Israel up out of their land. Such a statement appears as a blatant act of unbelief (though the writer does not call it such) and called for a specific test—the daily supply of manna and quail as well as the keeping of the Sabbath rest. Henceforth, throughout their forty years in the desert, the people had to depend daily on the provisions of the Lord. A pattern is thus established here that continues throughout the narratives of Israel's sojourn in the desert. As the people's trust in the Lord and in Moses waned, the need grew for stricter lessons.

Though it is true that the Israelites often had other sources of food (e.g., their flocks and herds), through the gathering of the manna and quail the Bible tells us the people witnessed daily miracles (Dt 8:3). For example, when the people went out to gather the manna, some gathered more than others. Each day, when they measured what they had gathered, the amount was just what each needed (Ex 16:17–18). This was another sign that God was intimately involved in providing for each one of his people.

Even amid the blessing of the manna and quail, some of the people did not obey the Lord's instructions for gathering it. They were to take only what they could eat for the day and not keep it for the next day. There were those, however, who stored some of what they had collected for the next day (v.20). Their disobedient efforts were to no avail because "maggots" rose up in the manna and it putrefied by morning. Their disobedience to God's good provisions provoked Moses to anger (v.20) and called for a rebuke from the Lord: "How long will you refuse to keep my commands and my instructions?" (v.28). This is yet another lesson of the failure of the people to obey God's will.

The mention of the forty years that they ate manna (v.35) anticipates God's judgment of this generation in Nu 14. It is worthy of note that the account in Nu 14 follows a second incident with manna and quail (Nu 11:4–35). Moreover, it was because of their lack of faith and trust in God (Nu 14:11) that Israel remained in the desert forty years and was not allowed to enter the Promised Land (Nu 14:21–23). Then, at the end of the forty years, on the day after the Passover when they entered the land of Canaan, "the manna stopped . . . but that year they ate of the produce of Canaan" (Jos 5:12).

Furthermore, it was by means of God's daily provisions for Israel that he taught them the importance of the Sabbath (vv.23–30). The daily gathering of the manna and quail was intended as a lesson in the importance of setting the seventh day apart for rest and remembrance. Not only would the double portion of manna keep over the sixth and seventh days, but also on the morning of the seventh day there was no manna.

The structure of the Sabbath week was thus already built into the gift of manna.

So great was the miraculous sign of the manna that provision was made for keeping an "omer of manna" as a witness for future generations (vv.32–34). Thus we are told here that when the ark was constructed, a jar of manna was kept in it "for the generations to come." Verse 34 is a comment by the writer that "updates" this narrative, telling us that Aaron did follow through with the Lord's command to store an omer of manna in the ark.

What is "manna"? Its description in this passage suggests it was not simply a kind of bread. Rather, it was akin to what we might call "pastries." Clearly, the Israelites had never seen or tasted anything like it before or since. They tried to describe its looks and taste by comparing it to "thin flakes like frost" (v.14), saying "it was white like coriander seed and tasted like wafers made with honey" (v.31). According to Nu 11:7–9, after eating manna for over a year, the Israelites developed new ways to prepare and cook it. It was ground or crushed and boiled in a pot or baked. It quickly rotted if left until morning (v.20), and "when the sun grew hot, it melted away" (v.21)—unless it was the Sabbath, in which case it was miraculously preserved (vv.23-27). In Ps 78:24, manna is called "the food of angels"; in Ne 9:20 it is associated with God's giving Israel his "good Spirit"; in 1Co 10:3 it is called "spiritual food."

The quail that God provided receives little attention in this chapter or elsewhere in Scripture (cf. Nu 11:31). Even in later allusions to these chapters, little (Ps 105:40) or no mention (e.g., Ne 9, 1Co 10) is made of them. There are numerous reports of migrating quail passing through the Sinai region from Africa. It is said that by the time the quail reach the desert they are so tired they can be captured by hand.

Within this chapter there is a curious reference to the people's seeing the "glory of the LORD appearing in the cloud" (v.10). On the face of it, the passage appears to recall a special and specific demonstration of God's glory "in the cloud" that served to underscore the importance of what the Lord was about to say to Moses. Some have suggested that the glory that the people saw in the cloud was a glorious appearance of Christ. The apostle Paul may have had this in mind when he wrote of Christ accompanying the Israelites in the wilderness when they were "under the cloud" (1Co 10:1–4).

## C. Water and War in the Desert (17:1–16)

### 1. Water from the rock (17:1–7)

Sometime before the third month (cf. 19:1), the Israelites left the Desert of Sin and traveled to Rephidim. That this place is in close proximity to Mount Sinai is clear from the fact that the rock from which they obtain water is located "in Horeb" (3:1; 17:6), that is, Sinai. They found water to be in short supply here, and though they already had a daily supply of food in the manna and the quail, they began to complain of thirst.

The incident recorded in this passage is similar to the incident in Nu 20:1–13, though there are marked differences as well. In both accounts, for example, the place is named Meribah because of the wordplay on the notion of "rebellion" (*rib*). Both incidents originated with the problem of a shortage of water and conclude with God's provision of water from a rock. In both narratives Moses gets water from the rock by striking it.

But in the present passage, Moses follows the Lord's instructions precisely, whereas in Nu 20 his striking the rock is seen as an evidence of his lack of faith. The chief difference between the two accounts lies in the fact that in

this passage *the people* are judged for an act of rebellion, whereas in Nu 20 *Moses and Aaron* are judged. The writer wants us to compare these two accounts. At the beginning of their time in the desert and again at the close of that time, God is the one who provided water from the rock for his rebellious people. Thus, by placing these two narratives about the rock both before the Sinai narrative and after, we are shown that the rock that gave them the water of life accompanied God's people from the beginning until the end of their time in the wilderness. Wherever they camped in the desert, the rock was with them. Perhaps this is what Paul meant when he identified Christ with the "rock that accompanied" the people in the desert (1Co 10:4).

When the people raised the question, "Is the LORD among us or not?" (v.7), they put God's promise to Moses in 3:12 to the test. God had promised, "I will be with you." As further confirmation of that promise, the Lord had said, "And this will be the sign to you that it is I who have sent you: When you have brought the people out of Egypt, you will worship God on this mountain" (3:12b). Here then, "at Horeb," the people find themselves "at Sinai." God's promise had been fulfilled, but they still questioned his presence.

### 2. The Amalekites defeated (17:8–16)

In this narrative is found the first mention of Joshua in the Pentateuch. Though in the remainder of the pentateuchal narratives he plays a relatively minor role, he was to be the next great leader in Israel, taking the place of Moses after his death (Dt 34:9) and leading God's people into Canaan along with the help of Eleazar, the son of Aaron. We can see then that the larger structure of the narratives in the Pentateuch continues to prepare the way for the events that lie yet in the future. Just as Joshua is introduced here after the first account of God's provision of "water from the rock," so also Eleazer is introduced in Nu 20 after the second. Within the narrative strategy of the Pentateuch, God's chosen leaders, whether king or priest, are thus closely associated with the "rock" that brings life to the people.

The Amalekites were the descendants of Amalek, the grandson of Esau (Edom, Ge 36:16). Their home was in southern Canaan (Nu 13:29). According to Dt 25:17ff., they attacked Israel when they were "weary and worn out" and cut off their stragglers without mercy. For this they were known as the "first among the nations" to wage war against God's people (Nu 24:20) and thus, according to God's promise in Ge 12:3, their memory was to be blotted out from under heaven (cf. Nu 24:20b; Dt 25:19). This was partially fulfilled during the time of Saul (1Sa 15) and Hezekiah (1Ch 4:43). But it was not until the death of Haman, the Agagite (Est 7; cf. 1Sa 15:8), that the last Amalekite was destroyed.

There are no indications of the Amalekites' specific act of treachery in the Exodus account. The narrative, rather, focuses on the means of their defeat. As long as Moses held up his hands, the battle favored the Israelites led by Joshua. Even when Moses' arms were tired and had to be propped up by Aaron and Hur (v. 12), the battle continued in Israel's favor. The significance of Moses' raised hands is given at the close of the chapter, "For hands were lifted up to the throne of the LORD." Hence the common interpretation of this picture of Moses is one of intercessory prayer.

The present narrative appears to have been shaped by its relationship to the events recorded in Nu 21:1–3, the destruction of Arad. Here in Ex 17, the people murmured over lack of water and Moses gave them water from the rock (vv. 1–7). They were attacked by the Amalekites but went on to defeat

them miraculously while Moses held up his hands. So also in the narrative in Nu 21, after an account of Israel's murmuring and of getting water from the rock (Nu 20:1–13), Israel was attacked but miraculously went on to defeat the Canaanites because of Israel's prayer (Nu 21:1–3).

## D. Jethro, Moses' Father-in-law (18:1–27)

The father-in-law of Moses goes by several names: Reuel in 2:16–22; Jether in 4:18; Jethro in 3:1; and Hobab in Nu 10:29. Moses had lived with his father-in-law as a shepherd (3:1). In Ex 3 he is called by God to return to Egypt. Although 4:19–20 makes it appear that Moses took his wife and two sons with him when he returned to Egypt, we learn from this passage that Moses had returned them to his father-in-law before going back to Egypt. Perhaps the purpose of the mysterious narrative in 4:24–26 is intended to give some motivation for the return of Moses' wife and family to Jethro.

The present narrative has many parallels with the account of Abraham's meeting with Melchizedek in Ge 14. Just as Melchizedek, the priest of Salem, met Abraham bearing gifts as he returned from battle (Ge 14:18ff.), so Jethro, the Midianite priest, came out with Moses's wife and sons to offer peace as Moses returned from the battle with the Amalekites. Melchizedek praised God for his rescue of Abraham from his enemies saying, "Blessed be Abram by God Most High . . . who delivered your enemies into your hand" (Ge 14:19), just as Jethro praised God saying "Blessed be the LORD, who rescued you from the hand of the Egyptians. . . . The LORD is greater than all other gods" (Ex 18:10). Melchizedek brought out bread and wine as a priest of God Most High and Abraham tithed to him (Ge 14:18ff.), and Jethro brought out a burnt offering and other sacrifices and ate bread with Moses and Aaron.

The purpose of such parallels appears to be to cast Jethro as another Melchizedek, the paradigm of the righteous Gentile. It is important that Jethro have such credentials because he plays a major role in this chapter, instructing Moses, the lawgiver himself, how to carry out the administration of God's law with Israel. Thus, just as Abraham was met by Melchizedek the priest (Ge 14), before God made a covenant with him in Ge 15, so Moses was met by Jethro, the priest (Ex 18), before God made a covenant with him at Sinai (Ex 19ff.).

# VI. The Covenant at Sinai (19:1–24:18)

## A. God Meets With Moses (19:1–25)

### 1. Arrival and encampment at Sinai (19:1–2)

The covenant at Sinai was established on the fiftieth day since the Exodus. The Israelites arrived at the Desert of Sinai the third day of the third month (Sivan). This would have been the forty-eighth day after Israel left Egypt. The next day they set up a new camp at the mountain (v.2b). The next morning, the fiftieth day, Moses went up to the mountain and received the covenant (see Dt 16:9–11; i.e., Pentecost; cf. Ex 34:22). The Israelites remained here for nearly one year, leaving on the twentieth day of the second month, in the second year (Nu 10:11).

### 2. The covenant announced (19:3–15)

On Mount Sinai, God made a covenant with Israel. This covenant called for obedience (v.5), and its purpose was to set Israel apart as a special people, a kingdom of priests and a holy nation (vv.5b–6). In chs. 20–23, the stipulations of the covenant are spelled out in great detail; much more is added in Leviticus, Numbers, and Deuteronomy. This covenant was intended as a fulfillment of the promises to Abraham, Isaac, and Jacob (2:24), but later in Exodus (ch. 32) it becomes clear that Israel could not obey this covenant, even while they were at Mount Sinai. Thus Israel broke this covenant (Dt 31:29–32:6, Jdg 2:10–13), and any hope for the future would have to rest in the establishment of a new covenant (Jer 31:31ff.).

Moses is the mediator of this covenant. God spoke to him on the mountain, and he carried these words back to Israel. When Israel agreed to enter the covenant, he carried their response back to God (Dt 5:5). Israel's acceptance of the covenant is called a mark of their faith ("trust") in God and Moses (v.9).

### 3. The Lord came down to Sinai (19:16–25)

The cloud that had led the people through the desert now appeared to rest on Mount Sinai. It was dark with smoke and foreboding, filled with fire and accompanied by loud bursts of thunder. Mysteriously amid the tumult, the blasts of trumpets could also be heard, growing louder every moment (v.16). The mountain where God had come was an inferno. This display of God's power was not lost on any of the people, for they feared greatly. As Moses explained it, "God has come to test you, so that the fear of God will be with you to keep you from sinning" (20:20). Later he again warned the people, "Be careful not to forget the covenant. . . . For the LORD your God is a consuming fire, a jealous God" (Dt 4:23–24).

The description of the setting of the giving of the Ten Commandments in v.25 is somewhat vague. There are at least two ways to view it. It appears on the one hand that God first spoke the Ten Commandments to Moses (v.19) and then he (Moses) gave these commandments to the people (v.25). The people were afraid to go near to hear God speak, and so they asked Moses to go for them (20:19). However, 19:25

can also be understood as saying the Lord first spoke the Ten Commandments to both Moses *and all the people* from the mountain. The people, after hearing God speak, then requested that God speak only to Moses and that Moses then speak to them (20:18–19; cf. also Dt 4:10–13; 10:4). The preface to the Ten Commandments in Dt 5:4–5, clarifies the issue further.

## B. The Decalogue (20:1–17)

Here the Bible refers to God's commands simply by the expression "these words" (v.1). Later they are called the "ten words" (34:28; Dt 4:13; 10:4) or "the covenant . . . which he commanded" Israel (Dt 4:13). These are thus the expression of God's will for his covenant people. The words were etched on both sides of two small stone documents (Ex 24:12). The documents, or tablets, were small enough for Moses to carry "in his hand" (32:15; Dt 9:15, 17). It is not clear whether all "ten words" were written on each tablet (with two complete copies), or whether some of the words were written on one tablet and some on the other. It is often maintained that the first group of commandments, dealing with a person's relationship to God, were written on the first tablet, and the second group, dealing with a person's relationships with one's fellow human beings, were written on the second tablet. There is no clear hint from the text of such a division.

Of particular interest is the question of the division of the "words" into *ten* commandments. Some have traditionally divided vv.3–6 into two commandments: the first (vv.2–3) taken as a call for absolute monotheism and the second (vv.4–6) as a command against idolatry. To arrive at a total number of ten commands, then, the last command must consist of the whole of v.17. Others, however, have read vv.2–6 as one command, a prohibition of idolatry, and count it as the first commandment (a

sense that "other gods" has elsewhere in Scripture). To arrive at ten commands in this case, v.17 is read as two. Finally, Jewish tradition reads v.2 as the first commandment and understands it as a call for a strict monotheism. Then vv.3–6 is taken as the second commandment, a prohibition against idolatry. While this debate cannot be decided with certainty, it is certain that the author of the Pentateuch understands the total number to be ten (cf. 34:28).

### 1. Prologue (20:1–2)

The basis of the call to obedience in the covenant was God's act of salvation in the Exodus. Thus the Lord identifies himself first not only as the only God but also as the God who delivered Israel from bondage.

### 2. The first commandment (20:3–6): You shall have no other gods.

In the rest of Scripture, the expression "other gods" refers to the wooden and stone idols of the nations around Israel; it does not refer to actual divine beings (Dt 28:36). This reference merely acknowledges that the other nations worship wooden and stone idols as their gods.

This commandment teaches that God is a jealous God, i.e., he will not tolerate anything short of wholehearted worship. He is a personal God and will not be satisfied with anything less than a personal relationship with men and women created in his image. To worship an image of God (an "idol") rather than God himself violates God's purpose for the creation of man and woman in his image (Ge 1:26). Thus God's will as expressed in these commandments is consistent with his purposes in creation.

The extended commentary on this commandment (vv.5–6) acknowledges that parents often pass on to their children the misdirected and ill advised patterns of life they learned from their own parents. Wrong notions about God and worship can be maintained for generations and can result in many hardships. On the positive side, however, the author also recognizes that, in God's grace, the love and obedience of a single generation can change the course of a family for thousands of future generations. In the historical books of the OT we see this pattern play itself out (e.g., see Jdg 2:10ff.). Part of the purpose of these books is to show that rebellion against the Lord was passed from one generation to another until ultimately the nation was sent into exile (2Ki 17:7–18a; 25).

The prophet Ezekiel asked the exiled Israelites the very question raised by the first commandment (Eze 18). Apparently some in his day felt that this commandment could be interpreted to mean that the accumulated sins of the parents were to be taken out on innocent children. A proverb had been coined in Israel, "The fathers eat sour grapes, and the children's teeth are set on edge." Ezekiel, however, argued over against such a proverb that "the soul who sins is the one who will die" (Eze 18:1–4). Ezekiel then raised the question of a righteous father and a wicked son and a wicked father and a righteous son and concluded that the reward or punishment of the son is not dependent on the deeds of the father (Eze 18:20).

### 3. The second commandment (20:7): You shall not misuse the name of the LORD your God.

God had revealed to Israel his name ("Yahweh"; see comment on ch. 3) and had given to them the corresponding privilege of calling on that name in worship and in time of need. Along with this privilege there came the responsibility of honor and respect. Israel was not to call on God's name "for no good purpose," i.e., they were not to presume upon their relationship with God to the point that he was merely at their beck and call. The whole of the instructions regarding the nature of Is-

rael's worship and the building of the tabernacle (chs. 25–31) was intended to teach Israel the proper way to call on God's name.

### 4. The third commandment (20:8–11): Remember the Sabbath day.

Under the covenant at Sinai, Israel was to set apart each seventh day of the week and keep it holy. In so doing they were following God's own pattern in creation (Ge 2:2–4). The purpose of the Sabbath day was to give rest from one's labor (Ex 23:12; Dt 5:14) and to provide an occasion for an assembly of the nation in a "holy convocation" (Lev 23:3).

### 5. The fourth commandment (20:12): Honor your father and your mother.

An important part of this commandment is the promise, "that you may live long in the land." This commandment is not addressed primarily to small children, admonishing them "to mind" their parents, though it no doubt includes that. The commandment is rather spoken to adults who are not dependent on their father and mother, but whose parents may even be dependent on them. They are to treat their parents with respect not only as long as *the parents* live, but also as long as *they themselves* live in the land the Lord God is giving them. Long after parents have departed, they must still be treated with respect by honoring and obeying this instruction. This is the basis of God's showing love to the thousands of generations of those "who love me and keep my commandments" (v.6).

### 6. The fifth commandment (20:13): You shall not murder.

The basis of this commandment prohibiting murder and manslaughter was laid down at Creation. The human race was created in God's image; thus, "Whoever sheds the blood of man, by man shall his blood be shed; for in the image of God has God made man" (Ge 9:6). That this commandment does not preclude capital punishment is clear from the fact that the death penalty is called for on numerous occasions in the OT law (e.g., 21:12; cf. Ge 9:5).

### 7. The sixth commandment (20:14): You shall not commit adultery.

Sexual intercourse outside of marriage is prohibited. This commandment is based on God's purposes for marriage as expressed in Ge 2:24. David, a man exemplary in most respects, nevertheless transgressed this commandment, and it marked the beginning of the end of his role as leader of God's people (2Sa 11).

### 8. The seventh commandment (20:15): You shall not steal.

The sense of the word "to steal" includes not only the act of taking what does not belong to one but also the deception involved in that act.

### 9. The eighth commandment (20:16): You shall not give false testimony.

Honesty and accuracy in the administration of justice and in everyday affairs is assumed here to be essential.

### 10. The ninth commandment (20:17a): You shall not covet your neighbor's house.

In Dt 5:21 this commandment is rendered, "You shall not covet your neighbor's wife." In other words, it exchanges one of the elements of the last part of the verse ("neighbor's wife") with the more general category of a "neighbor's house." The Deuteronomy passage also uses a different word for "covet" in the tenth command (the word "desire"). These changes suggest that the two parts of Ex 20:17 are understood in Deuteronomy as two separate statements, distinguishing one's "coveting" a neighbor's spouse from the "desiring" of a neighbor's property. Moreover, that these two statements in Exodus are, in fact, intended to be read as distinct is suggested by the repetition of the verb "covet" in v.17a and v.17b. If we allow Deuteronomy's interpreta-

tion to govern our understanding of the Exodus text, then the expression "coveting a neighbor's house," prohibited in the ninth commandment, is 'taken euphemistically in the sense of coveting a neighbor's spouse.

### 11. The tenth commandment (20:17b): You shall not covet . . . anything that belongs to your neighbor.

If we follow the interpretation given in Deuteronomy, this last commandment is a general prohibition of every kind of coveting. Its focus is on all types of covetousness, not on lusting after a neighbor's spouse.

## C. Worship and Idolatry (20:18–26)

The statement of the "ten words" (20:1–17) and the collection of "judgments" (21:1–23:13) are joined with a short narrative link (20:18–21). Here the report of the fear of the people is repeated, as well as the reason for the display of divine power at Sinai (see also Dt 5:22–33). The people were afraid to approach God at the mountain, so they made Moses the mediator of the covenant. Moses then explained that the proper response to a recognition of God's power was not a fear that caused them to flee from his presence but one that caused them to submit to him in godly living. Moses expressed the same idea in Dt 8:16, explaining that God's dealings with Israel in the wilderness were intended to humble and test them so that things might go well with them.

In vv.22–23, virtually the entire nature of the religion of the covenant is summarized, beginning with the warning against idolatry. Moses was to remind the Israelites that God had spoken to them directly and thus to warn them not to stray from God through worship of idols.

The simple description of true worship in vv.24–26 is intended to portray the essence of the Sinai covenant in terms that are virtually identical to that of the religion of the patriarchs—

earthen altars, burnt offerings, and simple devotion. If more than a simple earthen altar is desired (e.g., a stone altar), then it should not be defiled with carved stones and elaborate steps. The ultimate purpose of any such ritual is the covering of human nakedness that stems from the Fall (cf. Ge 3:7). The implication is that all ritual is only a reflection of that first gracious act of God in covering human nakedness with garments of skin (Ge 3:21). Later, in Ex 28:42, provision was made for the priests to wear linen undergarments "to cover their naked flesh" as they approached the altar.

It is notable that this picture of the nature of the "true religion" of the covenant should precede the countless details yet to be given for the construction of the tabernacle. The detailed and ornate description of the tabernacle seems a far cry from the simple worship envisioned here. These verses, however, play an important role in the lesson of the immediate narrative and ultimately that of the entire Pentateuch. They serve to focus our attention on the essential nature of the worship intended in the covenant. Israel's worship in the Sinai Covenant was to be the same as that of the patriarchs as described in the Genesis narratives. God would certainly be honored with all the gold and silver of the tabernacle that was to be built, but his honor was not to be at the expense of the simple call to obedience exemplified by the patriarchs.

## D. Judgments (21:1–23:12)

A selection of "judgments," totaling forty-two, is provided as a sample of the divine judgments that Moses gave the people. This number apparently stems from the fact that the Hebrew letters in the first word of the section, "and these," add up precisely to the number forty-two. There may also be a desire to have seven laws for each of the six days of work (cf. 20:11). Thus the sampling of laws in 21:1–23:12

should perhaps be understood as representing the whole Mosaic Law. The purpose of this selection was to provide a basis for teaching the nature of divine justice. By studying specific cases of the application of God's will in concrete situations, the reader of the Pentateuch could learn the basic principles undergirding the covenant relationship. Whereas the "Ten Commandments" provided a general statement of the basic principles of justice that God demanded of his people, the examples selected here further demonstrated how those principles, or ideals, were to be applied to real life situations.

## E. Prohibition of Idolatry (23:13)

The end of this section takes up again the first commandment, i.e., the warning against idolatry sounded at the beginning (20:22–23). The continual return to the theme of idolatry throughout this section of the book is preparation and background for an understanding of the incident of the golden calf (ch. 32). When Israel made the golden calf and set it up as an object of worship, they broke the first commandment and graphically demonstrated their inability to keep the covenant.

## F. Proper Forms of Worship: Feasts (23:14–19)

The ceremonial year is divided into three feasts. The Feast of Unleavened Bread has been described in 12:14–20; 13:3–9. The Feasts of Harvest (23:16a) and Ingathering (23:16b) are mentioned here for the first time (see also Lev 23:5ff.; Nu 28:26; Dt 16:9–12). At these three times of the year all the men of the community were to appear before the Lord (v.17).

A central regulation is then given for each of the three feasts. (1) For the Feast of Unleavened Bread nothing containing yeast was to accompany the sacrificial blood, and none of the Passover lamb (cf. 34:25b) was to be left over until morning (23:18). This was important because the Passover Feast was held on the previous day (12:8). (2) For the Feast of Harvest, it was the "best" of the firstfruits that were to be brought to the Lord's house. (3) For the Feast of Ingathering, only weaned animals were to be brought as offerings (cf. 22:29; Lev 22:27). A young goat "in its mother's milk" is one that still suckles from its mother. Thus the expression "do not boil a kid in its mother's milk" is an expression intended to state the principle that only weaned animals were to be used as offerings.

## G. Plans for Taking the Land (23:20–33)

God's care and guidance of the Israelites is here linked to his protection of the patriarchs. By means of explicit allusions to key passages in Genesis, the writer shows that what happened to the Israelites was the fulfillment of the promises God had made with the patriarchs. Jacob, for example, called God "the Angel who has delivered [him] from all harm" (Ge 48:16), just as God is here pictured as protecting his people with his "angel." A remarkable number of parallels between this section of text and Ge 15 show that God's promises to Abraham and the making of his covenant in that chapter are to be fulfilled in the promises of the Sinai Covenant. Abraham had foreseen the time when God would bring "fearful" (Ge 15:12; Ex 23:27) judgment on "the Amorites" (Ge 15:16; Ex 23:23) because of their iniquity. Though Israel was to "serve" (Ge 15:13–14) a foreign nation, they were not to "serve" (Ex 23:24) the gods of that nation. Rather, God would bless them (Ex 23:25) and they would not be barren (Ge 15:2–3; Ex 23:26). Their number would be great (Ge 15:5; Ex 23:26), and they would live in the land promised to the fathers (Ge 15:18–21; Ex 23:31). God had made a "covenant" with their fathers to give them the land (Ge 15:18), and they were not to make a "covenant" with those who lived in

the land (Ex 23:32–33). Though we must not overlook the fact that the failure of the people at Sinai (see Ex 32) meant postponing the fulfillment of these promises until the next generation (Nu 14), the intent of the covenant at Sinai is clearly seen in the relationship between this passage and the promises to the patriarchs.

After the sin of the golden calf and Moses' return to Mount Sinai, God again spoke of sending his angel before the people to give them the land, but, unlike the present text, at that point the promise of sending the angel contained an intimation of judgment (33:1–6). The angel was sent because the people were "stiff-necked" and unable to live in God's presence (33:5). Rather than representing God's presence with them, the angel had become a sign that God could not go with them personally (33:2–3). We should note here the frequent warnings against idolatry in this text dealing with God's promise to send his angel (e.g., 23:21, 24, 32, 33).

## H. Establishment of the Covenant (24:1–18)

As ch. 24 opens, we are reminded of God's instructions to Moses in 19:24, where God had said that Moses was to go down to the people, speak his words (i.e., 20:1–17) and judgments (i.e., 21:1–23:13), and return with Aaron. The priests and the people, however, were not to come up (19:24b). The writer now repeats in 24:3 that which had already been recounted in 19:25, that Moses went down and spoke God's words and judgments to the people. When the people heard Moses, with one accord they agreed to obey the covenant (v.3b), which was then ratified by the people in the ceremony at the foot of Sinai (vv.4–8).

After this ceremony, Moses and Aaron "went up" (v.9) to feast with Nadab and Abihu and the seventy elders (vv.10–11). The location of this feast is not certain, but it was most likely not on the mountain, because in the subsequent narratives God called Moses again to "come up the mountain" (v.12), and he, with Joshua, "went up" (v.13). Moses told the elders, Aaron, and Hur to remain until he and Joshua returned (v.14).

The elders were apparently not the same group as the priests since the text says the elders "went up" with Moses and Aaron but the priests were not to go up but rather were to remain with the people (19:24).

It should be noted that again it is stated in the text that Moses went up (without Joshua?) the mountain (v.15). The mountain was covered by the cloud. There Moses waited six days, and on the seventh day God called to him (v.16b). Moses again went up the mountain (v.18) and remained (alone, v.2) on the mountain for forty days and nights (v.18b). According to Dt 9:9, Moses fasted throughout this period of time (cf. 1Ki 19:8; Mt 4:2). Chapters 25–31 record God's words to Moses during this time on the mountain. At the close of these words of God, the narrative returns to Aaron, who is now standing with the people at the foot of the mountain (32:1). Moses (with Joshua; 32:17) then returns from the mountain to the people (32:15) at the foot of the mountain.

The text says that Moses and the elders "saw the God of Israel" (24:10–11). If we are to read this passage as it was apparently understood by the author of the Pentateuch (Dt 4:12, 15) and later interpreted (e.g., Jn 1:18), it probably is to be taken to mean they saw his glory, as in v.16, or they saw God in a vision. That they saw a *vision* of God is supported by the repetition of "they saw God" in v.11. In this repetition a different word for "to see" is used, one that in its other uses in the Pentateuch carries the sense of "to see in a vision" (Nu 24:4, 16).

## VII. The Tabernacle (25:1–31:18)

The instructions for the work of building the tabernacle provide an interesting parallel to God's own work of creation recorded in Ge 1–2. Just as that narrative portrayed God's creation of the heavens and earth as the arena in which God would have fellowship with humankind, so here the tabernacle is pictured as the means of restoring humanity's lost fellowship with God. There are, thus, several significant similarities.

(1) Note the overall structure of the two accounts. It is well known that the Creation account is structured around a series of seven acts of creation, each of which is marked by the divine speech, "And God said . . ." (Ge 1:3, 6, 9, 11, 14, 20, 24, 26, 28, 29). In the same way, the instruction for the building of the tabernacle is divided into seven acts, each introduced by the divine speech, "And the LORD said . . ." (Ex 25:1; 30:11, 17, 22, 34; 31:1, 12). Thus the tabernacle is portrayed as a reconstruction of God's good creation.

(2) The Garden of Eden is described in ways similar to that of the tabernacle. Both, for example, contained pure gold (Ge 2:12a) and precious jewels (Ge 2:12b) and were guarded by cherubim (Ge 3:24).

(3) At the close of the Creation account is the reminder that God rested on the seventh day (Ge 2:1–3). So also in the account of the building of the tabernacle, the last of the instructions is the reminder to observe the Lord's Sabbath (Ex 31:12–18).

(4) God concluded his last work of creation with an inspection and evaluation of all he had done (Ge 1:31) and with a blessing (v.28). Similarly, when the work on the tabernacle was done, Moses inspected and evaluated everything (Ex 39:43a) and blessed them (v.43b).

(5) The creation of man and woman was made according to a specific pat-

tern, the "image of God" (Ge 1:26–27). In the building of the tabernacle, the whole as well as the parts were to be made according to the "pattern" God had shown Moses (Ex 25:9).

(6) The Creation account is followed by the account of the Fall (Ge 3). At the center of the Fall account is humankind's disobedience of God's command not to eat of the Tree of Knowledge of Good and Evil. At the close of the instructions for the building of the tabernacle there is also a "Fall narrative," the account of Israel's sin of the golden calf (Ex 32). In both cases, disobedience to the divine command resulted in breaking God's covenant.

The fact that the tabernacle was to be built according to the "plan" or "pattern" that God had shown Moses on the mountain (Ex 25:9, 40; cf. 1Ch 28:11–12, 18–19) gives rise to a number of important points. (1) It suggests that the tabernacle was intended as a model or facsimile of God's heavenly abode. It thus was a kind of incarnation of God's presence with humankind. Through this "pattern" God was coming to dwell among his people. (2) The fact that the tabernacle was a "pattern" of something in heaven shows that it had a symbolic value as well as a practical purpose. Thus its various physical forms also had a spiritual meaning. There was thus a "typology" in the various features of the tabernacle. (3) The problem that faces the readers of the Pentateuch, however, is the fact that very little of the "heavenly" meaning of the tabernacle and its parts are explained in the text itself. Thus we, the readers, are invited to ponder over the description of the tabernacle with the expectation that they exhibit the pattern of the heavenly temple, but we are not given any help in explaining them. In other words, there is an intentional mystery about the tabernacle and the meaning of its parts. The fact that the NT writers explain many of its parts as "shadows" of the reality re-vealed in Christ (e.g., Heb 9:5) is in keeping with the larger purpose of these chapters. Through these explanations, we can know the spiritual explanation.

In the NT the tabernacle and the service associated with it in these texts is seen as a picture of the work of Christ (Jn 2:19–21; Heb 8:2; 9:11–12), the individual believer (1Co 6:19), and the church (1Ti 3:15; Heb 3:6; 10:21).

## A. Offerings for the Tabernacle (25:1–9)

Materials to be used in the construction of the tabernacle are enumerated first (see vv.3–7). It goes without saying that these materials were considered most precious and valuable to the Israelites; thus, no further explanation is needed why they were to be used (a more complete list is given later in 35:4–29).

After the list of building materials, the purpose of the tabernacle is explained. It was to be a sanctuary for God, his dwelling place among the people (v.8). In constructing the tabernacle, Israel was to follow the plan or "pattern" that God had shown Moses on the mountain (v.9).

## B. The Ark (25:10–22)

The ark was to be made of acacia wood (v.10a). Its size was three-and-a-half feet in length, two-and-a-half feet wide and high (v.10b). It was overlaid with gold, inside and out (v.11a) and was to have a gold border (v.11b). Four gold rings were to be attached to its sides for the acacia poles used to carry the ark (v.12–15).

The "Testimony" was to be put inside the ark (vv.16, 21b). The "Testimony" refers to the stone tablets on which were written the "Ten Commandments" (Dt 10:2–3; cf. 31:26).

A gold "atonement cover" the same size as the top of the ark (v.17) was put over the ark. Two gold cherubim were to be placed at either end of the "atonement cover" with outstretched wings covering the cover (vv.18–20).

The purpose of the ark is so that "above the cover between the two cherubim that are over the ark of the Testimony, I will meet with you and give you all my commands for the Israelites" (v.22). This promise was fulfilled after the dedication of the altar in Nu 7:89.

### C. The Table (25:23–30)

The table was to be made of acacia wood (v.23a). Its size was three feet long, one-and-a-half feet wide, and two-and-a-half feet high (v.23b). It was overlaid with pure gold and with golden borders (v.24). A golden rim was to be put on the borders (v.25). There were four gold rings, one by each leg (v.26). The acacia poles for carrying the table were to be overlaid with gold (vv.27–28). The utensils for the table were also made of gold (v.29). Its purpose was to hold "the bread of the Presence" (v.30).

### D. The Lampstand (25:31–40; Nu 8:1–4)

The lampstand was to be made of hammered gold (v.31a). It had six shafts on either side of a central shaft (v.32). Each shaft extending from the central shaft was to have three almond-blossom cups, a knob, and a bud (v.33). On the central shaft there were to be four almond-blossom cups with knobs and buds. A bud was to be placed at the point where each of the pairs of shafts joined the central shaft (vv.34–36). Seven lamps were to be put on each shaft (v.37). There were also gold snuffers and snuff-holders (v.38). The lampstand was not lighted until the dedication of the tabernacle (Nu 8:1–4).

### E. The Tabernacle (26:1–37)

The tabernacle itself consisted of curtains attached to wooden boards. There were three distinct structures involved, each of which was an integral part of the whole of the tabernacle, though each was also a distinct build-

ing. (1) The tabernacle proper consisted of the boards and a first layer of curtains surrounded by a large courtyard. It consisted of ten curtains joined together into two large sections of five curtains each (vv.1–6). Each curtain was to be forty-two feet long and six feet wide. On the edge of each large sections were fifty loops. The two sections were to be joined together with gold clasps by means of these fifty loops. Woven into the fabric of the curtains were images of cherubim, intended to recall the theme of "paradise lost" by alluding to the cherubim that guarded the "tree of life" in Ge 3:24.

(2) The second structure was a second layer of curtains made of goat hair (vv.7–14). There were eleven such curtains, made into two large sections— five for one and six for the other. These two sections were joined by fifty loops and bronze clasps. The extra curtain was to be folded over the entrance.

(3) A third structure consisted merely of a layer of ram skins dyed red that covered the tent, as well as an additional covering of the hides of "sea cows," an uncertain term indicating a material sometimes rendered "badgers' skins" or "porpoise skins."

The tabernacle was supported by upright boards of acacia wood, each about fifteen feet long and set into a pair of silver bases (vv.15–25). Along the length of the tabernacle were twenty frames. At the far end, opposite the entrance, were eight frames. The frames were overlaid with gold (v.29a).

Five sets of crossbars of acacia wood provided support for the frame of the tabernacle (vv.26–29). These crossbars were overlaid with gold and held in place by gold rings.

A curtain was to be set up within the tabernacle to separate the Holy Place from the Most Holy Place (vv.31–35). It was hung on four posts of acacia wood standing in silver bases. The ark and its atonement cover were to be placed behind the curtain in the Most Holy Place, and the table and lampstand were to be placed in front of the curtain. In the book of Hebrews, the inner curtain is taken as a symbol of Christ's body (Heb 10:20). It was this curtain, reconstructed for the Temple, that was "torn in two, from top to bottom" when Christ "yielded up his Spirit" on the cross (Mt 27:51; Mk 15:38; Lk 23:45). The point of the NT writers appears to have been to show that the death of Christ removed the necessity for the separation between God and his people.

Five posts of acacia wood were to be set up on bronze bases at the entrance of the tent and a finely embroidered curtain of blue, purple, and scarlet was hung on them (vv.36–37). This was to serve as the entrance to the tent and thus also the entrance to the tabernacle.

The final plan of the tabernacle was shown to Moses on Mount Sinai. He was to follow that plan in making the tabernacle (v.30).

## F. The Altar of Burnt Offering (27:1–8)

An altar which was seven-and-a-half feet square and four-and-a-half feet high was to be constructed of acacia wood and overlaid with bronze. It is not specifically said to be for "burnt offerings" but it is called that when constructed (38:1). The corners of the altar were made with raised tips, called "horns." The utensils used at the altar were also made of bronze. A bronze grating was to go with the altar, apparently placed on the inside of the altar to hold the ashes. The whole of the altar was carried with bronze rings and poles. In the book of Hebrews this altar is seen as a picture of the better altar of Christ (see Heb 13:10).

## G. The Courtyard of the Tabernacle (27:9–19)

A courtyard enclosed by curtains was to surround the tabernacle. Its opening faced east. It was about 150 feet long and 75 feet wide. The height of the curtains, which were attached to posts, was seven-and-a-half feet.

## H. The Oil for the Lampstands (27:20–21)

The people were to supply clear, pressed olive oil for burning the lamps. A note explaining the ordinance of maintaining the lamp is attached in v.21, assuming the appointment of Aaron and his sons as priests.

## I. The Priestly Garments (28:1–43)

Aaron and his sons were set apart from the rest of the Israelites as priests (vv.1–5). They were to wear special garments to give them "dignity and honor" and "to sanctify" them. The work was to be carried out by those whom God had filled with "the spirit of wisdom."

The first item described is the ephod (vv.6–14). After a general description of its color and material, its first notable feature is the two shoulder pieces studded with onyx stones. The names of the twelves tribes were engraved on these stones, six names on each stone. This was to show that in his role as high priest, Aaron bore these names as a memorial before the Lord; he was their representative. Just as Moses had been commanded to write down the events of the battle with the Amalekites (17:14) as a written memorial to Israel, so these stones would serve as a written memorial to the Lord. Two gold chains were to be attached to the two shoulder pieces.

The breastpiece (vv.15–30), also called the breastplate, was a small (nine inches by nine inches) pouch worn on the breast of the priest and attached by golden chains to the shoulder pieces. Engraved on its outer surface were the names of the twelve tribes of Israel. Each name was engraved on a different precious stone set in four rows on the breastpiece. As with the shoulder pieces, the purpose of these names was to be a written memorial to the Lord when the priest represented the people in the Holy of Holies. Inside the breast-piece were the Urim and Thummim, implements for deciding God's will; hence it is sometimes called the "breastpiece for making decisions" (v.15).

A blue tunic was to be worn over the shoulders of the high priest whenever he went into the Holy of Holies (vv.31–35). Gold bells were attached to the hem and could be heard while he was in the Holy Place. The purpose of the bells on the high priest's garments was that he might be heard going in and coming out of the Holy Place, "so that he will not die" (v.35). Perhaps in hearing the priest, those nearby in worship would be reminded to turn their attention to God. Or by means of the bells, the high priest would be distinguished from the other priests; thus it would be clear that it was he and no other when he entered the Holy Place.

A gold plate or plaque was to be worn on the priest's turban (vv.36–38). Engraved on this plaque were the words "HOLY TO THE LORD."

The basic garment of the priests was the tunic. It was to be woven of fine linen, as were the turban and sash (vv.39–41). There were two types of turbans—one for the high priest, and another kind, called a "headband," for the other priests. The purpose of such clothing was to "give [the priests] dignity and honor" (v.40b). A special act of consecration with anointing oil was necessary for these clothes to be worn and for the duties of the priesthood to be carried out.

The undergarments were made of plain linen (vv.42–43). Their purpose was to cover the body when the priests officiated at the Tent of Meeting or approached the altar—a function similar to the prohibition of steps on the altar, "lest your nakedness be exposed on it" (20:26). There is in this prescription for undergarments an allusion to the clothing that God made for Adam and Eve in the Garden of Eden (Ge 3:21).

## J. The Consecration of the Priests (29:1–46)

In the consecration of Aaron and the priests, they were first to be clothed in the garments described in the previous chapter. A "sacred diadem" (v.6) attached to the turban seems to be mentioned here for the first time. According to Lev 8:9, however, the "sacred diadem" was another name for the "gold plate" of 28:36.

A bull and two rams were required for the consecration of Aaron and the priests (vv.10–28). These animals were to be ritually slaughtered "before the Tent of Meeting." In Leviticus, the slaughter of the bull is called a "sin offering" (Lev 8:14), the slaughter of the first ram a "burnt offering" (Lev 8:18), and the slaughter of the second ram an "offering of ordination" (Lev 8:22), prepared as a sacred meal for Aaron and the priests (Ex 29:29–34). The offerings mentioned here in Ex 29, then, should be understood as "sin" offerings. This understanding is clearly anticipated at the close of this chapter (vv.35–37). Those verses also indicate that the whole ceremony was to be repeated for seven days.

Along with the seven-day consecration of Aaron and the priests, instructions are given for the daily sacrifice that is to be carried out perpetually for all generations (vv.38–46). Two yearling lambs are to be offered, one at morning and the other at twilight. This instruction is given here because, even though it would be a part of the consecration of the priests, it would continue on after that perpetually.

## K. The Altar of Incense (30:1–10)

An altar for burning incense was to be made of acacia wood. It was to be one-and-a-half feet square and three feet high. It was to have raised corners, or "horns," like the sacrificial altar (cf. 27:1–8) and was to be overlaid with gold. Two gold rings were attached to its sides for the acacia wood poles used to carry the altar. The altar of incense was to be put just in front of the curtain that separated the Holy of Holies from the remainder of the Holy Place. This altar was to provide a continual burning of incense before the presence of the Lord. The high priest was to burn the incense every morning and at twilight in the evening. Once a year the high priest made an atonement for this altar with the blood of the atonement.

## L. The Atonement Money (30:11–16)

The expense of the tabernacle service was to be shared equally among all Israelites, whether rich or poor. A census was taken, and from that, a donation of one half-shekel of silver per individual Israelite was required.

## M. The Basin for Washing (30:17–21)

A bronze basin was to be constructed for the priests' preparation for service at the altar. Before their work at the altar, they were to wash their hands and feet in the basin. The basin was placed between the altar and the Tent of Meeting.

## N. The Anointing Oil (30:22–33)

A special oil was to be mixed and used for anointing the various parts of the tabernacle, including the priests. The purpose of this was to set these persons and objects apart, to sanctify them. Thus, it was strictly forbidden to make and use the same oil for profane purposes.

## O. The Incense (30:34–38)

A special incense was to be mixed for the incense altar in front of the curtain of the Holy of Holies. Its purpose was to set the Tent of Meeting off as a special holy place. As with the anointing oil, the incense was not to be used for any profane purpose.

## P. Bezalel and Oholiab (31:1–11)

The work of God was to be done by means of the Spirit of God. Two skilled craftsmen were chosen by God—Bezalel from the tribe of Judah and Oholiab from the tribe of Dan. Though they were skilled men, the emphasis of the narrative is clearly on the fact that they were to do the work of building the tabernacle by means of the skills given them by the Spirit of God. In parallel with God's work of creation, just as God created by means of his Spirit (Ge 1:2–2:3), so also Israel was to do their work of building the tabernacle by God's Spirit. The parallels between God's work in creation and Israel's work on the tabernacle is part of a larger emphasis of the Pentateuch on the importance of the work of God's Spirit among his people. This is the same emphasis found in later biblical books where the "new covenant" notion of faith and internal change of heart are put at the center of one's relationship with God. Genuine obedience to the will of God comes only after the renewal of the human heart by the Spirit of God (cf. Eze 36:26–27).

## Q. The Sabbath (31:12–18)

The analogy between God's work of creation and Israel's construction of the tabernacle is drawn specifically into the open by the reference to the Sabbath at the close of the narrative. We are reminded that God did his work in six days and rested on the seventh day and that now Israel is to do likewise. Though it is clear that this pattern is taken up for all future generations (v.16), here the focus is on building the tabernacle. Just as God made the world, so Israel was to make the tabernacle. Like God's work, it was to be a holy work and was to be carried out by observing the holy times. Their work on the tabernacle was not holy merely because they were working on a holy structure. The work was holy because it was sanctified by the sign of the Sabbath.

Thus, the building of the tabernacle in the desert is a paradigm of all of Israel's life of work. By setting apart the Sabbath as a sign, the whole of their work was marked as a holy task.

### R. Conclusion (31:18)

This last verse returns our attention to the flow of narrative from ch. 24. Since ch. 24, God has been talking to Moses at the top of Mount Sinai. Now when he finishes, Moses is given the two stone tablets on which are written the Ten Commandments. In ch. 32, the narrative returns to the scene of ch. 24, picking up again with the people and Aaron at the foot of Mount Sinai. This verse is thus transitional, by means of which, we, the readers, are returned to the scene that Moses had left behind when he went up the mountain.

## VIII. The Golden Calf (32:1–35)

### A. The Making of the Calf (32:1–6)

The narrative returns to what was happening in the Israelite camp while Moses was receiving the covenant with the Ten Commandments on Mount Sinai. Ironically, at this very time Israel was in the process of breaking the first of those commandments. The writer goes to great lengths to show that Israel was unable to keep the covenant God had made with them. Throughout the remainder of the Pentateuch, the incident of the worship of the golden calf cast a dark shadow across Israel's relationship with God, in much the same way as the account of the Fall in Ge 3 marked a major turning point in God's dealing with humankind.

### B. Moses on the Mountain (32:7–14)

In the narrative of God's recounting to Moses the news of the golden calf, the reader is provided with three aspects of the divine perspective on Israel's sin. (1) God said, "They have been quick to turn away from what I

commanded them" (v.8). God had given the Ten Commandments, the first of which said, "You shall have no other gods before me" (20:2), and he had repeatedly warned them not to make or worship an idol (20:23; 23:13, 32–33). But now Israel had made for themselves just such an idol. (2) God said of Israel, "They are a stiff-necked people" (v.9). In their present state, Israel seemed incapable of obeying the covenant. He expressed a desire to destroy the people and start over by making a new nation with Moses (v.10). (3) But because of Moses' intercession and his appeal to the promises to the patriarchs, God had compassion on the people (v.14). A crucial role in this narrative, then, is played by the reference back to the promises made to the patriarchs (Ge 12:1–3).

These three points provide the basis of the subsequent narratives and God's further dealings with this people. Though a great act of God's judgment follows immediately (vv.27–35), the central themes focus on God's compassion and a new start for Israel.

### C. God's Judgment on Israel's Sin (32:15–35)

It is important to note that in this narrative, Moses, carrying out his role as mediator, acts and speaks on God's behalf. The divine wrath expressed in vv.9–12 was carried out by Moses and the Levites, "and that day about three thousand of the people died" (v.28). Moses, who had appealed for clemency on behalf of the people, now leads the vanguard of divine judgment. It is only in the last verse of the chapter that we see God himself acting directly in judgment, and this is by way of summary. The reason for this focus on Moses' role in judgment rather than God's is apparently the writer's desire to stress God's gracious response to Israel's sin. The central theme of the subsequent narrative is God's great mercy and compassion (33:19). God's further dealings with Israel henceforth emphasize that goodness and compassion. What the present narrative shows, however, is that God's gracious dealings with his people are not accomplished at the expense of a clear acknowledgment of his wrath.

At the close of this narrative we are reminded that as a result of the incident of the idolatrous golden calf, the people were "running wild" (v.25). This is a far cry from the picture of the people later in Nu 10:1ff. as they prepared to leave Sinai, when there is a marked order and care by which the people begin to move. Why the different picture of Israel under Moses' leadership? It should be noted that between the two narratives, that dealing with Israel's initial stay at Mount Sinai and that dealing with their departure, there lies an enormous series of collections of laws and regulations. What the narrative appears to be saying is that Israel's orderly departure from Mount Sinai was not an accident. It rather was the result of the countless "laws and regulations" given them by God at Sinai. Moreover, Ex 32 clearly helps to show that the laws given to Israel at Sinai were not mere arbitrary restrictions but necessary controls on an otherwise desperate and helpless situation.

## IX. The Restoration of Israel (33:1–34:35)

Moses returned to Mount Sinai and there, again, God spoke with him. Israel's relationship with God had been fundamentally affected by their "great sin" of worshiping the golden calf. There was now a growing distance between God and Israel that had not been there before. Each of the following sections of narrative specifically demonstrates the changes that have occurred in God's relationship to Israel. We should also note that the Levites are chosen in this narrative, and they replace the firstborn Israelites as priests in

Nu 3. This represents a further change in Israel's relationship with God in the Sinai covenant.

### A. The Angel (33:1–6)

The first intimation that the incident with the golden calf had changed the relationship of the Israelites with their God can be seen in the different emphasis given in the narrative to the "angel" that God sent before his people. In many respects, the passage is the same as 23:20–33, where God had previously promised to send his angel before his people (see especially 23:20). There the angel clearly represented God's presence among his people (23:23). Moreover, the Israelites were about to finalize their covenant with God at Sinai. It was precisely at that point that Moses was called to go up to the mountain to receive the covenant (24:1). Keep in mind too that, throughout that earlier narrative dealing with God's sending his angel, we find numerous warnings about the danger of idolatry (23:21, 24, 32–33).

Israel is once again waiting at the foot of Mount Sinai, and Moses is waiting to receive God's instruction on the mountain. The first instructions seem the same as before: Israel was to leave Sinai and enter the land promised to the patriarchs (33:1–3a), and God would send his angel before them (33:2). But in the present narrative, the reason for God's sending his angel to go before them has changed. God now said, "I will send an angel before you. . . . But I will not go with you, because you are a stiff-necked people and I might destroy you on the way" (vv.2–3). Whereas before, God had sent his angel to destroy *Israel's enemies* (23:23), now he would send his angel lest he destroy *Israel* (33:5). In the present narrative, the angel does not so much represent God's *presence* with Israel as his *separation* from them.

## B. The Tent of Meeting (33:7–11)

A further indication of Israel's growing separation from God as a result of the golden calf is the author's stress on the need for the construction of the Tent of Meeting. We know from the previous narrative that during the forty days on Mount Sinai, God had given Moses specific instructions for building the tabernacle (26:1–37). Its purpose was clearly stated by God: "Have them make a sanctuary for me, and I will dwell among them" (25:8). A part of the tabernacle was a goat hair covering over the inner curtains that was called simply "the tent" (26:7). Moreover, the whole of the tabernacle was sometimes called the "Tent of Meeting" (27:21; 28:43). Its purpose was to be the place where God could meet with his covenant people (see 29:42–43).

After the incident of the golden calf, however, the narrative tells of another "Tent of Meeting." This "tent" was not the same as the tabernacle. It was a meeting place with God that was "outside the camp some distance away" (33:7). That this was not the tabernacle is clear from the fact that at this point in the narrative the tabernacle was not yet built by Bezalel and his company of skilled workmen (36:8–38). Thus the "Tent of Meeting" in this passage was only for Moses and Joshua and was set apart from the people themselves. The people could only stand and watch from the distance of their own tents as Moses went out to enter the tent. The original idea of a "Tent of Meeting" by which God would dwell among his people had now become one of the means whereby God had been set apart from them.

## C. Moses and the Glory of the Lord (33:12–23)

A third indication of a change in Israel's relationship with God is the way in which God's glory is portrayed in this passage. A central feature of God's

original ascent upon Mount Sinai to speak with Moses was the great display of his glory before all the people: "and the glory of the LORD settled on Mount Sinai. For six days the cloud covered the mountain. . . . To the Israelites the glory of the LORD looked like a consuming fire on top of the mountain" (24:16–17). Now, however, when God spoke to Moses on the mountain, the display of his glory was significantly different. (1) There was no display of God's glory before all the people. Only Moses could look when God's glory passed by. (2) Even as he looked upon God's glory in this passage, Moses' face was covered by God's hand so he could see only the back parts of God's glory. (3) In ch. 34, it is recounted that the Israelite people only saw God's glory as it was reflected on the face of Moses when he returned from the mountain (34:29); they did not see God's glory itself. And just as God had covered the face of Moses lest he see too much of his glory, so Israel covered the face of Moses because "they were afraid to come near to him" (34:30).

Along with this change in the display of God's glory, there was also a change in the purpose of revealing God's glory. In the first revelation of God's glory at Sinai, Moses explained to the people that its purpose had been "to test you, so that the fear of God will be with you to keep you from sinning" (20:20). After the incident with the golden calf, however, the revelation of God's glory had a different purpose. When Moses asked to see God's glory, the Lord answered, "I will cause all my goodness to pass in front of you. . . . I will have mercy on whom I will have mercy, and I will have compassion on whom I will have compassion" (33:19). Surprisingly, what Moses learned about God's glory after the "great sin" (32:30) of the golden calf was not further fear of God but rather that he was a gracious God, full of much compassion. Consequently, in the next chapter, when the Ten Commandments were written on new stone tablets and a covenant was again established, a special emphasis is given to the importance of God's grace (see 34:6–7).

## D. The Stone Tablets (34:1–28)

Moses was told to prepare two stone tablets (vv.1–10); God would write the Ten Commandments on them, just as with the first tablets. Moses carried out God's command (v.4a) and took the two tablets with him back up the mountain (v.4b). Once on the mountain, however, God told Moses to write the "words" (v.27). This is followed by the statement that "he wrote the words of the covenant" on the tablets (v.28); the text is clear that it was the Ten Commandments that were written (v.28b). Yet in the parallel account in Dt 10:1–4, it was God, not Moses, who wrote the Ten Commandments on the two stone tablets.

How then are we to understand this present passage, which suggests that Moses wrote those words on the two tablets? An early, and, I believe, probable, explanation maintains that the Lord, not Moses, is the subject of the verb "he wrote" in v.28. Thus the words to be written by Moses in v.27 were not the same words as those which "[the Lord] wrote" in v.28. Moses was told to write "the words of the covenant" (i.e., the "covenant code" in 20:23–23:19), but these were not to be written on the two stone tablets. It was God who wrote the Ten Commandments on the stone tablets (v.28).

However the problem is resolved, what seems certain is that the covenant is established in this chapter on the basis of the original ten words that God himself had written on the tablets (v.1) as well as on the additional words that God commanded Moses to write (v.27). These additional words appear to have at least included those that God spoke to him during his second time on the mountain (vv.10–26). There are, interesting enough, "ten words" in this section as well. In some respects, these "ten words" have parallels in the Ten Commandments, but essentially they appear to be merely an expansion of the epilogue of the covenant code (see 23:13–19).

It is important to note that the twin themes of warning against idolatry and instructions for proper forms of worship played a significant role in the structure of the covenant code in chs. 20–24. Thus the making of a covenant in this chapter follows the same form as the old: (1) Warning against idolatry (34:11–17); (2) Instructions on true worship (34:18–26).

## E. The Glory on the Face of Moses (34:29–35)

Again as with the preceding narratives there is a significant reversal in Israel's relationship with God noted in the events of this narrative. Near the beginning of the earlier narrative of 32:15ff., Moses descended the mountain where he had been with God forty days and nights. In his hand were the two stone tablets. The text says, "When . . . he saw the calf and the dancing, his anger burned and he threw the tablets out of his hands" (32:19). Now, as Moses is shown again returning from the mountain with the two tablets in his hands, instead of Moses' amazement at what he saw in the camp, those in the camp were now amazed at what they saw in Moses—his radiant face—"and they were afraid" (v.30).

What had now happened to Moses was the beginning of the fulfillment of what God had earlier promised him on the mountain (see v.10). Henceforth, the covenant that God makes with Israel will focus on the role of the mediator. Through him God will display his glory to his people.

# X. The Construction of the Tabernacle (35:1–40:38)

## A. The Sabbath (35:1–3)

At the close of the instructions for the building of the tabernacle, Israel had been reminded of the necessity of keeping the Sabbath (31:12–17). All work, presumably that of the tabernacle as well, was to be suspended on the seventh day. After the narrative of Israel's great sin of the golden calf and before the description of the work on the tabernacle, there is again a reminder of the Sabbath rest.

## B. Materials for the Tabernacle (35:4–29)

A reckoning of the materials needed for building the tabernacle is narrated as well as the generosity of the people in giving and working "from a willing heart." The first part of the list is virtually verbatim that of 25:4–8. Since that list was only a general survey of materials needed, ch. 35 completes the list of all items actually gathered for every aspect of the building and recounts how the items were made. In the case of the yarn and linens, it says "every skilled woman spun with her hands and brought what she had spun—blue, purple or scarlet yarn or fine linen" (v.25). The emphasis in this section seems to be part of a larger focus on the role of women in Israel's worship (cf. 38:8).

## C. The Workmen: Bezalel and Oholiab (35:30–36:1)

God's preparation and choice of the skilled workers is repeated again in nearly verbatim fashion from 31:2–6. That which the Lord told Moses in ch. 31, Moses now repeats to the Israelites. There is one important difference, however. Since the description of the building of the tabernacle will focus not only on Bezalel and Oholiab but also on the many other skilled workers, Moses has given an interesting additional bit of information regarding God's preparation

of these men for his service. He writes that God had given both Bezalel and Oholiab "the ability to teach others" (v.34b). By adding this information to the narrative, Moses thus explains how the other workers obtained their skills for the work on the tabernacle. They were taught by the craftsmen God had gifted with his Spirit. Even their ability to teach others was a divine gift.

## D. The Response of the People (36:2–7)

The zeal of the people for the work of the tabernacle is graphically depicted in this brief narrative. When the workmen were brought together to begin the project, the people not only brought what they needed, but they also continued "to bring freewill offerings morning after morning." In fact, the people eventually had to be restrained from bringing any more.

## E. The Construction of the Tabernacle (36:8–38)

The order of recounting the construction of the parts of the tabernacle is not the same as that of the instructions in chs. 25–30. In the instructions, the individual items in the tabernacle were first described (the ark, table, lampstand) and then the tabernacle itself. Here, however, the writer begins with the tabernacle. The purpose for this change is perhaps to highlight the part of the work that involved "all the skilled workers" before moving on to that work that involved only Bezalel. Thus the picture that is given at the beginning of the narrative is that all the people participated.

The description of the building of the tabernacle follows closely that which was given earlier in the instructions. The major exception is, of course, that where the details are given as instructions in the first account (26:1–33), they are recorded here as accomplished. The purpose of such redundancy in the narrative is to show that the workmen carried out God's instructions *just as he had commanded.*

There are two major differences between the two accounts, however. (1) The present account states that the work was done by "all the skilled men among the workmen" (v.8). (2) Perhaps because of this additional information, the comment that the tabernacle was to follow the "plan" that Moses saw on the mountain (26:30) is missing in the present account. The focus is on the "skill" of the workmen. If only Moses saw the "plan," it follows that the workmen would have to be specially gifted if they were to follow it.

### F. The Ark (37:1–9)

The account given here of the construction of the ark follows closely the instructions given by Moses earlier in 25:10–22. There is, however, no mention of placing the "Testimony" in the ark after its completion (cf. 25:16, 21), nor is there any mention of placing the "atonement cover" on the ark (cf. 25:21). The reason for these omissions is that these two articles were put in place only after the tabernacle had been set up and dedicated with the anointing oil (40:20). It is specifically mentioned that Bezalel himself made the ark.

### G. The Table (37:10–16)

The construction of the table follows closely that of the instructions in 25:23–30. The Hebrew text is clear that Bezalel himself made the table.

### H. The Lampstand (37:17–24)

The construction of the lampstand follows closely that of the instructions in 25:31–40. As with the ark and the table, the text is clear that Bezalel himself made the lampstand. It is, of course, possible that he had assistance in the work, but the writer credits Bezalel himself. There is no mention of the lighting of the lampstand until the dedication of the tabernacle (Nu 8:1–4).

### I. The Altar of Incense, Anointing Oil, and Incense (37:25–29)

The account of the construction of the altar of incense, which fell near the end in the list of instructions (30:1–10), has been moved up with the other central articles of the tabernacle. Its construction follows the instructions verbatim. There is only a mere mention of the fact that they also made the anointing oil and the incense.

### J. The Altar of Burnt Offering (38:1–7)

Bezalel himself was responsible for building this altar (cf. NIV note). In the instructions for building it, the altar was not designated specifically for "burnt offerings," but here it is called "the altar of burnt offering." In the instructions for making this altar (27:8), Moses was told to make it "just as you were shown on the mountain." As is the case of the construction of the other articles, there is no mention of the workmen's following that pattern in this account of its construction. The focus is rather on the "skill" that God had given the workmen.

### K. The Basin for Washing (38:8)

The instructions for building the basin earlier in 30:17–21 were brief. The focus there was on the purpose for the basin and its location within the tabernacle. Here, however, an additional factor about the construction of the basin is given. It was made from the mirrors used by the "women who served at the entrance to the Tent of Meeting." Once again (cf. 35:25), the author appears to go out of his way to show that the women of Israel played an important role in the work of the tabernacle. Behind this concern to highlight what women did may lie the overall close association of "wisdom" and women in Scripture (cf. Ex 31:3; Pr 8:1ff; Ge 3:6).

The reference to the "Tent of Meeting" is probably to the tent that Moses had set up (33:7ff.) outside the camp, since the tabernacle had not yet been erected (cf. 40:2). In any case, the intent of the comment is to show the eagerness of the people to contribute freely to the construction of the tabernacle.

## L. The Courtyard (38:1–20)

The account of constructing the courtyard follows closely the instructions in 27:9–19.

## M. Atonement Money (38:21–31)

In 30:11–16 provision for financing the building of the tabernacle was laid out. Each individual adult counted in the census was to pay a half-shekel. When the census was carried out (38:26), the money collected was 301,775 shekels. Thus each of the 603,550 men (Nu 1:46) paid a half-shekel of silver, as required. The gold collected was 87,730 shekels, and the bronze was 212,400 shekels. The total collection amounted to several tons of precious metals.

## N. The Priestly Garments (39:1–31)

The description of the making of the ephod (vv.1–7) is in a somewhat abbreviated form from that of the instructions (28:6–14). It appears that it was not made by one individual but by several. It is stressed that Moses' instructions were followed precisely (v.5b).

Detailed instructions for the breastpiece (vv.8–21) are followed closely from 28:15–28. From the text it again appears that several workers were involved.

A few details are added concerning the way in which the robe was sewn (vv.22–26). It was, for example, made of "cloth—the work of a weaver." The tunic, turban, sash, and undergarments (vv.27–29) were made of cloth woven by a weaver; Moses' instructions were followed precisely in all the clothes (vv.26, 29).

The gold plate is identified as a "sacred diadem" (vv.30–31). Several workers were involved in making it,

and Moses' instructions were carefully followed.

## O. Moses Inspects the Tabernacle (39:32–43)

The description of the tabernacle given here repeats in large measure the command of Moses in 35:10–19. Its purpose is to show that the work was completed "just as the LORD had commanded Moses" (v.42). In a way that recalls God's own inspection of his work in Creation (Ge 1:31), "Moses inspected the work and saw that they had done it just as the LORD had commanded" (v.43). And as in God's work of Creation, a blessing followed the completion of the work (Ge 1:28), so also when the tabernacle was completed, Moses "blessed them" (39:43).

## P. Setting Up the Tabernacle (40:1–33)

This narrative begins with a description of the instructions given Moses for setting up the tabernacle. The Lord told him to set it up on the first day of the first month of the second year (v.17). First the ark was put in place and then covered with the curtains, i.e., the tents of the tabernacle and the curtain covering the Holy of Holies. Next came the table, the lampstand, the golden altar of incense, and the curtain covering the doorway to the tabernacle. The altar of burnt offering was then put before the doorway of the tabernacle, and the basin was put between the altar and the tent. The curtains making the courtyard were then put up all around, with a curtain providing a gateway to the courtyard. When all was in place, it was anointed with oil and the priests were brought in, dressed, and anointed.

Following the Lord's instruction, Moses now set up the tabernacle on the prescribed date. It had been only nine months since Israel arrived at Sinai (19:1), but the tabernacle was ready for the celebration of the first Passover that would have been only fourteen days off

(Nu 9:1–5). This careful attention of the writer to the chronology of the events shows that the restriction of the offering of the Passover lamb to the central worship center (Dt 16:1–8) could thus have already been carried out during this first celebration of the Passover in the desert.

Although the description of the erection of the tabernacle follows closely the instructions of vv.1–16, extra detail is given regarding the ark. The "Testimony," or stone tablets containing the Ten Commandments and other words spoken by God to Moses, was placed inside the ark, and the atonement cover was placed over it. It was apparently at this time that Aaron put the jar containing the manna "before" the ark (see 16:32–34; cf. Heb 9:4).

The Lord's approval of the work of building the tabernacle is shown by the fact that the cloud of his glory now took its place over the Tent of Meeting, i.e., the tabernacle. This was a visual reminder of the purpose of the tabernacle expressed in 25:8.

A final note is sounded in this narrative that prepares the way for the instructions that follow in Leviticus. We learn from the narrative that "Moses could not enter the Tent of Meeting because the cloud had settled upon it, and the glory of the LORD filled the tabernacle" (v.35). More provisions were thus necessary before they could enter into the tabernacle. Those provisions are given in the book of Leviticus.

# Leviticus

## Introduction

The book of Leviticus is a continuation of Exodus. Its name stems from the fact that in it the author focuses on the requirements of the covenant that relate to the "priests," who were from the tribe of Levi—hence, Leviticus.

Exodus 40 concluded with the completion of the tabernacle (40:17) in the first month of the second year, on the first day of the month. Numbers 1:1 begins on the first day of the second month of the second year after the Exodus. Leviticus, then, deals with those events that transpired during the intervening month. Its subject matter is the legislation given to Moses at the Tent of Meeting.

The central theme of the book is holiness. It intends to show how Israel was to fulfill its covenant responsibility to be "a kingdom of priests and a holy nation" (Ex 19:6; Lev 26:5).

## I. The Offerings and Sacrifices (1:1–17:16)

These chapters give a brief description of the various offerings and sacrifices used in the consecration of the priests and the people. They are not intended as an exhaustive explanation of the sacrificial system. These regulations provide background for the dedication of the tabernacle and the priesthood in chs. 8–9 as well as for the rest of the Pentateuch. They may be compared to the genealogies in Genesis, whose narrative purpose it is to introduce the main characters of the subsequent narratives.

An appreciation for the narrative purpose of these detailed regulations should lead us to focus on what the writer has put in these chapters rather than on what he has left out. That is, we should not attempt to reconstruct from these regulations the whole or even a part of the sacrificial procedures of ancient Israel. What is given is sufficient to enable us to understand the events recorded in the subsequent texts.

## A. The Laws of Sacrifice (1:1–7:38)

### 1. Introduction (1:1–2)

The first seven chapters have only a brief introduction. According to it, the instructions in this book give guidelines for bringing "an offering" to the Lord at the tabernacle. These instructions do not introduce the practice of offerings; rather, they provide regulations for existing practices of sacrifices and offerings among the Israelites in light of the newly established worship of God at the tabernacle. The narrative assumes that several types of offerings were already well known and practiced by this time among the Israelites (Ex 18:12). Moreover, various kinds of offerings had already been practiced by the earliest patriarchs (see Ge 4:3–4; 8:20; 46:1).

The narrative framework of Leviticus first shows that these instructions were given to Moses by the Lord at the "Tent of Meeting." This was probably the "tent" Moses set up outside the camp where God spoke to him (see comment on Ex 33:7–11). According to Ex 40:35, Moses could not enter the "Tent of Meeting" (i.e., the tabernacle); thus God continued to speak with him from the other tent outside the camp.

The instructions in Leviticus were designed to make that tabernacle accessible. Already here in the strategy of the author, we see the importance of the offerings and sacrifices and the dedication of the priesthood. Only after the dedication of the tabernacle and the priesthood were Moses and Aaron able to enter the tabernacle where God's glory dwelt (Lev 9:23). Thus, though at the opening of this section the "Tent of Meeting" refers to the one set up outside the camp, in the following chapters the "Tent of Meeting" refers to the tabernacle.

## 2. The burnt offering (1:3–17)

These instructions deal with three types of burnt offerings that could be brought to the tabernacle: (1) those from the herd (vv.3–9); (2) those from the flock (vv.10–13); and (3) those from the birds (vv.14–17). The offering was presented at the entrance of the Tent of Meeting, the tabernacle, where the offerer would lay his hand on the head of the offering and, if it were then accepted, it would "make atonement for him" (v.4b). If the animal was from the herd or flock, the offerer would slaughter and prepare it, and the priest would bring it and its blood to the altar where it would be completely burned. If the offering was a bird, it would be given over to the priests and prepared on the altar by them after it had been accepted. Further instructions on this offering are given in 6:8–13.

## 3. The grain offering (2:1–16)

A grain offering was an offering of flour prepared in any number of ways: fresh, baked, prepared on a griddle, or cooked in a pan. The offering was brought to the priest, who then took a small portion of it to burn on the altar. The rest was taken to be used by the priests. The grain offering could not contain yeast but was to be seasoned with salt. Further instructions are given in 6:14–18.

## 4. The fellowship offering (3:1–17)

Unlike the burnt offering, in which the whole of the offering was consumed by fire, in the fellowship offering only the "fat portions" and the blood were burned. The rest of the animal was prepared and eaten by the priests and the offerer. Here only the instructions regarding the offering of the "fat portions" are given. Instructions regarding the eating of the remaining portions are given in 7:11–36. The central issue in the handling of the fellowship offering is that none of the "fat portions" or the blood was to be eaten (3:17). Further instructions are given in 7:12, 16.

## 5. The sin offering (4:1–5:13)

The purpose of the sin offering was to atone for unintentionally breaking one of God's commandments (4:20, 26, 31, 35). Different forms of offerings and procedures were required, depending on the status or identity of the offender. For example, a sin offering for the high priest (4:3) or the community as a whole (4:13) required a young bull, whereas for an individual (4:27) or leader (4:22) in the community a goat or lamb was required. A poor person (4:7) was required to bring only two doves or two young pigeons (5:7). If one was still unable to afford this, a sin offering could be made of a tenth of an ephah of fine flour (5:11).

Like the burnt offering, one brought the appropriate offering to the tabernacle, laid his hands on the animal, and slaughtered it. The priest took the blood and sprinkled it on the altar. As with the fellowship offering, the "fat portions" were burned on the altar. When a priest was involved in the sin, the remainder of the sacrificial animal was carried outside the camp and burned on the ash heap (4:12, 21; 6:30). In cases where the officiating priest was not involved in the sin, the meat of the animal was not burned on the ash heap but was given to the priest to eat (6:26, 29; 7:7).

## 6. The guilt offering (5:14–6:7)

The guilt offering provided for the restitution of a wrong (5:16a; 6:5) along with atonement for the wrong itself (5:16b,18; 6:7). When restitution was made, the proper value was determined and a fifth (5:16; 6:5) of that was added to the repayment. The atonement in each case was the offering of a ram (5:15; 6:6).

## 7. Sacrificial instructions pertaining to priests (6:8–7:38)

The burnt offering (see comments on 1:3–17) lay on the altar throughout the night with the fire still burning. In the morning, the priest, properly dressed and consecrated, removed the ashes, placing them beside the altar while he changed his clothing. The priest then took the ashes outside the camp to a ceremonially clean disposal site.

The priests were to burn a designated portion of the grain offering (see comments on 2:1–16) on the altar with incense; the rest they could eat as their portion. It was to be eaten without yeast and could only be eaten by a "male descendant of Aaron" in the courtyard of the tabernacle. The grain offering was also the offering to be given on the day of the anointing of the high priest (6:19). It was prepared by the "son who was to succeed him as anointed priest." Unlike the usual grain offering, this particular offering was burned completely because it was a priest's offering (6:23).

Much has already been recorded regarding the sin offering in 4:1–5:13, though some important points are cleared up in this section. Here it is made explicit that the meat of the animals offered by individuals and leaders was to be eaten by the priests who performed the sacrifice (6:26, 29). Furthermore, a sin offering that was carried out as part of the cleansing of the tabernacle could not be eaten by the priest (6:30). Thus the principle is established that the sin offering could be eaten by the priests as long as the offering had not been given in any way on behalf of the priests.

The guilt offering (see comments on 5:14–6:7) had specific procedures for the slaughter of the animal and its presentation (7:1–10). The high priest is told to keep the skin of the sacrificed animal. The author may be alluding here to Ge 3:21, where the Lord gave animal skins to Adam and Eve for clothing.

In 7:12 and 16 it is assumed that a fellowship offering (see comments on 3:1–17) would be given "as an expression of thankfulness" (7:12), as part of

a vow (7:16), or as a freewill offering (7:16). One basic principle of eating the fellowship offering was that the fat and blood of the offering were devoted to God. The meat, i.e., the remainder of the offering after the "fat portions" were removed, could be eaten by anyone who was ceremonially clean (7:19). A second basic principle of this offering was that the priests were to have their share in the gifts. The breast belonged to Aaron and his sons, and the right leg belonged to the priest who offered the blood of that sacrifice at the altar.

## B. The Consecration of the Priests (8:1–9:24)

The instructions for consecrating the priests for work in the tabernacle were given in Ex 29:1–37. The execution of those instructions are carried out here, with little variation. In retelling these instructions, the writer is careful to label the various offerings according to the types of sacrifices described in the first part of the book. The bull, for example, is consistently called "the bull for the sin offering" (8:14–15; cf. Ex 29:14); the first ram is called "ram for the burnt offering" (8:18; cf. Ex 29:18); and the second ram is called "the ram for the ordination" (8:22; cf. Ex 29:23). The writer underscores the priests' careful attention to detail by reminding the reader that all was done "as the LORD commanded Moses" (8:17, 22, 29).

After the seven days of consecration for the priests, Moses gathered Aaron, his sons, and the elders of Israel and instructed them to prepare for the appearance of the glory of the Lord at the tabernacle. This appears to be the same group who "saw" God at Mount Sinai in Ex 24:9. The preparation consisted of offering several of the kinds of offerings described at the beginning of the book. When Moses gave the instructions, they followed his word to the letter. First the offerings were given for Aaron and the priests and then for the people.

At the conclusion, Moses and Aaron went into the Tent of Meeting (the tabernacle). In Ex 40:35 Moses could not enter the tabernacle because of the glory of the Lord. Moses and Aaron could now go in because of the sacrifices offered "as the LORD had commanded." When they came out again, "they blessed the people" (9:23). The fire from the Lord that consumed the burnt offering and the fat portions on the altar (9:24) was a sign to all the people that God had accepted their offerings. It is hereby established that by means of the priests' proper entry into the tabernacle, the nation was blessed. In the next chapter, we are given a negative lesson of the same truth in the example of Nadab and Abihu. Underlying both chapters is the same lesson: the blessing of God's people will come only through obedience to the divine pattern.

In the narrative itself, the response of the people echoes God's acceptance of them: "when all the people saw it, they shouted for joy and fell facedown" (9:24).

Surprisingly, Aaron's offering of the goat for the people's sin offering (9:15ff.) follows the instructions for the sin offering for a leader of the community, a male goat (4:22–26), rather than the sin offering for the whole community, a young bull (4:13–21), as might have been expected. Apparently this was because the whole community had not specifically sinned, and thus this offering was meant for any specific individual in the community in need of it. In any event, since the requirements for either sin offering varied, Aaron's offering led to some difficulty, as we see in 10:16ff.

## C. The Death of Nadab and Abihu (10:1–20)

Just as "the fire [that] came from the presence of the LORD" had been a sign

of God's approval of the dedication of the tabernacle and the priests in the previous chapter (9:24), so also the "fire [that] came from the presence of the LORD" in this chapter (10:2) was a sign of God's disapproval. The writer's purpose in putting these two narratives together was to show the importance God attached to obedience to his commands.

Immediately after the incident, Mishael and Elzaphan, the sons of Aaron's uncle Uzziel, were summoned to carry the bodies of Nadab and Abihu out of the tabernacle so that Aaron and his other sons would not become defiled.

It is important to note that Moses himself has interpreted the severe judgment of Nadab and Abihu by laying down the principle, "Among those who approach me [God] I will show myself holy. . . . I will be honored" (v.3). The purpose of the instructions for sacrifices was to provide a means of treating God as holy and honoring him before all the people. Thus behind the rebellious offering of Nadab and Abihu was a disobedient heart. They refused to come before him "as he had commanded." As such, the narrative is similar to that found in Samuel's response to Saul in 1Sa 15:22.

Within the course of this section, a question of the interpretation of the law arises. What should have been the procedure for Aaron's sons in carrying out the sin offering on this day of dedication? As Moses was reviewing the various offerings given at this dedication (vv.12–15), he could not find the part of the sin offering that was to have been eaten by Aaron and his sons (v.16). When he found that these parts had been burned and not eaten, he grew angry with Aaron (v.16b). According to Moses, Aaron's sons should have eaten the offering (10:17). Though the burning of the offering might have been justified on the grounds that it was a sin offering for the people (cf. 4:21; 9:15),

Moses apparently based his judgment on the fact that a goat, not a bull, was offered, making it an offering that should have been eaten (6:26).

Moreover, Moses appealed to the ruling in 6:30, which prohibited eating the sin offering only if the blood had been taken into the Tent of Meeting (10:18), which in this case had not happened (9:15). In his response, Aaron did not contest Moses' explanation of the regulations. He rather appealed to the deaths of his two sons, which, he argued, had rendered he and his other sons unfit for eating the holy food. But the concern for ritual purity had already been taken care of when Mishael and Elzaphan had carried the dead bodies out of the tabernacle (10:4). There was, then, no danger that Aaron and his sons were ritually unclean because they had touched dead bodies. Aaron had thus concluded that a mourner should not take part in a sacrificial meal. When Moses heard of Aaron's decision, he approved of it (10:20).

The overall lesson of this narrative plays an important role in delineating the ongoing responsibility of Aaron's priesthood, i.e., discerning between the holy and the profane, the clean and the unclean (vv.10–11; cf. Mal 2:7; Hag 2:11–12). In the chapters that follow, Moses will go into great detail in listing just these kinds of distinctions between the holy and the common, the unclean and the clean (11:47).

## D. The Laws of Purity and Impurity (11:1–15:33)

### 1. Regulations concerning animals (11:1–47)

This chapter contains a selected list of creatures, dividing each type into various classes of purity. It has regulations about four major groups of animals: land animals, birds or flying creatures, water animals, and "small creeping things." This is the same general classification of animal life found in the Creation account.

According to v.47, the determining category was whether a class of animals was unclean or clean. The goal was to determine whether or not an animal could be eaten. The notion of unclean and clean is specifically applied in this chapter to the question of holiness (vv.44–45). Violating any of the regulations relating to clean and unclean animals rendered one unclean and thus unable to enter into community worship (12:4b). Ultimately, the purpose of the chapter is to tie the concept of holiness to God's own example of holiness (11:45b).

The fact that some animals were clean and others were unclean does not imply that some animals are, in themselves, dirty. At the opening of the Pentateuch, for example, in the account of Creation, God saw all the animals he had created and at that time he said they were all "good" (Ge 1:21). This divine assessment of all creatures included even those animals called "detestable" here in Leviticus.

### 2. Purification relating to childbirth (12:1–8)

This is a short chapter and at first glance may appear to have been arbitrarily selected and placed here. It concerns only the case of purification related to a woman in childbirth. Why has the author chosen this specific topic and why he has placed it at this point in the narrative? When such questions are posed, it becomes clear that this chapter plays an important strategic role in relationship to the surrounding texts. It is in the regulations regarding childbirth that an explanation is given to the overall meaning of the notion of impurity throughout this whole section of legal texts: As long as the woman was unclean, "she must not touch anything sacred or go to the sanctuary" (v.4). In other words, impurity is defined with respect to the sanctuary (the tabernacle) and, more importantly, in terms of one's acceptability within the worshiping community. The sense of impurity is thus defined with respect to the goal of the covenant and the goal of Creation, i.e., the worship of God. As the man and woman were cast off from God's presence in the Garden of Eden (Ge 3:24–25), so the one who is unclean cannot come before God in his sanctuary. The writer has provided here a key to the notion of cleanness and uncleanness found throughout the rest of the book. Uncleanness meant one was barred from the worship life of the covenant community. In the present narrative, it may be that childbirth has been singled out in the discussion of purification because of its close association in the Pentateuch with both the blessing (Ge 3:15) and the curse (v.16).

### 3. Regulations dealing with skin diseases (13:1–14:57)

As is common in these collections of regulations, the description of the contents and purpose of the collection is placed at the end (14:56–57). There the contents of the chapter are described as "the instruction for all skin diseases, that for scabs, for clothing, for houses, raised spots, scabs and bright spots" (v.56). Its statement of purpose is "to teach the distinction between unclean and clean" (v.57). The various tests for skin disease are enumerated first, and then the cleansing procedures are described.

The first section deals with the various examinations for skin disease (13:1–46) and the detection of such diseases on one's clothing (13:47–59). When a skin disease was detected, there was no provision for healing the disease. Rather, the diseased person was required to "wear torn clothes, let his hair be unkempt, cover the lower part of his face and cry out, 'Unclean! Unclean!'" (v.45). That person was to live alone "outside the camp" (v.46). When clothing was found to be infected, it

was either washed and reexamined (v.54) or the article of clothing was destroyed (vv.52, 57).

Once again we see here echoes of the early chapters of Genesis. As the skin of the man and the woman was the focus of guilt and shame at the time of the Fall (i.e., in being "naked"; Ge 3:7), so now the writer of the Pentateuch uses the graphic horror of skin diseases found in these texts to depict a person's state of uncleanness before a holy God.

Along similar lines, it is significant that in the Genesis narratives the first man and woman, once they had sinned, suffered the same consequences for their contamination as the unclean person in Leviticus. If one were found to be unclean, "he must live outside the camp" (13:46). In the same way, Genesis shows that when Adam sinned, "the LORD God banished him from the Garden of Eden to work the ground from which he had been taken. [And] he drove the man out" (Ge 3:23–24).

The next unit of text in Leviticus (14:1–53) deals with provisions for cleansing from the diseases enumerated in the preceding passage. This "cleansing" was a procedure for pronouncing that one had been healed. First, the provisions for cleansing diseases on the flesh are given (vv.1–32) and then those for cleansing diseases from the house (vv.33–53). Both procedures are similar and follow the same pattern for pronouncing an object clean.

Though similar, there is a major difference between the two ceremonies in their treatment of that which was found to be diseased. For example, while there is no provision for actually healing the skin diseases, there is a provision for clearing a house of infection. Nevertheless, the two provisions are similar. The primary procedure for clearing a house of infection was, first, to close the house for seven days, and, second, if that did not remove the disease, the soiled stones of the house were removed and destroyed "outside the city" and then the house was to be replastered (vv.38–42). In the case of skin disease, the provisions for cleansing assumed at the start that the one to be cleansed had already been healed (v.3b). Like the soiled stones of the contaminated house, however, the diseased person must remain unclean and live "outside the camp" (13:46).

An important difference between a contaminated person and house was that there were offerings and sacrifices for the one healed of skin disease but not for the house that had been cleansed. It is understandable that sacrifices would not be offered for a house.

There are several features of the Flood narrative in Genesis that have parallels in the present text of Leviticus. (1) For example, God used water to cleanse the land of all flesh that had corrupted his way (Ge 6:12). The primary means of cleansing rituals in Leviticus was water. (2) Noah had to wait at the door of the ark for seven days (Ge 7:4, 10); the priest had to wait at the door of the house for seven days (Lev 14:38). (3) A sacrifice was offered at the conclusion of the Flood (Ge 6:20); a sacrifice was offered at the conclusion of a cleansing ritual (Lev 14:10, 21).

The significance of these parallels lies in the way they reveal the larger purpose and intention of the author of the Pentateuch. By following the patterns of the early narratives of Genesis, the author is able to show God's purpose in giving Israel these covenant regulations. They are God's way of effecting in the everyday life of his people the same goals and purposes he has for the entire human race. Sin and its contamination of worship and fellowship with God must be dealt with in God's way. As the Flood was once necessary to cleanse God's good creation from the evil that had contaminated it, so the ritual washings were a necessary

part of checking the spread of sin and its results in the covenant community.

### 4. Discharges Causing Uncleanness (15:1–33)

An outline and summary of the contents of this chapter is given in the final verses of the chapter (vv.32–33). The chapter begins with the basic premise of the regulations, "When anyone has a bodily discharge, the discharge is unclean" (v.2). There are two major sections. (1) There are regulations for a man with a discharge (vv.3–18). It begins with a description of the nature of the discharge (vv.4–12) and then follows with instructions for cleansing the discharge (vv.13–18). (2) There are regulations for a woman with a discharge (vv.19–30). It too begins with a description of the woman's discharge (vv.19–27) and then instructions for cleansing the discharge (vv.28–30). The instructions for cleansing are the same for both the man and the woman. They were to wait seven days after the discharge had ceased. Then they were to wash their clothes and themselves with fresh water. On the eighth day, they were to offer two doves or pigeons at the Tent of Meeting—one was a sin offering and the other a burnt offering.

The chapter ends with an important reminder of the purpose of the purity laws. The Lord told Moses that the ceremonial purity of the Israelite community must be maintained so that "they will not die in their uncleanness for defiling my dwelling place, which is among them" (v.31). In other words, these various conditions were not to be avoided because they were inherently evil, but because they disqualified one from participation in the worship of the community.

### E. The Day of Atonement (16:1–34)

Once a year, on the tenth day of the seventh month, a Sabbath was proclaimed and atonement was made for the sins of the whole nation. This was the Day of Atonement. The heart of the ceremony was the time when the high priest laid his hands on a live goat and confessed all the sins of the nation (v.21). The goat was then allowed to wander away from the camp and into the desert. Israel's sins were thus carried away. This was a lasting ordinance for Israel (v.34).

As a prelude to the instructions for this great day, the author recalls the tragic fate of Aaron's two sons, Nadab and Abihu (16:1). The fire that had consumed them serves as a vivid reminder that God must be approached with utmost reverence and holiness. The priests could not enter the tabernacle at their own whim. God's presence was "behind the curtain in front of the atonement cover on the ark," and any improper entry into the Tent would result in death (v.2).

The procedure for the celebration of the Day of Atonement consisted first of the consecration of the high priest (vv.3–4). Aaron, in linen garments (not his regular garments, cf. vv.23–24), was to take a young bull and a ram for himself, and two male goats and a ram for the Israelite community. First he offered the bull as his own sin offering. The bull was slaughtered and some of the blood was taken "behind the curtain" where it was sprinkled "on the front of the atonement cover" (vv.11–14). Incense was placed on the "fire before the LORD" (namely, the burning coals carried into the Holy of Holies by the priest's censer; v.12), and its smoke covered the atonement cover, shielding the high priest. Then he took the two goats for the community. One goat was marked by lot as belonging to the Lord and other as a "scapegoat."

The goat belonging to the Lord was offered as a sin offering for the people, and its blood was taken "behind the curtain" and sprinkled on the atonement cover (v.15). This sin offering made "atonement for the Most Holy Place

and the Tent of Meeting because of the uncleanness and rebellion of the Israelites" (v.16). Then blood from the bull and the first goat was sprinkled on the horns of the altar to cleanse the altar.

The second goat was preserved to make atonement by sending it into the desert, bearing the sins of the nation. The high priest laid his hands on the goat, confessed all of Israel's sins, and sent the goat away. The man who led the goat out (v.21b) then washed his clothes and bathed before coming back into the camp (v.26).

The high priest then changed into his regular priestly garments and sacrificed the second ram for a burnt offering for himself and the community's ram for a burnt offering for them. The bull and goat used for the sin offering were taken outside the camp and completely burned. The man assigned to burn them washed his clothes and bathed before coming back into the camp.

## F. Warnings Against Improper Actions (17:1–16)

Four specific warnings against improper actions are given in this chapter. (1) Animals for sacrifices were not to be slaughtered in places other than the Tent of Meeting (vv.2–9). What is prohibited is not every kind of slaughter but specifically slaughter for sacrifice (cf. vv.3–5, 13–14). Slaying animals for food in places other than the Tent of Meeting was of course permissible (cf. Dt 12:15). (2) Domestic animals were not to be eaten with their blood (vv.10–12). (3) Game animals were not to be eaten with their blood (vv.13–14). (4) An animal killed by a wild animal was not to be eaten (vv.15–16).

The writer's purpose in including this part at this point was to demonstrate the motive behind the strict rules regulating worship that are found throughout the following sections of the Pentateuch. As the writer himself tells us, "This is so the Israelites will bring to the LORD the sacrifices they are now making in the open fields" (v.5). Moreover, he adds, "They must no longer offer any of their sacrifices to the goat idols to whom they prostitute themselves" (v.7). Thus, the accumulation of laws regulating holiness has its motive in the prevention of further idolatry among the people. Just as the narrative about the incident of the golden calf revealed the imminent danger of Israel's falling into idolatry, so the present narrative demonstrates the ongoing threat. These two narratives, in fact, play an important role in the composition of this part of the Pentateuch.

We have already seen that the legislation describing Israel's priestly worship in the reinstituted Sinai Covenant (Ex 35–Lev 16) was prefaced by the narrative of the golden calf (Ex 32). The intent was to show the need for further regulations in Israel's worship. Idolatry was a real threat, and so specific regulations were needed to prevent it. Here, in Lev 17, at the close of that large section of priestly laws, the writer has attached another short narrative dealing with a similar problem. Once again the threat of idolatry can be seen in Israel's practice of sacrificing to the "goat idols." The two narratives showing the threat of idolatry form brackets around the detailed legislation dealing with the office of the priest—legislation primarily directed toward preventing further idolatry. The two narratives provide the priestly legislation with two vivid examples of Israel's falling away after "other gods." Thus, the writer provides justification for the legislation itself.

A further observation can be made regarding the larger structure of the arrangement of these laws. It has long been recognized that Lev 17 plays an important role with respect to the collection of laws that follow it (chs. 18–26), often called the Holiness Code. Characteristic of the these laws is the fact that they relate to the life of the av-

erage individual and not merely that of the priests. It shows how God's law regulates the everyday life of the individual Israelite. Chapter 17 forms a suitable introduction to the laws that immediately follow.

If we compare the two accounts of Israel's idolatry, Ex 32 and Lev 17, we see that each has a specific point of view. The incident of the golden calf clearly centers on the role of Aaron the priest. Throughout the narrative, the writer is careful to show that it was Aaron who led the people and made the idol.

On the other hand, in Lev 17 the threat of idolatry came solely from the Israelite people. The actual problem, in fact, was that the people were sacrificing "in the open fields" and not with the priests at the Tent of Meeting (vv.5, 7). By this time in the narrative strategy of the Pentateuch, the priests had been consecrated and were following the regulations given in Ex 35–Lev 19. What Lev 17:1–9 shows is that God's people at large had now begun to sacrifice to "goat idols," a form of false worship that led them away from the worship of God prescribed in the Sinai Covenant. What was needed, therefore, were more laws dealing with the everyday life of the people that would ensure that they remained holy and faithful to God. Thus, ch. 17 shows the necessity for this set of laws dealing with the everyday life of the people.

A basic principle of sacrifice is uncovered in 17:11: "For the life of a creature is in the blood, and I have given it to you to make atonement for yourselves on the altar." When the blood was drained from a sacrificial animal, its life was drained out and it died. Consequently, when the blood was shed, it signified death, which in turn "made atonement" in the sacrifice. The curse of death recounted in Ge 2:17 and 3:19 lies at the foundation of the sacrificial atonement. The death of the animal offered in sacrifice took the place of the one offering the sacrifice. In God's grace Israel's sins were atoned for by the offering of a substitute. In the NT the meaning of Christ's death on the cross is grounded in this view of sacrifice (Mt 26:28; 20:28; Eph 1:7; Col 1:20).

## II. Holiness in the Life of the People (18:1–27:34)

This section contains material concerned with the description and necessary instructions on how Israel was to become a holy nation—a nation set apart to God.

## A. The Conduct of God's People (18:1–20:27)

Several features of this passage parallel the two brief narratives of Ge 9:20–27 and 11:1–9. In the former, Noah's son Ham looked upon his father's nakedness; consequently the Canaanites, descendants of Ham, were cursed. So also in Lev 18:7 the warning is given not to look on one's father's nakedness, lest one be defiled like the inhabitants of the land of Canaan (18:24ff).

In the building of Babylon (Ge 11:1–9), God confused their language and dispersed the city's inhabitants because, he said, "nothing they plan to do will be impossible for them" (Ge 11:6). In the holiness laws in Lev 18–20, the noun form of the word "plan" occurs as a part of the explanation of the purpose of personal holiness. By means of these laws, the children of Israel were to ensure that there would be no "wickedness" (18:17; 19:29; 20:14; same root word as "plan") or "confusion" (18:23; 20:12; same root word as "Babylon") in the land. A parallel is drawn between the evils of the city of Babylon and Canaan. The purpose of the narrative is to warn the reader not to become wicked or confused like Babylon or Canaan.

### 1. Introduction (18:1–5)

In this introduction, the laws represented a way of life distinct from the "acts of Egypt" and the "acts of Canaan" (v.3). They were God's "judgments," and Israel was to "keep" them by "walking in them" (v.4). The result of keeping them was "life" (v.5). When this passage is quoted in Eze 20:11ff., the sense given to the notion of "life" is the same as that in the early chapters of Genesis—physical life as well as God's blessing of eternal life. Ezekiel saw Israel's time in the desert as a time of rebellion and failure to obey these laws. Consequently, he argued, the whole rebellious generation died in the desert and did not enter the Promised Land (Eze 20:13–14). Though Ezekiel goes on to show that God was compassionate to Israel and did not utterly destroy them, he is clear in his understanding that "to live" means here "to live and to enjoy God's covenant blessings in the Promised Land." As such Ezekiel correctly reflects the author's meaning in these narratives.

### 2. The defilements of the Canaanites (18:6–30)

The clue to the meaning of this segment is given at the close of the list of defilements. These laws were intended to distinguish the Israelites from the inhabitants of the land they were about to possess: "Do not defile yourselves in any of these ways, because this is how the nations that I am going to drive out before you became defiled" (v.24). Sexual relations are prohibited: (1) among family members (18:6–18)—since it is presupposed that the Israelites would not marry among the Canaanites (cf. Dt 7:3), strict regulations on marriage among their own people were necessary (cf. the basic rule in v.6, "No one is to approach any close relative to have sexual relations"); (2) during monthly period (v.19); (3) with a neighbor's wife (v.20); (4) in idolatry to Molech (v.21);

(5) in homosexual relations (v.22); and (6) in bestiality (v.23).

### 3. Statutes and judgments (19:1–37)

This section is introduced with the admonition, "Be holy because I, the LORD your God, am holy." The first section (vv.1–18) consists of a list of twenty-one (three times seven) laws. These laws are broken up into smaller units by a sevenfold repetition of the phrase "I am the LORD (your God)" (vv.3b, 4b, 10b, 12b, 14b, 16b, 18b).

The second section (vv.19–37) is introduced with the admonition, "You shall keep my statutes" (v.19a) and concludes with a similar admonition (v.37a) and the statement, "I am the LORD" (v.37b). Like the first section of laws, it consists of twenty-one (three times seven) laws, broken up into smaller units by a sevenfold repetition of the phrase, "I am the LORD (your God)" (vv. 25, 28, 30, 31, 32, 34, 36).

We have already seen a close relationship between the laws in the Pentateuch and the early sections of Genesis. A similar relationship between the procedures outlined for planting fruit trees here and in Ge 1 may occur. According to Lev 19, when fruit trees were planted, they could not to be eaten until the fifth year (in the fourth year they were holy). In the account of Creation, God created fruit trees on the third day (Ge 1:11–12), but there was not yet any person to eat from them. Taking the pattern of "days" in Ge 1 to correspond to a pattern of "years" in the present text, we see that humankind was created on the sixth day, the day when the fruit trees would be holy. On the next day, the Sabbath, they could eat from the fruit. Thus the writer of the Pentateuch portrays God as following the pattern of his own law.

### 4. Holiness laws (20:1–27)

This section of laws consists of fourteen (two times seven) laws, concluded by an extended appeal for holiness on the part of the nation when they took possession of the land of Canaan (vv.22–26). After the conclusion, one of the laws, the prohibition of mediums and spiritists (v.6), is restated (v.27).

## B. The Condition of Priests Within the Community (21:1–22:33)

### 1. Regulations for priests: First list (21:1–15)

The list has a brief introduction (v.1) and ends with the introduction to the next list (v.16). There are fourteen (two times seven) laws in the list.

### 2. Regulations for priests: Second list (21:16–24)

This list is introduced by the expression "The LORD said to Moses, 'Say to Aaron . . .'" (v.16) and is concluded by the expression, "So Moses told this to Aaron . . ." (v.24). There are fourteen (two times seven) laws in the list.

### 3. Regulations for priests: Third list (22:1–33)

The first nine verses discuss things that profane a priest. Between a short introduction (vv.1–2) and concluding statement (v.9), a selection of seven laws is given.

In vv.10–15, regulations on persons not authorized to eat the sacred offering are given. The basic principle was, "No one outside a priest's family may eat the sacred offering" (v.10). This principle is repeated on either side of the list of seven laws (vv.10, 13b). A brief statement regarding restitution for accidental eating of an offering is appended (vv.14–16).

Then follows a section on priestly offerings (vv.17–25). This selection of seven laws has the principle stated at the conclusion: these offerings "will not be accepted on your behalf, because they are deformed and have defects" (v.25b).

The chapter closes with a selection of seven laws regarding time intervals of sacrifices (vv.26–33).

## C. The Calendar of the Religious Seasons (23:1–24:23)

### 1. Seasonal Events (23:1–44)

Seven special seasons of the year are enumerated. This section has a clearly defined introduction (vv.1–2), which is repeated at the conclusion (v.44). The seven feasts described are the Sabbath, the Passover and Unleavened Bread, the Firstfruits, the Feast of Weeks, the Feast of Trumpets, the Day of Atonement, and the Feast of Tabernacles.

### 2. Continual offerings (24:1–9)

Two continual offerings are enumerated—the burning of oil in the golden lampstand (vv.1–4) and the preparation of the twelve loaves of bread on the golden table (vv.5–9). The bread was a regular part of the share of Aaron and his sons. They were to eat it within the tabernacle.

### 3. A blasphemer stoned and lex talionis (24:10–23)

Embedded in the narrative about the stoning of a blasphemer is a reminder of the penalty for murder. Note that the "whole congregation" was responsible for stoning the blasphemer (v.14). This may be the reason why there is a reminder of the penalty for murder, lex talionis, just at this point in the narrative. The author thus sets up a contrast between the whole congregation's acting to take the life of a blasphemer and a single individual acting as an individual taking "the life of a human being" (v.17). Thus an important distinction has been made between capital punishment and murder. Capital punishment was an act of the whole community, whereas murder was an individual act.

## D. The Sabbath and Jubilee Years (25:1–55)

At the close of the narratives dealing with God's speaking to Israel at Sinai, the writer recalls the setting of the giving of the Law: "The LORD said to Moses on Mount Sinai" (v.1; cf. 7:38).

It is important to remind us that all of these laws were given by God to Moses.

The central theme of this last set of instructions is that of restoration. Israel's life was to be governed by a pattern of seven-year periods, called Sabbath years. After seven periods of seven years, in the Year of Jubilee, there was to be total restoration for God's people.

### 1. The Sabbath year (25:1–7)

As had already been commanded (Ex 23:10–11), when the people entered the land, they were to sow and reap for six years and eat of the land's produce. In the seventh year, however, they were to leave the land fallow. The owner of the land was not to carry out any organized sowing and harvest. All the people of the land, rich and poor alike, were simply to live off the land (v.6). This provision was especially intended for the "poor of the people" (Ex 23:11). It was to be their year of plenty.

In the overall plan, the Sabbath year was to be a replication of God's provisions for the human race in the Garden of Eden. When God created Adam and put him into the Garden of Eden, he was not to work for his livelihood but was to worship (see comment on Ge 2:15). So also in the Sabbath year, humanity was to share equally in all the good of God's provision (v.6). In the garden, God provided for the human race an eternal rest and time of worship, the Sabbath. The Sabbath year was a foretaste of that time of rest and worship. Here, as on many other occasions, the writer of the Pentateuch has envisioned Israel's possession of the "good land" promised to them as a return to Eden.

### 2. The Jubilee year (25:8–55)

Every seven Sabbath years, Israel was to proclaim a special Sabbath, a Jubilee year. The basic idea of this year was that the fiftieth year was set apart as a holy year in which total restoration of land, property, and debts was made. If the nation was obedient to God's laws, he would bless them and increase the produce of their land so that they would have enough to live on for three years—through not only the Sabbath year (the forty-ninth year), but also the Jubilee year (the fiftieth) and from planting to harvest the next year (see v.21).

On the first day of the Jubilee year, a ram's horn was to be sounded and the Jubilee year proclaimed (v.9). The term "Jubilee" is a wordplay on the Hebrew term for "ram's horn" (*jobal*). All reckoning of the value of property and real estate was made relative to the time of the Jubilee year. The value was determined by how many years remained before the property would be released to its original owner.

In the Jubilee year, all property bought or sold would revert to its original owner. Thus the land could not be sold permanently (v.23). This restriction was because all the land belonged to God and the people of Israel were considered "tenants" on God's land.

There were two important exceptions to the Jubilee year provision. First, houses in walled cities could be sold permanently if the right of redemption had been forfeited by waiting one year (vv.29–31). Thus houses and property in the countryside and in unwalled cities were considered part of God's land and could not be sold permanently. The second exception had to do with the property of the Levites. Even in walled cities, if the city was a "Levitical town," i.e., a town set apart for the inheritance of the Levites (Nu 35:1–8), property had to be returned in the Jubilee year (25:32–34).

There were three primary concerns of the Jubilee year with respect to incurring debt (vv.35–55). (1) Israelites were to lend money without interest to fellow Israelites in need (vv.35–38). Such a provision would ensure that an Israelite would not lose his place among God's people. (2) A fellow Israelite could not be purchased as a slave. He could be

hired as a worker but would be released in the Jubilee year. Any slaves were to come from non-Israelite people (vv.39–46). (3) An Israelite could not be taken as a slave by a non-Israelite. He could be hired as a worker but was to be released in the Jubilee year (vv. 47–53).

### E. Final Conditions of the Covenant (26:1–46)

#### 1. Introduction (26:1–2)

The repetition of the term "covenant" here shows that what is intended is a summary of the conditions for the covenant reestablished after the incident of the golden calf. Thus, as has been the form throughout God's address to Israel on Mount Sinai, the statement of the conditions of the covenant is prefaced by a reminder of two central laws: the prohibition of idolatry (v.1) and the call to observe the Sabbath (v.2). It was through idolatry that Israel first broke the covenant at Sinai; the Sabbath was to be a sign of Israel's covenant relationship with God.

#### 2. General statement of the purpose of the covenant (26:3–13)

If Israel obeyed God's decrees and commands, they would live with great blessing in the Promised Land. The description of life in the land is reminiscent of God's original blessing in the Garden of Eden (see Ge 1:26, 28–29; 2:8; 3:8; 26:5–12).

#### 3. Warning of results of disobedience (26:14–39)

If Israel rejected God's decrees and commands they would experience divine punishment (vv.14–31), their land would be destroyed (v.32), and they would be sent into exile (vv.33–39).

#### 4. Hope for the future (26:40–45)

If Israel repented and humbled themselves, God would remember his covenant with Abraham, Isaac, and Jacob, and his promise of the land, and he would not break his covenant with them. At the time when Israel entered Egypt and was humbled under the hand of the king of Egypt, God remembered his covenant with Abraham and delivered them (Ex 2:24). Again in the future when Israel would humble themselves, God would remember his covenant and deliver his people.

### F. Vows and Tithes (27:1–34)

Just as the whole of the giving of the Law at Sinai began with Ten Commandments, so it now ends with a list of ten laws. The content of the ten laws deals with the process of payment of vows and tithes made to the Lord.

(1) *Persons dedicated to the Lord* (vv.1–8). The specific type of vow dealt with here is one that allowed for payment with a substitute. One gave his own worth in money to the Lord. This section does not relate to the vow so much as to the process of reckoning one's value in money.

(2) *Animals dedicated to the Lord* (vv.9–13). The concern in this law is with the status of an animal vowed in dedication to the Lord. Once an acceptable animal had been vowed, it could not be exchanged for a lesser animal. It was holy and remained so. If the animal became unclean and thus not acceptable for an offering, the priest was to set its value. It could then be reclaimed at one-fifth more value.

(3) *Houses dedicated to the Lord* (vv.14–15). This law describes the procedure for dedicating one's house to the Lord and then buying it back. When the house was vowed, the priest set its value and it could be bought back for one-fifth more money.

(4) *Inherited land dedicated to the Lord* (vv.16–21). When inherited land was dedicated by a vow, the value was set, based on the amount of produce of the land and the time remaining before the land would revert back to its owner in the Jubilee year. This land, once vowed, could be repurchased by the one who gave it as a vow. If the land was not redeemed, however, in the Jubilee year it would be deeded over to the priests.

(5) *Purchased land dedicated to the Lord* (vv.22–25). Land that one purchased could be dedicated to the Lord by a vow. Its value would be reckoned by the priest and paid by the one making the vow. In the Jubilee year the land would revert to the original owner.

(6) *Prohibition of dedication of firstborn* (vv.26–27). Since the firstborn animal was already dedicated to the Lord (Ex 13), it could not be given as a vow.

(7) *Procedure for total devotion to the Lord* (v.28). A heightened form of vow was called a devotion (*cherem*; see NIV note). In this vow the person or thing devoted was given without reservation to the Lord. Such a vow could not be reversed or substituted by a payment.

(8) *Procedure for total devotion of a person to the Lord* (v.29). This law represents a special instance of the previous total devotion. Under the law given at Mount Sinai, it was possible for one to commit an apostasy punishable by death (see Ex 22:20). Such a total devotion was irrevocable and could not be substituted by a payment.

(9) *Procedure for tithes from the produce of the land* (vv.30–31). The tithe could be repurchased for one-fifth more value.

(10) *Procedure for tithes from the livestock* (vv.32–33). A tenth of the livestock was given to the Lord. No provision was given for repurchasing this gift. The institution of the tithe was already established in Israel (cf. Ge 28:20–22; 14:20). In this passage the tithe is said to belong to the Lord. In Nu 18:8–32, the purpose and use of the tithe is explained. It was to be the means of support for the priests and the Levites at the sanctuary.

This book is briefly concluded with the statement that "these are the commands the LORD gave Moses on Mount Sinai for the Israelites" (v.34).

# Numbers

## Introduction

As is the case with the other books in the Pentateuch, Numbers is a section of the larger work. The English title "Numbers" is based on the "numbering," or census, of the people in the first chapters of the book.

The order of the material as it is arranged in the book is not strictly chronological. For example, 1:1 situates the events of the book on the first day of the second month of the second year after the Exodus. But 7:1 reverts back to the time of the setting up of the tabernacle, i.e., the first day of the first month of the second year (Ex 40:17). In 9:1–5 the time period of the material is that of the Passover celebration on the fourteenth day of the first month of the second year. Thus the arrangement of the book is as much topical as it is chronological.

Within the larger structure of the Pentateuch, however, there is a chronological order to most of the narrative. The events recorded fall into the time of the last days at Sinai and the period of Israel's sojourn in the desert. Within this larger time frame, the primary dividing point of the book is 14:45, the destruction and defeat of the disobedient Israelites in the hill country of the Amalekites. Thus there are two main divisions to the book, chs. 1–14 and chs. 15–36, each falling on either side of the account of Israel's failure to believe in God. In ch. 14 the people failed to trust in God; in ch. 20 Moses and Aaron failed to trust God. In both cases, the failure to believe resulted in failure to receive God's blessing of the land.

The location of the events recorded in the early chapters is the Sinai Desert. The people were encamped before Mount Sinai, and the tabernacle had been set up. Moses had received the laws with the covenant; plans were now being laid to leave Sinai and return to the Promised Land.

# I. The Census and the Organization of the People (1:1–2:34)

After the tabernacle had been set up, a census was taken in each of the tribes to determine who would serve in the military. Much of the material in these early chapters is devoted to the details of the census and the arrangement of the tribes for battle. The author wants to give the reader a full and accurate picture of the scale of operations and necessary preparations for Israel's return to the land.

In some respects this material justifies the scope of the laws given in the Pentateuch. With such a large nation, many detailed regulations were necessary. Moreover, there is a noticeable contrast between the orderly movement of the tribes from Sinai, as is shown here, and the picture of the people "running wild" in the account of the golden calf (Ex 32:25). Thus the laws God gave to Israel at Sinai had a salutary effect on the people.

## A. The Census (1:1–54)

Moses and Aaron were instructed to count all men in the camp twenty years old and up who were able to serve in the army. Twelve men, one from each tribe, were appointed to help with the count (see 1:5–15). Moses gathered the people together and counted them. The total from each tribe is listed in vv.16–46, giving a total of 603,550.

The Levites, those of the tribe of Levi, including Moses and Aaron, were not included in the census. Their task was separate from the rest of the Israelites, and thus they conducted their own census in 3:15 and 4:34ff. They were to keep charge of the tabernacle and Israel's worship. The purpose of setting the Levites apart and arranging them around the tabernacle was so that "wrath will not fall on the Israelite community" (v.53).

## B. The Arrangement of the Tribal Camps (2:1–34)

The tribes were arranged in orderly fashion around the tabernacle. According to v.34, their arrangement in camp was also the same order in which they were to travel.

If the list in this chapter is compared with that of the first chapter of Numbers, it becomes evident that the arrangement of the tribes around the tabernacle served to highlight the importance and centrality of the tribe of Judah, which has already gained the ascendancy over the other tribes (cf. Ge 49:1–27). It was from this tribe that the royal son would be born who would bring redemption to God's people.

Moreover, in the Genesis narratives, much attention is devoted to the notion of "the east," a theme that also appears important in the arrangement of the tribes. After the Fall, Adam and Eve, and then Cain, were cast out of God's good land toward the east (Ge 3:24; 4:16). Furthermore, Babylon was built in the east (Ge 11:2) and Sodom was east of the Promised Land (Ge 13:11). Throughout these narratives the hope is developed that God's redemption would come from the east and that it would be a time of restoration of God's original blessing and gift of the land in Creation. God's garden had been planted for Adam "in the east" of Eden (Ge 2:8), and it was there that God intended to pour out his blessing on him. It was not without purpose, then, that the arrangement of the tribes around the tabernacle should reflect the same imagery of hope and redemption, for Judah (along with Issachar and Zebulun) was on the east. On the south were Reuben, Simeon, and Gad. In the middle was the Tent of Meeting and the tribe of Levi. On the west were Ephraim, Manasseh, and Benjamin. On the north were Dan, Asher, and Naphtali.

## II. The Levites (3:1–4:49)

The identity and duties of the tribe of Levi are covered in detail in these two chapters. The writer begins by recounting the events that led to the death of two of Aaron's four sons, Nadab and Abihu (see Lev 10). In a way similar to the replacement of Reuben (the firstborn) and Simeon by Judah and Levi in the family of Jacob, Aaron's firstborn were replaced by Eleazar and Ithamar. The priesthood had already been firmly rooted in the family of Aaron (Ex 29:9). Thus, henceforth, the priests who served at the tabernacle could only be from the families of Eleazar and Ithamar (3:10).

In addition to the sons of Aaron, the Lord appointed the rest of the tribe of Levi to help the priests in the service at the tabernacle (3:7–8). The sons of Levi are identified specifically as the descendants of Levi's three sons, Gershon, Kohath, and Merari. Moses and Aaron are also included in this group since they were of the family of Kohath (Ex 6:18–20). Eleazar was the chief leader of the Levites.

Three previous incidents in Israel's history led to God's selection of the Levites as his servants in the work of the tabernacle. (1) Levi and Simeon had been rejected from participation with the tribes of Israel because with their "weapons of violence" they killed men in anger (Ge 49:5–6; cf. 34:25). (2) Certain members of the family of Levi had rallied behind Moses and the Lord after the incident of the golden calf (Ex 32:26). On that occasion the Lord chose the tribe of Levi for himself (Ex 32:29). (3) God claimed for himself every Israelite firstborn who had been "passed over" in the Exodus (Ex 13:1–2, 11–13). This claim was apparently intended at the start to be the means of establishing the priesthood in Israel (see comments on Ex 13:1–2); every firstborn son was to be a priest. Because of the Levites' faithfulness at the time of the golden calf, however, God relinquished his right to all firstborn Israelite males and put in their place the tribe of Levi (Nu 3:11–13).

The substitution of the firstborn Israelite males by Levites was carried out by means of a census. First, a census of the Levites was taken. Its total was 22,000. Then, all firstborn males among the Israelites were listed by name. That list totaled 22,273; this amounts to 273 more firstborn males than there were Levites. This surplus of firstborn Israelites was then replaced by the payment of a redemption price—five shekels each (cf. Lev 27:6).

The duties of the Levites were as follows:

(1) The Gershonites (camped to the west of the tabernacle) were responsible for care of the tabernacle, its coverings, the curtain at the entrance to the Tent of Meeting, the curtains of the courtyard, the curtain at the entrance to the courtyard, and the ropes (3:21–26).

(2) The Kohathites (camped to the south of the tabernacle) were responsible for the care of the sanctuary. This included care of the ark, the table, the lampstand, the altars, the articles of the sanctuary, and the curtain (3:27–32).

(3) When the tabernacle was moved, the priests (sons of Aaron), under the guidance of Eleazar (4:16), were to go into the sanctuary to prepare it to be moved. The various holy articles were wrapped in cloth and skins and readied for carrying. When all had been prepared, the Kohathites were brought in to carry the various articles.

(4) The Merarites (camped to the north of the tabernacle) were responsible for the frames of the tabernacle, the crossbars, posts, bases, tent pegs, and ropes (3:33–37).

## III. Holiness Among the People (5:1–6:27)

The focus of the writer now turns from the priests and Levites and their holiness to that of the individual Israelites. They also were to be a part of the holy nation (Ex 19:5). By means of a series of regulations and selected narratives, the writer demonstrates the importance of the total commitment of all the people to the requirements of God's covenant.

### A. The Purity of the Camp (5:1–4)

In Lev 13–15 Moses had instructed the priests how to examine and identify diseases. When a skin disease was detected, the diseased person was required to live alone "outside the camp" and to cry out "Unclean!" (Lev 13:45–46). As the camp became progressively purer, we notice that these commands were being carried out. This theme will not continue long, however, for the people quickly turned from God's way and failed to continue to trust in God.

### B. Treachery Against Others and God (5:5–10)

Moses had given Israel the guilt offering as a means of making restitution for an offense made against another Israelite (Lev 5:14–6:7). The narrative here recalls that law in order to demonstrate the wrongfulness of acting treacherously against one's neighbor. In describing an offense of a man or woman against a member of the community, the narrative specifically calls the one committing such an offense as "unfaithful to the LORD." Furthermore, the writer has included a special case of this offense to show that the act of treachery was committed not only against one's neighbor but also against the Lord. The point is clear—wrongs committed among God's people were actually wrongs committed against God himself.

### C. The Law of Jealousy (5:11–31)

The case of the jealous husband is a curious law that raises many questions about the nature of social relationships in ancient Israel. There is, however, not enough information given in this passage to allow even a sketchy reconstruction of the details of this ritual. This particular case is included here because it gives another illustration of God's personal involvement in the restitution of the sin of the nation. Within God's covenant with Israel, there could be no hidden sin among God's people. Neither could there be any hidden suspicion of sin.

## D. The Nazirite (6:1–21)

Little is known today regarding the origin and practice of the Nazirite vow in ancient Israel. The instruction Moses received was intended to regulate the practice of the vow, not establish it. The writer of the Pentateuch included these regulations in order to show that God made provisions not just for the priest but for all God's people to commit themselves wholly to God. By implication, all of God's nation could be totally committed to holiness.

The Nazirite vow entailed abstention from three things for a specified length of time: drinking wine or fermented drink (vv.3–4), cutting one's hair (v.5), and contacting a dead body (vv.6–7). At the conclusion of the vow, certain offerings were required (vv.13–20). An important provision was made for the Nazirite who, because of an emergency situation, had broken the vow (vv.9–12). In other words, some things in life superseded the requirements of the vow. After the emergency had passed, there were provisions for completing the vow (vv.9ff.).

The Nazirite's abstention from wine and strong drink is part of a larger picture in the Pentateuch of the association of strong drink with neglect for God's law. The priests were expressly prohibited from drinking wine and strong drink when they entered the Tent of Meeting (Lev 10:8). Perhaps Nadab and Abihu were drunk when they offered "strange fire" before the Lord. That, at least, would be consistent with

the fact that elsewhere in the Pentateuch, wine is shown as the cause of neglect and folly that ultimately leads to a curse (see Ge 9:20–27; 19:32ff.; Nu 22:1–3; Dt 23:3; cf. also Hab 2:5; Pr 3:6; 31:4–5).

## E. The Priestly Blessing (6:22–27)

At the close of this section dealing with the holiness of the people, the writer has attached the priestly blessing. By placing this text here, the writer shows that a central task of the priests was to be a source of blessing for God's people. Conversely, the text shows that the people were to find their blessing only in the priesthood, not apart from it. The holiness and blessing of the people was dependent on their recognition of the divine sanction of the priesthood.

# IV. The Dedication of the Tabernacle (7:1–10:10)

## A. The Dedication of the Altar (7:1–89)

The purpose of this section is to show that as the people had been generous in giving to the construction of the tabernacle (Ex 35:4–29), now they likewise showed the same generosity in its dedication. The whole of the nation gave sacrificially to the work of God.

The order of the gifts is the same as the appointment of the tribal leaders in ch. 2. Judah leads the list, as is consistent with the centrality of this tribe in the perspective of the writer of the Pentateuch (see comments on 2:1–34).

At the end of this long description of the dedication offerings for the altar is a verse about the fulfilled promise of God. In Ex 25:22 the plan and purpose of the "atonement cover" had been given to Moses along with the promise that God would speak with Moses between the two cherubim. The writer has intentionally delayed any mention of the fulfillment of this promise until the completion of the dedication of the altar.

## B. The Lighting of the Golden Lampstand (8:1–4)

At the construction of the golden lampstand (cf. Ex 25:32–40; 37:17–24), no mention was made of its lighting. The writer has waited until now to tell us that, as part of the dedication of the tabernacle, the lamps were lit.

## C. The Dedication of the Levites (8:5–26)

In chs. 3–4 the Levites were set apart to help the priests in the work of the tabernacle. However, they had not yet been consecrated for this work. Thus the writer includes here an account of their dedication as a part of the overall description of the dedication of the tabernacle. What is particularly striking about that dedication is the role that the whole congregation plays in the process. Unlike the consecration of the priests, in which the people merely looked on (Lev 8:3–4), the people play a central role by laying their hands on the Levites during their consecration (v.10).

The purpose of the narrative is to show that God first instructed Moses on how the Levites were to be consecrated (vv.5–19) and subsequently that those instructions were faithfully carried out (8:20–26).

## D. The Passover (9:1–14)

The Passover was celebrated on the fourteenth day of the first month of the second year as commanded by Moses (Ex 12). According to this passage, however, an unanticipated problem arose. Some men were unable to partake of the celebration because they were unclean. The purpose of this narrative is to show the reader how God's laws were carried out among the people. The response of Moses to this new situation demonstrates the way many of the laws in ancient Israel were carried out. When the Israelites realized a need for a further ruling, they took their request to Moses, and he then went before

the Lord. As it turned out in this case, God's answer conformed to the people's request. A second celebration was allowed for those who were unable to participate in the first Passover because they were ceremonially unclean. God's laws were not arbitrary and unreasonable. The Israelites themselves even played a part in their formulation.

## E. God's Leading in the Wilderness (9:15–23)

This section repeats Ex 40:34–38. As God led the Israelites to Sinai by the pillar of cloud by day and fire by night (Ex 13:21–22), so now he has begun to lead them into the Promised Land. The writer was intent on showing that at this point in their walk with the Lord, Israel was obedient and followed the Lord's guidance. Seven times in this brief narrative it is said that they obeyed "the LORD's command" and thus traveled when the cloud lifted from the tabernacle and moved (9:18, 20, 23; cf. Ex 17:1).

## F. The Departure From Sinai (10:11–12:16)

### 1. The silver trumpets (10:1–10)

As the people prepared to leave Sinai and travel to the Promised Land, a series of bugle calls was sounded for the sons of Aaron to help lead the people on their march through the desert. As the people followed the cloud that led them through the wilderness, the blasts of the bugle kept the order in their ranks. The tribe of Judah moved out at the first blast. The rest of the tribes followed in order at each successive call of the bugle.

### 2. Departure from Sinai (10:11–36)

The impression this narrative gives is that of an orderly and obedient departure from Sinai, a far cry from the scene that Moses saw when he first returned from the mountain and found the nation celebrating before the golden calf by "running wild" (Ex 32:25). After the golden calf, the Mosaic Law was able to bring order and obedience to the nation. The Law here seemed to be having its desired effect. As the narrative continues to unfold, however, it becomes apparent that the Law had not resulted in any fundamental change in the ways of the people. What lay ahead was a progressively worsening series of failures—failure both of the people and of their leaders. Something more than the Law was needed if the people were to follow God's will.

Moses asked his father-in-law (Hobab or Jethro) to remain with Israel because, being a native of the region, he knew the desert well and could help find suitable campsites (v.29); but he does not appear to have acceded to Moses' request. The Kohathites carried the ark ahead of the people "a journey of three days" (10:33), and the people followed as God (Dt 1:32–33) led them through the desert by means of the cloud (Nu 9:15–23). The three days' journey recalls the three days' journey requested by the Israelites while still in Egypt (Ex 3:18), the three days' journey from the Red Sea (Ex 15:22), and the three days' journey of Abraham to Moriah (Ge 22:4). The descendants of Moses' father-in-law later joined with Judah in taking possession of part of the land (Jdg 1:16).

### 3. Fire from the Lord (11:1–3)

In Ex 4:18, when Moses left both Sinai and his father-in-law to return to his people, he was mysteriously met by the Lord who, because Moses had not circumcised his son, sought to kill him (Ex 4:24–26). His wife, Zipporah, intervened, and the Lord quickly relented. In a curious repetition of this event, as Israel now left Sinai and again parted company with Moses' father-in-law, the Lord sent fire from above to destroy the outskirts of the camp. In this case Moses interceded and the Lord relented. Such incidents represent a turning point in the flow of events. They cast a foreboding mood over the course

of events about to be depicted. They show that all is not well, and hence they stir up an anticipation that something worse is yet to happen.

It is significant, then, that at the beginning of each of those large narrative segments of the Pentateuch that deal with Israel's departure to the Promised Land, they come face to face with God and the threat of his sudden wrath (cf. also Ge 32:22–32). In each case God threatens to put an immediate end to their venture, but also in each case God's action is averted and they are allowed to go on their way, so much the wiser if not wearier for their encounter.

### 4. Manna and the Spirit of God (11:4–35)

This section incorporates several distinct topics. It begins with the people's complaint about manna in the desert and their yearning to return to Egypt, where they imagine they could enjoy a variety of good foods in abundance (vv.4–9). The narrative then turns to Moses' discourse with God regarding the complaint of the people and God's response in promising to send his Spirit upon the select seventy elders (vv.10–17). In the following narrative, God adds to his promise to care for Israel the further word that the people's desire for the food of Egypt would not only be fulfilled but would be fulfilled to such an extent that it would actually have the effect of cursing them (vv.18–20); Moses is amazed (vv.21–23). Then comes the report of God's sending his Spirit upon the seventy elders (vv.24–30). At the close of the passage, God sends the people food in the form of quail, but as they are gathering the quail, this blessing suddenly becomes a kind of ironic punishment for those who had complained (vv.31–34).

What was the writer intending to teach in weaving the various aspects of these events together into one continuous account? Its central purpose appears to be to show the failure of

Moses' office as mediator for the people. The kind of leadership exhibited by Moses is placed alongside the role of the Spirit of God. The ideal leadership of God's people is shown in the example of the seventy elders. What is especially important to note is that this lesson comes from the lips of Moses himself. It is Moses who tells God, "I cannot carry all these people by myself; the burden is too heavy for me" (v.14), and it is God who responds by sending his Spirit on the seventy elders. Curiously enough, when Joshua complained that two men who were not a part of the selected group of seventy had also received the Spirit, Moses replied, "I wish that all the LORD's people were prophets and that the LORD would put his Spirit on them!" (v.29). In other words, Moses longed for a much different type of community than the one formed under the Law at Sinai. He longed for a community led not by a man like himself but a community mediated by God's Spirit.

The view expressed by Moses is precisely that of the later Israelite prophets in their description of the new covenant. Jeremiah, for example, looked forward to a time when the whole nation would have the Law written not on tablets of stone but on the hearts of the people, "from the least to the greatest" (Jer 31:31ff.). Joel and Ezekiel wrote in their visions of the fulfillment of Moses' ideal in the "last days" when God would pour out his spirit on "all flesh" (Joel 2:28) and put his Spirit in human hearts (Eze 36:22ff.). Then, at last, according to these prophets, God's people would walk in his ways and keep his commandments (Eze 11:20). The same view is developed further by Moses himself in Dt 30:6ff.

Thus, within the Pentateuch itself there seems to be a changing view of the role of Moses and the leadership he represents. Its shortcomings were becoming obvious and the failure of the people increasingly transparent. Consequently, as the narrative continues to unfold, a different type of rule, more akin to the kind of leadership seen in the Spirit-controlled office of the prophet, begins to emerge.

In light of what we have just said, however, it is important to note that in the next chapter (12:1–16) the issue of Moses' leadership is directly raised and contrasted with the kind of leadership provided by priests and prophets. Also in ch. 16 the question of Moses' leadership is still an issue to the writer of the Pentateuch.

## 5. Miriam and Aaron oppose Moses (12:1–16)

The narrative of Miriam and Aaron's opposition to the leadership of Moses is brief and leaves many details unexplained. Its meaning, however, is clear from its relation to the previous chapter. There Moses himself insinuated the superiority of this new form of leadership in saying, "Would that all the LORD's people were prophets" (11:29). In this way, the narrative manages to raise important questions about the role of a leader like Moses. Does this mean that Moses' leadership was, in fact, no better in God's eyes than that of other prophets like Miriam (see Ex 15:20)? Was Moses' role as leader not superior to that of the high priest, Aaron? The purpose of this chapter was to vindicate Moses' divinely given leadership and to brush aside any further suggestion that the type of leadership epitomized in Moses was no longer valid.

This vindication of Moses is the same as that given the people at the beginning of his leadership. Just as here the sign of Moses' leadership was Miriam's leprosy, so one of the first signs given to vindicate God's election of Moses as leader of his people was the sign of leprosy (Ex 4:6). In the earlier narratives dealing with the work of Moses, it was Moses himself who doubted his calling and who consequently became a leper. Here it is Miriam who doubted and thus became a leper. We should also note that the other sign given to vindicate the role of Moses in the earlier narrative was the serpent that came from Moses' staff (Ex 4:3). So also here, when Moses' authority is further questioned by the people at the end of their time in the desert (Nu 21:5), God responds by sending serpents against them (21:6ff.).

As the words of God to Aaron and Miriam show, God did speak to prophets, like Miriam, but not in the same way as he spoke to Moses. Moses the mediator was not a mere prophet, he was God's servant. God spoke to him not in visions and dreams, but "face to face" (vv.6–8).

Miriam was "confined outside the camp" for seven days, as was required of one with an infectious skin disease (Lev 13:4; Nu 5:2–4). Note that in the narrative portrayal of this incident we see that Moses waited for Miriam "from afar," as she once waited for him "from afar" in the bulrushes (Ex 2:4).

## VI. The Defeat of the First Generation (13:1–14:45)

This rather large section of narrative introduces the theme of the faithfulness of God in keeping the covenant and the unfaithfulness of human beings in trusting him. This is particularly notable in the account of sending the spies (chs. 13–14). The same theme is reintroduced in the account of Moses giving water to the people from the rock (20:1–13).

Following the account of the people's failure to believe in God in chs. 13–14, the writer has attached a further large set of laws dealing with sacrifice and the priesthood (15:1–19:22). Thus, as has been the case throughout the earlier parts of the Pentateuch (cf. Ex 32), after an account of Israel's unbelief, more laws are added as a response to

the failure of the people to trust God. Thus the structure and strategy of the narrative supports the apostle Paul's assessment of the giving of the law in Gal 3:19–23, that it "was added because of transgressions."

### A. Spying Out the Land of Canaan (13:1–25)

Moses was instructed by God to send spies from each of the tribes into the land. Moses sent twelve spies into the Negev and hill country to "see what the land is like and whether the people who live in it are strong or weak, few or many" (v.18). The spies spent forty days in the land and returned to Moses at Kadesh with fruit they had gathered from the land (cf. also Dt 1:22–23).

### B. The Report of the Spies (13:26–33)

The twelve spies reported that the land was filled with "milk and honey" and that there were strong fortified cities occupied by the descendants of Anak (v.28). However, they also gave a "bad report" saying, "We cannot attack those people; they are stronger than we are" (v.31). Only Joshua and Caleb were in favor of trusting God for his help in taking the land (v.30; 14:6–7).

### C. The Unbelief of the People (14:1–12)

In the midst of the crying of the people, the Lord spoke to Moses in the Tent of Meeting, "How long will this people treat me with contempt? How long will they refuse to believe in me, in spite of all the miraculous signs I have performed among them?" (vv.11–12). It is essential to note that the Lord calls their fearful response to the spies' report an act of "unbelief." In other words, the people failed to inherit the Promised Land and died in the desert without inheriting the blessing not so much for a specific act of disobedience or fear of the battles that lay ahead, but rather for the simple fact of their unbelief. They failed to trust in God. God was prepared to judge them with pestilence and to dispossess them severely for their lack of faith.

### D. Moses' Intercession (14:13–19)

But as has happened before in the narratives of the Pentateuch (e.g., Ex 32:11ff.), Moses interceded for Israel and replied to the Lord that his rejection of this people in the wilderness would have a lasting effect on the nations around them who had heard of what he had done in Egypt.

### E. The People Are Judged (14:20–38)

Israel had broken their covenant with the Lord, and he could have rightfully cast them off. But the Lord was gracious to them, "slow to anger, abounding in love" (v.18; cf. Ex 33:9). He heard Moses' plea on behalf of the people. Though Israel proved unfaithful, God remained faithful and gracious.

The end result of Israel's lack of faith is nevertheless severe. With the exception of Joshua and Caleb, that whole generation who did not believe died in the desert (v.29), that is, they were to dwell in the wilderness forty years until that generation had died (v.33).

### F. The Presumption of the People (14:39–45)

At the close of the narrative the writer recounts the aborted attempt of the people to take the land without the help of the Lord. This narrative shows the reverse side of their unbelief. Not only do they fail to trust God to give them the land, but in desperation they attempt to take it on their own. Their unbelief is manifest by their attempts to gain God's blessings apart from him.

In v.25 the Lord told Moses to "turn back tomorrow and set out toward the desert along the route to the Red Sea." When Moses told this to the people (v.39), they refused to obey the Lord, and "early the next morning they went up toward the high hill country" to take the land of Canaan (v.40)—the opposite direction of where God had told them to go. Thus they disobeyed the Lord's command (v.41) and were defeated by the Amalekites and Canaanites (cf. also Dt 1:34–46). They then dwelt in Kadesh many days (Dt 1:46), likely for the next thirty-eight years.

## VII. Laws Given During and at the Close of the Thrity-Eight Years (15:1–19:22)

### A. Seven Laws (15:1–36)

The section consists of a selected list of seven laws, the last of which is the penalty for a "defiant sin." The list is then followed by a narrative example of a "defiant sin," i.e., the willful disregard of God's Sabbath among the people. After this example of the neglect of God's law, the law regarding the wearing of tassels was placed because the "tassels" were, in fact, to serve as reminders to keep the law.

The laws here regarding grain offerings are not those of Lev 2, which were offered separately as a gift, but are here introduced for the first time and are to be offered along with either a burnt offering or fellowship offering.

In the case of the man caught gathering wood on the Sabbath (vv.32–36), it should be noted that Moses did not immediately put the offender to death, as stipulated in Ex 31:14 and 35:2. Rather, he put him away "because it was unclear what was to be done to him" (Nu 15:34). Since the punishment of death for "doing work" (Ex 35:2) or "profaning the Sabbath" (Ex 31:14) had already been given to Moses by this time, his uncertainty must have been either regarding the exact type of death penalty or whether gathering wood constituted "work." The Lord's answer (cf. Lev 24:10–23; Nu 9:7–8; 27:1–11) speaks to both questions, "The man must die. The whole assembly must stone him outside the camp" (v.35).

### B. Tassels (15:37–41)

The account of the command to make tassels for their garments demonstrates the underlying purpose of many of the laws given to Israel. It was by means of these tassels that the Israelites were to be reminded of the necessity of trusting God and obeying his commands. In many other ways as well, God provided reminders for his people. The very minutiae of the laws of God were a continual reminder that in every area of life God's people were to trust him and obey his word. God is concerned about the smallest details of a person's life.

### C. Rebellion and Reaffirmation (16:1–18:32)

Several narratives now follow that have in view specifically the role of Aaron and the priests. Also central to each one is the idea of a growing rebellion and dissatisfaction among the people of the covenant nation. As the laws increase and the constraints grow, the people seem less willing or less capable of following them. At this point we see that the whole of the order of the priesthood is thrown open to direct confrontation. What at first seemed so final and authoritative, i.e., God's word revealed at Sinai, was now being challenged on every side.

In the first narrative, 16:1–40, the Levites instigated an organized opposition to the authority of Aaron and the priests. Their contention was that in claiming the unique right and responsibility to represent the people before God, Moses and Aaron had "gone too far." (v.3). They based their argument against these two on the premise that "the whole community is holy, every one of them, and the LORD is with them" (v.3). Thus they asked, "Why then do you set yourselves above the LORD's assembly?" It was now no longer the "rabble" (11:4), i.e., the "mixed multitude," that stood behind

Israel's disobedience. It was now people from the tribe of Levi itself—the very tribe set apart and made ceremonially clean in 8:5–26.

This was probably not the first time, and certainly not the last, that God's servants have not been content with the ministries given them and have presumptuously sought for more status and power. God had established the house of Aaron, his sons, and their descendants as the priests among his people. They alone could officiate in the tabernacle (3:10). This was given as the expression of God's will at Sinai. The Levites had been set apart for work in the tabernacle (see chs. 3–4). Hence for them to try to obtain the rights and duties of the priesthood was a direct affront to God's will as revealed already in Scripture. That Moses was fully aware of this fact is shown by his response to the Levites: "You . . . have gone too far!" (16:8).

God told Aaron to gather the bronze censers of the rebellious Levites and overlay the altar with their metal. This was to remind all Israel "that no one except a descendant of Aaron should come to burn incense before the LORD, or he would become like Korah and his followers" (v.40).

To show that the rebellion of the Levites was not an isolated act but represented the mood of the whole community, the writer places immediately after this narrative an account of the opposition of the "whole Israelite community" (vv.41–50). This incident shows that rather than having felt contrition and repentance, the people grumbled at the Lord's punishment of the rebellious Levites. Their response is portrayed here in a way similar to Cain's anger when he perceived that his offering was not acceptable to God (Ge 4:5). From the writer's point of view, their actions spoke for their inner thoughts and feelings, just as Cain's killing of Abel revealed what was in his heart.

Ironically, as the narrative concludes, it is the intercession of Aaron and his priesthood that ultimately saves the lives of the people in the ensuing plague. Aaron "stood between the living and the dead, and the plague stopped" (v.48), and he "made atonement for them" (v.47).

As a continual reminder of the special office of priest and the importance of the house of Aaron, God gave Israel another "sign"—Aaron's budding staff (17:10). The point of this sign was to remind the people of the death of those who had tried to usurp the place of Aaron and his family and to go near to God in the tabernacle on their own. The Israelites got the message, for when they saw Aaron's budding staff, they said to Moses, "We will die! We are lost, we are all lost! Anyone who even comes near the tabernacle of the LORD will die" (vv.12–13). Their lament ends with a question, "Are we all going to die?" (v.13b).

This response of the people is much the same as those who stood at the foot of Mount Sinai when God made his presence known in a great display of fire and earthquakes (Ex 20:19). On that occasion, the people were afraid to go near to God, and Moses was appointed as a mediator for the people. Here, the people's fear of going near to God leads to a reaffirmation of the priesthood of Aaron and his sons in the immediately following narrative. The main difference in this narrative lies in the fact that it is not Moses but Aaron who now steps into the limelight as priest of God's people.

Much of the material covered in ch. 18, dealing with the roles of and provisions for the priests and the Levites, has already been given in chs. 2–3 and Lev 6. What is unique in the repetition of the material here is the fact that Moses is not mentioned in the instructions to the priests. Whereas earlier the Lord had spoken about the priests' duties to Moses as well as Aaron, here he speaks only to Aaron and his sons. Moses is not again addressed until 18:25.

What is to be made of the writer's exclusion of Moses in these priestly matters? The answer perhaps lies in the author's desire to tell us something about the role of Moses as leader of God's people. His role is not limited to the work of a priest, which Aaron for the most part assumes. Moses' role was becoming more distinct from the office of priest. His role as mediator of the covenant, already well-established throughout these narratives, was not merely a priestly one. He also functioned in the role of prophet and king, two themes that will be developed further in Dt 18:15; 33:5. Hence as the picture of Moses develops within the Pentateuch, it more closely resembles the future messianic ruler anticipated already in the Pentateuch as a prophet, a priest, and a king.

After a restatement of the distinct roles of the priests and Levites (18:1–7), there follows the provisions for the priests (vv.8–20) and the Levites (vv.21–32). The Levites were to be supported by the payment of a tithe (v.21). They in turn were to support the priests by paying a tithe of what was given to them (v.28). The responsibility of giving a tithe, a tenth of one's produce, had already been commanded for all the people in Lev 27:30–33. At that point it was said only that the tithe belonged to the Lord. This passage adds considerably to the purpose of the tithe; it is here commanded to be given to the Levites for their work at the tabernacle.

## D. Water of Cleansing (19:1–22)

At first sight there appears to be little connection between the material in ch. 18 and ch. 19, which deals with the rite of the red heifer, except that both concern the rites and responsibilities of the priests. It should be noted, however, that ch. 18 concludes with a warning about the consequences of sin and defilement, i.e., death (18:32). The fact that sin, defilement, and death are the central themes of the ritual of the red heifer suggests these two chapters have been intentionally linked by the author by means of the statement of these two themes in 18:32.

In ch. 19 provision is given for the preparation of the "water of cleansing" (vv.1–10). Following this passage are two examples of the use of this water: purification from contact with a dead body (vv.11–13), and purification after being in the same tent with a dead body (vv.14–22). Later, in 31:19–23, the "water of cleansing" is prescribed for those who had been in battle and had thus come into contact with the dead. In each of these contexts the use of the "water of cleansing" was for purification from association or contact with the dead. Thus, though the present passage does not specify its purpose, it is generally assumed that the "water of cleansing" was a special provision of purification for anyone who had come into contact with the dead.

The procedure for preparation of the water called for a "red heifer" without any blemish. The cow was never to have been yoked. It was to be taken outside the camp and slaughtered, and some of its blood was sprinkled "toward the front of the Tent of Meeting" (v.4). Note that the cow was not to be slaughtered by the high priest, but by his son, Eleazar (v.3). Nor was the slaughter to be carried out at the altar in the tabernacle, as would have been usual for a sin offering. It was, rather, to be taken outside the camp and was there to be killed. This fact has led many to argue that the red heifer was not slain as a sin offering. However, it is clear from the text that it was a sin offering (see v.9). The writer of Hebrews (Heb 9:13) groups this offering together with the "goats and bulls" of the sin offering, suggesting that he too understood it to be such.

This chapter and the larger context of the Pentateuch give significant clues to the meaning of the red heifer ritual. It is important to note that the description of the ritual itself (vv.1–10) is further elaborated and explained by the two examples of its use in vv.11–22. The two central features of the ritual are the "ashes" (vv.9–10) of the heifer and the "water of cleansing" (v.9) over which they are sprinkled. When the ritual is applied to the specific situations in vv. 11–22, however, the "ashes" of the red heifer are not called "ashes" but rather the "dust" of the heifer (v.17; NIV renders it "ashes," thus covering over the distinct clues in the text). Moreover, the "water" is not called merely "water" but rather it is called the "living water" (19:17; NIV "fresh water"). Thus the "dust" of the heifer was sprinkled over the "living water." By means of these two modifications, the author has elevated this rather obscure ritual to a much higher thematic plane, so that the ritual now reflects the contrast between the "dust" of death and the water of "life."

The narrative is thereby brought into alignment with other central narratives in the Pentateuch. Specifically, the notion of the "dust" of death and the water of "life" provides a specific link to the narrative of the Fall in Ge 3—two key terms there (see Ge 3:19, 24). Thus the ashes of the heifer come to exemplify the "return to dust"—that which characterized humanity's fall in Ge 3. The writer's concern for the ritual of the red heifer, then, finds its roots in the earliest narratives of Genesis where death itself is viewed as the ultimate defilement of God's good creation. Just as in the beginning, so now among God's covenant people, death is the archenemy. Just as death was alien to God's good creation, so also it is alien to all that God had intended in the covenant. There was to be no lingering over the bodies of the dead for God's people.

One could not even remain in the same tent with the dead. The focus of the covenant was blessing, i.e., life and not the curse of sin and death.

# VIII. Travel From Kadesh to the Border of Canaan (20:1–21:35)

It was now the first month of their last year in the desert. The Israelites had been wandering in the desert of Paran (13:3; 14:32–33) forty years (see comments on 14:39–45; Dt 1:46), and they were now encamped at Kadesh (20:1). By 22:1, Israel will have reached their final destination in their travels in the Pentateuch, the "Plains of Moab" (cf. 33:49).

There is a brief notice of the death of Miriam in 20:1b. The writer thus wants us to know that she died while the Israelites were in Kadesh in the fortieth year of their stay in the desert. Her death serves as a reminder that she did not enter the Promised Land with the new generation. At the end of ch. 20 is a report of the death of her brother Aaron. Not even Aaron, the high priest, was allowed to enter into the Promised Land (see also 33:38). The central concern of this chapter, however, is the reminder that Moses himself was not allowed to enter the Promised Land. What had happened to the people because of their unbelief in ch. 14 was now being repeated in Israel's leadership—Miriam, Aaron, and Moses were to die in the wilderness, not able to enjoy the blessings of the Sinai covenant, the gift of God's good land.

## A. Water From the Rock (20:1–13)

Though we often focus on Moses' action in this narrative as a means of determining just how and why he was denied the blessing of entering the Promised Land, it is important to note that the writer focuses instead on Moses' heart. He has deliberately withheld the details of Moses' failure. Commentators have traditionally attempted to describe precisely just what it was that

Moses and Aaron did to warrant God's displeasure. Some suppose Moses' act of unbelief was manifest in his striking the rock rather than speaking to it as God had said. Others suggest that Moses erred in striking the rock "twice," thus showing his anger and impatience. Still others argue that Moses' failure lay either in his speaking harshly to the people ("you rebels") or his attempt to take credit for the miracle by saying, "Must we [and not God] bring you water out of this rock?"

The fundamental problem with each of these explanations is that they go beyond what is given in the text itself and thus miss an important feature. It should be noted that just at the moment in the narrative where the writer could have described the actual misdeed of Moses and Aaron, it is interrupted by a word from the Lord. When he spoke to Moses and Aaron, the Lord did not say what they had done that was wrong but rather, and simply, that they had acted in unbelief ("Because you did not trust [i.e., believe] in me to treat me as holy before the Israelites"; v.12). By means of these words, we are allowed to see the underlying problem for what it was: the failure of Moses and Aaron to believe in the Lord and thus to treat him as holy before the people.

The writer no doubt wants us to get the larger message about the incident recorded here. He was not so much interested that we know the details of this or that act of Moses and Aaron that led to God's punishing their unbelief. Indeed, it could reasonably be argued that Moses and Aaron had not done anything specifically wrong. In some respects the narrative is like that of Cain and Abel's offerings (Ge 4:1–7), where we read simply that God accepted Abel's offering but not Cain's. The writer does not dwell on the nature of either offering; rather, he goes right to the heart of the question—to the Lord's evaluation of the offerers rather than the offerings. So also in this narrative is a clear statement from God as to why Moses and Aaron could not enter the land: they did not believe. Just as the people had failed to believe God and trust in him in ch. 14, so also Moses and Aaron come up short in the area of faith.

## B. Edom Denies Israel Passage (20:14–21)

A coherent sequence in the events of 20:14–21:4 is difficult to obtain from this narrative (omitted in Dt 2:1ff.). It may be the case that they are not listed in chronological order. Though it is not of decisive moment in the interpretation of this passage, we will try to reconstruct this sequence of events.

There are five distinct events that must be related. (1) Israel sent messengers to Edom to request permission from the king to pass through their land (vv.14–18). (2) Israel as a whole came to the borders of Edom to make a second request to pass through Edom on the road, but this too was denied (vv.19–21). Israel then turned away, presumably en route to the Promised Land on an alternate route. (3) Israel left Kadesh and came to Mount Hor, where Aaron died (vv.22–29). (4) Israel fought with Arad and decimated their cities (21:1–3). (5) Israel left Mount Hor and went around Edom by the "way of the sea" on their way to the land (21:4).

When listed in this textual order, chronological questions arise. According to 20:14–21, Israel left Kadesh to come to Edom and then left Edom to go to the land. However, after this, in v.22a, it is recounted that Israel left Kadesh and traveled to Mount Hor. Thus, after they had already left Kadesh, they appear to be back in Kadesh again where they leave for Mount Hor (v.22b). The events of vv.23–29, Aaron's death, take place at Mount Hor. The time and place of their battle with Arad is not given in the text

(21:1–3) but appears to come before Israel left Mount Hor in 21:4. When they left Mount Hor, Israel traveled around Edom on the "way of the Red Sea" (21:4); this appears to be the same event as 20:21 where Israel left the border of Edom to travel to the land.

There are at least two plausible orders of events to reconcile them. According to one suggestion, the order is as follows: (1) While living in Kadesh, Moses sent messengers to Edom (20:14–18); (2) Israel departed from Kadesh (20:22a); (3) Israel arrived at Mount Hor (20:22b), where there was the battle with Arad (21:1–3); the children of Israel made a second request to Edom and were turned away at the border (20:19ff.); (4) Israel departed from Mount Hor to go around Edom by way of the sea (21:4; 20:21b).

The second suggestion gives the following order: (1) While living in Kadesh, Moses sent messengers to Edom (20:14–18). At that time, the children of Israel made a second request to Edom, still by means of messengers, who were turned away at the border of Edom (20:19ff; 20:21b); (2) Israel departed from Kadesh (20:22a); (3) Israel arrived at Mount Hor (20:22b), and the battle with Arad took place (21:1–3); (4) Israel departed from Mount Hor to go around Edom by way of the sea (21:4).

It is difficult to decide which of these two explanations is more probable. There is no reason why we should insist that the narratives must be arranged in strict chronological order. The author is concerned about establishing patterns in these narrated events, and that fact sometimes causes him to link events out of their chronological order.

As noted above, Israel's failure to believe in ch. 14 is repeated in the story of Moses' unbelief (20:1–13). The complaints of the people (14:1–4; 20:2–5) lead the Lord to conclude that both Israel (14:11) and Moses (20:12) are lacking in faith. Moreover, both narratives are followed by an account of Israel's attempt to gain immediate entrance into the Promised Land—Israel's defeat by the Amalekites (14:40–45) and Edom's refusal to let Israel pass through their land (20:14–21). Thus the author shows the similarities between Israel's failure of faith and that of Moses. Both failed to believe God and hence could not go into the land.

## C. The Death of Aaron (20:22–29)

Surprisingly little is written of the death of Aaron. His death foreshadowed the death of Moses, perhaps because they were both guilty of the same sin, failure to trust the Lord (20:12), although here their sin is called "rebellion" (20:24; cf. Dt 32:48–50). Just as Moses would be commanded by the Lord to go to the top of a mountain and die (27:12; Dt 32:48–50; 34:5), so here Aaron was told to go up to Mount Hor and die. Just before the report of his death, however, there is a brief account of the investiture of the new high priest, Eleazar, the son of Aaron. In the same way, just before the death of Moses, Joshua was installed as the new leader to take his place (Nu 27:18ff.; Dt 34:9). These two new leaders, Joshua and Eleazar, were to take the place of those older leaders who were not permitted to enter into the Promised Land.

The priesthood of Eleazar and his family was to have a long succession throughout the remainder of Israelite history in the Bible. The descendants of Eleazar, i.e., Zadok and his sons (the Zadokites, 1Ch 24:3), were priests during the time of Solomon's kingdom, and they continued not only throughout the remainder of the biblical period but also beyond that to the time of the Maccabees.

During the time of the judges, however, the office of priesthood was occupied by the house of Eli (1Sa 1:1–4:22). There is no explanation when or how the priesthood was taken from the house of Eleazar and given to Eli's house. In 1 Samuel it is clear that Israel suffered greatly during this time; hence we may conclude the writer did not approve of that replacement. The narrative stresses that the priests, Eli's sons Hophni and Phinehas, abused their office (1Sa 2:12–17). During that time, God had few dealings with Israel (see 1Sa 3:1); an unnamed prophet proclaimed harsh words against Eli and his house and foretold the establishment of a more faithful line of priests (1Sa 2:27–36).

In the structure of the narratives in Numbers, a further pattern can be seen that anticipates and parallels the events of the establishment of the Davidic kingship in 1 Samuel. Shortly before David became king, the author records the reestablishment of the proper priesthood to the family of Eleazar. There is thus a concern to return to the themes and events of Nu 20–21. Furthermore, in the Balaam narratives that follow (chs. 22–24), the focus is on the coming king who would reign over Israel's enemies and bring about God's judgment on them for their treatment of Israel (cf. 24:9). The description of the coming king is remarkably similar to David. One of the last descriptions of this king was that he would bring an end to the Amalekites (24:20), who were Israel's "first" enemies (14:45) but who would "come to ruin at the last" (24:20). In 1 Samuel it was Saul's failure to carry out God's judgment against the Amalekites that marked his rejection as the true king (1Sa 15:1–26). Specifically, Saul spared Agag, the Amalekite king (1Sa 15:9), whereas in Balaam's prophecy the true king was to be exalted over Agag (Nu 24:7; cf. 1Sa 30; 2Sa 8:12).

These pentateuchal narratives, then, appear to foreshadow the time of the establishment of the Davidic kingship. It will become clear at the end of the Balaam oracles, however, that the time of the fulfillment of these prophecies looks far beyond David's own kingdom (see Nu 24:22–24) to the King who is yet to come.

## D. Arad Destroyed (21:1–3)

This narrative is shaped by its relationship to the events recorded in Ex 17. In Ex 17 the people murmured over lack of water, and Moses gave them water from the rock (vv.1–7). They were attacked by the Amalekites but went on to defeat them miraculously while Moses held up his hands (in prayer?). So also in the present narrative, after an account of Israel's murmuring and of gaining water from the rock (Nu 20:1–13), Israel was attacked but miraculously went on to defeat the Canaanites because of Israel's prayer (21:1–3).

The mention of Hormah at the conclusion of this story (v.3) provides a literary link with the earlier account of Israel's defeat at the hands of the Amalekites and Canaanites, "They beat them down all the way to Hormah" (14:45). Thus at the beginning of Israel's time in the desert, they are opposed by the Amalekites living in the land of Canaan (Ex 17), and at the end of their time there they are opposed again by the Canaanites (Nu 21). The parallels suggest an intentional identification of the Amalekites in the Exodus narratives and the Canaanites here. The structure of the narrative, thus, parallels Balaam's vision of the fate of the Amalekites in Nu 24:20. Amalek was the first nation to bring destruction upon Israel, but, as can be seen proleptically in the parallels inherent in the present narrative, in the end they too would be brought to destruction.

## E. The Bronze Serpent (21:4–9)

Here again the Pentateuch appears to follow a larger pattern by which events at the beginning of Israel's sojourn are repeated here at the close. When Moses first went before Israel to announce that God was about to deliver

them out of Egypt, he was given a sign to test and strengthen the people's faith. That sign was the snake that came from his staff (Ex 4:3, 30). Now, at the end of their sojourn in the desert, Israel again complained against God and Moses for bringing them out of Egypt. As in Ex 4, God gave Israel the same sign, a snake on a staff. The purpose of such parallels is to underscore the necessity of the people's response of faith in the sign. They must look to the sign in faith before they can be delivered (Ex 4:30–31; Nu 21:8). The NT writers were sensitive to these same themes. Jesus, for example, aptly applied the lesson of faith found in these narratives to the salvation brought about by his own death on the cross (Jn 3:14–15).

Some have thought it unusual that God would command Moses to make an image of a snake as a sign of Israel's faith since earlier on in the Pentateuch God had forbidden them to make a likeness "of anything in heaven above or on the earth beneath" (Ex 20:4). But the image commanded here in Nu 21 was not intended as an idol to be worshiped. We should note that at a later time in Israel's history, the people had begun to offer incense to this same image (2Ki 18:4); the bronze serpent was misunderstood by later generations as a venerable object of sorts. But God honored the object when it was put up before the people and they looked to it in faith. The bronze serpent is analogous to Gideon's gold ephod, which later generations worshiped (see Jdg 8:27).

## F. The Journey to Moab (21:10–20)

In this brief itinerary, the Israelites moved around Edom and into the territory of Moab. The writer has also included a selection from a book called the "Book of the Wars of the Lord." This book is not known apart from this one reference to it. The selection, though incomplete in its present excerpted form, was apparently given to verify that the Arnon River was the border of Moab. The land of Moab is the central focus of the next several chapters of Numbers.

## G. The Defeat of Sihon (21:21–32; cf. Dt 2:24–37)

Only the bare facts of the battle and its causes are noted here. Fortunately, the poetic sayings in the remainder of the narrative (e.g., vv.26ff.) include further details. These sayings focus on the previous military conquests of Sihon when he defeated Moab and captured their territory (v.26). By means of such historical notes, the writer justifies Israel's conquest of this area. They tell us that the land once occupied by Moab was at this time in the hands of the Amorites. According to God's instructions, the territory belonging to the Moabites was not to be disturbed by the conquering Israelites because they were the descendants of Lot (Dt 2:9). What now belonged to the Amorites, however, had been promised to Israel and was theirs for the taking.

These short notes provide the necessary introduction to the account of Balaam that follows (chs. 22–24). It was the Moabite king, Balak, who was to hire Balaam to curse Israel. God, however, was to overturn Balaam's curse so that it resulted in Israel's blessing. The case could perhaps have been made that Israel had unfairly taken Moab's land and thus Balak was justified in hiring Balaam. These notes, however, show that such was not the case.

## H. The Defeat of Og (21:33–35; Dt 3:1–11)

This brief narrative shows that what God had done for Israel in the past with their defeat of Sihon, he would continue to do with the rest of Israel's enemies (see 21:34). It provides an interpretive context for the events in the more detailed story that follows. We learn here that Israel's victories are from the hand of God. As ch. 21 shows, Israel was now a present threat to Moab. Chapter

22 reassures us that their king, Balak, was well aware of the threat (22:2–3), though his assessment of the cause of the threat is different from God's assessment. Balak then resorts to magic and incantations in his attempt to defeat God's people, but such means are futile against the plans of a sovereign God.

## IX. Balaam (22:1–24:25)

The Balaam narratives have long puzzled readers of the Bible. The primary enigma centers on Balaam himself. As a historical character, he fits quite well among other ancient Near Eastern religious men. As a biblical character, however, Balaam appears to be neither fish nor fowl. He was not an Israelite (22:5), yet he appeared to know God (22:8), and God spoke through him (24:2–4, 15–16). He practiced magic and incantations (24:1) and eventually led Israel into apostasy (31:16). In the end he was killed by the Israelites in their destruction of the Midianites (31:8).

In spite of the fact that we know so little about the man, the narratives dealing with Balaam play a strategic role in the overall message of the Pentateuch. Their placement at this point in the book is part of the writer's plan to develop a central theological thesis. The first planks of this thesis were laid down already in Ge 1, where the writer shows that at the center of God's purpose in creating the human race was his desire to bless them (see Ge 1:28). Even after the Fall, God let it be known that his plan for blessing humanity would not be thwarted by this act of disobedience, and he gave a promise that he would provide a means for restoring the blessing (see Ge 3:15).

God's concern for the human race continued. When he chose Abraham as the channel of the promised "seed" (Ge 12:1–3; cf. 3:15), his express purpose was to bless him and all the nations of the earth through this "seed." Abraham, like God's original intent for Adam in the beginning, was to become a great people and enjoy God's good land. When God's people were on the verge of entering into Egyptian bondage, God furthered his promise to Abraham by giving the patriarch Jacob a prophecy about one of his sons, Judah (Ge 49:8–12). Through the family of Judah, one would come who would be a king and restore God's blessing to Israel and all the nations. However, as God had forewarned Abraham (Ge 15:13–16), his people would first undergo a time of bondage and oppression. But after four generations, his "seed" would return to the land and again enjoy his blessing.

With this background in mind, we can now appreciate the plan of the writer of the Pentateuch and his concentration on the prophecies of Balaam. Underlying these narratives lies an interest in the promise God had made to Abraham, according to which those who bless his seed will be blessed and those who curse his seed will be cursed. Thus the narrative of Nu 22 opens with an account of Balak's dread of the great numbers of Israel. Balak, the king of Moab, had hired Balaam to curse the seed of Abraham, but as the story unfolds, God only permitted him to bless them. In spite of the nations' attempts to curse God's people, all that could ultimately happen is their blessing. Through Balaam the seed of Abraham is blessed and the seed of Moab is cursed (24:17).

The Balaam story, which lies at the close of Israel's sojourn in the wilderness, parallels many of the events and ideas of the story of the pharaoh at the beginning of Exodus. Both the pharaoh there and Balak here were kings of large and powerful nations that represented a major obstacle to Israel's entering the Promised Land. Israel was a threat to these nations only because God kept his promise to the fathers and had given them great increase in numbers. The pharaoh instigated plans to afflict Israel because he saw that they had become "much too numerous" (Ex 1:9), and his plan was to stop Israel from returning to their land (Ex 1:10)—i.e., to block the very blessing God had promised to Abraham (Ge 15:16). Like Pharaoh's plans, Balak's plans in the book of Numbers were also motivated by the fact that Israel had become "too numerous" (Nu 22:6; NIV, "too powerful"). Also like the pharaoh, Balak was intent on keeping the Israelites out of the land (Nu 22:6).

In the early narratives of Exodus, the pharaoh made three attempts to counteract the blessing and hence decrease the number of God's people. He put slave masters over the Israelites to oppress them (Ex 1:11–14); he commanded the Hebrew midwives to kill the male children (Ex 1:15–21); and he commanded that every male child be thrown into the Nile (Ex 1:22). Yet as the narrative unfolds, on each occasion God intervened, and the pharaoh's plan was turned into a blessing. Balak also made three attempts to thwart God's blessing for Israel (Nu 23:1–12, 13–26; 23:27–24:9), and each attempt was turned into a blessing (23:11–12, 25–26; 24:10–11). Just as after the third attempt of the pharaoh, the deliverer Moses was born, so after Balak's third attempt the author turns to the question of the birth of God's chosen Deliverer, the prophecy of the star that was to arise out of Jacob (Nu 24:12–25). Elsewhere in the Pentateuch Moses is cast as a figure of the coming King (Dt 33:5) and Prophet (Dt 18; 34; cf. also Hos 2:2).

Special messianic importance has been attached to the last oracles of Balaam (24:1–24). These are separated from the earlier ones by the introduction the author gives them (cf. the simple introduction to 23:7, 18 and the lengthy statements in 24:3, 15). Moreover, there are numerous allusions and parallels between the two sets of oracles. What is said about Israel's past in ch. 23, for example, is repeated in ch. 24, but here it describes the work of a future king (this is not always apparent in English translations). The writer views the reign of the future king in terms taken from God's great acts of salvation in the past. What God did for Israel in the past is seen as a type of what he will do for them in the future when he sends his promised king.

Not only do Balaam's final oracles allude to his own earlier ones, but also in speaking of the future king, Balaam alludes to, and in fact quotes, the earlier poetic sections in the Pentateuch. For example, in Nu 24:9 Balaam's reference to "lion" and "lioness" recalls similar references in Ge 49:9 (cf. also Nu 24:9 and Ge 12:3; 27:29; Nu 24:17b and Ge 3:15).

## X. The Establishment of the New Leadership in Israel: The Priests and the Prophets (25:1–27:23)

### A. The Failure of the Old Leaders: Moab Seduces Israel (25:1–18)

Though the introduction focuses on the daughters of Moab, the central narrative is about a Midianite woman, Cozbi, who leads the people away from the Lord (25:6, 14–15, 18). Moreover, in ch. 31, Midian is also held responsible for the actions of this chapter. According to 31:16, the whole of this incident was brought about by the counsel of Balaam.

Shittim (25:1) was located on the plains of Moab, the last campsite of the Israelites before entering into the land. Joshua sent the spies from here into Jericho (Jos 2:1).

As is often the case in the Bible, God's act of salvation is immediately followed by the apostasy of the people. In this case, "the men began to indulge in sexual immorality with Moabite women" (v.1); this led to their following after their gods. The similarities and contrasts between this narrative and the

book of Ruth suggests that both texts are dealing with similar ideas. The picture of Ruth, in fact, provides an excellent counter-example to that of the men of Israel in this episode. Ruth, a Moabitess, married an Israelite man and forsook her nation's gods to follow the Lord. For this she was given an inheritance in Israel. In this respect she is also like the daughters of Zelophehad in Nu 27:1–11, who also gained an inheritance among the men of Israel.

Amid this time of apostasy, the writer points to a specific incident that shows not only the horrible conditions among the Israelites but also the need for new forms of leadership. When Cozbi (v.15) was taken into the tent of an Israelite man before the eyes of Moses and the whole congregation, there was much distress but little action. Moses is remarkably ineffective in the face of a blatant transgression (v.6). The day was saved, however, by the decisive action of one from the next generation of priests, Phinehas, the grandson of Aaron. Through his zeal for the Lord, he stayed God's judgment, and the house of Phinehas was rewarded with a lasting "covenant of priesthood" (v.13).

### B. The Second Census (26:1–65)

This census took place in the plains of Moab (v.3), where the Israelites had camped just before the incident with Balak and Balaam (22:1). The author's purpose of going over the new census is stated in vv.64–65. None of the earlier generation had survived except for Joshua and Caleb, who were allowed to possess the land. Thus the text refers to the Lord's words of judgment in 14:22–24. What God had said there is shown to have been fulfilled. In other words, God's word is sure and certain. What he has promised, he will do. The writer is thus building a case about God: He is faithful both in judgment and salvation (cf. Ge 41:32).

In three places in the midst of this list of names and numbers (26:8–11, 19,

33) the writer includes a brief biographical fact. These comments have at least one feature in common—they deal with the continuance of a family line in spite of the death of the head of the family. (1) The mention of the incident of the rebellion of Dathan and Abiram (vv.8–11), for example, explains that the house of Korah did not die out when Korah and the others were destroyed; his "sons" survived. By reminding the reader of the large scale destruction of the house of Korah, this note also provides an explanation why the number of the men of Reuben was smaller in this census (cf. 1:21; Dt 33:6). (2) The mention that Er and Onan "died in the land of Canaan" (v.19) connects these two disobedient sons of Judah with the disobedient generation of Israelites who died in the wilderness (cf. v.65). It also explains that the house of Shelah survived and was reckoned in the census, even though there is no mention of his descendants in the earlier narratives (Ge 38). (3) The mention of Zelophehad (v.33) prepares the way for the account of Zelophehad's request for continuance of the rights of their father (27:1–11). Here, his house is already noted as continuing through his daughters after his death.

Instructions for the parceling out of the land by lot are given in vv.52–56.

## C. Zelophehad's Daughters (27:1–11)

In the previous chapter it was stated that the line of Korah did not die out (26:11), even though earlier in 16:32 the text said "all of Korah's men" had been swallowed by the earthquake. This raises the question: How could the line be preserved if there were no men to receive their father's name? The present narrative about the daughters of Zelophehad appears to raise this issue intentionally in order to speak precisely to the question. Here we are shown how it was possible to preserve a lineage in the absence of sons. According to the ruling in 27:8, the property rights and

family name were to go to the daughters if there were no sons in the family. If there were no daughters, the rights were to go to one of the brothers; and if no brothers, then the family rights were to go to the uncle or nearest of kin.

A close relationship between the situation of Zelophehad's daughters and the question of the survival of the line of Korah is further implied in the fact that the daughters themselves raise the example of Korah's death in the desert and compare their father's death with it. Behind the seemingly miscellaneous collection of narratives in this section of the Pentateuch, then, there is a conscious attempt to deal with the larger issue of the survival of the priestly line. Even in the midst of God's judgment, a remnant of the house of Korah is saved.

## D. Joshua Appointed Successor to Moses (27:12–23)

Earlier we drew attention to the similarities between the death of Moses and the death of Aaron as well as the connections between the installation of Eleazar as priest and the fall of the house of Eli in 1 Samuel (see comments on 20:22–29). Similar connections appear between the present narrative and future events. The portrayal of Moses passing his authority over to Joshua and Joshua's reception of the Spirit is noticeably similar to the transition of prophetic office from Elijah to Elisha in 2Ki 2:7–15. The writer of Kings seems to have intentionally worked certain of these themes into his narrative to draw out the comparison. For example, Elijah, like Moses at the Red Sea, divided the waters of the Jordan with his mantle (2Ki 2:8). After Elijah had been taken away and the Spirit that was on him had come upon Elisha, Elisha parted the same waters of the Jordan (2Ki 2:14). This follows the pattern of Moses and Joshua. After the glory of Moses had come upon Joshua, a man in whom the Spirit dwelt, he also went on to divide the waters of the Jordan as Moses had divided the Red Sea (see especially Jos 3:7).

In modeling the Elijah and Elisha narratives after the present narratives, the writer of Kings correctly followed their lead. The type of leadership characterized by Moses and Joshua is the same as that of Elijah and Elisha—a leadership guided by the Spirit of God. Later, in Dt 18:14ff., we see that the office of the prophet was patterned after God's work in Moses, "The LORD your God will raise up for you a prophet like me from among your own brothers. You must listen to him." Thus the succession of Moses and Joshua is cast as a succession of the prophetic office guided by the Spirit of God. It became a model for the succession of prophets at a later period. In light of the emphasis on the work of the prophetic Spirit in this section, it is appropriate that Moses refers to God in this passage as "the God of the spirits of all mankind" (v.16).

In v.21, the relationship between the two offices of priest and (prophetic) leader is described. The priest, Eleazar, was to enquire of the Lord by means of the Urim. The (prophetic) leader, Joshua, was to follow his advice.

## XI. Regular Celebrations (28:1–29:40)

The writer is aware that the instructions for the regular celebrations in Israel's worship calendar have thus far been mentioned at various points in the previous narratives but that there is still need of gathering these together into a summary statement and specifying the nature of their additional offerings. Thus what follows is a description of the regular offerings for each time of celebration. These offerings were to be given in addition to those required for each special feast.

The present list is drawn up primarily from the calendar of feasts in Lev 23. The effect of the present description is cumulative, i.e., there is a daily offering for each day of the year, a Sabbath offering for each Sabbath, an offering for the first day of each month, and offerings for each of the special feast days.

It may also be important that this list is given after the account of the death of the old generation and the conclusion of the new census. The religious duties are reiterated for the new generation who were now being called on to move into the Promised Land. Such a summary was needed. Though the Passover was celebrated at the time of the Exodus (Ex 12ff.) and the next year (Nu 9:1ff.), some, if not all, of the religious duties of the people were not kept during the years in the desert (see Jos 9:5–8).

### A. Daily Offerings (28:1–8)

These provisions, given in Ex 29:38–42, are repeated here for completeness, apparently because they had not been mentioned in Lev 23.

### B. Sabbath Offerings (28:9–10)

Observance of the Sabbath rest was grounded in creation when God himself "rested" from all his work (Ge 2:2–3). It was prescribed as part of the Decalogue in Ex 20:8–11 and was included as part of the regular celebrations in Lev 23:3. In Lev 23 no mention is made of the need to present specific offerings on this day; it is mentioned here for the first time (cf. Eze 46:1ff.).

### C. Monthly Offerings (28:11–15)

In the instructions for regular worship in Lev 23, setting apart the "first of the month" (the new moon) as a special day is not mentioned. In Nu 10:10, however, there is mention of the "first of the month" as a time set apart for celebration by the blowing of trumpets. Its inclusion here further shows that the earlier list in Leviticus is selective whereas the present list is intended to be comprehensive.

## D. Yearly Celebrations (28:16–29:40)

### 1. The Passover and Unleavened Bread (28:16–25)

The Passover as described in Lev 23:5–8 recounts that an offering of "fire" was to be presented to the Lord for each of the seven days of the Feast of Unleavened Bread. In the present passage, however, the nature of this "fire offering" is described (28:19–22). There was no need to list the Passover here since there are no specific offerings given for that day.

### 2. The Feast of Weeks (28:26–31; Dt 16:9–12)

Fifty days after the time of the "firstfruits" the Feast of Weeks was celebrated. In Lev 23:18, this feast already called for the offering of seven lambs, a bull, and two rams. Are the offerings listed here the same ones or are they additional offerings for the Feast of Weeks? As this passage is traditionally interpreted, the offerings described here (two bulls, a ram, and seven lambs) were to be given in addition to those noted in Lev 23.

### 3. The Feast of Trumpets (29:1–6)

The Feast of Trumpets, celebrated on the first day of the seventh month, is mentioned in Lev 23:23–25 as a time of special remembrance. The offerings for that day are listed here. (Shortly after the destruction of the Second Temple [A.D. 70], this feast was celebrated as Rosh Hashanah, the New Year's Day feast.)

### 4. The Day of Atonement (29:7–11)

Instructions for the celebration of the Day of Atonement on the tenth day of the seventh month are recorded in Lev 23:27–32; the "atonement" offerings are described in Lev 16. In the present chapter the writer lists only those offerings prescribed in addition to those of Lev 16. The Day of Atonement

was to have its own sin offering of a male goat (v.11).

### 5. The Feast of Tabernacles (29:12–38)

The Feast of Tabernacles is described in Lev 23:33–43. It was to be celebrated on the fifteenth day of the seventh month. In this passage it is called only "a festival," suggesting that it was a well-known and important yearly celebration. According to Lev 23:39 it was to mark the time of the "ingathering," or harvest, of crops and thus corresponds roughly to our Thanksgiving Day. The present chapter is devoted only to the special offerings for the eight days of its celebration. The sheer volume of the required offerings and sacrifices (thirteen bulls, two rams and fourteen lambs on the first day) suggests that this was considered the grandest of the early feast days. On each successive day of the feast, one less bull was offered.

## XII. Vows for Men and Women (30:1–16)

The arrangement and placement of this passage on vows at this point in the text is motivated by the mention of "vows" in 29:39. It focuses on the relationship between husbands and wives as well as fathers and daughters (see also Lev 27; Nu 6:1–21).

The section begins with a general statement of obligation in making vows: When a man made a vow, he was bound by it (v.2). It then asserts that a man was also responsible for vows made by women in his household. If he heard his daughter or his wife make a vow, a man could nullify the vow by speaking out. If he did not, however, the vow was left to stand. In the case of a widow or a divorced woman (i.e., where there was no father or husband), the word of the woman alone sufficed (v.9).

The assumed culpability of Adam in Ge 3 may stem from the principle behind this law. In Ge 3:6 Adam's wife makes a rash decision in his presence: "She took [from the tree] and ate it. She also gave some to her husband, who was with her, and he ate it." In light of Nu 30:1–16, Adam's silence in the narrative makes him culpable for his wife's action.

## XII. Battle With the Midianites (31:1–54)

The narrative now returns to the sin of the people at Baal Peor (ch. 25). There the Lord had instructed Moses to smite the Midianites for the cunning allurement of the Israelites by Cozbi, the daughter of a Midianite leader (25:6–15). Just as Phinehas was responsible for putting an end to the people's apostasy in ch. 25, so here he is called upon to carry out the revenge on the Midianites. In the ensuing battle, the 12,000 Israelite soldiers, under the command of Phinehas, killed "every man," including the five kings of Midian and Balaam, son of Beor.

By saving the women and children of Midian, the Israelite officers renewed the old threat of mixing with Canaanite women and thus forsaking the Lord. Hence they inadvertently return to the dangerous conditions of ch. 25. This time it is Moses, not Phinehas, who rises to the occasion and deals forcibly with the problem. His harsh solution is explained by a reference to the plague that struck 24,000 people during the previous apostasy with the Moabite and Midianite women (v.16b). The command that the army must ritually cleanse themselves after the battle is based on the instructions in 19:16–21. Such a command is also commensurate with the fact that their mission was one of carrying out the divine wrath upon the Midianites (cf. 25:16–17).

The "law that the Lord gave Moses," referred to by Eleazar in v.21, is not found elsewhere in the Pentateuch (but cf. ch. 19). This again suggests that the laws included in the Pentateuch are selective.

## XIV. The Transjordan Tribes (32:1–42)

This narrative provides a contrast between the earlier generation of Israelites who died in the desert and the new generation that was about to enter the land. The contrast comes as a result of Moses' misunderstanding the request for land by the tribes of Reuben and Gad. Moses at first interprets their request to remain on the far side of the Jordan as a source of "discouragement" to the people, just as the bad report of the spies had been in ch. 13. The willingness of these tribes to fight for the rest of the nation, however, shows that Moses was mistaken and that this generation was quite different than the one that had refused to enter the land.

The "half tribe" of Manasseh is not mentioned along with Reuben and Gad at the beginning of the narrative (they are mentioned for the first time in v.33). To clarify their also being allotted a portion of the area of the Transjordan, the writer concludes with an account of the conquests of the descendants of Manasseh in this region (vv.39–42).

The tribe of Manasseh was allotted Gilead (v.40), a parcel of land requested by Reuben and Gad (v.1). This implies that the initial request of Reuben and Gad included the allotment of Manasseh. Thus it appears that Gilead was given to both Reuben (v.1) and Manasseh (v.40). This difficulty is later explained: Half of Gilead went to the tribe of Reuben and half to Manasseh (Dt 3:3:12–13; cf. Jos 13:24–31). Apparently, the region of Gilead was not a specific location but a broad area of land in the central Transjordan.

## XV. Israel's Camps in the Desert (33:1–49)

The list of encampments in the desert begins with the Israelites' departure from Rameses on the fifteenth day of the first month and concludes with their encampment on the "plains of Moab" (see 22:1). Between these two are forty camps, perhaps reflecting the forty years spent in the desert. But the list is selective, since some sites recorded earlier are not included (e.g., Shur, Taberah, and Hormah, as well as sites mentioned in 21:11–13, 16–19).

Within the list of encampments are two short narratives that center on the work of Moses (vv.2–3) and Aaron (vv.38–39). In these two segments are found the only dates for Israel's journeys (vv.3, 38b), marking the beginning and end of the forty-year period in the desert. In both narratives is found the same comment that Moses and Aaron obeyed "the LORD's command." Thus one of the purposes of this list is a brief review of the work of these two great leaders. God used them and their obedience to lead the people in the desert for the forty years. That the positive side of their work is stressed can be seen from the fact that when Aaron's death is recorded here, there is no mention of the rebellion of Moses and Aaron, a theme stressed in other references to their deaths (cf. 20:24). In fact, in this passage, Aaron's death is portrayed as his last act of obedience, "At the LORD's command Aaron the priest went up Mount Hor, where he died" (v.38).

# XVI. Preparation for Possession of the Promised Land (33:50–36:13)

## A. The Division of the Land (33:50–34:29)

### 1. Instructions to drive out all the Canaanites (33:50–56)

The author is careful to point out here that Israel's possession of the land was an act of obedience to God's will. God was Lord of the land. He had created it "in the beginning" (Ge 1:1). He still owned it, and he gives it to whomever he pleases (cf. Jer 27:5). This passage shows that the Israelites were not

taking the land for their own gain but were acting as God's agents in punishing the idolatrous Canaanites. Thus they were to destroy all Canaanite idols and places of worship when they entered the land, and they were not to allow the Canaanites to remain among them. If Israel failed to obey God (which, in fact, proved to be the case), they too would become the objects of God's punishment. There is an ominous tone in the Lord's last words, "Then I will do to you what I plan to do to them" (v.56).

Joshua gave a similar warning to the nation of Israel after their initial success at taking the land (Jos 23:12), but already in his day God's command had not been carried out. For example, the Gibeonites deceived Israel into making a covenant with them (Jos 9:26). Later biblical writers looked back to the failure of Israel to carry out this command as a central cause of their apostasy (see Ps 106:34–39).

### 2. Description of the borders of the land (34:1–15)

Besides the obvious geographical markers, such as the Mediterranean Sea, many of the sites noted in this chapter are not identifiable today. A general outline of the area, however, can be obtained by following the natural boundaries of the land itself. These boundaries were never fully realized during Israel's subsequent history. The western boundaries of the Israelite nation, for example, never extended as far as the Mediterranean Sea. We should thus understand this list as a set of outside perimeters within which Israel was free to occupy territory.

The principal concern of the writer is not the exact identification of all these sites. His purpose, rather, is to show the work of God in allotting the land to his people. God is portrayed elsewhere in the Pentateuch as one who apportions the boundaries of all the nations (Ge 10; Dt 32:8), and here he is shown doing the same for his own people. The land was a gift from God, and Israel was to receive it with gratitude.

### 3. List of leaders responsible for dividing the land (34:16–29)

The first three names in this list are well known from the previous narratives—Joshua, Eleazar, and Caleb. The rest of the names are new. These men thus represent the new generation that was to take possession of the land. Each one is a tribal representative. The order of the tribes reflected in this list differs from that of the tribes in chs. 1 and 7, but follows somewhat the order of the allotment of the land in Jos 19. The tribes of Reuben and Gad are omitted since the focus is only on the region west of the Jordan.

### B. Cities for the Levites, Including Cities of Refuge (35:1–34)

A total of forty-eight cities were to be given to the tribe of Levi. Each lot was approximately 207 acres and consisted of a town and pasture. Six of these sites were to be cities of refuge. These instructions were carried out under Joshua's allotment of the land. In Jos 21 a list of these cities is given (see also 2Ch 31:15; Ezr 2:70). In the years before the Exile, Jeremiah, who was from a priestly family, lived in Anathoth, one of these levitical cities (see Jos 21:18).

After enumerating the provision for the cities of refuge, the writer inserts a complete description of the laws governing their use. The cities were to provide a shelter for anyone who committed a homicide. The natural assumption was that a close relative of a homicide victim would seek to avenge his death; thus provision was made to prevent this. Once the innocent "manslayer" had found a safe haven, a trial was to ensue. If it could be determined that he had intentionally slain the victim, it was to be ruled a capital offense and he was

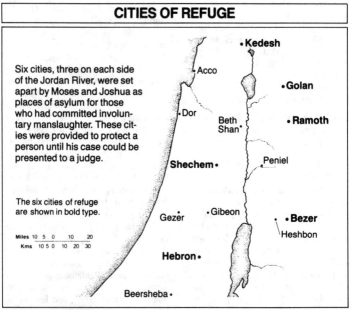

## CITIES OF REFUGE

Six cities, three on each side of the Jordan River, were set apart by Moses and Joshua as places of asylum for those who had committed involuntary manslaughter. These cities were provided to protect a person until his case could be presented to a judge.

The six cities of refuge are shown in bold type.

Miles 10 5 0 10 20
Kms 10 5 0 10 20 30

• **Kedesh**

Acco

• **Golan**

• Dor

Beth Shan•

• **Ramoth**

**Shechem** •

Peniel

Gezer •

• Gibeon

• **Bezer**

Heshbon

**Hebron** •

Beersheba •

to be put to death. If the death was ruled accidental, he was to remain under the protection of the city of refuge "until the death of the high priest" (v.25).

At the conclusion of the legislation, the underlying basis of this law is given: "Do not defile the land where you live and where I dwell, for I, the LORD, dwell among the Israelites" (v.34). In actual fact this principle was the basis of much of Israel's law. The uniqueness of biblical law lies in the fact that it represents the will of a personal God who graciously dwells among his own people.

## C. Inheritance of Zelophehad's Daughters (36:1–13)

The issue raised here stems from the decision regarding female inheritance in ch. 27. The problem and its solution are clear from the text. In order to prevent a tribe's loss of allotted inheritance in the event that it goes to a woman who then marries into another tribe, an additional stipulation was added to the ruling of ch. 27. The women of any tribe who have inherited property cannot marry into another tribe. Such a rule would ensure that a tribe's inheritance would not be taken into the inheritance of another tribe.

The reason this passage is placed here, rather than with ch. 27, is twofold. (1) It concerns the issue of tribal allotments, which is the focus of these last chapters of Numbers. (2) It is customary for large sections of the OT to conclude on a positive note. Thus the last words of this section (vv.10–12) provide an appropriate conclusion for the whole: "So Zelophehad's daughters did as the LORD commanded Moses . . . and their inheritance remained in their father's clan and tribe." These women provide a positive parting view of God's laws and the well-being of the people when they are carried out.

# Deuteronomy

## Introduction

The name "Deuteronomy" comes from the Greek rendering of Dt 17:18, where the phrase "copy of this law" was read as "a second Law" (*deuteronomion*). Though this was a misreading of the verse, the book continued to be called Deuteronomy because it gives the impression of being a "second Law." This is because much of the material it contains has already been recorded in the earlier sections of the Pentateuch (compare Ex 20 and Dt 5). On the other hand, one must not be left with the impression that the book merely repeats the earlier material in a redundant way. The key to understanding this repetition is Moses' statement of the purpose of the book in 1:5: "to expound this law." Deuteronomy is an explanation of the Law, not merely a repetition of it. It is like a commentary on the earlier passages of the Pentateuch. At the same time, it is not a separate book but an integral part of the Pentateuch.

## I. Introduction (1:1–5)

The opening section gives the setting of this part of the Pentateuch and its purpose. It is a collection of public addresses given by Moses to "all Israel." These addresses are the last words Moses spoke to the people as they were preparing to enter into the Promised Land, spoken across the Jordan, where the people were gathered after their forty years in the desert.

The purpose of the book is "to expound this law" (v.5). After the military struggles to gain the Transjordan, Moses devoted himself to making the law of God clear to the people as they entered the Promised Land (cf. 27:8; Hab 2:2). The book of Deuteronomy is the result of that work. It was to be their guide to the Law while living in the land.

The English term "law" is used to translate the Hebrew word *torah*. Unfortunately, the word "law" often carries the negative meaning of strict prohibition. *Torah*, however, is primarily positive. It is not so much prohibition as "instruction." Thus we should see here a reference to the divine instruction in God's will that Moses gives to the people as they prepare to enter into the land, telling them how they should live in God's land. Thus *torah* is to be learned, pondered, and applied to life. In light of this, Deuteronomy is not a book of laws, but rather a book that reveals and explains the will of God.

At the close of this book, when Moses presents this *torah* to the people, he represents it as God's way of restoring to them the divine view of "good and evil" that was lost in the Garden of Eden: "See, I set before you today life and prosperity [lit., good], death and destruction [lit., evil]. For I command you today to love the LORD your God, to walk in his ways, and to keep his commands, decrees and laws; then you will live and increase, and the LORD your God will bless you in the land you are entering to possess" (30:15–16). What humanity lost in the Garden of Eden is now restored to them in the *torah*, namely, God's plan for their good.

## II. Historical Review of the Earlier Narratives (1:6–3:29)

Moses begins his explanation of the Law with a historical review of God's gracious acts. The account begins with Israel's departure from Sinai (cf. Nu 10:11). It does not go back to the events of the Exodus or those at Mount Sinai, though in 1:30 Moses mentions the events in Egypt as something his listeners would recall. Moreover, the events of Mount Sinai are taken up in detail in chs. 9–10 and those of the Exodus in ch. 11. They are thus treated in reverse order of their occurrence in the earlier parts of the Pentateuch.

It should be pointed out here that when Moses reflects on the past, he does so with only few exceptions (see below) on the basis of the account of the past already written in the preceding narratives. Moses' view of the past is a "scriptural view." He does not recount events that were not recorded earlier. In other words, he does not assume a knowledge of Israel's history that is independent of the biblical account itself. His focus is on those events already present in the mind of the readers of the Pentateuch. This is important because it shows that his audience is not merely those Israelites whom Moses was addressing at a particular time on the plains of Moab. His audience is anyone who has read the earlier portions of the Pentateuch! Thus Moses' audience is always the contemporary reader.

An interesting confirmation of this feature can be found in those examples in Deuteronomy that do in fact refer to events not recorded earlier in the Pentateuch. For example, in 2:5, 9, 19, the writer mentions that the Lord had given certain sections of land to the descendants of Esau (2:5), the Moabites (2:9), and the Ammonites (2:19). Since none of these events is recorded earlier, the writer gives a brief historical account of the events leading up to God's giving these nations their inheritance (2:10–12, 20–23). In other words, when relevant historical information is missing, Moses supplies the reader with an account of those events.

The reason why Moses' speech focuses here only on the most recent events is that they concern the new generation that is to take possession of the Promised Land. In telling the earlier events, Moses wants to cast light on the situation of his own listeners (and that of the readers). They are the new generation. Their ancestors have all died in the desert. It is now their task to take up where those before them had failed. The past is not something that is done and over with; it is rather the beginning of the future. Throughout the narrative the stress is on the new beginnings of God's acts; Moses' call is for the people to "turn and get going" to take the Promised Land.

## A. Departure From Sinai (1:6–8; cf. Nu 10–20)

The speech begins by giving the basis of God's dealings with Israel, i.e., the promise of the land that God made to Abraham, Isaac, and Jacob. It should be noted that the boundaries of the land are those of the original promise in Ge 15:18–19.

## B. The Appointment of Leaders (1:9–18; cf. Ex 18; Nu 11)

Here Moses refers to Ex 18:13–26 (cf. Nu 11:16, 24), where Moses, on the advice of his father-in-law, appointed experienced officials to help in the administration of the nation. One of the central purposes of that narrative was to show that the need for additional leaders in Israel stemmed from God's faithfulness in blessing the nation (cf. Ge 12:2; 15:5; Ex 1:7; Nu 23:10). When Moses retells that event here, he does not follow the chronological order of Exodus (this event occurred prior to Moses' call to leave Mount Sinai in vv.6–8). Consequently, after this section about the appointment of leaders, the narrative returns to an account of Israel's leaving Mount Sinai (Horeb), thus picking up the events from 1:6ff.

## C. The Spies and Israel's Rebellion (1:19–46; cf. Nu 13–14)

The Israelites were en route to the "hill country of the Amorites" (v.19). They camped at the Desert of Paran or Kadesh (Nu 12:16; 13:26). Moses tells the events somewhat differently here than in Nu 13. Here the people ask to send spies in response to Moses' call to take the land, and Moses approves. In Nu 13, however, it is the Lord who commands that the spies be sent. This difference is usually explained by merging the two accounts in the following way (a scenario reflected already in the Samaritan Pentateuch, an early version of the Hebrew Bible): When challenged by Moses to take the land (Dt 1:20–21), the people, because of their lack of faith, requested that spies be sent first (v.22). Moses, who approved their plan (v.23a), took their request to the Lord (of which there is no mention in the text). The Lord also approved their plan and commanded Moses to appoint the spies (Nu 13:1ff.).

It is important to note how Moses heightens the foolishness of Israel's failure to trust God by picturing God's care for them as that of a father caring for his son (v.31). Often the lessons in Deuteronomy are brought home with vivid imagery, and sin is depicted not merely as evil but also as the height of folly. These narratives thus prepare the way for Moses' sermon at the close of this section (ch. 4), where he will argue that following the Law is "wisdom" (4:6). Hence he can depict sin as foolishness.

The failure of the people to take the land at the beginning of their sojourn in the desert is explained here the same way as it is mentioned in Nu 13–14: they "did not believe" (v.32; NIV, "did not trust"; cf. Nu 14:11). This is one of the few times in the Pentateuch when the reader is given an inside look at Israel's actions. In v.37 Moses added a parenthetical reference to his own failure to trust God, even though it happened much later (Nu 20).

In v.39 Moses refers first to the people's fear that their "children who do not yet know good from bad" would be taken as spoils of war, and then he refers to God's promise that they would see the Promised Land (Nu 14:31). His reason for stressing that part of the previous narratives lies in the fact that now, forty years later, as they stand on the banks of the Jordan preparing to go

into the land, the present generation to whom he is speaking were, in fact, those "little ones." By describing them as those who "do not yet know good from bad," Moses draws an important connection between entering the Promised Land and the original story of Adam and Eve in the Garden of Eden. It is as though Moses wanted to show that this new generation was now in much the same position as the first man and woman in the Garden of Eden. They "did not know good from bad" and thus had to depend on God to provide for them. Here again, as in v.31, the picture of God is that of a father providing for his child (cf. 32:6). The law that Moses gives to the people is the means whereby God provides for their good (cf. 30:15–16).

A recurring theme in these narratives is that of the Lord's promise to "fight for" his people. The purpose of stressing this theme is to encourage this new generation to trust God to do the same for them.

The Israelites came to Kadesh Barnea after leaving Mount Sinai (v.19). After their defeat at the hands of the Amorites (Amalekites and Canaanites) they returned to Kadesh (v.45) and, according to v.46, lived in Kadesh "many days." In 2:1 they wandered in the hill country of Seir for "a long time," then traveled beyond Seir (2:8) to Moab and across the Zered Valley (2:13; Nu 21:12). The total time from their stay in Kadesh to their arrival in the Zered Valley was thirty-eight years (2:14). Since, according to Nu 20:1, the Israelites were dwelling in Kadesh at the end of the forty years (compare Nu 20:28, Aaron died, apparently shortly after leaving Kadesh, and 33:38, Aaron died in the fortieth year of the Exodus), it is generally supposed either that they lived in Kadesh all thirty-eight years or that they, having left Kadesh after their defeat at the hands of the Amalekites (Nu 14), returned there a second time. It should be pointed out that though the Lord had told them to leave Kadesh (Nu 14:25), there is no mention of their doing so. Since Dt 1:43–46 states that they disobeyed the Lord and "marched up into the hill country" and that they "came back" after the battle and "stayed in Kadesh many days," the thirty-eight years were likely spent in Kadesh.

## D. Passing Through the Transjordan Desert (2:1–23)

The events of Israel's thirty-eight years in the desert are repeated by reminding the Israelites why the Edomite, Moabite, and Ammonite territories were not taken. The narratives in Genesis indicate that these three nations were related to the Israelites. Thus God said, "I will not give you any of their land" (vv.5, 9, 19; cf. Dt 19:14). This is the first time we learn that God had granted these nations a specific land to possess, along with that of Israel's. They had gained possession of these lands by defeating the former inhabitants and living there in their place (vv.10–12, 20–23). The author attributes the inheritance of these nations specifically to the work of the Lord: "The LORD destroyed them from before the Ammonites. . . . The LORD had done the same for the descendants of Esau" (vv.21b–22a).

It is also stressed in this section that the whole of the previous generation died during this time (vv.15–16).

The denial of Israel's request to pass through Edom (Nu 20:14–21) is omitted in Deuteronomy, but it is presupposed by the narrative. Moses recounts that they spent "many days going around the hill country of Seir" and that, after a time, the Lord instructed them to turn north and go past Edom ("the descendants of Esau") and not provoke them to war (vv.1–8).

## E. Conquest of the Transjordan (2:24–3:11)

### 1. Defeat of Sihon (2:24–37)

When Moses retells the story of the conquest of the land of King Sihon, he makes several significant additions. He first shows that Israel's request to pass through Sihon's land was made on the best of terms (cf. Nu 21:21). It was an offering of peace to the king (Dt 2:26), not an act of war. He adds that Israel had originally offered to buy supplies from Sihon (Dt 2:28), something not mentioned in Numbers. Furthermore, Israel's intention was not to take Sihon's land as their possession, but rather they wanted only to pass through his land on their way to the Promised Land (v.29; see comments on Nu 21:21–32).

But God had other intentions. He hardened Sihon's heart so that he resisted Israel. This was the first act of God in delivering the land over into Israel's hands (vv.30–31); as such it is remarkably similar to God's first act of delivering Israel from Egypt (Ex 7:3). Moses thus sees beyond the events previously recorded in Numbers to their underlying significance. God was at work here, bringing about his purposes. This stress on God's work helps account for the severity of Israel's actions in taking this land (v.34), a feature of the battle not mentioned in Numbers. Israel was clearly acting on God's behalf, and the destruction they wreaked on those in the land was the result of divine wrath on those people's sins (Ge 15:16). As Moses will go on to show in this book, Israel itself was not to be exempt from the same divine judgment (chs. 27–28) and was later to experience a similar fate (30:1ff.).

This event thus marks the beginning of God's work in giving the new generation of Israelites their inheritance (cf. "This very day I will begin . . .", v.25). The key terms in this section center on the idea of the new beginnings (2:25, 31; 3:23).

### 2. Defeat of Og (3:1–11)

Moses repeats the account of the defeat of Og from Nu 21:33–35 with one significant addition, "So the LORD our God also gave into our hands Og king of Bashan" (v.3). This remark stresses the theme of the account of the defeat of Sihon. The defeat of Og was also the Lord's work. Israel's success was not of their own making. This message could not fail to be lost on those who listened to Moses that day, nor does the author of the Pentateuch intend it to be lost on those who now read his book.

Verses 6–11 go beyond the earlier account of this battle in Nu 21:33–35, stressing the obedience and success of Israel in taking the Transjordan as well as the considerable size of the kingdom of Og. As was the case with the kingdom of Sihon, the whole of the kingdom of Og was destroyed.

### F. Transjordan Given to Reuben and Gad (3:12–20)

Recalling events from Nu 32, Moses reiterates the division of the land among Reuben, Gad, and Manasseh. He adds a note about the conquest of part of this land by Jair (see Nu 32:41). The Numbers passage had not specified that the region taken by Jair was part of the territory of Bashan; it had thus left the possible misimpression that Jair had taken the land of Gilead. Thus when recounted again here, the text adds specifically that Jair's conquest was in Bashan and thus was a part of the land given to the tribe of Manasseh (Dt 3:13). Later biblical writers (e.g., Jdg 10:4) identified Bashan and Gilead in such a way that Gilead appears as a more general area within which Bashan was situated (cf. Jos 13:30; 1Ki 4:13).

As Moses here looks back on the first stages of the conquest, he views God's plan for this people from a new perspective. Whereas in his earlier description he had stressed Israel's role in their taking the land (Nu 32), he now views this event from the perspective of the Lord's giving Israel rest (Dt 3:20). The expression "rest" is used again by Moses to portray Israel's entry into the Promised Land as a time of rest and enjoyment of God's blessing (12:10). This theme is clearly reminiscent of God's original intention of the "rest" enjoyed in the Garden of Eden (Ge 2:1–3; 2:15). The conquest of the land is viewed as a return to God's blessing in Eden.

### G. Joshua Replaces Moses (3:21–29)

Moses adds two important details regarding the events he has been recounting. The first is the reminder of the encouragement he had given to Joshua, "Do not be afraid of them; the LORD your God himself will fight for you" (v.22). Adding this element to the narrative is intended to provide the same encouragement for the readers. The second is Moses' prayer for clemency and permission to go into the Promised Land (vv.23–25). Though the request was denied, Moses was allowed to see the land from the top of Mount Pisgah. These two short narratives provide an important bridge to the subsequent books in the OT canon (cf. Jos 1:8–9). The central theme of the book of Joshua is grounded in these two speeches of Moses.

## III. Moses' Speech: Call to Obedience (4:1–40)

Having surveyed past events leading up to this moment, Moses is now about to part ways with the people and allow Joshua to take them into the land. He thus turns to explain the law they are to take with them. Since he will not enter the land and guide the people in God's law, he gives them his explanation of the Law. His central purpose is to draw out the chief ideas of the Sinai narratives (Ex 19–33).

## A. The Torah Is Wisdom (4:1–14)

As frequently happens in Deuteronomy, Moses focuses on only a few central ideas taken from the previous narratives. His purpose is to give a general summary. First he turns to the issue of obedience to the will of God. This he explains within the context of "wisdom." What other nations sought in attempting to gain wisdom, Israel had found in the revelation of God's will at Sinai. Just as in Ex 33:16 God's presence distinguished Israel from all the nations, so here it is divine wisdom given in the Law that singles them out. Moses reminds the Israelites that the great display of God's power in the giving of the law at Sinai (cf. Ex 20:18–19) was to underscore the foundation of their wisdom—the fear of the Lord (cf. Ex 20:20). As is frequently repeated in Scripture, "the fear of the LORD is the beginning of wisdom" (Ps 111:10).

## B. Warning Against Idolatry (4:15–24)

The second central idea that Moses stresses is the warning against idolatry. Just as Israel had easily slipped into idolatry, even while at Mount Sinai (Ex 32), so Moses is careful to warn them of the ever present danger of further apostasy. It should be recalled that the warning against idolatry is the first of the Ten Commandments (Ex 20:2–6) and the first command in the Covenant Code (Ex 20:23a). Referring to their failure to trust God in the desert (Nu 20), Moses for a second time here lays the responsibility of past failure on the shoulders of the people (v. 21; cf. 3:26). In Numbers it is clear that ultimately Moses was denied entry into the Promised Land because he (and Aaron) "did not believe" (Nu 20:12). Here, however, he reminds the people that it was their own murmuring and complaints that provided the occasion for his unbelief (Nu 20:3–6). Moses is not justifying his actions, nor is he seeking to cast the blame on the people. He seems rather to be laying a basis for reiterating a lesson found throughout the earlier narratives: even though Israel has had godly leadership (e.g., Moses or Joshua), if the people fail to trust God, it will be to no avail. Thus he warns them, "Be careful not to forget the covenant of the LORD your God" (v.23).

## C. The Exile (4:25–31)

In the same breath as he warns the people of the impending exile, Moses encourages the people by reminding them of God's great mercy. In no uncertain terms, he warns the Israelites that if they persist in idolatry, they will be taken off the land and scattered among all the nations in exile (vv.25–28). Then Moses turns his attention to Israel's return from exile. When they return to the Lord, the Lord will return them to the land promised to the fathers (vv.29–31). He gives expression to the same ideas underlying the narratives of Israel's first foray into idolatry, the golden calf (Ex 32). God was angry with them then and was ready to cast them off, but Moses intervened and the Lord showed himself to be long-suffering and forgiving (Ex 33:19).

## D. God's Presence With Israel (4:32–40)

Just as in Ex 33:15ff. the presence of God among his people marked them as a unique nation, so in the present narrative Moses returns to the theme of God's presence to underscore his mercy. Has there ever been a people who have heard the voice of the one true God speaking with them in their midst (vv.32–33; cf. Ex 19–20)? Has there ever been a people among whom God has displayed great signs and wonders and delivered them in mighty wars (v.34; cf. Ex 4–12)? God did all this for Israel because he loved them and had chosen them as far back as the time of the patriarchs (vv.37–38).

Why does Moses again stress God's love and mercy? Because it is the basis of the call for obedience (7:39–40). Moses' speech is punctuated with the call for wholehearted obedience to the will of God.

It is not without purpose that at this point in the speech Moses refers to the patriarchs (v.37). Throughout the Pentateuch the patriarchs, particularly Abraham, serve as examples of what it means to "keep God's laws" (Ge 26:5). Thus when the Pentateuch calls for obedience to God's "requirements" and "commands," it should be remembered that the foremost example of one who did this is Abraham (Ge 26:5), a man who lived by faith (Ge 15:6). Thus from the perspective of the whole of the Pentateuch, the reader is being called on to live a life like Abraham, a man of faith.

## IV. Cities of Refuge (4:41–43)

This section of text is actually a narrative insertion in the midst of Moses' speech, dealing with the allotment of cities of refuge to the tribes on the east side of the Jordan (cf. Nu 35:6, 9–34). Since this topic is treated in detail in ch. 19, it is curious that mention of it should be made here. There is, however, some justification for its being included here. First, Moses has been rehearsing the events dealing with the conquest of the area east of the Jordan. It is appropriate, then, to turn immediately to the legislation specifically relevant to that conquest. Second, since this narrative deals specifically with the question of a person who kills someone else, it is appropriately inserted immediately before the Ten Commandments. It provides a helpful qualification of the otherwise unqualified prohibition, "You shall not kill" (5:17). Thus the narrative plays an important role in providing an interpretive context for the law dealing with capital punishment.

## V. Giving of the Law (4:44–5:33)

### A. The Setting of the Law (4:44–49)

Much of what has already been recounted in chs. 1–3 is here repeated in summary form. It is cast in the form of a narration about Moses and is not a part of Moses' own discourse. The repetition found here is thus a part of the composition of the book and not that of Moses' speech to the people. As such this short summary plays an important role in guiding the reader through the book. Its purpose is to distinguish between the introductory material of the first three chapters and the exposition of the law itself in the subsequent chapters.

### B. The Introduction to the Law: The Covenant at Sinai (5:1–5):

Moses now gives an introduction that provides a context for his repetition of the earlier laws. He is particularly intent on driving home the point that God's covenant made with Israel at Sinai was the immediate responsibility of the present generation. It was not a covenant made to earlier generations ("our fathers") but to those of the present generation who had stood at the foot of Mount Sinai and heard the voice of God. This generation of Israelites were children when the original covenant was given at Sinai. Yet Moses rightfully treats them as those who were present and who could still recall vividly God's power. This generation is thus reminded that the Ten Commandments that follow have their primary goal in preserving the worship of God throughout the future generations.

### C. The Ten Commandments (5:6–22)

The Ten Commandments are repeated here to provide the context for Moses' explication of the law that follows. It is, as it were, the text for his sermon. It is repeated almost verbatim from Ex 20:1–17. However, as is true of most written texts in Scripture, the same material is here found in a different context, and thus its sense may vary slightly from its earlier statement. We should seek to understand these commandments in their new context of Moses' speech.

(1) The introductory words, "I am the LORD your God, who brought you out of Egypt" are the same as in Exodus, even though in the forty years that had intervened, the Lord had done many more things for Israel. Though the first three chapters of Deuteronomy have "updated" God's acts of grace and mercy toward his people, the basis of the call to obedience remains the same—one great act of deliverance of the people from Egypt.

(2) The prohibition of idolatry takes on a more realistic tone in this context. Exodus and Numbers have stressed Israel's continual backsliding into idolatry. Thus the relevancy of the prohibition of idolatry is not difficult to appreciate. Furthermore, the visitation of God's punishment on the "third and fourth generation" (v.9) takes on new meaning when spoken to the "second" generation, for the "third" generation was now living, a generation that had not seen God's great act of deliverance from Egypt. Thus this second generation must teach God's ways to the third generation (cf. 6:2, 6–9).

(3) The concept of "rest" on the seventh day is extended here to include one's whole household and servants. Israel must remember their time of service in Egypt and thus treat their own servants like themselves. In the same way, the reason for the Sabbath is now stated to be God's deliverance of the people from Egypt rather than God's rest at Creation. Thus God's special acts of deliverance are moved to the center of Israel's attention in the motivation given for keeping the law.

(4) In the commandment regarding honoring one's parents, the phrase "that it may go well with you" is added

(v.16). Though a seemingly minor addition, it shows that merely dwelling in the land was not God's ultimate goal for his people. He wanted their living in the land to be "good." This addition is consistent with the overall perspective of Deuteronomy that sees the land God is giving to Israel as the "good land" which they are to enjoy. In this way Moses is able to tie together the themes of God's "good land" in the early chapters of Genesis with Israel's enjoyment of the land in the Conquest. Israel is returning to God's "good land," created and prepared for them since the beginning.

(5) The Hebrew form of the last commandment (v.21) separates it into two distinct commandments (see comments on Ex 20:1–17), by using different words for "covet" and "desire." The object of the "desire" that is prohibited in the two commands in Ex 20:14 is reversed in Dt 5:21. According to the sense of v.21, two distinct prohibitions are being spoken. The first is that "you shall not covet your neighbor's wife," and the second is that "you shall not set your desire on your neighbor's house," etc. There is no possibility here of understanding the neighbor's wife as his property (as is left ambiguous in Ex 20:14).

## D. Moses Appointed as Mediator (5:23–33)

Referring back to the response of the people at Sinai in Ex 20:18ff., Moses recalls and expounds on their fear at hearing God's voice and his own consequent role as mediator between God and the people. In this text, the fear of the people is seen as a positive sign. Its purpose was to provoke them to seek after God and turn away from idols. It is stressed here because within the context of Deuteronomy, "fear" is central to the concept of divine wisdom and in the following exhortation the "fear of the LORD" is the foundation for obedience to God's will (e.g., 6:2).

The Lord's words in v.29, however, show that the fear exhibited at Sinai was not yet the kind of fear that would produce obedience.

## VI. General Principles of Law (6:1–11:32)

The speeches of Moses that follow show a conscious effort to develop the central ideas of the first of the Ten Commandments as given in ch. 5—whole-hearted worship of God and forsaking idols.

### A. Explication of Fearing God and Keeping His Commands (6:1–25)

Fear—i.e., a deeply felt respect for the Lord—must be taught to all generations as the basis for godly living and obedience. The result of obedience is blessing—living long and well in the land. The notion of blessing stressed here is that of Ge 1:28, "Be fruitful and increase in number; fill the earth." God's covenant with Israel was to be the fulfillment of God's original purposes in creation. The book of Joshua will show that though there were initial successes, the people ultimately were not able to keep the covenant and hence did not fully enjoy its blessings.

Ironically, the fear of God that produces obedience is here defined by "love"—"Love the LORD your God with all your heart . . ." (v.5). It is thus clear that the "fear of the LORD" that Moses has in mind is not that which flees from his presence but that which longs to do his will. It is a fear that produces not obeisance but obedience, not worry but worship (v.13). Clearly the central concern of Moses is the propensity of the people to fall into idolatry. Hence what he stresses beyond the need for love and reverence is the absolute "oneness" of God. There are no other gods beside him.

Thus Moses begins his exhortation with a summation of one of the most central ideas in all of Scripture, "Hear, O Israel: The LORD our God, the LORD

is one." This statement, called the "Shema" in later Jewish tradition, was referred to by Jesus as the "first" of all the commandments (Mk 12:29). Much discussion has centered on the meaning of the phrase "the LORD is one." Its sense becomes clear if read in light of the strict prohibition of idolatry and polytheism in the present text of Deuteronomy. It gives a clear statement of the principle of monotheism: there is one God and only one God exists.

It is important to note, however, that the stress on the uniqueness of God over against the worship of false idols is not stated in such a way as to exclude the equally important notion of the divine Trinity. The word used for "one" in this passage is not that which means "singleness" but "unity." The same word, for example, is used in Ge 2:24 where the husband and wife in marriage are said to be "one flesh." Thus, while this verse is intended as a clear and concise statement of monotheism, it was not intended to address or to exclude the concept of the Trinity.

### B. Explication of Separation From the Gods of Other Nations (7:1–26)

This passage weaves together sections of Ex 19:1–7; 23:20–33 as a means of elaborating on the importance of separation from the nations. Israel was called upon to forsake any possibility of following after the idols of the nations and to remember the only God who keeps "his covenant of love to a thousand generations of those who love him" (v.9). Moses stresses that separation from the gods of other nations necessarily entails separation from the nations themselves: "Make no treaty with them, and show them no mercy. Do not intermarry with them" (vv.2–3). These severe statements should be read in light of the narratives of Rahab and Ruth—both Canaanite women who married into the families of Israel (Jos 2:1ff.; Ruth). Moses' main concern is with the result of joining in marriage and treaties with the Canaanites who practice idolatry, "for they will turn your sons away from following me to serve other gods" (v.4). He is thus not speaking of those cases where Canaanites forsook their idols to follow the Lord. Furthermore, Moses also stresses that separation from these pagan gods also entails a refusal to allow the practice of their religion in their midst: "Break down their altars, smash their sacred stones . . ." (v.5).

Moses traces the underlying concern for Israel's worship of God back to their election. Israel was God's "treasured possession" (v.6). They were unique among the nations, just as God was unique among the false idols. He alone was God and Israel alone was his chosen people. However, lest there be any reason for Israel's pride to gain a foothold, Moses quickly adds, "The LORD did not set his affection on you and choose you because you were more numerous than other people, for you were the fewest of all peoples" (v.7). The basis of God's election of Israel was God's love, not Israel's greatness (v.8).

The fact that the total conquest of the land would not be quick has already been anticipated in Ex 23:27–33. Both here and in Exodus the reason given is the same: God would not allow them to totally destroy the land until they had grown to sufficient size in order to care for it adequately. Nevertheless, when Israel went in to take the land, it was promised that the defeat of the people of the land would be "quick" (Dt 4:26; 9:3). We know from later books of the Bible that in those lands where the Israelites fought powerfully, the enemy was quickly defeated. There were, however, some areas that remained unconquered for generations (cf. Jos 15:63).

## C. Warning Against Forgetting the Lord (8:1–20)

In this section, Moses first recalls God's provision for the people during

their sojourn of forty years in the desert. This time was a time of affliction and testing, "to know what was in your heart, whether or not you would keep his commands" (v.2). As in Exodus, the gift of manna was one of God's tests to see "whether they will follow [his] instructions" (Ex 16:4). Thus manna is similar to the Tree of Knowledge of Good and Evil in the Garden of Eden (Ge 2:16–17). It is also fitting, therefore, that Moses here describes the Promised Land and the blessings of the people living there in terms reminiscent of the Garden of Eden in Genesis: "So that you may live and increase and may enter and possess the land . . ." (v.1; cf. Ge 1:28); "For the LORD your God is bringing you into a good land—a land with streams and pools of water . . ." (vv.7ff.; cf. Ge 2:10ff.). Just as God's act of providing clothing for Adam and Eve was used to demonstrate his care for them after they were cast out of the Garden of Eden (Ge 3:21), so God's care for Israel in the desert is pictured here in his providing for their clothing (Dt 8:4).

If this link between manna and the Tree of Knowledge of Good and Evil is intentional, then it is all the more significant that Moses also links manna with the word of God (v.3). The story of God's sending the manna, then, relates back to the first test of the human race in the Garden of Eden . The manna was God's way of testing the Israelites in the desert, just as the tree was God's way of testing Adam and Eve in the garden. And what was lost in that garden is now being restored in the word of God. Thus at the close of the book of Deuteronomy, Moses depicts the Law as a return to that tree (see 30:15). Obedience to the Law is seen as the key to enjoying once again the blessings of the good land and of avoiding the curse of death (8:20).

## D. Illustrations From Israel's Past (9:1–10:11)

Moses now turns to illustrations from the past to support his central lesson that Israel should live a life of constant vigilance before God. He turns first to the incident of the golden calf recorded in Ex 32. The earlier rehearsals of past events have focused on God's faithfulness. The present illustrations focus on Israel's failure and faithlessness. They come primarily from Exodus and thus move further back in time than the earlier historical introduction in Dt 1–3, which began at Numbers.

### 1. Introduction (9:1–6)

Moses begins with a reminder of what the previous pentateuchal narratives have repeatedly stressed—Israel's possession of the land was not a reward given them on account of their own righteousness. The land was to be taken from the other nations "because of their wickedness" (v.5) and was to be given to Israel as a fulfillment of God's promise to the fathers (v.6). We should remember that a central part of the promise to the fathers was that "all the peoples on earth will be blessed through you" (Ge 12:3). Thus, in terms of God's ultimate purpose, his driving the nations out of the land and giving it to Israel was a part of his on-going plan to bless all nations, including, ironically, those now being driven out of the land.

In this speech, Moses leaves the people—and the reader—with a clear understanding that possession of the land was based on God's grace, not on Israel's own righteousness (v.6). He thus anticipates the views of the later prophets who based their hope in the future on God's faithfulness to his promises and not on the righteousness of "a stiff-necked people" (v.6b; see Eze 36:22–23). It is significant, then, that in this narrative, Moses closes his account of the incident of the golden calf by recounting his prayer not only for the

people of Israel, but also on behalf of the nations who have heard of God's dealings with his people (vv.26–29).

### 2. The golden calf (9:7–21)

In retelling the story of Sinai and Israel's breach of covenant in making an idol of the golden calf, Moses stresses how quickly the people fell into idolatry (v.12). His purpose is to emphasize the need for constant vigilance. The people's hearts can turn away from God when it is least expected. Certainly their standing at the foot of Mount Sinai while the prohibitions of idolatry were being written on the stone tablets was not a likely place for instigating the worship of the golden calf. Nevertheless it happened, and thus it serves as a cogent warning of how unexpectedly the hearts of the people go astray.

Moses also alludes to other places where Israel's failure to trust God was manifested: Taberah (v.22), Massah (v.22), and Kibroth Hattaavah (v.22); and then he turns briefly to Kadesh Barnea (vv.23–24). God's words to Israel there are important in this context because they express the central themes of the whole of the Pentateuch. At Kadesh, Israel rebelled against God's will and hence did not put their faith in him.

This reference to Israel's lack of "faith" (NIV, "trust") is central to the argument of the Pentateuch. The motivation for Israel's actions goes far deeper than mere "disobedience" to the law; it was symptomatic of a general lack of faith. Unlike Abraham, a man of faith (Ge 15:6), who is repeatedly alluded to in these texts, the people of Israel were unable or unwilling to walk with God in simple faith. This is the Israelites' chronic source of failure. Moses thus returns to the theme of faith and simple trust in God throughout these writings.

Returning to the incident at Sinai, Moses recounts his prayer on behalf of the people (vv.25–29). That prayer serves as a general statement of his concern for the people throughout the forty years in the desert. It is significant that Moses' prayer does not stress their "righteousness" but rather God's righteousness. Moreover, God's concerns for all the nations, a principal part of the Abrahamic covenant (Ge 12:3), can also be seen in Moses' words in v.28. Moses' prayer, then, becomes a means for him to turn our attention to the promises to Abraham and to view the present warnings from that broader perspective.

### 3. The new tablets at Sinai (10:1–5)

In order to show that the Lord heard the prayer of Moses and reestablished his covenant with them, Moses recounts the making of two new tablets for the Ten Commandments. He also says that in addition to the stone tablets he made a wooden chest in which to keep them. This wooden chest appears to be the Ark of the Covenant, which had not yet been made at this time. Presumably, before Moses went up the mountain to receive the new tablets, he began work on the chest—i.e., according to Ex 25:10, he had instructed Bezalel how to make it. After he returned back down the mountain, Bezalel completed the chest (the ark; Ex 37:1) and the new tablets were placed inside it (Ex 40:20). The parenthetical mention of the Ark of the Covenant in Dt 10:6–9 further suggests that the wooden chest in this passage should be identified with the Ark of the Covenant.

### 4. Parenthesis: Itinerary in the desert (10:6–9)

Moses is concerned to show that the priesthood of Aaron was also restored after the incident of the golden calf (cf. 9:20). He thus inserts this parenthetical narrative into the account of the events at Sinai. It recounts God's establishment of the house of Levi as priests before the Lord.

### 5. Conclusion: Dismissal from Mount Sinai (10:10–11)

At the conclusion of his speech, Moses states what his previous words have, in fact, already suggested. God was gracious to the people: "It was not his will to destroy [them]" (v.10). Furthermore, God intended them to enjoy the blessings of his promises to the fathers. God's past dealings with Israel have become the basis for their trust and obedience in the present.

### E. Admonition to Fear the Lord (10:12–22)

Moses now drives home the lesson of the preceding narrative. Israel is called upon to "fear the LORD, to walk in his ways, to love him, to serve the LORD your God with all your heart and with all your soul." These are the central ideas not only of the book of Deuteronomy, but the whole of the Pentateuch in its final shape. Because of God's grace and love for Israel, Israel was to be gracious and kind to others. In light of their immediate past, for Israel to follow in God's ways would mean a fundamental change of heart. Such a change of heart is described as "circumcision of the heart" (v.16), an idea to which Moses will return in 30:6, where his focus extends beyond the present events and his immediate generation. The ideas Moses is working with here and in ch. 30 are remarkably similar to those of the new covenant promises in the later prophets (see Jer 31:31ff.; Eze 36:22ff.). This is merely one more example of the frequent convergence of the message of the Pentateuch and that of the Prophets.

### F. Conclusion: Call to Love God and Obey His Will (11:1–32)

Thus far Moses has given an introduction to the collection of laws and judgments that will follow. His purpose has been to set forth two clear alternatives. Either Israel must obey God's will and love him with all their heart or they cannot continue to enjoy his blessings.

As Moses concludes his introduction to the collection of laws, he recalls what these people had seen God do to the Egyptians with their "own eyes" (v.7). He emphasizes that it was they "and not their children" who saw the mighty works of God. Recall that Moses is here addressing the "new generation," those whose parents had died in the wilderness. They had been only children when they saw God's mighty acts, and among them were the "firstborn" children whose lives had been delivered on the night of the Exodus (Ex 12:21).

Having reminded them of their own participation in God's work, Moses turns to their responsibility as parents and guardians of the next generation, their children who had not actually witnessed the great acts of God. For that generation and all subsequent ones, God's great acts would not be seen with their own eyes, but would be "seen" in the words of Scripture. It was to be in Moses' words here in the Pentateuch that the acts of God would be put before the eyes of their children, "Fix these words of mine in your hearts and minds . . . . Teach them to you children, talking about them when you sit at home and when you walk along the road, when you lie down and when you get up" (vv.18–19). The top priority is thus given to Scripture as the means of teaching the greatness and grace of God.

As a final means for driving home the importance of obedience and trust in God, Moses gives instructions for a ceremony that the people were to carry out when they entered the land (vv.29–32). They were to read the curses and blessings of the covenant on Mount Gerizim and Mount Ebal (see 27:1ff.). This ceremony was in fact initiated under Joshua in Jos 8:33ff.

## VIII. Instructions for Life in the New Land (12:1–26:19)

### A. Instruction for the Life of Worship (12:1–16:17)

#### 1. Central place of worship (12:1–32)

Moses begins by repeating his instructions (see 7:5) regarding what to do with the false worship centers after the Israelites had taken possession of the land of the Canaanites. They were to "destroy them completely" (v.2). Furthermore, Israel was to worship the Lord at a single, central place of worship. Not just any site would do (v.13)—only that site chosen by the Lord himself (v.14). Little is known about the location of this site before the time of David (cf. 1Sa 1–4), but since David's time, it has been Jerusalem (2Sa 6–7).

The provision in vv.15–25 that animals may be slaughtered for food at any place in the land clarifies the provision in Lev 17:1–7. There the slaughtering of animals for sacrifice could only be done at the Tent of Meeting. That implied, but did not specifically state, that the slaughter of animals for food could take place anywhere. This present passage makes this point explicit (see v.15). In so doing, the question of offering sacrifices other than at the one sanctuary chosen by the Lord was also clarified. All sacrifices must be carried out at the one central sanctuary.

The chapter ends with an oft-repeated warning against following after the gods of the nations (vv.29–32) and thus provides an appropriate introduction to the next chapter.

#### 2. Warning against those who entice others to follow "other gods" (13:1–18)

Three illustrations of possible temptations to follow other gods are enumerated. Under no circumstances are the Israelites to forsake the Lord their God. (1) If a prophet or dreamer, even one whose predictions come true, suggests that the people forsake the Lord by following other gods, his words must not be heeded (vv.1–5). According to 18:21–22, if a prophet's word comes true, it is a sign that he is a true prophet. Thus even though such signs may speak for the word of a prophet, if he attempts to persuade others to follow false gods, his words are to be rejected and he must be put to death (cf. 18:20). (2) If someone from one's own family entices him to follow other gods, such a one must be rejected (vv.6–11). The penalty again is death. (3) If an entire city forsakes the Lord and follows other gods, that city must be completely destroyed (vv.12–18).

### 3. The purity of the people (14:1–21)

A selection of regulations is placed here to show the measures that must be taken to maintain the holiness of the people. The repeated purpose of these regulations is to show that Israel was "a people holy to the LORD [their] God" (vv.2, 21).

(1) Israel was not to cut themselves or "shave the front of [their] heads" as a sign of mourning for the dead (v.1; cf. Lev 19:28; 21:5).

(2) A summary of clean and unclean animals is listed (vv.3–20), summarizing and explaining Lev 11:2–23. For example, in cases where the Leviticus passage only describes the kinds of clean animals that can be eaten (Lev 11:3), Deuteronomy lists specific examples (Dt 14:4–5). On the other hand, when examples are given in Leviticus (Lev 11:21–23), Deuteronomy lists only the general regulation (Dt 14:20).

(3) The prohibition of eating from a carcass is repeated from Ex 22:31 and Lev 17:15–16. In the present passage, however, such meat can be given to the "alien living in any of your towns" (Dt 14:21). However, since Lev 17:15–16 prohibits both the Israelite and the "alien" from eating the meat of a carcass, this passage must have a different sort of "outsider" in mind. Presumably

it was someone who had not joined with Israel in the covenant, i.e., one who was not a member of the "holy people" (v.21a). He is further identified in this passage by being associated with the "strangers."

(4) Moses repeats the prohibition of boiling a kid in its mother's milk (cf. Ex 23:19; 34:26).

### 4. Tithes (14:22–29)

A tithe is a tenth-part of one's produce, whether grain, fruit, oil, cattle, or sheep. In 12:6–8 Moses had commanded the people to bring their tithes and the "firstborn of [their] herds and flocks" to the sanctuary and to celebrate a joyous feast in thanksgiving for the Lord's blessings. Here he explains in more detail the procedures they were to follow.

Instructions regarding a tithe have already been given in Lev 27:30–33 and Nu 18:21–32. That tithe, usually called the "first tithe," was to be given for the support of the Levites who, in turn, gave a tenth of it to the priests. According to the present passage, a "second tithe" was also to be given by each Israelite "that you may learn to revere the LORD" (v.23). This tithe was to be given out of the remainder of the produce after the first tithe had been given to the Levites. A family celebration that included the Levites was to be held out of this tithe. Anyone who lived too far away to bring his tithe to the sanctuary was to sell his tithe and purchase food and drink for the celebration when he arrived (vv.24–27).

Every third year the tithe was to be given to the needy (cf. 26:12). Since the Levites are also mentioned here (14:28–29), this is probably a general statement that includes not only the "second tithe" spoken of here, but also that in Nu 18. Thus the Levites were to have their customary tithe, and the needy were to partake of this "second" tithe.

According to Ex 23:10–11, during the seventh year the land was to be "unplowed and unused" and available for the needy. Thus, in a cycle of seven years, during the first, second, fourth, and fifth years the tithe was eaten by the owner of the land; in the third and sixth years it was given to the needy; and in the seventh year the whole land was left for the needy.

### 5. Care for the poor (15:1–18)

The present passage further explains the Sabbath year release (see Ex 23:10; Lev 25:2–7). The premise of this exposition is that if the land was left unused in the Sabbath year, the landowner would not have this money to pay his debts. To alleviate this hardship, the debts were to be postponed for one year (the sense of the word translated "cancel" is "to postpone"). This provision did not apply to the "foreigner" (one who stayed temporarily in the land; v.3), but only to those who lived permanently in the land. In vv. 4–5 Moses qualifies his discussion of the "poor" in the land. He reminds the people that if they obeyed the Lord, they would have no need of laws dealing with the poor because God would so bless them that there would be no poor. They would, in fact, have such abundance that they would be the creditors of many nations.

The ideal is that there be no poor in the land; hence Moses ensures that in the event that there were needy people (as there surely would be; v.11), the Israelites would generously provide for them out of their own abundance. Out of the blessings of some the needs of others were to be met.

According to Lev 25:39ff., an Israelite could sell himself to another Israelite as a hired worker if he could not pay his debts. In light of such a provision, there was a need for a ruling regarding the length of such service; it was not to exceed six years (cf. Ex 21:2–7). This law applied equally to male and female servants.

### 6. Firstborn animals (15:19–23)

Laws regarding the firstborn were given in Ex 13:11–16; 22:29–27; Nu 18:15–18. In Nu 18, the firstlings were to be given to the priests as gifts, who presumably shared them with all those present at the celebration. In Dt 12:6–7 the firstlings were included in a list of offerings to be brought to the central worship site and eaten in a joyous convocation. This passage gives further regulations regarding firstborn cattle and sheep. They were not to be worked or sheared, as the other animals. Only those without blemish were to be brought to the place of worship and eaten by all of the people.

### 7. Feasts (16:1–17)

Moses now discusses the feasts during which the people were to appear before the Lord at the central worship site.

*Passover* (vv.1–8). Reference to the Passover has been made throughout the Pentateuch (see Ex 12:1–49; 23:18; 34:25; Lev 23:5; Nu 9:1–14; 28:16). Since several offerings were given during this feast, Moses refers generally to the sacrifice of "an animal from your flock or herd." The Passover itself required only a lamb (Ex 12:5). However, there were also additional mandated offerings during the Passover and subsequent seven days of the Feast of Unleavened Bread (Nu 28:19–25). Moreover, other offerings could be given as well (cf. 2Ch 35:7–8). In addition, what is anticipated by the completion of the tabernacle in Ex 40:17 is clarified here in vv.5–6: the Passover was no longer to be celebrated in each house (cf. Ex 12:46) but only at the central place of worship.

*Feast of Weeks* (vv.9–12). This feast day, also called the "Harvest Feast" (Ex 23:16) and "day of firstfruits" (Nu 28:26), is referred to several times in the Pentateuch. According to v.9 here, it must begin seven weeks after "the sickle [is put] to the standing grain." Depending on any particular season, this day could vary. In Lev 23:15, however, the time of reckoning the "seven full weeks," or fifty days (Pentecost) begins "on the next day" after the Sabbath. The purpose of this feast was to celebrate God's deliverance of the people from slavery in Egypt. It was a time of remembrance. Note that according to Ac 2, the "firstfruits of the Spirit" (Ro 8:23) were given on "Pentecost."

*Feast of Tabernacles or Booths* (vv.13–15). This feast is also called the "Feast of Ingathering" (Ex 23:16). In Lev 23:43 it is explained that the "booths" were to commemorate the huts the Israelites lived in when they came out of Egypt. As with other feasts, it was to be a time of great joy in remembrance.

*Summary* (vv.16–17). This summary repeats Ex 23:17. Here, however, Moses specifies that which has been the main point of this section of Deuteronomy—the feasts were to be celebrated only at the central place of worship.

## B. Instruction for Leadership (16:18–18:22)

### 1. Judges (16:18–20)

In 1:9–15 Moses recounted the occasion for the appointment of leaders for each of the tribes, here called "judges and officials." The work of governing God's people was too much for one man, Moses. Thus these judges were to carry on his work within each of the tribes and families. According to 17:8–13 these legal officials were to be organized at a local level as well as at a higher level for appeal.

The following section describes a series of occasions in which the need for a judge may arise. The judge was to play an important role in implementing and enforcing the prohibitions listed below.

### 2. Prohibition of wooden Asherah poles and pillars (16:21–22)

The Asherah poles and pillars have been mentioned in 7:5 as accouterments of Canaanite worship. They were to be destroyed when the Israelites moved into the land. In the present context the concern is that the central worship place not contain any traces of Canaanite worship.

### 3. Prohibition of defective sacrifice (17:1)

A defective sacrifice is here described as "detestable" to the Lord. The description of the defects listed here summarize Lev 1:3, 10; 22:17–26.

### 4. Penalty for worshiping other gods (17:2–7)

The penalty for worshiping other gods has been given already in Ex 22:20: "Whoever sacrifices to any god other than the LORD must be destroyed." Here the implementation of the penalty is closely described and applied to "any man or woman." The penalty is the same as that for one who seduces another to worship idols (Dt 13:7–12).

### 5. Law cases for the priests and judges (17:8–13)

The system of legal administration described here represents an implementation of that form of law established during Israel's time in the desert (Ex 18:21–23; Dt 1:16–17; 19:17–18). There were judges at the local level throughout the land as well as centralized at the place of worship. Obedience to the law is here presented as obedience to the will of God. Violation of the law is seen as rebellion against God.

### 6. The king (17:14–20)

The office of kingship has been anticipated since the Lord's promise to Abraham, "I will bless her [Sarah] so that she will be the mother of nations; kings of peoples will come from her" (Ge 17:16), and to Jacob, "kings will come from your body" (Ge 35:11; cf. 36:31). That this king would come from the tribe of Judah is clear from Ge 49:9–12. Key places in the Pentateuch refer to this king and his role in bringing about God's promises to Israel (e.g., Nu 24:7; Dt 33:5).

The ideal set forth in this passage is that of a king who is obedient to God's will, which he learns from reading the Law (vv.18–19). Thus he will "revere the LORD" and be humble (vv.19b–20). At a time when most ancient kings were virtually illiterate, Israel was to have a king who could make his own copy of the Law and study it daily. He was to be a scribe and scholar of Scripture.

The present passage anticipates the time when a king would be established over Israel and thus prescribes the kind of king they were to have. Central to this question is that he had to be one whom the Lord himself would choose (v.15), just as Israel was to worship God only at the place he chose. It is not difficult to see in these words the anticipation of King David, whose family God chose from among all the tribes (2Sa 7:18–24; Ps 78:70). Moreover, the warnings listed here regarding the dangers inherent in the kingship call to mind the downfall of Solomon, David's son.

Underlying these warnings is the larger issue that ultimately Israel was to look to God as their King and thus not put their trust in another. Their request for a king, in other words, should not arise out of a faltering faith and trust in the LORD. We should note here that when the day came that Israel did, in fact, request a king, God and his prophet Samuel saw in their request a veiled attempt to reject divine leadership (1Sa 8:6–9).

### 7. Offerings for the priests and Levites (18:1–8)

The role of the priests, chosen by God and separated apart as his servants, is summarized here. Their support was to come from a prescribed portion of the offerings given to the Lord. From the animals offered they were to receive "the shoulder, the jowls and the inner parts." From the rest of the offerings they were to be given "the firstfruits."

According to Lev 7:31–34, the priests normally received a portion of the fellowship offering, i.e., the breast and the right thigh of the animals offered. The portions for the priests described here were probably to be taken from the additional offerings prescribed in ch. 14.

### 8. Detestable practices (18:9–14)

Before introducing the office of the prophet, Moses emphatically prohibits all other means of knowing God's will. The office of the prophet was Israel's means of knowing that will; hence these other means must not be used to rival it.

### 9. The prophet (18:15–22)

Abraham is called a prophet in Ge 20:7, and the existence of prophets is presupposed in the Pentateuch (Ex 7:1; Nu 11:29; 12:6; Dt 13:2–3). But now, for the first time, the office of prophet becomes the specific subject of discussion.

The historical basis of this office is Israel's request for a mediator at Sinai (Ex 19:16–19; 20:19–21). Fearing to stand in God's presence, the people asked Moses to go before the Lord and return God's words to them. Thus the prophet was to be "like Moses." This suggests that the office of the prophet was to play an important role in the further history of God's dealings with Israel. Indeed, a major section of the OT canon is devoted to the work of the prophets (Isaiah–Malachi). The prophet was to be God's mouthpiece to the people. Just as Aaron spoke God's words to Moses and was thus called a prophet (Ex 7:1), so the prophet(s) whom the Lord would later raise up would speak to the people on God's behalf.

As a result of his position, a prophet's words were to be taken as the final authority. For this reason, strict measures were taken to ensure that false prophets would not arise among the people to lead them away from the Lord. The simple test of a true prophet was whether his words would come true. This suggests an important role of the prophet was "foretelling" the future.

In the NT v.18 is read in reference to the coming of the Messiah (Ac 3:22–23). But even within the OT itself this verse was taken to refer to a specific individual and not merely the succession of prophets that were to arise after Moses. In 34:10, for example, the final words of the book recall the promise of Moses in 18:18 and look far into the future to a single individual.

## C. Instructions for Order (19:1–23:14)

### 1. Cities of refuge (19:1–13)

According to Nu 35:9–34, Israel was to establish six "cities of refuge" to prevent the escalation of blood revenge and to provide the means for a fair trial in cases of homicide. Three of these cities were to be east of the Jordan and three west of the Jordan. The establishment of those cities east of the Jordan is recounted in Dt 4:41–43, whereas 19:1–7 looks at those west of the Jordan.

A third group of cities is envisioned in vv.8–9, but they were apparently never established. Because of Israel's continued disobedience, God never permanently increased their borders, and the cities were thus not needed. Since these cities were never built during Israel's historical past, the question of the fulfillment of these words of Moses arises. Some maintain that these cities will be built when the Messiah comes.

### 2. Boundary markers (19:14)

In the ancient world, territory was staked out by means of large stones bearing inscriptions that identified the owner of the property. These could easily be moved with a corresponding gain or loss of property. The notion of secretly or forcefully moving a neighbor's boundary marker thus became a proverbial expression for treachery and rebellion (Job 24:1–2; Pr 22:28). Its use here in Deuteronomy probably carries this same sense; that is, it is a warning against violating any standard set up by the "fathers" that has been ordained by God.

The "predecessors" here are either Joshua and the elders who cast lots for the various boundaries (Jos 13:6), or the patriarchs, such as Abraham (Ge 13:17) or Jacob (Ge 49), who through their travels and encampments had already surveyed and apportioned the land for their descendants. It may also refer to God's work of apportioning boundaries for all the nations (Dt 2:5, 9, 19; 32:8). Even these boundaries should be observed and honored.

### 3. Witnesses (19:15–21)

According to Nu 35:30 and Dt 17:6, more than one witness was required for a capital offense. This passage (and 17:6) specifies that two or three witnesses were enough. But it also raises another issue. What happens when the witness is false? Here Moses appeals to a provision stated earlier (17:8–13), to the effect that difficult cases were to be taken to the judges and priests at the central worship place. The accused and the suspected false witness were to stand before the Lord, and the case was to be thoroughly investigated by the judges. In other words, merely counting witnesses was not enough. If there was any suspicion of falsehood, as in the case of contradictory testimony, further investigation was required rather than merely adding more witnesses. The underlying concern of this text is the prevention of collusion.

### 4. War (20:1–20)

These regulations governing the conduct of war are not found elsewhere in the Pentateuch. Curiously, however, when Abraham wages war, he appears to follow these regulations in detail (see comments on Ge 14). Moreover, Moses himself follows these rules in Dt 2:24–3:11. The central purpose of these instructions is to emphasize that Israel's warfare was not intended for foreign aggression or personal wealth.

The Israelites were to carry out warfare with nations "afar off" (vv.10–15) differently than with those nations whose land they were to inherit through God's promises (vv.16–20). With the first group, they were first to offer terms of peace. It is assumed that the cause of the war was just and hence Israel would have been justified in destroying the city. Thus Israel was to act mercifully with the offending nations. If the terms of peace were not met, Israel was justified in waging war. This passage therefore allows for a just war with nations "afar off." The effect of these regulations can be seen in 1Ki 20:31, for Israel was known by their neighbors as a "merciful" people in warfare.

On the other hand, Israel was to take the Promised Land as a gift from the Lord. They were not to grow rich from their warfare there, but were to "completely destroy" all the spoils (v.17; cf. Jos 7). In this way Israel would also have no opportunity of learning the "detestable worship" of the Canaanites.

These regulations emphasize that there was no need in Israel of a large standing army (17:16). The Lord would fight for his people. The entire army was to have complete trust in the Lord and act in complete obedience to his will. If anyone was not completely devoted to the Lord and the task of war, he was to be taken out of the ranks and allowed to return home.

### 5. Unsolved murder (21:1–9)

This law is not given elsewhere in the Pentateuch. Its purpose is clear: Whenever innocent blood was shed, it was the responsibility of the people to carry out justice and punish the offender (cf. 19:1–14). In the event that the guilty party was unknown, justice

could not be adequately served and thus the people were still held responsible. The present law, then, was the means whereby the people as a whole could settle an unsolved murder.

### 6. Treatment of captive women (21:10–14)

In warfare with nations that were "afar off," the Israelites were not to take the lives of the women and children when capturing a city (20:14). The present law ensured the well-being of those captured women by giving them protection against being sold into slavery. It also provided for the assimilation of captive women into the Israelite society by allowing marriage to them. This, however, raises a question, since marriage to Canaanite women was already expressly forbidden in 7:3.

There is no mention in the present passage of the personal faith or religion of such a woman taken into the house of an Israelite. In light of the strict warnings against the dangers of foreign women leading Israel into idolatry and false religion (7:3–4), however, it seems reasonable to conclude that this case presumes the woman would accept Israel's covenant stipulations. In this sense, the law anticipates the case of Rahab (see Jos 6:25). That example may not specifically apply here, however, since she was not from a nation "afar off" but was from Jericho, one of the cities of Canaan.

### 7. Right of the firstborn (21:15–17)

This law is not mentioned elsewhere in the Pentateuch, though the right of the "firstborn" is assumed throughout the pentateuchal narratives (e.g., Ge 25:29–34; 49:3). The law is intended to protect the legitimate firstborn son, even though his mother may not have been a favorite wife. Polygamy is not sanctioned by this law; rather, its adverse effects are curtailed. The principle of monogamy has been assumed by the writer of the Pentateuch since the beginning (Ge 2:24). A double portion of inheritance was to be given to the firstborn.

### 8. A rebellious son (21:18–21)

According to Lev 20:9, a son who cursed his father and mother was to be put to death; in Ex 21:15, the same penalty was given to one who attacked his father or mother. The present law generalizes the offense to include any kind of refusal to obey and assumes the same stiff measures. The law here, however, provides an additional safeguard. The parents were required to bring the child before a council of elders. The council, not the parents, had to decide the case, administer the penalty, and so eliminate the evil influence of such a child from among the people (v.21). Moreover, it was also to provide a warning to parents and children alike of the consequences of disobedience and rebellion.

We should remember that laws such as this one are not held up to present-day readers of the Pentateuch as examples of how they should obey God and do his will. Rather, they are examples of what God required of Israel under the Sinai covenant. The author has already presented Abraham as his one clear example of what it meant to "keep the law" (Ge 26:5), even though Abraham did not have these "laws" of the Sinai covenant. Faith and trust in God is the author's answer to the question of what keeping the law is all about. In selecting various laws from the Sinai covenant, the author intends to give us, the readers, a glimpse of life under the covenant at Sinai. One can easily agree with the apostle Paul that such a law was a "yoke of bondage" (Gal 5:1).

### 9. Various laws (21:22–22:12)

After an execution, the body could hang on a tree as a public display of the consequences of disobedience (21:22–23). It was not, however, to remain on the tree overnight.

The general principle is then laid down that one cannot hide one's eyes from an obvious need (22:1–4; cf. Ex

23:4–5). It is one's duty to care for the lost property of a neighbor.

The next rule is sufficiently general to forbid a man's wearing any item of feminine clothing or ornamentation, or a woman's wearing any item of masculine clothing or ornamentation (v.5). The only reason given is that such a practice is detestable to the Lord.

The law in vv.6–7 both suggests the sense of fair play inherent in God's law and shows that God cares for the least among his creation.

In v.8 is another example of the importance of looking out for one's neighbor, even in seemingly insignificant places. No area of life fails to come under the scrutiny of God's will.

Breeding mixed cattle, sowing mixed crops, or sewing mixed threads was prohibited in Lev 19:19. In like manner, mixing two kinds of seed in an orchard, plowing with an ox and a donkey, and wearing mixed cloth are also prohibited here (vv.9–11). Their underlying assumption is set forth in the Creation account of Ge 1—God made everything "after its own kind," and any attempt to mix the created order is a violation of his will.

For v.12, see Nu 15:39.

### 10. Marriage, adultery, and rape (22:13–30)

If doubt were to arise as to the virginity of one's bride, a formal accusation was to be made to the "elders of the city" and proof of virginity was to be given by her parents (v.13). If the accusation was false, the husband was to pay a penalty. A wife is thus protected from any wantonness on the part of her husband. It is usually supposed that the proof consisted of a blood-stained cloth or clothing that the parents had kept since the night of the wedding.

The law prohibiting adultery in Lev 20:10 is restated here in v.22. Its purpose is further explained here by the addition of the phrase "to purge the evil from Israel."

Various conditions are given for deciding the penalty for rape. The first cases (vv.23–27) are those in which the young girl was already "pledged to be married." In this case she was considered a married woman, and thus the penalty for adultery applied. The only question is whether both the young girl and the man consented. The second case (vv.28–29) deals with the rape of a young girl who was not "pledged to be married." The law protected her and ensured her continued welfare.

In Lev 18 a number of marriages among relatives were forbidden. In the present text (v.30), only one is repeated—marriage to "the wife of one's father" (likely a stepmother).

### 11. Exclusion from the assembly (23:1–8)

Several conditions disqualify one from entering "the assembly of the LORD"—emasculation (v.1), offspring of a forbidden marriage (v.2), offspring of Ammonites or Moabites (vv.3–6), and, to a lesser extent, offspring of Edomites or Egyptians (vv.7–8). It is not entirely clear what "entering the assembly" means. It may have the limited sense of exclusion from public service or marriage into an Israelite family, or, more generally, it may mean exclusion from Israel's covenant relationship with God. In light of the fact that other biblical texts state clearly that foreigners could enjoy the same privileges in Israel's worship as native Israelites (see Nu 15:15), a more limited interpretation of this passage is warranted. It probably prohibited those concerned from participation in public worship at the Temple (La 1:10) or marriage to Israelites (cf. 7:3). The issue seems to be the threat of foreign influence in Israel's worship of God. Thus full participation of non-Israelites was accepted if they exhibited true faith in God. The book of Ruth provides a clear example of a believing Moabite who entered into the congregation of Israel and was allowed

to marry into the royal tribe of Judah. See also comments on Ezr 9 and Ne 13:1–3, 23–27.

### 12. Uncleanness in the battle camp (23:9–14)

In Nu 5:1–4 instructions were given for maintaining the purity of the whole Israelite camp. Here the concern is for the camps of the armies of Israel during the time of battle.

### D. Miscellaneous Laws (23:15–25:19)

At the close of this section, the author has selected twenty-one (seven times three) sample laws to further illustrate the nature of the requirements of living under the Sinai covenant.

(1) A fugitive slave (23:15–16) was not to be turned over to his master.

(2) Shrine prostitution (23:17–18) was forbidden.

(3) Lending money on interest (23:19–20) to an Israelite was forbidden but was allowed for foreigners (cf. Ex 22:25; Lev 25:36–37).

(4) Though vows (23:21–23) were made voluntarily, they were to be promptly kept.

(5) Farmers were to share their produce with the people of the land, but the people were not to profit from the farmer's generosity (23:24–25).

(6) Divorce (24:1–4) was permitted but restricted. The first part (vv.1–3) states the conditions on which the verdict (v.4) rested. If a man legally divorced his wife, if his wife then married another man, and if the new husband then divorced her or died, that woman could not return to her first husband.

(7) During the first year of marriage, a man was not responsible for military service or any other duty (24:5). He was to devote the first year of marriage to "bring[ing] happiness to the wife he has married."

(8) The millstones were not to be taken in pledge because a person's daily subsistence depended on them (24:6).

(9) Kidnapping, prohibited in Ex 21:16, is here repeated (24:7), with slight elaboration. The specific wording of the law is reminiscent of the story of Joseph (Ge 37:26–27; 40:15).

(10) A brief further warning regarding the plague of leprosy (24:8–9) is given. Reference is made to the earlier priestly teaching on the subject (Lev 13–14).

(11) Even in lending money, God's people were to act righteously (24:10–13). A "righteous" lender does not forcefully exact payment and allows a poor person to retain his pledge overnight if it is a necessity.

(12) Wages were to be paid promptly to hired workers (24:14–15).

(13) Punishment for a crime was to be born by only the offender (24:16). Family members were not held responsible for each other's crimes (cf. Eze 18:1–4).

(14) The administration of law should be carried out with equity for all members of society (24:17–18).

(15) The practice of allowing the needy to glean in the field is here grounded in remembrance of Israel's hard service in Egypt (24:19–22; cf. Lev 19:9; 23:22).

(16) Punishment was to be equitably carried out in the presence of the judges (25:1–3) and was limited to forty stripes.

(17) A concrete example is given to illustrate a general principle (25:4): A worker should be allowed to enjoy the fruit of his own labor. Paul applied this principle to Christian service in 1Co 9:9–10.

(18) Levirate marriage (25:5–10) is prescribed only here, though the earlier narratives presuppose it (e.g., Ge 38:8). It was used to preserve the name of a deceased brother.

(19) The consequence of the immodest act of 25:11–12 is the only example of punishment by mutilation in the Pentateuch.

(20) The weights and measures of trade were to be kept equitably (25:13–16). The motive was not only the blessing of long life in the land but also the fact that "the LORD your God detests anyone who does these things" (cf. Lev 19:35).

(21) The admonition to remember the treachery of the Amalekites is repeated to this new generation (25:17–19) just as it was to those who came out of Egypt (Ex 17:14; see also comments on Nu 22–24).

## E. Two Ceremonies: Firstfruits and Tithes (26:1–15)

### 1. Firstfruits (26:1–11)

The firstfruits of the produce of the land were to be given to the Lord (Ex 23:9–14; 34:26; Lev 27:30–33; Nu 18:12–13). They were to be brought to the priests as their inheritance (Dt 18:3–8) during the Feast of Harvest (Ex 34:22; Lev 23:15–17; Nu 28:26; Dt 16:9–10) and the Passover (Lev 2:14; 23:10). The present passage initiates a special ceremony to be carried out at this time, in which a portion of the firstfruits was set apart in a basket and brought to the priest in acknowledgment of God's gift of the good land. Also at this time the rehearsal of God's gracious dealings with the fathers was spoken before the Lord (vv.5–9).

### 2. Tithes (26:12–15)

Tithes were discussed earlier in 14:22–29. This passage describes the prayer offered at the giving of the second tithe. That prayer not only acknowledged payment of the tithe but also confessed general obedience to the Lord and an expectation of his blessing.

## F. Conclusion (26:16–19)

Moses' concluding words hark back to the beginning of the covenant at Sinai in Ex 19:5–6. If Israel obeyed the covenant, they would be God's prized possession, and he would make them an exalted and holy nation.

## VIII. The Covenant Ceremony in Moab (27:1–28:68)

### A. The Instructions Regarding the Stones and Altar on Mount Ebal (27:1–10)

When the people entered the land they were to set up large stones on Mount Ebal (vv.1–4), along with an altar for sacrifices, fellowship offerings, and a sacred meal (vv.5–8). The stones were to be plastered over and prepared for writing (a common method for public monuments in ancient Canaan). These stones appear to be the same stones as those used for the altar (v.8). The content of the writing is not specified; suggestions are the Ten Commandments, the blessings and curses of chs. 27–28, or the whole book of Deuteronomy. In Jos 8:32, when this command was carried out, Joshua "copied on stones the law of Moses" (the same expression translated "a copy of this law" in Dt 17:18). The purpose of this writing was to remind the people of the importance of obeying the covenant and its laws.

The ceremony described in this text is reminiscent of the covenant ceremony in Ex 24:4–8, where an altar was built with twelve stone pillars and God's words were written on the stone tablets and read before all the people.

### B. Twelve Curses (27:11–26)

A further ceremony was to be carried out when the people entered the land. It was to be held in the northern territory of the tribe of Manasseh near Shechem. There stood two mountains, Gerizim and Ebal. Half of the tribes of Israel (Simeon, Levi, Judah, Issachar, Joseph, and Benjamin) were to stand on Mount Gerizim to recount the blessings of the covenant, and the other half (Reuben, Gad, Asher, Zebulun, Dan, and Naphtali) were to stand on Mount Ebal to recount the curses (see vv.14–26 for the first set of twelve curses). Curiously enough, the "blessings" to be recited on Mount Gerizim are not recorded here. Perhaps this stresses that Israel did not prove themselves obedient to the covenant and hence did not enjoy the blessings.

### C. Blessings and Curses (28:1–68)

Another list of blessings and curses is given. These are not a continuation of the words to be recited at Ebal and Gerizim but are rather a further elaboration of the blessings and curses that would be incurred in the covenant. But it is implied in Jos 8:34 that these blessings and curses were also recited by the tribes at Ebal and Gerizim. If this "book of the law" in Jos 8:34 is our Pentateuch, then the blessings that were read on that occasion could only have been those of ch. 28, for no blessings are recorded in ch. 27.

Just as the curses were given more prominence in the ceremony of ch. 27, so the curses incurred by disobedience to the covenant are much more fully developed here. The writer of the Pentateuch hints that Israel would not prove faithful to the covenant (cf. Dt 31:16–18, 27) and thus would not enjoy its blessings.

The nature of the blessing is reminiscent of the blessing in the Garden of Eden: enjoyment of God's good land and many offspring (cf. Ge 1:28). The description of the curse, on the other hand, is reminiscent of the curse after the Fall (Ge 3:14–24): affliction and ultimately exile from God's land (see especially Dt 28:36, 64–68). The description of the curse also anticipates the fate of the nation at the time of the Babylonian captivity (Jer 43:7; 52:1–27).

## IX. The New Covenant (29:1–34:12)

### A. Introduction (29:1)

It is not entirely correct to speak here of a "renewal" of the covenant. This introductory verse states clearly that the covenant that Moses now speaks of is "in addition to the covenant he had made with them at Horeb [Sinai]." With these words, Moses is deliberately setting up a contrast between the covenant at Sinai and the covenant he envisions for Israel in the future. The past has ended in Israel's failure to keep the covenant and to trust in God. However, there is hope for the future; it is to this hope that Moses now turns. Thus the content of the following chapter focuses clearly on the themes of the new covenant. It is not by accident that it is precisely in these chapters that the NT writers see a prophecy regarding faith and the coming of Christ (e.g., Ro 10:6–13).

## B. Warnings Regarding the Covenant (29:2–28)

With a sober realism regarding Israel's failure to keep the covenant, Moses gives a final warning of the consequences of disobedience. In this section, the warnings are not so much designed to call Israel to obedience as to lay before them the tragic consequences of their repeated failure. This is not just one more call for obedience. That, of course, is something Deuteronomy already has plenty of. It is rather the groundwork for a new work of God that lies yet in the future. This new work is described in ch. 30. It is the work of faith and obedience that flows from a new heart (30:6).

Moses begins with a review of Israel's complete failure to see and understand God's work in their midst (v.4)—a review covering the same lessons as Dt 1–3. It begins with God's work in Egypt and continues to the conquest of the Transjordan (vv.2–8). Moses further grounds the work of God in the promises made to the "fathers, Abraham, Isaac and Jacob" (vv.9–13); thus he presupposes the lessons of Genesis.

As one example of these lessons, Moses turns to the story of Sodom and Gomorrah (v.23). His treatment of that narrative is an interesting reversal of

the themes found in Genesis. In Genesis, the account of the destruction of Sodom and Gomorrah was intended to show not only God's wrath against the wickedness of the pagan nations but also his salvation of the "righteous." The reminder that this same divine wrath could equally be turned against his own disobedient people is a startling thought here at the close of the Pentateuch. It redefines or, at least, clarifies what the Genesis narrative means when it speaks of the "righteous." It was not enough to be God's own people, or even to be a member of the covenant. Something more is required. Initially that "something more" is described negatively, as "they went off and worshiped other gods" (v.26). The next chapter stresses the positive side: "The LORD your God will circumcise your hearts and the hearts of your descendants, so that you may love him with all your heart and with all your soul and live" (30:6).

## C. Conclusion (29:29)

Moses closes these opening remarks abruptly with a statement about the limits of God's revelation. God has not revealed the whole of his wisdom and knowledge, but he has revealed "all the words of this law," and they are given to all generations. There is no end to the "secret mysteries" that one devises about God and his world. Moses, however, puts an end to all of them here by simply pointing to God's great act of grace in revealing his will in the law. The "secret things" simply refer to that which God has not revealed in Scripture.

## D. Future Blessing (30:1–20)

Before concluding this book, Moses takes a long look into the future of God's people. He speaks of a time when Israel's disobedience would lead to their captivity in a foreign land. He has already anticipated this view of Israel's future (see 28:36, 64–68), but now he looks beyond that time of judgment to a more distant time of restoration and redemption. At some point in the future, when Israel finds itself dispersed among the nations, they will again turn to the Lord, and the Lord will have compassion on them and restore them to the land (vv.1–5). At that time the Lord will give them a new heart (a "circumcised heart"; v.6, cf. 10:16), and they will "love him with all [their] heart and with all [their] soul, and live." Moses has in view the promise of the "new covenant" spoken of in Jer 31:31–34 and Eze 36:22–28. For these later prophets the hope still remained that in spite of Israel's repeated failure, God's promises to the fathers would ultimately be fulfilled, and that sometime in the future Israel would be restored to the land and the covenant.

In the time after the Babylonian captivity, when the Israelites were allowed to return to the land, much expectation arose regarding the fulfillment of this promise in ch. 30. The words of Nehemiah's prayer (Ne 9), for example, reflect his hope that in his own day the promise would be fulfilled. As the book of Nehemiah goes on to show, however, his hope was not realized, and the time of the return from the Exile was not to be the time of the fulfillment of Dt 30. In the NT, Simeon shows that at the time of Christ's coming, devout Israelites were still awaiting its fulfillment (Lk 2:25). Jesus himself said clearly that these texts in Deuteronomy and the Prophets, as well as many other Scriptures, were to be understood as pointers to his coming (e.g., Lk 24:25–27).

In explaining the nature of the new covenant, Moses compares it to the covenant at Sinai (vv.11–14). In that earlier covenant, the Law was written on tablets of stone that Moses went up Mount Sinai to receive and then took back to proclaim to the people. Thus, when he says in the present chapter,

"What I am commanding you . . . is not up in heaven, so that you have to ask, 'Who will ascend into heaven to get it and proclaim it to us so we may obey it?'" he means that in the new covenant the law would not be given again on tablets of stone but written on circumcised hearts, as in Eze 36:26. The view that Moses went "up to heaven" to receive the law has already been expressed in Deuteronomy. At Sinai, for example, God spoke directly to the people "from heaven" (4:36). Furthermore, his reference to going across "the sea to get [the commandment]" (30:13) alludes to Moses' leading the people across the Red Sea and to Sinai. Thus, in contrast to the giving of the Law in the Sinai covenant, in the covenant that Moses speaks of here, "the word is very near you; it is in your mouth and in your heart so that you may obey it" (v.14). This is again virtually identical to Jeremiah's view of the new covenant (Jer 31:31). Along similar lines, Paul interprets the present text as a reference to the coming of Christ and the emphasis in the new covenant on "faith" (Ro 10:6–9).

The word "today" in v.15 shows that at this point in the chapter, the perspective and focus of Moses' words are no longer that of the future time after the Exile. We are brought back to Moses and the people who are about to enter the land. Moses closes this section with several allusions to the first instance of the revelation of the will of God in the Scriptures, Adam in the Garden of Eden. He draws a comparison between the first work of God in providing a good land for his people and the situation of Israel as they were preparing to enter again into God's good land. Just as God had put "the tree of knowledge of good and evil" before the first man and woman in the garden (Ge 2:9b) and had commanded them not to eat from it on pain of death (Ge 2:17), so now Moses again presents to the people the choice of "good and evil" and "life and death" (Dt 30:16). Just as Adam and Eve were to depend on God's knowledge of "good and evil," so also in this covenant the people were to look to God's law as the pathway to the "good" and the means of regaining the "[tree of] life" that was lost in the Fall (Ge 3:22–24). And just as the godly were described in the Genesis narratives as those who "walked with God" (Ge 3:8; 5:22–24; 6:9; 17:1), so also here, keeping the covenant and enjoying God's blessings are described as "walking in his ways" (30:16). By carefully choosing his words to reflect back on these earlier themes in the Pentateuch, Moses skillfully draws his book to a conclusion by returning to its central themes.

The tragedy latent in these final words of hope is the fact that in the next chapter, Moses shows that the future choice of God's people would not be for the good but for the evil (see 31:16–17).

### E. Provisions for Maintaining the Leadership of Moses (31:1–29)

The work of Moses was to be maintained and continued in various ways after his death. The Lord himself would go before the people in battle with the Canaanites (vv.3–6), and Joshua was to be their new leader (vv.1–8, 14–18, 23). Moses was to write down the Law that God had given them and entrust it to the priests, who were to keep it in the Ark of the Covenant and read it publicly every seven years during the Feast of Tabernacles (vv.9–13, 24–27). Moses was also to write a song that would serve as a continual reminder of the message of the Law (vv.19–22; see 31:30–32:47).

The disobedience and failure of the people are repeatedly stressed in this section (vv.16–18, 27–29). According to v.29, it was because of the failure of the people that Moses wrote his song. It was to be a warning that "in the last days" ("in days to come," NIV) disaster would fall on God's people. It is impor-

tant to see that the introduction of this poem clearly sets its context as "the last days." It is not about something that would happen in the immediate future, but rather something that will take place "at the end of the days." It is not surprising, then, to find that there are no references to specific historical events in this poem. The description of the judgment of God on Israel and the nations is apocalyptic in scope and global in extent.

### F. The Song of Moses (31:30–32:47)

This song is another example of the way poetry is used in the Pentateuch to teach its major themes (see also Ge 49; Nu 24). The central theme of the poem is Israel's apostasy and God's threatening judgment. After a short introduction (vv.1–7), the poem begins with a description of God's election (vv.8–9) of Israel and his care for them from the time of the desert wanderings (vv.10–12) to their possession and initial enjoyment of the blessings in the land (vv.13–14). However, the poem turns quickly to Israel's presumptuous neglect of God's goodness and their apostasy (vv.15–21a). Once again it is idolatry that turns their heart from God. Then Moses gives a dramatic portrayal of God's future outpouring of wrath on his people (vv.21b–27) and Israel's continuing blindness in the face of it (vv.28–33). The emphasis on God's judgment of Israel raises the question of God's judgment of all the nations (vv.34–38). The vengeance stored up against Israel (v.34) is grounded in God's righteous vindication of the iniquity of all peoples (vv.35–42). In the end, however, God's judgment of Israel and the nations leads to a broader understanding of the concept of the people of God—not just Israel, but the nations, along with Israel, are called to praise God as "his people" (v.43).

Moses closes his song with a reminder to the people to pay close attention to these words he has put before them and to teach them carefully to their children (vv.45–47). These words are of central importance. They are the very life of the people as they now enter the Promised Land. Again it can be seen that the text portrays the Law as God's gift of life to his people in much the same way as the Tree of Life was put into the midst of the Garden of Eden (Ge 2:8–17). Just as obedience to the Lord's command not to eat of the Tree of the Knowledge of Good and Evil was the key to their access to the Tree of Life (Ge 2:16–17), so obedience to the Lord's command in the Law was to be Israel's key to "living long in the land" that God had prepared for them.

## G. God's Instructions to Moses to Die on Mount Nebo (32:48–52)

God repeats his instructions about Moses' death from Nu 27:12–14, only with more details. The purpose of this repetition is not clear, though perhaps it was to reestablish the general chronological sequence of events. In this way, we are aware that Deuteronomy is intended to be read as a discourse between Moses and Israel. At its close, the line of events is taken up again from the narrative at the end of Numbers. This section also anticipates the final chapter of this book, where Moses' death is recorded. His death was thus a fulfillment of God's words spoken in the present text.

## H. The Blessing of Moses (33:1–29)

These final words of Moses to the people are introduced as a "blessing." They begin with a brief introduction (vv.2–5) and, after listing the blessings for each of the tribes of Israel (vv.6–25), Simeon excluded, they conclude with a summary (vv.26–29).

### 1. The introduction (33:2–5)

Moses begins by returning to the central theme of the Pentateuch, the appearance of God among his people that was initiated at Mount Sinai and continued throughout their time in the desert.

This was a time when God showed Israel his love and cared for them with his holy angels. Through the Law given them by Moses Israel received God's instruction. The sense of the term "law" here is not so much the laws given at Sinai, but rather the "Book of the Law" that Moses wrote down and gave to the people (31:24–26). Moses' purpose was to show the importance of this book as divine instruction. Thus, in the blessing of the tribe of Levi, what is stressed is the responsibility given to the Levites of guarding the "Book of the Law" and teaching it to Israel (33:10). Already within the Pentateuch there is a clear distinction between the laws given Israel at Sinai and the Law (*torah*), represented by the Pentateuch itself.

Furthermore, Moses is here portrayed as a "king" among God's people. Though one can argue that the "king" in v.5 should be understood as the Lord, the immediate context strongly suggests that it is Moses. This is important in light of the fact that in the next chapter, Moses is viewed as a "prototype" of the coming prophet (see 18:15). Thus at the close of the Pentateuch, the two central messianic visions of the book, that of a coming king (Ge 49:10; Nu 24:7–9) and of a prophet (Dt 18:15), are united in the figure of Moses, the prophet-king.

We should also note that throughout the Pentateuch Moses also carries out the duties of priest. Thus in Moses, the OT brings together the offices of prophet, priest, and king. The text is always careful to note, however, that Moses was not a priest of the house of Aaron. His priesthood is of a different order than that pictured in the office of Moses. To find an analogy to Moses elsewhere in the Pentateuch, we need look no further than the figure of Melchizedek, the priest-king from Salem. Thus, as Melchizedek, the priest-king blessed Abraham at the beginning of the patriarchal narratives (compare Ge 14:19 and Dt 33:29), so here Moses the priest-king blessed the Israelites at the conclusion.

### 2. Blessings (33:6–25)

The blessings of each of the individual tribes are similar in many respects to the words of Jacob in Ge 49:1–27. Unlike Ge 49, however, where Judah is the central figure, the present passage pays rather scant attention to Judah and emphasizes instead the importance of Levi and Joseph. The Levites were given the role of teaching the Law to all Israel (vv.8–11), and the tribe of Joseph is pictured as enjoying the most abundant part of the land (vv.13–17). Clearly the intention of the blessings was to include the whole of Israel in God's blessing, both the tribes of the north, represented here in Joseph (Ephraim and Manasseh, v.17), and the priests, the house of Levi, who are otherwise excluded from the inheritance of the land.

We should not think, however, that the importance of the tribe of Judah has been diminished in this blessing. On the contrary, by focusing on the centrality of the "king" among the tribes of Israel, the introduction to the blessing draws heavily on the earlier blessings that stressed the role of Judah in God's future dealings with Israel (Ge 49:10; Nu 24:7–9).

### 3. Conclusion (33:26–29)

The final words of the blessing speak of the nation as a whole and of its enjoyment of God's good gift of the land. As we might expect, here at the end of the book, Moses pictures Israel's dwelling in the land as a reversal of the events of the early chapters of Genesis when Adam and Eve were cast out of the Garden of Eden. Just as God once "drove" the man from his good land (Ge 3:23) and "placed" cherubim to guard its entry, so he will again "drive" (v.27) the enemy from the good land and place Israel there to enjoy its bless-

ings (many of the words used are the same). In other words, the future that Moses envisions for the people of Israel is like that which God intended in the beginning.

### I. The Death of Moses (34:1–12)

The account of the death of Moses was probably added long after his death. By the time this chapter was written, his burial was so far in the past that the location of his grave was uncertain to the writer (v.6). Furthermore, a long succession of prophets had come and gone so that the writer could say, "Since then, no prophet has risen in Israel like Moses" (v.10). Though added later, this chapter plays a major role in the interpretation of the Pentateuch.

The chapter provides the final statement regarding the Lord's refusal to allow Moses to enter the Promised Land. It thus links up with the important theme that Moses, who lived under the law, was not allowed to enter into God's blessings because he failed "to trust" in God (Nu 20:12). According to this chapter, Moses did not die of old age (cf. v.7). His death was punishment, just like the generation that died in the wilderness during the forty years (Nu 14:22–23). Thus the life of Moses becomes the last example of the consequences of the fall of Adam and Eve. He, like they, was not allowed to enjoy the blessing of God's good land.

In contrast to Moses, however, this chapter also portrays Joshua as the new leader, ready and able to take the people into the Promised Land in obedience to God's commands. What is stressed here is the fact that Joshua was "filled with the spirit [or Spirit] of wisdom" (v.9) and was thus able to do the work of God. Like Joseph (Ge 41:37) and Bezalel (Ex 31:3), also filled with "the Spirit of God," Joshua was able to do God's work successfully. Thus this last chapter of the Pentateuch returns to a central theme, begun already in Ge 1: "the Spirit of God was hovering over the surface of the deep" (Ge 1:2). Only by God's Spirit can his work be done. Even when God himself does his work of creation, he does so by means of his Spirit.

Finally, this last chapter provides an important link to the rest of the books of the Bible that follow. By showing us that long after the time of Moses "the prophet like Moses" had not yet come (v.10), this chapter prepares us for reading the books that follow. It would be otherwise possible to read the book of Joshua, for example, and draw the conclusion that all the promises to Israel had been fulfilled in the successful conquest of the land under Joshua's leadership. This chapter, however, warns us that there is still more to God's promises than that which lay immediately ahead in Israel's history. In this respect it anticipates further statements in the book of Joshua (e.g., Jos 23:15–16) and Judges (Jdg 2:10–15) that show that the initial success of Israel under Joshua's leadership ended in failure, much as had been the case under the leadership of Moses. We are thus invited to look beyond those events to the coming of someone else—one like Joshua, and also one like Moses. In other words, this final chapter picks up the theme of the coming Messiah; and using Moses as a type, it turns our gaze beyond the immediate historical events to the future work of God in fulfilling his promises to the fathers.

# The Deuteronomic History

The concept of a "Deuteronomic History" is an important aspect of the OT historical books. Simply put, the concept is that in the writing of Joshua through 2 Kings, the overriding purpose was to teach and extol the basic message put forth in the book of Deuteronomy. Many biblical scholars hold that Joshua, Judges, 1 and 2 Samuel, and 1 and 2 Kings were originally written as one book, though this is by no means certain. What is important for our purposes, however, is the fact that these four books show a remarkable amount of similarity in theme and purpose and seem to have the same central message—one closely associated with the themes and message of Deuteronomy. It is this singularity of purpose that allows us to call this group of books the Deuteronomic History. In the following section we will look closely at the themes and purpose of this history.

## I. The Purpose of the Deuteronomic History

The purpose of this group of books is twofold. (1) The books are devoted to an explanation of Israel's exile in Babylon. The premise of the books is Dt 28: Israel had agreed to the covenant with God but had broken the stipulations. The punishment written there for such a breach of covenant was exile from the land. Thus these books explain that Israel went into exile not because God was unfaithful to the covenant, but because Israel had not kept it.

(2) These historical books also show Israel, and God's people generally, the way back to recovery and blessing. They are not merely an attempt to point out failure. They are more importantly a guidepost to repentance and faith. Again the premise is Dt 28:2: "All these blessings will come upon you and accompany you if you obey the LORD, your God." The message of these historical books is "Trust and Obey."

How do these books teach this message? By looking at how the books have been written, we can easily see the way in which this lesson is taught. The writers simply select certain events and persons whose lives and work in Israel's history either exemplified what it meant to trust and obey God (e.g., David) or what it meant not to trust and obey (e.g., Saul). The message is taught by contrasting the good examples with the bad. The reader is left to draw out the lesson from each of the historical examples given. Always, however, the lesson is to be drawn from the message of Deuteronomy. To "trust and obey" meant to do that which God had told them to do in the Book of the Law. We should, then, take a closer look at the central message of Deuteronomy.

## II. General Summary of the Message of Deuteronomy

(1) Deuteronomy first of all called for an absolute allegiance to the God of the covenant—"You shall have no other gods before me" (Dt 5:7). As can be easily seen from reading these books, one of the dominant recurring failures of Israel was their forsaking the Lord to follow after the gods of Canaan: "Then the Israelites did evil in the eyes of the LORD and served the Baals. They forsook the LORD, the God of their fathers, who had brought them out of Egypt. They followed and worshiped various gods of the peoples around them. They provoked the LORD to anger" (Jdg 2:11–13).

(2) Deuteronomy specified clearly and precisely the way in which Israel was to worship the God of the covenant. At the center of Israel's worship was the stipulation that God was to be worshiped at the place where he alone had chosen (Dt 12:1–14). Thus the

community's worship always rested in God's sovereign will.

(3) Israel's leadership was to be carried out by one man, a king, who was also to be a spiritual leader of God's people. Because the well-being of the nation was directly tied to the obedience of its leaders, the king was to be one who studied the law of God and was sensitive to the teaching of his word (see Dt 17:18–20).

(4) All Israelites—including the king—were to be careful to observe the words of the prophet whom God would send to speak to them his words (see Dt 18:14–19).

On the basis of these central ideas, the writers of Joshua, Judges, Samuel, and Kings set out to evaluate the failure of Israel and to provide the basis for a new hope of God's blessing for the future. We will now take a close look at three representative narratives from these books to see how these themes are developed.

## III. Representative Narratives

### A. Gideon (Jdg 6–8)

The narrative of Gideon is a part of the stories that take up the activities of Israel's leaders during the early stages of nationhood. Israel was a special kind of nation—a theocracy. Israel's real King was God. This meant that Israel's leaders had a special responsibility to rule the people in God's behalf. There could be no thought of an autonomous king: the Lord, alone, was Israel's King.

The story of Gideon was intended to show how an earthly ruler should govern God's people in light of the above-mentioned fact.

(1) God does not rely on the strength of a man to lead his people. This lesson is first seen in the fact that Gideon, like David, was of the smallest family in his tribe (Manasseh) and was the youngest of his father's house (Jdg 6:15; cf. 1Sa 16:1–13). The same lesson lies behind the narratives dealing with

Gideon's quest for a sign (Jdg 6:36–40). Gideon could be assured of a victory over the Midianites only if God was with him. God gave him that assurance by means of the signs.

Another incident with the same message is the narrative recounting the reduction of Gideon's army from 32,000 warriors down to 10,000, and then to 300 (7:1–8). On this occasion the lesson was stated explicitly: "The LORD said to Gideon, 'You have too many men for me to deliver Midian into their hands. In order that Israel may not boast against me that her own strength saved her, announce now to the people . . .'" (7:2–3).

Finally, it is important to note that Gideon's success depended on the same factor as all the other leaders in these historical books, namely, the work of the Spirit of God (6:34). The theme that echoes continuously throughout these narratives is that expressed later by the prophet Zechariah, "'Not by might nor by power, but by my Spirit,' says the LORD Almighty" (Zec 4:6).

(2) The leader of God's people must be zealous for the purity of the people's worship of God. Already in Dt 17:18–20, God said that the king was to lead the people in obeying God's law. In fact, the very existence of the nation was dependent on the spiritual well-being of the king.

Gideon showed great zeal for the Lord and the purity of his worship in Israel when he destroyed the altar of Baal and Asherah and erected in its place an altar to the Lord (Jdg 6:25–32). Gideon, in fact, is subsequently given the name Jerub-Baal, which means "Let Baal contend with him" (6:32). An interesting note in 6:27 indicates that because Gideon "was afraid of his family and the men of the town, he did it by night rather than in the daytime." The writer apparently wants to highlight Gideon's zeal for the Lord by revealing this insight into his actions. Even though he was afraid of the consequences, he did what God required.

(3) The leader of God's people must not usurp the right of God himself to rule his people. The leader must always remember that he only represents the real Leader—the Lord. This lesson can be seen in Gideon's refusal to accept the offer of kingship in Israel (see 8:22–23). It is important to keep in mind that this passage does not rule out the idea of a political kingship in Israel, but rather it shows that only a king whom God chooses can rightfully rule his people. It also shows that such a king must have the kind of attitude shown by Gideon—one that clearly acknowledges that the Lord is the only true King in Israel.

(4) There is also a negative lesson to be learned from the story of Gideon. No matter how successful the leader might have been, he cannot cease to diligently rule the people, lest they turn from following after God. This lesson is seen in the matter of Gideon's ephod (8:24–27). Gideon requested that his heroic deeds be rewarded by a share in the spoils of the Midianites. In a careless gesture, he made an ephod from the gold earrings of the Midianite spoils, and it became an object of worship in his own household (8:27).

This negative aspect of Gideon's story, as well as the negative moments of all the stories of God's leaders, serves a broader function in the whole Deuteronomic History. It creates a kind of anticipation, an expectation, of an ideal leader yet to come—a leader who would follow the lessons of the past and who would not fall short of the task of leading God's people in God's way. This expectation runs parallel to the growing concern of the prophetic literature—the disillusionment in the earthly leadership in Israel (prophet, priest, king) and the expectation of a "coming king" who would rule the people in righteousness and truth.

Along with this expectation of an ideal leader in the Deuteronomic History, there is the tendency to view certain leaders as more representative of the proper kind of leadership than others. Certainly David comes out on top as the closest approximation to the ideal—but he, too, had his faults (see 2Sa 11–12).

## B. Samson (Jdg 13–16)

The story of Samson is one of the most puzzling of all the biblical stories. When we look at all the events in his life, it becomes clear that many things he did could not be lessons of godly leadership. But what stands out most clearly is the zeal with which he fought against the enemies of God's people. He is, to this extent then, an example of the wholehearted zeal that God's leader is to have against the enemies of God.

## C. The Man of God at Bethel (1Ki 13)

Perhaps the story that best illustrates the intention of the author behind the selection of material in the Deuteronomic History is the story of the man of God sent to proclaim judgment upon Jeroboam's newly established altar at Bethel (1Ki 13). In this story, several of the deuteronomic themes are woven together.

In 1Ki 12 there are two primary events. (1) The kingdom has been divided, with Jeroboam becoming king of the northern kingdom (Israel). (2) This king, fearing that the people would return their loyalty to the Davidic king, established his own worship centers apart from the Temple at Jerusalem. He set up altars and golden calves at Bethel and Dan. Note how such an act cuts across the deuteronomic view of worship. Not only does Jeroboam relocate where Israel is to worship God (a direct violation of God's choice of Jerusalem in 2Sa 7); but also Jeroboam replaced the Levitical priests with priests from among the people and initiated new seasons and festivals. By instituting false worship, he was causing Israel to sin.

The following events are important in ch. 13. (1) It opens with the mission of a "man of God" to Bethel: he was to confront the king with God's word. Note how this follows the outline of the role of the prophet in Dt 18:18—to confront the king with the requirements of the covenant.

(2) When the prophet confronted Jeroboam and proved he was truly sent from God, Jeroboam had a change of heart toward the prophet—but it was not for the good. He wanted, rather, for the prophet to side with him in his new place of worship (13:7).

(3) But the prophet was under strict orders from the Lord. He was to return directly to his home. Thus he answered the king, "Even if you were to give me half your possessions, I would not go with you, nor would I eat bread or drink water here" (13:8).

(4) A new turn of events, however, faced the prophet on his return home: he was met by the old prophet from Bethel, who tried to persuade him that the Lord had told him that the man of God must return with him and eat with him. When he consented to the old prophet and ate with him, the man of God disobeyed the divine word given him, and it is interpreted as an act of rebellion. The lesson was clear: the man of God was to have absolute obedience to the word of God. He was not to let even a "new" word from God turn him from the word he had received.

The message of this section comes into even sharper focus when we view it against the background of the Exile. It was the duty of the prophets to warn the king and the people of their disobedience to the covenant. They did this by warning the nation of the impending exile. But there were always other prophets who proclaimed a different message (e.g., Hananiah in Jer 28). Most of the people followed the false prophets and turned away from the Lord, and their fate was thus sealed in the Exile. The experience of the man of God, then, was echoed many times over in the lives of those Israelites before the Exile.

# Joshua

## Introduction

The book receives its name from its central character, Joshua, the son of Nun (cf. 1Ch 7:20–28). He was from the tribe of Ephraim (Nu 13:8). We first learn of him in Ex 17:8–13, where he, with God's help, sorely defeated the Amalekites in battle.

Since it was not customary in the ancient world for a literary work to bear the name of its author, the book of Joshua is an anonymous work. Although many have supposed that Joshua wrote the book, and there is evidence of the use of "eyewitness" accounts in the book, there are also indications that the book, or at least part of it, was written a considerable time after the death of Joshua (e.g., the account of the death of Joshua in ch. 24). If we consider Joshua as the author, we must still say that the last chapter and several other sections were added to the book at a later date. Fortunately, however, it is not necessary to know the identity of the author of a work such as this in order to understand it.

From a close reading of the book we can see that the writer of Joshua intends to show that the Lord did, in fact, fulfill his promises to Abraham (Ge 13:15) and to Moses (Ex 3:8). As such, the book is a lesson of the faithfulness of God and his promises (cf. Jos 21:43–45; 23:14). At the same time, however, the book sets the stage for the beginning of a new era in God's dealings with Israel—namely, the history of Israel's failure to live up to their covenant obligations as God's people (cf. Jos 23:15–16). Thus two themes converge in this: (1) God's faithfulness to his promises; and (2) Israel's failure to trust and obey. In much of this book, the latter theme is kept in the background.

(1) That the overriding theme of Joshua is God's faithfulness to his covenant promises is seen in the summary statement in 21:43–45: "So the LORD gave Israel all the land he had sworn to give their forefathers, and they took possession of it and settled there. The LORD gave them rest on every side, just as he had sworn to their forefathers. Not one of all their enemies withstood them; the LORD handed all their enemies over to them. Not one of all the LORD's good promises to the house of Israel failed; every one was fulfilled."

(2) At the end of the book (23:15), however, we begin to hear the note of Israel's failure, "But just as every good promise of the LORD your God has come true, so the LORD will bring on you all the evil he has threatened, until he has destroyed you from this good land he has given you."

We cannot overlook the fact that throughout the narratives of this book, the man Joshua is presented in an exemplary way as a model of godly leadership. Not only are we, the readers, prepared by the pentateuchal narratives to accept Joshua's leadership as a replacement of Moses (Nu 27:18–23), but even more, we are repeatedly reminded that his leadership was characterized by the work of God's Spirit (Nu 27:18; Dt 34:9; cf. 11:16–30;).

Through a number of means, the writer of Joshua has deliberately linked this book to the Pentateuch. His success in doing so is evidenced by the fact that no one today would think of reading the book of Joshua apart from the context of the pentateuchal narratives. In the commentary that follows we will draw out the implications of a number of significant links between Joshua and the first five books of the Bible. In the present section, however, we will attempt to uncover some of the narrative means by which these two books are connected.

First, it is important to note that the book of Joshua begins with an explicit reference to the last event in the Pentateuch—the death of Moses (cf. Jos

1:1; Dt 34:5). It assumes that the readers are fully aware of who Moses was and that he has already died. Moreover, the writer of Joshua assumes his readers will be familiar with much of what Moses had commanded the nation of Israel. Joshua continually refers to "all the law my servant Moses gave you" (e.g., Jos 1:7, 13). In fact, already in 1:8 the Pentateuch is mentioned: "the Book of the Law."

Not only does Joshua contain these explicit references to the Pentateuch, but there are also indications that it assumes on the part of its readers a far more fundamental acquaintance with the material and message of the earlier work. For example, it casts its central characters and major events in roles and patterns that reflect the central characters and major events in the Pentateuch. The purpose of such shaping of the narratives is to establish a relationship between the events in the book of Joshua and those of the Pentateuch that can best be described as one of promise and fulfillment. In the Pentateuch it was clearly promised that what God had done for Moses and the Israelite people in the events of the Exodus and at Sinai, he would also do for the future generations. This we see carried out in the book of Joshua. Such is the theme, for example, in the Song of the Sea (Ex 15). The conclusion of the song in Ex 15:13–18 is a virtual outline of the events in the book of Joshua. Thus by drawing a parallel between those earlier events and the events in the life of Joshua, the writer is able to show that what God had promised was now being fulfilled.

The accompanying chart lists some significant parallels and links between Joshua and the Pentateuch.

| The Pentateuch | The Book of Joshua |
|---|---|
| (1) Crossing the Red Sea: "The waters were divided, and the Israelites went through the sea on dry ground" (Ex 14:21–22). | Crossing the Jordan River: "And the LORD said, 'Today I will begin to exalt you in the eyes of all Israel, so they may know that I am with you as I was with Moses" (Jos 3:7); "The whole nation had completed the crossing on dry ground" (Jos 3:17) ; "The LORD your God did to the Jordan just what he had done to the Red Sea" (Jos 4:23). |
| (2) Blood on the doorposts marking the houses of those who were to be saved in the Exodus (Ex 12:13). | Red cord marking the house of Rahab; anyone in the house would be saved in the conquest (Jos 2:7–20). |
| (3) Israelite males were saved from the command of the king by the resourceful and courageous Hebrew midwives (Ex 1:17–19); Moses' life was saved by his mother by being hidden from the king in the reeds (Ex 2:3); in the Song of the Sea, Moses says, "The people of Canaan will melt away" (Ex 15:15); God rewarded the midwives by giving them "houses of their own" (NIV, "families") (Ex 1:21). | Israelite spies were saved from the command of the king by the resourceful and courageous Canaanite harlot (Jos 2:3–4); Israelite spies were saved by Rahab by being hidden from the king in the stalks of flax (Jos 2:6); Rahab tells the spies, "All who live in this country are melting in fear" (Jos 2:9); Rahab was rewarded for her deeds by sparing her family among the Israelites (Jos 6:25). |

| The Pentateuch | The Book of Joshua |
|---|---|
| (4) Two spies gave a good report in taking the land (Nu 14:38). | Joshua sends out two spies (Jos 2:1); they return with a good report in taking the land (Jos 2:24). |
| (5) Moses meets the angel of the Lord in the burning bush before he leads the people out of Egypt (Ex 3:2–6): "Take off your sandals, for the place where you are standing is holy ground" (v.6). | Joshua meets an angel of the Lord near Jericho before he leads the people into the land (Jos 5:13–15): "Take off your sandals, for the place where you are standing is holy" (v.15). |
| (6) Moses must circumcise his son before the Exodus (Ex 4:24–26). | Joshua must circumcise the Israelite sons before the conquest (Jos 5:2–8). |
| (7) Moses and the Israelites celebrated the Passover before the Exodus (Ex 2:21). | Joshua and the Israelites celebrated the Passover before the conquest (Jos 5:10). |
| (8) Moses performed 13 signs before the Exodus (three signs, Ex 3:9; ten signs, Ex 7–11). | Joshua and the Israelites circled Jericho 13 times before the conquest (once each of the six days and then seven times on the last day, Jos 6:3–4). |
| (9) Moses held his staff raised until all the Amalekites were defeated (Ex 17:11). | Joshua held his javelin raised until all the Canaanites at Ai were defeated (Jos 8:26). |
| (10) After the victorious deliverance of the Exodus, the Israelites disobeyed God and failed in the wilderness (Nu 14). | After the victorious defeat of Jericho, the Israelites disobeyed and failed at Ai (Jos 7:1–5). |
| 11) Moses intercedes for the people of Israel after their failure in the desert: "The Egyptians will hear about it. . . . And they will tell the inhabitants of this land about it" (Nu 14:13–16). | Joshua intercedes for the people after their failure at Ai: "The Canaanites and the other people of the country will hear about this. . . ." (Jos 7:7–9). |

It is important to notice two elements at work in the events in Joshua. (1) The book stresses the miraculous nature of the events that resulted in Israel's possession of the land. The basis of such a perspective is the theology of the Pentateuch—the God of the covenant is the God of creation. God's power used on behalf of his people is the power of the Creator.

The notion of creation is important here for two reasons: (a) Creation is the basis of God's *right* to give the land to Israel. Genesis 1–2 establish the fact that God, the God of the covenant, created the land. Thus it is his land to give to whomever he pleases (see Ex 19:5). (b) Creation is also the basis of God's *power* to give the land to Israel. Throughout the narratives of Joshua there is the reminder that the God of the covenant uses his power over the natural forces (e.g., 3:14–16; 10:12–14) on behalf of his people.

The narratives of Joshua manifest a conscious effort to show that it is not Israel that takes the land, but rather the Lord who regains his land from the Canaanites and gives it to Israel (cf. Jos 24:13). Thus behind the scenes of battle there lies a mysterious figure, the "commander of the army of the LORD" (5:13–15). His presence is assumed throughout the narrative, ready to lead the people into the battles that follow. He is the true leader of the forces that take the land (see 24:12–13). Thus Israel must not trust in her own strength but look in faith to the God of the covenant and the God of creation—"the LORD Almighty."

(2) The book stresses the part each individual Israelite played in gaining the land. The Israelites did not wait at the Jordan until the Lord and his armies delivered the land to them. They were continually called upon by the Lord to enter the battle and, if need be, to die in order to secure the fulfillment of God's plan.

We see this idea dramatized in the book in both positive and negative ways. (a) Positively, Israel was called upon to circle Jericho seven days and then to shout and move in to take the city. The Lord took the city in his own way, but Israel too had to enter into the battle faithfully. (b) Negatively, Israel attempted to take the city of Ai on their own (8:7). They were overconfident and underprepared. They were, in effect, overstepping their role, and the result was fatal. Without the Lord fighting for them, their efforts were insufficient.

## I. Israel's Entry Into Canaan (1:1–4:24)

### A. The Commissioning of Joshua as a Replacement for Moses (1:1–18)

The narrative opens with the reminder of the death of Moses, the servant of the Lord (v.1; cf. Dt 34:5–12). The text thus consciously links itself with Deuteronomy and the Pentateuch.

In Deuteronomy Joshua had been duly commissioned by Moses, and the Israelites had accepted his leadership (Dt 34:9). As Moses had received a commissioning from the Lord while in the desert of Sinai (Ex 3:10), so now, at the beginning of the book of Joshua, Joshua also receives a direct commission from the Lord to lead his people in fulfillment of the divine promise to Abraham (Jos 1:6b; cf. Ge 12:1–3). God's specific words to Joshua allude not only to the divine promise to Moses (Ex 23:30–31; Dt 11:24–25) and Moses' instructions to Joshua in the Pentateuch (Dt 31:6–8) but also to God's promise to Abraham. As God had told Abraham, "Go, walk through the length and breadth of the land, for I am giving it to you" (Ge 13:17), so here God tells Joshua, "I will give you every place where you set your foot" (Jos 1:3). Moreover, as the Lord demonstrated his choice of Moses as leader of Israel with mighty deeds (Ex 4:30–31) and wonders, he now begins to display his power through Joshua, demonstrating his choice of Joshua as Israel's leader (Jos 3:7).

There is a pattern here that will recur throughout the remainder of the historical books:

a. **Commissioning by God's representative**

-Moses laid his hand upon Joshua (Dt 34:9)

-Samuel anointed Saul (1Sa 10:1)

-Samuel anointed David (1Sa 16:13)

-David commanded Zadok to anoint Solomon (1Ki 1:34)

b. **Demonstration of divine approval**

-Moses given signs to perform (Ex 4:30–31)

-Joshua given success in the conquest of Canaan (Jos 1:7)

-Saul given victory over the Ammonites (1Sa 11:11)

-David given victory over Goliath (1Sa 17)

-Solomon given great wisdom (1Ki 3:12)

c. **Popular recognition among God's people**

-The people see Moses' signs and believe (Ex 4:31)

-The people follow Joshua into battle (Jos 1:17; 24:15ff.)

-The people follow Saul (1Sa 11:12)

-The people recognize David's leadership (2Sa 2:4; 5:3)

-The people recognize Solomon's wisdom (1Ki 3:28)

As a demonstration of the fact that Joshua had replaced Moses as Israel's new leader, the writer appends the brief account of Joshua's ordering the people's preparation for battle and his speech to the tribes of Reuben, Gad, and Manasseh, both of which clearly allude to the work of Moses in the Pentateuch. (1) Joshua's first command, "Get your supplies ready. Three days from now you will cross the Jordan here to go in and take possession of the land" (v.11), is a clear reflection of God's command through Moses, "Be ready by the third day, because on that day the LORD will come down on Mount Sinai in the sight of all the people" (Ex 19:11).

(2) In Joshua's words to the tribes of Reuben, Gad, and Manasseh (vv.12–17), the writer directs our attention back to the earlier instructions given to them by Moses. Joshua begins (v.12) with a specific reference to the early words in the Torah, "Remember the command that Moses the servant of the LORD gave you" (see Nu 32:1–42; Dt 3:18–22). These words of Joshua also direct the reader's attention to Moses' own commissioning of Joshua (see Nu 32:28; Dt 3:21). In the words of the men from these tribes (v.17), we can hear the point being made by the writer, "Just as we fully obeyed Moses, so we will obey you. Only may the LORD your God be with you as he was with Moses."

The conscious references to the Pentateuch throughout the narratives in Joshua suggest that the writer wants us, at least initially, to view these events as a form of fulfillment of God's promises to the earlier generations. In doing so, however, the writer at the same time raises the question of whether these events are, in fact, to be understood as the actual fulfillment. We know, for example, from later biblical books that God's promises were not entirely fulfilled under the conquest of Joshua (e.g., see Jdg 1:19). Moreover, within the book of Joshua itself, in spite of the clearly positive view of the events of the Conquest expressed throughout the book (e.g., see Jos 21:43), a quite different view of these events surfaces at the close of the book: "But just as every good promise of the LORD your God has come true, so the LORD will bring on you all the evil he has threatened, until he has destroyed you from this good land he has given you" (23:15). The reader is thus left with the question of whether, or in what way, the conquest of the land under the leadership of Joshua is to be understood as a fulfillment of God's promises in the Pentateuch.

The answer to this question has frequently been sought in the historical circumstances of the Conquest. It is argued that at the time of the Conquest, the area actually taken by Joshua and his army (i.e., the central hill country) was not firmly held by the indigenous Canaanite populations. Because of the social organization of the land at that time, the Canaanites controlled only the large city-states in the valleys. These areas could be easily defended by chariot forces and thus offered no match for the ill equipped Israelites. Support for this view can be found not only in the statement of Jdg 1:19, "They were unable to drive the people from the plains, because they had iron chariots," but also from a general knowledge of the area gained from archaeology, which suggests that the technological superiority of the Canaanites with their chariots was neutralized by the mountainous terrain of Palestine's interior.

Though such an assessment of the historical and geographical situation at the time may no doubt be correct, it does not answer the question of why the writer of Joshua first deliberately represents the Conquest as a fulfillment of the promises in the Pentateuch (21:43–45) and then, at the last moment, seems to reverse himself and suggest that it was not complete and was to be only short-lived at best. The answer to this question lies not in a historical assessment of the events themselves but in an assessment of the literary strategy of the writer of the book. Viewed from this perspective, it seems clear that the writer, by deliberately stressing the fulfillment aspect of the Conquest under the leadership of Joshua, intentionally raises the larger question of whether it was, in fact, all that was intended in the promises to the fathers in the Pentateuch. In other words, he raises the question of whether the patriarchal promises were to be viewed merely within a historical frame or, in addition to that, also in a futuristic, or even eschatological, sense.

By retracing the strategy of the writer, then, we can see that he first leads the reader into concluding that the events of the Conquest may very well have been the fulfillment of the promises to the fathers. At the close of the book, however, the writer counters this possibility with the final words of Joshua, in which we begin to see that the events are not to be understood as the ultimate goal of the patriarchal promises. Something more comprehensive and certain still awaited in these promises for future generations. It is clear from his statement in 23:16, that,

at least from Joshua's own perspective, the fulfillment of the promises would have to wait until after the time of a yet future exile from the land (cf. Dt 30:1–5). There Joshua solemnly tells the people that "the LORD's anger will burn against you, and you will quickly perish from the good land he has given you." There is little doubt here that the author has in mind the future exile of the people in Babylon—a captivity that Moses has already warned the people of in Dt 4:25–26.

It is important to note that from Joshua's own words the possibility of apostasy and exile is only that—a possibility. From the viewpoint of the writer of the book, however, it has resolved itself into an eventuality. Not only do we, the readers, have the lesson of Israel's failure aptly demonstrated in the Pentateuch, which the book of Joshua presupposes its readers have, but also within the book of Joshua itself, the reader is given ample evidence that Israel would not likely remain faithful to God's covenant (cf. 7:1; 9:1–27). Finally, in Joshua's own words, the inevitable apostasy of the people is held up before the reader: "Joshua said to the people, 'You are not able to serve the LORD. He is a holy God; he is a jealous God. He will not forgive your rebellion and your sins'" (24:19).

The lesson of the book of Joshua, then, is that the Conquest was *not* to be understood as the final fulfillment of God's promises. A future fulfillment still awaited God's people. Israel's hope lay not in the past glories of Joshua but yet in the future with the coming of one like Joshua who would lead them in finally realizing God's promises. In the remainder of the Deuteronomic History, this anticipation of a future fulfillment of God's promises beyond the Babylonian captivity is developed into a central theme.

At the center of God's call and commissioning of Joshua is the command to obey the law (1:8). It is important to note here that what the writer has in mind is obedience to the *"Book of the Law"*—i.e., the Pentateuch. The reference to the Law in this passage is thus not to the various laws given to Israel in the Sinai covenant, but rather to the book that Moses had given to the people to read and meditate on. Joshua is here called upon to lead the people in the study of and meditation on the Law "day and night," much the same as the psalmist later presents the "blessed man" whose "delight is in the law of the LORD and on his law he meditates day and night" (Ps 1:2). Obedience to the will of God thus means in this case obedience to the will of God *as it is expressed in the Pentateuch.* This would include the lessons of the narratives as well as the laws. We have suggested earlier that the narrative lesson of the Pentateuch is primarily one of faith and trust in God. What God is here calling on Joshua to do is to meditate on the Law so that he can strengthen his faith and trust in God. The writer of the book of Hebrews saw this clearly and thus drew from the book of Joshua the lesson that it was "by faith" that the walls of Jericho fell down before the people of Israel (Heb 11:30).

## B. The Reconnaissance of Jericho (2:1–24)

The narrative now turns to Joshua's sending of the spies into the land and the account of their meeting with Rahab. We have already noted the close parallels between the account of Rahab and the spies and the Exodus from Egypt. Joshua is here being portrayed as a new Moses leading God's people into the land.

Two important points deserve special mention in the account of the spies' visit to Jericho. (1) Rahab's statement to the spies, "We have heard how the LORD dried up the water of the Red Sea" (v.10) raises the question of how the Canaanites had heard of what God had done for his people in Egypt. Unfortunately, the narrative does not allow us to answer this question with precision. We can only assume that the news had spread quickly throughout the land and that it had reached Jericho in a surprisingly accurate form. She even knew the name of the God of Israel, "the LORD." This helps put into perspective Moses' words in Nu 14:13–14, "The Egyptians will hear about it! . . . And they will tell the inhabitants of this land about it. They have already heard that you, O LORD, are with these people." Indeed, as Rahab's words show, the inhabitants of the land had heard what the Lord had done.

(2) Rahab is presented here as a model of Gentile faith. Her confession is noteworthy: "The LORD your God is God in heaven above and on earth below" (v.11). On the basis of this confession, the writer of Hebrews later wrote, "By faith the prostitute Rahab . . . was not killed with those who were disobedient" (Heb 11:31).

## C. The Crossing of the Jordan River (3:1–4:24)

Much attention is given in the narrative to the crossing of the Jordan River and its commemoration with the twelve stones. There can be no doubt that the writer intends us to see a parallel between this narrative and the crossing of the Red Sea with Moses. Joshua is portrayed as the new Moses leading a new generation of the sons of Israel into the land. This is a new beginning.

Two major developments come out of this event. (1) Joshua is shown to be God's leader: "Today I will begin to exalt you in the eyes of all Israel, so they may know I am with you as I was with Moses" (3:7). (2) Israel is given confidence that the Lord truly is able to give them the land: "This is how you will know that the living God is among you and that he will certainly drive out before you the Canaanites . . ." (3:10).

# CONQUEST OF CANAAN

When the Israelite tribes approached Canaan after four decades of desert existence, they first had to subdue the tribes in Transjordanian region, under Moses' leadership.

The military strategy of Joshua was brilliant in its simplicity. It had four goals: first, to cross the Jordan and gain a foothold in Canaan by seizing Jericho and its strategic plains, fords and roads; second, to capture the high ground around Bethel, Gibeon and Upper Beth Horon in order to dominate the hill country north and south of the ridge; third, to attack and neutralize lowland towns like Lachish; and finally, to break the power of the mighty urban coalition of northern towns led by Hazor. All of this took place about 1400 B.C.

## II. The Conquest (5:1–12:24)

### A. First Stage of the Conquest (5:1–8:35)

#### 1. Final preparations for battle (5:1–15)

Final preparations for the Conquest were now made. These included the rite of circumcision and the celebration of the Passover. Just as circumcision and the celebration of the Passover preceded the Exodus from Egypt (Ex 4:24–26; 12:1–13), so now they mark its conclusion. The Passover had not been celebrated since the Israelites were at Sinai, at the beginning of their second year in the wilderness (Nu 9:1–5). The significance of circumcision is explained by the Lord himself within this narrative, where he said to Joshua: "Today I have rolled away the reproach of Egypt from you" (v.9). Thus, circumcision was taken as a sign of God's purification of his people and their becoming fit for the new land. On the day after the Passover, the Israelites ate from the produce of the Promised Land. On that same day, the manna that had sustained them throughout their days in the wilderness stopped and they began to enjoy God's good provision of the land.

As a prelude to Israel's taking the city of Jericho and the rest of the land, we, the readers, are given a behind-the-scenes look at the real nature of the Conquest. Joshua met the captain of the Lord's army. Israel was not to take the land alone. They were to have the help of the armies of God. Though the narrative is short and leaves us with many unanswered questions, we see enough to know that God was at work in the actions that follow.

#### 2. The capture of Jericho (6:1–27)

In the battle of Jericho, the military strategy places the victory entirely in the hands of God. Even before the city was taken the Lord had said, "See, I have delivered Jericho into your hands" (v.2). At the pitch of battle Joshua told

Israel to "Shout! For the LORD has given you the city!" (v.16). The plan was dangerously simple. Israel was to circle the city silently once a day for six days. On the seventh day, they were to circle it seven times. Thus, Israel's role was purely and simply to represent the Lord before the people of the city. They had only to stand by and watch the Lord destroy the city walls. The presence of the Lord is clearly marked in the narrative by the Ark of the Covenant carried by the priests.

In contrast to the taking of Jericho, however, in the taking of Ai after the sin of Achan, Israel was called upon to perform a military stratagem—an ambush of the Canaanite occupants of Ai (8:1–23). We should not lose sight of the fact, however, that in both cases we are taught that it was the Lord who actually fought and won the battle. The situation with Achan's hidden sin only serves to show the important part that the Lord's help played in gaining the military victory. Without the Lord's help Israel would not have gained the land.

The lesson of this narrative is that it was solely by the strong arm of the Lord that Israel gained the land. Israel was called upon to trust completely in the Lord. Behind these events one can see the lesson of Proverbs being taught: "Trust in the LORD with all your heart and lean not on your own understanding; in all your ways acknowledge him, and he will make your paths straight" (Pr 3:5–6). At the conclusion of the battle we are reminded that the victory came because "the LORD was with Joshua" (v.27).

By recounting the rescue of Rahab twice within this one narrative (vv.17, 23), the writer underscores the importance of the theme of salvation in the midst of judgment. This was not a war of plunder or personal revenge against the Canaanites. It was, rather, the work of God's judgment against the people of the land (5:14). Those who helped the

Israelites, such as Rahab, were exempt from the divine judgment. One can see the Abrahamic promise at work in this narrative, "I will bless those who bless you" (Ge 12:3a). Rahab and her family continued to live in Israel long after this time (v.25). In this respect she is similar to Tamar (Ge 38), Ruth, and Bathsheba (2Sa 11:27), all non-Israelite women who, through faith, joined with the Israelites and thus played a central role in the house of David (cf. Ru 4:18–22; Mt 1:3, 5–6). In stark contrast to the faithful Rahab stands the deceitful Achan, from the house of Judah, who broke Joshua's ban and stole part of the forbidden plunder (7:1).

### 3. The overthrow of Ai (7:1–8:29)

When they entered the city of Jericho, Joshua had warned the people not to take from any of "the devoted things" of the city, lest they too become subject to the destruction (6:18). Achan, in disregard to Joshua's warning, took and hid a part of the plunder of the city in his tent. The result was a total defeat of the Israelites at the city of Ai.

Considerable attention is given to the mishap at Ai, which suggests an important lesson is contained in this narrative. The writer takes great pains to show (1) that the city should have been easily taken, and (2) that a carefully worked out plan ultimately succeeded. Thus it is in every way the reverse of the situation at Jericho. Nevertheless, the lesson of the narrative is clear. God's people must not have sin in the camp. They may hide their sins from each other, but God will find them out. Even a relatively easy victory like the capture of Ai would fail if the Lord were not fighting for Israel. Lying behind this narrative is the theme expressed in Dt 32:30, "How could one man chase a thousand, or two put ten thousand to flight, unless their Rock had sold them, unless the Lord had given them up?"

The elaborate plan ultimately necessary to take the small city of Ai suggests that Achan's sin had a more lasting effect on Israel's conquest of the land than we might otherwise have expected. No longer would Israel merely have to carry the ark before them and the walls of the cities would fall as at Jericho. A stratagem was necessary. Though the narrative is clear that the stratagem would fail without God's help, it is also apparent that Israel's failure to obey God's leader, Joshua, had ushered in a new stage in the Conquest—one that would finally result in an incomplete conquest (cf. 13:1) and failure (23:15–16).

### 4. Ceremony at Mount Ebal (8:30–35)

The narrative turns immediately to the ceremony at Mount Ebal. In accordance with the command of Moses in Dt 27:1–8, Joshua built an altar on Mount Ebal. Though this passage is only loosely connected with the events of the Conquest, it seems certain that its present location in the text is to be understood chronologically. That is, immediately after Israel had gained a foothold in the land, Joshua led the people to Mount Ebal to carry out Moses' command. The author wants to show that there was a genuine concern among all the people for obedience to God's law. It is also to be noted that his attention focuses on the copy of the Law prepared by Joshua and its public reading: "There was not a word of all that Moses had commanded that Joshua did not read" (v.35). Israel was now in the land; they had a copy of the Law that could be read by all; thus they were now ready to resume the Conquest and take the remainder of the land. Ironically, it was immediately after this event that we read of the fatal error of their entering into covenant with the Gibeonites.

The fact that this narrative places the Israelites relatively far north (Shechem) quite early in the Conquest has raised several historical questions.

How could they have reached this point without further battle? Did they make a peaceful alliance with the inhabitants of Shechem? Is this short narrative misplaced? Unfortunately, the present state of knowledge about the history and archaeology of this region during the time of the Conquest adds little to our understanding. A view that has wide acceptance is that the inhabitants of Shechem surrendered to the Israelites without a fight. Though possibly correct, we should not overlook the fact that the account of the Conquest in this book is a selective account. The author has deliberately chosen not to include many events and features. It is one thing to try to reconstruct the events of the Conquest, and it is quite another to attempt to understand the description of it given in the book of Joshua. The same question arises in the attempt to understand the relationship between the view of the Conquest in this book and that given in the first chapter of the book of Judges. As is the case with the four Gospels in the NT, we have varying accounts of the same events. While it is legitimate and important to attempt to harmonize them, both with each other and with history and archaeology, that is not the first task of Bible study. The focus of Bible study is the individual accounts and viewpoints of each of the books.

## B. Second Stage of the Conquest: The Fraud of the Gibeonites (9:1–27)

### 1. Introduction (9:1–2)

The author opens with a general statement about the effect of Israel's defeat of Jericho and Ai on the kings and nations of the land. He surveys a territory ("all the kings west of the Jordan"—in the hill country and the lowlands from one end of the country to the other, as far as Lebanon) much larger than the one encompassed by the events of the following narrative. He thus provides a wider context for the more limited narrative that follows. He returns to

this broader scope in the summary in 10:40–43.

### 2. Gibeonites' fraud (9:3–15)

The narrative of the pact with the Gibeonites takes up the course of events following the defeat of the city of Ai (8:24–29). Joshua had returned to his earlier camp in Gilgal (cf. 5:10). The Gibeonites, having heard of the defeat of both Jericho and Ai and fearing the worst for themselves, attempted a bold plan that the author compares to the kind of ruse the Israelites were able to play on the inhabitants of Ai.

What is to be noted in this narrative is the extent to which it presupposes the reader's awareness of God's law. This is shown in three distinct ways. (1) The basis of the Gibeonites' plan was the instructions for warfare given in Dt 20: It was permissible for Israel to enter into a peace treaty with those "nations afar off" (Dt 20:10–15). With the nations who lived in the Promised Land, however, it was forbidden. "Otherwise, they will teach you to follow all the detestable things they do in worshiping their gods, and you will sin against the LORD your God" (Dt 20:18). Thus the premise of the narrative is the curious circumstance of the Canaanites using the law to foil God's plans for Israel. (2) The narrative shows that Joshua and the leaders of Israel were aware of a possible fraud, and so they sought further evidence that the Gibeonites were not from the land. Thus Israel is shown here both as aware of the law and what it required for its correct application. Their problem, in other words, was not a lack of knowing the laws written in the Law. (3) But the author himself gives us an all-important clue to the meaning of the narrative when, at the conclusion, he states, "The men of Israel sampled their provisions but did not inquire of the LORD" (v.14). The fatal error of Joshua was his failure to "inquire of the LORD." The Law had clearly spelled out both the importance of seeking

God's will and the procedure for doing so, namely, the office of the prophet (Dt 18:14–22). As is common in the OT books that follow, at the heart of Israel's failure to follow God's will lies their neglect of the words of his prophets.

### 3. The consequences of the pact with the Gibeonites (9:16–27)

The author of the book clearly approves of the Israelite leaders' refusal to go back on their word, even though they had been tricked into making the treaty. From the point of view of the narrative, Israel was still at fault because they did not seek the will of God (v.14). Later it is recounted that Saul, "in his zeal for Israel and Judah" (2Sa 21:2), had reversed their actions here and "put the Gibeonites to death." This is seen as a grievous error, and David is credited for attempting to make amends for Saul's actions (2Sa 21:3, 14).

The events of this narrative play an important part in the larger thematic structure of the OT books. (1) Joshua's solution to the dilemma of what to do with the Gibeonites ("You are now under a curse. You will never cease to serve," v.23) follows precisely the instruction of Dt 20:11, "[They] shall be subject to forced labor and shall work for you." Thus Joshua is cast as a godly leader who knows God's law and applies it to life. (2) Joshua's words provide a link between the events in this narrative and the curse of the Canaanites in Ge 9:25, "Cursed be Canaan! The lowest of slaves will he be to his brothers." Thus in Joshua's words we see the fulfillment of the curse of Canaan. (3) But the fact that Joshua specified that the Gibeonites were to serve "in the house of my God" (v.25) adds a new dimension to his proposal. What he apparently had in mind may be illustrated by the later practice of "temple servants" initiated by David (Ezr 8:20). Thus capitalizing on the wordplay in Hebrew by which servants and worshipers are rendered by the same

word, what had begun as a curse ("You will not cease to serve") has become for them a blessing ("in the house of my God"). In making this addition, Joshua shows an awareness of a latent blessing in the curse of Canaan in Ge 9:26, "May Canaan be his slave" (i.e., the servant of the God of Shem"; cf. NIV note). As has happened so often in the biblical narratives, God's plans are not thwarted by human disobedience. His will is accomplished even though his people fail. Through Israel's thoughtless act of making a covenant with the Gibeonites, God's plan to bring all nations to himself is furthered (Ge 12:3).

### C. Third Stage of the Conquest: Victory Over the Southern Coalition (10:1–43)

#### 1. Defeat of the five kings (10:1–27)

The battle recounted in this chapter is between Israel and the five Amorite kings. The occasion was the peace treaty between Israel and the Gibeonites. The underlying cause was the Amorite kings' fear of Israel's victories at Jericho and Ai, as well as the fact that the Gibeonites had sided with them and they now posed a formidable threat.

Led by the king of Jerusalem, Adoni-Zedek, the five kings from Jerusalem, Hebron, Jarmuth, Lachish, and Eglon moved to punish the Gibeonites for making a treaty with Israel. In accordance with their treaty with Israel, the Gibeonites immediately appealed to Joshua for help (vv.3–7).

The writer makes it clear that the Amorite kings were summarily routed by the Israelites only because God fought for them (vv.8–27). To highlight the constant faithfulness of God in coming to Israel's aid, the Lord's words to Joshua deliberately allude to those of Moses: "Do not be afraid of them; I have given them into your hand. Not one of them will be able to withstand you" (v.8; cf. Dt 20:1–4). This same theme is repeated three times throughout this one narrative (vv.8, 19, 25), thus showing Joshua as a model of the kind of leadership God desired for his people. Joshua is the new Moses.

In the midst of the narrative, the writer has inserted a short account of God's sending hailstones upon the enemy and delaying the sun in the sky "till the nation avenged itself on its enemies" (vv.12–14). It should be noted that the section that describes the sun and moon as "standing still" in the midst of the sky is poetry and, as such, was not intended to be taken literally. As is the case in many places in Scripture, in this passage we are given both a narrative account of the battle (vv.7–11) and a poetic one (vv.12–14; cf. Ex 14–15; Jdg 4–5). In the narrative account we are told that Joshua "marched all night" to take the Amorites by surprise (v.9). This is expressed in the poetic version by saying, "The moon stopped, till the nation avenged itself on its enemies" (v.13a). Moreover, the narrative account of the battle concludes in v.27, with an account of the last act of Israel's avenging its enemies. Here it is expressly stated in the narrative that this last event happened "at sunset." The poetic expression of this fact is represented in the poetic line, "The sun stopped in the midst of the sky and delayed going down about a full day" (v.13b). Thus there are no grounds in the text for the oft-repeated view that the Bible reports that the sun and moon stood motionless for a period of a day while Israel defeated their foes. Once it is understood that the section stating this is poetic and that we have the description of actual historical events in the narrative itself, we can better appreciate the figurative nature of the language.

The concluding epilogue to the poetic text ("there has never been a day like it before or since," v.14) is often understood as a reference to an exceptionally long day and is thus taken to imply that the writer himself interpreted the poetry literally. A closer look at the statement, however, shows that what was unusual about this day was not its length, but the fact that on this day "the LORD listened to a man" and fought for Israel (v.14). This same theme is repeated at the conclusion of this chapter after the lengthy description of the cities and kings that Israel defeated (v.42).

### 2. Defeat of the seven cities (10:28–39)

As the summary of this section shows (vv.40–43), God fought for Israel and delivered the enemies into their hands. As is common in the Bible, the number seven functions as an expression of totality or completeness. Thus the writer lists the defeat of seven cities and leaves us with the sense of total victory.

At the conclusion (vv.40–43), the author returns to the larger picture of Israel's victories over all the land, reflecting the same perspective as at the opening of this section (vv.1–2). The point of these surveys is to show both that Israel's conquest of the land was wider in scope than the depiction of it in the narrative might suggest, and that behind it all was the fact that God had given them the victory. The writer is not as much interested in Israel's military prowess as he is the theological fact that the Lord had fought for them.

Curiously, after all these great victories, Joshua and the people returned to their camp at Gilgal (cf. 5:9–10; 9:6; 10:15). Much yet remained for them to do.

### D. Fourth Stage of the Conquest: Victory Over the Northern Coalition and Hazor (11:1–15)

Only one major battle among the northern territory is recounted in the book, the defeat of the northern coalition of kings at the Waters of Merom (vv.1–9). The writer begins with a list of the names of four kings, Jabin, Jobab, Shimron, and Acshaph (v.1), and then follows by giving only the places where the other kings ruled (v.2). These places seemed even to have been very ancient to the reader because the author explains them in the next verse (v.3): These are "the Canaanites in the east and west, . . . the Amorites, Hittites, Perizzites and Jebusites in the hill country; and . . . the Hivites." Two things should be noted about this explanation. (1) By means of it the author explains the place names by the well-known lists of inhabitants of Canaan associated with the promises to the patriarchs (cf. Ge 15:18–19). Thus the writer is careful to note that the land taken in this battle is still a part of that land promised to Abraham. (2) When this list occurs elsewhere, it usually contains seven or ten names, both numbers suggesting completeness and representing the whole of the population without being an exhaustive list. Here, however, the author lists only six names. It thus appears that he has intentionally left out one of the names so that the total with the previous four kings (v.1) would be ten, as in Ge 18:19. Thus, by keeping to the sense of his use of numbers, the author is able to show that this episode is only a representative instance of the whole conquest of the north. The absence of any round number in the list in ch. 12, however, suggests that the author there is giving an exhaustive list.

The description of the battle at the Waters of Merom (vv.4–14) is brief and clearly designed to highlight the role of Joshua as God's obedient servant. The battle is carried out along the lines prescribed in Dt 20. The enemy has come out "with all their troops and a large number of horses and chariots—a huge army" (v.4; see Dt 20:1). But Joshua is not afraid of them (again, see Dt 20:1), because the Lord is with them. Thus this narrative shows that under Joshua's leadership the people did not fear their enemy, but rather stood fast as the Lord delivered the enemy into their hands.

The swiftness of the victory ("suddenly," v.7) is matched by the briefness of the account. The author hurries to the conclusion that victory came because "Joshua did to them as the LORD had directed" (v.9). Although there is no mention of a "prophet," the notion of a divine spokesman in Dt 18 is nevertheless present in the text when it says, "The LORD said to Joshua" (v.6). It may be that Joshua is here being conceptualized as a prophet to whom God speaks his word (see comment on 9:3–15). In any event, Joshua followed the word that God spoke to him and the revelation of God's word in the Law (Dt 20). The author again stresses Joshua as God's obedient leader and goes on to note the success that follows from that (cf. 1:8–9).

The account of the destruction of the city of Hazor (vv.10–14), though important to the author in its own right as a continuing example of the success of the Israelites in the Conquest, also becomes a further vehicle to portray the nature and extent of Joshua's obedience to the will of God. After a brief description of his defeat of Hazor (vv.10–11), the author turns again to the question of Joshua's obedience. Three times in this brief section the author repeats the fact that Joshua obeyed God (vv.13, 15a, 15b).

What is particularly striking in v.15 is that the author ties Joshua's obedience specifically to those commands given in the Law by Moses, "as the LORD commanded his servant Moses." Clearly what is at work here in the narrative is the theme of the book expressed in 1:7, "Be careful to obey all the law my servant Moses gave you . . . that you may be successful wherever you go." Joshua "left nothing undone of all that the LORD had commanded Moses" (11:15); he did not "turn from it to the right or to the left" (1:7).

### E. Summary of Events (11:16–12:24)

The account of Israel's conquest of the land is brought to a conclusion with a sweeping summary. The attempt is not made here to summarize the preceding narrative accounts. They are left to stand on their own. What is here given is something quite different. It is a broad description of the conquest of the land of Canaan that reaches far back even into events recounted in the Pentateuch (e.g., Sihon and Og, 12:1–6). By means of this summary the narratives of the book of Joshua are linked as a unit to those of the Pentateuch. The author of this book appears to have deliberately written his book as a sequel to the work of Moses. It is hardly surprising then, that at the close of this book, the picture is given of Joshua himself already adding parts of this book to "the Book of the Law of God" (24:26).

In the two summaries that follow, the first (11:16–23) focuses on the territories taken by Israel and the second (12:1–24) on the kings they conquered.

#### 1. Territories taken by Israel (11:16–23)

The first point stressed by this summary is that the extent of the Conquest included all of the land of Canaan, "So Joshua took this entire land" (v.16). The enumeration of the various geographical areas (vv.16–17) makes it clear that the author means to say that all the land was taken. His stress on the fact that all the land had been conquered raises the question of the relationship of this statement to 13:2–6, where many areas are enumerated that, in the time of Joshua's old age, still remained to be taken. It also raises the question of the relationship of 11:16–17 with the statements in the Pentateuch that suggest the land would not be taken quickly, but rather in a slow, drawn out fashion (Ex 23:28–20; Dt 7:22).

Clearly the author of Joshua intends to say that though the land as a whole was taken in Joshua's day, much still re-

mained for the next generation to do. Indeed, it will be a part of his larger strategy to show that the next generation would not follow the lead of Joshua and thus would not be successful in taking the land. At the close of the book, Joshua himself tells the next generation, "You are not able to serve the LORD. . . . If you forsake the LORD and serve foreign gods, he will turn and bring disaster on you and make an end of you, after he has been good to you" (24:19–20). This book thus paves the way for Judges, which demonstrates in no uncertain terms that the next generation of Israelites after Joshua "forsook the LORD, the God of their fathers, who had brought them out of Egypt. They followed and worshiped various gods of the people around them" (Jdg 2:12).

Second, the summary now turns to the kings and cities of the land (vv.18–19) and assures the readers that they were all, except the Gibeonites (cf. 9:1–27), captured in "a long time." Here the author seems intent on expanding the reader's perception of the Conquest beyond merely the events covered in the preceding narratives. He does not want to leave the impression that his selective account of the Conquest was really all there was to it. It may also be that this reminder (that there was much more to the Conquest) serves to justify his cutting short the account at this point. By means of this summary we, the readers, are reassured that if more were to be given, it would be much like that which we have.

Third, the author makes an important theological point: "It was the LORD himself who hardened their hearts to wage war against Israel, so that he might destroy them totally" (v.20). This is a new idea in Joshua, though one that is known already in the Pentateuch (Ex 4:21; cf. chs. 7–12). Such a viewpoint throws a new light on the previous narratives. It shows an even deeper divine purpose behind the Conquest. Not only was it a fulfillment of God's promise to give Israel the land, but it was also a means whereby God's judgment could be brought to bear upon the Canaanites. In stressing this aspect of the purpose of God, the writer draws on themes that go back to the Abrahamic narratives in Genesis and the role his seed would play in the process of blessing and judgment of the nations. According to Ge 15:16, for example, Israel's sojourn in Egypt was intentionally delayed so that their entry into the Promised Land would coincide with God's judgment of the inhabitants of the land.

Inserted in this summary is an account of Joshua's conquest of the land of the Anakites in the hill country: Hebron, Debir, and Anab (vv.21–22). This narrative anticipates 14:6–15, where this same area was given to Caleb, and 15:13–19 where Caleb, with Joshua's blessing, is said to have taken Hebron (15:14), and Othniel, Caleb's brother, is said to have taken Debir (15:15–17). Thus, that which is here ascribed to Joshua in a general way is later specified as the work of Caleb and Othniel because they did it at Joshua's command (14:6).

In this short narrative, Joshua accomplishes precisely that which kept the original generation out of the land and in the desert for forty years, i.e., the defeat of the Anakites (cf. Nu 13:26–14:9). At that time, he, along with Caleb, encouraged the people to trust God and take the land, saying, "Do not be afraid of the people of the land, because we will swallow them up. Their protection is gone, but the LORD is with us" (Nu 14:9). It is appropriate, then, that the writer would include this notice in the summary of Israel's success under the leadership of Joshua. It is also appropriate that the same material would be repeated later in regard to Caleb to show his faithfulness as well (14:6–15).

A further function of this brief notice within the present summary may have been to identify more clearly the expression "mountains of Israel" in v.16. According to v.21, that expression refers to the whole mountain region to the north of the mountains in Judah. It thus expands the scope of Israel's success in taking the land under the leadership of Joshua.

An important statement falls at the close of this summary section: "Then the land had rest from war" (v.23). Its use here links the work of Joshua to that of the judges in Judges (Jdg 3:11, 30; 5:31; 8:28). While the judge was alive, Israel enjoyed peace in the land. This is stated again in the case of Caleb (14:15), whose brother Othniel was, in fact, a judge (Jdg 3:7–11).

### 2. Kings defeated by Israel (12:1–24)

Regarding the lands and kings east of the Jordan, the list of victories reaches back into the pentateuchal narratives to the accounts of the conquest of the East Jordan (v.1) area. As we have suggested above, by means of this summary the narratives of Joshua are linked as a unit to those of the Pentateuch. The author thus appears to have deliberately written his book as a sequel to the work of Moses.

Regarding the lands and kings west of the Jordan, a list of thirty-one kings forms the main body of this summary. Judging from those that can be identified from the previous narratives (e.g., Jericho, Ai, Jerusalem), the order of the list is intended to be taken as chronological. The list appears to be an exhaustive one and includes several sites not mentioned in the preceding narratives.

## III. The Distribution of the Tribal Territories (13:1–21:45)

### A. Introduction (13:1–7)

In 11:16–23 the author made the point that under the leadership of Joshua, Israel conquered "all the land of

Canaan" (11:16). This fact seems at odds with what the author states here in vv.2–6, that in the time of Joshua's old age, much of the land still remained to be taken. The key to understanding the passage lies in the opening remark of the writer, "Joshua was old and well advanced in years." This statement is not only to be compared to the same statement in 23:2, but also to 1Sa 8:1 ("When Samuel grew old") and 1Ki 1:1 ("When King David was old and well advanced in years"). In each of these passages, the special attention given to the old age of Israel's leader marks a transition in the leadership of God's people. Also in each case the nature of the transition is from the ideal leadership of a godly person to that of a less than ideal situation. We should not be surprised, then, to find that just after this transition in the narrative, we read of the less than ideal conditions that prevailed among God's people, namely, much of the land still remained to be taken. Thus, at this point in the text, the author attempts to show that much still remained for the next generation to do in taking the land and that much disappointment lay ahead. In the larger strategy of this book, the author intends to show that the next generation did not, in fact, follow the lead of Joshua and thus was not successful in taking the land.

## B. The Distribution of Land East of the Jordan (13:8–33)

The passage begins with a brief description of all the land east of the Jordan allotted to half of the tribe of Manasseh and to the tribes of Reuben and Gad (vv.8–13). There is then a short reminder of the fact that the Levites were not given an inheritance of land (v.14). What then follows is a detailed description of the allotment of land to Reuben (vv.15–23), Gad (vv.24–28), and the half-tribe of Manasseh (vv.29–32). At the close of this section is another reminder that the Levites were not given an inheritance of land (v.33).

## C. The Distribution of Land West of the Jordan (14:1–19:51)

### 1. Judah and Joseph (14:1–18:1)

Attention is first given to the two central tribes, Judah and Joseph. A short introduction (14:1–5) explains how the parcels of land were chosen ("assigned by lot," 14:2) and by whom ("Eleazar the priest, Joshua son of Nun and the heads of the tribal clans of Israel," 14:1).

Curiously, the allotment of territory to the house of Caleb, a non-Israelite, within the region of Judah is recounted first (14:6–15). The purpose of the writer in highlighting Caleb is to show that he, along with Joshua, was the only one among the earlier generation that proved faithful at taking God at his word. On that occasion, Moses had sworn to him, "The land on which your feet have walked will be your inheritance and that of your children forever, because you have followed the LORD my God wholeheartedly" (14:9). The success of Caleb in taking his allotment thus becomes a model of what the rest of the tribes were to do. Caleb even defeated the Anakites to gain his allotment (14:12, 15). They were the very people the Israelites feared most when they initially refused to take the land in Nu 13:28–33.

The lengthy description of the territory allotted to Judah (15:1–63) is broken up by only a few short, though important, narratives. (1) The writer notes that Jerusalem was a part of the territory of Judah (15:8). He makes this point by identifying "the Jebusite city" with the city of Jerusalem (cf. v.63). He does not leave this bit of information for the reader to discover on his own, but forthrightly inserts this explanation and identification of the ancient Jebusite city. By making this conscious effort to link Jerusalem to the tribe of Judah, the writer shows his awareness of the connection between the important themes that center in the house of Judah in the

# LAND OF THE TWELVE TRIBES

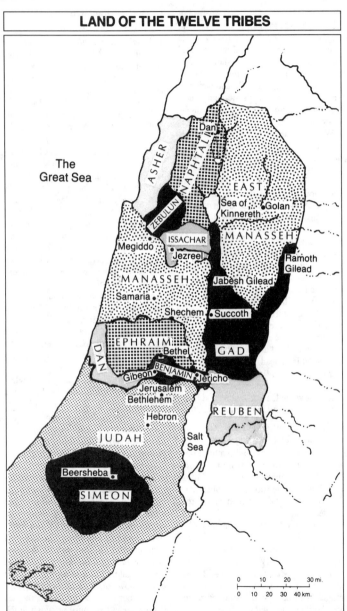

© 1994 The Zondervan Corporation.

Pentateuch (e.g., Ge 49:8–10; Nu 24:7–24) and those in the city of Jerusalem in the book of Samuel (2Sa 7). A larger concern is at work in the composition of this book. The importance of the city of Jerusalem is constantly being kept before the eye of the reader.

(2) The author also gives an account of Caleb's taking Hebron from the Anakites (15:13–19). This note allows the writer to give the details of how Caleb took Hebron (cf. 14:13) and Debir, two areas that were formerly taken by Joshua (11:21–22).

(3) At the close of the list, we are reminded that Judah could not take Jerusalem. The conquest was not complete. The land as a whole may be in their possession, but not the city of Jerusalem. More remained to be done. One can easily see here an anticipation of the time when that city would be taken by David (cf. 2Sa 5:6–10).

## 2. Sons of Joseph (16:1–17:18)

The introduction (16:1–4) begins with a general overview of the allotment of Joseph and ends with a reminder that this allotment was divided between Joseph's two sons, Manasseh and Ephraim (16:4). The allotment of Ephraim is listed in 16:5–10 and that of Manasseh in 17:1–13. After both lists the writer notes that the sons of Joseph were unable to drive the Canaanites completely out of the land (16:10; 17:12–13). Thus the lists conclude on the same thematic note as that of Judah (15:63), i.e., the failure of the people to drive out all of the Canaanites from the land.

An epilogue to these two lists (17:14–18) addresses the question of the division of Joseph's allotment between his two sons.

## 3. Tent at Shiloh (18:1)

The writer here inserts an important note that the whole congregation of Israel had gathered together at Shiloh and had established the tabernacle (the Tent of Meeting) there. Previously, that

meeting place may have been at Gilgal where the Israelites camped, though this is not specified by the writer. Moreover, we are told that "the country was brought under their control." There is a linguistic association of the idea of "peace and rest" with the name Shiloh. It is at least significant that this is the first reference to Shiloh and the "Tent of Meeting" in the book of Joshua, just at the point in the narrative where the writer stresses that Israel found peace. Moreover, it is possible that an allusion is intended to Jacob's prophecy about Judah in Ge 49:10, "The scepter will not depart from Judah . . . until he comes to Shiloh" (NIV, "to whom it belongs"). Both here and in Ge 49 the ideal of a peaceful enjoyment of God's good gift of the land finds expression. The writer of Joshua may, then, be deliberately alluding to the Genesis text as a way of showing that Israel, under Joshua, was now enjoying such a time as Jacob foresaw. The presence of such an allusion does not imply, however, that this was the fulfillment of Jacob's prophecy. In the Hebrew text, the word *Shiloh* in Ge 49 is generally distinguished in spelling from the place-name *Shiloh* where the tabernacle was built. The ark at Shiloh was later captured by the Philistines (1Sa 4), and the tabernacle built there by Joshua was destroyed (Ps 78:60; Jer 7:12).

## 4. Remaining seven tribes (18:2–19:51)

Though much has been recorded, there were still seven tribes who had not yet taken possession of their portion of the land. The writer thus turns to the task of describing, in cursory form, the conquest of the remaining parts of the land of Canaan. He begins with a survey of the land commissioned by Joshua (18:2–10).

It is possible to detect in Joshua's opening words a sense of delay on the part of the seven remaining tribes and some impatience on the part of Joshua.

Joshua said to them, "How long will you wait. . . ?" (18:3). The passage shows clearly that it was Joshua, not the individual tribes, who instigated the renewal of the Conquest. A team of surveyors were sent out to record the names of the cities yet to be taken. These names were written "on a scroll" (18:9) and divided into seven sections. From this list, lots were cast to determine the portions of land for each remaining tribe. The lists of cities and boundaries that follow give some indication of the nature of the scroll compiled by the surveyors. The seven sections of territory consisted of that for Benjamin (18:11–28), Simeon (19:1–9), Zebulun (19:10–16), Issachar (19:17–23), Asher (19:24–31), Naphtali (19:32–39), and Dan (19:40–48). In addition to these seven territories, Joshua was also given an allotment (19:49–50).

A formal conclusion (19:51) is given to this section covering the allotment of the tribes (14:1–19:51). The names of Joshua and Eleazar the priest are repeated from 14:1, along with the mention of the "heads of the tribal clans of Israel." Moreover we are reminded that the work was carried out "in the presence of the LORD at the entrance to the Tent of Meeting" in Shiloh. In this way the allotment is given official sanction. It could not be contested.

## D. The Cities of Refuge Appointed (20:1–9)

An abbreviated description of the purpose of the cities of refuge is given here (taken from Nu 35:6–34; Dt 4:41–43; 19:1–13). The author's purpose is to show that the people and Joshua followed God's instructions from the Law and appointed cities as he had commanded. There is, however, a subtle but nevertheless real hint of failure in this record of the six cities. In Dt 19:8–9 it was promised that if the Israelites were completely obedient in taking the land, the Lord would enlarge their territory

even more, and they would need "three more cities," making a total of nine cities of refuge for the land. Thus the fact that this book records only the six cities suggests that Israel had not carefully followed all of God's laws (Dt 9:9). Since these cities were never built during Israel's historical past, the question of the fulfillment of these words of Moses has attracted much attention among Christian and Jewish interpreters. Because the condition of Israel's obedience must first be met before the cities are built (Dt 19:8–9), it is often maintained that these cities will be built only when the Messiah comes.

## E. The Levitical Cities Appointed (21:1–42)

The writer shows here that the Israelites continued to obey the Law in their allotment of the land. Because the Levites were not given a territory of their own, they were allotted cities within the territories of the other tribes. Moses had commanded that each tribe give a portion of its land to the Levites (cf. Nu 35). Now these instructions are carried out by Joshua.

The three families of Levites were the descendants of the three sons of Levi—Kohath, Gershon, and Merari. Aaron was a descendant of Kohath (cf. Ex 6:18–20). Thus the Kohathites consisted both of the Aaronic priests (descendants of Aaron) and the remainder of the descendants of Kohath. The territories and cities allotted, forty-eight in all, are listed in this chapter. The first list is that of the territories within which each of the families of Levites were to have their cities. The descendants of Aaron were to have thirteen cities in the territories of Judah, Simeon, and Benjamin (v.4). The rest of the descendants of Kohath were to have ten cities in the territories of Ephraim, Dan, and the half-tribe of Manasseh (v.5). The descendants of Gershon were to have thirteen cities in the territories of Issachar, Asher, Naphtali, and the half-tribe of

Manasseh (v.6). The descendants of Merari were to have twelve cities in the territories of Reuben, Gad, and Zebulun (v.7). Each of these towns is then listed by name and territory: descendants of Aaron (vv.9–19), the rest of the Kohathite clans (vv.20–26), the descendants of Gershon (vv.27–33), and the descendants of Merari (vv.34–40).

In vv.11–12, the author of this book explains the relationship between the land in the territories of Judah and Simeon given to the Levites and that land in these territories previously given to Caleb and his descendants. The problem focuses on the city of Kiriath Arba, (also called Hebron). In 14:13–15 and 15:13 it is recounted that the city of Hebron was given to Caleb by Joshua. Thus, when this same city was given to the Levites, it raised the question of who owned the city. The writer shows that problem was resolved by giving the Levites the city of Hebron itself and allowing the descendants of Caleb to own and live in the surrounding villages (v.12).

## F. Summary (21:43–45)

The section on the distribution of the tribal territories is concluded by an important summary of its meaning to the author. Here we see clearly the theological message the writer has in mind for the book. Having conquered the land and allotted it among the tribes, it could now be said in these three verses that God's promises to the forefathers had been fulfilled. It is hard to imagine a more emphatic statement that the Conquest had been a success. Looking back to God's promise in 1:8, "Do not let this Book of the Law depart from your mouth. . . . Then you will be prosperous and successful," one can see that the writer has not only amply demonstrated that Joshua did what God commanded but also that God had been faithful and had given them the land. The purpose of the present summary

verses is to state this fact emphatically for the reader.

It is particularly important for the writer to make the point of Joshua's obedience and God's faithfulness to his promises at this point in the book, for here a shift in the author's focus can be detected. In the remaining chapters much of what he has established, especially with regard to Israel's successes in taking the land, begins to unravel and show signs of dissolution. The viewpoint of the book turns away from the current events of the Conquest and on to the future generations of God's people. Though the book ends on the high note of Israel's success under Joshua and God's faithfulness to his promises, a cloud can be seen forming on the distant horizon—one that portends of the disastrous events during the time of the Judges which ultimately lead to the exile of Israel from the land, the Babylonian captivity (2Ki 25). These words of warning about darker days ahead can be heard in the otherwise optimistic speeches of Joshua at the close of the book.

## IV. Final Speeches of Joshua (22:1–24:28)

### A. Joshua's Speech to the Two and One-half Tribes (22:1–34)

#### 1. The return of the Transjordan tribes (22:1–9)

The theology and basic lessons of the Pentateuch can be seen clearly in Joshua's words to the tribes of the Transjordan area, the Reubenites, Gadites, and the half-tribe of Manasseh. Their obedience has led to their success, and thus they can now return to their land and enjoy it as a good gift from God. When they settle down in their land, however, they must always be mindful that it is only by their faithful obedience to God's will expressed in the Pentateuch (the Law) that they can continue to enjoy God's gift. What does it mean to obey the Law? Joshua's answer is taken directly from the Pentateuch: "to love the LORD your God, to walk in all his ways, to obey his commands, to hold fast to him and to serve him with all your heart and all your soul" (v.5; cf. Dt 30:6–10). With this warning, Joshua blessed them and sent the tribes to their homes.

### 2. The altar at Geliloth (22:10–34)

Note what now happened. The writer of the book raises the problem of the altar these tribes built on their return home. "When they came to Geliloth . . . [they] built an imposing altar there by the Jordan" (v.10). The Law had clearly emphasized that only one altar was to be built and that was at the place where God had chosen (Dt 12). Shiloh was now that place, for it was there that the tabernacle had been built (18:1). Why, then, have the tribes of Reuben, Gad, and Manasseh built another altar at Geliloth? At this point, the reader is in much the same frame of mind as the rest of the tribes at Shiloh who were ready "to go to war against them" (v.12).

The narrative, however, takes a sudden turn. Before going to war against the Transjordan tribes, the Israelites sent Phinehas, the priest, as an emissary along with ten leaders, to enquire how these tribes could have carried out such a blatant act of rebellion (v.16). In the course of his speech, Phinehas even made reference to the sin of Peor, an event in which he played the central role (Nu 25). We should not overlook the fact that Phinehas's words to these tribes are not lost on either the writer of the book or the alert reader. In his words we hear repeated the basic message of the Pentateuch: "If you rebel against the LORD today, tomorrow he will be angry with the whole community of Israel" (v.18). We, the readers, hear this message now from the mouth of the high priest, Phinehas.

A further surprise awaits us as we listen to the reply of the Transjordan

tribes. Their new altar, they said, was not intended as a rival of the altar at Shiloh, but rather a reminder of the importance of all the tribes worshiping God together at that one place. The altar at Geliloth was to be a "witness between us and you and the generations that follow, that we will worship the LORD at his sanctuary" (v.27). Like the stones set up at the crossing of the Jordan (4:1–9), this altar was to remind future generations of the importance of obedience to the will of God in the Law.

## B. Joshua's Speech to the Elders and Leaders (23:1–16)

Two more speeches follow in rapid succession at the close of the book. These speeches serve not only as a conclusion to the book of Joshua but also provide an important link to the rest of Scripture. The first speech (ch. 23) serves specifically as a conclusion to Joshua, whereas the second (ch. 24) serves as a conclusion to the whole of the Pentateuch.

The first is Joshua's speech to the leaders of Israel. In it Joshua reviews the major events of the Conquest and draws out the central lesson: "Be very strong; be careful to obey all that is written in the Book of the Law of Moses" (v.6). These are the same words that the Lord spoke to Joshua himself at the beginning of the book (1:6–8). It is common within biblical narratives for the central themes to be stated at the opening of a book or section and then restated at the conclusion. Furthermore, Joshua repeats the theme of Israel's success in taking the land: "not one of all the good promises the LORD your God gave you has failed. Every promise has been fulfilled; not one has failed" (v.14).

Two new themes are also introduced in Joshua's speech. The first is the impending failure of the Israelites to carry out fully the aims of the Conquest: "But if you turn away . . . then you may be sure that the LORD your

God will no longer drive out these nations before you" (vv.12–13). This theme links the book of Joshua to the book of Judges. The second theme is Israel's coming exile: "If you violate the covenant of the LORD your God, which he commanded you, and go and serve other gods and bow down to them, the LORD's anger will burn against you, and you will quickly perish from the good land he has given you" (v.16).

## C. The Covenant at Shechem (24:1–28)

In the last of Joshua's speeches, we find the people of Israel renewing their covenant relationship with the Lord. He had now delivered the land into their hands. They had been duly warned of impending dangers and disasters. Now they are gathered at Shechem, where they had been in 8:30–35, being represented again by their tribal leaders. The form of the covenant follows that of ancient treaty documents.

In this speech, the author is able to link this book to the Pentateuch as a whole. Joshua begins this speech with a reference back to Abraham and the patriarchal narrative of Ge 24:2–4. He then rehearses the material of the Pentateuchal narratives down through his own day. In this respect, Joshua's speech is cast in the same form as that of Moses in the book of Deuteronomy (cf. chs. 1–3). Not only does this speech look far back into the Pentateuch for its lessons (vv.2–10), it also looks far into the future for its warnings: "If you forsake the LORD and serve foreign gods, he will turn and bring disaster on you and make an end of you" (v.20).

Furthermore, Joshua's speech bears remarkable similarity to the last speech of Moses in Dt 30–31. Just as Moses had called on the people to choose between following God and forsaking him (see Dt 30:19), so Joshua now confronts the people with the decision, "Choose for yourselves this day whom you will serve" (v.15). And just as

Moses was certain that the people would forsake God in the future (see Dt 31:29), so also Joshua was certain that the people would not succeed in following after God ("You are not able to serve the LORD" v.19).

There is, however, a slight contrast between the final speeches of Moses and Joshua. Moses appears more hopeful about the ultimate fulfillment to God's promises than does Joshua. Moses looks far beyond the events of the historical books that follow the Pentateuch (Dt 30:1–9). He even looks beyond the time of the Exile in Babylon recorded at the end of 2 Kings, directing our attention to what will happen to God's people after the Captivity (Dt 30:1–6), in much the same way as the later prophets do (e.g., Jer 31; Eze 36). Joshua, however, is only able to see what will happen to these people in the immediate days ahead (vv.21–27); he does not look beyond the Exile. For him the Exile is inevitable; and if there is yet hope, it rests only in God's faithfulness to his promises to the fathers. He does not see the light at the other end of the tunnel as Moses does in the Pentateuch.

## D. The Death of Joshua and Eleazar (24:28–33)

As the book of Joshua began with the death of Moses, so now it concludes with the death of Joshua (v.29) and Eleazar, the priest (v.33). Between the accounts of the death of these two leaders is the notice that Israel had faithfully carried out the instructions of Joseph in Ge 50:25 by burying his bones at Shechem. The author clearly means this to be taken as a sign that God was faithful to his promises and had given them the land. As such, this last notice in the book looks far beyond the impending disasters of the book of Judges to the future hope of the return from the Exile, much the same way as the prophet Ezekiel used the imagery of dry bones to picture the hope of future resurrection of God's people (Eze 37).

# Judges

## Introduction

The title of this book is taken from 2:16: "Then the Lord raised up judges, who saved them out of the hands of these raiders." During the time of both Moses and Joshua, there was a select group of leaders in Israel called "judges" (cf. Nu 25:5; Dt 1:16; Jos 8:33; 23:2; 24:1). According to Ex 2:14, there were already judges appointed among the Israelites in Egypt before Moses gave the Law.

In the Law of Moses, however, the office of the judge became an essential part of Israel's social and religious life (Ex 18:21ff.). In Dt 16–17, two kinds of judges were commissioned by Moses. (1) Moses appointed judges and officials for each Israelite town (Dt 16:18). (2) Moses appointed a higher court that was to be located at the site of the tabernacle where both judges and priests would officiate (Dt 17:8ff.). This second court would handle cases too difficult for the local courts, just as Moses in the desert handled cases too difficult for his judges (Dt 17:8; cf. Ex 18:22).

These Israelite judges were responsible both to maintain civil law and to see to it that Israel obeyed the laws of their covenant with the Lord, made at Mount Sinai. They were to lead the people in the way of the Lord (Ex 18:20). In this sense, the judges were precursors of the king. They did a king's work (cf. Dt 17:18ff.) until the coming of the monarchy.

As with the other historical books, the book of Judges does not contain the name of its author. However, it contains some clues as to the time when it was written. From 11:26, for example, we know that the book covers a time period of about three hundred years. Thus it is not likely that the book was written by an eyewitness to all the events. The book appears to be made up of many eyewitness accounts that were pre-

served in the author's own day and were apparently used by the author. The Song of Deborah (ch. 5), for example, is likely a song written at the time of the events it celebrates. The most obvious clue to the time period of the book's composition is the recurring phrase, "In those days Israel had no king. . . ." This remark suggests that the book was written during a time when there was a king in Israel, or perhaps even after the time of the kingship.

Both Jewish and Christian tradition have for the most part seen Samuel as the author of this book. There is, however, no evidence for this in the book itself. On the contrary, the reference to the "captivity of the land" in 18:30, which most likely refers either to the exile of the northern kingdom in 722 B.C. or of the southern kingdom in 586 B.C., would almost certainly rule out the time of Samuel. Fortunately, the meaning and authority of the books of the OT do not rest on our identification of their authors.

The close similarity between the judges and the later Israelite kings provides the basic motif of this book. In many respects it can be viewed as a manual for the kingship. After the death of Joshua, Israel was without a godly leader. Moses was dead; Joshua and the elders were dead (2:10). The writer intends to show that the only leadership that remained in Israel was vested in the office of the judge. As his personal representatives, the Lord raised up special leaders to fill the office of judge and to instruct the people in his law (2:16–19). Some of the judges were also raised up by God to meet emergency situations. Others seem only to have been raised up as lifelong teachers of the Law (10:1–5; 12:8–15). Whatever the particular case, the book of Judges demonstrates that in the time before the establishment of the kingship in Israel, God ruled his people through the office of the judge. The judge thus becomes a model or paradigm of God's rulership among his people.

In some cases, these judges were called on to provide heroic military leadership. Samson, for example, seemed to have provided little else. The normal pattern of the judge was to provide strong leadership for the needs of the nation at hand—either military or administrative.

If we ask why the writer of this book recounts the events of the lives of some judges but passes over the events of the lives of others, we find there are good reasons. He seems particularly interested in those judges with a dual responsibility: (1) military leadership against God's enemies (e.g., 2:16a), and (2) covenant leadership with God's people (2:16a).

Why these judges and not others? Because these judges—Othniel, Ehud, Deborah, Gideon, Jephthah, and Samson—most closely resembled the kind of king Israel should have in the eyes of the writer. For him, these men and women were the best models of godly leadership—not primarily because they were especially godly in every respect, but rather because they were those whom God could and did use, people who saw themselves as instruments in God's hands.

One of the most perfect expressions of this attitude in Judges is Gideon—"I will not rule over you, nor will my son rule over you. The LORD will rule over you" (8:23). These words clearly express the purpose of the author. Jephthah displayed the same attitude of dependence and submission to the Lord, seeing God alone as the true ruler in Israel. He declared to the sons of Ammon, "Let the LORD, the Judge, decide the dispute this day between the Israelites and the Ammonites" (11:27b). For Jephthah, the Lord alone was the true Judge and Leader of God's people.

Two further points should be noted regarding the function of the office of

the judge in the composition of this book. (1) It was the Lord alone who delivered Israel through the hand of the judge. (2) It was God's Spirit who gave the judge the power to perform his or her task. In this book we meet with essentially the same theme as the book of Joshua: The Lord will fight for his people. In Judges, however, we do not hear of the captain of the Lord's army (cf. Jos 5:13–15); rather we hear of God sending his Spirit.

There are two main lessons that come from this book. (1) The welfare of the Israelite nation is directly dependent on a knowledge of God's will, the Law. After the death of Joshua, we are told, a new generation arose who did not know the Lord nor the work that he had done for Israel (2:10). This ignorance of God's Word leads to the wickedness of the people and their eventual forsaking of the Lord and following other gods (vv.12–13). The point of these warnings is to emphasize the importance of God's law given to Moses and the importance of teaching that law to the next generation. Within this context, Judges is a graphic illustration of the need for instructing the future generations in God's Word (cf. Dt 6:6–7). This command stands in stark contrast to the picture in Judges of the generation who did not know what the Lord had done. Without biblical instruction the nation would crumble from within.

(2) God will punish his people for their unfaithfulness to his covenant. The principal stipulation of the covenant renewal at Shechem (Jos 24) was the commitment to serve the Lord alone and not serve other gods. As we see in Judges, however, Israel did not keep this promise. They forsook the Lord and served foreign gods (2:12), and they suffered severe consequences for their apostasy (see 2:14).

The book of Judges shows one of the clearest structures of any book in the Old Testament. All the sections of the book work together to express one primary idea—namely, the necessity of God-ordained leadership in Israel. The book functions in a series of cycles. Step 1 is the death of God's leader and the falling away of the people from following the Lord. Step 2 is the Lord sending oppressors upon the people. In Step 3, Israel calls out to the Lord for help. Then, as Step 4, God raises up a judge to help the people and lead them in the way of the Lord. The book closes with two vivid accounts of life during the days of the judges: the story of the wandering Levite priest (17:1–18:31) and the story of the Levite priest and his concubine (19:1–21:25). These two show the depths to which God's chosen people had fallen. The focus on the condition of the Levitical priests seems intended to contrast Israel's state with God's intention for them in Ex 19:6: "a kingdom of priests and a holy nation."

The book of Ruth (placed elsewhere in the Hebrew Bible) falls into the same period as the judges but contains a strikingly different perspective. It provides a picture of a Gentile's faith in the Lord in the midst of Israelite apostasy. Ruth provides an interesting parallel to the Rahab narratives that opened this section of the historical books (Jos 2). Moreover, the book of Ruth and the narratives about the Levite priests in Jdg 17–21 provide an introduction to the books of Samuel. Ruth, the faithful Gentile, was of the lineage of David. Thus, the great king and the dynasty founded by him in Judah arose from among the faithful of this dark period in Israel's history. On the other hand, the account of the Levitical priest in Jdg 19–21 took place in the hill country of Ephraim and resulted in the wholesale destruction of the Benjamites. The story underscores, then, the wickedness of the tribe of Benjamin, Saul's tribe, during the period of the judges. The two accounts tell of the ancestors of Israel's first two kings—Ruth and the future

King David; the Benjamites and the future King Saul (cf. 1Sa 9:1).

# I. Prologue (1:1–3:6)

## A. Survey of the Battles of the Conquest (1:1–36)

### 1. Death of Joshua (1:1)

The book opens with the notice of the death of Joshua. The purpose of this note is to set the context for the following description of the conquest of the land, showing that these were events that happened after Joshua died.

### 2. Judah and Simeon (1:2–20)

The central focus of the chapter is on the tribe of Judah. By immediately focusing on the conquests of this tribe, the writer suggests that Judah has begun to replace Joshua as God's leader. Just as Judah was the first to lead the tribes away from Sinai (Nu 2:3), so Judah leads in taking possession of the land. Clearly the writer has in mind the importance that the tribe of Judah enjoyed in the Pentateuch (e.g., Ge 49:8–12) and the role Judah would play in the subsequent events of the Davidic kingship (cf. 2Sa 7). The promise to Judah had been that the rulership would not pass from him until the true king would come. Thus the writer shows that God was continuing to use Judah as the leader of his people. God's promises were still intact.

The account of the defeat of Adoni-Bezek (vv.4–7) is intended to show that God's treatment of the inhabitants of the land was just. Without the confession of Adoni-Bezek that he justly deserved this divine punishment, one might raise the question of whether God's treatment of the inhabitants of the land was fair. Why should Israel be commanded to carry out such harsh judgment on these people? The writer uses Adoni-Bezek's own words to show that God's ways are just (see v.7).

The terse form of the description of the conquests in this chapter leaves the reader with some uncertainty about the course of events in the conquest of the city of Jerusalem. Because this city has such importance in the subsequent historical books, the writer takes special pains to show that it had not been permanently captured during this time. His purpose is to ensure a proper understanding of the subsequent narrative of 2Sa 6:5, where it is expressly stated that David captured the city of Jerusalem and dwelt there. According to vv.8–9, the men of Judah attacked Jerusalem and set it on fire. Later in the chapter, however, we are told that the tribe of Benjamin failed to drive the inhabitants of Jerusalem, the Jebusites, from the city and thus continued to live with the Jebusites. Furthermore, in Jos 15:63 we were told that the tribe of Judah could not dislodge the Jebusites from Jerusalem and that they also continued to live with them "to this day."

There are several ways to reconcile these verses. It appears that more than one attempt was made to capture Jerusalem and that it was not until the time of David that Israel was finally and permanently successful. Moreover, it appears that owing to its location immediately along the border between the tribal territories of Judah and Benjamin, Jerusalem could have been rightly claimed by either tribe. It was not unusual to assign a city to two territories (e.g., Beth Hoglah to Judah in Jos 15:61 and to Benjamin in 18:22; Kiriath Jearim to Judah in Jos 15:60; Jdg 18:12 and to Benjamin in Jos 18:28). Since Jerusalem was located in or between the territories of Judah and Benjamin, it appears that both Judah (Jos 15:8, 63) and Benjamin (Jos 18:16, 28) were awarded Jerusalem as part of their territory. The southern border of Benjamin, which included Jerusalem, was identical to the northern border of Judah, which also included Jerusalem. Neither tribe, however, was able to capture this city at this time, though both attacked it and Judah even burned it (Jdg 1:8).

David finally captured the city and took it from the Jebusites (2Sa 5:6). Even then, the Jebusites continued to live there (2Sa 24:16, 18; 1Ki 9:20; Ezr 9:1).

This narrative concludes with a summary statement that "the LORD was with the men of Judah" (v.19) and hence they had great success. They took the whole of the hill country in their allotted territory. The writer then makes a curious remark that the tribe of Judah took only the hill country and not the plains, because the people in the plains had iron chariots (v.19). This remark may have been made in anticipation of the Lord's purpose of leaving some nations in the land "to test all those Israelites who had not experienced any of the wars in Canaan" (3:1). It may also be intended to show that Judah took their allotted territories only with God's help, for otherwise they could not have taken them, since the inhabitants of these lands had iron chariots.

### 3. Battles by other tribes (1:21–36)

In the remainder of the chapter, the writer lists a series of battles by several of the remaining tribes: Benjamin (v.21), the house of Joseph (Manasseh, vv.27–28, and Ephraim, v.29), Zebulun (v.30), Asher (vv.31–32), Naphtali (v.33), Dan (v.34). For the most part these battles ended inconclusively with the Israelites living side by side with the people of the land.

## B. The Angel of the Lord at Bokim (2:1–5)

By means of the words of the angel of the Lord at Bokim, the failure of the Israelites is traced back to the covenant that they made with the Gibeonites (cf. Jos 9:1–27). There is a marked contrast between the message of the captain of the Lord's host who met Joshua at the beginning of the Conquest (Jos 5:13–15) and the words of the angel who met Israel at the close of the Conquest (Jdg 2:1–4). When Joshua met the angel of the Lord as they first entered the land to take Jericho, it was a time of great anticipation of victory. Now, after many years of battle and after the death of Joshua, the angel announces the failure of God's people to obey his will and their eventual failure to successfully take the land. The story of the Conquest concludes with Israel weeping over their past failures and offering sacrifices to the Lord in acknowledgment of their sins.

### C. The Apostasy of the Nation (2:6–3:6)

In summary fashion, the author establishes the pattern for the story of the judges that follows. Curiously enough, the narrative of vv.6–9 returns to the last scene in the book of Joshua (Jos 24:28), quoting directly from this section. Joshua himself was still alive, along with the whole generation who knew what the Lord had done for Israel. The theme of this summary is clear enough. Israel had demonstrated over and again their unwillingness to obey the commands of the Sinai covenant and thus were forced to endure God's wrath and punishment. When the writer says that "the hand of the LORD was against them to defeat them, just as he had sworn to them" (v.15), he is referring to the statement of the covenant in Lev 26:15, 17 and Dt 28:25. Their chief sin had been that of forsaking the true God and following after other gods (cf. Ex 20:1–6). But in spite of their repeated failure, God showed himself a compassionate and loving God whose punishment ultimately led to their salvation.

It is within this framework that the role of the judges is introduced. When the people found themselves "in great distress" (v.15) as a result of their unfaithfulness, the Lord raised up judges for them who "saved them out of the hands" of their enemies (v.16). For the most part, as long as they had a judge over them, the people walked in God's

way. As soon as the judge died, however, they again went their own way, forsaking God and following other gods. In fact, it sometimes happened that after the judge had saved them from their enemies, they still did not follow after him and serve the Lord (v.17).

The most startling aspect of this section is the comment that after Joshua and his generation died, "another generation grew up, who knew neither the LORD nor what he had done for Israel" (v.10). The writer wants it known that the sin of the people described in this was directly attributable to the fact that the nation did not know the Lord nor the Scriptures that told of what the Lord had done for Israel. Moreover, the writer implies that this new generation did not know the Lord because they had not been told about him and his great deeds for his people. The author's words recall the warning of Moses that a time was coming when the people of Israel would be "foolish and unwise" (Dt 32:6) and would have to again "consider the generations long past" (Dt 32:7) if they were to find God's will and blessing. The situation is reminiscent also of the last days in the period of the kings when the Scriptures were lost and unknown and, in fact, were inadvertently discovered while cleaning out the Temple (2Ki 22:8).

## II. The Judges (3:7–12:15)

### A. Othniel and Cushan-Rishathaim (3:7–11)

In this short narrative one can see quite clearly the pattern of the story of the judges that forms the major part of the rest of the book. We are told first that Israel had sinned and had fallen into idolatry. The Lord was angered and sold them into the hands of the Aramean king Cushan-Rishathaim. They served him eight years. When they cried out to the Lord, he raised up Othniel. By means of God's Spirit, Othniel defeated Cushan-Rishathaim and there was peace in the land for as long as Othniel lived (i.e., forty years).

It is clear that the author is primarily interested in the pattern and the lesson about God's grace and forgiveness that it teaches. He gives little else for the reader to think on. His purpose is to establish this pattern as straightforwardly as possible at the beginning. In the subsequent stories, the author will include many more historical details in each of the stories. By leaving out such details here at the beginning and concentrating only on the pattern of God's dealings, the author assures us that this pattern will not be lost to the reader amid the increasing details of each story.

## B. Ehud (3:12–30)

The narrative turns immediately to the next emergency situation and the rise of the second judge, Ehud. Israel fell back into sin (v.12) after the death of Othniel (v.11). God then raised up an oppressor, Eglon, the king of Moab (vv.12–13). After serving Eglon eighteen years (v.14), the Israelites cried out to the Lord (v.15) and he raised up a deliverer, Ehud (v.15). So far the story has followed the same pattern as before, but at this point, more details are added. The writer is intent on drawing the reader into the story by developing its dramatic qualities.

Though brief, the story of Ehud has all the makings of an adventure story. Ehud is a genuine hero who uses courage and resourcefulness to deliver God's people. What seems particularly important to the writer is the fact that Ehud used his own unique physical limitations to carry out the work of God. The whole of the story is built around his being left-handed, which to the writer is a limitation. In Hebrew, being left-handed is described as "restricted in his right hand." Ironically, Ehud was a left-handed man from the tribe of Benjamin, a name that means "son of my right hand" (see NIV note to Ge

35:18). In Ehud the author is able to show that God's leaders are those who use the talents and circumstances that God has given them to do his work, even when that entails some limitations.

## C. Shamgar (3:31)

Shamgar is not called a judge, but the text explicitly states that he "saved Israel," and thus he is included within the story of the judges. Like Samson, Shamgar fought the Philistines and delivered Israel by superhuman feats. Samson slew one thousand Philistines with the jawbone of a donkey (16:15), and Shamgar killed six hundred Philistines with an ox-goad.

## D. Deborah (4:1–5:31)

The story of Deborah fits neatly into the pattern of the judges. It begins with the notice that Israel has again done that which was evil in God's sight (4:1). God then sold them into the hands of their enemies (v.2), and the people cried out to God for help (v.3). God answered their cry by raising up a judge, Deborah (vv.4, 9), who defeated their oppressors (vv.16, 24); peace was restored to the land for forty years (5:31b).

Much material has been added to the narrative that highlights important subthemes of this story. Central to it is the notion that Deborah is a woman judge, a prophetess (4:4), and that Israel was delivered from their oppressors by two women, Deborah (v.8) and Jael (vv.9, 17–22). Both the narrative of ch. 4 and the poem of ch. 5 stress the part played by these two women in the defeat of Israel's oppressors. Moreover, both sections stress the courage and resourcefulness of Deborah and Jael at the expense of their male counterparts, Barak and Sisera. Thus the theme of God's handing Israel's enemy "over to a woman" (4:9; cf. 9:54) is twice repeated: Sisera was defeated because of Deborah's presence with Barak (4:8–16; 5:1–23), and he was killed by the hand of Jael (4:17–24; 5:24–30). The author's point in all this is not to elevate the virtues of women over those of men. Throughout the narrative he wants it made abundantly clear that it was God and God alone who delivered Israel's enemies into their hands (4:9, 14, 23; 5:31), working mightily through the resourcefulness of these two courageous women.

### E. Gideon (6:1–8:35)

The story of Gideon follows the essential pattern of the other judges. The narrative begins on the note that the Israelites again did what was evil in God's sight (6:1a) and that God gave them over to the Midianites (v.1b). The Israelites cried out to God from their oppression (v.6), and God sent a deliverer, Gideon (v.14). The enemy was defeated, and the land had rest for the forty years that Gideon ruled over Israel (8:28).

Much has been added to the story of Gideon. For the most part, the additional material emphasizes the fact that it was God alone, not the strength and power of Gideon, who had delivered Israel from their enemies. As the story begins to unfold, the words of the unknown prophet (6:7–10) review for the reader the fact that it was God alone who had brought the Israelites out of Egypt and into the Promised Land. Through this prophet God says, "I drove them from before you and gave you their land" (v.9). Moreover, Gideon's uncertainty and the details of his call (vv.11–24) further show that it was not in his own strength that he went into battle. He was, in fact, a reluctant warrior. In reply to the Lord's call, he said, "If the LORD is with us, why has all this happened to us? Where are all the wonders that our fathers told us about . . . ?" (v.13). Gideon insisted on the Lord's reassuring him with signs that he was with him.

Having been thus fully assured, Gideon obeyed God's call by destroy-

ing the altar of Baal in his father's city (vv.25–32). For this deed he earned the nickname Jerub-Baal, which means, "Let Baal contend with him" (v.32). It cannot be overlooked, however, that in spite of Gideon's valor, the author still takes pains to remind us that he waited for the cover of night to tear down the altar "because he was afraid of his family and the men of the town" (v.27).

Having passed the initial test, Gideon's major call to action came when the Midianites and their allies began to amass their armies for battle against Israel in the Valley of Jezreel (v.33). Through God's Spirit, Gideon was able to rally the tribes against their oppressors (vv.34–35). Once again, before going into battle, Gideon assured himself that God was with him by testing God with the fleece (vv.33–40). God responded to Gideon's request for a sign. He further put Gideon to the test by reducing his army from 32,000 down to 300 (7:1–8). God's purposes in this can be seen in the narrative itself, when he said to Gideon, "With the three hundred men that lapped I will save you and give the Midianites into your hands" (v.7).

The course of the battle itself shows that God is behind the successes of Gideon (vv.9–25). Gideon was encouraged by overhearing a Midianite soldier tell his companion that "God has given the Midianites and the whole camp into [Gideon's] hands" (v.14). Hearing this, he told his soldiers "the LORD has given the Midianite camp into your hands" (v.15). When the battle ensued, the writer assures us that "the LORD caused the men throughout the camp to turn on each other with their swords" (v.22). Thus, throughout the narrative the point is made that neither Gideon nor the Israelite armies delivered Israel from the Midianites. It was God and God alone.

The story of Gideon's battle against the Midianites trails off into an account of the series of events surrounding the pursuit of the fleeing Midianite kings, Zebah and Zalmunna (8:1–21). The central theme throughout these stories is that of the Israelite tribes' participation in the battle. The response of the Ephraimites, "Why didn't you call us when you went to fight Midian?" (vv.1–3), stands in stark contrast to that of the officials at Succoth, "Why should we give bread to your troops?" (v.6), and at Peniel, "They answered as the men of Succoth had" (v.8). Gideon appears to have had his hands full. Not only was he pressed for time and supplies in his pursuit of the enemy, but he received no cooperation from his own countrymen. Some complained because they were left out of the battle and others refused to join in. One cannot escape the conclusion that the writer intends to show that leading God's people was a thankless if not hopeless task. Through it all, though, we see Gideon faithfully accomplish his work under the power of God's Spirit (6:34).

It is within this context that one should understand Gideon's reply to the people's request that he rule over them: "I will not rule over you. . . . The LORD will rule over you" (8:22–24). His reply was not an empty gesture of modesty. Rather, it was a frank admission that God alone was the true King in Israel. As if to confirm the sense of the narrative that the situation in Israel was hopeless, the writer concludes the story of Gideon's great victory with two narratives. The first is the account of Gideon's leading the Israelites into the idolatrous worship of the gold ephod (vv.25–27) and the subsequent ruin of the people (8:22–35). This incident reflects back on Gideon's first statement, "I will not rule over you," by showing the ultimate failure of a human king. The second narrative is the contemptuous rule of Abimelech (Gideon's son) over Shechem (9:1–57). This incident reflects back on Gideon's second statement, "nor will my son rule over you"

(8:23), by showing the kind of rule Israel could expect from one's sons. The theme of a good man's wicked sons plays a prominent role in the subsequent historical books (e.g., Eli's two sons, 1Sa 2:12–36; Samuel's two sons, 1Sa 8:1–3; and David's two sons, 2Sa 13–18).

## F. Abimelech and Jotham (9:1–57)

Though the story of Abimelech and Jotham, the two sons of Gideon, is complicated, its message is clear enough. It is intended to teach that God truly reigned as King in Israel even in spite of the fact that Israel often forsook his ways and followed after other gods. Thus the story answers to Gideon's words in 8:23, "The LORD will rule over you." The point of the story is stated at its conclusion, "Thus God repaid the wickedness that Abimelech had done to his father. . . . God also made the men of Shechem pay for all their wickedness. The curse of Jotham son of Jerub-Baal came on them" (vv.56–57). Behind this story lies the hand of God patiently and powerfully working out his just purpose. As the events unfold, they at first give the impression that God's people, the Israelites, are ruled by a murderous anarchy. Abimelech hired certain reckless mercenaries, murdered Gideon's seventy sons, and as a consequence was anointed king. Only the youngest, Jotham, escaped (vv.1–6).

The narrative then turns to Jotham's speech. Jotham first tells the parable of the thornbush (vv.7–15) and then applies it to the city of Shechem and their king, Abimelech (vv.16–21). The point at which he applies the parable is the ultimatum at its conclusion, where the thornbush says: "If you really want to anoint me king over you, come and take refuge in my shade; but if not, then let fire come out of the thornbush and consume the cedars of Lebanon!" (v.15). According to Jotham's own explanation in vv.16–20, the parable applies to

Abimelech and the leaders of Shechem for their treatment of the seventy sons of Gideon. If they have done wrong, then fire should "come out from Abimelech and consume" them (v.20).

The author then recounts the downfall of Abimelech and Shechem. At key points we are shown that it is God's hand that lies behind the course of events. In vv.23–24, for example, God sent an "evil spirit between Abimelech and the citizens of Shechem," and "God did this in order that the crime against Jerub-Baal's seventy sons . . . might be avenged." Finally, at the end we are told that in the course of events "God repaid the wickedness that Abimelech had done to his father" and that "God also made the men of Shechem pay for all their wickedness" (vv.56–57). The narrative thus teaches the reality of divine retribution. This lesson falls in line with the larger purpose of the Deuteronomic History (see unit on "The Deuteronomic History" between Deuteronomy and Joshua).

### G. Tola (10:1–2)

A bare minimum is recounted about Tola. He saved Israel and judged for twenty-three years.

### H. Jair (10:3–5)

Jair had thirty sons who rode thirty donkeys and controlled thirty towns. He judged Israel twenty-two years.

### I. Jephthah (10:6–12:7)

As a prelude to the story of Jephthah the writer has placed an account of Israel's repentance (vv.6–16). It opens characteristically with a reminder of the fall of the Israelites into idolatry and the Lord's giving them over to their enemies. But when the Israelites cried out to the Lord in repentance, the Lord at first did not save them. He said, "You have forsaken me and served other gods, so I will no longer save you. Go and cry out to the gods you have chosen. Let them save you when you are in

trouble!" (vv.13–14). When they cried out again and removed their foreign gods from among them, the Lord was moved to compassion to save them. Thus the account of the deeds of Jephthah is presented as God's compassionate response to their pleas.

The story of Jephthah is complex; several lines of narrative fall together within the story. There is, for example, the matter of Jephthah's vow and his apparent faithfulness to it (see below). There is also the question of his illegitimate birth and his subsequent rise to the position of leader of the town of Gilead and judge of all Israel in spite of it. Moreover, throughout the narrative Jephthah shows many positive traits, not the least of which is his lengthy account of God's dealings with Israel since the time of the Exodus, which he delivered to the Ammonites. At the end of the story, in the wake of Jephthah's victory over the Ammonites, he was forced into war with the tribe of Ephraim, and 42,000 Ephraimites were killed.

Certain parallels between parts of the story suggest clues to their larger significance. The question of legitimacy, for example, appears to lie at the heart of several of the episodes. Jephthah, an illegitimate son, does not have an inheritance from his father. Similarly, Jephthah's daughter, because of his vow, does not provide a means of an inheritance for him. She died without children or was put away in perpetual virginity. Moreover, Jephthah's speech to the Ammonite king stresses that ownership of the land does not rest on inheritance but on the will of God: "Whatever the LORD our God has given us, we will possess" (11:24).

It appears, then, that a central theme of the Jephthah narrative is the sovereign will of God in choosing and using those whom he pleases. Jephthah's claim to rule in Israel was not based on birth, tact, or judgment. It was rather based solely on his zeal to trust God and do his will. In this regard, the story of Jephthah is remarkably similar to that of Samson.

The nature of Jephthah's vow (11:30–31) and its fulfillment (v.39) has occasioned much discussion. A common view is that Jephthah's apparent vow to sacrifice whatever or whoever came out to meet him when he returned from victory over the Ammonites meant that he sacrificed his own daughter, since she was the first one who met him. Such an interpretation, however, goes beyond the plain meaning of the text and overlooks important features in the original Hebrew. The words of Jephthah in 11:31 should be rendered, "whatever comes out of the door . . . will be the Lord's or I will sacrifice it as a burnt offering." In other words, Jephthah's vow contains two parts, dedication to the Lord or burnt offering. According to Lev 27 there were several categories of vows. The case frequently applied to Jephthah's vow is Lev 27:29, "No person devoted to destruction may be ransomed; he must be put to death." This text, however, relates to an entirely different kind of situation from this one, namely, treatment of God's enemies in a war commissioned by him. Moreover, the Hebrew terms used in Lev 27:29 are not those of Jdg 11:31.

The vows in Lev 27:1–13, however, *are* virtually identical to Jephthah's situation and use the same terminology. There are two types of vows here. The first is the dedication of a person to the service of the Lord (Lev 27:1–8); the second is the dedication of an animal for an offering to the Lord (Lev 27:9–13). In the second case, only a ceremonially clean animal could be offered to the Lord (Lev 27:11). Thus it is impossible for Jephthah to have vowed to offer as a burnt offering "whatever comes out of the door" of his house, at least according to Mosaic Law, which, given the fact that he uses the terminology of

the Mosaic Law (Lev 27:1–13), he surely intends to follow.

A further confirmation of this interpretation is the statement in 11:39. The text does not say "And he offered his daughter as a burnt offering." It says, rather, "And he did to her as he had vowed. And she was a virgin." The syntax of the two clauses suggests that the two actions are coterminus—i.e., his fulfilling of his vow consisted of her remaining a virgin. The text does not say she had not known a man up to this point, though that was no doubt the case, but rather that henceforth she did not have sexual relations with a man. Thus it assumes Jephthah's vow entailed the alternative of dedication to the Lord or burnt offering, and in the case of his daughter he fulfilled it by dedicating her to the Lord for life.

The recurring theme of "dedication to the Lord," found throughout the subsequent narratives, further supports this interpretation of Jephthah's vow as a dedication to lifelong service. For example, in the Samson narratives that follow (chs. 13–16), the central theme is that Samson has been dedicated to the Lord as a Nazirite (13:5–7). In the next narrative (chs. 17–18), the premise of the story of Micah the Ephraimite is his mother's dedication of the stolen silver to the Lord (17:3). In the narrative of Hannah's dedication of the last judge, Samuel, to the Lord for life (1Sa 1:22), close parallels can also be found to these earlier texts.

### J. Ibzan (12:8–10)

Ibzan, from Bethlehem, judged Israel seven years. He had thirty sons and daughters.

### K. Elon (12:11–13)

Elon, from Zebulun, judged Israel ten years.

### L. Abdon (12:14–15)

Abdon, from Ephraim, judged Israel eight years. He had forty sons and thirty grandsons who rode seventy donkeys.

## M. Samson (13:1–16:31)

The story of Samson is one of the most puzzling of all the biblical stories. What lesson does the story of this man have? When we look at all the events in the life of Samson, it becomes clear that many things he did could not be lessons of godly leadership. But what stands out most clearly is the zeal with which Samson fought against the enemies of God's people. He is, to this extent then, an example of the wholehearted zeal that God's leader is to have against the enemies of God (see the unit on "The Deuteronomic History" between Deuteronomy and Joshua).

## III. Epilogue (17:1–21:25)

The book closes with two extended narratives that serve to illustrate the almost unbelievable apostasy and degradation of the nation during this time: Micah's idolatry (17:1–18:31) and the Benjamite war (19:1–21:25). The primary thematic purpose of these narratives is suggested by the recurring phrase, "In those days Israel had no king; everyone did as he saw fit" (17:6; 18:1; 19:1; 21:25). Without the kind of leadership exemplified by the king in Dt 17:14–20, there was little hope of the people walking in God's ways.

The narratives in this section appear to have been deliberately cast so that they resemble events and narratives already recounted in the OT. The story of the Levite and his concubine (19:1–26) has many similarities with the Genesis account of the city of Sodom (Ge 19). The writer therefore shows that the state of the covenant nation had fallen to the level of the sins of Sodom and Gomorrah. The account of the battle with the Benjamites (20:1–48) shows remarkable similarities with the battle at the city of Ai (Jos 7–8) and the initial conquest of the land after the death of Joshua (Jdg 1:1–36). It is significant that these passages stress the people's failure to obey God and thus conquer the land. By casting these narratives to resemble the times of past failures, the writer shows that during the time of the judges, the people were unable or unwilling to obey the Lord, thus repeating the sins of their fathers. It is not hard to recognize in this a warning drawn from the lessons of the Pentateuch: "You shall not make for yourself an idol . . . for I, the LORD your God, am a jealous God, punishing the children for the sin of the fathers to the third and fourth generation of those who hate me. . ." (Ex 20:4–5).

# Ruth

## Introduction

In the English Bible, the book of Ruth has generally been considered an addendum to the book of Judges. Its opening words—"In the days when the judges ruled" (1:1)—have contributed much to that understanding. In the Hebrew Bible, however, the book is considered an addendum to the book of Proverbs. The character of Ruth is thus portrayed as a historical example of the "virtuous woman" of Pr 31:10–31. The poem in Proverbs is a Hebrew acrostic, each line beginning with a different letter of the Hebrew alphabet. The first line begins with the question "A wife of noble character who can find?" (v.10), and the last line is "let her works bring her praise at the city gate" (v.31). The only other book that uses the term "virtuous woman" or "wife of noble character" is the book of Ruth (3:11), where Boaz calls Ruth "a woman of noble character." In that same passage, Boaz says of Ruth, "All my fellow townsmen [lit., those at the city gate] know that you are a woman of noble character" (3:11). Boaz thus says of Ruth, the ancestress of David, precisely what the poem in Pr 31 says of the virtuous woman.

The author of the book is unknown, as is the time of its writing. According to the earliest traditions, the book was written by Samuel the prophet, but there is no compelling evidence to support that tradition.

The author had several goals in writing this story. (1) He wanted to show the rich heritage of the house of David, the source of the future messianic King. This book is full of messianic themes. Boaz and Ruth are presented as faithful members of the Davidic line who trusted God and sought to do his will. God was continuously at work in the lives of his godly remnant, even during the troubled and turbulent days of the judges. In fulfillment of the divine promises to the patriarchs (cf. Ge 3:15; 49:8–12; Nu 24:7, 17), God was being faithful to his word.

(2) The narrative of the book clearly shows that God works his plans in sovereign ways but not without the obedience of his chosen people. Ruth's good fortune, for example, came only because of her insistence on forsaking her own people, the Moabites, and following Naomi back to the people of Israel. God worked through her faithfulness and trust in God. The explanation of her deeds is given, within the story, by the words of Boaz, "May you be richly rewarded by the LORD, the God of Israel, under whose wings you have come to take refuge" (2:12). This concept of Ruth's trust in God is central to the book. We are also told how the ultimate outcome of the events being recorded was dependent on God alone. At the crucial point in the story, just as Ruth was about to meet her future husband, Boaz, the writer craftily suggests that "she just happened to be gleaning in the very field that belonged to her distant relative" Boaz (2:3, personal tr.). When the biblical writers speak of "happenstance," they invariably mean that God is at work in mysterious ways.

(3) We are taught in the book of Ruth that God's plans for the house of David were not limited to the people of Israel. Ruth, the faithful Moabite woman, played a key role in God's purpose. It can hardly be coincidental that in the central passages of the Pentateuch that speak of the promised Messiah (e.g., Nu 24:17), the enemy of God's kingdom is represented by the ungodly Moabites: "A star will come out of Jacob; a scepter will rise out of Israel. He will crush the foreheads of Moab" (cf. Dt 23:4). It thus comes as a great surprise to the reader to see that the house of David itself traced its lineage back to a Moabite. The key point of the book is to show that God desires

the worship of all humanity, not just a select or chosen people. The decisive difference between Ruth and the rest of the Moabites that were to be defeated by the coming Messiah, was that she exhibited faith and trust in God. She forsook the gods of her people and followed the one and only true God (see 1:16). Ruth, a foreigner by birth, followed the Lord (cf. Rahab in Jos 2) and became part of the lineage of the house of David.

The mention of David by name in the last chapter of Ruth suggests that this book was intended to be read in light of the role that David was to play in the monarchy. It is also significant that no other Davidic king who followed David is mentioned. In the book of Ruth, then, we have a picture of the faithful lineage of the house of David. At a time when the Israelites were forsaking the Lord and following the gods of the Canaanites and Moabites (Jdg 2:12–15), Ruth is shown forsaking those gods to follow the Lord.

## I. The Sojourn From the Promised Land (1:1–22)

The book opens with an account of the people of God in exile. They are in the land of Moab, it is in the days of the judges, and there is a famine in the land. The opening events of the book of Ruth are similar to the situation at the close of the book of Judges, where great numbers of the descendants of the tribe of Benjamin were killed (Jdg 20:1–48) and special measures were necessary to secure wives for them (Jdg 21:1–24). In the book of Ruth it is not the tribe of Benjamin, but the tribe of Judah that is at risk, and wives for them are sought in Moab. Judah is the tribe of David and also of the Messiah. Clearly the intent of the writer in recalling the days of the judges is to show that the story of Ruth begins with a most impossible situation.

Through the events of the story, however, we will see God take this hopeless situation and turn it to his purpose and glory. He does this by finding a faithful Moabitess, Ruth, who has married into the house of Judah. This is a most unlikely beginning to a story about the coming of the promised seed who will give Israel peace by "crushing the heads of the Moabites" (Nu 24:17).

## II. Ruth Meets Boaz (2:1–23)

In ch. 2 we begin to see the hand of God at work. Naomi returns from her sojourn in Moab to the land of Israel, and Ruth accompanies her. Though Ruth's deeds are not particularly extolled by the writer, later in this same chapter we learn from Boaz that her faithfulness and trust in God were well known throughout the whole region (v.11). We also learn that God was about to repay Ruth for her faithfulness (v.12). The firstfruits of God's blessing come to Ruth in the form of Boaz's special treatment of her and his provision for her family (vv.13–18). Finally, in the words of Naomi, we learn that God is behind all these events: "He has not stopped showing his kindness to the living and the dead" (v.20). Within the story itself, Naomi's words have the immediate sense of God's care for her, a widow, and her family. Within the larger context of the book, however, her words take on a further significance that relates to God's promises to the house of Judah (cf. Ge 49:8–12) and, specifically, to David (cf. 4:22; 2Sa 7:16).

## III. Ruth's Night at Boaz's Threshing Floor (3:1–18)

This chapter concentrates on one scene in the story of Ruth—her night visit to Boaz at the threshing floor. Fortunately, the sketchy details of the story and the customs involved do not effect the overall meaning of the story. It appears likely that the law of the levirate marriage lies behind the actions of Ruth and Boaz (see Dt 25:5–10; cf. Ge 38:8).

That law provided for the care of a widow by the closest of kin. The levirate marriage law may also be linked here to the law of the Year of Jubilee (Lev 25:10–28), which ensured that private property always remained the possession of a family or tribal group. In any event, Naomi's suggestion to Ruth that she force the hand of Boaz in obtaining for their family the right of inheritance is seen as an important step in God's faithfulness to the house of David.

The similarities between the story of Ruth and the story of Tamar (Ge 38) are hardly mere coincidence. Both Ruth and Tamar (Ge 38:12–26) employ a ruse to ensure that their rightful inheritance is granted them. Both are pronounced just and righteous for their actions (Ge 38:26; Ru 3:11), and both play a central role in the lineage of David (Ge 38:27–30; Ru 4:18–22). The story of Tamar is, in fact, mentioned at the close of the book of Ruth, and the concluding genealogy picks up that of Ge 38:27–30. In the Gospels it is precisely these two women who, along with Rahab and Bathsheba, are singled out for mention in the genealogy of Jesus (Mt 1:3, 5). The point of this similarity is to show that the same God is at work in both events. God's works may be mysterious, but they are revealing of his nature. As he has worked in the past, so also he always works in the lives of his people.

## IV. Ruth's Marriage to Boaz (4:1–22)

The details of the actual transaction are given at the close of the story (vv. 1–12). It is no surprise to the reader that the closest of kin forfeits his right to redeem Ruth's inheritance (vv. 1–6). Up to this point in the story the recurring theme has been God's faithfulness to the house of David and the confluence of human events to that purpose. Therefore, when the closest of kin refuses to buy Ruth's inheritance and take her as his wife, we see it as further evidence of God's providence. The words of the elders and those at the gate of the city provide a clear view of the central theme of the book. They focus the reader's attention on the promises that God had made to the forefathers, "May the LORD make the woman who is coming into your home like Rachel and Leah" (4:11); and they help to draw a line connecting those promises with the house of Judah, "Through the offspring the LORD gives you by this young woman, may your family be like that of Perez, whom Tamar bore to Judah" (v.12).

The purpose of the genealogy at the conclusion of the book is to make the final link between this story and the birth of David. We learn from this genealogy that the story we have just been reading is the story of the birth of David, the king of Israel, and the story of the birth of the Son of David, the Messiah.

# 1 Samuel

## Introduction

In the Hebrew Bible the title of the book is Samuel; there is no division between 1 and 2 Samuel. The title is derived from the principal character of the book, as was the case with the book of Joshua. Samuel, the prophet, was the founder of the Israelite monarchy.

Like the books of Joshua and Judges, we are not told the author of the book of Samuel. There are, however, clues to the time period within which the book was written. The length of time of the events of the book itself runs from the final days of the Judges to the final days of the life of David—over one hundred years. Thus the author was likely not an eyewitness to at least some of the events in the book.

That this is so is confirmed by the fact that the author often gives explanations of expressions and customs belonging to the time of Samuel and David. For example, in 1Sa 9:9 an explanation is given for the word "prophet," and in 2Sa 13:18 there is an explanation of Tamar's long-sleeved robe. If this book were written to people from the same time period, such explanations would not likely be necessary. One of the most interesting clues is the passage in 1Sa 27:6—"Ziklag . . . has belonged to the kings of Judah ever since." This suggests that the book was composed after the division of the nation into the two kingdoms of Judah and Israel.

There are also indications of the available sources that could have been used to compile the book. Mention is made, for example, to "the book of Jasher" in 2Sa 1:18 (cf. Jos 10:13). In 1Ch 29:29 there is mention of the "words" of Samuel, Nathan, and Gad, which were about the "acts of King David." These could also have been used by the writer of the book of Samuel. These references suggest there was a national archives of sorts during the time of David where records of important events of the kings were kept. According to 2Sa 8:16, David employed an official "recorder," Jehoshaphat son of Ahilud, and "secretary," Seraiah. These men no doubt had others working for them, and the works they produced would have been available to the writer of the book of Samuel.

The prophet Samuel was the last of the long succession of judges who had ruled over Israel and had led the people in the way of the Lord. In the person of the judge, the Lord ruled his people as their king. Gideon's rebuff of the offer to become king over Israel expresses well the theocratic ideal: "I will not rule over you, nor will my son rule over you. The LORD will rule over you" (Jdg 8:23).

Samuel, like Samson who preceded him as Israel's judge, was chosen and prepared for his service even before he was born (1:11). During his early years as a prophet and judge, Israel faced some of its darkest days—the Ark of the Covenant was captured by the Philistines, and Israel was overrun by their conquerors (4:11ff.; 7:14). Samuel was able to rally the people to renew their trust in the Lord and, like the earlier judges, was able to deliver Israel from its foreign oppressors—the Philistines (7:3–13).

As a prophet, Samuel played an important role in the larger thematic structure of the book of Samuel and in the Deuteronomic History. His importance for the writer of this book can be seen in the amount of space and detail devoted to him. Moreover, so important was Samuel that, in later tradition at least, the book received his name, even though he himself was not a character, or even alive, during the second half of the book (our 2 Samuel).

Why is the prophet Samuel so important in this book? To answer this question we have to look both at the situation that is addressed in the book as well as the larger theological context of the book. From what we can gather from the book itself, the original readers of the book of Samuel lived during a time of great discouragement or even exile. They also lived during a time of disobedience to God's covenant. Their disobedience had come primarily because their leaders, the prophets, priests, and kings, had led them in the ways of the nations around them and not in the ways of the Lord (Jer 8:4–12). God had warned the people by sending his prophets, but the nation would not listen and followed the word of the false prophets and weak kings instead (2Ki 17:7ff.). In sum, the problem of the exile was a crises in godly leadership. Israel had not understood the role of their leaders, the prophets and kings, and many of these leaders themselves did not understand their roles. In the book of Samuel, then, the author uses the prophet Samuel as a lesson in godly leadership. Samuel demonstrates by his actions the proper role of God's prophet as a leader of God's people. We can see a reflection of this in Ps 99:6, for example, where the prophet Samuel is held up, along with Moses and Aaron, as a model of the kind of leaders God desired for his people.

The kind of prophetic leadership exhibited by Samuel throughout this book is that which has been taught in Dt 18:14–22. Its message can be summarized in the following points. (1) Israel was to have access to the direct word of God in a way quite different from other nations (vv.9–14). God fundamentally rejected the ways of the nations (e.g., divination, sorcery, witchcraft). (2) The way Israel was to hear the word of God was limited to the word of the prophet. God was to give Israel an institution of prophets who were to speak his words to the people (v.15). Israel had requested this kind of word from God at Mount Sinai (vv.16–17) because they

had been afraid to speak with God face to face. (3) The prophet's word was to have absolute authority as God's word to the people (18:18–19). (4) The people were to be on constant guard against wrongly following the word of false prophets. They were to test their prophets to see if the word they spoke proved true over the course of time (vv.20–22). A true prophet was one whose words about the future were fulfilled.

Samuel the prophet is thus important to the writer because he exemplifies this deuteronomic teaching regarding the true prophet. Other features of the life of Samuel incorporate the deuteronomic teaching of the role of the priest and the king (see Dt 17:14–20). Samuel, like Moses in the Pentateuch, is an example of the role of the prophet, the priest, and the king.

# I. The Period of Samuel's Judgeship (1Sa 1:1–7:17)

## A. The Rise of Samuel and the Fall of Israel to the Philistines (1:1–4:22)

### 1. The story of Hannah (1:1–2:11a)

The main characters in the story are introduced at the beginning (1:1–3). Elkanah, Samuel's father, was from the hill country of Ephraim. According to 1Ch 6:33–34 he was a Levite. Elkanah had two wives, Hannah and Peninnah. Already in the introduction we are given the basis for the development of the plot of the story. Hannah was barren and Peninnah had many children (1:2b). As the story unfolds, we are told that Hannah was barren because the Lord had closed her womb (v.5). Eli, the priest, is mentioned only in passing at the beginning of the story. He is introduced as the father of Hophni and Phinehas. At the beginning of the story there is no hint of the negative role these two sons are to play in the subsequent narrative.

The introduction also sets the stage for the central events of the Hannah story, namely, the annual pilgrimage of

Elkanah and his family to the tabernacle at Shiloh (v.3). In this way the writer has linked Elkanah and his family to the instructions of Moses in Dt 16:16, which required that all Israelite men appear before the Lord three times each year to present an offering to the Lord. We thus see that Elkanah and his family are righteous, obedient Israelites, which makes the announcement of Hannah's barrenness all the more problematic.

The story begins to unfold by the development of conflict along two lines. First, there is the surface conflict between Hannah and Peninnah. Peninnah kept provoking Hannah "to irritate her" (v.6). At another level, however, we are told twice that the Lord had closed Hannah's womb (vv.5–6). As if to compensate for this, Elkanah customarily gave Hannah a double portion of food, "because he loved her" (v.5). From the very beginning, the story introduces this complex web of relationships, with little explanation of their underlying causes.

No explanation is given as to why the Lord had closed Hannah's womb or why Elkanah loved Hannah more than Peninnah. Elkanah's reply to Hannah's sadness, "Don't I mean more to you than ten sons?" (v.8) is probably to be taken as an honest evaluation of their relationship and not a self-delusion on his part, and thus shows that her lack of a child had not affected her relationship within Elkanah's household in the slightest. Thus, as the repeated reminder that it was the Lord who had closed her womb suggests, Hannah's concern for a child went beyond her natural desire for a child and the taunting of her rival. Her sadness was ultimately linked to her relationship with the Lord. By means of these features in the narrative, Hannah's barrenness is elevated to a significantly higher thematic level in the story. She appears to represent one whose suffering ultimately comes from God but for which

there is no visible cause. Hannah here in this story is not unlike Job. Both are faithful, yet both suffer at the hand of God.

In viewing these characteristics of the story we can begin to see the importance of Hannah for the writer of the book. She represents a significant portion of his readership. If we think of the book of Samuel as a narrative written to a people in distress and exile, or at least suffering under the hand of God's judgment, then Hannah easily becomes a source of identification for the godly remnant who innocently suffer along with the guilty. It thus makes sense that the story moves so quickly to its resolution by presenting Hannah praying intensely for a son in the presence of the high priest Eli (1:9ff.). In Dt 7:14 barrenness was a sign of God's judgment, and Isaiah the prophet even personified Israel in exile as the "barren woman" (Isa 49:21; 54:1). Eli's suggestion that her state was one of drunkenness may have been intended by the writer to link her troubles to those of the Exile. Jeremiah, for example, had used the notion of drunkenness to depict the effects of God's judgment (cf. Jer 13:13; cf. Isa 51:17–20). Thus, like Hannah, the exiled readers of this book would have prayed to the Lord out of a greatly distressed soul. They also would have prayed to a God who had caused their distress (cf. La 5:20–22).

The climax of the story comes with Eli's announcement that Hannah's prayer had been heard (1:17). She returned to her husband "and her face was no longer downcast" (v.18). In the same way that the narrative had earlier reminded the reader that the Lord had closed Hannah's womb, we are now told that "the LORD remembered her" (v.19) and "in the course of time Hannah conceived and gave birth to a son" (v.20). By the use of the vocabulary of "remembrance," reminiscent of earlier acts of God's deliverance (cf. Ge 8:1;

19:21; Ex 2:24), the writer further elevates the story to the level of God's saving acts for his people. It will be no surprise to the reader when Hannah herself turns to the same themes in the song that immediately follows this narrative.

The song of Hannah (2:1–10) is important for the interpretation of the story because, like most songs in the Bible, it is one of the ways the author uses to draw out thematic hot points of the story. The song follows the formal pattern of a praise song.

(1) Introductory announcement of praise (v.1a)

(2) Praise of the Lord's majesty (vv.1b–3)

(3) Praise of the Lord's grace (vv. 4–8b)

At its conclusion, however, the song contains a fragment of an eschatological hymn (vv.8c–10).

(4) Cause for praise (vv.8c–10a)

(5) Request (vv.10b-c)

As we will see, this additional element in Hannah's song plays an important role in developing the meaning of the narrative and ultimately the book.

According to Lev 7, the Mosaic Law provided for a formal acknowledgment of answered prayer by means of a sacrifice and a public statement. In her song and offering Hannah thus fulfilled her duty. The viewpoint of her song is basic to the development of the story. We see in the words of this song that for Hannah, God's answer to her prayer in giving her a son became an occasion for her to recall God's universal and eternal care for the oppressed. God's act on her behalf renewed in her a hope in God's promise of a coming messianic king. The sense of the song can best be seen in the ideas it expresses that go beyond Hannah's own immediate circumstances. At only one point, for example, does Hannah mention her barrenness (v.5b), and even here it seems only to be in the context of the formal imagery of the psalm itself. Clearly Hannah's attention in this song is on other matters—prompted, to be sure, by the Lord's hearing her own prayer for a son.

A prominent idea in Hannah's song is that of the Lord as a righteous judge. She uses much traditional imagery in her description of God. This can be seen by comparing her words and phrases with other psalms in the Bible (cf. v.3 with Ps 75:4–5; vv.6–7 with Ps 75:7, 10). For Hannah her answered prayer was a sign that the Lord is a righteous judge. He brought down the proud (Peninnah) and exalted the humble (Hannah). By means of this song, then, the idea of the Lord's judging the proud and exalting the humble is linked to the concepts of the barrenness and the blessing of children that are central to the theme of the narrative. Moreover, within the larger picture of the book, Hannah's barrenness and answered prayer becomes a vehicle for the theme of exile and deliverance. Quite naturally, this song assumes that she is the "righteous" one whom the Lord exalts, though it should be noted that it does not explain why she was in the right and Peninnah was wrong. But the narrative does explain why Hannah was just. She is the one who cried out to the Lord in her distress. Nothing, not even the care and attention given her by a loving husband, could console her desire for God's blessing, a son (cf. La 3:24–38). It is thus her zeal and love for God that is the mark of her righteousness before him.

Hannah's song takes an unusual turn at its conclusion. She adds an additional request: "O LORD, may those who oppose him be shattered; may he thunder against them from heaven; may the LORD judge the ends of the earth; and may he give strength to his king and exalt the horn of his anointed" (2:10). Though NIV has rendered the verbs in this section by the simple future tense, the form of the verbs in the Hebrew text is "volitional"; that is, they request that God will do something; they are not merely a prediction that he will. Thus, having proclaimed that the Lord is a righteous judge, Hannah continues by making a request to the Lord that he will now, or in the future, judge all of his creation. What she calls for, in other words, is the reign of God's kingdom upon the earth. She wants God's king and his Anointed One, the Messiah, to prosper and all the world to be judged. She is praying that God will send the promised Messiah. Such an expectation is not only sanctioned by the Pentateuch (cf. Ge 49:8–12; Nu 24:7–24; Dt 17:14ff.), but it is also the central theme of 1 and 2 Samuel (cf. 2Sa 7). This same hope of the coming of the Messiah flourished in the time of the Exile (cf. Da 7:13–14; Hag 2:20ff.; Zec 6–14).

### 2. The exile of the ark (2:11b–4:22)

In the first segment of this story (2:11b–4:1a) the author is primarily concerned with demonstrating that the priests, Eli's sons Hophni and Phinehas, are totally bereft of the ideals of God's law. He gives two reports of their misdeeds—the first demonstrating their greed (2:12–17) and the second their promiscuity (vv.22–25). This is then followed by two reports of God's judgment on the house of Eli. The first is the speech of the "man of God" (vv.27–36), and the second is the word of God given to Samuel (3:1–18). The fact that two accounts of their failure and two accounts of God's judgment are given is related to the requirement in Dt 19:15 that "a matter must be established by the testimony of two or three witnesses." Throughout this book the writer follows the same rule by reporting two distinct occasions for Israel's failure.

Also in this section the writer is concerned to report Samuel's call and verification as a true prophet. The call of Samuel is recounted in connection with the announcement of the downfall of the house of Eli (3:1–10). Here we see that it is Samuel who is first called as a prophet of God's judgment (vv.11–18). Like many prophets after him, he is called to announce the coming judgment of God. The verification of Samuel's call is recounted in 3:19–4:1a: "And all Israel from Dan to Beersheba recognized that Samuel was attested as a prophet of the LORD."

In the final segment of the story (4:1b–22), the narrative turns to the account of the exile of the Ark of the Covenant. The Israelites went out to meet the Philistines in battle and were summarily defeated in their first encounter (4:1b–2). Though the narrative provides no explanation for their defeat, the larger context suggests that it was because of the failure of their leadership, the ungodly priests. The author of Ps 78 draws the same conclusion from this story saying, "[They] rebelled against the Most High; they did not keep his statutes. Like their fathers they were disloyal and faithless" (Ps 78:56–64). After this defeat, the elders of Israel suggested that the ark be taken from the tabernacle in Shiloh and brought with them into battle. This was apparently to ensure that the Lord would give them victory (vv.3–4). But the result was further failure. In fact, it only served to increase the resolve of the Philistines. The ark was captured and Eli's sons were killed (vv.5–11), thus confirming the words of the man of God against the house of Eli (2:34). When Eli heard the news of the capture of the ark he died (4:12–18), and the wife of his son Phinehas gave birth to a son and named him Ichabod, i.e., "no glory" (vv.19–22).

There are several aspects of this story that contribute to its meaning in Samuel. (1) Samuel the prophet is nowhere to be found in the narrative itself; the story focuses only on Eli and his two sons. This appears to be the author's way of showing that Israel as a nation and their priests were operating without and apart from the word of God's prophet. The advice regarding the use of the ark in battle, which ultimately led to their total defeat, came not from the prophet Samuel but from the elders of the people. Moreover, the elders asked, "Why did the LORD bring defeat upon us?" (4:3), but they did not seek an answer from the prophet. Thus they were not acting in accordance with the prescriptions of Dt 18.

(2) The people, in taking the ark into battle, presumed upon the mere presence of the ark as a sign of the Lord's own presence and guaranteed help. That presumption was much like that of the Israelites who went into exile, in part because they had assumed that, regardless of how they lived, as long as the temple was in Jerusalem and God was in the temple, all would be well. The prophet Jeremiah said to them, "Do not trust in deceptive words and say, 'This is the temple of the LORD, the temple of the LORD, the temple of the LORD!' If you really change your ways and your actions and deal with each other justly . . . then I will live in this place" (Jer 7:4–7). This comparison between Israel's attitude toward the ark and their later attitude toward the temple would not have been lost on the readers of this book. Thus the sense of the story of the loss of the ark fits well into an exilic context for the book as a whole. It teaches that the failure of the priestly leaders of Israel caused the people to misunderstand God's promised presence in the covenant, and thus they forfeited their right to the Promised Land.

(3) The deaths of Hophni, Phinehas, and Eli show the gravity of the loss of the ark. With the loss of the ark went also the loss of Israel's priesthood. As a result, the priesthood of Eli was abolished. In a graphic picture of the departure of God's glory from the nation because of the failure of Eli's priesthood, this narrative ends with the naming of Eli's heir apparent to his priesthood as Ichabod. That is, the only surviving member of Eli's house was marked by his ignominious name, "Where is the glory?" The picture of the Lord's glory departing from his people in this story is reminiscent of the departure of that glory from the temple in Eze 9–10. Moreover, an interesting contrast is provided between the wife of Phinehas and Hannah. The births of Ichabod and Samuel are both presented as a sign that God had acted righteously with his people Israel. The son of the wife of Phinehas portends the eventual exile of the people from the land, whereas Hannah's son portends the time of the glorious return from that exile.

## B. The Return of the Ark and the Revival of the People (5:1–7:17)

### 1. The ark in exile and the return (5:1–7:1)

After they had captured the ark, the Philistines brought it to Ashdod to put it in the temple of their god, Dagon (5:1–2). The text does not state their reason for doing this, though it appears to have been put there as a trophy of sorts. It is also possible that they were expecting a blessing from it. In any case, as the story continues, the statue of Dagon was unable to stand before the ark. Twice it fell, and a plague broke out among those who kept it (vv.3–6). After passing the ark from city to city, the leaders decided to return it to Israel, devising a curious way to test whether their misfortunes were by chance or by the hand of the God of Israel (5:7–6:18). It should be noted that the Philistine priest and religious leaders were familiar with the story of the Exodus as it was told in the Pentateuch (6:6).

When the ark was returned, it was treated carelessly by the Israelites, and many died because of it (6:19). The ark was then given proper treatment according to the Law of Moses, and a priesthood was appointed to care for it (6:20–7:1).

To appreciate the meaning of this narrative we must remember that, according to the Pentateuch, the ark was the visual representation of the promise of God to dwell among his chosen people (Ex 25:22). The Israelites had misused this privilege by presuming upon it, and now the Philistines also attempt to turn their possession of the ark into a blessing for their land. But they too learned that the Lord's presence could not be manipulated in such a crass and selfish way. God's presence with the ark is a matter of grace.

Even though the Israelites had been judged by the removal of the ark, this narrative shows that God was still working on their behalf and waging war on their enemies, the Philistines. Thus God continued to judge Israel's enemies even though he had used their enemies as his instruments of judgment on his people (see the same lesson in Hab 1:12–13). Thus the God of Israel is one who both punishes and saves, but in punishment, the Lord's grace is actively at work on behalf of his people. It was in their punishment that God's people learned of his ever-renewed love for them (cf. La 3:22–23). Even when the ark was returned, Israel had to learn that their on-going relationship with the Lord continued to be one of grace. The Lord remains the sovereign God and must be treated as holy. The failure of the people to treat the ark rightly after its return is reminiscent of the failure of the people to rebuild the temple after the Exile in the days of Haggai and Zechariah (Hag 1:3).

### 2. The lesson of obedience (7:2–17)

After the ark had been returned and the Israelites had mourned their losses, Samuel gathered the people to call them to obedience (vv.2–3). The people responded by obeying the words of Sam-

uel and putting away all their foreign gods to follow the Lord alone (v.4). The scene is reminiscent of Jos 24:14–15, where under similar circumstances Joshua called on the people of Israel to "throw away the gods your forefathers worshiped beyond the River and in Egypt, and serve the LORD." Samuel then called an assembly at Mizpah, and the people fasted and confessed their sin (vv.5–6). Such a large assembly of Israelites attracted the attention of the Philistines, who thought they were gathering for war (v.7a). When the Israelites heard that the Philistines were preparing for war, they cried out to Samuel for help. Samuel responded by offering prayer and sacrifice, and the Lord answered him (vv.7b–10a). The Lord himself defeated the Philistines, who were no longer a threat to Israel all the remaining days of Samuel (vv.10b–17). The lesson of the narrative is clear: When the people followed the words of the prophet and obeyed the will of God, God gave them strength and fought against their enemies.

## II. The Beginning of the Israelite Monarchy (8:1–14:52)

### A. The Request for a King (8:1–22)

At the close of Samuel's life, after many years as the Lord's representative, a crisis developed over the kind of leaders Israel should have. Samuel had apparently retired as judge and had appointed his own sons to take his place (v.1). His sons, however, had abused the office and were using their position for worldly gain. The people, recognizing that Samuel's old age had hindered his ability to judge Israel, requested that he appoint a king over them to rule as the other nations around them (vv.4–5). Rather than wait for God to deliver by raising up a judge like Samuel, the people wanted to appoint a permanent leader, a king.

Samuel, however, was angered by this request and turned to the Lord for help. The Lord responded by explaining their request and instructing Samuel to acquiesce to their plan, even though the motives of the people were not right (v.7). Samuel then carried out their proposal and established the kingship in Israel with the house of Saul, but not without a solemn warning to remain faithful to the covenant and to remember that the Lord alone was the true king in Israel. The earthly monarch was merely the obedient servant of the Lord (vv.11–22; 12:14–15).

The seeming hesitation on the part of Samuel and God to provide Israel with a king is puzzling to some in view of the overall importance of the kingship in Israel's history and in God's own plans. In the Davidic covenant (2Sa 7), for example, God promised to establish an eternal Davidic kingship over Israel. Already in Ge 17:16; 49:10–12, God's plans for Israel's future appear to have included the kingship. Thus certain facts must be noted and correlated to alleviate the ambiguity. (1) According to Dt 17:14, the kingship in Israel was anticipated by Moses, and specific instructions were given regarding the kind of rule the king was to provide for the nation of Israel. It was to be a rule based on God's law. The king "is to read [God's law] all the days of his life so that he may learn to revere the LORD his God and follow carefully all the words of this law and these decrees" (Dt 17:19; cf. 1Ch 22:12–13; 2Ch 7:17ff.; 15:2; 31:20–21). Thus, long before the people requested a king in the days of Samuel, the Lord had already provided instructions regarding the kind of king they were to have. He was to be a king who would lead the people in the way of the Lord, much the same as the judges did during the early days of Israel's history.

(2) The people in Samuel's day appeared to have an incorrect notion of what their king should do. They wanted him to be like the kings of the other nations around them (vv.5, 20). As they explained to Samuel, they wanted a king who could maintain a standing army and who could fight their wars. In other words, they were seeking a military leader rather than a spiritual one. Their model for the kingship was shaped by the people around them and not by the word of God. It is an interesting fact that their first king, Saul, actually fit their description quite well. He gathered a standing army about him (10:26) and he, for the most part, proved courageous in battle (11:11). At the same time, the writer of Samuel shows that Saul failed precisely in the area of spiritual leadership by not keeping God's law (chs. 13–14).

(3) Samuel's act of displeasure over Israel's desire for a king stems from his misunderstanding of their motives. The Lord said to him, "Listen to all that the people are saying to you; it is not you they have rejected, but they have rejected me as their king" (v.7). Israel was not rejecting its present leader, Samuel. Rather, they were rejecting the kind of leadership God had given them, which up to this point had depended on God's sovereign selection and empowering and on the reliance of the people on the Lord to raise up a deliverer. But now with a king, such faith in the Lord's help was no longer necessary, and with a standing army, continuous trust in the Lord to raise up a deliverer would be rendered unnecessary. The people were wanting to exchange the "stone of help" (Ebenezer) as a sign of continual trust for the ready ability of the king to do their fighting.

(4) Regarding the way in which the people were given a king, at first glance it appears that Samuel and the Lord gave in to the desires of the people and that Israel was given a king as they demanded. But on closer look we see that Israel did not get precisely the king they demanded. Their king was still to be God's representative. He was anointed

by the Lord and Samuel his prophet, but not without certain stipulations. Along with giving them a king, Samuel sternly warned the nation: "If you fear the LORD and serve and obey him and do not rebel against his commands, and if both you and the king who reigns over you follow the LORD your God—good! But if you do not obey the LORD, and if you rebel against his commands, his hand will be against you" (12:14–15). In other words, Israel's king was to be the king anticipated in Dt 17. He was not to be a king like those of the other nations. He was to lead the people in the way of the Lord. He was to be a spiritual as well as a political leader.

## B. The Selection of Saul (9:1–10:16)

This narrative is one of the three accounts of the selection of Saul as king. In this one, Samuel anoints Saul while he is on a journey to find his father's donkeys; in the next narrative (10:17–27), Saul is appointed king of Israel by casting lots; then, following that, Saul is appointed king at Gilgal (11:1–15). This threefold pattern for the selection of Israel's leaders has been followed throughout much of the previous biblical texts (see comments on Jos 3). First there is a divine selection (9:1–10:16); then there is a public announcement (10:17–27); third, there is a divine demonstration of approval (11:1–11), followed by public acceptance (vv.12–15).

After a brief introduction to the family of Saul (9:1–2), the narrative begins with Saul's trek after his father's lost donkeys. Being unable to find them (vv.3–4), Saul sought the help of Samuel, the seer (vv.5–12). The note in v.9 gives an important explanation of the role of Samuel as a seer—that a "seer" was nothing more than a prophet. When Saul came to Samuel, Samuel had already been informed by God of his coming. Samuel recognized Saul and invited him to a feast (vv.13–24).

The next morning, as Saul was leaving the city, Samuel privately anointed him as a "prince," or king, in Israel (9:25–10:1). As a confirmation of his calling, Samuel gave Saul three signs that would be fulfilled (10:2–13), thus following the requirements for the confirmation of a prophet's words (see Dt 18). (1) Two men were to meet him by the grave of Rachel, who were to tell him where to find his father's donkeys. (2) Saul was to meet three men at the Oak of Tabor, going up to Bethel. They were to have three goats, three loaves of bread, and wine. (3) Saul was to meet a band of prophets coming down from a high place of worship at Gibeah. He was to be overcome by the Spirit of the Lord so that he would begin prophesying with these men. When these signs were fulfilled, which they were (v.9), it was to be taken as a confirmation that God had chosen Saul and that God was "with him" (v.7).

The picture of Saul prophesying is that of a new king with a new heart publicly proclaiming the great works of God among the people. The words of Deborah the prophetess in Jdg 5:2–31 give an insight into the nature of what Saul might have said as he was prophesying. The main role of the prophet's prophesying was to proclaim the mighty acts of God (Jdg 5:11). The people were amazed at Saul's doing this and so coined the expression, "Is Saul also among the prophets?" (10:11). The sense of this expression appears to be that God had done an unexpected act. Such reversals are a characteristic clue to the presence of a divine plan. The use of the expression in the present narrative provides an acknowledgment that Samuel's prophetic words had been fulfilled. Thus the acknowledgment that Saul is prophesying among the prophets is an acknowledgment that Samuel's words have been fulfilled.

## C. The Public Appointment of Saul (10:17–27)

A fascinating view of Saul is presented in this short narrative. Virtually all of it is positive, showing Saul's humility (v.22) and his great strength and acclaim: "There is no one like him among all the people" (v.24). Even the army he formed were "valiant men whose hearts God had touched" (v.26). Thus the people's request for "a king to lead us and to go out before us and fight our battles" (8:20) found the best possible candidate.

The author's purpose in stating such a positive note with Saul appears to be to clear the air regarding just what it was that went wrong with his kingship. When Saul failed as king, it was not because he was not a fit candidate for the job. His failure must be attributed to some other cause. As we shall see, that cause was Saul's failure to obey the word of the prophet.

## D. The Divine Confirmation of Saul (11:1–15)

To further set the stage for the account of Saul's failure, the writer provides one more narrative to show the people's and God's initial approval of him. Saul is presented as Israel's deliverer, remarkably similar to the judges. While all Israel cowered at the threat of the Ammonites, Saul rallied the tribes and defeated the enemy. Just as during the time of the judges, the Spirit of God came upon him and he had victory in the battle. At the conclusion of the story we see again that Saul's mighty deeds were known and acknowledged by the people.

It is in light of these narratives that the subsequent failure of Saul is explained. A valiant and mighty leader is not necessarily a godly one. God looked at the heart while the people saw only these superficial successes. The hearts of both Saul and David will be laid bare in the narratives that follow.

## E. Samuel's Speech (12:1–25)

Samuel had called the people together at Gilgal to celebrate Saul's victory over the Ammonites and to recon-

firm him as king (11:14). The author now includes a lengthy portion of Samuel's speech on that occasion. He began by declaring his own innocence in both the matter of the kingship and the matter of his role as judge over Israel. He then recounted God's "righteous acts" (12:7) for Israel, as recorded in the Pentateuch, beginning with God's sending Moses and Aaron to bring the people out of Israel and into the land (v.8). He then turned to the time of the judges, listing himself as the last judge (vv.9–11). His central point now follows: having a king would be no different than a judge. The success of the king, just like that of the judge, would depend on the obedience of the people of God (vv.14–15). Finally, he warned the nation that their present request for a king was a serious matter and that it greatly displeased the Lord. To demonstrate the point, Samuel called down a severe thunderstorm on the people, and they feared greatly (v.18).

In spite of the Lord's displeasure, however, there was still much hope for Israel. If they obeyed the Lord, he would bless them. If they rebelled, both they and their king would go into exile. The lesson of Samuel's speech is that of Moses in the book of Deuteronomy (e.g., Dt 4) and the prophet Ezekiel (e.g., Eze 36:22–32).

## F. Saul's Failure as King of the Lord's People (13:1–15:35)

The clearest example of the role that the king was to play in Israel comes from the account of Saul's failure. According to the narrative, Saul failed as king because he did not provide the spiritual leadership for the nation. He overstepped his bounds within God's established pattern for the king—he did not heed the words of God spoken by the prophet (13:9–14). Saul, as it turned out, was the kind of king Israel had wanted, for he could maintain a standing army, but he was not the kind of king the Lord wanted—he did not obey

God's will. Thus Saul was rejected as king and ultimately fell in defeat in battle (31:4).

After his rejection as king, Saul was not immediately taken away. Instead, he remained on the scene to provide a vivid contrast with the kind of king that the Lord wanted. The rest of 1 Samuel is devoted primarily to contrasting Saul and David, the new king who was a man after God's own heart. In short, Saul had the chance to provide the kind of leadership that God desired for his people, but he did not do so. He was thus rejected by God.

This raises the question of why God selected Saul as the first king. If he was not the right kind of king, why did God choose him? There is, unfortunately, not much in the text to give us an answer to that question. But a statement in 9:16 sheds some light on the question. According to that passage, Saul was chosen to deliver Israel from the hand of the Philistines. Thus at this point, the choice of Saul was related not so much to the people's request for a king as it was to their outcry because of the oppression of the Philistines. In other words, Saul is here likened to the judges, being chosen for the task of delivering God's people from their enemies, regardless of his particular spiritual traits.

The name "Saul" means in Hebrew "the one who was asked for"; thus his name appears to foreshadow the contrast between the king "asked for" by the people and the king chosen by God, i.e., David. Moreover, Saul was the son of Kish, of the tribe of Benjamin. This was the tribe responsible for the murder of the Levite's concubine in Jdg 19–20 and the tribe that fought against the other tribes and was defeated in Jdg 20. In Jdg 21 we are given an account of the way in which the tribe of Benjamin was saved from complete destruction. In contrast to the book of Ruth, which gives the faithful lineage of David, these last chapters of Judges give a sorry picture of the lineage of Saul.

It is clear from the narratives in Samuel that Saul had all the right external qualifications of a great leader and king. He was physically superior to the other men (10:23) and was courageous (11:1–11). But they also point to several of his traits that proved to be his downfall. The primary factor in his failure was his lack of covenant loyalty. Saul manifested a lack of covenant loyalty almost immediately after he was anointed, even though he did enjoy some military and political success for a period of time (13:8–14).

What eventually marked Saul's rejection as God's representative? The Philistines had gathered with 30,000 chariots and 6,000 horsemen to war with Saul (13:5). Saul's armies were deserting their ranks and fleeing from the Philistine threat (v.8). Samuel had given Saul instructions to wait for him before going into battle with the Philistines: "Go down ahead of me to Gilgal. I will come surely down to you to sacrifice burnt offerings and fellowship offerings, but you must wait seven days until I come to you and tell you what you are to do" (10:8). In other words, Samuel had put Saul and his leadership under the test of obedience to the word of God from the mouth of the prophet. This was the test of the true leader in Dt 18:15–16. It was, however, just this test that Saul failed—not waiting for Samuel to come.

A pattern is established here in Saul's rejection that was to remain throughout the rest of the period of the kingship. The relationship of the king and the prophet was one in which the relationship of the king to the covenant God himself was expressed. In God's kingdom, the king was to submit to the rulership of the Lord, the real King of God's people. The spokesman for God in this kingship was the prophet. Thus, as the king was submissive to the word of the prophet, he was found to be submissive to the Lord's will and consequently was acting as a true leader (see 12:23–24).

Saul, however, did not remain submissive to the word of Samuel. He was told to wait seven days and to wait for Samuel to come, but he did not (13:8). Under pressure and threat of defeat, Saul went on by himself. Saul had thus rejected the authority of the Lord and asserted himself above God's rule. He had taken the fate of God's people into his own hands. Such an act was a violation of the covenant and unforgivable for a godly leader.

Several later examples in Samuel and Kings illustrate this same lesson. David's submission to Nathan (2Sa 12), Hezekiah's submission to Isaiah (2Ki 19), and Asa's submission to Azariah (2Ch 15) are positive examples of godly leadership. Jeroboam's visit from the "man of God" (1Ki 13) provides a negative example like Saul. In such episodes, the writers intend to teach the lesson of the necessity of the leader's submission to the will of God. Without such an attitude of the heart, God cannot use the king.

### 1. Saul's first offense (13:1–15a)

This is the first of two accounts of Saul's failure to show godly leadership (see also 15:1–23). The fact that there are two accounts of Saul's failure is related to the requirement in Dt 19:15 that "a matter must be established by the testimony of two or three witnesses." Saul is being evaluated here by the standards of God's law. The course of events is simple: Samuel had instructed Saul to wait for him at Gilgal, and he would come in seven days to offer a sacrifice before the battle (v.8). Saul, however, feeling the threat and pressure of the Philistine forces who had gathered for battle, did not obey Samuel's words, and he offered the sacrifice before Samuel arrived (vv.8–9). As soon as he offered the sacrifice, Samuel ar-

rived (v.10). The meaning of the events for the writer is clear: Saul had preempted the authority of the Lord. He had disobeyed the word of the Lord's prophet (cf. Dt 18:18). Thus, according to Dt 17:20, he could no longer be king.

It is sometimes said that Saul's disobedience here was not that he disobeyed Samuel's call to wait, but that he, rather than a priest, offered a sacrifice. The expression "he offered the burnt offering," however, does not mean here that Saul himself carried out the offering but rather than he directed one of his priests to do the work (cf. 2Sa 24:25). Thus Saul's offense was not that he wrongfully did the duties of a priest, but that he disobeyed the word of the prophet of God. In this offense Saul demonstrated that he did not have the heart to rule God's people, as was required in the book of Deuteronomy.

This example of Saul, therefore, teaches the readers of this book to be completely dedicated to the work of the Lord and obey him with all their heart.

### 2. Saul's campaign against the Philistines (13:15b–14:52)

The narrative is quite complex. Many things happen within a short span of time. Saul reorganized his forces after many had fled (13:15b–16). The Israelite camp was at Geba, while the Philistines were camped at Micmash. At this time as well, the Philistines had sent out raiding parties throughout Israel (vv.17–18). The plight of the Israelites is intensified by the report that with the exception of Saul and Jonathan, his son, they had no weapons (vv.19–22). There was a Philistine outpost stationed at the crossing at Micmash (v.23). Jonathan secretly raided that outpost while Saul and his 600 men were at Gibeah, sitting "under a pomegranate tree" (14:2). The priest, Ahijah, was with him. When Saul and the other Israelite warriors heard the sound of the defeated Philistines, they rallied together to continue the battle (vv.15–23).

Just at this point an earthquake (v.15), sent by God, threw the Philistine camp into a great confusion, and they began fighting each other (v.20). As the battle progressed, the Israelites grew weary (v.24a), but Saul forbade them from eating until the battle was successfully over (v.24b). Jonathan, however, disobeyed Saul's order (vv.25–30) and ate some wild honey. After the battle, the Israelites ate the Philistine's provisions without a proper offering of thanks to God (vv.31–35). Saul then discovered Jonathan's disobedience and swore to put him to death (vv.36–44). The people, however, did not allow Saul to fulfill his oath (v.45). Thus, through the leadership of Saul, the Philistines were repelled, and wars were then waged against the Moabites, Ammonites, Edomites, Arameans, and Philistines.

The passage concludes with a summary of Saul's royal administration (vv.49–52).

We should first note that this narrative is positioned between the two accounts of Saul's rejection as king. It would seem likely, therefore, that the events of this narrative are intended to show the nature of Saul's unworthiness to lead the people of God. It is thus surprising to find that much of what Saul does in this narrative is positive and in line with the lessons of the book of Deuteronomy. He is, in fact, portrayed as a victorious king. The worst that can be said of Saul in this section is that he acts precipitously, but this is not portrayed by the writer as a major fault. It thus appears that the intent of the writer in this section is to show that from a general point of view, Saul was a desirable king and a worthy leader. Even the precipitous order for his armies not to eat until the end of the battle (14:24b) shows Saul's zeal to fight the battle with the Philistines.

Why such a positive view of Saul set between the two accounts of his rejection? In this way the writer has been

able to focus precisely on the central fault of Saul as king—his disobedience to the prophet. By recounting so many of his successes, the writer is able to highlight his one fault.

### 3. Saul's second failure as king of the Lord's people (15:1–35)

Samuel, the prophet, called on Saul to engage the Amalekites in a holy war, i.e., a war to carry out divine judgment upon the Lord's enemies (vv.1–3). The Amalekites had been Israel's enemies since the time of the Exodus from Egypt (Ex 17:8–16). They had attempted to hinder the Israelites from coming into the Promised Land (Ex 17:14), and it had been prophesied by Balaam in the Pentateuch that the future king of Israel would bring them to ruin (Nu 24:20). Thus Samuel's instruction to Saul was that no Amalekite was to survive (15:3). It is important to note that Samuel's words to Saul were the words of the Lord's prophet. It was the Lord, not merely Samuel, who had commanded him to go out against the Amalekites (vv.2–3).

Saul followed through and went out against the Amalekites. God gave him victory, but Saul did not fully carry out the word of the Lord. He "spared Agag and the best of the sheep and cattle, the fat calves and lambs—everything that was good. . . . But everything that was despised and weak they totally destroyed" (vv.8–9). In other words, Saul had turned a solemn commission of the Lord into an occasion for his own prosperity. Most importantly, he had disobeyed the word of the prophet. Because of this Samuel told Saul that he had disobeyed God and that the Lord was grieved (vv.10–19).

The heart of Saul is revealed in his protest to Samuel. It was not his fault, he said; it was the fault of his army (vv.20–21). Samuel replied to Saul's protest with a poetic lesson on what pleases God: "Does the LORD delight in burnt offerings and sacrifices as much as in obeying the voice of the LORD? To obey is better than sacrifice" (v.22). The purpose of Samuel's words is to show that God's leaders are to have a pure heart, one that is obedient to the will of the Lord. This Saul did not have. But there was one waiting in the wings who would have a heart like this. That one is David, introduced in the next chapter.

Saul confessed his sin of disobedience but to no avail (vv.24–26). Samuel told him, "You have rejected the word of the LORD, and the LORD has rejected you as king over Israel!" (v.26). When Samuel turned to leave Saul, Saul tore a piece of Samuel's cloak, providing the occasion for Samuel to tell Saul that the Lord had torn his kingdom away from him (vv.27–29). After Saul again confessed his disobedience, Samuel returned with him as an honor to his kingship (vv.30–31). Samuel then carried out the Lord's judgment against Agag with the verdict, "As your sword has made women childless, so will your mother be childless among women" (vv.32–33). Though it is not mentioned here, the narrative appears to have one eye on the words of Balaam in Nu 24:7 ("His [NIV, Their] king will be greater than Agag, his [NIV, their] kingdom will be exalted"), as if to say that Saul was not to be the fulfillment of these words. Someone else was yet to come. Thus, on two occasions, Saul had disobeyed the word of the prophet, and his kingdom was taken from him.

## III. The Decline of Saul and the Rise of David (16:1–31:13)

### A. David, the Man After God's Own Heart: The Early Years (16:1–30:31)

As the youngest son of Jesse, of the tribe of Judah, David was the second and the most successful king of Israel. Under him the Israelite nation reached its highest potential both spiritually and politically. David's descendants ruled the southern kingdom of Judah until the Babylonian exile. The NT refers to David fifty-eight times, many of which are references to the fact that Jesus Christ was a direct descendant of David and as such was the rightful heir to the throne (cf. Mt 1).

With the final acts of God's rejection of Saul as king, the process of the divine selection of a new king began. We are told far in advance that the new king will be one "after God's own heart" (13:14)—i.e., one who desired to walk in the way of the Lord. When David was selected, it was apparently this very feature that gained him the final approval of God. Even Samuel was willing to accept a leader on the basis of external judgment, but not God. The Lord looks into the heart of the man and selects his representatives on that basis (16:6–7).

Many episodes in the life of David are recorded prior to his becoming king in 2Sa 2:1–7. Contrary to what might have been expected, David did not immediately assume the kingship after the rejection of Saul. The text takes care to show that the same commissioning process initiated by Moses and Joshua was followed in the case of David. He was first commissioned as king by Samuel (16:13), then publicly confirmed by God in the slaying of Goliath (ch. 17), and finally was officially recognized as king by the people (2Sa 2:4; 5:1–5).

### 1. The selection of David (16:1–23)

The Lord instructed Samuel to go to the house of Jesse, David's father, to anoint the one whom he had chosen to replace Saul as king (vv.1–3). Again we can see the importance to the writer of Samuel, the prophet, as the one through whom the kingship was established. God's authority came through the prophet.

Jesse had eight sons, seven of whom he brought to Samuel for the selection. David remained with his father's sheep, not even considered as a possible choice. It was, of course, this

# DAVID'S FAMILY TREE

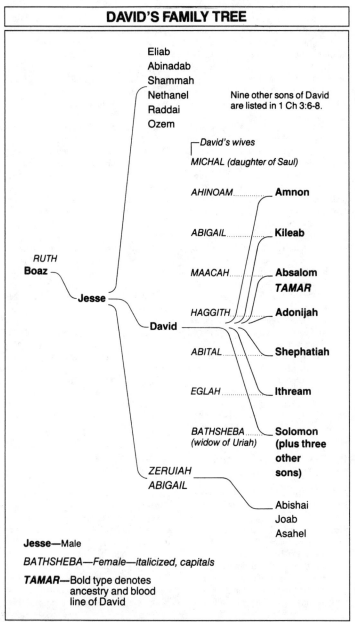

Eliab
Abinadab
Shammah
Nethanel
Raddai
Ozem

Nine other sons of David are listed in 1 Ch 3:6-8.

*David's wives*

*MICHAL (daughter of Saul)*

*AHINOAM* .............. **Amnon**

*ABIGAIL* .............. **Kileab**

*MAACAH* .............. **Absalom**
**TAMAR**

*HAGGITH* .............. **Adonijah**

*ABITAL* .............. **Shephatiah**

*EGLAH* .............. **Ithream**

*BATHSHEBA* .............. **Solomon**
*(widow of Uriah)* **(plus three other sons)**

*RUTH*
**Boaz**

**Jesse**

**David**

*ZERUIAH*
*ABIGAIL*

Abishai
Joab
Asahel

**Jesse**—Male

*BATHSHEBA*—Female—italicized, capitals

**TAMAR**—Bold type denotes ancestry and blood line of David

© 1989 The Zondervan Corporation.

David whom the Lord had chosen all along. Thus the narrative highlights its central theme—the Lord does not look on the outside, as a human being does, but at the heart (vv.4–13). As with Gideon (Jdg6:7–24), the choice of David is part of a continuing lesson that God works with human weakness to demonstrate his strength. David himself expressed this in Ps 8:2, "From the lips of children and infants you have established strength [NIV, ordained praise] because of your enemies, to silence the foe and the avenger."

David was immediately anointed king and, at that time, received the special endowment by the Spirit of God to carry out his role as king (v.13). At the same time, the Spirit left Saul (v.14)—he was thus no longer God's special representative, though he remained the "anointed" king. One of the most striking pictures of David in this book is his reluctance to force his way into his rightful position as king. He was the anointed king from 1Sa 16 on, but it is not until 2Sa 5 that he was recognized as king over all Israel. Throughout this period, David patiently waited for God's timing and tried as best he could to live peacefully with the jealous Saul.

The text says that Saul was troubled after the Spirit of God had departed from him. Ironically, in David's first appearance in the company of the king he is cast in the role of comforting the jealous Saul in his fits of rage. This picture of David curiously foreshadows his role throughout the remainder of the time of the monarchy. As Israel's psalmist, David sang and read to all who were in need of comfort. Unfortunately, like Saul, the future Davidic kings rejected the comfort provided by David in the Psalms and thus forfeited their only means of salvation and refreshment.

### 2. The confirmation of David (17:1–54)

The next major episode in David's rise to the kingship was his slaying of the giant Goliath. Many important insights regarding David are given in this narrative, the most important being the view we get of David's understanding of the Lord's role in a kingship. For David, Israel could not be protected by mere spears and swords (v.47); the Lord gave the battle into their hands. David is the writer's example of a leader who puts his trust wholly in the Lord.

Where did David learn this lesson? He has been reading the Word of God. He knew the lesson of the Law that God's people find security not by trusting in their own resources, but by trusting in the Lord to save them (e.g., Ex 23:31).

We should note here how often this same aspect of David's faith is reflected throughout the Psalms (e.g., see Pss 19:14; 31). Saul must have listened only to the music and not the words of these songs of praise and trust in the Lord that David sang to him.

### 3. The public recognition of David (17:55–18:16)

There are three short narratives that follow the account of David's slaying Goliath. The purpose of these stories is to show the extent of David's growing recognition among the people. The first narrative shows the special recognition given David by Saul and his officers (17:55–18:5); the second is that of the celebration of Saul and David's victory by the women of the city (18:6–11); and the third is the summary of David's success with the people (18:12–16).

In the first account, Saul wanted to know the family line of David, apparently to see what potential power or rivalry the family of this young warrior might present to him. The story thus contrasts David, who had just defeated Goliath by God's power, and Saul, who was concerned about the natural succession of power in the family of David. To emphasize the difference between the two leaders, the writer tells us that as Saul was asking David about his family, David stood before him, "still holding the Philistine's head" (17:57). This is a contrast of two, quite different, kinds of kingship, one that derived its power from God, the other from natural kinship.

### 4. The beginning of opposition from Saul (18:17–30)

In this narrative a familiar theme is taken up to show that God was with David and not with Saul. Try as he might, Saul could not curb David's successes nor his growing popularity with the people (cf. Ex 1–2). Saul concocted a scheme to deliver David into the hand of the Philistines. He had to prove he was a mighty warrior to win the hand of Saul's older daughter in marriage (v.17). This was apparently to fulfill his promise (17:25) that anyone who would slay Goliath would have his daughter in marriage. David refused his first offer of his oldest daughter but then accepted the offer of Michal, who loved him (18:20, 28). Saul's plan, however, backfired. Far from being the means by which David was delivered into the hands of the Philistines, in slaying the Philistines to win Saul's daughter, David's popularity with the people increased all the more. As the summary at the conclusion of the passage shows (v.30), David's "name became well known" from his battle with the Philistines.

### 5. The intensification of Saul's opposition (19:1–24)

In the previous narrative, Saul had secretly tried to do away with David (18:17b). When that failed, Saul openly attempted to have David removed. In his first overt attempt to take David's life, Saul's son Jonathan was able to ameliorate his anger (19:1–7). As David continued to have military success and thus gained wider recognition among the people, Saul's troubled spirit returned and his efforts to kill David were renewed (vv.8–17). This time it was Michal, Saul's daughter, who res-

cued David (vv.12–16). The thematic elements of the narrative are reminiscent of the early chapters of Exodus where Moses was delivered from the decrees of Pharaoh by Pharaoh's own household.

In the third phase of Saul's attempt on David's life, his plan was averted through the Spirit of God (vv.18–24). Saul, seeking to take the life of David, was prevented from doing so when the Spirit of God came upon him. Saul prophesied all night while David escaped.

### 6. Jonathan allied with David against Saul (20:1–42)

This long and carefully detailed narrative shows that David, the new king, made a peaceful transition from the old dynasty. He did not gain the throne by force or rebellion. Rather, it came to him with the full acknowledgment of the legitimacy of the old regime. This idea becomes particularly important in the final segments of narrative in 1 Samuel. There we see that when given the opportunity to take the kingdom by force, David repeatedly refused (cf. 24:1–22).

### 7. David's flight from Saul (21:1–27:12)

The biblical writer now gives a loosely connected account of David's marshaling of his army and of his initial rise to power. There is nothing particularly glamorous about it. Rather, it shows that David rose to power by simple trust and obedience to the Lord's guidance. The central theme running throughout these narratives is the picture of the future king, David, following the words of the prophet Gad and inquiring of the will of God by means of the priests. This is how he gained the support of all the people, even Israel's neighbors.

In his flight from Saul, David's first stop was at Nob (21:1–9). In order to get help from the priests at Nob, it was necessary for David to fabricate the story that he was on a secret mission for Saul. The writer gives the details of this account without passing judgment on David's actions or words. Only later does he inform us that David regretted misleading the priest (22:22).

The events of this section are linked with those of the next chapter by the presence of Doeg, the Edomite (21:7). Doeg reported to Saul that the priests aided David's escape; thus, Saul had all the priests put to death (22:9–19).

David then fled to Achish, king of Gath, where Goliath had come from (21:10–15). Here it was necessary, out of fear for his life, for David to deceive Achish into thinking he was insane (21:13–15). Only then was he able to escape harm.

When he left Gath, he went to Adullam, where he gathered about him an army of 400 men. This group consisted of those who had been mistreated or were otherwise in distress. In this he seemed to be following the pattern of Gideon (Jdg 7:7) and Jephthah (Jdg 11:3), who also were used by God to deliver the nation though their forces were weak and scraggly.

David then left Judah to take refuge in the land of Moab (22:3–5). He brought his mother and father with him to live with the king of Moab, "until I learn what God will do for me" (22:3). David was also accompanied by the prophet Gad, David's seer (2Sa 24:11). Gad advised him not to remain in Moab with the king, and David obeyed the words of Gad. In other words, during this time David was being guided and instructed by the Lord through his prophet and was patiently obeying God's leading.

The narrative now moves to Saul's brutal act of revenge on the priests at Nob. All were killed (22:6–19) except for the young priest Abiathar, who escaped and joined with David (vv.20–23). In contrast to David, who had the growing support of the people and priests, Saul had only the support of Doeg, the Edomite. With his support, Saul waged war even against the Lord's own priests. Thus this narrative shows that Saul had become Israel's enemy. By contrast, David was now accompanied by the prophet Gad and the priest Abiathar.

Next (23:1–29) David was rescued by God because he had the priest and the ephod with him. This section gives an important example of the way God's leaders were guided by the Lord.

In the next narrative (23:15–29) God was at work protecting his servant David. Through no resourcefulness of his own, David was saved from the hands of Saul: "Saul was going along one side of the mountain, and David and his men were on the other side, hurrying to get away" (v.26). Just as Saul's men were closing in on David, Saul received word to turn quickly from the pursuit because the Philistines were raiding the land (v.27).

In the next incident, Saul was again chasing David and stopped at the very cave where David was hiding (24:1–3). He went into the cave and was close enough for David to strike him. David, however, refused to do so. Instead, he took Saul's coat that he had laid nearby (vv.4–7). After Saul had left the cave, David called out to him with Saul's coat in his hand, showing full well that he could have killed him if he had wanted (vv.8–15). David said regarding this incident, "I will not lift my hand against my master, because he is the LORD's anointed." He even rebuked his own men for suggesting that he should take the kingdom by an act of violence. Saul then himself acknowledged David's innocence by saying to him, "You are more righteous than I. . . . You have treated me well, but I have treated you badly. . . . May the LORD reward you well for the way you treated me today. I know that you will surely be king and that the kingdom of Israel will be established in your hands" (cf. vv.16–22). Thus, even Saul acknowledged David's right as king.

By this point in the narrative, several key characters have acknowledged the legitimacy of David's kingship: Jonathan, the heir of Saul's own dynasty; the prophets Samuel and Gad; the priest Abiathar; and King Saul. The narrative now turns to the recognition of David's kingship among various private individuals and shows that the wise men and women among God's people were quick to see in him a godly leader. The foolish, on the other hand, fail to acknowledge his rule. This point is particularly stressed in the story of the fool, Nabal, and his wise wife, Abigail (ch. 25).

Chapter 25 opens with a brief notice of the death of Samuel. Then both Nabal and Abigail are introduced. We are told that Nabal was very wealthy, but "surly and mean in his dealings" (v.3). Abigail, on the other hand, was "an intelligent and beautiful woman." David had provided protection for Nabal's herdsmen (cf. v.16), and now that they were shearing their sheep, David sent messengers to Nabal asking for a reward (vv.4–9). Nabal flatly refused to reward David, charging that David was one of many rebellious renegades (vv.10–11). David immediately prepared to avenge himself in an attack against Nabal (vv.13).

When Abigail heard of it, however, she quickly made arrangements to comply with David's request and, in fact, did so (vv.14–20). We should note that the writer has strategically inserted here an account of the oath David had taken regarding Nabal and his household (vv.21–22), swearing, "May God deal with David, be it ever so severely, if by morning I leave alive one male of all who belong to him!" (v.22). Abigail, however, met David and spoke to him with words that reveal her wise heart (vv.23–31). In speaking to David, she

first took the guilt of her husband on herself (v.24) and then dismissed his actions as nothing but the work of a fool. Her point was that such a fool is not worthy of David's attention (v.25).

Abigail then attempted to win David's favor. First, she suggested that the Lord was using her to prevent David from avenging himself (v.26). Next she urged David to acknowledge that the Lord alone is the avenger of the wicked (v.26): "[May] all who intend to harm my master be like Nabal [the fool]." The sense of her words is related to the recurring theme that fools will eventually be the cause of their own ruin. In other words, since Nabal, her husband, was a fool, David need not avenge himself—his own foolishness would get the best of him and bring him down. One cannot help but recognize in Abigail's words a veiled reference to David and Saul. When she says "all who intend to harm my servant" she, of course, meant Nabal, but within the larger narrative context this applies equally well to Saul. Thus in her wise words are both an explanation and a theological justification for David's own actions toward Saul. That this was not lost on David is shown in the next chapter, where David applies Abigail's words to his treatment of Saul (26:10–11), and Saul acknowledges that he has "acted like a fool" (26:21).

Abigail concluded her words with what amounts to a virtual prophecy of David's impending kingship (25:28–31). Her point was to remind David that he was the Lord's chosen one and that he should not err now by seeking to avenge himself against Nabal.

David acknowledged the wisdom of Abigail's words and sent her away unharmed (vv.32–35). We take it, then, that David would not harm Nabal. As a confirmation of David's promise, as well as Abigail's wise words about allowing the Lord to avenge one's enemies, we read that when Abigail returned home, Nabal was stricken by the Lord and he died (vv.36–38). When David heard the news of his death, he acknowledged that the Lord had avenged his enemy and "brought Nabal's wrongdoing down on his own head" (v.39). David then married Abigail and took her into his house (vv.39c–42).

The overall meaning of this narrative about Nabal and Abigail within the context of the book of Samuel is threefold. (1) Those who resisted the Davidic kingship were like Nabal, i.e., foolish (see v.26b). (2) Those who were wise and understanding among the people recognized that the Lord was with David, "for the LORD will certainly make a lasting dynasty for my lord, because he fights the LORD's battles" (v.28b). (3) David was a leader who listened to wise counsel. He was persuaded here by the words of this wise woman. This stood in stark contrast to Saul's refusal to listen to the similarly wise words of Ahimelech (22:14–15). There is a curious similarity between Abigail's approach to David and that of a prophet's. Her words were like the words of a prophet, though they were in fact the words of a wise person. In any event, David heeded them as God's words to him.

The story in ch. 26 is similar in general outline to that of David's refusal to take Saul's life in ch. 24. David and Abishai secretly crept into Saul's camp at night "and there was Saul, lying asleep inside the camp with his spear stuck in the ground near his head" (v.7). David, however, refused to "lay a hand on the LORD's anointed" (v.9), knowing full well that "the LORD himself will strike him; either his time will come and he will die, or he will go into battle and perish" (v.10). So David took Saul's spear and water jug to demonstrate that he had again had opportunity to take Saul's life but had not done so (vv.11–20). On hearing this, Saul repented again and acknowledged David's innocence (vv.21–25). Saul's words, "I have acted like a fool," recall the words of Abigail in 25:26. Thus David had learned the lesson of Abigail's speech: Do not avenge yourself, for the Lord will avenge his own in due time.

There are several curious features about the story in 27:1–12. (1) David is portrayed as the king in exile in Philistia: "David and his men settled in Gath with Achish" (v.3). (2) Even though in exile, David remained loyal to God's people in Israel. He continued to fight against their enemies (vv.8–9). (3) Yet David led Achish to believe that he was loyal to the Philistines against Israel (vv.10–11); thus he is portrayed as an ally of Achish (v.12).

The natural question that this story raises is why, or for what purpose, the writer included it in his book. The answer lies in a comparison of David's actions with those of Saul in ch. 28. There Saul is portrayed as one who was disloyal to God or his people even while living in the land. David, by contrast, is here portrayed as one who remained loyal to the Lord and his people even though living in exile. This picture reminds one of Daniel and his three friends (Da 1–6).

The narrative of ch. 27 continues in ch. 29, after an interruption of an account of the last events dealing with Saul.

### 8. An interlude: Samuel's final word to Saul (28:1–25)

As v.1 suggests, the events of this chapter occurred during the time that David was in exile and Saul was waging war with the Philistines. A parenthetical note tells us that Samuel was dead and that Saul had expelled all mediums and spiritists from the land. In seeking guidance for battle, Saul sought a message from the Lord through all legitimate means—dreams, Urim, and prophets—but there was no answer (vv.4–6). Thus Saul turned to an illegitimate one, the witch of Endor (vv.7–14). Curiously, when Saul sought the Lord through the prophets, he received no word. When he turned to the medium, however, he received a word from the prophet Samuel. There is clear irony in this story. The word he received from Samuel proved only to further confirm God's original words to Saul that his kingdom would be taken away from him (vv.17–18). Moreover, Samuel's prediction of Saul's death also served to confirm the word of Samuel as a true prophet (v.19).

This passage of Scripture has given rise to many questions. How, for example, should we understand the appearance of Samuel long after his death? And what was the medium's role in Samuel's appearance? The narrative clue of this passage is the medium's surprise when she saw Samuel (v.12). Moreover, the text never says that the woman brought up Samuel. It says only that Saul requested to see Samuel (v.11), and then immediately it states that the woman saw Samuel and was shocked (v.12). Thus the writer appears careful to avoid attributing the event to the woman. But Saul did talk with Samuel at this time (vv.15–19).

In this narrative, then, the prophet Samuel gives his last word on Saul. His kingdom would be destroyed and David would become king. Saul had committed the final sin. He had sought the word of a medium, expressly forbidden in Dt 18:9–14, and had received a word of judgment from the prophet (Dt 18:15–22). Saul's only consolation came from those who were, in the words of Deuteronomy, an abomination to the Lord.

### 9. David is saved from fighting for (or against) Saul (29:1–11)

David had joined the ranks of the Philistines and was preparing for battle with Saul (vv.1–2). The Philistine commanders, however, raised an objection to David's participation (vv.3–5), for they did not trust this Israelite in their ranks. The narrative does not state expressly whether these commanders were correct in their assessment of David's motives, but the larger context suggests that they were. In 27:8–12 we were told that David had deliberately misled Achish into thinking that he was the enemy of Saul and Israel. Thus it appears that Achish was wrong about David. David would indeed have joined with Israel against the Philistines (v.4). The Philistines' reference to "taking the heads of our own men" is likely a direct allusion to David's taking Goliath's head (17:46, 51, 57).

David was thus sent back from the battle and not allowed to fight (vv.6–11), preventing him from rescuing Saul from the hand of the Philistines as he had done with Goliath (ch. 17). We can see here that God was working providentially with David. He was prevented from rescuing Saul, using the mistrust of the Philistines to bring about his plan. It should also be noted that through this decision of the Philistine commanders, God also allowed David to return to Ziklag in time to rescue his own family (ch. 30).

### 10. David defeats his enemy and restores his kingdom (30:1–31)

When David and his men returned to Ziklag, they found it had been plundered and destroyed by the Amalekites (vv.1–5). David's wives, along with those of the others, were taken captive. In their grief, David's men were near rebellion, but David responded by seeking the Lord's guidance (vv.6–8). After receiving guidance, David and his 600 men pursued the Amalekites, leaving behind 200 of them exhausted at Besor Ravine (vv.9–10). In his pursuit, David found a sick Egyptian slave who had been left behind by the Amalekites and who led them to the raiders (vv.11–16). David then smote the Amalekite raiders and rescued all his own family and property (vv.17–20). When they returned to the 200 men they had left behind, a dispute arose over who should receive the rescued property (vv.21–25). Some of those who went with David argued that the others who were too tired to go into battle should not receive their share of the property (v.22). David, however, answered that it was the Lord who had given them the victory and not those who had gone into battle; thus all of the men should share equally in the results. David then divided the spoils of the war with all the Judean cities that had suffered loss (vv.26–31). Clearly this was the kind of king God desired for his people.

This chapter marks the turning point in the writer's portrayal of David. Although still fleeing Saul, David now began to take the steps that would lead him to the kingdom. He was saving God's people from their enemies, and his successes in battle came clearly from the Lord. David took his men from near rebellion to total victory over the Amalekites. The key to his success is given in v.6b: "But David found strength in the LORD, his God." This attitude of confidence in the Lord is expressed also in the matter of the division of the spoils. David reminded his men that it was the Lord alone who had given them victory in the battle and who had given them all the spoils (vv.23–24).

The initial work of David in unifying his kingdom can be seen in his returning the spoils to all of Judah. We should never underestimate the impor-

tance in God's plan of unifying the whole kingdom (cf. Ps 133:1). David was the only king of Judah who was able to do this, and in this narrative we see why. He was a king who ruled God's people justly and righteously.

## B. The Death of Saul (31:1–13)

The battle at Gilboa was a decisive battle in the war between Israel and the Philistines. What was at stake in the battle was nothing less than the control of Saul's kingdom. If Gilboa was lost, the Philistines would succeed in dividing the nation in half. Although the details of the battle are not known, the Philistines did gain the upper hand, and Saul's army was defeated. Added to the account in the book of Chronicles is an explanation of the cause of Saul's defeat: "Saul died because he was unfaithful to the LORD; he did not keep the word of the LORD and even consulted a medium for guidance, and did not inquire of the LORD. So the LORD put him to death and turned the kingdom over to David son of Jesse" (1Ch 10:13–14). That explanation assumes that we are familiar with the whole story of the reign of Saul given in 1 Samuel. Twice Saul did not keep the word of the Lord that was spoken through the prophet Samuel (1Sa 13:1–23; 15:1–35). And Saul sought the counsel of a medium on one occasion (1Sa 28). Behind this condemnation is the clear teaching of Dt 18:10–22. Israel was not to seek the will of God in the counsel of mediums or in the words of false prophets but in his own word, spoken by the prophets whom he had raised up.

# 2 Samuel

## Introduction

See introduction to 1 Samuel.

## I. David's Rise to the Kingship in Jerusalem (1:1–6:23)

### A. Saul, Abner, and Joab (1:1–3:39)

The last stages of David's rise to the kingship over all of Israel were marked by two apparent mishaps; in both of them, however, the writer of the book is careful to show that David was innocent. The first mishap was the death of Saul. In 1Sa 31 we are given the actual account of the death of Saul, written from the point of view of the biblical writer. In 2Sa 1, however, a contrasting account is given by an Amalekite. As readers who have just read 1Sa 31, we cannot help but be suspicious of the Amalekite's version here. The facts do not line up. Whereas in 1Sa 31, Saul is said to have died by falling on his sword, here in 2Sa 1 the Amalekite says that he killed Saul. He mentions nothing about Saul's armor-bearer who was with Saul when he died, nor does his story of the pursuing Philistines (2Sa 1:6) match that of the narrative of 1Sa 31.

When the Amalekite brings Saul's crown and bracelet to David, he appears to be offering the symbols of Saul's kingship. David's response to the Amalekite assures the readers that he was not seeking to gain the throne through the unfortunate fate of Saul (2Sa 1:11). David's lament for Saul and Jonathan (vv.19–27) reveals the depth of his loss for both of them. It thus removes any doubt that David saw in their death an occasion for his own rise to power.

Only after seeking the Lord's guidance did David return to the land of Israel. In obedience to the Lord's word, David returned to Hebron and was there made king over the house of Judah. Immediately he set out to restore unity to God's people by promising to reward the respectful deed of the men of Jabesh Gilead who had buried Saul and Jonathan's bodies (2:4–7).

The second unfortunate mishap en route to David's becoming king was Joab's murder of Abner (2:18–3:39). Joab was the leader of David's armies in his battles with Saul's son Ish-Bosheth (2:12–17). Abner was general under Saul and continued under Ish-Bosheth. Although he tried hard to avoid it, Abner killed Joab's brother Asahel in battle (vv.21–23). Joab waited for the right opportunity and then took revenge on Abner for the death of his brother (vv.23–27). Although the removal of Abner led to David's acceptance as king by the entire nation, the narrative clearly shows that David was innocent of any guilt in his death (vv.31–39). David made Joab his general but did not leave this deed unpunished (v.29). What is significant about David throughout this narrative is that he does not continue the blood revenge cycle that led to Abner's death. David was content to leave vengeance in God's hands. David's refusal to eat on the day of Abner's burial was a sign to all the people (vv.36–37), and to the reader, that his heart was truly grieved by Abner's loss. Only at the end of his life—and for good reason—is Joab punished (1Ki 2:5ff.).

It is important to note the state of the nation of Israel immediately preceding David's assuming the kingship. The nation of Israel was divided into two separate kingdoms. David was already ruling the southern tribe of Judah, while Saul's son Ish-Bosheth was ruling the north, the area called simply Israel. In other words, the situation was similar to that of the nation after Solomon. It becomes clear, then, from these narratives that the nation was only truly united during the reigns of David and Solomon, his son. From this viewpoint it becomes apparent that David's and Solomon's kingships were times when the nation was truly a united kingdom. Unlike David, a major weakness of Solomon's kingship was his inability to provide a successor who could hold the nation together (cf. 1Ki 11:26–39).

## B. The Death of Ish-Bosheth (4:1–12)

As is clear in the case of the Amalekite's supposed slaying of Saul in ch. 1, David did not take the kingship from Saul by force. The treacherous deed of Saul's captains, Baanah and Recab, removed Ish-Bosheth from the throne and thus paved the way for David's rule over the northern tribes. Their action was not rewarded by David but severely punished. These narratives are intended to show that David's heart was right before God and that he did not seek to promote himself to the throne.

## C. David Becomes King Over All Israel (5:1–5)

David had already been anointed king over the tribe of Judah in Hebron (2:4). After the death of Ish-Bosheth, the elders of the northern tribes ruled by the house of Saul came to David at Hebron and there anointed him king over all Israel. Again we see that it was not David who sought this honor but the leaders of Israel's tribes who sought David.

## D. David Captures Jerusalem (5:6–16)

Though Israel had long lived in the land, the city of Jerusalem had not been permanently captured (see comments on Jos 15; Jdg 1:2–20). Now David took the city for his own. Henceforth, Jerusalem was the "City of David."

The king of Tyre, who would later contribute to the building of the temple in Jerusalem, here provides materials for David's house. Hiram's contribution to building that house is seen as a sign that confirms the fact for David that "the LORD had established him as king over Israel and had exalted his kingdom for the sake of his people Is-

rael" (v.12). The reason for this has already been expressed in the Song of Moses (Ex 15:1–18), where the promise had been given that the Lord would establish a place for his dwelling when the people entered the land (Ex 15:17). The sign of the fulfillment of this promise was to be that the nations around about Israel would stand in fear of them and be delivered into their hands. This promise was a repetition of that made by Jacob that a kingdom would be established in the tribe of Judah that would have "the obedience of the nations" (Ge 49:10). Moreover, this same promise occurs again in the prophecy of Balaam that a king (Nu 24:7, 17) would arise who would crush the foreheads of Moab and conquer the cities of Edom. David thus had good grounds for seeing Hiram's gift as a sign of the Lord's beginning to fulfill these earlier promises by establishing his kingdom in Jerusalem. The picture of the nations of the world contributing to the glory of Jerusalem is a common theme in the subsequent biblical texts (cf. Ps 72:15; Hag 2:7–8).

As if to give additional confirmation of David's assessment of these events, the writer includes an account of David's defeat of the Philistines. In this narrative the Lord tells David, "I will surely hand the Philistines over to you" (v.19). This appears to be an allusion to Moses' song in Ex 15:14–18: "anguish will grip the people of Philistia. . . . By the power of your arm they will be as still as a stone. . . . You will bring them in and plant them on the mountain of your inheritance—the place, O LORD, you made for your dwelling." Thus, as is often the case, the writer builds his narrative on the biblical texts and themes from the Pentateuch.

## E. The Ark Is Brought to Jerusalem (6:1–23)

The narrative of David's moving the Ark of the Covenant to Jerusalem teaches the seriousness and reality of God's presence. God's presence among his people was not to be taken lightly. God had graciously promised to be near his people, and Moses had instructed them how the ark was to be treated (Ex 25–31). There was much celebration before the ark as David and the people attempted to move it to Jerusalem; however, not all was carried out as had been commanded. The people were carrying the ark of God on a cart pulled by oxen (v.3)—ironically, just as the Philistines had done when they returned it to Israel (1Sa 6:7). Moses, however, had taught that the Levites (the sons of Kohath) were to carry the ark with the carrying poles inserted in the rings on either side of the ark, so that no one would "touch the holy objects" and die (Nu 4:15).

It was failure to be faithful in that small matter that led to the great tragedy recorded here (cf. 1Ch 13:9–10). Uzzah put out his hand to hold the ark because the oxen stumbled, and "the LORD's anger burned against Uzzah because of his irreverent act; therefore God struck him down and he died there beside the ark of God" (v.7). That event took its sudden, tragic turn unexpectedly while the people were rejoicing over the return of the ark. David responded in anger and fear, not knowing whether to carry on or to postpone the moving of the ark. Having decided out of apparent desperation to postpone any further moving of the ark, David left it at the home of Obed-Edom, along the way to Jerusalem.

When he later continued the task of moving the ark to Jerusalem, David took great care that the law of God was followed. His dancing and leaping before the ark was an indication of the joy he felt for the ark and God's presence there. Michal's response also revealed her heart: "When she saw King David leaping and dancing before the LORD, she despised him in her heart" (v.16).

The author's focus on David's response to Michal's belittling his dancing for joy suggests that the real issue in the narrative was the demonstration of David's gratitude for the Lord's giving him the kingdom and his wholehearted devotion to serve him. Michal's attitude is presented as the final spiteful word from the house of Saul. Thus, the "daughter of Saul had no children to the day of her death" (v.23).

The ark was placed in a tent (v.17), but in the next chapter David makes plans to build a house for it.

## II. The Davidic Covenant (7:1–29)

The opening of ch. 7 makes it clear that by now David had succeeded in becoming king of Israel. He had rest from his enemies and a united kingdom. He had now set his mind on building a "house" (i.e., a temple) for the Ark of the Covenant. But the Lord had other plans. He sent the prophet Nathan to ask David, "Are you the one to build me a house to dwell in?" (v.5). David was not to build a "house" for the Lord; rather, the Lord would build a "house" for him (v.22). The kind of house that the Lord was to build for David was a continuing line of kings, a dynasty over all Israel and the tribe of Judah—a dynasty of the "offspring" of David (vv.7:12ff.).

We must first ask who this "offspring" or "house" was to be. Was it one of the earthly, political kings that ruled Judah after David's death? Or was it a future messianic king from the lineage of David? The OT prophets and the NT writers see this promise of an "offspring" or "seed" as a messianic promise of a future king (see Isa 42:1, 6; 49:9; 55:3,4; Mal 3:1; Lk 1:32–33; Ac 2:30–36). How does the writer of Samuel see it? This is, in fact, the question to which the remainder of the book is primarily addressed.

A good case can be made that the writer of this book has set up Solomon as the object of the promise that one of David's own "offspring" would build the temple and rule in peace. The writer does this by first showing that none of the other sons of David survived the conflicts and intrigues that surrounded the house of David days following the Davidic covenant. Within the narrative itself, Solomon even takes the view that the Lord's covenant with David was to be fulfilled in him (see 1Ki 8:20).

But we must be careful not to identify Solomon's viewpoint with that of the writer of the book of Samuel. The narrative itself is quick to remind us that Solomon proved unfaithful and thus the promise was not fulfilled in him (1Ki 11:9–12). This same passage in Kings, however, tells us that God's promise to the house of David remained even though Solomon proved unfit. The Lord told Solomon, "Yet I will not tear the whole kingdom from him, but will give him one tribe for the sake of David my servant and for the sake of Jerusalem, which I have chosen" (1Ki 11:13). Thus within the strategy of the books of Samuel and Kings, the writer is able to show that the promise made to David goes beyond Solomon to another "offspring" yet in the future.

The word "forever" is repeated three times in this narrative. Part of the plan of the remainder of the books of Samuel and Kings is to show that none of the descendants of David lived up to the test of faithfulness to God's covenant that was required for the fulfillment of the promise (cf. 1Ki 6:11–13). Thus the "house" that is to be built extends far beyond the temple built by Solomon and the temple built after the return from Babylonian exile (see Ezra and Nehemiah). The fullest expression of the future fulfillment of this promise is found in the book of Daniel. In several of the dreams and visions of that book the eternal Davidic kingdom is

pictured as a divine kingdom that rules over all the earth and puts an end to the kingdoms of humankind. It is the kingdom established by the "one like a son of man" who comes in the clouds to establish an eternal kingdom upon this earth (Da 7:13–14). This is also the view of the Chronicler (see comments on 1Ch 17) and the NT, where this promise extends to Jesus, the Messiah, the Son of David (cf. Jn 2:19–21; Rev 20).

## III. The Decline of the House of David (8:1–24:25)

The rest of the 2 Samuel deals with several significant events from the life of David. The writer begins with a general description of his conquests.

### A. David's Conquests (8:1–18)

The picture presented here of David's reign appears to be shaped by the vision of Balaam in Nu 24:17–20. Balaam had prophesied that a king (Nu 24:7) would arise in Israel who would conquer Israel's enemies, the Moabites, Edomites, and Amalekites. The writer of the present book focuses on these and other nearby nations to show that David at least met much of this prophecy. It is in this sense that we should understand the description of David in v.15: "David reigned over all Israel, doing what was just and right for all his people." David was one who fulfilled many of the prophecies of the promised king.

What is particularly important about this account, however, is that the writer limits David's conquest to the regions around Israel's borders. His kingdom extended only as far as Damascus. The NIV suggests that David's victories went all the way to the Euphrates River (v.3), but the Hebrew text says only that David restored his control to "a river," not otherwise specified. The later tradition that this was the Euphrates River is motivated by the parallel text of 1Ch 18:3, which mentions the Euphrates.

# DAVID'S CONQUESTS

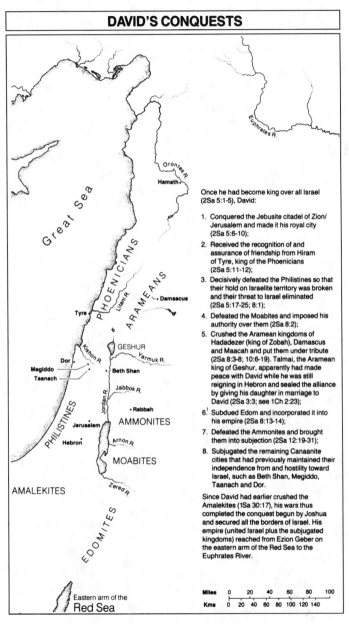

Once he had become king over all Israel (2Sa 5:1-5), David:

1. Conquered the Jebusite citadel of Zion/Jerusalem and made it his royal city (2Sa 5:6-10);

2. Received the recognition of and assurance of friendship from Hiram of Tyre, king of the Phoenicians (2Sa 5:11-12);

3. Decisively defeated the Philistines so that their hold on Israelite territory was broken and their threat to Israel eliminated (2Sa 5:17-25; 8:1);

4. Defeated the Moabites and imposed his authority over them (2Sa 8:2);

5. Crushed the Aramean kingdoms of Hadadezer (king of Zobah), Damascus and Maacah and put them under tribute (2Sa 8:3-8; 10:6-19). Talmai, the Aramean king of Geshur, apparently had made peace with David while he was still reigning in Hebron and sealed the alliance by giving his daughter in marriage to David (2Sa 3:3; see 1Ch 2:23);

6. Subdued Edom and incorporated it into his empire (2Sa 8:13-14);

7. Defeated the Ammonites and brought them into subjection (2Sa 12:19-31);

8. Subjugated the remaining Canaanite cities that had previously maintained their independence from and hostility toward Israel, such as Beth Shan, Megiddo, Taanach and Dor.

Since David had earlier crushed the Amalekites (1Sa 30:17), his wars thus completed the conquest begun by Joshua and secured all the borders of Israel. His empire (united Israel plus the subjugated kingdoms) reached from Ezion Geber on the eastern arm of the Red Sea to the Euphrates River.

But it is important to note that in that passage the focus is not on the border of the territory David was "restoring" but that which he was attempting "to reach." In other words the two texts are not about the same situation. In any event, neither text appears to set the Euphrates River as the border of David's kingdom.

The question at stake is whether, or to what extent, David's kingdom approximated the fulfillment of God's promise to Abraham in Ge 15:18 and Balaam's prophecy in Nu 24:17–24. The answer that comes from this text is that David's kingdom did not reach those promised boundaries. In fact, by specifying the boundaries it did reach, the writer makes certain that we understand that David's kingdom did *not* reach those of the kingdom spoken of by Balaam.

By way of summary, the writer reports that "The LORD gave David victory wherever he went" (v.6; repeated in v.14). This is the main point of the accounts of David's conquests.

The statement at the conclusion of the chapter that "David's sons were priests" (NIV, "royal advisers") is important in showing that David's kingship was envisioned by the author of Samuel as a form of priesthood. Certainly it was not of the Levitical priests since Zadok and Ahimelech were the Levitical priests. The kind of priests identified with the sons of David was apparently that which was already represented in Melchizedek, a priest-king (Ge 14:18–20). According to Ps 110, David himself recognized in the Davidic covenant of ch. 7 a divine promise that his descendants were to be priests "in the order of Melchizedek" (Ps 110:4). Also in the postexilic period, the hope of the restoration of the Davidic kingship centered on the expectation of a king who would also be a priest (cf. Zec 6:9–15).

## B. David Provided for the House of Saul (9:1–13)

In the midst of his account of the conquests of David, the writer has inserted a note about David's faithfulness to his promise to Jonathan that he would always care for his household (cf. 1Sa 20:14). Its appropriateness here amid the narratives of David's defeat of his enemies stems from the fact that Jonathan, Saul's son, had asked David to remember his household "even when the LORD has cut off every one of David's enemies from the face of the earth" (1Sa 20:15). Thus, as he is recounting David's successes against his enemies, he also recounts David's faithfulness to his word to Jonathan, particularly in caring for Mephibosheth. In this way, David's victories are cast as the fulfillment of Jonathan's words, "May the LORD call David's enemies to account" (1Sa 20:16).

## C. David Defeats the Ammonites (10:1–22)

The descriptions of the wars of David continue with an account of the subjugation of the Ammonites. The battle with the Ammonites further involved the Arameans, a group of city states already defeated by David (cf. 8:5–6). In that battle, Hadadezer, king of Zobah (an Aramean state just north of Israel), obtained the help of the Arameans in Damascus, and David, in defeating them, gained control of that city as well (8:5–6). In the present case, Hadadezer and his soldiers were hired by the Ammonites to fend off David's attack. When Israel proved victorious, Hadadezer sought further help from the Arameans beyond the Euphrates River (10:16), though they appear to have offered him little assistance. David defeated them as well (v.18). In the end, David subdued the Ammonites and continued to exercise his rule over the Aramean state controlled by Hadadezer (v.19). The text does not imply that those Arameans "beyond the [Euphrates] River" were subsequently a part of David's kingdom. The focus of the passage is on the Aramean states of Zobah and Damascus.

## D. David's Sin With Bathsheba (11:1–27)

This narrative focuses the reader's attention on the role of the prophet Nathan in confronting the king with his need to follow the justice prescribed in the covenant. According to Deuteronomy, the prophet was to guard the covenant responsibilities of the king; he was never to side with the king against the requirements of the covenant. We could give several other examples of the exercise of such covenant responsibilities by the prophets (e.g., Samuel confronted Saul in 1Sa 15; the man of God [prophet] confronted Jeroboam in 1Ki 13; Elijah confronted Ahab in 1Ki 18). See unit on "The Deuteronomic History" between Deuteronomy and Joshua and comments on 1Sa 1–7 for a discussion on the role of the prophet in the Deuteronomic History.

## E. David's Repentance (12:1–25)

The account of David's repentance after the incident with Bathsheba (12:1–25) is intended to show that he truly was a man after God's own heart. He listened to the rebuke of the prophet, something neither Saul nor most of the latter Davidic dynasty were ever willing to do. Thus we learn that David followed the prescriptions of Deuteronomy, even in times of weakness and failure. The narrative ends on the positive note of the birth of Solomon, whose name means "he has made peace." There is also the added note that "the LORD loved him" and thus instructed Nathan to name him Jedidiah, "beloved of the LORD" (vv.24–25). In this respect, the narratives of the book of Samuel anticipate those of the book of Kings. Their focus is on the identifi-cation of the offspring of the house of David and the next king, Solomon.

The account of the further defeat of the Ammonites at the end of the story (vv.26–31) is the writer's way of showing that David's repentance had been accepted by God and that he continued to give David success.

## F. Amnon and Tamar (13:1–22)

This narrative is intended to show how the sin of David and Bathsheba was repeated or duplicated in the lives of David's sons. Thus Amnon's rape of Tamar has its parallel in David's adultery with Bathsheba. It is significant that Amnon's plan was suggested by a "very wise man," Jonadab (NIV, "very shrewd man," v.3). The author of this book lays the blame for Amnon's wicked transgression at the feet of those who claim to be wise. In the same way, the story of the Fall in Ge 3 is linked to the "wise" counsel of the serpent (cf. Ge 3:1, 6). Thus the author attempts to link the fall of the house of David with the fall in the Garden of Eden; in both narratives, the attempt to gain through wisdom that which was forbidden is the central motif. Moreover, in both narratives the transgression occurs when the woman offers food to the man to eat (cf. vv.10–11 with Ge 3:6). In the case of David and Bathsheba, Joab's report of the death of Uriah alludes to the death of Abimelech by the hand of a woman (11:21) and thus links the theme of David's downfall to that of Abimelech's, by the hand of a woman.

Parallels such as this are signals of larger thematic links. This general merging of the themes in these various "Fall" narratives finds additional support in the fact that the result of Amnon's actions proves to be identical to that of the biblical story of Cain and Abel, which ends on the tragic note of brother slaying brother (13:23–39). Note that in ch. 14 the wise woman from Tekoa describes the death of Amnon in words drawn directly from Ge 4.

## G. The Wise Woman From Tekoa (14:1–33)

Once again David is saved from making a fatal mistake by the words of a wise woman (cf. Abigail in 1Sa 25). The narrative account is written in such a way that the woman's description of the events of Amnon's death at the hand of Absalom does not follow the actual account given in ch. 13, but rather the story of Cain and Abel in Ge 4. In both stories the two sons were "in the field" and the one rose up against the other and killed him. As in the case of Cain in Ge 4, the immediate concern in the woman's story is for avenging the death of the son and putting an end to the family of the murderer. The woman's words, "Let the king invoke the LORD his God to prevent the avenger of blood from adding to the destruction, so that my son will not be destroyed" (v.11) sounds remarkably similar to Cain's, "My guilt [NIV, punishment] is more than I can bear. . . . I will be a restless wanderer on the earth, and whoever finds me will kill me" (Ge 4:13–14). David's response, "Not one hair of your son's head will fall to the ground" (v.11b) is like that of the Lord to Cain, "Not so; if anyone kills Cain, he will suffer vengeance seven times over" (Ge 4:15).

These parallels are intended to show that David has a heart like God. They both respond with wise compassion. The woman was quick to drive home the point, "When the king says this, does he not convict himself, for the king has not brought back his banished son? . . . God does not take away life; instead, he devises ways so that a banished person may not remain estranged from him" (v.13). This is a lesson right out of the OT law. David had the heart of God, and the woman acknowledged this by saying, "My lord the king is like an angel of God in discerning good and evil" (v.17).

As the story continues, David displayed even greater discernment by seeing the work of Joab behind the woman's words. This was again recognized by the wise woman: "My lord has wisdom like that of an angel of God— he knows everything that happens in the land" (v.20).

At the conclusion of the story, the parallels between David's response to Absalom and God's response to Cain are further reinforced. Just as Cain "went out from the face of the LORD [NIV, from the LORD's presence, Ge 4:16]," so Absalom "went to his own house and did not see the face of the king" (v.24). Then as the narrative tells us that Cain was blessed with descendants (Ge 4:17–22), so also in Samuel we are told of Absalom's family. Finally, as the last statement in the story of Cain (Ge 4:26b) makes clear, there was a restitution of fellowship with God in those days, just as Absalom was restored to fellowship with his father David (vv.32–33).

These parallels between the two stories of Cain and Abel and Amnon and Absalom are part of a larger pattern of narration in the Bible that attempts to show that God's work with his people in the present can be illuminated by reflection on his work with his people in the past. God's ways teach God's will. We may be sure that what he has done for the fathers, he will do for us.

## H. Rebellion Within the House of David (15:1–20:26)

### 1. Absalom's rebellion (15:1–19:43)

This narrative demonstrates David's trust in God's faithfulness. Even in the face of the rebellion of the "offspring" of his own house, David trusted God fully to secure his promise. Statements and examples to this effect are found throughout the narrative. The clearest statement of David's trust in God is in 15:25. When driven from Jerusalem by Absalom's rebellion,

David did not seek to fight for the city. He said simply, "If I find favor in the LORD's eyes, he will bring me back and let me see it and his dwelling place again." When Shimei from the family of Saul came out to curse David, David's response was to leave the entire matter in the Lord's hands, "Leave him alone; let him curse, for the LORD has told him to" (16:11). David showed complete confidence in the Lord's provisions, "It may be that the LORD will see my distress and repay me with good for the cursing I am receiving today" (v.12).

One can easily see the relevance of this example of David to the readers of the book of Samuel. When, after the Babylonian captivity, the people returned to the land to rebuild the temple in Jerusalem, they faced similar opposition from those living in the land (cf. Ne 4:1–3). What better example could be given them of a leader who trusted wholly in the Lord's protection and help? Above all, David's concern was for the ark of the Lord and the priests. They were to remain in Jerusalem with the ark (15:25). Thus David's heart is set on God's promise in 2Sa 7, that the Lord's house, the temple, and David's house, the offspring of David, would dwell in Jerusalem forever. Further insight into David's trust in God is seen in Ps 3, which he wrote "when he fled from his son Absalom."

### 2. Sheba's rebellion (20:1–22)

This narrative raises the question of whether David's kingdom could be replaced by someone from another tribe. Sheba, from the tribe of Benjamin, instigated a revolt against David, calling into question his right to rule all Israel. In effect, Sheba raised the larger question of the role of the earlier pentateuchal texts in legitimatizing the kingdom of David. The promises to the fathers in the Pentateuch had specifically named the tribe of Judah as the only legitimate home of the promised

kingdom (cf. Ge 49:8–12). As has been characteristic of the Samuel narrative since the beginning, the author of the book rests his case for the legitimacy of the house of David in the work and words of a wise woman. The wise among God's people stand behind the Davidic kingship. Only the fool like Sheba would dare question what had been so clearly promised in Scripture.

### 3. Peace restored (20:23–26)

In the end, peace is restored, and this section closes with a listing of David's government officials.

### I. David Avenges the Gibeonites (21:1–14)

There was a famine throughout the land for three years. The writer shows that David knew what to do—he "sought the face of the LORD"—i.e., he inquired of the prophet (cf. God's command in Dt 18:14–22). The narrative also shows that David was quick to respond to God's answer. This famine came because the iniquity of Saul against the Gibeonites had not been avenged. Interestingly enough, just as David did not know the cause of the famine without the word of the prophet, so the reader also has no possible clue. Since the previous narratives in the book do not record such an event, we have no independent knowledge of Saul's "putting the Gibeonites to death." This is not a new feature of the biblical narratives (cf. comments on Dt 2:10–12, 20–23). In any case, we see David in this narrative careful to carry out God's word from the prophet, and we see that God honored David's response (v.14b). David's compassionate heart is also manifest (vv.13–14).

### J. David's Victories Against the Philistines (21:15–22)

In order to confirm that the Lord had forgiven David and was now again fighting for him, the writer recounts a series of victories of David and his men over the Philistines. In his descriptions of the Philistines, the writer seems to go out of his way to draw a connection between these final battles of David against the Philistines and his first battle with Goliath. One of the Philistines defeated by Abishai, for example, was Ishbi-Benob, "whose bronze spearhead weighed three hundred shekels" (v.16), bringing to mind Goliath's bronze coat of armor "weighing five thousand shekels" (1Sa 17:5). Another Philistine slain by David's men is described as "a huge man" (v.20), just as Goliath was described as "over nine feet tall" (1Sa 17:4).

At one point in the narrative, the writer draws such a close parallel between David's slaying Goliath (1Sa 17) and Elhanan's slaying the brother of Goliath (cf. 2Sa 21:19 with 1Ch 20:5) that he records simply that Elhanan slew Goliath. Some have taken this to be a copyist's error, inadvertently omitting the words "brother of [Goliath]" in the Samuel passage. Though this is possible, it is more likely that the writer intended to say that by slaying Goliath's brother (named Lahmi in 1Ch 20:5), Elhanan was, in fact, finishing David's work of smiting Goliath. This would be consistent with the suggestion that the five stones taken by David when he slew Goliath (1Sa 17:40) anticipate the defeat of the four remaining Philistine giants recorded here in 2Sa 21 (cf. v.22).

## K. David's Final Song (22:1–51)

It is fitting that the David narratives be concluded by one of his many songs from the book of Psalms—in this case, Ps 18. The psalm is a celebration of God's faithfulness to David and his house. Its central message falls in the final lines: "He gives his king great victories; he shows unfailing kindness to his anointed, to David and his descendants forever" (v.51). What is unusual, however, is that the song has been placed where it has within the book of Samuel. If the focus of the psalm is on

the victories of David, as it appears to be, then why is it placed after the accounts of the failures and rebellions of his sons? One would have expected it to be placed after ch. 7.

The answer lies in the meaning of the last lines. Who is the "king" and "anointed [one]" in v.51? It has been common to take this to refer to David and his descendants, mentioned in the second part of the verse. The problem, however, is that the terms "his king" and "his anointed" are singular and thus do not likely refer to David and his descendants. On the contrary, this in all likelihood refers to the promised "seed" (NIV, "offspring"), the Messiah of 7:12. If this is so, then the position of this song after the record of David's own failure, along with that of his sons, makes sense. Within the larger strategy of the book, the song shows that David's trust in God's faithfulness to his promise has not wavered in the face of the seeming impossibility of its fulfillment. Thus, at the end of his life, David looked back in faith at God's promises and forward in hope to their fulfillment in the coming of a future "king" and "anointed one."

In order to make this point more clearly, the author of the book attaches the last words of David (23:1–7) to this song. The two texts are joined by linking them with the key words "anointed one" (22:51; 23:1). Thus the last words of David open with his focus on the Lord's "anointed" (23:2).

## L. The Lord's Anointed (23:1–7)

In these last words of David, we are shown David's own evaluation of God's promise in ch. 7 and what it means in light of the failure of his own house to fulfill it. David begins with a brief description of the "man anointed by the God of Jacob" (v.1), about whom David wrote so many of his psalms. He makes the claim that in these psalms, the Lord spoke through him by "the Spirit of the LORD," putting his word on

David's tongue (v.2). What did David write of in these psalms? He says he wrote of the Anointed One who "rules over men in righteousness . . . in the fear of God" (v.3). This passage has long been understood by Christians and early Judaism to refer to the Messiah.

There are good grounds to interpreting it in this manner. The crux of David's words lies in v.5. In many English versions, David says, "Is not my house right with God? . . . Will he not bring to fruition my salvation and grant me my every desire?" In the Hebrew text, however, David says simply, "Because my house has not been thus with God . . . he will not bring to fruition my salvation and all my desire." What David means is that his house has not ruled over people in righteousness and in the fear of God, and thus they have not received the fulfillment of the promise of an eternal kingdom made in ch. 7.

There is a great difference between these two readings of David's words. The most important point to be made is that within the logic of the larger narrative, the Hebrew text makes very good sense. We have seen that the narratives that follow God's promise to the house of David in ch. 7 have focused on the failure of David and his house, as well as on David's trust that God would be faithful to his promise. That is, in fact, the point of David's words here. In spite of the fact that his own household has failed, God has made "an everlasting covenant, arranged and secured in every part" (v.5). David's words thus show that there is continued hope for the future that God would remain faithful to his promises and send the eternal King, the Anointed One.

If this passage is read in light of the continued story of the failure of the house of David in 1 and 2 Kings, then David's words prove also to be prophetic. We find that none of the historical kings fulfilled the prophetic promise of the Anointed One that David wrote of in the Psalms. Moreover, David's words fall in line with the strategy of the narratives in the books of Kings, in that they conclude on this same note (see comments on 2Ki 25:27–30).

## M. David's Mighty Men (23:8–39)

The list of David's thirty-seven mighty warriors serves a dual purpose. (1) The names of these men and the brief accounts of their military prowess show that God has given David help on all sides. One cannot read these exploits without drawing the conclusion that God had given these men to King David. (2) At the same time, however, the focus on their exploits, rather than on David's, appears to push David out of center stage. It thus prepares the way for the view of David that emerges in the next chapter—the view of one who has lost his confidence in God to help him in time of trouble and who has begun to rely instead on his own strength.

It can hardly be accidental that the list of mighty warriors in ch. 23 ends with the name Uriah the Hittite. The reader is immediately reminded of David's sin with Bathsheba, his first failure to obey God's will in ruling his people. Thus we are brought back to David's first failure as an introduction to his last failure, the numbering of his army.

## N. David's Numbering of His Army (24:1–25)

This chapter records David's second failure to trust God and live according to Dt 17:14–21. The fact that two accounts of David's failure are given is related to the requirement in Dt 19:15 that "a matter must be established by the testimony of two or three witnesses"; this principle has been operative throughout 1 and 2 Samuel. It is the writer's way of showing that David did not live up to the requirement of the king in Deuteronomy and thus he was not the promised king. David's numbering his armies is related to the injunction not to "acquire great numbers of horses for himself" (Dt 17:16). The intention of Deuteronomy was the same as the present narrative, i.e., prohibition of trusting in a large army for security rather than in the Lord.

When the writer says, "The anger of the LORD . . . incited David" to number his armies, he is saying that God sold them into the hands of their enemies because of their unfaithfulness. The mention of Uriah the Hittite in the preceding verse (23:39) is a narrative clue to the underlying cause of David's deed.

When David saw the angel striking down the people of Israel, he quickly confessed the wrong he had done and asked the Lord to let his hand fall upon him and his house (v.17). He purchased the threshing floor of Araunah where, in God's grace, the plague had been stopped. David built an altar at this location and the Lord answered his prayer (v.25). The writer puts much emphasis on this location, because it was to be the site of the temple. Thus in this final act of David, the first step toward the fulfillment of the promise in ch. 7 was accomplished. God had chosen the place where his name was to dwell. Thus the book ends with one question resolved, i.e., where the temple was to be built; but with another question unresolved, who was to build it? That question was to be addressed in the next book, the book of Kings.

# 1 Kings

## Introduction

In the Hebrew Bible the title of the book is Kings; there is no division between 1 and 2 Kings. The date and the author of this book are unknown. Early tradition ascribed the book to the prophet Jeremiah, but there is no sound basis for that assertion. The last event recorded in the book is the release of King Jehoiachin from prison in Babylon and the daily ration of food given him "as long as he lived" (2Ki 25:27–30). Thus the book was written a considerable period of time after the Exile in 586 B.C.

## I. Solomon (1:1–11:43)

### A. Adonijah's Rebellion and Solomon Accession (1:1–53)

The book of Kings opens immediately with the continuation of the question of who would succeed David as king and thus fulfill the Lord's promise in 2Sa 7:12–13, "I will raise up your offspring to succeed you. . . . He is the one who will build a house for my Name." With David now near death, the question of his successor was urgent. Absalom was dead, and the oldest son was Adonijah, David's fourth son (2Sa 3:4).

Adonijah conspired with members of David's court (1Ki 1:9) to take the throne. Bathsheba, Zadok the priest, Nathan the prophet, and Benaiah (v.26) the captain of the guard, however, took countermeasures, seeking to make Solomon king. While Adonijah and those with him were celebrating their impending success, Solomon was quickly escorted to the Spring of Gihon (v.38) and anointed king by Zadok before all the people (v.39).

The pattern of Solomon's inauguration is similar to Israel's leadership in the past: anointing, public acceptance, and divine demonstration of approval:

1. **Commissioning by God's representative**

-Moses laid his hand upon Joshua (Dt 34:9)

-Samuel anointed Saul (1Sa 10:1)

-Samuel anointed David (1Sa 16:13)

-David commanded Zadok to anoint Solomon (1Ki 1:34)

2. **Demonstration of divine approval**

-Moses given signs to perform (Ex 4:30–31)

-Joshua given success in the Conquest (Jos 1:7)

-Saul given victory over Ammonites (1Sa 11:11)

-David given victory over Goliath (1Sa 17)

-Solomon given great wisdom (1Ki 3:12)

3. **Popular recognition among God's people**

-The people see Moses' signs and believe (Ex 4:31)

-The people follow Joshua into battle (Jos 1:17; 24:15ff.)

-The people follow Saul (1Sa 11:12)

-The people recognize David's leadership (2Sa 2:4; 5:3)

-The people recognize Solomon's wisdom (1Ki 3:28)

### B. David's Last Words (2:1–12)

David's last words to Solomon (2:1–9) carry a great deal of weight in light of the message of the whole of the book of Kings. In the first place, they provide a specific link to the preceding book of Samuel and to the major theme of the last part of that book: the Davidic promise (2Sa 7). David's words also refer back to a number of unfinished incidents from 1 and 2 Samuel, clarifying and specifying two important features of the promise. (1) David raises the issue of obedience as a condition of the fulfillment of God's promise: "Walk in his ways, and keep his decrees and commands, his laws and requirements, as written in the Law of Moses . . . that the Lord may keep his promise to me" (vv.2–4). Though the promise had already been recorded in 2Sa 7:12–16, this is the first time that conditions and the importance of obedience to the Law of Moses is mentioned. In the earlier account of the promise, there was only a slight hint that conditions were laid out for the fulfillment of the promise (cf. 2Sa 7:14b). Thus David's words become essential for understanding the nature of the fulfillment of the Davidic promise. They set the stage for determining who the promised offspring of David would be, or more importantly for the book of Kings, who the promised seed would *not* be. As we will see, the writer uses these words to demonstrate to his readers that none of the historical descendants of David during the period of the monarchy were, in fact, the fulfillment of the divine promise.

(2) As long as the descendants of David remained faithful to God's commandments, they would "not be cut off" (NIV, "never fail to have a man on the throne of Israel"). Here, in both a negative and a positive way, David's words anticipate the central theme as well as the conclusion of the book of Kings. The book ends, of course, with the house of David and the nation of Israel going into Babylonian captivity. Thus David's words already begin to provide the basis for explaining the Exile: the Davidic kings did not remain faithful to the Lord or obedient to the Law of Moses. This point will be driven home numerous times throughout the book. However, the positive contribution that David's words make to the book as a whole relates to the final words of the book of Kings (2Ki 25:27–30), where it is recounted that even in Babylon the house of David did survive and was doing well. There was thus still hope for the fulfillment of the promise. God's promise to David remained intact.

## C. Solomon's Kingdom Established (2:13–46)

### 1. Adonijah's second rebellion (2:13–25)

After the death of David, Adonijah made another attempt for the throne. This time the attempt was more subtle, but Solomon was not to be fooled. He knew the true intent of Adonijah's request for Abishag, the Shunammite. It was a veiled attempt to gain legitimacy to David's throne through marriage to Abishag (v.22). Adonijah was therefore executed (v.25). We should note, however, that the writer of Kings uses Adonijah's own words to vindicate Solomon's kingship. He said to Bathsheba, "The kingdom has gone to my brother [Solomon]; for it has come to him from the LORD" (v.15b).

### 2. Old debts are settled (2:26–46)

After this, Solomon dealt with those who had followed Adonijah. Abiathar was replaced as high priest by Zadok (vv.27, 35), Joab was executed (v.34), and Shimei was killed (v.46). In each of these three cases, the theme is that of fulfillment. Zadok and his lineage henceforth assume the office of high priest in fulfillment of God's word to Samuel (1Sa 3); Joab is punished for the murder of Abner (2Sa 3:27) and Amasa (2Sa 20:10); and David is avenged for the mistreatment he received from Shimei (v.44b; cf. 2Sa 16:5–12). Moreover, in these acts Solomon also fulfilled David's last instructions to him (cf. vv.5–9).

## D. Solomon's Wisdom (3:1–4:34)

Solomon went to Gibeon to offer sacrifices at the large "high place" that had been erected there. The author of Kings appears somewhat apologetic for Solomon's actions, assuring us that Solomon, appearances to the contrary, loved God and was obedient to his commandments (3:3). In any event, he is careful to distinguish these offerings at the high place from the appearance of

God in Solomon's dream (3:5–14) at Gibeon. God gave Solomon great wisdom in the context of the dream, not within the context of the high place. It is significant that after this dream, Solomon returned to Jerusalem and there presented himself before the Lord at the Ark of the Covenant (3:15). The Chronicler offers more details about this incident, showing that the Tent of Meeting, the tabernacle, and the bronze altar were at Gibeon at this time, and thus Solomon's sacrifices were in line with the Law of Moses (see 2Ch 1:1–13).

Recognizing the scope of the task that lay before him, Solomon asked God for the wisdom to rule his people: "So give your servant a discerning heart to govern your people and to distinguish between right and wrong" (3:9). The writer goes on to give us an example of Solomon's wisdom in the ruling concerning the two prostitutes (vv.16–28). His wise decision in this case vindicated the divine gift that had been given him: "all Israel . . . saw that he had wisdom from God to administer justice" (v.28).

### E. Solomon's Temple (5:1–9:28)

The writer has two primary purposes in his account of Solomon's preparation for building the temple. (1) He wants to continue to direct the reader's attention to the possibility that Solomon's temple was the fulfillment of God's promise to David (2Sa 7). In this passage it is Solomon's own words to the king of Tyre that turn our attention back to God's promise to David, "I intend, therefore, to build a temple for the Name of the LORD my God, as the LORD told my father David" (5:5). There can be no doubt here that Solomon believed he was the promised offspring. It was on that basis that he planned to build the temple. The patient reader will soon learn, however, that in God's plan, Solomon was not the promised offspring (11:9–13). When the conditions for the fulfillment of the

promise to David are reiterated to Solomon (see 6:12), we realize by the end of the story of Solomon that he did not meet these conditions (11:9–13). Thus within the flow of the narrative, our attention, though initially directed to consider Solomon as a possible fulfillment of God's promise to David, is redirected to look far beyond him for the fulfillment of the promise. It is in this sense that these texts in the book of Kings are to be considered messianic texts. They develop the theme of the promised offspring of David and they attempt to show that none of the historical kings in the house of David met the condition of obedience that was to be the characteristic sign of the Promised One.

(2) The writer wants us to realize that Solomon's work on the temple is a picture or image of the ultimate fulfillment of God's promise to David. The promised offspring will be like Solomon when he comes. By this point in Scripture, it had long been promised that the nations, along with Israel, would play a significant role in the kingdom of God promised to David (cf. Ge 49:10c; Nu 24:7–24). This was also to become a central theme in the writings of the prophets (cf. Isa 2:2–4; Hag 2:7). Along with these other biblical writers, the author of Kings pictures this in his account of the building of Solomon's temple. With Hiram, king of Tyre, at the beginning of the account of the temple's building (5:1–18), and the visit of the queen of Sheba at its conclusion (10:1–13), the writer portrays the nations playing an important role in Solomon's kingdom, both in supplying their own wealth for building the temple (cf. Hag 2:7) and in appreciating its glory and splendor (cf. Isa 2:2–4).

There are distinct features of the building of the temple that the writer stresses in particular. The first is the exact time and duration of the building of the temple. Solomon began to build the temple 480 years after Israel had come out of Egypt (6:1), and it was completed in seven years (6:38b). Whether we take 480 symbolically for twelve generations of forty years each or literally, this much is certain: by means of this chronological note, the writer consciously links the building of the temple with a larger chronological understanding of Israel's history. He uses chronology not for its own sake, but for a theological purpose. He conceptualizes Israel's history in terms of the major time periods when God was dwelling with his people in the tabernacle and temple.

The clue to the chronology is found in the 430 years Israel was in Egypt (Ex 12:40). If the number of years from the Judges to the arrival of the ark in Jerusalem (1Sa 7:2) are added, without attention to overlapping periods, the total is also 430 (410 years of Judges plus the 20 years the ark was at Kiriath Jearim, 1Sa 7:2). Moreover, if the number of years of the kings of Judah are added from the time of the building of the temple, the total is also 430. Thus the scheme yields three periods of 430 years each: The time before the ark, the time before the temple, and the time before the temple is rebuilt—a total of 1,290 years.

Since the biblical text specifies the seven years that Solomon's temple was completed (6:38) and the thirty-three years that David reigned in Jerusalem with the ark (2Sa 5:5), we have nearly all the numbers for a chronological link with Israel's dwelling in the land with the tabernacle before the building of the temple (430 + 33 + 7 = 470). The missing number is the duration of Joshua's conquest of the land. The number 480 suggests the time of the Conquest was reckoned by the author of Kings to be ten years.

Interestingly enough, the ten years allotted here is the same assumed for the Conquest in Ac 13:18–19, which gives the total figure of 450 years—400 years in Egypt (Ac 7:6) + 40 years in the wilderness (Ac 13:18) + the time God "overthrew the seven nations in Canaan and gave their land to his people as their inheritance" (i.e., the Conquest under Joshua). The number 480 years in 1Ki 6:1 probably takes its starting point from the time of the Conquest, since the phrase "came up out of Egypt" can refer either to the crossing of the Red Sea (Ex 19:1; 33:38) or the crossing of the Jordan River (2Ch 6:5; Ps 114:1–3; Jer 32:21).

A great deal of attention to detail is given by the writer to the building plans of the temple. Although modern readers are preoccupied with how the temple may have looked, the writer's focus is not on that. He is more interested in the effect the temple would have on those who worshiped there. One can clearly see by reading through the account that his emphasis is on the cedar paneling, gold, palm trees, lions, bulls, and the cherubim that made up the decor of the temple. Why these specific features? Because it is precisely these features of the temple that were features of the Garden of Eden in the Genesis narratives and in later prophetic texts—the very thing that the tabernacle and temple were intended to recall. In Ge 1–2, the writer goes to great lengths to show that humankind was created to worship God and to enjoy his fellowship amid the trees, animals, gold and precious stones that God had put in the garden. Within the Pentateuch itself, the Garden of Eden is cast as a prototype of the tabernacle and temple. Thus the temple, at least in the eyes of the writer of Kings, was constructed and decorated to serve as a type of God's original intent for humanity of worship and fellowship. The temple was God's way of restoring the fellowship and worship that was lost through human disobedience in the garden. The effect of worship in Solomon's temple would be comparable to that of entering the Cistine Chapel today and being drawn into the imagery of the biblical narratives by means of the decorations on the walls and the ceiling. In both cases the worshipers' attention is focused on the biblical narratives of Creation.

There is a hint within these narratives, however, that all was not well. Solmon devoted seven years to building the temple, the house of God, but thirteen years to completing his own house. Had Solomon's later life not shown a fundamental flaw in his walk with the Lord, the reader may be tempted to overlook the excessive care he took on his own house. But in light of the fact that, in the end, it was his divided heart that disqualified him from receiving the divine promise—i.e., "his heart was not fully devoted to the LORD his God" (11:4) it hardly seems accidental that the writer interrupted his account of the building of the temple to recount Solomon's attention to his own house (7:1–12). This interruption serves as a concrete reminder of the fragmentation of Solomon's own heart.

Having given an account of the ark's entry into the temple (8:1–9), and the cloud of God's glory that accompanied it (vv.10–11), the writer allows Solomon to speak once more about God's promise to David (vv.12–21). Solomon spoke without hesitation of the fulfillment of God's promise to David; hence, the writer of the book and its readers know that all was not to be as Solomon supposed. As if to seal his fate with his own words, the writer recounts at length in ch. 8 Solomon's prayer of dedication, providing a clear hint of his own eventual failure to keep God's law, as well as that of the nation as a whole (vv.22–53).

In this prayer we see the emergence of a slightly different Solomon, one who was ready to concede that much more remained of God's promise to David than the completion of the temple that he was now celebrating. There was still the matter of obedience that stood between himself and God's fulfillment of the promise. Solomon prayed, "Now LORD, God of Israel, keep for your servant David my father the promises you made to him when you said, 'You shall never fail to have a man to sit before me on the throne of Israel, if only your sons are careful in all they do to walk before me as you have done'" (v.25). It was precisely on this point that Solomon himself would fall short of God's requirement and hence block the fulfillment of God's promise (11:6). Thus his following request, "And now, O God of Israel, let your word that you promised your servant David my father come true" (8:26), takes on a quite different set of possibilities. God had promised David both blessing, if his sons proved obedient (2Sa 7:12–14a), and punishment, if his sons proved disobedient (2Sa 7:14b).

Though the ultimate outcome would bring eternal blessing (2Sa 15–16), there was no guarantee of the fulfillment of the promise in the historical descendants of David during the time of the monarchy. Unknown to Solomon, he and his descendants were embarking on the road to punishment and exile rather than blessing and eternal kingdom. The account of that road to exile will occupy the writer of the book of Kings to the conclusion of the book. We will see, however, that through it all, the writer never takes his eyes off the ultimate fulfillment of the promise. His hope, however, was not centered in the historical kings of the house of David, but in the One yet to come who was a rightful heir to that throne. That is why, at the conclusion of his book, he was content to note that even through the Babylonian exile, the house of David remained intact (25:27–30) and thus contained within it the hope of the future fulfillment of God's promise to David.

In keeping with the writer's awareness of the eventual judgment and exile of God's people, it is significant that much of Solomon's dedicatory prayer deals with the question of judgment, restoration, and return from the Exile. Anyone of God's people who sins and disobeys God is to repent before him at the temple. Throughout the prayer the focus of Solomon's dedication is not on the worship of God at the temple but on the repentance of God's people and divine forgiveness. The key sins and divine judgments recited in the prayer are precisely those on which this writer will focus in the subsequent narratives. For example, in the Elijah-Elisha narratives (1Ki 17:1–2Ki 2:12), "the heavens are shut up and there is no rain because your people have sinned" (1Ki 8:35; cf. 17:1) and there is "famine or plague . . . [and] an enemy besieges them" (8:37; cf. 2Ki 6:24–8:20).

Moreover, exile from the land, a major theme in 2 Kings, is also a central concern of Solomon's prayer (8:34, 44–53). It is, in fact, the last section of Solomon's prayer that provides the theological basis for the hope that ultimately grows out of the book of Kings. Solomon, drawing on the promises of God in Dt 30:1–6, looks beyond the time of Israel's exile to the time of God's mercy on Israel and their return. As in Dt 30:2, the basis of God's forgiveness and restoration of his people is their own recognition of their sin and repentance (1Ki 8:47–50). Though the book of Kings ends with the people of Israel in exile, it does not end on a note of despair, because the words of Solomon's prayer have already looked far beyond that event. In a real sense, this dedicatory prayer of Solomon speaks the last words of the book.

Another key theme in Solomon's prayer is the conversion of the nations (vv.41–43). The temple was to be a center to which all the nations could come and worship God: "so that all the peoples of the earth may know your name and fear you, as do your own people Israel" (v.43). This theme is in keeping with the words of Jacob in Ge 49:10, that the king of the tribe of Judah would enjoy the "obedience of the nations" (cf. Ps 72:8–15).

At the close of his prayer, Solomon blessed the congregation. In this blessing there is another reminder of his own impending failure. He tells the people, "Your hearts must be fully committed to the LORD our God" (v.61), which is the exact reversal of what the writer says about Solomon himself three chapters later: "His heart was not fully devoted to the LORD his God" (11:4). He is convicted by his own words.

As confirmation of where the narrative is taking Solomon, the writer inserts an account of the Lord's second appearance to Solomon (9:1–9). The Lord focuses on the question of fulfilling his promise to David. He tells Solomon: "If you walk before me in integrity of heart and uprightness, as David your father did, and do all I command and observe my decrees and laws, I will establish your royal throne over Israel forever, as I promised David your father" (vv.4–5). But then the Lord adds a negative side to the promise: "If you or your sons turn away from me and do not observe the commands and decrees I have given you . . . then I will cut off Israel from the land I have given them and will reject this temple I have consecrated for my Name" (vv.6–7). Once again the events of this book take a turn in the direction of judgment and exile.

Within the narrative itself there is an immediate hint that already something was awry. The relationship between Solomon and Hiram, a token of divine blessing in the previous chapters (5:1–12), began to deteriorate into a squabble over the value of property (9:10–14). Furthermore, we now learn that Solomon had a foreign wife, the daughter of Pharaoh—innocent enough here, but two chapters later this became the source of his eventual downfall (11:4). Finally, the mention in 9:15–28 of Solomon's great material wealth (vv.18, 26–28), his great number of horses (vv.19, 22), and his alliance with Egypt (vv.16, 24) suggests that he was already beginning to fall short of being the ideal king envisioned in Dt 17:14–17. These are only hints, however, for the writer continues to extol Solomon's greatness for at least another chapter. But after that, when the final verdict on the life of Solomon is given, its fundamentally negative character should not take us by surprise. Solomon reaped that which he had already sown in these earlier chapters.

## F. Solomon's Wealth and Glory (10:1–11:8)

The writer's purpose here is not merely to show how close Solomon came to being the ideal king envisioned in Dt 17 and 2Sa 7, but also to present him as a figure or picture of the ideal king. Though ultimately Solomon's kingship, like that of the rest of the Davidic kings, ended in ruin and division, his rule in particular came closer to the ideal than any of the others. It is for that reason that the writer elaborates on the glories and splendor of that kingdom. Solomon was the greatest king, and a picture of the promised King who would be even greater than Solomon. The writer of the book of Chronicles goes even further than the book of Kings in this regard.

For the writer of the book of Kings, the aspect of Solomon's kingdom that most characteristically pictured the ideal king was the acclaim of his wisdom throughout all the world. Thus the visit by the queen of Sheba becomes virtually proverbial in its meaning for the writer. In her words and in her actions the queen of Sheba epitomizes all those nations of the world who would one day in the future come to pay homage to the eternal kingdom of the Son of Man (cf. Da 7:14). The ideal of God's law as presented in the Pentateuch was that in it Israel was to exhibit divine wisdom among the nations. If Israel kept God's instructions, all the nations would hear of it and say, "Surely this great nation is a wise and understanding people" (Dt 4:6). Moreover, the king was to be the wisest of them all. He was to have his own copy of the Scriptures and was "to read it all the days of his life" (Dt 17:19). Only then would "he and his descendants . . . reign a long time over his kingdom in Israel" (Dt 17:20).

The queen of Sheba, visiting the wise King Solomon, had her hard questions with which she tested his wisdom (10:1), and Solomon "answered all her questions; nothing was too hard for the king to explain to her" (v.3). The queen was overwhelmed and confessed, "Indeed, not even half was told me; in wisdom and wealth you have far exceeded the report I heard" (v.7). From the author's point of view we know that she was not merely testing Solomon's wisdom, but she was testing God's wisdom as well (cf. 4:29–34). Her response, then, was not only an evaluation of Solomon's wisdom but also an evaluation of the source of his wisdom, i.e., divine instruction found in Scripture. She herself arrived at this same conclusion by exclaiming, "Praise be to the LORD your God, who . . . has made you king, to maintain justice and righteousness" (10:9). For the writer of the book of Kings, her great wealth, along with the wealth from Hiram's ships (which he inserts just at this point in the narrative, vv.11–12), is a picture of the "wealth of the nations" (Hag 2:7; NIV, "desire of all nations"; cf. Isa 60:5ff.) that would one day be brought to the future Son of David reigning in Jerusalem. What the prophet Haggai had pictured in his vision of the future, the writer of this book depicted in images drawn from the greatest days of Israel's past glories.

In the summary of Solomon's wealth that now follows (10:23–11:8), one can clearly see the narrator's strategy. He begins by extolling the wisdom God had given Solomon, but before he has finished, we see that it was just this wealth and wisdom that led to Solomon's downfall. He was "greater in riches and wisdom than all the other kings of the earth. The whole world sought audience with Solomon to hear the wisdom God had put in his heart" (10:23–24). This summary looks back to God's earlier promise to Solomon that through the wisdom God gave him, he would "have no equal among kings" (3:12–13).

In this earlier passage, however, God warned Solomon that if he was to continue to enjoy God's blessing, he must "walk in my ways and obey my statutes and commands as David your father did" (v.14). Curiously, it was just at that moment that "Solomon awoke—and he realized it had been a dream" (v.15). This may be an initial hint by the writer that Solomon's wisdom and blessing might one day vanish in the same way as his dream did. This is suggested by the fact that in the same abrupt fashion as Solomon awoke from his dream in ch. 3, the writer's description of Solomon's wealth and divine blessing in ch. 10 turns abruptly to the tragic reality with which he ended his reign (10:25–11:8). Although after 10:24 the description continues in what appears to be a positive vein—"Year after year, everyone who came brought a gift—articles of silver and gold . . . horses and mules. Solomon accumulated chariots and horses. . . . The king made silver as common in Jerusalem as stones. . . . [His] horses were imported from Egypt. . . . [He], however, loved many foreign women besides Pharaoh's daughter . . . [and they] turned his heart after other gods" (10:25–11:4)—the reader who is aware of Dt 17:16–17 will immediately recognize that the list

enumerated here is precisely that which God's ideal king is warned against (see Dt 17:16–17). Solomon became ensnared by his own wisdom and disobeyed God's commands. Thus the writer turns to an account of God's judgment of Solomon in the next section.

## G. Solomon's Fall (11:9–43)

The Lord had specifically commanded Moses in Dt 17:17 that the king "must not take many wives, or his heart will be led astray." Solomon clearly violated this commandment, and the writer has taken great pains to show it. The reason it is important to the writer of Kings to show that Solomon had transgressed this specific command of God is because he wants to show that Solomon was *not* the "offspring" promised to David in 2Sa 7. According to that promise, David was to have a son who would rule after him and build a temple in Jerusalem (7:12–13). What better candidate for fulfillment of that promise than Solomon? We have seen that within the narrative, Solomon himself even applied the Davidic promise to his work of building the temple (1Ki 5:5). As readers we must be careful not to identify Solomon's understanding of the Davidic promise with the writer's and hence with God's, for the narrative continues, implying that Solomon was not the promised offspring. He thought he was, but he was not. That promise remained yet to be fulfilled with a future seed of David.

How does the writer of Kings demonstrate this point? He does so first by repeating the promise God had made to David in 2Sa 7 (see 1Ki 5:3–5). But then God himself clarified the fact that there were necessary conditions for the fulfillment of the promise, namely, following God's decrees and keeping his commandments (see 6:12–13)—conditions not recorded earlier. From that narrative we learn that unless these conditions were met, Solomon's kingdom would not fulfill the promise to David.

Having made this initial point, the writer then proceeds to show that Solomon did not, in fact, meet the conditions. By multiplying horses, returning to Egypt, taking foreign wives, and accumulating great wealth, he violated God's command to Moses regarding the conduct of the king. Thus God could say to Solomon, "You have not kept my covenant and my decrees, which I commanded you, [and] I will most certainly tear the kingdom away from you and give it to one of your subordinates" (11:11).

God had promised David that he would never take his love away from David's descendants, as he did when he removed the kingdom of Saul (2Sa 7:15). On the contrary, God had said to David, "Your house and your kingdom will endure forever before me; your throne will be established forever" (v.16). In conjunction with this eternal promise, God here also reminded Solomon that though his kingdom would be divided and reduced to one tribe (i.e., Judah, including the members of the tribe of Benjamin, 12:21), that tribe would remain.

As if to confirm his own word by the mouth of a second witness (cf. Dt 19:15), God sent the prophet Ahijah from Shiloh to Jeroboam, son of Nebat, who had rebelled against the kingdom of Solomon (1Ki 11:26–29). Jeroboam was to have that part of the kingdom that was torn from Solomon (vv.30–39). With a view to the events of the remainder of the book of Kings, the prophet says, God would "humble David's descendants because of this, but not forever" (v.39). The humbling of the house of David began immediately with the rise of Solomon's adversaries, Hadad the Edomite (vv.14–22), Rezon, son of Eliada (vv.23–25), and the rebellion of Jeroboam (11:26–12:20).

After the death of Solomon, Rehoboam his son succeeded him as king (11:43).

## II. The Divided Kingdom (12:1–22:53)

### A. Israel 1: Jeroboam (12:1–14:20)

After the death of Solomon, his kingdom was divided. The northern tribes rebelled against the Davidic dynasty in Jerusalem and established an independent kingdom. Jeroboam, the son of Nebat, from the tribe of Ephraim, who had once rebelled against Solomon (11:26) was chosen as king (12:20). The writer shows that the divided kingdom was the result of a foolish decision of the young king Rehoboam. The elders who had counseled his father, Solomon, advised him "to be a servant to these people and serve them and . . . they will always be your servants" (v.7). Rehoboam, however, rejected their counsel and followed the harsh advice of "the young men who had grown up with him" (vv.10–14). Nevertheless, the writer makes it clear that behind this act of folly were the workings of the sovereign hand of God: "the king did not listen to the people, for this turn of events was from the LORD, to fulfill the word the LORD had spoken to Jeroboam" by the prophet Ahijah (v.15). Moreover, when confronted with a second word from God (vv.22–24a), Rehoboam wisely "obeyed the word of the LORD" and thus averted more calamity (v.24b).

In contrast to the Davidic king Rehoboam, who proved obedient in the end, the king of Israel, Jeroboam, began an apostasy that was to plague the northern kingdom throughout all its years, ultimately leading not only to the ruin of his own dynasty (13:34), but to the destruction of the entire northern kingdom (2Ki 17:21–23). Jeroboam established two rival worship centers, one at Bethel and the other at Dan (1Ki 12:25–33). At these centers he established a new priesthood and new feast days "of his own choosing" (v.33), and he set up two golden caves (cf. Ex 32:4) before which the people offered sacrifices. All this was intended to rival the true worship of God at Jerusalem (v.27).

Since Jeroboam's apostasy was in direct violation of God's covenant with Israel, God raised up a prophet to confront the king. The story of the unknown man of God is recounted in 13:1–34. Not only did the prophet condemn Jeroboam's apostasy, but he also foretold the coming of the Judean king, Josiah (2Ki 22:1–23:30), who would be the one to put an end to it. Not only did the prophet perform a sign to confirm his word (1Ki 13:3–5), but also within this book the author notes the exact fulfillment of his word when it occurred (2Ki 23:16).

The story of the man of God who confronted Jeroboam and whose signs and words proved true, takes a curious turn after his initial success. Although he wisely rejected the offer of reward from the king (v.8), he unwisely took the counsel of an old prophet from Bethel (vv.18–19), and it proved his undoing. Twice we are told that the man of God was not to eat or remain in Bethel, but to return directly back to his home in Judah (vv.9, 17). The man of God, however, was caught unawares when an old prophet from Bethel, whose word he trusted, deceived him with a false word from the Lord (v.18). While eating with the old prophet, the fate of the man of God was sealed by an authentic word of the Lord that came, ironically, to the old prophet (vv.21–22). The point of this story becomes clearer at its conclusion. The remarkable events of the death of the man of God, thus fulfilling the word of the old prophet, make it inescapable that this man of God was a true prophet and that his words against the apostasy of Jeroboam were true. Even the old prophet from Bethel recognized this (vv.31–32). In spite of

such confirmation, however, "Jeroboam did not change his evil ways" (v.33a) but continued in his apostasy (v.33b).

The author of Kings includes a second account of a prophet who testified against Jeroboam, the prophet Ahijah (14:1–16). His word confirms what was said by the man of God in ch. 13, but it also adds considerably to it. The man of God had spoken against the apostasy of Jeroboam and had foretold its final ruin. Ahijah, on the other hand, foretold the eventual downfall of the entire northern kingdom of Israel. Jeroboam's apostasy was the first and most fundamental cause of Israel's ruin at the hands of the Assyrians (2Ki 17:7–23). It should be noted, however, that in 2Ki 17:7–23, when the writer of Kings reviews the litany of evils that brought on the destruction of the nation, the fundamental problem underlying all of them was Israel's lack of faith: "They did not believe in the LORD their God" (2Ki 17:14b; NIV, "did not trust"). Thus for this writer, as bad as Jeroboam's apostasy was, it was only symptomatic of a more fundamental problem of faith. In this regard, the writer of Kings shares the same outlook on Israel's apostasy as Isaiah (cf. comment on Isa 7:9) and the author of Hebrews (ch. 11).

## B. Judah 1 (14:21–15:24)

With the covenant that God made with David (2Sa 7:16) came the assurance that only a descendant of David could legitimately rule over God's people. Thus a line of succession was established after David and continued until the time of the Exile. Even during and after the Exile, the royal lineage of the house of David remained intact (cf. 2Ki 25:30). Part of the writer's purpose in treating the kings of the house of David in this book is to show God's faithfulness to his word in Ge 49:10, "The scepter will not depart from Judah nor the ruler's staff from between his feet, until he comes to whom it belongs."

The writer devotes most of his attention to the ruin and loss in the Davidic kingdom after the death of Solomon. There was much apostasy in Judah (14:22–24). Not only did Rehoboam lose most of his father's kingdom, he also lost most of his father's wealth (vv.25–28). Moreover, there was continual warfare between Israel and Judah during this time (vv.29–31).

The narrative makes it clear that conditions did not improve during the subsequent reign of Abijah (15:1–8). It also is clear about why this was the case. The heart of the king was "not fully devoted to the LORD his God, as the heart of David his forefather had been" (v.3). David was the standard by which all the subsequent rulers of Judah were judged. The very survival of the kingdom during this time was due only to God's faithfulness to his promise to David (v.4; cf. 2Sa 7:16).

The kingship of Asa (15:9–24) represents a turn for the better. He "did what was right in the eyes of the LORD, as his father David had done" (v.11). Consequently, he gained the upper hand against the northern kingdom of Israel and had peace with his neighbors (vv.16–22). The only drawback to Asa's reign was that he failed to remove the "high places" (v.14) from the northern kingdom (cf. comment on 2Ch 15:17), i.e., the false worship centers at Bethel and Dan. The writer mentioned this not to find fault with Asa, but to reinforce the word of the man of God who had prophesied that Josiah would be the one to remove them (1Ki 13:2).

## C. Israel 2 (15:25–22:40)

The narrative returns here to the events of the kings of Israel in the north. Nadab, the son of Jeroboam and an evil king like his father, reigned only two years (15:25–32). The "sin which [Jeroboam] had caused Israel to commit" (v.26) was the establishment of false worship centers at Bethel and Dan. Nadab was killed by Baasha (15:33–16:7), who destroyed not only Nadab, but all the descendants of Jeroboam and thus began his own dynasty. The writer of Kings sees Baasha's revenge as a fulfillment of the word of the prophet (cf. 13:34).

The writer makes it clear, however, that Baasha was no better than those of the house of Jeroboam (15:34). Thus the Lord raised up the prophet Jehu (16:1) to announce the downfall and ruin of the house of Baasha. Jehu's prophetic word was fulfilled when Baasha's son and successor, Elah, was killed by Zimri, one of his own officials (16:8–14).

Zimri, who made himself king (16:20), reigned only seven days (vv.15–20). Then the people of Israel choose Omri as their king. Omri put an end to Zimri's rebellion but fared no better than those he had deposed (vv.21–28). To Omri goes the credit of moving the royal city from Tirzah to Samaria (v.24).

The writer of Kings was particularly interested in the reign of Omri's son, Ahab (16:29–22:40). The kingdom of Israel reached a new low with his reign (16:30), principally because of the influence of Jezebel, the daughter of the king of Sidon (v.31). Ahab introduced Baal worship in Israel as well as the use of sacred poles (Asherahs) in worship (the exact nature of these sacred poles is still not certain). Asa, in Jerusalem, had "deposed his grandmother Maacah from her position as queen mother, because she had made a repulsive Asherah pole" (15:13). In the present context it is clear that they represented a foreign element that was extremely repulsive to the writer of Kings. Ahab also build a temple to Baal in Samaria (16:32–33).

The writer of Kings is constantly on alert for evidence of fulfilled prophecy. Thus, recalling the "solemn oath" of

Joshua in which he stated that anyone who rebuilt Jericho would do so "at the cost of his firstborn . . . and youngest" (Jos 6:26), he notes here its fulfillment in the death of the firstborn and youngest sons of Hiel while rebuilding Jericho (1Ki 16:34).

Embedded in the narratives of Ahab and Jezebel and extending somewhat beyond them is the account of the prophet Elijah (1Ki 17:1–2Ki 2:12). Elijah waged what appears to be a one-man battle against the apostasy of Ahab's kingdom. For the writer of Kings he represents everything that was good and necessary in God's establishment of the office of prophet (Dt 18:14–22). Elijah followed the script of the Pentateuch so well that he virtually spoke and acted as Moses would have, had he lived in that time. The fact that he lived a life as an outsider, in constant threat of imprisonment and persecution, witnesses to the state of apostasy that reigned in the land. When God told Elijah that there were 7,000 others like him "whose knees have not bowed down to Baal" (19:18), we, the readers, are as surprised as Elijah.

The writer of Kings appears to have deliberately cast the story of Elijah as a parallel to that of Moses. (1) As Moses went before the pharaoh to announce the plagues (Ex 7–11), so Elijah went before Ahab to announce that "neither dew nor rain" would fall except by his word (1Ki 17:1).

(2) When Moses stretched out his hand over the Red Sea, "the waters were divided, and the Israelites went through the sea on dry ground, with a wall of water on their right and on their left" (Ex 14:21–22). Elijah struck the waters of the Jordan River and "the water divided to the right and to the left, and [they] crossed over on dry ground" (2Ki 2:8).

(3) As Moses and the Israelites were kept in the desert beyond the Jordan by a daily supply of manna from heaven in the morning and meat in the evening (Ex 16), and drank from the water supplied by God (Ex 17), so Elijah was kept "east of the Jordan" and "the ravens brought him bread and meat in the morning and . . . in the evening, and he drank from the brook" (1Ki 17:5–6). In the same way, when the brook dried up, Elijah was fed from the meager resources of the widow at Zarephath whose jar of flour and jug of oil, just like the manna and the rock in the desert (Ex 16:35), was not used up nor ran dry (1Ki 17:15–16).

(4) Just as by fire God had demonstrated his choice of Moses at Mount Sinai (Ex 20:18; 32:35) and at the rebellion of Korah (Nu 16:35), so God demonstrated his choice of Elijah at Mount Carmel (1Ki 18:16–40): "The god who answers by fire—he is God" (v.24).

(5) Just as Moses fled Egypt and hid in the wilderness in fear for his own life (Ex 2:14), so Elijah fled Israel in fear to seek refuge in the desert (1Ki 19:1–5).

(6) The angel of the Lord met Moses at the burning bush on Mount Sinai (Ex 3:2), and an angel met Elijah at the broom tree (1Ki 19:4) and strengthened him for his journey of "forty days and forty nights" to Mount Horeb, which is Sinai (v.8).

(7) On Sinai, Moses stood "in a cleft in the rock" and watched God's glory pass by (Ex 33:21–23). It is perhaps just this passage that the writer of Kings has in mind when he says that Elijah slept in "the cave" (1Ki 19:9; NIV, "a cave") and from "the mouth of the cave" saw the Lord pass by (vv.11–13).

(8) As Moses was given Aaron (Ex 4:14–16) and Joshua (Ex 17:10) to assist him in the work of the Lord, so Elijah was given Elisha and Jehu (1Ki 19:16–17).

(9) Moses was given the curious assistance of the Arameans, i.e., Balaam from the land of Aram (Dt 23:4; Nu 22–24). Similarly, Elijah was curiously

assisted by Hazael, king of the Arameans (1Ki 19:15).

(10) At the end of his life, Moses stood on the eastern bank of the Jordan River looking into the Promised Land on the other side (Dt 34:1–4). There he died in the presence of the Lord and, curiously, there was no site where his burial could be commemorated (Dt 34:5). Unlike the patriarchs (Ge 23:19; 25:10; 35:19–20, 29; 50:12–13, 24–26; Jos 24:32) and others of his own generation (Jos 24:29–30, 33; cf. Nu 20:28), "to this day no one knows where his grave is" (Dt 34:6). Elijah too, at the end of his life, stood on the eastern bank of the Jordan River and from there was taken up to heaven in a chariot of fire (2Ki 2:11). Hence, like Moses, there was no burial site for Elijah.

Why did the writer of Kings go to such lengths to parallel the lives of these two men? The answer lies in Moses' prophecy regarding "the prophet" in Dt 18:17–18, "The LORD said to me . . . I will raise up for them a prophet like you from among their brothers," and in the final words of the Pentateuch, after the death of Moses, "Since then, no prophet has risen in Israel like Moses, whom the LORD knew face to face, who did all those miraculous signs and wonders. . . . For no one has ever shown the mighty power or performed the awesome deeds that Moses did in the sight of all Israel" (Dt 34:10–12). Clearly the message of the Pentateuch is that God was going to send another prophet like Moses, who would do the same great signs and wonders as Moses. It also seems evident that the writer of Kings is interested in the fact that Elijah was "like Moses."

The question is, however, does the writer intend to show that Elijah was that prophet spoken of by Moses, or does he intend to show that Elijah was not that prophet? Taken as a whole, it is unlikely that the book of Kings intended to say that Elijah was the prophet of which Moses spoke. As we will see, part of the writer's purpose was to show that Elisha's work was double that of Elijah. For the writer of Kings, Elijah, like Moses, was a further example of the future prophet who was for the Pentateuch, as well as for Kings, a messianic figure. The writer wants his readers to look for the coming of a prophet like Moses and like Elijah, though he would be greater than both. The book of Malachi provides an interesting glimpse into the way the book of Kings was being read close to the time it was written: "Remember the law of my servant Moses, the decrees and laws I gave him at Horeb for all Israel. See, I will send you the prophet Elijah before that great and dreadful day of the LORD comes" (Mal 4:4). In other words, both Moses and Elijah are viewed as those who are to prepare the way for the coming of the Day of the Lord.

The narrative of the war between King Ahab of Israel and King Ben-Hadad of Aram (20:1–43) is intended to show how far Ahab was from being willing or able to do the work of God. The assumption upon which the story turns is that Ahab's armies were called to do the work of God in bringing judgment upon the Arameans. Moreover, it was through this work of judgment that the Lord intended to reveal himself to Israel. He said to Ahab, "I will deliver this vast army into your hands, and you will know that I am the LORD" (v.28; cf. v.13). The writer expends considerable effort in showing how wicked and deserving of judgment the Arameans were (vv.1–12). By way of contrast, Ben-Hadad's officials acknowledged that "the kings of the house of Israel are merciful" (v.31). As the story is told, king Ahab, disregarding the word of the prophet, fell victim to Ben-Hadad's scheme in a way reminiscent both of the Gibeonites' deception of Joshua (Jos 9) and Saul's failure to heed the word of Samuel after the battle with the Amalekites (1Sa 15:9–33). In both cases, as well as the one here, the writer stresses the act of disobedience, not the apparent mercy shown by the deed. In the dramatic confrontation between Ahab and the prophet (vv.35–43), the writer uses Ahab's own words to convict him of his wrong. From the writer's perspective, Ahab was guilty because he had "set free a man [the LORD] had determined should die" (v.42).

As if to insure that the reader does not draw the conclusion that Ahab was the "merciful" king that Ben-Hadad's officials took him to be (v.31), the writer of Kings recounts the incident of Naboth's vineyard (21:1–26) to reveal the heart of king Ahab. The king may have attempted to spare the life of Ben-Hadad, but he would not lift a finger to save the life and inheritance of a fellow Israelite whose property he coveted. Thus the writer's verdict is that "there was never a man like Ahab, who sold himself to do evil in the eyes of the LORD, urged on by Jezebel his wife" (v.25). For these two acts of disobedience, Ahab's kingdom was rejected (vv.21–22).

Unexpectedly, Ahab repented and humbled himself at the hearing of God's judgment (v.27). God responded to Ahab's act of contrition and postponed the ruin of his kingdom (vv.28–29). There is a clear lesson on the nature of God's grace at the close of this story. Having just stated that Ahab was the "vilest" idolater, "like the Amorites the LORD drove out before Israel" (v.26), when he repented, the writer is quick to show God's compassion and forgiveness.

The end of Ahab's life is told in a remarkable story that highlights the sovereign hand of God in the affairs of his chosen people (22:1–41). The heavens open before the eyes of the reader as the prophet Micaiah tells of a divine plan to "entice Ahab into attacking Ramoth Gilead and going to his death there" (v.20). Ahab, ignoring Micaiah's warning, went into battle (22:29)—but with the precaution of taking on a disguise (v.30). In the midst of battle, the army of Arameans searched for Ahab throughout the Israelite ranks, under specific instructions from their king to fight with no one "great or small, except the king of Israel" (v.31). The Aramean soldiers thought they found him in the person of King Jehoshaphat of Judah, but once they discovered he was not Ahab, they turned back from pursuing him (vv.32–33). Then, without warning, a single arrow shot "at random" decided the outcome of the battle and the fate of Ahab's kingdom (vv.34–38). At the close of the story, even the trivial details of Ahab's death reveal the truth of the word of the prophet (v.38; cf. 21:19).

### D. Judah 2: Jehoshaphat (22:41–50)

Jehoshaphat, like his father Asa, was a good king. Also like his father, he did not remove "the high places" (v.43). These may refer to the false worship centers at Bethel and Dan set up by Jeroboam. The Chronicler (2Ch 17–20) devotes much attention to Jehoshaphat because of the many good aspects of his reign. The writer of Kings, perhaps for the same reason, passes over Jehoshaphat rather quickly. Unlike the Chronicler, his interest is more on the failures of these kings than on their successes.

# 2 Kings

## Introduction

See the introduction to 1 Kings.

## I. The Divided Kingdom (Continued) (1:1–17:41)

### A. Israel 3 (1Ki 22:51–2Ki 8:15)

#### 1. Ahaziah (1Ki 22:51–2Ki 1:18)

The book of 1 Kings closes with a brief notice of the reign of Ahaziah (1Ki 22:51–53). As with the other kings of Israel, Ahaziah "did evil in the eyes of the LORD" by following in the ways of Jeroboam (v.52). What the writer means by this is that he continued to maintain and encourage the priests, ceremonies, and worship centers established by Jeroboam at Bethel and Dan (1Ki 12:25–33).

Ahaziah was the only other Israelite king whom Elijah confronted (2Ki 1:1–18). Like his father Ahab, Ahaziah followed the gods of Israel's neighbors and forsook the God of Israel. Just as Elijah had challenged Ahab with fire from heaven (1Ki 18:24), so now he challenged Ahaziah (2Ki 1:10). The lesson of the story is clear. The king, along with all of God's people, must obey the words of God's prophet. As Moses had commanded, "The LORD your God will raise up for you a prophet like me from among your own brothers. You must listen to him" (Dt 18:15). Curiously enough, Moses had reminded Israel in this same passage that they themselves at Mount Horeb (Sinai) had asked God to let Moses be their prophet because they were afraid of the fire that had come down from heaven onto the mountain. In light of the central importance of the fire from heaven in Elijah's acts, it is significant that Elijah himself departed in a chariot of fire (2Ki 2:11).

#### 2. Elisha (2:1–13:10)

After the account of the departure of Elijah (2:1–2), the writer has inserted a major section of narratives dealing with the acts of his successor, Elisha (2:13–8:15). When Elisha asked Elijah for a "double portion of your spirit" (2:9b) he was not only asking to continue the work of Elijah but to increase it as well. To show that his wish was granted, the writer has structured and selected the narratives about Elijah and Elisha so that there are twice as many miracles recorded for Elisha (sixteen in all) as those of Elijah (eight in all).

**Miracles in the life of Elijah**

(1) fed by ravens (1Ki 17:5–6)

(2) provision of food for the widow at Zarephath (17:7–16)

(3) widow's dead son revived (17:17–24)

(4) stops and sends rain (17:1; 18:1,41–45)

(5) fire from heaven on prophets of Baal (18:16–40)

(6) food supplied by an angel (19:5–9)

(7) fire from heaven on messengers of the king (2Ki 1:10–15)

(8) parting the Jordan River (2:8)

**Miracles in the life of Elisha**

(1) parting the waters of the Jordan River (2Ki 2:13–14)

(2) healing of the water (2:19–22)

(3) bear consumed forty-two youths (2:23–25)

(4) flowing water in the desert (3:15–20)

(5) defeat of Moabites (3:21–25)

(6) the widow's oil (4:1–7)

(7) the barren woman's son (4:8–17)

(8) the woman's dead son revived (4:18–37)

(9) the death taken from the stew (4:38–41)

(10) feeding of the hundred men (4:42–44)

(11) the healing of Naaman (5:1–19a)

(12) the judgment of leprosy on the servant Gehazi (5:19b-27)

(13) the floating axehead (6:1–7)

(14) knowledge of king of Aram's plans (6:8–12)

(15) the blindness and capture of the king of Aram's army (6:13–23)

(16) the lifting of the siege of Samaria (6:24–7:20)

### 3. Joram (Jehoram) (3:1–9:26)

After a brief report on the wickedness of Joram (3:1–3), the writer incorporates a major portion of the story of Elisha into the account of his reign. For the most part, Joram remains in the background, described only as "the king of Israel" throughout these narratives (e.g., 5:6; 6:10). In fulfillment of the word of the Lord spoken by Elijah to his father Ahab (1Ki 21:29), God ultimately brought judgment on the house of Ahab in the death of his son Joram. This came by the hand of Jehu (2Ki 9:24–26), who was specifically chosen as an agent of God's judgment (1Ki 19:16).

### 4. Hazael (8:7–15)

In 1Ki 19:15 the Lord had commanded Elijah to anoint Hazael as king over Aram. Though it is not recorded in the book of Kings, the present text, which records Elisha's journey to Hazael in Damascus, assumes that Elijah did, in fact, anoint him. From Elisha's troubled response to the prospect of Hazael's kingship (2Ki 8:12), it is apparent that Hazael had been anointed to inflict judgment on Israel. In that sense he was like the "adversaries" that the Lord raised up against Solomon (1Ki 11:14, 23) and the Assyrians whom God would use to judge Israel for their idolatry (2Ki 17:7–23). The writer of Kings makes frequent mention of the hardships that Hazael inflicted on Israel and Judah (8:28–29; 9:14–15; 10:32b; 12:17–18; 13:3, 22) until the time of his death (13:24).

### B. Judah 3 (8:16–9:29)

### 1. Jehoram (Joram) (8:16–24)

The attention of the writer now shifts to the kingdom of Judah and the reign of Jehoram, the son of Jehoshaphat. Jehoram married a daughter of Ahab and thus followed the ways of the house of Ahab (8:18). His treachery served as an occasion for the writer to recall God's faithfulness to his promise to David: "for the sake of his servant David, the LORD was not willing to destroy Judah. He had promised to maintain a lamp for David and his descendants forever" (v.19; cf. 2Sa 7:16). This is really the heart of the theological message of the book of Kings: God's faithfulness to the house of David and the hope in the eternal kingdom. One can see that we are not far here from the theology that lies behind later passages of Scriptures such as Da 7:9–14, and much of the NT—the hope of an eternal, Davidic kingdom.

The seemingly insignificant note that in Jehoram's day "Edom rebelled against Judah and set up its own king" (8:20) and that "to this day Edom has been in rebellion against Judah" (v.22) plays an important role in the overall message of the book of Kings. In the Pentateuch, the future king promised to reign over the house of Judah was to be specifically identified by his dominance over Edom (Nu 24:18). The nation of Edom became a symbol of the reign of the messianic king because in the Hebrew language, there is a simple wordplay between "Edom" and the Hebrew word for humankind, "Adam." Thus, the writer here notes that any messianic hopes for the present house of David were quickly fading away with the loss of sovereignty over the kingdom of Edom.

### 2. Ahaziah (8:25–9:29)

Ahaziah, like his father Jehoram, was related to the house of Ahab (8:27), or as the writer reminds us, the house of Omri (v.26; cf. 1Ki 16:21–28). Amid the account of the reign of Ahaziah, the writer of Kings has inserted the narratives that treat Jehu, the son of Jehoshaphat, the son of Nimshi.

## C. Israel 4: Jehu (9:1–10:36)

Jehu, the son of Jehoshaphat, the son of Nimshi, had been singled out as an instrument of God's judgment already in 1Ki 19:15. Now he would carry out that task under the aegis of the prophet Elisha. Thus he was anointed king of Israel with the specific task of destroying the remainder of the house of Ahab (2Ki 9:1–13).

First Jehu killed Joram (9:14–26) and Ahaziah (vv.27–29). Then he went out after Jezebel, the wife of Ahab, and, with the help of the inhabitants of Jezreel, killed her (vv.30–37). With the death of Jezebel the word of the prophet Elijah was fulfilled (v.36; cf. 1Ki 21:23–24). There follows the account of Jehu's total eradication of the house of Ahab, including Ahab's seventy sons in Samaria (2Ki 10:1–10) and all who remained in Jezreel, including "his chief men, his close friends and his priests" (v.11). He traveled through the countryside seeking out and executing any survivors (vv.12–17). Jehu then turned against the priests and the servants of Baal and "destroyed Baal worship in Israel (vv.18–29).

Though recounting these events in graphic detail, the writer takes pains to show that Jehu acted according to the will of the Lord and as the instrument of divine justice against the idolatry of the nation (v.30). Already in the Sinai covenant and in the Law, Moses had taught Israel, both by example (Ex 32:27–28) and by precept (Dt 13:1–18), that idolatry would not be tolerated among God's people.

In spite of Jehu's zeal against idolatry, he did not remove the false worship centers of Bethel and Dan, and hence he continued in "the sins of Jeroboam" (vv.29, 31). For this neglect, God sent an adversary, Hazael, against his kingdom (cf. 1Ki 19:15b; 2Ki 8:7–15). Ironically, it was Hazael whom Elijah anointed along with Jehu as God's instruments of judgment (1Ki 19:17).

## D. Judah 4: Joash (11:1–12:21)

When Ahaziah was killed (9:27), his mother, Athaliah, assumed the throne in Jerusalem, thinking she had killed all possible rivals (11:1–3). However, Joash, the son of Ahaziah, had been hidden away in the temple, and there he remained until he was old enough to rule (vv.3, 21). When Joash reached the necessary age, Jehoiada, a priest at the temple (cf. v.9), secretly executed a plan to make the young crown prince king and thus secure his rightful throne (vv.4–21). This plan was successful, and Athaliah was put to death (vv.15–16). Jehoiada then made a covenant between the Lord and the people, and the temple of Baal, with its priests and its altars, was destroyed (vv.17–18a).

Because of the godly instruction of Jehoiada, the young king "did what was right in the eyes of the LORD" (12:2). As had all the kings who preceded him in Judah, however, Joash failed to remove the "high places" at Bethel and Dan (cf. 10:29; 1Ki 12:25–33); thus he never lived up to the ideal of David in uniting the people in the worship of God at Jerusalem. Joash did, however, devote much attention to the repair and care for the temple, and for that, the writer of Kings gives him high marks (2Ki 12:4–16). Care and concern for the temple in Jerusalem was an integral part of the Davidic covenant (1Sa 7:13). Later biblical writers went so far as to see in this royal responsibility a priestly role for the Davidic king (1Ch 17:14; Zec 6:13). The idea was not new, however, since it was already expressed by David in Ps 110:4, "The LORD has sworn ... 'You are a priest forever, in the order of Melchizedek,'" and this was a central part of the Pentateuch's messianic future (see comment on Ge 14).

Joash was eventually assassinated by two of his officials (2Ki 12:20).

## E. Israel 5 (13:1–25)

### 1. Jehoahaz (13:1–9)

Jehoahaz was the son of Jehu (v.1). Like those before him, he did not remove the high places at Bethel and Dan that Jeroboam had set up (v.2); thus God sent Hazael king of Aram against him (v.3; cf. 8:12; 1Ki 19:15). Jehoahaz, however, repented and sought the Lord, and God sent Israel a deliverer (2Ki 13:4–5). The writer of Kings was not so much interested in the identity of the deliverer as he was in the fact that God sent him. It may be that Jehoash, the son of Jehoahaz, was understood as the deliverer in that he "recaptured from Ben-Hadad son of Hazael the towns he had taken in battle from his father Jehoahaz" (v.25). The writer notes that he did this because "the LORD was gracious to them and had compassion" (v.23). A similar situation occurred for much the same reason during the reign of his son, Jeroboam II (14:25–27). God had compassion on Israel in spite of their sins.

### 2. Jehoash (13:10–25; 14:15–16)

Though in the estimation of the writer of Kings, Jehoash did not rise above the other kings of Israel, several important events occurred during his reign that are recorded in the book. Elisha became ill and died during the reign of Jehoash. The king's sorrowful response to Elisha's illness is a witness to the high regard with which he was held even by a king who did evil in God's eyes. When he saw the deathly ill Elisha, Jehoash exclaimed, "My father! . . . The chariots and horsemen of Israel!" (13:14), apparently with the sense of "You are worth more to Israel than all her chariots and horsemen combined." A testimony to the unusual power of Elisha is found in the brief episode of the dead man disposed of in haste in Elisha's grave (13:20b–21).

The writer interjects a lesson in the midst of his account of Jehoash that sheds much light on the entire history of God's dealings with Israel. Israel was oppressed by Hazael, king of Aram, during the reign of Jehoash, but God was "gracious to them and had compassion" on Israel. Thus he did not let Hazael destroy his people. The writer is clear that God's actions were not motivated by anything Israel had done. It was rather "because of his covenant with Abraham, Isaac and Jacob" (v.23). Thus the writer of Kings reaches back into the earliest sections of the Pentateuch, to the narratives of God's promises to the patriarchs, for his lesson on God's work with his people. In his patience and longsuffering with Israel, God was being faithful to his promises.

## F. Judah 5: Amaziah (14:1–22)

As with most of the kings of Judah, Amaziah did many good things, but he failed to put an end to the false worship centers in Bethel and Dan. Only one king would do this and that was Josiah (23:15), the king prophesied on the day those centers were dedicated (1Ki 13:2).

It is interesting to note that the writer specifically mentions that in his administration of the kingdom, King Amaziah obeyed the "Book of the Law of Moses," quoting Dt 24:16. Amaziah thus approximated in his life the ideal of the kingship as spelled out in Dt 17:18–19. Having mentioned his obedience to the law, the writer then notes that Amaziah defeated the Edomites, another sign that he was approximating the ideal king (see comments on 2Ki 8:16–24).

Amaziah was subsequently defeated by Jehoash, the king of Israel (14:8–14), and fell prey to an internal conspiracy (vv.19–20). If we are to take Jehoash's word for it, Amaziah's downfall came as a result of pride and arrogance (v.10).

## G. Israel 6: Jeroboam II (14:23–29)

Jeroboam II followed in the footsteps of his namesake, Jeroboam the son of Nebat. The prophet Jonah lived during or before his reign and had given a prophecy regarding God's compassion on his people Israel (v.25). God fulfilled the prophecy through Jeroboam II. By inserting these notes about the early work of the prophets, the writer of Kings is preparing the reader for the lesson that will come in ch. 17. When, at last, God rejected Israel and sent them into exile, the writer of Kings assures us that it was only after much patience and compassionate warnings on God's part: "The LORD warned Israel and Judah through all his prophets and seers" (17:13). God had sent Israel a continuous line of prophets to warn the nation of the consequences of their sin and idolatry, but Israel failed to take heed.

## H. Judah 6: Azariah (15:1–7)

Azariah obeyed God but did not remove the false worship places at Bethel and Dan. Azariah was stricken with leprosy in the latter part of his life, which the writer of Kings saw as the result of divine judgment (v.5).

## I. Israel 7 (15:8–31)

Zechariah (vv.8–12) was the fourth generation of the house of Jehu. His assassination at the hand of Shallum was a fulfillment of God's word to Jehu (10:30). As a reward for his father Jehu's obedience to his divine commission (1Ki 19:16–17; 2Ki 10:30), God had allowed Jehu's dynasty to remain four generations. With Zechariah, however, Jehu's dynasty ended.

After Zechariah, the leadership of the northern kingdom began to disintegrate. Shallum (2Ki 15:13–16), Zechariah's assassin, was assassinated by Menahem after only one month (v.14a). Israel endured the hard rule of Menahem (vv.17–22) for ten years. During his reign the king of Assyria, God's ap-

pointed instrument of judgment first came on the scene (v.19). Peace could now only be obtained with the price of silver and the taxation of every Israelite, particularly the wealthy.

With Pekahiah (vv.23–26), Pekah (vv.27–31), and Hoshea (17:1–6), the northern kingdom of Israel came to an end. These kings fared no better than their predecessors in the eyes of the writer of Kings. They continued to support and encourage the false worship of the golden calves at Bethel and Dan. Pekahiah was assassinated by one of his chief officers, Pekah (v.25). In Pekah's day the Assyrian king Tiglath-Pileser captured a major portion of his territory (v.29). Pekah was assassinated by Hoshea, who succeeded him as king (v.30). The account of the fall of Hoshea's kingdom to the Assyrians is given in ch. 17.

## J. Judah 7 (15:32–16:20)

Jotham, the son of Uzziah (or Azariah; cf. 2Ki 15:7), did what was right in the eyes of the Lord—i.e., he obeyed the Law and the word of the prophets (vv.32–38). Like the kings of Judah before him, however, he did not remove the calf images and sanctuaries that Jeroboam had built in the northern kingdom.

Jotham resisted an initial attack on Judah's northern border from Pekah, king of Israel, and the Aramean king Rezin (v.37). After Jotham's death (v.38), Ahaz became king of Judah (16:1–20). During his reign Pekah and Rezin attacked Jerusalem and besieged the city (v.5). Ahaz, a wicked king in the eyes of the writer of Kings (vv.2–4), appealed to the Assyrian king, Tiglath-Pileser, for help (v.7). This king complied and, after being paid off with the silver and gold from the temple at Jerusalem (v.8), he attacked and defeated Damascus (v.9; see also Isa 7:1–8:18).

While in Damascus with Tiglath-Pileser, Ahaz was impressed with a large altar he saw there, and sending a drawing of it back to Jerusalem, he commissioned the building of a similar altar and the reconstruction of the temple to accommodate it (16:10–18). The writer of Kings is curiously quiet about this act, though it is beyond doubt that he considered it a gross violation of the Mosaic Law. On the eve of the fall of the northern kingdom, the kingdom of Judah was beginning to pick up where Jeroboam left off—corrupting the true worship of God as prescribed in the Law. Instead of a foreign altar at Bethel and Dan, Ahaz now put a foreign one within the Jerusalem temple itself.

### K. Israel 8 (17:1–41)

The last king to reign in Israel was Hoshea (vv.1–6), who did evil in God's sight, "but not like the kings of Israel who preceded him" (v.2). This perhaps means that the actions of kings like Pekahiah and Pekah who preceded Hoshea had reached such depths that it was impossible to sink any lower. To leave the impression that Hoshea did something worse than, or just as bad as, them would diminish the evil of their actions.

The fall of the northern kingdom came during the reign of Hoshea (vv.7–41). A brief description of the event is given in vv.3–6, followed by the writer's lengthy lesson on its cause (vv.7–23) and aftermath (vv.24–41).

Caught in a political crossfire between Assyria and Egypt, Hoshea was attacked and imprisoned by the new king of Assyria, Shalmaneser V (vv.3–4). After a long siege of Israel's capital city, Samaria, and a wholesale invasion of the land, the Assyrians captured the city and sent the Israelites living in the northern kingdom into exile. The writer of Kings does not mention the name of the Assyrian king at the time of the invasion, but it was probably Sargon II who, in 722 B.C., had replaced Shalmaneser V.

For the writer of the book of Kings there was only one explanation for this event: "All this took place because the Israelites had sinned against the LORD their God, who had brought them up out of Egypt" (v.7). After enumerating some of the blatant sins that Israel had repeatedly committed (vv.8–12), the writer concludes with a short summary: Israel (and Judah) had disobeyed the words of their prophets and had thus broken the Mosaic Law (v.13). At the heart of their problem, he adds, was their lack of faith: "They would not listen and were as stiff-necked as their fathers, who did not believe [NIV, trust] in the LORD their God" (v.14). This is then followed by a litany of Israel's past failures, all of which stemmed from their lack of trust in God (vv.15–17). The "great sin" (v.21) of both Israel and Judah was their continuing to follow the sin of Jeroboam, who established false centers of worship at Bethel and Dan in opposition to God's command to worship him in Jerusalem (vv.18–23; cf. Dt 12; 2Sa 7).

The Assyrians resettled the northern kingdom with people from other parts of their empire (v.24). The writer of Kings is aghast at the religious syncretism of the resettled population (vv.25–34a). His purpose, however, was not to denigrate this new group of settlers, who he suggests could not have known any better (e.g., v.27), but rather to drive a lesson home to his readers, who were familiar with the Scriptures and the law of God (vv.34b–41).

## II. Judah After the End of the Northern Kingdom (18:1–25:30)

### A. Hezekiah (18:1–20:21)

Hezekiah is given high marks by the writer of Kings (18:1–8). He was king of Judah during the time the Assyrians attacked and deported the northern kingdom (vv.9–12). During his reign, the Assyrians also invaded the land of Judah and captured many cities (v.13), threatening even to lay siege to Jerusalem (18:14–19:34). God intervened and the Assyrians were defeated (19:35–37). The story of Hezekiah's courage and trust in God serves as a backdrop for the writer's central message.

At first Hezekiah seemed ready to acquiesce to the demands of the Assyrians (18:14–16). The messengers of the king of Assyria, however, began to raise the stakes in front of all the people. Not only did they want a complete capitulation of the city of Jerusalem, but they presented their demands as an affront to Judah's trust in God ("On whom are you depending, that you rebel against me?" v.20) and the word of their prophets ("The LORD himself told me to march against this country and destroy it," v.25). The Assyrian messengers then shouted in Hebrew to the people of the city, "Do not let Hezekiah persuade you to trust in the LORD" (v.30). Finally they pitted themselves against God himself, "Has the god of any nation ever delivered his land from the hand of the king of Assyria? . . . How then can the LORD deliver Jerusalem from my hand?" (vv.33–35).

Hezekiah's response is paradigmatic of the leadership God desired for his people. He went immediately to the temple of the Lord and sent for the prophet Isaiah (19:1–2). Isaiah's word to the king was one of trust in God and assurance of his deliverance (vv.5–7). In the midst of his speech, Isaiah foretold the fate God had in store for the king of Assyria (v.7): he would "return to his own country, and there I will have him cut down with the sword" (v.7); this was fulfilled at the close of the narrative (vv.35–37).

The writer concludes his account with a report of Hezekiah's prayer (vv.14–19) and God's answer through the prophet Isaiah (vv.20–34). In both of these the central themes of the book of Kings find expression. God would

deliver his people if they turned to him in trust (vv.19a, 29–34), and he would destroy all those who turned away from him and followed the ways of the nations (vv.17–18, 27–28). God's plans for blessing all the nations would be accomplished (vv.19b, 25–26, 34b).

In the story of Hezekiah's illness (20:1–11), the writer of Kings shows that God hears the prayers of the righteous and gives them years of blessing if they call on him. The prophet first said to the king, "You will not recover" (v.1b), but after Isaiah's prayer, the Lord told him to go back to Hezekiah and tell him, "I have heard your prayer and seen your tears; I will heal you" (v.5). Surely, from the viewpoint of the writer, God's words are directed as much to the reader as they are to Isaiah.

God's last words to Hezekiah, however, portended a divine judgment on the house of David that lay in the future. Hezekiah's visit by the Babylonian envoys (vv.12–18) provided an apt setting for a preview of the events that lay just ahead for the nation of Judah. Judah would go into captivity in Babylon (vv.16–18). Hezekiah replied to Isaiah's prophecy by saying, "The word of the LORD you have spoken is good. . . . Will there not be peace and security in my lifetime?" (v.19). Such a positive, and ostensively selfish, response to Isaiah's word of judgment is difficult to gauge in light of what Hezekiah had said and done earlier in the narrative. These words do not appear as those of one who had risked life and property for God's people and God's honor. In light of this larger context, then, we should probably understand Hezekiah to mean that it was good there would be continued peace in his days so that all might see how God rewarded faithfulness. Hezekiah was thus not speaking of the good that such a word held for him personally, but for the people of God, giving them a lesson from the time of peace in that day.

### B. Manasseh (21:1–18)

The last days of Judah have come. Manasseh led the people in such apostasy (vv.2–11) that the Lord determined to bring destruction and exile on Judah and Jerusalem (vv.12–16). The writer of Kings makes it clear that the basis of God's complaint against Judah was their failure to keep the Law of Moses (vv.8–9). A measure of the severity of God's anger against Manasseh can be seen in that when Judah later repented and put away their idolatry during the time of Josiah (chs. 22–23), God did "not turn away from the heat of his fierce anger, which burned against Judah because of all that Manasseh had done to provoke him to anger" (23:26).

### C. Amon (21:19–26)

Amon was a carbon copy of his father Manasseh. He fell victim to a conspiracy and assassination (v.23) after only two years on the throne (v.19).

### D. Josiah (22:1–23:30)

Josiah was a good king in the eyes of the writer of the book of Kings (22:1–2). As such, he was actively engaged in the upkeep and repair of the temple (vv.3–7). In the process of cleaning the temple, the high priest, Hilkiah, found "the Book of the Law" (v.8). This book was apparently a copy, or the copy, of what we now have as the Pentateuch (cf. v.25). When the book was brought before the king and read, it caused an instant revival (vv.9–11). The king set out at once to obey the words written in the book and to avert the anger of the Lord so clearly spelled out in it (vv.12–13). The first thing he did was to send for a prophet, Huldah the prophetess (v.14), to inquire of the meaning of what he had read in the book. Huldah replied first that the Lord was about "to bring disaster on this place and its people, according to everything written in the book" (v.16). She then added that the Lord had heard and seen the repentance of Josiah and thus judgment would not come in his days (vv.18–20).

Josiah then read the "Book of the Covenant" (Ex 24:7) before all the people (23:1–2), and they renewed their covenant with the Lord (v.3). The temple was cleaned out, all foreign objects of worship were burned outside Jerusalem, and the ashes taken to Bethel (v.4). All forms of pagan religion were removed from Jerusalem (vv.5–7). Josiah then sent word throughout his kingdom that all pagan worship was to be totally eradicated (vv.8–20). In the process of clearing away the foreign altars, Josiah came to Bethel and "even that altar and high place he demolished" (v.15). He defiled these altars with the bones of the nearby tombs, just as the man of God had foretold (v.16; cf. 1Ki 13:2). With this act, Josiah distinguished himself from all other kings in Israel and Judah. He had destroyed the altar set up by Jeroboam at Bethel. Josiah also led the people in the celebration of the Passover (2Ki 23:21–23) and followed all the commandments of the "Law of Moses" (vv.24–25; cf. Jos 1:7).

As good as Josiah's reform was, it came too late. The base sins of the people during the time of Manasseh had provoked the Lord to such anger against Judah that the coming exile foretold by Isaiah (20:16–18) could not be averted (23:26–27). Josiah himself was suddenly taken from the scene in the midst of the battle with the Egyptian pharaoh Neco (23:29–30).

### E. The Last Kings of Judah (23:36–25:7)

Jehoahaz (23:31–35) reigned as king in Judah only three months. He was displaced and imprisoned by the Egyptian pharaoh Neco. The pharaoh appointed Eliakim, son of Josiah, as king, changing his name to Jehoiakim (23:36–24:7). During the riegn of Jehoiakim's, the Babylonian king Nebuchadnezzar first invaded Judah (24:1). The Lord also sent other raiders—

Babylonian, Aramean, Moabite, and Ammonite—against Judah during his reign "because of the sins of Manasseh" (vv.2–4). From the viewpoint of the writer of Kings, these things were happening to Judah just as the prophets had long ago foretold (v.3).

Though Jehoiakim's son, Jehoiachin, reigned in Jerusalem only three months (24:8–25:30), he continued as "king of Judah" well into the Babylonian captivity (25:27–30). Jehoiachin surrendered Jerusalem to Nebuchadnezzar and his army (24:10–12a) and was taken prisoner to Babylon (vv.12b, 15). Nebuchadnezzar removed the royal treasures and temple artifacts to Babylon, along with all but the poorest inhabitants of the city. He then made Mattaniah, Jehoiachin's uncle, king in Judah, changing his name to Zedekiah (v.17). Though by now the reader of this book will surely know it, the writer attaches a brief note to this account: "It was because of the LORD's anger that all this happened to Jerusalem and Judah, and in the end he thrust them from his presence" (v.20).

### F. Exile to Babylon (24:18–25:26)

The last days of the kingdom are recounted almost matter of factly. During the reign of Zedekiah (24:18–25:7), Nebuchadnezzar returned to plunder and destroy Jerusalem (25:1–17). The temple and the royal palace were burnt (v.9), the walls were broken down (v.10), and the people were taken into exile (v.11). All of the valuable utensils and temple equipment were taken to Babylon, including the precious metals from the temple decor (vv.16–17). The chief priest and the leading men of the city were executed (vv.18–21).

Nebuchadnezzar appointed Gedaliah (vv.22–25) as governor over the people who remained in Judah, but he was quickly assassinated (v.25). Fearing Babylonian reprisals, those who had remained in the land fled to Egypt (v.26).

### G. Epilogue (25:27–30)

For the writer of the book of Kings, the destruction and judgment of the Exile was not the last word. There was still hope in God's promises to the house of David because it was an eternal promise (2Sa 7:16). Thus, at the close of this book, he turns to the future, noting that the house of David was not only still intact but flourishing in the house of the king of Babylon. Jehoiachin, the heir to the throne of David and the promises of God, was sitting on "a seat of honor higher than those of the other kings who were with him in Babylon" (v.28). Clearly this was meant to inspire hope in God's faithfulness to his promises. In a similar manner, the prophet Amos closes his book of God's judgment on Israel and Judah with a reminder that after the judgment of exile, the fallen house of David would be restored and would once again possess the remnant of Edom and all the nations (Am 9:11–12). The hope of the coming Messiah filled the air.

# 1 Chronicles

## 1. Introduction

The earliest title known for the books of Chronicles is "The Things Left Behind." This seems to mean simply that these books contained material not included in the other historical books. Very early, that title was also taken more positively to mean that the books contained important summaries of other biblical books. They were a condensed version of the rest of the OT historical books.

But why retell the same events? There are two basic answers to that question. (1) The writer wanted to give his readers another version of those events. Anyone who has both witnessed an event and read a news report of it knows how much the meaning and sense of that event lies in the reporting. By providing a second picture of Israel's history, therefore, a fuller appreciation and understanding of those events is given by the Chronicler. In that respect, his purpose can be compared with the four gospels in the NT. Each gospel gives a picture of Jesus Christ. Each has its point of view and presents the life and teachings of Jesus from that perspective. The result of the four gospels is a deeper and richer picture of Jesus.

(2) The author intended not simply to retell these events but to explain and expound on their meaning in the context of Israel's history. These two books form a sort of commentary on the other historical books.

This message of Chronicles is "messianic"; i.e., it looks forward to the coming King who will rule over God's people forever. In the historical books, the Psalms, and the Prophets, the term *Messiah* stands for the Davidic King. It is the Messiah, the Christ, the Son of David, who will bring peace to his own people and blessing to all people. In the NT this King's name is revealed as Jesus.

To their own generation, the books of Chronicles were a vivid reminder of the hope that rested in the faithfulness of God. They were reminders that the Lord had made a promise to the world and to the house of David. The promise was of peace and prosperity, and the channel of the fulfillment of the promise was the covenant people of God, Israel. The books, in that setting, were a call for trust and obedience on the part of God's people (see 2Ch 7:14).

## I. Names and Genealogies (1:1–10:14)

### A. The Lineage of David (1:1–3:24)

The writer begins his work with an introduction to the house of David. The use of genealogical lists to set the stage of historical narrative is well known in both the OT (Genesis) and the NT (Matthew and Luke). Just as Luke's gospel traces the lineage of Jesus (the Son of David) back to Adam (Lk 3:38), so also the writer traces David's lineage to Adam.

One of the overarching themes of 1 and 2 Chronicles is that the Davidic kingship is to be the instrument of God's promised salvation and blessing. In these genealogies the writer seems especially concerned to show that this salvation and blessing is not just for God's people, Israel, but also for all humankind. That is shown throughout these books in a number of ways. Here, at the outset, it is made clear that the house of David is of the house of Abraham, a descendant of Adam. By working through the descendants of David, God is reaching to the entire human race. By recognizing the house of David as also of the lineage of Adam, the Chronicler is very close in his thinking to the apostle Paul, who saw in Jesus Christ "the last Adam" (1Co 15:45).

## B. The House of Israel (4:1–7:40)

Having placed the line of David firmly within the context of the families of humankind, the author now begins to mark off the line of promise. The line of the promise is that elect nation through whom God intended to bring blessing and salvation to a lost world. He takes great pains to tell us that the nation is Israel, the descendants of the sons of Jacob.

### 1. The family of Judah (4:1–23)

The list of the sons of Israel begins with the family of Judah. According to the prophecy of his father Israel (Ge 49:8–12), Judah was to be the leader of the families of Israel, and the promised blessing was to come to Israel and the nations through that family. With that promise in mind, the Chronicler begins his enumeration of the household of Israel. The thought that the Davidic dynasty represents that chosen leadership is a central theme in the books of Chronicles. It should not go by without notice that the central themes of these books are being prepared in these opening genealogies. The stage is being set, and the actors in the great drama to follow are given their proper introduction.

### 2. The family of Simeon (4:24–43)

Simeon and his descendants come next in the list, probably because the family of Simeon shared the territory allotted to the family of Judah (Jos 19:9).

### 3. The families of the Transjordan: Reuben, Gad, and the half-tribe of Manasseh (5:1–16)

The list of names is expanded to give a short history of the families that settled along the eastern banks of the Jordan. When the Israelites settled in the land of Canaan, three families remained on the east side of the Jordan: the families of Reuben, Gad, and half of the family of Manasseh (Nu 32; Jos 13:8–33).

Reuben, the firstborn, had forfeited his birthright through immorality (Ge 35:22; 49:4). Possession of the birthright meant preeminence among the families. The sons of Joseph, Ephraim and Manasseh, now enjoyed that privilege. In spite of that right of the firstborn, however, it was from the house of Judah, the family of David, that the true leader of the sons of Israel was to come (1Ch 5:1–2).

Chapter 5 ends with another reminder of God's faithfulness (5:25–26). This time, however, the result is not salvation but judgment: the exile of the families of Reuben, Gad, and the half-tribe of Manasseh. God's faithfulness cuts both ways. He is gracious and forgiving to those who put their trust in him; but those who forsake him to follow other gods he will punish. God stirred up the heart of the Assyrian king Tilgath-Pileser, and he carried the Transjordanian tribes into exile. When God did that, he was only acting out of faithfulness to his covenant with Israel. According to the covenant, trust would bring blessing, but disobedience would bring exile (Dt 28).

### 4. The family of Levi (6:1–81)

The list of the names of the family of Levi is carefully constructed. Its purpose is to make clear the line of descent of the priests and Levites. The list begins with the levitical line that traces its descent from Aaron, the first priest (6:1–15). The Chronicler begins with this line because only those Levites (descendants of Levi) who were descended from Aaron could legitimately do the work of a priest at the temple (6:49; Nu 3:5–38) and could carry out the duties of the sacrificial system. The importance of that distinction is seen after the rebuilding of the temple during the return from exile. If a priest could not establish that he was a descendant of Aaron, he could not serve in the new temple as a priest (Ne 7:63–65).

The next section, the list of the descendants of Levi, is a general enumeration of the levitical family (vv.16–53). The purpose of this list may be seen from the descendants of Levi who are selected and emphasized: Samuel, Heman, Asaph, and Ethan. What do these "Levites" have in common? Elsewhere we know that these men and their descendants were the prophets who served God at the temple (1Sa 3:21; 1Ch 25:1). They are the counterparts of the priests. Together with the priests, those prophets and their descendants maintained the relationship and fellowship between God and Israel at the temple. Along with the Davidic king, those prophets and priests provided the basis of God's rule among his people; they were the basis of the kingdom of God.

The Chronicler's interest in the family of Levi includes not only the physical lineage of the descendants, but also the geographical borders of their inheritance (vv.54–81). God's kingdom was a place as well as an exercise of power. God ruled within a realm, the land of promise. His rule, however, was not limited to that realm (see 2Ch 6:18).

## 5. The remaining families of Israel (7:1–44)

The Chronicler ends his genealogical and historical survey of the families of Israel by tracing briefly the descendants of Issachar, Benjamin, Naphtali, Manasseh, Ephraim, and Asher.

Two families are omitted from that list: those of Dan (Ge 30:1–6) and Zebulun (Ge 30:19–20). Those omissions are not without purpose. The writer is concerned to show that the house of Israel still consists of the twelve families of the sons of Jacob. Since he has counted the half-tribe of Manasseh as a complete family (5:23–24) and has counted the Levites as part of the twelve families (6:1– 81), the omission of Dan and Zebulun is required to maintain the number twelve.

## C. The House of Saul (8:1–9:44)

The last list of names serves as a transition into the first narrative section, the death of Saul (10:1–14). Continuing the genealogical style, the Chronicler prepares the way for the opening of his narrative by giving the lineage of Israel's first king, Saul (8:1–40). What does the last list of names tell about Saul? For what purpose have those names been included? The answer lies in the way the lists of names are arranged in chs. 8 and 9. In both chapters, those "who lived in Jerusalem" (8:28; 9:34) are distinguished from those who lived in Gibeon (8:29; 9:35). The purpose of that distinction is to show that Saul was from that part of the family of Benjamin that was from Gibeon, not Jerusalem. There were Benjamites who lived in Jerusalem, but Saul was not of that group.

Those two cities, Gibeon and Jerusalem, were important centers. Jerusalem was the city of David. It was also Zion, the place where God's temple had been built. It was the city where Israel met with God and was the center of all God's blessing and salvation (2Ch 6:6). Gibeon was where the tabernacle of the Lord was kept. There Zadok the high priest served the Lord, and there the musicians Heman and Jeduthun sang praises to the Lord, while the burnt offerings were being sacrificed (1Ch 16:39–41). Gibeon was an important place of worship for Israel, and even Solomon went there on one occasion to worship (2Ch 1:3–6).

Gibeon, however, was not God's chosen place. Gibeon was chosen by Israel as the place where the tabernacle could be kept. But God had chosen Jerusalem as the place where his name would dwell (2Ch 6:6). Not only was Jerusalem God's choice, but so was the house of David. Jerusalem and David are the two components of God's plan of salvation and blessing in the books of Chronicles; Saul and Gibeon are not.

By drawing the line connecting Gibeon and Saul, the way is prepared for the story of Saul that follows. Saul and Gibeon were chosen by Israel. Although God approved of both, neither succeeded in gaining a central place in his plan of salvation. God's plan must be carried out by God's people in God's way and by God's choice. That way was David and Jerusalem.

## D. The Death of Saul (10:1–14)

Saul was Israel's first king. He was anointed by Samuel (1Sa 10:1) and fought valiantly against the Philistines and other enemies of God's people. Saul's kingship, however, ended in defeat as he proved to be a king not worthy to lead God's people (1Sa 13:13–14). Because the house of Saul was not God's chosen instrument of salvation, the Chronicler is interested only in the last and most significant event in Saul's reign as king: the defeat of Saul and his army by the Philistines at Gilboa. The account is almost a verbatim report of Saul's defeat in 1Sa 31.

An important recurring lesson in the books of Samuel and the books of Chronicles is the importance of the leaders of God's people to follow the word of the Lord. Leadership is serious business. There is no room for only partial obedience.

## II. David (11:1–29:30)

David is a central figure in 1 and 2 Chronicles. The theme of salvation and blessing was personified in his reign over Israel. As a result, David became the standard by which all future kings were measured. A good king was one who did "just as his father David had done" (2Ch 29:2). Moreover, David was the king who most epitomized the promised Messiah. For many of the biblical writers, to talk of David was to talk of the Messiah (e.g., Eze 35:23–24). Judging from some of his own psalms (e.g., Ps. 22), David even entertained that view about himself. Such a view of

David seems also to have been the viewpoint of the Chronicler. As he writes about David and evaluates later kings by the standards of David, he has in mind not just the David who was king, but also the "David" that would yet be king, the Messiah. In that sense much of the perspective of the books of Chronicles is messianic. They look forward with anticipation to the coming King who will bring in God's final salvation and blessing.

## A. David Becomes King Over Israel (11:1–3)

It was a foregone conclusion that David would be king. His struggle to rise to power and the setback under the reign of King Saul that loom so large in 1 Samuel are passed over, except for a simple comment from those who had gathered to make David king (see v.2).

The account of David's anointing at Hebron contains only one addition to the account in 2Sa 5:1–3. In support of his emphasis on the power of God in bringing about his plans, the writer adds the comment that everything happened "as the LORD had promised through Samuel" (v.3). By that comment we see the real cause of David's anointing. His kingship was a fulfillment of the words of Samuel the prophet. The events of Israel's history—the death of Saul, the reign of David and Solomon, and the downfall of the kingdom—were not merely the result of the political, economic, and social conditions of the day. They owed their cause to the acts of God in the history of his people. God was working in the history of that people and in the lives of its leaders. He revealed the meaning of that history to his prophets, so that when his words came to pass, the people could see the plan of God. This view toward the events is the same as that of the prophet Amos: "Surely the Sovereign LORD does nothing without revealing his plan to his servants the prophets" (Am 3:7).

David's kingship found confirmation in three ways: (1) the consent of God's people (vv.2–3); (2) the word of the prophet Samuel; and (3) the victories he received from the hand of God.

## B. The Capture of Jerusalem (11:4–8)

The account of David's capture of Jerusalem is brief. With David in possession of Jerusalem, the kingdom was given a centrally located capital with the best natural defenses in the area. Mount Zion, the city of David, became a citadel that symbolized God's eternal care and protection of his people. Psalmists often sang the praises of God and his holy city (e.g., Ps 48:1–3).

## C. David's Mighty Men (11:9–12:40)

A person is known by the company he or she keeps. That is the idea behind the enumeration of the mighty men who surrounded David and aided his establishment of the kingship. The Chronicler has already described the mighty deed of David's commander, Joab. Now he turns to describe David's army. The list of mighty men is given in three sections: the chiefs among David's men (11:10–25); the mighty men in David's army (11:26–47); and the mighty men who joined David in Ziklag, while he was still fleeing Saul (12:1–40).

The point of the detailed enumeration of the names and exploits of those men is to show that David was a leader who had gained the full confidence and support of the best men in Israel. Those were men who had received the medal of honor in service to David and his kingdom.

The Chronicler has selected an interesting episode that serves to demonstrate why David attracted the loyalty of those men (11:15–19). When three men, at the risk of their own lives, broke through enemy lines to draw water from a well for David, David showed remarkable sensitivity to dangers his men faced in battle. Pouring the water out as an offering to the Lord, David said, "God forbid that I should do this! . . . Should I drink the blood of these men who went at the risk of their lives?" (11:19). David cares sincerely for those entrusted to his care.

The list of mighty men who came to David at Ziklag is given only in 12:1–40. There are several points that seem to be emphasized by the inclusion of that list. (1) The men who joined David and supported his kingship were from "all Israel." (2) The number of the men following David was very large (12:22). (3) That large number represented an even larger group of kinsmen who stayed behind but gave their full support to those who went to join David (12:39–40). Indeed, there was great joy in Israel over the leadership of David and over the support that the people expressed for David. (4) Even relatives of Saul came out to join David (12:1–2, 16, 29). (5) The support given to David was not merely military assistance. The Chronicler states explicitly why those men joined David: "to turn Saul's kingdom over to him, as the LORD had said" (12:23). Through those mighty men God was at work fulfilling the word he had spoken about David by the prophet Samuel (1Sa 16:12).

## D. David and the Ark of the Covenant (13:1–16:43)

The Ark of the Covenant plays a central role in these chapters. The ark was a wooden chest overlaid with gold. It was handcrafted by Israelite artisans during the period of desert wanderings. The pattern for building the ark was given to Moses at Mount Sinai, and it became one of the most important components of Israel's worship (Ex 25:9–22). By means of the ark, the invisible presence of the God of the covenant was visualized. The ark was no mere symbol of God's presence. It was the place where God had chosen to center his presence among his people (Ex 25:22).

The Chronicler's concern with the whereabouts of the ark during the reign of David is a reflection of the importance that the Ark of the Covenant held for Israel. The first official duties of David in 1 Chronicles concern the care for the ark. The ark had been captured by the Philistines (1Sa 4:11) but had subsequently been returned to Israel and was being kept in the house of Abinadab in the city of Kiriath Jearim (1Sa 7:1).

David's desire to bring the ark to Jerusalem to be near the center of God's people shows his concern for God's presence to be with his people and in his kingdom. David had taken seriously the promise of the covenant God to dwell among his people (Ex 19:3–6; 25:8). He also had seen the need of the people to reestablish their relationship with God. They had not sought the ark of God in the days of Saul (1Ch 13:3), and David's concern was that God's people again seek the Lord at the ark, which meant to come before God at the ark and pray (2Ch 6:19–21).

The account of the movement of the ark to Jerusalem is given in stages. Each stage contributes to the lesson intended for the reader.

## 1. Removing the ark from Kiriath Jearim (13:1–14)

The first stage of David's moving the ark to Jerusalem teaches an awesome lesson: the seriousness and reality of God's holy presence among his people. That presence was not, and is not, to be taken lightly. God had graciously promised to be in the midst of his people. His presence was real and was not to be treated as merely symbolic. God's holiness can never be treated with mere empty ritualism.

In the Pentateuch, God had instructed Israel how to respond appropriately to his presence (Ex 25–31). Much of that instruction consisted in performing special acts at special times and places. There was always the danger that by performing those actions an empty ritual would replace a true respect for God's presence. The Chronicler, like many of the prophets, is particularly concerned to warn the people against taking those sacred actions and holy objects lightly. Here in ch. 13 he reminds readers that the ark is the ark of God the Lord, "who is enthroned between the cherubim—the ark that is called by the Name" (v.6).

There was much celebration before the ark as David and the people moved it along the hilly roadways to Jerusalem (v.8). However, all was not well. God's word was not obeyed. The joy was there, the excitement was there, the music and celebration were great, but God's presence was not being properly acknowledged. All the music and singing were a hollow substitute for an attitude of deep respect for the presence of God. The people had carried the ark of God on a cart pulled by oxen (vv.7, 9). That may have been a way suitable for the Philistines to carry the ark (1Sa 6:7), but God had instructed Israel to carry it in a very specific and different manner: the Levites (sons of Kohath) were to carry the ark with the "carrying poles" inserted in the rings on either side of the ark, so that no one would touch the holy objects and die (Nu 4:15).

It was the failure to be faithful in that little matter that led to the great tragedy in vv.9–10, the death of Uzzah as he touched the ark when the oxen stumbled. That event took its sudden, tragic turn while the people were rejoicing over the return of the ark. Things happened so unexpectedly that David responded in anger and fear, not knowing whether to carry on or to postpone moving the ark. Having decided out of apparent desperation for the latter option, he left it at the home of Obed-Edom, along the way to Jerusalem.

Almost as suddenly as it had come, the perplexing tragedy of this account ends. The story concludes with one of the central themes of salvation in the books of Chronicles: the blessing of the Lord—in this case on the family of Obed-Edom (v.14).

## 2. Restoring fellowship with God (14:1–17)

Not only had the Lord restored the blessing of his presence at the ark in the house of Obed-Edom (13:14), but David's kingdom also was again experiencing God's blessing. The Chronicler singles out three events from David's life to show that the Lord was blessing his kingdom. These events in ch. 14 are to be read as a direct consequence of David's taking proper care for the ark of God. Blessing from God follows obedience to God's Word.

(1) The Chronicler recounts the tribute paid to David by the surrounding nations. Hiram, king of Tyre, sent messengers bearing materials and workmen who were to build a house for David. To David that was a sign that the Lord was establishing David's kingdom (vv.1–2). The Lord had made David's house great.

(2) The Chronicler takes up the theme of David's sons and daughters (vv.3–7). In a manner reminiscent of the godly men in the early chapters of Genesis, the writer shows God's blessing on David by the enumeration of the births of his children. We can almost hear the words of Genesis echoing in the account of David's family: "God blessed them and said to them, 'Be fruitful and increase in number'" (Ge 1:28).

(3) David continued being victorious over the enemies of God's people, the Philistines (vv.8–17). By the hand of the Lord, he defeated them, and "David's fame spread throughout every land, and the LORD made all the nations fear him" (v 17)

In the account of the ark, two things are emphasized—God's presence and God's power. Both must be taken seri-

ously if one is to reckon with the living God. The overall purpose in the Chronicler's stressing just those two points in connection with the Ark of the Covenant is that the ark marked the point of prayer and communion between God and Israel (cf. 2Ch 6:1–42). God's presence and God's power give sense to prayer and make it effective. The Chronicler, then, is laying serious theological groundwork here by stressing the importance of obedience in fellowship and the importance of God's presence and power in prayer.

## 3. The ark rests in Jerusalem (15:1–16:43)

With the events of chs. 13 and 14, David had learned many important lessons. He now returns to his original intentions of moving the ark to Jerusalem and restoring the presence of God to its rightful place—in the midst of God's people. Chapters 15 and 16 now stress three important points.

(1) The centrality of the priests and the Levites (15:1–15). David had learned that the proper way to approach God in fellowship and worship was in the manner prescribed by God himself. He prepared a place for the ark of God and there set up a tent (v.1). David was following the instruction that God had given to Moses at Mount Sinai (Ex 26:7ff.). He then commanded that only the Levites were to carry the ark, and that they were to carry it in the prescribed way (vv.2–15). The importance of that point is shown by the detail supplied in these verses. To show that his heart was in the right place, David carried out God's will to the letter. The key phrases here are "in the prescribed way" (v.13) and "as Moses had commanded in accordance with the word of the LORD" (v.15).

(2) The joy of God's presence (15:16–16:6). The description of David's preparation for worship in 15:16–29 clearly shows the extent of joy and praise he intended for his newly

established center for worship. In today's categories, David was providing a full orchestra and choir. What better description of worship could be given than that in 15:16—"to sing joyful songs"?

(3) *Telling God's glory among the nations* (16:7–43). As part of the joy of worshiping in God's presence, a hymn was sung on the day of dedication of the ark. The hymn is, in fact, a medley of hymns from the book of Psalms and is so arranged to give emphasis to one central idea: the intended result of Israel's worship of God is the salvation of the nations so that they, too, may worship God at his temple. Israel's worship was evangelical: it was to include all people of all lands (cf. Zec 2:10–11).

The hymn begins, as most hymns, with a call to worship (vv.8–13). It is especially striking that the hymn turns almost immediately to the theme of the nations' (Gentiles') participation in that worship: "Make known among the nations what he has done" (v.8b). The terminology used here calls to mind the kind of worship seen in the stories of Abraham where, having built an altar in the land of Canaan among its inhabitants, he "called on the name of the LORD" (Ge 12:8).

After the call to worship, the hymn extols the greatness and the grace of God (vv.14–22). The theme of God's grace is recalled in the remembrance of his covenant with Abraham. When Israel was only a small family moving from nation to nation, God promised to give them the land of Canaan and protected them among the nations (see especially vv.21b–22). After a renewed call to worship (vv.23–24), the hymn extols the greatness of God over the vain idols of the nations (vv.25–26) and recalls the power and glory of God, the Creator (vv.27–30). The hymn ends with a call to all creation to turn to the Lord in trust and obedience because he

is coming in judgment and in salvation (vv.31–36).

It is significant for the message of the Chronicler that he recounts this hymn as the exemplary hymn of the dedication of the ark. He shows that in David's day, Israel's worship was directed outward toward the nations as well as upward toward God, as it had been in the time of Abraham and would be in the days of the Messiah (see Isa 12:1–6).

## E. David and the Promise (17:1–29:30)

In these chapters we find the single most important event in the life of David—God's covenant promise to give him an eternal kingdom. By sheer repetition (three times), the point is made clear that the house of David is God's chosen vehicle for bringing salvation to the nations. The Messiah will be a son of David.

### 1. The first account of God's promise to David (17:1–21:30)

There are several important components to the promise that God makes to David in this first account of the promise (the Davidic covenant). The focus is clearly on those features of the promises that relate to David. The Chronicler throws light on the fulfillment of the specific promises to David in his own lifetime. In other respects, however, the promises concern a descendant who will do for Israel far more than his father David. By showing God's faithfulness in his promises to David, the Chronicler is giving a basis for trust in God's faithfulness concerning the future Son of David, the Messiah, who is in the center of the message of hope.

First Chronicles 17:8–9 helps to show the outline that follows the first account. In v.8 God promises to give victory to David from all his enemies, so the account of David's victories is recorded in chs. 18–20. In v.9 God promises that through David he will establish a place for his people, Israel. As the following verses and Dt 12:1–11 make clear, the Lord has in mind primarily a place for his temple. Thus, ch. 21 records the events leading up to the selection of the site for the temple—the threshing floor of Ornan.

(1) *The promise* (17:1–15). When David determined to build God a permanent house (temple), his plans had to undergo some modification. David could not build the house; David's descendant, a later king, would build the house. What was so wrong with David? Why could he not build the temple? The answer comes from God's reply to David's plan: "I have never had need of a house in which to dwell. From the earliest times a simple tent for my dwelling has been all I asked for. Did I ever ask any of my leaders to make me a permanent house? When I want a house, I'll choose who will build it for me" (vv.5–6, author's paraphrase). In other words, as Moses had said in Dt 12:5, God alone must choose the place for his dwelling.

After rejecting David's plan to build the temple, God announced his own plan (vv.11–15): a son of David, a Davidic king whom God himself would choose, would build God's house, the temple. When this son came, he would not only build God's house, he would be ruler of a kingdom established by God forever—God's eternal kingdom.

To see the importance of this promise it is necessary to contrast this passage with 2Sa 7:1–17. In that account, the author is interested in the Messiah who will rule over God's eternal kingdom, but he is also interested in the short-range implications of God's promise, especially as it concerns Solomon. Solomon was David's son, he built the temple, and he was a man of peace. To what extent does Solomon figure in this promise of an eternal King to follow David? The rest of 2 Samuel and the book of Kings is an attempt to answer that question. The answer is that

the immediate descendants of David, Solomon through the last king before the Exile, Zedekiah, did not fulfill the promise. Had the promise rested in them alone, Israel's hope would have led to despair. The author of 2 Samuel prepared his readers for that inevitable conclusion by including the words of God to David, "When he does wrong, I will punish him with the rod of men, with floggings inflicted by men" (2Sa 7:14b). Those words clearly imply that the immediate descendant of David would not measure up to the standards of the One ultimately envisioned in that promise. As God later makes clear, the promise to David had attached to it the obligation of obedience (see 1Ki 6:11–12). Prophets like Isaiah made it clear that, in spite of the failure of the descendants of David, God's promise would still be fulfilled in the son of David who was to come (see Isa 9:6).

It is from that prophetic perspective of hope that the Chronicler draws out the significance of God's promise to David—not overlooking the role of Solomon and the other Davidic kings in that promise, but looking beyond them to the future fulfillment. The Chronicler has his mind set, not on the disobedient Davidic kings that led his people to exile, but on him who said, "My food . . . is to do the will of him who sent me and to finish his work" (Jn 4:34).

(2) *David's response* (17:16–27). In David's response to God's promise, two qualities of his heart are apparent: humility and trust in God. His first response was, "Who am I, O LORD God, and what is my family, that you have brought me this far?" (v.16). But having considered what God had just promised, David went on to say that his rise from a shepherd to a king was a very small thing compared to the high status God had now bestowed upon him. What God had now promised regarding the One to come was beyond any of David's expectations, and he realized

that its fulfillment was beyond his own powers: "What glory can David add to that which you, O Lord, have chosen to do with your servant?" (v.18, author's paraphrase).

Flowing naturally out of that realization of his own powerlessness, David's prayer turns to the praise of Israel's Redeemer and his confidence in God to accomplish what he had promised (vv.20–27). What better way was there for the Chronicler to reaffirm Israel's hope and trust in the coming Deliverer than to recount for his readers the trust and confidence with which David responded to the promise of his coming?

(3) *The defeat of the enemy* (18:1–20:8). With a broad brush and occasional detail, the Chronicler paints a vivid picture of David's military victories. The theme of these chapters is stated twice: "The LORD gave David victory wherever he went" (18:6b, 13b).

As he had promised (1Ch 17:8), God was with David and delivered him from all his enemies and made a great name for David among all the people of the land. In ch. 19, his wars are not viewed as wars of aggression, for it was necessary that he defend himself against humiliating acts of aggression by his enemies (19:7).

(4) *God's establishment of a place to live* (21:1–30). Having demonstrated the fulfillment of God's promise to David that he would cut off his enemies from before him, the Chronicler recounts the fulfillment of the second portion of God's promise to David: "I will provide a place for my people Israel" (17:9). The words of God are referring not merely to a place to dwell, but the place where God himself would dwell, namely, the temple, whose site was chosen by the Lord himself (ch. 21). That the temple is preeminently in view in God's promise in 17:9 can be seen in the verses that follow. The central task

of the promised descendant is that he should build a temple for the Lord (17:12).

God's choice of the temple site, however, was carried out through the instrumentality of his servant David. The occasion of the selection of that site is recorded in great detail, because the events point out in remarkable clarity the ultimate purpose for the temple: God's salvation for his people.

David had angered God by numbering his army (21:1–7). That was apparently a reflection of David's lack of trust in God to save his people. Although David confessed his sin, he was required to bear the consequences of that sin (vv.8–12). After thousands fell by the plague that the Lord had sent upon his people, he was grieved and called his messenger of destruction to a halt (v.15). At the site where the messenger halted, the threshing floor of Ornan the Jebusite, David fell down before the Lord and pled to let the punishment fall upon him and his house rather than on the people (vv.16–17). But God commanded David to build an altar on that site and offer up the sacrifice he had provided in his Law. That site was where God had chosen to build his house (21:18–22:1). In a dramatic and climactic way, the purpose of the building of the temple was given. It was not to be a religious shrine, but the place where sinful human beings would meet with a righteous and holy God and where God would genuinely show that his mercies were great.

In 21:1 the Hebrew word *satan* (without the definite article) means simply "an adversary." It is a common word in the historical books to describe the enemies of Israel (cf. 1Sa 29:4; 2Sa 19:23; 1Ki 5:4; 11:9–14, 23, 25). The text appears to be suggesting that a new uprising of Israel's enemies had precipitated David's move to number his army. That seems to be borne out by v.12 (which mentions the impending threat of Israel's enemies) and by the parallel passage in 2Sa 24:1–25 (which connects David's numbering his army with the anger of the Lord that burned against Israel). The association of an attack from external enemies and the anger of the Lord is not immediately clear until it is noted that, for the biblical historians, the Lord's anger against Israel commonly resulted in oppression from her enemies. As the anger of the Lord burned against Israel, he gave them into the hands of plunderers, who looted them; and he sold them into the hands of their enemies around them, so that they could no longer stand before their enemies. This passage, then, should be read as a commentary on 2Sa 24 and on *satan*, the Hebrew word for "adversary."

## 2. The second account of God's promise to David (22:1–27:34)

In the first account of God's promise to David (17:1–21:30), we saw God's faithfulness to his promise by what he had accomplished through those aspects of the promise that specifically concerned David. In the second account of the promise to David, we will see how David himself made preparations for the fulfillment of those aspects of the promise that extended beyond his own reign. David prepared for the future fulfillment of the promise, and he did so in very concrete, specific terms: he gathered the material for building the temple (22:1–19) and appointed the officials who would administer the kingdom after him (23:1–27:34).

Embodied in David's zealous activity in these chapters is an important lesson: the preoccupation of God's people with the hope of God's promise. David showed by his actions that his uppermost desire was to see God's promise fulfilled. The focus of the promise was the building of the house of God.

(1) *Preparations for the temple building* (22:1–19). This section does not have a parallel in the other historical books. The Chronicler, drawing on his own sources of information (perhaps royal records), shows that David was responsible for gathering the building materials and workers (vv.1–4, 14–19) and for ensuring that the temple plans corresponded to the promise of God (vv.5–13).

By including the charge of David to Solomon, the Chronicler has added to the reasons David himself was not to build the temple. The temple was to be built by a man of peace, not by one who had shed much blood (v.8). Therefore his son Solomon, a man of peace (*shalom*), was to build the temple.

But, in David's charge to Solomon an even more important qualification to God's promise is given: obedience to the will of God (v.13). The right to be God's leader demands the responsibility to be obedient to his will. Only then will the king prosper. As the Chronicler and the biblical historians are quick to point out, even Solomon, a man of great wisdom and understanding, would not measure up to that qualification (1Ki 11:1–13). In fact, after the Chronicler has penned his final sentence (2Ch 36:23), still occupying the center of attention is the question: Who will be the one to build the Lord's temple? Apart from the NT, that question remains unanswered, even today.

(2) *The administration of the temple and the kingdom* (23:1–27:34). In 23:1–2 we have the outline for the remaining chapters of 1 Chronicles: "When David was old and full of years, he made his son Solomon king over Israel. He also gathered together [organized] all the leaders of Israel, as well as the priests and Levites." In reverse order, that summary is the basis for the account of David's organization of the Levites (23:1–32; 24:20–31), the priests (24:1–19), the musicians and doorkeepers (25:1–26:32), and the princes of Israel (27:1–34), and for the account of the

enthronement of Solomon (28:1–29:30).

David did not originate the special status of the Levites among the families of Israel, nor did he for the first time appoint them as servants in the worship of God. That was done by God through Moses on Mount Sinai (Nu 3). But David was alert to God's will and planned that the temple be administered according to it.

The arrangement of ch. 23 is simple and straightforward. The names of the heads of the family of Levi are listed (23:3–24; Gershom, Kohath, and Merari), and then the duties specified by David are enumerated (23:25–32). Those duties included all the work of the temple worship, with the exception of the work only a priest (a son of Aaron) could do. Previously, the major task of the Levites had been to carry the parts and utensils of the tabernacle (cf. Nu 3:1–4:49). But now that the Lord had established peace for Israel through David and had chosen to dwell in Jerusalem, the work of the Levites was changed to that of caring for the temple.

Because the work of the priests (sons of Aaron) has been mentioned in connection with the duties of the Levites (23:28), the subject of the duties of the priests is briefly mentioned in ch. 24. The priesthood in Israel could be carried out only by a descendant of the house of Aaron (Nu 18:7). The duty of the priest was to attend to the altar and to perform service "inside the veil," i.e., within the temple itself (cf. Nu 18:1–7). David, with the priests Zadok and Ahimelech, organized the work of the priests into groups of twenty-four. Each group of priests was to carry out the service of worship for one week (2Ch 23:8).

Regarding ch. 25, it is clear from the genealogies that Asaph (6:39–43), Heman (6:33), and Jeduthun or Ethan (6:44–47) were Levites. David was responsible for organizing their families into the orders of temple musicians. Their responsibilities are described as "prophesying, accompanied by harps, lyres and cymbals" (25:1). Praise and worship at the temple were accompanied by musical instruments. The Chronicler traces the origins of this service back to David.

The account of David's organization of the Levites is concluded by summarizing the duties of three further groups of Levites: the gatekeepers (26:1–19), the treasury guards (26:20–28), and the ministers of external affairs (26:29–32). The gatekeepers were the temple guards. David had wisely selected them from families whose leaders were capable men, able to do the job (26:8). Just as it was important to assign musicians to lead the worship and praise (25:7), so also it was important to find "able men" (warriors) to guard the gate day and night (26:7). The writer's concern for detail led him to include even the number of guards at each of the gates around the temple (26:17–18). The need for security at the temple is understandable, in light of the treasures stored in its treasury (26:27–28).

This section concludes with an account of the organization of the princes of Israel (27:1–34): his army (27:1–15), tribal leaders (27:16–24), administrators (27:25–31), and counselors (27:32–34).

### 3. The third account of God's promise to David (28:1–29:30)

The Chronicler's primary concern in recounting events in the life of David has been the promise of a coming King to reign over God's people. God made a promise to David that one of his descendants would rule over his kingdom forever and build a house for him. In his own day, the promise had still not been fulfilled. His emphasis on the promise of God is seen in his repeating the account of the promise three times. In this third account, the promise is recounted to be announced to a congregation of the leaders of Israel (28:1).

In both the second (22:7–13) and third accounts, Solomon is taken to be the descendant of the promise by virtue of his being a man of peace and his building the temple. From David's perspective there seemed little doubt that God's promise was about to be fulfilled in the reign of Solomon (28:5–7). Certainly the preparations made for the building of the temple showed that David had little doubt that Solomon was the one.

If the Chronicler is still waiting in hope for the fulfillment of the promise to David, then he, contrary to David, certainly does *not* believe Solomon was the son promised. Solomon was "a son" of David and he built a temple, but he is not "the Son" of David; and, as the Chronicler sees it, a future temple is yet to be built (2Ch 36:23).

(1) *The public announcement of Solomon's kingship* (28:1–10). The third announcement of the promise was given as a public proclamation of Solomon's kingship before the leaders of Israel. The account is without parallels in the other historical books of the Bible. David announced that his plans had been to build the temple, but because he was a warrior and not a man of peace, God had promised him a descendant who would build God's temple. Publicly, David announced that God had chosen Solomon from among all his sons. As long as Solomon remained obedient, God promised David that his kingdom would stand firm (v.7). On the basis of that promise, David admonished the leaders of Israel (v.8) and Solomon (v.9) to keep God's commandments and obey his will.

Of special importance is the inclusion of the explanation David gave for wholehearted obedience: "for the LORD searches every heart and understands every motive behind the thoughts" (v.9b). Because the Chronicler is re-

cording David's establishment of the public and external forms for worship, the temple, and the altar, the matter of inner sincerity is of utmost importance.

(2) *The temple plan* (28:11–19). David had received a plan for the temple from the Lord (v.19), and now he passed the plan on to the builder, Solomon. Some idea of the contents of this plan outlined by David can be seen in the description of the completed temple (2Ch 3–4).

(3) *Work on the temple commissioned by David* (28:20–29:9). The Chronicler takes great pains to make clear David's role in the building of the temple. David's words to Solomon, admonishing and exhorting him to build the temple, sound much like the words of Haggai, the prophet after the Exile, who stirred up the hearts of the people and the leaders to rebuild the temple that lay in ruins (see Hag 2:4– 5).

(4) *David's blessing* (29:10–19). These are David's final words—his last address to his people and last official word to his son Solomon. The first of his themes is the greatness of God (vv.11–13): everything belongs to God. David then turns in amazement to what God's people have been able to donate willingly for the temple. He has been thinking about Israel's history; in their growth from a small family of shepherds to a kingdom of international importance, he has seen God's hand at work (vv.14–16).

As his next words suggest (v.17), David seems to see, in the growth of the nation Israel, the course of his own life's journey from shepherd to king. David's prayer (1Ch 29:18–19) is that the people and new king, Solomon, not lose sight of the centrality of a pure heart as they plan and build this magnificent temple. The secret of David's leadership was not power and wealth, but trust in a God to whom belongs all power and wealth (cf. Ps. 19:10). The people's willingness to donate their wealth to build the temple is a sure sign that their heart is pure. His prayer is that the Lord will preserve this desire of their heart. With that, David commits his people and their new king into the hand of his sovereign Lord.

(5) *The coronation of Solomon* (29:20–25). A comparison of the accounts of Solomon's coronation here and in 1Ki 1 shows clearly that the two books have different emphasis. The writer of Samuel and Kings is concerned with the conflict that lay behind the selection of David's successor. Solomon's kingship was accomplished at great personal cost to David and his household. Ultimately, God's will prevailed and the man of peace, Solomon, did ascend to the throne (29:22; 1Ki 1:39).

Assuming his readers are aware of the tragic details that preceded Solomon's coronation, the Chronicler writes only of the final victory. That he assumes his readers know of the events of 1Ki 1 is clearly seen in his notice that 1Ch 29:22 is the "second" coronation of Solomon. The first coronation, before only David's entourage from Jerusalem, is recorded in 1Ki 1.

(6) *The death of David* (29:26–30). The account of David's reign ends with a notice of the years he served as king and a reference to other works that contain more information about the acts of King David. It is not clear if those works are the books of 1 and 2 Samuel and 1 and 2 Kings, or if the Chronicler had other sources that are no longer available.

# 2 Chronicles

## Introduction

See introduction to 1 Chronicles.

## III. Solomon and the Descendants of David (1:1–36:23)

Solomon's major accomplishment was the building of the temple in Jerusalem. The Chronicler's interest in that aspect of Solomon's reign can be seen clearly by comparing the account of his reign here and in 1Ki 1:1–11:43. The Chronicles account is a shorter work overall, and with few exceptions it includes only those events that serve to show Solomon's concern and care for the building of the temple. In that respect, the Chronicler's treatment of Solomon is similar to his treatment of David and his treatment of the Davidic dynasty in the remainder of the book. In recounting the deeds of the kings of Israel and Judah, he is concerned primarily with their care for the temple of God.

Why does the king's concern for the temple loom so large in this section? There are at least two answers to that question. (1) By the Chronicler's day the question of the temple was perhaps the central issue of Israel's faith. The first temple had been destroyed by the Babylonians. The people had returned from exile and faced the prospect of rebuilding the temple in Jerusalem.

(2) The prophets saw that Israel's only hope for the future lay in God's sending the promised messianic King to rule the world in peace and righteousness (Isa 9:6–7). The historical books have provided the basis for that hope in the account of the Davidic covenant (2Sa 7; 1Ch 17), according to which the promised King (the Messiah) would be a descendant of David and would build a house (temple) for God. The Messiah would not only be a political leader, but a religious leader as well. He would be king and priest; and although of the family of David and the tribe of Judah, he would not be of the priestly line of Aaron. Nevertheless, his concern for the proper worship and fellowship with God through the temple would characterize him as one who had priestly concerns.

King David epitomized that kind of king. But it is clear that David was not that king, for he was a man of war and bloodshed, and the King to come would be a man of peace (1Ch 22:7–9). Nevertheless, David's kingdom characterized the rule of the promised King. Henceforth, all kings in Jerusalem would find their measure in the degree to which they were like or unlike David. David's rule was characterized by a concern for temple worship. Indeed, the whole plan of the building and the order of the service was established by David's command. Thus, if a king was to measure up to David, he had to have a zeal for the house of God (cf. Jn 2:17). It was part of the Chronicler's primary concern to take a historical inventory of the descendants of David. He, in effect, asks: How did the promise to David fare? Did the Promised Seed come?

Was God's promise fulfilled? The Chronicler's answer, although hesitant in his account of Solomon, is a resounding no. There were good kings and bad kings in the inventory, but when the story has ended and the last king is in exile, the Promised One has not yet come. His concern, however, is not to lament the fall of the last king, but to point to the future to the One who is yet to come.

### A. Solomon (1:1–9:31)

By any standards, Solomon was a great king. David had bequeathed to him a large and stable kingdom. In this passage, the major interest is in how Solomon went about his task of building the temple. Whatever his weaknesses, Solomon had true greatness, and that greatness was seen in his devotion to the worship of God at the temple. He devoted himself to providing for the presence of God among his people. In that respect Solomon was like the promised King.

### 1. Solomon's preparation (1:1–17)

The first official act of Solomon was his journey to Gibeon with his entourage. His reason for going was that "God's Tent of Meeting" was there (v.3). Therefore, Solomon's first official act was in essence one of worship. The Chronicler carefully points out that worship at Gibeon was legitimate because all the accoutrements of worship prepared by Moses' instruction, except the ark, were kept here.

The wisdom and wealth that characterized Solomon's kingship were a gift from God. It is important to see the nature of the wisdom that Solomon requested. He asked for wisdom and knowledge "that I may lead this people" and "govern" them (v.10). Both the Chronicler and the writer of the parallel passage in 1Ki 3 had in view here the requirement of the king in Dt 17:18–20. The king was expected to know the law of God, fear God, and observe God's will as expressed in the Law. In the words of Moses in Dt 4:5–8, the law is wisdom and understanding.

### 2. Preparations for building the temple (2:1–18)

Although the Chronicler enumerates some details of the construction materials, his primary interest in the temple preparations lies clearly in the written exchange between Solomon and Hiram of Tyre.

Solomon's letter to Hiram provides a telling glance into his intention in building the temple. He saw the temple, not as a place to contain the God of the universe, but a place where he and his people could celebrate God's presence.

Solomon's letter also reveals his purpose for wanting the best craftsmen and the most precious materials: "the temple I am going to build will be great, because our God is greater than all other gods" (v.5).

Hiram's reply to Solomon (vv.11–16) is significant in light of the overall purpose of the books of Chronicles. One of the central themes is the place of the Gentile nations in the worship of God. That reply to Solomon serves to show that even in Solomon's day there were Gentiles who recognized the Lord as the Creator and whose contribution to the temple was welcomed by God's people. That is still a far cry, however, from Haggai's wealth of all nations (cf. Hag 2:7) or the vision of Zechariah of many peoples and mighty nations coming to seek the Lord in Jerusalem and to entreat his favor (Zec 8:22–23).

### 3. The temple is built (3:1–5:1)

The site of the temple, Mount Moriah, is identified both with the threshing floor of Ornan, which David purchased (1Ch 21:18–30) and with the mountains where Abraham offered up his son Isaac (Ge 22:2, 14). Since in Ge 22:14 the theme is God's provision of a substitutionary sacrifice, the Chronicler is reminding his readers that Solomon's temple site was on the same mountain. For sinful humanity to come into God's presence, a sacrifice was necessary. By grace, God provided the sacrifice.

No accurate picture of the temple can be drawn from Chronicles, since the account here is merely a rough sketch. The structure was about 90 feet long, 30 feet wide, and a little over 40 feet high—about the size and shape of a large suburban home. The glory of the temple lay not in its impressive size but in the quality and craftsmanship of its construction and furnishings.

### 4. The dedication of the temple (5:2–7:11)

The Chronicler gives the account of the temple dedication in four parts.

(1) *The ceremony of the ark* (5:2–14). David had brought the Ark of the Covenant to Jerusalem (1Ch 16:1). At

that time Jerusalem, called Zion, was only a small, well-fortified hill. Solomon built the temple to the north of the city and extended the limits of the city to include the temple. Consequently, it was necessary to move the ark "up to" the temple from its resting place in the city of David.

(2) *Solomon's speech* (6:1–11). Once more the Davidic covenant promise was repeated (see ch. 4). This time Solomon expressly applied the promise to himself and his completion of the temple (vv.4, 10). Although Solomon was no doubt correct in his assessment of the Lord's fulfilling his promise to David that his son would build the temple, he did not know that his own disobedience would lead to his downfall. He may have been the one in view in the promise, but he was not the One envisioned in the promise. The Chronicler's purpose is not to show that the promise failed in the past, but to show why the promise still holds good for the future.

(3) *Solomon's prayer* (6:12–7:3). The point of Solomon's prayer is clear: God is present among his people and hears their prayer when they, in obedience, call out to him (cf. v.14, the prayer's beginning). Solomon's enumeration of situations in which God's people may call out to him culminates in the prayer of those who have been taken into exile (vv.36–39). The problem of the prayers of the exiles is important, as the conclusion of this book suggests. Although this book ends on the note of the nation in exile, the one ray of hope is the rebuilding of the temple (36:23).

The theological basis of Solomon's prayer is important to note. In Solomon's words, God's "Name" dwelled in the temple he had built (v.20). Solomon's idea of what that meant can be seen in his address to God in v.18: "Will God indeed dwell on earth with men? The heavens, even the highest heavens,

cannot contain you. How much less this temple I have built." God did not live in the temple as people live in their houses. He was present in the temple, but the whole universe cannot contain him. Solomon brings together two important attributes of God. He is transcendent—the whole world does not limit him. But he is also present. His presence can really be thought of as especially accessible at the temple. That is what is meant by the phrase "put your Name there" (v.20).

To the biblical writers, the name of God, like his glory, was a way of speaking about God's attentive presence at the temple. Solomon's choice of words shows that he has clearly thought the issue through: God, who dwells in heaven, hears the prayers given at the temple, because there his Name dwells (v.21). Even when his people pray toward the temple in a far-off land, God hears their prayers from heaven offered at the temple (vv.38–39). Such an attitude toward God's presence at the temple was a hallmark of the King on whom the Chronicler had set his hope (Jn 2:16).

The conclusion to Solomon's prayer is the same as that of Elijah's prayer at Mount Carmel (1Ki 18:38–39): "Fire came down from heaven and consumed the burnt offering and the sacrifices, and the glory of the LORD filled the temple" (7:1).

(4) *The dedication ceremony* (7:4–11). A seven-day feast for the dedication of the altar was coupled with the seven-day Feast of Tabernacles. The number of animals sacrificed during the dedication, though large, is not improbable. Even larger numbers of animal sacrifices are known from ancient times.

### 5. Solomon's night vision (7:12–22)

Solomon received a confirmation of his prayer in a night vision (perhaps a dream). But he also received a stern warning of the importance of obeying

God's will. Solomon's kingdom would be established if he was obedient to that will; if not, the nation would be exiled and the temple destroyed.

The Chronicler certainly knows that the Davidic kings were not obedient. His history has helped to make that fact indelible. But his purpose is not to rub salt in old wounds; rather it is to show how to avoid the consequences of disobedience. When the nation suffers because of disobedience, the proper recourse of the people is repentance. God's people can always pray, repent, and seek forgiveness; he is always ready to hear and forgive (7:14–15).

### 6. Solomon's kingdom is established (8:1–18)

The Lord had appeared to Solomon and had reaffirmed the Davidic promise to him. When the Chronicler recounted the initial promise to David (1Ch 17:1–21:30), he stressed several features of David's kingdom that demonstrated God's fulfillment of specific promises in the life of David. After the Davidic promise was reaffirmed to Solomon, the Chronicler recounts several features of Solomon's realm that demonstrate the Lord's words "I will establish your royal throne" (7:18). Narratively, the Chronicler has shown that God is faithful to his word.

### 7. Solomon's wealth and wisdom are acclaimed (9:1–28)

Not only had the Lord given Solomon a great kingdom in fulfillment of the promise to David, but he also had given Solomon much wealth and wisdom, as he had promised at Gibeon (1:12). Solomon asked first for wisdom, and God also gave him wealth.

Not only had the queen of Sheba heard of Solomon's great wisdom, but when she met him in person, she discovered "half the greatness" of his wisdom had not been told (v.6). This picture of Solomon's fame and the distant nations coming to hear him, bearing gifts, is reminiscent of the kind of messianic hope characteristic of the Chronicler's day (Hag 2:7). Long before that time, however, the prophet Isaiah had voiced much the same hope that the Messiah's reign would show forth in such brilliance (see Isa 60:3, 5–6). In fact, all nations will come to Jerusalem when the promised Son of David comes (see Isa 2:3).

The queen of Sheba who came to Jerusalem with much wealth and found that she had only imagined half of the king's wisdom gives a dramatic picture of the hope that the Chronicler, along with the prophets, had vested in the Davidic kingship. What the prophets had voiced in their visions of the future, the Chronicler narrated in his glimpses from the past.

The theme of Solomon's relationship to the other nations continues in vv.13–28, showing how they contributed greatly to Solomon's wealth. Certainly his wealth was the result of good trade relations and wise use of resources, but it was something more. All of that wealth was the wealth of the nations, and they were bringing it to the son of David (see especially vv.22–24).

Behind this portrayal of Solomon's wealth lay a clearly defined hope in what God will again do through the Davidic kingship. One like Solomon will come again, and the nations will bring their wealth to him (see the prophecy in Ps 2:7–8).

### 8. Solomon's death (9:29–31)

What is surprising about the portrayal of Solomon is that it concludes without any notice of the misfortune that befell him in his later years. The Chronicler's reason for omitting those details involves two factors. (1) He assumed the details were known by the reader from 1 Kings and felt no need to repeat them since they were not important to his overall purpose. (2) His interest in Solomon was primarily "exemplary." Solomon was an example of the promised descendant of David who, in the Chronicler's day, had not yet come. Insofar as the reign of Solomon represented the reign of the Promised One, the Chronicler's interest was served. He was content to let the other biblical writers give the more rounded picture. His goal was to build hope for the future rather than to lament the past.

### B. Rehoboam (10:1–12:16)

Following his death Solomon's kingdom was divided. Ten tribes to the north rebelled against the Davidic dynasty in Jerusalem and established an independent state. For the most part the Chronicler concentrates only on the Davidic kings in Jerusalem. He was seeking not a comprehensive understanding of the past but a theological perspective on the present and future.

### 1. The rebellion of the northern tribes (10:1–11:4)

A number of interesting lessons can be drawn from this account, taken almost verbatim from 1Ki 12. (1) Solomon's son Rehoboam did not act wisely and lost his kingdom. Taking counsel from the young men and rejecting the counsel of the elders is the ultimate in the lack of wisdom.

(2) Another lesson has been inserted in the account that is crucial to this book: "So the king did not listen to the people, for this turn of events was from God, to fulfill the word the LORD had spoken to Jeroboam son of Nebat through Ahijah the Shilonite" (10:15). The course of events had been announced beforehand by God, and Rehoboam's actions proved to be in conformity to what the prophet had said. Nothing can stand in the way of God's purposes. What he has promised, he will bring to pass. Even a disastrous situation such as the division of the kingdom and the loss of ten tribes of Israel was not without its place in God's plan for his people.

By making that point, the Chronicler is giving his readers a basis for understanding the Exile. If the loss of ten tribes was no threat to the purpose of God, much less is the loss of the remaining two. The Exile did not mean the end to God's plan. The word of the prophet remains firm. God will establish it. To reinforce that point is the account of the prophet Shemaiah (11:2–4), who gave God's reevaluation of the rebellion: "Go home, for this is my doing."

### 2. Rehoboam's kingdom (11:5–23)

The material covered in this section has no parallel in the other historical books. The section gives an important glimpse of the Chronicler's evaluation both of the northern kingdom, Israel, and of the southern kingdom, Judah. He clearly views the northern kingdom as having been led into apostasy by their new king, Jeroboam (v.15). Thus, no one who still professed to seek the Lord could be a part of such worship. They had to come to worship God at Jerusalem (v.6).

On the other hand, the Chronicler not only views the southern kingdom as the place of true worship, but he also sees it as now being made up of all those from all the tribes of Israel who worshiped the true God (v.16). The "remnant" of the true Israel, from all the tribes, has returned, and Judah is the true Israel.

In the southern kingdom, little had been lost of the kingdom of David and Solomon. However, that would last only "three years" (v.17)—an ominous reminder that Rehoboam was not to be the Promised One.

### 3. Shishak's invasion (12:1–12)

The invasion of the southern kingdom by the Egyptian army under Shishak offers two lessons: (1) Unfaithfulness brings punishment if you are God's people; (2) God looks upon a repentant heart with grace (cf. Ps 51:17b).

### 4. The conclusion to Rehoboam's reign (12:13–16)

The summary of the reign of Rehoboam is to the point: "He did evil because he had not set his heart on seeking the LORD" (v.14). That is, he did not properly worship the Lord by caring for the temple and leading his people in God's law.

### C. Abijah (13:1–14:1)

In contrast to the rather brief notice of the reign of Abijah in 1Ki 15:1–8, the Chronicler seems to have taken special interest in Abijah's short reign. The writer of 1 Kings grouped Abijah along with those kings who "committed all the sins his father had done before him" (1Ki 15:3). The Chronicler, on the other hand, puts Abijah in a better light by virtue of his concern for the temple, the priests, and the Levites. He undoubtedly concurred with the assessment of the writer of 1 Kings, but that did not prevent him from pointing to at least one redeeming act of Abijah.

This chapter represents the primary statement regarding the northern kingdom—the Chronicler's only such assessment of the "sin of the north." He then turns his attention away from the apostasy of the northern kingdom and focuses the remainder of his attention on the Davidic kings of the southern kingdom.

### D. Asa (14:2–16:14)

### 1. General character of Asa's reign (14:2–8)

The 1 Kings account of the reign of Asa has been considerably expanded in this section. Both authors agree at the start that "Asa did what was good and right in the eyes of the LORD his God" (14:2; cf. 1Ki 15:11). The writer of Kings is content not to detract from that general assessment. However, the Chronicler finds several features of Asa's reign that both support that general view and, to some extent, temper it with the picture of a reign characterized by spiritual defeat. The strength of Asa's reign lay in his concern for the renewal of the temple and its worship and the courageous faith that Asa had in his Lord.

### 2. The invasion of Asa's kingdom (14:9–15)

The invader Zerah was a Cushite (Ethiopian), probably in the service of the Egyptians who held nominal control over the southern borders of Asa's kingdom. The Chronicler is interested in one aspect of the invasion—its demonstration of the power of God to deliver his people from the enemy. Although Asa was clearly outnumbered, he recognized in those unfortunate odds opportunity to trust in the power of God to deliver (v.11). The Chronicler's summary statement tells the rest of the story: "The LORD struck down the Cushites before Asa and Judah. The Cushites fled" (v.12).

Asa acknowledged as the basis of his trust and courage that human beings cannot hold back the plans and purposes of God.

### 3. Asa's revival (15:1–19)

As with many religious revivals, the revival in Asa's day was started by the words of a preacher, the prophet Azariah. His message was straightforward: seek the Lord while he can be found (v.2). Azariah drew his lesson from the past and evidently had in mind the period of the judges, although his description could fit many periods in Israel's history (vv.3–7).

Asa's response to the message of Azariah was immediate. He, in effect, rededicated the temple and celebrated the renewal of the covenant of the Feast of Weeks (Pentecost), which later Jewish tradition also used for commemorating the covenant. Again, the emphasis was the direct connection between the king's spiritual leadership and his concern for the worship of God at the temple. Here, Asa's actions were an intimation of the final work of the One who is to come (Jn 2:15–16).

### 4. War with the northern kingdom (16:1–10)

Again the Chronicler adds considerable detail to the account of 1Ki 15:17–22, casting a shadow across Asa's victory over the northern kingdom. The account of the war between Judah and Israel in 1 Kings is given without much editorializing on the part of the Chronicler. His inclusion of the prophecy of Hanani (vv.7–9) shows that he, too, considers Asa's alliance with Ben-Hadad to have been an unfortunate mistake. As with the invasion by Zerah the Cushite, Asa should have trusted in the Lord, for the Lord would have delivered him (v.8). How easy it is, in Asa's shoes, to forget the help of God in the past and to falter in our trust in him today. The prophet's words remain our only source of comfort as they should have been to Asa: "The eyes of the LORD range throughout the earth to strengthen those whose hearts are fully committed to him" (v.9). Curiously, Asa was angered at the prophet's suggestion that he had acted foolishly. His lack of trust in God resulted in his despotic oppression of his own kingdom (v.10).

### 5. The conclusion of Asa's kingdom (16:11–14)

The conclusion of the acts of Asa calls to mind the final failure of the Davidic kings as a whole, again reminding the reader that Israel's hope was in One who was yet to come. Why did Asa's reign end in the shadow of God's judgment rather than in the light of God's help? The answer is given in the statement about Asa's diseased feet: "Though his disease was severe, even in his illness he did not seek help from the LORD, but only from the physicians" (v.12). Asa again failed to trust God.

### E. Jehoshaphat (17:1–20:37)

Jehoshaphat's name means "the Lord will rule [judge]." The account of his reign seems to be governed by that same theme. All that he accomplished was based on the reality of a living God actively at work among his people, instructing them in the way they should go and defending them when they put their trust in him.

### 1. Introductory summary of Jehoshaphat's reign (17:1–6)

The account of Jehoshaphat's reign begins with an assessment of the king that measures him by the deeds of David. According to accounts, Jehoshaphat did well.

### 2. Jehoshaphat's administration of the kingdom (17:7–19)

Here we find a survey, not included in 1 Kings, of the administrative accomplishments of King Jehoshaphat. He was concerned that his kingdom be properly instructed in the law of God. As his name implies, he desired that the will of the Lord might rule among his people, and so appointed officials and Levites to travel throughout Judah to teach the people the law (vv.7–9). The people could not be expected to walk in God's way if they had never been instructed in God's will. As he built walls to fortify his cities, so also he built spiritual walls to ensure obedience to God. Although those walls were not made of stone and mortar, they would still be standing long after the last bricks had crumbled in his fortified cities, for "the word of our God stands forever" (Isa 40:8).

The evidence of the Lord's approval of Jehoshaphat's reign is given by the description of the fear his enemies had for him. They did not make war on him because they feared the Lord. Their ancient enemies the Philistines even brought Judah "gifts and silver" (v.11).

### 3. Jehoshaphat and King Ahab (18:1–34)

This chapter describes a war between Ahab's northern kingdom and the Arameans over the disputed Transjordan lands around Ramoth Gilead. The unsuccessful attempt on Ahab's part to gain control of Ramoth Gilead was the third major confrontation between Ahab and his Aramean rivals. The battle ended with Israel's defeat and Ahab's death.

Jehoshaphat first made his mark on the situation when he insisted that Ahab inquire first for the word of the Lord before he went into battle (v.4). Jehoshaphat wanted to do only the will of God. Not convinced that Ahab's four hundred prophets had really spoken the will of God, Jehoshaphat insisted further that a "prophet of the LORD" be found to inquire of the Lord (v.6). Reluctantly, Ahab had the only prophet of the Lord available to him, Micaiah, brought before them and, as he had guessed, Ahab heard only an evil report from that prophet. Clearly the Lord was not with Ahab (vv.16–22). Ahab's defeat in battle was confirmation that the words of Micaiah were true.

### 4. Jehoshaphat's appointment of judges (19:1–11)

Jehoshaphat returned home safely after a close brush with death in his alliance with Ahab. When he returned home a prophet, Jehu, son of Hanani, was waiting with a word from the Lord: "Should you help the wicked and love those who hate the LORD? Because of this, the wrath of the LORD is upon you" (v.2). Jehu's words clearly referred to Jehoshaphat's alliance with Ahab and his close call with death. In light of Jehoshaphat's appointment of judges in this chapter, it seems likely that the Chronicler also intended Jehu's words to apply to his present task, for his prophecy is a fitting statement of the theme of ch. 19: Jehoshaphat's appointment of judges.

The judges were to administer God's will among the people. Theirs was the awesome task of deciding between the guilty and the innocent. The judge was the representative of God, and in his decisions he gave the will of God. It was of utmost importance, then, that the judge not align himself with the wicked by taking a bribe, but that he always carry out his work in "the fear of the LORD," i.e., in obedience to the will of God alone (v.7). It is important to note that Jehoshaphat himself was actively involved in that system of justice and saw his task as teaching and preaching the word of the Lord (v.4).

### 5. Jehoshaphat's war with the Moabites and Ammonites (20:1–30)

This event is recorded only here and truly typifies Jehoshaphat's reign and name: "The Lord will rule [judge]." The salvation of God is put in its clearest light in this narrative. As the prophet Jahaziel put it, "You will not have to fight this battle. Take your positions; stand firm and see the deliverance the LORD will give you, O Judah and Jerusalem" (v.17).

The account of Jehoshaphat's prayer is reminiscent of the dedication of the temple by Solomon (6:12–42). The nation was in danger of attack by its enemies, and the king rallied the people at the temple to ask God's help. The basis of his prayer was God's promise to be present at the temple and to give the land to Abraham's descendants (vv.5–9). Jehoshaphat's request was straightforward and can aptly fit the request of the godly in any age: "O our God, will you not judge them? For we have no power to face this vast army that is attacking us. We do not know what to do, but our eyes are upon you" (v.12). Jehoshaphat was not asking for vengeance; he was only calling on God for help.

The reply of the prophet Jahaziel reinforced Jehoshaphat's reliance on the Lord: "The battle is not yours but

God's" (v.15). In those words we can hear not only the prophet speaking to Jehoshaphat and his people, but also the Chronicler speaking to his own day: "Have faith in the LORD your God and you will be upheld; have faith in his prophets and you will be successful" (v.20). Surely God's people today need to hear that same word.

### F. Jehoram (21:1–20)

The reign of Jehoram is a classic example of forsaking the Lord. He murdered his own brothers for no apparent reason and followed the idolatrous practices of the kings of Israel to the north, to whose family he was related by marriage (v.6). His kingdom began to crumble before his own eyes as kingdoms on the east and west of him rebelled (vv.8–10) and invaded his own kingdom (vv.16–17). His life ended with a terrible illness, and when he died it was "to no one's regret" (v.10). All this was the result of Jehoram's forsaking the Lord and doing evil in God's sight.

Yet, there is another point to make in the account of Jehoram's reign. No matter how low the house of David may fall, God is not unfaithful to his promise: "Nevertheless, because of the covenant the LORD made with David, the LORD was not willing to destroy the house of David" (21:7). It is to be noted that Jehoram was not confronted by a prophet from his own kingdom, the nation of Judah. Unlike all the other Davidic kings, he was opposed by Elijah, the great prophet whose call was to proclaim God's word against the apostate northern kingdom of Israel. What a comment on the wickedness of Jehoram that God's prophet to apostate Israel should send a message against him as well (vv.12–15).

### G. Ahaziah (22:1–9)

Ahaziah, like his father, Jehoram, and his mother, Athaliah, had close ties with the northern kingdom. His mother was the granddaughter of the wicked Israelite king Omri and was the daughter of Ahab. The influence of his close relationship with Israel and with his own mother ultimately meant destruction for Ahaziah (22:4).

This is a greatly abbreviated story of the end of the dynasty of Ahab that is recorded in 2Ki 9–10. The Chronicler has given only the facts relevant to Ahaziah's death. Because of his close association with Ahab's son Jehoram, Ahaziah was slain along with Jehoram by Jehu, God's anointed. That meant that Ahaziah's death was also from God (v.7).

### H. Athaliah (22:10–23:21)

At the beginning of Athaliah's reign she had killed all the heirs to the throne of David, with the exception of Ahaziah's young son Joash. This young boy had been hidden in the temple by his aunt Jehosheba, the wife of the high priest Jehoiada. Chapter 23 takes up the events that marked the end of Athaliah's six-year reign and the enthronement of Joash. Because she was not a son of David, the Chronicler is not interested in the events of her reign. It should not be forgotten that she was the daughter of Ahab, the wicked king of Israel (21:6; 22:3).

The events of ch. 23 are crucial to the message of 1 and 2 Chronicles. For the most part, the Chronicler has paid attention to the role of the Davidic king in protecting and caring for the proper worship of God at the temple. When the true, promised King comes, he will "build the house of the LORD."

The events of this chapter, however, have reversed the usual order of things. Now the king was not the protector of the temple; he was the protected. The temple was the vital link in the preservation of the Davidic dynasty; without it, there would be no hope of the fulfillment of the promise to David.

That reversal was not without its significance to the Chronicler's own day, which was much like the time of Queen Athaliah. A Davidic king was not on the throne. The hope of the fulfillment of God's promise to David rested on what was left of the house of David. Little could be done at the moment to restore David's kingdom because Judah and Israel were no longer sovereign states. They were mere provinces of a massive empire, Persia. All that remained of God's promise to David was the remnant of the house of David and the reestablished house of God. It is clear that the focus of the hope of the fulfillment of God's promise to David was centered on the temple. As long as it remained, there was hope that the Messiah would come to care for it. So, as in the time of Queen Athaliah, the temple was the protector of the promise to David.

## I. Joash (24:1–27)

The account of the reign of Joash, tragic as it is, provides a classic example of the lesson the Chronicler has in mind throughout these two books: God will fulfill his promise of peace by sending a son of David to reign successfully on the throne; his success will depend on his obedience to God's will; that obedience will be measured in terms of concern for the worship of God at the temple. The priests and Levites were to play a central role in the promise because through their teaching of God's law to the king and the people, obedience was accomplished. Jehoiada, the godly priest, was able to lead the young king in God's will as long as he was alive. But when he died, the king and his kingdom fell into apostasy (vv.2, 15–18).

The lesson does not end here. When the people fell away, God did not abandon them; he sent his prophets to warn them that they would be given over into the hands of their enemies as punishment (vv.20–22). When the king and the people rejected the word of the

prophets, God's warning of punishment came true (vv.23–24).

Behind the tragedy of Joash's reign, however, a message of hope pervades 1 and 2 Chronicles. If the people would only listen to the prophets and if they would turn to God, the Lord would restore their blessing, and their latter glory would be greater than the former glory (cf. 6:24–25).

## J. Amaziah (25:1–28)

At first glance the account of the reign of Amaziah appears sketchy and disjointed. A closer look, however, reveals that there are three carefully collected events from his reign that deal with the issue of obedience to God's will. Those events teach the familiar lesson of this book: God helps his people when they obey; but when they disobey, God's people can expect punishment. The purpose of such punishment is to bring them back to him and away from serving other gods (25:16).

The first event noted in Amaziah's reign is the justice carried out by the king against the slayers of his father (vv.3–4). The Chronicler draws an immediate point that the king was, at the start of his reign, a good king—he obeyed the law of Moses (v.4; the law required that guilty individuals be held responsible for a murder, Dt 24:16).

The second incident is the battle with the Edomites, Judah's eastern neighbors (25:5–13). In this account as well, Amaziah was a faithful king. He obeyed the word of the prophet who warned him not to ally himself with the sinful northern kingdom. Although it meant less military strength, Amaziah went into battle without that help, and God gave him the victory.

In spite of those two accounts that portray Amaziah as a king who honored God's word, a third account shows that Amaziah's reign ended in failure because he did not continue to put his trust in God (vv.14–24). In the midst of his victory over the Edomites, Amaziah met his downfall—he brought back the gods of the Edomites and set them up as his own (v.14).

The Chronicler has wisely chosen the ironic words of the prophet to expose his utter dismay at the folly of idolatry: "Why do you consult this people's gods, which could not save their own people from your hand?" (v.15). Idolatry simply makes no sense. God had just delivered their enemy into their hand, and they responded by serving the gods of the enemy!

Amaziah's blindness was a lesson in the dangers of idolatry; his defeat at the hands of the northern kingdom was from God, "because they sought the gods of Edom" (v.20). The sin of idolatry was considered extremely dangerous by the biblical writers. Idolatry struck at the very heart of the relationship between God and his people. The basis of the covenant, after all, was the personal fellowship between humankind and the Creator. Idolatry meant that some object was put in the place of the personal God, and nothing was more of an affront to God than that. As he himself instructed the people, "I, the LORD your God, am a jealous God" (Ex 20:5).

### K. Uzziah (26:1–23)

In 2Ki 15:1–7 we have only a bare sketch of the reign of Uzziah (or Azariah), noting that "the Lord struck the king, so that he was a leper to the day of his death" (2Ki 15:5). The Chronicler has included much more material regarding Uzziah's leprosy to show that it was a result of the king's pride and presumption.

The first part of the account stresses that Uzziah's fame was well known and well deserved. He had built a great and prosperous kingdom because he had continued to seek God (v.5). To seek God meant primarily to carry out the proper worship of the Lord at the temple.

Uzziah's reign, however, took a decided turn for the worse in the account of the king's usurping the role of the priest (vv.16–21). When Uzziah became strong, he became proud and was no longer careful to obey God's law (v.16). Only the priests were allowed to officiate at the altar in the temple (Nu 3:10, 38), but Uzziah dared to challenge God's will and, by force, set his mind to offer incense at the altar. The result of that act of rebellion was that he was stricken with leprosy the remainder of his life.

The significance of Uzziah's leprosy is brought out clearly: He was "excluded from the house of the LORD" (v.21). What a distance had been traversed from the promise of a coming son of David who would build a house for God (1Ch 17:12) to the Davidic king Uzziah who could not even enter the Lord's house because he was unclean.

### L. Jotham (27:1–9)

Jotham was a good king. He cared for the temple (v.3), and his reign was recognized even by his neighbors (v.5). In summary, "Jotham grew powerful because he walked steadfastly before the LORD his God" (v.6). All of that should have added up to an important and influential reign. It is, however, surprising that the Chronicler has devoted so little to the reign of this king. One clue may lie in the comment that "the people . . . continued their corrupt practices" during his reign (v.2). Such a reign does not serve to build hope in the fulfillment of the Davidic promise. Jotham was a great king, but in his day there was no revival of his people. The kings that interest the Chronicler are those who bring revival.

### M. Ahaz (28:1–27)

The account of the reign of Ahaz provides the first evidence of the Chronicler's response to the question of the purpose of the Exile. This account is by and large supplementary to the one recorded in 2Ki 19:1–37. Only three major events are selected: (1) Ahaz's idolatry (28:2–15); (2) Ahaz's appeal for help from the Assyrian king Tiglath-Pileser (vv.16–21); (3) Ahaz's closing of the temple (vv.22–25).

Although Ahaz fell far short of God's will, he did not turn to God in repentance when chastisement came, as other kings had done. On the contrary, God's chastisement served only to harden him in his unfaithfulness: "In the time of trouble King Ahaz became even more unfaithful to the LORD" (v.22). Certainly there were other kings who did not heed the call of God and did not repent when they were punished. What is important to see at this stage in the narrative is that the Chronicler has made a special point of bringing that feature of Ahaz's reign into the light. In doing so he is saying that the end of the house of David in the Exile was a result of the kind of hardness of heart exemplified in Ahaz.

### N. Hezekiah (29:1–32:33)

Although much material is devoted to Hezekiah's reign, the main point of the narrative is simple: when the son of David cares for the temple and the worship of God there, God brings peace to his kingdom. The length of the Chronicler's treatment of Hezekiah's reign is due to his concern for detail, which is his way of driving home his point. He gives a detailed account of the rededication of the temple (29:1–36), the celebration of the Passover (30:1–27), and the reestablishment of the orders of priests and Levites (31:1–21). This revival of the worship of God is followed by one of the most stunning of God's victories in all of Scripture—the defeat of the Assyrian Sennacherib (32:1–33).

Hezekiah's reign appears to have sparked a new hope in the house of David. He led the people in a genuine revival, and God heard their prayer and healed their land (30:20). Yet the Chronicler makes it clear that he is not intending to rekindle a new hope in the present Davidic dynasty. Hezekiah grew proud, like many of the other kings, though he also repented, was forgiven, and averted God's wrath (32:26). Nevertheless, his reign was not the time of promised eternal peace, but rather, the calm before the storm.

### 1. The temple rededication (29:1–36)

According to 28:24, Ahaz had closed the doors of the temple and had set up worship centers throughout Jerusalem and the other cities of Judah. Hezekiah's first important task was to open the temple for worship and to reconsecrate it with a solemn assembly.

### 2. The Passover (30:1–27)

The revival that began in the heart of the king spread to the leaders and was proclaimed throughout the land. For those remaining in the north and for those still in need of repentance in the south, the celebration of the Passover would mark the establishment of a renewed covenant and a return to the "God of Abraham, Isaac and Israel" (v.6).

Hezekiah's proclamation to the north shows that repentance would mean a return from exile of many of those captives in Assyria (v.9). The basis of his call for repentance was the appeal to a God who is "gracious and compassionate. He will not turn his face from you if you return to him" (v.9).

Hezekiah's prayer for the people (vv.18–20) allows a helpful glimpse into the heart of both this godly king and the Chronicler. Both were sincerely concerned for the proper exercise of worship at the temple. Carelessness in this regard would be the last thing either would tolerate. At the same time they were both concerned ultimately with the question of a right heart attitude. Mere ritualism is not the goal of temple worship (30:19; cf. Ps 15).

### 3. The priests and the Levites (31:1–21)

Like David and Solomon before him, Hezekiah took a personal interest in the organization and welfare of the priests and Levites. The Chronicler's particular interest seems to show that when the people tithe, there is abundance, with plenty left over (v.10).

### 4. The invasion of Sennacherib (32:1–33)

The Assyrian king Sennacherib was one of that country's most powerful kings. He led several military campaigns against the lands around Judah, and on more than one occasion his armies threatened the kingdom of Judah. Sennacherib recorded his version of the events in ch. 32 in his own royal archives.

Hezekiah's encouraging words strengthened not only those in Jerusalem in his own day, but continue to give courage to failing hearts in every age: "Be strong and courageous. Do not be afraid or discouraged because of the king of Assyria and the vast army with him, for there is a greater power with us than with him. With him is only the arm of flesh, but with us is the LORD our God to help us and to fight our battles" (vv.7–8).

### O. Manasseh (33:1–20)

Manasseh's reign represents one of the most dramatic turnabouts in 1 and 2 Chronicles. He began as an extremely evil king and led the hearts of the people away from the Lord (vv.2–9). Other biblical writers see his reign as the point of no return, leading to the Exile (see 2Ki 23:26; Jer 15:4). The Chronicler, however, gives an account of Manasseh's repentance and the reparations that resulted from his tortuous exile to Babylon. What happened to him personally in Babylon would soon happen to the whole nation.

Because the Chronicler is more interested in the question of how to get his people out of the Exile than how they got in, he dwells only on the results of Manasseh's repentance. Certainly Manasseh's early sins had devastating consequences for his people and his kingdom. In spite of his repentance, the people still continued in his old ways (v.17), and his son Amon multiplied the earlier sins of his father (v.23). The Chronicler agrees wholeheartedly with the other biblical writers that Manasseh's reign and influence did mark the turning point toward exile. However, he has left that point for others to make. For him, Manasseh's repentance is a dramatic lesson in God's grace.

### P. Amon (33:21–25)

The reign of Amon was short; the Chronicler devotes little time to it. Its primary significance lay in Amon's failure to repent as his father Manasseh had. This failure was a direct result of his father's earlier sins. In other words, Manasseh's sins continued to affect God's people and, in particular, his own son.

### Q. Josiah (34:1–35:27)

The reign of Josiah was tragic. He was one of the few godly kings of the line of David. He ushered in widespread reform throughout his kingdom, including the land to the north (34:6). At the peak of his reign, he was slain in battle (35:22–24). The account of the reign of Josiah emphasizes two important events: (1) the discovery and reading of the Law of Moses (34:14–33); and (2) the celebration of the Passover (35:1–19).

### 1. The law of Moses (34:1–33)

The loss of the Law of Moses in Josiah's day was not a new problem. In fact, the problem appears to have been at the very root of Israel's failure to keep her covenant obligations and to obey God's will. Already in the earliest stages of her history as a nation, after the death of Joshua and his generation, "another generation grew up, who knew neither the LORD nor what he had done for Israel" (Jdg 2:10). A new generation cannot live on a legacy. They must learn afresh who the Lord is and what he has done for them. When the Law of Moses was read, its words became God's final sentence against his disobedient people: "My anger will be poured out on this place and will not be quenched" (34:25)—a reference to the coming Babylonian exile (36:17–21).

Josiah is seen as an exemplary Davidic king. He led the people in God's way and, "as long as he lived, they did not fail to follow the LORD, the God of their fathers" (34:33).

It should be noted again that the temple was at the center of this time of revival. It was as the people were repairing the temple that they discovered the law. As the temple once protected the house of David (22:10–12), so now it protected the Law of Moses. The temple had preserved from destruction the two foundational pillars of Israel's faith, God's law and the king. It also served as the rallying point of Israel's faith in the coming Messiah. The God whose Name dwells in the temple is a living God and has promised to send an eternal King to rule his kingdom in peace and righteousness.

### 2. The Passover (35:1–19)

Again the intensity of the Chronicler's interest in Josiah's care for the worship of God at the temple can be measured in his attention to detail. Josiah's reign pictures vividly the reign of the coming King. When he comes, he will be like Josiah. He will lead his people in the worship of God at the temple.

### 3. The death of Josiah (35:20–27)

The Chronicler is not concerned with the details of the battle that resulted in Josiah's death. The battle at Carchemish involved two major empires of the ancient Near East, Babylon and Egypt. Josiah met his end while attempting to oppose the Egyptian forces en route to the battle. Because he did

not listen to Neco's message, he was killed. Josiah, a great king whose reign was characterized by obedience and godliness, in the end did not heed God's warning and fell in battle. At this last moment in his book, the Chronicler reminds his readers that the Promised Seed of David has not yet come. Even Josiah failed at a crucial moment to obey God's will. The words of David regarding the promise of an eternal kingdom lie behind Josiah's tragic end: "If you seek him, he will be found by you; but if you forsake him, he will reject you forever" (1Ch 28:9).

### R. The Conclusion (36:1–23)

The Chronicler ends with a cursory review of the last kings who reigned over the kingdom of their father David (vv.1–13); a short sermon on the cause of the Exile (vv.14–21); and Cyrus's edict, marking the start of the temple rebuilding (vv.22–23).

### 1. The last kings (36:1–13)

The Chronicler's emphasis in recounting the days of the last Davidic kings is to show that their dominion was finished and that the real power now rested in the hands of foreign empires—Egypt and Babylon. What a great distance from the expectation that the Son of David would rule from sea to sea with the nations as his inheritance (Ps 2). The point is that the historical kingdom of David was not the reign envisioned in the promise to David. That kingdom ended in failure. To explain that further, a concluding sermon is added to this account of the last kings—kings whose reigns typified much of the house of David before them.

### 2. The Chronicler's sermon (36:14–21)

The theme of the Chronicler's concluding remarks is expressed awesomely in v.16: "They mocked the messengers of God, despised his words and scoffed at his prophets until the wrath of the LORD arose against his people and there was no remedy." God gave his people over into the hands of their enemies, and those enemies burned the house of God (v.19) and carried his people into captivity in Babylon (v.20). All that is the opposite of what the Chronicler hopes for. The past lies in ruins, but the future lies in the promise of God as stated in 7:14. When the temple is again rebuilt and the people pray, even though they are in exile (6:36–39), God will hear their prayer and restore their peace. All is made to rest on the rebuilding of the temple.

### 3. The edict of Cyrus (36:22–23)

The last two verses of 2 Chronicles ultimately determine the mood of both books. They are not about human failure, but about the power and promises of God. Out of the ruins of human effort, the Chronicler shows that God's purposes can never fail and that all he intends to do will be accomplished (see Isa 9:7). The Exile and the destruction of the temple may have seemed to put an end to the promise that God would rule his people through the house of David, but the Chronicler's purpose has been to show that God is still at work and that the hearts of the mightiest rulers are in his hand. If need be, God will stir up the spirit of Cyrus, the king of Persia, to accomplish his purpose (see comment on 1Ch 28:20–29:9); the edict of Cyrus, published in the Chronicler's day, seems to him to be just such an occasion (see Isa 44:28). God is at work in history and in the course of events that are shaping history. What some may have read as an interesting and much-welcomed headline, the Chronicler sees as proof that God's "compassions never fail. They are new every morning; great is [his] faithfulness" (La 3:22– 23).

# Ezra

## Introduction

The date and authorship of the book of Ezra are unknown.

## I. The Return (1:1–6:22)

### A. Rebuilding the Temple in Jerusalem (1:1–4:24)

#### 1. Cyrus allows Jews to return to Jerusalem (1:1–4)

The book of Ezra begins with a fulfilled prophecy from the book of Jeremiah. Jeremiah had foretold that Judah would go into exile to Babylon (Jer 25:8–10) and that this exile would last for seventy years (25:11). At the end of this period, Judah would return to the land (29:10–14). The writer of the book of Ezra, referring to Jeremiah's prophecy, sees its fulfillment in the first group of Jews who returned to Jerusalem under the leadership of Zerubbabel and Jeshua the high priest. The primary task of that group was the reconstruction of the temple. Part of the strategy of this book is to show that though there was initial fulfillment, much more remained of God's promises in the future.

It is important to note that the writer stresses that these events are the result of the sovereign work of God. It was God who "moved the heart" of Cyrus to allow the Jews to return (v.1), and it was God who "moved" the heart of the people to leave Babylon and return to Jerusalem to build the temple (v.5).

#### 2. Preparation for the return to build the temple (1:5–2:70)

The leaders of the exiles made the necessary preparations for the journey and the construction of the temple (1:5–6). This included regaining possession of the original utensils of the temple that had been taken by Nebuchadnezzar (vv.7–11). These treasures were put in the care of Sheshbazzar (v.8; 5:14), who was appointed governor of the region (5:14).

Some indication of the extent of the undertaking can be seen in the list of returning exiles (2:1–67). At the head of the list were twelve leaders, including Zerubbabel and Jeshua, the high priest (v.2). These are followed by a list of "the men of the people of Israel" (vv.2b–20, 70b; cf. 3:1). Thus in the writer's view, this group included among them a remnant of the original "Israel" that once occupied the northern kingdom. The return is pictured as a comprehensive return of God's people. A list of priests (vv.36–39), Levites (v.40), singers (v.41), gatekeepers (v.42), temple servants (vv.43–54), and descendants of the servants of Solomon (vv.55–58) follows. There were also many whose lineage could not be clearly established (vv.59–60), even from among the priests (vv.61–63).

When they arrived in Jerusalem, the returning exiles and their leaders were eager to begin work on the temple. They gave freely from their own wealth (vv.68–70).

#### 3. Beginning the work (3:1–13)

The first act of restoration was the rebuilding of the altar at the site of the temple (vv.1–6), accomplished under the leadership of Zerubbabel and Jeshua. Zerubbabel was a descendant of the Davidic kingship through his father Shealtiel (v.8), and Jeshua was the high priest (Hag 1:1; Zec 3:1). The altar was built according to the prescriptions in the Law of Moses (v.2). The altar was first used for the evening and morning sacrifices (v.3) and the burnt offerings for the Feast of Tabernacles (v.4). Thereafter it was used for all regular feasts and celebrations (v.5).

Since the altar had been built before the temple, it was necessary to begin work on the foundation of the temple (vv.7–13). The writer's emphasis on laying that foundation during the time of Cyrus is intended to cast the work on the temple as a fulfillment of Isaiah, who wrote: "I am the LORD ... who says of Cyrus, 'He . . . will say of Jerusalem, "Let it be rebuilt," and of the temple, "Let its foundations be laid"'" (Isa 44:28). Just as Solomon obtained materials for his temple from Tyre (1Ki 5:1–11), so the material for the new temple was also obtained from "Sidon and Tyre" (Ezr 3:7). Work on the temple began in the second month of the second year after the return. Zerubbabel and Jeshua, along with the priests and Levites, carried out the work (v.8). There was great celebration with the laying of the foundation (vv.10–11). Those who had seen the former temple, built by Solomon, wept in sorrow, while others shouted for joy (vv.12–13). Already Solomon's temple was being idealized, and the present one could not match it. Though there was joy in what God had done in the present, there was still room for hope that greater blessing was possible in the future.

### 4. Opposition to the rebuilding of the temple (4:1–24)

When Zerubbabel and those working on the temple refused to allow the local inhabitants of the land to participate in the building, "counselors" were hired "to frustrate their plans" (v.5) to build the temple. This effectively halted the work on the temple throughout the reign of Cyrus and into the reign of the next king, Darius (vv.4–5, 24; 5:16b).

At this point in the narrative, the writer includes a verbatim copy of a complaint written by the leaders of Samaria at a later date, and on another occasion, to the Persian king Artaxerxes (vv.8–16). The primary charge against the people of Judah at that time was that their refortification of Jerusalem was an effort to instigate a tax rebellion against the Persians (vv.12–13). To corroborate their charges, the Samaritan leaders appeal to the Persian records of Jerusalem's past rebellions (v.15). At the time the letter was written, it proved successful, and the building on the city was halted (v.24). Although not written dur-

ing the time of Zerubbabel's building of the temple, the letter provides a glimpse into the ongoing rivalry between the Jews and the inhabitants of Samaria throughout this period.

### B. Renewal of the Rebuilding of the Temple (5:1–6:22)

After a long delay, the rebuilding of the temple was again underway. There were two causes for this renewed effort. The first was the prophetic encouragement of Haggai and Zechariah (5:1–2). The second was a letter sent to Darius (5:3–6:12). The writer clearly intends us to see a link between these two causes. When the people followed the words of the prophet (cf. Dt 18:18), God brought them success. Not only was Tattenai's bureaucratic bumbling (5:3–17) squelched by Darius's reply (6:1–12), but also it led to the expenses of the building being covered by the king's own treasury. In Haggai's own prophecy, he had spoken of the "wealth of the nations" (NIV, "the desired of all nations") contributing to the building of the future temple (Hag 2:7).

The temple was completed in the sixth year of Darius (6:13–15). The Levitical priesthood was installed during an elaborate dedication of the temple (6:16–18), and in the same year they celebrated the Passover (6:19–22).

## II. Ezra (7:1–10:44)

### A. Ezra Prepares to Leave for Jerusalem (7:1–14)

Ezra was a priest of the house of Aaron (7:1–5) and was "well versed in the Law of Moses" (v.6). Apparently because of his wisdom and knowledge of Israelite law, he enjoyed the favor of the king (v.6). Ezra came to Jerusalem with a letter of introduction from King Artaxerxes, commissioning him to administer the land of Judah according to God's law (7:11–28). He was accompanied by seventy men who returned with him to Jerusalem (8:1–36).

## B. Problem of Intermarriage (9:1–10:44)

A major problem faced Ezra on his return to Jerusalem to administer the law. The people, and especially their leaders, had "not kept themselves separate from the neighboring peoples with their detestable practices" (9:1). Although the problem involved intermarriage (v.2) among the sons and daughters of the nations, the difficulty lay with their "unfaithfulness" to God (vv.3–4).

Ezra, in his prayer of confession, cast this sin of the people within the larger context of Israel's covenant relationship with God. This was another instance of Israel's unbelief (v.7). The people had been warned by God's prophets (vv.10–12), but they had disregarded God's words and were guilty (v.15). God had remained faithful to his promises, and the people had found grace in their return from captivity (vv.8–9), but having returned and found God's grace, they once again joined in apostasy with the people of the land. God's people were no further along than in the days of Joshua when they disobeyed God and made a covenant with the Gibeonites (Jos 9).

Ezra's prayer answers another central question in the book of Ezra. At the beginning of the book the author linked the return from exile with Jeremiah's prophecy of seventy years. The return was the fulfillment of that prophecy. Ezra's prayer, however, shows that the fulfillment was short-lived at best. God was faithful, but Israel proved unfaithful. Jeremiah's prophecy, therefore, remained to be fulfilled in the future (cf. Da 9:1–2). A similar theme is found in the book of the prophet Zechariah. According to him, God's promises would be fulfilled only when Israel turned in obedience to God's commands (Zec 6:9–15).

When the people heard Ezra's prayer, they joined him in confessing their sins (10:1–2) and resolved to obey God's law (vv.3–6). They then resolved to put away their foreign wives (vv.7–11), not en masse, but orderly and on an individual basis (vv.12–17). To give some idea of the magnitude of the problem, the writer concludes the book with a list of those guilty of intermarriage (vv.18–44).

# Nehemiah

## Introduction

The date and authorship of the book of Nehemiah is unknown. Though Nehemiah speaks in the first person throughout the book, there is no direct evidence that he is the author since he is also a part of the narrative (e.g., 8:9). In the Hebrew text, the books of Ezra and Nehemiah are a single book, hence the heading "The words of Nehemiah son of Macaliah" (1:1) marks a section of the book only. It is not a title.

## I. Nehemiah's Return (1:1–4:23)

This book opens with the godly Nehemiah hearing of the despicable condition of the city of Jerusalem (1:1–4). The walls lay in ruin and the gates were torn down. Because he held a high office in the court of the Persian king Artaxerxes I, Nehemiah was able to do something about it—but not without the Lord's help. He went immediately to prayer (vv.5–11).

In his prayer, Nehemiah looked back to Israel's failure to keep God's law and the subsequent destruction and exile to Babylon. He confessed the sins of his fathers as well as his own: "We have not obeyed the commands, decrees and laws you gave your servant Moses" (v.7). Throughout his prayer, however, there is a clear sense of hope. Just as God was faithful to his covenant promises to bring judgment upon the nation, so there was the hope that he would also remain true to his promises to bring salvation and blessing (v.9). The basis of Nehemiah's hope is God's promise in Dt 30:1–6, which he paraphrased in this prayer: "When you and your children return to the LORD your God and obey him with all your heart and with all your soul according to everything I command you today, then the LORD your God will restore your fortunes" (Dt 30:2–3).

Having obtained permission and assistance from Artaxerxes I to return and rebuild the city of Jerusalem, Nehemiah left to go to the city (2:1–9) and began to inspect the walls (vv.11–16). But there was trouble already brewing among the enemies of God's people—Sanballat and Tobiah "were very much disturbed that someone had come to promote the welfare of the Israelites" (v.10). To the writer of the book of Nehemiah, however, these two leaders represented the ancient enemies of Israel, the Ammonites (1:10; cf. Dt 23:3, "No Ammonite or Moabite or any of his descendants may enter the assembly of the LORD").

As the rebuilding of Jerusalem began (2:17–18), opposition immediately arose (vv.19–20). The people were mocked and taunted by their enemies, but it served only as an occasion for Nehemiah to give a renewed commitment to the faithfulness of God: "The God of heaven will give us success" (v.20). As a demonstration of the truth of Nehemiah's confession, the writer records, at length, the success of the builders (3:1–32). The report of further opposition only highlighted the success that the Israelites were enjoying from the hand of God (4:1–23).

What lay at the heart of their success? The writer's answer is not hard to find in the narrative: "We prayed to our God and posted a guard day and night to meet this threat" (4:9). The lasting image that arises out of this text is that of the builders of the city of Jerusalem who "did their work with one hand and held a weapon in the other" (v.17). There is a practical realism in the piety exemplified in this book.

## II. Problems Among the People of God (5:1–19)

Amid his description of the rebuilding of Jerusalem's walls, the writer inserts two brief narratives that show the quality of Nehemiah's godly leadership. The first deals with the fact that some Israelites were charging interest to their fellow Israelites and that this had led to poverty and economic slavery (5:1–13). Nehemiah's solution was to apply the Law of Moses to the problem. According to Dt 23:20, Israelites could "charge a foreigner interest, but not a brother Israelite."

Nehemiah's godly leadership is further exemplified in his not requiring the food allottment that was rightfully his as governor of the province (5:14–19). Though previous governors had insisted on their allottment and had thus placed heavy demands on the people, Nehemiah did not (v.18). His prayer, "Remember me with favor, O my God, for all I have done for these people" (v.19), is not intended as an appeal to self-righteous favor in God's sight, but as a statement of fact that God looks with favor on those who do his will.

## III. Conspiracy Against Nehemiah (6:1–7:3)

The narrative resumes the opposition of Sanballat and Tobiah to the work of Nehemiah (vv.1–14). Nehemiah refused to be intimidated at the threats and antics of his enemies. He met each case of opposition by trusting God and striving to be obedient to his word. He let God take care of the opposition (v.14). Hence the wall was completed in fifty-two days (vv.15–16)—a vivid demonstration to the nations around them that the work had been done with the help of God (v.16). Even though important leaders in Judah and men close to Nehemiah had sided with the opposition (vv.17–19), God gave him success and thwarted all their plans. Jerusalem was protected (7:1–3).

## IV. Registration of Families: List of Returnees (7:4–73)

The city walls now complete, Nehemiah turned to the problem of restoring the city itself. He began by taking a census of the people living in the land who had returned from Babylon. The writer includes the original list of those who had returned to rebuild the temple (vv.6–73), a virtual duplicate of the list in Ezr 2. For the next three chapters, the writer devotes his attention to the religious life of the city and the growing importance of the Law of Moses among the people. In ch. 11 the narrative returns to Nehemiah's efforts to restore city life in Jerusalem.

## V. Ezra and the Law (8:1–10:39)

### A. Ezra Reads the Law (8:1–12)

On the first day of the seventh month Ezra stood on a high wooden platform and read aloud the "Book of the Law of Moses." This book was apparently the same document as our modern-day Pentateuch. This day was a special day of rest (Sabbath) and was celebrated as the Feast of Trumpets (Lev 23:23–25; Nu 29:1–6). All the people stood as Ezra read the book, and "he read it aloud from daybreak till noon" (8:3). The people wept as they listened to the words of the Law (v.9); the Levites (Jeshua and the twelve) also explained the Law to the people who were standing nearby, "giving the meaning so that the people could understand what was being read" (v.8). Thus the people celebrated "with great joy, because they now understood the words that had been made known to them" (v.12).

### B. The Response of the People (8:13–10:39)

Ezra continued to teach the Law to the people (8:13), fulfilling the task for which he had been sent to Jerusalem (cf. Ezr 7:10, 25b–26). Moreover, he led them in the celebration of the Feast of Booths (8:13–18). As a result of their reading the Law of Moses, a special day of fasting and repentence was called on the twenty-fourth day of the same month (9:1). On this day the Israelites "had separated themselves from all foreigners," "stood in their places, and confessed their sins and the wickedness of their fathers" (v.2). The writer of Nehemiah appears intent on showing that by this time the people had reached the same state of repentance and godly sorrow as Nehemiah had at the beginning of the book (cf. 1:4–11).

In the people's prayer of confession and praise that follows (9:1–37), the reader is given an interpreted overview of the teaching of the Pentateuch and the historical books of the OT. The summary begins with God's creation of the world, just as the Pentateuch begins with Creation. It concludes, appropriately, with the events of the books of Kings, Ezra, and Nehemiah. This confession is one of the most complete summaries of the OT to be found within the OT itself (cf. Ps 78; Stephen's speech in Ac 7). The central theme of this summary is God's faithfulness to Israel and Israel's continual failure to trust in him.

At the conclusion of their confession (9:38–10:39), the people "bind themselves with a curse and an oath to follow the Law of God given through Moses the servant of God and to obey carefully all the commands, regulations and decrees of the LORD our God" (10:29). The writer also includes a brief description of several specific regulations to show more precisely what the people's oath actually entailed—e.g., no marriage of children to foreigners (v.30), keeping the Sabbath (v.31), paying the temple tax (v.32–33), priestly contribution of wood (v.35), and first-fruits and tithes (v.36–39).

## VI. Residents of the New Land (11:1–13:3)

A registration of families who had returned from Babylon apparently showed that far too few people had settled in Jerusalem. Nehemiah thus provided for an orderly resettlement in the city by casting "lots to bring one out of every ten to live in Jerusalem" (11:1).

The writer includes a list of those who settled in Jerusalem (vv.4–73) as well as the rest of the cities (vv.25–36). This is followed by a list of priests and Levites (12:1–26), divided into those who served in the time of Zerubbabel and Jeshua (vv.1–11), Joiakim, Jeshua's son (vv.12–21), and Eliashib, Jeshua's grandson (v.22).

The effect of these lists is to show the nature and extent of Nehemiah's godly leadership. The "great trouble and disgrace" of the "Jewish remnant that survived the exile" in Jerusalem, which was the initial concern of Nehemiah at the opening of the book (1:1–11), has now been cared for, and Nehemiah's visit has proven successful. It is fitting then, that at the close of the book, the author would give an account of the dedication of the wall in Jerusalem (12:27–43). It was the report of the ruined walls of the city that had been the focus of Nehemiah's initial concern (1:4). Now, instead of the "great trouble and disgrace" in Jerusalem, "the sound of rejoicing in Jerusalem could be heard far away" (12:43). Once again order was restored in Jerusalem and worship was carried out as "in the days of David" (v.46) and Moses (v.47b). Moreover, as in the days of Balaam's attempt to curse God's people, Israel was again a separated people (13:1–3).

## VII. Nehemiah's Final Reforms (13:4–31)

According to v.6, Nehemiah had returned to King Artaxerxes in the thirty-second year of that king's reign. "Some time later" (v.6b) Nehemiah returned a second time to Jerusalem and found that many of his reforms had taken a downward turn. There was thus need for further reform. The book concludes with the personal account of Nehemiah about his additional reforms. He restored the temple storerooms to their rightful use (vv.4–9), rectified the proper servies and support of the

Levites (vv.10–14), enforced observance of the Sabbath laws (vv.15–22), rebuked the people for allowing mixed marriages with "women from Ashdod, Ammon and Moab" (vv.23–27), expelled the son-in-law of Sanballat from the office of the priesthood (vv.28–29), and "purified the priests and Levites of everything foreign" and clearly defined their proper duties (vv.29–31).

The last words of the book focus ironically on God's blessing of the individual Nehemiah, "Remember me with favor, O my God" (v.31b), and decidedly not on the people as a whole. The reader has learned that though there were godly persons like Nehemiah among God's people, the nation as a whole was not any different than it had been in the days of King Solomon, who "was led into sin by foreign women" (vv.26–27).

This last chapter of the book plays an important role in the strategy of the writer. Without this chapter, the book of Nehemiah portrays a steady upward progression of God's people in Jerusalem after the time of the Babylonian exile. The reader is given the impression that in that return, all God's promises to David and the forefathers were being fulfilled in those days. A similar strategy was at work in the composition of the book of Joshua. With the last chapter of Nehemiah, however, as with the book of Joshua, the reader is given another view of these events: much remained of God's promises to his people. The historical return from exile was a part of God's plan of blessing his people, but it was not the last word. God had remained faithful, but the people had failed to trust and obey him. The book thus looks forward to a time when God would fulfill his promises to Israel and the people would respond in obedience. It would be like the time of Nehemiah, but it was not that time itself. There is, in other words, a noticeable eschatology in the strategy of this book. Its focus is not on the past but on the future blessing of God's people.

The same message can be seen in several other books written during and after the time of the Babylonian captivity. Apart from the historical books of Joshua, Judges, Samuel, and Kings, all of which have this same perspective on Israel's history, the book of the prophet Malachi stresses heavily the failure of God's people to trust him and obey his word after the blessing that came in the return to Jerusalem. The book of Daniel is likewise concerned with this question. There, the expected fulfillment of God's promises is extended far beyond the time of the return from Babylon (cf. comments on Da 9) and is clearly messianic in its central focus (see comments on Da 7).

# Esther

## Introduction

The date and authorship of the book of Esther is unknown. Tradition ascribed the book to the "Men of the Great Synagogue," but there is no independent confirmation of that fact. Like many biblical books, the work is anonymous.

The central part of the book of Esther is devoted to telling the story of Esther, the Jewish queen of Persia (1:1–9:17), and the last section deals with the origin of the Jewish Feast of Purim (9:18–10:3).

The outline of the story of Esther is similar to other stories in the Bible, such as the story of Joseph (Ge 37–50), Moses (Ex 2), David (1Sa 29–30), Daniel, and Ezra and Nehemiah. In each of these stories, a gifted Israelite is taken into the palace of a foreign king and is there granted an opportunity to preserve the life of God's people. Each of these stories makes its own contribution to the larger question of God's providential care for his people. The unique feature of the story of Esther is that it teaches this lesson without ever mentioning God. In this book, God remains the unspoken "actor" in an otherwise entirely human drama. Or, to put it another way, God is not so much an implied actor in the drama as he is the author of the script. Given the continuous series of "coincidences" at key moments in the story, the reader is left no room for doubt that the events happened as they did because they were planned that way by God. Mordecai as much as says this in his challenge to Esther at the peak of the story: "Who knows but that you have come to royal position for such a time as this?" (4:14).

## I. The Story of Esther (1:1–9:17)

### A. Royal Banquet (1:1–22)

The story opens with a royal banquet given by the Persian King Xerxes (vv.1–9). It was during this banquet that the queen, Vashti, refused the request of the king to attend his banquet and thus forfeited her claim to the throne (vv.10–22). In telling the story, the writer goes to some length to show that the loss of the queen was regrettable to everyone, especially the king, and thus could not be explained in human terms other than a highly unfortunate series of events. It is precisely in these kinds of events that the writer casts God as the unseen mover behind the events of human history. There may even be an appeal to comedy in the writer's depiction of the king and his nobles scrambling to come up with a plan to ensure that "all the women will obey him respect their husbands" (v.20) and that "every man should be ruler over his own household" (v.22). As the story unfolds it becomes clear that the kingdom prospers only when the king listens to the wise counsel of his wife.

### B. Esther Becomes Queen (2:1–23)

Again there is irony in the way the story is told. The king, searching for a queen who will obey him (vv.1–4), finds Esther (vv.5–7), a queen who at the moment of crisis would have the courage to disobey him. She was taken into the king's palace and chosen as queen (vv.8–18).

Within the course of telling the story, the writer carefully introduces Esther to his readers. Not only are we told that Esther "was lovely in form and features" (v.7), but also we see that her beauty and charm were immediately recognized by Hegai, the one in charge of the king's harem (v.9a). His excessive concern for her (v.9b) leaves no doubt in the reader's mind that she will be chosen by the king. It is really no contest. The writer's depiction of Esther's moral courage, however, will take more time. Here at the beginning of the story we learn only that Esther was raised by "a Jew of the tribe of Benjamin, named Mordecai," one of the exiles from Jerusalem (vv.5–7). Her resolute obedience to the word of Mordecai (v.10) already drops a hint of the kind of woman she will prove to be. Moreover, Mordecai's courage in exposing the assassination plot against the king (vv.19–23), shows that Esther is following good counsel.

## C. The Moment of Crisis (2:19–5:8)

Ironically it was Mordecai's refusal to pay honor to Haman that incited him against the Jews (3:1–15). Thus the story teaches more than perseverance through suffering. As is also the case in the book of Daniel, this story teaches steadfast loyalty to one's beliefs, even in the face of recriminations. It is not hard to see in Mordecai's refusal to bow before Haman, the equally bold refusal of Shadrach, Meshach, and Abednego to bow down to Nebuchadnezzar's golden image (Da 3:16–18), or Daniel's continued daily prayers in the face of Darius's prohibition (Da 6:10). In each case there was a willingness to accept the consequences and, at the same time, an implicit trust that God would intervene.

Unlike the situations of Daniel and his three friends who were rescued miraculously the mouths of the lions or from the fiery furnace, the deliverance that came to God's people in the book of Esther was the result of a courageous act of a young woman, an intricate series of events and intrigues, and the wise counsel of Mordecai. The writer's point is to show that the hand of God can be seen in the one case just as clearly as the other. God can not only stop the mouths of lions, he can also determine the destiny of kings and queens, if need be, for the sake of his chosen people.

Mordecai's initial response to Haman's decree does not reveal the underlying stratagem that later surfaces. He was simply overwhelmed with grief and horror (4:1–5). In his pleading with

Esther to confront the king, however, we see the well-laid plans of a wise counselor (vv.6–17). Mordecai's words to Esther also focus the reader's attention on the central lesson of the book: "If you remain silent at this time, relief and deliverance for the Jews will arise from another place" (v.14). Though God's plans depend on human efforts, they are not limited by those efforts. Human decisions do not determine God's plan; they are only the means by which one becomes a part of those plans. Thus Esther chose to go before the king (5:1–8) and become a part of God's plan for his people.

The reader can immediately see the events begin to take shape. Haman's boasting and preparation for the death of Mordecai would prove to be nothing more than a confirmation that God was honoring Esther's courage (5:9–14; cf. 7:9–10). The same is true for the king's sleepless night and his plans to honor Mordecai on the next day (6:1–14). All too quickly, for Haman's sake at least, the crucial pieces of his fate fell into place. By his own selfish words, Haman pronounced a blessing on Mordecai and the Jews (6:6–13), reminiscent of Balaam's constrained blessings of Israel in the days of Moses (see comments on Nu 22–24). Not only did Haman inadvertently bless God's people, but he was hanged on the very gallows he had designed for Mordecai (7:1–10), his estate was put into the hands of Esther and Mordecai (8:1–2), his plans to destroy the Jews were reversed by a royal edict (8:3–17), and the Jews were given free reign to protect themselves against the hatred of their enemies that had been stirred up by Haman (9:1–17).

In mounting up such a multilayered set of "coincidences," the writer builds his case to the reader that God is at work in the world both to will and to do his good pleasure, and that all things work together for good for those who trust in him. After a similar set of "coincidences" in the life of Joseph, the author of the Pentateuch offered the following explanation in Joseph's speech to his brothers: "You intended to harm me, but God intended it for good to accomplish what is now being done, the saving of many lives" (Ge 50:20).

## II. The Feast of Purim (9:18–32)

The writer of the book of Esther now turns to the meaning of the Jewish festival Purim. So great was the deliverance of God's people that an annual feast was commissioned for its remembrance.

## III. A Final Word About Mordecai (10:1–3)

Curiously, the book concludes with a final word about Mordecai rather than Esther. Though Esther was the crucial link in the working out of God's blessing for Israel, the writer concludes by saying that it was Mordecai who "worked for the good of his people and spoke up for the welfare of all the Jews" (v.3b). Though tradition has tended to remember the single act of courage of the beautiful queen Esther, the writer himself calls our attention back to Mordecai.

# Job

## Introduction

The book of Job is named for its principal character, Job. The name means "the persecuted one." The author of the book is unknown, as is the time of its composition. It has been attributed both to Moses and to Solomon, but with little solid evidence for support. The most that can be said is that the book and its central themes are a part of the "wisdom books" of the OT. Job is presented as a nearly perfect example of a wise man. What happens to him in this book and what he learns from it are presented as a model for the life of the people of God.

The following outline gives the structure of the book.

I. Prologue (1:1–2:13)

II. Job's Lamentation (3:1–16)

III. Job's Discourses (4:1–42:6)

   A. Job and his Friends: Eliphaz, Bildad, Zophar (4:1–31:40)

   B. Elihu's Speeches (32:1–37:24)

   C. The Lord's Speeches (38:1–42:6)

IV. Epilogue (42:7–17)

Rather than look at all of the passages in the book one by one, we will instead summarize the argument of the book as a whole.

## Summary of the Argument of the Book

As part of the biblical wisdom books (Job to Song of Songs), the book of Job presents the man Job as an example of a perfectly wise man. He is described by the Lord himself as "blameless and upright, a man who fears God and shuns evil" (1:8). What especially marked Job as a wise man was the fact that he feared God (1:8–9). The fundamental and essential quality of biblical wisdom is "the fear of the LORD" (cf. Ps 111:10; Pr 1:7). As the perfect example of the kind of wisdom that God intended his people to seek and to have,

Job became the target of a great challenge. Satan attacked God in the first chapter of the book by challenging the validity of divine wisdom. Like Goliath (1Sa 17), God's adversary, Satan, challenged the validity of true godly wisdom.

We must bear in mind that we, as readers of the book of Job, are at an advantage. Neither Job nor his friends had access to the information given us in the prologue to the book. Job did not know that his troubles were the result of "a test" of his wisdom. Nor did he know that his troubles did not come as a result of divine punishment for sin or unrighteousness. Thus, as readers, we know the truth about Job's troubles. We know that he was righteous, even though throughout most of the book, Job's friends accused him of unrighteousness. We must not read the book as though Job knew he was being tested. All that Job knew was that he was living a perfectly good life and, all of a sudden, trouble came down on him in heaps.

It is generally held that the primary purpose of the book is to explain why God's people suffer or why the righteous suffer. Though there are lessons in the book about suffering, it is a mistake to read the book as an explanation for that. Strictly speaking, the book explains only why Job suffered. We, the readers know from the prologue that he was the wisest man on earth and as such was selected as an object of Satan's attack. He was a test case for divine wisdom.

The central purpose of the book of Job is to give a practical demonstration of the value of divine wisdom. Thus the first question posed in the book was God's question to Satan: "Have you considered my servant Job . . . a man who fears God and shuns evil?" (1:8). To this Satan responded, "Does Job fear God for nothing?" (v.9), meaning by implication that Job feared God for what he got out of it. Here is the central concern of the book. What motivates the kind of godly living exemplified in the righteous man Job? Is it the possessions and security that God has given him? Or would a truly wise man continue to live a godly life, even in the face of material loss and suffering? Satan's answer was "No! Take away his blessings and Job will not continue to live a godly life." God, however, knowing that true wisdom is its own reward, answered "yes" in Job's behalf. A truly wise man seeks to live a godly life regardless of the earthly rewards.

The theme of the quality and motivation of Job's wisdom is developed in the book along two lines. (1) There was the challenge and the test of Job's wisdom, recorded in the prologue. Job was tested twice (1:13–19; 2:7–10), and on both occasions he proved by his actions that his fear of God, his wisdom, was genuine (1:20–22; 2:10).

(2) In the main body of the book of Job, we see Job learning deeper lessons about God and one's relationship to him. The lessons that Job learned all point to the central theme of the book: true wisdom, true godliness, comes from complete submission to God's rule, regardless of temporary rewards or suffering. We hear Job echo this conclusion in the final scene of the book: "I know that you can do all things; no plan of yours can be thwarted. . . . My ears had heard of you but now my eyes have seen you. Therefore I retract [NIV, despise myself] and repent in dust and ashes" (42:2–6). What did Job repent of? Was it the unrighteousness that had caused his suffering? No, for it was not unrighteousness that had brought on Job's troubles; he was a "righteous" man (1:8). Job repented here of his own limiting of God's sovereign will and the limitations he had placed on God' authority: "Surely I spoke of things I did not understand, things too wonderful for me to know" (42:3). Job learned that

true wisdom came only with total submission to God's rule; i.e., Job learned the fear of the Lord.

The series of discourses that developed between Job and his friends is based on a common assumption they shared. Job and his friends were equally convinced that Job's suffering came from God and that there was a lesson to be learned from it. We the readers know that this assumption was only partially correct. The writer of the book has thus put us in the position of having to evaluate critically the various positions of Job and his friends. The reader is thus pulled into the discourse as one who knows more than the participants themselves.

Job's three friends held essentially the same view of Job's sufferings. For them Job's troubles were a matter of divine retribution. They each in turn made the point that no one, including Job, was free from sin and thus absolutely righteous before God. Moreover, they held, in agreement with the rest of Scripture, that God punishes sin. Thus they concluded, each in his own way, that Job ought to examine his life more carefully to see what sin or sins might have caused his troubles. Their advice was always the same: "If you return to the Almighty, you will be restored" (22:23; cf. 5:8–17; 8:20; 11:13–15; 22:21–30; 36:8–11). As readers we can see that their advice was good but misplaced. Nevertheless, in the end, Job did repent (42:6).

Elihu's position was that Job's troubles were intended to provide him with divine discipline and instruction. He began his discourse by maintaining the position that a person cannot question the justice of God (34:16). He also maintained, in opposition to the three friends, that Job's problems could be explained by other means than by assuming that Job had sinned (33:13–30). God might allow misfortune in one's life as correction or to keep someone from foolish pride. Since Job apparently did not know what purpose God had in mind in these troubles, Elihu concluded that Job's only safe response was "to fear" the Lord and trust his justice (37:23–24). As readers who have all the necessary facts of the case, we can easily see that Elihu's position was much nearer to the point than Job's three friends.

In response to such advice, Job persistently maintained his innocence. He was convinced that he had done nothing to merit the magnitude of his troubles (9:21; 16:12; 23:10–12; 27:2, 4–6). Job, for his part, wanted a hearing with God (13:3,14; 23:3–5). As readers we know that Job's suffering was not caused by sin, but we learn from the text itself that his continuous accusations against God came dangerously close to attributing injustice to God. The Lord himself responded to his pleads with the warning, "Would you discredit my justice? Would you condemn me to justify yourself?" (40:8). In any event, when Job did get his hearing with God, he found that he could not plead innocence. He might plead the fact that he had lived a righteous life and had feared God; but when anyone does come into God's presence, these things do not seem to count. When standing in God's mighty presence, Job learned that his righteous living and his fear of God were only the obvious response of a creature before his Creator. They did not serve as merit to be presented to God.

Job's conclusion is also the lesson of the book as a whole: "I am unworthy—how can I reply to you? I put my hand over my mouth" (40:4). "Therefore," he continues, "I retract [NIV, despise myself] and repent in dust and ashes" (42:6).

We have looked at the events of the book of Job from the perspective of Job and his friends. There is, however, another perspective on these events offered by this book—the divine perspective. By means of the prologue (chs. 1–2), the divine speech (chs. 38–41), and the epilogue (ch. 42), the reader himself is put in the position of seeing the events from the divine perspective. From that point of view, Job was right in his claim that there was no sin in his life that merited the magnitude of suffering he had experienced (1:8). From the divine perspective, however, we also know that Job was wrong when, to justify himself, he accused God of being unjust (40:8). Here the lesson of Job is that a person does not have all the resources nor the right to call God's justice into question. In the end, however, Job's wisdom prevailed. He retracted his accusations against God's justice (42:6), submitted to the rule of God, and was accepted again and blessed by God (vv.7–17).

The book of Job thus shows that the truly wise man, like Job, is one who submits to the will of God and who does not call God's justice into question. God is the Creator, human beings are the creatures, and, in the final analysis, their role is to submit to the divine authority. This is not to say that the book teaches that whatever God does is just, simply because he has the right to do it. It is, rather, to say that God always does justice, even though we cannot always see it from our limited perspective. As represented in the character of Job, the proper response of God's people is to submit to God's will and wait for the return of divine blessing.

# Psalms

## Introduction

The book of Psalms can be read as a single book with each individual psalm intentionally arranged within the book in a meaningful way. Underlying the arrangement of the psalms within the book is the view that they are to be read as pointing to the messianic King.

## I. Introduction (1–2)

### Psalm 1

The first psalm serves as an introduction to the whole book. It establishes the central theme of the book—meditation on Scripture as the way of the righteous. In God's written Word, the righteous will find blessing.

### Psalm 2

The second psalm is attached to the first as a means of further qualifying its central theme. The psalm is a messianic psalm based on the promise to David in 2Sa 7:16 (see comments on 2Sa 7). The effect of attaching it to the first psalm is to show that meditation on Scripture ultimately leads to trusting in the Messiah (v.12).

## II. David and the Promised Seed (3–9)

### Psalm 3

The link to the earlier psalms is provided by the superscription, "A psalm of David. When he fled from his son Absalom." This superscription informs the reader that the theme of this psalm continues to be that of the messianic promise to David in 2Sa 7:16. In the case of Ps 3, the question is raised as to how David himself understood God's promise when his own son, Absalom, rebelled against the house of David (2Sa 15). The words of David here show that his trust in God's promise did not waiver, even in the face of a grievous obstacle to the fulfillment of that promise. In spite of overwhelming odds

against him, and thus against God's own promise to him, David says, "From the LORD comes deliverance" (v.8). Within the book of Psalms, this psalm is thus intended as an encouragement to the reader to imitate David's faith in God's promises and not to let one's faith in God waiver even though God's promised Messiah had not yet come.

The superscription in Ps 7, which speaks of the news David received of Absalom's death, serves as a bracket to show the reader that Pss 4–6 must also be understood in light of the rebellion of Absalom. The superscriptions thus provide an important key to the context within which these psalms are to be read and understood. They also point to the overall messianic sense given to these psalms.

### Psalm 4

Continuing from Ps 3 (see comment), this psalm shows David's constant pleading for God to act on his behalf—"Answer me when I call to you, O my righteous God. Give me relief from my distress" (v.1). When read within the larger context of the book of Psalms, David's words express the composer's own longing for the coming of the promised Messiah. This theme continues throughout the book.

### Psalm 5

David, the king, addresses God, the King, waiting in eager expectation of God's reply. Here he asks that his enemies, who "have rebelled against" God (v.10b), be brought to their knees. The superscriptions of Pss 3 and 7 have helped identify David's plight historically as Absalom's rebellion. The introduction to the book of Psalms (Pss 1–2), however, has directed the reader to understand David's words in light of the promised Messiah. The righteous that David prays for in v.12 are thus the "blessed" ones who "put their trust [NIV, take refuge] in him" (v.12), i.e., the Lord's "Anointed One" (v.2).

## Psalm 6

Again David returns to the theme of waiting patiently for God's response. David is in anguish as he waits for God to act, "How long, O LORD, how long?" (v.3), but still he knows that God has promised to save him (v.4) and that the Lord has heard his prayer (v.9). The terminology that David uses in v.4, "because of your unfailing love," shows that his thoughts are on God's promise to send an eternal king in 2Sa 7.

## Psalm 7

The superscription provides the key to the links between the first several psalms. This psalm represents David's response to the word of Absalom's death, which he heard from the Cushite (2Sa 18:21–33). On hearing the news, David was greatly distressed and said, "O my son Absalom! My son, my son Absalom! If only I had died instead of you" (18:33). In a similar fashion here, David disclaims all guilt in the matter, saying, "If I have done evil to him . . . let him trample my life to the ground and make me sleep in the dust" (vv.4–5). David appeals to God, the "righteous judge" (v.11), and turns his eyes toward God's final judgment of the ungodly: "He has prepared his deadly weapons; he makes ready his flaming arrows" (v.13).

At the close of the psalm, David vows to "sing praise to the name of the LORD Most High" (v.17). The composer of the book of Psalms has thus placed a Davidic praise psalm immediately after this. Psalm 8 opens with the praise of the name of God.

## Psalm 8

The NT writers saw this psalm as a prophecy of Jesus Christ (Heb 2:6–8). The fact that within the strategy of the book of Psalms this psalm is linked to the divine promise to David of a future Messiah (Ps 2:2), suggests that the composer also understood it messianically. The "son of man" (v.4b) would

then be understood in light of "the son" in 2:12, "Kiss the Son." In such a context, the psalm was probably to be understood as a praise of the "Son of man" who, "crowned . . . with glory and honor" was "a little lower than God [see NIV note]" (v.5). He is thus a royal figure, much like the "son of man" in Da 7:10–14, and has dominion over all of God's creation (v.6).

The writer of Hebrews, in relating this psalm to Jesus, says that the Son was "crowned with glory and honor because he suffered death" (Heb 2:9b). Though there is no mention of the death of this heavenly King in Ps 8, the superscription to the following psalm expressly mentions "To the tune of 'The Death of the Son'" (see comment on the next psalm).

## Psalm 9

In the NIV superscription to this psalm, the phrase "To the tune of" has been added by the translators and is not in the Hebrew text. Thus, the title of the psalm is simply, "Concerning the death of the son." This note provides an interesting link between Pss 8 and 9. The composer of the book of Psalms has intentionally identified the words of this psalm with the notion of the death of "the son of man" in Ps 8. It can hardly be coincidental that in the NT, the "glory and honor" with which the "son of man" is crowned (8:5b) is also linked to the death of the Son of God (Heb 2:9b). There appears to be a consistent messianic reading of these psalms within the strategy and structure of the book of Psalms. A similar reading of these psalms is reflected in the NT.

We have already noted that the superscription of Ps 7 had focused the words of that psalm on the death of David's son, Absalom. This raises the question of whether the "death of the son" was intended to refer to Absalom. However, because of the intervening mention of the "son of man" in Ps 8, the "death of the son" here is surely intended to refer to that son (8:4) rather than to Absalom (7:1; cf. 3:1). The position and sequence of the psalms thus play an important role in the sense they have in the larger context of the book.

In light of the messianic and eschatological sense that this psalm has within the book of Psalms, it is fitting that the theme of Ps 9 is the eternal kingship of God: "The LORD reigns forever; he has established his throne for judgment. He will judge the world in righteousness" (vv.7–8). Moreover, the theme of Zion as the place of God's kingship, an essential part of the Davidic promise (2Sa 7), plays an important role in this psalm (9:11, 14) and many others within the book. The central theme of the psalm is the judgment of the wicked nations (vv.15, 17, 19–20) and the divine salvation of the righteous (vv.9, 18); it ends on a high note of triumph and praise. As we will see, however, the next psalm takes a sharp turn in another direction and hence shifts the thematic focus of the book as a whole.

## III. Times of Trouble for the House of David (10–41)

### Psalm 10

The opening lines of this psalm set the tone for the next series of psalms: "Why, O LORD, do you stand far off? Why do you hide yourself in times of trouble?" (v.1). In stark contrast to the victorious praise of Ps 9, the focus of Ps 10 is the times of trouble when the wicked one prospers (vv.1–11). There is hope at the end of the psalm, however, and it consists of the same hope in the coming kingdom of God: "The LORD is King for ever and ever; the nations will perish from his land" (v.16).

### Psalm 11

Like Ps 10, the focus of the psalm is on the question of what the righteous should do during the times of trouble when the wicked prosper: "When the foundations are being destroyed, what can the righteous do?" (v.3). The answer given by the psalm lies in the patient expectation of the righteous for the coming of the divine King (vv.4–7). The opening line of the psalm, "In the LORD I trust [NIV, take refuge]," is a reference back to the introductory theme of trust in God's promise to send the Anointed One (Ps 2:2, 12).

### Psalm 12

This psalm adds significantly to the general theme of the surrounding psalms. It too focuses on times of trouble for God's people (vv.1–4). Rather than looking into the future to the time of the establishment of God's kingdom, however, it stresses God's present comfort and care for the righteous (vv.5–8): The Lord "will keep us safe and protect us" (v.7).

### Psalm 13

This psalm looks internally at the heart of the righteous who must wait patiently for God's salvation. As such it expresses the despair that often accompanies such waiting: "How long, O LORD? Will you forget me forever?" (v.1). The psalm concludes by recalling God's "unfailing love" (v.5), the use of which term in Hebrew links the psalmist's hope to God's promise of a deliverer from the house of David (2Sa 7:16).

### Psalm 14

As in the introduction to the book of Psalms (Pss 1–2), the hope in God's messianic promises to the house of David is cast in terms of the wise man and the fool. The "fool" is one who has given up hope that God will punish the wicked and deliver the righteous (vv.1–5a). The wise, however, are those who continue to long "that salvation for Israel would come out of Zion!" (v.7a).

The context makes it clear that the fool's words, "There is no God," are not those of an atheist who doubts God's existence, but rather they are the words of the wicked who think they can get away unscathed with their evil deeds. The psalmist calls not for proof of God's existence but confidence in his presence, "for God is present in the company of the righteous" (v.5b).

## Psalm 15

Having raised the question of the righteous who wait for the fulfillment of God's promise in Ps 14, the composer now offers a description of true righteousness (vv.2–5a).

## Psalm 16

As a model of faithfulness and trust in God's messianic promise, the composer includes one of David's own reflections on the Davidic promise (2Sa 7:16). At the center of his thoughts is David's confidence in the resurrection. In Ps 16 David contemplates his own trust in God (vv.1–4) and the blessing he had received from God's hand (vv.5–6; cf. 2Sa 7). The source of his rejoicing is God's promise of eternal blessings (vv.7–11). David knows that God will not abandon him and his descendants in the grave, and he keeps the promise of an eternal king and kingdom before him at all times (v.8). David's confidence in his own resurrection stems from his trust in the resurrection of his Promised Seed: "nor will you let your Holy One see decay" (v.10).

The apostle Peter saw numerous aspects of this psalm fulfilled in the death and resurrection of Jesus (Ac 2:24–32). When read within the context of the book of Psalms, there is much in this psalm that bears out Peter's interpretation. His understanding is further born out by the fact that the next psalm lays great stress on the theme of resurrection.

## Psalm 17

This psalm is a prayer of David, but its content focuses the reader's attention on the theme of resurrection. For the most part the psalm recalls the laments of David as he was being pursued by his enemies. At the close of the psalm, however, David's thoughts look beyond his immediate enemies, resting his hope in the fact that one day he will see God's face: "When I awake, I will be satisfied with seeing your likeness" (v.15b).

To the extent that the composer of the book of Psalms sees David as a messianic figure, his words in this psalm give expression to the hope of the resurrection of the Messiah found in the previous psalm.

## Psalm 18

The superscription locates this psalm in an earlier period of David's life when he fled from Saul and his army (the same psalm is found in 2Sa 22). The psalm begins with David's expression of trust in God (vv.1–3) and follows with a lament (vv.4–5), a call to God for help (v.6a) and God's answer (v.6b). The central part of the psalm consists of a description of God's rescue of David cast in the form of a theophany, i.e., an awesome display of God's power as Creator (vv.7–19). In the remainder of the psalm, David casts himself as a figure of the promised messianic King, God's "anointed" (v.50), seeing in his own divinely wrought victories a portrait of his eternal descendant (v.50b).

## Psalm 19

Two themes come together in Ps 19: the revelation of God in creation (vv.1–6) and the revelation of God in his Word (vv.7–14). God's glory is displayed in creation and God's grace is displayed in his Word. Within the whole of the book of Psalms, three major psalms stress the importance of the revelation of God's will in his Word: Pss 1, 19, and 119. Each of these is immediately followed by a distinctly messianic psalm or group of messianic psalms: Pss 2, 20–21, 120–133. This suggests that within the whole of the book, the composer intends to balance the one theme, God's Word, with that of the other, God's Anointed—the Messiah. The Word of God and the Anointed One, the Messiah, are thus represented as God's two primary means for bringing salvation and redemption. The feature that makes God's Word "more precious than gold" (v.10) is that it points to the Redeemer (v.14b).

## Psalm 20

Psalm 20 is a blessing (vv.1–5) in behalf of the Anointed King of the house of David (v.6). Its aim is the fulfillment of the promises to David as described in Ps 2 and 2Sa 7:16. Though meaningful in its own right, the psalm functions as a thematic marker within the structure of the whole book. It establishes the context of the surrounding psalms by linking them to the messianic themes developed in the introduction to the book (Pss 1–2) and to the messianic promise in 2Sa 7.

## Psalm 21

Psalm 21 takes up the theme of the king's trust in God (v.1) introduced in Ps 20:7. Further links between the two psalms can be seen by comparing 20:4, "May he give you the desire of your heart," and 21:2, "You have granted him the desire of his heart."

There are, moreover, links in Ps 21 with several of the preceding psalms. The purpose of such links is to elevate the portrait of the "king" taken up from the preceding psalms to a much higher plane. The psalmist, for example, tells God, "Surely you have granted [the king] eternal blessings and made him glad with the joy of your presence" (v.6). The king is thus one who dwells in God's presence and enjoys eternal blessings. Furthermore, by addressing the king directly in vv. 8–12, the psalm connects the idea of God's future judgment (v.9b) with the coming of the "king" (v.9a). The king is thus not one

of David's historical descendants but rather the messianic king promised to David. In this way Ps 21 plays an important role within this book by focusing the reader's attention on the future of the house of David instead of on its past. For the Davidic king, the time of the fulfillment of the hope expressed in the psalms still lies in the future, in the hope of the coming of the Messiah.

## Psalm 22

The first part of the psalm (vv.1–22) is a lament of "the afflicted one" (v.24a). Though David is the author of this psalm, he is not to be understood as the one who is speaking in the psalm itself. A careful look at it shows that David as author begins to speak only at v.23, where he addresses the congregation, speaking about the "suffering of the afflicted one" (v.24), which has been recorded in the first part of the psalm. David, speaking about the "afflicted one," says that God "has listened to his cry for help" (v.24b). In v.25 he turns to address the "afflicted one" saying, "From you comes the theme of my praise in the great assembly." By speaking *about* the Lord, not *to* him, in vv.25–26, the author shows that he is addressing the Afflicted One. Continuing to address him in the following verse, David says "all the families of the nations will bow down before you [NIV, him]" (v.27b), using an image that recalls the "son of man" in Da 7:13–14. Finally, looking into the distant future, David concludes by saying, "Posterity will serve him; future generations will be told about the Lord. They will proclaim his righteousness" (vv.30–31).

As the psalm now stands, it represents David's proclamation to the congregation regarding the suffering of the "afflicted one" and his ultimate victory over death. The description of his suffering (vv.7–18) has, for good reason, long been associated with the crucifixion of Jesus (see Jn 19:24).

## Psalm 23

Following closely on the heels of the Suffering One in Ps 22, who feels "forsaken" by God at his moment of trial (22:1), the present psalm is centered on the theme of God's presence in the face of death. The psalm is about the "anointed" one who enjoys God's presence forever (v.6). In the Hebrew text of this psalm, the speaker says, "I will return to the house of the LORD," rather than "I will dwell in the house of the LORD." The "house of the LORD" refers to the temple in Jerusalem. This psalm thus looks forward to the time when the Anointed One returns to the temple. Within the OT, this is a common messianic image (cf. Zec 9:8–9). It is thus fitting that the following psalm is a celebration of the return of the "King of glory" to the temple in Jerusalem.

## Psalm 24

The victorious return of the glorious King to the house of the Lord is celebrated in this psalm. His kingdom is "the world, and all who live in it" (v.1). The King is met by those who have a pure heart (v.4) and are blessed of the Lord (v.5). They sing to the gates of Jerusalem and the temple to open for the entrance of the victorious King. In this psalm the King is identified as the Lord himself. It is not uncommon in the Bible to refer to the King Messiah as God (cf. Ps 45:6; Isa 9:6).

## Psalm 25

During the time that the book of Psalms was being composed in its final form and the psalms were being arranged in the order in which we now have them, a prominent theme in Israel's messianic hope was that Israel and the nations would return to Jerusalem and the temple, and would there be taught God's truth, the Law (cf. Zec 8:20–23). This expectation was rooted in the words of such prophets as Isaiah: "In the last days . . . many people will come and say, 'Come, let us go up to the mountain of the LORD, to the house of the God of Jacob. He will teach us his ways'" (Isa 2:2–3). The placement of Ps 25 after Ps 24 appears to reflect this messianic picture. Having come to the temple in Jerusalem to receive the King of glory (Ps 24), the psalmist now asks, "Guide me in your truth and teach me, for you are God my Savior, and my hope is in you all day long" (v.5). The psalm, written as an acrostic of the Hebrew alphabet, repeatedly raises the request for the Lord's instruction. The last line of the psalm expresses its central theme, the eager hope for the coming of Israel's Redeemer (v.22).

## Psalm 26

Continuing the theme of the enjoyment of God's presence in the temple, the psalmist praises God for his protection and care. He loves God's house, the temple, where God's glory dwells (v.8). Echoing the themes of God's instruction from both Pss 1 and 25, he confesses that he walks in God's truth and does not "consort with hypocrites . . . evildoers and . . . the wicked" (vv.3–5). Like many of Israel's prophets (e.g., Isa 29:13), the psalmist stresses the importance of sincerity of heart in worship (vv.6–11).

## Psalm 27

Once again, following the theme established in Ps 23, the focus of the psalmist is on God's presence in the temple and his loving protection of the righteous. The psalmist looks forward with hope and expectation to the time when he will again "dwell in the house of the LORD all the days of [his] life" (v.4), clearly, within the book of Psalms, an allusion to Ps 23:6. An added exhortation is attached to the end of this psalm, giving it a note of urgency: "Wait for the LORD; be strong and take heart and wait for the LORD" (27:14). Here David's words are being presented to the reader as an example to follow. We are called upon to be like

David and "be strong and take heart and wait for the LORD."

## Psalm 28

Within the arrangement of the psalms in this section of the book, Ps 28 plays a key thematic role. It not only takes up the theme of God's presence in the temple, which is found in the preceding psalms, but, more importantly in light of the whole of the book, it ties it into the overarching theme of hope in the coming of the Messiah.

In the preceding psalms, readers are admonished to be like David and to place their hope in God. In the present psalm, that hope is focused in God's sending his Anointed One (v.8). Though David is the author of the psalm, his own words appear to conclude with the confession in v.7, "The LORD is my strength and my shield. . . . I will give thanks to him in song." The psalm continues, however, with an application of David's words to a specific situation in the life of the people, namely, their waiting for the salvation and blessing of the "anointed one" (vv.8–9).

## Psalm 29

In Ps 28:7 David says, "I will give thanks to [the Lord] in song." The links between Pss 28 and 29 (e.g., 28:8a; 29:11a) suggest that the composer of the book intends us to read the present psalm as that praise that David sang to God. In this psalm the Lord is praised both as the Creator and Sustainer of all creation (vv.1–9a) and as the King who dwells among his people in his temple (vv.9b–11).

## Psalm 30

In the title of this psalm we are told that this psalm was used "for the dedication of the temple." Since these titles are a part of the book and often serve to link the various psalms to other biblical texts and to each other, we should pay close attention to the sense intended by this title. We have seen that the continuing theme of the psalms in this section is the enjoyment of God's presence in the temple (cf. 23:6). Since this psalm refers to a divine rescue of David and his return to the temple, the mention of the dedication of the temple most naturally recalls the return of the Israelites from the Babylonian captivity and the rebuilding of the temple in Jerusalem. God's rescue and restoration of David after a season of trials is thus made into a picture of Israel's recovery from exile. A similar use of David's psalms can be seen in Ps 51.

## Psalm 31

As in Ps 30, David's prayers for help from the Lord are presented as exemplary models of faithfulness. David took refuge in the Lord (vv.1–9), and though he suffered greatly (vv.10–13), he did not lose heart (vv.14–22). At the close of the psalm, the "saints" of the Lord are addressed in terms reminiscent of the first psalm: "The LORD preserves the faithful, but the proud he pays back in full" (v.23; cf. 1:6). The final words of the psalm, "Be strong and take heart" (v.24), recall God's challenge to Joshua, "Be strong and courageous" (Jos 1:6).

## Psalm 32

David rejoiced in God's forgiving grace (vv.1–2). It did not come easy, however. He agonized greatly before openly confessing his need for God's forgiveness (vv.3–5). His joy at God's forgiveness leads him to call upon others to seek the Lord's grace while he can still be found (vv.6–10; cf. 95:7b). As with many of the preceding psalms, at the close of this psalm a further application of David's words is made on behalf of the "righteous" and "upright in heart" (v.11). The "righteous" are those to whom the book of Psalms as a whole is addressed (cf. 1:6).

## Psalm 33

This psalm follows closely and is linked to Ps 32 by addressing its readers as "righteous" and "upright" (v.1; cf. 32:11). It is a praise (vv.1–5) to God the Creator (vv.6–9) and the sovereign Lord of the nations (vv.10–19). At the close of the psalm we hear the voice of God's people responding to the word of praise: "We wait in hope for the LORD; he is our help and our shield" (vv.20–22). Within the compositional strategy of the book of Psalms, David's words of praise have given expression to the people's hope for future deliverance.

## Psalm 34

By means of the superscription, the composer of the book of Psalms links this psalm with a specific situation in the life of David, "when he pretended to be insane before Abimelech [i.e., Achish], who drove him away, and he left" (cf. 1Sa 21:14). At that time David was fleeing from Saul and sought refuge with the Philistines. God delivered him both from Saul and the Philistines.

The psalm is an alphabetic acrostic on the theme of God's deliverance. The final line (v.22), which is added to the acrostic, focuses the reader's attention on God's redemption of his servants who take refuge in him. In doing so, this line links the psalm to the larger messianic theme established in Ps 2:12, "Kiss the Son. . . . Blessed are all who take refuge in him."

## Psalm 35

This psalm is concerned almost entirely with the theme of the Lord's vindication of his faithful servant (v.27). The psalmist does not find the source of his hope in his own righteousness but in God's concern for the poor and the weak (v.10) and for the unjust treatment he has received (vv.11–18).

## Psalm 36

The psalmist's attention turns from the righteous sufferer in Ps 35 to the wiles of the wicked (vv.1–4) and God's protection of the righteous (vv.5–12).

## Psalm 37

In its general themes, Ps 37 can be classed as a wisdom psalm; that is, it is concerned with proper actions and outlooks among God's people. Its message is "Do not fret because of evil men" (v.1), and, "Trust in the LORD and do good" (v.3). The Lord will work all things out for the good of the righteous, and the wicked will not succeed. The optimistic tone of the psalm is tempered, however, by the way in which it deliberately postpones the reward of the righteous and the judgment of the wicked. The righteous are directed to "wait patiently" for the Lord to act (v.7). The wicked, though they now prosper, will be cut off in "a little while" (v.10). Ultimately, the vindication of the righteous and the punishment of evil will come in the day of the final judgment, known only to the Lord (v.13). For the present time, the wicked continue to prosper, but their days are numbered. The righteous, on the other hand, are upheld by the Lord's hand (v.24).

Who are the righteous in this psalm? They are those in whose heart is the law of God (v.31; cf. 1:2) and who "take refuge in him" (v.40; cf. 2:12b). The psalm is thus a restatement of the central themes of Pss 1–2 and the whole book.

## Psalm 38

This psalm appears to be placed here as a vivid example of David's own "fretting" over evil men (vv.12, 16–20), the very attitude warned against in Ps 37. Psalm 37 closed with the promise that the Lord will "help" and "save" (NIV, "deliver") the righteous from the hand of the wicked (37:40), and Ps 38 closes with the desperate call to the "Savior" to come quickly to "help" (v.22). In the midst of his lament, however, David sees the hand of God (v.2b), even in his afflictions (vv.1–11). As admonished in 37:34, "Wait for the LORD and keep his way," David has resolved to "wait" for God to answer him (38:15).

## Psalm 39

In this psalm, David's afflictions are viewed from a new vantage point, the divine viewpoint of eternity. When David saw how short were his days (v.4) and the vanity of human life and wealth (v.6), he could not but confess his hope in God alone (v.7) and his sense of alienation in this world (v.12b). Curiously, the psalm concludes on a note of despair (v.13), but it is important to note that it is followed in the next psalm by an account of God's answer to David's prayer and the reassurance of God's promise to send a deliverer (Ps 40).

## Psalm 40

David, the psalmist, begins by recounting deliverance from the Lord (vv.1–3a), seeing his salvation as an example to others to "put their trust in the LORD" (v.3b). David then raises his own experience to the level of a general principle: "Blessed is the man who makes the LORD his trust" (v.4a). Moreover, he views his experience of deliverance in light of God's great "wonders" accomplished for his people in the past (v.5a) and yet promised for the future (v.5b).

With the mention of God's future deliverance, David recalls that which was written "in the scroll of the book" about God's promised deliverer (vv.6–8). He does so by speaking, in the first person, in behalf of the deliverer. The "scroll" to which he refers appears to be the Pentateuch, the book of Moses. In it, Israel was taught that God did not desire "sacrifice and offering" but rather service, exemplified by the sign of piercing the ear of a slave to denote his devotion to his master (Ex 21:6). Such

obedience comes from the heart (40:8; Dt 30:6).

David confesses God's faithfulness and salvation before the whole of the great assembly (v.10). On this basis, he calls out for God to accomplish salvation for his people and the defeat of their enemies (vv.11–17).

## Psalm 41

Following the call for help and deliverance in the previous psalm, the composer of the book of Psalms concludes the first major section with a Davidic psalm of trust. In this psalm David gives expression to the unfailing faithfulness of the Lord in behalf of his own. God is closer than a trusted friend (v.9).

The final words of the psalm, "Praise be to the LORD, the God of Israel, from everlasting to everlasting. Amen and Amen" (v.13), are part of the structure of the book of Psalms. This recurring phrase divides the book into five sections (cf. 72:19; 89:52; 106:48).

## IV. The Prayers of the Sons of Korah (42–49)

## Psalm 42

This psalm is the first of eight prayers and songs of the sons of Korah. When read in sequence, a thematic development can be seen in the arrangement of the psalms. Psalm 42 begins with a plea for restoration and return to God's favor. The psalmist has been cast away from God's presence and longs to return to him and again "go with the multitude, leading the procession to the house of God, with shouts of joy and thanksgiving among the festive throng" (v.4). Though his soul is downcast (vv.5, 11), he strengthens himself in the hope that he will yet praise God among the worshipers at the temple.

## Psalm 43

This psalm continues the same line of thought and development as the previous psalm, a castaway seeking to return to God's presence. The same phraseology is found in both psalms (cf. 42:6a, 11 and 43:5a; 42:9 and 43:2). Since this psalm has no title, it was probably intended to be read together with Ps 42 as a single psalm. Like Ps 42, the psalmist finds himself "oppressed by the enemy" (43:2b; cf. 42:9b). In Ps 42 he sees himself as "forgotten" by God (42:9a), but now he adds the significant thought that he has been cast away by God himself: "You are God my stronghold. Why have you rejected me?" (v.2). The cause of his separation from God now lies in divine rejection, implying fault on the part of the psalmist. With this added sense of guilt, the psalmist's notion of God as his "Savior" (43:5b; cf. 42:11b) implies the further need of divine forgiveness. In the next psalm, the psalmist's laments focus precisely on the question of human guilt.

## Psalm 44

This psalm begins with the words of the congregation, "We" (v.1), reflecting back on God's deliverance and help of their fathers (vv.1–8). It should be noted that in the midst of these reflections, the psalmist inserts his personal thoughts into the words of the congregation, thus providing an explanation of God's past help: "You are my King and my God, who decrees victories for Jacob" (v.4), and "I do not trust in my bow, my sword does not bring me victory" (v.6). These two insertions prove helpful in explaining the unusually strong complaint against the Lord expressed by the congregation in the remainder of the psalm (vv.9–26). The complaint continues along the same lines as Ps 42–43, "But now you have rejected and humbled us" (v.9; cf. 42:9; 43:2).

The congregation's complaint is that God had rejected and humbled them (vv.9–16) for no apparent reason (vv.17–25): "Our hearts had not turned back; our feet had not strayed from your path" (v.18). They had been faithful to

God's commandments and had not fallen into idolatry (v.20). In spite of this, God had hidden his face and forgotten them (v.24). However, if we read their complaint in light of the earlier acknowledgment of the psalmist, "I do not trust in my bow" (v.6), we are led to the conclusion that, though outwardly obedient, they still lacked trust in God. When the psalmist says, "I do not trust in my bow" (v.6), rather than "we do not trust in our bows," he implies that the congregation has yet to learn this lesson. In this respect the sense of the psalm is similar to that of 51:16–17, that what pleases God is not just outward obedience to his commandments, but also "a broken and contrite heart" (51:17b).

The call of the congregation for divine redemption (v.26) is answered by the promise of a divine Redeemer in the next psalm.

## Psalm 45

The call of the people of God for divine redemption in the previous psalm (44:26) finds its answer in this psalm. Using as a motif the image of an ideal earthly king, the psalmist envisions the coming of the divine King (45:6) to defeat the enemies of his people. He first describes the excellence and glory of the Warrior-King (vv.2–3) who will "ride forth victoriously in behalf of truth, humility and righteousness" (v.4) and will defeat the enemy (v.5). He then describes the King as the one who occupies the eternal throne of God (v.6) and rules exalted over other royal figures as the Anointed of God (vv.7–9).

On this the King's wedding day, the psalmist admonishes the bride to "worship" (v.11b; NIV, "honor") the King as her "Sovereign" (v.11b; NIV, "lord"). The use of such language in describing the bride's relationship to the king strongly suggests that she is to be taken as a figure of the congregation's faithful trust in the King. In the same manner, the beauty and purity of the bride are portrayed (vv.13–15) as exemplary of those who enter into his presence, namely, the listening congregation.

## Psalm 46

The portrayal of the coming of the ideal King (Ps 45) is followed by a description of the King's city, Jerusalem, at the time of his coming. When God dwells in his temple in Jerusalem, there is no reason to fear, "The LORD Almighty is with us" (v.7a).

## Psalm 47

This psalm continues the line of thought from the previous psalms by portraying God's reign as King in Jerusalem as extending beyond that of his own chosen people to include all the earth. God, who "is seated on his holy throne" (v.8; cf. 45:6), "reigns over the nations" (v.8).

## Psalm 48

The description of Jerusalem at peace under God's protective care continues from the previous psalms. Jerusalem, like Sinai, is God's holy mountain (vv.1–3). It is safe from all threats (vv.4–7), and his people live there securely (v.8). Within God's protective care, his people meditate on his "unfailing love" and rejoice over his judgments (vv.9–11). Jerusalem is secure with God as their guide, even unto death (vv.12–14; NIV, "the end").

## Psalm 49

Having raised the question of God's care and protection "even to the end" (48:14b; i.e., "death"), this "wisdom" psalm extends the promise of God's care *beyond* the grave. Human beings cannot redeem their own lives (vv.7–9). They cannot add days to it. Wise people and fools, each in their own time, will die (vv.10–14). But the godly should have no cause for worry in the face of death (v.5), because "God will redeem my life from the grave; he will surely take me to himself" (v.15).

The key to life is "understanding" (v.20). Wealth and glory will quickly fade away (vv.16–19). This is the "wisdom" (v.3a) that the psalmist calls upon all to hear (v.1).

## V. The Prayer of Asaph (50)

### Psalm 50

The psalm is divided into two parts, the first being addressed to the righteous (vv.1–15) and the second to the wicked (vv.16–23). To the righteous, the Lord says two things. (1) God will come in judgment to punish the wicked and gather to himself the "consecrated ones who made a covenant with [him] by sacrifice" (vv.1–6).This is no doubt a reference to the covenant sacrifice at Sinai (Ex 24:4–8). (2) In light of the role of sacrifices in establishing the covenant, the psalmist warns the people against undue dependence on it (vv.7–15). God does not need our sacrifices (vv.8–13). What he wants from his people is simple trust: "Call upon me in the day of trouble; I will deliver you, and you will honor me" (v.15).

Turning to the wicked, however, God warns them against undue trust in the law and the covenant (v.16). Though they may give sacrificial offerings, their hearts are disobedient and their tongue speaks evil (vv.17–20). What pleases God is a grateful heart (vv.21–23). This theme leads naturally into David's prayer in the next psalm.

## VI. The Prayers of David (51–65)

### Psalm 51

The occasion of this psalm was the rebuke of David by the prophet Nathan after David had committed adultery with Bathsheba (see the superscription). David calls to God for mercy (vv.1–3). He confesses his guilt against the commandments of God (v.4) and sees it as a part of an even larger guilt that extended back through his parents, before his own birth (v.5). It is for the remission of this guilt that David now cries out to God, "Wash me, and I will be whiter than snow" (v.7), knowing that the only remedy is a new heart: "Create in me a pure heart, O God, and renew a steadfast spirit within me" (vv.8–13). In these words David expresses the living hope of the new covenant (cf. Dt 30:6; Jer 31:31–34; Eze 36:24–27).

David acknowledges that the sacrifices of the old covenant cannot purge him of guilt before God (vv.13–16; cf. 50:9–13). The sacrifice that opens the way to fellowship with God is "a broken spirit" and "a broken and contrite heart" (v.17; cf. 50:14–15).

## Psalm 52

The "evil one" whom David addresses in this psalm is identified in the superscription as Doeg the Edomite. The account of this event is found in 1Sa 21:7 and 22:9–23. The story itself sheds little light on this psalm. The note about Doeg is probably intended to bring David's words into the larger messianic picture of the fall of the house of Edom at the hands of the house of David (cf. Nu 24:18). It had long been an important part of the messianic hope of Israel that the Messiah's coming would be marked by the destruction of Israel's enemies, principally, the Edomites (e.g., Am 9:12; Ob 18). Edom was particularly singled out, not because they were excessively evil, but for what was in fact a literary reason: "Edom," similar to the Hebrew word for humankind ("Adam"), was used in order to form a wordplay. Hence, in speaking of the defeat of Edom (v.5), the psalmist naturally calls to mind God's judgment of all humanity. It is only natural, then, that the next psalm focuses on God's universal judgment of humankind.

## Psalm 53

The psalmist, who sees that the "sons of men" (v.2) have turned away from God and do not fear his judgment

(vv.3–5), concludes that they are "fools" (v.1). When they say, "There is no God," they mean that God will not punish their sins with judgment. They ignore his laws and oppress his people (vv.2–4); but to their surprise, God does act, putting to shame those who attack his people (v.5). In light of his confidence in God's care for Israel, the psalmist calls for God to fulfill his messianic promise to David (cf. 2Sa 7:16), "Oh, that salvation for Israel would come out of Zion!" (v.6).

## Psalm 54

According to the superscription, David wrote this psalm when he had been betrayed to Saul by the "Ziphites." In the psalm itself he calls these men "strangers" and "ruthless men . . . without regard for God" (v.3). They are thus identified with the "fools" in 53:1 who say, "There is no God." In contrast to them, David confesses, "Surely God is my help, the Lord is the one who sustains me" (v.4).

## Psalm 55

At the beginning of this prayer psalm, David calls out for help from the Lord (vv.1–2a) amid deep periods of anguish and rejection (vv.2b–11). Even his own closest friends have turned against him (vv.12–14, 20–21). As the psalm progresses, however, his mood shifts from one of despair to one of trust and resolve to put his confidence in the Lord (vv.16–19). David concludes by admonishing others to imitate himself and put their trust in God (vv.22–23).

## Psalm 56

Having called on others to imitate himself and always trust God, despite the severity of their situation, David now recalls a specific time in his life when he was called upon to do this very thing. It is an account of his prayer "when the Philistines had seized him in Gath" (cf. 1Sa 21:10–15). We learn from this psalm that on that occasion,

David did not hesitate to call out to God for help (vv.1–2), and God heard his call (v.13). He acknowledged his fear (v.3a) as well as his trust in God (vv.3b–5). David describes his troubles in images general enough to apply to virtually any difficult situation. The recurring theme of the psalm is the contrast between God's faithfulness: "In God I trust" (vv.4, 11), and human powerlessness: "What can mortal man do to me?" (cf. vv.4b, 11b).

## Psalm 57

As in the previous psalm, the superscription provides us with a particular setting—David sang this psalm when he "had fled from Saul into the cave" and there found deliverance (1Sa 24:1–4). Amid the dangers of fleeing from the enemy (vv.1–6), David remained firm in his trust in the Lord (vv.7–11).

## Psalm 58

As if turning to address the enemies who have pursued him in the two previous psalms, David begins here by asking, "Do you rulers indeed speak justly?" (v.1a). His answer is based as much on his knowledge of human nature as on his own sense of innocence: "In your heart you devise injustice" (vv.2–5). He knows their accusations against him are unjust (v.2a) and that their attacks on him stem from a wicked heart (vv.3–5). On this basis David calls to God for help, using bold, forthright, imagery (vv.6–9)—drawing on the picture of the defeat of the unrighteous as the slaying of a wild beast (v.6) and the drying up of a mighty river (v.7). David's purpose is to set before the reader a vivid picture of God's righteous vindication of the oppressed (v.10a) and thus to encourage them in the faith that "there is a God who judges the earth" (v.11b).

## Psalm 59

This psalm returns to the specific historical incident "when Saul had sent

men to watch David's house in order to kill him" (cf. 1Sa 19:11). Like most superscriptions, the details of the specific event shed little light on the sense of the psalm itself, but serve rather to show that David's words arose out of real life situations. These are not the musings of a cloistered poet.

Within the psalm itself, David is cast as one hiding from evil, and violent men are those who "return at evening, snarling like dogs, and prowl about the city" (vv.6, 14). But David knows he is safe because he lies within the mighty fortress of a "loving God" (vv.9–10, 16–17). David is confident that he has done no wrong (v.4); thus God will deliver him from these unjust men (vv.5, 10) and will severely punish them (vv.11b–13). David asks God not to bring punishment on them so quickly that the lesson would be lost on the godly (v.11a). It needs to be shown, he suggests, that God's wrath has come upon these ungodly men because of their sin and pride (vv.12–13).

## Psalm 60

By means of the superscription, the psalm is placed in the time period of David's conquests against Aram Naharaim and Aram Zobah (cf. 2Sa 8; 1Ch 18). At that time also David had defeated the Edomites (2Sa 8:12–13). This psalm is particularly focused on that victory. Edom looms large in importance in these psalms because of its role in the early messianic hope that surrounded the house of David (cf. comments on Nu 24:18). Edom is also important in the imagery of the biblical writers as a cipher for all humanity (see comments on Ps 52).

David begins with a confession of Israel's transgressions and the acknowledgment of God's righteous anger against them (vv.1–3). In spite of their experience of divine wrath, he has hope for the faithful that God will save them (vv.4–5), a hope grounded in God's faithful care for his chosen people

Israel (vv.6–7) and his ultimate judgment of their enemies (vv.8–12).

## Psalm 61

Having raised the notion of God's final victory over his enemies in the previous psalm, David here prays in behalf of God's eternal King: "May he be enthroned in God's presence forever" (v.7). David appears in this psalm to reflect on God's promise in 2Sa 7:16, the promise of an eternal kingdom and an eternal King. This is the decree of the Lord mentioned in Ps 2:7. As in 2:8, David here pictures the domain of this King in universal terms: "From the ends of the earth I call to you" (v.2). Moreover, as in 2:12, God's promise to raise up an eternal King to the house of David is the only source of refuge for those who fear him (vv.4–5).

## Psalm 62

Continuing his focus on God's promise to the house of David (2Sa 7:16), which has been an important part of the thematic structure of the book of Psalms, the psalmist turns his attention to God's faithfulness and power: "My soul rests in God alone; my salvation comes from him" (v.1). As it now stands, this psalm does not mention the messianic king, though the notion of salvation (vv.1–2, 6–7), God's loyal love (v.12), and future reward (62:12) bring it within the thematic range of the messianic hope found in the Psalms. When read within the context of Psalms, David's words point specifically to the future salvation of God's people and the promise of a future Messiah. Its linkage to Pss 61 and 63, which in fact take up the theme of the future promised King, suggests that the composer of Psalms saw in David's words in this psalm an expression of hope in the Messiah.

## Psalm 63

The superscription tells us merely that David wrote this psalm "when he was in the desert." This notice, however, provides the setting for much of the imagery and thematic development of the psalm, especially within the context of the book as a whole. In the first place, the notion of David in the desert is the appropriate context for the imagery of his thirsting after God "in a dry and weary land where there is not water" with which the psalm begins (v.1). Moreover, the notion of waiting for God while in the desert recalls the imagery of Israel's sojourn in the desert and their hope of entering into the Promised Land. Thus, this psalm of David is brought into the larger pentateuchal picture of salvation and redemption for Israel, and certain of his words can be seen to echo those of Moses and the Israelites in the desert. When David says, "My soul will be satisfied as with the richest of foods" (v.5), he recalls Israel's daily enjoyment of the divine provision of manna (Ex 16). Moreover, when David says, "They who seek my life will be destroyed; they will go down to the depths of the earth" (v.9), one cannot help but think of the fate of those who opposed Moses in the desert (Nu 16:32–33). Finally, the sudden mention of "the king" at the conclusion of the psalm brings to mind the Pentateuch's focus on the victorious King of the future who would arise from the tribe of Judah and bring peace and salvation to God's people (Ge 49:8–12; Nu 24:7, 17).

It seems reasonable to conclude, then, that the composer of the book of Psalms saw in David's desert prayer a reflection of Israel's hope in the coming of "the King."

## Psalm 64

As with the preceding psalm, within the larger context of the entire book, David's words express faith and hope in God's promise of future salvation for "all mankind" (v.9). He begins with a prayer in his own behalf (vv.1–6), expressing confidence that God will rescue him (vv.7–8). This leads him to an expression of confidence that one day "all mankind" will fear God and proclaim his wonderful works (v.9). He thus concludes by calling on "the righteous to rejoice in the LORD and take refuge in him" (v.10). These last words bring David's psalm into alignment with the central theme of Psalms: "Pay homage to [NIV, Kiss] the Son. . . . Blessed are all who take refuge in him" (2:12).

### Psalm 65

Taking up the theme from 64:9 of God's universal rule, David writes a song of praise to God who dwells in Zion (i.e., Jerusalem) and who rules over all the earth. "All men will come" to Zion (v.2) and will be forgiven their transgressions (v.3). God will be the "Savior, the hope of all the ends of the earth and of the farthest seas" (v.5). He is the Creator (v.6), the Redeemer who brought his people through the Red Sea (v.7), and the Sustainer of his people (vv.8–13).

## VII. Anonymous Psalms (66–67)

### Psalm 66

Following David's description of God's universal reign in Ps 65, the composer of the book of Psalms inserts two anonymous psalms. This first one calls on all the world to sing praises to God for his wonderful deeds (vv.1–4). The psalmist, recalling the theme of the Exodus, tells of what God did for his people in delivering them from bondage in Egypt (vv.5–12). This is a recollection of God's salvation of Israel and his gift of the Promised Land and Jerusalem. While bringing his burnt offering before the Lord at the temple (vv.13–15), the psalmist acknowledges the need for confession of sin (vv.16–18), and he praises God for his answer to prayer (vv.19–20).

### Psalm 67

In the second anonymous psalm, God's salvation of the nations reaches its full expression. It opens with a blessing, "May God be gracious to us and bless us and make his face shine upon us" (v.1). It then turns immediately to the theme of the salvation of the nations, "that your ways may be known on earth, your salvation among all nations" (v.2). The theme of salvation is then extended to encompass God's universal reign over all the world: "May the nations be glad and sing for joy, for you rule the peoples justly and guide the nations of the earth" (v.4). The God of Israel is the God of all the earth (vv.5–7).

These two anonymous psalms have paved the way for the central theme of Ps 68, the coming of the universal King to Zion.

## VII. Prayers of David (68–72)

### Psalm 68

David opens with a call for the coming of the divine King (v.1a) and the defeat of his enemies (vv.1b–2). Turning to the righteous people of his own nation, David calls on them to sing praises to the Lord, who is in his holy dwelling (vv.3–6). He then recounts the appearance of the Lord in his glorious victories in behalf of his people (vv.7–10) when he gave them the Promised Land (vv.11–14). The conquest of the land was great indeed (v.15), but it paled in comparison to God's triumph over Zion, "the mountain where God chooses to reign, where the LORD himself will dwell forever" (v.16). When he has conquered Zion, all nations will come to worship him and bring their gifts (vv.17–18). They will sing praises to God, the King and their Savior (v.19), who will give them life (v.20). When the Lord comes, the enemy will be destroyed (vv.21–23); the Lord will be accompanied by a great procession into the sanctuary (vv.24–26), which will include not only his people Israel (v.27) but also the kings of the earth (vv.28–31).

With this hope in view, David calls on the kingdoms of the earth to sing praises to the Lord, the God of Israel, who is awesome in his sanctuary (vv.32–35).

## Psalm 69

At first glance, the central theme of this psalm appears to contrast sharply with that of the previous psalm. When one reads through the entire psalm, however, it becomes apparent that the two psalms are quite similar—they both express the fervent desire of the psalmist for God's salvation of Zion and the establishment of his kingdom (vv.34–36). In other words, both look back to God's promise to David (cf. Ps 2:7; 2Sa 7:16) and eagerly await its fulfillment in Zion. In the present psalm, however, David focuses his attention on the miserable state of God's people as they await the fulfillment of the promise. They, like David, have sunk "in the miry depths where there is no foothold" (vv.1–3) and have many enemies without cause (v.4). Like David, they are willing to admit their guilt (v.5) and place their hope in the Lord (vv.6–12). They call out for deliverance and salvation (vv.13–18), but they find no one to comfort them (vv.19–21). Thus they beseech the Lord in graphic terms for deliverance and the destruction of their oppressors (vv.22–28). In the end, they, like David, will rest content in the hope that "God will save Zion and rebuild the cities of Judah . . . and those who love his name will dwell there" (vv.29–36).

## Psalm 70

This psalm serves as a fitting request for a speedy answer to David's call for salvation in Ps 69. David begins with an anxious call to God, "Hasten, O God, to save me; O LORD, come quickly to help me" (v.1), and he concludes on the same note, "Come

quickly to me, O God . . . do not delay" (v.5).

By itself, in isolation from its context within the book of Psalms, this psalm is a simple call for help in an unnamed emergency. When read as a follow-up to Ps 69 and as a prelude to Pss 71–72, it is a call for God's swift return to establish his universal kingdom and to send his eternal King.

## Psalm 71

The section of the book of Psalms recounting the prayers of David, which began with his reflections on God's promise of a messianic Seed (cf. Ps 2), is now drawing to a close (cf. 72:20). This is the last prayer of David; Ps 72 is by Solomon. In it David, now as an old man (vv.9, 18), looks back over a lifetime of God's faithfulness (vv.5–6, 17). Though he still has enemies (vv.4, 11, 13) and is still in need of God's protection (vv.1–3, 12), his long years of trusting God have become a new source for his assurance that God will care for him. Thus his years of old age are devoted to praising the Lord (vv.14–16) and to proclaiming his righteousness (vv.19–24).

As David's last word about himself and God's promised Messiah, this psalm plays an important role in the strategy of Psalms. Just as this section began in Ps 3 with an expression of David's trust in God's promise (Ps 2; cf. 2Sa 7), so now it concludes with a similar statement of trust. It can hardly be accidental that this psalm, with David's reflective glance over his long life, was placed at the conclusion of his prayers.

## Psalm 72

One can see evidence of a literary strategy in the composition of the book of Psalms in the way Pss 2 and 72 are linked. Just as Ps 2 provided a vivid reminder to the reader of God's messianic promise (2Sa 7), so Ps 72 returns to a restatement of that promise. Furthermore, just as the superscription of Ps 3 provided the historical setting for these psalms by placing them within the context of the rebellion of David's son Absalom (3:1), so the superscription of Ps 72 returns the reader to David's son Solomon, another likely heir to the promise. According to the superscription, Solomon wrote this psalm. The fact that it was written by Solomon rather than David shows that Solomon was not the fulfillment of the promise. Like his father David, Solomon looked forward to the time when God would fulfill his promise and send the Messiah. That is the theme of Ps 72.

The psalm begins with a request for justice and righteousness on behalf of the King (vv.1–4) and is reminiscent of Solomon's own request for wisdom to rule God's people (1Ki 3:9). The psalm then turns to a request that shows the psalmist can only be thinking of the future Messiah: "May he be feared as long as the sun endures" (v.5; NIV, "He will endure as long as the sun"). He continues with a description of the earthly reign of the messianic King (vv.6–14), which he envisions as a time of universal prosperity (vv.15–17). John, in the book of Revelation, depicts this rule as a one-thousand-year reign of Christ, the Millennium. The psalm concludes with praise to God, who alone will accomplish his promise (vv.18–19).

The last verse in this psalm (v.20) belongs to the composer of the book of Psalms. It ties together the entire first half of the book, from Ps 3 through 72, and shows that all these psalms are to be read as prayers on behalf of God's promise of a Messiah. Psalm 72 thus fits within this group because it also focuses on the divine promise. It is important to note that the next group of psalms are not by David. There are only scattered Davidic psalms or groups of psalms in the remainder of the book (Pss 86; 101; 103; 108–110; 138–145).

## VIII. Psalms of Asaph (73–83)

### Psalm 73

Beginning with the overall thought of the psalm, "Surely God is good to Israel, to those who are pure in heart" (v.1), Asaph turns his attention to the seemingly endless prosperity of the rich and famous. How well off they are compared to the suffering and daily misery of the common man (vv.2–12)! Looking at them, one would think it does one little to live for the Lord and keep a pure heart (vv.13–16). But Asaph, a choir leader at the temple, stops himself in the midst of such thoughts and recalls the true state of the matter that is represented by the presence of God at the temple. When he entered the temple and contemplated God's presence there, it was clear to him that the rich and famous have a passing treasure, "as a dream when one awakes" (vv.17–20). God is with his people, and he is their strength forever (vv.21–26). What a contrast to the godless who will ultimately perish apart from God (v.27). It is "good to be near God" (v.28). For Asaph this meant coming before God in the temple. For the Christian it means enjoying God's presence throughout the daily affairs of life.

The strong confidence in God's presence in this psalm stands in sharp contrast to the estrangement from God expressed in the following psalm. Again there is evidence here of an overall strategy on the part of the composer of the book of Psalms who, like the author of Ecclesiastes, juxtaposes rather hard sayings like Ps 74 with comforting reassurances such as Ps 73.

### Psalm 74

In stark contrast to the assurance of God's presence just expressed by Asaph in Ps 73, the psalmist (probably a later descendant of Asaph) begins his psalm with the despairing words, "Why have you rejected us forever, O God?" (v.1).

The cause of his despair is made clear from the beginning: the temple has been destroyed and now lies in ruins (vv.3–8). For the psalmist, the chief problem is God's lack of help: "We are given no miraculous signs; no prophets are left, and none of us knows how long this will be" (v.9). It is not a problem for him personally, but rather it is a possible cause for derision on the part of God's enemies (v.10). The psalmist has no doubts that God can and will act to vindicate his promises to Israel (vv.11–17). God has made a covenant with them (v.20), and thus he prays for God's quick action on their behalf (vv.21–23). God's response comes in the following psalm.

## Psalm 75

This psalm is placed here as a direct response to the lament of Ps 74, where Asaph had asked God, "How long will you wait to vindicate God's people?" In this psalm he recounts God's words, "I choose the appointed time; it is I who judge uprightly" (v.2). Though it is important for God's people to call out to him for salvation (Ps 74), they must remember that God always acts according to his own time schedule (Ps 75). Both psalms also show vividly that God always acts in response to the prayers of the upright. God in effect tells Asaph to keep praying until the appointed time comes. The example of the psalmist is very much like that of the prophet Habakkuk who, when praying for God's quick judgment, had to learn the lesson of patience (Hab 2:1–4).

## Psalm 76

Following closely on the themes of the preceding Asaph psalms, this psalm describes God and his time for judgment. With Ps 73, he is the God whose dwelling place is Zion, the site of the temple. With Ps 74, he is the God who comes in judgment upon those who have oppressed the godly. With Ps 75, he is the God who acts at his appointed time and thus is the one who is to be feared (v.11).

## Psalm 77

This psalm expresses the psalmist's confidence in the midst of his prayers for divine action. Though there were no miraculous deeds in his own day (cf. 74:9), his resolve is to meditate on God's glorious deeds in the past (77:5–12). This is what gives him resolve to continue to seek God's justice in the present.

The psalm concludes with a brief, general description of God's past deeds as recorded in the Scriptures (vv.13–20). It is followed by a detailed account of God's past deeds on Israel's behalf (Ps 78).

## Psalm 78

This psalm, which recounts in poetic form the major events of the biblical narratives, is suitably placed after Ps 77, where the psalmist vowed to remember and meditate on God's past deeds. It begins with a description of the psalmist's purpose: "I will utter hidden things, things from of old" (v.2b) in order to "tell the next generation the praiseworthy deeds of the LORD, his power, and the wonders he has done" (v.4). In other words, he is going to recount the narratives of Scripture in poetic form.

The first act of God he records is not creation, nor is it the call of Abraham—both of which we might have expected from reading the Pentateuch. He begins rather with the giving of the Law at Sinai. The purpose of the Law, he says, was to teach the next generations to know God, i.e., to know his will for them (v.6). That, he says, would lead, or should have led, to their trusting God (v.7). It did not, however—either for the first generation whom God delivered from Egypt (vv.8–56) or for the succeeding ones whom God gave the Promised Land (vv.57–66). In the end, God rejected this people, except for the one tribe of Judah (vv.67–68). There he chose Jerusalem as the city of his dwelling place (v.69) and the house of David as the kingdom through whom the promised royal Seed would come (vv.70–72). Once again we can see how the messianic theme of 2Sa 7 has dominated the viewpoint of the psalms.

## Psalm 79

As a sequel to Ps 78, in which the rejection and exile of the northern kingdom is recounted along with God's special care for the tribe of Judah and the temple at Jerusalem, Ps 79 recounts the ultimate downfall of the southern kingdom and the destruction of the temple. The point of the composer of the book of Psalms was to show that neither of the historical kingdoms proved faithful to God, and thus both were subject to God's judgment.

The psalm begins with a graphic depiction of the destruction of Jerusalem and the temple (vv.1–4). This is followed by the call of a survivor, "How long, O LORD? Will you be angry forever?" (v.5). The psalmist acknowledges God's justice in bringing destruction on his own sinful people (vv.7–8), but he prays for mercy on his generation, the sons and daughters of those who failed to obey God (vv.9–11). The basis of his appeal is not his own righteousness, but rather the vindication of God's holy name (v.12) and God's election of Israel as his own people (v.13).

## Psalm 80

This psalm turns directly to the question of the restoration of the house of David in the postexilic period. Like the psalms that have preceded it, the psalmist calls out for God's help and deliverance. His focus, however, is on the restoration of the Davidic kingdom, which had flourished in the preexilic period like a lush vine planted by God. At the center of his hope is the "son of man," whom God was to raise up himself (v.17). The hope and expectation of

this psalm is virtually identical to that of Da 7 and together with it forms an important basis for the NT's understanding of the Messiah.

This psalm thus plays an important role within the book of Psalms. It focuses the reader's attention on the continuing hope and trust in God's promise to David during the postexilic period. The downfall of the Davidic monarchy did not mean an end to the hope in God's promises. Those promises all along were directed toward a greater Seed of David than Solomon or any other leader. The promises always were directed toward the heavenly Messiah whom we see so clearly here and in Da 7—the Man at God's right hand (v.19).

## Psalm 81

In response to the prayer for help and salvation in the previous psalm, the Lord now replies in Pss 81–82. His words to his people are clear enough. If they want deliverance, they must obey his word: "If my people would but listen to me . . . how quickly would I subdue their enemies" (vv.13–14). Israel has been disobedient and God has given "them over to their stubborn hearts to follow their own devices" (v.12). If only they would follow him, says the Lord, "You would be fed with the finest of wheat; with honey from the rock I would satisfy you" (v.16).

## Psalm 82

The Lord continues (from Ps 81) to reply to the prayers of Israel, calling on them to obey his word. This psalm reminds us of the theme heard many times in prophetic literature that obedience to God's will should be translated into acts of kindness and mercy (vv.3–4; cf. Mic 6:8).

## Psalm 83

This psalm concludes the Asaph psalms (Pss 73–83) by again calling on God to deliver his people (the central theme of these psalms). The temple lies in ruins (74:7), and the city of Jerusalem is laid bare (79:1). Thus the psalmist now cannot keep quiet until God has acted on their behalf and destroyed the enemy (vv.2–17). This psalm ends on the note that behind the psalmist's call for vindication lies the hope that in their judgment the nations may come to know that God alone is "the Most High over all the earth" (v.18).

# XI. Psalms of the Sons of Korah (84–85)

Little is known of the family of Korah, apart from the well-known incident of divine judgment on their ancestor in Nu 16. In the days of David, members of this family played an important role in the musical celebration at the tabernacle and later the temple. These psalms appear to stem from that era.

## Psalm 84

This psalm is a celebration of the joy of worshiping in God's presence at the temple. Whereas the earlier Asaph psalms had lamented the destruction of the temple, these psalms are placed here as expressions of the yearnings of God's people for its restoration.

When written, this psalm expressed the excitement and anticipation of the pilgrimage to the temple to celebrate the annual feast days (cf. Lev 23). It recounts the journey to Jerusalem (vv.5–7) as well as the recollections of former visits to the temple (vv.1–2). The psalmist even envies the sparrow who makes his nest in the rafters of the temple and raises her young there. She is always near to God's altar (vv.3–4). In its present context within the book of Psalms, this psalm expresses the longing hope for the rebuilding of the temple and the exhortation to prepare for it. Humility (vv.8–10), godliness (v.11), and trust (v.12) are the prerequisites for enjoying God's presence and protection.

## Psalm 85

This psalm voices the request and hope for God's ultimate restoration of his people. Salvation is near for those who fear him, but there is a need for righteousness to prepare for his coming. God has forgiven Israel their transgressions in the past, and thus there is grounds for hope in the future. For the psalmist there is great comfort in the fact that God's anger against his people will not last forever.

It is interesting to note how this psalm appears to cast the specter of hope into the more remote future, with expressions such as, "Will you be angry with us forever? Will you prolong your anger through all generations?" (v.5). The viewpoint of the psalm is toward a more seasoned hope in God's deliverance. Salvation is near, but only to those who fear him (v.9). Before the salvation of the Lord occurs, righteousness must prepare the way (v.13). The example of David is given in the next psalm.

# X. Psalm of David (86)

## Psalm 86

The composer of the book of Psalms may well have intended this Davidic psalm as an example of how God heard the prayers of the righteous in the past and answered them with deliverance. Thus he inserted it in the midst of the Korahite psalms. Here David gives expression to the central themes of Pss 84–85, divine forgiveness for the righteous: "You are forgiving and good, O Lord, abounding in love to all who call to you" (v.5). These words appear as a concrete confirmation of Ps 85:2, "You forgave the iniquity of your people and covered all their sins."

David's words also provide a pattern for obtaining divine forgiveness: "Teach me your way, O LORD, and I will walk in your truth; give me an undivided heart, that I may fear your name" (v.11). If one longs for God's mercy, one must long to walk as David walked before the Lord. Here David is set forth as an example of a truly godly Israelite, in the same way that he serves as an example of a truly godly king in the book of Kings. The past is presented as the pathway to the future.

## XI. Psalms of the Sons of Korah (87–88)

### Psalm 87

This psalm gives us a glorious picture of a restored Zion. In that day, says the psalmist, even Babylon and Philistia, the two archenemies of Jerusalem, will acknowledge the presence of God in Zion. This song embodies in a few brief images the hope that is set forth throughout the Korahite psalms and, indeed, throughout the Psalms as a whole: the restoration of the city of Jerusalem in the days when God fulfills his promises to David (cf. 2Sa 7). Hence the meaning of the phrase, "Glorious things are said of you, O city of God," is a reference to the time of the Messiah's reign in Jerusalem over the nations of the world.

### Psalm 88

The psalmist, Heman the Ezrahite, one of the sons of Korah, opens with a lament for his suffering from divine judgment (vv.1–9a). He says to the Lord, "You have put me in the lowest pit.... Your wrath lies heavily upon me" (vv.6–7). Though he acknowledges that his "trouble" comes from God, he nevertheless calls out to God for deliverance (vv.9b–14). He cries out, "Why, O LORD, do you reject me and hide your face from me?" (v.14). The depth of his torment can be seen in his statement, "From my youth I have been afflicted.... I have suffered your terrors and am in despair" (v.15). He continues, "Your wrath has swept over me; your terrors have destroyed me" (v.16), and he concludes on a note of despair, "The darkness is my closest friend" (v.18).

Clearly the intent of the composer of the book of Psalms is to use Heman's desperate pleas to God as a picture of those still awaiting the fulfillment of the divine promise. Heman is one who knows of the restoration spoken of in Ps 87, but who must also wait for God's timing in accomplishing it. In the NT, Luke writes of Simeon, a man who was righteous and devout, that "he was waiting for the consolation of Israel" (Lk 2:25). In light of this psalm, one can appreciate Simeon's joy at taking the baby Jesus in his arms and crying out, "Sovereign Lord, as you have promised, you now dismiss your servant in peace. For my eyes have seen your salvation" (Lk 2:29–30).

## XII. Psalm of Ethan the Ezrahite (89)

### Psalm 89

In stark contrast to the despair of Ps 88, Ps 89 opens with a praise of "the Lord's great love" (v.1). The composer of the book of Psalms intends the readers to look beyond the suffering expressed in Ps 88 to the joy that awaits the faithful when God sends the deliverer to Zion (cf. Ps 87). This praise song is thus intended to be read in anticipation of that fulfillment and serves to comfort those who, like the psalmist in Ps 88, have not yet experienced God's fulfilled promises. Fittingly, the psalm is a celebration of the Lord's promise to David (vv.3–4; cf. 2Sa 7), that the Lord would raise up a seed from the house of David and establish his throne forever (vv.4, 29, 36; cf. 2Sa 7:13). The psalmist extols God's faithfulness to his covenant promises and puts the Davidic covenant at the center of his trust. This is the covenant by which God was to send the Messiah to Israel.

Midway through the psalm, however, there is a break in the mood of praise and expectation. The psalmist suddenly turns to the sorrows of his own day: "But you [O God] have rejected, you have spurned, you have been very angry with your anointed one. You have renounced the covenant with your servant" (vv.38–39). The following verses show that the psalmist has in mind the destruction of Jerusalem and the Babylonian captivity. Thus at the close of the psalm, he returns to the theme of lament and prayer for God's intervention and deliverance: "How long, O LORD? Will you hide yourself forever?" (v.46). Reflecting over the glories of the past in the days of David and the sorrow and rejection of his own day, he calls on God to act in restoring Zion to its former glory. For the composer of Psalms, this psalmist's honest prayer becomes the voice and expression of the countless generations of God's faithful who long to see his kingdom established and the taunts of the enemy silenced (v.51).

## XIII. Psalm of Moses (90)

**Psalm 90**

At this point in the book of Psalms, the attentive reader is in need of comfort and reassurance in God's eternal care. The psalm of Moses provides such a word. Just as in writing the Pentateuch, Moses here includes in his picture of God's power and care a reflection on the creation (vv.1–2; cf. Ge 1), the fall of humankind (vv.3–6, cf. Ge 3), divine judgment (vv.7–9; cf. Ge 6–9; 19), and human frailty (v.10; cf. Ge 47:10). In light of such a view of God and the human condition, Moses returns to the theme of this portion of the book of Psalms and calls on God to have compassion on his people and send a deliverer (vv.13–17).

## XIV. Anonymous Psalms (91–100)

**Psalm 91**

Following on the theme of Ps 90, "Lord, you have been our dwelling place throughout all generations" (90:1), Ps 91 gives a word of comfort for those who have not yet seen the fulfillment of all of God's promises: "He who dwells in the shelter of the Most High will rest in the shadow of the Almighty" (v.1). Rather than call for an end to the ever-present threat to God's people, as the earlier psalms have done, this psalm calls on its readers to seek refuge in the Lord amid their present troubles. The presence of this psalm within the book of Psalms shows that the composer wants his readers to settle in for the long run. Though they pray earnestly for the Lord to send salvation to Zion, as in the earlier psalms, the readers should also seek comfort and protection in trusting the Lord. God will protect them even while they wait for his deliverance.

In this psalm the idea of angels plays an important role (v.11). God commands them to guard his people and protect them from harm and danger (cf. Heb 1:14).

**Psalm 92**

We have seen that with Pss 90 and 91 the mood and focus of the psalms has shifted to that of extolling the greatness and grace of God. This psalm carries that theme to a new height and as such prepares the way for the theocratic hymns that follow (Pss 93–99). In Ps 92 the psalmist looks at God's love and faithfulness (vv.1–3), his power in the created world around him (vv.4–5a), and the profundity of his thoughts in God's Word (v.5b) which the foolish do not understand (vv.6–7). In light of these certainties of God's provision, the godly need not fret over the deeds of the wicked (vv.9–11). They will flourish because God is their Rock (vv.12–15).

**Psalm 93**

In this psalm and several that follow (93–99), the Lord's eternal theocratic rule over the world is celebrated. In Ps 93 the focus is on God's rule over the great powers of creation, specifically the waters of the sea (vv.3–4). The psalm closes with a reminder of the steadfastness of God's eternal Word (v.5). God, like the earthly king in Dt 17:18, is pictured as one who rules according to his own divine statutes.

## Psalm 94

Having introduced God as universal King (Ps 93), the composer of the book of Psalms inserts a psalm that focuses on his role as "Judge of the earth" (v.2). To him, an important implication of God's kingly rule is his judgment of the wicked (vv.3–11). Again, as in the earlier psalms, God's work in the world turns on what he has revealed in his Word: "Blessed is the man you discipline, O LORD, the man you teach from your law" (v.12). The way to avoid God's judgment of the world is to seek to live by the principles of his Word (vv.13–15). Consolation, strength, and joy come from meditation on that Word (vv.16–19). In this way, by understanding God's Word, the godly take refuge from the wicked (vv.20–23).

## Psalm 95

Psalm 95 begins in a usual way, calling on God's people to praise him as their eternal King (vv.1–7a). He is "the Rock of our salvation" (v.1; cf. 92:12–15), the Creator who made the earth and the sea (vv.3–5), and the One who is to be worshiped as our Maker (vv.6–7). At v.7b, however, the psalm takes an abrupt turn from praise to warning, calling on its readers to obey the Word of God and not rebel as Israel had in the desert (vv.7b–11). God's power and grace are great, but for the psalmist, the most important implication for his people is obedience to his will. Note how this psalm follows the basic outline of the Pentateuch, beginning with the portrayal of God as Creator, then moving to the response of his people in worship, and ending on a note of their failure to trust.

## Psalm 96

Once again in this psalm the twin themes of God's theocratic rule and divine judgment are brought together. The psalm begins with a call for all the nations to praise and worship the eternal King (vv.1–13a); and it closes with a warning that when he comes, he will "judge the world in righteousness" (v.13b). Over and over in these psalms the reader is reminded of the important implication of divine kingship. It requires a response of both praise and obedience. The following psalm (Ps 97) focuses on God's coming in judgment.

## Psalm 97

The psalm begins like the other theocratic psalms with a celebration of God's kingly rule: "The LORD reigns, let the earth be glad" (v.1). It turns quickly to the theme of judgment: "Clouds and thick darkness surround him; righteousness and justice are the foundation of his throne" (v.2). The righteous should rejoice at his coming (vv.8–12), but the wicked should tremble at the thought of it (vv.3–7).

## Psalm 98

Following Ps 97, which ended on the note of the rejoicing of the righteous at the coming of the Lord, this psalm continues on that theme. God's judgment of the wicked means salvation for the righteous (vv.1–3). Therefore all creation should rejoice to see God's righteous judgment of the wicked (vv.4–9).

## Psalm 99

This psalm marks an important transition within the book of Psalms. The central theme of the theocratic psalms (Pss 93–99) has been the universal rule of God over all his creation. Now the focus begins to shift to the special and unique care that God has taken for his chosen people Israel. The focus turns to God's universal reign "in Zion" (v.2) and his election of the patriarchs (v.4), Moses and Aaron (v.6a), and the prophets (v.6b). This will be the central theme of the psalms that follow.

## Psalm 100

The eternal and universal King praised in the preceding theocratic hymns (Pss 93–99) is now extolled as the God of Israel, his chosen people. Universal creation is seen in terms of the divine election of Israel: "It is he who made us, and we are his; we are his people, the sheep of his pasture" (v.3). The praise of God comes from the courtyards of his temple in Jerusalem (v.4). His covenant with Israel is celebrated as an eternal manifestation of his love (v.5).

## XV. Psalm of David (101)

### Psalm 101

It is in keeping with the particular focus of this part of the book of Psalms that the composer has included a personal, pietistic psalm of David. We do not see David the king here. Rather, we see David the individual believer, seeking to do the will of God in his everyday life. The love and justice of God that was celebrated in universal terms in the theocratic psalms (Pss 93–99) are here pictured in the godly life of one of God's chosen people. David says, "I will be careful to lead a blameless life. . . . I will walk in my house with a blameless heart" (v.2). The virtues he extols are humility, honesty, and goodness (vv.3–8).

## XVI. Psalm of an Afflicted Man (102)

### Psalm 102

Again within the book of Psalms the note of the restoration of the city of Zion is sounded. Between two Davidic psalms, this work of an anonymous sufferer expresses the repeated yearning for the Lord to "rebuild Zion and appear in his glory" (v.16). The fact that this psalm accompanies two Davidic

psalms is probably not accidental. It was to David that the original promise to restore Zion and send the Messiah was given (cf. 2Sa 7). The insertion of this "Zion song" within a section of the book that focuses on personal piety was perhaps intended by the composer to blend together the two themes of personal godliness and eager anticipation of the work of God in the world. These two themes are often found together in the Bible. God's people are to wait eagerly for the coming of the Lord; yet, while doing so, they are to live as though he were already here.

## XVII. Psalm of David (103)

### Psalm 103

Taking its lead from the Scriptures themselves (Ex 34:6), this psalm of David focuses the reader's attention on the compassion and great love of God. Its chief concern is the Lord's forgiveness of the sins (v.3) of those "who keep his covenant and remember to obey his precepts" (v.18). God, whose throne is in heaven (v.19), will not "harbor his anger forever" (v.9). Forgiveness will come for a disobedient people, but it will come only because of God's great compassion (v.13).

With these themes in mind we can see how this psalm fits within its present context in the book of Psalms. By this time in the book, the reader has been led to identify with the godly who suffer from divine judgment because of the sins of a disobedient people. The godly are called upon to wait patiently and expectantly for the coming of the Lord. That coming is expressed, as in Ps 102, by notion of the rebuilding of Zion, i.e., the fulfillment of the promise to David that one of his descendants will rule over the house of David and over Jerusalem (Zion) forever. When read from this perspective, the whole of these psalms are messianic in a true sense of the term. They look forward to the coming of an individual Davidic king who will rule the nations and God's people and who will usher in a time of great prosperity for all God's creation (v.22).

# XVIII. Anonymous Psalms (104–107)

## Psalm 104

This psalm is a hymn of praise to God as the Creator and the Sustainer of all life. The psalmist begins by extolling God's work of creation (vv.1–9). He then turns to recount the many ways in which God continues to sustain his creation. He gives water to all his creatures (vv.10–12) and to his creation (v.13), so that the earth brings forth food and shelter for the animals and for people (vv.14–18). The sun and the moon mark off the seasons of human life (v.19). Even the time of darkness provides the means whereby some animals receive their food (vv.20–21), leaving the daytime safe for human beings and their labor (vv.22–23). There is a "wisdom" in all this that the psalmist wants his readers to see (v.24)—a wisdom that is a constant reminder of God's power and care for his creation (vv.25–30). It is this wisdom that gives occasion for displaying God's glory in the present psalm (vv.31–34).

Tucked into that last line of this psalm is a note that ties this psalm in with those around it—the call for the coming of God's judgment on the wicked (v.35). Continually the reader is reminded that things are not yet as they should be. Though God's creation is good and displays his glory, there must still be future judgment. Creation still awaits its final redemption.

## Psalm 105

This psalm is a poetic summary of the message of the Pentateuch. It centers on God's promise to Abraham to give his descendants the land of Canaan (Ge 15:18–19). It begins by recounting that promise (vv.1–11) and ends by re-

counting its fulfillment, or lack of fulfillment, in Israel's conquest of the land (v.44). There is some uncertainty at the close of the psalm that is caused by the sudden mention of obedience (v.45). The Israelites were brought into the land to obey God. Does the psalmist see the conquest of Canaan as the fulfillment of the Abrahamic promise? Or does his mention of the importance of obedience suggest that he sees the Conquest as a failure on the part of the people to claim the promise? This uncertainty reflects the same ambiguity that lies within the book of Joshua (see commentary). Both Joshua and this psalm see Israel's conquest of Canaan in the context of God's promise to Abraham. Both also see the people's own disobedience as their undoing. Although the people were brought into the land "that they might keep his precepts and observe his laws" (v.45), they did not do so (cf. Jos 9). Apparently the psalmist, in his dependence on the Pentateuch, assumes his readers were aware that Israel failed (cf. Jos 24:19–20). In any event, the sudden mention of the importance of obedience at the close of the psalm appears to qualify this otherwise optimistic psalm.

## Psalm 106

Like Ps 105, this psalm is a poetic summary of the message of the Pentateuch. The key to the psalmist's understanding of its events lies in his opening statement: "We have sinned, even as our fathers did" (v.6). The psalmist writes during a time when Israel was under divine judgment for their disobedience. He looks back at the events of the Pentateuch to find parallels for his own day. His final plea is that somehow things would turn out differently in his day from that of old. He concludes by calling out to the Lord for salvation for his people, though he acknowledges that God is just in punishing them. Like Daniel (cf. Da 9:4–19), the psalmist prays in the midst of exile that God would restore his people to their land (v.47).

## Psalm 107

The previous psalm closes with a call for God to gather his people from the nations (106:47). The present psalm, appropriately, expresses the thanksgiving of "those he gathered from the lands, from east and west, from north and south" (vv.1–3). As in the days of the desert wandering, when the people cried out to the Lord, he heard their cry and "led them by a straight way to a city where they could settle" (v.7). Similarly, this psalmist acknowledges that God was just in sending his people into exile (v.11). But when they cried out to him, he heard their prayer and "brought them out of darkness and the deepest gloom and broke away their chains" (v.14). The psalmist illustrates this from several biblical examples.

The intent of the psalm is stated precisely at its close: "Whoever is wise, let him heed these things and consider the great love of the LORD" (v.43). Biblical narratives are the source of reflection on God's goodness, even when they recount stories of judgment and trouble. The "wise" person addressed at the close of this psalm is the one who, as in Ps 1, meditates on God's Word day and night.

## XIX. Psalms of David (108–110)

Three quite different psalms of David have been inserted into the book of Psalms at this point. What they have in common is both the perspective from which they were written (that of the oppression of God's people at the hand of their enemies) and the goal to which they are directed (divine deliverance and salvation through the coming of the kingdom of God).

## Psalm 108

This psalm begins with an expression of praise (vv.1–5) and moves quickly to a request for help in the midst of defeat (v.6). David's experience in this psalm is portrayed as a model for the righteous at all times. God answered his prayer (vv.7–9), and thus all Israel knows that they "shall gain the victory" when he tramples down the enemy (v.13).

## Psalm 109

In this psalm, David calls for God's righteous judgment against "wicked and deceitful men" (v.2). In effect he asks that God send someone to do to them what they have done to him. David is not trying to get even with those who have mistreated him. He wants only for God to act and "not remain silent" (v.1) in the face of injustice.

The poetic imagery used throughout this psalm employs many overstatements and exaggerated metaphors. He says of the wicked, for example, "May his children be fatherless and his wife a widow" (v.9). In using such imagery, David is not wishing evil of innocent children and wives. Rather, he employs picturesque, even graphic, language to make his point; but he is writing poetry, not prose. His words should not be taken literally here, anymore than when he says, "My heart is wounded within me" (v.22) or "I fade away like an evening shadow" (v.23).

## Psalm 110

The last Davidic psalm in this series of three focuses on the messianic promise that God made to David in 2Sa 7. This was a promise of a royal descendant and an eternal kingship. As in other psalms that take up this same theme (e.g., Pss 2; 72), the present psalm views David's kingship in universal and victorious terms, "You will rule in the midst of your enemies" (v.2b). But the focus of this psalm is not on the kingship of the Davidic Son alone. David's recounting of God's promise also takes up and develops the theme of the priesthood of his descendant, "You are a priest forever, in the order of Melchizedek" (110:4b). In 2Sa 7 God had told David that his promised descendant would build "a house," (i.e., a temple) for the Lord (2Sa 7:13); according to Chronicles, God also promised to establish this descendant over both his "house" (the temple) and over his kingdom (1Ch 17:14). Like Melchizedek (Ge 14:18), he would be a king-priest. This psalm is a celebration of both aspects of God's promise.

No other psalm in the book of Psalms is as clear about the identity of the Promised Seed as this one. As Christ himself once reminded the Pharisees in his day, David called this descendant "my Lord" (v.1). How then could this "Son of David" be one of the "sons of David," i.e., one of the earthly monarchs who ruled the kingdom of David after him?

# XX. Anonymous Psalms (111–121)

## Psalm 111

This psalm is an acrostic (i.e., each of its stanzas begins with a different letter of the Hebrew alphabet). The purpose of an acrostic is to expand the psalmist's exposition of a single theme. In effect, it forces the psalmist to repeat a single idea twenty-two times, one time for each letter of the alphabet. The theme of this psalm is God's faithfulness to his covenant. It thus plays an important role in following the account of the Davidic covenant in Ps 110.

## Psalm 112

This psalm is also an acrostic. Its central theme is God's faithfulness to the righteous. Though David is not mentioned in the psalm, its context within the book of Psalms suggests that the composer of the book had David primarily in mind. The psalm is thus a reassurance of God's faithfulness to the house of David: "His children will be mighty in the land ... and his righteousness endures forever" (vv.2–3).

## Psalm 113

This is a hymn of praise for God's gracious care for his people. It focuses particularly on God's choosing a leader for them by raising him out of the humblest circumstances and seating him with princes. This must without doubt refer to David's words in 2Sa 7:18, "Who am I, O Sovereign LORD, and what is my family, that you have brought me this far?"

## Psalm 114

Though brief, this psalm makes an important contribution to the ongoing theme of the book of Psalms. First, it links God's deliverance of Israel from Egypt (v.1), the conquest of the land of Canaan (vv.3–6), and the establishment of the temple in Jerusalem (114:2) in a continuous seam of divine activity on Israel's behalf. Second, it links these divine acts with "the God of Jacob, who turned the rock into a pool, the hard rock into springs of water" (vv.7b–8). Thus, through the imagery of this psalm, the three major covenants in the OT (the Abrahamic, Ge 15; the Mosaic, Ex 24; and the Davidic, 2Sa 7) are united and identified with the "springs of water" that God gave Israel in the desert (v.8).

## Psalm 115

In this psalm, the "God of Jacob" of Ps 116 is contrasted with the idols of the nations (vv.4–8). The nations may ask, "Where is their God?" (v.2), but the psalmist knows that God is not to be seen by human eyes. He is not made of "silver and gold" (v.4). The true God dwells "in heaven" (v.3) and is sovereign over all his creation (v.3b). In his grace, God has created "the land" (v.15) and has given it to human beings as their place to live (v.16).

## Psalm 116

The psalmist, facing a present danger, looks back at God's gracious deliverance in the past (vv.1–10). Though others have failed him (vv.9–11), God has proved faithful (vv.12–16) and is thus the focus of the psalmist's hope for the future (vv.17–18). The addition of v.19 shows that for the composer of Psalms, Israel's future hope lies in the restoration of the temple, the house of God, in Jerusalem. The hope thus expressed in this psalm is that of the fulfillment of the Davidic covenant (see 2Sa 7).

## Psalm 117

This short psalm plays an important role within the larger structure of the book of Psalms. The previous psalm focused the reader's attention on the future fulfillment of God's promise to David through the coming of the Messiah. This one shows that the scope of that promise is all the nations of the world. The promise to David was of a universal kingdom. Thus the psalmist calls on all the nations to sing praises to God. His great love is toward all.

## Psalm 118

In this psalm, the central themes of the preceding section are summarized and restated. The psalm opens on the same note as it closes: God's love for Israel and the nations "endures forever" (vv.1, 29). The speakers within the psalm are identified first as Israel (v.2), then as the priests (v.3), and finally all "those who fear the LORD" (v.4). Thus the words of the psalm apply to the nations as well as to Israel. The key is whether the nations fear the Lord (v.4) or fight against him (vv.5–12). If they are on God's side, then they, like Israel, can put their hope in God's deliverance (vv.13–14). The righteous of this psalm are thus defined as those who fear the Lord and call out to him (vv.15–21). Their salvation has come about because of the "stone the builders rejected" (v.22). This stone has become the "capstone" of the new gates of the temple in Jerusalem (vv.22–26). He is the Blessed One who comes in the name of the Lord (v.26a). Though the psalm itself does not identify who this One is, the larger context within Psalms makes it clear that he is the Promised Seed of the house of David, the Messiah. It is for this reason that this psalm is frequently alluded to in the NT (Mt 21:42; Mk 12:10–11, Lk 20:17, Ac 4:11; Eph 2:20; 1Pe 2:7).

## Psalm 119

Though the longest psalm in the book, the central theme of Ps 119 is quite simple. It is a celebration of God's gift of the Law (the Torah) to his people. It is an acrostic, containing twenty-two sections of eight verses, each verse of each section beginning with a letter of the Hebrew alphabet in sequence. The term "law" in this psalm should be understood as the Hebrew Scriptures themselves—i.e., the Pentateuch, the Prophetic books, and even the book of Psalms (cf. Ps 1). This psalm is thus a celebration of God's gift of the Scriptures. It is through reading and studying the Scriptures that the psalmist grows in his relationship with God. Walking with God means reading his Word. God's Word is a light along the pathway of one's life (v.105). It is through that Word that one may "keep his way pure" (v.9).

There are three psalms that focus directly on the Scriptures as the means of living a righteous life before God: Pss 1; 19; and 119. Each of them is followed within the book by a unit that focuses on the coming Messiah: Pss 2; 20; 120–134 (the Psalms of Ascents). It is as if the composer of the book of Psalms were telling the readers that if they search the Scriptures, they will find the Christ. The OT Scriptures point beyond themselves to the coming Messiah. Reinforcing this strategy is the further fact that Ps 119 ends with the curious image of a "lost sheep" who has strayed from the flock (v.176). This provides an important link with the messianic Psalms of Ascents, which begins precisely on the note of wandering, lost, in a strange land (cf. Ps 120).

# XXI. Psalms of Ascents (120–134)

The Psalms of Ascents are a carefully selected group of psalms, arranged around the theme of God's messianic promise to David (Ps 132). The word "Ascents" has been variously interpreted. It could refer to the "steps" leading up the temple altar, in which case these psalms would have been sung at the time of an offering or sacrifice. The term could also refer to the people's "going up" to Jerusalem during one of the annual pilgrimages (cf. Lev 23), suggesting these psalms were sung during one such festival. If we look at the term within the book of Psalms, however, the word appears to refer to Israel's "coming up" out of exile, thus setting the theme of these psalms within the context of Israel's return from Babylonian captivity.

Throughout the OT, the notion of the return from Babylonian captivity is seen as a picture of the times of the Messiah (cf. Isa 40). The Psalms of Ascents are thus to be read within Psalms as an expression of the hope of God's faithfulness to David and the fulfillment of his messianic promise. Such a reading of these psalms is consistent with their internal structure. The central psalm is Ps 132, which specifically recounts the Davidic covenant of 2Sa 7.

## Psalm 120

This psalm picks up with the theme with which Ps 119 curiously ended, the picture of a "lost sheep" who has strayed from the Lord. The psalmist finds himself dwelling in Meshech, "among the tents of Kedar" (v.5). Like the psalmist in Ps 119, he is lost and calls out to the Lord in his distress (v.1).

## Psalm 121

Following closely on Ps 120, the psalmist affirms his hope and trust in the Lord, the Creator of the heavens and earth (v.2). His hope is not in the mountains (v.1), but in the Maker of the mountains. Though lost and in need of deliverance, the psalmist remains confident in the Lord's salvation.

## Psalm 122

The salvation hoped for in Ps 121 is here depicted as the rebuilding of the city of Jerusalem and the house of David. In other words, it is here depicted as the fulfillment of the Davidic covenant (2Sa 7). To pray for the peace of Jerusalem (v.6) is to pray for the coming of the Promised Seed of David, the Messiah.

## Psalm 123

The psalmist expresses his confidence that only the Lord himself is able to bring salvation. He waits patiently for any and every act of God on behalf of his promise. He is like a servant who waits intently for any movement of the master's hand. His hope is filled with eager anticipation.

## Psalm 124

The central theme of the previous psalm is repeated again here. God alone is the One who will bring Israel's salvation. Just as he saved Israel from the waters of the Red Sea (Ex 14–15), so their future redemption will come before their enemies destroy them.

## Psalm 125

Again in this psalm, as throughout the Psalms of Ascents, the future blessing of God's people, Israel, is pictured in terms of the Davidic covenant, i.e., the restoration of the city of Jerusalem (vv.1–2). The eternal restoration of Jerusalem was promised to David along with the reign of an eternal Seed (2Sa 7). A renewed and rebuilt Jerusalem is thus the centerpiece of Israel's future hope. "The scepter of the wicked will not remain over the land allotted to the righteous" (v.3), because "the LORD will banish" the wicked and bring peace to Israel.

## Psalm 126

Within the present context of the Psalms of Ascents, it is not difficult to see why the psalmist raises the specter of Israel's return from captivity. In this psalm, however, the picture of the return from Babylon is an image drawn from Israel's *past*. It was, indeed, a time of great rejoicing and celebration—so much so that it now has become a picture of Israel's future blessing. Just as Israel went into captivity in weeping and returned with songs of joy, so also, when God finally restores their fortunes, they will again be like "those who sow in tears" and "reap with songs of joy" (v.5).

We should not overlook the importance of this psalm for the overall interpretation of the Psalms of Ascents. This psalm, with its direct allusion to the return from Babylon, shows that Israel's troubles remain. God has still to fulfill his promise to David. The Messiah has not yet come. Nevertheless, the righteous remain faithful in their trust in God's promises. They await the songs of joy that will come with the arrival of the Messiah.

## Psalm 127

Although the sense of this psalm has a personal application in the life of every parent ("sons are a heritage from the LORD"), the context of the Psalms of Ascents suggests that the composer of the book has the house of David and the Promised Seed particularly in mind. God alone will raise up that house and watch over the city of Jerusalem. God's people cannot hurry the coming of the Messiah. They can only wait for the Lord to act and thus to establish his kingdom. It is vain to attempt to do otherwise.

## Psalm 128

In this psalm, a personal blessing (vv.1–4) is turned into an expression of hope for the coming of the Messiah (vv.5–6). The key phrase is "may you see the prosperity of Jerusalem" (v.5b). It is one thing to have a prosperous life and large family (vv.2–3), but it is quite another thing to enjoy such blessings within the context of the reign of the Promised Seed of David (v.5b). The psalm in its present form within Psalms uses imagery from the former to express the latter.

## Psalm 129

As with the two previous psalms, the individual hopes and trials of the psalmist are cast in such a way that they express the hope of the people in God. Just as the psalmist was "greatly oppressed" from his youth (v.1a), so "let Israel say—they have greatly oppressed me from my youth" (v.1b–2a). Just as the Lord has remained faithful to the psalmist, so he will not neglect his promises to Israel.

## Psalm 130

The psalmist presents his own patient waiting on the Lord (vv.1–6) as a model for Israel's hope in their own redemption (vv.7–8).

## Psalm 131

As in the preceding psalms, the psalmist calls upon Israel to hope in the Lord's promised redemption (v.3), using his own patient waiting as their example (vv.1–2).

## Psalm 132

This psalm is the centerpiece of the Psalms of Ascents. In it we see that the focus of Israel's future hope is God's promise to David: "O LORD, remember David" (v.1). The psalm follows closely the account of the Davidic covenant in 2Sa 7. David, wanting to make a place for God to dwell (vv.2–10), received an oath from the Lord that his own descendants would rule over his throne forever (vv.11–12). David's descendants were not faithful, however, and thus were removed from the throne. But God had chosen David and the city of Jerusalem (Zion), and thus he promised to raise up a future Seed to the house of David, the Anointed One, the Messiah (vv.13–17). Psalm 132 is a reminder that God's promise to David remains intact and that it has become the basis upon which Israel's future hope lies. When the Chosen Seed of David comes, God promises, "I will clothe his enemies with shame, but the crown on his head will be resplendent" (v.18).

### Psalm 133

In the terse imagery of this psalm, the composer of the book of Psalms is able to link and interweave several basic themes. Following Ps 132, it is clearly to be read as an expression of the blessing that the Promised Seed of David will bring to his people. When he comes, it will mean that "brothers live together in unity" (v.1), no doubt a reference to the united kingdom that Israel enjoyed during the reign of David and will once again enjoy during the reign of the Messiah. Moreover, the coming of the promised Seed of David will mean a return of the glorious worship of God on Mount Zion (v.3), pictured here in the image of precious oil running down the beard of Aaron (v.2). Most importantly, however, the blessing that the Promised Seed will bring to God's people is pictured here as an eternal blessing—the gift of "life forevermore" (v.3). We should not fail to see that for the psalmist, and for the composer of the book of Psalms, God will offer his people eternal life in the sending of the promised Son of David (cf. Jn 3:16).

### Psalm 134

This psalm forms a natural conclusion to the Psalms of Ascents. It calls on all who worship God at Zion to praise the Lord, the Creator, and to look for his blessing to come from Zion. Its call for praise (v.1) is answered in the following two psalms (135–136).

## XXII. Anonymous Psalms (135–137)

### Psalm 135

In response to the call to praise in Ps 134:1, this praise psalm recounts the greatness of God as it is displayed in his creation (vv.5–7), and the grace of God as it was displayed in his deliverance of Israel from Egypt and their possession of the land (vv.8–12). It closes with a reminder of the futility of idolatry (vv.13–18).

### Psalm 136

In further response to the call to praise in Ps 134:1, this praise psalm, like the previous one, recounts the greatness of God displayed in creation (vv.4–9) and the grace of God displayed in his deliverance of Israel from Egypt (vv.10–16) and their possession of the land (vv.17–22).

### Psalm 137

This psalm returns the reader to the point of exile and despair expressed in Ps 120. It, along with Ps 120, thus function as "bookends" for the Psalms of Ascents. Their purpose is to clarify for the reader the fact that this psalm is to be read within the context of Israel's return from Babylonian captivity. When read within that context, the Psalms of Ascents express Israel's renewed hope for the fulfillment of the Davidic covenant. Even though God's promise to David to rebuild his kingdom and send the Messiah did not find its fulfillment in the return from Babylonian captivity, that return did provide a renewed basis for hope in the ultimate fulfillment of the promise. God was still at work among his people. He was involved in their lives, proving to them that he would remain faithful to his word. Though present events were difficult and were like those of the Captivity itself, Israel could remember earlier days when God proved faithful and could thus continue to remember God's promises to restore Jerusalem.

The sentiments expressed in this psalm should be understood in light of the fact that the psalm itself is poetry. Biblical poetry, like most poetry, employs graphic imagery to portray and express its ideas. When the psalmist says, "Happy is he who repays you . . . who seizes your infants and dashes them against the rocks" (vv.8–9), he is intending to say only that "happy is he who brings peace to Jerusalem." This imagery is no more intended to be taken literally than elsewhere in the psalms where the psalmists speak of rivers clapping their hands and mountains singing for joy.

# XXIII. Psalms of David (138–145)

Fittingly, as the book of Psalms nears its end, we find a group of Davidic psalms, reaffirming David's own confidence in God's promise. Such a focus clearly betrays the messianic interest of the composer of Psalms. This book was no doubt composed during a time when the righteous were suffering at the hands of the wicked. This could, of course, have been at any time in Israel's history. Thus, one of the central purposes of the book was to provide the example of David, who in his own day suffered unjustly but continued to keep his focus on God and his promises.

## Psalm 138

In this psalm David calls both on his own people at the temple to sing praises to God (vv.1–3) and on "all the kings of the earth" (vv.4–5). The scope of the Davidic covenant is thus extended far beyond the borders of ancient Israel (cf. 2:8–12). At the conclusion of this psalm David gives a renewed expression of his hope in the fulfillment of God's promise: "The LORD will fulfill his purpose for me; your love, O LORD, endures forever" (v.8). The purpose of the

composer of the book is to portray David's faith as a model for the reader. In spite of all his trouble and evidence to the contrary, David's faith in God's promised Messiah never wavered!

But why does David have such faith in God? The composer of Psalms seeks to answer that question in the next psalm.

## Psalm 139

In this psalm we are given an intimate look at the substance of David's faith in God. We hear in his own words about the God in whom David put his trust. This psalm is David's own personal description of his God. As Moses gave a poetic description of God in Ex 15, so here David gives a poetic "theology" of God.

We learn first that God searches and knows the heart of David intimately (vv.1–4). And not only that, God is also intimately involved in David's life (vv.5–6). There is no place he can go where God is not present with him (vv.7–10). Not even the darkness can hide David from God's searching presence (vv.11–12). David knows God as his Creator (vv.13–16a) and Sustainer (v.16b). Though he loves to meditate on God's greatness, David also knows that his knowledge of God does not even begin to scratch the surface of God's own thoughts (vv.17–18). Finally, David's God is a God of judgment against sin, and at the end of this psalm David himself vents his sense of divine anger against those "bloodthirsty men" who speak evil against God (vv.19–24). As the next psalm shows, however, David is content to leave such evil people in the hands of God.

## Psalm 140

Following closely on David's lament against evil people in Ps 139, this psalm develops further the portrait of David as the righteous sufferer who is content to leave the wicked in God's hands for judgment. After lamenting the slanderous deeds of ungodly men (vv.1–11), David concludes by voicing his confidence that "the LORD secures justice for the poor and upholds the cause of the needy" (vv.12–13).

## Psalm 141

Like those that precede it, this psalm is a model of simple piety and trust in God. The composer of the book of Psalms has no doubt put it here as an example of how his readers may respond to evil in their own world. Here David laments the unjust treatment he has received at the hands of the wicked. He knows that God is just and that their deeds will ultimately come back to judge them. In the meantime, however, David is content to fix his eyes on the Lord and "let the wicked fall into their own nets" (v.10).

## Psalm 142

The theme of this psalm is the same as those around it. David has come to the end of his rope, but his faith and trust in God have not wavered. Though his spirit grows faint within him, he waits for God to act and anticipates the time when the righteous will prevail.

## Psalm 143

Though essentially the same in content and general theme as the preceding psalms of David in this section of the book (140–142), this psalm adds significantly to the overall message of Psalms. It first of all adds the dimension of seeking God's will amid trials and troubles. Here David not only laments his troubles, but he also meditates on God's Word, seeking to understand his ways (v.5). In this respect, the psalm is similar to the introductory psalm (Ps 1), where the counsel is given to meditate on God's Word day and night as the means of finding success and blessing in this life.

Second, this psalm adds the notion of God's leading by his Spirit (v.10). Throughout the Scriptures we are taught that the godly must depend on God's Spirit for guidance, wisdom, and strength. In this psalm, David is presented as a model of such dependence. The concepts presented here are clearly those of the new covenant (cf. Eze 36:27; Ro 8:4).

## Psalm 144

Continuing in the same vein as the preceding Davidic psalms (140–143), David now calls on the Lord to come to the rescue of the righteous. In the imagery used here by David, however, a new dimension is given to his prayers. There is a clear note of imminency sounded in this psalm, coupled with a widening of his vision of God's intervention. David prays that God would "part the heavens . . . and come down; touch the mountains, so that they smoke" (v.5). Elsewhere in the Scriptures such language is usually reserved for the descriptions of the Lord's victorious coming at the end of the ages (cf. Da 7:14; Hab 3:3–6). In light of the fact that the book of Psalms has increasingly focused the reader's attention on the imminent hope of the coming of the Lord, it seems likely that the composer sees in David's poetic imagery an expression of the same hope. He intends for us to draw the conclusion that David himself shared the hope of the Lord's glorious and victorious return. Certainly the picture David paints at the close of this psalm shows that he expected God's intervention on his behalf to do more than to restore normalcy. He expected the Lord's return to establish a kingdom of peace and prosperity unequaled by anything Israel had yet experienced (144:12–15).

## Psalm 145

This is the last Davidic psalm in the book—David's last words, so to speak. It is thus fitting that this is a praise psalm—one unlike any that David has sung before! In it David lists and extols the mighty attributes of God. He begins by instructing each generation to continue to proclaim the greatness of God (vv.1–7). Each generation is to commend God's works to another (v.4a) by telling of his "mighty acts" (v.4b). They are to meditate on God's "wonderful works" (v.5b) and celebrate his "abundant goodness" (v.7a). The remainder of the psalm does just that.

Central to this psalm is the idea of God's kingdom (vv.11–13). The concept of that kingdom here adds a new element to the hope expressed in David's words throughout the Psalms. It brings into sharp focus that which has been just below the surface. God's promise in 2Sa 7 was not merely the restoration of David's kingdom, but rather the establishment of God's own kingdom here on earth. The book of Chronicles laid heavy stress on precisely this point in its account of the Davidic covenant (cf. comments on 1Ch 17). Thus, when David says in this psalm that "the LORD is faithful to all his promises" (v.13), he has in mind the establishment of God's "everlasting kingdom," which "endures through all generations" (v.13). This is a kingdom that includes "all men" (v.12), not just the house of Israel.

Here, then, at the close of the book of Psalms, the composer inserts a psalm of David that specifically expresses his own hope in God's promises. It is a hope remarkably similar to that found in Da 7:10–14 and later in the NT—the establishment of the glorious kingdom of the Lord's Messiah.

## XXIV. Anonymous Psalms (146–150)

The book of psalms appropriately ends on the note of praise. The composer of Psalms has placed five anonymous praise psalms as the conclusion of the book.

### Psalm 146

In this psalm is repeated all of the major themes of the book of Psalms:

God's power that is demonstrated in his creation and care of the universe (v.6); God's grace in his love and care for his people (vv.7–9); God's kingdom that he has promised to David (v.10) and will establish in Zion (v.10).

### Psalm 147

In his praise of God's grace and care for his people, the psalmist turns to the picture of the return of Jerusalem at the time of the return of the people from captivity (v.2). As is the case throughout the book of Psalms, God's act of deliverance in returning his people to the land is seen as a continual reminder of God's special care for Israel (vv.3–11). A second reminder is the fact that he gives peace and prosperity to Jerusalem (vv.12–18). A final reminder is that God has given Israel "his word" (v.19). This emphasis on God's Word, at the close of the book of Psalms, is intended to pick up the same theme introduced at the beginning (cf. Ps 1:2) and throughout the book (cf. Pss 19 and 119). It is of obvious interest to the composer of Psalms to put stress on the fact that God has revealed his will to Israel in his Word. The book of Psalms itself is a part of that revelation.

### Psalm 148

The psalmist calls on all creation to praise God. The focus of his praise is the "horn" that God has raised up for his people (v.14). The identification of this "horn" is not certain within this psalm itself. If one has been reading the book of Psalms attentively up to this point, however, there is little question that the psalmist is referring to the Promised Seed of David (cf. 110:7). The fact that the following psalm lays its stress precisely at this point further confirms the reader's judgment and gives additional evidence that the book of Psalms, as a literary work in its own right, is thoroughly messianic in purpose. When Jesus and the NT writers read it in just this way (Lk 24:44; Ac

2:25–31), they were following the lead of the composer.

## Psalm 149

The central theme of this psalm is the praise and celebration of the people of Israel at the time of the restoration of Zion and the establishment of the kingdom (v.2). Zion is restored, the King is ruling, and the nation has set out "to inflict vengeance on the nations and punishment on the peoples" (v.7). This is the same vision of the future that we find depicted so eloquently in Da 7 and so dramatically in the book of Revelation. It is yet to be fulfilled at the return of Christ (cf. Rev 19). This psalm, along with the final words of praise in Ps 150, is a fitting conclusion to the book of Psalms, for it ends with an expression of celebration of the restoration of Zion and the return of her King.

## Psalm 150

The book of Psalms ends with this praise psalm. God in his sanctuary (v.1) is surrounded by the praises of his saints. This is precisely the picture of the reigning king in Rev 4 and Da 7:27. Once again, we see that the composer of the book of Psalms had a larger purpose in mind in composing this book. These psalms are not placed randomly within the book. They show a clear focus and intention to present the hymns of Israel as expressions of the hope that God would fulfill his promises to David and send the Messiah.

# Proverbs

## Introduction

The title of the book of Proverbs in the Hebrew Bible is "The Proverbs of Solomon." There are, of course, other proverbs in the book that were not written by Solomon (cf. 24:23; 30:1; 31:1), and there is clear indication within the book that Solomon was not the author of the book as a whole. According to 25:1, for example, editors during the reign of King Hezekiah, who lived long after the time of Solomon, copied and added more of Solomon's proverbs to an earlier version of the book. Thus the title of the book is intended to show that it was written as a showpiece of the wisdom of Solomon; a major part of the book consists of his own proverbs. According to 1Ki 4:32, Solomon was known to have produced at least three thousand proverbs. Some three to four hundred of these have been preserved in this book.

There has been much discussion of the precise meaning of the word "proverb" as it is used in this book. Most would agree, however, that a proverb is a terse, apt expression of a truth about life. Such "proverbs" are intended as counsel and guides for living wisely. As the prologue to the book makes clear, these proverbs are intended to make fools wise. If a fool takes heed of the wisdom expressed in these proverbs, he or she will no longer be a fool but will, instead, become wise.

Many suggestions have been made about the time and the process by which the book of Proverbs achieved its present shape. Some have wondered if perhaps Solomon wrote the initial book and later generations of wise men added to it. Others have attempted to argue that one of Israel's prophets, such as Isaiah or Ezekiel, wrote the book from an earlier collection of Solomonic proverbs. It has even been suggested that the names "Agur" (30:1) and "Lemuel" (31:1) are nicknames of Solomon himself, and thus the book as a whole, in its present shape, was the work of Solomon. This view seems unlikely in light of the clear references within the book to later generations of wise men (24:23; 25:1).

Recent studies of the book of Proverbs have emphasized that the work in its present form has a discernible shape that reveals a specific purpose. Its prologue (chs. 1–9) is an extended apologetic for the value and importance of seeking wisdom. The body of the book (chs. 10–24), to which an addition has been made (chs. 25–29), is intended as a selection of wise sayings, gathered for the purpose of study and meditation. The conclusion of the book, which consists of three parts (30:1–33; 31:1–9; 31:10–31), is an effort to show the application in specific situations of the wisdom embodied in the book.

One can see a careful interplay between "common sense" and "divine wisdom" at work throughout the book. In the first place, the central role of Solomon throughout the book indicates that the author of the book sees a close relationship between common sense and divine wisdom. In 1Ki 3:1–15, Solomon is shown to have had the good sense to seek divine wisdom in governing the people of God. When God said that he would grant Solomon any wish, Solomon responded by asking for divine wisdom. He was thus given a "wise and discerning heart" (1Ki 3:12). In this passage, divine wisdom is closely linked to God's "statutes and commands" (v.14), i.e., the law of God. As far as the biblical authors were concerned, therefore, the text that they had in their hands was the most perfect statement of divine wisdom (cf. Ps 119:9). Thus the man Solomon perfectly embodies the ideal of one who has common sense, divinely given wisdom, and a knowledge of God's Word.

Another way in which the book of Proverbs links common sense and divine wisdom can be seen in the overall strategy that lies behind the arrangement of the proverbs within the book. A close reading of the Hebrew text suggests several discernible patterns by which various proverbs are linked. Often it amounts to little more than grouping proverbs together that use similar words, i.e., key-word associations. This type of arrangement of literary works was not uncommon in the ancient world and continues to be used today (cf. *Nave's Topical Bible*).

For the most part, however, the arrangement and groupings of the proverbs defy any attempt to demonstrate a coherent structure. It is better to appreciate this fact than to attempt to overlay the text with an artificial construct. This very lack of a coherent structure, in fact, forces the reader to concentrate on each individual proverb in its own right. There is no getting around it. One must read the book of Proverbs one proverb at a time and meditate on it apart from the context of the rest of the book. It is this aspect of the book's structure that most accurately reflects its overall strategy.

There is one more related point that can be raised about the strategy of the present composition of the book of Proverbs. The lack of a literary context within the book forces the reader to provide a context for interpretation from his or her own life. Behind the apparent randomness of the arrangement of the book, therefore, is the goal of forcing the reader to apply the wisdom of the proverbs to one's own life. This is consistent with the overall purpose of biblical wisdom, i.e., the application of divine truth to everyday life.

## I. Prologue (1:1–7)

The prologue sets forth the intent of the book in no uncertain terms: "for attaining wisdom and discipline . . . for

giving prudence to the simple, knowledge and discretion to the young" (vv.2–4). From the beginning the prologue makes it clear that the wisdom intended here is divine wisdom: "The fear of the LORD is the beginning of knowledge" (v.7). Its goal is daily living, but its origin is from heaven.

The prologue also clearly establishes its opposition: "fools despise wisdom and discipline" (v.7b). Divine wisdom is not for everyone. Some people reject it. There is, however, no neutral ground. For the writer of this book, those who reject its central purpose of seeking wisdom are fools. It is precisely this concern to win over the fool to the importance of wisdom that lies behind the first major section of the book, the apologetic for wisdom.

## II. Apologetic for Wisdom (1:8–9:18)

This defense for the importance of seeking wisdom is cast in the form of parental counsel. Those addressed are called "sons," and the counsel given is referred to as "your father's instruction" and "your mothers teaching" (1:8). Though not clear in English translation, it should be pointed out that the word for "teaching" is the Hebrew word *torah*, a word used to refer to God's "law." Thus, part of the divine wisdom of this book is that parental instruction is referred to by the same word as divine instruction. Behind such usage lies the admonition of Moses in Dt 6, that parents' primary responsibility is to teach their children God's law, the Torah.

In his defense of divine wisdom, the writer turns first to the dangers of the evil influence of sinners and the devastating influence they can have on the young (1:10–19). At this point in the book, the writer looks only at the human consequences of following the wicked. His counsel is that the evil deeds of the wicked will one day catch up with them and be the very cause of their own misery. The writer, in other words, does not at this point directly raise the question of divine judgment. His perspective is limited to the consequences of sin. The world is so constructed, he argues, that sin has its own consequences. Lying behind such counsel is a view of the world as created by a righteous God who has chosen to run the affairs of this world by his own just standards.

Turning to the metaphor of wisdom as a woman, the writer speaks of her crying aloud in the streets (1:20). The image is intriguing. Why is this woman crying aloud in the streets? The picture that most naturally comes to mind is that of a mother seeking her wayward son, or a wife calling out to her unfaithful husband. She looks for him in the very streets and public squares where he has abandoned her. Her words to the young man are not comforting words; rather, they are words of warning and rebuke. The son who leaves the counsel of his father and mother cannot so easily return to them. Wisdom, as it is pictured here, is a way of life. One chooses a pathway of life that leads to either life or death. As the woman fully knows, when the wayward son looks for wisdom along the calamitous pathway he has chosen (1:27), they will not find her (1:28).

The metaphor of wisdom as a woman continues throughout this introductory section of Proverbs by being contrasted with "the adulterous" woman, the unfaithful wife (2:16–22; 5:1–14; 6:20–7:27; 9:13–18). By contrast, finding wisdom is like finding a virtuous wife (3:13–18; 5:15–23; 8:1–21; 9:1–11). Such wisdom God himself possessed in creating the universe (3:19–20; 8:22–31), and he rewards those who possess it (3:21–35; 8:32–36). As the verses just cited show, the repetition of these themes form the central argument of the apologetic for wisdom.

As part of the strategy of the prologue to Proverbs, the speaker himself reflects on the process of his own obtaining of godly wisdom from his father (4:1–27). In a pattern strikingly reminiscent of Dt 6, the father tells his son that his own father taught him wisdom from the time of his youth. When he was just a boy, his father set him down in his house and taught him wise sayings. The examples given (4:4–27) show that his father's proverbs were much like those that are about to be offered in this book. The book of Proverbs is thus shown to be a tool that preserves in literary form the process of learning wisdom from one's godly parents. Just as in Dt 6, the Scriptures are presented as a tool for, not a replacement of, the process of inculcating wisdom and values to the next generation.

With these exhortations and examples as backdrop, the book opens up into the full array of Solomonic proverbs.

## III. Collection of Solomonic Proverbs (10:1–29:27)

### A. Proverbs of Solomon (10:1–24:22)

The first collection of proverbs consists of a loose grouping of nearly fifteen chapters of individual proverbs. In these proverbs the whole range of human life is covered, such as relationships among family members, business partners, neighbors, friends, and enemies. All levels of human social activities are also covered. Clearly the attempt has been to provide a sample collection of wise sayings and judgments on every aspect of human life.

This first group of proverbs is specifically labeled as the "Proverbs of Solomon" (10:1). They are primarily characterized by their "antithetical" nature. An antithetical proverb first makes a statement of a general truth and then follows it by a statement of its antithesis. For example, the first saying is "A wise son brings joy to his father, but a foolish son grief to his mother" (10:1). The purpose of such a style is to expand the reader's understanding of an aspect of life. The antithetical process forces the reader to look at the truth of the saying from more than one perspective, just as we might say today, "There's good news and there's bad news. Do you want the good news first or the bad news?" Truth about life resides in both the good parts of life and the bad. Such thinking about wisdom is rooted in the biblical doctrine of the fall of humankind. Practical wisdom must look at all sides of life.

Within these strictly Solomonic proverbs there are two groups. The first group consists primarily of short, single line sayings (10:1–22:29). The second group expands the sayings somewhat by developing certain central ideas of the first group. The final verse in the first group (22:29) acts both as a summary of the goal of wisdom—becoming a "man skilled in his work"—and a transition to the next section—"He will serve before kings." Taking up the theme of serving before kings, 23:1 discusses "when you sit to dine with a ruler. . . ." Thus, although there is little sign of structure within the groups of proverbs, there are clear signs of structure and compositional strategy at the seams.

The primary contribution of this secondary, expansive collection of proverbs is to introduce a new dimension into the discussion of wisdom. This new dimension is that of divine judgment and future punishment. Throughout most of the proverbs and sayings in the book up to this point, the idea of divine retribution has remained below the surface. Their focus has been primarily on the rewards of wisdom itself and the perils of folly. With the expanded proverbs and sayings of 23:1–24:22, however, there is a noticeable

emphasis on rewards and punishment in the future.

In this section the father tells his son that if he is wise, it will not only make his father glad (23:15; cf. 10:1) but also, "There is surely a future hope for you, and your hope will not be cut off" (23:18). Not only is there mockery in folly (24:9), but also divine punishment: God "will repay each person according to what he has done" (24:12).

This section closes with the admonition to "fear the LORD and the king," because the destruction of the wicked will arise suddenly and without warning (24:21–22; cf. Ps 2:12). It appears clear that the everyday deeds of God's people, whether they be good or bad, are here being viewed from the eternal perspective of a holy God intent on bringing the entire human race into account for their rebellious deeds—a quite new outlook on the wisdom sayings from the first part of the book, but a familiar theme in biblical literature in general.

## B. Sayings of the Wise (24:23–34)

This short addition to the words of Solomon is attributed simply to "the wise." The expression used here may also mean "for the wise." In any event, these sayings are given as further elaboration of the words of Solomon. What do they add? A brief glance at the content of these sayings shows that their focus is on the practical affairs of everyday life: the courtroom (24:23b–25, 28–29), interpersonal relationships (24:26), domestic work (24:27), and business (24:30–34). Thus they provide a few test cases for the application of the general wisdom statements that preceded them. In this respect they resemble much of the laws in the Pentateuch. They do not so much express the general rule, but rather illustrate it by example.

## C. More Proverbs of Solomon (25:1–29:27)

This collection of wise sayings is prefaced with a rare notice of its authorship. They are the proverbs of Solomon that were gathered by court officials during the reign of King Hezekiah (25:1). It is thus noteworthy that the content of nearly all of these sayings relates to political rule or governance. The application of these principles applies, of course, to private as well as public life. The focus, however, is clearly public life. One could entitle this section, "Principles of Leadership." Once again, within this book, there is little recognizable structure to aid in the interpretation of each saying. The reader is forced to read each individual saying apart from any literary context and, in seeking an appropriate context, must search within the context of his or her own life for an application. It may have been for just this reason that the compiler of Proverbs closes the book with a close-up account of three individuals, Agur (30:1–33), Lemuel (31:1–9), and "a wife of noble character" (31:10–31). We thus see the wisdom embodied in the chapters of this book through the lens of the lives of these three individuals. They become the model for the reader's own life-application of wisdom.

## IV. Sayings of Agur (30:1–33)

Agur's sayings are by far the most unusual and interesting in the entire book. They are, in fact, more than merely "wisdom sayings." They are also called "an oracle" (30:1). An oracle is quite a different kind of writing than a wise saying. Whereas a wisdom saying is a conclusion drawn from the observation of everyday life, an oracle is a word from God. While it is true that Solomon received his wisdom from God (1Ki 3:12), his wisdom was nevertheless mediated through his own observation of the world around him.

Agur's wisdom, however, came to him by direct revelation from God. It is for that reason that the content of his "saying" goes beyond what has been given in the book so far.

A comment is due on the NIV translation of v.3, "I have not learned wisdom, nor have I knowledge of the Holy One." Though this is a possible translation, the Hebrew text says, "I have not learned wisdom, but I have knowledge of the Holy One." In other words, though Agur is not a wise man, he is a prophet of sorts and thus can lay claim to oracular knowledge of God.

It is important to note that in Agur's words we are given a further interpretation of several earlier passages of Scripture. When Agur asks the question in v.4, "Who has gone up to heaven and come down?" he is alluding to Moses' words in Dt 30:12, "Who will ascend into heaven?" (cf. Ro 10:6). When he asks, "Who has gathered up the wind in the hollow of his hands. . . ? Who has established all the ends of the earth?" (v.4), he is alluding to the role of "wisdom" personified as an "architect" or "craftsman" in Pr 8:27–30. In fact, in both passages Agur appears to be raising the question of the identity of the One who is with God and who brings wisdom from God to the human race.

In the following verses (vv.4a–6), Agur goes on to identify this One as the Son of God (v.4d) and the "word of God" (v.5). The picture Agur gives us of the Son of God, dwelling with God as Wisdom personified and bringing the Word of God to us, is much like that in Da 7:14, where the Son of Man, who is with God in the heavenlies, brings God's kingdom to humankind in the last days. Through the words of Agur, in other words, the compiler of the book of Proverbs turns the reader's attention to Israel's future messianic hopes. The wisdom portrayed here and embodied in the sayings of Solomon thus becomes emblematic of the Wisdom of the divine Son of God known in the other biblical texts. The practical wisdom of the book of Proverbs is thus made to serve an even higher purpose than that of getting along well in this life. It provides the way of escape in the coming day of judgment: "Every word of God is flawless; he is a shield to those who take refuge in him" (v.5).

Agur's words thus reinforce the tendency we noted in the earlier parts of the book of Proverbs—that of directing the reader's attention beyond the everyday consequences of one's action to that future day when God will hold one accountable for all his or her deeds in the last days (24:12).

## V. Sayings of Lemuel (31:1–9)

Lemuel's words are, like Agur's, called an "oracle," given to him by his mother. It shows little sign of being a prophetic oracle, however. In most respects, it is similar to the oracle of Agur. It focuses on the practical application of the general principles embodied in the book of Proverbs. Unlike most of the collections of sayings in Proverbs, the oracle of Lemuel's mother focuses on only a couple brief themes: the dangers of a profligate life (vv.1–7) and defending the rights of the poor (vv.8–9).

## VI. Poem to a Virtuous Woman (31:10–31)

The book of Proverbs closes with an ode to a virtuous woman. Throughout the book, a central theme has been the personification of wisdom as a virtuous wife (3:13–18; 5:15–23; 8:1–21; 9:1–11). It is thus fitting that the book should close with an extended example of such a wife. She is the embodiment of the wisdom portrayed throughout this book. The poem itself is an acrostic; each line begins with a different letter of the Hebrew alphabet. The first line begins with the question "A wife of noble character who can find?" (v.10); the last line of the poem is "let her works bring her praise at the city gate" (31:31). Apart from the book of Proverbs, the term "wife of noble character" is used only in the book of Ruth (Ru 3:11), where Boaz calls Ruth "a wife of noble character" (see introduction to Ruth for more on this subject). In the Hebrew Bible, the book of Ruth follows Proverbs directly. As the ancestress of David, Ruth is treated as an historical example of the virtuous woman mentioned here.

# Ecclesiastes

## Introduction

The Hebrew title of the book means "the preacher" and is rendered in English by way of the Greek word for "preacher," *ecclesiastes*. The preacher (NIV, "teacher") is the primary character of the book. The book is, in fact, a monologue of this man. Though not expressly stated, he is probably to be identified as Solomon, "son of David, king in Jerusalem" (1:1).

We must not think, however, that the preacher was also the author of the book. The book is *about* the preacher but not necessarily *by* the preacher. This can be seen clearly at the close of the book where the author cuts into the preacher's monologue and brings the book to its conclusion (12:9–14). As a matter of fact, in his final remarks, the author of the book stands somewhat in judgment over the words of the preacher, both evaluating them and attempting to see them in a larger context. From the author's standpoint, the words of the preacher are wise words, "upright and true" (12:9–10), and as such are like those of other wise men (v.11); but taken in themselves, these words do not state the whole of the matter. They are the truth but not the whole truth. For the writer of Ecclesiastes, one can become weary in seeking out wisdom from the books of the wise (v.12). The simple truth that one should live by is "Fear God and keep his commandments, for this is the whole duty of man. For God will bring every deed into judgment" (vv.13–14). Human wisdom has its limits. In the end, only God's commandments as they have been revealed in Scripture can find ultimate reward. This viewpoint is the same as that of Moses in Dt 4:6, where he identified the Law with wisdom: "For this [the Law] will show your wisdom and understanding."

It is important to keep the author's perspective in mind as we try to understand the message of the book. The author does not agree with everything the preacher says; otherwise said, the author often records the words of the preacher and then adds his own qualification to them. His primary qualification lies in the fact that the preacher's words are intended to be understood as conclusions drawn from the point of view of human wisdom. They are not intended as the last word. The last word on the matter is always God's perspective. In 3:19, for example, the preacher says "Man's fate is like that of the animals; the same fate awaits them both: As one dies, so dies the other . . . man has no advantage over the animal. Everything is meaningless." In itself, the preacher's words sound pessimistic. The author, however, will not let these words stand alone. To show what the preacher meant, he prefaces these words with the more general reminder that "God will bring to judgment both the righteous and the wicked, for there will be a time [of judgment] for every activity, a time [of judgment] for every deed" (v.17). This attitude considerably softens and modifies the following words of the preacher. It shows that he is speaking on two levels. In the one case he is speaking as a wise man who views the world around him with all the limitations of human existence (v.19). In the other case, the author adds the words of the preacher with respect to the divine perspective of judgment and eternal reward for the righteous (v.17). These are not so much contradictory statements as they are evaluations of human existence from two quite different perspectives, the human and the divine.

## The Message of Ecclesiastes

To get a sense of the overall message of the book of Ecclesiastes it is important to see it from the point of view of the OT wisdom literature (see unit on "Wisdom Literature"). Ecclesiastes is concerned with the major themes of OT wisdom. At its heart is the notion of the fear of the Lord and its value in everyday life. Moreover, the book clearly has a "this-worldly" orientation. It is concerned with the practical application of God's law in the life of the righteous. Furthermore, it consists of an extended evaluation of alternative lifestyles. Wisdom literature in general was keenly aware of varying ways of living and often sought to determine the "best" way. In the last analysis, however, there were only two ways: the way of the righteous and the way of the wicked (cf. Ps 1). The way of the righteous, for the author of this book, consisted not so much in finding wisdom per se, as in finding wisdom in obeying God's law. Underlying the "wisdom" taught here is the biblical idea of the fear of the Lord as taught, for example, in Ex 20:18–20: The fear of God is intended "to keep you from sinning."

In this context we can see that the author of the book follows closely the monologue of the preacher as he recounts his exploration of human wisdom (1:12). The preacher does not test wisdom in isolation from life, but within life itself. Thus he evaluates human wisdom in comparison with "madness and folly" (1:17).

The preacher's conclusion is repeatedly stated in the most extreme terms: "'Meaningless! Meaningless!' says the Teacher. 'Utterly meaningless! Everything is meaningless!'" (1:2). Given the fact that the preacher's words speak only of human wisdom, the author of this book stands behind his negative assessment. He is not willing, however, to let these negative conclusions be the last word, or at least the only word. Repeatedly we are reminded of the limitations of the preacher's assessment. He is speaking of life "under the sun": "Yet when I surveyed all that my hands had done and what I had toiled to achieve, everything was mean-

ingless, a chasing after the wind; nothing was gained under the sun" (2:11).

A few verses later, lest we think that this is the preacher's final word on the matter, the author adds the further and much more positive words of the preacher: "To the man who pleases him, God gives wisdom, knowledge and happiness, but to the sinner he gives the task of gathering and storing up wealth to hand it over to the one who pleases God. This too is meaningless, a chasing after the wind" (2:26). By putting these two sets of sayings of the preacher together, the author shows that life is meaningless only to those who do not do the will of God. To the man who pleases God there is "wisdom, knowledge and happiness."

At the heart of the preacher's view of God's creation lies his assessment of time: "There is a time for everything, and a season for every activity under heaven" (3:1). After enumerating twenty-eight (seven times four) examples of "times" God has created (vv.2–8), the preacher concludes with the simple statement that God "has made everything beautiful in its time" (v.11). What is more—only God, not a human being, can know all his times "from beginning to end" (v.11). A person's greatest good lies in enjoying the time God has given and in doing good (vv.12–13). God's purpose behind it all is "that men will fear [NIV, revere] him" (v.14). Why should they do so? Because "God will bring to judgment both the righteous and the wicked, for there will be a time for every activity, a time for every deed" (3:17).

There are, then, two levels of assessment of wisdom in the book of Ecclesiastes. First, there is a comparison of wisdom with other ways of life as they are seen "under the sun." Second, there is a view of true wisdom seen from God's perspective. Human wisdom, when viewed simply from the perspective of this life, appears to offer very little beyond those other ways that human beings have devised for themselves. The preacher concludes, "Then I thought in my heart, 'The fate of the fool will overtake me also. What then do I gain by being wise?' I said in my heart, 'This too is meaningless'" (2:15). "Like the fool, the wise man too must die!" (2:16b).

In light of a sovereign God to whom one submits in fear, however, wisdom is of far greater value than any other alternative way of life. In the last analysis, humankind will be held accountable to God and will be rewarded for obedience to his will. Thus the preacher concludes, "Although a wicked man commits a hundred crimes and still lives a long time, I know that it will go better with God-fearing men, who are reverent before God" (8:12).

# Song of Songs

Though the first verse of the book is usually translated "Solomon's Song of Songs," it could be understood either as a song that Solomon wrote or a song about Solomon (cf. Ps 72:1). In light of the fact that Solomon is referred to within the book itself (e.g., 3:7), it seems more likely that it is a poem about Solomon and one of his young lovers (cf. 1Ki 11:3).

The book's straightforward depiction of human love in all its aspects gave rise to various figurative interpretations at an early stage in its history. Jewish interpreters of the Song of Songs understand it as a picture of God's relationship to his beloved Israel, whereas Christians have commonly understood it in terms of Christ and his church. In modern times there have been many interpreters of the book who have understood it "literally" and simply as an ode to human love. Although it is, on the face of it, just that—an ode to human love—one must ask whether it was originally intended to be read as such by its first audience. There are some indications within the book itself that suggest it was not. For example, the book is poetic and, as such, much of its visual imagery is intended to portray themes and ideas that lie outside the range of the poetic images themselves. There is no question that the book is a poetic drama of a lover's longing for his beloved and of her willing complicity. To suggest, however, that this drama of two lovers is, in fact, the intent of the book is to confuse the poetic imagery with the purpose of the poem.

To say this about the book, however, is not to justify the wholesale allegorizations of the poem that have characterized much of its history. Though it does serve as a wonderful picture of God's relationship to Israel and of Christ's relationship to the church, there are no clues within the book itself

to support such a reading. In the last analysis, one's interpretation of this book should come from within the book itself, and preferably from the clues given by the author himself.

One such set of clues is that of the overall structure of the book. It is evident from a simple reading of the book that the "reflections on love" of the lover and the beloved do not progress and build in intensity in the course of the poem itself. Rather, the intensity of their love for each other remains at a feverishly high pitch from the beginning of the poem to its end. Compare, for example, the beloved's opening words, "your love is more delightful than wine" (1:2) with her words at the end of the poem, "May the wine go straight to my lover, flowing gently over lips and teeth" (7:9b). This is therefore not a "love story" as such. It is not about a boy who meets a girl and they fall in love and live happily together.

Furthermore, it should be noted that, though the poetic imagery comes close at times to suggesting the lover and his beloved have in fact come together and joined themselves in that union that they so longingly describe, the structure of the book itself suggests that has not yet happened. The book, in fact, closes with the words of the beloved, still wooing her lover to come away with her and be "like a young stag on the spice-laden mountains" (8:14). That which they both long for has not yet happened. It lies yet in the future. The poem itself focuses on the quest of the lovers and says very little about the obtainment of their goal. If anything, it leaves the reader with the sense that the goal itself is unattainable. The lovers' quest is an ideal, a longed-for desire that lies beyond their own grasp.

There is another structural clue to the poem's meaning in the composition of the book. Though the goals of the lover and his beloved do not progress in the course of the poem, there is a progress and larger structural movement given to the poem by the author. It consists in the refrain, "Do not arouse or awaken love until she [NIV, it] so desires" (2:7b; 3:5b; 8:4b). The refrain itself is densely ambiguous. Were it not for the larger structural links in the book, its meaning would be virtually unattainable.

As it turns out, however, at the close of the book, the author links this refrain to the last series of statements of the beloved by the words, "Under the apple tree I roused you; there your mother conceived you, there she who was in labor gave you birth" (8:5b). In itself, this statement appears to do little more than identify the beloved as the "one who aroused" the love in her lover "under the apple tree." This proves to be an important identification, however, in that the cluster of terminology used by the beloved in this passage also suggests the author has in mind an allusion to at least two other key biblical texts: (1) the prologue to the book of Proverbs and (2) the account of the Fall in Ge 3. Both passages show obvious signs of influence from the wisdom literature of the OT. If an illusion is intended to these passages, it suggests that "the beloved" in the Song of Solomon is intended to be understood as a personification of "wisdom" and Solomon, or "the lover," is intended as a picture of the "promised seed" of Ge 3:15, i.e., the Messiah. It is in keeping with the wisdom texts in the OT generally that the Song of Songs would have been composed as a poetic picture of the Messiah's love for wisdom and of wisdom's quest for the "seed" promised in the Scriptures, for it is in the Wisdom Literature generally that such messianic themes abound.

What appears to have happened in the composition of the Song of Songs is that the author has seen in this love-song the possibility of a portrait of Israel's long-awaited messianic king. Solomon, the son of David (cf. 2Sa 7:16), whose quest for wisdom characterizes the central core of the book of Proverbs, speaks in the prologue of that book of binding wisdom to himself and on his heart (Pr 3:3; 7:1–3) in the same way that in this book the beloved says, "Place me like a seal over your heart, like a seal on your arm" (8:6). Moreover, in Proverbs Solomon says, "Say to wisdom, 'You are my sister'" (Pr 7:4), just as here the beloved says, "If only you were to me like a brother" (8:1). An extended comparison of these two books suggests that these are not mere coincidental similarities of words and phrases, but rather a deliberate "inter-textuality," or allusion of one text to another. Such verbal links and allusions between the personified Dame Wisdom in the book of Proverbs and the young beloved in the Song of Songs invite our attempts to see a larger purpose behind this love song. I have suggested that such a purpose is to be found in the growing messianic hope found in these sections of the OT.

We may summarize by saying the Song of Songs is intended as a portrait of the promised Messiah's love for divine wisdom. The Messiah is here pictured by Solomon, and "wisdom" is personified by the young and beautiful beloved. Throughout the poem the notion of love is idealized by the fact that its obtainment lies in the future. The quest for wisdom was aroused "under the apple tree" (8:4a), probably an allusion to the time of the Garden of Eden when the first woman "saw that the fruit of the tree was . . . desirable for gaining wisdom [and] she took some and ate it" (Ge 3:6). The obtainment of wisdom, however, will come only when one like Solomon comes to claim his beloved.

If this interpretation is correct and the phrase "under the apple tree" is a reference to the "tree of the knowledge of good and evil" in Ge 2–3, then not only does this offer an early interpretation of the tree as an "apple tree" (interesting in itself but not terribly important), but also the reference to "there your mother conceived you, there she who was in labor gave you birth" (8:5b) would suggest that the author of the Song of Songs also understood both the promised "seed" in Ge 3:15 and the reference to Eve as "the mother of all living" (Ge 3:20) messianically. Such a link, if it was intended by the author of this book, would place this song on a quite different level than that of an ode to human love. It would, in fact, give credence to the traditional attempts to see more in this poem than meets the eye. It would also provide some guidelines along which the symbolism of the book is to be read. Finally, such a reading of the book would also provide needed insight into the underlying justification for the book's inclusion into the OT. There is general recognition today that the time of the formation of the OT canon coincided with a significant surge in the hope of the imminent return of the messianic king. This book was included in the canon, one might say, because it was intended as a picture of the Messiah.

# The Prophetic Literature

## Classification of the Prophetic Literature

| Major Prophets | Minor Prophets | |
|---|---|---|
| Isaiah | Hosea | Joel |
| Jeremiah | Amos | Obadiah |
| Ezekiel | Jonah | Micah |
| Daniel | Nahum | Habakkuk |
| | Zephaniah | Haggai |
| | Zechariah | Malachi |

| Preexilic Prophets | Exilic Prophets | Postexilic Prophets |
|---|---|---|
| Isaiah | Ezekiel | Haggai |
| Jeremiah | Daniel | Zechariah |
| Hosea – | | Malachi |
| Zephaniah | | |

## The Message of the Prophetic Literature

In approaching the question of the central message of prophetic literature, we should begin with the understanding of the prophets as messengers of the covenant God. Sent to a disobedient people, they were like modern-day revivalists, calling the people back to the faith of the fathers, the faith of the covenant promises to Abraham, Moses, and David. Thus they were not so much innovators as revivalists.

In their day, the people of the covenant had largely failed to keep its commands. They had fallen away from God and his covenant. The problem that the prophetic literature faces is that Israel did not realize or did not want to realize that they were living in apostasy. They had mistaken the blessings of the covenant (God's presence at the Temple) for the requirements of the covenant (their own obedience). Rather than returning to the Lord in repentance and in obedience to his law, the people presumed upon God's presence among them saying, "Is not the LORD in our midst? Calamity will not come upon us" (Mic 3:11; cf. Jer 7:1–7).

In the face of such false security, the prophets brought the startling word that God was not on the side of his own covenant people. They had forsaken his covenant, and now he was to send judgment on them. A dominant theme, then, in the prophets is that one day all of Israel's objects of comfort and religious support would be taken away and God would come in judgment upon their disobedience—"See now, the Lord, the LORD Almighty, is about to take from Jerusalem and Judah both supply and support . . . the hero and the warrior, the judge and the prophet. . . . Jerusalem staggers; Judah is falling; their words and deeds are against the LORD, defying his glorious presence" (Isa 3:1–8). The message of divine judgment on his own people is central to the prophetic literature.

Interwoven in these themes of judgment, however, are many strands of a counter-theme, the theme of divine blessing and salvation. God had promised "the fathers" that through their offspring would come blessing to all humankind. Thus, in spite of the imminent judgment that was to come on the people, there was yet hope for the future.

There are many texts throughout the prophetic literature that speak of this hope of salvation in the midst of judgment, but the following is a list of the most important:

(1) Isa 4:2–6
(2) Isa 9:2–7
(3) Jer 31:31–34
(4) Eze 36:22–28
(5) Hos 1:8–2:2
(6) Mic 7:18–20

# Isaiah

## Introduction

The book of Isaiah is an anonymous work. Its title, "The vision . . . that Isaiah son of Amoz saw," does not indicate its authorship so much as it does its content. It is a book composed of the prophetic words of the prophet Isaiah. It is clear from reading the book, however, that the author intends it to be read from the perspective of its original context in Isaiah's own day. Both his naming of the Persian King Cyrus and the prediction of his release of the Jewish captives in Babylon long before its time forms a central part of the message of the book (cf. chs. 44–46). That these prophecies are authentic, therefore, is essential to their meaning.

## I. Introduction (1:1)

Isaiah the prophet prophesied from the days of king Uzziah (791–740 B.C.) to Hezekiah (716–687). His call to the office of prophet came in the year that King Uzziah died (6:1).

## II. Judgment and Salvation for God's People (1:2–12:6)

The first theme taken up by the book of Isaiah is the rebellion and apostasy of God's people, Israel (1:2–6:13). Israel had forsaken God and thus stood in danger of divine wrath. Interwoven into this theme of judgment is the theme of salvation and God's faithfulness. Jerusalem would be left desolate (1:7), but there would be a remnant that survives (v.9). Though Jerusalem had become a harlot (v.21), it would once again be called "the City of Righteousness" (v.26b). In the future, the "last days," Jerusalem would be the center of God's work among the nations of the world. The nations would stream into it and from there they would learn God's will (2:1–5). At that time God would judge all the nations and punish them for trusting in their idols (vv.6–22).

Divine wrath would come even on God's people in Jerusalem and Judah (3:1–4:2), but God would send a deliverer (4:2–6). The portrait of the divine deliverer, "the Branch of the Lord" (v.2), is modeled on that of Moses who brought God's people through the desert with "a cloud of smoke by day and a glow of flaming fire by night" (v.5; cf. Ex 14:19–20). God had prepared Israel and Judah to be a choice vineyard, but they refused to obey his will, and thus he was going to send them into exile (5:1–30). For Isaiah, the rise of the Assyrian Empire was seen as an act of God, preparing an instrument of wrath against his disobedient people Israel and Judah (10:5ff.). This nation, however, is not identified in the early portions of the book. The prophet states only that God "whistles for those at the ends of the earth" (5:26a) and "they come swiftly and speedily" (v.26b) to do his work.

In the face of such divine wrath and impending judgment against his own people, God called the prophet Isaiah. Isaiah was taken into the very throne room of the holy God (6:1–13). There he was purified and commissioned to speak God's words of judgment and salvation. He was warned, however, that God's people would not heed his words and that his message would only serve to harden them further and seal them for divine judgment. Even then, however, a "holy seed" (6:13) would survive God's day of wrath and a remnant would return.

The writer of the book of Isaiah inserts a brief narrative of Isaiah's confrontation with King Ahaz of Judah (7:1–25). Ahaz was under attack by King Rezin of Aram and King Pekah of Israel, the northern kingdom. Isaiah's message to the king of Judah was to trust in God: "If you do not stand firm in your faith, you will not stand at all" (v.9). As it turned out, Ahaz did not trust in God. He rejected God's offer to give him a sign under the guise of piety: "I will not put the LORD to the test" (v.12). God, however, responded with a show of his own faithfulness. He gave Ahaz and the house of David a sign to prove his determination to deliver his people from trouble. The sign was a promise of a son of David born of a virgin. The child would be born in a time of distress for God's people when they would be under the rule of an oppressor much like the king of Assyria (vv.14–15). It was a sign of blessing and salvation, however, since the birth of that child would be a sign that God was with his people Israel ("Immanuel," i.e., "God with us"). Having given Ahaz and his descendants the sign, Isaiah then foretold the coming of the Assyrians as a divine appointed instrument of wrath (vv.16–25). Henceforth, God's people would not live freely, but would live under the domination of the great foreign powers. Because Ahaz had rejected God's offer, the sign was not given for his own day. It was given to the future generations who were to await God's sending the promised Son.

There was another sign given to Ahaz, but it was not a sign of blessing. It was a sign of impending and swift judgment (8:1–3). The sign was the birth of Isaiah's own son, "Maher-Shalal-Hash-Baz," whose name means "quick to the plunder, swift to the spoil" (v.3; see NIV note). The birth of this son would mark the impending destruction of the northern kingdom of Israel (Samaria) and the Aramean kingdom of Damascus (v.4), as well as the devastation and subjugation of Judah by the Assyrians (vv.5–8).

Because God was with Judah, however, Assyria's plans to destroy Jerusalem would not succeed (vv.9–15). Having given this testimony, Isaiah was instructed to entrust it to his disciples so it would be preserved until the time of its fulfillment (vv.16–17). In the future, when others turned to mediums and

spiritists, God's people were to turn to his law and the testimonies of his prophets (vv.18–20a). At that time, these prophecies would provide light and comfort for God's people. They were to show that God's promises are sure, and thus they would give hope in the midst of darkness. That hope would be the promise of the coming Son of David (9:1–7). He would come like the sunrise at dawn, destroy the enemy, and establish God's kingdom and "reign on David's throne and over his kingdom ... forever" (9:7).

Israel, the northern kingdom and enemy of Jerusalem, would perish at the hand of the Assyrians (9:8–10:4). God had continually warned them, yet they would not turn back to him. Moreover, Isaiah's prophecies looked beyond the punishment brought on by the Assyrians to a time when the Lord would turn in judgment against Assyria (10:5–11, 13–19, 23–34) and thus bring peace to his people again (vv.12, 20–22). The future salvation of Jerusalem is seen most clearly in the prophecies of 11:1–12:6. Here Isaiah describes the coming of the Son of David (11:1), filled with God's Spirit (v.2). He would judge the nations in righteousness (vv.3–5) and bring peace to the world (vv.6–9). When he came, he would gather the lost remnant of Israel from among all the nations (vv.10–13) and reclaim the Promised Land to its original boundaries from Assyria to Egypt (vv.14–16; cf. Ge 15:18). In that day Israel would sing praise to God for his great salvation (12:1–6).

## III. Judgment and Salvation for the Nations (13:1–23:18)

The time when God would punish the nations and bring peace to Israel involved not only the Assyrians but all the nations of the world (chs. 13–23). The judgment of these nations would one day result in establishing a final peace (cf. 18:7; 19:21–25).

The writer of the book of Isaiah begins his selection of divine judgments against the nations with Isaiah's oracle against Babylon (13:1–14:23). The Lord would bring a mighty nation from a far land against Babylon (13:1–8). It would destroy Babylon in a mighty conflagration (vv.9–16). Isaiah identified this nation as the Medes (vv.17–19). After its destruction, Babylon would never rise again (vv.20–22). At that time, Israel would again dwell in their own land (14:1–2) and sing taunt songs against Babylon, their former oppressor (vv.3–23).

In the same way that Babylon would fall by God's hand, God would also destroy Assyria (14:24–27), Philistia (14:28–32), Moab (15:1–16:14), Damascus (17:1–14), Cush (18:1–8), Egypt (19:1–17; 20:1–6), the Desert by the Sea (21:1–10), Dumah, i.e., Edom, (21:11–12), Arabia (21:13–17), Jerusalem (22:1–25), and Tyre (23:1–16). In the midst of all these prophecies of judgment, however, there is a word of salvation and blessing for the nations: Moab (16:5), Damascus (17:7), Cush (18:9), Egypt (19:18–25), and Tyre (23:17–18).

## IV. Isaiah's Apocalyptic Vision (24:1–35:10)

Having enumerated the destruction of Israel's historical enemies, the writer of the book of Isaiah now turns to an apocalyptic vision of the destruction of all nations and humankind (24:1–13): "See, the LORD is going to lay waste the earth and devastate it; he will ruin its face and scatter its inhabitants" (v.1). At this time God's kingdom would be established in Jerusalem and "the LORD Almighty will reign on Mount Zion and in Jerusalem" (v.23).

In response to his vision of the future reign of God's King, Isaiah breaks out into praise (25:1–12). In his praise, he envisions the time when God would establish his kingdom on Mount Zion

and hold a great banquet for all the nations (v.6). Moreover, "he will swallow up death forever. The Sovereign LORD will wipe away the tears from all faces" (v.8). In that day the people of the earth would say, "Surely this is our God, we trusted in him, and he saved us" (v.9). The inhabitants of Judah would also sing praises to the King in that day (26:1–21). They would be the "righteous nation . . . that keeps faith" (v.2). They would arise from the dead, shout for joy (v.19), and wait for the Lord "to punish the people of the earth for their sins" (v.21).

God's destruction of the enemy in that day is compared to a battle with the "Leviathan, the coiling serpent . . . the monster of the sea" (27:1). God watches over his people Israel, caring for them like a gardener cares for his vineyard (vv.2–5). One day Israel would take root and blossom again "and fill all the world with fruit" (v.6). After a time of desolation and abandonment, God would again gather his people from Assyria and Egypt and they would "come and worship the LORD on the holy mountain in Jerusalem" (vv.12–13).

Isaiah then turns to Ephraim, the northern kingdom, which was about to be taken into exile by Assyria. His oracle warned them of God's impending judgment (28:1–29). The destruction and captivity that Assyria would bring on Israel was ordained by God (v.2). Assyria was a nation through which God spoke to his people "with foreign lips and strange tongues" (v.11). Israel would not listen to God, so he brought against them a people they could not understand.

In the midst of his oracle of the destruction of the northern kingdom, Isaiah turns to address those in Judah who were glibly looking on with a false sense of security (28:14–16). The only true security for God's people, was to put their trust in the "precious cornerstone" and the "sure foundation" that the Lord himself would lay in Zion (v.16a): "the one who trusts [in him] will never be dismayed" (v.16b).

Having forewarned the northern kingdom of their impending doom, Isaiah turns to address his oracle of woe to "Ariel," i.e., Jerusalem, the city of David (29:1–24). It too would be besieged by Assyria, the instrument of God's wrath (vv.2–4). But, unlike the kingdom of the north, God would rescue Judah and Jerusalem (v.5–8) for the sake of his promises to David (v.1a). When God did this wonderful work of salvation among them, however, those in Jerusalem would be blinded to it as if they were in a "deep sleep" (vv.9–10). The prophecies of this book would be "sealed in a scroll" so that it could not be read (vv.11–12). The heart of the people would be far from God, though outwardly they would continue to worship him as the age-old traditions of their elders have mandated (v.13). God would thus bring further woe upon his people to open their eyes and ears so that they would "hear the words of the scroll and out of gloom and darkness the eyes of the blind will see" (v.18). At that time God would bring salvation to Jerusalem (vv.19–24).

In light of the hope of such a great salvation, Isaiah pronounced judgment upon Jerusalem for their failure to trust God (30:1–7). They would rather look to the strength of Egypt than to God in the time of need. Egypt, however, would bring them "only shame and disgrace" (v.5), and their help would be "utterly useless" (v.7).

Isaiah was instructed to record his oracles of judgment against Jerusalem in writing as "an everlasting witness" against the rebellious people of Judah (v.8). The people in Isaiah's own day did not want to hear the words of the prophets (vv.9–11), so the words were written down for a future generation to read (vv.12–18). Included in God's

words of judgment for Jerusalem were also words of comfort and salvation (vv.19–26). There would come a time when the people of Jerusalem would "weep no more" (v.19). The oracle of salvation for Israel is followed by an oracle that depicts the coming of God in judgment on the nations (vv.27–33), identified here with Assyria (30:31).

In the time of judgment, Jerusalem should not seek help in Egypt (31:1–3): "the Egyptians are men and not God" (v.3a). When the nations surrounded Jerusalem, God, not human beings, would rescue it (vv.4–5). Therefore, argues Isaiah, Israel should turn to him and forsake their idols because when the time of judgment came they would surely forsake them (vv.6–9).

In that day there would be a righteous king in Jerusalem (32:1), and God's people would see and understand the word of the Lord and their salvation (vv.2–8). But destruction and devastation had to come first (vv.9–14). After that, the Spirit of God would be poured out on his people and righteousness would prevail in the kingdom (vv.15–20). God would put an end to the enemy that destroys his people (33:1) and restore his blessing to Zion (vv.2–12). Who are God's people? Isaiah identifies them with those who do God's will (vv.13–16): "He who walks righteously and speaks what is right" (v.15). These are the people who would see God's Savior, the King (v.17), coming to destroy the wicked (vv.18–19) and bringing peace to Jerusalem (vv.20–24).

All nations are then warned of the day when God would bring retribution on them (34:1–17) "to uphold Zion's cause" (v.8). The prophet singles out Edom in particular as Israel's archenemy (vv.9–15). When this judgment came upon Edom and the nations, the "scroll of the LORD" would testify that all these things had been foretold and came to pass just as it was written (v.16). As in 8:20 and 30:8, the writer of the book of Isaiah is conscious of the effect his work would have on later generations of readers who would know of the events being foretold in this book. At that time all the nations would "see the glory of the LORD" (35:2) coming "with divine retribution" (v.4) to save his people: "Then will the eyes of the blind be opened and the ears of the deaf unstopped" (v.5; cf. 6:9–10). Those who have been redeemed out of captivity would return to Zion (v.10) on a highway called "the Way of Holiness" (v.8).

## V. Isaiah's Historical Insertion (36:1–39:8)

The invasion of Judah by the Assyrians marked an important moment for Isaiah's prophecies (chs. 36–39). It was at this time that God began to turn against Assyria, the instrument of his wrath, and brought destruction upon it (37:36–38). That which Isaiah had announced in 10:12 now seemed to be happening: "When the LORD has finished all his work against Mount Zion and Jerusalem, he will say, 'I will punish the king of Assyria for the willful pride of his heart and the haughty look in his eyes.'" Assyria had now become the object of God's anger. No longer was it a threat to Jerusalem.

However, the end that Isaiah had seen coming at this time did not come. Where was the Son who was to mark the end of the age? (cf. 9:1–7) Where was the "shoot of Jesse" who was to bring peace to the world (ch. 11)? Therefore, at this point in the book of Isaiah, the writer must address this central question that the prophecies of Isaiah have inevitably raised: When would these things happen? Was the prophet speaking of events in his own day? Or did he look forward in time to a future judgment and salvation of God's people (cf. Ac 8:34)?

He answers that question with this lengthy insertion of historical narrative

into the words of Isaiah (chs. 36–39). The narrative (virtually identical to 2Ki 18:13–20:19) recounts Assyria's invasion of Judah. It thus shows that many of Isaiah's prophecies had that particular historical event in mind. But the strategic role this narrative plays within the context of the book as a whole shows that the author had a larger purpose. The narrative inserted into Isaiah goes beyond the time of the Assyrian invasion of Jerusalem and ends abruptly with Isaiah's warning of a future exile of Jerusalem to Babylon (39:6). Babylon, not Assyria, is the actual focus of the narrative. By means of the narrative, then, the author projects the reader's vision beyond the immediate events in the life of Isaiah to the time of the Babylonian invasion of Jerusalem. The judgment and salvation of the oracles that precede and follow this narrative must thus be viewed in light of the Babylonian captivity of Jerusalem, not merely the Assyrian invasion. The point of this shift in reference of the prophecies of Isaiah is to locate them in the future rather than the past or the present. In other words, as is suggested at numerous points in the prophecies themselves, their scope is messianic and eschatological. They look forward to a time after the exile in Babylon when God would judge the nations and bring peace to Jerusalem by means of his promised King.

In refocusing the reader's perspective on these oracles of Isaiah, the author raises another question that he has yet to deal with: What about the events that followed the return of Israel to Jerusalem after the Babylonian captivity? Were the events of that period the actual reference of these prophecies, or did they refer to events still beyond those? This is a question that many of the OT prophetic books are concerned with. We will see that Isaiah's answer was similar to the others. The prophets were speaking of events that lay far beyond the scope of Israel's immediate history. The prophets spoke about the times of the end, the messianic times, which involved all nations in God's plan of blessing.

The clearest expression of that concern of the prophets is the vision of the kingdom of the Son of Man in Da 7:9–14. If we judge Isaiah's prophecies in light of their literary context within this book, then both he and Daniel, as well as the rest of the prophets, were looking to the distant future reign of the Messiah. Peter appears to have read the prophetic books in this way: "Concerning this salvation, the prophets, who spoke of the grace that was to come to you, searched intently and with the greatest care, trying to find out the time and circumstances to which the Spirit of Christ in them was pointing when he predicted the sufferings of Christ and the glories that would follow. It was revealed to them that they were not serving themselves but you, when they spoke of the things that have now been told you by those who have preached the gospel to you by the Holy Spirit sent from heaven" (1Pe 1:10–12).

Hezekiah was king of Judah during the time that the Assyrians attacked and deported the northern kingdom (2Ki 17:1–6). During his reign, the Assyrians also invaded Judah and captured many cities (Isa 36:1–3; 2Ki 18:13), threatening also to lay siege to Jerusalem (Isa 36:4–37:35; 2Ki 18:14–19:34). God intervened, and the Assyrians were defeated (Isa 37:36–38; 2Ki 19:35–37).

Hezekiah is seen by Isaiah as a model of faith and trust in the Lord. It is significant that his portrayal of the events of Assyria's invasion in this book omits any mention of Hezekiah's first attempt to acquiesce to the demands of the Assyrians (2Ki 18:14–16). Isaiah begins his account with the messengers of the king of Assyria sent to demand a complete capitulation of the city of Jerusalem (36:2–20). The Assyrian messengers presented their demands as an affront to Judah's trust in God ("On whom are you depending, that you rebel against me?" vv.2–9; cf. 2Ki 18:17–24) and the word of their prophets ("The LORD himself told me to march against this country and destroy it," v.10; cf. 2Ki 18:25). The Assyrian messengers then shouted in Hebrew to the people of the city, "Do not let Hezekiah persuade you to trust in the LORD" (v.15; cf. 2Ki 18:30). Finally the messengers pitted themselves against God himself: "Has the god of any nation ever delivered his land from the hand of the king of Assyria? . . . How then can the LORD deliver Jerusalem from my hand?" (vv.18–20).

Hezekiah's response is paradigmatic of the leadership God desired for his people. He went immediately to the temple of the Lord and sent for the prophet Isaiah (37:1–2; cf. 2Ki 19:1–2). Isaiah's word to the king was one of trust in God and assurance of his deliverance (vv.5–7; cf. 2Ki 19:5–7). In the midst of his words to Hezekiah, Isaiah foretold the fate of the king of Assyria (v.7; cf. 2Ki 19:7). That fate—that he would "return to his own country, and there [be] cut down with the sword" (v.7; cf. 2Ki 19:7)—was fulfilled at the close of the narrative (vv.36–38; cf. 2Ki 19:35–37).

The writer concludes his account with a report of Hezekiah's prayer (vv.14–20; cf. 2Ki 19:14–19) and God's answer through the prophet Isaiah (vv.21–35; cf. 2Ki 19:20–34). In both Hezekiah's prayer and the Lord's answer the central theme is that God would deliver his people if they turned to him in trust. God would destroy all those who turned away from him and followed the ways of the nations. God's plans for blessing all the nations would be accomplished.

In the story of Hezekiah's illness (38:1–8; cf. 2Ki 20:1–11) the writer of this book shows that God hears the prayers of the righteous and promises them years of blessing if they call on him. The prophet Isaiah had said to Hezekiah, "You will not recover" (38:1; cf. 2Ki 20:1b). After Hezekiah's prayer (vv.2–3), however, the Lord told Hezekiah that he would live fifteen more years" (v.5). The message of this text is clear: The Lord answers prayer. The narrative in the book of Isaiah includes a section written by King Hezekiah himself (vv.9–20) that is not in 2 Kings. In it Hezekiah acknowledged his gratitude for God's healing and vowed to spend the remainder of his life in praise at the Temple (v.20). The healing of Hezekiah thus pictured the faithful among God's people who call out to him in their distress and are healed. They are the ones who will return to the Temple and worship God. Note that the remainder of the book of Isaiah focuses his prophetic word on the healing of God's people and their return to worship God at the Temple.

God's last words to Hezekiah portend of a divine judgment on the house of David that lay in the future. Hezekiah's visit by the Babylonian envoys (39:1–7; cf. 2Ki 20:12–18) provided an apt setting for the background of the rest of Isaiah. Judah would go into Babylonian captivity (vv.5–7; cf. 2Ki 20:16–18), though not during Hezekiah's lifetime. Hezekiah replied to Isaiah's prophecy by saying, "The word of the LORD you have spoken is good. . . . There will be peace and security in my lifetime" (v.8; cf. 2Ki 20:19). It is precisely at this point that the narrative halts and the prophecies relating to the return from Babylonian captivity begin (chs. 40–55). Hezekiah is thus presented as an example of one, like those who would return from exile, who would have peace in his days.

These verses thus provide the explicit backdrop for the remainder of the book of Isaiah. After the defeat of As-syria, the narrative tells us, a new cloud loomed on the horizon, the growing empire of Babylon: "The time will surely come when everything in your palace, and all that your fathers have stored up until this day, will be carried off to Babylon. Nothing will be left, says the LORD. And some of your descendants, your own flesh and blood who will be born to you, will be taken away, and they shall become eunuchs in the palace of the king of Babylon" (39:6–7).

It is from this perspective that the book of Isaiah develops the hope of the coming redemption of Israel—the time of peace and blessing for God's people and for the nations of the earth. It is this message that would give comfort (40:1ff.) to Jerusalem and that forms the central focus of the remainder of Isaiah's prophecies.

## VI. Prophecies Relating to the Return From Babylon (40:1–55:13)

Isaiah, speaking words of comfort to the exiles who were ready to return to the land of Judah (40:1–2), recounts God's promise to prepare their way and bring them home (vv.3–5). Humanity's feeble efforts to thwart God's promises are like grass that withers and falls when "the breath of the LORD blows on them" (v.7). The word of God, promised long beforehand and recorded by the prophet Isaiah (8:20; 30:8; 34:16), however, has remained firm and "stands forever" (40:8b). The coming of the Sovereign Lord to judge the nations and restore Jerusalem was now in sight (v.10). No one could stand in his way: "Surely the nations are like a drop in a bucket" (v.15). He is incomparable, and no skilled craftsman can fashion an image of him (vv.18–20). He is sovereign over all the nations (vv.21–25) and the creator of the universe (vv.26–30). He gives strength to those who place their hope in him (v.31).

Looking now at events that lie far in the future, Isaiah begins to describe the coming of a mighty king who would do God's work of judgment upon the nations and return Israel to their land (41:1–3). In 45:1 Isaiah would identify this king as the Persian king Cyrus. For the present his identity remains veiled in the imagery of Isaiah's poetic verse: "Who has stirred up one from the east, calling him in righteousness to his service?" (41:2). The passage in ch. 41 of Isaiah introduces several related ideas. The first is that a deliverer was emerging on the horizon who would save God's people (vv.2–3, 5–7, 11–13, 25). The second is that God himself had raised him up and had promised to do so long before in the distant past (vv.4, 21–29). The third is that God would do this in behalf of his chosen servant, Israel (vv.8–10, 14–20).

In 41:8 God calls Israel "my servant," as he also called many individuals in Scripture (e.g., Moses in Jos 1:2; Job in Job 2:3). In 42:1–4, this "servant" is a single individual who would "bring justice to the nations" (v.1b) by establishing "his law" among all the peoples of the world (v.4b). As described here, this servant would be a new Moses who, like Moses in the desert, would give God's law to the people. Isaiah deliberately drew from the imagery of the messianic prophet "like Moses" that was the focus of the Pentateuch's eschatology (cf. Dt 34:10–12). He also added considerably to the picture. The "mighty power" and "awesome deeds" that the prophet like Moses would do (Dt 34:12), are identified by Isaiah as opening the eyes of the blind and, like Moses, freeing the captives from prison (42:7; cf. Ex 3:10). With the coming of this servant, the Lord would do "new things" and, as a confirmation of it, he was here announcing them long before they would happen (v.9). Therefore, all nations

would rejoice at his victorious coming (vv.10–17).

Having described the messianic Servant of the Lord who was sent to open the eyes of the blind, Isaiah returns to the image of Israel as God's servant and identifies them as the blind and the deaf (vv.18–20). It would be precisely their eyes whom the messianic Servant would open and they whom he would release from captivity (cf. vv.19, 22). Isaiah was thus describing in detail the blindness and exile of Israel, from which the Lord's Servant would rescue them (vv.21–25).

Again using the imagery of Moses and Israel's exodus from Egypt ("When you pass through the rivers, they will not sweep over you," 43:2), Isaiah describes God's deliverance of his servant, Israel, from future exile (vv.1–8). God's power and glory is manifest in the fact that long before he acts to deliver Israel, he has announced his intentions through the prophetic word (vv.9–13). The Lord names Babylon specifically as both the agent and object of his wrath (vv.14–15). They would be treated just as the Lord had treated the Egyptians when he brought Israel out of bondage (vv.16–17). Whereas in the past God turned the waters into dry land in behalf of his people (Ex 14), in the future he would bring springs of water for his people in the dry desert (vv.18–21). In spite of God's deliverance of Israel in the past, they had not followed him in worship and repentance (vv.22–24). God, nevertheless, would blot out their transgressions "for [his] own sake" (v.25), though they would first have to face his wrath (vv.26–28).

Though Israel would suffer divine punishment, they would not be forsaken (44:1–2). A time of great blessing and restoration awaited them in the future (vv.3–5). God would pour out his Spirit on Israel and bless their descendants (v.3b). It would not be the dumb idols that would deliver Israel, it would be "Israel's King and Redeemer, the LORD Almighty" (v.6). The ultimate proof of God's power would be the fulfillment of his word (vv.7–8). Idols are nothing but lifeless images made by human imagination (vv.9–20). God alone would rescue and redeem his servant Israel (44:21–23). Jerusalem would lay in ruins, but one day the Lord would restore it and it would again be a great city (vv.24–27).

This would happen in the day that the Lord raised up the Persian king Cyrus (v.28; cf. Ezr 1–3). Cyrus would be God's anointed one, chosen to redeem God's people from captivity and rebuild the temple (45:1). God would raise him up and give him great victories for the sake of his chosen people, Israel (vv.2–6), and for the sake of the nations of the world: "so that from the rising of the sun to the place of its setting men may know there is none besides me" (v.6). Just as God created the heavens and the earth in the beginning and waters above and below (Ge 1:1–8), so he would create a new heavens and new earth in which righteousness would rain down from the heavens and salvation would spring up from the earth (45:7–8).

God's plans are just and right. If he chose to raise up Cyrus to rebuild Jerusalem and set the exiles free (v.13), there was no one who could question him or quarrel with him (v.9). He is the sovereign Lord, the Creator of the universe and the Savior of his people (vv.10–25). He has cared for Israel since the days of their birth in Egypt (46:1–4). He is the living God, unlike the idols of the nations who were carried about on platforms and which were themselves taken into captivity (vv.3–4). God is the eternal One who makes "known the end from the beginning, from ancient times, what is still to come" (vv.8–10). He would summon Cyrus from the east like a bird of prey and perform his will (v.11). His ulti-

mate goal was the salvation and restoration of Zion, the city of his own dwelling place, the Temple (vv.12–13).

The prophet's vision now turns to Babylon, the nation that would take Israel from Jerusalem and into captivity (47:1–15). God used Babylon against Israel as an instrument of his wrath (v.6), but Babylon was a proud and wicked nation. With the rise of Cyrus, their glory would come to an end. Their ruin would be evident to all.

As for the Israelites, the inhabitants of Judah, God's righteous anger against them was well deserved (48:1). They did not seek the Lord "in truth or righteousness" (vv.1–2), and they were warned far in advance so they would know it was God alone who had brought about their calamity (vv.3–6a). But God would also do "new things" that were not announced by the prophets in ages past (vv.6b–8). What are the "new things"? It appears that Isaiah intends the following verse as a description of these: "I will delay my wrath; for the sake of my praise I hold it back from you, so as not to cut you off" (v.9). The sense of this passage is similar to that of Da 9, where Jeremiah's prophecy of divine retribution for Israel after seventy years is extended to seven times seventy years "to finish transgression, to put an end to sin, to atone for wickedness, to bring in everlasting righteousness" (Da 9:24). The time of God's judgment would be delayed and thus extended past present events and into the distant future. Even though God's words to the prophets in the past were now being fulfilled in the fall of Babylon at the hand of Cyrus (vv.12–22), God's wrath would be delayed and Israel would not yet be cut off.

The two servants of the Lord now speak. In light of the preceding prophecies of judgment against God's people, the first servant, Israel, confesses, "I have labored to no purpose, I have spent my strength in vain and for nothing" (49:4). By way of contrast, the Servant who speaks in vv.5–7 cannot be Israel because he has been called "to bring Jacob back to him and gather Israel to himself" (v.5a). This Servant would not only restore Israel (v.6), but also God would make him a "light for the Gentiles" to bring "salvation to the ends of the earth" (v.6). This Servant would take Israel from captivity and restore them in the land (vv.8–26).

The Lord now addresses a disobedient Israel as the son of a divorced wife (50:1–3). They were sold into slavery because of their own sins (v.1b), not because their Father was unable to ransom them (v.2b). God would send a Redeemer to Israel, the Servant, but they would reject him (vv.4–11). Nevertheless, God would send his salvation to those who "listen" to him, "pursue righteousness," and "seek the LORD" (51:1): "The LORD will surely comfort Zion and will look with compassion on all her ruins" (v.3). God's future redemption of Israel would be like his great acts of creation and redemption in the past (vv.9–16). Therefore, though they would suffer much at the hand of the Lord for their transgressions, those who lived in Jerusalem should rejoice in the expectation of their salvation (vv.17–23). When God sent their deliverance and cleansed the city, Jerusalem would never again be defiled again (52:1). It would be oppressed, but the Lord would return to Zion and proclaim peace and salvation (vv.2–9). When that happened, "all the ends of the earth" would see "the salvation of our God" (v.10).

Israel's salvation would be the work of God's Servant (52:13–53:12). He would accomplish his goal and be highly exalted (52:13), but in the process the Servant would be marred and so disfigured that many would be as appalled at him as they were of Israel in their captivity (v.14). He would offer himself as an atonement sacrifice for Is-

rael and the nations (v.15). In his own day, no one would believe his message, though they would later turn to him and marvel at their former unbelief (53:1). He would be ignored (v.2), rejected (v.3a), and despised (v.3b). Yet he would take upon himself the afflictions and sorrows of others and give his life as a sin offering (vv.4–12).

By means of the offering of his Servant, the Lord would redeem Israel and the nations. When they turned to him in faith and trust, the Lord would never again cast them off (54:1–17). His "covenant of peace" with Israel and the nations would last forever (vv.10). Thus the invitation is given to all nations to accept the Lord's offer of life through his "everlasting covenant" with David (55:1–3; cf. comments on 2Sa 7). Through the messianic Seed of David and the eternal kingdom promised him, the Lord would have mercy on all nations (vv.4–7). God's word never fails, and his promises achieve their purpose (vv.8–13).

# VII. Isaiah's Final Prophecies (56:1–66:24)

Because God's salvation was close at hand, he would call on his people to "maintain justice and do what is right" (56:1). For the Israelite who lived under the Mosaic covenant, this meant strict observance of the Sabbath day of rest (v.2). Even foreigners and others excluded from the people were to be included in Israel's worship if they kept God's Sabbath and his covenant (vv.3–7). God's salvation extends to more than a select few (v.8).

In Isaiah's day, the Israelites did not show much sign of repentance (vv.9–12). There were few who lived righteously (57:1), and those who did suffered for it (v.2). The rest had forsaken the Lord and followed after idols and false gods (vv.3–11). When the day of distress came upon God's people and they were carried off in exile, their only refuge would be their trust in the Lord (vv.12–13). God would look upon their contrite heart and forgive them, but if they persisted in their wickedness, there would be no peace for them (vv.14–21). The kind of repentance God required of his people is a contrite heart and a life of good works. There was little value in fasting if one's life did not reflect compassion and obedience to the will of God (58:1–14). Israel's troubles were not due to God's inability to help them. Their sins had separated them from God (59:1–8). In behalf of God's people, Isaiah the prophet acknowledges their guilt (vv.9–15). Israel could not help themselves, so God himself would come to their defense (vv.16–19) and send his Redeemer to Zion (v.20). That Isaiah's prophecy has the new covenant (Jer 31:31; Eze 36:26) specifically in mind here is clear from what the Lord says in v.21: "'This is my covenant with them,' says the LORD. 'My Spirit, who is on you, and my words that I have put in your mouth will not depart from your mouth, or from the mouths of your children . . . forever,' says the LORD."

When God would establish his covenant with Israel and send his Spirit upon them, all the nations would see their light and stream into Jerusalem (60:1–14). Isaiah's oracle in vv.1–4 is an expansion of his vision in 2:2–4. In that day Israel, though once poor and destitute, would receive great wealth from the nations and Jerusalem would be rebuilt (60:15–18). God himself would dwell among his people in Jerusalem, and all his people would be righteous (vv.19–22).

In that day one anointed by God's Spirit would come "to preach good news to the poor" (61:1) and "to proclaim the year of the LORD's favor and the day of vengeance of our God" (v.2). This would be a time of restoration and rebuilding of Jerusalem (vv.3–4) and great reward for God's people (vv.5–9). The Anointed One would make Jerusalem a site of righteousness and praise before all the nations (vv.10–11). Jerusalem, the Daughter of Zion, would be known among the nations as the new bride of the coming Savior (62:1–12).

Upon the arrival of the Savior, he would trample over Jerusalem's enemies as one treads a winepress (63:1–6). Yet the Lord would be kind to the house of Israel (vv.7–8), just as he had been with them in the past: "In his love and mercy he redeemed them; he lifted them up and carried them all the days of old" (v.9). As in the past, the Lord would also turn and become Israel's enemy if they rebelled against him (v.10). At this point, the writer inserts a lengthy recollection of God's dealings in Israel's past and present (63:11–65:16). The perspective is that of the exiles in Babylon (see comments on 39:5–7): "Why, O LORD, do you make us wander from your ways? . . . For a little while your people possessed your holy place, but now our enemies have trampled down your sanctuary" (63:17–18). "Even Zion is a desert, Jerusalem a desolation" (64:10). "Our holy and glorious temple . . . has been burned with fire" (v.11). They acknowledged their guilt and called upon God for help (64:1–7, 12).

In the past, God warned Israel and pleaded with them to turn from their wicked ways (65:1–7). God, however, still saw a good remnant among the people in Israel, and he determined not to destroy all of them (v.8). The faithful remnant, his "servants," would yet enjoy God's blessing (vv.9–10), but the rest "who forsake the LORD and forget [his] holy mountain [Zion]" (v.11) would be destined for the sword and would be forgotten (v.12–16).

In God's future for Israel and the nations, he would create "new heavens and a new earth" (v.17a), and "the former things will not be remembered" (v.17b). God would delight in Jerusalem. As in the early chapters of Genesis

(Ge 5), human life would be extended so that "he who dies at a hundred will be thought a mere youth" (65:20). The years of their lives would be like that of a tree (v.22). There would be peace and harmony in God's creation as it was in the beginning (v.25), though "dust will be the serpent's food" (v.25b). The punishment of the serpent at the Fall of the human race (Ge 3:17) would still be in effect.

At that time God would not seek the one who worshiped in the temple with sacrifices (66:1–4). The true worshiper would be "he who is humble and contrite in spirit, and trembles at [his] word" (v.2). The peace of Jerusalem would flow like a river (v.12). It would be the place where all nations would see God's glory (vv.18–21). Those who repented and turned to the Lord would live forever (v.22) in God's presence (v.23), but those who rebelled against him would perish (v.24).

# Jeremiah

## Introduction

Jeremiah prophesied from the time of Josiah to the time of the Babylonian captivity (cf. 1:2). The leading political power in his day was Babylon under King Nebuchadnezzar. The end of the Assyrian Empire had come with the fall of Nineveh (612 B.C.) and the battle of Carchemish (605 B.C.). The last kings of Jerusalem (Jehoiakim, Jehoiachin, and Zedekiah) were defeated by Babylon, and Jerusalem was destroyed in 587 B.C.

In the face of this Babylonian threat, Jeremiah was charged with the message that Babylon was the instrument of God's wrath, sent to punish the wicked nation of Judah. The only remedy, Jeremiah announced, was to accept God's punishment by submitting to the yoke of Babylon. Those who opposed Jeremiah, on the other hand, could and did raise the objection that God would never abandon his people Israel, nor would he let the house of David and the city of Jerusalem be destroyed. Rather, as the false prophets proclaimed, God would soon restore the fortunes of the house of David and of Jerusalem, and they would return to their former glory (see 28:1–4).

Jeremiah's reply to their argument was simply an appeal to the terms of the Sinai covenant. Israel had sinned, and God, being a righteous God, would soon bring judgment against the sinful nation (cf. Dt 27–29). However, like most of the prophets, Jeremiah also had a word of hope and salvation. The time would come when God would again bless his people. This time would come after the return of the people from the Babylonian captivity—a captivity that would last seventy years (cf. 25:11–12; 29:10).

The basic structure of the book of Jeremiah is also reflected in that of Isaiah and Ezekiel:

(1) Prophecies of doom against Judah;

(2) Prophecies of doom against the nations;

(3) Prophecies of hope for Israel and Judah.

## I. Introduction (1:1–19)

### A. Title (1:1)

The title of this book is descriptive of its contents—the "words," or "matters," of Jeremiah. According to 36:32a, Jeremiah dictated to his scribe, Baruch, much of the material in this book. Moreover, according to 36:32b, "many similar words were added to them." The "words" of the title (1:1) are divided into two sections, 1:2–39:18 and 40:1–51:64a. The subscription, "The words of Jeremiah end here" (51:64b), marks the end of that segment of the book that begins with "the words" of Jeremiah (1:1). The book itself, however, is extended by a further account of the fall of Jerusalem (52:1–30) and the release of Jehoiachin after the Exile (52:31–34).

### B. Summary (1:2–3)

The book opens with a brief chronological note regarding the time of Jeremiah's ministry in Judah. He prophesied from the thirteenth year of Josiah to the exile to Babylon. There are many other historical notes throughout the book. The author's purpose in giving these notes is to make sure that the reader views Jeremiah's message within the context of the exile to Babylon. In so doing, the book raises the question of whether the prophecies of Jeremiah, both the judgments and the anticipated blessings, were to be understood as fulfilled in the events of his own day, or whether they, in fact, found their reference in events that lay in the future. For the most part, the NT writers saw Jeremiah's prophecies concerning the future as relating to the time of the coming of Jesus Christ. We will see that this was also the viewpoint of the author of the book. An important part of

Jeremiah's strategy in relating his words to historical events of his own day was to show that these events came and went, and yet his words were not fulfilled in them. Their fulfillment related to an event still to come, namely, the appearance of the Messiah.

## C. Jeremiah's Call (1:4–19)

The whole of Jeremiah's message is summarized in his call. He was chosen before he was born and given the task to announce the impending divine judgment against Judah and Jerusalem. The nature of that judgment would be an overwhelming defeat of the nation by "the peoples of the northern kingdoms" (v.14). As we continue to read the book, we find that this is pictured in the destruction of Jerusalem by the Babylonians. Before we reach its end, however, we learn that God's words look far beyond that particular historical event to a future time of judgment for Israel identified later in the book of Daniel as the "abomination that causes desolation" (Da 9:27).

## II. Prophecies of Doom Against Judah, Jerusalem, and the Nations (1:1–25:38)

The book of Jeremiah begins with a lengthy indictment of the unfaithfulness of the people of Israel, beginning with the early days when God cared for them in the desert, but concentrating on the sins of Judah and Jerusalem in Jeremiah's own day (2:1–3:5). Judah did not heed the lesson of the destruction of the northern kingdom (3:6–10) and thus, in God's sight, were more guilty than Israel whom God had cut off (v.11). Just as God would be merciful to Judah and Jerusalem, he would also forgive Israel, and thus both kingdoms would again be reunited and dwell together in the land (3:12–4:2). If Judah did not repent and return to the Lord, however, God would send a mighty nation "from the north" against them, just as he did to Israel, their land would be desolated, and they would be taken into captivity (4:3–31). Because of the extent of Judah's sins (5:1–11), there was little hope that they would escape divine judgment (5:1b). Their chief problem was that they did not listen to or believe the words of the prophets God had sent to them (5:12–31; cf. Dt 18:14–22). Given the certainty of divine judgment, the destruction of Zion was inevitable (6:1–30).

In ch. 7 Jeremiah raises the question of the basis of Judah's refusal to listen to God's prophets. They have presumed upon God's Sinai covenant with Israel and his promise to dwell in Solomon's temple. What they failed to realize, however, was that there were conditions attached to God's promise. God's people were to live godly lives in obedience to his will. They were not to presume that God would bless them and protect them even though they forsook his covenant and broke his laws (7:1–11). Jeremiah appeals to them, and hence to the readers, to look at God's dealings with Israel in the past. They should take note of what happened to the house of God at Shiloh, which was destroyed because the people had not obeyed the word of God (vv.12–15). In the same way God would destroy Jerusalem and Judah (vv.16–20). His intention for his people Israel was never to bless them without requiring sincere obedience to his law. Even when he brought them out of Egypt, it was not to give them sacrifices and offerings as mere duties to perform (vv.21–22). Rather, it was that they might walk in his ways and do his will (v.23). Israel, however, did not obey, and to that day, they had not trusted God and obeyed his law. Judgment and punishment upon them, therefore, was certain (7:24–9:26).

Two central themes stand out amid Jeremiah's many words of judgment. (1) God's people Israel were "uncircumcised in heart" (9:26). This is a hint of the promise in the Mosaic covenant that in the future, after a time of judgment and exile, God's people would be given a new heart, a "circumcised heart" (Dt 30:6). Thus Jeremiah is building a case for the new covenant as a fulfillment of the promise of Moses in Dt 30. (2) Israel had been involved in idolatry (10:1–16). This too relates to a central message of the Pentateuch. The first commandment stated that Israel was to worship God alone and was not to bow down to idols (Ex 20:2–6). Moreover, God's power and majesty had been clearly demonstrated in the Creation account in Ge 1. God alone created the heavens and earth. The idols were therefore worthless imitations (Jer 10:11–16). The same power God had demonstrated in Creation would one day soon be turned against his own disobedient people. They would be carried away into exile by an invasion "from the north" (vv.17–25) because they had broken the covenant that their forefathers had made with God when he brought them out of Egypt (11:1–10), and because they had followed other gods (vv.11–17).

It is no wonder that with such a message of unmitigated divine judgment, Jeremiah's words were not only unpopular but were considered dangerous. On at least one occasion, God had to intervene and save him from a plot against his life (11:18–23). Jeremiah's impatience at God's delay of judgment against the wicked (12:1–4) became an index of God's patience and love for his people. It was not easy for God to give those whom he loved into the hands of their enemies (v.7b). Even after the land had been devastated, God would punish the nations who carried out his divine wrath (vv.8–14). Moreover, after his wrath was poured on all nations, he would turn again to them in compassion and "bring each of them back to his own inheritance and his own country" (v.15). "If they learn well the ways of

my people and swear by my name," God said, "then they will be established among my people" (v.16). God's concern extends beyond his people Israel to the nations of the world.

Though God's ultimate plans for Judah and Jerusalem were for blessing, their pride and arrogance would lead them into judgment (13:1–14). Hence Jeremiah repeated his warning of the coming destruction of the land by the armies of the north (vv.15–27) and added to it a vision of impending drought and famine (14:1–12).

As Jeremiah proclaimed God's words of judgment against Israel, he could not help but plead to the Lord in their behalf (vv.7–9). The Lord, however, rebuked Jeremiah for siding with the people. Though other prophets in Jeremiah's day had words of comfort for the people, they were "prophesying lies" in God's name and deluding the people into believing judgment would not come (vv.14–18). Still, Jeremiah continued to plead on behalf of the people (vv.19–22). Reminiscent of Moses' pleading for Israel in the wilderness (Nu 14:13–19), Jeremiah called on the Lord to remember his covenant and "for the sake of your name do not despise us" (14:21). God's answer, however, was adamant: "Even if Moses and Samuel were to stand before me, my heart would not go out to this people" (15:1). The die had been cast; the people had to be delivered into the hands of Babylon and go into captivity (vv.2–14). Only Jeremiah, if he repented, would be rescued, for he was an obedient servant (vv.15–21). As for the rest of God's people, God had withdrawn his blessing, love, and pity from them (16:5); they would go into captivity because they trusted in their idol gods (16:1–18).

As is common in the prophetic literature, in the midst of the lengthy oracles of judgment, there are a few precious words of comfort and hope. Just as

Israel's deliverance from Egypt had become a paradigm of divine grace and salvation, one day in the future God's deliverance of Israel from "the land of the north," Babylon, would also serve as a reminder of God's saving grace (16:14–15). Regardless of the inevitable punishment of the wicked, those whose trust was in the Lord did not need to fear in the time of distress, for God would watch over them (17:7–8). If only the people would honor God and keep his Sabbath, as he commanded, there would be peace and prosperity in the land and the house of David would flourish (vv.19–27).

Jeremiah learned from the example of the potter who refashioned his ruined pot that God would relent his plans of judgment and bless his people if only they would repent and hearken to his warning (18:1–12). Israel did not repent, however, and they did not heed the words of Jeremiah (vv.13–17). Instead, they made plans to kill the prophet so that their own wise men and prophets would prosper (vv.18–23). Jeremiah responded by renewing his message of divine judgment against Jerusalem (19:1–15).

These renewed attacks on the false hopes of the nation earned Jeremiah nothing but persecution (20:1–2). In the face of such persecution, however, he refused to change his message. If anything, he intensified it by referring for the first time to the kingdom of Babylon (vv.3–6). Henceforth in the book of Jeremiah, the nation that would destroy Jerusalem "from the north" is identified as Babylon. Though Jeremiah regretted greatly the fact that God had called him to proclaim bitter words of judgment against Jerusalem, he gratefully acknowledged God's ever-present help and strength in the midst of the persecution it brought him (vv.7–18).

For some time now Jeremiah had been warning those in Judah and Jerusalem of an impending attack on their land by the great nation "from the north," Babylon. Now they had come and the city of Jerusalem was surrounded by the armies of Nebuchadnezzar. King Zedekiah sent for Jeremiah in hopes that he had a good word of salvation for him and his city. He said, "Perhaps the LORD will perform wonders for us as in times past so that he will withdraw from us" (21:2). Jeremiah, however, had only a word of judgment for the king (vv.3–14). The city would be destroyed. Ironically, the only hope for the people lay in their surrender to the king of Babylon (v.9).

There was hope for the house of David, if they ruled God's people righteously and kept God's commands (22:1–4). But if they continued as they were now, they could expect nothing but destruction and captivity from the hand of the Lord (vv.5–9). Jeremiah offered the examples of the two kings, Josiah and his son, Shallum (Jehoahaz). All had gone well for Josiah, who kept God's covenant, but Shallum, who had not obeyed the Lord, died in exile (vv.10–17). Therefore, the last Davidic kings in Jerusalem, Jehoiakim and Jehoiachin, could expect only exile and death outside the Promised Land (vv.18–27). The whole house of Jehoiachin, for that matter, would never again "sit on the throne of David or rule anymore in Judah" (vv.28–30).

In the midst of this word of judgment, however, Jeremiah spoke a word of hope—there would be to the house of David "a righteous branch, a King who will reign wisely and do what is just and right in the land. . ." (23:5–8). Here Jeremiah looked forward to a return of God's people from their captivity (v.3). At that time a Davidic King would again reign over them in Jerusalem. Judah and Israel would be reunited as in the days of David.

The false prophets who had arisen among the people were saying that God's judgment would not come against the people of Judah (vv.17a, 25–32). What calamities had already befallen the people were the worst of it. Soon God would rectify even that and all would be well (23:17b). Such prophets, Jeremiah argued, were filling the people with "false hopes" (vv.16, 18–24). They themselves, however, were going to suffer even greater judgment: "Their path will become slippery; they will be banished to darkness and there they will fall" (23:12, cf. vv.19–20, 30–32). Though their lies gave great comfort to the people, they also did great harm to them because they took away the incentive to repent, with the result that "no one turns from his wickedness" (vv.14b). Thus "from the prophets of Jerusalem ungodliness has spread throughout the land" (vv.15). There were so many false prophets, each claiming to have received a word from the Lord, that God had taken away all prophetic oracles from his people (vv.33–40). Anyone who claimed to have an oracle from the Lord would be punished as a false prophet (v.34).

In the vision of the two baskets of figs (24:1–10), Jeremiah was shown what would happen to two groups of exiles in Judah. The first group were those who had been taken to Babylon with the Davidic king Jehoiakim in the first deportation by Nebuchadnezzar (24:1; cf. 2Ki 24:15–16). This group would return to the land and find God's blessing after the Exile (Jer 24:4–7). Though not stated directly by Jeremiah, the basis of this promise of future blessing was the Davidic covenant (2Sa 7). God had promised an eternal kingdom to the house of David, and thus the final word for the Davidic kingship could only be blessing. In light of this prophetic word, it is significant that the book of Jeremiah concludes with a word about King Jehoiakin and his release from prison during the last days of the Exile (52:31–34).

There was no word of hope for the second group of exiles, however (24:8–10)—the group that remained in the land with Nebuchadnezzar's puppet king, Zedekiah (v.8; cf. 2Ki 24:17); they would perish outside the land. Before the book of Jeremiah ends, we will have learned that Zedekiah died a humiliating death in Babylon (Jer 52:7–11), and all those who had remained in Judah were exiled (vv.12–30). This stands in stark contrast with the ultimate blessing of King Jehoiakin (52:31–34).

With ch. 25, we come to a major turning point in the book of Jeremiah. Using the words of Jeremiah's earlier oracles (25:1), the writer begins to focus beyond the immediate events of the destruction of Jerusalem by Nebuchadnezzar to the return of God's people and the punishment of the Babylonians. The writer's use of earlier prophecies from the days of Jehoiakim is occasioned by the fact that during the reign of Jehoiachin, Jehoiakim's son, God had warned all prophets not to speak oracles in his name (23:33–36). Thus the writer shows by his use of these earlier prophecies of Jeremiah that, long before, he had prophesied that there would be a limit to the judgment of God's people by Babylon—seventy years (25:11). After that time, Babylon itself would be destroyed (v.12), just as the other nations who had cursed God's people (vv.13–38).

## III. Prophecies of Salvation for Israel and Judah (26:1–35:19)

This is the section of the book containing the prophecies of the "new covenant" (31:31ff.).

When Jeremiah had prophesied his earlier oracles (26:1), there was still hope for God's people if they repented (vv.2–6). They had not repented, however; and what is more, the priests and prophets now set out to kill Jeremiah because of his strong words of judgment (vv.7–15). Though another prophet, Uriah son of Shemaiah, had already met with a similar fate (vv.20–23), Jeremiah was rescued by an appeal to the example of Hezekiah's reverential treatment of the prophet Micah (vv.16–19).

Jeremiah's prophecies (27:1–22), given during the reign of Jehoiakim (NIV, Zedekiah; cf. NIV note), raised the heat of his words against Judah one more notch. Not only had the people been warned of the coming destruction of their land by the hand of the Babylonians, but now they were also being told to submit willingly to the yoke of Babylon. They were to take their punishment by Babylon as from the Lord. Whereas before Jeremiah had warned that God's judgment was coming upon the people for disobeying God's law, now even more punishment would come for refusing to accept God's judgment (v.8). Submitting to the heavy yoke of Babylon would be a sign of their trust in God's faithfulness to Jerusalem (vv.11–12).

Only the false prophets had words of comfort in those days (vv.9–10, 14–15). The point of contention between Jeremiah and the false prophets centered on the temple utensils that had already been carried off to Babylon. The false prophets comforted the people with the words that these vessels would be returned quickly and peace would be restored (v.16). Jeremiah had warned, however, that the vessels of the temple would be returned only after a period of seventy years, when the full measure of God's wrath was spent against Judah and the nations (cf. 25:12–14). Not only would the vessels already taken not be returned quickly (27:16), but also those valuables left behind would be taken to Babylon and remain there until, in God's timing, he brought them back (vv.18–22; cf. Da 5:1–2).

Jeremiah met head-on with the false prophet Hananiah over the issue of the return of the temple vessels. Hananiah claimed to have received an oracle after the time in which God had ceased giving them (23:34–38). The text, then, has already marked his words as his own and not God's. Moreover, his words contradicted those of Jeremiah. Hananiah assured the people that God would "break the yoke of the king of Babylon" (28:2) and "within two years" return all the temple articles and King Jehoiachin himself from Babylon (vv.3–4). Although Jeremiah wished Hananiah's words were true (vv.5–6), he knew quite well that God had determined otherwise (vv.7–9). Because of the obvious apostasy of Israel and the nations, prophecies of divine judgment were the stock and trade of true prophets (v.8). For a prophecy of hope and blessing to be proved true, however, one had to wait for its fulfillment (v.9). Hananiah's attempt to cover his false prophecy with more of the same kind (vv.10–11) only served to heighten God's punishment. Instead of a wooden yoke from Babylon on Judah, the nation would be put into a yoke of iron (vv.12–14). Moreover, Hananiah was altogether removed by his death from causing further damage to God's people (vv.15–17). Ironically, Jeremiah's word as a true prophet was confirmed.

In conformity to his words against the false prophets, Jeremiah sent a letter to the exiles in Babylon (29:1–23). They were not to expect to return quickly, as Hananiah and the false prophets had said. They should "build houses and settle down; plant gardens and eat what they produce" (vv.4–5). They would be in Babylon for seventy years (v.10). Added to the stark reality of Jeremiah's words of prolonged judgment against Israel (vv.4–9, 15–23, 24–32), there were also words of comfort and promises of eventual blessing (vv.10–14).

In ch. 30 Jeremiah breaks out into a full description of the divine blessings that lay ahead for Israel and Judah. There would be "a time of trouble" for God's people, the descendants of Jacob, but after that, both the people of the northern kingdom of Israel and Judah would come back into the Promised Land. At that time, the promise to David that one of his descendants would reign over an eternal kingdom (2Sa 7:16) would be fulfilled (30:9) and he would bring peace to God's people (v.10). God's wrath against Israel would not destroy them. It would only serve as the Lord's discipline (v.11). The punishment that God would bring against them was, by now, inevitable (vv.12–15), but blessing and salvation still lay ahead (vv.16–22). God's wrath against Israel and Judah would only be understood from the viewpoint of his great blessing that would follow it (vv.23–24).

Jeremiah adds to his vision of Israel's future blessing the notion of a "new covenant" (31:31). Just as God had brought Israel out of Egypt and had entered a covenant with them at Sinai (Ex 19), so when he restored them to the land again it would be on the basis of a covenant. This new covenant, however, would not be like the Sinai covenant. In that covenant, Israel had been given the law on tablets of stone. Moreover, in the incident of the golden calf, they had broken the covenant and Moses dashed into pieces the tablets of stone (v.32; cf. Ex 32). But in the new covenant, Israel would be given the law written on their hearts.

Jeremiah's view of the new covenant is much like that of Moses in Dt 30. Moses also looked to a time after the Babylonian captivity (Dt 30:1–2) when God would give Israel a new heart. They would follow God's laws and love God with all their heart (Dt 30:3–6). In the new covenant, not only would the people have the law written on their hearts, they would also know God and enjoy his forgiveness (Jer 31:34). Because of this covenant, God promised that Jacob's descendants would never cease to be a nation (v.36). Like Jeremiah's portion of land purchased at the time of the Babylonians' siege of Jerusalem, the Lord had preserved Israel's right to the land. They would return to the land after a time of captivity and enjoy its blessings forever. His covenant with them would be "an everlasting covenant" (32:1–44).

In ch. 33 the writer of this book links Jeremiah's words about the new covenant with his earlier emphasis on God's promise to David (2Sa 7:16): "In those days and at that time I will make a righteous Branch sprout from David's line; he will do what is just and right in the land" (Jer 33:15). In those days there would be both an eternal kingship and an eternal priesthood (vv.17–18). God's covenant with David was as certain and eternal as his appointment of the times of day and night (vv.19–22). Through his promise to David, God would restore all the descendants of Abraham, Isaac, and Jacob (vv.23–26).

As if to show that in the final days before the fall of Jerusalem, the people of Judah had not forsaken their disobedient ways, the writer of the book records their breech of solemn covenant with their slaves (34:1–22). Even though they had repented and returned to the law of God, freeing their slaves as the law had commanded (vv.8–10), the leaders of the people soon changed their minds and forced their slaves back into service (v.11). Similarly, God would take away Israel's freedom by turning them over to their masters in Babylon (vv.12–22).

The only example of faithfulness to a solemn covenant and obedience among the people of Judah was that of the Recabites. This enigmatic group who lived only in tents and followed faithfully the vows their forefathers had made, provided a perfect example of what God required of his own people.

As a lesson to a disobedient and unfaithful Israel, God blessed the family of Jonadab son of Recab with the blessing that should have gone to the sons of Israel (35:1–19).

## IV. Baruch's Narrative of the Suffering of Jeremiah (36:1–45:5)

The account of the first edition of Jeremiah's book (36:2) sheds much light on the purpose and strategy of the present edition. God had spoken many times to the inhabitants of Judah, but they had not heeded his words. Jeremiah was thus instructed to write out in full all the words that he had spoken from the days of Josiah to those of Jehoiakim. Perhaps the cumulative effect of all these words would have a more lasting effect on them (v.3). This need for a cumulative effect helps explain the unusually complete record of divine judgments against Judah and Jerusalem in the first part of the book of Jeremiah. That it achieves this goal is clear to anyone who reads through these words of judgment in a single sitting.

Jeremiah carried out the Lord's command and dictated his words to Baruch, his scribe (36:4–26). Those who heard the words of Jeremiah written in the scroll immediately understood the fear of God that these words would engender in the people (vv.16–19). King Jehoiakim also understood the importance of Jeremiah's scroll and thus destroyed it immediately (vv.20–26). The king's response to that scroll appears only to have confirmed the importance of such a written document. Thus Jeremiah, at the Lord's command, dictated another copy of the scroll and added many similar things (v.32b). The reference to "many similar words" is probably a comment on the nature of the book of Jeremiah that we now have in the Bible. It not only contains many words of Jeremiah, but also other things as well. Particularly striking in the present book are the many personal narratives about the life of Jeremiah (chs. 37–38, 40–45) and the historical narratives of the fall of Jerusalem at its conclusion (cf. 39:1–10; 52:1–34). It is significant that these added things are placed immediately after the remark in 36:32b.

The added narratives about the life and ministry of Jeremiah begin with the story of his imprisonment (ch. 37). After Zedekiah had been placed over Judah by Nebuchadnezzar, Jeremiah's fate took a turn for the worse. Since his message had always been that the Babylonians were the instrument of divine wrath and that the Israelites should submit to their rule, it appeared to many that he had sided with the enemy, Babylon, and was attempting to discourage any further resistance. Jeremiah was thus imprisoned on what amounted to a charge of treason (37:11–15; 38:1–6). King Zedekiah, however, showed signs of complicity with Jeremiah. Specifically, he sent word to Jeremiah "to pray to the LORD our God" in behalf of the nation (37:3) and, with the help of Ebed-Melech (38:7–13), he protected Jeremiah's life (37:16–21; 38:28). Though this gained the king some reprieve from Babylon (37:4–5), it was only short-lived (37:6–8). Judah's sins were too great for their punishment to be averted at this late stage (vv.9–10). Jeremiah's personal word for Zedekiah during this crisis was the same as he had counseled all Israel: "If you surrender to the officers of the king of Babylon, your life will be spared and this city will not be burned down; you and your family will live" (38:17). However, unlike Ebed-Melech (39:15–18), Zedekiah was afraid to put his trust in God (38:19), in spite of the continued encouragement of Jeremiah (vv.20–23). This fear and uncertainty is dramatized in the fact that he even concealed from his officers his consultation with Jeremiah (vv.24–27).

The fall of Jerusalem finally came in Zedekiah's ninth year (39:1–10). This book of Jeremiah gives the account of the fall of Jerusalem in a slightly shorter version of 2Ki 25:1–12 (see also Jer 52:4–16). At this point in the book, the writer's primary interest lies both in the fact that God's word through Jeremiah was fulfilled and that Jeremiah himself, along with those who had sided with him, escaped the fate of the others. Jeremiah, who had counseled submission to Babylon as a recognition of God's just retribution against Israel, was protected and cared for by the Babylonian king (39:11–14). Ebed-Melech the Cushite, who had saved Jeremiah's life (38:7–13), was also saved from the destruction of the Babylonians because he had "trusted" in the Lord (39:15–18).

Curiously, as if to add insult to injury, the fulfillment of Jeremiah's own words against Jerusalem is stated by the general of the Babylonian army, Nebuzaradan: "The LORD your God decreed this disaster for this place. And now the LORD has brought it about; he has done just as he said he would" (40:2–3). The fact that these are Nebuzaradan's words of judgment against Jerusalem and the temple is similar to the fact that it was Cyrus in Ezr 1:2 who announced the fulfillment of Jeremiah's promise that the temple would be rebuilt. That is, the fulfillment of Jeremiah's words of judgment against Jerusalem and the temple was recognized and announced by the Gentile powers. Clearly the biblical writers intend to show the wider recognition of God's work with his people. The implications extend far beyond the immediate concerns of the people of Israel.

Those from Judah who were left behind by the Babylonians recognized Gedaliah as their leader. This man had been appointed by the Babylonians as an overseer of the region (40:5). Though he was well liked among the Jews (vv.7–16) and the people were beginning to prosper under his leadership (vv.10, 12), Gedaliah was assassinated and many leaders were killed by an Ammonite-led rebellion against Babylon (41:1–12). Through the leadership of Johanan, son of Kareah, and his remnant of an army, the survivors were liberated.

These Jewish survivors, led by Johanan, banded together with Jeremiah to serve the Lord and obey his word (41:16–42:6)—intent on fleeing to Egypt to escape Babylonian reprisals (41:16–18). Through Jeremiah, however, the Lord warned these people not to go down to Egypt, but rather to remain in the land and seek the Lord's help and protection from the Babylonians (42:7–18). If they fled to Egypt the same divine judgment that had overtaken Jerusalem would come to them in Egypt. Jeremiah himself pleaded with them to heed God's word (vv.19–22).

As if they had learned nothing from the events of the immediate past, the people forsook the word of the prophet Jeremiah and went to Egypt (43:1–7) anyway, forcibly taking Jeremiah with them (43:6). En route, Jeremiah prophesied that Nebuchadnezzar would destroy Egypt on account of the Jews who had taken refuge there (vv.8–14, 20–30). The people, however, did not listen to his words (44:19). Only Baruch (45:1–5) and a small remnant (44:28) would survive the divine wrath about to come upon the people in Egypt.

## V. Prophecies of Doom Against the Nations (46:1–51:64)

The last major section of the book of Jeremiah consists of a series of judgments against the enemies of Israel: Egypt (46:1–26), the Philistines (47:1–7), Moab (48:1–46), the Ammonites (49:1–5), Edom (49:7–22), Damascus (49:23–27), Kedar and Hazor (49:28–33), and Elam (49:34–38). This series culminates in an extended word of judgment against Babylon (50:1–64a), in which the rise of the empire of the Medes is specifically foretold (51:11, 28). It is clear that for the writer of the book of Jeremiah, the enumeration of these various judgments against Israel's enemies was a way to express the certitude of God's promise of salvation for Israel (49:2b; 50:4–8, 17–20, 33–34; 51:5–6, 10, 24, 35–39, 45–53). Thus, while they represent the certitude of divine judgment on Israel's enemies, they also express the certitude of divine blessing and salvation for Israel. Moreover, interspersed in these words of judgment are words of hope and salvation for Israel (46:27–28) as well as for Moab (48:47), the Ammonites (49:6), and Elam (49:39).

## VI. Conclusion (52:1–34)

The book of Jeremiah closes with two narratives from the book of Kings. The first is a lengthy reiteration of the account of the fall of Jerusalem (52:1–30), taken almost verbatim from 2Ki 24:18–25:21. This serves to put the pre-ceding prophecies of judgment against Babylon (50:1–51:58) in their proper perspective. Even though Babylon was an instrument of judgment in God's hand (51:7), they had wantonly destroyed Jerusalem and God's temple (v.11b), and thus God was raising up the Medes to punish them (50:41–44; 51:11).

The second narrative, which closes the book (52:31–34), is a verbatim account of the restitution of the royal prerogatives of King Jehoiachin in the palace of the Babylonian king Evil-Merodach (taken from 2Ki 25:27–30). The purpose of this narrative, positioned as it is at the close of the book, is to show that God's purposes for Israel and his promises to David (2Sa 7) were still being carried out, even though the city had been destroyed and the king was living in exile in Babylon. The promised Redeemer had not yet arisen, but one could see in the events of this brief narrative that God was still at work. This book thus ends on a note of hope and expectancy of the fulfillment of God's blessing for Israel.

# Lamentations

## Introduction

The impact of the Exile on the thought and life of the Jewish people is best seen in the document that came directly from the time of the fall of Jerusalem, the book of Lamentations. The writer of the book is not identified in the text; many think it may be Jeremiah (based on 2Ch 35:25, though the "laments" mentioned there for King Josiah are not the laments in this book of the Bible).

The book of Lamentations is a theological explanation of the Exile and destruction of Jerusalem. The meaning it gives to the Exile is clear: It meant that the days of Israel's reliance on the Lord's covenant, established with Israel at Sinai, were over. The covenant, or rather, Israel's disobedience to the covenant, had led to the punishment of the Exile. Even though the Sinai covenant was broken, however, Israel's relationship with the Lord was not over. The Lord would be faithful to his promises to David and the Davidic covenant (2Sa 7:16). There was thus hope for the future. The faithful were to put their hope in God's promises and wait patiently for the Lord's salvation (cf. Isa 40:31). When Israel's punishment was complete, he would leave his people in exile no longer (4:22; cf. Isa 40:2). Thus restoration becomes the major theme on which the book concludes: "Restore us to yourself, O LORD, that we may return; renew our days as of old" (5:22).

## I. The City of Jerusalem (1:1–22)

The author begins by describing Jerusalem as it lay in ruins after the Babylonian destruction (vv.1–4). Jerusalem, like a forsaken widow, weeps bitterly in the night, with no one to comfort her (1:1–2). There were no more appointed feasts (v.4), all her gates were desolate (v.4), her priests were groaning (v.4), and she had become the slave of her enemies (v.5).

The author is quick to point out, however, that there was a reason behind Jerusalem's misfortune: "The LORD has brought her grief because of her many sins" (v.5). This viewpoint of the author is the same as that of the Deuteronomistic writer (see unit on "The Deuteronomistic History" betweeen Deuteronomy and Joshua).

## II. Israel's Enemy (2:1–22)

In ch. 2 the author gives full vent to the notion that Israel's enemy has now become the Lord himself: "The Lord is like an enemy; he has swallowed up Israel. He has swallowed up all her palaces and destroyed her strongholds. He has multiplied mourning and lamentation for the Daughter of Judah" (v.5).

## III. Despair and Comfort (3:1–66)

In ch. 3 the author again expresses the idea that it was the Lord himself who brought on the destruction of Jerusalem; this brings him to the brink of despair: "I have been deprived of peace; I have forgotten what prosperity is. So I say, 'My splendor is gone and all that I had hoped from the LORD'" (3:17–18).

At this very point, however, the writer pauses to remember that all hope is not lost. There is still one last source of comfort—God's loyal love, his covenant faithfulness, and his compassion never cease (v.22). "This I call to mind," he says, "and therefore I have hope" (v.21). Out of the midst of the deepest despair of the Exile spring new rays of hope: "Great is your faithfulness" (v.22). With this hope comes a new call to life and faith in the Lord.

There is thus hope for the reader of these lamentations, but the Exile is, nevertheless, real. The judgments they contain must be endured. But a new way of life is called for in the light of this new hope in God's promises—a life of waiting silently for the salvation of God: "It is good to wait quietly for the salvation of the LORD. . . . Let him offer his cheek to one who would strike him, and let him be filled with disgrace. For men are not cast off by the Lord forever" (vv.26–31).

Thus in vv.39–42, the writer calls for repentance and confession of guilt, and then lapses again into the grief of the present hour—the horror of the Exile and of the destruction of Jerusalem (vv.43-48).

In the last sections of ch. 3, a new note is heard amid the voice of ruin, a call for God to recompense those who brought on this destruction (i.e., the Babylonians): "You have seen, O LORD, the wrong done to me. Uphold my cause!" (v.59); "Pay them back what they deserve, O LORD, for what their hands have done" (v.64); "Pursue them in anger and destroy them from under the heavens of the LORD" (v.66).

## IV. Anticipation of Return (4:1–22)

In ch. 4 the poet continues his description of the tremendous devastation that took place in the Promised Land, concentrating especially on the effects of the siege of Jerusalem on the people here. But there is also the anticipation of a return from this exile: "O Daughter of Zion, your punishment will end; he will not prolong your exile" (v.22a).

## V. The Poet's Prayer (5:12–22)

The final chapter of Lamentations is in the form of a prayer. The author asks the Lord to look on what has been happening to his people. He acknowledges that it was decades of sin that caused this pain and suffering (v.7). He closes his prayer by asserting God's eternity (v.19) and by asking God to restore and renew his chastised people (vv.20--22).

# Ezekiel

## Introduction

Ezekiel began his prophetic ministry in the fifth year of Jehoiachin's exile (1:2; 592 B.C.). The latest date in the book is the twenty-seventh year of Jehoiachin's exile (29:17; 570 B.C.). Ezekiel was among the exiles in Babylon and carried out his prophetic ministry there (1:1).

The historical events that are important in the book are both the rise of the Babylonian empire and the rise of the nation of "Gog"—the next Gentile ruling nation of importance. Gog is mentioned as the "prince of Rosh" in 38:2, but it is not easily identified from historical records. It may be intended as a symbol of a great empire that was yet to rise and take a stand against God's people in the prophet's own day or in the eschatological future.

As the book of Ezekiel opens, the first exile to Babylon had taken place and the second was pending (cf. 1:2; 2Ki 24:12ff.).

There were at least two distinct parts to Ezekiel's message to the exiles. (1) He warned them not to follow the words of the false prophets who (as had happened with Jeremiah) spoke of the peace and blessing that was in store for them. Ezekiel, like Jeremiah, warned the exiles that ruin, not peace, loomed on their horizon. The people had rebelled against God and had broken his covenant; consequently, they could only expect God's judgment. (2) Ezekiel also prophesied that peace and blessing would still come to Israel some day in the future—after the time of judgment and destruction. Two major sections of Ezekiel deal with these prophecies of hope: chs. 36–39 (the restoration of God's people) and chs. 40–48 (the restoration of God's temple).

## I. Introduction (1:1–3)

For the most part the book of Ezekiel is written in the first person, with the prophet himself as the narrator. Although that is also the case in 1:1, vv.2–3 are clearly the work of an author other than the prophet. Speaking of Ezekiel the author says, "The hand of the LORD was upon him" (v.3). The purpose of the author's interrupting Ezekiel, the narrator, was to clarify the otherwise ambiguous date in 1:1, "in the thirtieth year." Some have supposed that the thirtieth year was a reference to the age of Ezekiel when he first received his vision; but there is no evidence to support such a theory. According to the author in v.2, the "thirtieth year" was the fifth year of the exile of King Jehoiachin (593 B.C.). Thus, five years after the first group of exiles were taken from Judah, Ezekiel, one of the exiles himself, saw the heavens opened and received "visions of God."

The first group of visions recorded in the book of Ezekiel contain mostly words of judgment against the people of God who still remained in Judah and Jerusalem. These were the people who would later be taken captive by the Babylonian king Nebuchadnezzar. Interspersed in these words of doom and judgment are also many words of comfort and hope. Beginning in ch. 34, these become the major focus of the book.

## II. Judgment Against God's People Israel and Judah (1:4–24:27)

### A. Ezekiel's Call (1:4–3:11)

The book opens with a description of Ezekiel's divine call. From the midst of "a windstorm coming out of the north," Ezekiel saw the appearance of the glory of God (1:4–28). Falling facedown, he heard a voice saying that he was to go to the rebellious nation of Israel (2:1–8) and to proclaim to them the words of "lament and mourning and woe," written for him on a scroll (2:9–3:11). Ezekiel was then taken by the Spirit "to the exiles who lived at Tel Abib" (3:12–15). Here he was given the task of being a "watchman" for the people. The guilt of the people was upon his shoulders if he failed to warn them of their need to repent (vv.16–27). His mouth was closed so he could not rebuke the people on his own (v.26). He could speak only when God put his words in his mouth (v.27). After the destruction of Jerusalem, when God had words of comfort for his people, Ezekiel's mouth was opened (33:22).

## B. The Announcement of the Fall of Jerusalem (4:1–7:27)

Ezekiel's first words of warning come as a series of symbolic acts, each picturing some aspect of the impending destruction of Jerusalem. He first laid siege to the city of Jerusalem inscribed on a clay tablet (4:1–3). He then lay on his side for 430 days (vv.4–8; cf. comments on 1Ki 6:1), eating wheat and barley to symbolize the defiled food the Israelites would eat while living among the nations in exile (vv.9–17). Then he shaved his hair and beard, burning some of it and scattering the rest in all directions (5:1–4), symbolizing Jerusalem's destruction and scattering among the nations (vv.5–17). The small portion of hair that Ezekiel was told to "tuck away in the folds of [his] garment" (v.3) apparently was meant to symbolize the eventual salvation of a remnant after God's anger had ceased and his wrath against Israel subsided (v.13).

In graphic detail, the prophet describes the impending destruction of Judah and its structures of idolatry (6:1–7:27). The destruction would come from "sword, famine and plague" (6:11). It would be "an unheard-of disaster" that would mark "the end" of Israel's possession of the land (7:5–6). What Ezekiel may have in mind was the final destruction of the kingdom by the Babylonians, "the most wicked of the nations to take possession of their houses" (v.24), though it is important to note that this word of judgment does not specifically mention Babylon by name. It may, in other words, already be viewing the destruction of Jerusalem in eschatological terms and not merely in terms of the immediate destruction by Nebuchadnezzar. That the book of Ezekiel has a perspective on the final days of history is clear from passages such as chs. 36–39.

## C. The Temple Vision (8:1–11:25)

While in exile, in the sixth year of the first captivity of Jerusalem, Ezekiel was lifted up in a vision and taken to the city of Jerusalem. He was shown the various forms of apostasy within Jerusalem itself (8:4–18). There was an idol at the entrance to north gate of the altar (vv.5–6). Seventy elders were in the temple, each with a shrine to his own idol (vv.7–13). Women were mourning for Tammuz, a foreign deity, at the entrance to the north gate of the temple (vv.14–15), and twenty-five Israelite men were bowing down to the sun in the east (vv.16–18). It was because of such things that the Lord was angry with Israel and determined to bring down his wrath upon them (v.18).

It was also because of such things that the glory of the Lord departed from the temple (9:1–11:25). When Solomon built the temple and the Ark of the Covenant was brought into it (1Ki 8:1–9), "the glory of the LORD filled his temple" (1Ki 8:10). Now, because of the extreme wickedness and apostasy of the people, the Lord's glory was taken away. Ezekiel first saw God's glory move from above the cherubim to the threshold of the temple (9:3). It was then transported by the wings of the cherubim to the entrance of the east gate (10:18–19), where it left the temple and the city (11:22–25). It was through the east gate that the glory of the Lord would again return to the temple in the "last days" when Israel would be restored and the temple rebuilt (43:4).

At the same time that he saw the glory departing from the temple, Ezekiel saw a graphic vision of the destruction of the idolatrous people of the city (9:1–11). Within the book, this provides the context for a prophetic word warning of the impending exile (11:1–15) and the promise of a future return (vv.16–21).

After the vision, Ezekiel packed his belongings and, in full view of the people, set out on a journey to symbolize the coming exile of Jerusalem (12:1–20). He dug through the walls of the city and carried his belongings on his shoulders (v.7). To the curious onlookers, Ezekiel explained the meaning of his act: "This oracle concerns the prince in Jerusalem and the whole house of Israel who are there. . . . As I have done, so it will be done to them. They will go into exile as captives" (vv.10–11).

## D. Popular Sayings Explained (13:1–19:14)

The next major section of this book gathers together a series of responses to popular sayings among the exiles. These sayings were apparently used by those in exile to justify their complacency in following God's law. Ezekiel thus set out to refute the sayings and thereby to turn the people's attention back to God.

**Saying 1.** "The days go by and every vision comes to nothing" (12:21–23). Clearly the purpose of this saying was to call into question the validity of the prophet's word of judgment in light of the fact that Jerusalem still lay intact and unharmed. But Ezekiel's word was that God would soon "put an end to this proverb" (v.23). The day of judgment was near, "it shall be fulfilled without delay" (v.23b). The source of the saying appears to have been the false prophets who continued to prophesy peace for

Jerusalem (13:1–23). Unlike these false prophets, however, God's prophets foretold that he would quickly send destruction (v.16).

**Saying 2.** "These men have set up idols in their hearts and put wicked stumbling blocks before their faces. Should I let them inquire of me at all?" (14:1–11) The saying is cast in the form of a question, a puzzle. Its answer is ironic. Such idolatrous people may inquire of the Lord, but the Lord would answer them with severe judgment. God requires repentance from those who inquire of him (v.6).

**Saying 3.** "Even if these three men—Noah, Daniel and Job—were in it, they could save only themselves by their righteousness" (v.14). The saying assumes that the people were relying on the righteousness of some among them or of their forefathers for their security with God. God's response, however, is that divine judgment cannot be averted merely by the righteousness of a select few. The righteous will be saved but the wicked will perish (vv.12–23).

**Saying 4.** "How is the wood of a vine better than that of a branch on any of the trees in the forest?" (15:1–8). This saying assumes a knowledge of the value of the wood of a vine and that of a tree. The wood of a vine, like Jerusalem, is good for nothing but burning.

**Saying 5.** "Your father was an Amorite and your mother a Hittite" (16:3, 45). This saying introduces an extended allegory of God's dealings with Judah and Jerusalem (vv.1–63). It is explained by means of another proverbial saying: "Like mother, like daughter" (v.44). Judah and Jerusalem are seen as part and parcel of their Canaanite and pagan neighbors. The review of Israel's past, seen in this allegory, provides an occasion to recall God's covenant promises of blessing to Israel "in the days of [their] youth" (v.60). Thus the prophetic word of judgment ends on the positive note of a prophecy of hope (vv.60–63).

**Saying 6**. "A great eagle with powerful wings, long feathers and full plumage of varied colors came to Lebanon. . . . He took some of the seed of your land and put it in fertile soil . . . and it sprouted and became a low, spreading vine. . . . But there was another great eagle with powerful wings and full plumage. . ." (17:1–24). This saying consists of an allegory (vv.1–10) with an interpretation (17:11–21). Within the allegory, the first eagle is Babylon, the vine is Israel taken into captivity, and the second eagle is Egypt, to whom Israel looked for help instead of trusting in God. The picture of Israel as a vine builds on the earlier saying that compared the worthless value of the wood of a vine to that of a tree (15:1–8). Moreover, the image of Israel as a vine growing in the soil of Babylon and reaching for the soil of Egypt gives rise to another allegory, picturing a redeemed Israel as a young shoot of a cedar tree planted "on a high and lofty mountain" (17:22–24; cf. Isa 4:2).

**Saying 7**. "The fathers eat sour grapes, and the children's teeth are set on edge" (18:1–32). This saying appears to acknowledge the validity of the prophet's announcement of impending judgment, expressing a fatalistic interpretation of it: What can the sons do about divine judgment if it comes because of the sin of the fathers? In this saying the whole ethical demands of the prophet's message were undercut. Ezekiel's response was to counter this saying with another: "The soul who sins is the one who will die" (v.4). God's judgment could be averted only through repentance: "Rid yourselves of all the offenses you have committed, and get a new heart and a new spirit. Why will you die, O house of Israel? . . . Repent and live!" (vv.31–32).

**Saying 8**. "What a lioness was your mother among the lions!" (19:1–9).

This saying, and the one that follows, are based on an ironic application of the prophecy of Jacob in Ge 49:8–12 to the kings of Judah. In his prophecy of the future of the tribe of Judah, Jacob had called Judah "a lioness" from whom the scepter and ruler's staff would come (Ge 49:9–10). Ezekiel recalls that Judah did become a young lion (Eze 19:3; cf. Ge 49:9), but, he adds, Judah was soon carried off to Egypt with no hope of wielding the scepter. Another strong lion came from the tribe of Judah, however. This was the house of David. It too was carried into captivity without the authority of its scepter. It is important to note that Ezekiel was not saying that Jacob's prophecy had failed. He was rather saying that the prophecy had not yet been fulfilled. He looked to the future for the fulfillment of Jacob's prophecy. In the next section (Eze 21:27), Ezekiel again alludes to Jacob's prophecy when he speaks of the restoration of the kingship in the house of David: "It will not be restored until he comes to whom it rightfully belongs." The expression "to whom it rightfully belongs" is a virtual quotation of Jacob's words in Ge 49:10, "The scepter will not depart from Judah . . . until he comes to whom it belongs."

**Saying 9**. "Your mother was like a vine in your vineyard planted by the water" (19:10–14). Ezekiel had already used the imagery of a "vine" to describe Judah's apostasy and weakness (15:1–8; 17:6). Here he links the image to Jacob's prophecy as well. Jacob had pictured the mighty ruler from the tribe of Judah tethering "his donkey to a vine, his colt to the choicest branch" (Ge 49:11). Thus, looking at the kingship in the time of David, Ezekiel says of Judah, "Your mother was like a vine. . . . Its branches were strong, fit for a ruler's scepter" (19:10–11). But in the Exile, the house of David "was uprooted in fury and thrown to the ground. . . . No strong branch is left on it fit for a ruler's scepter" (vv.12–14).

## E. God's Dealings With Israel (20:1–44)

Having raised the question of God's dealings with Israel since the days of old, Ezekiel now surveys Israel's history with a view toward "the detestable practices of their fathers" (20:4b). He begins with the time of Israel's sojourn in Egypt (vv.1–9). What Ezekiel records here is not recorded elsewhere in the OT. The Pentateuch passes over this period in Israel's history with little or no comment (Ex 1:1–7). According to Ezekiel, the Israelites had forsaken God and followed after the gods of Egypt during their time there. They had set their eyes on "the vile images" and "the idols of Egypt" (Eze 20:7).

The situation was no better during their time in the desert (vv.10–26). The people rebelled against God, rejected his laws, and did not follow his decrees (v.13). Their hearts were still turned toward their idols (v.16b). God thus gave them stringent laws when they were in the wilderness—laws intended to keep them from forsaking him altogether (vv.21–26; cf. Gal 3:19). When Israel entered the land, the situation went from bad to worse (vv.27–29).

Turning to his own day, Ezekiel envisioned a new exodus for the people of God (vv.30–38), one that included both judgment (vv.34–36) and the hope of salvation in the form of a new "covenant" (vv.37–38). We should note that at this stage in the book of Ezekiel, the return from Babylonian captivity is not in view as a time of salvation for the people of God. This time is rather a time of purging God's people of "those who revolt and rebel" against God (v.38); "they will not enter the land of Israel."

In the future, however, the entire house of Israel would turn to the Lord in obedience and with "holy sacrifices" (vv.39–44). God would accept them v.41), and they would be brought back into the land (v.42) by divine grace (v.44). In this prophetic word, Ezekiel anticipates the whole of the prophecies of Israel's future in chs. 34–48, including the notion of a restored temple and sacrifices offered during the future reign of the Davidic king.

## F. Impending Judgment (20:45–24:14)

Having presented the main lines of judgment and salvation that awaited the people of God, Ezekiel now turned to describe in more detail the specific aspects of the divine judgment. He looked first at the divine judgment that was about to fall on the southern regions of the land, i.e., the land of Judah (20:45–49). He then centered his prophetic word on the city of Jerusalem and the temple (21:1–27).

As 21:19 makes clear, the divine judgment that Ezekiel had in view was that of the destruction of the city by the Babylonians. The king of Babylon cast lots to decide whether he should invade Jerusalem or the Ammonite city of Rabbah, and the lot fell on Jerusalem (vv.20–22). God had determined the lot in order to bring judgment on the "profane and wicked prince of Israel" (v.25). The king of Judah would be removed until the true King came to claim the throne promised him long ago in the days of the forefathers (v.27; cf. Ge 49:10). Even though the lot of the Babylonian king fell on Jerusalem, the Ammonites would not escape God's wrath (vv.28–32).

Why was Jerusalem singled out among these nations? Because it was a "city of bloodshed," and its people had not kept God's laws (22:1–16). The first commandment in the Sinai covenant was the prohibition of idolatry (Ex 20:2–6). Thus Ezekiel's indictment of the people was that they had become defiled by the idols they had made (22:4). Furthermore, Ezekiel charged them with breaking virtually the whole of the Ten Commandments (vv.6–12).

Turning to the remnant of the "house of Israel," Ezekiel describes the fate they would share with the inhabitants of Jerusalem (vv.17–22) as the result of the sins of the rest of "the land" (vv.23–31). With this broader perspective of the sins of the whole nation in view, Ezekiel recounts an extended allegory of the "two sisters," Oholah and Oholibah. These two names characterized that which was distinct about the two kingdoms. The name of the northern kingdom, Oholah, means "she who dwells in her own tent [tabernacle]." It thus views the northern kingdom from the perspective of the false worship centers set up by Jeroboam I (cf. 1Ki 12–13). The name of the southern kingdom, Oholibah, means "My tent [tabernacle] is with her," thus looking at the fact that the true temple of God was in Jerusalem. In this allegory, the two kingdoms of Samaria (the northern kingdom of Israel) and Judah (the southern kingdom) are portrayed as promiscuous young women flirting with their foreign lovers, Assyria and Babylon. In disgust, God had given them over to their lovers, and their lovers had brutally abused them (23:1–49). Like a large cooking pot that cannot be cleansed of the years of stain and residue, Israel's and Judah's sins were indelible (24:1–14).

The visions of Ezekiel regarding the divine judgment against Jerusalem and the temple close with a striking image of the horror and disbelief of the people on hearing of the temple's ruin. The temple was "their stronghold, their joy and glory, the delight of their eyes, their heart's desire" (v.25). The numbness that Ezekiel felt on hearing of his wife's death, "the delight of [his] eyes," was intended to symbolize the people's own "quiet groaning" (v.17) on hearing of the ruin of the temple (vv. 15–27).

## III. Judgment Against the Nations (25:1–32:32)

Ezekiel now announces divine judgment against the nations for their mistreatment of Israel. The basis of his oracles against the nations was God's promise to Abraham, "whoever curses you I will curse" (Ge 12:3). The nations enumerated in this list of oracles were to be destroyed because they rejoiced at the destruction of God's people: Ammon (25:1–7), Moab (vv.8–11), Edom (vv.12–14), Philistia (vv.15–17), Tyre (26:1–28:19), Sidon (28:20–23), and Egypt (29:1–32:32). Imbedded in these oracles of judgment against the nations is a reminder of the hope that still lay ahead for the people of Israel (28:24–26); this section anticipates the theme of the second half of the book (chs. 33–48).

The oracles against Tyre (26:1–28:19) and against Egypt (29:1–32:32) are exceptionally lengthy. The oracle against Tyre includes a description of the Babylonians' destruction of that city (26:1–21), a lament for the fallen city (27:1–36), an indictment against the pride of the prince of the city of Tyre (28:1–10; using the imagery of a fallen angel in the Garden of "Eden," cf. v.13), and a lament for the prince of Tyre (vv.11–19). The oracle against Egypt also includes a description of the Babylonians' destruction of the land of Egypt (29:1–21), a lament for the fallen land (30:1–26), an indictment against the pride of the pharaoh of Egypt, using the imagery of a fallen tree in the "garden of God" (31:1–18), and a lament for the pharaoh of Egypt (32:1–32).

## IV. Future Blessing for Israel (33:1–48:35)

### A. Summary (33:1–20)

Two central themes of the preceding chapters are restated and summarized here. Ezekiel's role as a watchman for Israel is recast in 33:7–9 as a virtual restatement of 3:17–19, and the expression of God's desire for the repentance of the sinner (33:11–20) is repeated from 18:23–29. Thus, as a prelude to the oracles of hope and salvation, the writer of the book of Ezekiel returns to the importance of Israel's repentance. The basis of his grounding Israel's salvation in their repentance can be found in the theology of Ge 18:19—if the descendants of Abraham would "keep the way of the LORD by doing what is right and just," God would fulfill his promises to the fathers. This is the theology of the new covenant that is so clearly expressed in the second half of Ezekiel (cf. 36:27).

## B. Restoration of the House of David (34:1–35:15)

With the announcement of the fall of Jerusalem (33:21–33) and thus the fulfillment of Ezekiel's oracles of divine judgment, the prophet's visions turn to that of the restoration of the house of David (34:1–31). The fulfillment of Ezekiel's oracles serve to demonstrate the validity of his role as a prophet (33:33). That, in turn, within the strategy of the book, serves as a basis for the reader's hope in the fulfillment of Ezekiel's words of blessing.

Ezekiel's words of hope and blessing lie in his vision of the restoration of the house of David. Based on God's promise to David in 2Sa 7:16, Ezekiel saw a time in Israel's future when they would be regathered from exile among all the nations and returned to the land (34:13–22). At that time God would place his servant David over them as shepherd (v.23) and prince (v.24). Undoubtedly Ezekiel used the notion of the kingship of David as a figure of that of the Messiah. This is particularly clear in the idyllic scene described in 34:25–31, a virtual return to the conditions of the Garden of Eden.

In keeping with the picture of David's kingship as a messianic figure, the writer of this book records a prophetic oracle against Edom (35:1–15).

Not only was David the king who successfully conquered and ruled over the land of Edom (2Sa 8:14), but also this was specifically prophesied of the Messiah in Nu 24:18. Thus by focusing on the ruin of Edom at this point in the book, the writer shows that the prophecy in Nu 24 still had its fulfillment in the future—when Edom would be destroyed.

## C. Restoration of the People of God (36:1–39:29)

Not only would the house of David be restored and Israel's enemies be defeated, but also the people of God would be returned to the land and given a new heart (36:1–38). This is the new covenant, pictured here as a fulfillment of God's promise through Moses in Dt 30:4–6, "Even if you have been banished to the most distant land under the heavens, from there the LORD your God will gather you and bring you back. . . . The LORD your God will circumcise your hearts and the hearts of your descendants, so that you may love him with all your heart and with all your soul, and live."

The restoration of God's people in the last days is graphically pictured in the scene of the valley of dry bones (37:1–10) and its explanation (37:11–14). Ezekiel prophesied that, at that time, all Israel would again be united in a new Davidic kingdom as in the days of David (37:15–28). In those days Israel's enemies would be sorely defeated (38:1–39:24) and God's people would enjoy peace and safety at last in their own land (39:25–29).

## D. Restoration of the Temple (40:1–48:35)

The final vision in the book of Ezekiel is that of the new temple in Jerusalem. The writer of the book gives much attention to detail, holding the grand picture of this temple before the eyes of the reader as long as possible— for most modern readers, too long! In any event, for the writer of the book, the restoration of the temple meant the culmination of all God's promises of blessing and fellowship. One can sense the same intensity of feeling toward the implications of the new temple here in Ezekiel as one feels in the depiction of the New Jerusalem in the book of Revelation. The temple and the New Jerusalem are both pictures of the same reality—the human race's enjoyment of God's presence and fellowship. It is a return to God's original intent for the human race in the Garden of Eden (Ge 1–2).

For the writer of Ezekiel this could only be expressed in terms of the Mosaic covenant—the tabernacle and the temple. For John in Revelation, however, this could only be expressed by the incarnation of the Lamb of God and the replacement of the temple with the New Jerusalem (see Rev 21:22). He saw that God was present with his people in the whole city (Rev 21:23–27), not merely in the temple, as is depicted in Ezekiel (Eze 48:32). The two visions of Ezekiel and John express the same ideas, but they use different imagery. It is important to note that John's images also are derived from the OT. According to the prophet Zechariah, "on that day HOLY TO THE LORD will be inscribed on the bells of the horses. . . . Every pot in Jerusalem and Judah will be holy to the LORD Almighty" (Zec 14:20–21).

The description of the new temple and its environs is given with little or no comment from the author of the book. From the mere description of it one is intended to get a sense of its majesty and glory. The design and magnitude of the temple is left to speak for itself. Unlike the old temple that was destroyed by the Babylonian army, from which God's glory had departed (10:18–19), the glory of God filled this temple (43:1–11). Like the old temple, however, this temple also was decorated

with images of God's Garden in Eden (41:17–19; 47:1–12; cf. comments on 1Ki 6).

The description of the temple consists of the following major sections:

1. Measurements of the court of the new temple (40:5–47)

    a. Wall around temple area (v.5)

    b. East gate in wall (vv.6–16)

    c. Outer Court (vv.17–19)

    d. North Gate (vv.20–23)

    e. South Gate (vv.24–27)

    f. Inner Court (vv.28–37)

    g. Rooms for preparing sacrifices within the inner gateway to the altar (vv.38–43)

    h. Priests' (sons of Zadok) rooms outside inner gateway to the altar (vv.44–47)

2. Measurements of the new temple (40:48–41:26)

3. Measurements of the rooms for priests (42:1–14)

4. Measurements around the outside of the temple area (42:15–20)

5. The glory of the Lord returns to the temple (43:1–11)

6. "The law of the temple" (43:12–27)

    a. The altar (vv.13–17)

    b. The offerings (vv.18–27)

7. The glory of the Lord fills the temple (44:1–4)

8. "The regulations" of the temple (44:5–31)

9. Dividing the land (45:1–12)

    a. The "sacred district" (vv.1–5)

    b. City property (v.6)

    c. Land of the Prince (vv.7–12)

10. Offerings and holy days (45:13–46:24)

11. The river coming out of the temple (47:1–12)

12. Boundaries of the land (47:13–23)

13. Allotment of the land (48:1–29)

14. The gates of the city (48:30–35)

# EZEKIEL'S TEMPLE

**A.** Wall (40:5,16-20)
**B.** East gate (40:6-14,16)
**C.** Portico (40:8)
**D.** Outer court (40:17)
**E.** Pavement (40:17)
**F.** Inner court (40:19)
**G.** North gate (40:20-22)
**H.** Inner court (40:23)
**I.** South gate (40:24-26)
**J.** South inner court (40:27)
**K.** Gateway (40:28-31)
**L.** Gateway (40:32-34)
**M.** Gateway (40:35-38)
**N.** Priests' rooms (40:44-45)

**O.** Court (40:47)
**P.** Temple portico (40:48-49)
**Q.** Outer sanctuary (41:1-2)
**R.** Most Holy Place (41:3-4)
**S.** Temple walls (41:5-7, 9, 11)
**T.** Base (41:8)
**U.** Open area (41:10)
**V.** West building (41:12)
**W.** Priests' rooms (42:1-10)
**X.** Altar (43:13-17)

**AA.** Rooms for preparing
        sacrifices (40:39-43)
**BB.** Ovens (46:19-20)
**CC.** Kitchens (46:21-24)

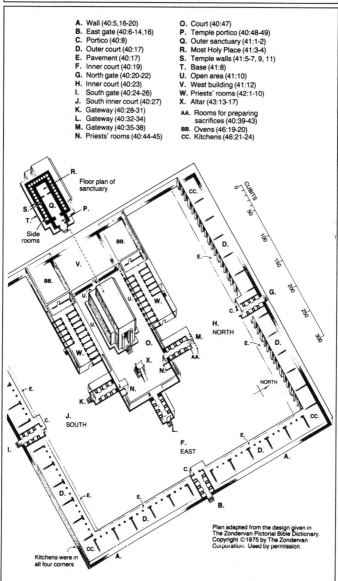

Floor plan of
sanctuary

Side
rooms

CUBITS

0
50
100
150
200
250
300

NORTH

NORTH

J.
SOUTH

F.
EAST

Plan adapted from the design given in
The Zondervan Pictorial Bible Dictionary.
Copyright © 1975 by The Zondervan
Corporation. Used by permission.

Kitchens were in
all four corners

# Daniel

## Introduction

In the English Bible, the book of Daniel is listed with the prophets. Not so in the Hebrew Bible. There, the book is placed after the book of Esther and before Ezra. Both in content and chronology, Daniel is suited for either position. The prophet Daniel was a contemporary of the prophet Ezekiel. He is even mentioned in Eze 14:14, 20 and 28:3. Although he lived somewhat earlier than Esther, the events in his life were similar to hers. Both Daniel and Esther (and Joseph too) rose to a place of high position in the court of a foreign king. God used their positions to save his people from annihilation. In the lives of these three individuals we can see the hand of God at work in the details of everyday life.

The book of Daniel, however, goes far beyond Genesis and Esther in its perception of the hand of God at work in the world. In Daniel the work of God is seen on a global scale. Not only did God rescue his people through their courageous faith; he also promised to rescue and vindicate his people in an ultimate way and on a cosmic scale in the days of the Messiah.

Daniel is called "Apocalyptic Literature," meaning literature that "reveals" the plans and mysteries of God. In it we see beyond the veil of everyday experience. The plan of God for the ages is unrolled before our eyes. As is often the case in such literature, the mysteries are revealed in highly symbolic images. One must guard against a too facile interpretation of these images. We can do that by paying careful attention to the interpretations provided within the narrative of the book. In this commentary, we will interpret the various visions of Daniel and the Babylonian kings always and only as they are interpreted within the book itself. It is always tempting to try to second-guess what this or that vision may signify. That is all well and good, but in the last analysis, we must pay most attention to the interpretations provided within the texts themselves and, where there are none, to refrain from straying too far in our own suppositions.

In the charts that accompany the text of this commentary, we will attempt to distinguish the visions and dreams from the interpretations of them given in the text. The content of the dreams and visions will be listed within the boxes, and the interpretations of them given in the text will be listed alongside them on the right.

## I. An Introduction to the Book (1:1–21)

The first chapter of the book of Daniel serves as a fitting introduction to the whole book. It clarifies a number of features of this unique book and gives a broader context to the events recorded. The abrupt change in language from Hebrew to the language of the Chaldeans (Aramaic) in 2:4, for example, is anticipated and, at least in part, explained by the story of Daniel and his friends learning this language (see 1:4b). Moreover, the chief characters of the book—Daniel, Shadrach, Meshach, Abednego, and Nebuchadnezzar, the king of Babylon—are each introduced, along with the general setting of the rest of the book, the court of King Nebuchadnezzar.

Interestingly enough, the Hebrew names of these four men are given along with their Babylonian names. The Hebrew reader would not understand the meaning of the latter, but the meaning of their Hebrew names is clear. Thus this chapter casts further light on the narratives that follow (see comments on ch. 3). Furthermore, the integrity of Daniel and his three friends is fully established here. Their refusal to eat the rich foods of the Babylonian king shows them to be true Israelites who remain faithful to God's law even in the most adverse circumstances. Finally, the origin of the superior wisdom of Daniel and his friends, as well as the unusual favor that they found with their enemies, is explained in this chapter: both were given to them by the God of Israel (vv.9, 17).

## II. Nebuchadnezzar's Dream (2:1–49)

The narrative of ch. 2 contains the account of Nebuchadnezzar's dream and Daniel's interpretation. This dream and its interpretation provide the conceptual framework for most of the other events and visions that follow. According to Daniel's interpretation, God has shown in Nebuchadnezzar's dream not only the whole panorama of the future of his and subsequent human kingdoms in this world but also the plan that God has for his own chosen people. The dream is about what will happen "in the last days" (v.28); he who reveals mysteries has shown "what will be" (v.29).

Figure 1 presents the central elements of Nebuchadnezzar's dream (vv.31–35), with the corresponding interpretation given by Daniel (2:36–45).

Figure 1

| The Vision | The Interpretation (within the passage) |
|---|---|
| –A huge shining statue | |
| –Head of pure gold. | –Nebuchadnezzar represents world domination (2:37-38). |
| –Chest and arms of silver. | –Another kingdom (downward or limited) (2:39a). |
| –Belly and thighs of bronze. | –A third kingdom which will be over all the world (2:39b). |
| –Legs of iron. | –A fourth kingdom which will be stronger than for others (2:40). |
| –Feet of iron and pottery. | –A divided kingdom will arise, still characterized by the strength of iron but weakened by being part pottery in the [ten] toes (2:41-42). |
| | –There will be mixing of the seed of man and lack of cohesion in the kingdom (2:43). |
| –Rock cut out, not by human hands; it struck the statue on the feet of iron and clay and crushed them. | –"In the days of those kings" God will raise up an eternal kingdom (2:44a). |
| –The whole statue was pulverized and was swept away by the wind. It could no longer be found. | –God's kingdom will destroy "all kingdoms" and will stand forever (2:44b). |
| –The rock became a large mountain and filled the whole land. | –Daniel and his three friends given authority over all of Babylon just as the saints in God's kingdom will take over the authority of the four kings (2:48-49). |
| | –The fact that Daniel was able to recount the dream shows that God is revealing these future events and that the interpretation is true (2:45). |

According to Daniel's interpretation, the statue in Nebuchadnezzar's dream was intended to represent the flow of events of human history up to and including the time when God would destroy all the kingdoms of the earth and establish his own eternal kingdom. It should be noted that only Nebuchadnezzar's reign is identified by Daniel—he was the head of gold. Though numerous attempts have been made to identify the other kingdoms, we should not lose sight of the fact that the text itself does not do so and, it would appear, should be understood without such an identification. Rather than attempting to identify each of the four kingdoms, it makes more sense to take the entire statue as a representation of all earthly kingdoms and to ask the question of what Daniel's interpretation says about these kingdoms.

An interesting feature about Daniel's description of Nebuchadnezzar's kingdom seems to support such a reading of the dream statue. When he describes the reign of Nebuchadnezzar, Daniel relies heavily on concepts and terminology from Genesis, i.e., God's words to the first man and woman in Ge 1:26–28. Daniel says that God has given Nebuchadnezzar dominion and power and glory. He has placed the beasts of the field and the birds of the air under his authority. In other words, Daniel's interpretation of the dream sees Nebuchadnezzar's reign as king of Babylon as a reflection of the dominion God had given humankind over all his creation. In making this identification, Daniel's interpretation appears to follow an identical line of thought within the book of Genesis that links the dominion given to the first man to the establishment of the city of Babylon in Ge 11:1–9. The building of that city represents the last major human attempt to fulfill God's good plan gone awry through human disobedience. In other words, the city of Babylon functions for the writer of the Pentateuch as an image of human efforts to gain God's blessing on their own and apart from God.

Daniel's interpretation of Nebuchadnezzar's dream points in this direction. The statue and the kingdoms represented in it are intended as an image of failed attempts by human beings to find God's blessing. This is why the various aspects of the statue all show a marked deterioration in value and strength. The metals decrease in value; the second kingdom is "inferior" (v.39) to the first; the last kingdom is a mixture of iron and clay and "will not remain united, any more than iron mixes with clay" (v.43). Thus humanity's efforts to unite and find divine blessing are to become increasingly weaker and more chaotic until the end comes, when God's kingdom will replace those of humankind. God's kingdom will remain forever.

I have attempted here to explain Daniel's interpretation of the dream along only those lines given in the book itself. I believe that is the best way to understand this difficult text. In the history of the interpretation of this passage, however, there has been no end to the attempts to go beyond Daniel's interpretation and to identify from history the kingdoms represented in the dream. In what follows we will attempt to give a brief overview of the interpretation of the four kingdoms in Da 2.

A common approach has been to identify the four metals with the kingdoms of Babylon, Medo-Persia, Greece, and Rome. The effect of this line of interpretation is to locate the establishment of the fifth kingdom, the falling rock that became a huge mountain, during or after the time of the Roman Empire. Such a reading of the dream is commonly found in Christian interpretations of Daniel because the birth of Jesus and the establishment of the church come during the time of the Roman Empire. A similar view is also held by early Jewish commentators, especially those who lived before the final collapse of the Rome Empire (A.D. 1453).

There is, however, a further problem in identifying the fourth kingdom as Rome. According to the dream and its interpretation, the fourth kingdom was destroyed by the falling rock, which is the establishment of the fifth kingdom. The problem comes when it is seen that the Roman Empire was not destroyed by the coming of Jesus and the establishment of his church. A common response to this problem has been to maintain that the fifth kingdom, the kingdom of God, was "spiritual" and thus ultimately defeated the Roman Empire by eradicating its idolatry and false religion. In other words, the dream and Daniel's interpretation, though understood literally and historically, is applied spiritually. In support of such an interpretation some have pointed to Jesus' words to Pilate in Jn 18:36, "My kingdom is not of this world." The context of John's gospel, however, suggests that Jesus' words were not so much intended as a comment on the spiritual nature of his kingdom as they were a statement about how his kingdom would be established. He said in effect, "My kingdom is not *from* this world. If it were, my servants would fight to prevent my arrest. . . ." Thus his kingdom comes from God and is not dependent on human effort for its establishment.

A typical response to a spiritual interpretation of the fifth kingdom has been to point to the fact that if one understands the first four kingdoms literally and historically as four physical kingdoms, the last being Rome, then there seems little basis for saying the fifth kingdom is not also a physical one. This has, in fact, been a common contention of Jewish interpreters of Daniel's dream. Jewish interpreters, however, have not been under the same constraints as Christian interpreters of this passage, because in their view, the messianic fifth kingdom has not yet been established.

There are others, however, who do hold both that the fourth kingdom is Rome and that the fifth kingdom is a physical kingdom. In their view, the Roman Empire, which is to be destroyed by the falling rock, is to be a distant descendant of the original Roman state revived or reestablished in the last days before the second coming of Christ. In other words, the fulfillment of Nebuchadnezzar's dream lies in the future and will be a part of the series of events during that time.

In many modern commentaries the fourth kingdom in Nebuchadnezzar's dream is identified with Greece. Thus the four kingdoms are Babylon, Media, Persia, and Greece. For the most part the rationale for this lies in the assumption that the book was written during the time of the Greek Empire and thus recounts events only up to its own day. An identification of the fourth kingdom with Greece creates serious problems for a direct association of the fifth kingdom with the coming of Christ, or with any future expectation of the kingdom. Jesus was born and the church was established a considerable time after the fall of the Greek Empire; in any event it did not appear to be historically linked to it. Thus, those who hold to the identification of the fourth kingdom as Greece generally relate the fifth kingdom to the revival of the Judean state during the time of the Maccabees (164 B.C.) and later. The reference to Christ is then taken as another fulfillment of the prophecy.

If, however, we understand the interpretation of the dream apart from any attempt to identify the four kingdoms as specific historical empires, then not only is the question of the relationship between the fall of the fourth kingdom and the rise of the fifth resolved, but so are several other difficult features of the dream. In the first place, such an understanding of the image explains why the dream casts Babylon in such an untypically positive light. It is a well-known fact that the view of Babylon as the head of gold contrasts sharply with the usual picture of Babylon in the Bible and in the book of Daniel. If the whole of the statue is understood as a representation of biblical Babylon as developed already in the Pentateuch (e.g., Ge 11:1–9), then we can see the point of both the positive and negative aspects of the image. The positive, the head of gold, reflects God's original intention of giving humankind dominion over all his creation (Ge 1:26–28). The negative decline and deterioration of the statue and the final division of the kingdoms in the iron and clay can then be seen as a reflection of the division of Babylon in the confusion of languages (Ge 11:8–9; cf. 10:25).

Moreover, by viewing Nebuchadnezzar's image in terms of itself rather than in terms of the events of external history, we are in a better position to understand the sense of the central notion of the "mixture" of the people (2:43). There have been many, largely unsuccessful, attempts to identify this "mixture" in the events of ancient and modern history, as if the meaning of the interpretation depended on our knowing what event in human history this refers to. The meaning, however, is given quite clearly in the text: humankind "will not remain united" (v.43). The sense of the "mixture" thus is related to the progressive deterioration of the strength of the image as manifested in the golden head. The term "mixture" refers elsewhere in Scripture to intermarrying (Ezr 9:2), and "seed of man" denotes "common people" (1Sa 1:11) or "nonroyalty"; thus what Daniel appears to have in mind is that there will be a progressive breakdown in royal authority. The world will grow worse and worse until it is restored by Christ.

When, in the dream, the rock strikes the feet of the statue and the statue falls to the ground, it is a picture of the final defeat of all human efforts to counterfeit God's blessing. When this happens and Christ's kingdom is established, it can be said, as is recorded in the book of Revelation, "Fallen! Fallen is Babylon the Great!" (Rev 18:2). The meaning of this vision is not dependent on whether the last kingdom is Greece or Rome. In fact, the last kingdom will be any human government that attempts to carry out God's mandate to have dominion over all creation without relying on God's plan and power.

The narrative of Nebuchadnezzar's dream in ch. 2 is followed in the next four chapters (chs. 3–6) by four key episodes in the lives of the kings of Daniel's day. Each of these events has features that appear intentionally to parallel aspects of Nebuchadnezzar's dream in ch. 2. Thus the four kings and kingdoms of the statue serve as an outline or pattern for the narratives that follow in chs. 3–6. The first episode in ch. 3, for example, is that of the gold image Nebuchadnezzar set up in his kingdom. This image is clearly intended to be a reflection of that image with the gold head that Nebuchadnezzar saw in his dream in ch. 2. In ch. 4 Nebuchadnezzar's kingdom is likened to a tree that grows till "it [is] visible to the ends of the earth" (4:11). All this was then reduced to ruin by the God who "is sovereign over the kingdoms of men and gives them to anyone he wishes" (4:17). Thus Nebuchadnezzar's kingdom in ch. 4 is contrasted with the kingdom of God, which begins as a stone and becomes a mountain that fills the whole earth. In ch. 5 Belshazzar's kingdom "is divided and given to the Medes and Persians" (5:28), suggesting an intentional link with the "divided kingdom" of iron and clay in Nebuchadnezzar's dream (2:41). At the close of the fourth episode in ch. 6, Darius proclaims that God "is the living God and he endures forever; his kingdom will not be destroyed" (6:26), using the very words of Daniel's interpretation of Nebuchadnezzar's dream in 2:44.

## III. Nebuchadnezzar's Image (3:1–30)

In ch. 3 the statue set up by Nebuchadnezzar appears to be intentionally linked to the dream in ch. 2. Some have suggested that the dream is what gave Nebuchadnezzar the idea for a statue, though such explanations go far beyond the legitimate bounds of the interpreter. The task is to recognize what lies in the text, not to speculate on what is not there. The author's point is simply to link the two chapters by a common subject, the image, and thereby to cast the events of ch. 3 in such a light that they become an instance in the larger meaning of the dream. We thus see in the events of ch. 3 a picture of what is required of the faithful who are called upon to wait patiently for the coming of God's kingdom. While waiting, God's people are to be like Shadrach, Meshach, and Abednego and not bow the knee to any human kingdoms. The reader, in the face of the worsening conditions of humankind forecast in the dream of ch. 2, is given the example of these three men. Their words to Nebuchadnezzar are a thematic reminder of the message of the book as a whole: "If we are thrown into the blazing furnace, the God we serve is able to save us from it, and he will rescue us from your hand" (v.16). Moreover, the three men go on to tell Nebuchadnezzar, the head of gold from the earlier chapter, "even if [God] does not [save us], we want you to know, O king, that we will not serve your gods or worship the image of gold you have set up."

There may also be a link between the events in ch. 3 and the vision in ch. 7. In ch. 3 the men who cast the faithful three into the furnace are consumed by the fire, while in ch. 7 the fourth beast who makes war with the saints is destroyed by fire. Moreover, in ch. 6 the king's counselors are crushed and destroyed by the lions just as the nations are crushed and destroyed by the fourth beast in ch. 7.

It should be noted that the names of these three men, Shadrach, Meshach, and Abednego, are Babylonian names and would not be meaningful to the Hebrew reader. In the first chapter, however, we have been given their Hebrew names, and these would suit well their circumstances in this chapter. Shadrach is Hananiah, "the Lord shows grace"; Meshach is Mishael, "Who is what God is?" and Abednego is Azariah, "The Lord is [my] help." The first chapter thus plays an important role in the meaning of the present narrative.

## IV. Nebuchadnezzar's Second Dream (4:1–37)

As mentioned earlier, in this narrative Nebuchadnezzar's kingdom is likened to a tree that grows till "it [is] visible to the ends of the earth" (v.11). It is thus contrasted with the kingdom of God, which begins as a stone and becomes a mountain that fills the whole earth (2:34–35). There are also striking parallels between Daniel and King Nebuchadnezzar here and Joseph and the pharaoh in Ge 37–42. For example, quite apart from the general similarity between the two narratives, just as Pharaoh was given two dreams to underscore the certainty of their fulfillment (Ge 41:32), Nebuchadnezzar also had two dreams, each signifying the same basic idea: the contrast of the kingdom of God and the kingdoms of humankind. Both Pharaoh's dreams and Nebuchadnezzar's are centered on a period of divine blessing and abundance followed by a period of divine judgment. Both conclude with a warning about a period of seven years of judgment (Ge 41:27). In both narratives the pharaoh and Nebuchadnezzar are called upon to acknowledge that their greatness has come only through the grace and power of the God of heaven (Ge 41:32–39; Da 4:27).

The sense of the narrative as well as the meaning behind the parallels with Joseph and Pharaoh is to show that the kingdoms of this world stand or fall by the will of God, "The Most High is sovereign over the kingdoms of men and gives them to anyone he wishes" (v.17).

## V. Belshazzar's Feast (5:1–31)

In ch. 5 Belshazzar's kingdom "is divided and given to the Medes and Persians" (v.28), suggesting an intentional link with the "divided kingdom" of iron and clay in Nebuchadnezzar's dream (2:41). Moreover, in his interpretation of the handwriting on the wall, Daniel contrasts Belshazzar's divided kingdom with the splendor and glory of his father Nebuchadnezzar's (vv.18–23). Thus in this chapter, just as in the dream of ch. 2, the "greatness and glory" of the kingdom of Nebuchadnezzar is contrasted with the "divided" and "wanting" kingdom that marks the end (2:41–43; 5:29).

## VI. Daniel in the Lion's Den (6:1–28)

At the close of the fourth episode in ch. 6, Darius proclaimed that God "is the living God and he endures forever; his kingdom will not be destroyed" (v.26). These words, which are identical to those in Daniel's interpretation of Nebuchadnezzar's dream in 2:44, serve further to link the events of this chapter to the interpretation of the dream in ch. 2. Just as the focus of Daniel's interpretation of the dream was the eternal kingdom of God, so the focus of the series of narratives that follow is also the eternal kingdom of God. The message of the narratives thus continuously reinforces Daniel's interpretation of the dream.

There is also a link between the events of ch. 6 and Daniel's vision in ch. 7. Just as Nebuchadnezzar dreamed of a statue with a golden head (ch. 2) and then made a golden statue (ch. 3), so also in ch. 6 Daniel was thrown into a den of lions and then, in ch. 7, saw a vision of wild beasts, the first of which was a lion. Moreover, Daniel is rescued from the wild beasts, just as the saints of the Most High are to be rescued from the fourth beast (7:21–22).

## VII. The Visions of the Four Beasts, the Son of Man, and the Ancient of Days (7:1–28)

For the explanation of the vision in ch. 7, see Figure 2.

The visions in ch. 7 are not only central in importance to the book of Daniel but they also provide the basis for much of the eschatological and messianic hope in the remainder of the Bible. Almost anywhere in the Bible where the Messiah is spoken of one will find that the basic imagery and central concepts are shaped by the visions of this chapter. Central to these visions is the appearance of the Son of Man coming in the clouds to receive the eternal kingdom from the Ancient of Days (vv.13–14). The imagery and ideas found here are not themselves new. They are taken from earlier biblical texts in the Pentateuch and the historical books. Chief among these is 2Sa 7, the promise of an eternal kingship in Jerusalem that God made to the house of David.

In general terms the visions of this chapter are arranged to show a contrast between the kingdoms of humankind and the kingdom of God. The four beasts, which represent human kingdoms, are viewed as they rise up from the sea. Over against these we find the "one like the son of man" descending down out of the clouds. The viewpoint of the description of the four beasts is viewed, as it were, from sea level, the

Figure 2

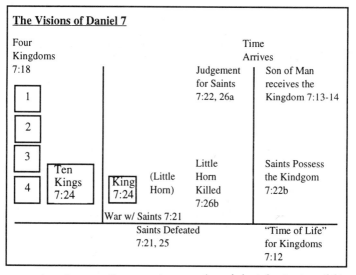

perspective of one standing on earth, whereas we look upon the scene of the "son of man" and "Ancient of Days" as if we ourselves were standing in the throne room in heaven.

There appears to be an intentional link between the visions in chs. 2 and 7. Both chapters present the kingdoms of humanity in stark contrast to the kingdom of God. Both represent human government in four stages, each stage becoming more brutal and chaotic and ending in total defeat and replacement by the kingdom of God. For the most part these kingdoms are not to be identified with specific kingdoms in antiquity, though there is no end to the attempts to make such identifications. Our concern in ch. 7 will not be with what kingdoms may or may not be alluded to in these visions. Rather, we will focus on what these visions are intended to tell us about human government and the ultimate victory of the kingdom of God.

A word about the structure of this chapter is in order before proceeding with an analysis of the visions. As is the case elsewhere in Daniel, the visions in ch. 7 are followed by an interpretation. There are, however, unique features to the visions in this chapter. (1) A close reading of the Aramaic text suggests that there is more than one vision in this chapter. Though this is not of major concern, we will nevertheless attempt to follow the pattern of multiple visions in the analysis below.

(2) There is a twofold interpretation given to the visions: A general interpretation is given in vv.17–18, followed by Daniel's seeking added information about certain aspects of the visions in vv.19–22. In the process of seeking additional information, however, Daniel recounts further details of his vision that were not mentioned earlier. As it turns out, these features are just those that play a major role in the subsequent interpretation (vv.23–27). We have sought to clarify this point in the charts

of the visions that follow. We have put the initial descriptions of each of the visions (vv.2–14) in large boxes and the interpretation of the visions (vv.17–18, 23–27) in the right-hand column. The additions to the visions have been enclosed in smaller boxes and put within the large boxes. A glance at the material in these boxes is quite informative in that it shows more precisely the particular focus and interest of the chapter. One observation that immediately stands out is that the "saints," who are identified as those who receive the kingdom from the Ancient of Days, are introduced into the description of the vision only in the secondary versions (i.e., within the smaller boxes). This suggests that while the primary focus of the visions was on the Son of Man's reception of the kingdom, the focus of the interpretation has been to show the role of the "saints" in receiving the kingdom.

(3) A third structural feature of ch. 7 is that the vision of the Son of Man appears to have been strategically placed in the exact center of the chapter. It is often the case that within the compositional strategy of biblical texts, the center position is reserved for the central thematic elements. Thus the author intends to give prominence to the Son of Man. He wants to highlight both the fact that the kingdom of God is received from the Ancient of Days by the Son of Man, and the fact that the saints play an important role, for they too receive the kingdom. The interpreter is deliberately ambiguous regarding who the saints receive the kingdom from. In the last analysis it seems likely that we are to understand it to mean that the Son of Man receives the kingdom from the Ancient of Days, and the saints, in turn, receive it from him.

## A. The First Vision (7:1–6)

As Figure 3 shows, very little in this first vision is interpreted in the text. The imagery of the four winds of heaven blowing over the great sea (v.2) has many parallels in the OT (cf. Ge 1:2; 8:1; Ex 14:21; 15:10; Eze 1:4), thus a certain appreciation for the rest of the OT seems prerequisite to the vision. The four beasts arising out of the great sea, each one different than the other (v.3) contrast with that of the son of man, who arises out of heaven. In Ge 1:20–25 the beasts (living creatures) also arise out of the sea, each according to its own kind, i.e., differing one from another (cf. Isa 27:1), in contrast with human beings created in God's image (Ge 1:26). Thus, as was the case in the

Figure 3

| The Vision | The Interpretation (within the passage) |
|---|---|
| –Four winds blowing into the sea.<br>–Four beasts rising out of the sea (3).<br>–1st like a lion with eagles' wings.<br>–Wings plucked out; lifted off ground; stood on ground like a man; heart like a man given to it.<br>–2d like a bear; one side lifted; three ribs in its mouth. They said to it, "eat much flesh."<br>–Another (3d) like a leopard; four wings on its back; four heads; authority given to it. | –These are four kingdoms rising from the land (7:17). |

imagery of Nebuchadnezzar's statue in ch. 2, this first vision appears intentionally to take up the central themes of the early chapters of the Pentateuch. These themes set the scope of the visions to the same parameters as that of the Creation narratives. The last days will be like the first. The God of history is the Creator of the universe. Later in this chapter, these four beasts are explained as four kings who arise out of the earth or land (v.17). In the end, their kingdom is to be given over to the saints of the Most High (v.18).

The first beast was like a lion, with eagle's wings (v.4). As Daniel watched, the beast's wings were plucked out, it was raised off the ground, set upon feet like a human being, and a human heart was given to it. No further description of the first beast is given, nor is there a subsequent interpretation of the meaning of this beast. If correlated with the vision in ch. 2, this beast is the head of

gold, Babylon (Nebuchadnezzar; cf. 2:38). Perhaps the lifting of the lion upon the feet of a human being is an allusion to the image in ch. 2 that stood upon its feet. According to one commentator, the plucking of the beast's wings denotes the fall of Babylon and his lifting up denotes the removal of its kingdom.

The second beast, resembling a bear (v.5), is usually identified with Persia or Medo-Persia (cf. 8:20), though the text does not make this identification. It has been suggested that it was raised on one side because after the fall of Babylon, the kingdom of Persian waited one year for the reign of the Medes. No interpretation is given for the three ribs in its mouth, though it is often held that the three ribs represented three regions that were in perennial rebellion against Persia. Others see the ribs as symbolizing those kings who were instrumental in building the second temple, especially

Figure 4

| The Vision | The Interpretation (within the passage) |
|---|---|
| −Fourth beast exceedingly dreadful.<br>−Large iron teeth.<br><br>   −Claws of bronze (7:19). | −Fourth kingdom will be in the land (23a). |
| −Consuming, crushing the others with its feet. | −Will consume, tread, crush (23b). |
| −Different from the others.<br>−Ten horns.<br>−Another, little horn, coming up among the ten horns.<br>−Little horn uprooted three of the ten horns.<br>−Little horn has eyes like a man.<br>−Little horn speaks great (words). | −Will be different (23a).<br>−Ten kings will arise (24a).<br>−Another king will arise among the ten kings (24b).<br>−He will defeat three of the kings (25b).<br><br><br>−He will speak against the most high (25a). |
|    −Little horn made war with the saints (7:21).<br>   −Little horn prevailed against saints (7:21). | −He will wear away (harass) the saints (25a).<br>−He will intend to change times and law (25b).<br>−They (saints) will be put in his hands for a time, times, half a time (25b). |

Figure 5

| The Vision | The Interpretation (within the passage) |
|---|---|
| –Thrones set up; Ancient of days sits.<br>–Ancient of days wears white garments and has hair white as wool.<br>–His throne surrounded by fire; has wheels of fire and a river of fire.<br>–Multitudes surround the throne.<br>–Judgment (court) sits.<br><br>   –Judgment given for the saints (7:22).<br><br>–Books are opened. | –Judgment will sit (26a). |

since "ribs" is used frequently in the Bible to denote the "side supports" of the temple walls.

The beast with four wings and four heads (v.6) is commonly identified as Alexander the Great who divided his kingdom into four rulers when he died. Others identify this beast with Persia. It may be that the four wings and heads are intended to represent Greece as a whole. In any event, it should be stressed that the text does not identify the king or the kingdom represented by this beast, nor is there any indication that we are to seek an identification. The beasts, like the metals in the statue in chapter 2, appear only collectively to represent human government in its entirety. It is to this kingdom that the kingdom given to the Son of Man stands in opposition.

**B. Elements of the Second Vision(s) (7:7–12)**

*1. The fourth beast (7:7–8)*

The fourth beast (see Fig. 4) has no likeness to a known animal. Perhaps something like the beast in Isa 27:1 is in view. It is possible that the vision of the fourth beast occurs on a different night than the previous three beasts (cf. v. 7). Some say that the ten horns represent the ten kings of Rome preceding Vespasian, who destroyed the second temple, and that the little horn is Titus who, according to tradition, defiled the temple.

*2. The ancient of days (7:9–10)*

This is God who now sits in judgment upon the fourth beast and those that preceded it and who have oppressed his children (see Fig. 5). The books contain the transgressions and evils they have committed.

Figure 6

| The Vision | The Interpretation (within the passage) |
|---|---|
| –Little horn speaking great words.<br>–The (4th) beast was killed; his body destroyed; thrown into fire.<br>–The other beasts lost their power and were given a time of life "until a time, times, and half a time."<br><br>  –Until the time arrived (7:22b). | –His authority removed (26b).<br>–He is destroyed until the end (26b). |

Figure 7

| **The Vision** | **The Interpretation**<br>**(within the passage)** |
|---|---|
| –One like a son of man comes in the clouds.<br>–He comes up to the Ancient of days.<br>–Authority and kingship is given to him (7:14).<br><br>    –Saints possess the king-<br>    dom (7:22).<br><br>–All nations worship him.<br>–His authority is forever.<br>–His kingdom will not pass away. | <br><br><br>–saints receive the kingdom (7:18).<br><br>–the kingdom and authority is given to the people of the saints (27a).<br><br><br>–All authorities will worship him (27b).<br><br>–His kingdom is forever (27b). |

### 3. Part 3 (7:11–12)

The little horn speaking proud words is removed, and the kingdom of the rest of the kings is removed (see Fig. 6). Some relate this part to Rev 19:20, where the Beast and the False Prophet are cast alive into the lake of fire at the time of Christ's second coming. It appears in v.12 that the rest of the beasts are still around after the destruction of the fourth beast. A time in life is given to them until the appointed day of the battle of Gog and Magog. According to others, v.12 precedes v.11 in time so that by the time the fourth beast is destroyed, the other beasts have used up their extension of time. The sense is that each kingdom has its time of rule, followed by a survival after its downfall and transition to the next kingdom.

### C. Elements of the Third Vision (7:13–27)

Figure 7 shows the interpretation within the text for this third vision.

### 1. The kingdom given to the Son of Man (7:13–14)

The one like "the son of man," the Messiah, comes to the Ancient of Days, who is sitting in judgment on the nations. The kingdoms of the nations are given to this same person. He is likened to the beasts (possessing all dominion), and the Israelites are likened to the son of man, humble and pure.

Some recognize that the figure of the son of man in ch. 7 does not entirely fit a collective interpretation (i.e., the Israelites as a whole); they argue that this chapter is the result of a reinterpretation of an original individual figure and its application to the nation as a whole. The nation is viewed in the figure of the eschatological individual.

Note first that, according to v.14, the kingdom is given to the son of man. In v.18, however, it is "the saints of the Most High" who are to receive the kingdom. When, in v.22, the vision of vv.13–14 is reiterated, we are told that judgment is given to the saints of the Most High and that they are to possess the kingdom. Thus, in v.22, additions are made to the original vision of v.14 that correspond to the subsequent interpretation in v.18.

The further interpretation of v.14 that follows in this chapter (v.27) is inconclusive. First, it may be read either as "the people of the saints of the Most High" are to be given the kingdom, or "the people, the saints" are to be given the kingdom (v.27). The first reading suggests that the people and the saints are not the same entities and thus, if the saint(s) of the Most High is the son of man, then the people of the son of man are given the kingdom. The clearest indication that an individual divine figure is in view in v.14 is the fact that the one to whom the kingdom is given will be worshiped by "all people, nations and men of every language" (v.14). It is unlikely that Daniel would envision this for the people of the kingdom.

### 2. The interpretation (7:15–27)

We offer two classic interpretations here. An older Jewish interpretation sees Israel as taking the land from Edom, which is the fourth kingdom, Rome. The horn of v.8 made war with Israel (the saints). The ten horns are ten kings from the same kingdom. After these kings, another will arise, who is Titus. He will oppress Israel and attempt to get them to transgress their feast days and laws. No one knows how long this will prevail ("a time, times and half a time").

A modern interpretation sees the "saints" as the saved of all ages as well as the holy angels. The kingdom possessed by "the saints of the Most High," while eternal, may easily include the millennial kingdom and the eternal rule of God that follows. The little horn is the outstanding person at the end of the ages who will be destroyed when the kingdom comes from heaven. "A time, times, and half a time" refer to the last three and one-half years preceding the second advent of Christ, who will bring in the final form of God's kingdom on earth. There is nothing in ch. 7 of Daniel to alter the conclusion that the fourth empire is Rome, that its final state has not yet been fulfilled, and that it is a genuine prophetic revelation of God's program for human history.

## VIII. Additional Visions (8:1–27)

On the visions of ch. 8, see Figures 8 and 9.

The goat with four prominent horns is interpreted as four kingdoms from a nation, but without that nation's power (v.22). The parallel sense of "power" in ch. 7 is political "authority" (7:6, 12). The leopard with four heads "was given" its political authority. Since this authority is not mentioned of the other beasts in ch. 7, it appears to match the special mention of "without its own

Figure 8

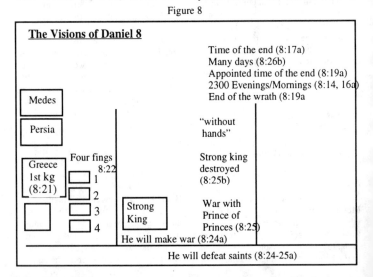

**The Visions of Daniel 8**

| Medes | | | Time of the end (8:17a)<br>Many days (8:26b)<br>Appointed time of the end (8:19a)<br>2300 Evenings/Mornings (8:14, 16a)<br>End of the wrath (8:19a |
| Persia | | | "without hands" |
| Greece 1st kg (8:21) | Four fings 8:22<br>1<br>2 | | Strong king destroyed (8:25b) |
| | 3<br>4 | Strong King | War with Prince of Princes (8:25) |
| | | He will make war (8:24a) | |
| He will defeat saints (8:24–25a) | | | |

Figure 9

| The Vision | The Interpretation (within the passage) |
|---|---|
| | –Vision for time of the end (8:17). –What will be at the end of the wrath (8:19). |
| –A ram with two horns, beside the canal. One horn longer. –Ram charged west, north and south. –Goat with prominent horn came from the west. | –Ram is kings of Medes and Persia (8:20). –Goat is king of Greece, the big horn is first king (8:21). |
| –Goat charged ram in great rage, shattering his two horns, knocking him to the ground and trampling on him. –Goat became great, but large horn was broken off. –Goat grew four prominent horns in its place. –A little horn came out from them and grew large. | –It was broken (8:22). –Four kingdoms from a nation (8:22). –At end of their kingdom, when transgressors have finished (it = their kingdom), a strong king will arise (8:23). |
| –It became great to the hosts of the heavens. –It caused to fall from the hosts and from the stars and trampled them. | –In his heart he became great (8:25a). –He will destroy mighty men and holy people (8:24b). –When they are at rest, he will destroy many (8:25a). |
| –It was great up to the Prince of the hosts. –The continual offerings were removed. –The holy place was destroyed. –The hosts was given upon the continual offerings in transgression. –It cast truth to the ground and made great success. | –Against the Prince of princes he will stand (8:25b). –He will cause astounding devastation will succeed in whatever he does (8:24). –In 2300 evenings and mornings, the holy place will be sanctified (8:14). |
| ┌─────────────────────────────┐ │ –How long? (8:13) │ │ *Vision of the offering. │ │ *Transgression that destroys. │ │ *Giving of Holy place. │ │ *Trampling of the host.. │ └─────────────────────────────┘ | –Without hands he will be destroyed (8:25b). |

power" in the present chapter. This suggests that the four kingdoms are not all considered from the authority and power of this one nation and hence leaves open the identity of at least one of the four kingdoms as not from the lineage of the one nation, Greece. If so, then the little horn that comes from one of these four kingdoms in ch. 8 may be the same as the little horn of ch. 7, which comes from the fourth beast, Rome. This would solve the problem of having to identify the four kingdoms with a particular moment in time when the rulers of Greece were in fact, four (usually, the number of Greek rulers during this period exceeded four); thus the number of four kingdoms here may have been determined from the general schema of four kingdoms throughout the book of Daniel.

A little horn came out from them and grew large (v.9). This is interpreted that when the reign of the four kings ends, a strong king will arise and will increase in wickedness (v.23). Some identify "their kingdom" and the transgressors as Israel, and the end of their kingdom and the completion of their transgression as the destruction of the second temple in A.D. 70. If this is so, then the strong king is Titus. Others see the "their kingdom" as Israel but see the strong king as Antiochus IV Epiphanes.

Note that the ram with two horns refers to the two kings of Medes and Persia (v.20)—thus one animal but two king(dom)s.

## IX. The Messiah Is Cut Off (9:1–27)

Approaching ch. 9 from the viewpoint of the meaning of the book as a whole leads us to ask what particular contribution it makes. We should note that there are several significant new features introduced here. (1) Chapter 9 does not contain a vision or a dream of events. It rather focuses on the interpretation of a previous text of Scripture, i.e., Jer 25:11, which speaks of Israel's seventy years of exile. This is an important distinction, showing that the book of Daniel has already begun the process of moving beyond new visions and dreams to that of interpreting authoritative Scripture. (2) God's people, Israel, are quite differently characterized here than in the other parts of Daniel. Throughout the whole of the book, they are primarily represented in the characters of Daniel and his three friends. As such, God's people are faithful and true to his law in the face of the most dire circumstances. In ch. 9, however, Israel as a whole is characterized as a sinful and rebellious people, justly in need of divine punishment (vv.15–16). Thus, somewhat suddenly into a picture of God's faithful and righteous people who suffer at the hands of the Gentile nations, ch. 9 introduces a picture of an unrighteous, sinful people who are facing God's righteous wrath. (3) Also new and important is the death or defeat of an "Anointed One" (v.26). In each of the other visions, God's kingdom is shown as utterly victorious without the slightest hint of defeat or failure. In ch. 9, however, no sooner is the figure of the Anointed One introduced (v.25) than he is suddenly and without explanation "cut off" (v.26).

From these unique features one can readily see that ch. 9 makes a major contribution to the sense of the book. Up to this point, the theme of the establishment of God's eternal kingdom has been the central focus of the writer. His emphasis has been on the gradual decline of human kingdoms and the expectation of the sudden rise of the divine kingdom. The question that has accompanied this picture of the coming kingdom is the time of its fulfillment. Will it be at the return from Babylonian captivity, as may have been suggested by Jeremiah's prophecy? Or, will it come at a much later period? Daniel now provides the answer to this question by extending the seventy years of

Jeremiah's prophecy by a multiple of seven. An anointed one will come to establish an eternal kingdom after a time of seven and sixty-two weeks. With this chapter also comes a new idea of a delay in the establishment of the divine kingdom. When the Anointed One does come to establish the kingdom, he will be cut off; thus the fulfillment of the vision in Jeremiah is to be extended still further into the future, to the seventieth week.

It is important to note the major themes in Daniel's prayer of confession (vv.5–19), for they provide the basis not only for the delay in the fulfillment of God's promises but also for God's continued faithfulness to his promises. Daniel opens his prayer with a reminder of God's continual watchfulness over his people and his promises. He then recounts the sin of the people of Israel and their continued disobedience to God's covenant. Repeatedly, Daniel returns to the themes of the Pentateuch, particularly to Deuteronomy, stressing that Israel had failed to listen to the warnings of God's prophets and had thus been cast off from the land in exile. Daniel, moreover, acknowledges that Israel deserved the exile in which they now have found themselves. But, he continues, God is faithful and compassionate. He has chosen this people and the city of Jerusalem, and he will not abandon them now. Daniel thus earnestly prays for divine forgiveness and restoration of his people and his city Jerusalem.

The words of the angel Gabriel (vv.20–27) are presented as a direct response to Daniel's prayer. God will forgive and restore Jerusalem, but it will not be at the end of the Babylonian captivity, i.e., in Daniel's own day. It will come in the distant future, after a time of seventy weeks of years, in which the full measure of God's judgment of Israel will be expended. Moreover, when the time of the fulfillment of Jeremiah's

vision comes, it will still not mark the final fulfillment of the visions of Daniel, i.e., the establishment of the eternal kingdom of God. Unlike what we might have expected from the visions of the book so far, particularly Da 7, when the king comes, he will not receive the kingdom; rather, he will be cut off (vv.25–26). In the final week of years, the seventieth week, one final enemy will come who will destroy the city of Jerusalem and the temple and commit a great sin of sacrilege against the God of heaven. The optimistic visions of the earlier part of the book of Daniel and the prophecies of Jeremiah are thus tempered by the realistic hope presented in this chapter. Much remains of the suffering and sorrow, but the end of the enemy "is decreed" (v.27) by an all-knowing and all-powerful God.

What is to be made of the time period covered by the sixty-nine weeks of years referred to in this passage? If we know how to identify the starting time, it is not difficult to calculate the time of the coming of the "Anointed One," but the starting point is not specified. It says merely, "From the issuing of the decree to restore and rebuild Jerusalem until the Anointed One, the ruler, comes, there will be seven 'sevens,' and sixty-two 'sevens'" (v.25). Fortunately, the author of Nehemiah has provided a link between the events of his book and those here in Daniel. By alluding to this prophecy, Nehemiah provides the date of the twentieth year of King Artaxerxes (445 B.C.) as the time when the word was issued to rebuild the city of Jerusalem (Ne 2:1–9).

Having thus directed the focus of Daniel's vision beyond the events of his own day, the author in the next chapter turns to a description of the intervening years. Consequently, the last of Daniel's visions takes us through the subsequent history of the people of God, covering the events that are to happen before the coming of the Anointed One, the Messiah.

## X. The Last Vision (10:1–11:45)
### A. Introduction (10:1–11:1)

The vision in ch. 11 is given a lengthy introduction in ch. 10. Its purpose is stated succinctly in v.14, "I have come to explain to you what will happen to your people in the last days [NIV, future], for the vision concerns a time yet to come." Thus not only is the vision about the future, but it is specifically about the eschatological future, the last days.

### B. The Vision Itself (11:2–45)

The vision in ch. 11 follows the same basic pattern as those in chs. 2, 7, and 8 (see Fig. 10).

The vision begins with four kings who appear to parallel the four kingdoms of the earlier visions. These kings are all from the empire of Persia. They

are followed by the kingdom of Greece. As in ch. 8, the vision focuses on the one strong Greek king and the subsequent division of his kingdom into four parts. The major political events of these four kingdoms are then enumerated through the reigns of ten kings (vv.5–35). There seems to be little doubt or disagreement that the fulfillment of this part of the vision came during the history of Israel in the Hellenistic age. The last of the ten kings is Antiochus IV, or perhaps Rome.

At the conclusion of the vision (vv.36–45), Daniel's attention is directed to another king, distinct from the kings of the North and the South that have thus far been the concern of the vision. This king will exalt himself against God and seek to overcome the other kingdoms and the Holy Land itself. The time of the coming of this king will be "the time of the end" (v.40). He

Figure 10

| The Visions of Daniel 11 | | | |
|---|---|---|---|
| | | Comes to his end (11:45b) | In that time (12:1a) |
| | | | Michael, great prince, will arise (12:1a) |
| | | Time of the end (11:40) | |
| Persia (11:1) | | Blasphemous acts (11:36-39) | Time of distress (12:1a) |
| 1  2  3  4 (11:2) | | Invasion of Land (11:40) | |
| | | Enters Land, many fall (11:41) | In that time (12:1b) |
| Greece (11:3a) | | Other lands defeated (11:42) | Your people will escape (12:1b) |
| Greece 1st Kg (8:21) | 10 Kings  1  2  3  4 | Gathers much wealth (11:43) | Resurrection (12:2) |
| | 11:5, 6, 7, 9, 10, 11, 13, 15, 20, 21 | Conquests (11:44) | |
| | | Encamps between seas and holy mountain (11:45a) | |
| | | He will make war (8:24a) | |
| (11:4a) | | He will defeat saints 8:24-25a | |

is thus to be identified with the final king and kingdom known in the other visions as the "little horn" (ch. 7), the "strong king" (ch. 8), and the statue that fell when the uncut stone struck it (ch. 2). At this time he will engage in a great war against the other nations and God's people (vv.40–45). The fact that he is not to be identified with Antiochus IV or any of the kings of the previous period can be seen in the fact that in v.40, this king engages in war with both "the king of the North" and "the king of the South." This king is thus neither the king of the North or of the South. He thus cannot be Antiochus IV, who was a king of the South. Moreover, according to ch. 12, "at that time" there is to be a great distress and a resurrection in which Daniel's people will be delivered. This seems to point far beyond the time of Antiochus IV or any period in Israel's history.

## XI. A Time of Distress (12:1–13)

The angel continues to speak in ch. 12; he expressly refers to the time of the events of the vision in ch. 11 as "at that time" (12:1). According to this section, in the days of the last king there will be a time of distress for Daniel's people, but they will be delivered by a great resurrection (v.2). With this, the vision of the end is abruptly halted and sealed "until the time of the end" (v.4).

In a final segment of the vision, the question of the time of the fulfillment of the vision is raised: "How long will it be before these astonishing things are fulfilled?" (v.6). An enigmatic answer is given, "When the power of the holy people has been finally broken" (v.7); this is linked to the oft-repeated phrase "a time, times and half a time." To this Daniel himself replies, "I heard, but I did not understand," and he is instructed again to seal up the vision until the time of the end. A final clue is given to "those who are wise" (v.11). The numerical pattern of this clue refers the reader back to Gabriel's explanation of Jeremiah's seventy weeks in 9:27, thus showing that the fulfillment will come in the second part of the seventieth week.

As an example for all believers, Daniel is told to carry on until the time of the end when he will be resurrected with the rest of those who will receive their eternal reward.

# Hosea

## Introduction

In the Hebrew Bible, the last twelve books (the Minor Prophets) are considered as a single book. Hosea is the first of these minor prophets. He probably began his prophetic ministry during the reign of Jeroboam II (the last king of the house of Jehu, cf. 1:4; 2Ki 15:8–31). The book records the Lord's relationship to Israel in terms of Hosea's own unfortunate marriage. The Lord's love for Israel was characterized as "loyal love"—a determined, steadfast love for his own chosen people. It was a love that was determined to remain faithful to the covenant, regardless of Israel's unfaithfulness.

Hosea's prophecy against Israel was based squarely on the stipulations of the Mosaic Law (Ex 20:1–6)—the Lord is a jealous God, and Israel was to have no other gods before him. Moreover, the Lord is a loving God who shows his "loyal love" to thousands of generations who obey and love him. In spite of all that was to happen to Israel, the Lord's love for them could not be quenched (Hos 11:8–11). The Lord's punishment of Israel was not rejection. After the judgment of exile, the Lord would again bring his people back into the Promised Land and care for them as at the beginning (2:16–25; 3:5; 11:8–11; 14:2–10).

## I. Hosea's Marriage (1:2–3:5)

### A. Hosea's First Marriage to a Harlot (1:2–2:23)

This first marriage of Hosea symbolized Israel's and Judah's apostasy. The faithfulness of Hosea to his wife, however, symbolized God's faithfulness to Israel.

The first chapter is not only a programmatic introduction to the book, but it is also a fitting introduction to the whole of the Minor Prophets. It begins with the notion that Israel has sinned and would be cast away from God's presence (1:4). Moreover, in the coming judgment on the northern kingdom, Judah would be delivered from Israel's fate (v.7). In the future, however, God would have compassion on Israel and regather them from among the nations and, together with Judah, they would again dwell in the land (v.11).

Chapter 2 gives more details about the judgment introduced in 1:4, as well as the salvation mentioned in 1:11. Israel had forsaken God to follow Baal (2:1–13), but God would allure her back to himself, "as in the day she came up out of Egypt" (vv.14–23). As in other prophetic literature, the Exodus from Egypt is used as a picture of their future salvation.

### B. Hosea's Second Marriage to a Harlot (3:1–5)

The prophet's second marriage to a harlot was intended to cure her of her harlotry, thus symbolizing God's use of the Exile to cure Israel of apostasy. We should understand 3:4–5 as a programmatic introduction to the theme of Israel's messianic hope. This hope runs throughout the Minor Prophets. Simply stated, it was the messianic hope derived from God's promise to David in 2Sa 7:16—the Messiah was to be a king of the house of David, and when he came he would rule like David. David was an idealization of the messianic hope. Thus Hosea, who lived long after the time of David's kingdom, could still look forward to the time when Israel would "return and seek the LORD their God and David their king" (3:5).

## II. Israel's and Judah's Present Sins (4:1–9:9)

This section is a catalog of Israel's sins, interspersed with the reminder of God's faithfulness and future redemption for Israel (5:15–6:3). For Hosea, Israel's sin consisted primarily in their looking to other nations for help rather than seeking help from the Lord. In

7:11, for example, Israel was said to seek the help of Egypt and Assyria. In 8:8–9 they sought Assyria's aid, and in 8:13 the Exile is called a "return to Egypt." Israel was to go into exile to Assyria—seen as a return to the bondage of Egypt (8:13; 9:3, 6; cf. 11:5).

## III. Israel's and Judah's Past Sins (9:10–14:9)

The past sins of Israel and Judah provide the context for viewing their present sin and for showing God's long-suffering love for Israel. God had long endured his disobedient people, but his love for them still remained. In spite of Israel's past sins, their future remained hopeful because God would not forsake them (11:8–11). The future held for Israel a "new exodus" from Egypt (11:11; cf. 11:2; 12:13).

The book of Hosea thus deliberately casts the future messianic age in imagery drawn from Israel's past deliverance from Egypt (see especially 12:10). The Messiah was to be a new Moses (cf. 2:2), who would once again lead God's people up out of the land of their bondage and captivity. That is, what God did to deliver his people from Egypt in the past, he would do again in the future (12:9). In his use of this imagery, the writer of Hosea follows the lead of the writer of the Pentateuch (see comments on Nu 24), where the future is an antitype of the past.

Furthermore, in 3:5 this future messianic leader is said to be of the house of David. Thus the writer also draws from the divine promise in 2Sa 7 (see commentary). At the conclusion of the book, the writer calls upon the reader to understand his book with wisdom and discernment (14:9). In the same way, the book of Joel, which follows Hosea, picks up this line of thought and appeals directly to the elders of the people to instruct the children of the next generation in the ways of the Lord. The books of the Minor Prophets, then, appear to be directed specifically to the "wise" among the people of God.

What all this suggests is that when Matthew sees a fulfillment of Hosea's words in the coming of the Christ and his own return out of Egypt (Mt 2:15), he was reading the book of Hosea as it had originally been intended. Matthew was not reading into the OT ideas and themes that were not really there; he was drawing his themes from the OT itself.

# Joel

## Introduction

It is not possible to assign a date to the book of Joel or to the time of Joel's ministry. The fact that it is placed between Hosea and Amos in the Hebrew Bible may be a clue that its message should be read in context with the message of those two books. The book of Joel begins with a call to the wise (elders) to seek understanding and pass it on to their children (1:2–3). This follows on the heels of Hosea's admonition to the wise (Hos 14:9), which immediately precedes Joel in the OT. Throughout Joel the reader is continually reminded of the impending "day of the LORD," a phrase that serves as a unifying factor throughout the entire book (1:15; 2:1, 11, 31; 3:14).

## I. Introduction (1:1–3)

By means of its introduction the book is cast in the form of wisdom instruction. It addresses the readers as "elders," calling on them to "tell it to your children" (1:2). The purpose of such an introduction is to make sure that the reader understands the content of the book as "wisdom."

## II. Locust Plague (1:4–20)

The description of the devastation of a locust plague is recounted as a symbolic anticipation of the coming day of the Lord (v.15). As in Hos 12:10, the great events of the past are used as images of the future. The point of Joel's description is that all the normal divine provisions that Israel enjoyed were to be removed in an instant. As in Ps 37, Joel's admonition to prepare for the coming judgment was directly to the wise and the discerning (cf. also Da 12:3); they must repent (Joel 2:13–15).

## III. Invasion (2:1–11)

The day of the Lord would soon come as an invasion that overtook the land by surprise. "Like dawn spreading across the mountains a large and mighty army comes" (v.1b). In his description of this invasion, the prophets words reach epic proportions: "Before them fire devours, behind them a flame blazes" (v.3). The purpose of this sort of description was to insure his reader that the mighty hand of God lay behind this scene. The earth shook, the sky trembled, "the sun and moon [were] darkened, and the stars no longer [shone]" (v.10). This was the army of God (v.11); this was the "day of the LORD" (v.11b).

## IV. Call to Repentance (2:12–20)

The only way for Israel to avert the impending divine judgment was to repent and turn to God. This section of the book was intended to call the reader to a decision to repent (see v.13). The book was here addressing all generations of God's people as they await the coming of divine judgment on the world. The basis of Joel's call to repent was the wonderful grace and compassion of God: "He is gracious and compassionate, slow to anger and abounding in love" (v.13b). If the people repented, the Lord would "take pity on his people" (v.18) and drive the northern army far from them (v.20).

## V. Future Salvation (2:21–27)

In spite of the impending doom, there was still hope for Israel in the future. God would restore their blessing. There was no need for fear and sorrow. There was hope for the future. God had not forsaken his people. Hence, the "people of Zion" should rejoice and be glad (v.23); "never again will my people be shamed" (vv.26–27).

## VI. The Coming of the Spirit (2:28–32)

Before "the day of the LORD," God would pour out his Spirit upon the entire human race. Salvation would come from Zion, i.e., Jerusalem. God's work in the future would be marked by a new outpouring of his Spirit upon all people. As in the days when Israel was in the desert (cf. Nu 11), God would again pour out his Spirit, and his people would prophesy (Nu 11:25), dream dreams, and see visions (Nu 12:6). God would also, in that day, give evidence of his power through signs in the heavens and deliverance for Jerusalem (2:31–32). This same theme of the work of the Spirit and Israel's obedience can be found in Eze 36:24–27.

## VII. Judgment of the Nations (3:1–16c)

When blessing would be restored to Israel, God would judge the nations for their treatment of Israel (cf. Eze 38–39). This would be the fulfillment of God's promise to Abraham: "I will bless those who bless you, and whoever curses you I will curse" (Ge 12:3). The nations had mistreated Israel, and God would repay them with judgment. The place of this judgment would be the "Valley of Jehoshaphat" (v.12).

## VIII. Salvation for Zion (Jerusalem) (3:16d–21)

Two themes dominate this segment of Joel: (1) salvation and blessing would come from Zion (cf. Ge 14; 2Sa 7), and (2) the Lord was present in Zion (cf. Ps 133). The emphasis on Zion as God's habitation stems from the promise that God made to David in 2Sa 7. There, in Zion, he would establish his kingdom, and there he would dwell in his temple. This promise was never fulfilled in David's day, nor was it ever fulfilled during the times of their kings. The basis of Israel's hope for the future lay in the eternal faithfulness of God to this promise. Coupled with this promise was the further hope that God's original purposes in creation would once again be played out on this earth. Thus the book of Joel ends on a reflective note of the return of God's blessings in Eden (v.18) and the final destruction of the enemies of God's people (vv.19–21). This theme of God's judgment against the nations is continued in the following book of Amos.

# Amos

## Introduction

This book is about the prophet Amos, a sheepherder from Tekoa, in Judah, who was called by God to prophesy to the people of Israel (7:15) in the days of Jeroboam II (1:1; cf. 2Ki 14:23–29). He apparently carried out most of his mission at the worship center at Bethel—a sanctuary of the king and palace (Am 7:13). Amos preached fearful words of impending doom, summarized by the priest Amaziah as: "Jeroboam will die by the sword, and Israel will surely go into exile, away from their native land" (7:11).

Within the book itself, Amos stressed the moral ruin of God's people (2:6–8; 3:9–10; 5:7–12) and their mistaken presumption that since they were the elect, nothing bad could happen to them (3:2; 9:7). According to him, God's people mistakenly presumed that as long as they kept up their external forms of worship, the Lord would not let them perish (5:4–6; 5:21–23; 6:1; 8:14). At the close of the book (9:11–15), however, there is a word of hope and salvation. God would not forget his promises to the house of David. He would send the promised Messiah after a time of judgment.

## I. Introduction (1:1–2)

The book picks up remarkably well from the book of Joel (Joel 3:16), where the theme was God's judgment against the nations.

## II. Oracles Against the Nations (1:3–2:16)

The theological basis of these judgments is Ge 12:3. The irony of Amos' words, however, is that Israel and Judah were themselves included among those who were to be judged. Amos' intent was to show how far Israel and Judah had strayed from the covenant. They too would be treated like those outside the covenant.

## III. God's Word Against Israel and Judah (3:1–4:13)

This series of sayings draws out the implications of the previous oracles against the nations. If God would punish the nations for their wickedness, how much more would he punish Israel and Judah, who ought to have known better, given their special status before God (3:1–2, 7).

## IV. Three Woes (5:7–14)

The first woe (5:7–17) is an enumeration of the sin of injustice and a call to repentance. The second woe (5:18–27), enumerates the sin of hypocrisy in worship and issues a call to repentance. The third woe (6:1–14) focuses on the sin of arrogance.

## V. Five Visions (7:1–9:15)

The first vision (7:1–3) is that of the devastation of the land by a swarms of locusts. The second (7:4–6) is that of the devastation of the land by fire. The third (7:7–9) is that of the Lord measuring the deeds of the people of Israel as a builder, using a plumb line, measures the wall of a city. The fourth vision (8:1–3) is of a basket of ripe fruit, indicating to Israel that the time was ripe for the coming of judgment. The fifth vision (9:1–15) is of utter devastation of the people of Israel by the judgment of God, though it closes with a message of salvation.

Amid these five visions, the author of the book has placed an important narrative of Amos's prophetic ministry (7:10–17). This narrative provides a historical reference point for the prophecies that precede and follow it. It shows that Amos's words refer to the sins of the king (Jeroboam) and his false worship center at Bethel, as well as the failure of the prophets to speak out against them. The prophets of Israel had so failed in their task that it was necessary for God to call a farmer to deliver his words. The narrative, moreover, shows that the reference of Amos's words was the impending exile (7:17) and thus that Israel's hope lay still in the future, beyond the time of captivity that faced them in the immediate future (cf. Isa 36–39). Thus the narrative provides the interpretive framework for understanding the words of the prophet within the context of this book.

The final vision in the series (9:1–15) stands in marked contrast to the first four visions. It not only contains a word of stern judgment, but it is also a word of salvation. The judgment serves to put the salvation into the perspective of God's wrath and mercy. Note also that the word of salvation is based on God's promise to David in 2Sa 7 (the Davidic covenant). The "fallen booth of David" (Am 9:11) would rise up again at a time of future blessing and salvation. This refers to the restoration of the Davidic house and the coming of the messianic king. The kingdom of Judah had been destroyed by the Exile and the house of David had been decimated. There was hope for the future, however, because God had made an eternal promise to the house of David.

At that time Israel would "possess the remnant of Edom and all the nations that bear my name" (9:12). What this meant within the immediate context is that the nations, here pictured as Edom, would one day be a part of God's kingdom. Edom was characteristically used to represent the "nations" in the OT because the spelling of the name *Edon* in Hebrew is virtually identical to the Hebrew word for "nations." For Israel "to possess" the nations is the same as for the nations "to seek" the Lord.

This interpretation of the words of Amos, which is found in the LXX, the early Greek translation of the OT, and in Ac 15:17, is made more certain in the following book, Obadiah. In that book, the returning exiles of Israel "will possess" the land of Edom, thereby extending the Lord's kingdom beyond the boundaries of Israel to include all the nations (Ob 20–21). It is thus fitting that this prophecy of hope at the close of the book of Amos is followed by the book of Obadiah. The message of one book (Obadiah) is thus used to explain the imagery of another (Amos).

# Obadiah

## Introduction

Within the context of the Minor Prophets, the words of Obadiah against Edom (v.1) pick up the lead of Joel 3:19 and Am 1:11. In these two books, the people of Edom represented the nations who were the professed enemies of God's people Israel. This also follows from Hos 12, where Jacob was presented as representative of the people of Israel in his struggles with his brother Esau (Edom, Hos 12:3). The book of Obadiah portrays God's judgment on these nations. In contrast to this, the book of Jonah, which follows Obadiah, portrays God's blessing and salvation of the nations. Thus, together, the two books give the full picture of God's concern for the nations. He would judge the nations who turned against his people (Obadiah); but he would bless the nations who heeded the words of his prophets (Jonah).

## I. Judgment Against Edom (1–16)

The book of Obadiah falls naturally into two parts. The first section (vv.1–16) recounts the words of God's judgment against the nation of Edom for their mistreatment of the people of Judah. The complaint of the prophet against Edom is that they rejoiced to see destruction come upon Jerusalem and Judah. They "stood aloof while strangers carried off [Israel's] wealth and foreigners entered [their] gates and cast lots for Jerusalem" (v.11). They rejoiced on the day Judah was destroyed (12) and waited "at the crossroads to cut down their fugitives" (v.14).

## II. Deliverance for God's People (17–21)

The second section of Obadiah (vv.17–21) turns to the theme of salvation and deliverance for the people of God. Here we find a common theme in the prophets: salvation will come to Zion (v.17a) and the people of God will receive their due inheritance (v.17b). On that day, the nation of Israel will turn the tables on Edom and conquer them (v.18). This will be a fulfillment of the prophecy of Balaam in Nu 24:18 and will thus signal the coming of the messianic age. In the logic of the imagery of this book, the picture of Israel's conquering Edom is taken to mean that Edom, and thus all "nations," will, in that day, become a part of God's kingdom. When the Deliverer(s) who rules on Mount Zion governs the mountains of Edom (v.21a), it will mean that Edom will have become a part of God's kingdom (cf. comment on Am 9:12).

# Jonah

## Introduction

The book of Jonah narrates one prophet's dealings with God and the nations. The primary focus of this story is on Jonah and on what it reveals about the character of God. The central message of the narrative contains several points.

(1) God answered the prayers of confession of the pagan sailors as they cried out for help in a time of need. God answered Gentile sailors, just as he answered the prayers of Jonah in his time of need. There is no distinction with God. He hears and answers all who cry out to him. A central concern of the book, then, is to show that God's mercy and salvation is to extend to all the nations. Jonah, the reluctant prophet, is slow to appreciate this feature of God's grace—or, to say it another way, Jonah is slow to agree with God. Jonah seems to have a clear understanding of God's grace and how it extends to the nations (cf. 4:2). His problem is that he does not agree with God on this point and would like, rather, to see God's grace and mercy limited to his own people.

(2) God's plan to reach the city of Nineveh with his word of judgment could not be thwarted by the disobedience of Jonah. Throughout the whole of the narrative God was actively at work bringing his plans to fruition. Much like the narratives of Genesis, God's plan was established in spite of the disobedience of his chosen ones. Jonah could not escape God's call. Whether in the bottom of the ship or at the bottom of the sea, Jonah could not escape God.

(3) God had mercy on the Ninevites when they repented and believed, and he rebuked his own (Jonah) for his hardness of heart. Clearly the focus of this book is on the reluctance of Jonah to acknowledge the universal scope of God's grace. Indeed, we are never really sure at the end of the book that

Jonah himself got the message. The book, however, is clear—God has compassion on all his creatures. We see this message played out in the events of the book itself.

## I. Scene One: Jonah's Adventure (1:1–17)

### A. Jonah's Call (1:1–2)

The book opens with God's call to Jonah to preach against the wickedness of the city of Nineveh. The city in this story represents the great kingdoms of this world that stand in opposition to God's people and his kingdom.

### B. Jonah's Response (1:3)

Jonah responded to God's call with disobedience. He set out in the opposite direction, "headed for Tarshish" (v.3). We are not given the motives for his disobedience at this point in the story. We are tempted to suppose that he was afraid to carry out God's plan because Nineveh was a "great city" (v.2). We will see, however, that this was not the reason. The real reason is kept concealed by the writer until ch. 4, at which time we discover that Jonah disobeyed God because he did not want Nineveh to receive God's grace (4:2).

### C. God's Response (1:4–17)

God responded to Jonah's disobedience by throwing up obstacles into his way. First he hurled (v.:4) a great storm into the sea where Jonah was fleeing. This resulted in Jonah himself being hurled (v.15) into the sea, only there to be found by a great fish that God had appointed "to swallow Jonah" (v.17). God was in control of his world, and Jonah could not hide from him. Jonah's disobedience, in fact, became the very means whereby God's grace was extended to the Gentiles. When they saw God's calming of the sea on Jonah's behalf, "the men greatly feared the LORD, and they offered a sacrifice to the LORD and made vows to him" (v.16). This is the writer's way of saying that the men put their trust in God. Jonah's rejection had led to the salvation of the Gentiles.

## II. Scene Two: Jonah's Rescue (2:1–10)

The second scene takes place in the belly of the great fish, where we overhear Jonah's rejoicing at being rescued. The word's of his psalm clearly show that Jonah, and thus also the author of the book, saw the great fish as an instrument of God's salvation. Jonah was safe in the belly of the fish, and in this psalm he gave thanks to God. The psalm also thematizes what Jonah's salvation meant: "Those who cling to worthless idols forfeit the grace that could be theirs" (v.8). This refers to the sailors who forsook their trust in idols and turned to the living God. To such people God will be gracious. There is, then, a broad scope to God's salvation. It stands in sharp contrast to the narrow self-interest exhibited by Jonah. The irony of the story is that Jonah, blinded to the fact of God's grace, did not seem to appreciate the sense of his own words.

## III. Scene Three: The Salvation of Nineveh (3:1–10)

Jonah did not have to preach long before the entire city of Nineveh turned from their idols and put their trust in God. Literally, the narrative says "The Ninevites believed God" (v.5). This is a strong statement in the OT narratives, identical to Ge 15:6, where Abraham, the father of the people of Israel, "believed God" and was thereby counted as righteous. Like Abraham, these Ninevites did not have to go through an elaborate ritual or a long initiation to become a part of the people of God. They simply believed God's words, spoken by his prophet. The genuineness of their response was characterized in their repentance and fasting (vv.5b–9). They even put sackcloth on their cattle

(v.8). When God saw such sincere repentance, "he had compassion and did not bring upon them the destruction he had threatened" (v.10).

## IV. Scene Four: Jonah's Lesson (4:1–11)

It was now time for Jonah to learn his lesson. First we are shown the real motive behind Jonah's reluctance to obey God. Jonah said, "That is why I was so quick to flee to Tarshish. I knew that you are a gracious and compassionate God, slow to anger and abounding in love, a God who relents from sending calamity" (v.2). His words are revealing in more than one way. As far as the sense of the book is concerned, however, the central role these words play is to explain God's gracious response to the faith of the Ninevites. No wonder God forgave them when they repented (cf. v.10). Jonah's words show that this is a part of his nature; he is a compassionate and gracious God.

Jonah's words also show the short-sighted vision of the prophet himself. In a real sense this book is an indictment of precisely such attitudes, be they those of the prophets or not. Jonah was focused on himself and his own people. His petty concern for the vine that shielded him from the sun (vv.6–8) was a picture of Israel's own self pity and lack of concern for the nations. God's question at the close of the book, "Should I not be concerned about that great city?" (v.11), confronts anew each reader of the book. We are not given any encouragement that Jonah responded well to this question. The writer did not intend to tell us about Jonah but to put God's question clearly before the reader. While we are tempted to inveigh against Jonah for his petty selfishness, we must also be aware that we are looking at a picture of our own frailties.

# Micah

## Introduction

The book of Micah is about the prophet Micah, a contemporary of Isaiah. Like Amos, Micah was particularly forceful in his denunciation of the social morality in Judah. His prophecies contain a heavy emphasis on attacking the mere externality of the people's worship. This attack reaches a high point in the oft-repeated words of Mic 6:6–8, "With what shall I come to the LORD . . . ? And what does the LORD require of you? To act justly and to love mercy and to walk humbly with your God." Such statements should not be understood as a mere indictment of Israel's worship. They are rather a call for justice along with worship and true morality.

Micah's warning to Judah was that "Zion [Jerusalem] will be plowed like a field, Jerusalem will become a heap of rubble, the temple hill a mound overgrown with thickets" (3:12). Thus, like Isaiah and the other prophets, Micah envisioned a time in the future when the temple in Jerusalem would be destroyed. Likewise, this prophet put much emphasis on Israel's hope in the future. The central passage in this regard is 5:2. Note how this passage was applied to Jesus in Mt 2:5–6.

## I. Introduction (1:1)

This verse introduces us to Micah and to the time in which he prophesied.

## II. Judgment Against Israel (1:2–2:11)

The book begins with the image of the Lord as the Judge of all the earth coming to judge his own people, Israel. The problem that Micah confronted was the sin of idolatry (1:5ff.) and injustice (2:1ff.). Like Isaiah, he saw the instrument of God's wrath as the nation of Assyria. The identity of this nation, however, was concealed in the first pronouncement of judgment. In 1:15 the nation of Assyria is called "a conqueror" (cf. 5:5). The punishment that awaited the sinful people was the punishment of exile from the land (1:16; 2:3–5)—a remedy already anticipated by Micah. The people were to live so that their "ways are upright" before God (2:7; cf. 6:8).

## II. Salvation for Israel (2:12–13)

Abruptly the book turns from judgment to salvation. The theme of this section on salvation is the return of the people from exile. Micah envisioned a time in the future when Israel would return from captivity, led by their king, the Lord their God (cf. Isa 40:3ff.).

## III. Judgment Against Israel (3:1–12)

Just as abruptly the book returns to the theme of judgment against the unjust and against the leaders of God's people who presumed upon God's grace (v.11). Again the punishment was exile (v.12).

## IV. Salvation for Israel (4:1–5:15)

This section of the book consists of five pronouncements of salvation: salvation for the nations at Zion (4:1–5); salvation for the regathered remnant (vv.:6–7); salvation for the victorious remnant (vv.8–13); salvation for the ruler of the remnant (5:1–5a); and salvation for the nations of the earth (vv.5b–9).

The promised ruler in 5:1–5a would come from Bethlehem and lead the victorious remnant in defeat of the enemy. The theme of this section expresses the idea that the small would overcome the mighty "in the strength of the LORD" (v.4).

The nature of Assyria's guilt is clearly described in 5:10–15 and is summed up in the phrase "upon the nations that have not obeyed me" (v.15b). Any nation (Assyria or Israel) that did not obey God would be judged.

## V. Judgment Against Israel (6:1–7:6)

This section contains several short sayings against the wickedness of Israel. These sayings contrast their sins with the simplicity of pleasing God: "act justly and love mercy and walk humbly with your God" (6:8).

## VI. Salvation for Israel (7:7–20)

There are several components in the meaning of this final section. (1) One must wait for God's salvation. Salvation for God's people did not lie on the immediate horizon; it was eschatological (v.7). (2) Judgment had to precede salvation because God's people had sinned grievously (v.9). (3) The enemy would ultimately be destroyed (v.10). When that time came, however, all the nations would also enjoy God's salvation (v.12). This future salvation was as sure as Israel's past salvation because God is faithful to his promises (vv.14–20).

It is important to see that the book closes with a reference to the Abrahamic covenant, God's promise to Abraham of a great nation and possession of the land (Ge 12:1–9). The basis of Micah's hope is thus the message of the Pentateuch. God's promises are sure. He will fulfill them just as he has promised the fathers "in days long ago" (7:20).

# Nahum

## Introduction

The book is about the prophet Nahum, who prophesied in the southern kingdom of Judah during the last decades of their kings. Very little else is known about him and his ministry. It begins with a short poetic message, proclaiming the Lord as a mighty and righteous God who rules not only among his own people but also over all of his universe (1:1–14). Thus Nahum saw God's relationship to Israel through the lens of both the covenant and creation. Nahum proclaimed comfort (his name means "comfort") to Judah in his message that the Lord would bring righteous judgment upon their bitter enemy, the Assyrians. This mighty nation, which had by now overrun Judah and Israel for many years, had transgressed God's edict. God had promised Abraham that "those who curse you, I will curse" (Ge 12:3). Thus Assyria stood under the impending judgment of God and would quickly pass from the scene of world history: "No more will the wicked one invade you; they will be completely destroyed" (1:15b).

## I. Introduction (1:1)

This first verse introduces us to the book of Nahum the prophet, whose words and message become the focus of the book. According to this verse, the prophet saw a great vision regarding the destiny of the nation of Assyria, particularly the city of Nineveh.

## II. Hymn (1:2–11)

The book opens with a hymn depicting the glory of the Lord coming in judgment. The hymn is an acrostic (alphabetic psalm). It has been altered, however, by the addition of vv.9–11 midway through the hymn—three verses that make an application of the message of the hymn to God's judgment of Nineveh. Thus the general theme of God's judgment of the nations is particularized in his judging of Nineveh. It is fitting that this book is grouped along with Jonah and Micah, two books that also focus on the destiny of Assyria.

## III. Salvation for Judah (1:12–2:2)

The implication of Nineveh's destruction is drawn out for Judah. Simply put, Nineveh's destruction meant the salvation of Judah. The point of this section was to show that God's universal judgment of the nations would result in salvation for his own people (1:15; 2:2). There was always a note of salvation in the midst of God's threats of judgment. Here the reader's attention is directed to the "one who brings good news, who proclaims peace" (1:15). This focus on an individual deliverer "who proclaims peace" draws on the imagery and hope firmly established in the earliest of the OT books (cf. Ge 49:10; Isa 9:6).

## IV. Destruction of Nineveh (2:3–13)

In graphic detail the destruction of Nineveh and of the Neo-Assyrian Empire is portrayed. The point of this depiction was to emphasize that it was the Lord who had brought this against them. The prophet saw behind it the mighty hand of God: "'I am against you,' declares the LORD Almighty. 'I will burn up your chariots in smoke'" (v.13). Moreover, the book intends to show that God had done this great thing in order to "restore the splendor of Jacob" (v.2). That is, behind the events of history stood the sovereign power of God, and behind that power stood God's purpose. The nations had mistreated Israel, and God would not let that go unpunished. This was the lesson of God's covenant with Abraham (see Ge 12:3).

# V. Destruction of Nineveh (3:1–19)

The fall of Nineveh is again recounted in order to put it in the context of God's on-going work of judgment against the nations (3:8–11ff.). What God had done to Nineveh was merely an example of his actions among the other nations. No nation, not even the mighty Assyrian Empire, could escape the chastening hand of God. Assyria had scattered God's people, and now they themselves were "scattered on the mountains with no one to gather them" (v.19).

# Habakkuk

## Introduction

Very little is known about the prophet Habakkuk. The message of the book of Habakkuk, however, is clear. As far as can be gathered from the book, Habakkuk lived and proclaimed his words during the time of the downfall of the Assyrian Empire and the rise of Babylon.

As the book depicts Habakkuk, two tensions were created in his mind as he surveyed the scene before him. (1) He saw the evident wickedness of his own nation Israel, which seemed to go by unnoticed or at least unpunished (1:2–4). It is not clear whether the violence and lawlessness that Habakkuk lamented in the opening chapter was being carried out by a foreign oppressor or by Habakkuk's own countrymen, though most likely Habakkuk and his countrymen were under siege by an outside power. (2) God had used a very wicked nation, Babylon, to punish his own people (1:5–17).

Habakkuk's response is a model for the righteous of all ages. As he looked at the evil around him, he called out to God for action, but he then waited on God who he knew would do what was right (2:1). In this regard Habakkuk exemplifies the message of Isa 40:31, "Those who wait [NIV, hope] upon the Lord will renew their strength."

God's own response to Habakkuk's laments in ch. 1 was a promise to reward such faithful waiting (2:2–5). God had set limits for the oppressor. His time of judgment would come and the wicked too would face divine judgment (vv.6–20). The righteous were to live in constant faith in God's justice and power: "The righteous in his faith shall live" (2:4; NIV, "the righteous will live by his faith").

The book of Habakkuk concludes with a hymn of praise, which depicts God's mighty and glorious appearance in salvation (3:3–15). It is this victorious coming of the Lord in judgment and salvation that gives the book, in its final shape, its relevance and meaning for today. At the beginning of the book Habakkuk lamented in bewilderment of all the evil he saw around him. At the end of the book, after the depiction of God's glorious victory in ch. 3, Habakkuk was content to wait on God and to rejoice in his salvation (3:16–19).

## I. The Laments of Habakkuk (1:1–17)

The book of Habakkuk opens with a short account of Habakkuk's laments (vv.1–4). Looking around him he saw nothing but violence and distress. It is difficult to say precisely what it was that he saw. The purpose of the book is to keep his words as general as possible, thus making Habakkuk's words applicable to all times. The prophet spoke for any and all righteous ones who are distressed by the rampant disregard of God's law on all sides. His central concern was to know "How long?" God was going to tolerate such evil without sending judgment.

Habakkuk's lament was interrupted by a word from God, in which he said, in effect, "A work is being done which many will not believe in when they hear of it" (v.5). These words challenged even Habakkuk to look more closely at what he was lamenting to see if he might not see something of the work of God already being accomplished in his midst. The "work" that God spoke of here is not clearly defined. In the immediate context it consists of God's sending a great and fearful nation against Habakkuk's own countrymen (vv.6–11) as a work of judgment (v.12b). Later biblical writers identified this "work" of God with the coming of the Messiah and his sacrificial death on the cross (Ac 13:41). Since the book of Habakkuk itself links the "work" of God in v.5 with the messianic eschatological "work" of God in salvation (3:2; NIV, "deeds"), the NT interpretation of this passage appears to be right on the money. Habakkuk, like the faithful in every age, was being challenged to wait patiently and faithfully for God to fulfill his promise to send the deliverer, the Messiah.

## II. God's Response (2:2–20)

Thus the revelation that Habakkuk received from God awaited "an appointed time" and would "not prove false" (v.3). Evil men and mighty nations would come and go (vv.5–19). The Lord would see to it that they reaped the wages of their wicked deeds (vv.13, 16b). There lay yet in the future, however, an appointed time (v.3).

## III. A Hymn of Praise (3:1–19)

At that time the Lord would come in great glory and bring final salvation to the faithful (vv.3–15). Habakkuk, when he heard of this, called on God to do it in his own day: "I stand in awe of your work [NIV, deeds], O LORD. Renew [it] in our day, in our time make [it] known" (v.2). Though he called for God's action now, Habakkuk was willing to "wait patiently" (v.16b) because the Lord is his strength (v.19). In him was his joy (v.18). The final lesson of the book, then, is for the godly to wait. God is already at work. The faithful can see the hand of God in the events around them. Their task is to wait for God's appointed time and to rejoice in his salvation.

It is fitting that the following book, Zephaniah, is devoted in its entirety to the theme of "the day of the LORD"—the same day recounted here at the close of the book of Habakkuk.

# Zephaniah

## Introduction

This book is about the prophet Zephaniah, who prophesied in the days of King Josiah (639–609 B.C.). The central theme of the book is the announcement of the coming "Day of the LORD." As such this book appropriately follows the book of Habakkuk, which concluded on this very theme.

## I. Introduction (1:1)

This first verse introduces us to the book of Zephaniah the prophet. The book itself is a literary work about the prophet and his message. It is more than merely a record of Zephaniah's words. These words are arranged within the book in order to convey a message to the reader.

## II. The Day of the Lord (1:2–18)

The book opens with the announcement of the impending "day" of judgment against "all who live in the earth" (v.18). The focus of the pronouncement, however, is that Israel too, along with Jerusalem, stood under God's wrath (vv.10–11). As such the scope of the book is the whole people of God. In God's plan there is a future for the whole of the seed of Abraham (cf. Ge 12:2–3).

The cosmic scope of the divine judgment announced in this book is established at the beginning by means of a series of allusions to the creation account in Genesis. Just as God filled the whole of his creation with animals, birds, fish, and humankind (Ge 1), so also in judgment he will wipe out all of these creatures, even including the human race (Zep 1:2–3). Just as the focus of the creation account in Genesis is the "land," so also here the focus of God's judgment is the "land" (Zep 1:4–13). Judah stood under God's wrath because they had forsaken him and followed after gods of their own making (vv.5, 9b).

The description of the "day of the LORD" here in vv.14–18 is remarkably similar to that in Hab 3:3–15. It is no accident that these two books have been placed together in the Hebrew Bible.

## III. Call to the Righteous (2:1–3)

At the conclusion of the description of the "day of the LORD" is a brief call to the righteous to seek the Lord and find refuge in him from the wrath to come (v.3). As in Habakkuk, the righteous are those who put their trust in God during these days of distress. They wait for the "appointed time" to come by seeking righteousness and humility (v.3b).

## IV. Judgments Against the Nations (2:4–15)

The nations are now brought into the sphere of the Day of the Lord. God's judgment extends beyond his people Israel to all the nations. The nations that have historically oppressed Israel are selected and warned of the coming day of divine wrath: Philistia (vv.4–7), Moab and Ammon (vv.8–11); Cush, i.e., Egypt (v.12), and Assyria (vv.13–15).

## V. Woe to Jerusalem (3:1–7)

The prophet now turns to Jerusalem, which "does not trust in the LORD" (3:1b). God's people have not learned from the experiences of the other nations, and so they too will suffer God's judgment (v.7). A righteous God dwells within their midst (v.5), and thus they are as subject to his wrath as are the rest of the nations (vv.5b–7).

## VI. Salvation to the Nations (3:8–13)

The purpose of divine judgment is salvation. God plans to purify the nations "that all of them may call on [i.e., worship] the name of the Lord" (v.9). In that day, the nations will be purified of the proud and arrogant and only the humble will remain along with the remnant of Israel (vv.12–13).

## VII. Salvation to Israel (3:14–20)

After judgment comes salvation. Israel's blessing will be restored, and the exiles will be returned to Jerusalem (v.20). The focus of the message of salvation, therefore, is the hope of the return from Babylonian captivity. The hope expressed in the book, however, extends far beyond that return. As is true of most of the prophetic literature, the return from Babylon is used as an image of the future coming of the messianic age. The book of Haggai, which follows this book in the Hebrew Bible, is devoted specifically to the question of the return from Babylon and the fulfillment of God's messianic promises. Haggai, along with Zechariah and Malachi, attempt to show that the time of the return from Babylon did not bring in the messianic age because the people of Israel did not respond in faith. As the Lord had told Habakkuk, a work was being done in their day in which they did not believe (Hab 1:5).

# Haggai

## Introduction

The book records the prophecies of the prophet Haggai, who preached to those who had returned from Babylonian captivity and were living in Jerusalem (ca. 520 B.C.). It not only records the prophecies of this great man, but also portrays him as a model of faithfulness and commitment to God's work. Haggai is one who knew what God required and was ready to exhort those around him to do it. In his case it was the building of the temple. He knew that God had promised that the Messiah would come when the temple was restored. This was a part of his promise made to the house of David (2Sa 7).

At the time of the return from Babylon the temple lay in ruins. Haggai was called upon to exhort the people to rebuild the temple and prepare for the coming of God's Messiah. The book concludes before we see a full picture of the people's response. In Zechariah and Malachi, however, we are given a view of God's people that helps explain the lack of fulfillment of God's promise in their day. The people were still not ready to accept the work of God in their midst. They did not believe, and thus the promise was not yet fulfilled. It was the intent of these three books to explain why God's promise had not yet been fulfilled. The clear message was that all these events were part of the larger plan of God to postpone the fulfillment of his promise until "the appointed time."

The book of Daniel played an important role in the interpretation of these books. It showed that God had a master plan for the ages. The postponement of his promise was for the sake of the nations. The messianic promises made long ago to Abraham and his seed was for the salvation of all the nations of the earth (Ge 12:2–3). The delay in fulfillment of this promise had a larger purpose, precisely the point made by Peter: "The Lord is not slow in keeping his promise. . . . He is patient with you, not wanting anyone to perish, but everyone to come to repentance" (2Pe 3:9).

## I. First Oracle (1:1–11)

This oracle immediately sets the tone for the interpretation of the return from the Exile. God's people had returned to Jerusalem, but the temple still lay desolate (v.9). Haggai's main point here was to show that the Israel that returned from the Exile was really no different from the Israel that had gone into exile. Both stood under God's judgment (vv.10–11).

## II. Narrative (1:12–15)

In response to Haggai's word, Israel's leaders (Zerubbabel and Joshua) and the remnant began work on the temple. These faithful few served as a model for what had to be done to receive God's promised blessing.

## III. Second Oracle (2:1–9)

As the remnant worked on rebuilding the temple, the second oracle developed a renewed future hope for them. A temple even more glorious than Solomon's would be built from the wealth of the nations (vv.6–9). The second oracle makes the future rebuilding of the temple the focus of Israel's trust and confidence in God and his promises.

The oracle was addressed to Zerubbabel, son of Shealtiel, who was the scion of the house of David and thus heir to the messianic promise (2Sa 7:14–16). The time was ripe for fulfillment. The oracle was also addressed to the high priest, Joshua. According to Zec 6:9–15 (cf. Ps 110:4), the high priest was also to play an important role in the fulfillment of the Davidic promise in the messianic age. The Messiah was to be a king and a priest. The connection between these two came from the fact that the central role of the king was to care for the temple, the house of the Lord. Both Solomon and David were models of the Messiah in this regard.

The concern for the building of the temple in the messianic age can be seen in the prophet word of vv.6–7: "'In a little while I will once more shake the heavens and the earth, the sea and the dry land . . . and the desired of all nations will come, and I will fill this house with glory,' says the LORD Almighty." Clearly the event the prophet had in view was the future messianic kingdom. But who or what is the "desired of all nations?" Some take this to mean simply the gold and precious materials gathered from the nations that would be used to build the temple. It is more likely, however, that this refers to the Messiah himself, the one whom all nations desired. When the temple was built, it would signal his coming.

## IV. Third Oracle (2:10–19)

This oracle provides the important interpretive clue to the relationship between the present temple and the future, or eschatological, one. The present temple was not the temple of the future because the present remnant (returned Israel in Haggai's day) was not yet like the future, eschatological remnant. The present remnant was unclean, and so was the work of their hands, the present temple (v.14). Thus, for Haggai, the long-awaited blessing was still future (v.19). Nevertheless, the present temple was a concrete, physical sign that the future temple would surely be built (vv.15, 18).

## V. Fourth Oracle (2:20–23)

As the present temple had become the focus of the future (eschatological) temple, so also the present leader (Zerubbabel) was the sign of the future leader (the Messiah). Thus, the historical return from Babylonian captivity in 539 B.C. and the rebuilding of the temple by Zerubbabel was not the fulfillment of the hope of the prophets (e.g., Isa 40; Zep 3:20). The Israel of the historical return was "unclean" (unfaithful); but in their response to the words of the prophet and their willingness to begin work on the temple, they were a model of the faithful remnant of the future who would one day follow the Messiah and rebuild the temple in Jerusalem; at that time all the promises of the prophets would be fulfilled.

For a full understanding of the sense of this book we need to look at the following book, the book of Zechariah.

# Zechariah

## Introduction

The prophet Zechariah was a contemporary of Haggai. The book of Haggai concludes, curiously, with the possibility that one of Israel's present political leaders (Zerubbabel) may have been *the* Messiah. Zechariah shows that the Messiah would come only when Israel had completely obeyed God's will. The fulfillment is conditional: "This will happen if you diligently obey the LORD your God" (6:15). Since the Israel and Jerusalem of his own day failed to meet that standard, Zechariah leaves us with the message that the coming of the Messiah and the promised "return" from captivity was to be reckoned as something yet to happen in the future.

The book of Zechariah thus plays a crucial role, like that of the book of Daniel, in the interpretation of the prophetic books. It shows that the references to the coming Messiah are not to be understood in a political, historical sense, but rather in an eschatological, future sense. The messianic promises are still intact and look toward the future.

## I. Introduction (1:1)

This verse introduces us to the time of Zechariah's prophecy and thus provides an important link to the preceding book, the book of Haggai (cf. Hag 1:1).

## II. Warning to Repent (1:2–6)

Immediately following Haggai's "great expectations" (Hag 2:20–23), the book of Zechariah shows the true nature of the present "return" from the Exile. The nation that had returned from Babylon to the Promised Land was thrust into the same situation as those who lived before the Exile. They had to turn from their wicked ways and live righteously if God was to dwell in their midst. This introductory warning sets the stage for the rest of the book:

the blessing of the messianic age would come only when God's people had turned to him in obedience and righteousness (cf. 3:7; 6:15; 7:9–14; 8:14–17; cf. Eze 36:24–28).

## III. Eight Night Visions (1:7–6:8)

(1) The Man on the Red Horse (1:7–17). The seventy years were nearly complete and the temple was about to be rebuilt.

(2) Four Horns/Four Craftsman (1:18–21). Israel's enemies would be destroyed.

(3) The Measuring Line (2:1–13). Jerusalem would be rebuilt as a habitation for all nations.

(4) New Garments for Joshua (3:1–10). Israel must obey God to enjoy the promised blessing (cf. Hag 2:13–14; also Ge 18:19).

(5) Gold Lampstand/Two Olive Trees (4:1–14). The work of God in establishing his kingdom would be by the power of his Spirit (v.6; cf. Ge 1:2; Ex 31:3–6).

(6) The Flying Scroll (5:1–4). Justice would be administered throughout the whole land.

(7) The Woman With an Ephah (5:5–11). Wickedness would be removed from the land and taken to Babylon.

(8) The Four Chariots Between Two Bronze Mountains (6:1–8). God's wrath would be vented against the land of the north (Babylon/Assyria).

## IV. The Crowning of Joshua (6:9–15)

Joshua, the high priest, was a symbol of the "priest-king" who was yet to come. His title was "the Branch." All of God's promises to the house of David, which included a "priest-king" ruler (Ps 110), would come to pass when Israel obeyed the will of God (6:15).

This is a crucial section of the book and a crucial section of the OT. Here we see that the fulfillment of the messianic promise is conditional. That fulfillment required a king who would obey the will of God perfectly. The book of Zechariah is here building on the theme of 1Ki 6:12, where Solomon himself was told by the Lord that the fulfillment of the promise to David was contingent on his obedience. Solomon, of course, did not fulfill the requirement to obey God's laws, and thus the Lord did not reckon his building of the temple as a fulfillment of the promise to David (see 1Ki 11:11). Nevertheless, the promise of God remained intact (1Ki 6:12–13), just as God had said it would (2Sa 7:14b–16). Thus there was hope yet for the future.

## V. Judgment of Israel (7:1–14)

Immediately following the call for obedience in 6:15, the book turns to Zechariah's accusation that the people of his day were just as disobedient as those who went into exile. The point of this section is that those who returned to Jerusalem in Zechariah's day and their leaders (e.g., Zerubbabel and Joshua) were not to be understood as the final fulfillment of God's promises. A future fulfillment yet awaited them.

## VI. Salvation for Israel (8:1–23)

Having disqualified the events in his own day as the time of the fulfillment of God's promises, Zechariah now turns to elaborate on the true nature of the kingdom that was yet to come. This chapter presents a panoramic view of the events in the messianic age. The prophet foresaw that God would again dwell in Jerusalem, and that Jerusalem would again be called a "City of Truth" (v.3). This city would be a place of joy and salvation (vv.4–8), peace (vv.9–11), prosperity (v.12), and blessing (v.13). Worship of the true God would be restored to Zion, and peoples from all nations and tribes of the world would come to Jerusalem to worship him (vv.20–23).

## VII. Judgment and Salvation for the Nations (9:1–7)

God would purge the nations so that they too would become his people. His judgment upon the nations is seen here primarily as a prelude to the coming of the King (cf. Isa 9:1–6). It should be noted just how little attention has been given to this theme in Zechariah. Its predominate emphasis lies on the salvation of Israel and Jerusalem.

## VIII. Salvation for Israel (9:8–10:12)

At the center of Zechariah's vision of salvation for Israel was the coming of the King to Jerusalem—the King who would rule the nations in peace and righteousness (9:9–10; cf. Pss 2; 72). The prophet took this picture of the coming King from the prophecies of the Pentateuch. The King whom he foresaw riding on a donkey was that Lion of the tribe of Judah who would rule the nations and the people of God (Ge 49:8–12). Zechariah also borrowed part of his imagery from Isa 63:1–6. The images used here were then borrowed and developed by the writers of the NT (cf. Mt 21:5; Rev 19:11–16).

The central theme of this section is Israel's coming victory over their enemies at the hand of this victorious King. These images can ultimately be traced back to the promise to Eve in Ge 3:15—the victorious "seed" of the woman who would crush the head of the enemy.

## IX. The Shepherds (11:1–17)

This chapter opens with a poetic prelude to the theme of Israel's shepherds (vv.1–3). Here the image of the shepherd represents the divinely appointed leaders of the people. At first God appointed a good shepherd to rule his people. This shepherd is represented by the prophet Zechariah, who guided the people with the two staffs "Favor" and "Union." The primary focus of the passage is on a shepherd who was yet to come. But the people did not want to be ruled by this good shepherd. They rebelled and dismissed him for "thirty pieces of silver" (v.12). The picture finds its fulfillment in the coming of Christ and in his rejection.

Zechariah was then appointed to represent the rule of "a foolish shepherd" (v.15), whom God would appoint over his people after their rejection of the good shepherd (v.16). This worthless shepherd would lead them to slaughter as part of God's judgment against his disobedient people. Zechariah here envisions the divine judgment that would come upon the people of God because of their rejection of the good shepherd. That divine judgment is commonly identified with the treatment given to the Jewish people under the Roman empire.

## X. Jerusalem and the Nations (12:1–14:21)

A future day was coming when God would restore the peace of Jerusalem, as in the days of David, preceded by a great battle. Jerusalem would be surrounded by many nations, but God would deliver his city and the tribe of Judah for the sake of the promise made to David (2Sa 7). As in David's days, there would be peace in all the world. At this time God's people would look back at their treatment of the rejected shepherd, and there would be great weeping (12:10–13:6). When the shepherd was struck down, the people scattered and perished (13:7–9).

At this time, events would happen much like those connected with the return from Babylonian captivity in Zechariah's day. It would be preceded by an attack on Jerusalem by all the nations, but God would defend his city against them (14:1–15).

The book concludes with a picture of eternal peace and blessing enjoyed by all the surviving nations (14:16–21). They would all come to Jerusalem to worship God at the temple (vv.16–19), just as formerly only Israel enjoyed that privilege. Zechariah pictures the future in images drawn from the past. The whole world would be the people of God. All of Jerusalem would be holy (vv.20–21), not just the courtyards of the temple. Even the cooking pots in Jerusalem would be like the sacred bowls of the temple.

Zechariah's mention of the "Angel of the LORD" who would go before the people of God preparing the way of salvation (12:8b) provides the link to the final book in the Minor Prophets, Malachi—meaning "my angel" or "my messenger." That book focuses precisely on the role of this angel.

# Malachi

## Introduction

This book is by the prophet Malachi, who carried out his prophetic work during the days after the return from Babylonian captivity. There is a symbolic reminder in the name of Malachi ("my messenger") in that it anticipates the prophecy regarding the final messenger ("my messenger") announced in 3:1 and the prophecy about the return of Elijah in 4:5. This future prophet would be much like the present Malachi in that he would prepare the nation for the coming of God's kingdom.

The "angel" in the book of Malachi also continues the thought of the book of Zechariah, which had briefly focused on the "Angel of the Lord" who went before the people of God to prepare the way of salvation (Zec 12:8). Ultimately, these allusions can be traced back to the "angel" in Ex 23:20, who went before the people of God in the desert and prepared the way for them.

Thus the book as a whole, which contains words of warning to the present sinful nation, is a model of the warning to be announced by God's messenger who was yet to come. Upon his arrival, that messenger would carry out a rule similar to that of Malachi.

The book itself is arranged around a series of disputes between Malachi and the people during the time of the return from captivity. In these disputes, the prophet was building a case against the people, demonstrating that they were not yet ready for the coming of the promised King.

## I. Introduction (1:1)

According to this verse, the material in this book must be read as an "oracle," i.e., a prophetic word from God. Malachi, whose name means "my messenger," is the name of the prophet. As is often the case in the OT, the name of a prophet signifies the role he would play. His role anticipated that of the future prophet who would prepare the way for the coming of the Messiah. At the close of the book, that prophet is identified as Elijah; in the NT he is identified as John the Baptist.

## II. Disputes (1:2–4:3)

The case that Malachi presents against the people of God consists of six "disputes."

*Dispute #1 (1:2–5).* God had cared for Israel throughout the past, but Israel did not recognize or appreciate God's care. Israel was ungrateful.

*Dispute #2 (1:6–2:9).* Israel treated their offerings carelessly and thus dishonored God.

*Dispute #3 (2:10–16).* Israel profaned their covenant with God by marrying pagan women.

*Dispute #4 (2:17–3:5).* Though Israel might think that God would never carry out his plan of judgment against unrighteousness, God would soon send his messenger.

*Dispute #5 (3:6–12).* Israel withheld their tithes and offerings from the Lord. If they gave to God, he would abundantly bless their land.

*Dispute #6 (3:13–4:3).* Israel was tired of waiting for God's blessing, but those who did wait would have a part in the divine blessing to come.

## III. Warning (4:4–6)

The time of judgment was yet to come. There was hope, however, for those among God's people who feared his name. Waiting consisted in obediently trusting God to fulfill his promises and to send his future prophet—the prophet who would prepare the people for the coming of God's kingdom.

# Matthew

## Introduction

The gospel of Matthew does not mention its author. Although the title, "According to Matthew" is found with the earliest complete manuscripts, it is generally supposed to date back only to about A.D. 125. The chief source for our knowledge of the authorship of this gospel is a quotation of the early church writer Papias (ca. 60–130). It is probably best to retain the notion that this book was an anonymous work. Fortunately, we do not need to know the identity of the writer to understand the work itself.

The gospel itself gives no clear indication of the date of its composition. Since it was quoted by two early Christian writers, Ignatius (c. 35–c. 107) and the Didache (c. 100), thus we can be assured it was already in existence before the second century A.D.

This gospel has a clearly marked structure, consisting of an alternation of narratives about the life of Jesus and discourses that give account of his teaching. Each discourse section closes with a similar formula that also introduces a narrative section: "When Jesus had finished saying these things. . ." (7:28; 11:1; 13:53; 19:9; 26:1). Because there are five discourse sections, some have argued that Matthew's gospel is structured on the analogy of the Pentateuch. Although this may have been the case, not much can be made of it for illuminating the book itself.

Since one of the main features of Matthew is its use of OT quotations, the purpose of the gospel has generally been assumed to be a presentation of Christ as a fulfillment of OT prophecies. There are other indications within Matthew that it was also intended to be a Christian apologetic. The details that Matthew supplies of Jesus' birth, for example, would answer any charge that Jesus' birth was illegitimate; it would

also show that he did not become the Son of God at some point later in his life and ministry, but rather he was the Son of God before he was born of a virgin. Moreover, the account of the trip to Egypt and the return to Nazareth would explain why Jesus resided in Nazareth rather than Bethlehem; and the account of the bribing of the tomb guards would counter any claim that the disciples had stolen the body.

It is widely held today that Matthew's gospel had at least two primary functions within the early church community: (1) It served as a collection of Jesus' sayings and actions that were a part of the community worship of the early church; (2) it was also a manual for teaching Christian leaders in the early church.

## I. The Beginning (1:1–4:25)

### A. Early History (1:1–2:23)

The book of Matthew begins with a record of the genealogy of Jesus (1:1–17), tracing his lineage back through David to Abraham. The purpose of this genealogy is to show that Jesus was the son of David (hence, a legitimate heir to the title of Messiah; cf. Ps 2) and a descendant or seed of Abraham (hence, a legitimate heir to the blessing of Abraham; cf. Ge 12:1–3). The author then moves directly to give a full account of the birth of Jesus. His primary focus is on the Virgin Birth (1:18–25) and the world-wide recognition of this birth, i.e., the Magi from the east (2:1–12).

One additional narrative is included by Matthew to show the Lord's protection of the young Jesus during his early years. Like Israel in the OT, Jesus had sojourned in Egypt. When Jesus, with his family, came up out of Egypt, Matthew saw the providential hand of God not only in protecting him from Herod's murderous attempt against him, but also in fulfilling the words of the prophet Hosea (Hos 11:1): "Out of Egypt I called my son." Matthew thus saw in Israel's exodus from Egypt a picture of God's future redemption. In this respect, he was like Moses, the author of the Pentateuch, who also saw Israel's exodus as a picture of God's future work of redemption (see comment on Nu 24:8).

Herod's brutal order to "kill all the boys in Bethlehem and its vicinity who were two years old and under" (2:16) parallels the order of Pharaoh, "Every boy that is born, you must throw into the Nile" (Ex 1:22). The similarity is not lost on Matthew. By means of this portrayal of the events in his early life, Jesus is cast in the role of a new Moses, prepared in Egypt to lead his people into the Promised Land and thus to fulfill the blessings of Abraham.

## B. Preparation (3:1–4:25)

Matthew records three events out of the early period of preparation in Jesus' ministry. (1) The beginning of Jesus' ministry is marked by the appearance of John the Baptist, preaching a message that the kingdom of heaven was near (3:1–12). He thus called upon Israel to repent in preparation for it. Matthew stresses the fact that there was a great response in Jerusalem and Judea to John's preaching. In John's words to the Pharisees and Sadducees Matthew finds a thematic statement of the whole of his book. First there is the note of impending judgment on the nation of Israel: "Who warned you to flee from the coming wrath?" (v.7). Second, John says, "Produce fruit in keeping with repentance" (v.8); hence, Matthew's emphasis on true discipleship finds expression in the negative example of these religious leaders. Finally, there is John's statement that "the ax is already at the root of the trees" (v.10), anticipating the fact that by the time the book is complete, Matthew will have chronicled the rejection of Israel and the establishment of the church as "stones" that God would raise up for the "children of Abraham" (v.9). Matthew no doubt has

in mind Jesus' later statement to Peter, "Upon this rock I will build my church" (16:18).

(2) Matthew now turns to what amounts to a second introduction of Jesus, now as an adult, ready to do the work of God. He does so in the context of John's baptism in the Jordan. Jesus, like the rest of those in the region, came to John to be baptized (3:13–17). John recognized Jesus and hesitated to baptize him, knowing that his baptism was one of repentance. But Jesus insisted, saying to John, "It is proper for us to do this to fulfill all righteousness" (v.15). We learn what Jesus meant by this in the following section, when the heavens opened and a voice from heaven said, "This is my Son, whom I love; with him I am well pleased" (v.17). Thus it was by means of John's baptism that Jesus was declared publicly to be the Son of God. These words confirm what Matthew has already shown in his gospel, namely, that Jesus is the eternal Son of God (cf. 1:23; 2:15).

(3) It is precisely on the question of Jesus' sonship that the Devil now opens his temptation of Jesus (4:1–11), "If you are the Son of God, tell these stones to become bread" (v.3). Jesus, who, in a similar fashion to that of Israel in the Exodus, had been in the wilderness without food for forty days and nights, is taunted by the Devil to produce bread for himself, like the manna that God had given Israel (Ex 16). Jesus replied to the Devil by quoting Dt 8:3, in which Moses had interpreted the manna as a sign that doing the will of God was more important than meeting physical needs.

Jesus fends off two additional attacks on his sonship by taking recourse to the Scriptures. Matthew not only is concerned to show that Jesus is, indeed, the Son of God, but also to show by example how his Christian readers can themselves fend off the attacks of the Devil. Jesus, the Son of God, did not use his own powers or wisdom to meet the attacks of Satan. He, rather, relied on God's Word.

## II. Jesus in Galilee (4:12–20:34)

### A. The Sermon on the Mount (4:12–7:29)

As an introduction to Jesus' sermon on the mountain, Matthew records a summary of Jesus' ministry in Galilee. This includes the account of his choosing his first disciples (4:18–22). Matthew first demonstrates from the OT that Galilee was the most appropriate place for Jesus to begin his ministry (Isa 9:1–2). He has already shown that Jesus fulfilled the OT prophecies that the Messiah would be born in Bethlehem, the city of David (2:6). It was just as important for Matthew to show that Galilee was the appropriate starting point for his ministry. In the quotation from Isaiah, Galilee is especially called "Galilee of the Gentiles"; hence, Matthew is again anticipating the shift that would take place in his gospel from Israel to all the nations (cf. Mt 28:19). The picture of Jesus here is reminiscent of Ezra in the OT, who once stood on a high wooden platform and read aloud the "Book of the Law of Moses . . . from daybreak till noon" (Ne 8:1–3). The picture here of Jesus and the Twelve may have been modeled on that of "Jeshua" and the twelve (Ne 8:7), who explained the Law to the people, "giving the meaning so that the people could understand what was being read" (Ne 8:8).

Matthew's account of the Sermon on the Mount is presented in summary form. Jesus had been preaching in synagogues throughout the cities of Galilee (4:23–25). His message was, like that of John the Baptist, one of repentance and the nearness of the kingdom of heaven (v.17). Matthew summarizes Jesus' message with the title "good news," i.e., the Gospel (v.23). Now in his summary of Jesus' Sermon on the Mount, Matthew's concern is to show the nature of the content of Jesus' teaching.

Jesus begins his sermon with the OT theme of "blessing," a pattern visible in Psalms such as Ps 1:1. The focus of his teaching is set on the future. The kingdom that Jesus announces is one for which its members must suffer in the present, but who will find great reward "in heaven" (5:12). Jesus' sermon anticipates his later teaching on the kingdom of heaven in ch. 13. That kingdom, which was then and there being established by Jesus, would find its ultimate victory only after a time of suffering and ignominy.

It is in light of the notion of waiting for the consummation of the kingdom that Jesus here teaches his disciples how to live in God's blessing and joy. Such a life, Jesus says, should serve as a beacon to the world, giving glory to the heavenly Father (v.16). It is a life that does not abolish the teaching of the Scriptures, but rather fulfills God's intentions in giving his Word to Israel. It calls for a righteousness that goes far beyond that of the scribes and the Pharisees (vv.17–20). The righteousness of God's kingdom, for example, does not stop at the prohibition of murder. It goes beyond obvious acts of violence to the inner, secret sins of anger and slander, "But anyone who says, 'You fool!' will be in danger of the fire of hell" (v.22). If it is wrong to commit adultery, it is also grievously wrong even "to look at a woman lustfully" (vv.27–28). In drawing these distinctions, Jesus clearly reflects the OT's own emphasis on the fundamental evil of "little sins," such as hatred and slander (see Pr 6:25, 27; 11:12–13).

The standard of righteousness that Jesus appeals to in this sermon is not that of human wisdom or traditional values (v.47). Jesus states clearly at the conclusion of this section of his sermon that members of the kingdom of heaven are to "be perfect, therefore, as [their] heavenly Father is perfect" (v.48).

With the call to righteous living comes the warning of self-righteousness and hypocrisy (6:1–7:5; 7:15–27). The central theme of this second half of the sermon is service to God, "who sees what is done in secret" (6:4, 6, 18) rather than service before other people. In the midst of these repeated warnings against hypocrisy, Jesus calls for an absolute trust in the heavenly Father and commitment to his kingdom (6:25–34; 7:7–13).

Matthew closes the account of Jesus' teaching with a description of the people's response. They were astonished by they way he taught and were struck by the difference between his authority and that of their own teachers of the law (7:28–29).

## B. Jesus' Great Deeds (8:1–9:38)

To illustrate the authority of Jesus, Matthew now records several incidents in Jesus' ministry that focus on the recognition of his authority among the people and the Jewish leaders. These are not random incidents, however. The specific examples of Jesus' acts recorded here correspond to the list of evidences given to the imprisoned John the Baptist (11:2–6). John had sought from Jesus a confirmation that he was, in fact, the promised Messiah. Jesus answered John by pointing to his deeds: "The blind receive sight [cf. 9:27–31], the lame walk [9:2–7], those who have leprosy are cured [8:1–4], the deaf hear [9:32–34], the dead are raised [9:18–26], and the good news is preached to the poor [10:5–42]" (11:5).

In the account of the healing of the leper (8:1–4), the man says simply, "Lord, if you are willing, you can make me clean" (v.2). There is no question of Jesus' ability to heal. All depends on his sovereign will. Jesus replied, "I am willing, be clean!" To show that Jesus' teaching did not abolish the importance of the Law of Moses, Matthew adds Jesus' instructions to the leper that he now show himself to the priest, "and offer the gift Moses commanded" (v.4). It may be significant, however, that the purpose for obeying what Moses commanded was to be "a testimony to them [i.e., the priests]" (v.4).

The account of Jesus' encounter with the centurion (vv.5–13) demonstrates clearly that even the Gentiles recognized his authority. When a Gentile centurion came to Jesus regarding his sick servant, he said simply, "Just say the word, and my servant will be healed" (v.8). The centurion's faith in Jesus' authority amazed even Jesus, who said, "I have not found anyone in Israel with such great faith" (v.10). On seeing such faith among the Gentiles, Jesus returned briefly to a familiar theme throughout this gospel, namely, the rejection of Israel and the Gentiles' inheritance of the kingdom of heaven (vv.11–12).

In the account of Jesus' authority over diseases, Matthew stresses the power of "his word" to heal. He healed Peter's mother-in-law (vv.14–15) and cast out the spirits "with a word" (v.16). Matthew sees this as another example of fulfilled prophecy (v.17).

In the narrative that follows, Matthew shows that Jesus demanded absolute authority over those who wanted to follow him (vv.18–22). To the one follower who vowed to follow Jesus "wherever" he goes, Jesus replied, "The Son of Man has no place to lay his head" (v.20). Though terse, the sense of Jesus' reply seems to be that the commitment to follow Jesus should have no qualifiers attached to it. In his words, at least, the teacher of the law left the impression that in his commitment he assumed he would have a place to lay his head. The second disciple's request to bury his father before he followed Jesus was met head on with the call for immediate obedience, "Follow me, and let the dead bury their own dead" (v.22). In both incidents, Jesus' call is for unqualified obedience.

Jesus' authority extended even to the forces of nature (vv.23–27). When he calmed the storm at sea, his disciples observed, "Even the winds and the waves obey him!" (v.27). When Jesus cast the demons out of two men and allowed them to go into a herd of swine, the whole town pleaded with him to leave their region (vv.28–34). Matthew does not explain why they made such a request, but the likely reason is that they were unable to reckon with such authority. They saw the authority of Jesus as a threat to their present way of life and hence rejected him.

In the narrative that follows (9:1–8), Matthew brings out the most important implication of Jesus' authority, i.e., the power to forgive sin. What requires more power—to heal the sick or to forgive sin? Both, says Jesus, are the work of God, not of a human being. Thus Jesus healed the paralytic "that you may know that the Son of Man has authority on earth to forgive sins" (v.6).

Within the context of Jesus' call for absolute obedience, the narrative of his call of Matthew finds its most appropriate setting (v.9). Matthew is someone who gave up all and followed Jesus (vv.9–13). When the Pharisees questioned the character of those who, like Matthew, followed the Lord, Jesus referred to a well known OT theme to answer their complaint (v.13): God desires mercy, not sacrifice (Hos 6:6). In the question of fasting that immediately follows (9:14–17), this theme is further pursued to the point of the need to break with the traditions of the past to follow and serve Jesus. New wine must be put in new wineskins (v.17). There is an additional hint in Jesus' words to the time when "the bridegroom will be taken from them" (v.15). Within the book of Matthew, this surely refers to the death of Jesus and the new covenant (26:28). Thus the contrast between the old and

the new in these two proverbs should be taken to be a contrast between the old covenant, established between God and Israel at Mount Sinai, and the gift of the new covenant to the church, established at Golgatha (27:32–56).

Matthew continues to recount stories that stress the authority of Jesus in his power to heal the sick and raise the dead (9:18–34). He gives a striking picture of Jesus' authority in v.18 by showing one of the "rulers" bowing down at Jesus' feet. The section concludes with the opinion of two groups of eyewitnesses. The first group, the crowd who witnessed the work of Jesus, said, "Nothing like this has ever been seen in Israel" (v.33); the second group, the Pharisees, concluded, "It is by the prince of demons that he drives out demons" (v.34). They did not question his power to do the works that the crowd had witnessed, but they did question the source of that power. The stage was being set for the leaders of Israel to reject their promised Messiah. In this account of the explanation of Jesus' authority, Matthew has given us a perceptive view of their rejection. These leaders did not reject Jesus because they were unconvinced of his authority, but because they did not accept and submit to it.

Matthew closes this section of his gospel with a summary of the activity of Jesus during this time: "Jesus went through all the towns and villages, teaching in their synagogues, preaching the good news of the kingdom and healing every disease and sickness" (v.35). Jesus' response to the crowds that he attracted was one of compassion. In an allusion to an OT description of Israel in the days of the Messiah, Jesus called them "sheep without a shepherd" (v.36; cf. Zec 10:2). Jesus' call to "ask the Lord of the harvest to send out workers into his harvest field" sets the stage for the discourse that follows (10:1–42).

## C. Sending of the Twelve (10:1–42)

As a link to the narratives that precede, Matthew states that Jesus "gave [the disciples] authority to drive out evil spirits and to heal every disease and sickness" (10:1). Thus the same divine authority that the preceding narratives demonstrated as operative in the life of Jesus was now given to his disciples. Consistent with the notion that the people of Israel were like "sheep without a shepherd" (9:36), Jesus sent his disciples only to "the lost sheep of Israel" (10:6). Their message was that the kingdom of heaven was near (v.7), and they were to "heal the sick, raise the dead, cleanse those who have leprosy, drive out demons" (v.8). When Israel eventually rejected their Messiah, the offer of the kingdom was extended to all nations (cf. 28:19).

Jesus sent his disciples throughout the land of Israel to announce the coming of the messianic King. In Matthew's gospel this is the prelude to the people's rejection of this King. Matthew, however, records Jesus' instructions to his disciples in such a way that they provide a guide to the evangelistic mission of his own readers in the early church. Thus many of the instructions Jesus gave his disciples in this section have a larger application in the life of the readers of this gospel. The gospel is a virtual manual for evangelism and discipleship. This is particularly true of the instructions in vv.17–25, which resemble closely the instructions in 24:9–14.

## D. Jesus and His Opponents (11:1–12:50)

The brief narrative of John's seeking a confirmation of Jesus' calling serves as a summary of the preceding chapters. The list of his deeds that Jesus gave John is a summary of the preceding accounts of his miracles (cf. comment on 8:1). Thus these miracles serve the purpose of demonstrating the identity of Jesus. They are his credentials that verify that he was the chosen one promised in the OT Scriptures and announced by John.

Jesus now gives his own understanding of John the Baptist (11:7–15). John was the last of the line of prophets that extended from the OT period (vv.7–9a), but he was more as well. He was also the first of the fulfillment of that which was promised by the OT prophets (vv.9b–11). Thus the mission of John signaled the coming of the promised kingdom of God (vv.12–15).

Jesus continues to show that the treatment John received, as well as the treatment that lay in store for him in the near future, was a sign that the kingdom announced by John was being rejected by God's people. Judgment, rather than blessing, awaited the present generation. At this point in this gospel, the attention turns away from the present establishment of the kingdom of heaven to its rejection by Israel. Whether one speaks of a "postponement" of this kingdom or of a mere inauguration of the kingdom with a delayed consummation, the fact remains that a shift takes place here that ultimately leads to the establishment of the church (16:18) and the opening of the Gospel to all nations (28:19).

The shift in Jesus' message is unmistakable in 11:20–24, where he reflects back on his earlier works in the cities of Israel and, as the prophets before him (e.g., Isa 1:9), turns to the imagery of Sodom (Ge 19) to describe God's judgment on Israel. In these cities Jesus did the works of God, but the people did not repent. The only explanation of such hardness of heart, Jesus says, is God's wisdom and his good pleasure (11:26) in not revealing himself "to the wise and learned" (v.25a) but to "little children" (v.25b). God's will was being accomplished in Israel's rejection of the Messiah. Jesus' perspective was later reflected in the words of Paul in Ac 28:26, where he said of

Israel, "You will be ever hearing but never understanding." Paul saw in Israel's rejection the plan of God to offer salvation to the Gentiles (Ac 28:28).

The rejection of Jesus by the leaders of Israel is shown in ch. 12. They first accuse Jesus and his disciples of breaking the Law of Moses (vv.1–14). Jesus appeals to his own authority over the Mosaic Law: "The Son of Man is Lord of the Sabbath" (v.8), as well as to a proper understanding of the Law itself: "It is lawful to do good on the Sabbath" (v.12). This is the point in Matthew where the plot to kill Jesus begins to move into play. It is also at this point that Jesus becomes identified as the Servant of the Lord. Henceforth, a central theme of the book is that of the death of the Servant, "in [whose] name the nations will put their hope" (v.21).

The final turning point in the ministry of Jesus comes when the Pharisees attribute Jesus' works to the work of Satan: "It is only by Beelzebub, the prince of demons, that this fellow drives out demons" (v.24). Jesus responds to them not only by pointing out the desperate absurdity of their charge ("every kingdom divided against itself will be ruined"; v.25), but also by cautioning them of the seriousness of their rejection of God's offer: "by your words you will be acquitted, and by your words you will be condemned" (v.37). In these stern words to the Pharisees, Matthew may also be warning his readers of the seriousness of rejecting Jesus. Jesus' words to the Pharisees are cast in such a way to include anyone confronted with the similar question: Who is Jesus? Jesus says, "I tell you that men will have to give account on the day of judgment for every careless word they have spoken" (v.36). Thus Matthew shows that rejection of Jesus means rejection of God's Servant sent to die for human sin (v.18). How much better the offer Jesus gives to those who believe in him: "Come to me, all you who are weary and burdened, and I will give you rest . . . and you will find rest for your souls" (11:28–29).

One cannot read Jesus' final words to the Pharisees in this section (vv.38–45) without sensing the turning point in Jesus' message: "A wicked and adulterous generation asks for a miraculous sign! But none will be given it except the sign of the prophet Jonah" (v.39). The "sign of Jonah," Jesus explains, is to be Jesus' own resurrection. As in the days of Jonah and Solomon, the nations will receive the sign and come from the ends of the earth (vv.40–42), but "this wicked generation" that has rejected the kingdom offered by Jesus will go from bad to worse (vv.43–45).

As the last narrative in this section shows, membership in God's kingdom was not to be based on family relationships, as had been the case in the initial offer of the kingdom. Jesus had said to his disciples, "Do not go among the Gentiles or enter any town of the Samaritans. Go rather to the lost sheep of Israel" (10:5–6). This is consistent with the OT view of the kingdom that was promised to Israel and the house of David (2Sa 7:16; Isa 9:7). But now Jesus says, "Whoever does the will of my Father in heaven is my brother and sister and mother" (12:50). At the close of the next section of parables, Matthew returns to the family of Jesus and reiterates this same point, only from the perspective of those in his home town. His close acquaintances ask, "Isn't his mother's name Mary, and aren't his brothers James, Joseph, Simon and Judas? Aren't all his sisters with us?" (13:55–56). They did not understand, Jesus concludes, "because of their lack of faith" (v.58).

### E. Seven Parables of the Kingdom (13:1–58)

The kingdom that Jesus offered to all those who would accept it is now illustrated in seven parables: the sower (13:1–23), the weeds (13:24–30, 36–

43), the mustard seed (13:31–32), the yeast (13:33–35), the hidden treasure (13:44), the pearl (13:45), and the net (13:50). Though each parable makes its own contribution to the reader's understanding of the kingdom, each also expresses the same basic truth. Jesus came to establish the kingdom promised in the OT prophetic literature, and he was, in fact, about to fulfill his mission. That kingdom, however—which was to be a visible, universal rule of the Messiah—would begin in a small, almost imperceptible, form, as a mustard seed or as a piece of yeast in a lump of dough. Unlike what might have been anticipated from reading the OT, there was to be a delay between the coming of the King and the consummation of the kingdom. During that delay, kingdom members were to live in expectation of the return of the King and the final establishment of the kingdom at the "end of the age" (vv.39, 40, 49).

That this was a fulfillment of the OT hope in a way that differed from what might have been expected is suggested by Jesus' last remarks in this section: "Every teacher of the law who has been instructed about the kingdom of heaven is like the owner of a house who brings out of his storeroom new treasures as well as old" (v.52). Jesus' view of the kingdom has some elements that are a part of the OT's view and some that are new.

Matthew then returns to the family of Jesus and reiterates the point made at the beginning of this section: membership in God's kingdom is not to be based on family relationships, as had been the case in the initial offer of the kingdom. But his own close acquaintances did not understand "because of their lack of faith" (v.58).

## F. The Itinerate Ministry of Jesus (14:1–16:12)

Matthew includes a selection of the works of Jesus along an itinerary through Galilee. He begins with what appears to have been the cause of Jesus' moving throughout the region, the beheading of John the Baptist (14:1–14). He first reviews the events in Jerusalem that led to the death of John. We are thus given a preview of what is going on there, and we quickly learn that all is not well in Jerusalem. In a word, Matthew shows that the prophets are still being killed in Jerusalem. Jerusalem has not changed since the days of the OT.

Jesus, on hearing of the death of John, went into the desert (NIV, "solitary place," 14:13). He was not hiding from Herod, who had killed John, but, like John, he was preparing the people in the desert for the coming of God's kingdom (3:1–3). Thus, as Israel was fed manna to sustain them in the desert until they entered the Promised Land (Ex 16), Jesus fed bread to the 5,000 (14:15–21). As Moses brought the people through the Red Sea to teach the people to trust God (Ex 14:31), Jesus brought Peter "upon the sea" to teach his disciples faith (14:22–33). Matthew seems particularly interested in the parallels with Israel's exodus as recorded in the OT. Just as the Scriptures stress that God brought his people through the sea with his "mighty hand and outstretched arm" (Dt 7:19) and kept them from sinking "to the depths like a stone," like the Egyptians who did not believe (Ex 15:5), so Jesus "reached out his hand" to keep Peter from sinking into the sea (14:30–31) and brought him to the boat in safety (v.32). Moses said, "Do not be afraid. Stand firm and you will see the deliverance the LORD will bring you today" (Ex 14:13); Jesus said, "It is I. Don't be afraid" (14:27).

Jesus now enters the area of Gennesaret (14:34–15:28). Matthew gives a short summary account of Jesus' activity there. The stress is on the fact that he healed many sick (14:34–36). Here also we are given a foretaste of the situation in Jerusalem. Jesus is met by Pharisees and teachers of the law who are scandalized by Jesus' disciples' apparent disregard for their "traditions." Jesus answers their accusations with his own exposition of the importance of the word of God over against tradition. What makes for purity and righteousness is not conformity to external rules and regulations, but rather a clean heart (15:1–20).

In his brief journey to Tyre and Sidon (vv.21–28), regions outside of the land of Israel, Jesus explained the goal of his preaching about the kingdom. At least at this point in the book of Matthew, it is clear that Jesus envisioned the kingdom of God along much the same lines as the OT prophets. Jesus told the Canaanite woman that he "was sent only to the lost sheep of Israel" (v.24). It is part of Matthew's purpose to show that as this kingdom was rejected by Israel, the offer was extended to "all nations" (cf. 28:19). Thus, seeing the woman's great faith, Jesus healed her daughter. The Gentile woman's faith stands out in great contrast in these narratives. Even the disciples, for example, have "little faith" (14:31).

Matthew closes his portrayal of the Galilean ministry of Jesus with a summary of his healing "the lame, the blind, the crippled, the mute and many others" (15:29–31), an account of the feeding of the 4,000 (vv.32–38), and Jesus' journey to Magadan (15:39–16:12). Here, having been tested by the Pharisees and Sadducees (16:1–4), Jesus warns his disciples of the yeast, i.e., the teaching (v.12), of the Pharisees and Sadducees (vv.5–12).

## G. The Church (16:13–20:34)

Jesus' question to his disciples, "Who do people say the Son of Man is?" marks a major turning point in this gospel. As their answer shows, the people are still in the dark about the identity of Jesus: "Some say John the Baptist; others say Elijah; and still others, Jeremiah or one of the prophets" (16:14). Peter's answer, however, is right on target: "You are the Christ, the Son of the living God" (v.16). Thus, Jesus says, on this confession ("this rock") he will build his church. The church has now come into full view in this gospel. Access ("the keys") into the kingdom of heaven will henceforth come through the church.

Having raised the issue of the building of the church, Jesus moves immediately to the means by which it will be built. He "must go to Jerusalem and suffer many things . . . and be killed and on the third day be raised to life" (v.21). Even Peter, to whom the Father in heaven had revealed the identity of Jesus (v.17), has not come up to full speed. He does not understand how the victorious reign of the Christ, the Son of the living God, could come through death and suffering. Jesus thus explains that through the death and resurrection of Jesus, the OT promise of the reign of the Son of Man (Da 7:9–14) will be accomplished. Though it is not explained, Jesus' statement that "some who are standing here will not taste death before they see the Son of Man coming in his kingdom" (16:28) may be a reference to early martyrs like Stephen who, at death, saw "heaven open and the Son of Man standing at the right hand of God" (Ac 7:56).

The following two chapters consist of a collection of Jesus' deeds and sayings that establish policies and procedures for the ongoing administration of the church. The gospel of Matthew, and especially this section, is thus intended as a guidebook or manual for the church after the Resurrection (cf. 17:9).

The first subject dealt with is the essential and close relationship between Jesus' kingdom and the OT prophets. The Transfiguration (17:1–13) is a vivid reminder of the unity of God's work with Israel and the church. At the same time, it shows that there is also a distinction between God's work with

Israel and his church that is here being inaugurated. In the Transfiguration, Moses and Elijah are presented as witnesses to Jesus' present work but not participants. Peter's desire to build "three tabernacles" (NIV, "shelters") is rebuffed by the voice from heaven. While Peter is still speaking, the Father acknowledges only Jesus as the one in whom he is well pleased. "Listen to him!" (v.5). It is not difficult to see in this a focus on the priority of the work of Jesus over against Moses and Elijah.

When the disciples raise the question of Elijah's role in the coming kingdom, Jesus replies by saying that John the Baptist was the "Elijah" who announced the coming Messiah (v.13). Thus the church, which Jesus is now inaugurating, shares with Moses and Elijah in God's kingdom, but Moses and Elijah do not share in the church. The place of Moses and Elijah is taken by "Jesus only" (cf. v.8).

In the following story of Jesus' healing the boy with a demon (vv.14–21), a further parallel between Jesus and Israel is drawn. Jesus says, "O unbelieving and perverse generation . . . how long shall I stay with you? How long shall I put up with you?" (v.17). These words readily evoke the image of Israel's failure to believe God in the desert: "The LORD said to Moses, 'How long will these people treat me with contempt? How long will they refuse to believe in me, in spite of all the miraculous signs I have performed among them?'" (Nu 14:11; cf. Ps 95:10). Faith was the missing factor in Israel's relationship with God, and it could threaten to be the missing factor in the church. With faith, however, "nothing will be impossible" (v.21). It is tempting to see in Jesus' words about faith moving mountains (v.20) an allusion to the mountain represented earlier by Moses and Elijah, i.e., Mount Sinai or Horeb (Ex 19:1; 1Ki 19:8).

In the account of Jesus paying taxes (vv.22–27), Matthew teaches by precept and example that Jesus' followers were to pay taxes in order not to "offend" (v.27). In the miraculous nature of the payment, there may be the suggestion that God will provide for such faithfulness. Moreover, in the church that Jesus has founded, whoever comes as a little child will be the greatest (18:1–4), and "whoever welcomes a little child" in Jesus' name, welcomes Jesus (vv.5–9). The importance of having regard for the meek and humble lies in the fact that the heavenly Father cares for each one of them (vv.10–14). There will be strife among God's people; thus, Jesus gives specific procedures for dealing with it (vv.15–17). The church as a body acts in Jesus' behalf because they have been gathered in his name (vv.18–20). The central rule that governs the various relationships within the church is that of forgiveness (vv.21–35).

Matthew seems particularly concerned to show that marriage (19:1–12) and the family (vv.13–15) stand at the heart of most relationships within the church. He also shows that Jesus allowed for exceptions. In the case of divorce, "marital unfaithfulness" (v.9), and in the case of marriage, "renouncing marriage for the sake of the kingdom of heaven" (v.12), call for exceptions from the rule. As in the OT (e.g., Dt 6:7), Jesus focused the attention of the church on the children—the next generation (v.14).

Jesus' teaching regarding wealth was followed closely by the early church in Jerusalem. Jesus said, "If you want to be perfect, go, sell your possessions and give to the poor" (v.21). In the church in Acts, "all the believers were together and had everything in common. Selling their possessions and goods, they gave to anyone as he had need" (Ac 2:44–45). In both Matthew and Acts, this is emphasized not as the standard but as the ideal: "If you want to be *perfect*" (v.21, emphasis mine). Though it is hard for a rich man to enter the kingdom of heaven (v.23), it is not impossible (v.26). In the last analysis, salvation does not depend on a person's wealth, or lack of it, for "with God all things are possible" (v.26). The parable of the vineyard workers shows that reward will not depend on the amount of work done, but on the generous grace of God. Those who put themselves first, however, "will be last in the kingdom of heaven, and many who are last will be first" (v.30; 20:16).

Jesus himself set the supreme example of his teaching in willingly giving up his own life (20:17–19). Though his disciples may want to gain equal honor with Jesus in his kingdom, only Jesus knows the real price that must be paid: "to give his life as a ransom for many" (v.28). The glorious and victorious Son of Man (Da 7:9–14) must first become the Suffering Servant (Isa 53:8). Only the blind will see him (20:19–34).

## III. Jesus in Jerusalem (21:1–27:66)

### A. The Last Works of Jesus (21:1–22:46)

When Jesus arrived at Jerusalem, the crowds were ready, and he entered just as the prophets had foretold the Messiah would come: "See, your king comes to you, gentle and riding on a donkey" (21:5). But when asked who Jesus was, they reveal their lingering lack of understanding: "This is Jesus, the prophet from Nazareth in Galilee" (v.11). Their answer stands in sharp contrast to that of Peter's: "You are the Christ, the Son of the living God" (16:16). The importance of this difference can be seen in the fact that the church is built on Peter's confession (v.18), whereas at the trial of Jesus a week later, this same crowd shouted "Crucify him!" (27:22).

As had been promised in the OT, the Messiah would be recognized for his zeal for the house of God, the temple (1Ch 17:12; Zec 6:11–13). The children welcomed Jesus as the "Son of David" (21:15), but the chief priests "were indignant" (v.15) and sought to undermine his authority (v.23). Jesus again looked to the work of John the Baptist as the one who announced his coming (vv.23–27; cf. 3:1–17; 11:1–19; 14:1–12). The chief priests and the elders feigned repentance at the preaching of John and thus, in Jesus' parable, were like the son who agreed to work for his father but did not go out into the field (21:28–32). On the other hand, the true members of God's kingdom were those who repented at John's preaching, like "the tax collectors and the prostitutes" (v.31). Repentance at John's preaching is that which led to faith in Jesus (v.32).

Like a landowner who casts away his dishonest and treacherous tenants, God will cast off the chief priests and elders of Israel and give his kingdom to another people (vv.33–46). When those invited to the wedding banquet refuse to come, the king will send his army and destroy those who refuse his invitation (22:1–7). He will then send his servants "to the street corners and invite to the banquet anyone" willing to come (vv.8–14).

Jesus' teaching, directed at the leadership in Jerusalem (21:45), provoked great opposition, both in the form of hidden plans to take his life (v.46) and of open "plans to trap him in his words" (22:15). The first plan, brought forth by the Pharisees, was to trap him with the civil authorities: "Is it right to pay taxes to Caesar or not?" (v.17). But they were caught in their own trap in that his reply only served to demonstrate his wisdom: "Give to Caesar what is Caesar's, and to God what is God's" (v.21).

The second plan, that of the Sadducees, sought to trap Jesus in a matter of the Mosaic Law. When a man follows the Mosaic Law and marries the wife of his deceased brother (Dt 25:5), "in the resurrection, whose wife will she be?" (22:28). Again, the plan fails, and the crowds are "astonished at his teaching" (v.33).

The Pharisees then return with a third question: "Which is the greatest commandment?" But Jesus' answer leaves them without any objections (vv.34–40). Moreover, he redirects their questions about his understanding of the Mosaic Law to a question about their understanding of Scripture: "What do you think about the Christ? Whose son is he?" (vv.41–42). When they answer merely that the Messiah was to be the son of David, Jesus shows that their answer cannot stand the test of the OT. Calling their attention to the Psalms, Jesus showed that David himself called the Messiah his Lord (Ps 110:1), so how can he be merely his son (vv.43–45)? Jesus' understanding of himself as the Christ, the Son of God, is revealed in his answer, and, in the process, the inadequacy of the Pharisees' response is exposed.

## B. The Last Works of Jesus (23:1–25:46)

Taking the occasion of the attempts of the Pharisees to trap him in a matter of the law, Jesus turns to the crowd and his own disciples to censure the hypocrisy of "the teachers of the law" (23:1–38). He begins by acknowledging the legitimate office held by these teachers as interpreters of Mosaic Law: they "sit in Moses' seat" (v.2). Thus what they teach, in so far as it is the teaching of Mosaic Law, must be obeyed by those under the Mosaic covenant (v.3). The problem does not lie in what they teach but in their own lack of obedience. They teach one thing and do another. As Jesus had repeatedly taught in this gospel, the teaching of the Law is directed to the heart (see 15:18). As for the teachers of the Law and the Pharisees, however, "everything they do is done

for men to see" (23:5). Jesus then drove home his point with a scathing series of seven "woes" (vv.13–36).

Jesus extended his condemnation of the teachers of the Law and the Pharisees to the whole of Jerusalem and the nation (vv.37–39). They were like the nation of old who suffered God's judgment in the Babylonian captivity (2Ki 25). They had killed the prophets and rejected God's messengers. Hence, like Israel of old, they would also be "left desolate" (v.38; 24:1–2). Jesus, however, continued to speak of a time in the future when Jerusalem would again turn to him and say, "Blessed is he who comes in the name of the Lord" (23:39). The crowds in Jerusalem had greeted him with these words when he entered Jerusalem only days before (21:9), but a time remained in the future when the whole city would join in.

On the Mount of Olives, alone with his disciples, Jesus began to teach them about his future return (24:3–25:46). Before he returned, many false messiahs would come, deceiving many into following them. There would be wars, famines, and earthquakes, but these would only be the harbingers of his return; they would not mark "the end" itself. His followers would suffer much persecution and apostasy, but the gospel of the kingdom was to be preached throughout all the world. Only then would the end come. As the book of Daniel (Da 9:27; 11:31; 12:11) had foretold, the central event that would mark the return of Christ would be a great act of sacrilege at the site of the temple, that is, "the abomination that causes desolation." Though false prophets and false messiahs would abound during this time, the faithful were to wait patiently for the coming of the true Messiah, the Son of Man, who would come openly, in the clouds, before the eyes of all, as Daniel had foretold (Da 7:9–14). When he came, he would send his angels to gather his own from all the corners of the world. The people of Israel, God's chosen people, would "certainly not pass away," they would remain "until all these things have happened" (24:34).

The time of Christ's return is known to no one, "not even the angels in heaven, nor the Son, but only the Father" (v.36). It will happen, as with the flood in Noah's day (Ge 6–9), when it is least expected. Therefore, God's people must watch and remain faithful (24:42), like a homeowner guarding his house (vv.43–45), like a wise servant waiting for the return of his master (vv.46–51), like wise bridesmaids with lamps filled and ready for the coming of the bridegroom (25:1–13), and like the "good and faithful servant" who invests his talents while waiting for his master's return (vv.14–30).

As Daniel had also foretold (Da 7:9–10), when the Son of Man returns, he will judge all the nations. Those who have been faithful to him in his absence will inherit "the kingdom prepared for [them] since the creation of the world" (25:34). Those who have rejected him will be sent "into the eternal fire prepared for the devil and his angels" (v.41).

## C. The Death of Jesus (26:1–27:66)

Matthew is careful to note that the death of Jesus happened at the time of the Jewish Passover. Thus two central themes from the OT are linked in Jesus' death: The Messianic Son of Man (Da 7:9–14) is identified as the Passover lamb (Ex 12–13). Matthew thus reflects the same understanding of the death of Christ as the apostle Paul, who wrote, "Christ, our Passover lamb, has been sacrificed" (1Co 5:7). That Jesus was fully aware of his impending death is evident from his response to the woman "with an alabaster jar of very expensive perfume, which she poured on his head as he was reclining at the table" (26:7). Jesus saw this as a preparation for his burial (v.12). At this same time, Judas

Iscariot sought an opportunity to betray Jesus to the chief priests (vv.14–16).

Jesus celebrated the Passover meal with his disciples on the evening he was betrayed (vv.17–35). During the meal, he identified his own death with the bread and wine of the Passover meal (vv.26–29). At the same time he identified his death as the fulfillment of a covenant "for many for the forgiveness of sins" (v.28).

As Jesus and his disciples left the place of the meal and moved toward Gethsemane, Matthew, as the other gospels, stresses that Jesus was to face his death alone. He left his closest disciples and then, in the garden, he anticipated his separation even from the Father. Though Jesus was fully aware of what was about to happen to him in Jerusalem, the disciples were sleepy and tired of waiting, and they quickly fell asleep. Jesus' admonition, "Watch and pray so that you will not fall into temptation" (v.41) seems directed as much to Matthew's readers as to the disciples. His words echo the warning he gave to those awaiting his second coming, "Keep watch. . . . [You] must be ready, because the Son of Man will come at an hour when you do not expect him" (24:42–44).

Matthew stresses that Jesus voluntarily gave himself over to his enemies because he saw it as a fulfillment of Scripture (26:54, 56). He was first taken to Caiaphas, the high priest, where he was interrogated by the teachers of the law and the elders (v.57). With Peter looking on, or at least nearby (v.58), false witnesses were brought forward to testify against him (vv.59–63). When asked directly by the high priest if he was "the Christ, the Son of God," Jesus said, "Yes, it is as you say" (v.64). Looking beyond his crucifixion, Jesus stated that he, the messianic Son of Man, would yet return in the future "coming on the clouds of heaven" (v.64). On the basis of that statement, the high priest condemned Jesus of blasphemy. Peter, as Jesus had foretold (vv.31–35), denied him three times.

Having condemned Jesus to death, the chief priests and elders handed him over to the Roman governor, Pilate (27:1–2). Matthew goes to great lengths to demonstrate Jesus' innocence. Before taking his own life, for example, Judas, his betrayer, confessed he had "betrayed innocent blood" (v.4), but the chief priests were unwilling to take back their money, confessing it to be "blood money" (v.6). Pilate, in "great amazement" (v.14), was unable to find a valid charge against Jesus. Pilate's wife sent him a message to have nothing "to do with that innocent man" (v.19). The crowd called for the freedom of a murderer, Barabbas, over that of Jesus (vv.15–21), choosing instead to have Jesus crucified (v.22) for no apparent reason (v.23). Finally Pilot, washing his hands before the crowd, stated, "I am innocent of this man's blood. . . . It is your responsibility" (v.24). The crowd readily consented, "Let his blood be on us and on our children!" (v.25).

In utter humiliation (vv.27–31, 41–44), Jesus was crucified (vv.32–56). At the moment of his death, the curtain of the temple was torn (v.51), the earth shook (v.51), the tombs broke open, "and the bodies of many holy people who had died were raised to life" (v.52). The Roman centurion and guards, terrified, said, "Surely he was the Son of God" (v.54). These events bear a marked similarity to those of Daniel's vision of the coming of the Son of Man: "There will be a time of distress. . . . Multitudes who sleep in the dust of the earth will awake" (Da 12:1–2). The Messiah was cut off (Da 9:26) and, as Jesus had said (Mt 24:1–2), "the people of the ruler who will come will destroy the city and the sanctuary. The end will come like a flood" (Da 9:26). Matthew surely has an eye on the text of Daniel as he records these events of the death of Jesus.

## IV. The Resurrection (28:1–20)

Matthew assures his readers that Jesus' tomb was secured, lest "his disciples come and steal the body and tell the people that he [had] been raised from the dead" (27:64). Thus, when he writes of the Resurrection, there can be no talk of hoax. As the angel first announced the birth of Jesus to his mother, Mary (1:18), so now the angel announced his resurrection to the two Marys at the tomb (28:1). While the guards were being paid off to tell a different story (vv.11–15), the women, having seen Jesus on their way back to Jerusalem (vv.9–10), were joyfully telling the disciples what they had seen.

Jesus, having met his disciples in Galilee, sent his disciples out to "make disciples of all nations," promising to be with them till the end of the age (vv.19–20). Matthew's gospel has reached its climax, the end toward which it was heading—the good news was now to be proclaimed to Gentiles as well as to the Jews.

# Mark

## Introduction

The gospel of Mark makes no mention of its author. The title, "According to Mark," is found on the earliest manuscripts of this gospel, but these manuscripts date from the fourth century A.D. The book is thus an anonymous work and was apparently intended to be read as such. Early tradition places the writing of this gospel in Rome, after the persecutions of Nero (A.D. 64)—i.e., about 65–70. Whatever we might conclude regarding the accuracy of these earliest traditions, we should in no case allow them to influence our understanding of the book itself. It is enough that we know the book was already in circulation in the first stages of the early church.

The argument of Mark can be seen both in its content and in the overall structure or shape that the author gives to the book. We should note a few points about the content of Mark's gospel, both in terms of what is in the book and what is not. Many of the aspects of the ministry of Jesus that are found in the other gospels are not included in Mark. There is no discussion of his birth, early life, family, and genealogy. The gospel begins with the ministry of John the Baptist, who announced the coming of the Messiah (1:2–8). Moreover, little attention is paid to the teaching of Jesus. Mark focuses on the actions and events of his life, such as his death and resurrection. The only important exception to this is Jesus' eschatological discourse in ch. 13. The inclusion of this material betrays Mark's interest in the "last days" and the role of Jesus in fulfilling the eschatological hope of ancient Israel.

Mark's primary interest lies in the key events of the last week in the ministry of Jesus Christ, i.e., in Christ's death and resurrection. The proportionally large final section of the book (chs. 11–16) is devoted solely to Christ's last seven days in Jerusalem.

The major turning point in the book's portrayal of Jesus comes with Peter's confession in 8:29, "You are the Christ." After this the focus of this gospel is on the death and resurrection of Christ (see 8:31).

Throughout the book itself, the author strategically focuses the reader's attention on key, theologically important aspects of the ministry of Christ by means of summary statements and repetition. Mark begins with the statement that Jesus is the "Christ, the Son of God" (1:1). At the close of the first section (the account of the ministry of John the Baptist), the confirmation of Jesus as the messianic Son of God is again stated by a voice from heaven, "You are my Son, whom I love; with you I am well pleased" (1:11). At the center of the book, on the Mount of Transfiguration, a voice from heaven again says, "This is my Son. Listen to him!" (9:7). Then at the end of the book, the Roman centurion exclaims, "Surely this man was the Son of God!" (15:39).

Thus Mark's gospel is concerned with the question of the identity of Jesus as the messianic Son of God. Not only is this reinforced through the divine voice that spoke from heaven at the time his baptism and transfiguration, but it is also acknowledged by the Gentile centurion at the cross. At the center of the book, Jesus himself raises the question: "Who do people say I am?" (8:27). Though Peter and the other disciples recognized him and confessed him to be the Messiah, it is clear from Mark's gospel that the leaders of God's people, the Jews, did not. The picture of Jesus in Mark, therefore, seems consciously modeled on that of the Messiah in the OT. He is One who came to deliver his own people but whom they rejected and scorned (see Isa 53:3).

# I. The Beginning (1:1–13)

## A. The Prologue (1:1)

Mark describes Jesus from the very start as the "Son of God" (v.1). Is this verse a title of the book as a whole or only of the first section of Mark (1:2–13)? The context suggests that Mark intended this first verse both as an introduction to the book and as a description of its first major section, the ministry of John the Baptist, which is, strictly speaking, "the beginning" of the gospel (cf. Ac 1:22). It may be a part of Mark's larger purpose to fill out the content of the gospel to include its "beginning" with John. This would have the effect of including, as well, all the works of Christ during his earthly ministry as part of "the gospel."

## B. John the Baptist 1:2–8

Mark begins his account of the ministry of John the Baptist with a quotation that combines three OT passages: Ex 23:20; Mal 3:1; (4:5); Isa 40:3. These passages identify John the Baptist as the fulfillment of the promise of a "messenger" who was to come in preparation for the Messiah. According to Mal 4:5, the messenger was to be the prophet Elijah. Mark appears to understand that to mean the "messenger" would be a prophet "like Elijah," in the same way that the Messiah was to be a prophet "like Moses" (cf. Dt 18:15; 34:10).

Central to Mark's description of John is his emphasis on the forgiveness of sins. John's baptism was "a baptism of repentance for the forgiveness of sins" (v.4). Already Mark is preparing the way for his presentation of Jesus as the servant of the Lord who would take away the sin of the world. John's words, "I baptize you with water, but he will baptize you with the Holy Spirit" (v.8) should be understood in light of the OT view of the messianic kingdom. Upon the coming of the Messiah, God would gather the people of Israel, sprinkle

them clean with water, and put his spirit within them (Eze 36:24–28).

## C. The Baptism and Temptation of Jesus (1:9–13)

Mark introduces Jesus in v.9 with an account of his baptism and the descent of the Spirit upon him. Jesus, identifying with his sinful nation, was baptized by John. As he came up out of the water, the heavens were "torn open," the Spirit descended upon him as a dove, and a voice was heard to say, "You are my Son, whom I love; with you I am well pleased" (v.11). In these events and words there is an identification of Jesus as the Spirit-filled messianic prophet of Isa 61:1, the messianic Davidic King in Ps. 2:7, and the Servant of the Lord in Isa 42:1.

# II. The Beginnings of the Galilean Ministry (1:14–3:6)

## A. Summary Statement (1:14–15)

Verses 14–15 establish the framework of the events of Jesus' Galilean ministry. Mark telescopes into a short span the ministry of Jesus that took place before the imprisonment of John the Baptist. A similar summary statement is found at the beginning of the other major sections of Mark's gospel (3:7–12; 6:6b).

Mark gives a summary of the message that Christ preached: "The time has come. . . . The kingdom of God is near. Repent and believe the good news." Jesus preached the good news of the impending kingdom of God. In fulfillment of Isa 9:1, Jesus preached this message first in Galilee. As the concept of the kingdom of God comes into clearer focus throughout the book of Mark, we will see that it is fundamentally shaped by Daniel's vision of the messianic Son of Man who was to receive God's kingdom and rule over all nations "in the last days" (see coments on Da 7:10–14).

### B. The Call of the Disciples (1:16–20)

Four disciples were called: Peter, Andrew, James, and John. They were all fishermen. Mark's purpose is clearly to highlight Jesus' promise to make his disciples "fishers of men." Mark returns to the theme of the call to discipleship at the opening of each of the subsequent major sections (3:13–19; 6:7–13). We can thus see that Mark's gospel, like Matthew's, was intended as instruction in discipleship. Jesus is presented as a model for Christian discipleship.

### C. Jesus in the Synagogue at Capernaum (1:21–28)

Mark wants to show that the message of Jesus regarding the coming of the kingdom of God was backed up by divine authority. The demons recognized Jesus' authority and so did those who saw Jesus' miraculous deeds. The words of the demons reveal the age-old battle that was beginning to come to a head in the ministry of Jesus: "Have you come to destroy us?" (v.24). These words show that they were aware of the battle foretold in Ge 3:15 and now moving into its final stage. Mark also demonstrates here, however, that though the battle has begun, the victory lies yet in the future. The ultimate defeat of the Devil would wait until the final victory over sin and death, i.e., in Jesus' own death and resurrection.

### D. Jesus Heals the Sick (1:29–34)

The purpose of the narrative of the first healing miracle of Jesus, Peter's mother-in-law (vv.29–31), is to demonstrate that Jesus had authority over physical disease. Mark also notes that Jesus would not permit the demons to speak "because they knew who he was." Mark thus asserts that Jesus had the authority to quiet the evil spirits; his victory over them is assured. The coming of the kingdom of God was not to be announced by the powers of evil. It was sufficient to show that their defeat meant that the kingdom was at hand.

### E. Jesus' Prayer and Departure (1:35–39)

Though the news of Jesus' miracles had attracted large crowds, Jesus went out alone to pray. Already Jesus' mission was beginning to baffle his disciples and we the readers as well. Finding Jesus in solitude they said, "Everyone is looking for you!" (v.37). Jesus, who knew well what his mission was, calmly explained that he had come to preach in the synagogues throughout the region of Galilee and that was what he intended to do. The reader is thus advised to listen more closely as the narrative unfolds to what Jesus' mission entailed. Jesus was not looking for large crowds. He was not looking for a great following built on his miracle-working. Jesus, as he explained to Peter, was sent by God to proclaim his message throughout all the land (v.38). Thus Jesus left Capernaum and traveled throughout Galilee "preaching and casting out demons" (v.39).

### F. The Healing of the Leper (1:40–45)

Jesus was approached by a leper and healed him. Mark no doubt intends this account as further evidence of Jesus' divine authority. His warning to the leper to keep silent about this deed, to go to the priest, and to offer the necessary gift for cleansing shows that Jesus followed all the requirements of the Mosaic Law. He did not offer a new way of approaching God. Rather, he saw himself as the fulfillment of the old.

### G. Conflicts (2:1–3:35)

In chs. 2–3 Mark brings together a series of isolated incidents, each of which involves Jesus in a conflict with the Jewish leaders. Mark has grouped these accounts closely together, concentrating on the developing conflict between Jesus and the religious leaders. As a background to this conflict, we can also see the growing popularity of Jesus with the common people. Mark has made it clear that Jesus did not seek popular approval. In fact, he constantly discouraged it. But as his popularity grew, so did the opposition. Mark concludes these accounts with the ultimate confrontation between Jesus and the Jewish leaders—their accusation that Jesus was in collusion with Beelzebub (3:20–30).

The first dispute between Jesus and the Jewish leaders is set within the context of the account of healing of the paralytic (2:1–12). The account shows clearly Mark's overall purpose in writing this gospel—to show that Jesus came to forgive sins and that he did so with divine authority. The issue is raised by the Jewish leaders who were offended by Jesus' claim to forgive the paralytic's sin (v.5). In his answer to their questioning of his authority, Jesus showed that his power over disease was tantamount to authority to forgive sins. Their questions also served to demonstrate Jesus' divine authority. They asked, "Who can forgive sins but God alone?" (v.7). If one can heal disease, which is beyond dispute after the events of ch. 1, then it follows that he can forgive sins, since both of these powers are worthy of God alone.

The second conflict story (2:13–17) is set within the context of the call of the tax-collector Matthew and the banquet at his house. The conflict began (v.16) when the "teachers of the law" saw Jesus eating with "tax-collectors and 'sinners'" and were ostensively offended. In his reply to them Jesus used the proverb: "It is not the healthy who need a doctor, but the sick" (v.17). In this reply, Jesus gave a clear, though veiled, indication of his mission—to call sinners to God.

The question of fasting (2:18–22) provides the next conflict story. The question is that of religious practice, specifically, obedience to the OT law. In treating this question, Mark provides the reader with an assessment of the relationship of Jesus both to the traditional Jewish interpretation of the law and to that of John the Baptist. Jesus again answered their question by stating a proverb: "How can the guests of the bridegroom fast while he is with them?" (v.19). Jesus is thus saying that his gospel is fundamentally different from what John offered his disciples or from what the Pharisees offered theirs. What John's disciples were waiting for in their fasting has already come. Jesus is that salvation that John preached. Jesus' words thus reinforced the central theme of ch. 1.

In vv.21–22 Jesus gave two additional proverbs that illustrate the truth that he had just stated. The time of expectation and the time of realization are distinct. They are like new cloth and old garments, or new wine in old wineskins. The two "times" do not overlap. Thus Jesus' disciples need not fast as an act of expectation, but rather they should rejoice that the time is at hand.

In v. 20 Jesus adds a comment that goes beyond the question asked him. A time will come, he says, when the bridegroom will be taken away. Then his disciples will fast. At his baptism, Mark presented Jesus in the role of the suffering servant of Isaiah. Here again Mark alludes to the events that lie ahead. Jesus will be taken away by his crucifixion. The reference to this future time is veiled within Jesus' use of parables. Only later would his disciples look back at this statement and see what he meant. Mark's gospel is, in fact, a part of, or a result of, that later reflection.

The next conflict story (2:23–28) arises out of an incident in which Jesus and his disciples were passing through a grain field on the Sabbath. His disciples took some of the grain as they passed by and began to eat it. The Pharisees, who were following along with the crowd, interpreted this as work and thus saw the disciples as violating the Sabbath. Jesus answered their accusation by an appeal to a scriptural example—David's flight from Saul at Nob (1Sa. 21). The key words in the 1 Samuel passage are "not lawful." David also did that which was unlawful, but the Scriptures do not condemn him for it. In this passage, then, Jesus provides an example of an appeal to a higher principle than the strictly legalistic application of the Sabbath or any other law. That higher principle is embodied in the proverb: "The Sabbath was made for man, not man for the Sabbath" (v.27). Jesus appeals here to Ge 1–2. In the logic of that passage, God's setting apart the seventh day as a day of rest, the Sabbath (Ge 2:3), is viewed as his final gift to his newly created human beings. Adam and Eve were not created to work for God but to worship God.

After another conflict story (3:1–6), the Jewish leaders began to plan how to destroy Jesus. That story took its occasion from a healing in a synagogue on the Sabbath. Mark informs his readers that the Jewish leaders were watching to see if Jesus would heal a man with a shriveled hand on the Sabbath so that they could accuse him. From Mark's perspective, these leaders had clearly misunderstood the law of the Sabbath. When Jesus put the issue clearly before them, they were silent. Angered by their silence, Jesus healed the man by restoring his hand. This incident goes far beyond the previous Sabbath controversy. The question here was not one of need; the withered hand could be healed the next day with no significant difference. The issue now was the more general question of doing good. This story shows that the legalism of the scribes had so bound the law that it had become impossible to do good by keeping it.

It is this event that marked the beginning of the plots to destroy Jesus (3:6). With the hatching of these plots Mark concludes this section. The die is being cast for the death of Jesus, the Servant of the Lord.

## III. Later Stages of the Galilean Ministry (3:7–6:29)

### A. Summary Statement (3:7–12)

The latter part of Jesus' Galilean ministry is described in summary fashion. Jesus had withdrawn from the city to the Sea of Galilee. Large crowds followed him there. Also large crowds came to him from all parts of Palestine. Mark reiterates Jesus' authority over the unclean spirits and his preventing them from revealing his identity.

### B. Appointment of the Twelve (3:13–19)

The twelve disciples are appointed by name. Mark notes specifically that the Twelve were also appointed as "apostles" (v.14), thus clarifying the identity of an apostle as one sent from the beginning to preach with authority (cf. comment on Ac 1:22).

### C. Opposition From Jerusalem (3:20–35)

This account gives an assessment of the judgments that were being formed about Jesus—by his kinsmen and by the religious leaders in Jerusalem. The charge made by the teachers of the law from Jerusalem is stated in v.22—"He is possessed by Beelzebub! By the prince of demons he is driving out demons." Jesus demonstrates that such a charge was gravely dangerous and false (vv.23–27). The parable is concluded with a stern warning that blasphemy against the Holy Spirit is unforgivable (v.29).

Mark, apparently sensing the severity of Jesus' words, adds the explanation in v.30 that Jesus had warned the scribes in this instance because "they were saying, 'He has an unclean spirit'" (v.30). This passage has troubled many people throughout the history of the church and, given Mark's special attention to it, must have been a question already in his day: What is blasphemy against the Holy Spirit? On this issue we can say five things:

(1) There is a warning here against speaking evil of the Holy Spirit. This should not be minimized.

(2) It should always be born in mind that the blasphemy spoken of here is an overt, calloused attack against the Spirit. Thus it can be a matter of absolute certainty that anyone who is afraid he or she has committed this sin should be comforted by the very concern itself. There is a distinct contrast between speaking against the Son of Man and speaking against the Spirit. The point is that even blasphemy against the Son of Man is forgivable, but not so against the Spirit. Thus blasphemy against the Spirit is evil in the extreme.

(3) The use of the verb tense here indicates that the sin of the scribes was not just the uttering of a sentence, but rather a "fixed attitude of mind." Both Matthew and Luke add, "Knowing their thoughts he said to them. . . ."

(4) It is not said that the scribes had actually committed this sin already, and it may be that Jesus is warning them that what they are saying comes close to blasphemy if they persist. It is true that later on many of these same people would hear the preaching of Peter, and Peter would call upon them to repent and follow Christ.

(5) Finally, there is the example of Paul (Saul) who said in 1Ti 1:13, "Even though I was once a blasphemer and a persecutor and a violent man, I was shown mercy because I acted in ignorance and unbelief."

## D. The Parables of the Kingdom (4:1–34)

This section of Mark's gospel represents a major turning point in the ministry of Jesus. Jesus had come teaching that "the kingdom of God is at hand" (1:15). His message, however, had not been widely received by the people to whom the kingdom had been promised in the OT. At the end of ch. 3, Mark shows that the leaders of the people had rejected the kingdom that Jesus offered them. Mark's narrative has made it clear that their rejection of Jesus did not take him by surprise. There was to be a time when the bridegroom would be taken away from his own (2:20). Nevertheless, the idea that the kingdom could come and yet be rejected by God's people was a new idea in the Bible's eschatology. Mark thus gives his readers a sampling of Jesus' parables to help explain the nature of this new idea.

The parable of the sower (vv.3–20) shows that only a few of those who hear the word of Christ will accept it. The parable of the lamp set on a stand (vv.21–25) teaches that even though the message of Christ is a mystery to some, it should be proclaimed to all. The parable of the growing seed (vv.26–29) teaches that God alone is responsible for the growth of Christ's kingdom. The parable of the mustard seed (vv.30–32) shows that the ultimate success of Christ's kingdom is assured precisely because God will give it its growth.

Verse 11 introduces two important terms: "mystery" and "the kingdom of God." A "mystery" is a truth previously unknown that now has been revealed. Jesus distinguishes between those who know the "mystery" of the kingdom of God and those who only receive the parable. In other words, the parable is a way of both revealing and concealing the truth about God's kingdom (see v.12).

"The kingdom of God" is not a term upon which all agree. Some make a distinction between the kingdom of heaven (the rule of God over earth, excluding angels and other creatures) and the kingdom of God (God's rule over all creatures and things, including the kingdom of heaven). In this schema, the domain of the kingdom of heaven is only a part of the kingdom of God. It is the messianic kingdom that will be realized on earth during the Millennium.

This kingdom of heaven was offered to the Jewish nation at the time of Christ, but it was rejected by them; thus its realization as a fulfillment of the OT prophecies was postponed.

Others identify the kingdom of heaven with the kingdom of God. According to them, the kingdom of God is God's redemptive reign whereby he establishes his rule among humankind. This kingdom, which will appear fully at the end of the age, has already come into human history in the person and mission of Jesus. Thus there is a dual aspect to the kingdom of God. It has a fulfillment within history (the first coming of Christ) and a consummation at the end of history (the second coming of Christ). The "mystery" of the kingdom is its first stage of coming into history prior to its final fulfillment—a teaching that the OT writers did not speak about; they saw only the one aspect of consummation of the kingdom. The first stage was as a mustard seed. Later the kingdom would come as a large tree filling all the earth. The church is the community of the kingdom but not the kingdom itself.

### E. Jesus' Power over the Enemies of Humankind (4:35–5:43)

In each of the next four accounts Jesus is portrayed as one who has authority over our great enemies: storms, spirits, disease, and death.

### 1. The calming of the storm (4:35–41)

The significance of Jesus' calming the raging sea lies in the role that the sea played in the OT. It was the great sea that God first divided to allow the dry lands to appear on behalf of humankind (Ge 1). When Adam and Eve forsook God's way, God was grieved and sent the sea back over the whole earth and all living beings (Ge 6–9). When God wanted to make known his power to save his people, he brought them to the Red Sea, and there "he rebuked the Red Sea, and it dried up" (Ps 106:9). Thus,

when Jesus stilled the raging sea, he was demonstrating that he had authority over humankind's and Israel's age-old enemy, the sea (cf. Ps 89:9; Isa 69:2, 15; 18:16).

The most prominent feature of this account is the question it leaves in the minds of the disciples: "Who is this? Even the wind and the waves obey him!" (4:41). Mark leaves the question unanswered in the minds of the disciples and his readers, but the answer is clear in light of the OT emphasis on God's power over the sea (cf. Job 38:8–11). There is no clearer demonstration of the deity of Jesus in the NT. He has the power of the Creator who can rebuke the sea and wind and bring calm.

### 2. The healing of the demoniac from Gerasenes (5:1–20)

The demoniac, like the sea, raged out of control, posing a threat to all who walked by. When Jesus confronted him, the man, like the sea, became calm, "sitting there, dressed and in his right mind" (v.15). When the people of the region saw the work of Jesus, they, like the disciples earlier in the boat, "were afraid" and "began to plead with Jesus to leave their region." Those who heard the news from the demoniac himself "were amazed" (v.20). Mark's purpose is to show that Jesus had begun to do the mighty works of God among the people of Israel and the nations. He thus gives clear evidence that the kingdom of God was at hand.

### 3. The healing of the woman with an issue of blood and the raising of the dead girl (5:21–43)

Mark begins the narrative with the call to Jesus by Jairus, the lay leader of the synagogue. On his way to heal the ruler's daughter, Jesus was met by a woman with a bleeding problem, a condition that had lasted twelve years. She secretly touched Jesus in the crowd, hoping to be made well (v.28). Mark has already shown that many had come to Jesus to be healed just by touching him (3:10; cf. 6:56). Thus the narrative itself has informed us that the woman, as many had done already, wanted to be healed by touching his garments. Upon being touched, Jesus perceived that the power went forth from him (v.40). Jesus knew the woman had been healed when she touched him.

While Jesus was speaking to the woman, the servants of the ruler's household came to tell him that his daughter was dead (v.35). They asked: "Why bother the Teacher any more?" concluding that Jesus had no authority over death. When Jesus told them that the child was not dead but only sleeping, they laughed at him. But Jesus, knowing his authority even over death, knew that he had power to raise her. The people, who saw Jesus as a healer and miracle worker, were "completely astonished" at his demonstration of power even over death. Thus this section of Mark's gospel closes with an exhibition of the authority of Jesus over the greatest of our enemies—death.

### F. Rejection of Jesus at Nazareth (6:1–6a)

Mark concludes his narrative of the ministry of Jesus in Galilee by an account of his rejection in his own city. The words of the close friends of Jesus' family ("Isn't this Mary's son?") provide a striking contrast to Mark's overall presentation of Jesus as "the Son of God" (e.g., 1:1, 11). Their question, which remains unanswered within this narrative, receives a resounding reply in the words of the centurion standing beneath the cross when Jesus died: "Surely this man was the Son of God" (15:39).

Jesus used a proverb to explain his rejection: "Only in his hometown, among his relatives and in his own house is a prophet without honor" (v.4). Through this proverb, Mark gives further proof that Jesus' claims were true. His rejection in his own city proves he was a true prophet!

## IV. Jesus Goes Outside Galilee (6:6b–8:26)

### A. Summary Statement (6:6b)

Mark now begins to move the narrative away from Galilee and in the direction of Jerusalem. As yet it is imperceptible, but as the events unfold, that final destination comes into sharper focus.

### B. Sending of the Twelve (6:7–13)

In 3:14 we were told that Jesus chose his disciples "that he might send them out to preach and to have authority to drive out demons." Jesus now began to use them for this purpose. Mark presents them as those sent ahead of Jesus to prepare the way for his coming. This sending immediately began to draw fire from Jerusalem (cf. 3:22). Thus Mark turns our attention to Herod in the next section and gives us a glimpse of the spread of God's kingdom from within the enemy camp.

### C. Opposition From Jerusalem (6:14–29)

The account of the death of John the Baptist is inserted here within that of the sending of the Twelve (which concludes in 6:30), even though that death happened much earlier. Mark places the death of John here because it is of strategic importance to him. The opposition that Jesus was beginning to face from Herod is the same as that which John the Baptist had already received. Just as Herod and those in Jerusalem had opposed John, a true prophet sent from God, so also they were now plotting against Jesus. The conclusion is transparent: Jesus also is a true prophet. Curiously, Herod himself acknowledged that John was a true prophet in that he believed that John had "been raised from the dead" (6:16).

### D. Feeding of the Five Thousand (6:30–44)

The account of the feeding of five thousand is linked to the sending of the

Twelve (6:7–13) in v. 30. When the Twelve returned to Jesus they reported all they had accomplished and taught. Together, Jesus and the Twelve withdrew into the desert to rest. While there a large crowd gathered to hear Jesus teach. Mark's description of the crowd as "sheep without a shepherd" seems intended to link this scene with that of Israel in the desert (Nu 27:17); thus it provides a further link between the manna that the Israelites received in the desert and this account of the feeding of the five thousand.

Mark's reminder that after all had eaten their fill, there still remained twelve basketfuls of bread and fish (v.43) may be intended to show that Jesus' miracle even surpassed that in the days of Moses. In Moses' day "each one gathered as much [manna] as he needed" (Ex 16:18) but "no one [was] to keep any of it until morning" (Ex 16:19).

### E. Walking on the Sea (6:45–52)

Jesus' power over the sea is reminiscent of the Lord's use of Moses to conquer the Red Sea in the desert (Ex 14:21). Once again there appears to be a contrast between Moses' dividing the sea and walking through it on dry ground and Jesus "walking on the lake" (6:49). Just as Moses shouted to the people "Do not be afraid. Stand firm and you will see the deliverance the LORD will bring you today" (Ex 14:13), so Jesus tells his terrified disciples, "Take courage! It is I. Don't be afraid" (6:50).

Once again, Jesus' miracle seems to go beyond that of the events of Israel in the desert. As is the case of the desert narratives in the Pentateuch (see comments on Nu 14 and 21), Mark's conclusion here highlights the unbelief and hardness of heart of the disciples: "They had not understood about the loaves; their hearts were hardened" (6:52).

### F. Summary of Healings (6:53–56)

As an introduction to Mark's stress on the growing opposition of the leaders from Jerusalem, Mark gives a summary account of the crowds that Jesus' deeds were beginning to attract. It is, in fact, from within these large crowds that Jesus met opposition from "the Pharisees and some of the teachers of the law who had come from Jerusalem" (7:1).

### G. Teaching Against the Rules of the Pharisees (7:1–23)

A question about "washings" provides an occasion for a discourse on religious rites and rules. The Pharisees asked a specific question that assumes common ground with Jesus regarding the validity of the "traditions of the elders." Before recounting his answer, Mark clarifies for the reader that the tradition spoken of here is not that of the OT. It is rather Jewish custom (vv.3–4). Such a clarification is important because Jesus' answer undermines the basic premise of the Pharisees' question by rejecting the validity of their tradition: "Thus you nullify the word of God by your tradition" (v.13).

Once alone with his disciples, Jesus extends his teaching to the larger question of religious purity and purity of the heart (vv.18–23). It is possible that Jesus is here still speaking only of the Jewish customs relating to handwashings and not to the broader issue of the continuing relevance of the Mosaic food laws (in the OT). The author's comment in v.19b, however, clearly draws the broader conclusion from Jesus' words: "In saying this, Jesus declared all foods 'clean.'" Thus Mark sees in Jesus' words to his disciples a basis for the loosening, or even the abrogation, of the Mosaic dietary laws Such a message became much clearer in God's later revelation to Peter (see (Ac 10:9–16).

## H. Syrophoenician Woman (7:24–30)

We can clearly see the skill of the author in his selection of this short narrative to follow Jesus' discussion of the Jewish laws. Here a Gentile woman finds acceptance with God through her faith, apart from any dependence on the Jewish purity laws. Moreover, her request is for Jesus to cast an "evil [lit., unclean] spirit" out of her daughter. The narrative thus graphically illustrates the need to purify the heart. This is precisely the theme of the preceding passage, where Jesus said, "All these evils come from inside and make a man 'unclean'" (7:23).

## I. Deaf Man Healed (7:31–37)

According to the prophet Isaiah, when the promised Messiah comes, "the eyes of the blind will be opened and the ears of the deaf unstopped" (Isa 35:5). The following narratives provide specific examples of the fulfillment of this prophecy in the ministry of Jesus. The deaf man can hear (vv.31–37) and the blind man can see (8:22–26). Not only does Mark provide proof that this was fulfilled in the ministry of Jesus, but also it shows that the people in Jesus' day, both Jews and Gentiles, recognized this "with amazement."

## J. Blindness Removed (8:1–26)

In this section Mark has arranged several scenes to show the gradual process of Jesus' removing the blindness of those around him. First he recounts Jesus' feeding the four thousand (vv.1–9). As with the earlier story of feeding the five thousand (6:30–44), Mark's emphasis falls on the similarity between Jesus' miracle and God's gift of manna to the Israelites in the desert (Ex 16). Mark also emphasizes that unlike the manna, the bread provided by Jesus can be "left over" for continual provision. It is, in fact, this very point that Jesus stresses to his disciples in the next section when they are again worried that they have no bread to eat.

Mark's point is to show that unlike Moses in the desert, Jesus provides continuously over and above what they will need. This is what the disciples "still do not understand" (vv.14–21).

To show that such an understanding comes as a gradual process, Mark recounts the story of the healing of the blind man at Bethsaida (vv.22–26). When this man was "healed," he could see, but only partially (v.24). This man's sight provides the perfect picture of Mark's view of the disciples' faith. Only when Jesus touches him again he can see perfectly (v.25).

The growing faith of the disciples is contrasted with the permanent blindness of the Pharisees. They do not receive a sign from heaven because they come to test Jesus (vv.11–12). Thus when the disciples fail to appreciate the significance of Jesus' providing bread for the four thousand and five thousand and begin to worry that they have no bread (v.14), Jesus warns them of the "yeast of the Pharisees and that of Herod." That yeast was their hardness of heart and failure to understand what they saw and heard (vv.17–19).

In the following section (vv.27–30), Peter provides the perfect example of one who truly understands what he sees and hears. When asked by Jesus, "Who do you say I am?" Peter replies without hesitation, "You are the Christ." The disciples are like the blind man who sees, but only partially. Peter is like the man after Jesus has given him a second touch. He sees "everything clearly" (v.25).

## V. The Way to Jerusalem (8:27–10:52)

This section is the turning point of the book. Up to now Jesus has been silent about his full intentions to be delivered up to be killed and to suffer for the sins of the human race. There have been allusions and hints that he is the Servant of the Lord, but his disciples have not fully grasped the significance of his mission. He does many things they do not understand, and we must assume Mark's readers are not yet intended to understand. Here, at the turning point in the understanding of the disciples, is also the turning point of the understanding of Mark's readers. They too begin to see things "more clearly." From here on, the mission of Jesus becomes clear: He must be delivered up to die and to be raised again as the Messiah.

## A. Peter's Confession—the Turning Point (8:27–30)

While traveling outside Galilee, in Caesarea Philippi, Jesus began to ask the disciples what the people were saying about his ministry. It is clear from their answer that the people still had little understanding of who Jesus was. Jesus then asked the disciples: "But who do you say that I am?" It was Peter who answered, "You are the Christ" (v.21). Mark leaves this confession as the climax of the account.

Following Peter's confession, Jesus began to teach the disciples the full significance of what the title Messiah would mean. What follows, then, is a concentrated effort on the part of Jesus to instruct his disciples, and Mark his readers, concerning the immediate implications of his being the Messiah.

## B. Jesus' Teaching on the Messiah (8:31–33)

The chief element in the teaching of Jesus is the emphasis on the suffering and death of the Messiah: "The Son of Man must suffer many things and . . . be killed" (v.31). The primary OT passage underlying Jesus' teaching is Isa 53, where the messianic figure of the "servant of the Lord" pours out his soul in death for the sins of the people. For Mark, then, the crucifixion of Jesus, which he will record at the end of his book, is the means whereby Jesus gave his life as a ransom for many. It was the sacrificial death of the Son of God.

## C. Events on the Way to Jerusalem (9:1–10:52)

### 1. The Transfiguration (9:1–13)

Jesus said to his disciples, "Some who are standing here will not taste death before they see the kingdom of God come with power" (v.1). To show what Jesus had meant, Mark attached the account of the transfiguration of Christ in which Peter, James, and John "see the kingdom of God come with power." This brief glimpse of Jesus' future glory is only a foretaste of the kingdom, but it clearly demonstrates for the reader the nature of the kingdom and its power. Like Moses at Mount Sinai (Ex 34:29–35), Jesus "was transfigured" and became "dazzling white" (vv.2–3). Moses and Elijah, one of the two great prophets promised to return to announce the coming of the Messiah (cf. Dt 18:15; 34:10; Mal 4:4–5), appeared along with Jesus. Peter, out of fear and not knowing what to say, wanted to memorialize the presence of these three great men of the Bible, but within an instant the Transfiguration, with its glimpse of the future, ended. Mark thus shows that the time of the establishment of the kingdom had not yet come. Jesus himself warned the three disciples that the time would not come until after the Resurrection (vv.9–10). That the time was at hand, however, is made clear by Jesus' own explanation that Elijah, the prophet who would prepare his people for the coming of the Messiah, had already come. It seems certain, within the context of the gospel of Mark, that Jesus was referring to John the Baptist (cf. 1:1–8).

### 2. The healing of the possessed boy (9:14–32)

The story of the healing of the possessed boy turns on two different but related points. It first shows that faith is the key to God's work and power. When the disciples were unable to drive out the evil spirit, Jesus replied, "O unbelieving generation . . . how long shall I stay with you?" This at first appears to be addressed only to the disciples, but then Jesus, turning further to the boy's father, said, "Everything is possible for him who believes." The father confessed, "I do believe," but then added, "help me overcome my unbelief!" Thus without placing the blame directly on either the disciples or the father, Jesus stressed the central importance of faith.

The second issue at play within this narrative comes from the father's further request, "Help me overcome my unbelief!" and from Jesus' final statement to the disciples, "This kind can come out only by prayer." Behind the call to faith is a further call for more faith. Faith must grow to maturity. Though an element of faith was present with the disciples and the father, it was not sufficient to cast out the evil spirit. Both the father and the disciples needed a stronger faith. Mark is here challenging his readers to go beyond an initial recognition of Jesus as the Son of God; they must strengthen their faith through prayer. What kind of prayer? The answer lies in the father's request, "Help me overcome my unbelief!" (v.24). When the father asked for more faith, the son was healed. Thus Mark sees the need for prayer as a need to seek more faith.

The need for more faith, both on the part of the disciples and the readers of Mark's gospel, is reinforced in the following segment, vv.30–32. Here Jesus again reminds the disciples of his impending betrayal and death. The disciples, however, "did not understand what he meant and were afraid to ask him about it." The readiness of the boy's father to ask Jesus for more faith is thus contrasted with the disciples' reticence to ask Jesus for more understanding.

### 3. Questions (9:33–10:12)

Mark has grouped a series of narratives that focus on questions the disciples and followers of Christ will face in the future. At the same time, he has interwoven several warnings of Jesus regarding his impending death in Jerusalem (9:31; 10:32–34, 38, 45). The picture of Jesus that emerges is of one who has an immediate mission but who, at the same time, is well aware of the fact that the consequences of that mission extend far into the future. He is preparing his disciples for both. Mark, of course, also has his eye on both for the sake of the reader.

The first question raised by the disciples is, "Who is the greatest?" (9:33–37). Jesus' answer is simply that those who would be great must come to him as a little child. John then raises the question of those who work in Jesus' name but who do not associate with the disciples (vv.38–50). Jesus' answer is presented in the form of a proverb: "Whoever is not against us is for us." He then explains this to mean that anything done in Jesus' name will be rewarded (vv.39–41). Conversely, anything done to hinder belief in Jesus will be punished (vv.42–50).

The Pharisees now raise the question of divorce (10:1–12). Mark says specifically that their intent was to test Jesus, apparently about the meaning of the law. Mark uses the occasion to teach his readers about Jesus' use of the law. The law regarding divorce, he says, was given "because your hearts were hard" (v.5); it was not God's intent from the beginning (v.6). The emphasis regarding the purpose of the law for Israel is similar to that of Paul in Gal 3:19.

### 4. Discourses on the Kingdom of God (10:13–52)

Mark now records five narratives that focus on the nature of the kingdom of God. The kingdom is to be received as a little child (vv.13–16). The rich will enter the kingdom only with great difficulty (vv.17–27). Discipleship will have its reward in the kingdom (vv.28–31). Greatness in the kingdom will be characterized by service, not by privilege (vv.32–45). The King of the kingdom is the promised Son of David (vv.46–52). Salvation comes to those who have faith in this King: "Your faith has saved [NIV, healed] you" (10:52; cf. Ps 2:12).

# VI. Ministry in Jerusalem (11:1–13:37)

## A. The Entry into Jerusalem (11:1–11)

With the entry of Jesus into Jerusalem on a donkey, the Messiah promised in the prophets is officially presented to the Jews. His coming into Jerusalem fulfilled the prophecy of Zec 9:9. In that passage the Messiah is depicted as a victorious King, bringing salvation and peace to a rejoicing nation. Zechariah's king was "gentle and riding on a donkey," but his dominion "will extend from sea to sea" (cf. Zec 9:9–10). In drawing on the OT image of the coming messianic king, Mark focuses our attention on the promised King of the House of Judah (Ge 49:8–12) coming in meekness to his people but also in victory over his enemies.

In 11:10 the crowd shouts, "Blessed is the coming kingdom of our father David," but already by v.11 the crowd is gone as quickly as it came. With only his disciples, Jesus left the city he had just entered and returned to Bethany alone. Thus very quickly Mark has turned our attention to the rejection of Jesus. He has not dwelled long on the initial, and short-lived, reception. The narratives that follow will provide more details about what happened to the people's hope. This is the first and last popular show of support for Jesus in Jerusalem. Like the fig tree, they had withered from the root by the next day (11:12–14, 20–21). In the entry into Jerusalem, then, we have the official presentation of the King to his people and their consequent failure to accept his kingdom. The King leaves Jerusalem without his people.

## B. The Barren Fig Tree and the Cleansing of the Temple (11:12–25)

The fig tree is cursed for not producing fruit. Mark adds the explanation that the figs were not in season—thus Jesus was cursing the tree, not simply because it had not produced fruit, but because it was a symbol of the unfaithfulness of the people of God.

Like the fig tree, the worship of the people at the temple was not pleasing to God. There was no faith there. Jesus drove out those who focused on the external aspects of Israel's worship. His actions were a warning of impending judgment on this people.

## C. Controversy at the Temple (11:27–12:34)

Mark includes five brief narratives that show the nature of the controversy that arose between Jesus and the Jewish leaders. Most of the discussion takes place within the temple courts. Several different groups approach Jesus with their questions: the chief priests, the teachers of the law, the elders, the Pharisees and Herodians, and the Sadducees. The section ends with the brief and curious interchange between Jesus and "one of the teachers of the law" who approached him individually after the others. Unlike the others, Jesus said to this one, "You are not far from the kingdom of God." Thus there are two main groups represented in these controversies: the religious leaders who sought only to find fault in Jesus' teaching and the one who truly seeks wisdom.

### 1. Question of Jesus' authority (11:27–33)

Mark begins with the question of the authority of Jesus. The chief priests, the teachers of the law, and the elders asked Jesus, "By what authority are you doing these things?" Mark shows that they were caught off guard by Jesus' reply. Jesus related the question of his authority to the larger question of the ministry of John the Baptist. The Jerusalem leaders were unwilling to commit themselves on this subject before the crowds. In developing this narrative, Mark has a double purpose. (1) He wants to expose the hypocrisy of the religious leaders. We, the readers, are given the necessary inside information to see through their answer about John the Baptist: "They feared the people, for everyone held that John really was a prophet" (v.32). Thus we see that their answer in v.33 is only a political retreat. (2) Mark is able again to establish at least a tacit connection between John the Baptist and Jesus, a recurrent theme in this gospel since the beginning (1:2–8). A new aspect is added, however, in that here Mark shows that even the leaders in Jerusalem were willing to concede the connection. By their silence they left unchallenged Jesus' implicit claim to the same authority as John.

### 2. The wicked tenants (12:1–12)

Having identified the key characters in the controversy that now ensues, Mark carries it a step further by recounting Jesus' parable of the wicked tenants. This parable, Mark says, was addressed to these same leaders (v.1). That Jesus was in fact speaking about them is transparent from the parable itself, but Mark nevertheless tells us that the religious leaders recognized themselves in what Jesus had said (v.12). It is important to note that in this parable Jesus continues to draw a connection between himself and John the Baptist. The parable is about Israel's treatment of the prophets (including John) throughout their long history; "some of them they beat, others they killed" (v.5). It is also important to see that in this parable Jesus again anticipates his own death at their hands (see vv.7–8). The parable thus exposes the plans of the chief priests and teachers of the law who, Mark has already informed us, were "looking for a way to kill him" (11:18).

### 3. Question of taxes to Caesar (12:13–17)

This narrative addresses an issue that must have been crucial in Mark's day, if not also in Jesus' day. Did Jesus' controversy with the leaders in Jerusalem also pit him against the Roman authorities? Unwittingly on their part, the attempt of the Pharisees and Herodians to catch Jesus in his words only served to further Mark's purpose to show that Jesus bore no malice against Rome. He was not a rebel; he was a revivalist. Again, as elsewhere in Mark, Jesus answered his accusers with a proverb: "Give to Caesar what is Caesar's and to God what is God's" (v.17).

### 4. Question of the resurrection (12:18–27)

We might well ask if Mark has a clear strategy for including this particular narrative at this point in the book. The question raised by the Sadducees is apparently intended as an argument against the notion of a resurrection, since, as Mark tells us, they "say there is no resurrection." Jesus does not answer their specific question in v.23 but rather assails the apparent lack of understanding that lies behind it. What they failed to see is that the Scriptures speak of a future that is to be altogether different than the past or the present. To understand God's work in Scripture, one cannot merely project the present order into the future. The resurrection will be a totally different life than present human existence; "they will be like the angels in heaven" (v.25).

In Jesus' answer, we see Mark's purpose. Jesus reads Moses and the OT Scriptures differently than the Jewish leaders. The resurrection will not mean a return to the status quo; it will mean a new order of life. Jesus' own resurrection, which he has anticipated numerous times already in the book, will mark the beginning of that new order.

## 5. The great commandment (12:28–34)

Mark concludes this section of controversies on the positive note of agreement between Jesus and one of the scribes. Jesus is approached by one of the teachers of the law who saw that Jesus "had given them a good answer." He then posed a question to Jesus, apparently out of sincere interest, and not merely to trap him. His question goes to the heart of Jesus' own teaching: What is the essence of the Law? When Jesus replied that the Law's essence is to love God and your neighbor, the scribe agreed and added by way of confirmation a central teaching from the OT Scriptures, "to love [God] . . . and to love your neighbor . . . is more important than all burnt offerings and sacrifices" (cf. Hos 6:6; Mic 6:8).

Such a view that love of God and one's neighbor is "more important" than the "burnt offerings and sacrifices" at the temple is considerably different than that of the Jews in Jesus' own day. Though many readily agreed that love of God and one's neighbor was "as important as" temple worship, the view of this particular scribe is unique. Seeing that he answered "wisely," Jesus said, "You are not far from the kingdom of God." Jesus does not mean that this scribe is "in" the kingdom of God, but rather, in his stress of the importance of love over burnt offerings, he has come near.

## D. Teaching at the Temple (12:35–44)

Mark concludes his account of Jesus' discourses at the temple with three examples of his teaching. In the first (vv.35–37), Jesus raises the issue of the Messiah as the Son of God. Referring to Ps 110, he asks, How can the scribes say that the Messiah is only an earthly king if David himself calls him Lord? The issue raised here lies at the base of Jesus' teaching about the kingdom of God that comes in ch. 13. The kingdom of God he proclaims is not an earthly kingdom. It is the heavenly kingdom, the reign of the Son of Man, that will be established here on earth in the last days.

A further lesson about the nature of the kingdom of God comes next in the form of a warning: Beware of teachers of the law who seek their own power and glory (vv.38–40). When the kingdom comes, "such men will be punished most severely."

Finally, Jesus gives the object lesson of the widow's penny (vv.41–44). The contrast is between the wealthy of this world who give only a portion of themselves to the work of God and the widow who gave "all she had to live on." Such is the nature of the kingdom of God. Mark now turns to Jesus' teaching regarding the time and nature of its coming.

## E. The End of the Age (13:1–37)

This is Mark's longest treatment of the teaching of Jesus. It clearly shows the importance he attaches to the subject. From the perspective of the readers of this gospel, one can see its central importance. It relates to their own hope and expectation of the return of Christ. Thus Mark devotes much space to Jesus' own treatment of the subject.

Jesus and the disciples have left the temple, and Jesus is speaking only with his followers. The discourse begins from an observation of the beauty of the temple by one of the disciples. Jesus then foretells the destruction of the temple, something that did, in fact, happen in A.D. 70 by the Romans.

Later, on the Mount of Olives, four of his disciples asked him, "When will these things happen? And what will be the sign that they are all about to be fulfilled?" As the subsequent discussion of Jesus shows, the disciples' question relates not to the time of the destruction of the temple but rather to the time of the appearance of the Son of Man (v.26). In response to these questions, Jesus immediately calls for discernment. They will have to distinguish between false claims that the times have arrived and true signs that the times are near. Jesus' key point at the opening of the discourse is that when they see the world around them go from bad to worse, they should take heed that this is not yet the end (v.7); it is only "the beginning" of the end (v.8). That is, there will be a specific time period of great distress before "the end" comes. When it does, only "he who stands firm to the end will be saved" (v.13).

Jesus now begins to describe what the "beginning" of the end will be like (vv.9–13). His description resembles some of the events that happened to the early Christians in the book of Acts: "You will be handed over to the local councils [Sanhedrins] and flogged in the synagogues" (v.9). But much of it goes far beyond those events, such as the event that Jesus describes in v.14, "'the abomination that causes desolation' standing where it does not belong." This event will signal the final moments before the end, a time of "distress [tribulation] unequaled from the beginning, when God created the world, until now—and never to be equaled again" (vv.19–25). The Lord, in his mercy on the elect, will cut this time period short (v.20), and at its conclusion the Son of Man will come in the clouds, gather the elect, and establish his kingdom (vv.26–27).

What is the "abomination that causes desolation"? Mark himself inserts a comment to the reader at this point in the text, calling on him to take special note. Why? Because the "abomination that causes desolation" is specifically developed elsewhere in Scripture (Da 9:25–27), and he wants his readers to draw on that passage for understanding of this one. Mark thus presupposes a general knowledge of "the events of the end." His intent is not to restate such matters, but rather to provide the reader with Jesus' own warn-

ings and admonitions about how his followers should live up to and during these days.

It is true that Christians through the ages have gained great strength and comfort from just these words of admonition. The world has never been without a time when much of what Jesus here speaks of was in evidence—e.g., wars and rumors of wars, earthquakes, and famines (vv.7–8). Indeed, individual Christians and groups of all kinds have believed strongly that this or that series of events in their own day was the signal of the end of which Jesus here speaks. Nevertheless, at no time in history have all of these events come together in a way that permits one to say Jesus' words have already been fulfilled. They still await fulfillment, along with all those unfulfilled prophecies from the OT Scriptures to which Jesus here alludes.

Thus Mark's purpose has not been lost on the church in their reading of this gospel. He concludes Jesus' discourse with the reminder, "No one knows about that day or hour"—not even the Son (v.32)! Therefore, Jesus says, "What I say to you, I say to everyone: 'Watch!'" (v.37).

## VII. The Death of Jesus (14:1–15:47)

### A. Events Leading up to His Death (14:1–52)

The chief priests and teachers of the law were plotting to kill Jesus (vv.1–2). Jesus was in Bethany at the home of Simon the leper (vv.3–9). Here a woman came to him with a vial of costly perfume and poured it over his head. Jesus interpreted her action as a prophetic act announcing his coming death. Thus Mark includes it here in his gospel as an introduction to the account of Jesus' death. At this same time, Judas was with the Jewish leaders giving them Jesus' whereabouts (vv.10–11).

In his account of the Last Supper (vv.12–26), Mark takes special note of the fact that the time of the Passover was at hand. He thus stresses the fact that the Last Supper was the Passover meal. This account of the meal serves two purposes within his gospel. (1) It demonstrates that the salvation of the Lord, which was commemorated in the Passover meal, was now about to be realized in the death of Jesus, and that it too was to be commemorated by God's people. This is especially seen in the interpretation of the meal given by Jesus, when he says, "This is my body"; "This is my blood of the covenant."

(2) Mark's account demonstrates that the death of Jesus was not a catastrophe that overtook Jesus, but rather something for which he had long prepared. Not only was Jesus' death anticipated by Jesus himself, but, Mark shows, the scattering of the disciples after his death was also known beforehand (v.27; Zec 13:7). Jesus also prepared them for his resurrection by his promise to go before them to Galilee after he had been raised (v.28).

In the account of Jesus' prayer in the garden (vv.33–42), one can again see the failure of Jesus' disciples to understand his mission. This was the time prepared by God, before the foundation of the world, when the ultimate sacrifice of his Son would be offered, but the disciples were asleep. They were slow to comprehend what was about to take place: "their eyes were heavy. They did not know what to say to him" (v.40). After the third time, still finding the disciples sleeping, Jesus said, "Are you still sleeping and resting? Enough! The hour has come" (v.41). At least part of Mark's purpose in developing this scene is to offer some explanation of the disciples' denial and abandonment of Jesus during the Crucifixion: "Then everyone deserted him and fled" (v.50). Just as Jesus found Peter sleeping three times, so also Peter publicly denied

Jesus three times (vv.66–72). There is a lesson here for Mark's readers: "Watch and pray so that you will not fall into temptation" (v.38).

The portrayal of Jesus' betrayal in Mark's gospel is guided by the author's intent to demonstrate that, as the Servant of the Lord (Isa 53), Jesus voluntarily gave himself as an offering. Though the guards came out for him armed with swords and weapons, Jesus reminded them that he was not a criminal to be taken by force; "Every day I was with you, teaching in the temple courts, and you did not arrest me" (v.49). He then stated that he was being taken because "the Scriptures must be fulfilled." This is one of many references to Isa 53: "He was led like a lamb to the slaughter . . . so he did not open his mouth. By oppression and judgment he was taken away" (Isa 53:7–8).

Mark gives a brief account of the "nakedness" of one of Jesus' followers who fled when he was arrested (vv.51–52). Mark may have in mind the Fall narrative, in which human nakedness is used as a picture of sin and the need for atonement, i.e., covering (Ge 3:7, 21).

## B. The Trial of Jesus (14:53–15:15)

After being arrested in the garden, Jesus was immediately taken to the home of the high priest, where the chief priests, elders, and teachers of the law had gathered. The council was the Sanhedrin, the official ruling body of the Jews in Palestine. The first stage of the trial consisted of testimonies against Jesus. In it, however, they were unable to find the necessary agreement among the witnesses to put Jesus to death (14:55). Mark adds the comment, "Many testified falsely against him." Jesus was not guilty of any charge. Like the Servant of the Lord (Isa 53), Jesus did not die for his own guilt but was delivered up on our behalf.

Seeing that the witnesses against Jesus could not convict Jesus, the high priest (Caiaphas) stepped forward to question him. Jesus remained silent, and Caiaphas asked: "Are you the Christ, the Son of the Blessed One?" (v.61). Jesus gave the simple answer, "I am," and he continued with quotations from Da 7:13 and Ps 110:1, both of which contain messianic prophecies. Thus Jesus acknowledged himself as the Messiah to the high priest.

Following the verdict, some of the men present began to mock Jesus for his messianic claim. At this same time, Mark recounts, Peter was below in the courtyard, denying Jesus: "He began to call down curses on himself, 'I don't know this man you're talking about'" (v.71). Peter thus serves as a stern reminder to Mark's readers of the need to remain faithful to Jesus in spite of the severest adversity.

Early the next morning the Sanhedrin met again to present their case against Jesus to Pilate (15:1–15). Jesus was charged with being the "king of the Jews." Jesus replied to this charge cryptically: "It is as you say [but I wouldn't put it that way myself]." In effect, Jesus remained silent throughout the entire ordeal (v.5). Behind Mark's emphasis on the silence of Jesus before his accusers lies the picture of the silent Suffering Servant of Isa 53:7. Before Pilate condemned Jesus to death, he made an additional effort to persuade the crowd against condemning Jesus, offering to release him as part of the festival custom. The crowd refused, asking for Barabbas to be released instead. For Mark this event was unmistakable testimony to the innocence of Jesus. Pilate, the Roman official, representing Roman law and jurisprudence, did all he could to free Jesus because he could find no fault with him. In the end, Pilate refused to condemn Jesus, turning him over instead to the crowd for a decision. The crowd shouted, "Crucify him!" (v.13). Pilate felt he had no choice but to deliver Jesus over to be crucified.

## C. The Crucifixion (15:16–41)

Roman law mandated that a conviction of capital punishment be carried out immediately. Capital punishment included not only beating and mistreatment before the execution, but also the victim was mocked and ridiculed as well. Jesus was forced to carry his cross to the site of his death, Golgotha. Jesus was offered a mixture of wine and myrrh, but he refused. Mark says, in summary fashion, only that "they crucified him" (v.24a). The narrative stresses the personal shame and sorrow of the crucifixion rather than physical pain. It thus lays great stress on the theological aspects of Christ's death and not merely the physical.

From noon ("the sixth hour") until mid-afternoon ("the ninth hour") a darkness fell over the whole land. At the end of that time, Jesus cried out, "My God, my God, why have you forsaken me?" and with another cry he died (v.37). These words come from Ps 22:1; they express the cry of the righteous Messiah for God's help as he bears the sin of the world.

In characteristic fashion, Mark immediately focuses on the crowds who mistakenly understood Jesus to be crying for Elijah. A Roman centurion standing near looked at Jesus and said: "Surely this man was the Son of God!" (v.39). Here Mark gives another witness to the genuineness of Jesus. In the words of this Roman officer, Mark sees the summation of his gospel: Jesus is the Son of God (cf. 1:1, 11).

Mark is not through with the story of Jesus, however. In fact, at this point he has completed only the first part of the creedal statement of the Gospel found in 1Co 15:3–8, i.e., Jesus, the Christ, the Son of God, died for our sins according to the Scriptures. He now turns to the remaining part of that creed, i.e., he was buried and rose again and appeared to Peter and then to the Twelve.

### D. The Burial (15:42–47)

Mark takes special care to report the details of Jesus' burial. A wealthy Jewish leader, Joseph of Arimathea, "who was himself waiting for the kingdom of God," courageously asked permission to bury Jesus. When Pilate learned that Jesus had died, he gave the body to Joseph (15:45). Mark, in recalling this incident, may have had Isa 53:9 in mind: "He was assigned a grave with the wicked, and with the rich in his death."

## VIII. The Resurrection of Jesus (16:1–8)

The main body of the gospel of Mark concludes with an account of the resurrection of Jesus. Mark focuses only on the empty tomb and the angel who announced to the women that Jesus had risen from the dead. The angel told the women to tell the disciples and Peter that they would see Jesus in Galilee, as he had told them (14:28). The women fled from the tomb "trembling and bewildered" and, out of great fear, told no one what they had seen and heard (16:8). The ending of Mark found in the NIV (vv.9–20) is not attested by the earliest manuscripts. Most believe it was attached to the end of the book at a much later date. It summarizes the last events of Jesus' time on earth after the Resurrection. Most of the material can be found in Matthew, Luke, and Acts.

# Luke

## A. Introduction

The gospel of Luke has the same author as the book of Acts. Both contain a prologue addressed to the same man—Theophilus. In Ac 1:1 the writer refers to "my former book" that he wrote to Theophilus, one concerning "all that Jesus began to do and teach until the day he was taken up." This description of the former account fits Luke precisely. A close study of the language and style of Luke and Acts shows that they were written by the same author. Neither book, however, names Luke as the author.

If we can reconstruct the identity of the author of Acts, then we can know the author of Luke. The author of the book of Acts is usually established on the basis of certain passages in which the author recounts events in the first person—the "we-sections." For example, Ac 1:1–16:9 is recounted in the third person, but at 16:10 the narrator uses the pronoun "we." Thus it is usually concluded that the author of Acts joined Paul at Troas and remained with him until Philippi (16:17). On the basis of a similar change from third to first person at 20:5, it appears that Paul was again joined by the author at Philippi and continued with Paul until they arrived in Jerusalem (21:17). After this time the author appears not to have been with Paul until 27:2, when he accompanied Paul aboard ship enroute to Rome. He arrived with Paul in Rome in 28:16.

Taking these "we-sections" as the starting point, then, by process of elimination, the identity of the writer who accompanied Paul can be established. (1) All individuals mentioned with Paul in the "we-sections" are eliminated on the assumption that since the writer is referring to himself in the first person, he would not otherwise give his name. (2) Then we must list all individuals

whom Paul mentions as being with him in Rome (in the Prison Letters; see Col 4:14; Phm 24; 2Ti 4:11) but who are not in the first group. This leaves Mark, Jesus Justus, Epaphras, Demas, Luke, and Epaphroditus. Such a process does not establish beyond doubt that Luke is the author of Luke-Acts, but it does show that he is a probable candidate. Here we must turn to the records of the early church. These records provide as straightforward evidence as possible that Luke was the companion of Paul who wrote Luke-Acts.

There is no indication of when the gospel of Luke was written. Those who deny the possibility of genuine prophecy date the gospel after A.D. 70, since they suppose this is the event spoken of by Christ in Lk 21:20–21: "When you see Jerusalem surrounded with armies, then you will know that its desolation is near. . . ."

According to Ac 1:1, Luke was written before Acts, though there is no indication of how long before. The book of Acts concludes with Paul staying in a Roman prison for two years in relatively good conditions (Ac 28:30). It may be that the author concludes at that point because he was at that point in Rome with Paul. Moreover, there are no indications of the persecutions under Nero (A.D. 64) or of the destruction of Jerusalem (A.D. 70). Thus, Luke may have been written some time prior to A.D. 64. How much earlier, we cannot say.

## I. Early History of the Forerunner and of the Messiah (1:1–2:52)

The purpose of this gospel is clearly stated in 1:1–4. The author states that there had been other similar works written about Jesus, some by eyewitnesses and others that relied on accounts handed down from eyewitnesses. Although he acknowledges that these works were written by "servants of the word" and hence of great value, he himself intends to go beyond them to give a more strictly chronological (NIV, "orderly," 1:3) account. In this way he intends his gospel to provide a firm basis for Christian teaching.

Reflecting this concern, Luke begins with John the Baptist, the first key figure in the series of events in the unfolding of the message of the gospel of Christ. Luke, however, begins not with John himself, nor with his call and ministry, but with his family heritage and birth. Like Jesus, John's birth was announced to his parents by an angel. As with the great prophets and patriarchs of the past (e.g., Isaac, Ge 11:30; Judah, Ge 29:31–35; Samuel, 1Sa 1:5–20), before his conception John's mother, Elizabeth, was barren (Lk 1:7). His birth was thus a miraculous sign that God was beginning to work among his people. There are numerous parallels between the birth of John and that of the prophet Samuel (1Sa 1:1–2:10). For example, Samuel was the forerunner of King David, just as John was the forerunner of the Son of David, the King.

Before recording the birth of John, Luke turns to the announcement of the birth of Jesus (1:26–56). The announcement and births of both key figures are closely intertwined in this gospel. The same angel, Gabriel, announced both births. John, in his mother's womb, "leaped for joy" (v.44) at the sound of the voice of Jesus' mother. John is like the prophet Jeremiah, set apart while still in his mother's womb (Jer 1:5). Even before the two sons were born, John acknowledged the coming of Jesus. We thus learn from Luke's gospel why it was that all Israel came out to hear John's message. He was a prophet of God, set apart with authentic biblical signs: "The Lord's hand was with him" (v 66). It was the prophet, the last of a long line, who was to announce the birth of Jesus, the Messiah.

All these events were the direct work of the Holy Spirit. John was to be "filled with the Holy Spirit even from birth" (v.15). Jesus was born of a virgin because of the Holy Spirit (v.35). Elizabeth, filled with the Holy Spirit, announced the blessing of the child Jesus, to be born to Mary (vv.41–42). Zechariah, John's father, prophesied by the Holy Spirit about the ministry of his son, John (v.67). And Simeon, moved by the Holy Spirit, recognized Jesus as the Savior (2:25–32). The work of the Holy Spirit in the early stages of the unfolding gospel finds a parallel in the work of the Holy Spirit in founding the church (Ac 2).

Mary's song (1:46–55), like that of Hannah's (1Sa 2:1–10), sees her promise of a son as a sign that in the birth of this son, God was fulfilling his blessing to Abraham (v.55; 1Sa 2:10). Zechariah's song (vv.67–79) sees the birth of John as a sign that God was fulfilling his blessing to Abraham (v.73) and to David (v.69). The birth of Jesus was the fulfillment of the OT promises to Israel.

In line with Luke's intent to tell the story of Jesus chronologically (see comment on 1:3), he places Jesus' birth within the context of Roman history. Jesus was born in the days of Caesar Augustus, the first Roman emperor, when "Quirinius was governor of Syria" (2:1–2). Being from the line of David, Joseph was required to register in a census at his ancestral birthplace, Bethlehem. Jesus was born there, as it had been foretold by the prophet Micah (Mic 5:2). He was born "in a manger," and his birth was announced to shepherds who lived out in the fields (2:1–20). What could be more lowly and unassuming? As with John the Baptist (1:65–66), the news of his birth spread throughout the countryside (2:17–18).

As the Mosaic Law stipulated, on the eighth day Jesus was circumcised (Lev 12:3). He was taken to the Temple (thirty-three days later, according to the

Law; Lev 12:4) to be presented as the firstborn (Ex 13:2,12; cf. 1Sa 1:21–28), and his mother fulfilled the necessary rites for purification (Lev 12). Throughout the narrative (2:22–24, 27, 39, 41), Luke stresses that all was accomplished according to what "the custom of the Law required" (v.27). In Simeon (vv.25–32) and the prophetess Anna (vv.36–38), he shows that those from Israel whom God had prepared and who were waiting for the promised Messiah were quick to recognize Jesus as that Messiah. Luke's stress on the fact that Simeon and Anna were both advanced in age (vv.29b, 36) underscores that Israel had been waiting a long time for the coming of Christ.

In a rare glimpse of Jesus' childhood, Luke shows that Jesus was well aware of his identity and calling from the Father. At twelve years old, he was found among the teachers at the Temple, "listening to them and asking them questions" (v.46). Moreover, "everyone who heard him was amazed at his understanding and his answers" (v.47). When his parents scolded him, Jesus replied, "Didn't you know I had to be in my Father's house?" (v.49). Though as yet his parents did not understand what this meant (v.50), this was apparently a reference to the central role the Messiah was to have in the worship of God at the temple. In 2Sa 7:13, for example, David was promised that the Messiah would build a temple (NIV, "house") "for my Name." The Chronicler adds that God's covenant with David also included the promise that God would "set him [the Messiah] over the temple [NIV, my house] and my kingdom forever" (1Ch 17:14). Along these same lines, the prophet Zechariah had foretold that the Messiah would "build the temple of the LORD . . . and he will be a priest on his throne" (Zec 6:12–13).

In spite of Jesus' self-awareness as the Son of God, he "was obedient" to his earthly parents. Luke closes his brief view of this time in Jesus' life with the summary statement: "Jesus grew in wisdom and stature, and in favor with God and men" (2:52).

## II. The Beginning (3:1–4:13)

Again being careful to place the gospel story in a historical and chronological context (cf. 1:1–4), Luke dates the beginning of the ministry of John the Baptist in the "fifteenth year of the Roman Caesar Tiberius" (3:1). On the basis of the Roman calendar, this date would be A.D. 29.

### A. John the Baptist, Forerunner of the Messiah (3:1–23)

In line with his earlier emphasis on the birth of Jesus as fulfilling God's promises to Abraham, Luke focuses his account of John's ministry on the question, Who is the seed of Abraham? John's answer to this question is twofold. (1) No one can claim a right to the Abrahamic promises by mere natural lineage. If God chooses to do so, he can raise up children for Abraham from dead stones. (2) The seed of Abraham will be known by their fruit. They are those who do the same righteous deeds reflected in the life of Abraham.

Many saw in John's ministry the possibility that he might be the Messiah (v.15). But John moved quickly to dispel such ideas. As Luke stresses by quoting Isa 40 (see 3:4–6), John was the forerunner of the Messiah. His baptism of repentance and preparation was to be the occasion for the announcement of the Messiah. At his baptism, Jesus was thus declared to be the Son of God by a voice from heaven (v.22). With the arrival of the Messiah, the ministry of the forerunner was quickly cut off (v.20).

### B. The Genealogy of Jesus (3:23–38)

As in the narratives of the OT, the central character of Luke's gospel, Jesus, is introduced by means of a genealogy (cf. Ge 5:28–29). It is important to note how Luke uses this genealogy.

Jesus has just been identified as the Son of God in the previous verse (3:22). Moreover, in the next chapter, his own townsfolk will ask themselves, "Isn't this Joseph's son?" (4:22). Thus Luke strategically places his genealogy here to show that Jesus' lineage does, indeed, trace back to God and not to Joseph. In the Greek text of Luke, the expression "son of" is grammatically linked to Jesus throughout the genealogy. Thus Jesus is first called, "so it was thought," the son of Joseph (v.23a). Then, in v.23b Jesus, *not* Joseph, is called the son of Heli. Also Jesus, *not* Heli, is the son of Matthat (v.24a), and so on. The importance of this observation lies in the fact that at the conclusion of the genealogy, Jesus, not Adam, is called the "son of God" (v.38b). Thus, what was stated at the beginning of the genealogy, that Jesus is the Son of God, is confirmed at its conclusion.

In reading the genealogy this way, an age-old question is also resolved— Whose genealogy is represented by Luke, Joseph's or Mary's? Since Joseph's genealogy is recorded in Matthew, and it differs from Luke's at key points, it has generally been supposed that Luke represents Mary's lineage. This would not be possible, however, if Heli were the father of Joseph. It would seem, then, that Luke intends to give a different genealogy of Joseph than Matthew did. If Luke's genealogy identifies Heli as the father of Jesus and not Joseph, then it squares with the traditional harmonization of the two genealogies. Matthew gives the genealogy of Jesus through the line of Joseph, and Luke gives the genealogy of Jesus through the line of Mary's father, Heli.

## C. The Preparation of the Messiah (4:1–13)

Luke again stresses the role of the Holy Spirit in the work of Jesus: He was "led by the Spirit in the desert" (v.1). As Israel in the OT was led by the cloud in the wilderness forty years,

Jesus was led by the Spirit in the desert where he was then tested by the Devil forty days. The first test came when Jesus had not eaten and was hungry. The Devil said to Jesus, "If you are the Son of God, tell this stone to become bread" (v.3). When God sent Israel manna in the desert, it was "to test them and see whether they will follow [his] instructions" (Ex 16:4). Thus, here in Luke's gospel, Jesus answered the Devil's temptation with the lesson Moses himself drew from Israel's test of manna (as reflected in Dt 8:3).

Jesus, unlike Israel in the past, did not succumb to the temptation. By means of God's Word, he successfully deflected the attacks of the Devil. Luke reminds the reader, however, that though defeated this time, the Devil only made a strategic withdrawal: "he left [Jesus] until an opportune time" (v.13). Thus the remainder of Jesus' ministry is here characterized as an ongoing battle with the Devil.

## III. Jesus in Galilee (4:14–9:50)

The Spirit led Jesus back to Galilee (4:14). There he taught in the Jewish synagogues and was highly acclaimed. Luke recounts for his readers a series of events that help summarize and characterize Jesus' ministry in Galilee.

At Nazareth (4:14–30), his hometown, Jesus went to his own synagogue and there, participated in the regular Sabbath reading. Turning to a well-known messianic text, Isa 61, Jesus openly and unambiguously declared that the passage was fulfilled in him (v.21). The hearers responded with predictable amazement, even raising the same question with which Luke himself was concerned in writing Jesus' genealogy: "Isn't this Joseph's son?" (v.22). Anyone who has been reading the book of Luke up to this point is prepared to answer that question. Jesus was not the son of Joseph; he was the Son of God. Moreover, their failure to see this had numerous antecedents in the lives of OT prophets, such as Elijah. The people's anger was particularly aroused by Jesus' inference that their rejection of him "in his own country" had its roots in OT times when God sent his prophets to Gentiles rather than to the rebellious Israelites (vv.25–27). The people's attempt to kill Jesus on this occasion anticipates the account of the stoning of Stephen in Ac 7:54–58 following a similar accusation (Ac 7:1–53).

The amazement of the people continued in Capernaum (4:31–44). There Jesus quieted a man possessed by a demon and demonstrated his authority over "evil spirits" by casting the demon out. At the home of Simon's (i.e., Peter's) mother-in-law, Jesus healed many people and cast out many demons. He continued preaching "the good news of the kingdom of God" in all the synagogues of the region.

Luke begins his account of the calling of Jesus' disciples with Simon Peter, James, and John by the Lake of Gennesaret (5:1–11). The occasion of casting nets for fish is taken as a picture of their work as disciples. When they obeyed Jesus' instructions and cast their nets on the other side of the boat, "they caught such a large number of fish that their nets began to break" (v.6). While they were all astonished at the number of fish they had caught, Peter, falling on his knees before him, saw the broader implication: "Go away from me, Lord; I am a sinful man!" (v.8). Pulling their boats on shore, "They left everything and followed him" (v.11).

In spite of Jesus' own efforts to carry on a quiet ministry of healing and preaching the good news in the synagogues of Galilee, news of such healings as the leper (vv.12–14) and the paralytic (vv.17–26) quickly spread through the region, and Jesus began to attract large crowds. Along with them also came increasing opposition from the leaders of the people (vv.17, 21).

Jesus was careful to pay respect to and obey the Mosaic Law (v.14), but he nevertheless drew sharp attacks from the Pharisees and the teachers of the law. Their opposition, however, only served to further confirm his identity. When the Pharisees asked, "Who can forgive sins but God alone?" (v.21), Jesus responded with the explanation that it was for precisely this reason that he healed the sick—"that you may know that the Son of Man has authority on earth to forgive sins" (v.24). His miracles were signs of his identity as the Son of God.

Furthermore, when the Pharisees asked, "Why do you eat and drink with tax collectors and sinners?" Jesus responded by saying it was, in fact, just to these sinners that he had been sent: "I have not come to call the righteous, but sinners to repentance" (v.32). When the Pharisees continued to ask why his disciples did not fast, it served as an occasion for Jesus to explain his own relationship with the religious rites and duties of the past: "New wine must be poured into new wineskins" (v.38).

This was true not only for fasting, but also for such central practices as the Sabbath. The Pharisees asked Jesus, "Why are you doing what is unlawful on the Sabbath?" (6:2). Jesus answered their question by appealing to OT narratives. David himself "ate what is lawful only for priests to eat" (v.4). To confirm this thesis, Luke adds another similar incident, Jesus healing on the Sabbath (vv.6–11). In this narrative Jesus' words clarify his earlier answer: "I ask you, which is lawful on the Sabbath: to do good or to do evil, to save life or to destroy it?" (v.9). Thus, what David and he had done was to fulfill the intent of the Sabbath that God gave Israel. Such answers to the questions of the Pharisees became the ground from which further opposition grew (v.11).

In summary fashion, Luke recounts that Jesus, having called twelve disciples and designated them as apostles, taught them the central ideas of the kingdom of God (vv.20–49). He first defined the nature of God's blessing (vv.20–26), then stressed the central importance of love (vv.27–36), forgiveness (vv.37–42), sincerity (vv.43–45), and obedience (vv.46–49).

Jesus then returned to Capernaum (7:1), where Luke records two miracles. Jesus healed the centurion's servant (vv.1–10) and raised the widow's son in Nain (vv.11–15). The centurion, a Gentile, came to Jesus in faith, believing that Jesus could heal his servant. As such he became an object lesson in the faith of the nations around Israel and thus a contrast to the kind of faith that Jesus found in Israel (v.9). Nevertheless, the result of Jesus' healing the widow's son was a heightened sense in Israel that God had sent a great prophet (vv.16–17). The similarities between the account of Jesus' deed and that of the prophet Elisha (2Ki 4:32–35) are no doubt intended by Luke to strengthen the people's conclusion.

The miracles that Jesus performed were the decisive proof to John the Baptist that he was the chosen one promised in the OT Scriptures and announced by John (vv.18–23). John was the last of the line of OT prophets and the first fulfillment of the promises of the OT prophets (vv.24–28). His word carried much weight with the people who were baptized by John (v.29) but not with the Pharisees and experts in the law who rejected John's baptism (v.30). The treatment John received at their hand, similar to that which Jesus received, was a sign that the kingdom announced by John was being rejected by God's people. Judgment, rather than blessing, awaited the present generation (vv.31–35).

Jesus' own explanation for his rejection by the religious leaders is disclosed in the act of the sinful woman who washed his feet with her tears,

"wiped them with her hair, kissed them and poured perfume on them" (vv.36–50). The Pharisee who had invited Jesus to his house was unable to understand such devotion to Jesus because, unlike this woman, he had not experienced the depth of forgiveness that this woman had. Besides the twelve apostles, several women also followed Jesus (8:1–3). These, like the woman who washed Jesus' feet, had been forgiven much and had been "cured of evil spirits and diseases" (v.2). Some also were wealthy (v.3). These followers of Jesus were like the seed that landed on the good soil who heard Jesus' word, retained it, and were persevering in producing a crop (vv.4–15). They would be richly rewarded (vv.16–18) and were considered closer than Jesus' own family (vv.19–21).

In each new event, the disciples learned something new about Jesus that left them "in fear and amazement" (v.25). When he calmed the storm (vv.22–25), for example, they asked, "Who is this? He commands the winds and the waters, and they obey him." Luke's readers, of course, know the answer to their question: Jesus is "Christ the Lord," whom the angels announced at the beginning of the book (2:11). These events, then, for the reader, serve as a confirmation of the words of the angels who announced the birth of Jesus. Moreover, he has authority over a legion of demons, who begged Jesus not to send them "into the Abyss." In a graphic demonstration of his power, Jesus sent them into a herd of swine, who then rushed over a steep cliff into a lake and drowned (vv.26–39). Jesus healed a woman sick for twelve years whom no one could heal, and he raised a twelve-year-old girl who lay dead in her father's house (vv.40–56).

This same authority of Jesus was given over to the disciples, and they went from village to village preaching the gospel and healing sick (9:1–6).

When the news of Jesus' deeds reached Jerusalem, the leaders were dismayed (vv.8–9). Herod was left with only the question, "Who, then, is this I hear such things about?"

Even after their return from preaching and healing in the villages throughout the region, the disciples were still dependent on Jesus for their daily bread (vv.10–17). When they obeyed his word, however, their needs were met, and there were twelve basketfuls left over.

The last great lesson the disciples had to learn was that Jesus had come to give his life in preparation for the kingdom of God. Unlike many in the crowds, Peter understood that Jesus was the Messiah (NIV, "Christ") of God (vv.18–20). But Jesus also had to tell Peter that as the Christ, he had to be rejected, killed, and raised to life before the establishment of the kingdom of God (vv.21–27). As a foretaste of that kingdom, Jesus took Peter, John, and James to the Mount of Transfiguration. These disciples saw a glimpse of the future kingdom, with Moses and Elijah talking to Jesus "about his departure, which he was about to bring to fulfillment at Jerusalem" (v.31). They also heard a voice from heaven that proclaimed Jesus as the Son of God. At a crucial turning point in the book of Luke, the readers are given a clear perspective for viewing the events in the remainder of the book. Jesus is about to "set his face toward Jerusalem" (v.51), and there is no doubt in the mind of the readers as to what would happen to him there.

The disciples were still unable to do all the works of Jesus. For example, a boy was brought to Jesus to heal whom the disciples were unable to help (9:37–43a). Moreover, there was still much about Jesus that the disciples did not understand and "were afraid to ask" (vv.43b-45). Their argument over "which of them would be the greatest"

(v.46) reveals just how far they had to go before they learned the standard of greatness in God's kingdom—"he who is least among [them] is the greatest" (vv.46–50).

## IV. Jesus' Journey to Jerusalem (9:51–19:27)

Jesus now resolutely begins his journey to Jerusalem. His purpose is clear, and he has made it known to his disciples: "The Son of Man is going to be betrayed into the hands of men" (9:44). He "must suffer many things and be rejected . . . killed and . . . raised to life" (9:22).

In Luke's gospel, Jesus arrives in Jerusalem in 19:28. There are thus ten chapters devoted to his journey to Jerusalem. Much in these chapters recounts his teaching to his disciples as well as his deeds.

Luke first recounts that Jesus, on his way to Jerusalem, passed through Samaria (9:51–56). Luke perhaps mentions this because of the similar pattern to the spread of the Gospel in the early church. In Acts, Jesus told the disciples to preach the Gospel "in Jerusalem, and in all Judea and Samaria, and to the ends of the earth" (Ac 1:8). Thus, as Luke presents it, Jesus' ministry had already prepared the way for the Gospel by starting in Galilee and moving to Samaria, Judea, and then to Jerusalem.

As he traveled to Jerusalem, the focus of Jesus' teaching turned to the kingdom of God. In the OT promises, Jerusalem was to be the center of the kingdom (cf. Isa 2:2–4). There was a price to pay for those who would enjoy the blessings of God's kingdom. The disciples had to count the cost (9:57–62). Moreover, those who were sent out to proclaim the Gospel of the kingdom had to go as representatives of the King. Jesus thus gave his disciples strict instructions on how to carry out his work (10:1–24). Representatives of God's kingdom must be like lambs amid wolves (v.3). They are not to seek personal gain, but are to rely on the Lord's provision and accept the help and support of those who serve him (vv.4–16). Their message is simple: "The kingdom of God is near you" (v.9). If they are rejected, it is only because they have represented Jesus (v.16).

Luke includes these instructions in his gospel because they were still needed in the spread of the Gospel in the church. If Jesus "saw Satan fall like lightning from heaven" (v.18) as a result of the preaching of these seventy-two disciples, what must he see in the work of the churches to whom Luke writes his gospel? Whatever opposition they might meet with on the way, the words of Christ would be a constant source of comfort: "I praise you, Father, Lord of heaven and earth, because you have hidden these things from the wise and learned, and revealed them to little children" (v.21). The work of building God's kingdom is God's work. Those who participate in it are more blessed than prophets and kings of old who wanted to hear and see these things but did not (vv.23–24).

Jesus' teaching on the kingdom of God did not replace the teaching of the OT Scriptures. It was rather an application of the message of those Scriptures in light of the central importance of the love of God and of one's neighbor. Jesus taught that one's neighbor included even those who could be considered one's enemies (vv.25–37). The Samaritan, the enemy of the Jews, showed love to the man from Jerusalem. As such he demonstrated, over against the narrow focus of the priest and the Levite, that in God's kingdom, the command to love one's neighbor extended far beyond narrowly defined human boundaries. Furthermore, in the kingdom of God, only one thing was of lasting importance—this is pictured in the single devotion of Mary who sat listening at the feet of Jesus (vv.38–42).

Prayer is central to the members of God's kingdom (11:1–13). Jesus gave his disciples a simple pattern by which to pray (vv.1–4). He then taught them about the importance of persistent and expectant prayer (vv.5–13).

The mood of the growing crowd is reflected (1) in their accusation that "by Beelzebub, the prince of demons, [Jesus] is driving out demons" (v.15), and (2) in their asking "for a sign from heaven" (v.16). Jesus met the first charge with a proverb: "A kingdom divided against itself will be ruined" (vv.17–23). Moreover, failure to appreciate the spiritual battle at stake could lead to a lack of vigilance and result in one's "final condition . . . [being] worse than the first" (vv.24–26). God's kingdom rests on the power of God's word (vv.27–28).

Jesus met the second charge by rejecting the crowd's request for a miraculous sign from heaven. The sign given to "a wicked generation" was only that which Jonah represented to the Ninevites, i.e., the threat of impending destruction (vv.29–32). The crowd would reject that sign because their eyes were blinded (vv.33–36). Nevertheless, Jesus proclaimed judgment against the leaders of the people in a series of six woes (vv.37–52). This further hardened them against Jesus, and they sought to entrap him in his teaching (vv.53–54).

With the ever-growing crowd pressing in on him, Jesus began to warn his disciples about the importance of sincerity and honesty before God (12:1–12). Greed and possessions can keep one from the kingdom of God (vv.13–21). One must trust in God, not wealth (vv.22–34), and live in constant expectation of the coming Son of Man (vv.35–40). These exhortations are clearly directed by Luke to the concerns and needs of the early church. Jesus spoke here as one who was looking ahead to a future coming of the Son of Man. That is, he was looking beyond his own rejection in Jerusalem to the future time of his return. This is one of many ways in which Luke's gospel shares the perspective of the early church reflected in the book of Acts.

Luke's perspective of Jesus is highlighted by Peter's question, "Lord, are you telling this parable to us, or to everyone?" (v.41). This question is precisely that of the inquisitive reader of Luke's gospel. Who is Jesus speaking to here? To his disciples or to a much wider audience? His answer further directs his message to those in the early church awaiting the second coming of the Son of Man. The faithful and wise servant, Jesus says, is one whom the master finds doing his will when he returns (vv.42–48). Jesus has "a baptism to undergo" that will "bring fire on the earth." He has not come to bring peace, but division (vv.49–53). The disciples, and Luke's readers, will have to learn to "interpret this present time" (vv.54–56). A time is yet coming when one will need wisdom and judgment to escape prison (vv.57–59). It must be remembered that when Luke wrote his gospel and its sequel, the early church knew quite well of the things of which Jesus was here speaking.

Thus Jesus called on the crowd to repent (13:1–5). Those in Jerusalem were under the same divine judgment as those in Galilee. If they had been spared thus far, it was only because they were being given another opportunity to repent (vv.6–9). The prospect of Jerusalem being given a second chance to repent suggests that Luke has in mind the preaching of Peter and the early church in Ac 2, when Jerusalem was called to repent. Part of Luke's purpose in Acts is to show that when the people refused this second offer, God turned to the nations and offered his kingdom to them (Ac 28:28).

The kingdom that Jesus offered to Israel represented a break with the ideas of God's kingdom current in his own day. The difference often centered on the meaning of the Sabbath. The religious leaders' understanding of the kingdom was reflected in their anger that Jesus would heal a crippled woman on the Sabbath (13:10–14). Jesus, however, argued that the Sabbath was a time to be set free from bondage (vv.15–17). The kingdom of God, rejected in Jesus' own time, would one day fill all the world (vv.18–21). Jesus' teaching contains a note of warning to those in Israel: Once the kingdom was rejected, the door would be closed. They would see "Abraham, Isaac and Jacob and all the prophets in the kingdom of God," but they would be cast out (vv.22–30). In that day, people would join the kingdom "from east and west and north and south." Luke clearly has in mind here the offer of the kingdom to the Gentiles recounted in Acts (cf. Ac 11:1). Jesus, however, did not leave Jerusalem without hope. The time would come, he said, when they would again see Jesus coming to Jerusalem in the name of the Lord (vv.31–35); the imagery is that of Da 7:9–14.

In the meantime, the Pharisees continued to cling to their own understanding of the law and the Sabbath and thus failed to understand the nature of the kingdom that Jesus preached (14:1–6). As Jesus understood it, the kingdom was not for the proud, but for the humble (vv.7–11); not for the rich and exclusive, but for the poor, the crippled, the lame, and the blind (vv.12–14). While the kingdom would not intentionally exclude the proud and the rich, they would refuse the invitation to come (vv.15–24). Those who do come must count the cost, forsake all, and follow Jesus as his disciples (vv.25–35).

The chief stumbling block among those who considered themselves righteous and thus already members of the kingdom of God was that Jesus had extended the offer of the kingdom to those whom they had excluded. The Pharisees said, "This man welcomes sinners and eats with them" (15:2). Jesus, however, warned them that the purpose of the kingdom was to provide redemption for the lost, not a mere haven for the righteous. He illustrated this with three parables: the lost sheep (vv.3–7), the lost coin (vv.8–10), and the lost son (vv.11–32). In each of these Jesus focused on the salvation of the lost and the joy their acceptance into the kingdom should engender. Rather than seek to exclude such new members from the kingdom, Jesus admonished his disciples to court friendly ties with those on the outside as a means of winning their acceptance (16:1–15). Luke no doubt intended Jesus' words, "Use worldly wealth to gain friends for yourselves, so that when it is gone, you will be welcomed into eternal dwellings" (v.9), to speak to the situation in the early church that is reflected in Acts, where the early believers shared their worldly goods with one another (see Ac 2:44–47; 4:32–37).

There may also be a word here to groups such as those in the Jerusalem church ("the party of the Pharisees," Ac 15:5) who insisted that "the Gentiles must be circumcised and required to obey the law of Moses." If directed at groups such as this, Jesus' parable of the shrewd manager would be saying to them that as they leave their old master, their legal traditions, they had better release some of the debt that their new associates (the Gentiles) owe, in order to be "welcome . . . into their houses" (Lk 16:4). This is, in fact, the same argument the apostle Paul used in Ac 15 when he stated that Christians in Jerusalem should not put "on the necks of the disciples a yoke that neither we nor our fathers have been able to bear" (Ac 15:10); and it was the conclusion of the Jerusalem church: "We should not make it difficult for the Gentiles who are turning to God" (Ac 15:19). Both Jesus and the early church based their

conclusions on the same principle: "God knows your hearts" (Lk 16:15; Ac 15:8).

In the next section (16:16–18) Luke shows that Jesus' words must not be understood as canceling the validity of the OT Scriptures: "It is easier for heaven and earth to disappear than for the least stroke of a pen to drop out of the Law" (v.17). While in the past ("until John," v.16) the requirement, even for Gentiles, was to follow the "Law and the Prophets," now "the good news of the kingdom of God is being preached, and everyone is forcing his way into it" (v.16). As in the early church, Jewish Christians "should not make it difficult for the Gentiles who are turning to God" (Ac 15:19). The Scriptures were to lead sinners to God's kingdom (16:19–29), not to keep them out. If people do not listen to Scripture, "they will not be convinced even if someone rises from the dead" (v.31). It is significant that in Luke's gospel, even after his own resurrection, Jesus devoted his time to teaching the disciples the Law and the Prophets (24:13–49), and he "opened their minds so they could understand the Scriptures" (v.45).

Forgiveness and faith must characterize the life of a disciple (17:1–6); this is the duty of a servant (vv.7–10) and arises out of a grateful heart (vv.11–19). Though the Pharisees were expecting to see the coming of the kingdom of God in their own day, Jesus warned them that it was already in their midst and they had rejected it (vv.20–21). There was to be a future return of the Son of Man to establish his kingdom (cf. Da 7:9–14), but first it was necessary that Jesus "suffer many things and be rejected by this generation" (v.25). No one knows the time of that coming (vv.26–37). Nevertheless, those who trust in Jesus are to continually offer up prayer that God's kingdom will come (18:1–5). They must not lose heart: "Will not God bring about justice for his chosen ones, who cry out to him day and night?" (v.7). God will "see that they get justice, and quickly" (v.8). The larger question is whether, when he comes, the Son of Man will find anyone continually praying in this way (v.8). Prayer of this sort must be offered in humility. It is characterized by the words of the tax collector: "God, have mercy on me, a sinner" (vv.9–14). One must come to God as a little child (vv.15–17). Such faith is difficult for the rich and the proud, but with God, it is not impossible (vv.18–29).

Jesus' own disciples did not understand his teaching regarding his death and resurrection in Jerusalem (vv.31–33); its meaning was hidden from them (v.34). The blind beggar whom Jesus passed on his way to Jerusalem, however, knew that Jesus was the "Son of David" (vv.38–39). Even when rebuked, he persistently called out all the more to Jesus for mercy (v.39). Jesus answered his call, and he was healed because of his faith (vv.40–43). In the same way the chief tax collector, Zacchaeus, persistently pursued Jesus, gave half of his possessions to the poor, and righted those he had wronged. Such a man, Jesus said, was a "son of Abraham," whom the Son of Man came to save (19:1–10).

As Jesus neared Jerusalem, the expectation arose among the people that the kingdom of God would soon be established. Jesus warned them, however, that the time had not yet come. There was to be a delay, and those who would enter the kingdom had to wait faithfully until the return of the King (vv.11–27).

## V. Jesus in Jerusalem (19:28–21:38)

The King came to Jerusalem, but the kingdom was rejected (19:28–37, 41). Only his disciples recognized him as "the king who comes in the name of the Lord" (v.38). To the rest "it was hidden" (v.42). Jesus wept, knowing what

great blessings there could have been for Israel and what great judgment lay ahead (vv.41–45). As Jesus taught in the temple, events turned quickly and decisively against him (vv.45–48).

The first question raised by the chief priests, the teachers of the law, and the elders was "by what authority" Jesus preached (20:1–8). Jesus related the question of his authority to the larger question of the ministry of John the Baptist. The leaders in Jerusalem were willing to concede the connection between John and Jesus, and by their silence, they left unchallenged Jesus' implicit claim to the same authority as John. In the following narrative, Jesus continued to link his ministry to that of John the Baptist. The parable of the tenants (vv.9–19) is about Israel's treatment of the prophets, God's servants, throughout their long history. John was the last of these. Finally the landlord's son was sent, and "they threw him out of the vineyard and killed him" (v.15). In this parable Jesus again anticipated his own death at their hands. Moreover, the parable exposed the plans of the chief priests and teachers of the law who "looked for a way to arrest him immediately" (v.19). Jesus foiled their further plans of trapping him unfairly by an appeal to a proverb: "Give to Caesar what is Caesar's, and to God what is God's" (vv.20–26).

With the resurrection of Jesus only days away, the Sadducees unwittingly raised a central question (vv.27–40). Jesus assailed the apparent lack of understanding that lay behind their lack of belief in the Resurrection. What they failed to see was that the Scriptures speak of a future that will be altogether different from the past or the present. To understand God's work in Scripture, one cannot merely project the present order into the future. The Resurrection will be a totally different life from present human existence; "they are like the angels" (v.36). Jesus read Moses and the OT Scriptures quite differently than the leaders at Jerusalem. The Resurrection would not mean a return to the status quo; rather, it would mean a new order of life. Jesus' own resurrection would mark the beginning of that new order.

The Christ foretold in the OT as the Son of David was not a mere descendant of David. He was David's Lord (vv.41–44), and David humbly submitted to him. The Jewish teachers of the law, however, were proud and loved to hear the praises that they received from the people (vv.45–47). In contrast to them and any others who gave out of their wealth, the poor widow depicted here, who gave all she had, exemplifies the kind of worship that pleases God (21:1–4).

Though the present temple had great physical beauty, a time was coming when it would be destroyed and left abandoned (vv.5–6). No one knew the time when this would happen, but many signs would precede it. There would be wars, Jerusalem would be destroyed and "trampled on by the Gentiles," and her people would be "taken as prisoners to all the nations" (v.24). This would extend "until the times of the Gentiles are fulfilled" (v.24). After this, Jesus continues, the Son of Man will return, as foretold in the book of Daniel, "in a cloud with power and great glory" (v.27). When these things begin to happen, "the kingdom of God is near" (v.31). The nation of Israel will not pass away until "all these things have happened" (v.32).

The central concern of those who are waiting faithfully for the return of the Son of Man is vigilance: "Be careful, or your hearts will be weighed down with dissipation, drunkenness and the anxieties of life, and that day will close on you unexpectedly like a trap" (v.34).

## VI. Crucifixion and Resurrection (22:1–24:53)

Jesus was betrayed during the time of the Passover celebration (22:1–6). On the night of the Passover feast, Jesus gathered with his disciples for a last supper before his death (vv.7–38). During the meal, Jesus spoke of his impending death and of his future return to establish his kingdom. His death meant the sacrifice of his own body for his disciples and for all who would become his disciples (v.19), and the shedding of his blood was the beginning of the "new covenant" (v.20), promised by the OT prophets (Jer 31:31; Eze 36:26). Its coming signaled the end of the old covenant between God and Israel at Sinai (Jer 31:32). Though the disciples were commanded to celebrate the new covenant death of Christ as a "remembrance" (v.19b), Jesus would not again celebrate it until he came again in his kingdom (vv.16, 18).

Jesus explained to his disciples that his death was to be understood in terms of the "servant" prophecy of Isa 53, which "must be fulfilled" in him (v.37). The disciples were to follow his example of service and not seek to lord over others, as Gentile kings do (vv.24–28). Their time to rule would come when Jesus returned to establish his kingdom (vv.29–30). Though the disciples were willing even to go to death for Jesus (vv.31–38), in the hour of temptation they slept (vv.39–46), and later Peter disowned him (vv.54–62). Jesus, however, knew that he would be alone in this hour (v.34). His concern was for the disciples' ongoing ministry after his resurrection and return to the Father: "I have prayed for you, Simon, that your faith may not fail. And when you have turned back, strengthen your brothers" (v.32). The perspective is clearly that of the events in Acts, in Peter's central role in building the church in that book. Luke writes this gospel with his second book in mind.

In the mission of Jesus' disciples during his own ministry, their work was temporary and had its goal in the final days in Jerusalem (cf. 10:1–16). Jesus now commissioned the disciples for the much larger task of waiting for his return: "But now if you have a purse, take it, and also a bag. . ." (v.36). They were even told to purchase a sword, though not for taking the kingdom by storm (see vv.49–50); apparently, the swords were only to be used for protection (cf. Ne 4:17). In stressing the ongoing nature of the disciples' commission and the idea of self-support and protection entailed in Jesus' instructions, Luke perhaps has in mind the example of the apostle Paul, who in his travels and work of evangelism supported himself by making tents (Ac 18:3).

Jesus was first taken by the chief priests and temple guards into the house of the high priest (vv.52–54). Peter, waiting in the courtyard, denied any association with Jesus (vv.55–60). When the rooster crowed and Peter had denied him three times, Jesus was close enough to him to be able to cast a knowing glance in his direction (v.61), filling him with a sense not only of the emptiness of his own vows, "Lord, I am ready to go with you to prison and to death" (v.33), but also with Jesus' faithfulness, "I have prayed for you, Simon, that your faith may not fail" (v.32).

At the high priest's house, the guards mocked and beat Jesus (vv.63–65). At daybreak Jesus stood before the council to face the charges they brought against him. Jesus refused an outright claim to be the Messiah, saying, "If I tell you, you will not believe me, and if I asked you, you would not answer" (vv.67–68), adding, "from now on, the Son of Man will be seated at the right hand of the mighty God" (v.69). Luke's readers can see that Jesus' words refer to the establishment of the church in Ac 2:33 and thus are a positive answer to the council's question. In avoiding a direct answer, Jesus prevents any linkage between his own idea of the Messiah and that of the Jewish leaders.

When they asked further, "Are you then the Son of God?" (v.70), his answer at first glance seems even more evasive ("You say so"), but Luke shows that they understood it as a positive answer or at least enough to hang an indictment on (v.71). Armed with this "confession," the Jewish leaders took Jesus to Pilate, the Roman governor, and offered this charge, "He claims to be Christ" (23:1–2). When Pilate asked for confirmation, Jesus again replied with an ambiguous answer, "You say so" (less ambiguous in the NIV: "Yes, it is as you say," v.3). Thus Pilate could find "no basis for a charge against" Jesus (v.4).

When Pilate discovered that Jesus was a Galilean and hence under the jurisdiction of Herod, he sent Jesus before him. Herod, having heard much about Jesus, wanted to see him perform a miracle (vv.5–8). Jesus, however, refused to answer any of Herod's questions (v.9).

Luke goes to some pains to show that Pilate found Jesus to be innocent of the charges brought against him (vv.10–25). Instead, it was the crowd who wanted Jesus crucified (vv.18–23). In the end, Pilate gave in to their wish (vv.24–25).

Even as they led Jesus off to be crucified, Jesus spoke of the impending destruction of Jerusalem (vv.26–31). On the cross, however, Jesus said, "Father, forgive them, for they do not know what they are doing" (v.34). Luke no doubt has in mind a link between these words of Jesus on the cross and Peter's appeal to the people of Jerusalem after the Resurrection: "God has made this Jesus, whom you crucified, both Lord and Christ. . . . Repent and be baptized, every one of you, in the name of Jesus Christ for the forgiveness of your sins" (Ac 2:36–38).

On the cross, Jesus was surrounded by scoffers. There were three notable exceptions. (1) One of the criminals crucified with Jesus said, "Jesus, remember me when you come into your kingdom" (23:40–43) and thus became the first to enjoy the new covenant. (2) The centurion guarding Jesus said, "Surely this was a righteous man" (v.47). (3) A member of the council that had turned Jesus over to Pilate, Joseph of Arimathea, took the body of Jesus and laid it in his own tomb (vv.50–54). Each one of these in his own way understood who Jesus was and openly confessed allegiance to him. The rest of the crowd "beat their breasts and went away" (v.48), leaving his followers watching "at a distance" (v.49). Only the women who had been with Jesus followed to see where the body of Jesus was being laid (v.55).

When the women returned two days later to prepare the body of Jesus for burial, they found the tomb empty. Two angels announced to them that Jesus had risen (24:1–8). When the women reported to the disciples what they had seen, no one believed them. Luke gives a revealing picture of the state of mind of Jesus' followers on the day of the Resurrection. Peter ran to the tomb and found it empty. He left the tomb "wondering to himself what had happened" (vv.9–12).

Two of Jesus' disciples, enroute to the village of Emmaus, confessed to their unknown inquisitor, "We had hoped that [Jesus] was the one who was going to redeem Israel" (v.21). Moreover, they said, it had been three days since the Crucifixion, and all they had heard was the report of the women's vision at the empty tomb that Jesus was alive (vv.22–24). It was not until Jesus explained the OT Scriptures to the disciples and broke bread with them that "their eyes were opened and they recognized him" as the risen Lord (vv.25–32). It is no doubt significant that pre-

cisely these two features of the witness of the early church are likewise stressed in the book of Acts: proof from Scripture (Ac 2:14–28) and fellowship around the breaking of the bread (Ac 2:42).

The two men returned to Jerusalem with the news of Jesus' resurrection, only to be told by the rest of the disciples that Jesus had appeared to Simon Peter as well (vv.33–35). Suddenly Jesus himself appeared in their midst. They were still slow to believe (v.38), at first because they were "startled and frightened, thinking they saw a ghost" (v.37) and then because of their joy and amazement (v.41). The disciples looked on as Jesus took a piece of broiled fish "and ate it in their presence" (vv.42–43). As with the two men on the road to Emmaus, however, it was not until Jesus explained to them the Scriptures that they understood the events that had just taken place.

Jesus went on to say that because of his sacrificial death as the Messiah and because of his resurrection from the dead (v.46), "repentance and forgiveness of sins will be preached in his name to all nations" (v.47). The disciples themselves were to wait in Jerusalem until Jesus sent the Holy Spirit whom the Father had promised (v.49). After that, they were to be powerful witnesses of what God had done in Christ Jesus (v.48).

Consequently, in obedience to the command of Jesus, the disciples remained in Jerusalem and worshiped regularly at the temple (vv.50–53). Luke continues with the account of the witness of this early group of disciples in the book of Acts.

It is probably not without purpose that in the order of the books of the NT, the book of Acts does not immediately follow after Luke. The gospel of John falls between Luke's two books. This appears due to the obvious fact that the Gospels are grouped together. But that could have been accomplished by putting Luke after the gospel of John. John seems to have been intentionally placed between the end of Luke and the beginning of Acts. One major reason for this could have been John's emphasis on the role of the Holy Spirit. Luke ends on the note of Jesus sending the Holy Spirit. Acts begins on the same note. John devotes much of his attention to the theological development of the role of the Spirit in the life of the Christian.

# John

## Introduction

The author of the book is described as "the disciple whom Jesus loved" (21:20–24). Within the book itself there is an early verification of the authenticity of the gospel of John by eyewitnesses, who affirm that the facts are true: "This is the disciple who testifies to these things and wrote them down. We know that his testimony is true" (v.24). Though it is not certain who these eyewitnesses were, they do attest to the truthfulness of what this disciple wrote about Jesus.

The more important identification is that of "the disciple whom Jesus loved." According to 21:20, he is "the one who also had leaned back against "Jesus' breast at the supper." Unfortunately, in 13:23 that disciple's name is not mentioned. It thus appears that the writer of the book of John, a disciple of Jesus, has carefully avoided using his own name anywhere in the gospel. We do know, however, that he was one of the disciples and that he was one of the closest associates of Jesus among the disciples. Since Peter is mentioned in the gospel, this leaves only James and John of Jesus' inner circle of three. James, we know from Acts, died early (Ac 12:2). Thus, the most likely candidate is John. Furthermore, in the early writings of the church from the NT, the fourth gospel is unanimously attributed to John. The first reference to his authorship is found in the writings of Theophilus of Antioch (c. A.D. 180). Irenaeus (c. 130–c. 200), a student of Polycarp (a friend of John), also credits John with the authorship of this gospel.

The most prevalent date assigned to John's gospel is the last decade of the first century. The basis of the late first-century date is primarily the lack of the mention of the destruction of Jerusalem in John. It must have been written much later than A.D. 70, after the memory of this event had died out, though some use this argument to propose a date prior to 70. There is nothing to prohibit dating John before A.D. 50.

John states clearly his intention in writing this gospel: "that you may believe that Jesus is the Christ, the Son of God, and that by believing you may have life in his name" (20:31). John's concept of "believe" is a central factor in the gospel—to believe is to have eternal life (3:16). The gospel of John was written to present the early church with a collection of signs that Jesus performed which could be used in evangelism.

## I. Prologue (1:1–14)

The gospel of John begins with an introduction to Jesus that goes far beyond the other Gospels. Jesus is the Word that was with God before the creation of the world. By him all things were created. This same view of Creation is found in the OT book of Proverbs (Pr 8:22–36). Relying heavily on the images of Creation from Genesis, John deliberately blends his images so that he also describes the new creation, i.e., the Gospel and new life that Jesus brought to all humankind. He describes Jesus as the light that shone upon the darkness on the first day of Creation (Ge 1:3). As the darkness was unable to hold back that first light, so the darkness of sin in human hearts (cf. 3:19) could not hold Jesus back. That light gave life to all humankind.

As the Word of God, Jesus became flesh and lived among God's people Israel. Those who believed in him were given the right to be God's children. Israel had been given a revelation of God's will in the Law of Moses, but they had not seen God. God lived in the tabernacle that Moses built, but his glory was concealed within the Holy of Holies. Jesus revealed God's grace and truth by living among his people. In him they saw God's glory.

## II. The Revelation of Jesus to the World (1:15–12:50)

### A. The Witness of John the Baptist (1:15–3:36)

John the Baptist plays a key role in linking the old with the new, for he was the prophet sent from God to announce the coming of the Messiah—i.e., an OT prophet announced the coming of the NT Messiah. Moreover, for John, the author of this gospel, the words of John the Baptist provide the necessary link between the prologue and the narrative of Jesus' ministry that follows. When John the Baptist tells the messengers from the Pharisees in Jerusalem that "among you stands one you do not know" (1:26), he identifies for the readers, at least, Jesus as the light who "came to that which was his own, but his own did not receive him" (v.11).

John the Baptist also introduces Jesus as the OT Passover Lamb (see comments on Ex 12–13), seen as a sacrifice to "take away the sin of the world" (1:29). Through John the Baptist's identification of Jesus, the central thematic structure of the gospel of John is established. Jesus is the Messiah foretold in the OT. He came to Israel and was rejected, but in this rejection, others received him; thus God offered a Passover Lamb for the whole world, through whom they could have forgiveness for sin.

The author moves quickly to identify those among God's people Israel who received the light—the first disciples (1:35–51). When they heard John the Baptist identify Jesus as the Lamb of God, they simply turned and followed him (vv.36–37). Jesus then said, "Come," and "they went" (v.39). The simplicity of this first call is no doubt intended to illustrate what Jesus would later teach: "My sheep listen to my voice; I know them, and they follow me" (10:27).

When Andrew brought his brother Simon to Jesus, Jesus already knew him: "You are Simon son of John" (1:42). When Jesus said to Philip, "Follow me" (v.43), Philip heard his voice and knew him: "We have found the one Moses wrote about in the Law, and about who the prophets also wrote" (v.45). When Philip brought Nathaniel to Jesus, Jesus already knew him as "a true Israelite, in whom there is nothing false" (v.47). He in turn knew Jesus as "the Son of God" and "the King of Israel" (v.49).

Having shown the reader the nature of the "true Israelites" who followed Jesus, the author now turns to the picture of Jesus among the Israelites who would ultimately reject him. In the first narrative, the marriage at Cana (2:1–12), Jesus "revealed his glory" (v.11), but only "his disciples put their faith in him" (v.11). The master of the banquet knew that the new wine was "the best," but "he did not realize where it had come from" (vv.9–10). Since it is elsewhere the author's practice to allow his character's words to say more than they actually intended (cf. 11:49–53), the banquet master's words may be intended to characterize the blindness of those who rejected Jesus (cf. 9:35–41).

In the account of Jesus' cleansing the temple (2:13–25), a more dramatic picture of those in Jerusalem is given. Jesus said they had turned "my Father's house into a market!" (v.16). A central feature of the OT's picture of the Messiah is the building of God's temple (2Sa 7:13; Zec 6:12–13). In John's gospel this is extended to include the Resurrection. Even the disciples did not understand Jesus' words until "after he was raised from the dead" (v.22a); then "they believed the Scripture and the words that Jesus had spoken" (v.22b). Thus the author shows that the words of Jesus must often be understood in light of later events that uncover their real intent. The author does this not to encourage his readers to look for such hidden meanings on their own, but rather to alert them to appreciate the meanings that he himself intends. In this case, John understands the OT promise that the Messiah would build a temple for God's people in terms of the priesthood of Jesus that is grounded in the Resurrection. Through his exaltation to the right hand of the Father, Jesus, the High Priest, will make obsolete the old order at the temple. This is the same view as the writer of the book of Hebrews (see Heb 9:11–12). Later Jesus would tell the Samaritan woman that "a time is coming and has now come when the true worshipers will worship the Father in spirit and truth, for they are the kind of worshipers the Father seeks" (4:23).

Having introduced the notion of a spiritual understanding of the temple and the new people of God, John now moves to an extended discussion between Jesus and Nicodemus, "a member of the Jewish ruling council" (3:1), which centers on "heavenly things" (v.12). To see the kingdom of God one must be "born again," or "born from above" (v.3, cf. NIV note), i.e., be "born of water and the Spirit" (v.5). Within this gospel, this discussion is intended to clarify Jesus' spiritual understanding of the people of God. The basic thesis put forth in this discussion is that such an understanding of the people of God was already foretold in the OT (Eze 36:24–27), and a leader in Israel, such as Nicodemus, "should not be surprised" to hear of it (vv.7, 10). Membership in God's spiritual kingdom will not be limited to the OT people of God. Physical birth is neither a requirement nor a guarantee. God sent his Son to die for the whole world. The only requirement and guarantee is faith (vv.16, 18).

In his account of the final witness of John the Baptist to Jesus (vv.22–36), the author of this gospel shows that John was in full accord with Jesus' teaching about the kingdom. John, who continued to baptize, saw his own ministry fading out as Jesus' continually increased. Jesus was the Son of God, the bridegroom to whom the bride belonged. In him there is eternal life.

## B. Jesus and the Samaritans (4:1–42)

In the account of the woman at the well, John continues his explication of Jesus' teaching on the Spirit. The central theme is the "living water" (v.10) that gives eternal life (v.14). Like Nicodemus in ch. 3, the Samaritan woman can only understand Jesus in the context of the well of water from which Jacob drank. But Jesus reminds her that "everyone who drinks this water will be thirsty again" (v.13). If she wants the water that Jesus offered, she must set straight her deeds before God. Jesus said to her, "The fact is, you have had five husbands, and the man you now have is not your husband" (v.18). Jesus has raised the issue of eternal life to the level of the woman's behavior. The author no doubt intends this as an illustration of Jesus' words in the previous chapter: "Whoever lives by the truth comes into the light" and "his deeds will be exposed" (3:20–21). When the woman came to Jesus, her deeds were exposed. Only then could she receive the living water.

John does not explain what led to the woman's question regarding the dispute between the Jews and the Samaritans about the place of worship (4:19–20). The more important issue is that her question provided a context for raising once again the idea of spiritual worship: "the true worshipers will worship the Father in spirit and truth" (v.23). Just as Jacob's well could not quench thirst forever, a physical temple could not provide lasting worship.

When the disciples raised a similar question about Jesus' need for physical food, Jesus told them, "I have food to eat that you know nothing about" (v.32). What food? His disciples were perplexed. "My food," Jesus said, "is to do the will of him who sent me and to finish his work" (v.34). As readers, we know that Jesus was referring to his death (19:30) and resurrection, the work he did finish.

John concludes this section with an account of many Samaritans coming to faith in Jesus (4:39–42). Thus Jesus was recognized as more than the Redeemer of Israel; he was "the Savior of the world" (v.42). This is further demonstrated in the next section where Jesus, a prophet without honor "in his own country," traveled further into Galilee and healed the son of a Gentile official (vv.43–54).

## C. Miracles and Signs; Jesus and the Old Testament (5:1–6:71)

Back again in Jerusalem, Jesus went to the Pool of Bethesda and there healed a man who had been crippled thirty-eight years. It being the Sabbath day, when the man walked away carrying his own mat, the Jews who saw him were scandalized that he was doing work on the Sabbath. Jesus justified doing work on the Sabbath by appealing to the fact that God, his Father, did not cease work on the Sabbath and "is always at his work to this very day" (v.17). This answer served only to heighten the anger of these devout Jews against Jesus: "not only was he breaking the Sabbath, but he was even calling God his own Father, making himself equal with God" (v.17).

Jesus replied to them in a rather lengthy discourse on what it means to be the Son of God (vv.19–47). The context of this discourse is the Son of Man passage in Da 7:10–14. In the messianic text of Da 7, it is the Son of Man who carries out the task of judgment given him by the "Ancient of Days." Thus Jesus says, "The Father judges no one, but has entrusted all judgment to the Son" (5:22). As the Daniel passage shows, all nations are to honor the Son with the same honor as given to the Father (v.23). Daniel wrote of the Son of

Man, "He was given authority, glory and sovereign power; all peoples, nations and men of every language worshiped him" (Da 9:14). Having identified himself as the Son of Man in Daniel, it was natural for Jesus to turn to the idea of the resurrection from the dead (Jn 5:25), for the coming of the Son of Man in Daniel is signaled by the resurrection from the dead (Da 12:2). Thus Jesus' defense against the accusation that he made himself equal to the Father was his appeal to the Scriptures. He could rightly claim that they "testify" that the Son of Man is equal with the Father (5:39). When he completes the work that the Father has given him, i.e., his death on the cross (19:30), that work will testify "that the Father has sent" him (19:36) and that he is in fact the promised Son of Man. The only question that remains is whether those accusing him will accept the authority of the OT. Jesus says, "If you believed Moses, you would believe me, for he wrote about me" (5:46).

After Jesus appealed to the OT Scriptures as the foundation of his messianic claim, John, the author of the book, now adds the account of Jesus' feeding the five thousand (6:1–15) and his walking on the sea (vv.16–24), the two miracles that most closely represent the work of Moses in the OT (cf. comments on Mt 14:1–33). Moses gave the people manna in the desert (Ex 16) and brought them through the sea (Ex 14). It is thus significant that when the people saw Jesus feed the five thousand, they immediately believed in Jesus as "the Prophet who is to come into the world" (6:14). This Prophet was the one "like Moses . . . who did all those miraculous signs and wonders" (Dt 34:10–11).

In light of these allusions to Moses in the works and words of Jesus, it is significant that, in the next section, those following him raise the question of the manna in the desert and the work of Moses (6:25–71). In response to their questions, Jesus reminded them that it was not Moses who gave Israel the manna, but rather the "Father who gives you the true bread from heaven" (v.32). Moreover, Jesus added, the true bread from heaven is not that which Israel ate of and was hungry again the next day, "for the bread of God is he who comes down from heaven and gives life to the world" (v.33). In other words, Jesus taught that the OT narratives of Israel receiving the manna were a picture of God the Father giving life to his people through the Son. He said, "I am the bread of life. . . . For I have come down from heaven" (vv.35, 38).

When the crowd questioned how Jesus, "the son of Joseph, whose father and mother we know" (v.42), could be the one who came down from heaven, Jesus explained that he came from the heavenly Father: "No one has seen the Father except the one who is from God; only he has seen the Father" (v.46). Though his hearers remain perplexed at Jesus' words, the readers of John's gospel know what he is saying because John, in his prologue (1:1–14), has already introduced Jesus as the Word who was with God and who was God (1:1).

In light of his identification of himself as the Son of God, Jesus now explains his allusion to the OT manna narratives: "Your forefathers ate the manna in the desert, yet they died. But here is the bread that comes down from heaven, which a man may eat and not die. I am the living bread that came down from heaven. If anyone eats of this bread, he will live forever. This bread is my flesh, which I will give for the life of the world" (vv.49–51). Just as Jesus would give the world the "living water" that was eternal life (4:14), so in his own death for their sins, Jesus would give his body and flesh as the manna that would be eternal life for the world (6:51).

Once again, those listening to Jesus did not understand (vv.52, 60). The readers of this gospel, however, have only to keep reading, and they will understand what Jesus means. Jesus was speaking of his death on the cross by which he would give life to the world. Jesus explained to those listening that his words were to be understood spiritually. Only those who were called by the Father could come to him (v.65). Hence many turned away "and no longer followed him" (v.66). In contrast to those, Peter, speaking for the rest of the Twelve, who remained with Jesus, said, "You have the words of eternal life. We believe and know that you are the Holy One of God" (v.68).

## D. Jesus at the Temple (7:1–8:59)

John now gives an extended summary of various discourses of Jesus at the temple. In it we see a wide range of responses among the people and the Jewish leaders to the claims of Jesus. John begins with an inside look at Jesus from the point of view of his own brothers, who "did not believe in him" (7:1–9). There is a mocking tone to their remarks. Before he began to speak publicly at the temple, the crowds had already formed opinions about Jesus. Some said he was a good man, others said he "deceives the people" (v.12). In the midst of the celebration of the Feast of Tabernacles, Jesus began to speak and the diverse responses multiplied.

In his summary list of Jesus' discourses, John returns to the same or similar topics. On repeated occasions Jesus addressed the question of the source of his teaching, stressing each time that his message came from God and that he himself had come from God (7:16–19, 28–29; 8:12–20, 48–59). It is on these themes that the discourses concluded, at which time the people "picked up stones to stone him" (8:59). Jesus also gave a defense for healing on the Sabbath (7:21–24), in which he called for the use of "right judgment" in making such decisions (v.24).

Another topic that comes up throughout these summaries is that of Jesus' departure to be with the Father (7:33–36; 8:21–30). This is coupled with the notion that the "time" for his departure had been definitively set but had not yet come (7:6–8, 30). It is not surprising that those who heard him were continually perplexed by this, though we, the readers, have little difficulty understanding him. We have John's prologue to tell us that Jesus was with the Father in eternity, and we have the rest of the book to point us to the Resurrection.

It is interesting to note how John adds a particularly helpful explanation to one of Jesus' discourses. Jesus said, "Whoever believes in me, as the Scripture has said, streams of living water will flow from within him" (vv.37–38). John adds, "By this he meant the Spirit, whom those who believe in him were later to receive. Up to that time the Spirit had not been given, since Jesus had not yet been glorified" (v.39). With this explanation, we are enabled to link Jesus' words to the OT's promise of the Spirit (Eze 36:26) as well as to understand the relationship between Jesus' work and the sending of the Spirit at Pentecost in Ac 2. John later records several of Jesus' references to the sending of the Spirit after his departure (16:7; 20:22). In this instance, however, it is John, the author of the book, who makes the comment. Thus we are given an inspired comment on the event at Pentecost after it had happened.

Throughout Jesus' discourses, the opinions remained divided about his identity (7:40–52). Jesus also turned the tables on his opponents and questioned their identity. They claimed to be the children of Abraham, but that would be true only if they did the works that Abraham did (8:31–41). But if they did the works of the Devil, they ran the risk of becoming children of the Devil (vv.42–47).

During this time, the teachers of the law attempted to trap Jesus in a matter of legal interpretation. They brought to him a woman caught in adultery (7:53–8:11). Their question was whether the stringent requirements of the Mosaic Law should be applied in their day. Jesus' answer was straightforward. Although the law should be carried out, it could not justly be applied. Its administration required a kind of righteousness that did not exist in Israel at that time: "If any one of you is without sin, let him be the first to throw a stone at her" (8:7).

## E. Healing of the Man Born Blind (9:1–10:42)

The failure of his opponents to understand is dramatically portrayed in Jesus' healing the man blind from birth. The meaning John intends for this story is found in Jesus' last words to the Pharisees: "If you were blind, you would not be guilty of sin; but now that you claim you can see, your guilt remains" (9:41). There are none so blind as those who will not see. Because the blind man knew he was blind, he also knew when he received sight (v.25). Those who could see, however, were in danger of confusing their sight with understanding. The blind man could easily draw the conclusion from his healing that Jesus was sent from God: "If this man were not from God, he could do nothing" (v.33). The Pharisees saw with their eyes but refused to believe (v.34). It was to judge such spiritual blindness that Jesus came into the world (v.39).

The blind man could not see, but he heard the voice of Jesus and was healed. Jesus is the good shepherd (10:1–21). Like the blind man, his sheep hear his voice and follow him. They do not follow the thief who comes only to steal and destroy. When they hear Jesus and follow him, he gives them life. Though the Pharisees and those listening to these parables do not understand them (v.6), the reader has the advantage of having the whole book of John before him. Jesus' parables make much more sense when read from that perspective. Again, it is the prologue to John's gospel that provides the key. Jesus is the one sent from God who came to his own people but who was rejected by them (1:11–12). He was the light of the world that "shines in the darkness, but the darkness has not understood it" (v.5); hence, he gives sight to the blind. The light that Jesus gives is life: "In him was life, and that life was the light of men" (v.4). Though his own rejected him (v.11), there were many who would accept him (v.12), hence, Jesus has other sheep that will listen to his voice (10:16).

Jesus' words in ch. 10 also anticipate the events of his death recorded at the conclusion of the gospel (19:1–37). Repeatedly Jesus turns to the theme of the good shepherd who "lays down his life for the sheep" (10:11, 15, 17–18). He gave his life of "[his] own accord," at "the command" of the Father (v.18). This understanding of Jesus' mission is found throughout John's gospel. Jesus was with the Father in eternity past (1:1). There was a council in heaven before the foundations of the world: "I have brought you glory on earth by completing the work you gave me to do" (17:4). God rewarded the obedience of the Son by giving him a kingdom: "I have revealed you to those whom you gave me out of the world" (17:6); "they are not of the world, even as I am not of it" (v.16). As is true throughout the Gospels, Jesus' understanding of his mission is fundamentally shaped by the vision of the Son of Man recorded in Da 7:9–14.

It is not hard to see why those who heard Jesus speak "were divided" over his meaning (10:19). They had to judge by the signs they had: "Can a demon open the eyes of the blind?" (v.21). The reader of the gospel of John, however, has much more to go on. Seen from the perspective of God's eternal plan laid out by John in this gospel (e.g., 3:16), Jesus' words not only make sense but place Jesus himself at the center of God's eternal decrees for the salvation of people.

At the Feast of Dedication, Jesus continued these themes among those who did not believe. His miracles were to demonstrate that he was sent from God; in spite of them, not all believed (10:25), but only those whom the Father had given to Jesus (v.29). They were the sheep who heard the voice of the shepherd (vv.26–27). The crowd that picked up stones to kill Jesus showed by their actions that they understood his claims: "You, a mere man, claim to be God" (v.33), but they did not believe him or his message (vv.38–39). They found themselves fighting against what was written in their own law (v.34).

## F. The Raising of Lazarus (11:1–12:11)

The key to John's understanding of the story of Jesus' raising Lazarus lies in the mourners' response to his death: "Could not he who opened the eyes of the blind man have kept this man from dying?" (11:37). In contrast to their shortsighted lament, Jesus saw the death of Lazarus as an occasion to demonstrate that he was "the resurrection and the life" (v.25). Though all who were present believed that Lazarus would "rise again in the resurrection at the last day" (v.24), John shows that those "last days" had arrived in the person of Jesus, the Son of God. He said to them, "He who believes in me will live, even though he dies; and whoever lives and believes in me will never die" (vv.25–26).

As a result of this miracle, many present believed in Jesus (v.45). Ironically, the resurrection of Lazarus also became the turning point for the Jewish leaders. Henceforth, they made plans to kill Jesus (vv.47–57). In their very plans, however, the will of God was to be accomplished. Caiaphas, the high priest, "prophesied" unwittingly that Jesus would give his life "for the Jewish nation" (v.51) as well as for "the scattered children of God" (v.52).

John gives a brief account of Jesus at Bethany having dinner with Lazarus and his family (12:1–11). This narrative provides a transition point for his last journey into Jerusalem. It was the last supper before the Last Supper (see 13:1–17). On this occasion, Mary poured expensive perfume on Jesus' feet and wiped them with her hair. Over Judas' objection, Jesus praised Mary, seeing her action as a preparation for his own burial, when he would be taken away from them.

## G. Entry into Jerusalem (12:12–50)

There were great crowds in Jerusalem for the celebration of the Passover (11:55). They had been looking for Jesus to come (v.56) and had been alerted by their leaders to report it to them (v.57). When Jesus came, however, the crowds rushed into the street, gathering palm branches and shouting "Hosanna! .. Blessed is the King of Israel" (12:13). Even his own disciples did not understand the significance of Jesus' entry into Jerusalem. Only after his death and resurrection did they understand, for then they saw the whole of his ministry in light of the OT Scriptures (v.16).

John, the author of this gospel, however, keeps the reader fully informed as the events happen by supplying the relevant OT texts (here Zec 9:9, quoted in Jn 12:15). Jesus was the King foretold by the OT prophets. He was the son of David, promised in 2Sa 7, and he was the Son of Man, promised in Da 7:9–14. The fact that the author continually reminds his readers that the time in which Jesus' entered Jerusalem was

the time of the Passover (11:55; 12:12, 20) is likewise intended to show that Jesus fulfilled the OT; he was the Passover Lamb. The words of John the Baptist, the last of Israel's prophets, were also being fulfilled: "John saw Jesus coming toward him and said, 'Look, the Lamb of God, who takes away the sin of the world!'" (1:29).

When Gentile Greeks came to Jesus during the time of the Feast (12:20–23), Jesus saw this as a sign that the Son of Man was to be glorified. Within the strategy of the book, John probably has in mind the fact that in Da 7, the glorification of the Son of Man is marked by "all peoples, nations and men of every language" coming to worship him (Da 7:14). Thus Jesus later says, "I, when I am lifted up from the earth, will draw all men to myself" (12:32).

In 12:37–50, John gives a final summary of the response to Jesus' self-revelation (1:15–12:50). The Jews' rejection of Jesus is explained from the Jewish Scriptures themselves. The greatest of the OT prophets, Isaiah, had long ago seen "Jesus' glory and spoke about him" (12:41). John explains Jesus' rejection, first as a fulfillment of Isaiah's prophecy that the people of Israel would reject their Messiah in unbelief (v.38, quoting Isa 53:1). Second, John shows that according to Isaiah, the reason for the people's unbelief lay in God's blinding their eyes (v.40). Though stated in particularly strong terms, John was not content to let this be the last word. He immediately added the fact that "many even among the leaders believed in him" (v.42). According to this explanation, the unbelief of the people was not caused by God. It lay rather in the heart of those who had rejected Jesus: "for they loved praise from men more than praise from God" (v.43). Those with such a heart were blinded lest they turn to him and be forgiven (v.40).

## III. The Revelation of Jesus Before His Own (13:1–20:29)

### A. The Last Supper (13:1–17:26)

John understood Jesus' death as the death of Isaiah's Servant of the Lord (Isa 52:13–53:12). Thus it was important for him to show that Jesus carried out the role of the Lord's Servant in all respects. This is the central theme of the narrative of Jesus washing the feet of his disciples (13:1–20). The Servant, who gives himself for God's chosen ones, cleanses them thoroughly by his sacrificial death: "Unless I wash you, you have no part with me" (v.8). The disciples, having already put their faith in Jesus, are clean. Presumably the Servant's death has already cleansed them. They have need only that their feet be washed (v.10). They will continue to need their feet washed, and so Jesus sets the example for them: "You also should wash one another's feet" (v.14). By this he apparently means that the disciples ought to continue to encourage one another in their walk with the Lord and in striving for godliness. Or, as he later explains, "A new command I give you: Love one another. As I have loved you, so you must love one another" (v.34). As in many of John's narratives, the sense is directed more to the readers of John's gospel than to the disciples within the narratives as such. Thus Jesus tells them, "You do not realize now what I am doing, but later you will understand" (v.7).

Judas plays an important role in this narrative. He was the exception to all that Jesus spoke of in this text. He was the one who was not clean (vv.10–11) and had need of washing his whole body. As Jesus washed their feet, Judas was the one who "lifted up his heel against [him]" (v.18). But the presence of the betrayer among his disciples also demonstrates the truthfulness of Jesus' claims. As the quotation from the OT shows, Judas' betrayal of Jesus was also a sign of fulfilled prophecy (v.18).

John records Jesus' farewell discourse at length (14:1–16:33) and concludes with Jesus' prayer for his disciples (17:1–26). In both the discourse and the prayer, Jesus' words look far beyond the specific needs and concerns of his disciples on the night of his death. They look to the whole of the subsequent history of the church. The background to his words is the teaching of Jesus found throughout the gospel of John. Jesus is the Son of God and the Son of Man. As the Son of God, he had come to fulfill the command of the Father to redeem his chosen people. As the Son of Man, he had come to establish God's kingdom.

The specific issue that the lengthy discourse addresses is the fact that Jesus is about to return to the Father and hence will no longer be physically present with his disciples. They will continue to follow him, however, and wait for his future return. It is this time of waiting and watching that Jesus specifically has in mind throughout the discourse. What are the disciples to do? and, How are they to carry on his work until he returns?

Jesus begins his discourse with words of comfort that look far beyond the events of the next twenty-four hours to those of eternity. His departure means a further step in the progress of God's purpose. He goes to prepare a place for his people in the heavenly temple ("my Father's house"). Here Jesus draws on the prophet Ezekiel's concept of a new temple with rooms for the priests who will dwell with God (Eze 40:38–47). Later, in Revelation, John will see a vision of "the new Jerusalem, coming down out of heaven from God, prepared as a bride beautifully dressed for her husband" (Rev 21:2). At that time there will no longer be a temple in this city "because the Lord God Almighty and the Lamb are its temple"

(Rev 21:22). The father's house, the temple, will be replaced by the new Jerusalem, and there God's people will dwell forever with the Lamb.

The key to the meaning of the discourse is given at its conclusion. Jesus said, "I came from the Father and entered the world; now I am leaving the world and going back to the Father" (16:28). At this point the disciples, who have been quite puzzled throughout the discourse, openly proclaim both their understanding of what Jesus has been saying and their faith in him (vv.29–30). The discourse, then, is an explanation of what will happen to the disciples and the early church in the time between Jesus' death and his return to establish his kingdom. Jesus will not be physically present among them. He will be with the Father in heaven. He will send the Holy Spirit to guide them and comfort them. They will continue to have fellowship with Jesus through the Spirit. They will have the life he promised them through the work of the Spirit. The Spirit will take his place, convicting the world of sin, righteousness, and judgment. The Spirit will guide the believing community "into all truth" (v.13).

The one rule of faith that will define the disciples as a believing community will be their love for each other. This love will be the fruit of the Spirit who lives in them. One can easily see that the kind of community that Jesus here envisions is precisely that which unfolds in the book of Acts. This gospel of John presupposes and anticipates the establishment of the church. It hardly seems accidental that in the shape of the NT, the gospel of John has been placed just prior to the book of Acts.

Thus, in this discourse, Jesus defines more clearly the nature of his community during the time he will be with the Father. It will be the spiritual community of the church. Each individual will be indwelt with the Spirit of God and will have life and bear fruit as a branch on a vine (15:1–7). It is this form of spiritual life that Jesus had spoken about to the Samaritan woman: "The true worshipers will worship the Father in spirit and truth" (4:23). It was this that Jesus spoke of on the day of the feast when he said, "Whoever believes in me, as the Scripture has said, streams of living water will flow from within him" (7:38)—to which John explained, "By this he meant the Spirit, whom those who believed in him were later to receive" (v.39).

In Jesus' final prayer (ch. 17), the whole of his ministry and purpose is summarized and explained to the reader. Jesus was returning to the Father. He was sent to those whom the Father had chosen (v.2). He had found them and had revealed to them the knowledge of the only true God (v.3). All that he had done was in fulfillment of "the work [the Father] gave [Jesus] to do" (v.4). Now Jesus was returning to the state of glory with the Father that he had "before the world began" (v.5). One can see that the view Jesus had is identical to that of the prologue of John's gospel (1:1–14).

As Jesus was now about to leave his disciples, he prayed for their protection in the world (17:6–12) and their continued joy and sanctification (vv.13–19). And Jesus looked beyond these disciples to their disciples and prayed on their behalf (vv.20–22). His central concern was that these future generations of disciples would continue in unity and love for one another (v.23). Finally, Jesus looked to the time of his return to gather his community to himself. Thus the prayer ends ("I want those you have given me to be with me where I am," v.24) where the discourse began ("I go to prepare a place for you . . . that you also may be where I am," 14:2–3).

## B. Death and Resurrection
(18:1–20:29)

### 1. Jesus' arrest, trial, death, and burial
(18:1–19:42)

The narrative picks up from 13:30 with the betrayal of Jesus by Judas (18:1–11). He was taken both to Annas and to the high priest Caiaphas and questioned "about his disciples and his teaching." During this time Peter denied Jesus three times (vv.12–27). John, overlooking the remorse of Peter, stresses the fact that Jesus had predicted Peter's denial in 13:38 (cf. also 18:9, 32). Thus John's focus is not so much on the personal effect of these events in the lives of Jesus' disciples as on their eternal implications. Everything was happening as planned. God was at work in every detail.

Jesus was then taken before Pilate (18:28–19:16a). Here John stresses the time of Jesus' death and correlates it with the Jewish Passover. John had introduced Jesus with the words of John the Baptist, "Behold the Lamb of God" (1:29); now he returns to that imagery in his account of Jesus' death. Moreover, in Jesus' reply to Pilate, the earthly ruler representing Rome, he stresses the spiritual aspects of his kingdom: "My kingdom is not of this world. . . . [It] is from another place" (18:36). By now the readers of John's gospel have a fairly good understanding of what Jesus meant, having pondered the words of Jesus in chs. 14–17. The spiritual kingdom is the community that Jesus promised his disciples in his absence.

John is particularly concerned to show that Pilate only very reluctantly had Jesus crucified. It was only at the Jews' insistence that he finally had it carried out. Thus even at this late stage in the book, John still has the theme in mind with which he began the book: "his own did not receive him" (1:11). Jesus was the Servant of the Lord who

was "despised and rejected" (Isa 53:3) by his own people.

John recounts the crucifixion of Jesus (19:16b–37) in such a way that its fulfillment of OT prophecies is highlighted (e.g., vv.23–24). Particularly important to John is the identification of Jesus as the King of the Jews (vv.19–22). Thus in the title given Jesus at his death, he was recognized as the Davidic King, the Messiah, and the Son of Man who received the kingdom (Da 7:9–14). More importantly, it was a Gentile Roman official who called him "King of the Jews," just as in the book of Daniel it is the Gentile nations who acknowledge the Son of Man as king of the Jews (Da 7:14, 27).

In keeping with John's emphasis on the work that Jesus was sent into the world to do, the final words of Jesus he records are simply "It is finished" (19:30). Jesus had completed the work of the Father. John's focus on the fact that the Roman guards did not break Jesus' legs (vv.31, 33) but instead pierced his side (vv.34–35) is linked to his desire to show that even in the smallest details, the fulfillment of OT prophecies (vv.36–37; cf. v.24) give witness to Jesus as the Messiah (cf. 20:31).

In his account of the burial of Jesus, John shows that two "secret" Jewish believers, Joseph of Arimathea and Nicodemus, openly acknowledged their faith in Jesus (19:38–42). There may be a suggestion here that many more such believers were to be found among even the leaders of the people (cf. 12:42).

### 2. Jesus' resurrection (20:1–29)

John stresses the empty tomb throughout his account of the Resurrection. He gives the names of the first witnesses, Mary Magdalene, Simon Peter, and himself (anonymously, as "the other disciple"; vv.4, 8). John shows that the level of the disciples' understanding of Jesus was still incomplete—the disciples "still did not understand from Scripture that Jesus had to rise from the dead" (v.9). In doing so he gives some justification for his own gospel. A large part of the focus of the gospel has been to show how, in God's eternal plan, it was necessary that the Messiah "rise from the dead."

As an instance of the disciples' failure to understand the Resurrection, John records the events of Mary's surprise meeting with Jesus (vv.11–18). In a scene reminiscent of the healing of the blind man (9:1–10:42), Mary did not "see" (20:14) Jesus, but she knew his voice (v.16; cf. 10:14). As Jesus had promised on the night of his arrest (16:7), he again tells the disciples to "receive the Holy Spirit" after his departure. This gospel anticipates the events recorded in the early chapters of Acts (Ac 2:1–4).

The concern of Thomas to feel and touch the wounds in the body of the risen Lord is an important element in John's gospel. Later, in his first letter, John refers to the events of the Lord's resurrection as that which "we have looked at and our hands have touched" (1Jn 1:1). Jesus fully appreciates Thomas's concern: "Put your finger here; see my hands. Reach out your hand and put it into my side. Stop doubting and believe" (20:27).

## IV. Conclusion (20:30–21:25)

At the conclusion of this gospel, John summarizes his purpose in writing (20:30–31). He has given the reader an account of the signs and miracles that Jesus did, proving that Jesus is the Christ, the Son of God. By believing in Jesus, life is offered in his name. Thus, in the epilogue of this book, John returns to the theme of life in Christ that was the focus of the prologue: "In him was life, and that life was the light of men. . . . To all who received him, to those who believed in his name, he gave the right to become children of God" (1:4, 12).

The account of the third and last appearance of Jesus in Galilee (21:1–25) presents a picture of the future ministry of the disciples as fishers of people. The meaning John intends is transparent. When the disciples follow the words of Jesus, they will make many disciples (v.6). John clearly intends his gospel to be a guide to the words of Jesus. Jesus had said, "I, when I am lifted up from the earth, will draw all men to myself" (12:32). By means of this book, the message of Jesus will be heard and received by many.

Jesus' final instruction to the disciples is to care for his growing number of disciples: "Feed my sheep" (21:17). Jesus' first word to his disciples was, "Follow me" (1:43); that was also his last (21:19). In his farewell discourse Jesus had warned the disciples: "In this world you will have trouble" (16:33). Now he again warns them of trouble, even anticipating the kind of death (21:18) Peter would die. Just as in this gospel Jesus had anticipated other tragic events as part of God's larger plan, so now Peter's own death was also shown to be in God's plan.

Attached to the end of John's gospel is a verification of the truthfulness of the author and the reliability of his work (vv.24–25).

# Acts

## Introduction

Both the gospel of Luke and Acts contain a prologue addressed to "Theophilus." In Ac 1:1 the writer refers to "my former book" which he had written to Theophilus, one that concerned "all that Jesus began to do and teach until the day he was taken up to heaven." This description fits Luke precisely. A close study of the language and style of Luke and Acts shows that they were written by the same author. While both books are anonymous, Luke is a plausible author for both (see introduction to Luke).

Acts concludes with Paul having stayed in Roman prison two years under relatively good conditions (Ac 28:30). Presumably the author concludes at that point because he was with Paul in Rome at that time. There are no indications in the book of the persecutions under Nero or of the destruction of Jerusalem. Hence, a date prior to A.D. 64 seems most likely.

## I. Prologue (1:1–11)

The book of Acts begins with an explicit reference to the gospel of Luke. The author calls it "my former book." The present book is a continuation of that gospel. In that gospel, the events in the life of Jesus are recounted up to the time of his resurrection and ascension. Acts, after a brief introduction, continues with the events of the early church after Jesus' ascension. The focus of the book is on the work of Christ carried on in the church by the Holy Spirit.

Thematically, the Lord's last words to his disciples (v.8) provide the structure and argument of the book. After his ascension into heaven, Jesus told his disciples that they would "receive power when the Holy Spirit [came] on" them. They were then to be Christ's witnesses. The spread of the Gospel was to begin in Jerusalem, then follow a course into Judea and Samaria and finally to the ends of the earth, i.e., Rome. In following this pattern, Acts begins with an account of events in Jerusalem (1:12–5:42), then focuses on Judea and Samaria (6:1–12:25), and concludes with the early missionary journeys to the "ends of the earth" (13:1–28:31). The book closes with an account of Paul's evangelism and teaching in Rome.

Luke is careful to tell us that Jesus spent much time (forty days) teaching his disciples about the kingdom of God before his ascension (1:3). In this section, the disciples raise a central question: "Lord, are you at this time going to restore the kingdom to Israel?" (v.6). The book of Acts as a whole is intended as an answer to this question. We should note that at the end of the book (28:31) Paul was in Rome preaching "the kingdom of God" and teaching about the Lord Jesus Christ. Thus there seems little question that the establishment of the church and the spread of the Gospel is intended to be understood as the beginning of the reign of the kingdom of God.

On the other hand, Paul was preaching about the kingdom of God in Rome, the capital of the Gentile world, not in Jerusalem. This book takes great pains to show that the center of the church, and hence the kingdom of God, moved from Jerusalem to Rome. Thus the book answers the disciples' question negatively. The kingdom has been established but not yet restored to Israel. As Jesus himself answered, "It is not for you to know the times or dates the Father has set by his own authority" (1:7). The restoration of the kingdom to Israel lay yet in the future. This is the kingdom promised to David (2Sa 7) and already developed in Luke's account of the birth of Jesus: "The Lord God will give him the throne of his father David, and he will reign over the house of Jacob forever; his kingdom will never end" (Lk 1:33). The book of Acts is about the establishment of the church.

## II. The Early Church (1:12–12:25)

### A. The Early Congregation (1:12–5:42)

To highlight the role of the church in the kingdom of God, the opening section of the book (1:12–26) focuses on the replacement of Judas as one of the Twelve—a number that from the gospel of Luke continues to reflect the twelve-tribe unity of the nation of Israel.

The events of Pentecost (2:1–47) are cast in such a way as to show that they represent the fulfillment of the OT promises of the Davidic messianic kingdom. The central OT text is 2Sa 7:4–17, though, as the several OT quotations in this chapter show, there were other passages as well. As in 2Sa 7, the locus of the messianic kingdom is Jerusalem. The coming of the Spirit was promised throughout the OT (e.g., see Eze 36:27). In 2:17–21, Peter gives an extended quotation from Joel 2:28–32. In 2:25–28 he links it with another quotation from Ps 16:8–11, and in 2:34–35 with Ps 110. Luke uses Peter's sermon to establish his main point at the opening of this book: the messianic kingdom of David was now being offered again to Israel. It had been offered to Israel by Jesus before his death (Lk 13:34–35; 23:3), and it was now being offered again (Ac 2:36; 3:19–26). This offer was a fulfillment of Jesus' last request on the cross: "Father, forgive them, for they do not know what they are doing" (Lk 23:34).

Thus Peter tells those looking on the events of Pentecost, "This is what was spoken by the prophet Joel" (Ac 2:16). Peter announced that Joel's prophecy was being fulfilled, just as the angel Gabriel had announced at the birth of Jesus that the prophecies of Isaiah were being fulfilled (see Lk 1:32–

33). In both cases, however, the people of Israel rejected the King and the kingdom (Lk 23:18–38; Ac 3:23; 4:1–12). Only a remnant from the house of Israel followed Jesus (Ac 2:37–41). This became the seed from which the early church grew. The new Christians devoted themselves to "the apostles' teaching and to the fellowship, to the breaking of bread and to prayer" (v.42). The apostles performed "many wonders and miraculous signs" (v.43), and "all the believers were together and had everything in common" (v.44). Though they met for fellowship in their own homes, they "continued to meet together in the temple courts" (v.46).

Luke then recounts a particularly important example of a miracle performed by the apostles, the healing of the crippled beggar (3:1–10). Peter performed miracles just as Jesus had in the gospel of Luke. He was the central figure representing the early church at this time. The healing of the crippled beggar became the occasion for Peter's second sermon in Jerusalem (3:11–26). He began by identifying Jesus as the one promised and sent by "the God of Abraham, Isaac and Jacob." He is the "Holy and Righteous One" whom Israel rejected and handed over to the Romans "to be killed" (vv.13–14). But God raised him from the dead, and it is by faith in him that the crippled beggar was healed (v.16). Because Israel acted in ignorance when they rejected Jesus, Peter offered them another chance to repent and turn to God (v.19). If they did so, their sins would be forgiven and the Lord would send "the times of refreshing" (v.19), i.e., "the Christ, who has been appointed for you—even Jesus" (v.20). He will "remain in heaven until the time comes for God to restore everything, as he promised long ago through his holy prophets" (v.21).

Although Luke does not include an account of the response of the people, he does give a detailed report of the reaction of the leaders of the Jews to Peter and John (4:1–22). Unable to deny that Peter and John had worked a miracle (v.16), the "rulers, elders and teachers of the law," along with the high priest and others of his family (vv.5–6), warned the apostles "to speak no longer to anyone" in the name of Jesus (v.17). Not knowing "how to punish them" (v.21), they then released them. The rejection of Jesus by these leaders was interpreted by the apostles as a fulfillment of the words of Ps 2:1–2: "The kings of the earth take their stand and the rulers gather together against the Lord and against his Anointed One" (vv.25–26).

Luke goes to some length to show that God was working in this small group of believers. They prayed for boldness to speak the word and for God to perform "signs and wonders through the name of" Jesus (vv.23–30). God answered their prayer by filling them with the Holy Spirit so that they "spoke the word of God boldly" (v.31), and by doing great signs among them through the apostles (v.33; 5:12–16). Amid the great signs, however, God still looked upon the heart of each of these believers. Some, like Barnabas, selflessly shared all that they owned with the church (4:32–37). Others, like Ananias and Sapphira, lied both to the apostles and to God and were severely punished (5:1–10).

The result of the growth of the early church was an increasing opposition from the leaders in Jerusalem. The apostles were arrested by "the high priest and all his associates, who were members of the party of the Sadducees" (v.17). But an angel released them during the night, and at daybreak the apostles were again proclaiming the Gospel in the temple courts. Taken once more to the high priests, again it was Peter who defended the apostles before the Sanhedrin (vv.29–32). The Jewish leaders charged him with inciting the people against them by making them responsible for the death of Jesus (v.28).

Peter and the apostles, however, responded with the defense, "We must obey God rather than men!" (v.29). Jesus had been sent by God, and both the apostles and the works that they did in his name were ample evidence that his word was true. At the last moment, the cautious words of the Pharisee Gamaliel won the day. There had been similar occurrences and claims made in the past, Gamaliel argued, and nothing ever came of them. "Leave [the apostles] alone. . . . For if their purpose or activity is of human origin, it will fail. But if it is from God, you will not be able to stop these men; you will only find yourselves fighting against God" (vv.38–39).

Gamaliel's words provide the apologetic background to the remainder of the book of Acts. In their own words, the Jewish leaders had settled on a criterion. If the spread of the early church failed, it was only the work of human beings. Luke is thus intent on showing that, far from failing, the early church continued to grow, not only in Jerusalem, but in Judea and to the ends of the earth. It was, in other words, the work of God, "Day after day, in the temple courts and from house to house, they never stopped teaching and proclaiming the good news that Jesus is the Christ" (v.42).

## B. The Early Spread of the Church (6:1–12:25)

The focus of the book of Acts turns now to key individuals instrumental in the spread of the early church: Stephen (6:1–8:3), Philip (8:4–40), Saul (i.e., Paul; 9:1–31), and Peter (9:32–11:18). The first two men, Stephen and Philip, were not of the Twelve. They were numbered with the seven "deacons" who had been appointed to help administer the daily needs of the growing church (6:1–7).

## 1. The Hellenists, Stephen, and Persecution (6:12–8:3)

Stephen, "a man full of faith and of the Holy Spirit" (6:5), "did great wonders and miraculous signs among the people" (v.8). Opposition to his teaching broke out among Jews from the Greek-speaking world: Cyrene, Alexandria, Cilicia, and Asia. When argumentation failed, men from these groups stirred up widespread resentment against Stephen, based on false witnesses. Their charge was that Stephen was speaking against the temple and the Law of Moses (vv.13–14). Stephen gave a lengthy explanation and defense of his teaching before the Sanhedrin (6:15–7:53), at the conclusion of which, he charged Jerusalem's leaders with being a "stiff-necked people, with uncircumcised hearts and ears" (7:51). For this, Stephen was dragged out of the city and stoned (v.57).

Stephen's speech before the Sanhedrin was a masterful appeal to the whole of the OT Scriptures in defense of the Gospel. In it Stephen stressed the promised blessings of God and their continual delay because of the people's unfaithfulness. He began with God's call of Abraham out of Mesopotamia and his promise to give the land to Abraham and his descendants (vv.1–5). With that promise, there was also the threat of exile and postponement of the blessing (vv.6–8). God gave Abraham "the covenant of circumcision" as a sign of the promise. The first exile and delay of the promise came when the patriarchs "were jealous of Joseph" and sold him into Egypt (v.9). God, however, rescued Joseph and made him a ruler of a great Gentile nation, Egypt (v.10). As such, Joseph was able to save the chosen seed of Abraham by bringing them down to Egypt (vv.11–16).

As the time of fulfillment grew near, oppression increased for God's people in Egypt, but God sent a deliverer, Moses (vv.17–36). Moses had

given Israel "living words" to pass on to future generations (v.38) and the promise of the coming of another prophet, like him (v.37; cf. Dt 18:15; 34:10). Having delivered the people from Egypt, however, the fulfillment of God's promise to Abraham was delayed again because of the sin of the golden calf: "God turned away and gave them over to the worship of the heavenly bodies" (vv.39–43). In spite of the sin of the golden calf, Israel enjoyed God's presence at the tabernacle that God had given to Moses. Those who "enjoyed God's favor" continued to meet with God at the tabernacle up to the time of David and Solomon, when the temple was built (vv.44–47). The temple, however, was not God's original intent for living with his people: "The Most High does not live in houses made by men" (v.48). The prophets had long ago spoken of the inadequacy of the temple (vv.49–50), but their message had been rejected and the messengers persecuted, just as now, in Stephen's own day, the promises were to be delayed, the message rejected, and the messenger persecuted (vv.51–53). Only Stephen saw the promise fulfilled—"heaven open and the Son of Man standing at the right hand of God" (vv.54–56). Unwittingly mimicking the words of judgment against Israel spoken by the prophet Isaiah ("make their ears dull. . . . Otherwise they might hear with their ears, understand with their hearts, and turn and be healed," Isa 6:10), the people "covered their ears" and stoned him (vv.57–58a).

Standing at their side was the young man, Saul (later to become the apostle Paul), who himself would say of Israel's rejection of Jesus, "they hardly hear with their ears. . . . Otherwise they might . . . hear with their ears, understand with their hearts and turn" (28:25–27). From the time of Stephen on, a great persecution arose against the church; Saul led the field in trying to "destroy" it (8:1–3). But as in the time of the Exodus, "the more they were oppressed, the more they multiplied and spread" (Ex 1:12).

## 2. The mission of Philip (8:4–40)

The ministry of Philip is an example of the spread of the Gospel during a time of oppression. Philip, forced to flee from Jerusalem to Samaria, preached the Gospel there and performed miraculous signs (vv.4–8). Many believed and were baptized (vv.9–12), including a sorcerer, Simon (v.13). The Gospel had now been offered to and accepted by the Samaritans; so the leaders of the church in Jerusalem sent Peter and John to confirm these new believers in the faith. When Peter and John prayed for them, these Samaritan believers received the Holy Spirit (cf. Ac 2), confirming that they had been accepted by the Lord into the church. Thus, in Luke's overall strategy within Acts, the church was beginning to expand beyond its initial stages in Jerusalem. Moreover, it was all carried out under the watchful eyes of the apostles in Jerusalem and the work of the Spirit of God.

Luke records the incident of Simon the sorcerer's attempt to purchase the ability to impart the Holy Spirit (vv.18–24) in order to drive the point home to the reader: The work of God *cannot* be purchased with money. One whose heart is set on gaining wealth from the ministry can have no share in it (v.21). Though Peter's words to such a one are a stern warning to the readers of this book, his call for repentance and forgiveness is also meant as a source of great comfort (vv.22–23).

The Gospel now spread to Ethiopia (vv.26–40). Just as the angel of the Lord had led Israel through the desert (Ex 23:20), so here Philip was led in "the desert road that goes down . . . to Gaza" (Ac 8:26). Just as Stephen had drawn the message of the gospel from a thorough review of the OT Scriptures (7:1–

50), so Philip began with the words of Isa 53 and "told [the eunuch] the good news about Jesus" (Ac 8:35).

## 3. The conversion of Paul (9:1–31)

This is the first of four times Luke recounts Paul's conversion (9:3–6, 27; 22:3–21; 26:12–18). For Luke it was a decisive stage in the spread and development of the early church. It meant a new direction for the spread of the Gospel. Paul was to be the apostle to the Gentiles: "This man is my chosen instrument to carry my name before the Gentiles and their kings and before the people of Israel" (9:15).

Arising out of the persecutions aroused by the stoning of Stephen (8:1–3), Saul (Paul) was actively engaged in pursuing the spread of the Gospel into Damascus. In an ironic role, reminiscent of his future ministry of carrying the Gospel to foreign soil, he had prepared to hunt down and stamp out any trace of the nascent church in Damascus (9:1–2). He never made it there, however—at least not in the capacity of one who would persecute the church. On the way to Damascus, Saul met Jesus, and ironically, he who had been blind to the Gospel (8:1) was now blind to the world (9:8). After he had received the Holy Spirit, "something like scales fell from Saul's eyes, and he could see again" (v.18). For Luke, Saul is a paradigm of the Israelite who, once blind, now, with his eyes opened, could see Jesus (cf. 28:26–27). He immediately began to preach the Gospel in the synagogues (9:20), proving that "Jesus is the Christ" (v.22). As would be the case throughout the remainder of Acts, Paul was forced to flee Damascus because of the opposition he faced from his teaching.

Returning to Jerusalem, Saul "moved about freely . . . speaking boldly in the name of the Lord" (v.28). In due time, his teaching aroused the anger of his fellow Jews and he had to flee again, first to Caesarea and then to Tarsus (v.30).

### 4. The mission of Peter (9:32–11:18)

With Paul safely in Tarsus and the church in Judea, Galilee, and Samaria growing in numbers and strength (9:31), Luke turns to the ministry of Peter. He records the details of two miracles that Peter performed: the healing of the paralytic Aeneas (vv.32–35) and the raising of the disciple Dorcas (vv.36–43). It is important for Luke to show the apostolic credentials of Peter at this point in the narrative because, in the next section, at God's command, Peter initiates a major transition in the nature of the early church. The church will not only be opened to Gentiles, but also the stringent requirements of the Mosaic Law will be lifted. Though the Gospels show that Jesus had already taught the temporary nature of the Mosaic Law (Mt 19:8; Mk 7:19), Luke gives the historical record of God's bringing this about in the early church.

An angel appeared to a Roman centurion in Caesarea named Cornelius. He was a devout man who offered prayers to God and gave gifts to the poor. The angel directed him to find Peter in Joppa and return him to Caesarea. While they were coming to Joppa, Peter also received a vision. In the vision, the Lord commanded Peter to eat from an array of animals that had been declared unclean in the Mosaic Law. In the vision, Peter refused to eat the unclean food, but the Lord insisted three times.

While he was still puzzling over the meaning of that vision, Peter received the messengers from Cornelius. Peter was then directed by the Spirit to go with the men to Cornelius. Something of the state of mind of Peter and the early church can be seen in his remarks at meeting Cornelius. He tells him that "it is against our law for a Jew to associate with a Gentile or visit him" (10:28). Up to this point, Peter, a Christian, still considered himself a Jew with all the responsibilities that entailed. It would have been unthinkable for him to have gone to the house of Cornelius without the express command of the Lord in the vision. Even then, Peter resisted. A further insight into the gravity of Peter's action can be seen in the reaction of the "circumcised believers" in Jerusalem. Upon hearing what Peter had done, they criticized him, saying, "You went into the house of uncircumcised men and ate with them" (11:2–3). To Luke, however, a change had taken place in Peter's thinking: "God has shown me that I should not call any man impure or unclean" (10:28). "I now realize how true it is that God does not show favoritism but accepts men from every nation" (vv.34–35).

When Cornelius asked Peter what it was the Lord had commanded him to say, Peter began to retell the story of the Gospel. He began with the life and ministry of John the Baptist, then spoke about Jesus' ministry, death, and resurrection, and concluded with the spread of the Gospel in the early church (vv.36–42). He assumed that Cornelius, a Roman official, was already for the most part aware of what he was recounting. It is interesting to note just how parochial Peter's presentation of the Gospel was. He viewed the Gospel as God's message "to the people of Israel" (v.36) and understood his commission to be "to preach to the people" (v.42), presumedly, the Israelite people. Only when he came to a summary of the message of the OT prophets did the scope of Peter's presentation of the Gospel begin to open beyond that of the people of Israel: "All the prophets testify about him that everyone who believes in him receives forgiveness of sins through his name" (v.43). At this point, "while Peter was still speaking" (v.44), the Holy Spirit came upon Cornelius and those with him, leaving the "circumcised believers who had come with Peter . . . astonished that the gift of the Holy Spirit had been poured out even on the Gentiles" (v.45). It could not be denied because "they heard them speaking in tongues and praising God" (v.46). Not knowing what else to do, Peter ordered that these new believers also be "baptized in the name of Jesus Christ" (v.48).

Peter had much explaining to do on his return to the Jerusalem church (11:1–18). When criticized for eating with Gentiles (and we may assume for baptizing them), Peter offered only a mere description of the events as his defense (vv.4–15). He then added the earlier words of Jesus (v.16) and the witness of the Holy Spirit, which was the same as that which they themselves had received on Pentecost (v.17). His conclusion, and hence also Luke's in the argument of the book of Acts, was, "Who was I to think that I could oppose God?" Thus the offer of the Gospel to Gentiles as well as Jews was not a planned strategy of outreach on the part of the early church. Rather, God "granted even the Gentiles repentance unto life," and the early church could only praise God and offer "no further objections" (v.18).

## 5. The congregation at Antioch (11:19–30)

In 11:19–26, Luke quickly adds an explanation that Peter's experience was not isolated. Even though, for the most part, Christians were spreading the Gospel "only to Jews" (v.19), some were also evangelizing the Greeks in Antioch (v.20). Though recounted only in summary form, we can see that the Jerusalem church followed the same procedure as with Peter. In sending Barnabas to Antioch, the church in Jerusalem was content with "the evidence of the grace of God" that he saw there (vv.22–24). It was at this time also that Paul (Saul) came to Antioch, with Barnabas, and both of them remained there for a full year, teaching "great numbers of people" (vv.25–26). Here

they were first called "Christians" (v.26b). At this time Barnabas and Saul were also sent to Judea (i.e., Jerusalem) with a gift of provisions for the churches there (vv.27–30).

## 6. Persecution of the early community by Agrippa (12:1–25)

Barnabas and Saul returned to Antioch when they "had finished their mission ... taking with them John, also called Mark" (v.25). During this time Peter was imprisoned and miraculously rescued (vv.1–19). Luke has carefully woven the two narratives together to emphasize the dual leadership of Peter and Paul in the church at Jerusalem. After ch. 12, we hear of Peter only once again in Acts, during the Jerusalem Council (15:7). Peter is a transition figure in the book. He led the Jerusalem church and represented the early Jewish Christians. But Luke's purpose in this book is to show that the church expanded beyond this initial group of believers. Thus, after the Gospel had spread to the Gentiles, the focus of Luke moves beyond Jerusalem to Paul and his missionary journeys among the Gentiles. It is significant that in Ac 15, Peter is the one who gives a decisive defense of the Gentile mission of the church: "God, who knows the heart, showed that he accepted [the Gentiles] by giving the Holy Spirit to them, just as he did to us" (15:8). The spread of the Gospel to the Gentiles was not the result of Paul, the apostle to the Gentiles, but rather Peter, the leader of the Jewish church in Jerusalem.

As his last word on the situation in Jerusalem, Luke includes a brief account of the death of Herod (12:19b–25), one in a long line of kings who opposed Jesus and the church (cf. Lk 9:9; 13:31–33; 23:7–12). Luke perhaps intends this narrative as a commentary on the fate of the Jewish leaders who, in response to the growing church, "did not give praise to God" (Ac 12:22). Behind this narrative stand the words of

Gamaliel, recorded earlier in Acts (see 5:38–39). These leaders had had ample time to see that the work of Jesus had not failed, thus they should have concluded that it was the work of God. From this point on in the book, the Gospel begins to spread to the ends of the earth—ironically, through the work of Paul, a student of Gamaliel (22:3).

## III. The Mission of the Early Church (13:1–28:31)

### A. The First Missionary Journey (13:1–14:28)

The leaders of the church at Antioch, having been led by the Holy Spirit, sent Barnabas and Saul on a missionary journey to Cyprus (13:4–12), Pisidian Antioch (13:13–52), Iconium (14:1–5), and Lystra and Derbe (14:6–20). They then returned to Antioch (14:21–28). They took John Mark with them (13:5b; cf. 12:25), but he returned to Jerusalem after a short time into the journey (13:13). According to 15:38, Paul saw this as a desertion of their work (cf. 15:36–41).

In recounting the narrative of this journey, Luke focuses on the work of Saul, whom he begins to call Paul in 13:9. Clearly Luke's interest is in the central role played by Paul in evangelizing the Gentiles. On this journey, Paul and those with him "proclaimed the word of God" in the Jewish synagogues (13:5, 14–44; 14:1), but they were nearly always forced to go outside the narrow limits of Judaism to gain a hearing (13:6–12, 45–52; 14:2, 19). The result was that both Jews and Gentiles came to faith in Jesus as the Messiah. The opposition of the Jewish sorcerer and false prophet, Bar-Jesus, for example, resulted in the conversion of the Roman proconsul, Sergius Paulus (13:6–12).

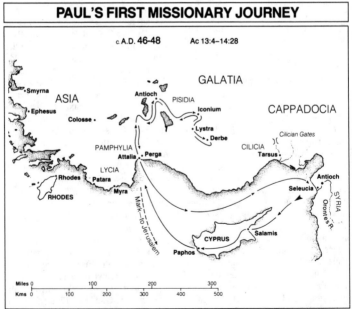

## PAUL'S FIRST MISSIONARY JOURNEY

c.A.D. 46-48      Ac 13:4–14:28

Luke includes a lengthy summary of one of Paul's synagogue sermons (13:16–41). The sermon was addressed to those of Israel and to "Gentiles who worship God" (v.16). He began with God's call of "the fathers," i.e., Abraham, Isaac, and Jacob. But he moved immediately to God's deliverance of Israel from Egypt and their time in the desert. Though subtle, Paul cast Israel's time in the desert in a rather negative light, saying, God "endured their conduct for about forty years in the desert" (v.18). This is the same view of the wanderings in the desert reflected in Stephen's speech in 7:39–43, and it stems from the interpretation of this time in Israel's history found in the prophetic books (e.g., Am 5:25–27). Ultimately, this view is derived from the Pentateuch itself (see comments on Ex 32). This was an important feature of Paul's reading of the OT, fitting in with the negative direction he would take at the conclusion of his sermon with Israel's rejection of Jesus. Just as Israel rejected Moses in the desert and God endured them for forty years, so Israel rejected Jesus, but God was continuing to endure them.

The time of the Conquest, the judges, Samuel, and King Saul were briefly alluded to, leaving the central focus of Paul's summary of the OT Scriptures on David and his descendant, Jesus. Jesus was the fulfillment of God's promise to David that from among his descendants would come Israel's Savior (cf. 2Sa 7:12). Moreover, Paul stressed, Jesus was given the full endorsement of John the Baptist, a man clearly recognized throughout the Jewish community in Judea as a true prophet (Lk 20:6). Jesus, however, had been rejected by "the people of Jerusalem and their rulers" (13:27). This led to his crucifixion. But God raised him from the dead, and many of his followers had seen him and were now bearing witness of him to the people of Israel.

The resurrection of Jesus had been promised by David in the Scriptures. To read the Scriptures as about David himself rather than the Messiah, Paul argued, was to miss the very meaning of the words themselves. David died, was buried, and his body had decayed. Thus David's words, "You will not let your Holy One see decay," could not be about him, but had to be about the Messiah, who would be raised from the dead (vv.34–37). Moreover, Jesus' death meant justification from sin, which was not possible by the Law of Moses (vv.38–39). Anyone who might scoff at such claims should take warning of the words of the prophets themselves: "I am going to do something in your days that you will not believe [NIV, that you would never believe]" (v.41b).

Luke records that "many of the Jews and devout converts to Judaism" accepted Paul's words about Jesus and were encouraged by Paul and Barnabas to "continue in the grace of God" (v.43). The next week, however, Paul and Barnabas met with stiff opposition, leading them to turn to the Gentiles (vv.44–48). Paul saw this not as a strategical retreat, but as a central part of God's plan to bring the Gospel to the Gentiles. Even the prophets had spoke of God's messengers as "a light for the Gentiles" (v.47). In this way "all who were appointed for eternal life" were presented with the Gospel and believed (v.48). Thus, even when they were persecuted and forced to flee the region, Paul and Barnabas "were filled with joy and with the Holy Spirit" (v.52).

As their journey progressed, Paul and Barnabas came to Iconium and there, "spoke so effectively that a great number of Jews and Gentiles believed" (14:1). There was also great opposition (vv.2–5), but it only served to further the spread of the Gospel (vv.6–7). So successful were they in Lystra that the local residents thought them to be

Greek gods (vv.8–13). Paul responded with the warning that although such ideas about "worthless" idols had been tolerated among the Gentiles in the past, all nations were now to turn from them to the worship of the living God. Paul's response to the people's desire to deify them (vv.15–18) stands in sharp contrast to that of Herod when the crowd called out, "This is the voice of a god, not of a man" (12:22).

Paul and Barnabas returned to Antioch by ret    ing their journey and encouraged the new Christians "to remain true to the faith" (14:21–22). They also appointed elders in each of the new churches (v.23). On their arrival in Antioch they reported all that had happened to them, stressing the fact that God "had opened the door of faith to the Gentiles" (v.27). It was this fact that erupted into the Jerusalem Council (ch. 15).

### B. The Jerusalem Council (15:1–35)

Among the new Christians in Antioch were some Christians from Jerusalem teaching the necessity of circumcision and obedience to the Law of Moses for salvation (15:1). Paul and Barnabas, who were at Antioch at that time, opposed their teaching vehemently. The church in Antioch sent Paul and Barnabas to Jerusalem to seek the advice of the apostles and elders there (vv.2–4).

When the council was convened, the two sides were quickly drawn. A group of Pharisees who were believers stated their case: "The Gentiles must be circumcised and required to obey the law of Moses" (v.5). Luke records that there was "much discussion" on this issue (v.7). At its conclusion, Peter, the erstwhile representative of the Jewish believers, in his last appearance in the book of Acts, stated what was to become the consensus of the council: "Why do you try to test God by putting on the necks of the disciples a yoke that neither we nor our fathers have been able to bear? No! We believe it is

through the grace of our Lord Jesus that we are saved, just as [the Gentiles] are" (vv.10–11). Paul and Barnabas followed Peter's words with a report of what God had done among the Gentiles on their missionary journey to Asia Minor (v.12). At the conclusion, James voiced the decision of the council (vv.13–19), and a letter was sent to Antioch recording the decision: In agreement with the words of the prophets themselves, the Gentiles who had come to faith in Jesus did not have to fulfill the Law of Moses. Out of respect for the Jews, however, they should abstain from those things that were particularly offensive (v.20).

Luke thus shows in this incident that the early church was careful and thoughtful of the central issues at work in the development of the early church. They did not tolerate unauthorized preaching, as had originally stirred up the problem in Antioch, and they were prepared to discuss the questions openly. The bases of their decision were the Scriptures, the teaching of Jesus, and the work of the Holy Spirit. All sides were given an opportunity to speak, and a consensus was reached. Luke writes as if he intended this account to provide an example for further decisions in the church.

### C. The Second Missionary Journey (15:36–18:22)

Paul and Barnabas made plans for a return trip to the churches they had founded in Asia Minor. Because of a "sharp disagreement" over including John Mark on the journey, Paul and Barnabas parted company (15:36–39). Barnabas, with John Mark, went by sea to the churches in Cyprus, and Paul, with Silas, went by land through Syria and Cilicia. Luke intends to show that even in adversity and struggle, God's work was carried out.

Paul and Silas, continuing on their journey through Asia Minor, met Timothy at Lystra. Timothy was circumcised by Paul—apparently in accordance with the Jerusalem Council's decision (16:4). Timothy, whose mother was Jewish, was a Jewish Christian, but he had not been circumcised because his father was Greek. Together with Silas and Timothy, Paul traveled to Troas (15:40–16:10). They did not preach on the way (16:6), and, though intending to head north and west to Mysia and Bithynia, by the Spirit's direction they set sail for Macedonia.

Events on this journey stand in sharp contrast with those of the first. At Philippi, Paul preached "on the Sabbath," but not in a synagogue. He went "outside the city gate to the river," at a "place of prayer" (v.13). The fact that the meeting for prayer was on the Sab-

bath suggests that this was a Jewish group. There they met Lydia, a tradeswoman who heard Paul preach the Gospel and believed in Jesus. Ironically, the people of the city charged Paul and Silas with being "Jews" and "advocating customs unlawful for us Romans to accept or practice" (vv.20–21). Behind their charge lay the simple fact that Paul had cast a "spirit" out of a slave girl who had earned her owners a great deal of money by fortune-telling. For this, Paul and Silas were stripped, beaten, and thrown into jail without a trial (vv.37–39). While in jail, they "were praying and singing hymns to God, and the other prisoners were listening to them" (vv.25). Through their courage and compassion, the jailer believed in Jesus and was saved.

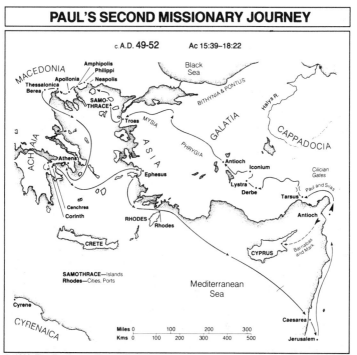

## PAUL'S SECOND MISSIONARY JOURNEY

c.A.D. 49-52          Ac 15:39–18:22

SAMOTHRACE—Islands
Rhodes—Cities, Ports

Miles 0    100    200    300
Kms 0  100  200  300  400  500

At Thessalonica, the disciples were back in a synagogue, preaching and reasoning "with them from the Scriptures, explaining and proving that the Christ had to suffer and rise from the dead" (17:1–9). Some were persuaded, including many Gentiles and prominent women. As many times already, Luke stresses that Jewish opposition to Paul's teaching led to trouble with the city officials. Here, as at Philippi, the charge was that they were "defying Caesar's decrees" and calling Jesus a king (v.7).

Arriving at Berea, Paul again went to a Jewish synagogue where, this time, his message was well received. His hearers "examined the Scriptures every day to see if what Paul said was true" (v.11). Many Jews and Gentiles believed in Jesus (vv.10–15). Again, further opposition meant they had to leave these new converts and move on to the next city, Athens.

In Athens (vv.16–34), Paul not only "reasoned in the synagogues with the Jews and God-fearing Greeks," but he also went to the marketplace "day by day" to speak with those who gathered there. His presence aroused the curiosity of the philosophers of the city, and they sought from him an explanation of his teaching. Luke records a summary of Paul's address with them at the Areopagus (vv.22–31), a place where they customarily gathered to discuss "the latest ideas."

Although Luke tells us that Paul was "greatly distressed" at the idolatry he found in Athens, there is no mention of this in his speech. Rather, he stressed the positive side of their "objects of worship" and saw in them a link to the message of the gospel: the altar inscribed "TO AN UNKNOWN GOD" (v.23). It was of the worship of this God that Paul spoke. When Paul identified God as the one "who made the world and everything in it" and who "gives all men life and breath," and when he stated that "from one man he made every nation of

men" (vv.24–26), he unmistakably relied on the view of God revealed in the OT (Ge 1–11). Thus he showed that, even here in Greece, an understanding of the God of the OT was fundamental to an appreciation of the Gospel. He did not build on a Greek foundation. He found a link with the Greeks' "UNKNOWN GOD," but by its very nature, such a link could not be a basis on which to develop his message. His Gospel was about the God who made himself known in Scripture.

At the same time, Paul showed a remarkable willingness to quote their own Greek poets (v.28). He did so, however, not to support the message of the Gospel, but to show the fallacy of their idolatry (v.29). Such ignorance might have been overlooked in the past, but the time had come for its judgment. Paul clearly recognized the implications of the Gospel's being offered to the Gentiles—a central point of Acts: They were now responsible to its claims.

The urgency of Paul's message came from his appeal to the eschatological aspects of the OT Scriptures: God "has set a day when he will judge the world with justice by the man he has appointed" (v.31). Paul had begun with the Genesis narratives, and he now concluded with ideas derived directly out of later texts of the OT (e.g., Da 7:9–14). Hence, for him, the decisive proof of God's work was the Resurrection (cf. Da 12:2). This was also the point at which Paul's hearers broke in on him: "Some of them sneered, but others said, 'We want to hear you again on this subject'" (17:32). Luke records that a few believed in Jesus after hearing Paul's sermon, including "Dionysius, a member of the Areopagus, also a woman named Damaris" (v.34).

On the next leg of the journey, Paul was in Corinth and back in the synagogue, "trying to persuade Jews and Greeks" (18:1–17). Paul's focus was "testifying to the Jews that Jesus was the Christ" (v.5). His associates at Corinth were fellow tentmakers Aquila and his wife, Priscilla, Jews who had recently been expelled from Rome, and Silas and Timothy, who had joined him from Macedonia.

Again meeting stiff opposition from the Jews, Paul left the synagogue and moved to the house next door to continue his teaching (v.7). Luke adds the remarkable notice that during this time the leader of the synagogue, Crispus, his entire household, and many others in Corinth "believed in the Lord" and were baptized (v.8). Having received encouragement from the Lord in a vision, Paul remained teaching in Corinth for a year and a half (vv.9–11).

In Paul's vision, the Lord had said, "No one is going to attack and harm you" (v.10). To illustrate what this meant, Luke includes a brief narrative of an attempt made by the Jews to silence Paul by appealing to Gallio, the Roman proconsul of that district. Gallio summarily refused to harm Paul and "had [the Jews] ejected from the court" (vv.14–16).

Luke gives only a summary of Paul's return to Antioch (vv.18–22). He continues to stress, however, that Paul's primary focus remained the synagogue, where he "reasoned with the Jews" (v.19).

## D. The Third Missionary Journey (18:23–21:16)

Luke turns immediately to Paul's third missionary journey. Having spent some time in Antioch, he traveled throughout the regions of Galatia and Phrygia (18:23) before moving on to Ephesus.

In Ephesus Paul met some disciples of John the Baptist (19:1–7). They may have been those who had followed Apollos, an Alexandrian Jew (18:24–28) with a thorough knowledge of the OT Scriptures. Apollos had been educated in "the way of the Lord" and had an accurate knowledge of Jesus. Priscilla and Aquila, who had remained at Ephesus during Paul's second journey (v.19), needed only to explain to him "the way of God more adequately" (v.26). Apollos had moved on to Achaia, where he "vigorously refuted the Jews in public debate" (v.28).

When Paul returned to Ephesus, he apparently met with a remnant of Apollos's earlier "disciples." They were Christians, but they had not yet been baptized by the Spirit into the church. When Paul did baptize them and lay his hands on them, just as the first Christians at Jerusalem, "the Holy Spirit came on them, and they spoke in tongues and prophesied" (19:6). Moreover, Luke stresses that they numbered about "twelve men" (cf. 1:26). Luke's purpose in highlighting the conversion of these men appears to be to give justification and explanation for the inclusion of all the various transitional groups into the early church. It may also have been to provide limits for any further claims for legitimate inclusion into the church. In Luke's day, there were no doubt many groups that sought legitimacy under the umbrella of the early church. By carefully identifying those groups that were in fact included, Luke provides a basis for the exclusion of all others. The fact that these twelve disciples were indirectly linked by Luke to Apollos, an Alexandrian Jew, suggests that Luke may also be addressing the question of the legitimacy of the church in Alexandria. Those who represented that church, which otherwise remains unmentioned by Luke, are here noted as being essentially at one with the growing church in Jerusalem and Asia.

In Ephesus, Paul also taught in the synagogue (19:8). When opposition arose, Paul left the synagogue and held daily discussions in "the lecture hall of Tyrannus" (v.9). He continued there for two years and enjoyed a widespread audience (v.10). Luke seems concerned to stress the "extraordinary miracles" that God did through Paul during this time (v.11). Miracles are already extraordinary, but Luke describes these miracles at Ephesus as "extraordinary" miracles! The reader quickly understands what Luke meant by his giving two examples of such miracles. In the first, "even handkerchiefs and aprons that had touched [Paul] were taken to the sick, and their illnesses were cured and the evil spirits left them" (v.12). In the second, when Jewish exorcists attempted to cast out evil spirits "in the name of Jesus, whom Paul preaches," not only were they unsuccessful, but they were attacked and overpowered by the spirits so fiercely that the inhabitants of the city were "seized with fear,

and the name of the Lord Jesus was held in high honor" (v.17). These were not ordinary miracles!

With great success, however, came great opposition. Luke gives a vivid account of such opposition that faced Paul in Ephesus (vv.23–41). The shift in Luke's focus away from the synagogue and toward the pagan Gentile world is clearly noticeable in this section. Paul's opposition came not from the leaders of the synagogue, as was so common in the earlier parts of this book, but from the pagan workers who traded in the business of idolatry. Even when the Jews attempted to become involved by pushing their spokesman to the front (v.33), the crowd would have nothing to do with them (v.34). Thus Luke shows that this disturbance had nothing to do

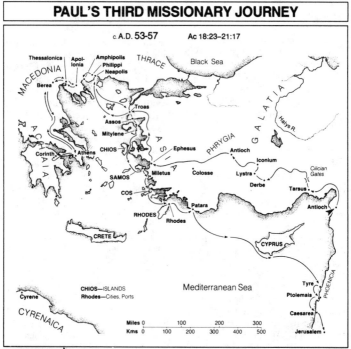

## PAUL'S THIRD MISSIONARY JOURNEY

c. A.D. 53-57    Ac 18:23–21:17

CHIOS—ISLANDS
Rhodes—Cities, Ports

Mediterranean Sea

Miles 0    100    200    300
Kms 0    100    200    300    400    500

© 1989 The Zondervan Corporation.

with the erstwhile struggle between the Jewish leaders and the early church. Rather, this was a struggle between the Gospel and the pagan world. In the end, however, it was again the Roman government that calmed the opposition and returned peace to the city (vv.35–41). The city clerk spoke in behalf of the administration of Rome when he said, "We are in danger of being charged with rioting because of today's events" (v.40).

Paul journeyed from Ephesus to Macedonia to Greece and back to Troas (20:1–6). After a brief stay in Troas (vv.7–12), he went to Miletus (vv.13–16). Calling the elders of the church at Ephesus, Paul bid them farewell (vv.17–38) and continued on to Jerusalem (21:1–16).

Luke's portrayal of Paul's ministry now bears close resemblance to that of Jesus. Just as Jesus resolutely set his mind on going to Jerusalem (Lk 9:51), so here Paul "was in a hurry to reach Jerusalem" (Ac 20:16). Just as Jesus prayed into the night while his disciples slept (Lk 22:39–46), so Paul at Troas "kept on talking until midnight" while Eutychus "was sinking into a deep sleep" (20:7–9). Paul, like Jesus (Lk 22:7–38), delivered a farewell address to his disciples before going to Jerusalem (Ac 20:13–48). Arrest and trial awaited both Jesus (Lk 22:1–6) and Paul (Ac 21:4–13) in Jerusalem, though both had resolved to die if it be "the Lord's will" (Lk 22:42; Ac 20:23–24; 21:14). In this way Luke shows his readers that, though events may appear otherwise, Paul's life was following God's plan and his will was being accomplished. As it had been with Jesus, Paul's journey to Jerusalem was not so much the end of his life as it was its goal (20:24).

## E. Arrest (21:17–23:10)

Paul faced controversy with fellow Christians in the Jerusalem church immediately on his return to Jerusalem (21:17–26). The newly converted Jewish Christians, who were zealous for the law, were concerned with reports they had heard that Paul taught Jewish Christians outside Jerusalem "not to circumcise their children or live according to [Jewish] customs" (v.21). Paul was advised by the leaders of the Jerusalem church to join in purification rites at the temple so "everybody will know there is no truth in these reports about you, but that you yourself are living in obedience to the law" (v.24). Paul conceded to their wishes and the conflict was avoided.

What does Luke have in mind by including this brief episode between Paul and these Jewish Christians? He has clearly distinguished between the expectations of Jewish Christians and Gentile Christians. As v.25 shows, the issue of the Gentile Christians' requirement to obey the law and Jewish customs had been resolved at the Jerusalem Council (ch. 15). That was not the question here. Rather, the question was whether Jewish Christians also had to abandon the requirements of the Law. The elders of the church in Jerusalem did not think so, and Paul went along with them. Moreover, Luke was clear that their intent was not limited to Jews in Jerusalem. They wanted it known that the report that Paul taught Jews outside Jerusalem "to turn away from Moses" (21:21) was not only completely false, but also that Paul himself was "living in obedience to the law" (v.24). Luke's purpose, then, was to show that the development of the Gentile church did not mean the end of God's work with his chosen people Israel. God had not cast Israel off when he opened the doors of the church to the Gentiles. A remnant of Israel was saved. As Paul later wrote, "God did not reject his people, whom he foreknew. . . . At the present time there is a remnant chosen by grace" (Ro 11:2–5).

An additional purpose Luke may have had in mind with this narrative was to expose the error of the Asian Jews' accusation against Paul in the next section. They said, "This is the man who teaches all men everywhere against our people and our law and this place" (21:28). The fact that Paul had just gone out of his way to demonstrate that he had been "living in obedience to the law" (v.24) shows the reader that their accusation was false.

Nevertheless, Paul was arrested on the false charge of teaching against Israel and the law (vv.27–40). Once again it was the Romans who intervened and saved his life (vv.31–32). Through them Paul was given another chance to speak and defend himself before the Jews at Jerusalem (22:1–21). In his defense, Paul stressed that he was a faithful Jew, with a high regard for the law. He began by speaking to them in Aramaic. Under Gamaliel he "was thoroughly trained in the law of our fathers and was just as zealous for God as any of you are today" (v.3). Moreover, he himself persecuted the early Christians (v.4). Paul then told the story of his vision of Jesus and his conversion. He included several new features that reinforced his contention that he was an obedient Jew. For example, the man whom Jesus sent to confirm him after the vision, Ananias, "was a devout observer of the law and highly respected by all the Jews living" in Damascus (v.12; cf. 9:10, where Ananias was simply called "a disciple"). Also, Paul added that on a later return to Jerusalem, while he was praying at the temple, he again saw the Lord in a vision; it was then that he was sent "far away to the Gentiles" (vv.17–21).

At the mention of his commission to preach to the Gentiles, the crowd's patience was expended, and as at the time of the stoning of Stephen (v.20), of which Paul had been a part, the people began casting off their coats to stone

him. Paul was rescued only by an appeal to his Roman citizenship (vv.26–29). It may be a part of Luke's strategy to draw out the irony of Paul's situation. Amid all the talk of the Law of Moses, it was only by appealing to Roman law that he could get a fair trial (vv.29–30). Paul's response to the high priest reinforces such an intention: "You sit there to judge me according to the law, yet you yourself violate the law by commanding that I be struck!" (23:3). Moreover, Paul's own innocence is shown by his immediate recognition that he himself had violated the law in "insulting God's high priest" (v.4). In his response, Paul also acknowledged the validity of the high priest (v.5).

In his defense before the Sanhedrin (vv.6–10), Paul's appeal to the Resurrection did more than merely put an effective end to his trial. For Luke's account in the book of Acts, it plays a central role in developing the explanation for Jerusalem's rejection of Jesus. The division of the Jewish leaders over the question of the Resurrection pointed to the real issue at stake in the message of the Gospel. The Sadducees, who did not believe in the Resurrection, were not prepared to accept the Gospel message that the early church preached. Peter's first sermon in Acts had set the tone of the book's overall theme. David had foreseen the resurrection of the Messiah (2:25–31), and "God raised this Jesus to life, and we are all witnesses of the fact" (v.32). The basis of the Gospel was God's exaltation of Jesus in the Resurrection. It was through the Resurrection that God fulfilled his promises to David to establish an eternal kingdom (vv.34–36).

## F. Journey to Rome (23:11–28:31)

The course of events now took a major and final turn, signaled by a word from Jesus: "As you have testified about me in Jerusalem, so you must also testify in Rome" (23:11). We thus are shown that the events recorded by

Luke follow a determined purpose. The Lord is behind all that happens, and it is for his purpose (cf. Ro 8:28).

The first instance of this truth was a desperate and deadly plot against Paul (23:12–22). Paul was rescued and taken to the Roman governor, Felix, for safety (vv.23–35). In his account of Paul's rescue, Luke's appreciation for the Romans is unmistakable. He even recounted a full report of the Roman commander's letter to Felix (vv.26–30)! Luke's purpose was to highlight the fact that in this trial, all sides were "able to learn the truth about all these charges" brought against Paul (24:8). Felix himself was almost persuaded of the truth of Paul's words, but he pushed the decision aside. Luke adds the reason why: It had nothing to do with the strength of Paul's argument, nor with Felix's own lack of conviction at what he heard Paul speak. Rather, Felix was "afraid" when he heard Paul's words about "the judgment to come" (v.25). He rejected the offer of the Gospel, Luke intimates, because of the duplicity of his heart: "he was hoping that Paul would offer him a bribe, so he sent for him frequently and talked with him"

(v.26). Felix is like several characters in the book of Acts who come near the Gospel but fall short because of the attitude of their heart (e.g., Ananias and Sapphira in 5:1–10; Simon the sorcerer in 8:9–24). They want to gain personal advancement at the expense of the Gospel.

Paul remained in prison in Caesarea for two years, until Felix was replaced by Festus (24:27). Again, the Roman government gave providential protection to Paul (25:1–6) and a fair trial (vv.6–12). In the end it was his appeal to Caesar that provided his rescue (vv.12, 21; 26:32) and ultimately his journey to Rome (25:25). On the negative side, the central point stressed in Luke's various summaries of the proceedings is that Paul had broken no laws and that the charges against him were trifle matters dealing with the Jewish law (25:8, 19, 25–27; 26:31). The positive point stressed in Paul's own defense was the centrality of Jesus' resurrection: "Why should any of you consider it incredible that God raises the dead?" (26:8, 23). Jesus was the one promised by the OT prophets. He suffered, died, and rose again as a

**PAUL'S JOURNEY TO ROME**

"light to his own people and to the Gentiles" (v.23).

Luke recounts the two responses to Paul's defense. The response of Felix was to conclude that Paul was "out of his mind" from too much study (v.24). Agrippa's response, however, was more cautious and, in fact, ambiguous. It served to show the reader Paul's zeal for the Gospel more than Agrippa's own assessment of the truth of what Paul had spoken. He said to Paul, "Do you think in such a short time you can persuade me to be a Christian?" (v.28), and then left the room saying, "This man is not doing anything that deserves death or imprisonment" (v.31).

Luke spends much literary effort in his account of Paul's journey to Rome. There are similarities between this account and the narrative of the book of Jonah. Both accounts stress the guidance, through peril, of a sovereign God bringing his plan to completion. Jonah was reluctant to go to Nineveh to proclaim repentance to the Gentiles, and Paul went to Rome in chains. Paul did not originally set out to preach to the Gentiles, but, as with Jonah, God had other plans. Both of them experienced God's sovereign guidance in the great storm at sea. Like Jonah, Paul encouraged the men on board ship to have faith in God, and God rescued them. Luke, it appears, has deliberately fashioned his account after that of the prophet Jonah to cast Paul in the role of the prophet to the Gentiles as Jonah was in the OT.

After the shipwreck, Paul arrived on the island of Malta (28:1–10). To show the desperate need of the Gentile nations, Luke tells the story of the islanders of Malta and their fickle and hopeless superstition (vv.1–6). As they attempted to understand the unusual events that Paul brought to their island, they could not see behind these events to the work of the one God. They recognized the presence of a divine work, but they could only conclude that Paul must be a god (v.6). Unlike his treatment in Jerusalem, however, Luke shows that Paul was received here "with hospitality" (vv.7–10). One cannot help but see in this island narrative Luke's attempt to demonstrate the spread of the Gospel to the "ends of the earth" (cf. 1:8). As if to highlight further the need of these Gentiles, Luke tells us that Paul sailed into Rome on a ship "with the figurehead of the twin gods Castor and Pollux" (28:11).

Once in Rome (vv.17–31), Paul continued his practice of meeting with "the leaders of the Jews" (v.17), and "from morning till evening he explained and declared to them the kingdom of God and tried to convince them about Jesus from the Law of Moses and from the Prophets" (v.23). Some believed, but others disputed. As Luke concludes the book, the verdict of Paul is allowed to remain as the verdict of the book itself: "God's salvation has been sent to the Gentiles, and they will listen!" (28:28).

# Romans

## Introduction

The title of this letter "to the Romans" is found in the earliest complete NT manuscripts. Its writer is the apostle Paul. At the end of his third missionary journey (Ac 20:1–5), he was in Macedonia and Achaia, taking up a collection for the poor among the saints in Jerusalem (Ro 15:25–32). It is usually assumed that Paul was in Corinth when he wrote this letter, where he remained three months (Ac 20:3). This dates the book at about A.D. 58.

Like the other works of Paul in the Bible, the book of Romans is formally a letter. It is written to a specific church (Rome), has an introductory greeting (1:1–7), and gives a list of personal notes at the end (16:1–27). For the most part, however, this is where the similarity ends. The book is, in fact, an extended treatise on the nature of the Gospel, with a sustained argumentation throughout. Paul reasons, argues, gives examples, and exhorts his readers—all with the intent of making them strong in the faith. What he wanted to do in person (cf. 1:11), Paul accomplishes by this letter, "that you and I may be mutually encouraged by each other's faith" (1:12).

The central line of thought in the book is justification by faith. God has declared all those who put their faith in Christ to be righteous. There is no other way to obtain righteousness before him than through accepting God's gift in Christ. Humankind apart from God cannot find peace with God. Judaism's reliance on the Law of the Sinai covenant does not result in a right standing before God. All people have fallen short of God's standards of righteousness, and all their efforts are futile. The good news is that God, in his great grace, has sent his own Son Jesus Christ as a sin offering for humanity, and through faith in him, all are made righteous.

Having built the above case for the Gospel in the first eight chapters of the book, Paul turns to two major questions. The first is God's continued faithfulness to the people of Israel: How does God's message in Christ affect Israel's covenant promises? His answer in chs. 9–11 is that God still intends to keep his covenant promises to Israel and that one day they will turn to Christ in faith (11:12–32). The second question is the practical effect that the Gospel is to have in the everyday life of the church (see chs. 12–15). His answer is that the righteousness imparted freely to every believer is to be worked out in every aspect of the believer's life. The guiding principle is mutual love for one another and mutual concern for the spiritual growth of the church.

## I. Opening Greeting (1:1–7)

Paul's opening greeting, which constitutes a single sentence, introduces four primary subjects: (1) Paul, the writer; (2) the Gospel of God; (3) the Son of God; and (4) the Christians in Rome.

It was the normal Greek epistolary style for the sender to begin a letter with his own name. Paul calls himself a "servant" of Christ Jesus. This would have immediately identified him with the great men of past biblical history, such as Moses (e.g., Nu 12:7). Paul also describes himself as an "apostle." Again he uses a term steeped in OT meaning. In Isa 51:2, for example, God says of Abraham, "I called him"; and in Isa 49:1, the Servant of the Lord says, "Before I was born the LORD called me." By using the word "called," Paul emphasizes that he did not gain apostleship through his own striving, but rather like the prophets in the OT, God called him.

What Paul is writing about is "the gospel"—the good news about Jesus Christ. In vv.1–4 Paul summarizes the contents of his message (for other such summaries, see 1Co 15:1ff.; Ro 2:16; 16:25; 2Ti 2:8; cf. Ac 26:22–23).

Paul stresses certain aspects of the Gospel that are important for the argument of the book. Paul, being a Jew, was conscious of the Jewish accusations against the Gospel as something new, something that did not belong to the OT Scriptures. Thus here, in 3:21, and 1Co 15:3–4, he is careful to point out that the Gospel was announced beforehand in the Scriptures. The phrase "his prophets" was a common way of referring to the writers of the OT; it means not just "the prophets" per se but all of the writers of Scriptures.

Paul now defines more clearly the content of the Gospel—it is concerning God's Son, Jesus Christ. There are two ways in which to understand the title "Son of God." (1) It denotes for Paul the eternal relationship that existed between God the Father and God the Son, the second person of the Trinity. It is in this sense that Paul most often uses this designation of Christ, namely, to denote his eternal preexistence with the Father (cf. Ro 8:3). (2) But there is also the sense in which at Paul's time the promised Messiah was designated as "the Son of God."

Paul adds two statements regarding the Son. (1) He was of the seed of David (v.3). The expectation that the Messiah would come from the seed of David was without question in the OT and in the Judaism of the NT (see 2Sa 7; Zec 6:12; Lk 1:32). (2) He was shown to be the Son of God by virtue of the Resurrection. He was not merely declared to be the Son of God by the Resurrection, but he was declared to be the *Son-of-God-in-power* since the Resurrection. In contrast to the apparent weakness of his earthly ministry, here Jesus is shown in power.

Paul addresses himself to the question of his writing to the church in Rome, a church he had never visited. Since he had received the apostleship to the Gentiles, Rome was a reasonable audience to address. The Roman church, though not founded by him, was nevertheless within the sphere of his apostolic commission; therefore, he had a right to address it as he did.

## II. Personal Notes Regarding Paul and the Church at Rome (1:8–15)

### A. Paul's Thanksgiving to God for the Faith of the Roman Christians (1:8)

Paul begins the body of this letter with a personal note regarding the faith of the Roman Christians. The Roman church is known throughout the world as a church that is obedient to the faith.

### B. Paul's Desire to Visit the Church at Rome (1:9–15)

Paul lays great stress on his desire to visit the church at Rome. In typical OT fashion (1Sa 12:5; Ps 89:38; Jer 42:5) he calls on God as his witness that he has prayed constantly that he might be allowed to come to Rome (vv.9–10); but so far, he has been hindered (v.13) from coming. Paul's reason for wanting to visit Rome is simply his eagerness to impart to the Romans "some spiritual gift" (v.11) to strengthen them, and, at the same time, to be strengthened by them also (v.12). He seems to be purposely ambiguous here regarding the nature of the spiritual gift he wishes to bestow (cf. "some" gift). His intention, however, is clear—"to make you strong" (v.11). In v.13 Paul goes on to describe his desire to have some fruit among the Roman Christians as he has had among the other Gentiles.

In vv.14–15, Paul gives a further reason why he is eager to come to Rome: he is under obligation to preach the gospel to them as he has been to preach it to all people—the wise and unwise, Greeks and barbarians. But thus far he has been hindered from coming (v.13). He knows that he cannot come in the near future, because he is presently on his way to Jerusalem (15:25); and there seems to be some doubt in his mind as to when, or if, he will eventually travel to Rome (15:30–31). So in this letter he develops the message that he intends to preach to them when the time comes.

What Paul intends to preach to the Roman Christians is the "gospel." The "gospel" is more than the message that Christ died for your sins. The Christians in Rome already believed that, and their faith was known throughout the world (v.8). The message that Paul intends to preach is an expanded and developed explication of the Gospel in all its ramifications as we find it in the book of Romans. It is the gospel of the "righteousness of God" by faith.

## III. Paul's Statement of the Theme of the Book (1:16–17)

Paul begins with a statement that sets the tone for the remainder of this letter: "I am not ashamed of the gospel." Paul may be suspecting a certain reticence on the part of the Roman Christians to preach the Gospel. So Paul writes this letter to make them strong, since he cannot do so in person. Behind all he writes there are these words: "I am not ashamed of the gospel." As he systematically works through the reasons why he is not ashamed, he continually stresses one main point—it all makes sense! There's nothing here to be ashamed of!

When Paul has completed his defense (11:36), he still has not completed his letter. There is still a "therefore" to be tacked onto his defense of the Gospel. He urges Christians to present themselves wholly to God, serving God in a manner that is worthy of God's people (12:1–2).

In presenting the theme of his letter, Paul presents a capsule view of the relationship of salvation and faith. He begins with the term "the gospel" (1:16), which has its source in the power of God, not himself. Paul adds that this power is a power to save those who believe, both Jew and Gentile. Having said this much, Paul has introduced the important proposition: salvation by faith.

How does Paul use the term "salvation"? (1) He uses it only when he is speaking of the relationship between God and humankind. (2) He uses this word primarily in reference to a future event; salvation will come (e.g., Ro 5:9; 1Co 5:5). (3) Paul writes of salvation from the wrath of God. In his writings he repeatedly refers to the coming wrath of God that will be poured out on all sin at a definite time in the future, a day called "the day of God's wrath" (Ro 2:5). On this day the righteous judgment of God against all sin will be executed (2:5; 5:9, 16, 18; 8:1; cf. Eph. 5:6; Col 3:6). Salvation is the deliverance from the wrath of God.

This salvation from God's wrath comes by faith, i.e., to those who believe in Jesus. Paul's use of both the verb "to believe" and the noun "faith" shows that he understands the word to be one of action. He does not use this word in the sense of "to have faith," but "to believe something." Thus the idea of faith always has with it the idea of a message that one believes. We could summarize Paul's point by saying that faith is a response to a particular message—in this case, the gospel.

What kind of response is faith? It is a response of obedience. The idea of faith as obedience is of central importance to Paul's idea of faith (cf. "obedience that comes from faith" in 1:5); he repeats the same point in 16:26. In light of this idea of faith, Paul can also speak of unbelief as "disobedience"—being disobedient to the gospel (10:16). So close are the ideas of faith and obedience that Paul can use the two terms interchangeably. In 1:8, for example, he writes, "Your faith is being reported all over the world"; and in 16:19, he says, "Everyone has heard about your obedience." Obedience to the Gospel is submission to God's grace displayed in the Gospel of Christ (Jn 3:16).

Having said that salvation is by faith, Paul now enters the main topic of his discussion: the righteousness of God (v.17). Verse 17 is the basis for the proposition introduced in v.16 about the Gospel being the power of God unto salvation by faith. In God's gracious act of sending his Son to die for the human race, God has revealed his righteousness completely by faith. Those who are righteous will not fall under God's wrath but will be saved. They will not be destroyed in the day of God's wrath. As a support, Paul quotes Hab 2:4, "The righteous will live by faith," i.e., will be saved or remain living in the day of wrath.

The phrase "the righteousness of God" can have two possible meanings in the NT. (1) It can refer to a righteousness that is an attribute of God—the kind of righteousness that we refer to when we say, "God is righteous" (cf. 3:5, 25–26). (2) The phrase can refer to a human condition that has been brought about by God, thus meaning "a righteousness from God" (10:3). Which of the two possible meanings fits best here? The answer can only come from a study of the context. If we look at the structure of Paul's argument in 1:18–8:39, we see that he focuses his attention most directly on the second meaning: the righteousness that God gives to people by faith (see 2:13; 3:20, 24, 28; 4:2, 13; 5:1, 9, 19).

It is important to get a clear idea of what Paul means by the term "righteousness." Does he use the term with its meaning in the Greek language, or is the Greek term merely a translational term for the underlying Hebrew word? "Righteousness" in Greek is similar to the way we use it: it describes one's ethical conduct. The meaning of the corresponding Hebrew word, on the other hand, was different. In the OT, the word for "righteousness" is a legal term, not an ethical one, and it was used primarily within the context of the OT system of law and judgment. "Righteousness" was not something one could have in and of itself; it was rather something one had in relationship to a system of law, a standard. It meant "conformity to a norm." In the OT the standard was Torah, the revelation of the will of God. One who is righteous is shown to be in conformity to God's standard, God's Torah.

## IV. The Revelation of the Righteousness Which Is From God Alone (1:18–4:25)

The central section of Paul's argument is stated in 3:21–26, namely, that the righteousness that makes one acceptable before God has been made available to all who believe. It is not available in any other way, i.e., it is not obtainable by works. This central section is preceded by two longer sections (1:18–32 and 2:1–3:20), in which Paul shows not simply that all people are sinners and thus under God's wrath, but, more specifically, emphasizes that the Jew, who trusts in human works, is under God's wrath in just the same way as the idolatrous Gentile. Paul's argument is not simply "justification by faith" but also the denial of its opposite, "justification by works."

How does Paul structure his argument? First, in 1:18–32, he paints a picture of humanity apart from God. In ch. 2 he turns his argument against the Jewish reader by saying, in effect, "You too are guilty, because you do not keep the law. Having discussed the unrighteousness of the Jew who trusts in works of law, Paul then turns to answer the obvious question: "What advantage, then, is there in being a Jew?" (3:1). His answer is that there are many advantages, but salvation by good works is not one of them, for "no one will be declared righteous in his sight by observing the law" (3:20). This leads naturally to the statement of Paul's main thesis in 3:21, that the righteousness of God has been manifested apart from the law, through faith in Jesus Christ (3:22).

Paul concludes this section with a discussion of a related problem: that of boasting, i.e., pride in one's own works. In 3:27–31 he demonstrates that pride has no place in a system built on faith-righteousness, and in ch. 4 he illustrates this point in the life of Abraham.

## A. The Portrait of the Pagan Gentile (1:18–32)

Paul's argument assumes a revelation in nature. God has made himself known to the human race in nature: "What may be know about God is plain to them, because God has made it plain to them" (v.19). Moreover, "since the creation of the world God's invisible qualities—his eternal power and divine nature—have been clearly seen" (v.20). Nevertheless, humankind fell into idolatry (v.21); people have "exchanged the glory of the immortal God for images made to look like mortal man and birds and animals and reptiles" (v.23). Accordingly, God abandoned the human race to gross sins and perversion: "he gave them over to a depraved mind" (vv.28–39). Paul thus concludes that the Gentile pagan is without excuse (v.20).

Paul's point is that the pagans are without excuse because they have willfully and with a clear knowledge rejected God's revelation to him. Paul intends to use this evidence gathered from the pagan's verdict, against the Jewish reader in ch. 2. The case he is building is this: one is held responsible for the "law" that has been given him or her. Anyone who breaks that law is without excuse. He states this clearly in vv.12–14: "All who sin apart from the law will also perish apart from the law, and those who sin under the law will be judged by the law. . . . When Gentiles, who do not have the law, do by nature things required by the law, they are a law for themselves, even though they do not have the law."

When Paul turns to his Jewish reader in ch. 2, he is ready to draw a simple logical conclusion, saying as it were, "Therefore, you who are condemning the pagan Gentiles in ch. 1 are also without excuse for the same reason that they are without excuse—namely, you are breaking the clearly revealed will of God in the law."

## B. The Failure of Judaism (2:1–3:20)

That Paul has a Jewish reader in mind is clear from 2:17, where he specifically addresses the reader as a Jew. Paul is quick to call upon this reader to take a sober look at himself with respect to the law of God he purports to teach. Does he himself keep this law? The answer Paul confidently appears to expect is no. As in ch. 7, Paul may here be speaking from his own experience in Judaism. He knew what it meant to be an instructor in God's law and yet to be guilty of breaking it.

Having painted this portrait of the nature and failure of the law, as exemplified in Judaism, Paul goes on to show that in reality the Jew is in the same position as the pagan Gentile. Both have a law but neither has truly kept it (see especially 2:26–27).

Paul's conclusion leads naturally to the question he raises in 3:1: "What advantage, then, is there in being a Jew?" Paul goes on to deal with several important objections to what he has been saying. The first of these objections is the value of being a Jew in light of Paul's statements about Judaism and circumcision in 2:25–29. Paul has said that merely being a Jew or merely being circumcised ultimately has no value before God; what matters is obedience to God. What, then, is the value of being a Jew, and what value is the covenant that is signaled by circumcision? Paul's answer is cut short after discussing only one "advantage" to being a Jew—namely, that the Jews were entrusted with "the very words of God" (he again picks up the question in ch. 9). "Very words" (or "oracles") refers to the OT in general. In other words, the chief advantage of being a Jew, over against a Gentile, was the gift of the Torah. They had the revelation of God's will.

Having said this much, Paul goes on to another objection. He says: "What if some did not have faith? Will their lack of faith nullify God's faithfulness?" The way Paul has asked this question shows that he expects a negative answer, but he goes on to answer the objection specifically: "Not at all! Let God be true and every man a liar" (3:4). In other words, Israel's unbelief cannot cancel God's plan that is working through this people.

The next obvious question is this one: What if the Jews did not carry out their responsibility? Would the plan fail? Paul's answer is "No!" Israel's unbelief cannot cancel God's plan. "Let God be true, and every man a liar" (3:4).

Paul then raises another objection (3:5): If our unrighteousness demonstrates so clearly God's righteousness, is God then unrighteous when he judges and inflicts wrath? Paul's answer is an emphatic "No!" The explanation he gives is in the form of another question: "How could God judge the world?" The force of the answer can only be appreciated when we see it in light of the common ground Paul shows with his objector: both assume that God will judge the world. It does not follow that God is unjust when he judges unrighteousness, because otherwise one of the most important ideas in the Bible, that God is judge of the unrighteous, would not be true.

At this point (3:7–8), Paul introduces a further objection, similar to 3:5 but viewed with the sinner in mind rather than God's righteousness. If

God's truth is made more abundant by my lie, then why am I still being judged as a sinner? Is it fair for a person to be blamed for his falsehood, when it has actually resulted in God's glory?

Paul continues in v.8: "Why not say ... 'Let us do evil that good may come?'" This, he says, is what some have slanderously reported about his teaching. Paul's answer to this objection is a virtual silence. He simply says, "Their condemnation is deserved." The fallacy of the statement, "Let us do evil that good may come," is self-evident.

If there is still any doubt that the Jews have no special status of merit before God and that they stand equally in need of God's grace, Paul finalizes it all with a series of OT passages that describe all people as guilty before God (3:9–18). He then summarizes and draws the conclusion in 3:19–20: "Now we know that whatever the law says, it says to those who are under the law, so that every mouth may be silenced and the whole world held accountable to God. Therefore no one will be declared righteous in his sight by observing the law; rather, through the law we become conscious of sin."

## C. The Righteousness That Is From God (3:21–26)

Paul begins this statement of his major thesis by asserting that the righteousness of God apart from any righteousness gained by observing the law has just recently been made manifest in the life, death, and resurrection of Jesus Christ. This "righteousness of God" is the righteousness that a person may receive from God. The phrase "apart from law" refers to the preceding phrase in v.20, "no one will be declared righteous ... by observing the law." "Apart from law" thus means apart from the works of the law.

Again (as in 1:2) Paul stresses that this "righteousness from God" is found witnessed to in the OT. Paul has in mind the example of Abraham (Ge 15:6). In

3:22 he states that this "righteousness from God, apart from law," is a "righteousness from God [that] comes through faith in Jesus Christ." Clearly, Paul is contrasting a supposed righteousness gained by observing the law and a righteousness gained as a free gift to all who believe.

In vv.22–24 Paul continues to describe the righteousness that comes apart from works. He states first that it is "to all who believe" (see 1:16). Thus he implies that those who do not believe do not have this righteousness from God. To "fall short of the glory of God" means to fail to receive the glory God bestows. In v.24, the word "redemption" means "to ransom by the payment of a price." Its usage is primarily from the slave market in the ancient world. Slaves could be bought out of slavery by the payment of a price by an individual or a country.

The NT uses this word to express the freeing of someone from slavery to sin by the payment of the ransom price, the blood of Christ (see 1Co 6:20, Eph 1:7; cf. Mk 10:45). That is, Paul uses "redemption" to describe the work of Christ on behalf of believers—they are bought out of slavery by the death of Christ as the ransom payment.

Paul states in v.25 that God has "presented" Christ to be a propitiation (NIV "sacrifice of atonement") by his blood. He is here introducing us to the realm of the OT sacrificial system. He says, in effect, that God has made Christ our sacrifice. The system of sacrifice in the OT was based on the notion of the wrath of God and the giving of an offering. God's wrath is simply the reverse side of his holy love. As a holy God, the Lord will not tolerate sin in his creation. That refusal to tolerate sin is what the Bible calls God's wrath. It is portrayed in the Bible not by a mere outburst of passion, but is rather characterized as an essential element in his being. Both wrath and love are attributes of the biblical God.

OT sacrifice was not a bribe to the deity to buy off God's wrath. It was, rather, a means whereby one acknowledged total reliance on God's mercy. As such it stood for the provision that God had given his people whereby they could restore and maintain fellowship with him that had been broken by sin. God graciously accepted the sacrificial gift as a substitute. The basis of the OT sacrificial system was the grace of God in giving a person a means of acknowledging reliance on God's forgiveness.

The word Paul uses to express the idea of the gift offering here is the noun "propitiation" ("sacrifice of atonement"). In using this word Paul immediately associates the death of Christ with the sacrificial system in Leviticus. The word denotes a substitute given to bear God's wrath. Paul adds that this atonement was done by means of "his blood," i.e., the death of Christ on the cross. The intended result of God's presenting his Son as a propitiation was to demonstrate that he was not being unrighteous in passing over past sins.

## D. The Exclusion of Boasting (3:27–31)

Having said that one can be made righteous by faith, apart from works, Paul draws the natural conclusion that one cannot claim any merit before God on the basis of one's works. Boasting is excluded by the law of faith. Paul then turns to the one individual who might conceivably claim a right to boast, i.e., the patriarch Abraham, and he shows that he too has no right before God.

## E. The Case of Abraham (4:1–25)

Abraham cannot claim any merit before God because the Scriptures clearly teach that he was justified by faith, not by works (vv.1–5). David himself talked about the possibility of God declaring one's sins forgiven and pronouncing him righteous (vv.6–8).

Abraham was righteous by faith before he entered into the covenant with God that was marked by circumcision. The promises to him were given while he was yet uncircumcised; thus they too were based on faith (vv.13–14). If they had been based on law, they would not have been sure promises, because the law could not be maintained (v.15). Having been based on faith, the promises were a matter of God's grace and thus were made certain (v.16). The nature of Abraham's faith was such that he believed God was able to give life to himself and Sarah, in spite of the obvious physical impossibility of their age (vv.17–22). Thus Abraham's faith is a model for our own faith and demonstrates that we too cannot lay claim to any boasting before the finished work of God's grace (vv.23–25).

# V. Implications of Righteousness in the Life of the Believer (5:1–8:39)

## A. Reconciliation (5:1–21)

Paul begins a new phase of his argument in ch. 5. The phrase "since we have been justified by faith" (v.1) sums up what he has stated in 1:18–4:25. He continues with the assertion "we have peace with God."

The ideas presented in this section center around the NT conception of reconciliation. Reconciliation is the doing away of enmity, the bridging over of a quarrel. It implies that the parties involved were at one time hostile to one another. The cause of the enmity between God and humanity is sin. God's holiness demands that we be without sin. When Adam sinned, a barrier was set up between God and us. The process of reconciliation is the removing of the cause of that barrier, namely, the removal of human sin by the substitutionary death of Christ. Thus, by the death of Christ, human sin is truly removed; the human race and God are again "at peace."

This section speaks of *justification* and *reconciliation* as two distinct elements in the work of the death of Christ. Christ's death for believers removed their sin. On the basis of this death God can declare that believers are righteous. That is justification. On the basis of Christ's death God's wrath was satisfied, i.e., the cause of the enmity between God and humanity, sin, was removed, thus making peace. In v.2 Paul describes "peace" with God in terms that call to mind the sacrificial terms of the OT. In Christ, by faith, we have obtained the right to be present before God.

In vv.12–21 Paul presents a detailed discussion of the work of Christ in relationship to sinful humanity at enmity with God. He does this by a carefully constructed argument based on the participation of all humanity in the sin of Adam. Paul begins his comparison of Christ and Adam with a statement of the work of Adam (v.12): (1) "Sin entered the world through one man"; (2) "death [came] through sin"; (3) "in this way death came to all men"; (4) "because all sinned."

A great deal of discussion has centered around this last phrase, "because all sinned." Some interpret the phrase as meaning that death comes to all people because all have sinned, just as death came to Adam because Adam sinned. Others, however, understand Paul to be saying that death came to all people because when Adam sinned, all sinned in connection with him. The structure of Paul's argument supports this latter view, that all people sinned in Adam's sin. Paul is arguing that what one man (Adam) did affected all, just as what one man (Christ) did affected all. Paul's conclusion then is that all people sinned in Adam; thus "in Adam all died" (cf. 1Co 15:22).

Verses 13–14 are a parenthesis, intended to further demonstrate that all people sinned in Adam (cf. v.12). Paul begins by saying that sin was already in the world before God gave Moses the Law on Mount Sinai (v.13). But it was sin that was not taken into account because as yet there was no law. Sin is a meaningful concept only if there is a law to transgress. Paul's evidence for the presence of this sin in the world is the fact of death. Since there is death in the world, there must also be sin (v.14). Thus the sin that brought death was not personal transgression of law but the sin that all sinned in Adam (v.12). Between the time of Adam and Moses, in other words, sin was imputed.

In vv.15–17 Paul develops another parenthetical argument before returning to his main point introduced in v.12. Paul's purpose in this parenthesis is to emphasize the important dissimilarities between Adam and Christ before drawing out the details of the similarity in vv.18–21. He begins with the statement that the grace of God received in Christ is "not like the trespass." The difference is one of kind. The process by which Adam's sin resulted in death to all was one of legal consequences. Adam, as the head of the race, decided the consequences of everyone. Christ, on the other hand, provided a different process that did not operate merely within a context of legal consequences. It rather worked in the context of grace. The death of Christ for the many was a legal satisfaction for sin, but it was "much more" than that—it was based on God's grace. So the penalty of death was the penalty that resulted from the application of the law, while the gift of righteousness was a free gift of God's grace.

In vv.18–21, Paul returns to his comparison of Adam and Christ. His point lies in the fact that both Christ and Adam held a special and unique relationship to all humanity. Adam was the father of all humanity; but more than this, Adam was the head of all humanity in a special and God-ordained way.

How Adam lived had legal consequences for all of humanity. We can see this not only in the writings of Paul (1Co 15:22), but the idea of representation is also in the Genesis narrative Paul uses. In Ge 3:14–15, for example, the serpent is cursed, as a representative of all serpents: "You will crawl on your belly and you will eat dust" (Ge 3:14). The woman is cursed, as a representative of all women: "I will greatly increase your pain in childbearing" (v.16). Adam is cursed, as a representative of all men: "Cursed is the ground because of you" (vv.17–19).

The question naturally arises: How is this sin transmitted to all people? The answer to the nature of all humanity's participation in the sin of Adam lies in the comparison of Adam and Christ. Paul's argument is that just as Adam's sin was passed to all, so Christ's righteousness is passed to all. The method of transaction is the same. Paul has already argued that Christ's righteousness (the righteousness of God) is passed to all by their being declared righteous by faith. On this analogy, then, it seems best to view Adam's sin as imputed to all because Adam was the representative head of all people.

But Adam was not the only one to stand in the position as representative of all people. Adam, Paul has said, was a "pattern of the one to come" (v.14). Paul's argument, then, continues on the supposition that the second person of the Trinity, the Son of God, became the representative of all humanity and thus through him, God's righteousness passed to all. The basis of the work of Christ, then, is the Incarnation. Because there is a real link between all humankind and Christ, a real imputation of righteousness can occur. Adam's sin results in a common relationship of sin among all humanity; Christ's incarnation results in a common relationship of righteousness with all humanity.

## B. Sanctification (6:1–8:39)

### 1. Dying to sin (6:1–14)

Paul now turns to the question of the believer's relationship to the power of sin (6:1–23). He begins with the concept of dying to sin (vv.1–14). This question arises naturally from Paul's argument in ch. 5. Paul has said that "where sin increased, grace increased all the more" (5:20). From this he raises the question posed by the antinomialist: "Shall we go on sinning so that grace may increase?" His answer is an emphatic "By no means!" This question, however, is more than a mere objection of the antinomialist. It is also an introduction to the question of the relationship of the believer to the power of sin.

Paul begins his discussion of this question with the emphatic assertion that the believer has "died to sin," and thus the idea of one's continuing to live in sin is absurd (v.2). To demonstrate what he means that the believer has "died to sin," Paul reminds the reader of the significance behind the act of Christian baptism (v.3). To be baptized into Christ is to be baptized into his death. Baptism is the outward sign that one is "in Christ"; thus Paul speaks of baptism when he raises the issue of being in Christ (cf. 1Co 12:13). Paul's point is that the believer who is "in Christ" has died to sin in the death of Christ and is alive to newness of life as Christ also arose from his death (vv.3–4).

What does Paul mean by saying believers have "died to sin" and therefore will not "live in it any longer"? Does it mean that believers no longer *can* sin? no longer *will* sin? or no longer *should* sin? To say believers no longer *can* sin contradicts what Paul says about himself in 7:15, "What I want to do I do not do," and in 7:21, "When I want to do good, evil is right there with me." Moreover, to say that believers *will* no longer sin contradicts Paul's continuous exhortations not to let sin have dominion over them. The last possibility alone, that believers *should* no longer sin, is consistent with both the idea that believers still experience a warfare with sin and are called upon to continue to wage the war against sin's dominion as well as the fact that believers are provided with the necessary power to wage that war, namely, the Holy Spirit (8:4).

In his argument at this point in the book, Paul is looking primarily at the work of Christ in his death for sin as a substitutionary sacrifice. This, Paul states, is the one basic fact of the life of all believers. Before God they are without sin. Thus, it is absurd that they should continue to live in sin that grace may abound. Rather, they should go on to live without service to sin (v.6); they should "count [themselves] dead to sin but alive to God in Christ Jesus" (v.11).

Paul does not yet tell how this is to be done in the everyday life of the believer; this comes in ch. 8.

### 2. Slaves to righteousness (6:15–23)

In vv.15–23 Paul draws a comparison between two kinds of lifestyles: slaves to sin and slaves to righteousness. Paul's point is that one is a slave to what one submits oneself, whether to sin or to righteousness. Formerly, Paul's readers were slaves of sin, and their obedience to sin involved all of their lives. They gave themselves fully to sin (v.17a). In the same way, Paul argues, they ought now to submit fully to righteousness (v.19). Again, Paul postpones any explanation of how this is to be done. Before he raises that question (ch. 8), he moves to the problems involved in attempting to live righteously in one's own power (ch. 7); from there, he discusses the value of the Law.

### 3. The believer's relationship to the power of God's law (7:1–6)

In 6:14 Paul has stated: "You are not under law, but under grace." He now turns to demonstrate why this is true in the life of the believer. His argument is that the law of God applies to one who is alive. Death, in other words, cancels the authority of that law. To illustrate the point, Paul appeals to the marriage law that bound a husband and wife together for life. If the husband died, the wife was free to remarry (vv.2–3). Thus, Paul concludes, the believer who died in Christ to the law (as a law of works) is free from the law and can belong to another, namely, to Christ (v.4)

In v.6 Paul contrasts two states: "the new way of the Spirit" and "the old way of the written code." By dying with Christ, the believer is freed from binding service to the Mosaic Law and is thus freed to serve God apart from that law. Paul returns to these categories again in ch. 8, but he halts his argument here temporarily to discuss the value of the Law in light of the work of Christ.

### 4. The nature and function of God's law in relationship to the believer (7:7–25)

From all that Paul has said regarding the law thus far, an important question arises, "Is the law sin?" (v.7). He emphatically denies this. Far from being a sinful instrument, Paul states that the law has, in fact, a positive role in the life of the believer. First of all, it is the means whereby sin can clearly be revealed: "I would not have known what sin was except through the law" (v.7b). Paul does not mean that one does not sin without the law; rather, one's sins are not clearly shown to be rebellion against God's will except where that will has been revealed. The example he gives comes from the tenth commandment, "Do not covet." He would not have known that this was against the will of God, had God not said, "Do not covet."

We might ask how this feature of the law can be considered a "positive" role. The answer is that Paul is viewing God's law from the point of view of grace—justification by faith, apart from observing the law. The law shows to those who are justified by faith the will of the God who saved them. From this point of view the law is positive. But Paul also recognizes that this feature of the law carries with it a negative factor, namely, it gives occasion for rebellion against God's will. The moment God's will is made known, one has the occasion both to honor it in obedience or to rebel against it. Paul says that it is sin that takes the occasion presented by the law to produce rebellion (v.8). Apart from the law sin has no occasion to exist; it is dead. A second positive role of the law is to show sin for what it really is: "utterly sinful" (v.13). The law exposes sin.

If the law is not sinful but indeed is "spiritual," then why does it pose such a threat in the life of the believer? Paul addresses himself to this question in the following verses (vv.14–25). Much discussion has centered on the meaning and application of these verses. Does Paul refer to himself here as a Christian, or is he speaking of his condition before he became a Christian? We agree with those who say that the experience pictured here is not wholly autobiographical; rather, Paul is attempting to demonstrate what would indeed be the situation if those who are faced with the demands of the law and the power of sin in their lives were to try to solve their problem independently of the power of Christ and the enablement of the Spirit. In other words, Paul is describing hypothetically what our relationship would be to the law's demands if we did not have the power of the Spirit. This is not then a mere description of a "carnal Christian" but rather a description of a hypothetical Christian without the Spirit. Such a Christian desires to live as a Christian and not to let sin reign, but, hypothetically, he or she does not have the power: "I myself in my mind am a slave to God's law, but in the sinful nature a slave to the law of sin" (v.25b).

This leads naturally to the emphasis of ch. 8, namely, Paul's emphasis on the source of the Christian's power to live a godly life, the Holy Spirit.

We began vv.14–25 with the question, "If God's law is not sinful, then why is it such a threat to the Christian?" Now we can discuss Paul's answer. The law is a threat because of the weakness of the sinful human nature, i.e., the flesh. If we had only the flesh to rely on, then the law would indeed be a heavy weight on us. But "thanks be to God," Paul says (v.25), for "there is now no condemnation for those who are in Christ Jesus, because through Christ Jesus the law of the Spirit of life has set me free from the law of sin and death . . . that the righteous requirements of the law might be fully met in us, who do not live according to the sinful nature but according to the Spirit" (8:1–4).

Paul states in 7:14b, "I am unspiritual [lit., fleshly]," i.e., "I belong to the realm of the flesh insofar as it is weak and sinful. This is not the same as being "in the flesh," which for Paul refers to the state of unbelief (7:5, 8:8). Rather, this is the "fleshly" (NIV, "worldly") of 1Co 3:1, "Brothers, I could not address you as spiritual but as worldly—mere infants in Christ."

Second, Paul says he is "sold as a slave to sin" (7:14b). This expression is Paul's term for what he is about to describe in vv.15–23. That is, there is a power of sin that dwells in Paul's own human nature that if left to itself, without any help from the power of the Spirit, would not allow Paul, or any Christian, to be obedient to the will of God.

### 5. The leading of God's Spirit (8:1–39)

Having discussed the nature of the law and the believer's relationship to it, Paul now continues the argument from 7:6 by discussing the implications of the believer's death in Christ. The primary implication of the believer's death to sin is the fact that now, by the power of the Spirit of God, one is able to live

in fulfillment of the requirements of the law (vv.1–4). Grace, in other words, does not free the Christian from living according to God's will; rather, it makes it possible for one to live according to God's will. The law, in other words, is not the means of justification or sanctification, but it is the end of both salvation and sanctification. This is the teaching of the new covenant found in the OT prophets (cf. Jer 31:31–34; Eze 36:27).

Sanctification, then, is a process whereby believers by the power of the Spirit come to live more and more in conformity to the law of God (God's will). We should be careful to understand correctly the phrase at the end of v.4: "who do not live according to the sinful nature but according to the Spirit." Paul does not state this as a condition, as though he were saying, "The requirement of the law may be fulfilled in us if we do not live according to the sinful nature but according to the Spirit." Rather, the phrase describes the manner in which the requirement of the law may be fulfilled, i.e., by not living according to the sinful nature but according to the Spirit. The law's requirement will be fulfilled by our relying on the Spirit's power, instead of the flesh.

In vv.5–11, Paul gives a lengthy explanation of the phrase "us, who do not live according to the sinful nature but according to the Spirit." He has said that it is possible that the will of God may be fulfilled by those who live in the Spirit, not in the flesh, and now he will explain why this is so. There is a basic difference between one who Paul describes as living "according to the sinful nature" and one who lives "according to the Spirit" (vv.5–8). The former cannot please God by keeping his law (v.7). Such a person is unable to keep God's law and thus is unable to please God (cf. 7:14–25). According to 8:7–8, one who walks "according to the sinful nature" is unable to submit to and please God. Moreover, Paul stresses the inner working of the Spirit of God in the life of the believer as the power to live a life pleasing to God (v.11). It is the Spirit who lives within the believer that raised Christ from the dead and who will also make alive the mortal body of the believer. Here Paul alludes back to his example of Christian baptism, where he compared the believer's death in Christ to the symbolic act of baptism and the believer's new life with the new life of Christ in the Resurrection (6:1–4).

Furthermore, the life of the Spirit is not limited to only a few Christians (vv.9–10); all Christians have the life-giving Spirit within them. Thus, Paul can say to Christians that they are not to see themselves as living according to "the sinful nature" (v.9); they must live according to the Spirit (vv.12–14).

In vv.12–14 Paul draws the various lines of his argument together into a summary involving two important ideas. (1) The nature of the Christian's being indwelt by the Spirit of God obligates him or her to a certain pattern of life, i.e., walking in the Spirit. This lifestyle includes such characteristics as not living according to the flesh (v.13), i.e., putting "to death the misdeeds of the body." From Paul's comments in 7:14–25, it is clear that one cannot put to death the deeds of the body on one's own. The Christian must be "led by the Spirit of God" (8:14). The name Paul gives to this way of life is that of being "sons of God" (v.14). The idea of being led by the Spirit, then, is the process of continuing to put to death the deeds of the flesh by means of the Spirit. Paul stresses both the human responsibility ("putting to death") and the divine enablement ("led by the Spirit").

(2) The way of life that Paul describes is not optional. Paul says, "If you live according to the sinful nature, you will die" (v.13). What does he mean when he says, "You will die"? He

apparently means the opposite of what he means in the second half of the verse: "You will live." To "live" means essentially the same as "to be saved." Thus "to die" must mean the opposite, to be lost. Paul's point is not that one would lose one's salvation if one were to live according to the sinful nature. Paul's point is, rather, that the Christian has no other choice but to live according to the Spirit; holiness is a matter of necessity.

In the next section of ch. 8, Paul discusses the element of hope that makes up the life in the Spirit (vv.15–30). He introduces this topic with a brief discussion of the sonship of those led by the Spirit (vv.15–17). Because all Christians have the Spirit, Paul calls the Spirit "the Spirit of sonship." "Abba" is an Aramaic word having the connotation of familiarity and devotion. The feature of sonship that Paul then draws upon (vv.16–17) is that of inheritance: "If we are children, then we are heirs." The topic of the inheritance and blessings of the believer's sonship takes Paul into the realm of the hope that marks the life of the Christian. The "present sufferings" do not compare with the future blessings, i.e., "the glory that will be revealed in us" (v.18). These "sufferings" are the sufferings that Christians incur as followers of Christ in this world.

Paul calls to mind the state of all creation and draws from it a pattern of hope in tribulation for the believer (vv.19–23). He states that the whole creation eagerly awaits the time when God will reveal his glory. The present order of creation has been thrown off center by the Fall and will be restored at the time when the children of God are revealed in glory. Paul certainly has in mind here the curses of Ge 3 on the ground, but there is another sense in which Paul is speaking of matters not immediately discernible to us. From the point of view of Ge 1–3, Paul is saying that creation is no longer "good." In speaking of a future time of restoration of creation from its present state, he is speaking along the same lines as Peter in 2Pe 3:12–13, who predicts the destruction of the present world and the creation of "a new heaven and a new earth, the home of righteousness" (cf. Rev 21:1). Paul's point is that believers should also have this eager expectation of the coming redemption of the body—the bodily resurrection when all things will become new (v.23). The basis of this expectation is a "hope" that our redemption will come (v.24).

What kind of hope should Christians have (vv.24–30)? Our hope is in something that we presently cannot see. It is rather a patient, but eager, expectation (v.25). This hope is a hope that is supported by the work of the Spirit (vv.26–27). It is a hope founded on a view of the absolute sovereignty of God, who is actively at work in the world to bring about his own purpose (8:28–30).

## VI. The Question of Israel (9:1–11:36)

### A. Introduction of the Problem (9:1–6a)

Paul begins with a description of his personal attitude toward Israel (vv.1–3). He is grieved by the fact that the nation of Israel has rejected the new covenant and does not now experience what he has been describing in ch. 8. In v.6a Paul raises the question indirectly: "It is not as though the word of God has failed." He feels the tension in the mind of his readers as to how to explain Israel's rejection of the new covenant in light of the sovereignty of God and the power of his eternal promises. The direction of his answer is determined by the fact that in spite of what may appear, God's promises have not fallen. Why? For two reasons: the Gentiles owe their salvation to the rejection of Israel; and, in the long term, God's pur-

poses embrace his own people. Before going into these two points, Paul lays the groundwork for his answer to the problem by clarifying some of the basic concepts involved in the solution.

### B. The Clarification of the True Israel (9:6b–13)

Paul states: "For not all who are descended from Israel are Israel" (v.6b), and "nor because they are his descendants are they all Abraham's children" (v.7). Having said this, Paul then begins to describe the concept of a "true Israel" that is formed by the sovereign election of God: "It is through Isaac that your offspring will be reckoned" (v.7b). Israel's existence, at least as a theological entity, is not determined by mere natural lineage. Rather, it is based on the promise given by a sovereign God (vv.8–13).

Note that Paul uses the term "Israel" as opposed to the term "Jew" throughout this section. Strictly speaking, he is not discussing what happened to Jews in God's program, but rather, what happened to "Israel." Thus he is not merely speaking of the Jews of his day who had rejected the Gospel. He is talking about the larger entity, the chosen people Israel, through whom God promised to fulfill his sovereign plan of redemption. Paul's categories are theological and biblical, not national and political.

### C. Divine Sovereignty and Israel's Election (9:14–29)

Having introduced the concept of God's sovereign will in his definition of the term "Israel," Paul is compelled to discuss divine sovereignty and Israel's election (vv.14–29). "Is God unjust?" (NIV)—or better: "God certainly is not unjust, is he?" It is important to see how Paul answers this question. He does not present a logical argument intended to "prove" the justice of God in light of his sovereignty. Rather, he simply quotes a passage in Scripture that states that God is merciful in his sovereign election. The argument is simply that since the Scriptures state God is merciful in his sovereign election, he cannot possibly be unjust.

Paul anticipates another question in v.19: "Why then does God still blame us?" The sense of the question is, "Why does God hold humanity responsible when in light of his sovereignty, no one can oppose his will?" In his answer, Paul again appeals to Scripture, to a common biblical notion that no creature of God has the right to question the justice of the Creator. The true "first cause" is God's own personal will. Humanity, the creature, is in no position to question the propriety of God's will (vv.20–22). As an example of the sovereign will of God to display his glory, Paul comes back to the central issue of this section and speaks of God's plan to elect not only some out of the Jews but also some out of the Gentiles. Thus, in v.23 Paul again raises the question of God's election of his chosen people—not just Jews but Gentiles also. That this was God's plan all along is demonstrated from the references to it in the OT passages he quotes (vv.25–29).

To summarize—not all descendants of Israel are Israelites (vv.6–8); not all Jews are God's chosen (v.24); and not all God's chosen are Jews (v.24).

## D. Israel's Unbelief (9:30–10:21)

At the close of ch. 9, Paul summarizes the question that he has raised: the Gentiles were made righteous by faith, but the Israelites could not attain to righteousness because they sought it through works rather than faith (vv.30–33). Paul devotes all of ch. 10 to a discussion of Israel's failure to respond to the Gospel in faith. True Israel is distinguished on the basis of faith (9:30–33); historical Israel failed in faith (10:1–21). Yet God's plan for Israel did not fail; rather, it was enlarged to include the Gentiles (11:1).

## E. Israel's Present and Future Status in God's Plan (11:1–36)

In ch. 11, having laid the groundwork in chs. 9–10, Paul is prepared to discuss the primary question of Israel's present and future status in God's plan.

### 1. The concept of a remnant in Israel (11:1–7b)

Paul begins with a question that is really a statement of fact: "God has not rejected his people, has he?" (v.1). His answer is emphatic: "By no means!" His first line of evidence for this is the fact that Paul himself, an Israelite, has not been cast off by God (v.1b). Therefore, Paul concludes, "God did not reject his people, whom he foreknew" (v.2a). But he does not stop here. He goes on to show that the idea of a few being chosen out of the whole (i.e., the concept of a remnant) is not new. It can be seen already in the OT, such as in the account of Elijah at Mount Horeb (vv.2b–4). In v.5 Paul draws the conclusion, "So too, at the present time there is a remnant chosen by grace."

Israel as a whole did not attain to righteousness because they sought it out of works (v.7). The elect remnant, however, did attain to righteousness, but it was solely out of grace.

### 2. The hardening of the rest (11:7c–10)

Paul, still speaking of the present Israel, groups the entire nation into a second category—the nonelect. These, he argues, have been hardened, or made insensitive (v.7c). Paul quotes the OT again to demonstrate the nature of this hardening of the nonremnant, using the passive voice. Thus Paul has avoided attributing this hardness to God. Nevertheless, the Scriptures that Paul quotes state explicitly that it was God who gave Israel a "spirit of stupor" (v.8). The primary passage being quoted is Dt 29:3. Here the context is Israel's experience in the desert and their continual unfaithfulness in the face of the miraculous provision from God. In spite of all his provision for them, the Israelites proved unfaithful, and God responded in judgment by refusing to give them further understanding. A second passage quoted by Paul is Isa 29:10, "The LORD has brought over you a deep sleep." Here again the context speaks of Israel's unbelief that is followed by God's punishment—the spirit of "a deep sleep" (cf. Isa 29:11–14). Finally, quoting Ps 69:23, Paul states that their table became a "snare and a trap."

### 3. The result of Israel's hardening (11:11–24)

The result of the hardening of Israel, Paul makes clear, was salvation to the Gentiles. He begins with a question to which he will return in v.25: "Did they [the Jews] stumble so as to fall beyond recovery?" His answer is clear: "Not at all!" But their fall, he argues, did have a good outcome in God's program. It resulted in the salvation of the Gentiles, a salvation that also has its purpose in light of God's plan with Israel. It is to make Israel jealous and stir them up (v.11c). But their fall was not a total fall, and thus we await "their fullness," which will bring even greater riches to the nations (vv.12–16).

In vv.17–24, Paul discusses the Gentiles' position as part of God's elect over against the position of the Israelites who have fallen out of this position. The image he uses is that of the grafted wild olive branch and the natural olive branch that has been cut off. The Israelite is the natural olive branch that grows out of the "nourishing sap from the olive root" (v.17). This root is the Abrahamic covenant promise, which, from the beginning, has been the basis of God's dealing with Israel and which also forms the basis of God's dealings with Gentiles (Ge 12:1–3). The wild olive branch is the Gentile who is now grafted into the root—namely, the promised blessings of Abraham. The basis of Israel's being cut off and the Gentiles' being grafted in was and is

faith (v.20). The result of the hardening of Israel to salvation by faith is, then, a worldwide body of elect from every nation who are the spiritual heirs of the covenant promises to Abraham. The notion that the Gentiles could be "grafted" into the covenant promises of Abraham, however, opens the question about the efficacy of the promises yet to Israel. It is, then, to this question that Paul turns in v.25.

### 4. The future of Israel (11:25–36)

In v.25 Paul speaks of a "mystery." This mystery is the fact of the hardening of a part of the Israelites "until the full number of the Gentiles has come in." That the nation of Israel would experience a partial hardening for a period of time to allow for the inclusion of the Gentiles into God's plan was unknown in the OT Scriptures. It is now revealed in the NT. The expression "full number [lit., fullness] of the Gentiles" apparently refers to the total number of Gentiles who will be included in God's plan during the time of Israel's hardening. After this "fullness" has come in, then "all Israel will be saved."

It is generally agreed that this refers to Israel as a national entity; they will yet be saved in the future. It is also generally agreed that Israel as a national unit will be saved by believing in Christ as Savior. There is, however, a difference of opinion about the status of this believing nation of Israel in God's overall program. Some hold that upon believing, the nation of Israel becomes a part of the true Israel, the church. Others hold that the belief of the national Israel will mark the fulfillment of the OT promises to physical Israel (Isa 2:2–4; 60:1ff.; 62:2; Zec 9:22–23).

## VII. Exhortations (12:1–15:13)

### A. Introduction (12:1–2)

Paul begins describing the Christian life by using an analogy to the OT sacrificial system: "Offer your bodies as living sacrifices" to God (v.1). The motive for doing so is stated emphatically: "in view of God's mercy"; that is, the basis of obedience is God's mercy. In a similar fashion (see Ex 20:2; Dt 6:12), the basis of Israel's obedience was the gracious act of God in delivering them from slavery in Egypt.

God is interested in the whole of a person's life, both body and soul. For Paul, the body was the battleground of spirituality, to the extent that he could even summarize the spiritual life as putting to death the deeds of the body by means of the Spirit (8:13). Paul does not merely say to present one's body to God. He says, in addition, "offer your bodies as living sacrifices" to God—sacrifices that are "pleasing" to him. In light of the context of the book of Romans, Paul means by this that the Christian should be free from the imperatives of the deeds of the sinful nature (cf. 6:13). He calls this a "spiritual act of worship"—i.e., a kind of worship that is carried out with a conscious intention of pleasing God.

In v.2 Paul continues to admonish his readers to "renew" their minds so that they can rightly know how to please God in their daily worship or service. He writes, "Do not conform any longer to the pattern of this world," i.e., do not let this world determine what is "pleasing to God." Rather, let your minds be "transformed" by the will of God.

## B. A List of Admonitions (12:3–21)

### 1. A realistic look at oneself within the body of Christ (12:3–8)

The danger Paul anticipates in the church at Rome is a growing polarity within the body of Christ—some members usurping more than their share in the work, and consequently others within the same body doing less than their share. To Paul, each member has been given a "measure of faith" (cf. Eph 4:7), a specific sphere where one's faith is exercised. Paul illustrates this

by using the physical body (vv.4–5; cf. 2Co 10:13–15). Whatever your gift, use it as the exercise of the faith given you by God.

### 2. General principles (12:9–27)

Paul then list a series of examples of general principles that are to govern the Christian's life.

## C. Obedience to Authorities (13:1–7)

The general principle laid down here is that all Christians are to submit to the government authorities because they are commissioned by God to provide peace and stability within society. Paul has qualified the kind of government he is speaking of by focusing on government in the ideal sense. The authority of human government is given by God, and its purpose is to maintain the good. When a government does this, it is fulfilling its God-ordained role, and Christians are to submit to it. If a government fails to do this, it loses its God-ordained status as government, and the Christian is not obligated to submit to it. There is a higher standard by which Christians may judge whether a particular government is, in fact, carrying out its God-given role, namely, whether it is "God's servant to do you good." This demands that Christians have a legitimate sense of what "the good" is—i.e., that which conforms to God's will. Christians should be continually evaluating the role of their government in providing and protecting "the good."

## D. The Centrality of Love in the Life of Christians (13:8–10)

The general idea of Paul's statement in v.8 is clear. Christians are to pay all that they owe. In this context the reference is to taxes, revenue, respect, and honor (v.7). In a modern society built on a credit economy, Paul's statement would be difficult to follow. Thus the NIV has translated this verse as, "Let no debt remain outstanding." Christians are not to refuse to pay that which by agreement they are obligated to pay.

The second idea Paul raises is the obligation of Christians to love others. This debt can never be fully paid.

## E. The Christian's Perspective on Time (13:11–14)

The central idea of these verses is that the Christian's eyes should ultimately be on the expectation of the coming of Christ; "the day is almost here" (v.12). All of this life should be viewed in the light of the next life, the one lived with Christ. Paul does not attempt to argue that the return of Christ is near. He, in fact, does not even state it here. Nevertheless, lying behind his instructions is the idea that each day brings us closer to Christ's return (v.11). In light of the return of Christ, Paul admonishes his readers to live as those who are soon to be with him.

## F. The Question of Doubtful Things (14:1–15:13)

Though Paul is here discussing "questionable" areas of conduct, they are not explicitly defined by him. He lists only three examples: (a) eating meat or vegetables; (b) observing special days; (c) drinking wine (14:21). These questionable areas are "religious" in nature, in that they are considered to be done "to the Lord" (v.6). The background of these matters is perhaps the pattern of clean and unclean instructions known from the OT and Judaism. They relate to the worship of God, not to one's personal salvation. Paul's verdict on these things is: "I am fully convinced that no food is unclean in itself. But if anyone regards something as unclean, then for him it is unclean" (v.14).

Paul also raises the question of the "weaker" Christian in this passage. He describes such a one as holding to a particular kind of religious observance as a means of expressing devotion to God. Weaker Christians do not believe that their observance of this act holds any salvific merit with God. Paul would not allow that to remain questionable.

A third line of thought in this passage is the discussion of one "who has faith" or (cf. 15:1), one who is strong enough "to bear with the failings of the weak." Paul includes himself in this group of the strong. Such a person sees beyond specific acts to the acts of one's whole life as a devotion to God. For example, a strong person "considers every day alike" (14:5), "for if we live, we live for the Lord; and if we die, we die for the Lord. So, whether we live or die, we belong to the Lord" (v.8).

In light of such issues, Paul formulates the principle that Christians must not judge one another in questionable areas of conduct because God himself will judge each one according to one's own standard of devotion (14:10–12). More important than judging others, Paul says, is the rule of loving others and bearing their weaknesses. This means acknowledging that a particular act has special significance to some and that by performing it one might cause someone else to stumble (v.21). The goal of this kind of love is both the strengthening of the weaker brother (15:2) and unity in the church (v.6).

In 15:7 Paul generalizes this principle of acceptance within the church: all whom Christ has received should be accepted. Paul then applies the principle to the situation that he has been concerned with throughout the letter, the Jew and the Gentile together in one body (vv.8–12).

## VIII. Closing Words (15:14–16:27)

Paul again reminds the Romans that he had long intended to come to their city but had been hindered (15:22–23). He had been in Macedonia and Achaia, where a collection was being made for the poverty-stricken saints in Jerusalem (15:25–33). He closes the letter with numerous greetings.

# 1 Corinthians

## Introduction

Although this letter is given the title 1 Corinthians, in actual fact Paul had already written an earlier letter to the church in the city of Corinth (see 5:9), but that letter has not been preserved in the NT. We know of a total of four letters that Paul wrote to the church at Corinth: (1) 1Co 5:9; (2) 1 Corinthians; (3) 2Co 2:3; (4) 2 Corinthians.

The apostle Paul, as indicated within this letter itself (1:1), was the author of this letter. He wrote it while ministering and teaching in the city of Ephesus (16:8). According to Ac 20:31, he spent nearly three years at Ephesus. Paul had been in Corinth for a year and a half on his second missionary journey (Ac 18:1–18). If it was written at the end of Paul's time in Ephesus (16:7), the date of the letter would be around A.D. 54–56.

The argument of 1 Corinthians is closely tied to its occasion. The report (1:11) Paul had received about the divisions and quarreling within the church at Corinth necessitated his addressing specific problems and questions decisively and with apostolic authority. The book itself, then, is structured around those issues.

The theme Paul returns to throughout the book is that of the unity of the church, the body of Christ, and the importance of each member's concern and care for others. All things are to be done for the sake of building up the body of Christ. For Paul, this meant the Christian life finds its reward in the blessing that awaits the people of God at the return of Christ. The hope of the resurrection thus lies behind most, if not all, of Paul's discussion.

## I. Introduction (1:1–9)

Paul begins the letter with a strong assertion of the steadfast faithfulness of the church at Corinth. They "do not lack any spiritual gift" (v.7a), and they "eagerly wait for our Lord Jesus Christ to be revealed" (v.7b). Paul's confidence lies in the Lord's faithfulness in keeping the Corinthian church strong.

## II. Divisions Within the Church (1:10–4:21)

Paul turns quickly to the problems and questions within the Corinthian church, the very questions that had given rise to his letter. The first of these was the growing quarrels and divisions among its members. Each group had its own leaders. These leaders were apparently arrogantly asserting their own learned views on the nature and implications of Paul's gospel.

Paul's response is complex, but underlying all of his remarks is the fact that, for him, the message of the Gospel is simple and can be understood in the ordinary language of common people. Though the wisdom of God displayed in the Gospel is sublime, God's wisdom is easily distorted when forced into categories of human wisdom. The Gospel, in fact, becomes foolishness when seen within that context. Paul himself, in presenting the Gospel at Corinth, had not attempted to dress it in "eloquence and superior wisdom" (2:1). The simple fact of Jesus' death on the cross was sufficient to demonstrate the life-giving power of God. It is the Spirit of God that enlightens the hearts of believers and enables them to "understand what God has freely given" (v.12). Without the Spirit, such simple truths would not be acceptable to the average person, for he or she simply would not understand them.

If the leaders of the Corinthian church want to assume a role of importance, then they should follow the example of Paul himself and of the other apostles and church leaders (such as Apollos, whom Paul considers a coworker, not a rival). God's leaders are, in fact, servants. They do not receive great acclaim for their work and their faithfulness. They do not receive great wealth and power. For the sake of the Gospel, these leaders of the church have given all and are content with serving the Lord.

## III. Moral Scandals in the Church (5:1–6:20)

In ch. 5 Paul turns to the question of sexual immorality within the Corinthian church, i.e., the problem of incest. Paul argues that not only was such behavior expressly forbidden in the OT (Lev 18:6), but it was even abhorrent to pagans. To make matters worse, the Corinthians were proud of such behavior in their own midst (5:2)! This could mean that they were proud of their liberty in Christ, so that such behavior was looked to as a sign of this liberty. Or it could mean that the Corinthian church had been so blinded by the stellar qualities of some among them that they overlooked obvious instances of immorality in the lives of these people. In any event, Paul argues that such a situation should have been recognized and dealt with summarily. For their own good, such offenders should be put out of the church where, presumably, they would learn their lesson, repent, and be "saved on the day of the Lord" (v.5).

From this example, Paul draws a larger principle. Christians are not to associate with one who claims to be a Christian and yet is "sexually immoral or greedy, an idolater or a slanderer, a drunkard or a swindler" (v.11). In this way, Christians should exercise judgment among themselves (v.12). Paul leaves to God the judgment of those outside the church (v.13).

The fact that Christians are to judge one another within the church leads Paul to the second moral problem at Corinth—Christians were taking other Christians to court. Paul appeals to the Son of Man passage in Da 7 to show that "the saints" (i.e., Christians) will one day judge the world with Christ. Why, then, do they not now judge one another? For Paul, the Christian's life was to be characterized by a striving to live out the principles of God's kingdom in the present age. That often means being mistreated and cheated. But that is far better than violating God's will. The ultimate question for Paul was the future inheritance of the kingdom of God. Overlooking the implications of the kingdom in one's everyday life could be a sign that one is not a member of that kingdom.

For Paul, as in the OT (Da 12:2), the coming of the future kingdom of God would be initiated by the physical resurrection of the body from the dead (6:14). Thus, sexual immorality, a sin of the body, is particularly damaging to the Christian's life in Christ. God prizes the body so much, Paul argues, that those who have lost their bodies in death will rise again to receive their bodies just as Jesus did in his resurrection. The body belongs to God as one of the "members of Christ" (v.15). In Creation he raised it out of the dust (Ge 2:7), and in the Resurrection he will again raise it out of the dust (Da 12:2). The body is a temple of the Holy Spirit. Thus sexual immorality is tantamount to the desecration of the Lord's temple, a veritable "abomination that causes desolation" (Da 12:11). Paul's imagery here is in keeping with the OT prophets' view of idolatry and apostasy as prostitution (cf. Dt 31:16).

## IV. Questions Regarding Marriage (7:1–40)

Having discussed sexual immorality and the importance of the body, Paul moves naturally to the topic of sexuality and marriage, responding to questions that had been asked of him by the Corinthian church (7:1). Paul's advice is at once practical and realistic. Although he wishes Christian men and women would not marry (vv.1, 7), presumably because there is no marriage in the resurrection (Mt 22:30), Paul knows that in real life—this side of the resurrection—men and women have God-given physical desires. Paul knows that the Scriptures teach that marriage is a part of this world (Ge 2:24) and that God himself had said, "It is not good for the man to be alone" (Ge 2:18). Paul, however, has his eyes set on the return of Christ and the establishment of his kingdom. He knows that Jesus could return at any moment: "The time is short. . . . For this world in its present form is passing away" (7:29–31). For those whose sights are set that high, there is little time for the everyday concerns that marriage naturally entails: "To the unmarried and the widows I say: It is good for them to stay unmarried" (v.8).

Paul, however, is not an ascetic. He knows that not all have the same focus; many are consumed with other desires. Thus, "if they cannot control themselves, they should marry, for it is better to marry than to burn with passion" (v.9).

That Paul has a much larger question in mind is evident from the fact that he extends his principle on marriage to include virtually every aspect of the Christian's life (vv.17–40): "Each one should remain in the situation which he was in when God called him" (v.20; cf. vv.17, 24).

## V. Questionable Issues in the Church (8:1–11:1)

To the question of eating meat offered to idols, Paul develops for his readers and applies two key biblical principles: "'Everything is permissible'—but not everything is beneficial" (10:23); and, "Nobody should seek his own good, but the good of others" (v.24). His practical interest is evident in the fact that he applies these two principles in the context of evangelism and Christian maturity, i.e., the weaker brother.

Whether Christians should eat meat which had been offered to idols was apparently a pressing question in the church at Corinth. For Paul, however, the more important question was how such issues were dealt with by the church. It had become a matter of pride on both sides of the question, so Paul begins at that point (8:1–3). As the OT teaches throughout (e.g., "All who make idols are nothing, and the things they treasure are worthless," Isa 44:9), Paul affirms that idols are "nothing at all" (8:4) and hence not a serious threat in themselves. (This is not to say that idolatry cannot be an occasion for the worship of demons, as Paul later suggests in 10:20.) If, however, a Christian brother should think otherwise, it would be wrong for him to eat meat offered to an idol. Moreover, if that person were to see another Christian eat meat that in his mind was "defiled," it would surely send the wrong signal. It could very easily be interpreted by him as a license to do even that which one knows, or thinks, to be wrong. This would "wound [the] weak conscience" of the weaker brother (8:12) and thus make his conscience less effective in important matters of behavior. For the sake of such persons, one should not eat meat offered to idols or do anything else that may be wrongly interpreted.

Paul gives his own situation as an example of putting aside individual rights out of concern for others. As an apostle, Paul had all the rights and privileges of an apostle. For the sake of the Gospel, however, he relinquished those rights. Everything Paul did was for a higher purpose, i.e., "for the sake of the gospel" (9:23). His mind was set on the prize at the end of the race—the coming of the kingdom of God that he looked for at any moment. Paul did not want to be found "disqualified" when he faced the risen Lord (v.27).

Was it possible that someone like Paul could be disqualified? In answer to that question, he gives the example of the Israelites in the desert. They "were all under the cloud" and "passed through the sea" (10:1); moreover, "they were all baptized into Moses in the cloud and in the sea" (v.2). If anyone could have claimed to have made it, it would have been those Israelites—they even "drank from the spiritual rock that accompanied them, and that rock was Christ" (v.4). Most of them, however, were disqualified; "their bodies were scattered over the desert" (v.5), and they did not enter the Promised Land. As with the OT prophets (Nu 20:9–12; Am 5:25–26), Paul looks at Israel's sojourn in the desert as a time of failure. Only Joshua and Caleb were found faithful (Nu 14). Moses himself died in the desert and could not enter the land (Nu 20:12). Thus, these OT narratives are as lessons for those who now live during the days of fulfillment (10:11), lest they too test the Lord's forbearance and fall, as it were, in the desert. Paul, apparently sensing the stringency of his warning, quickly adds the comforting promise that God is faithful and will not allow anyone to be tempted beyond what one is able to bear (v.13).

The warning, nevertheless, remains, that Christians are not to presume upon their rights and privileges, but are to act responsibly toward the mutual good of all (v.33). Their freedom in Christ should not be turned against the weaker members of the church.

## VI. Questions of Public Worship (11:2–34)

Paul addresses two procedural problems in the public worship services of the Corinthian church: (1) the proper procedure for covering one's head in prayer (vv.2–16), and (2) the proper procedure for commemorating the Lord's Supper (vv.17–34). Like the earlier sections of this letter, Paul appeals to general principles, but here he also cites both custom and precedent to support his case.

In the case of head coverings, Paul appeals to the general principle of headship: "the head of every man is Christ, and the head of the woman is man, and the head of Christ is God" (v.3). This principle, based on the pattern of the creation of the man and woman in the Genesis narratives (Ge 2:7–24), had been used to support a well-known custom in the early church (v.16). When men prayed in public worship, they uncovered their heads, whereas women prayed with their heads covered. To do otherwise was considered dishonorable (vv.4–7). This was ultimately a question of authority (v.10), and, as Paul maintained in 1 Ti. 2:12, women should not have authority over men in the church.

The situation with the Lord's Supper was an entirely different matter. The practice of commemorating the Lord's Supper in the Corinthian church is censured strongly by Paul. He says, "Your meetings do more harm than good" (v.17), meaning, apparently, that their disruptive "divisions" and their practice of greedy feasting and drunkenness obscured the purpose of their commemoration. The bread and cup are intended to "proclaim the Lord's death until he comes" (v.26) and thus are symbols of his own body: "For anyone who eats and drinks without recognizing the body of the Lord eats and drinks judgment on himself" (v.29). The purpose of the meal was not to satisfy hunger, but to remember the work of Christ. Failure to recognize or presume upon Christ's work brings one under God's judgment. What was the remedy for their abuse in the practice of the Supper? When they came together to eat, they were to "wait for each other" (v.33), thus acknowledging that the meal was not to satisfy hunger but was a commemoration.

## VII. Questions of Spiritual Gifts (12:1–14:40)

Paul's discussion of spiritual gifts follows closely the central theme of the book, as well as the particular point raised in connection with the Lord's Supper. The exercise of spiritual gifts should be for the "common good" (12:7) of the whole of the church, and it should center on the worship of Christ (v.3). The church, as Christ's body, has many parts. One Spirit has baptized all members into the same body (v.13). God has arranged the parts of the body to fulfill his plan and purposes. Though each part plays a vital role in God's design, some parts (or gifts) in the body are more honorable than others. The honor bestowed on some gifts, such as apostleship, prophecy, and teaching, is for the sake of unity and mutual concern (v.25). Not all, however, are given these gifts, nor is any single individual given all of the gifts; but everyone can eagerly desire to have "the greater gifts" (v.31).

There is, however, a "more excellent way" (12:31), one that transcends the exercise of each and every one of the gifts that God gives. That is the way of love. Without love, the exercise of even divinely given gifts is "nothing" (13:2). Love is the manner and the goal of exercising spiritual gifts. Gifts are important but temporary. They are provisions that God has given to his church, like the helps that small children need in growing to maturity. Love, on the other hand, is like the sound mind of an adult. It always knows the right thing to do and does it. Such maturity is the result of being properly nourished on the gifts of the Spirit.

Thus, for Paul, the Christian's life should be characterized by a striving for spiritual gifts, practiced in the spirit of love. That would result in harmony and order in the life of the Christian and in the life of the church. In the everyday exercise of a gift, one's concern should be the building up of others, not self-satisfaction and fulfillment. When applied to specific gifts, such a rule suggests that a gift like prophecy, which is speaking to others "for their strengthening, encouragement and comfort" (14:3), has greater value for the church (vv.4–5) than tongues, which "does not speak to men but to God" (vv.2, 4). If, however, someone interprets the tongues, the church can thereby profit (v.5b). In the church community, one must be conscious of speaking clear "intelligible words" (vv.6–9) that "build up the church" (v.12). Thus if the gift of tongues is exercised in the church, one should also pray that God will give the gift of interpretation so that others may be strengthened and encouraged by what is said (vv.13–19).

The gift of speaking in tongues, as the OT shows, was given to the church as a sign for unbelievers. Judging from Paul's quotation from Isa 28:11–12, the unbelievers he has in mind are Jews. His description of the purpose of the gift of tongues follows the example of Ac 2. In Acts, the gift of the Spirit resulted in the disciples speaking "in other tongues as the Spirit enabled them" (Ac 2:4). Each of the "God-fearing Jews from every nation under heaven" (v.5) heard "them speaking in his own language" and were "utterly amazed" (vv.6–7). They asked, "How is it that each of us hears them in his own native language?" (v.8). The Acts passage is a concrete example of the role the gift of tongues played as a sign to Jews that the OT prophecies were being fulfilled in their day. As Peter said on that occasion, "Fellow Jews . . . this is what was spoken by the prophet Joel" (vv.14–16).

The worship of the church was to be characterized by singing hymns and using words of instruction, revelations, and tongues with interpretation (1Co 14:26). The focus of the service was "the strengthening of the church" (v.26). Only two or three persons were to speak in tongues consecutively, with interpretations, or to prophesy (vv.27–29). The others were to "weigh carefully what is said" (v.29). The women were to "remain silent" (v.34). Paul warns of stringent consequences for those who ignore his teaching (v.38).

An enlightening example of an early worship service such as this is found in Acts. Paul and Barnabas were "worshiping the Lord" in the church at Antioch (Ac 13:2) when the Holy Spirit spoke, apparently through one of the prophets there (v.1). In this case, however, the goal was not edification, but direction for the spread of the Gospel into Asia.

## VIII. Questions About the Resurrection (15:1–58)

Paul's last topic is the Resurrection. As we have seen, his hope in the resurrection has governed the nature of his teaching throughout this letter (see comments on chs. 8–10). Paul was eagerly awaiting the return of Christ and the resurrection of the dead, which, according to OT prophecy (e.g., Da 12:2), would accompany it. It was imperative for him to address the question raised by those who doubted the Resurrection. There were many in early Judaism who taught that there was no resurrection. In the Gospels, these people were associated with the school of the Sadducees (Mt 22:23). Paul, like Jesus, believed strongly in the Resurrection. For him, the hope of a future bodily resurrection of all Christians was founded on the central facts of the Gospel, i.e., that Jesus died for our sins, was buried, and rose again (15:1–4, 12–23). Not only was this taught in the OT Scriptures (v.4), but it had also been witnessed by the founders of the apostolic church (vv.5–8), of which he himself was one

(vv.9–11). It was the fact that he had seen the risen Lord on the road to Damascus that turned Paul from a persecutor of the church to one of its leading apostles (see Ac 9).

Central to Paul's understanding of the return of Christ and the future establishment of God's kingdom is the concept of the resurrection (vv.23–28). Paul follows the OT closely in his explanation of the events of the last days, the return of Christ, and the resurrection. As with Jesus, his basic text is the Son of Man passage in the book of Daniel (chs. 7, 12). When Christ returns (15:23b), those who belong to him will arise from the dead (v.23c). This will mark the coming of the end (v.24a). Christ will return to destroy "all dominion, authority and power" (v.24c), reign until the time he "has put all his enemies under his feet" (v.25), including death itself (v.26), and then hand "over the kingdom to God the Father" (vv.24b, 28). Paul's view of the future kingdom is the same as that of Jesus in Mt 24 and John in Rev 19–20.

Paul's next argument for the necessity of the resurrection has been variously interpreted: "Now if there is no resurrection, what will those do who are baptized for the dead?" i.e., "Why are people baptized for them?" (v.29). What Paul means by this expression may be demonstrated in the next verse: "And as for us, why do we endanger ourselves every hour?" (v.30). The expression "baptism for the dead" may then refer to the martyrdom that many Christians in Paul's day suffered for the sake of Christ and for those who had died before them. This is the sense of "baptism" in Mk 10:38: "Jesus said, 'Can you drink the cup I drink or be baptized with the baptism I am baptized with?'" Jesus refers to his own death by the term "baptism." Thus Paul tells the Corinthians that such sacrifices as he and others are making by daily risking and losing their own lives are futile if there is no resurrection (15:32).

A major objection to the notion of a resurrection was the question of the kind of body the dead would have (v.35). The objection, as Paul answers it, centers on the fact that the dead no longer have bodies because their physical bodies have decayed and rotted away. Paul responds by showing that in nature itself, dust and decay precede regeneration: "What you sow does not come to life unless it dies" (v.36). Just as in nature, Paul continues, so also in the resurrection "God gives it a body as he has determined" (v.38). We need not worry about the bodies of the dead that have decayed and lie in ashes. God will give them a body that will never decay again (vv.42–44), just as he has given all creatures in his universe the kind of body fit for them (vv.39–41). The chief characteristic of the new body given to those in the resurrection is its spiritual nature; that is, bearing "the likeness of the man from heaven" (v.49), it will be an imperishable body that will not have "the sting of death," which is sin (v.56).

Because of the resurrection of the body, a Christian's work, done for the Lord, will never be in vain (v.58).

## IX. Personal Matters (16:1–24)

Paul closes the letter with a reminder of the collection for God's people in Jerusalem, the churches which were in need of assistance. He closes the letter with some final admonitions and greetings.

# 2 Corinthians

## Introduction

This letter is really the fourth letter that Paul wrote to the Christians in Corinth (see introduction to 1 Corinthians), though the letter mentioned in 2Co 2:3 may be our 1 Corinthians.

The apostle Paul, as indicated within this letter itself (1:1), was the author of the letter. He wrote it during his travels in Macedonia (2:13; 7:5; 9:2). The date it was written is dependent on that of 1 Corinthians, since both letters were written within a short span of time. If 1 Corinthians was written at the end of Paul's time in Ephesus (1Co 16:7) and is dated around A.D. 54–56, then the present letter was written a short time later in the same year.

This letter is a unique and remarkable piece of literature. It is a letter; yet more than that, it is a monologue, with Paul delivering a veritable barrage of words to his readers in Corinth—sometimes lamenting their misunderstanding of his motives, sometimes castigating those among them who were stirring up strife, and sometimes praising God for the blessings and edification that had come through his personal afflictions. Yet, at the same time, with this unrelenting war of words as a backdrop, Paul also manages to raise and masterfully handle some of the most thorny issues of the Gospel in all the NT. With much repetition and pathos running throughout the book, one has to read the book at two levels. The first is the emotive level, at which the reader is forced to absorb the full range of Paul's anxiety and trauma at the response of the Corinthians to his previous letter. There comes a point, however, where this part of the book has to be tuned out slightly to allow the reader to focus on the weighty issues of the Gospel that Paul raises in the midst of his personal turmoil. The comments in this commentary will focus on both aspects.

## I. Introduction (1:1–11)

Paul immediately sets the tone of his letter with a reminder of the great suffering he has endured for the sake of the Christians at Corinth (vv.3–11). All the essential elements of the remainder of the letter are found in this opening volley. As in 1 Corinthians, the hope that sustained Paul in the midst of "great pressure" was that of the resurrection (cf. comments on 1Co 8–10; 15). God was faithful and answered the prayers of many on Paul's behalf, and now Paul has been spared to write this letter of comfort to the church at Corinth. For Paul, behind all the misfortune he has endured, there lies the all-encompassing divine compassion: "If we are distressed, it is for your comfort and salvation" (v.6). There is a purpose for all that has happened, and Paul is not going to let it go by unnoticed!

## II. Change of Plans and Delay (1:12–2:13)

The first matter Paul turns to is his change of plans in visiting the Corinthian church. He had planned to visit Corinth, but sent a letter instead—a letter that had caused them sorrow (7:8). That letter was either what we now call 1 Corinthians or, more likely, a letter that has not been preserved in the NT. In any event, it is to the Corinthians' painful response to that letter that Paul now addresses himself. First on his agenda is the restoration of one of their members who had been disciplined (2:5–11). Paul instructs that he should now be restored and comforted "so that he will not be overwhelmed by excessive sorrow" (v.7).

## III. Paul's Apostolic Ministry (2:14–7:16)

Paul digresses at this point in the letter to put his personal situation in a larger context for his readers. That larger context is the apostolic ministry to which he has been called within the new covenant. The concept of the new covenant, promised in the OT (Jer 31:31–34; Eze 36:22–32), becomes a particularly apt way for Paul to address the problems in the Corinthian church. In the new covenant, the external law of God written on tablets of stone was replaced by the law of God written on the hearts of God's people (Jer 31:33). Thus, as Jesus taught in the Gospels and as Paul repeatedly stresses, Christians are those who love God and serve him with their whole heart. Since the Spirit of God dwells in them (Eze 36:27), they are God's temple, the "aroma of Christ among those who are being saved" (2:15). They themselves are a testimony, a letter of recommendation, of Paul's apostleship, "written not with ink but with the Spirit of the living God, not on tablets of stone but on tablets of human hearts" (3:3). Thus, the very lives of the Christians at Corinth testify to Paul's new covenant apostleship.

To reassure his readers of the real difference the new covenant has made in their lives, Paul contrasts their experience of God's glory in the new covenant with the fading and fearful response of Israel at Mount Sinai, i.e., in the old covenant. His main point is the great superiority of the glory of the new covenant (vv.9–11).

Paul assumes that the old covenant at Sinai had failed to produce a righteous people of God. It is important to note that Paul is not referring to the OT Scriptures here. Rather, he is referring to the Mosaic covenant that God made with Israel at Mount Sinai, which is described in the OT. As Paul shows in his reference to the veil of Moses in Ex 34, the OT itself shares his view of the fading glory of the old covenant. After being with God on the mountain, Moses had to wear a veil over his face to shield God's glory from those who looked at him—"The Israelites could not look steadily at the face of Moses because of its glory" (v.7). Paul, however, sees a

second aspect to the veil that Moses wore. It not only shielded the Israelites from facing God's glory, but it also hid from them the fact that the glory on Moses' face was fading (v.13). To this very day, he argues, "the same veil remains when the old covenant is read" (v.14); that is, "when Moses is read, a veil covers their hearts" (v.15). For Paul, the veil that was on the face of Moses now lays over the face of the OT Scriptures and hides its meaning from anyone who reads it without turning to the Lord. With believers who have the Spirit of God in the new covenant, however, the veil is taken away. They both see God's glory revealed and reflect that glory "with unveiled faces" (vv.17–18).

It is important to note here that Paul is not endorsing a "spiritual" or "allegorical" reading of the Scriptures as a way of seeing Jesus in the OT. He is, in fact, saying just the opposite. He is arguing that the truths of the new covenant are already there in the OT Scriptures, so much so that those who do not see it are blinded by a veil. The truth is there, but they cannot see it. Paul is not saying we should "spiritualize" the OT; he is rather saying we should read the OT with "spiritual eyes."

What kind of glory do Christians reflect? Lest his readers begin to look around themselves for shining faces, Paul immediately points to the ways in which God's glory radiates from the faces of new covenant believers. It is, first of all, by their renouncing "secret and shameful ways" (4:2a), not using deception (v.2b), not distorting God's Word (v.2c); it is by living a life with a clear conscience in the sight of God (v.2d). The light that "shines out of the darkness" is the work of Christ that is seen in the actions of Christians (vv.3–6); the glory does not radiate from Christians in themselves. They "have this treasure in jars of clay" (v.7). The glory shines from these jars of clay so that all may see that "this all-surpassing power is from God and not from us" (v.7). Paul, looking at his own inglorious circumstances, concludes that it is in just these kinds of circumstances that "his life may be revealed in our mortal body" (v.11). It is the truth of the new covenant gospel that keeps Paul from losing heart when he looks at those things happening to him all around (vv.16–18). It also gives him hope for the eternal dwelling that awaits him when his temporary, earthly clay jar has passed away (5:1–5). We can learn to be content in our present state, but our lasting hope is for that time when we are "away from the body and at home with the Lord" (vv.6–10).

The importance of Paul's concentration on the new covenant concept of a new heart can be seen in his description of those at Corinth who were turning the church against his apostolic leadership. They were "those who take pride in what is seen rather than in what is in the heart" (v.12). This was not merely an attack on Paul's authority, it was a distortion of the very Gospel that Paul had preached to them. Thus what lies behind Paul's assertions of his apostolic authority is the love of Christ and the truth of the Gospel (5:13–6:2). That Gospel is one of "God . . . reconciling the world to himself in Christ, not counting men's sins against them" (5:19). It is the gospel of grace (5:21–6:1). Such a gospel should be kept clear at all times (6:3–13) and never linked with unbelief of any kind (vv.14–18). It demands purity of life (7:1) and open acceptance of one another (vv.2–4).

As an example of the ministry of reconciliation, Paul recounts the example of Titus (vv.5–16), the Macedonian churches (8:1–9), and the Corinthians' own actions in the past (vv.10–15). The pressing current example, which Paul addresses in 8:1–9:15, is the collection he was taking among the churches for the needy churches in Jerusalem (8:1).

## IV. Defense of Paul's Apostolic Ministry (10:1–12:21)

Having described his apostolic calling and presented his immediate reason for writing, Paul turns now to a passionate defense of his apostolic ministry. Paul is first of all concerned that the Corinthians do not confuse his defense of his apostolic authority with boasting, though he readily admits that much of what he has to say could be construed as boasting (10:1–18). Thus he vows he "will not boast beyond proper limits, but will confine our boasting to the field God has assigned to us, a field that reaches even to you" (v.13).

Paul's major concern with what he has heard of the church at Corinth is the presence there of false apostles (11:13) and their attempt to undermine his own authority as an apostle in order to gain that authority in Corinth. The threat to the church is that someone may present them with a "Jesus other than the Jesus [Paul] preached" (v.4) and that their "minds may somehow be led astray from your sincere and pure devotion to Christ" (v.3). In defending himself before the church at Corinth, Paul is determined not to adopt the methods of these "super-apostles" (cf. 12:11), and yet he is not going to let them outboast him in matters that clearly demonstrate the sincerity of his ministry (11:6–12:10). Lest anyone mistake his motives, Paul reminds his readers that his boasting has been entirely limited "to things that show [his] weakness" (11:30).

## V. Paul's Apostolic Ministry Exercised (13:1–10)

Though continuing at the same pitch, Paul brings the letter to a close with a stern warning lest his intentions and plans be misunderstood or deliberately misconstrued. His desire to be weak in Christ must not be interpreted as weakness. The matter was one that required serious reflection: "Examine yourselves to see whether you are in the faith; test yourselves" (v.5). Paul was no longer under examination, his readers were. For him, this letter was proof that he had not failed the test (cf. v.5); it was now time for the church at Corinth to see if they had (v.5). The question was not "Who is right?" but whether they would "do what is right" (v.7). In the end, Paul is confident that truth would prevail because the apostolic authority that the Lord gave him was "for building you up, not for tearing you down" (v.10).

## VI. Conclusion (13:11–14)

As a conclusion Paul summarizes the underlying exhortation of his letter: "Aim for perfection, listen to my appeal, be of one mind, live in peace" (v.11). He closes with one of the most beautiful benedictions in the NT, reflecting the qualities of the Triune God.

# Galatians

## Introduction

In the early NT manuscripts this letter, written by the apostle Paul (1:1), is entitled "To the Galatians." As with most NT books, the date this letter was written cannot be determined with precision. For one thing, the destination, Galatia, is not a precise geographical term and could be located in more than one of Paul's missionary journeys. But it is clear from the content of the letter that it was written during Paul's active ministry in Asia Minor and that it deals with a central question in the early church, the role of the Mosaic Law in the life of the Gentile Christian. This is the same issue that arose in Ac 15.

Certain teachers in the churches of Galatia had challenged the Gospel Paul had previously preached in these churches. They were attempting to persuade the Gentile Christians in those churches to live by the requirements of the Mosaic Law rather than by grace. For Paul, this represented "another gospel," different from the one he had preached. Thus, the purpose of this letter was to set straight the nature of the Gospel entrusted to them in the beginning and to give a justification for it, based on his calling as an apostle.

## I. Introduction (1:1–10)

Paul begins immediately in his introduction to establish the main line of argument in the book. His apostleship was "not from men nor by man, but by Jesus Christ and God the Father who raised him from the dead" (v.1). It is important for Paul to demonstrate that he was directly and divinely appointed as an apostle. The Gospel he preached is the only Gospel; there is no other (vv.6–10). There were some in the churches in Galatia who, in Paul's view, preached another gospel, which was "really no gospel at all" (v.7). It meant "deserting

the one who called [them] by the grace of Christ" (v.6).

## II. The Divine Origin of Paul's Gospel (1:11–2:10)

Paul then sets out to demonstrate that the Gospel he preached was the one and only true Gospel. He received it "by revelation from Jesus Christ" (1:12), and it was confirmed by the early church leaders. The reference to the revelation Paul received is to the vision of Jesus that he saw on his way to Damascus (Ac 9). After he received this revelation, Paul did not consult with the other apostles in Jerusalem for three years. Only after three years in Arabia and Damascus did he go to Jerusalem to meet with Peter and James for fifteen days. But these were the only apostles he met with.

After fourteen years of continuous ministry, Paul later returned to Jerusalem and, at that time, was privately examined by the leaders of the church there. The issue centered on the place of the Mosaic Law in the preaching of the Gospel and, specifically, the question of whether Gentile Christians should be circumcised. Paul held stringently to the view that Gentiles were not to be made subject to the stipulations of the Mosaic Law. The resolution of that meeting was that Paul's message was well suited for his commission as an apostle to the Gentiles and that Peter's message was suited for his ministry to the Jews. On that basis, the leaders of the Jerusalem church—James, Peter, and John—agreed and gave Paul "the right hand of fellowship" (2:9).

## III. The Statement of the Problem (2:11–16)

The flashpoint came with Peter's actions in Antioch. Although initially content to live free of the law (i.e., according to Paul's gospel), Peter later "began to draw back and separate himself from the Gentiles because he was afraid of those who belonged to the circumcision group" (v.12). In other words, Peter, who knew better, disregarded the Gospel and buckled under pressure from "the circumcision group" from Jerusalem. Others, including even Barnabas, followed his example (v.13).

Paul confronted Peter with the charge of hypocrisy. While in Antioch, he had been willing to live like a Gentile, free from the restrictions of the Mosaic Law, but when representatives from Jerusalem came, he gave in to pressure and began insisting that Gentiles follow the Mosaic Law (v.14). Something was wrong!

## IV. Statement of the Gospel (2:17–21)

Peter's actions were contrary to the basic message of the Gospel, Paul argues. Even Jewish Christians knew that "a man is not justified by observing the law, but by faith in Jesus Christ" (v.16). The question, as Paul puts it, is clearly centered on salvation. According to his Gospel, salvation is not dependent on keeping the Mosaic Law, "because by observing the law no one will be justified" (v.16). Ultimately it boils down to the question of the work of Christ on the cross, concludes Paul: "I have been crucified with Christ. . . . If righteousness could be gained through the law, Christ died for nothing!" (vv.20–21).

## IV. Sanctification by Faith and Freedom From Law (3:1–5:12)

Paul now turns to the question of the Christian's way of life. Having begun by faith and not obedience to the law, should one now turn back to the law? Is it the Spirit or human effort that empowers the Christian's life (3:3)? That question, says Paul, is answered for us in a number of ways. Does God give Christians his Spirit and work miracles by the law or by faith? The answer is either too obvious for Paul to give or it is rolled over into the next example, Abraham. Here Paul quotes directly from Ge 15:6, "He believed God, and it

was credited to him as righteousness" (3:6). In this very example, Paul argues, the Scriptures themselves are looking to this point of time when the Gentiles, apart from the law, would receive the gift of righteousness through faith (vv.7–9).

Having given two examples to prove the point that righteousness comes by faith, not by law, Paul now turns to the reverse side of the question. What is life like under the law? Here again Paul relies on a direct quote from the OT: "Cursed is everyone who does not continue to do everything written in the Book of the Law" (v.10; cf. Dt 27:26). Thus no one is righteous before God by the law (vv.11). Moreover, Paul states, "the law is not based on faith" (v.12). It is just the opposite: "The man who does these things will live by them" (v.12, a quotation from Lev 18:5). Thus it is by faith that Gentiles were given Abraham's blessing, and it is by faith that we receive the promise of the Spirit (v.14).

God made a covenant promise to Abraham that the Gentiles would be blessed in the Messiah, who would come from his descendants (vv.15–16). That promise was made four centuries before the law was given (v.17), and hence the law could not nullify it. If, once the law was given, the blessing of Abraham was based on that law, it would mean that the promise had been done away with. But even within human society, promises cannot be nullified. They must be kept. Thus the law cannot replace or add to the original promise made to Abraham.

The law did have a definite purpose, related to Israel's need for guidelines and help in their weakness. They needed the law for their own survival. Their numerous transgressions in the desert, especially that of the golden calf (Ex 32), proved their need for special measures. It was not given them to impart life and fulfill the promises of blessing. Rather, it had a distinct purpose of holding them, as it were, as prisoners until the time when "faith should be revealed" (v.23). Now that faith in Christ has come, Paul says, "we are no longer under the supervision of the law" (v.25).

Thus in Christ all have been made children of God (v.26). No longer are there to be distinctions such as Jews and Gentiles, slave and free, male and female. In Christ all are Abraham's descendants. Before the coming of Christ, God's people were heirs of the promises to Abraham, but they were "subject to guardians and trustees," i.e., the law (4:1–2). In the divine plan of the ages, God sent Jesus to redeem his people from the law and to give them their full rights as his children (vv.3–7). The Gentiles were in no better position before the coming of Christ. They were enslaved to false gods in ignorance (v.8). Now that Christ has come to set all of us free, why would anyone want to go back to this former state of slavery (vv.9–20)?

For Paul the issue comes down to the biblical example of Hagar and Sarah and the two covenants they represent, the Sinai covenant and the new covenant. Hagar, the slave, represents the covenant at Sinai (vv.24–25), and, in Paul's day, the Jews in Jerusalem. They were under the guardianship of the law. Sarah, however, the wife of Abraham, represents a different Jerusalem, one from above. She is the mother of those who enjoy the blessings of Abraham in Christ (vv.26–28). Then, as now, the son of the slave persecuted "the son born by the power of the Spirit" (v.29). Then, as now, Paul continues, Christians should not forfeit their freedom in Christ by going back into the state of bondage to the law (4:30–5:12).

## V. Living by the Spirit (5:13–6:10)

The fact that Christians are not under the Mosaic Law should not be taken to mean they are free to live as they please. There is a higher law, the law of Christ (6:2): "Love your neighbor as yourself" (5:14). Those who live by the Spirit will not "gratify the desires of the sinful nature" (5:16–21; 6:8a) but will exhibit the "fruit of the Spirit" (5:22–6:6; 6:8b–10).

## VI. Conclusion (6:11–18)

Paul concludes with a brief summary of the letter, saying that the real motive of those who were attempting to push obedience to the law upon Gentile Christians was fear of persecution (v.12). Paul's parting thought is that believers enjoy God's peace and mercy, not by circumcision or uncircumcision, but rather by being "new creatures" in Christ (vv.14–15).

# Ephesians

## Introduction

In early NT manuscripts this letter is entitled "To the Ephesians," but since some early manuscripts do not have "in Ephesus" in 1:1, the title may be a later addition. The apostle Paul is identified as the author. Because he calls himself a "prisoner" in this letter (3:1; 4:1), it is assumed to have been written around A.D. 60, the time of Paul's imprisonment in Rome.

Paul's primary focus in this letter is the status of the Gentile Christians within God's eternal plan. For Paul, the work of Christ in his death and resurrection resulted in a new direction taken in God's plan. Gentiles were being united together with Jews in the church as a single people of God. This was not, however, something new to God. He knew it from ages past, but after the Resurrection he revealed it to the apostles and prophets of the NT church. Paul's purpose in this letter was to explain and present this new direction in God's eternal plan.

The first three chapters are devoted to explaining God's eternal plan and the Gentiles' position in it. In the last three chapters Paul gives practical guidelines for living the Christian life in light of God's eternal plan.

## I. Introduction (1:1–2)

Paul gives little personal introduction, either of himself or his readers. His concern appears to be merely to identify himself. Moreover, the phrase "in Ephesus" is not found in some of the earliest and best NT manuscripts. The letter may have been written as a circular letter to be read by many churches throughout the early church.

The crucial bit of information given about the readers is simply that they are "saints," i.e., Christians, and that they have faith in Christ Jesus (v.1). This is assumed by Paul throughout the letter and is one of its essential features. It is written to Christians to explain and expound their status as Christians within the larger context of God's plan for the ages.

## II. The Gentile Church in God's Plan (1:3–3:21)

### A. God's Accomplishment of the Plan (1:3–14)

Paul begins the body of his letter with a sweeping panoramic view of God's plan for humankind, beginning in eternity past before Creation. He first looks at a Christian's divine blessings "in the heavenly realms" (v.3). Paul presents the Christian's life in Christ as one that draws on a treasure of inherited wealth stored in heaven under God's safekeeping. The Christian has this inheritance solely because of God's eternal plan for the human race and for creation. Before he created the world, God chose each individual believer to be adopted as his own child, to be redeemed, and to inherit the heavenly wealth of his only Son. Why? Because he loved them. God's plan involved the death of his Son, Jesus. God also determined to reveal his plan to humankind and to set a specific time when that plan would be carried out. The ultimate goal of his plan was to bring praise to himself. As each individual Christian turns to Christ in faith, he or she is included in God's plan and marked with the seal of the Holy Spirit, thus guaranteeing an inheritance when the time comes.

### B. Implication of the Plan for Gentiles (1:15–23)

Paul's immediate concern for his readers is that they properly understand and appreciate what their inheritance is and what it means for their daily living. Much of what they need to know comes from a deeper knowledge of the spiritual things that must be given the Christian by God himself. The "eyes of their heart" (v.18) need to be enlightened for them to know "the riches of their glorious inheritance" (v.18). Thus Paul knows all he can do is pray that God will give his readers an understanding of these things as he himself sets out to explain them.

He begins his explanation with Jesus' resurrection (vv.19–23), by which God exalted Christ to his right hand, giving him dominion over all things. Paul assumes his readers will recognize the imagery from the Son of Man passages in Da 7:9–14. The Son of Man receives the kingdom from the Ancient of Days, and all nations are put in subjection to him. Thus, Paul's revelation of this great mystery comes from his own eyes having been enlightened as he read and poured over the OT Scriptures. For him, Daniel's vision of the promise of a messianic King ruling over all the world (Da 7:9–14) has been realized "in the heavenly realms" in Christ's resurrection; it has also meant Christ's becoming the head of the church.

## C. Description of the Plan (2:1–3:13)

Central to Daniel's vision of the kingdom of the Son of Man is the fact that those who belong to that kingdom include not only the OT Jewish "saints of the Most High" (Da 7:27) but also the Gentiles, i.e., "all peoples, nations and men of every language" who will worship the Son (Da 7:14). With an eye particularly on the Gentiles, Paul begins by describing the mutual condition of all humankind before the coming of Christ (2:1–10). The Gentiles "were dead in transgressions and sins" because they "followed the ways of this world" (vv.1–2). But so also were the Jews: "All of us also lived among them at one time, gratifying the cravings of our sinful nature. . . . Like the rest, we were by nature objects of wrath" (v.3). Thus, in Paul's view, both Jews and Gentiles were "objects of [divine] wrath" and in need of the grace of God (v.8). When God raised Jesus from the

dead, he also made believers "alive in Christ," even while they were still "dead in transgressions" (v.5). All this came by grace in order to demonstrate "the incomparable riches of his grace" (vv.6–7).

In describing God's plan to the Gentile churches in Asia Minor, then, Paul turns specifically to the divine inheritance of the Gentiles (vv.11–12). Before Christ, the Gentiles were not a part of God's people. They were "excluded from citizenship in Israel and foreigners to the covenants of the promise"; they were "without hope and without God" (v.12). In the death of Christ, the shedding of his blood, the Gentiles were brought into the people of God (v.13). The death of Christ did this by abolishing the Mosaic Law "with its commandments and regulations," thus destroying "the barrier, the dividing wall of hostility" (v.14). In Christ both Jews and Gentiles are one, with one sacrifice giving them all access to God. Thus in the church, Gentiles are now "fellow citizens with God's people and members of God's household" (v.19).

## D. The Revelation of the Mystery (3:1–13)

Earlier generations of God's people did not understand God's plan for the Gentiles as Paul now did. They were unaware that Jews and Gentiles were to be united as one people of God in Christ (v.6). Now, says Paul, this "mystery" has been revealed "to God's holy apostles and prophets" (v.5). It was Paul's specific calling to make this mystery clear, since it had been "for ages past . . . kept hidden in God" (v.9). Paul specifies more clearly what he means in v.10: God's "intent was that now, through the church, the manifold wisdom of God should be made known." Thus, though God's specific work with the nations through the church was not previously known, it had now been revealed to Paul and to others. Earlier generations knew from the OT that

God's kingdom would include the Gentiles (e.g., Isa 2:2–5; Da 7:9–14), but in those texts, the plan of God was portrayed in terms of the kingdom of Israel (e.g., Da 7:27). The concept of the church as the body of Christ remained hidden with God until the coming of Jesus.

### E. Riches and Power (3:14–21)

Paul returns to the theme of the riches stored up for those who are in Christ (cf. 1:3–14), though now he views the riches as spiritual power in living the Christian life (3:16). The resources of the Christian's inheritance in Christ is "his power that is at work within us" (v.20). Thus, Paul now turns to his instruction on how Christ's power is to be lived out in the everyday life of the Christian and the church.

## III. The Way of Life for the Church (4:1–6:20)

### A. The Unity of the Church as the Basis and Goal of Life (4:1–16)

Paul begins with a description of the general goal of the Christian life: exhibiting the love of Christ with one another, thereby arriving at "unity in the faith" (v.13a) and "attaining to the whole measure of the fullness of Christ" (v.13b). This is accomplished in the church by a proper application of the gifts each member of the body has received (vv.11–12) and by achieving maturity in the knowledge of the truth (vv.14–16).

### B. Warning Against Worldly Practice (4:17–24)

An understanding of what God has done in Christ should lead to a transformed life. Former ways of thinking, developed apart from the new life in Christ, should be consciously put aside and replaced by the practice of "true righteousness and holiness" (v.23). In the next section, Paul lists specific examples of such true righteousness.

### C. Examples of True Righteousness (4:25–6:9)

Paul begins with a general summary of the nature of true righteousness. This includes speaking the truth; controlling anger; not stealing; doing hard work; sharing with others; using clean talk; mutually building up others; honoring the Spirit; ridding oneself of bitterness, rage, anger, brawling, and slander; being kind; and forgiving one another (4:25–32). He stresses further the importance of avoiding sexual immorality, obscenity, foolish talk, coarse joking, and greediness. Such acts and attitudes are not a part of God's purpose for the Christian's life but are, rather, habits of his or her former way of life (5:1–20).

Paul then applies these principles to key areas of life, beginning with the family. Wives are to submit to their husbands as they submit to Christ. The husband is the head of the wife as Christ is the head of the church (vv.22–24). Husbands are to love their wives as Christ loves the church (vv.25–33). Children are to obey their parents, and parents are to be kind to their children (6:1–4). Slaves are to obey their masters sincerely, and masters will be held accountable before the Lord for how they treat their slaves (vv.5–9).

### D. Divine Equipping for Spiritual Warfare (6:10–20)

Paul concludes with a reminder of the spiritual warfare that exists in a Christian's life. The kind of equipment needed for daily struggles with the old way of life are precisely those gifts that the Spirit gives to the church.

## IV. Conclusion (6:21–24)

Paul, in asking for prayer at the conclusion, reminds his readers that he is now in prison for proclaiming the mystery that he has just explained to them in this letter. It is a vivid reminder for them that the world was not ready to receive the message of the kingdom.

# Philippians

## Introduction

In the early NT manuscripts the book is entitled "To the Philippians." The apostle Paul is identified as the author in 1:1. Because he was "in chains" when he wrote this letter (1:12–14), it is commonly assumed to have been written around A.D. 60, the time of Paul's imprisonment in Rome.

Paul wrote this letter to the church in Philippi, with specific issues in mind. His primary concern was that they not veer away from the genuineness and sincerity of their faith. There were forces at work within the church that threatened to do just that, and Paul goes to great lengths in this letter to persuade the church and its leaders not to follow them. He leads them by encouragement and example. He stresses throughout that they have done well in the faith up to this point, but as in his own ministry, the greatest tests lay ahead. The key to the direction they should take lies primarily in the example of Christ (2:1–18), but also in Timothy and Epaphroditus (2:19–30), Paul himself (3:1–21), and their own past acts of faithfulness (4:10–20). Paul also uses this letter to give a word of thanks to the church in Philippi for some gifts they had sent to him.

## I. Introduction (1:1–11)

Paul addresses the "saints," i.e., the Christians, at Philippi and their leaders. Judging from his tone and the points he stresses in his opening remarks, Paul is concerned with the direction the church is about to take. He is confident that their walk with the Lord has been exemplary up to this point, but there are forces at work in the church that could alter or even reverse that direction. Thus Paul's primary interest is in encouraging them to continue in the direction they have been going. For this they will also need discernment.

## II. Encouragement of the Community (1:12–3:1)

### A. Report of Imprisonment (1:12–26)

One of the factors at work within the church at Philippi was their concern for Paul's imprisonment and what it meant for the Gospel. Paul assures them that, however perilous his troubles have been, they have resulted in the effective spread of the Gospel and thus are a cause for joy. He casts his own situation in terms that reflect those of the church at Philippi. He has weathered much and has seen the progress of the Gospel in his struggles. Like the Philippians, the crucial moment for Paul is what lies just ahead. For that he needs discernment. Thinking aloud, he asks, "What shall I choose? I do not know!" (v.22). He is at a crossroads and must resolve to continue on faithfully as he has in the past (vv.23–30). They also should follow his example, he tells them, "since you are going through the same struggle you saw I had, and now hear that I still have" (v.30).

### B. Continue in Humility (1:27–3:1)

Another factor at work within the Philippian church was an impending and menacing factionalism. Paul turns to the example of Jesus himself to stress the importance of humility, "doing nothing out of selfish ambition or vain conceit" (2:3). Jesus, "being in very nature God," did not hesitate to make "himself nothing, taking the very nature of a servant" (vv.6–7). It was only through such deep humility that "God exalted him to the highest place" (v.9).

Having presented Christ, the highest example of humility and concern for others, Paul presents two additional examples from their own midst, Timothy and Epaphroditus (2:19–30). These two men embody the kind of humility and love for the church that Paul wishes the Philippians themselves had.

## III. Warning Against False Teaching (3:2–4:1)

In his warning against the false teachers or leaders among them—those who were threatening to turn the church in the wrong direction—we can see the reason for Paul's focus on humility. These would-be leaders were beginning to stress "confidence in the flesh" (3:3), i.e., elevating the importance of personal achievement and status over dependence on the work of Christ. Paul's argument against such claims stems from his own personal experience. Although he has more to boast about than any of them in matters relating to personal achievement, he considers it all as "loss for the sake of Christ" (v.7). Paul wants only a righteousness "that comes from God and is by faith" (v.9).

As with his other letters, Paul's ultimate goal is to "know Christ and the power of his resurrection" (v.10). Again casting his own experience in terms that relate to the Philippians, Paul acknowledges that he has not yet obtained this goal. It will, however, continue to be the focus of his Christian walk in the days that lie ahead: "Forgetting what is behind and straining toward what is ahead, I press on toward the goal to win the prize for which God has called me heavenward in Christ Jesus" (vv.13–14). This attitude, Paul states, is the mark of Christian maturity (v.15). Rather than follow those "enemies of the cross of Christ" among them who stress personal achievement and self-gratification (vv.18–19), Paul exhorts his readers to follow his example and to seek as their leaders those among them who also "live according to the pattern we gave you" (v.17). The key difference between the two kinds of leaders is their ultimate goal. The would-be leaders set their minds "on earthly things" (v.19), but Paul eagerly awaits the coming of Christ and the resurrection (3:20–4:1).

## IV. Exhortations (4:2–20)

Paul speaks specifically to a problem of dissension between two faithful Christian women, Euodia and Syntyche (vv.2–3). He then broadens out his appeal in the most general terms: rejoice, be gentle, do not be anxious, give thanks in everything, and think on that which is true, noble, lovely, admirable, excellent, and praiseworthy (vv.3–8). Paul appeals to his own example and teaching as their guide in Christian living (v.9), as well as to the example of the Philippians themselves in the help they had given him (vv.10–20).

## V. Conclusion (4:21–23)

Paul closes with a brief greeting to all the "saints" at Philippi from the "saints" that are with him.

# Colossians

## Introduction

In the early NT manuscripts this book is entitled "To the Colossians." The apostle Paul is identified as the author in 1:1. The date that he wrote this letter is uncertain. Most date it at the same time as Ephesians, i.e., around A.D. 60, while Paul was in Rome.

Paul's primary concern for the church at Colosse was the threat of false teachers in their midst. He was convinced that the church had been thoroughly grounded in sound doctrine, but he saw a need for greater understanding on their part. Central to that need was a proper knowledge of the supremacy of Christ. Thus Paul explains his own understanding of Christ, the true image of God, through whom the world was created, his sacrificial death, and the power of his resurrection. He then warns the church of the dangers of human philosophy and religion. Finally, he exhorts them to godly living.

In this letter Paul reveals some of his deepest thoughts about Christ, showing a rich background of reading and reflection on the OT. Jesus is the Son of God (Ps 2), by whom God made all things (Ge 1:1). He is the very image of the invisible God (Ge 1:26).

## I. Introduction (1:1–8)

Paul begins with an acknowledgment of the strong faith and love of the "saints" in the church at Colosse. It is a faith and love rooted in hope (v.5). He then speaks of their need for further "knowledge of [God's] will through all spiritual wisdom and understanding" (v.9); the sense is that this letter will direct itself to that end. To Paul, quality Christian living is engendered by a proper understanding of the Gospel (vv.10–11). Christians are members of and share an inheritance in "the kingdom of the Son" (vv.12–14). As such, they have redemption and the forgiveness of sins, and they shine as lights in a dark world.

## II. The Lordship of Christ Over the World (1:9–2:23)

### A. Christ, Creator and Savior of the World (1:12–23)

For Christians to have a proper understanding of their inheritance in "the kingdom of the Son," Paul knows it is essential for them to understand the identity of Jesus, the Son of God. Thus he rehearses for them a short Christian hymn (vv.15–18a). Scholars today are virtually unanimous in holding that Paul quotes an early Christian hymn already in use in the early church. This tribute to the supremacy of Christ finds its origin in the Creation account in the book of Genesis, and it shows a great deal of thoughtful reflection on the theme of Jesus in the OT. In the early church there was much discussion, particularly with Jewish Christians, about the first word in the Hebrew Bible—"in the beginning." Jews had long seen in this word a reference to "Israel," God's firstborn. Paul's hymn suggests that early Christians followed this line of thinking, only making the obvious shift from "Israel" to "Jesus" as the reference of the first word. Such "homiletical" interpretations of the OT are not uncommon in the NT and Judaism. They are not meant to prove a point but to illustrate and elaborate a theme.

According to Paul's hymn, Jesus is the "image of the invisible God" (cf. Ge 1:26), the "firstborn over all creation." The notion of Jesus as the "firstborn" in Ge 1:1 probably stems from the fact that the Hebrew word for "beginning" can also be translated "firstborn," as it was frequently understood by Jews. Moreover, when Paul's hymn says that "by him all things were created," it shows an awareness that the Hebrew preposition "in" in Ge 1:1 ("in the beginning") can also be rendered as "by"; hence, Ge 1:1 can be read as: "By the firstborn, God created the heavens and the earth." The reference to "things in heaven and on earth" is clearly linked to Ge 1:1, "the heavens and the earth," and Paul's all-inclusive terms "visible and invisible" come from the fact that in Ge 1:2, the expressions "formless and void" were interpreted as "visible and invisible" by Jewish interpreters of the Greek OT.

The affirmation that "thrones or powers or rulers or authorities" were created by Christ stems from reading the account of Ge 1 in light of Ps 8:5–6, "You crowned him with glory and honor. You made him ruler over the works of your hands." The statement that "he is before all things" is derived from linking the traditional reading of Ge 1:1 as "in the beginning" to the homiletical "by the firstborn"; thus, if the world was created by the firstborn in the beginning, then he was before all things.

Paul then adds, "He is the head of the body, the church," alluding to the fact that the Hebrew word for "beginning" can also be rendered "head" and was, in fact, also translated that way by early Greek translators. Finally, the same Hebrew word also has the sense of "supremacy"; thus Paul adds, "that in everything he might have the supremacy" (1:18). Here the hymn leaves off and the allusions to Ge 1:1 cease. The hymn thus gives us a fascinating glimpse into the early church's understanding of Jesus and the OT.

Paul continues to speak about Christ, turning to his work of redemption on the cross (vv.19–20). For Paul, the practical implication of Christ's shed blood is that through it, Christians, who were once "alienated from God" (v.21) have now been reconciled to God and made "holy in his sight and free from accusation" (v.22)—clearly an allusion to the sacrificial lamb of the Passover Feast (cf. Ex 12:5).

## B. The Apostle as Minister of the Gospel and Church (1:24–2:5)

Paul, concerned about the spread of false doctrine at Colosse, briefly recounts his calling as an apostle and gives a summary description of the nature of the church. The church is the community of saints, both Jews and Gentiles, in whom Christ dwells (1:27). This "mystery" was not made known "for ages" (v.26), i.e., it was not revealed in the OT Scriptures. Paul's commission as an apostle to the Gentiles was, in part, intended to make this mystery known (see the book of Ephesians). The importance that he attached to that commission is shown by the many afflictions he had suffered for the sake of the Gospel (1:28–2:5).

## C. Warning of False Doctrine (2:6–23)

Part of Paul's responsibility as an apostle, sent to reveal the "full riches of complete understanding" of the Gospel (2:2), involved his confronting all forms of false doctrine. Those who had "received Christ Jesus as Lord" (v.6) needed to be exhorted to "continue to live in him, rooted and built up in him, strengthened in the faith" (v.7). Paul wanted a firm foundation in the faith, with no slippage into areas of false doctrine or false practice.

He therefore first warns the Christians at Colosse of the dangers of "hollow and deceptive philosophy, which depends on human tradition and basic principles of this world rather than on Christ" (v.8). He contrasts these things with the "fullness of the Deity" that is found in Christ. For the Christian, knowing Christ is all-sufficient. In him is the power of God to save sinners and give them a new heart. Such power can never be found in human wisdom, no matter how subtle or high-minded it may be.

The central focus of the Christian's life is not an elaborate philosophy (v.8), traditions, a list of rules (v.14), or religious festivals (v.16); the center is the simple message of the crucified Christ (vv.13–15). The religious celebrations of the past, found throughout the OT, all pointed to the death of Christ and the new life found in him (v.17); but they were shadows and should never be allowed to eclipse the central importance of Christ's death in the Gospel (vv.16–23).

## II. Instructions (3:1–4:6)

Paul now turns to elaborate on what it means to live a new life in Christ. In the first place, it means looking forward with eager expectation to the return of Christ (3:4). Second, it means no longer living according to the standards and patterns of one's former life (vv.5–11).

Finally, it means practicing godly virtues in the church (vv.12–17), in the home (vv.18–21), and at work (3:22–4:1)—always aware and ready to proclaim the Gospel to others (4:2–6).

## III. Conclusion (4:7–18)

Paul closes the letter with a somewhat lengthy series of greetings. Curiously, he mentions both Mark (v.10) and Luke (v.14), two individuals who, according to early tradition, were writers of the second and third gospels. He also gives instructions that this letter to the Colossians be circulated to the church at Laodicea (v.16), and for them, in turn, to read the letter that he had sent to Laodicea. It is sometimes thought that the letter sent to Laodicea was the letter Paul wrote to the Ephesian church.

# 1 Thessalonians

## Introduction

The apostle Paul is identified as the author in the first verse (1:1). The letter is usually dated at A.D. 51 and thus was the first of Paul's letters in the NT. It is written to the church in Thessalonica, one of the churches that Paul began on his second missionary journey (see Ac 17:1–7). The argument of this letter is simple and straightforward. Paul was writing to this early church, which had suffered much for the sake of the Gospel. He knew that they had weathered the persecution well, but he wanted to encourage them further. The central focus of the book is the eager expectation of churches everywhere for the return of the Lord. One matter that needed further clarification was the timing of the Lord's return and the sequence of events. Paul addressed these questions in 4:13–5:11.

## I. Introduction (1:1)

Although three men are listed in the opening verse of this letter, the apostle Paul is usually considered to be the one who wrote it. He greets the Christians in Thessalonica with the simplest of Christian greetings: "Grace and peace."

## II. Praise Section (1:2–3:13)

### A. The Return of the Son and the Coming Wrath (1:2–10)

Paul begins with a glowing report of the faith and endurance of the Thessalonian Christians. They have begun well and have demonstrated their faith throughout the whole region. Moreover, they are awaiting the return of Jesus, the Son of God, "from heaven," who will rescue them "from the coming wrath" (v.10). Paul ends on this important note, and he will return to it again. The picture he draws on is that of Da 7:1–14, the coming of the Son of Man to receive the kingdom from God.

### B. Previous Persecutions for Christ (2:1–3:13)

Paul, grateful for the faithfulness of the Thessalonian Christians, reminds them of both his and their past persecutions. In his earlier visit, he had delivered the Gospel to them under great persecution (2:1–12). These afflictions, in fact, proved to be a demonstration of his commitment to Christ and of his love for the Thessalonians—the love of a "mother caring for her little children" (v.7). Moreover, the Thessalonians "suffered from [their] own countrymen" when they received the Gospel (2:13–16). Paul aptly draws a comparison between their suffering and the suffering of the early Christians, Jesus, and the prophets among OT Israel (vv.14–15). Persecution can, in fact, be expected of all true followers of Christ (3:3–5).

But having heard the recent report from Timothy that their faith was strong in spite of their tribulation, Paul was overjoyed: "For now we really live, since you are standing firm in the Lord" (v.8). Throughout this section of the letter, Paul returns to his expectation of the Lord's return (e.g., 2:19; 3:13).

## III. Waiting for the Lord's Return (4:1–5:22)

### A. Ethical Exhortations (4:1–12)

In light of the return of the Lord and the hope of his appearing, Paul stresses the importance of godly living. It is God's will that the Christians in Thessalonica be holy and abstain from sexual immorality (v.3). No one should wrong or take advantage of a fellow believer (v.6); rather, each one should practice brotherly love (vv.9–10), attempting to live a quiet life by working with one's own hands (v.11). Such a life will not only win the respect of those outside the church, but also enable one "not [to] be dependent on anybody" (v.12).

## B. The Coming of the Lord (4:13–5:11)

Apparently some in the church of Thessalonica had become discouraged at the deaths of several of their members. They wondered whether perhaps the hope of these believers for being raised from the dead ceased. As an answer to their concern and as an encouragement for their continued faithfulness and patience, Paul summarizes the events that will surround the return of Christ. Jesus, who himself died and rose again, will return with those who have died (4:13–14). First, Jesus will come down out of heaven, with a shout and the sound of a trumpet, and the "dead in Christ" will rise from their graves to meet him (vv.15–16). After that, those Christians still alive at the time of his coming will be gathered up into the air to meet him as well (v.17).

When will Christ return? No one knows. His coming will take most by surprise, but his true followers will be ready. They are those who are watching and waiting for his return. They are those who will not lose faith in waiting (5:1–11).

## C. Instructions for Community Life (5:12–22)

Paul closes the body of this letter with several instructions for maintaining unity in the church: respect your leaders (vv.12–13), work hard, be patient, be kind to one another, always be joyful, pray continually, and give thanks in all circumstances (vv.14–18).

## IV. Conclusion (5:23–28)

Paul concludes with a reminder of the importance of holy living in light of the Lord's return (v.23).

# 2 Thessalonians

## Introduction

Like 1 Thessalonians, the apostle Paul wrote this letter to the church that he had begun in Thessalonica. It was written shortly after the first one and thus was also one of the first NT letters that Paul wrote (about A.D. 51).

The Thessalonian church continued to experience great hardship and persecution. They remained steadfast in their faith in Christ but were in need of encouragement. In the midst of their troubles, rumors and reports were circulating that Jesus had already returned. Paul thus wrote this letter to comfort these faithful Christians and to affirm that though Jesus had not yet appeared, their hope in his imminent return was not misplaced. Jesus would return, establish his kingdom, and judge the world.

## I. Introduction (1:1–12)

As with his first letter to the Thessalonians, Paul begins with a glowing report of the faith and endurance of the Thessalonian Christians. They have demonstrated their faith throughout the ˑˑˡ ᴊle region by persevering "in all the ⸝ersecutions" (vv.3–4). Paul's focus, however, immediately shifts to the return of the Lord. The suffering of the Thessalonians shows that they were "counted worthy of the kingdom of God" for which they were suffering (v.5). God is just, and their sufferings would be redressed "when the Lord Jesus is revealed from heaven in blazing fire with his powerful angels" (vv.6–7).

The imagery of Da 7:9–14 is unmistakable in Paul's description. The Son of Man will come in the clouds (v.7; cf. Da 7:13) and in flames of fire (v.7; cf. Da 7.9), surrounded by his angels (v.7; cf. Da 7:10). He will judge the nations (vv.8–9; cf. Da 7:10) and establish his kingdom for the saints of the Most

High, a holy people (v.10; cf. Da 7:27). Thus the hope that Paul now holds out to the Thessalonian Christians in the midst of their suffering is precisely that given to Daniel when God's people were in exile in Babylon. They too had been waiting for the coming of the promised King and his kingdom.

## II. Instruction Regarding the Return of Christ (2:1–12)

Apparently letters purporting to be from Paul had circulated among the churches announcing that Jesus had already returned to establish the kingdom, and that the Thessalonian Christians had been bypassed. Paul disclaims any authenticity to those letters and argues strenuously against the truthfulness of what they reported. His argument against the Lord's having already come is simply that "the man of lawlessness" and his rebellion have not yet occurred (v.3). This is an argument based on the proper sequence of events.

His defense for the proper sequence is strictly biblical. He had already taught them about these events and the return of the Lord when he was with them in person (v.5). Though we do not have further record of that teaching, it is clear that Paul's text was Daniel. Throughout the book of Daniel, the coming of the kingdom of God is preceded by an individual or powerful nation that exalts "himself over everything that is called God" (v.4). In Daniel he was called the "fourth kingdom, strong as iron—for iron breaks and smashes everything" (Da 2:40); the "fourth beast—terrifying and frightening and very powerful" (Da 7:7); "the little horn" that came out of the fourth beast (Da 7:8); "the ruler who will come [and] destroy the city" (Da 9:26); or the king who "will exalt and magnify himself above every god and will say unheard of things against the God of gods" (Da 11:36). In Daniel's visions, this ruler rebels against God and his people for a little while, but after that the Son of Man will come from heaven to destroy him and establish an eternal kingdom (Da 7:23–28).

Paul's reference to the "man of lawlessness" setting himself up in the temple and proclaiming himself to be God (v.4) is a reference to Da 9:27, "And on a wing [of the temple] he will set up an abomination that causes desolation." This will continue "until the end that is decreed is poured out on him" (Da 9:27b). Paul's point is clear. Though "the secret power of lawlessness is already at work," this individual has not yet been revealed. Therefore, the Lord cannot yet have returned.

Paul continues by stressing that when this "lawless one" does come, he will do such "counterfeit miracles, signs and wonders" that all who are not true followers of Christ will be deceived by him and perish with him (vv.9–12).

## III. Paul's Confidence in Their Steadfastness (2:13–3:5)

Paul is confident that the Thessalonian Christians will not be deceived by "the man of lawlessness." God has chosen them, and they will stand firm in that day by holding on to the teaching they have received from him.

## IV. Instructions (3:6–15)

Paul warns the church to keep away from those teachers who do not, like him, work with their own hands for a living.

## V. Conclusion (3:16–18)

In light of the fact that there were letters in circulation falsely purporting to be from him (2:2), Paul is careful to mark this letter with his own "distinguishing mark" (3:17).

# 1 Timothy

## Introduction

This is the first letter that the apostle Paul wrote to his dear friend and co-worker, Timothy. Together with 2 Timothy and Titus, these letters are called "The Pastoral Letters," because they deal with instructions given by Paul to two young men in pastoral situations. There is no clear indication of the date of the writing of 1 Timothy. It is usually dated late in Paul's life, sometime after his imprisonment in Rome in A.D. 60–62 (Ac 28:30).

In this letter, Paul writes a summary manual to the young pastor and overseer, Timothy. He stresses the importance of sound doctrine that leads to godly living. Moreover, he warns Timothy of the inherent dangers of church life in a fallen world. There will be false teachers and false doctrine. Thus the church and its leadership should prepare themselves well for the work of the ministry, both by choosing competent leaders and by avoiding dishonest and unethical persons. The only true guide for solving or avoiding problems in the church is the test of Scripture and a proven godly life.

## I. Introduction (1:1–2)

Rather than addressing a church or group of churches, which has characterized Paul's letters up to this point, Paul addresses Timothy personally. Thus this is a pastoral letter, i.e., a letter addressed specifically to pastors or leaders of the churches. This is reflected throughout the remainder of the letter. Paul greets Timothy as his "true son in the faith," meaning that he was the "father" who had led Timothy to faith in Christ (cf. 1Co 4:15–17).

## II. False Teachers (1:3–20)

Timothy was in Ephesus (v.3) and was representing Paul in that church. But there were also teachers of false doctrine there. Thus Paul's first instructions to Timothy concern what he should do and say to these teachers. Paul approaches the problem by principle and example. The principle that he gives Timothy is the "goal of this instruction" (1:5, NIV, "this command"). Timothy must examine his teaching and that of others by the criterion of the life produced by the instruction. Correct teaching will result in godly living, i.e., "love, which comes from a pure heart and a good conscience and a sincere faith" (v.5).

The first example that Paul gives Timothy is the negative result of the false teachers who "wandered away [from sincere faith] . . . and turned to meaningless talk" (v.6). They have no understanding of the things they are teaching. The positive example comes from Paul's own experience. The grace of God that Paul learned in the Gospel resulted in "faith and love that are in Christ Jesus" (v.14). Thus, as a result of the instruction he received, his former wicked way of life was transformed "as an example for those who would believe on [Jesus Christ] and receive eternal life" (v.16).

## III. Church Order (2:1–3:16)

### A. Prayer in the Church (2:1–15)

Paul turns to the matter of prayer in the church. As is typical of his concerns throughout his letters, he admonishes Timothy to ensure that the life of the church be maintained and sustained through prayer. They must pray for everyone, even for kings and those in authority, not merely for each other. Prayer for kings and authorities will enable Christians to live "peaceful and quiet lives in all godliness and holiness" (v.2) and, by implication, will result in the wider spread of the Gospel (vv.3–4).

The men of the church were to pray "without anger or disputing" (v.8). The women were to attend the worship services dressed modestly, i.e., "with decency and propriety, not with braided hair or gold or pearls or expensive clothes" (v.9). They were to clothe themselves with good deeds (v.10). What this should entail, Paul explains, was "learning in quietness and full submission" (v.11). Women were not "to teach or to have authority over a man" but were to "be silent" in the worship service (v.12).

Paul gave warrant for his instruction regarding the primacy of the husband's role in public worship from the Creation narratives in Genesis. Adam was created first, and then his wife, Eve; hence, the Scriptures assign to the husband a primary responsibility for his family's well-being (v.13). Paul's rationale is based on the role of the firstborn in the Genesis narratives. If Adam was created first, that makes him the firstborn, and thus he bears the responsibility for the family.

Paul also derives his warrant for the importance of the wife's modest dress and demeanor from the Genesis narratives. In Ge 3:15, God promised that a son would be born of the woman, who would crush the head of the serpent and restore God's blessing. Thus, Paul asserts, salvation for all humankind was promised "through childbirth [NIV, childbearing]—if they continue in faith, love and holiness with propriety" (vv.14–15). Paul seems to derive the importance of modest clothing from the fact that in the Genesis narrative, God provided the man and the woman with clothing to cover the shame of their nakedness (v.21). Hence, for Paul, modesty was a sign of continual dependence on God's provision.

## B. Qualification for Leadership in the Church (3:1–16)

### 1. Elders (3:1–7)

Paul lists, in summary fashion, the requirements of an "overseer" or elder in the church. The description is of a sober-minded, amiable family man who knows Scripture and how to apply it to the life of the church. Paul does not explain what the elders were to do in the church, though undoubtedly he assumes that they, like Timothy, were to provide the central leadership. Hence, the instruction Paul gives to Timothy throughout this letter can be taken as a

## QUALIFICATIONS FOR ELDERS/OVERSEERS AND DEACONS

| | | | | | |
|---|---|---|---|---|---|
| Self-controlled | ELDER | ITi 3:2; Tit 1:8 | Temperate | ELDER | ITi 3:2; Tit 1:7 |
| Hospitable | ELDER | ITi 3:2; Tit 1:8 | | DEACON | ITi 3:8 |
| Able to teach | ELDER | ITi 3:2; 5:17; Tit 1:9 | Respectable | ELDER | ITi 3:2 |
| Not violent but gentle | ELDER | ITi 3:3; Tit 1:7 | | DEACON | ITi 3:8 |
| Not quarrelsome | ELDER | ITi 3:3 | Not given to drunkenness | ELDER | ITi 3:3; Tit 1:7 |
| Not a lover of money | ELDER | ITi 3:3 | | DEACON | ITi 3:8 |
| Not a recent convert | ELDER | ITi 3:6 | Manages his own family well | ELDER | ITi 3:4 |
| Has a good reputation with outsiders | ELDER | ITi 3:7 | | DEACON | ITi 3:12 |
| | | | Sees that his children obey him | ELDER | ITi 3:4-5; Tit 1:6 |
| Not overbearing | ELDER | Tit 1:7 | | DEACON | ITi 3:12 |
| Not quick-tempered | ELDER | Tit 1:7 | Does not pursue dishonest gain | ELDER | Tit 1:7 |
| Loves what is good | ELDER | Tit 1:8 | | DEACON | ITi 3:8 |
| Upright, holy | ELDER | Tit 1:8 | Keeps hold of the deep truths | ELDER | Tit 1:9 |
| Disciplined | ELDER | Tit 1:8 | | DEACON | ITi 3:9 |
| Above reproach (blameless) | ELDER | ITi 3:2; Tit 1:6 | Sincere | DEACON | ITi 3:8 |
| | DEACON | ITi 3:9 | Tested | DEACON | ITi 3:10 |
| Husband of one wife | ELDER | ITi 3:2; Tit 1:6 | | | |
| | DEACON | ITi 3:12 | | | |

guide to elders. An important part of their responsibility lay in teaching sound doctrine and combating false teachers. They were to devote themselves "to the public reading of Scripture, to preaching and to teaching" (4:13).

### 2. Deacons (3:8–16)

Since elders are distinguished from deacons in this chapter, the analogy of Ac 6:1–6 seems appropriate. Just as the elders were to provide the teaching and general oversight of the congregation, the deacons were to attend to the everyday business of the church. Their requirements are essentially the same as those for the elders, though with a different emphasis. For deacons, Paul highlights characteristics of trustworthiness and a proven track record, both important in light of the day-to-day concerns entrusted to them. Their wives must also be trustworthy and worthy of respect.

## IV. Combating False Teachers (4:1–16)

### A. The Importance of Sound Doctrine (4:1–11)

Realistically, Paul argues, church leaders can expect that "some will abandon the faith and follow deceiving spirits" (v.1). Characteristic of such teaching is that it was a perversion of God's good gifts. Paul alludes to the early chapters of Genesis to show that "everything God created is good" (v.4; cf. Ge 1:31). Just as the serpent had wrongly suggested that God said, "You must not eat from any tree in the garden" (Ge 3:1), so these false teachers were perverting God's good gifts and forbidding one's enjoyment of them (vv.3–5). The task of Timothy and other pastors, who have been "brought up in the truths of the faith and of the good teaching" (v.6), is to "point these things out to the brothers" (v.6) and to live them out in their own lives (4:7).

### B. The Importance of Timothy's Example (4:12–16)

Paul wants a living example of his teaching among the churches. Timothy is to be that example, just as all pastors should be. What is thus required is diligence and devotion in both sound doctrine and godly living. This is what will "save both yourself and your hearers" (v.16).

## V. Instructions for Church Life (5:1–6:2)

Paul goes on to give Timothy sound, practical advice on how to treat various members of the church (5:1–2). The treatment of widows requires special attention (vv.3–16). Judgment is necessary to determine those who have a genuine need and those for whom help is available elsewhere.

The basic principle for supporting teaching elders is that they should be given double honor (vv.17–19). This entails both financial support and clear investigation in cases where their honor has been challenged. They must receive twice as much support for their work in teaching, and twice as many witnesses are required to convict them of any wrongdoing. If any elders are found to be in the wrong, they must be publicly rebuked.

Servants must give their masters respect and honor (6:1–2). The servants Paul has in mind are the household servants who were supported by their masters as part of their employment. That Paul is not here endorsing involuntary slavery is clear from the fact that in 1:10 he has condemned it in the harshest of terms. Paul does not deal with the other side of the question here, such as how masters should treat their servants. Paul's letter to Philemon, however, addresses precisely that point. He also gives instruction to masters as part of his list of general household instructions in Eph 6:9 and Col 4:1.

## VI. Warnings and Admonitions (6:3–21)

Paul concludes his letter with a renewed warning against false teachers who seek to make a profit from their teaching (vv.3–10). Such men are "conceited and understand nothing" (v.4). Teachers should pursue godliness and sound doctrine, being content with the support given them from the church (5:17–18). In that way they will "fight the good fight of faith" (6:12) and be found faithful when the Lord returns.

If the wealthy want lasting treasures, they should generously share their riches with those less fortunate (vv.17–19). Wealth is uncertain, but God is a lasting source of hope.

In a final word to Timothy, Paul charges him to guard that which has been entrusted to him. To go beyond that to seek "what is falsely called knowledge" (v.20) is to risk departing from the faith. Though it is difficult to determine precisely what "knowledge" Paul is referring to, the general sense of this letter would suggest it was knowledge gained apart from the Scriptures (cf. 4:13). Paul's second letter to Timothy has more to say about this.

## 2 Timothy

### Introduction

This is the second letter that the apostle Paul wrote to his dear friend and coworker, Timothy. There is no clear indication of the date of 2 Timothy. About all that can safely be said is that, from the content of the letter itself (cf. 4:6), it was written late in Paul's life. This was probably his last letter.

Paul, nearing the end of his ministry, writes to encourage Timothy to remain faithful to the Gospel he had received from him. As a backdrop to this appeal, he gives a stern warning about false teachers and treacherous opponents of the Gospel. Such men will grow more numerous as the Lord's return approaches, but that should not deflect one's attention from the main task of the Gospel, which is teaching and proclaiming faith in Christ as it is taught in the Scriptures.

### I. Introduction (1:1–14)

Paul's second letter to Timothy has the distinct note to it that conditions in the churches were becoming troublesome and more urgent. On the one hand, godly leaders such as Timothy were coming close to losing heart. On the other hand, false teachers were becoming more and more impudent in their teaching and actions. Thus Paul begins his letter with an impassioned appeal to Timothy to "fan into flame the gift of God" and to not be timid, but to have a "spirit of power, of love and of self-discipline" (vv.6–7). Paul admonishes him to not be ashamed to testify about the Lord (v.7).

Paul's solution to Timothy's need for encouragement is to stress the dimensions of the grace of God given him in the Gospel. The Gospel was not a new idea. It was a grace planned and given by God "before the beginning of time" (v.9) and has now been revealed through the appearing of Jesus (v.10).

Thus the scope of the Gospel that Paul preached was the same as that of the OT Scriptures themselves. It extended back beyond the beginning (Ge 1:1). Jesus' death, which destroyed death (Ge 3:15), has brought life and immortality (1:10; cf. Ge 3:23–24). Such a message inevitably stirs up opposition and invites distortion (v.12). All the more important, then, is it to remain faithful to the teaching Timothy received from Paul (vv.13–14).

### II. Warnings to Timothy (1:15–4:8)

In warning Timothy of the perils of remaining faithful to God's Word, Paul reminds him that throughout Asia even he himself had been deserted (1:15–18). But Paul remained faithful, and so now he pleads with Timothy to remain faithful and strong in Paul's teaching (2:1–2). Like a good soldier, a successful athlete, or a hard-working farmer, Timothy must focus on the work of the Lord rather than on worldly affairs (vv.3–7).

In times of trouble, Paul warns, it is important to focus on the essentials of the Gospel (vv.8–13). One needs to know precisely why and for what he is suffering. In this case it centers on the resurrection of Jesus and on his claim to be the Davidic Messiah (v.8). Moreover, Paul's confidence in God's election enables him to "endure everything" (v.10).

Timothy's task is to keep reminding those in the church of the teaching of God's Word (vv.14–26). He should study it well, focus on the central points, and know how to answer when serious questions arise. Those who oppose his instruction, "he must gently instruct," leaving the task of changing their minds to God (v.25).

Some groups, however, are impossible to teach. They are the godless who will arise in increasing numbers as the return of the Lord approaches (3:1–9).

Timothy should have nothing to do with them; their motives are impure (v.6), they are unteachable (vv.7–8), and "their folly will be clear to everyone" (v.9).

Paul's teaching, on the other hand, has been thoroughly tested and proven by his way of life and the troubles he has endured (vv.10–13). Therefore, Timothy should continue in the teaching that he has learned from Paul, knowing that it is grounded in the OT Scriptures (vv.14–17). For Paul, the Scriptures are a central witness to the truth of the Gospel because they are inspired (i.e., "God-breathed," v.16); in them the salvation that comes through faith in Christ Jesus is taught (v.15b).

Therefore, Timothy must "preach the Word" at all times, exercising great patience and careful instruction (4:1–2). He must continue in God's Word even if and when the time comes that those who hear his teaching will not be able to endure it (vv.3–5). They will leave him and instead follow teachers who say what they want to hear. That experience, Paul suggests, has already begun to happen to him (vv.6–8; cf. 1:15; 4:16).

## III. Personal Notes (4:9–22)

In his final personal instructions, Paul appropriately asks for his "scrolls and parchments" (v.12), i.e., his copy of the Scriptures. Paul, a rabbi by training, would have had much of the Scripture committed to memory, but, true to his instructions to Timothy, he wants to search the God-breathed Scriptures.

# Titus

## Introduction

The apostle Paul wrote this letter to his dear friend and coworker, Titus. Together with 1 and 2 Timothy, these letters are called "The Pastoral Letters." There is no clear indication of the date of the writing of Titus. It is safe to say that Paul wrote it after his imprisonment in Rome, i.e., after A.D. 62.

Paul gives Titus general and specific instructions in carrying out his ministry on Crete, much like Paul had given to Timothy in 1 Timothy. Paul's central concern was combating false teachers. In the face of this challenge, he stresses that Christians can make a certain defense of the Gospel only by living a life that is beyond reproach. If each member of the church pays close attention to self-control and godliness—and keeps the return of the Lord in view—the church will grow in sound doctrine and God's work will prosper.

## I. Introduction (1:1–4)

Paul considerably expands the introduction of this letter, not so much in length as in depth. He speaks of the hope of eternal life "which God, who does not lie, promised before the beginning of time" (v.2), and which at the appointed time was entrusted to him "by the command of God" (v.3). A Christian's life should be lived in light of this hope. Paul emphasizes the Christian's hope at the beginning because in the course of his argument, it is the "blessed hope" of Christ's return that motivates the Christian to live a godly life (cf. 2:13).

## II. Task of Titus at Crete (1:5–16)

Paul begins the body of his letter with instructions for Titus, who is serving as pastor on the island of Crete. There is work left undone there that Titus must complete. He must appoint elders in very town; hence, Paul reviews

for him the qualifications he should look for in those elders (vv.6–9). This is necessary because numerous false teachers are ruining the churches and seeking dishonest gain by their teaching. These teachers have to be dealt with decisively before they can do any further damage (vv.10–16).

## III. Order of Community (2:1–3:11)

What must Titus do to combat the false teachers? Paul's answer is simple: "You must teach what is in accord with sound doctrine" (2:1). Older men are to be taught to act worthy of respect (v.2). Older women are to live in reverence, not slandering others, but teaching what is good (v.3). The younger women are to "love their husbands and children" and provide a good home for them (vv.4–5). The young men are to be self-controlled (vv.6–8). Household servants are to carry out their duties faithfully and honestly (vv.9–10).

In every relationship, Christians must reject ungodliness and live "self-controlled, upright and godly lives," eagerly awaiting the return of Christ (vv.11–15). Meanwhile, Christians are to live in subjection to the "rulers and authorities" and always be ready to do what is good (3:1–3). Paul grounds his call to godliness in the nature of the Gospel itself. God saved sinners, not because of their righteousness, but in order to produce good works in their lives. In Christ, Christians have been washed and renewed by the Holy Spirit and made fit "to devote themselves to doing what is good" (vv.4–8).

## IV. Conclusion (3:12–15)

Along with personal greetings, Paul concludes with an explanation of the practical importance of sound doctrine: "Our people must learn to devote themselves to doing what is good, in order that they may provide for daily necessities and not live unproductive lives" (3:14).

# Philemon

## Introduction

This letter to Philemon is identified in the NT as written by the apostle Paul. From the letter itself it is clear that it was written during one of Paul's imprisonments—presumably his imprisonment in Rome in A.D. 60–62 (i.e., the same time that he wrote Ephesians and Colossians). Paul writes an appeal to the Christian leader Philemon to receive back Onesimus, his former servant who had run away.

## I. Introduction (1–7)

After a brief greeting, Paul begins his appeal to Philemon by acknowledging the work of God in Philemon's life and ministry (he was a resident of Colosse; see Col 4:9). Based on his "love for all the saints" (v.5), Paul appeals to Philemon for a gracious reception of Onesimus, his former slave, whom Paul is sending back to him. If Philemon were not to accept Onesimus back, much of what Paul says in this introductory word would be contradicted.

## II. Request for Reception of Onesimus (8–20)

The main point of the letter is Paul's appeal to Philemon on behalf of Onesimus. Although he does not explain the circumstances behind Onesimus's need for Paul's letter, we can gather from the letter itself that Onesimus was a former household servant of Philemon (v.16). He had apparently escaped from or deserted Philemon, but he had subsequently met Paul and heard the Gospel. Thus both Philemon and Onesimus were in Paul's eternal debt.

Paul writes this letter to urge Philemon pastorally to accept Onesimus, his former servant, back as a brother (v.16). He may mean to accept him back as a servant and, as such, to treat him as a brother in Christ, or Paul may mean to release Onesimus from his status as a servant. In either case, it would be a great display of the power of the Gospel within the context of the ancient world. Paul, with apostolic authority, says he could order Philemon to accept Onesimus, but that would hardly have the effect of a voluntary act of brotherly love. Paul wanted Philemon's actions to be "spontaneous and not forced" (v.14). Paul was fully confident that Philemon would accept Onesimus with open arms (v.16); nevertheless, he offered to pay any outstanding debts or penalties Onesimus might owe.

This short book clearly owes its acceptance within the NT canon to the fact that it speaks directly to an issue that lies not too far beneath the surface throughout the NT—i.e., the effect of the Gospel on the existing social structures of the ancient world. The Bible is clear in its opposition to involuntary slavery. In 1Ti 1:10, for example, Paul reckons "slave traders" along with "the ungodly and sinful, the unholy and irreligious." But what was the impact of the Gospel on those economic structures of the sort that included servants who were bound to their masters under the full force of the law? Paul's letter to Timothy states that servants should treat their masters with respect, including believing masters (1Ti 6:1–2). But what about believing masters' treatment of believing servants? It is just at this point that this letter provides an answer. It becomes the occasion for Paul to urge that just as Christian servants must respect their Christian masters, so Christian masters are to accept and respect their Christian servants as brothers, even if they have wronged them.

## III. Conclusion (21–25)

We do not have Philemon's response, but Paul's confidence expressed at the conclusion makes its absence immaterial. The very existence of this letter suggests that Philemon heeded Paul's request.

# Hebrews

## Introduction

The title "To the Hebrews" is found in the earliest complete manuscripts of the NT. This was probably not intended as a description of the particular community to which the book was addressed, but rather, like most of the titles in the NT, a description of the content of the book. The term "Hebrews" was a name for Jews as opposed to Gentiles. Thus this is a book dealing with matters that relate to the Jews, or more specifically, probably Jewish Christians.

The authorship of this book is unknown. The fact that the writer refers to the temple worship as still being practiced strongly suggests that it was written before the destruction of the temple in A.D. 70.

The central theme of the book is the work of Jesus Christ as the mediator of the new covenant. The writer first introduces Jesus as the eternal Son of God, a messianic title from the OT. From there, he develops an extended argument that both the messianic promise in the OT and the resurrection of Jesus prove him to be a priest of an order different from and superior to that prescribed in the Mosaic covenant. His priesthood is that prefigured in the OT narratives and prophecies about Melchizedek.

As a high priest and mediator of the new covenant, Jesus offered the supreme sacrifice of his own blood and thus atoned for sin once and for all. This was accomplished after his resurrection when he entered the Holy of Holies in the heavenly tabernacle. In this never-to-be repeated sacrificial act, Jesus initiated the new covenant promised in the OT, purifying the hearts of God's people and giving them renewed power to live godly and faithful lives. On this basis, the writer pleads with his readers not to forsake such a great salvation and to persevere until the time when Jesus returns to establish his kingdom.

## I. Introduction (1:1–6:20)

### A. The Work of the Son of God (1:1–2:4)

The book begins with an exposition of the work of Jesus Christ, the Son of God. The revelation of the salvation of God, promised in the OT Scriptures, has now been made known by Jesus, the Son of God. The Son was with God already at Creation and is the "exact representation of his being" (1:3). He "provided purification for sins" and was then exalted to "the right hand of the Majesty in heaven." In making these points, the writer has summarized the work of Christ in terms of the OT's messianic hope. The Messiah is the Son of God who reigns with God in his eternal kingdom (Ps 2; Da 7), as well as the sacrificial lamb of God who gave his life for the sins of humanity (Isa 53). As such the Son of God is the only mediator between humanity and God. As a mediator, he is far superior to angels, who are "ministering spirits sent to serve those who will inherit salvation" (v.14).

With such a momentous event unfolding before one's eyes, confirmed by signs and miracles, neglect or failure to appreciate it constitutes the worst kind of rejection. Thus the writer urges his readers not to "ignore such a great salvation" (2:1–4).

### B. The Incarnation and Exaltation of Christ as Prerequisite to His Role as a Merciful High Priest (2:5–4:16)

In the passage from Ps 8:4–6 that is quoted here, there are two central ideas. (1) God made the Son lower than the angels "for a little while" (see NIV note). (2) God "crowned him with glory and honor and put everything under his feet." The "little while" in Ps 8:5 is interpreted here as the time of the incarnation of Christ, i.e., the time of Jesus' earthly ministry. Thus, after his death and resurrection, Jesus was "crowned with glory and honor," and through his death, he has brought "many sons to glory" (2:10). These ideas, when applied to the work of Christ, show that God first made Jesus suffer with humanity before he made him a high priest. Jesus is thus a "merciful and faithful high priest" (v.17) who "is able to help those who are being tempted" (v.18), because "he himself suffered when he was tempted" (v.18).

Moses established the high priesthood of the house of Aaron; but Jesus, by his incarnation and resurrection to the right hand of God, became a high priest "of the same family" (v.11) as all humanity. He is a high priest who can claim to be a brother to everyone, not merely those who are of the house of Aaron. In this respect, the priesthood of Jesus can claim superiority to that of Aaron (3:1–6).

In the same way, those who trust in Jesus as their high priest should take heed to the warnings and lessons of God's people in the desert (3:7–4:13). The lesson is drawn from Ps 95:7–11, which shows that Israel's heart grew hard during the time they were in the desert. Their time there was one of "rebellion" (3:8) and testing God; thus God "was angry with that generation" (v.10), and they did not inherit "the rest" in the land promised to them (v.11). For the Christian, the warning is to guard against "a sinful, unbelieving heart that turns away from the living God" (v.12). The example of the Israelites, God's own people who died in the desert, shows that there is no one who should feel exempt from the warning of sin and unbelief (3:13–4:2). In explaining the harsh wording of Ps 95, the writer makes a subtle appeal to Nu 20:12 by raising the issue of faith, an issue not mentioned in Ps 95. In Nu 20 it is explicitly noted that Israel's failure to enjoy God's rest was because of their unbelief (see comments on Nu 20). Thus, as in the Pentateuch, only those "who have believed enter that rest" (4:3).

Though many Israelites in Moses' day did not find the divine rest promised them, David's words in Ps 95 show that a rest still remained for them in the future (vv.3–9). The rest given the new generation under Joshua was not the promised rest (v.8). David, long after the time of Joshua, was still looking for a rest for God's people. It is that rest that the writer of Hebrews sets before his readers: "Let us, therefore, make every effort to enter that rest" (4:11). This is the message of the "word of God" (v.12).

## C. Jesus as High Priest (5:1–6:20)

The writer begins this section with a description of the central duties of a high priest. The high priest was selected as a representative before God to offer sacrifices and gifts (5:1). It was necessary for him to be human in order to represent humankind adequately before God. Jesus met this requirement in his incarnation and earthly life. Moreover, the high priest must be called by God (v.4). Jesus was also called by God, as Ps 2 demonstrates. By quoting the messianic Ps 2, the writer of Hebrews links the role of Jesus as high priest to that of Davidic Messiah. In Ps 110, which he quotes next, these two features of the OT's theology, the Messiah and the priesthood, are already linked (5:6). In Ps 110, however, it is not the Aaronic priesthood that was in view, but that of Melchizedek. Melchizedek was both a king and a priest (Ge 14:18); hence he was particularly apt for an image of Christ's priesthood. Melchizedek was also a king of Jerusalem and thus a perfect picture of the Davidic kingship through which the promise of a Messiah had come (5:6–10; 6:20).

The writer interrupts his train of thought at this point in the book (5:11–6:20) in order to clarify for his present readers the direction he is about to take. He clearly shows that his plans in the remainder of the book are to present an in-depth exposition of the nature of Christ's high priesthood (7:1–10:10). He is aware, however, that not all of his readers are prepared to follow his argumentation and thus derive benefit from his exposition. He warns them not only of his intention to delve deeper into the "solid food" for the spiritually mature, but also, pastorally, of their need for "someone to teach you the elementary truths of God's word all over again" (5:12). Judging from his summary of the areas and topics of the "elementary teachings" (6:1) that he gives in 6:1–3, the writer has in mind the kind of teaching found in the NT letters, especially those of the apostle Paul.

In the case of this letter, there are two main reasons why the writer intends to move beyond these elementary truths. (1) He is confident that his readers are not bereft of the kind of maturity that befits a growing Christian (vv.9–12). They are ready to move on in their understanding, even though they are still in need of prodding (v.12). (2) If some "fall away," it is impossible for them "to be brought back to repentance" (v.6). The exact sense of this text is uncertain when viewed in the context of the whole of Scripture. Some say this passage teaches that Christians can lose their salvation if they fall away. Such an interpretation, however, does not square with those passages in Scripture that speak unambiguously of Christians being chosen in Christ "before the creation of the world to be holy and blameless in his sight" (Eph 1:4; cf. Ro 8:31–39). Consequently, others have argued that the writer of Hebrews must be speaking hypothetically; that is, if it ever were possible for Christians to fall away, it would be impossible to renew them to repentance. A third option is that the writer is speaking hyperbolically, taking "impossible" to mean that

it is "very difficult" to renew them to repentance. Finally, some interpret this reference to mean that if professing Christians fall away from the faith, it only serves to prove that the faith of these people was not genuine in the first place (cf. 1Jn 2:19). In any case, on the pattern of Mk 10:27, we should always acknowledge that "all things are possible with God."

Having given his readers one of the sternest warnings in all the NT (6:4–8), the writer concludes with an emphasis on the faithfulness of God (vv.9–19). Inheritance of the promises is based both on the sure word of God who made the promise (vv.13–19) and on the faith and patient obedience of his people (vv.9–12).

## II. The High Priesthood of the Son (7:1–10:18)

### A. The Priesthood of Melchizedek (7:1–28)

The priesthood of Jesus, the Son of God, was not that of the house of Aaron established in the Mosaic covenant. It was, rather, a priesthood offered as one of the functions of the messianic descendant of David promised in Ps 110. The writer of the book of Hebrews demonstrates from the OT Scriptures, first, that the messianic priesthood, exemplified in biblical Melchizedek, was superior to that priesthood of the house of Aaron and, second, that the priesthood of Aaron was always and only a temporary priesthood and, as such, was in need of being superseded. The primary basis of his argument is the eternal nature of the Messiah-Priest promised to David (Ps 110), which far exceeded the priesthood of Aaron established by Moses. Much of his argument hinges on the simple fact that the priesthood spoken of in Ps 110 implies that already in the OT the temporary nature of the Aaronic priesthood was recognized.

Behind the argument of this chapter is the underlying distinction between a priest as such and the priesthood that any given priest represents. Melchizedek was a priest who represented a specific type of priesthood, while Aaron was a priest who represented a different type of priesthood. The writer turns first to Ge 14 to show that the priesthood of Melchizedek was distinct in many ways from the Aaronic priesthood. Abraham paid tithes to him (v.2), and Melchizedek bore special names, such as "king of righteousness" and "king of peace" (v.2), suggesting the special nature of his priesthood. But fundamentally, the distinction of Melchizedek lay in the fact that his priesthood was not limited to specific genealogical factors (v.3). In the Pentateuchal narratives, unlike Aaron (Ex 6:13–27), Melchizedek is introduced without a list of his ancestors; this is taken byt he author of Hebrews to mean that his priesthood was not dependent on his family line, and thus his role as high priest did not pass from one family to another or from one member of the family to another. He remained "a [high] priest continually" (v.3; NIV, "forever"), i.e., for as long as he lived.

Having established this essential characteristic of Melchizedek's priesthood, the writer turns to Ps 110 to show that David was promised an eternal descendant to occupy the office of Melchizedek's priesthood. If the priesthood that he represented was unlimited, then an eternal priest such as that promised to the house of David could serve eternally. Thus in the office of priest occupied by Jesus, there is both an eternal priesthood and an eternal priest. The promise of an eternal priest in Ps 110 thus marks a major turning point in God's plan. It means not only the end of a particular kind of priesthood (i.e., the Aaronic priesthood), but also an end to the system of law of which it was a part (i.e., the Sinai covenant and the Mosaic

Law; v.12). Jesus is thus a priest of "a better covenant" (v.22) and "a permanent priesthood" (v.24), one already anticipated in the OT itself.

## B. The High Priestly Service (8:1–10:18)

### 1. The service of the new covenant (8:1–13)

Christ, the Son of God, being an eternal high priest, does not offer sacrifices in a sanctuary made "by man" but in "the true tabernacle set up by the Lord" in heaven (vv.1–2). The earthly temple, with its priesthood, is but a shadow or copy of this heavenly sanctuary, made according to the pattern shown to Moses on Mount Sinai (v.5). The contrast between the earthly temple and its priests, and the heavenly temple and its eternal High Priest, is that which the prophet Jeremiah spoke of in contrasting the old covenant and the new (vv.6–12). The new covenant, promised already in the OT, has made the old covenant obsolete (v.13).

The long quotation from Jer 31:31–34 in 8:8–12, the longest OT quotation in the NT, plays an important role in the writer's overall strategy. Not only does it show the temporal nature of the old covenant and the superiority of the new covenant, but it also shows that the chief characteristic of the new covenant is its renewal of the heart and the mind: "I will put my laws in their minds and write them on their hearts" (v.10). Hence, in the following section, when the external regulations of the old covenant are contrasted with the internal renewal of the heart in the new covenant, it will be seen as something already anticipated in the OT (cf. 9:10, 14).

### 2. Exposition of the new covenant (9:1–10:18)

The details of Israel's worship at the tabernacle contained many spiritual lessons. Central to them all was the necessity of the yearly atonement of blood sacrifice offered by the high priest. The fact that it was to be repeated yearly and was offered not only for the people, but also for the high priest himself, was intended by God to show its inadequacy. Though necessary for atonement at that time, it was ultimately intended to reveal that "the gifts and sacrifices being offered were not able to clear the conscience of the worshiper" (9:9). There were merely "external regulations applying until the time of the new order" (v.10).

Just as in the old covenant the high priest continually offered the blood of sacrificial animals as redemption from sin, in a once and for all act as High Priest of the new covenant, Christ offered his own blood as a sacrifice in the Holy of Holies of the true tabernacle, the heavenly one. Christ thus became the mediator of the new covenant between God and his chosen people, offering eternal salvation through his death (vv.11–15).

The Greek word for "covenant" that is used throughout this section of Hebrews also has the sense of "last will and testament." Thus, in vv.16–17, the writer of Hebrews draws on the analogy of a "will" to illustrate the necessity of Christ's death in establishing the new covenant. For a "will" to go into effect, there must be the death of the one who made the will (v.18). Even in the old covenant, the slaying of animals was necesary; the author takes this as a picture of the death requried so that of those entering the "will" might receive the inheritance. When the will went into effect, their sins were forgiven by the Lord (vv.19–22).

What was formerly practiced under the old covenant by way of a "copy," or foreshadowing of heavenly realities, was accomplished once and for all by Christ in the heavenly temple itself (vv.23–28). The sacrificial death of the eternal Son of God does not need to be repeated for each act of sin. Being an eternal offering, it is sufficient for every act of sin since the creation of the world; thus, "at the end of the ages," it did away with all sin.

Like the apostle Paul and the other NT writers, the final hope of the writer of Hebrews lies in the return of Jesus Christ "to bring salvation to those who are waiting for him" (v.28). It is at this time that Jesus will judge the world (v.27). The conceptual imagery of the writer is clearly informed by the prophetic vision of Da 7:9–14, the coming of the Son of Man to establish the eternal kingdom of God.

The very fact that the rituals of the old covenant had to be repeated on a yearly cycle is evidence of their temporality and ultimate inability to cleanse the human heart from sin (10:1–2, 11). After all, if the rituals of the old covenant had been effectual, why were they repeated year after year? Their value lay not in their final effect but in the reminder of human sin and guilt that they provided (v.3). The justice of God could not be settled by the offering of animal sacrifice (v.4). The guilt of humankind lay in the transgression of Adam, for which the penalty was death (Ge 2:17b). Consequently, humankind must die (Ge 3:19b). The writer of Hebrews reveals the divine solution in his quotation of Ps 40:6—Christ, when he came into the world, said, "A body you prepared for me." Thus, "we have been made holy through the sacrifice of the body of Jesus Christ once for all" (10:10).

Having performed his eternal sacrifice, the Son of God takes his seat "at the right hand of God" (v.12; cf. the Son of Man in Da 7:9–14) and awaits the time of the arrival of his kingdom (10:13). Meanwhile, the work of the new covenant in perfecting the saints and writing the law on their hearts is already at work.

## III. The Consequences (10:19–13:17)

### A. Application of the New Covenant in the Life of the Christian (10:19–39)

Several features of this book remind one of the apostle Paul. It was no accident that until quite recently, most Bible scholars assumed that Paul was in fact the author. In any case, like Paul, the writer of Hebrews turns immediately to the practical application of what he has been developing at length in the first section of this letter. That application consists both of the exhortation to live the Christian life in accordance with the new heart given to a person in Christ (vv.19–25), and of the warning of judgment to come for neglecting Christ's sacrifice (vv.26–31).

The immediate readers of this letter have fared well in their faith in past times, but they face an uncertain future. Therefore, the writer calls them in all earnestness to continue in well-doing and not to "shrink back" from receiving the promises. He holds out to them both the hope of the imminent return of Christ (vv.35–39) and the commendable examples of faithfulness in the past (11:1–40).

### B. The Nature of Faith (11:1–40)

The writer of this letter has repeatedly demonstrated the importance of looking to the OT Scriptures not only for instruction in God's plan of salvation but also as a source of comfort in the life of the Christian. Hebrews 11 is a paradigm for the Christian's reading and meditation on Scripture. It is an example of Paul's dictum that the OT narratives "were written as instruction [NIV, warnings] for us, on whom the fulfillment of the ages has come" (1Co 10:11). He first defines the nature of biblical faith (v.1) and then illustrates it from the examples of Scripture (vv.2–38). He follows the order of events as depicted in the OT.

Faith is being confident in what is hoped for but not yet seen (v.1). The first example of faith from the OT comes from the Creation account in Ge 1. The Bible teaches that "the universe was formed at God's command, so that what is seen was not made out of what was visible" (v.3). For the writer of Hebrews, faith accepts the biblical view of Creation as God's word because this is what the Scriptures teach. The list continues with Abel (v.4), Enoch (v.5–6), Noah (v.7), Abraham (vv.8–19), Isaac (v.20), Jacob (v.21), Joseph (v.22), Moses' parents (v.23), Moses (vv.24–28), Israel in the Exodus (v.29), Israel in the Conquest (v.30), Rahab (v.31), Gideon, Barak, Samson, Jephthah, David, Samuel, and the prophets (vv.32–38).

The list is an interesting one, both for what it says and what it does not say. For the most part, it does not assume that the reader will merely submit to the selection as a valid demonstration of faith. Rather, it provides a running commentary on the lives of several individuals selected and thereby demonstrates the life of faith that they lived. In the case of Enoch, for example, the writer reasons that since the biblical text in Genesis states that Enoch "was commended as one who pleased God" (v.5b), he must have had faith because "without faith it is impossible to please God" (v.6a). The Genesis narratives, however, do not explicitly state that Enoch "pleased God." What they do state is that Enoch "walked with God" (Ge 5:22, 24). But since the Genesis narratives also state that Noah "walked with God" (Ge 6:9b) and that "Noah found favor in the eyes of the Lord" (Ge 6:8), the writer of Hebrews concludes that the expression "to walk with God" means "to find favor with God." In other words, the list in ch. 11 is evidence of a great deal of thoughtful meditation on Scripture, in which the author links words and ideas in one passage to those of another. It is precisely this kind of reading that the authors of the OT Scriptures anticipated when they composed their writings. Moreover, it was the importance of "faith" that many, if not all, of the OT writers wanted most to elucidate.

There are some names on the list that are identified within the OT text itself as having faith: for example, Abraham (Ge 15:6) and Israel in the Exodus (Ex 4:31a; 14:31b). In the case of Moses (Heb 11:24–29), there is no explicit statement that he "believed" God, though the fact of his faith may have been drawn from the statement about him in Nu 12:7, "he is faithful in all my house" (cf. Heb 3:2). It is significant, however, that the writer of Hebrews omits from his list of the faithful any mention of the time of Israel's desert wandering. He has already portrayed that period in Israel's history, like the Pentateuch itself (Nu 14:11; 20:12), as a time of unbelief (Heb 3:7–19).

## C. Exhortation to Holiness (12:1–29)

The writer returns here to the central theme of the book: perseverance in the face of adversity. In his exhortation to put away "the sin that so easily entangles," he appeals both to the example of Jesus (vv.1–4) and to the implication of Christians being children of God (vv.5–13)—cf. "the Lord disciplines those he loves" (v.6). Finally he turns to the implication that the believer's holiness should have within the context of the new covenant (vv.14–29). God has not changed. He is still the same "consuming fire" (vv.18, 29) that Israel experienced at Mount Sinai with the giving of the Law of Moses (12:18–21). What has changed, however, is the relationship between God and his people in the new covenant. Mount Zion, the heavenly Jerusalem, the "joyful assembly," has replaced Mount Sinai, the place where even Moses was "trembling with fear" (v.21).

## D. Instructions in Practical Holiness (13:1–17)

The implications of Christ's work as mediator of the new covenant are spelled out here by means of concrete examples: brotherly love (v.1), hospitality (v.2), visiting the imprisoned and mistreated (v.3), faithfulness in marriage (v.4), contentment (v.5), trust in God (v.6), teachability (v.7), doctrinal stability (v.9), bearing disgrace for Christ's sake (v.11–13), hope (v.14), offering praise (v.15), sharing with others (v.16), and obedience and submission to authority (v.17).

## IV. Conclusion (13:18–25)

After a short doxology (vv.20–21), the writer makes a final appeal for a hearing in the difficult matters he has raised in this letter (v.22). The concluding greetings are reminiscent of the letters of Paul.

# James

## Introduction

The name of the author of this book is given simply as "James, a servant of God and of the Lord Jesus Christ" (1:1). Most likely this James was the son of Mary and Joseph, the half-brother of Jesus (cf. Mk 6:3). After Peter left Jerusalem in Ac 12:17, James took over the leadership of the church in Jerusalem (see Ac 15:13). No certain date can be obtained for the composition of this book. Most biblical scholars date it among the earliest NT books.

The book of James is a treatise on divine wisdom. It is considerably dependent on the wisdom literature and wisdom themes of the OT. Like wisdom texts such as Ps 37, it deals with the practical problem of living according to God's will in a fallen and hostile world. Moreover, also like Ps 37 and other wisdom biblical texts, its final solution rests in the eschatological hope of the return of the messianic kingdom. Only then will God's righteous judgment be exercised on the ungodly and the godly be rewarded. Until then, the task of the wise is to live godly lives and to trust God in every area of life. This is emphasized in the book of James by an appeal to the humility and purity of heart that characterizes those who already enjoy the benefits of the new covenant.

## I. Introduction (1:1)

The book of James begins very simply with the introduction of its author, James, and a brief description of its audience, "the twelve tribes scattered among the nations." Since the name of the leader of the Jerusalem church was James (Ac 15:13) and the early apostles numbered twelve (Ac 1:26), it has frequently been assumed that this letter was written by the James at Jerusalem and that the designation "the twelve tribes" was an early expression for the Jewish church. The general "wisdom"

nature of the letter, however, suggests that the ambiguity of the addressees as "the twelve tribes" may be a deliberate attempt on the part of the writer to give the book a wide and general circulation and at the same time retain its position as wisdom within the context of the biblical canon. The wisdom contained in this book, in other words, is not intended to be generic wisdom, as wisdom tends to be, but wisdom addressed to the people of God, i.e., "the twelve tribes" and hence is biblical wisdom.

## II. Divine Wisdom (1:2–27)

James gives an exposition of divine wisdom dealing with two specific areas of the Christian's life: trials (1:2–18) and obedience to Scripture (1:19–27).

### A. On Trials (1:2–18)

Curiously, the book of James begins precisely at the point where the book of Hebrews concludes, exhortation to perseverance in a time of trials (cf. Heb 12:1). Its lesson is the same: God will use testing and trials as a way of perfecting faith (v.4; cf. Heb 12:5–6). What one should seek in the midst of trials is the "wisdom" that God intends to teach by means of trials. Unlike worldly wisdom, divine wisdom does not come from mere observation. It comes from much prayer and divine illumination (v.5), as well as from an unwavering faith (vv.6–8).

Like biblical wisdom in general, James' wisdom shows signs of reflection on OT Scripture. The exaltation of the humble and the decline of the proud (vv.9–10), for example, is a common theme in the OT (cf. 1Sa 2:7–8), as is the passing glory of wealth in the face of divine judgment (cf. Ps 37:1–2; Isa 40:6–8). The blessed person is the one who remains faithful through trials (cf. Ps 37:5–7).

Moreover, James' discourse on the origin of trials and sin is taken directly from the Genesis narrative of the fall of Adam and Eve (Ge 3:1–13). God did not tempt our first parents; it was their own desire that enticed them (v.13; cf. Ge 3:6), led them astray, and ultimately resulted in their death (vv.12–15; cf. Ge 3:19). "Don't be deceived" (v.16; cf. Ge 3:13b), God, "the Father of the heavenly lights" (v.17; cf. Ge 1:3), gives only that which is good (v.17; cf. Ge 1:31). He "does not change like the shifting shadows" (v.17; cf. Ge 1:2).

### B. On Obedience to Scripture (1:19–27)

As James has just demonstrated, divine wisdom comes from reflective listening to God's Word, implanted in a godly life (vv.19–21). Not merely listening, but doing what God's Word teaches leads to blessing. Again James comes close to the central themes of Hebrews in stressing the new covenant ideal of the law written on the heart (cf. Heb 8:10).

## III. Application of Divine Wisdom (2:1–3:12)

James now gives three sets of examples of the application of the divine wisdom described in ch. 1. It is the divine wisdom that comes from having the law written on the heart.

### A. Humility (2:1–13)

In 1:9–11, James put forth a basic tenet of divine wisdom: it is the humble, not the rich and prideful, who can expect to enjoy God's blessing. He now turns to a concrete example of the application of this truth in the life of the church: relations between the rich and the poor in the church. Giving preferential treatment to the wealthy and mistreating the poor is a violation of the central message of the law: "Love your neighbor as yourself" (v.8).

### B. Faith and Works (2:14–26)

In 1:22 James warned against merely listening to the Word of God and not doing it. He now applies this truth to the concrete situation of a living faith. The faith by which one claims to be

saved (v.14) is a living faith that produces action (v.17). Thus works of love serve as evidence of saving faith. Abraham's offering of Isaac, which he did in Ge 22, is an example of the faith by which he was declared righteous in Ge 15:6. God called him to a specific action (Ge 22:1–2), and when he obeyed (22:3–10), Abraham showed evidence of his faith—"his faith was made complete by what he did" (Jas 2:22).

### C. On the Tongue (3:1–12)

In 1:19 James admonished the reader to be "slow to speak." He now turns to the concrete example of the power of the tongue. Teachers have to talk; they cannot merely listen. Thus they risk a stricter judgment and should be doubly careful of what they say (cf. 2:12), knowing, however, that they are not perfect and "stumble in many ways" (3:2). The real problem of the tongue lies in a lack of control (vv.3–8). It is an instrument that can be used for both praise and cursing (vv.9–12); Christians are called to use it to bless God and other people.

## IV. Further Lessons in Wisdom (3:13–5:11)

### A. Divine Wisdom (3:13–18)

The test of divine wisdom lies in the results it produces in life situations. Earthly wisdom stems from envy and selfish ambition and produces disorder (3:14–16). Divine wisdom stems from a pure heart and produces peace and righteousness (vv.17–18).

### B. Admonition to Follow Divine Wisdom (4:1–5:11)

Behind the instruction of biblical wisdom lies the overwhelming confidence in divine justice. It is God and God alone who metes out reward and retribution for human action: "God opposes the proud but gives grace to the humble" (4:6); therefore, "Humble yourselves before the Lord, and he will lift you up" (v.10). There is nothing the wise Christian can do that will facilitate God's righteous judgment. All one can do is rest in the all-encompassing will of God (vv.11–16) and do that which one knows to be good (v.17).

Where, then, does the hope of the Christian lie? Like all biblical wisdom (cf. Ecc 12:13–14), for James the hope lies in the future fulfillment of God's eternal plan: "Be patient, then, brothers, until the Lord's coming" (5:7). The rich and the proud, though they prosper now, are only storing up divine judgment for themselves when Christ returns (vv.1–6). The book of Job is a paradigm of God's ultimate vindication of the righteous wise man (v.11).

## V. Concluding Examples of Wisdom (5:12–20)

The wise person is one who trusts God in all things and waits for him to fulfill his promises. Nevertheless, there is still much room for prayer (vv.13–15) and confession of sin (v.16). Elijah (1Ki 17–18) is a biblical example of the effective prayer of a righteous man (vv.16–18). Moreover, there is also room for admonishing one another to walk in God's wisdom (5:19–20).

# 1 Peter

## Introduction

The author of this letter is identified in 1:1 as the apostle Peter. No definite date can be assigned to the writing of the book.

This book was written to give hope and encouragement to Christians who were suffering for the sake of Christ. Their hope lies in the joy that awaits them at the return of Christ. The encouragement Peter offers them comes from the fact that in their suffering they share in the sufferings of Christ. Throughout the book Peter draws on the analogy between the people of God in the OT and members of the present church. Like Israel, the church is called to holiness as a new people of God. It is their godly lives in a wicked world that draw the fire of persecution. Their suffering therefore is a clear indication of their faithfulness to Christ. The situation of the readers of Peter's letter is similar to the readers of both the OT and the NT, where it is assumed that God's people will suffer for righteousness' sake. From the events in the life of Joseph in Egypt to that of Daniel in Babylon, the biblical narratives present God's people as sojourners—just like Peter's readers, whom he calls "aliens and strangers in the world" (2:11)

## I. Introduction (1:1–2)

Peter introduces his central theme here at the beginning of the book. He writes to "God's elect" who are "strangers in the world" (v.1). They are strangers in that they, with Peter, eagerly await the return of the Lord to establish his kingdom (cf. 1:17; 4:7). In this world they suffer painful trials (4:12), but they have a better hope when Christ's "glory is revealed" (4:13). It is with this backdrop in mind that Peter writes his letter. Moreover, Peter calls them "God's elect" because they "have been chosen according to the foreknowledge of God" for "obedience to Jesus Christ" (1:2). All that has and is happening to these Christians in the world is part of God's "sanctifying work" for them.

## II. The New People of God (1:3–4:11)

### A. Election and Sanctification (1:3–2:10)

#### 1. The return of Christ (1:3–12)

Peter's starting point for hope in the Christian life is the resurrection of Christ (v.3), but the focus of his hope is clearly set on Christ's second coming (v.5). There are present sufferings, but there is also a sustaining hope of future glory in the return of Christ. The present sufferings have their place in God's plan. They are intended, in God's wisdom, to prove their faith to be true (v.7). The OT prophets searched intently their own writings to know the time and circumstances of Christ's coming, though they were well aware that what they wrote of was not to be in their own day but was yet for the future (vv.10–12).

#### 2. The Christian's holy life (1:13–21)

Peter's emphasis on the return of Christ is geared to his appeal for holy living. Christians are to live in light of the hope of Christ's imminent return. That means they should not live according to the standards of this world. They are strangers in this world (v.17), where values are measured in terms of silver and gold (v.18); but they are at home in the presence of a holy God who purchased them "with the precious blood of Christ" (v.19).

Throughout this book, Peter returns to the imagery of the OT to describe the Christian's relationship to Christ. Here he uses the imagery of the first Passover celebration in the Exodus, when a sacrificial lamb without blemish or defect was set apart four days before the feast to be offered as a substitute for the death of the firstborn (Ex 12:2–6). In the same way, Christ was set apart "before the creation of the world" to be "revealed in these last times for your sake" (v.20).

### 3. A holy people (1:22–2:10)

God's intent in his covenant with Israel given on Mount Sinai was that they would be a "kingdom of priests and a holy nation" (see Ex 19:6). Thus he revealed his word to them through Moses (Ex 19:6b), written on tablets of stone (Ex 24:12). Drawing on the images of these Exodus narratives, Peter views the church as those who have been born of the word of God; they are a "spiritual house to be a holy priesthood" (2:5). In light of the new covenant promises in the prophetic books, Peter sees that God's word is now written on their hearts of flesh (Jer 31:33) by God's Spirit (Eze 36:26). They have been born again "through the living and enduring word of God" (1:23). They are "living stones" (2:5), offering "spiritual sacrifices" (v.5b); they are a "chosen people, a royal priesthood, a holy nation" (v.9).

### B. Instructions (2:11–4:11)

In light of their standing as a new "people of God" (2:10), Peter instructs Christians to "live such good lives among the pagans" so that many will turn to the Lord in faith and thus "glorify God on the day he visits us," i.e., at the coming of Christ (v.12). What does it mean to "live good lives"? It means abstaining from worldly desires (vv.11–12), submitting to authority (vv.13–17), submitting to one's master and thus following the example of Christ (vv.18–25), submitting to husbands (3:1–6) and thus following the example of Sarah, respecting wives (v.7), and living in harmony with one another (vv.8–12).

If Christians live in this manner, they will call attention to themselves in a wicked world. They should be ready, then, at all times "to give an answer to everyone who asks" the reason for their hope (vv.13–15), and they should be

ready to suffer for doing good (vv.16–17). In a similar way, Christ himself preached salvation to a wicked audience when he "preached to the spirits in prison who disobeyed long ago when God waited patiently in the days of Noah" (vv.19–20). Noah and those with him in the ark were saved from their own wicked generation by the Flood, symbolizing how the water of Christian baptism saves Christians from the world and, in the Resurrection, makes them alive to Christ (vv.21–22). Through the Resurrection, Christians become members of Christ's kingdom, over which he reigns at the right hand of God (v.22). As members of that kingdom they are to live according to God's will and not in the ways of their former lives (4:1–6). Their one and only hope should be fixed on the return of Christ (vv.7–11).

## III. Suffering for Christ (4:12–5:11)

It should be no surprise if Christians must suffer for Christ in this world. Christ himself suffered. Christians themselves should rejoice that they "participate in the sufferings of Christ" (4:12–19).

As Jesus' last words to Peter were "Feed my sheep" (Jn 21:17b), so Peter's last words to his readers are, "Be shepherds of God's flock. . . . And when the Chief Shepherd appears, you will receive the crown of glory" (5:1–2). Elders are to oversee the church not by lording over them or being greedy for earthly gain, but "as examples to the flock" (vv.3–4). Young men are to serve in submission to older men. All are to be humble and self-controlled (vv.6–9), trusting God for strength and power (vv.10–11).

## IV. Conclusion (5:12–14)

Peter concludes his letter with a cryptic reference to "she who is in Babylon, chosen together with you" (v.13). This is no doubt a reference to the Christian community in the city from which he is writing this letter, but it is not clear which city. In the literature of the Bible, the city of Babylon is a virtual code word for any city or nation united against God, i.e., the Antichrist (cf. Rev 18). Peter probably uses the term to identify himself with the saints of all ages who live in a world united against God and his Christ.

# 2 Peter

## Introduction

The author of this letter is identified as the apostle Peter (1:1). No definite date can be assigned to the writing of the book.

Peter writes a second letter to the churches scattered throughout Asia Minor (cf. 1Pe 1:1) to address the specific problem of false teachers. There were some among the churches who had lapsed back into their former ungodly ways and were apparently teaching that God's lack of judgment on them was a sign of his approval. Peter argues that such thinking is counter to all that the Scriptures teach about God's righteous judgment of sin. It is merely a ruse on the part of the false teachers to cover their own greed. The fact that the Lord has not returned to judge the wicked and reward the righteous is not a sign that God has gone back on his promises. It is rather a sign of God's mercy even for the ungodly. God's delay is intended to give time for everyone to repent.

Like Peter's first letter, this one also draws on the central theme of patiently "waiting on God," found throughout the writings of Scripture. It is, in fact, the Scriptures themselves that Peter holds out to his readers as the basis of their hope and trust in God. God has always remained faithful. He has an appointed time; "though it linger; wait for it, it will certainly come and will not delay" (Hab 2:3)

## I. Introduction (1:1–2)

In the opening greeting of this letter, no specific churches, cities, or individuals are mentioned. The book appears to be consciously addressed to virtually every Christian reader, though it is also true that the same audience is assumed for this letter as for his first one (cf. 2Pe 3:1). The central theme is established in the formal greeting.

Grace and peace are to be found in abundance "through the knowledge of God and of Jesus our Lord" (v.2). Peter's purpose in this brief work is to strengthen the reader's knowledge of God and Jesus through an emphasis on the importance of sound doctrine.

## II. Defense of Christian Eschatology (1:3–3:13)

### A. Effective Knowledge of Jesus (1:3–11)

Peter begins with a brief discussion of the importance of a well-balanced knowledge. For him, knowledge of Jesus is an important link in the Christian's possession of divine power (v.3). The starting point is faith (v.5) and the goal is love (v.7), but to both of these must be added goodness, knowledge, self-control, perseverance, godliness, and brotherly kindness (vv.5–8). Such qualities of life will keep Christians "from being ineffective and unproductive in [their] knowledge" of the Lord Jesus Christ (v.8).

### B. Witnesses of Christ's Divine Power (1:12–21)

Christians need be to continually reminded of the knowledge of Christ's power in their lives (vv.12–15). That, in part, is Peter's purpose in writing this letter. The apostle, who at this time was about to give his life as a martyr for the Lord (cf. Jn 21:18–19), reminds his readers that he was an eyewitness to the honor and glory Christ received from his Father at his transfiguration (cf. Mt 17:5; Mk 9:7; Lk 9:35): "We ourselves heard this voice that came from heaven when we were with him on the sacred mountain" (v.18). Peter's words are similar to those of John in the next book: "That which we have heard, which we have seen with our eyes . . . this we proclaim" (1Jn 1:1).

Not only can Peter claim his own eyewitness account of Christ's glory, but there is also "the word of the [OT] prophets" that has proved even more certain (v.19). God's prophetic word is like "a light shining in a dark place" (v.19b; cf. Ps 119:105). In the imagery Peter uses here (cf. Ge 1:3; Isa 9:2), his point is that reading and meditating on Scripture dispels the darkness of the mind in the same way that the sunrise brings the clear light of day. The prophets themselves did not devise these prophecies about Jesus on their own. They were "carried along by the Holy Spirit" (vv.20–21). Thus a primary source for the Christian's knowledge of Jesus is the prophetic word of the OT Scriptures. Peter demonstrates the importance of this statement in the many allusions and references he makes to the OT in this very book.

## C. Warnings of False Doctrine (2:1–22)

Just as there were true prophets and false prophets in OT times, so also, Peter warns, there are false teachers in the church who bring swift destruction by their teaching (vv.1–4). The motivation for these false teachers is greed (v.3). They "have secretly introduced destructive heresies, even denying the sovereign Lord" (v.1b). The fact that these false teachers exist and their ungodly lives are not punished by divine judgment should not be taken to mean that God does not judge such people. Drawing on lessons from the OT, Peter argues that, though it may delay, God's judgment always falls on the ungodly. The pages of the OT that he turns to concern the fallen angels in the Garden of Eden (v.4; cf. Eze 28:11–19), the Flood in the days of Noah (v.5; cf. Ge 6–9), the destruction of Sodom and Gomorrah (vv.6–14), the story of Balaam (vv.15–16), and certain proverbs (v.22; cf. Pr 26:11).

It should be noted that Peter follows the sequence of events of divine judgment as they are presented in the OT. He begins with the fall of Satan and his angels in Eden. The primary biblical source for Peter is the prophecy against the king of Tyre in Eze 28. Ezekiel, threatening the swift destruction of the king of Tyre, much like Peter, drew on a close reading of the Garden of Eden narratives in Ge 2–3 to show that the fate of the king of Tyre would be the same as that of the fallen angels. According to Peter, when the angels "sinned" (v.4a; cf. Eze 28:16a), they were expelled from the Garden of God (v.4b; cf. Eze 28:16b) and cast into a consuming fire (v.4b; cf. Eze 28:18).

In his account of the destruction of Sodom and Gomorrah, Peter expands on the treatment of Lot and his angelic visitors (vv.8–14) because it provides a particularly graphic and apt example of Christians living within an ungodly world. His description of Lot in Sodom intentionally blends with his description of the ungodly in his own day. In v.8, Peter describes Lot among the wicked at Sodom, but then in vv.9–10a, he turns to the unrighteous in his own day. In v.10b, however, Peter returns to the Sodom narratives in Genesis where the men of Sodom were "not afraid to slander celestial beings" (cf. Ge 19:5)—all the while Peter has his eye on the wicked of his own day (vv.12–14). Though the angels who visited Lot were "stronger and more powerful" (v.11; cf. Ge 19:10–11), they did "not bring slanderous accusations against" the men of the city "in the presence of the Lord" (v.11b). This is apparently a reference to the fact that in Ge 18:20–21, the angels were sent only to confirm the outcry against Sodom that had already come up before the Lord and did not themselves make the accusations against the cities.

Peter concludes with a stern warning to have nothing to do with these false teachers. They have turned away from Christ and, because they have perverted the Gospel message, they are worse off now than before they had any knowledge of it (vv.17–22).

### D. The Return of the Lord (3:1–13)

In his first letter, Peter had repeatedly urged his readers to look forward to the return of Christ and to live in eager expectation of it. Lest he leave the impression that Christ's return must and will happen only in the immediate future, he now turns to explain the necessity of God's delay in sending his Son.

The argument Peter particularly addresses in this section is one that says God will not intervene in judgment in the affairs of humankind and creation because he has never done so in the past (vv.3–4). The error of such thinking is that it overlooks the obvious biblical fact that God did intervene in human affairs and creation to bring judgment in the days of the Flood. God made the earth from the waters, and he destroyed it from the same waters (vv.5–6). The same divine word that brought the world into existence has promised to bring the judgment of fire upon this world and the destruction of the ungodly (v.7).

In the delay of his coming, God is not slow to keep his promise. He is patient, wanting to give everyone, even the ungodly, time to repent and turn to him. God reckons time differently than human beings do. With God "a day is like a thousand years, and a thousand years are like a day" (v.8). God is waiting, giving time for repentance, because he does not desire "anyone to perish, but everyone to come to repentance" (v.9). The end will come, however, and when it does, the ungodly and all God's creation will be destroyed by fire (vv.10–12).

This planned destruction of the wicked does not mean the end of God's plan for the righteous. It is only the beginning. In keeping with his promise, there will be a new heaven and a new earth (cf. Isa 65:17), which, unlike the old fallen one, will be "the home of righteousness" (v.13).

### III. Concluding Warnings (3:14–18)

The hope of Christians is the return of Christ to establish his kingdom. It is in light of this hope that God's people should strive to live godly and pure lives. The apostle Paul has already written about these same things (e.g., 1Co 15; 2Th 1–2). Nevertheless, some easily distort his writings, along with the rest of the Scriptures, and thus constant attention to these doctrines are the only defense against error.

# 1 John

## Introduction

The author of the letter is not identified in the text. Its close association with the fourth gospel has led to the identification of its author as John. It is best to keep in mind, however, that the book is anonymous. No definite date can be assigned to the writing of this book.

Like the fourth gospel, 1 John is primarily concerned with the identity of Jesus as the Son of God. Central to the author's understanding of the Gospel is the new covenant ideal of the new heart indwelt by God's Spirit. Through Christ the believer has forgiveness of sins, fellowship with God, and hope of eternal life.

Another part of the author's purpose is to warn true believers of the perils of false teaching. The external tests of false doctrine are the identity of Jesus as the Christ and love for one's fellow Christians. The internal test is the witness of the indwelling Spirit.

## I. Introduction (1:1–4)

The author begins with the claim of being an eyewitness to "the Word of life" (1:1–2). With clear allusions to the prologue to the Gospel of John, he says the Word was "from the beginning" (v.1; cf. Jn 1:1) and "with the Father" (v.2; cf. Jn 1:2), but also that he saw and touched the Word and now testifies to it. What is the Word? It is that which the author now proclaims in this book. The goal of his writing is that he might have fellowship in the Word with his readers (1:3).

## II. Fellowship With God (1:5–2:17)

The message that this letter proclaims is that Jesus is "the atoning sacrifice" (2:2) for sin. He assumes without further explanation that his readers understand both the nature and impor-

tance of Christ's death as a sacrifice for sin. He assumes, in other words, the kind of developed theology found in Heb 9. Through the blood of Jesus, God's Son, those who walk in God's light are purified from all sin (1:7). Those who do not walk in God's light are liars, even though they may claim to have fellowship with him (v.6). No one can claim to be without sin, though walking in fellowship entails a continuous confession of sin and dependence on Jesus' atoning death.

The way of life pictured here is cast in such a way to reflect the life of God's people under the Mosaic covenant, though obviously under the new provisions of Christ's death and the new covenant. The Christian, like the Israelite, comes into God's presence only on the basis of the shed blood of a sacrifice. For John, Jesus is that "atoning sacrifice" (2:2). Moreover, the Christian, like the Israelite, must continually maintain an upright relationship with God through confession and repentance (1:9). By drawing on these analogies, John does not identify the Mosaic covenant with the new covenant; rather, like the writer of the book of Hebrews, he is showing the superiority of the new covenant by virtue of its eternal sacrifice and priesthood. In the new covenant, Jesus is not only the "one who speaks to the Father in our defense" (2:1) but also "he is the atoning sacrifice" (v.2).

Under the Mosaic covenant, the Israelites were expected to exhibit their fellowship in their obedience to the Mosaic Law; so, John says, Christians must obey Christ's commands and "walk as Jesus did" (2:6). For John, walking as Jesus walked is not "a new commandment but an old one" (v.7), which they "have had since the beginning" (v.7b), i.e., the command to love one another (cf. Lev 19:18; Dt 30:6b). The fact, however, that the truth of this commandment was revealed in Jesus and can be realized in the Christian through the light that shines through him, makes this a "new command" (v.8). Therefore, if one lives in the light, then one will "love his brother" (vv.9–11). John closes this section with a poetic summary of the believer's position in Christ (vv.12–17).

## III. The Apostasy of Those Who Turned Away From Christ (2:18–27)

John is concerned about those among the churches who had fallen away from the Gospel and were attempting to lead others astray with them. The fact that they have fallen away, John says, is evidence that they never truly belonged to Christ (b.19). Those who have a genuine "anointing from the Holy One" will not fall away, though they are always in need of a warning (v.26). The only safeguard against falling away is holding firm to the teaching of Jesus just as it has been taught (v.27).

The central question for anyone's teaching about Jesus is whether one believes him to be the Christ, i.e., the Messiah (v.22). John's conception of the Christ is clearly that expressed in the OT Scriptures as well as throughout the NT books, namely, Jesus is the heavenly Son of Man who, in his death and resurrection, has received the kingdom and the people promised him before the foundation of the earth (cf. Da 7:9–14; Jn 17:1–5). Thus to deny that Jesus is the Christ is to deny "the Father and the Son" (v.22). In other words, for John, to accept Jesus as the Christ is to accept the Trinitarian confession of Jesus as Lord.

## IV. The Test of True Faith (2:28–3:24)

Having described the marks of the false teachers, John turns to the distinguishing characteristics of the true children of God. The primary characteris-

tics of the Christian are righteousness (2:29–3:10), love (3:11–20), and faith (3:21–24).

Christians are to test the spirits of prophets who profess to speak in God's name (4:1–6). The test is whether they acknowledge that "Jesus Christ has come in the flesh," or "Jesus, as Christ come in the flesh" (v.2). Every spirit that "does not [thus] acknowledge Jesus is not from God" but is "the spirit of the antichrist" (v.3). According to 2:22, the one who is an antichrist "denies that Jesus is the Christ," whereas here the antichrist denies "Jesus, as Christ come in the flesh." In 4:15, however, the one who is of God "acknowledges that Jesus is the Son of God"; and in 5:1 "everyone who believes that Jesus is the Christ is born of God"; and in 5:5 the one who overcomes the world is "he who believes that Jesus is the Son of God." It is not clear whether a distinction is intended in the different wording of these verses or a more general denial of the claims of the Gospel that encompasses them all is in view.

In 4:4–6 John himself moves beyond this confessional test to give a more general criterion for distinguishing the true from the false: "We are from God, and whoever knows God listens to us; but whoever is not from God does not listen to us. This is how we recognize the Spirit of truth and the spirit of falsehood" (v.6). To this John adds the test of love in 4:7–5:4: "Whoever does not love does not know God, because God is love" (4:7–8).

## V. The Witness of the Spirit (5:5–13)

At this point in the book, John's line of thought regarding Christ reaches its highest point in the confession that "Jesus is the Son of God" (v.5). As the Son of God, Jesus "is the one who came by water and blood" (v.6), i.e., he came in the flesh (cf. 4:2). Moreover, it is the Spirit that bears witness to him (v.6b) by means of an internal testimony: "Anyone who believes in the Son of God has this testimony in his heart" (v.10). What is the testimony? It is the eternal life given in the Son (v.11): "He who has the Son has life" (v.12).

## VI. Conclusion (5:14–21)

John has written this letter to those who believe in Jesus as the Son of God. His purpose was to give them assurance that their faith in him was true (v.13). In such an assurance there is also confidence that God hears and answers the Christian's prayer (vv.14–15).

In light of all that John has written about Jesus, the Son of God, it follows that at the close he would identify him as "the true God and eternal life," and then conclude with a warning against idolatry. Idolatry is the worship of false god(s).

# 2 John

## Introduction

The author of this brief letter is identified only as "the elder" (v.1). The close association of this book with the fourth gospel and 1 John has led to the identification of its author as John. It is best to keep in mind, however, that the book is anonymous. No definite date can be assigned to the writing of this book.

It is reasonably clear that this letter was intended as a summary of 1 John. Its specific contribution lies in the fact that it succinctly focuses on the main points of that letter (walking in Christ, brotherly love, and false doctrine), and adds the warning against inadvertently sharing in the work of the antichrists (vv.10–11). It should be noted that the letter of 3 John takes these same themes and applies them to a specific church situation.

## I. Introduction (1–3)

The book is addressed to "the chosen lady and her children" (v.1). This is usually taken to be a reference to a local church, though some take it to refer to a specific house church in the home of a prominent woman. The fact that the letter closes with a greeting from "the children of your chosen sister" strongly suggests that these are titles given to various church bodies and not specific individuals.

John opens the letter with a greeting that focuses on the central themes of his first letter (1 John), i.e., the Trinitarian notion of Jesus Christ as God's Son and the twin themes of truth and love (v.3).

The remainder of the letter serves as a sort of summary of the major points of 1 John.

## II. Summary Themes (4–11)

As in 1Jn 1:5–2:2, the writer begins with an emphasis on the importance of maintaining a consistent walk with Christ (v.4). The importance of one's personal walk with Christ is then extended to include the command to love one another (v.5; cf. 1Jn 2:7). Walking in the light also means walking in love (v.6; cf. 1Jn 5:3).

Love involves trust, and thus John warns his readers to "watch out" for the "many deceivers, who do not acknowledge Jesus Christ as coming in the flesh" (v.7; cf. 1Jn 4:2–3), and who would cause them to lose their reward (v.8). The test of true discipleship is continuing "in the teaching of Christ," i.e., in the teaching about Jesus as the Son of God who has come in bodily form to give himself as an "atoning sacrifice for our sins" (1Jn 2:2, 22). John heightens his warning regarding these false teachers by urging his readers to give no support whatever to them. To welcome such teachers is to participate in their work (v.11).

## III. Conclusion (12–13)

The close of the letter anticipates John's third letter. In stating that he still has "much to write," the writer suggests that more is yet to come, even though his clear immediate intention is to visit them "and talk face to face" (v.12). Moreover, this final note is an acknowledgment of the incontestable brevity of this letter.

# 3 John

## Introduction

Like 2 John, the author of this letter is identified only as "the elder" (v.1). The close association of the book with 1 and 2 John has led to the identification of its author as John. It is best to keep in mind, however, that the book is anonymous. No definite date can be assigned to the writing of this book.

The similarities between 3 John and 2 John are striking. The present letter is a virtual replay of 2 John, only with the difference that where 2 John deals with general principles, this one gives concrete examples in the life of a specific church. As in 2 John, its three primary themes are walking in Christ, brotherly love, and false doctrine.

## I. Introduction (1)

The letter is addressed to a specific individual, Gaius, who was apparently a leader in a local church. Though brief, the introduction establishes clearly the fact that the writer and Gaius are in fundamental agreement in the teaching of Christ. John says of him, "whom I love in the truth." Love and truth are the central themes of all three of John's letters. These themes are set alongside that of false doctrine.

## II. Walking in the Truth (2–4)

In both 1Jn 1:5–2:2 and 2Jn 4, the writer began with an emphasis on the importance of maintaining a consistent walk with Christ. Here he commends Gaius for his continuing "to walk in the truth" (v.3). Thus Gaius is here presented as a concrete example of John's teaching in the other letters.

## III. Brotherly Love (5–8)

In the other two letters of John, the importance of one's personal walk with Christ is extended to include the command to love one another (1Jn 2:7; 2Jn 5). Walking in the light also means walking in love (1Jn 5:3; 2Jn 6). Thus,

again, Gaius is presented in this letter as a concrete example of brotherly love that stems from walking in the truth.

## IV. The Test of False Teachers (9–12)

In his previous letters, John has repeatedly warned his readers of false teachers. There are two kinds of tests. The first is doctrinal: Do they acknowledge Jesus as coming in the flesh (1Jn 4:2–3; 2Jn 7)? The second is practical: Do they exercise love (1Jn 4:7–12)? John thus presents Gaius here with two opposing examples of professing teachers in the church, Diotrephes and Demetrius. He must apply John's tests to distinguish between the two.

John begins with a description of Diotrephes, "who loves to be first" and "will have nothing to do with us" (v.9). He is "gossiping maliciously" and "refuses to welcome the brothers" (v.10). On the other hand, Demetrius "is well spoken of by everyone—and even by the truth itself" (v.12). John apparently means by this that Demetrius's life is consistent with the teaching of Christ. The choice between these two teachers, then, is clear-cut: "Anyone who does what is good is from God" (v.11). The test has been applied, the example of Diotrephes rejected, and the example of Demetrius is to be imitated (v.11).

## V. Conclusion (1:13–14)

Within the present canonical order of the NT books, the writer's concluding statement that he still has "much to write" (cf. 2Jn 12) anticipates the book of Revelation, the final work of John. It may also be a veiled apology for the extreme brevity of the letter. It is clear from the letter itself, however, that the writer ostensibly means by this remark only that his desire is to talk to his readers "face to face" rather than write any further (v.14).

# Jude

## Introduction

The author is identified as Jude, a brother of James (v.1). This James is most likely the half-brother of Jesus (see Mk 6:3, where "Judas" means "Jude"), the man who eventually became the leader of the church in Jerusalem (cf. Ac 15:13; 21:18). No definite date can be assigned to the writing of this letter.

The letter of Jude has a distinct focus. The author warns his readers against the clever devices of the false teachers among them. Their false teaching may be new, but their error, manifested by their ungodly manner of life, is as old as time. For Jude, the question boils down to the authority by which these men claim to teach. They claim their own authority, whereas Jude warns his readers to remain faithful to the doctrine that they have already been taught.

## I. Introduction (1–2)

Jude does not address his letter to a specific audience. He writes "to those who have been called" (v.1). In v.18 he refers to and quotes from 2Pe 3:3; thus we may assume he had the same general audience in mind as Peter did (cf. 1Pe 1:1). In any event, this letter is remarkable for its "strictly business" approach, concluding only with a formal doxology (vv.24–25).

## II. False Doctrine (3–23)

### A. Contend for the Faith (3–4)

Jude begins cordially enough ("Dear friends"), with a plea to "contend for the faith that was once for all entrusted to the saints" (v.3). But he moves quickly into a scathing denunciation of false teachers (v.4). What was at stake was nothing less than a perversion of God's grace into "license for immorality" (v.4b) and a denial of Jesus (v.4c).

## B. Beware of False Teachers (5–16)

The threat to the church posed by these false teachers was the same as the apostasy of Israel in the desert. Those whom God delivered from Egypt, he later destroyed because they did not believe (v.5; cf. Nu 14:11; 20:12). Likewise the angels, who were created to be with God, "did not keep their positions of authority" and were subsequently "bound with everlasting chains for judgment" (v.6). Jude, like Peter (2Pe 2:4), probably has in mind here the fall of Satan and his angels alluded to by Ezekiel in his prophecy against the king of Tyre (Eze 28:11–19). As a third example, Jude mentions Sodom and Gomorrah, whom God once delivered through Abraham (Ge 14:11–24), but who "gave themselves up to sexual immorality and perversion" (v.7; cf. Ge 19:5) and God destroyed them (Ge 19:24).

Jude warns that the false teachers among the churches "pollute their own bodies, reject authority and slander celestial beings" in the same way as the people of Sodom (v.8; cf. Ge 19:5–9). They apparently rejected all authority but their own; thus, in Jude's mind, these men assumed more authority than even Michael the archangel. According to a popular story about the death of Moses, known to Jude and his readers but no longer extant, Michael refused to condemn Satan in his dispute about the body of Moses, being content to call upon God to rebuke him (v.9). Such respect for divine authority was not to be found with these false teachers (v.10). They were like Cain, who refused to pay heed to God's warning (Ge 4:6–12), and like Balaam and Korah, who sought gain from destroying the work of God (v.11).

Jude goes on to give a vivid description of the modus operandi of these false teachers. They have no qualms about blatantly seeking their own profit among God's people (v.12–17). Jude, quoting a first-century work about the patriarch Enoch (1 Enoch 1:9), reassures his readers that divine judgment is awaiting these ungodly men (vv.14–16). The reason Jude appeals to the book of Enoch rather than a book from the OT may lie in the fact that the word "ungodly" occurs repeatedly in this quote and hence forcefully drives home his main point throughout the whole of the letter: "They are godless men . . ." (v.4). The same word, "ungodly," also occurs in Jude's quotation of the apostle Peter (v.18).

### C. Importance of Sound Doctrine (17–23)

Jude's final appeal is to the authority of Jesus and the apostles—in this case, Peter's reference to the words of Jesus in 2Pe 3:2–3: "In the last times there will be scoffers who will follow their own ungodly desires" (vv.18–19). Jude then elaborates, describing them as those who divide the people, who follow their own "natural instincts," and do not have the Spirit (v.19). In opposition to such men, Jude says, his readers should build themselves up by paying attention to doctrine ("faith"), prayer, love, and mercy (vv.20–23).

### III. Conclusion (1:24–25)

Jude closes the letter with a formal doxology that stresses God's power to preserve believers until the time that Christ returns.

# Revelation

## Introduction

Though this matter is disputed by some, it seems best for a number of reasons to consider the author of this book to be the apostle John, the same one who most likely wrote the gospel of John and the three letters of John. The date of the writing of this book was probably toward the end of the first century A.D, when John was exiled on the island of Patmos because of his Christian faith and witness.

The subject of this book is "eschatology," i.e., the doctrine of the last things. It ends with the return of Jesus Christ, the destruction of the Devil and all his cohorts, and the creation of the new heavens and the new earth. One of the most common ways in which John structures his book is according to the number seven: for example, seven letters, seven seals, seven trumpets, and seven bowls. In many of John's divisions of seven, the sets are divided into a set of four, and then a set of three.

It is accepted by all futurists that the book of Revelation deals primarily with the Tribulation period, prior to the second coming of Christ. The primary basis for this reading of Revelation comes from the correlation of chs. 6–19 with the prophecy of Daniel's seventy weeks in Da 9:24–27. We can note the following features of the seventy weeks from this passage in Daniel:

(1) The entire prophecy has to do with Daniel's people and Daniel's city, namely, Israel and Jerusalem (Da 9:24).

(2) Two distinct rulers are mentioned in Da 9: "the Anointed One, the ruler" (9:25) and "the ruler who will come" (9:26).

(3) The time period involved is exactly seventy weeks (Da 9:24). These seventy weeks are further divided into three lesser periods: seven weeks, sixty-two weeks, and one week.

(4) The beginning of the period is at "the issuing of a decree to restore and rebuild Jerusalem" (Da 9:25).

(5) The end of the seven plus sixty-two (or sixty-nine) weeks will be marked by the appearance of "the Anointed One, the ruler" (Da 9:25).

(6) At a later time, after sixty-nine weeks, the Anointed One will be cut off, and Jerusalem will again be destroyed by the people of another "ruler who will come" (Da 9:26).

(7) After these two important events, the seventieth week occurs. The beginning of this week is marked by the establishment of a firm covenant of one week between the coming ruler and Israel (Da 9:27).

(8) Halfway through the seventieth week, the coming ruler will halt the practice of sacrifice, and a time of great wrath and desolation will ensue (Da 9:27).

(9) After the seventy weeks is complete, a time of blessing will come for the nation of Israel (Da 9:24).

We can arrange these events in the following sequence:

(1) The first sixty-nine weeks, which are taken as prophetic years (1 year = 360 days), began March 14, 445 B.C., with the issuing of a decree to rebuild Jerusalem in the reign of the Persian king Artaxerxes (Ne 2:1–8).

(2) The period of sixty-nine years ended in April 6, A.D. 32, when Jesus entered Jerusalem on a donkey.

(3) The question that now arises is what to do with the seventieth week. There are two interpretations. The first is the *continuous* view, which holds that the whole seventy weeks are to be understood as a continuous and unbroken sequence. This would put the seventieth week, a time of seven years, within the time period of the book of Acts. There may be some indication of this expectation in Peter's words to the nation of Israel in Ac 3:19–21, "Repent, then, and turn to God, so that your sins may be

wiped out, that times of refreshing may come from the Lord, and that he may send the Christ, who has been appointed for you—even Jesus. He must remain in heaven until the time comes for God to restore everything, as he promised long ago through his holy prophets." The second view, the *gap* view, holds that there is an indefinite time period between the sixty-ninth week and the seventieth week. Appeal is usually made to the fact that in Da 9:26 the death of Christ and the destruction of Jerusalem are said to happen "after" the sixty-ninth week and, at least by implication, before the seventieth week. There appears to be, then, a gap of sorts, since the city of Jerusalem was not destroyed until A.D. 70. If this gap exists, there is no reason why a much larger gap may also be assumed. Thus the seventieth week is separated from the sixty-ninth week by a large gap of uncharted time (almost two thousand years already) and lies still in the future from our perspective today.

Regarding the seventieth week itself, we may say the following things:

(1) It is a period of seven years that lies between the rapture of the church and the return of the Lord Jesus Christ (cf. Mt 24:15–30).

(2) This week of seven years provides the exact chronological framework for the great events of chs. 6–19. The several references to time periods in Revelation are at face value the equivalent of three and one-half prophetic years—years of 360 days each: "a time, times and half a time" (12:14); "42 months" (11:2; 13:5); and "1,260 days" (11:3; 12:6).

How does one account for the two sets of three and one-half years? The three and one-half years of 11:2 seem to be the last half of the seventieth week because it states there that during this time, the Gentiles will tread the holy city underfoot. This appears to coincide with Da 9:27, where, "in the middle of

the week," the sacrifices at the temple will be halted. Thus, the three and one-half years of 11:3 are the first half of the seventieth week because the two witnesses bear their testimony during this period, and they cannot be slain until the Roman beast comes to the height of his power (11:7; 13:7). Note, however, that others hold that the two witnesses carry out their work during the last half of the Tribulation.

Chapters 4–19 contain a rich assortment of events, all of which, in some way or another, fall into the period of the Tribulation, i.e., Daniel's seventieth week. One of the central questions facing anyone who wishes to understand the book is that of the order of the events recorded. Does John write these events in the order that they are to occur? Or are the events simply listed without regard for their actual sequence? One of the difficulties of understanding the order in which these events are to occur is the fact that most of the events are portrayed in highly symbolic language and their meaning is thus not self-evident. Before we can understand their order, we must understand what it is that these events portray. Another element that further complicates this problem is that the symbolic events of Revelation owe their interpretation to other portions of Scripture, such as Mt 24 and Eze 38–39. To make the process of understanding these events as little complicated as possible, one should first survey the events of the book alone, viewing the events recorded here only in their symbolic dress, without interpretation. After a sense of the order of the book is obtained, then we can proceed to develop the order and the meaning of the figurative events.

The following is a list of the principal and distinct events of chs. 4–19:

(1) Vision of the throne in heaven (ch. 4)

(2) The sealed book and the Lamb (ch. 5)

(3) Opening of the first six seals (ch. 6)

(4) Sealing of the 144,000 from the tribes of Israel (7:1–8)

(5) Triumph of innumerable multitude (7:9–17)

(6) Opening of the seventh seal (8:1–13)

(a) Half-hour silence (8:1)

(b) First four trumpet blasts (8:2–13)

(7) Fifth trumpet blast = first woe (9:1–12)

(8) Sixth trumpet blast = second woe (9:13–21)

(9) Preparations for the seventh trumpet blast (10:1–11:14)

(a) Vision of the angel with the open booklet (ch. 10)

(b) Measuring the temple (11:1–2)

(c) Testimony of the two witnesses (11:3–14)

(10) Seventh trumpet blast = third woe (11:15–19)

(11) Woman with the child and the great red dragon (ch. 12)

(12) Beast from the sea (13:1–10)

(13) Beast from the earth (13:11–18)

(14) Vision of the 144,000 on Mount Zion (14:1–5)

(15) Three angelic proclamations and a voice from heaven (14:6–13)

(16) Vision of the harvest and vintage from heaven (14:14–20)

(17) Preparation for the last seven plagues (15:1–8)

(18) Pouring out of the seven bowls (16:1–21)

(19) Vision of Babylon seated on the beast (17:1–6)

(20) Interpretation of the vision of Babylon and the beast (17:7–18)

(21) Doom of Babylon (18:1–24)

(22) Triumph in heaven (19:1–10)

(a) Two hallelujah psalms (19:1–8)

(b) An angelic message (19:9–10)

(23) Vision of crowned warrior (19:11–16)

(24) Overthrow and end of the beast and the false prophet (19:17–21)

What is the sequence of these events? Their most natural reading is that they occur in the same chronological sequence as they appear in the book (see Fig. 1). Others hold that these judgment events are not consecutive but, rather, come to a conclusion at the precisely same point in time. Thus each group of judgments amounts to a

| Seals | 1 2 3 4 5 6 7 | | | | | | | | | | | | | Second |
| | Trumpets | | 1 2 3 4 5 6 7 | | | | | | | | | | Coming |
| | | Bowls | | 1 2 3 4 5 6 7 | | | | | | | | |

*Fig 1*

| Seals | 1 | | 2 | 3 | 4 | 5 | 6 | 7 | Second |
| | Trumpets | 1 | 2 | 3 | 4 | 5 | 6 | 7 | Coming |
| | Bowls | 1 | 2 | 3 | 4 | 5 | 6 | 7 | |

*Fig. 2*

| Seals | 1 | 2 | 3 | 4 | 5 | 6 | 7 | | Second |
| | Trumpets | 1 | 2 | 3 4 5 6 7 | | | | | Coming |
| | | Bowls 1 2 3 4 5 6 7 | | | | | | |

*Fig. 3*

"stepping back" from the end of the preceding sequence (see Fig. 2).

It has frequently been noted that considerable overlap can be seen between various parts of these events. In 6:17, for example, the sixth seal appears to signal the arrival of the final event of the great day of wrath. Furthermore, already in 11:15, the seventh trumpet signals the arrival of the end: "The kingdom of the world has become the kingdom of our Lord and of his Christ." Such parallels have led many to suppose that the events of the book are arranged in a sort of "recapitulation" of a single series of events.

There are other aspects of the events of the book that further support this contention. For example, the seventh seal (8:1), unlike the first six seals, contains no plague or judgment. The same is true of the seventh trumpet (11:15). In both cases it is possible to say that the events that follow are to be read as a further description or supplementation of the events recounted earlier. The seven trumpets (8:6–11:19), for example, can be read as representing the missing judgments of the seventh seal (8:1), and the seven bowls (16) as representing the missing judgments of the seventh trumpet (see Fig. 3).

It should be noted that almost every interpreter of the book of Revelation holds that these three sets of seven judgments provide the overall chronological framework of the book of Revelation. Within this framework John has woven several further episodes or visions relating to various aspects of the Tribulation period. These single episodes are presented as short glimpses of events within the time frame of the Tribulation.

(1) In 7:1–8 John presents the sealing of the 144,000 from the twelve tribes of Israel. This apparently takes place at the beginning of the judgments, in that four angels are commanded to hold back any harm until the 144,000 had been sealed.

(2) Immediately following this episode, John sees a great multitude from every nation, tribe, and people standing before the throne and before the Lamb (7:9ff.). These are identified as those "who have come out of the great tribulation; they have washed their robes and made them white in the blood of the Lamb" (7:14). Here the time seems clearly to be after the Tribulation period.

Some of these vision episodes are highly figurative: for example, the woman with the child and the red dragon (ch. 12); the two beasts, one from the sea and one from the earth (ch. 13); and the woman sitting on the red beast (ch. 17). Some of the elements of these visions are interpreted for John. The red dragon who attacks the woman about to have a child is called "that ancient serpent called the devil, and Satan" (12:9). The interpretation of the beast from the earth is given in the form of the cryptic number of his name, 666. As is not uncommon, the explanation given in the text serves as much to conceal as to reveal. The "mystery of the woman and of the beast she rides" is given in detail to John (17:7ff.), but still much is left unexplained.

Some aspects of the visions are left without an explanation. Who, for example, is the "woman clothed with the sun" in 12:1? Or the male child whom she bears (12:5)? Or the beast who comes out of the sea (13:1)?

# I. Introduction to the Book (1:1–3)

The book describes itself as a "revelation of Jesus Christ," given to John by God. Its contents are described as "what must soon take place" (v.1). God the Father is the ultimate source of the revelation, while Jesus Christ, the Son of God, is the mediator of that revelation. Through him it passes on to an angel and then to his servant John. This is the pattern of revelation throughout this book (cf. 1:18; 3:35; 5:20ff.; 7:16; 8:28; 12:49).

John's use of the expression "what must soon take place" provides us with a helpful model for viewing the manner in which the book of Revelation relies on and uses the OT. In many commentaries and editions of the NT, this phrase is cast as a quotation of a similar phrase in Da 2:28, 45, "what will happen in the days to come." It is true that John does not use words to introduce this phrase as a quotation from the book of Daniel as most other NT writers would have done. But the Greek phrase used here is identical with the phrase in the Greek translation of Daniel, and it is a kind of stock phrase that John uses throughout Revelation (1:19; 4:1; 22:6, 16). This raises the possibility that John is indeed quoting from or alluding to the book of Daniel and is sending his readers a message that he is expecting them to read Revelation in light of the Daniel passage.

One difficulty this idea presents us with, however, is that both Revelation and the Greek translation of the book of Daniel say more than the original Aramaic text of Daniel. The difference lies in the addition of the word "must." The Aramaic text of Daniel says only that God has made known "what will happen in the days to come," not what "must" happen. It may be a small point, but John and the Greek translators of Daniel appear to have added the notion of necessity ("must") as an interpretation of the Daniel passage. In light of the fact that both the book of Daniel, and this passage stress the role of God's sovereignty behind future events being forecast in the book, we would probably be wise to see the additional interpretation added by John as a valid and important emphasis of the book of Revelation. Not only does God reveal what "will" happen, but from a biblical per-

spective, because they are his revelation, these things "must" happen.

If John is in fact referring to Da 2 in his use of this phrase, how does he intend it to be understood within the book of Revelation? Is it simply a matter of biblical phraseology, like someone who says "Am I my brother's keeper?" may be using the words of Ge 3 but not intending any particular reference to that text? Or, does John expect us to bring an understanding of the book of Daniel with us when we read the book of Revelation? Ordinarily this may be a difficult question to resolve, but because there are many other correspondences between Daniel and Revelation, it therefore seems likely that John intends us to make a connection. If so, then we can ask how the Daniel passage helps us understand or appreciate John's use of the same, or nearly the same, phraseology. One clue to John's meaning is to note the fact that he has substituted Daniel's term "latter days" with the term "soon." In Daniel, the term "latter days" can be understood as that whole scope of world history that runs from about 600 B.C. to the second coming of Christ. John has considerably narrowed the range of this term by stating simply that the revelation that John has received is about that which will "soon" take place.

John's use of the term "soon" raises another question. Does he mean that the events recorded in this book are to take place within the first century (his own time)? If so, the book is a highly stylized and dramatized version of the persecution of the church in the first century. It seems more likely, however, that the things prophesied in Revelation go far beyond any known historical situation in the first century. Thus we are faced with a dilemma. John writes as if the events of the book are to happen "soon"; yet we know from history that they did not. Ladd gives a helpful explanation in his commentary on Revelation.

> The Old Testament prophets blended the near and the distant perspective so as to form a single canvas. Biblical prophecy is not primarily three-dimensional but two; it has height and breadth but is little concerned about depth, i.e., the chronology of future events. There is in biblical prophecy a tension between the immediate and the distant future. It is true that the early church lived in expectancy of the return of the Lord, and it is the nature of biblical prophecy to make it possible for every generation to live in expectancy of the end.

It is also possible to read the term "soon" as "quickly," thus describing how, rather than when, these events were to take place. John would thus be saying, once these events begin, they will quickly run their course.

This opening section ends by making an appeal to those congregations to whom the book is addressed, as well as to all Christian churches everywhere. The appeal is to read and obey the prophecies contained in the book. Those who do so are called "blessed." This word is common in the NT and has a distinct meaning. The Greek word itself means "joyful," but the kind of joy contained in the word is of special significance. In general it refers to the joy one has from the expectation of the coming kingdom of God. In the Sermon on the Mount, for example, Jesus taught that those who lived in the expectation of God's kingdom were "blessed" because whatever their present sorrow or trouble might be, they would one day live in God's kingdom. In like manner, those who read this book and remain faithful to God are blessed because they will one day live in God's kingdom.

John adds a special dimension to his appeal to the readers in the words "the time is near" (v.3). Here again, as in v.1, John stresses the fact that the events recorded in this revelation are impending. There is no prophetic event standing in the way of their fulfillment. In effect, John is reminding his readers that they are in the last days, the days preceding the time of the end. In light of this, John calls on his readers to pay close attention to the words of this prophecy. Again, the particular perspective of biblical prophecy is in view here. John does not look at the possible interval of time between his readers and the events of the book but rather stresses the most important truth of all, namely, "Be on guard! Be alert! You do not know when that time will come" (Mk 13:33).

## II. Summary of the Contents of the Book (1:4–8)

John begins by introducing himself and identifying his readers. This was the customary form of greeting for a letter in the first century (see especially the way in which Paul introduces such letters as Galatians, 1 and 2 Corinthians, and 1 and 2 Thessalonians). Thus the book of Revelation is, in fact, a letter, an epistle. This feature sets the book of Revelation apart from all Jewish apocalyptic literature and firmly anchors the book in history.

Why John writes only to these seven churches in his greeting has puzzled many commentators. The book was surely intended to have a wider circulation. This address to the seven churches in Asia may be related to John's frequent literary use of the number "seven" as a way of arranging and organizing his material (1:4, 12, 16; 4:5; 5:1, 6; 7:2; 10:3; 11:13; 12:3; 13:1; 14:64). This number often implies the idea of completeness and thus may be intended here to express the idea that the letter is addressed to all churches everywhere. This would conform to v.3, which is not addressed specifically to the seven churches but to anyone who "reads the words of this prophecy."

John's greeting contains an exalted praise of God the Father. The apostle

Paul began his letters with the greeting "grace to you and peace from God our Father" (Ro 1:7; 1Co 1:3). John writes "grace to you and peace from him who is, and who was, and who is to come" (v.4). It seems clear that this extended reference to God the Father stems from the description of God in Ex 3:14 and Dt 32:39. This language John uses bears close similarity to ancient Greek and Aramaic versions of the OT. It must be remembered that at the time John was writing, he had already seen the visions recorded in this book. These visions firmly set in John's mind the view of God as the ever-present sovereign God who controls the universe. It is as if here, John is so taken by the power and majesty of God that he cannot restrain himself from the praise that wells up in his heart.

John adds, "and from the seven spirits before his throne." Some have understood this to be a reference to angelic beings such as those in 8:2. Other considerations, however, suggest that this is John's description of the Holy Spirit. First, there is a close association of these seven spirits with both God and Jesus Christ. In this context, grace and peace are dispensed from him who is, was, and will be (the Father), from Jesus Christ (v.5), and from the seven spirits. Second, there is a possible allusion here to Isa 11:2, where the Spirit of God is given a sevenfold title. He is the Spirit of the Lord, of wisdom and understanding, of counsel and power, and of knowledge and the fear of the Lord. Thus John's reference to seven spirits may be a reference to the various roles of the Spirit of God (cf. "the sevenfold Spirit" in NIV note). Moreover, it is possible that the number seven may, again, be intended as an expression of completeness.

After the mention of the Father and the sevenfold Spirit, John turns to Jesus Christ, his central concern throughout this book. The title "Christ" occurs seven times in the book of Revelation. The title identifies Jesus as the messianic king of the house of David, the "Anointed One." As important as this title is, the more common title of Jesus in this book is that of the Lamb.

Jesus is then designated by three further titles: "the faithful witness, the firstborn from the dead, and the ruler of the kings of the earth." Apart from this passage and a similar one in 3:14, Jesus is never referred to as a "witness." The meaning of this title can be seen in the use John makes of the word elsewhere in this book. In 2:13 the "faithful witness" is one who held to the name of Christ in time of trouble and was slain for his faithfulness. In 11:3 John writes of two "witnesses" who were to prophesy for 1,260 days and then be slain. Again in 17:6 John writes of many "witnesses" who have died for their faith in Christ. The word "witness," then, as John uses it, denotes one who loses one's life for the sake of Christ. Not all members of God's people who are killed can rightly be called "witnesses"—only those who die in the evangelistic service of Jesus. This meaning can easily be fitted to 1:5, where Christ himself is called "the faithful witness." Here Christ is called that title because he himself proclaimed his message and died in the course of that witness. Christ is thus the true witness. John, who knows the visions of the future events that await God's people, stresses at the beginning of his letter that Jesus Christ himself was the true witness, the first to die for the cause of the Gospel. The title of "witness" that John gives to Jesus, then, represents his earthly work of giving his life for the many.

The second title that John gives to Jesus is "the firstborn of the dead." In NT theology, the work of Christ is thought of in three stages: his death, resurrection, and ascension. Within this framework, the title "firstborn of the dead" is commonly associated with the Resurrection. Though it is correct to see it as such, the idea of the "firstborn" implies that there is more to it. It includes the notion of the exaltation of Christ to Lordship over all creation, as well as the expression of his authority over the dead and the promise of their redemption. This sense of the term "firstborn" can be seen in Ge 49:3, where Reuben, the firstborn, is "preeminent in power." Also in Col 1:18, Christ, the firstborn from the dead, is also the head of the body, the church. Thus the title "firstborn of the dead" designates the rulership and authority of Christ over those for whom he died. This authority is demonstrated in his resurrection and exaltation to the right hand of the Father. Such a view of Christ is important for the readers of John's book. John does not merely look back to the historical fact of the Resurrection. He also looks at the present and future consequences of it—that Jesus is Lord over the church and reigns now at the right hand of the Father.

Finally, Jesus is designated "the ruler of the kings of the earth." The phrase "kings of the earth" is a characteristic phrase from the OT and, in the book of Revelation, denotes the enemies of Christ and his people (cf. 6:15; 17:2, 18; 18:3, 9; 19:19). Throughout the book it is these "kings of the earth" who align themselves with the beast and with the prostitute of Babylon to oppose God and his people. Thus, John here designates Christ as the one who has authority over all these powers and who has destroyed the power of the "rulers of this age" (1Co 2:8).

We can thus see that John has given Jesus Christ a threefold title that stresses his death, resurrection, and exaltation over believers as well as his ultimate victory and exaltation over the nations. These are important elements in the doctrine of Christ in the NT and are especially important in light of the

vision John has received regarding coming events. As with John's use of the title for God the Father, so also his title for Christ the Son stresses that the coming events described in his book are all under the absolute control of the sovereign God.

John's greeting turns now to doxology (vv.5b–6; cf. 5:9–10). Again he lists three aspects of Christ's work on behalf of believers. (1) He loves the church. (2) He has released believers from their sin by his shed blood. Here, as in 5:9, the central deed of Christ was his work of redemption on the cross. The church has been bought out of its sins by the price of Christ's blood, much as a slave in NT times was bought out of slavery with a price. The church was purchased out of its slavery to sin and put in a new relationship of service to God. (3) This new relationship is described as Christ making us into "a kingdom and priests to serve his God and Father" (v.6a). The allusion to Ex 19:6 could not be clearer. In Exodus, Israel was called upon to obey the stipulation of the Lord's covenant so that they could be his people and he would be their King. As John now sees it, the church is made a member of God's kingdom by the blood of Christ, the free work of his grace toward sinners.

Before recounting the vision that he had received, John announces the nature of his letter. It is to announce that Jesus Christ is returning (v.7). The picture John gives of Christ's return is drawn from two important OT passages, Da 7:9–14 (in which the Son of Man is pictured coming to receive an eternal kingdom from the Ancient of Days) and Zec 12:10 (where the coming one is pictured as one who has been "pierced" by those for whom he is coming). This image of Christ sets the stage for the visions that follow. At the center of the visions is the one who comes in the clouds to receive the divine kingdom. This one is the Lamb slain before the foundation of the world (5:9–12). Just as in the OT texts he relies on, John shows a curious disregard to distinguish carefully between the one who comes for the kingdom, the Son of Man, and the one who gives him the kingdom, the Ancient of Days. As is the case throughout this book, John stresses the role of the sovereign God, who rules all things. He is the true author of the coming events described in this book.

## III. Seven Visions for the Churches (1:9–22:6)

### A. The First Vision: One Like the Son of Man Who Comes to Judge the Saints (1:9–3:22)

It is important to note that the vision of the coming of the Son of Man in Da 7, which is the OT background for the present text, consists of two distinct scenes. In Da 7:9–10 is a picture of the coming of the Ancient of Days to bring judgment, and in Da 7:13–14 is a portrayal of the Ancient of Days giving the eternal kingdom over to the Son of Man. First judgment, then the kingdom. John appears to follow this same pattern by presenting Jesus as first coming to judge the churches (chs. 2–3) and then coming to judge the nations (6:1–20:10). The role that the vision of the Son of Man and the Ancient of Days in Daniel has played in shaping the present text is explained in the next section: Christ is described both as one like the Son of Man and the Ancient of Days.

#### 1. John's call vision (1:9–20)

As is common in the prophetic books, John recounts the call he received and the means whereby God gave him his revelation of things to come. He first tells us that he had been exiled to the island of Patmos, just off the southwest coast of Asia Minor. His exile had resulted from his preaching the Gospel. He had himself, in other words, suffered the kind of persecution that awaited the whole of God's people

in the near future. He thus writes his letter to others who were also facing tribulation, and he calls himself a "companion in the suffering."

Next John states that he was "in the Spirit" on "the Lord's Day" (v.10). The phrase "in the Spirit" suggests that John had been overcome by the Spirit so that he was ready to receive the divine visions that follow. Such a description of his state at the time helps set the stage for our appreciation of the nature of the visions. These are not the result of John's imagination; he really saw these things. They were given to John by the Spirit of God. They are thus divine revelations. The phrase "the Lord's Day" refers to the celebration of the first day of the week, Sunday, as a reminder of the day on which the Lord was raised from the dead (Mt 28:1). It is thus fitting that John should see a vision of the resurrected Christ on the day set apart to commemorate this event.

John heard a voice behind him, telling him to write in a book the things he would see and to send it to the seven churches. These things constitute the whole of the rest of the book of Revelation. In other words, the things that John had to send to the seven churches go far beyond the specific messages to the seven churches. This is clear from the fact that in 4:1, after the close of the messages to the seven churches, John continues to recount the visions he saw on this day.

When John turned to see who was speaking, he saw a vision of Christ. The appearance of Christ is the same as that of the Ancient of Days in Da 7:9–10, yet John identifies him as "one like the Son of Man" (v.13; cf. Da 7:13–14).

In this vision, John is given the meaning of only two features of the vision of "one like the Son of Man." The first is the mystery of the seven stars. They are the angels of the seven churches (v.20). It is apparently to these angels that John is instructed to write in chs. 2–3. Who are these "angels"? The term itself can refer to heavenly beings or earthly officials. Thus they can be identified either as heavenly beings who represent each local church in the heavenly courts or as actual church officials within each church. It is common today to think of them as analogous to the leaders in the early Jewish synagogues who were called "those sent from the congregation."

The second feature of the vision of Christ explained to John was the mystery of the seven lampstands. These represented the seven churches (v.20). The other features of the vision are left unexplained, perhaps because their meaning is self-evident or can be determined from other passages where they reoccur within the book. What appears certain from the vision itself, however, is that the images are all intended to portray the majesty and lordship of the Savior. The response of John within the narrative of the book is presented as the only fitting response to such a vision— "When I saw him, I fell at his feet as though dead" (v.17). In this respect, John's actions anticipate the response of all the saints in the rest of the book (cf. 4:11).

After describing the vision, John records the words of Christ (1:17b–3:22). What gives these words their special importance is the fact that they constitute a major portion of the words of Jesus spoken after the Resurrection.

Jesus first identifies himself by means of two titles taken largely from the OT. The first one is "I am the First and the Last." The phrase "First and Last" is used again in 2:8, where it likewise refers to Christ, the one sending the letter to the seven churches. In 22:13 the same expression is accompanied by two similar ones, "the Alpha and Omega" and "the Beginning and the End." The expression "the Alpha and Omega" is used to designate God in 1:8 and 21:6. The expression "the Be-

ginning and the End" is also used of God in 21:6. In the OT the phrase "First and Last" is a self-designation of the Lord. The Lord says in 44:6, "I am the first and I am the last" (cf. Isa 48:12). In these contexts, the sense of the expression appears to be "the eternal One."

The expression "I am the Living One" is also a designation of God in the OT (e.g., Da 6:26–27), as well as in the book of Revelation (4:9; 10:6; 15:7). The title "Living God" in the OT stresses the fact that God is alive and actively working in the affairs of humankind. In Da 6:26–27, "the living God" delivers and rescues Daniel from the mouth of the lions (cf. Dt 32:40; Jos 3:10).

In this vision of Jesus, we are given three additional statements by which he identifies himself. In the expression "I was dead," Jesus looks back to his own death on the cross, a theme stressed throughout Revelation. Then by the phrase "I am alive forevermore," he looks at his eternality. Finally he looks at his power over life and death: "I have the keys of death and Hades." In Jewish thinking, God alone possessed the keys to death. He thus was able to give life to the dead. Possession of the keys of death meant having authority over death. For Christ to claim that he had the keys to death and Hades was, in effect, another claim to equal authority with God.

John is then given the instruction to write down the things that he has seen—the things that are now and the things that shall take place after these things (v.19). This verse is often taken as the key to the structure and argument of the entire book of Revelation. Those who hold a futuristic, pretribulational interpretation of the book point to this verse as an indication of the chronological sequence of the book. "What you have seen" is identified as the vision of Christ that has just been described (vv.9–20). "What is now" is taken as a reference to the words of Christ to the seven churches (2:1–3:22). "What will take place later," then, refers to that which is to happen in the future, after the church age, i.e., during the time of the Great Tribulation described in the rest of this book. It is important to see the role that the phrase translated "later" has for the pretribulational view. If the "what is now" (2:1–3:22) refers to the church age, then we can expect "what will take place later" to refer to what happens after the church age, namely, during the Tribulation (4:1–19:21). Since chs. 2–3 are written specifically to churches during the present age, then what happens "after this" (4:1) must relate to the Tribulation that takes place after the church age.

The pretribulational view finds further support in the repetition of this same phrase twice in 4:1. A common interpretation of the first occurrence of the phrase "after this" in 4:1 is that it refers to a time after the completion or fulfillment of the prophecies spoken of in 2:1–3:22. Posttribulationalists, however, argue that this phrase refers only to the time of the vision that John saw. After the vision of 2:1–3:22 he saw the vision of 4:1ff. Thus the first "after this" in 4:1 means simply that after John saw the vision concerning the churches, he saw the vision of the heavenly throne room in 4:1ff.

The key question, however, is the meaning of the second occurrence of the phrase "after this" in 4:1. It may be a mere restatement of the first phrase or it may be an introduction to the remainder of the book. If it is the latter, then its sense must be understood eschatologically, "in the last days." An important point to consider is that this phrase seems to be borrowed from the OT book of Daniel. In Da 2:29 Daniel is told that Nebuchadnezzar's dream is intended to reveal "what is going to happen." A study of Jewish thinking on the OT and of their translations of the OT

suggest that in John's day the phrase "after this" was understood eschatologically as referring to a time in the future when God would draw to an end his dealings with humankind.

What then is the meaning of 1:19? We should first note that the phrase "what will take place later" refers to the same phrase in 4:1. In making this connection we are thus suggesting that John's visions are about the eschatological future. The phrase "what is now" points to the entirety of John's first vision, i.e., to the vision of Christ that includes his messages to the seven churches (chs. 2–3). The phrase "what you have seen" is a general statement that refers to all the visions that John has seen and has recorded within the book of Revelation. A slightly paraphrased version of the NIV would be: "Write, therefore, what you have seen [about] what is happening now and what will take place in the last days."

## 2. The seven letters (2:1–3:22)

It is frequently held that the seven churches in chs. 2–3 represent the "spiritual history" of the church during the last nearly two thousand years. The church at Ephesus (2:1–7) represents the church of the first century; Smyrna (vv.8–11), the church under persecution (A.D. 100–316); Pergamum (vv.12–17), the church mixing with the world in the Middle Ages; Thyatira (vv.18–29), the time of decline in the pre-Reformation period; Sardis (3:1–6), the time of the Reformation; Philadelphia (vv.7–13), period of revivalism in the church; and Laodicea (vv.14–22), final state of apostasy in the visible church.

There are, of course, many variations in this view. Some today see the seven churches as representing progressive stages in the history of the church. Each church represents a new feature of the church that continues into the next stage. The aspects of the church of Ephesus, for example, do not cease after the first century but become a part of the next phase and continue throughout the remainder of the history of the church. The fact that only the last four churches are warned about Christ's return (Thyatira, 2:22, 24; Sardis, 3:3–4; Philadelphia, 3:10; Laodicea, 3:16) has led others to suggest that only these last four churches have aspects that continue unto the last days.

Another common view of these letters is that they represent the specific historical churches to whom the book of Revelation was written. The fact that there are seven churches is commonly taken as an indication that these churches were chosen to represent all the churches at that time and thus the book of Revelation was intended for a much larger audience.

The phrase "he who overcomes," which occurs in each of the messages to the seven churches, is in need of some clarification. Some suggest that these "overcomers" are those who endure the Tribulation faithfully. They are thus an indication that the church will be present on earth during the time of the Tribulation. In 15:2 the "overcomers" seem to be victims of persecution during the Tribulation because of their faithfulness to Christ. Others, however, argue that the word "overcoming" is John's expression for "faith" (see especially 1Jn 5:4) The "overcomer" then, in the language of John's writings, generally refers to anyone who is victorious in faith. Overcomers are true members of the people of God. Such an understanding fits well the description of the "overcomers" in 21:7, where they are those who will drink of the water of life forever, in contrast to "the cowardly and the unbelieving" (21:8).

**B. The Second Vision: The Throne, the Lamb, and the Book With Seven Seals (4:1–8:1)**

John first receives a vision of the "throne in heaven," with various creatures around it (on "after this" in 4:1, see comments on 1:19). Then John sees

a "scroll with writing on both sides and sealed with seven seals." This is a two-part document that has an initial summary written on one side with seven seals (6:1–8:1). When the seals are opened, the full description is given on the inside of the scroll (8:2–22:5).

### 1. Theophany: The throne scene (4:1–11)

Before John sees the vision of the Tribulation wrath, he is introduced to a scene from heaven. A few of the features of the heavenly vision are identified. The seven lamps of fire are the "seven spirits of God" (v.5). The seven eyes of the Lamb are also the seven spirits of God (v.6). Several of the features of the vision are obvious and are thus not given an interpretation. The one sitting upon the throne (vv.2–3), for example, is clearly God. The scene is an allusion to the "Ancient of Days" in Da 7:9–10. The throne (4:2) appears to represent God's sovereignty and kingship.

There are other features of the vision that leave us on our own for an explanation. The identity of the twenty-four elders, for example, is not given and is not immediately obvious. It seems most likely that they represent the church in that they are distinct from the angels in 5:11 and are shown offering up the prayers of the saints (5:8). Their white garments and crowns of gold are presumably symbols of their purity and rewards (cf. Isa 24:23b).

Some elements of the visions cannot be identified at all. These include the rainbow (v.3), the flashes of lightning and peals of thunder (v.5), the sea of glass (v.6), and the four living creatures (v.7).

### 2. The Lamb and the book with seven seals: (5:1–14)

The Lamb is identified as "the Lion of the tribe of Judah, the Root of David" (v.5). The "Lion of the tribe of Judah" is an allusion to Ge 49:9–10; "the Root of David" to Isa 11:1. The golden bowls of the twenty-four elders are identified as "the prayers of the saints" (v.8), and the scroll in v.1 is identified as a scroll of judgment in 6:1.

### 3. The vision of the seven seals (6:1–8:1)

On virtually all reckonings, the vision of the seven seals provides the book with its essential outline spanning the whole of the seventieth week of Da 9:27. The first four seals compose a unit within themselves (6:1–8). The fifth seal is distinct (vv.9–11), as is also the sixth seal (vv.12–17). The sixth seal seems to relate especially to a time called "the great day of their wrath." The seventh seal, which is separated from the preceding seal by the parenthetical events of ch. 7, introduces the coming trumpet judgments (8:1ff.).

There are definite features of the *first four seals* that suggest these belong together as a distinct unit within the seven seals. They are each introduced by one of the four living creatures (6:1, 3, 5, 7). Each of the first four seals is preceded by the call to "come," and each contains the image of a horse and rider (vv.2, 4, 5, 8). There is, moreover, a progression of the meaning given for each of the four seals: conquering (v.2), making war (v.4), famine (vv.5–6), and death (v.8).

The four living creatures are known from 4:6–7. They are (1) one like a lion, (2) one like a calf, (3) one like a man, and (4) one like a flying eagle. Each creature is "covered with eyes," has six wings, and speaks endlessly the words, "Holy, holy, holy is the Lord God Almighty, who was, and is, and is to come." There are many attempts to explain the significance of these living creatures. The similarities between these creatures and the "four living beings" in the vision of the first chapter of Ezekiel has frequently been pointed out. If there is a connection between the Ezekiel vision and the creatures in Revelation, then Ezekiel's identification of them as cherubim is a help (Eze 10:1).

They may also be identified with the seraphim in Isa 6:1–3.

The most plausible interpretation of these creatures appears to be that they represent all the living creatures that God created in the Genesis account (Ge 1): the lion represents the wild animals; the calf, the domesticated animals; man, humankind; and the eagle, the fowl of the air. Certainly in these points there is a close agreement between the two biblical passages. The fact that these creatures were appointed to continuously give praise to God suggests that the theme of Ps 19 is also present in the imagery of the four seals. Reflecting on Ge 1, Ps 19 presents God's creation as a continuous reminder of God's glory. It should be noted that missing here is an important group of animals from Ge 1, the sea creatures. It may be that the vision has this group in mind in the mention of the "sea of glass" (4:6). On the other hand, the mention of the creatures of the sea may have been deliberately avoided because of the predominately negative view of the sea throughout the book of Revelation (cf. 21:1) and the fact that the creature who comes out of the sea in 13:1 is the Beast, the Antichrist.

Before each seal is broken by the Lamb, each living creature calls out respectively, "Come!" There are various possible interpretations of this call. It could be a call to John to come closer and look at the vision. It may also be a directive on the part of the living creature to call forth the various horsemen in the vision. An equally plausible explanation, however, comes from the fact that the same expression, "Come!" occurs at the close of the book (22:17, 20). There the call to "come" represents John's eager anticipation of the return of Christ, "Come! Lord Jesus" (22:20). It may be, then, that in the vision of the first four seals, the living creatures begin their respective roles of ushering in divine judgment with a call for the return of Christ. If such is the case, then the role of the living creatures as symbolizing all of God's creatures is similar to that of all creation in Ro 8:19, where Paul writes that all creation waits eagerly in anxious longing for the glory that accompanies the revelation of Christ.

The composite picture presented by the four horsemen is that of divine judgment poured out upon the earth. It anticipates the final judgment of the sixth seal and the trumpets (8:1ff.). Much has been said about the identity of the rider on the white horse, the question being the similarity between the description of this rider and that of the coming of Christ in 19:11ff. But the identity of this rider is not given in this text. Regardless of who the rider is, his task is clear: "He rode out as a conqueror bent on conquest" (6:2). Within the larger structure of the book itself, it seems likely that the two visions of the rider on a white horse are intended to offset each other.

In these first four seals John sees a time of increasing warfare, famine, pestilence, and death by wild beasts. As this vision unfolds, he hears the groans of the four living creatures, symbolizing Creation itself as it cries out to God for its redemption. The cry of the four living creatures is amplified in the cries of the martyrs of the fifth seal (6:9–11).

The scene introduced by the *fifth seal* raises the question of the relationship between the events it records and the first four seals. The martyred souls in the fifth seal vision appear to be those who have suffered and died for the Gospel during the time of the first four seals. We are thus given a brief glimpse of what has been happening on earth during these days of wrath. The powers of earth have been under God's wrath, but they continued to slay his saints and reject his Gospel message.

Who are the saints who have been martyred (v.9)? It is generally agreed that they are a specific group of believers who have been martyred during the time of the Tribulation. They are, however, only the first group to be martyred. They are explicitly told that more were to join their ranks (v.11). A more precise identification of these martyrs is not possible from the text itself, though it is possible to link them to the martyrs who have come out of the Great Tribulation in 7:9ff. and with those who do not take upon themselves the mark of the Beast in 13:15ff.

The content of the *sixth seal* is different from that of the earlier seals. John writes that there was a great earthquake (6:12), accompanied by four cosmic phenomena. The sun became black, the moon red as blood, the stars fell from heaven as figs shaken from a fig tree by the wind (v.13), and the sky was split open as a scroll rolled up (v.14). Finally, John records the response of the people of the earth. He lists seven groups of human beings, covering all classes of society, thus stressing the universal scope of the sixth seal. These people hide from the one who sits on the throne and from the Lamb, because the great day of wrath has come.

Some hold that the events of this seal are too cosmic to be taken literally. The earthquakes, for example, may refer to the shaking of all political and ecclesiastical institutions. Others, however, take these images literally. Just as the sun was darkened before the day of the exodus from Egypt (Ex 10:22), it is argued, so also during this time the sun will actually lose its light. The stars falling from heaven may refer to some meteoric manifestation.

Finally, there are those who hold that the language used to describe these events is, in fact, symbolic, but the events themselves are real cosmic events. There is similarity, for example, between the events of the sixth seal and the description of the end times in the OT prophetic literature (Isa 34:4; Joel

2:31; 3:15; Hag 2:6) and in Mt 24:29. They see the language used here as poetic or symbolic, even though real cosmic catastrophes are described, not mere spiritual realities.

What method or procedure should we employ to determine the best interpretation of these visions? The major drawback to a symbolic interpretation is that it leaves us with no controls over the meaning of the passage. Interpretations of pure symbols easily become arbitrary. On the other hand, a strictly literal interpretation runs the risk of overlooking the obviously symbolic nature of John's vision. The first four seals, for example, are manifestly symbolic. The fifth seal, whether it is an actual event or not, still contains many symbolic features, such as the altar, the position of the saints under the altar, and their white robes. It seems reasonable that if there are clear symbolic features in the visions of the first five seals, then there would be symbolic features in the sixth. John himself uses symbolic terminology in the description of the vision. He says, for example, "the sky receded like a scroll" (6:14).

In 7:1–8, we are introduced to two groups of people. The first group consists of 144,000 "servants of our God" who have been sealed by him. The group consists of 12,000 from each of the twelve tribes of Israel, and the names of the tribes are listed. There is no universal agreement on the actual identity of this group; some identify them with the actual physical descendants of these early Israelite tribes, while others understand them as a symbolic reference to the church, the new Israel.

It has often been noted that John's list of the twelve tribes varies somewhat from the usual listing in the OT. Specifically, Dan and Ephraim are omitted, and Joseph has been added. Since John does not give us his reasons for this arrangement, there are many attempts to provide a solution. Some see in this "irregularity" a motive for viewing the list as spiritual Israel or the church. Others argue that John associated Dan with the idolatry of Jdg 18:30 and thus felt compelled to omit that tribe in this context, which is decidedly anti-idolatry. It should be noted, however, that a "normative" list of the tribes of Israel is not to be found in the OT. There are, in fact, some twenty different orders and lists of Israel's tribes. Only once is the same list repeated (Nu 2:7; 10:14–29). The most important element is the stress on the number twelve, which reflects an interest in the identification of this group with OT Israel.

The pretribulational view of Revelation identifies this group as representing the godly remnant of Israel on earth during the Great Tribulation. These are Jews who will be saved and who will be physically protected during the Tribulation. The role of this large group will be to proclaim the message of the Gospel. The result of their preaching will be a great multitude of Jewish and Gentile believers.

Posttribulationalists identify the 144,000 as "spiritual Israel," i.e., the church, though some suggest that they form a Jewish remnant—not members of the church and therefore not to be raptured at the end of the Tribulation. They are orthodox but unconverted Jews who will resist the seductions of the Antichrist.

Apart from the fact that the 144,000 are identified as coming from the twelve tribes of Israel, the strongest argument that they are to be understood as physical Israel lies in the distinction John makes between this group and the great multitude that follows (7:9–14).

The "great multitude" is described as consisting of those "from every nation, tribe, people and language" (v.9). They are thus non-Israelites who have "come out of the great tribulation" (v.14). It seems clear from this passage that many will turn to Christ during the Tribulation period and will suffer martyrdom for the sake of the Gospel. The scene that John sees here appears to come after the end of the Tribulation. It finds its parallel in the scene at ch. 21, the new Jerusalem.

Regarding the seventh seal (8:1), it has no content: "When he opened the seventh seal, there was silence in heaven for about half an hour." The apparent purpose of the seal and the silence was to provide a link to the next set of seven events, the seven trumpets.

## C. The Third Vision: Seven Trumpets (8:2–11:19)

### 1. The first four trumpets (8:2–13)

This vision opens with a depiction of seven angels being given seven trumpets and another angel burning incense on the altar before the throne of God (8:2–5). In John's vision, each angel prepared to blast his trumpet (v.6). The first four trumpets signaled four great catastrophes upon the earth: hail and fire mixed with blood (v.7); something like a huge mountain being hurled blazing into the sea (vv.8–9); a great star falling from the sky (vv.10–11); and the sun and moon being stricken and unable to give a third of their light (v.12). The last three trumpet blasts were preceded by a special warning about their severity (v.13).

### 2. The fifth trumpet (9:1–12)

The fifth trumpet signaled the onset of several simultaneous catastrophes. When it sounded, a star fell from heaven and was given the key to the Abyss. Smoke arose out of the Abyss and darkened the sky. Locusts came out of the smoke and tormented all those who did not have the seal of God on their foreheads.

### 3. The sixth trumpet (9:13–10:11)

At the sound of the sixth trumpet (9:13–21) the command was given to release the four angels who were bound at the great river Euphrates. At this, 200

million horses and riders were released to slay a third of humankind. Those not slain by these horsemen did not repent but remained in their idolatry and immorality.

### 4. Interlude before the seventh trumpet (11:1–14)

Before the sounding of the seventh trumpet, three additional scenes are recounted: the angel with a scroll (10:1–11), the temple (11:1–2), and the two witnesses (vv.3–14). The apparent purpose of the account of the angel with the scroll was to show that there was a limit to the apocalyptic visions given to John. There could have been more, but God called it to a halt. The book with the seven thunders was not to be recorded by John. He was, instead, to eat the book and thus keep its contents entirely to himself.

The account of the measurement of the temple and the story of the two witnesses are related by the reference to a three-and-one-half year time period in each. The temple was to be trampled by the Gentiles for 42 months (11:2), and the two witnesses were to prophesy for 1,260 days (v.3). Each period represents half of the final seven-year Tribulation prophesied in Da 9:24–27. The appearance of the Beast (11:7; 13:1) and the death of the two witness is thus correlated with the "abomination that causes desolation" (see Da 9:27; Mt 24:15).

Though the text does not identify the two witnesses, they have often been associated with Moses and Elijah. As with these two witnesses, Elijah was given power to shut up the sky (1Ki 17:1), and Moses turned the waters of Egypt into blood (Ex 7:17).

### 5. The seventh trumpet (11:15–19)

The seventh trumpet signals a time of great praise and celebration in heaven. It marks the beginning of the reign of God's kingdom.

## D. The Fourth Vision: The Battle With the Wicked Powers (12:1–14:20)

### 1. The vision of the dragon and the woman with child (12:1–17)

John saw a woman about to give birth to a male child and an enormous red dragon with seven heads and ten horns standing ready to devour the child when he was born. When the child was born, he was snatched up to God, and the woman was protected for 1,260 days. This was followed by a war in heaven, in which Michael and his angels defeated the dragon and cast him out upon the earth. In heaven there was great celebration that with the defeat of the dragon, "that ancient serpent called the devil, or Satan," God's kingdom had finally been established. Only on earth was there still cause for concern. The dragon was still making war with the woman and "the rest of her offspring" (v.17).

### 2. The two beasts (13:1–18)

As his vision continued, John saw two beasts. The first one arose out of the sea; it represented the Antichrist (vv.1–10). To it was given the authority, power, and kingship of the dragon. It was thus able to make war with the saints and to conquer them. All nations worshiped the Beast, except those whose names were written in the book of life belonging to the Lamb. This beast is the fourth beast of Da 7.

The second beast in this chapter (the third one that John saw in this fourth vision) arose out of the earth; it represented the False Prophet (vv.11–18). It had two horns like a lamb, but it spoke like a dragon. It had all the authority of the first beast and performed great, miraculous signs, deceiving all the earth. It set up an image of the first beast and killed all those who refused to worship it—clearly an allusion to the story of Nebuchadnezzar's image in Da 3. The number of the beast was 666.

### 3. The coming of the Son of Man (14:1–20)

John first saw the Lamb standing on Mount Zion with the 144,000. This was followed by the vision of an angel flying in midair, proclaiming the eternal Gospel to every nation on earth. A second angel was seen proclaiming the fall of Babylon. A third angel followed them with the warning not to receive the mark of the Beast. In this context, John saw a vision of one like the Son of Man seated on a white cloud (cf. Da 7:9–14). A sickle was put into his hands to harvest the earth. The harvested grapes from the earth's vineyards were then put into the great winepress of God's wrath, where they were trampled outside the city (cf. Isa 63:2–6).

### E. The Fifth Vision: The Seven Plagues (15:1–16:21)

In 15:1–16:1 John recounts the preparation for the last of the series of seven judgments. He first saw a heavenly scene of those who had not served the Beast and who were now worshiping and praising God before his throne. His attention then turned to the heavenly temple, where he watched one of the four living creatures fill seven bowls with the wrath of God and give them to the seven angels.

In 16:2–21 John recounts the judgments wrought on the earth by these seven bowls of God's wrath. Throughout this section we are reminded that those who suffered these judgments refused to turn to God in repentance (vv.9, 11, 21). When the *first bowl* was poured out, ugly and painful sores were found on those who had taken the mark of the beast (v.2). With the *second bowl*, the sea turned to blood and every living creature in it died (v.3). The *third bowl* caused the rivers and springs to turn to blood (vv.4–7). An explanation and vindication of this judgment is then given, similar to the vindication of God's turning the Nile waters into blood in Ex 7:14–24. The Egyptians had killed all male children by having them thrown into the Nile (Ex 1:22), and so God had sent a plague against them and the Nile. So the bloodshed of the nations against God's saints and his prophets is vindicated by giving the nations "blood to drink" (v.6). The conclusion is expressly stated, "Yes, Lord God Almighty, true and just are your judgments" (v.7). During the *fourth bowl*, the sun became extremely hot and seared the inhabitants of the earth with its intense heat. With the *fifth bowl*, the kingdom of the beast was plunged into darkness. When the *sixth bowl* was poured out, the Euphrates River was dried up and the kings from the East came across it to gather for battle at Armageddon (vv.12–16). The *seventh bowl* marked the final stage of God's judgment. There was a great earthquake, thunder and lightning, and huge hailstones. The city of Babylon and the cities of the nations were destroyed (vv.17–21).

## F. The Fall of Babylon (17:1–19:10)

Next, John is given a closer look at the judgment and fall of the city of Babylon. The city is depicted as a prostitute sitting on many waters. Then John sees another vision of the woman—in the desert sitting on a red beast. She is called "Mystery Babylon the Great," and she is described as being "drunk with the blood of the saints" who bore testimony to Jesus (17:1–6).

John is then given the interpretation of this vision, beginning with the beast on which the woman was riding. The beast has seven heads and ten horns. He "once was, now is not, and will come up out of the Abyss and go to his destruction" (v.8; cf. Da 7). The angel who gave John the interpretation acknowledges that understanding it "calls for a mind with wisdom" (v.9). This perhaps is a reference to the fact that much of the imagery comes from OT passages such as Da 7 and thus requires

a knowledge and understanding of those texts.

The seven heads are "seven hills on which the woman sits," and they are "seven kings" (vv.9–10). Five of these seven kings have now passed away. The sixth king "is," and the seventh "has not yet come" (v.10). The beast itself represents "an eighth king" (v.11). From this it is apparent that the meaning of the description of the beast as something that "was, is, and will be" is that this beast represents the last king of a kingdom that has ruled in the past and in John's own day and will rule again in the future. The ten horns of the beast are ten kings who have yet to rule along with the beast, i.e., the eighth king. These kings and the beast will make war against the Lamb, who will be accompanied by his "faithful followers" (v.14; cf. Da 7:21). The waters that John saw in the first part of the vision are interpreted as the peoples of the earth (v.15). The woman who sat upon the beast represents "the great city that rules over the kings of the earth" (v.18). This city is apparently Babylon. The beast and the ten kings will destroy her as God's instruments of judgment (vv.16–17).

The sudden ruin of the city of Babylon is victoriously described by the angels (18:1–24), and the saints, apostles, and prophets are called on to rejoice over it (v.20).

In response to the angels' call, the saints in heaven lift up their voices in praise and thanksgiving for the defeat of the great prostitute and for the avenging of their own shed blood (19:1–10).

## G. The Destruction of the Godless Forces (19:11–20:15)

### 1. The victorious Messiah (19:11–21)

The fall of Babylon is accompanied by a battle of the armies of heaven, led by the one mounted on a white horse whose name is "the Word of God" (vv.11–16). This is clearly a picture of Christ (cf. 20:4), "KING OF KINGS AND

LORD OF LORDS" (19:16). At his appearance he mounted an attack on the Antichrist, the False Prophet, and the kings (vv.17–21). The Antichrist and the False Prophet were captured and thrown into "the fiery lake of burning sulfur" (v.20). The kings who followed them into battle were slain by the sword of the one mounted on the white horse.

### 2. The defeat of the dragon (20:1–10)

First an angel from heaven was sent to seize the dragon, bind him in chains, and cast him into the Abyss for one thousand years (vv.1–3). Then there was a resurrection. The resurrected were those martyred by the Beast. They reigned with Christ for one thousand years (v.4). Another resurrection was announced at the end of the one thousand years (v.5). At that time Satan (the dragon) was released. He gathered all the nations (Gog and Magog) together and mounted an attack against Jerusalem. He was defeated by fire from heaven and cast into the same burning lake as the Beast and the False Prophet were (vv.7–10).

### 3. The Great White Throne Judgment (20:11–15)

The last act of judgment that John saw in this vision was a great court session in which all of the dead were gathered and the deeds of each were read off from the books kept in the court (cf. Da 7:10). Death itself was thrown into the lake of fire, along with Hades. Then another book was opened in the court, "the book of life." Anyone whose name was not written in this book was also cast into that lake. A description of these individuals is given in 21.8.

### H. The New Heaven and the New Earth (21:1–22:5)

John's vision takes up again the theme of Ge 1: God created a new heaven and a new earth (21:1–8). In the midst of this vision, John saw a new Jerusalem in which God would again dwell with humankind, just as in the Garden of Eden (Ge 2). This city is described in detail in 21:9–27. Just as in the Garden of Eden, a river flowed through the city and watered the Tree of Life (22:1–2). In this city the curse of Ge 3 has been removed (v.3) and God once again dwells with his people in an eternal kingdom (vv.4–5).

## IV. Conclusion (22:6–21)

John concludes his book with two further sayings of Jesus that stress his imminent return (vv.6–17). John then warns against adding anything further to the visions or sayings that he has recorded (vv.18–20). He concludes with a salutation to his readers (v.21).